MW01628908

Modern Compliance

BEST PRACTICES FOR SECURITIES & FINANCE

Volume II

Compiled and Edited by
David H. Lui
John H. Walsh
Jason K. Mitchell

This book is a summary for general information only.
It is not a full analysis of the matters presented and should not be relied upon as legal advice.

ISBN 978-0-8080-4822-0

Printed in the United States of America.

For Amy, Debbie and Jill,
whose endless patience and encouragement
continue to make this project a reality.

In any moment of decision,
the best thing you can do is the right thing,
the next best thing is the wrong thing,
and the worst thing you can do is nothing.

— Theodore Roosevelt

Modern Compliance Volume II Editorial Board Members

We would like to express our appreciation to the following individuals for their work as members of the Editorial Review Board for Volume II of Modern Compliance. Their guidance and feedback assured that Volume II adhered to the highest standards for scholarship, relevance to the Compliance mission and readability. Without their help, this book would not have been possible.

About the Editors

JOHN H. WALSH

Mr. Walsh was a key regulator at the SEC for 23 years, serving as Chief Counsel and Acting Director of the Office of Compliance, Inspections and Examinations. In that capacity he was instrumental in creating OCIE and one of the key figures overseeing the development of the standards governing securities compliance. In 2016 Mr. Walsh was elected to membership in the American Law Institute, the leading independent organization in the United States dedicated to clarifying, modernizing, and improving the law. Mr. Walsh has a Ph.D. in History from Boston College, and a juris doctor degree from Georgetown University. He is currently a Partner at Eversheds Sutherland and admitted to practice in New York and the District of Columbia.

DAVID H. LUI

Mr. Lui was chair of the industry's trade group, the National Society of Compliance Professionals, and has been a chief compliance officer for some of America's largest investment advisers, including Charles Schwab Investment Management, Franklin Advisers (Franklin Templeton), U.S. Bancorp Asset Management, and Galliard Capital Management, an $85 Billion subsidiary of Wells Fargo. Mr. Lui is currently a Principal with Galliard Capital Management. Mr. Lui is a graduate of Brown University with a bachelor of arts degree with Honors in History and a juris doctor degree from the University of California, Hastings College of the Law. He is admitted to practice in California and Minnesota.

JASON K. MITCHELL

Jason K. Mitchell serves as the CCO for Summit Creek Advisors, LLC in Minneapolis. Mr. Mitchell entered the financial services industry in 1999, and dedicated himself to the compliance profession in 2004. Prior to joining Summit Creek Advisors, Mr. Mitchell served as a senior compliance associate for Galliard Capital Management, overseeing the investment advisory functions of the firm. He also previously served as a compliance manager at U.S. Bancorp Asset Management, where he supervised the firm's compliance training program, as well as code of ethics administration and SEC examination coordination responsibilities. He graduated with a bachelor of arts degree in Economics and Management from the University of Minnesota, Morris.

Foreword

By Marc Wyatt
Former Director, Office of Compliance Inspections and Examinations
U.S. Securities and Exchange Commission

As the former director of the Office of Compliance, Inspections, and Examinations (OCIE) at the Securities and Exchange Commission (SEC), I am honored to be writing the foreword to the second volume of *Modern Compliance.*

During my time at the SEC, I witnessed how investor protection is front and center in everything OCIE does. Based on my time in industry, I believe investor protection should be of paramount importance to all firms operating in the financial services industry. Indeed, how can a firm go wrong by doing what is best for its customers? Growth and profits are generated by producing strong investment returns for clients and fostering a reputation of fairness. These client relationships have the potential to span many decades and different phases of life. It is a noble pursuit: helping the young invest for their first home, helping parents invest so that their children might attend college, helping in the preparation for retirement, and helping current retirees afford to meet the challenges of retirement and the goals of passing on a legacy to their children. In many ways, the government's interests in protecting investors are very much aligned with those of industry as it strives to provide quality services. These interests all intersect in what we call "compliance." But how do we get there?

In my experience, effective compliance requires a blend of leadership, business unit involvement, and a mindset of continuous improvement within a compliance program. The compliance program rules for investment advisers and investment companies became effective in 2004. Although these rules have only just reached their "teenage" years, they have helped to revolutionize compliance practice across the financial services industry; from a regulatory perspective, they were truly game-changers. Among other things, the rules prompted the creation and elevation of the role of chief compliance officer (CCO) at firms, and established requirements such as annual reviews. But perhaps the most important factor driving an organization's compliance efforts is the mindset of its leaders. "Tone at the top" is a powerful predictor of whether an organization has a culture of compliance that permeates the organization. To be effective, compliance must be integrated throughout an organization's business lines; it cannot simply reside in an isolated office or be an afterthought to key business decisions.

Financial services often attract entrepreneurial professionals who look to grow profitable businesses by creating value for their clients. Many readers of this book may find themselves working at firms at which investment professionals are comfortable taking risks and have utmost confidence in their view of appropriate risk/return frameworks. Sometimes these frameworks may not translate into appropriate decisions regarding compliance because these business leaders lack a thorough understanding of what is required under the federal securities laws. Leadership may also become blind to conflicts of interest that cloud their decision making and their interpretation of facts. Effective compliance officers will recognize that these human factors are present in their organizations and work diligently to educate, inform, and persuade business leaders about legal requirements and to help establish best practices in both compliance and firm governance. In short, the effective compliance officer helps others in the organization see what they do, leading to conditions that help an organization's senior leaders set the right tone for the people under them. The most effective compliance officers demonstrate lasting value to their firms by building compliance programs that are adept at identifying and raising both compliance and operational risks to business leaders, by taking steps to design processes to mitigate those risks, and by taking action to address smaller problems before they mushroom into larger ones. The rapid changes we are witnessing in the financial services industry make staying on top of these risks all the more important.

For those securities industry professionals working in organizations with leaders who care deeply about compliance, I hope that you appreciate and value the fact that your organizations are better positioned for success than organizations that are less focused on compliance. A firm that does not value compliance risks the loss of customers, employees, and reputation, as well as faces increased liability and potentially loses the ability to participate in the industry. Strong compliance is good for business!

As a compliance professional, you will have challenges. Sometimes they will feel insurmountable. Sometimes you may be seen as a hurdle to increasing profitability or expanding into new product areas. You likely will be asked to do more with less but asked to make sure you don't "miss anything." You may feel like you have sold the world a lookback option. These are the realities, and it will take patience and resiliency to overcome these challenges and to reach the right balance with the business units pushing or pulling you in directions you are reluctant to go. In sum, working in compliance does have special challenges: tough internal customers, a message that may be unpopular and/or costly, and regular regulatory scrutiny. I think the best advice I can offer to compliance professionals is not to jeopardize your reputation and career for another's reckless desire for short-term profit or purported glory. Although getting to "yes" can sometimes appear critical to a firm's growth or profitability, having the courage to find a better way, or even to say "no," may be imperative to your professional development and preservation—and often, as argued above, to the preservation and growth of long-term profits for the entity. The law will be on your side.

We all are aware of how technology and innovation have changed the markets; the resultant pace of change in how firms operate and how they interact with clients is rapid, and the resulting compliance issues complex and in flux. It is crucial that firms understand how these technological advancements change and shape compliance risks. At the same time, technology is expanding the toolkit for compliance professionals. We have witnessed the development of new tools enhancing firms' abilities to supervise employees and surveil for potential compliance issues. Although it is still early days in the overall evolution of this space, there is a lot of excitement about the ability to use technology more effectively to enhance compliance efforts.

The securities industry is constantly evolving to meet the needs of investors, often at breakneck speed. Your role and responsibilities will likely also expand exponentially. Just as financial technology or "FinTech" is permeating throughout our industry, you may have to deploy regulatory technology or "RegTech" to keep up. As the volume of data and the size of systems increase, you will have to become more efficient and effective about how you identify anomalies, monitor the activities of your employees, and identify suspicious activity. You may also need to include more information technology (IT) professionals in your Compliance and Legal Departments. This is the changing face of compliance. Data analytics, modeling, and detection will become part of your parlance, if they haven't already. Understanding the interplay among these areas and the various business units at your organization is critical. Technology advances will hopefully mean the ability to identify and monitor more information and data, and to automate more functions with big data analytics and artificial intelligence. I encourage you to embrace these emerging solutions as the industry continues to evolve. As one of my favorite poets wrote, "Changes aren't permanent. But change is."

Examiners are often asked to report back on their impressions about the riskiness of the firms they examine. More often than not, firms that have a straightforward business model and can demonstrate an effective compliance program are deemed lower risk, and thus are less likely to receive repeated examinations. Among other things, regulators like to see compliance programs that routinely identify and assess risk, policies and procedures that effectively address risk and compliance with the law, compliance staff who actively take steps to monitor processes and to conduct forensic testing, and meaningful compliance training and educational outreach to firm personnel.

In my experience, examiners recognize that there are no perfect compliance programs, but they expect to see compliance officers who demonstrate that they are engaged in efforts to continually improve their programs. Moreover, the compliance officer who is candid, is straightforward, and discloses the steps that were taken to correct errors, mistakes, and compliance breaches will develop a reputation for trustworthiness. The SEC's website is full of cases in which enforcement actions were taken against firms and individuals who failed in fulfilling their obligations to clients. What is unfortunately not seen are the day-to-day actions of the diligent, reputable individuals serving as compliance officers who are able to keep their firms out of the SEC's crosshairs through well-designed programs, robust implementation, and open dialogue with regulators.

I hope this book, whose contributors include some of the most experienced compliance and legal professionals in the field, will help to inform the choices you make as you work to develop and refine your career as a compliance professional and the compliance program for which you are responsible.

Marc Wyatt is currently the Head of Global Trading at T. Rowe Price. Before joining T. Rowe Price in February 2017, Mr. Wyatt was the Director of the Office of Compliance Inspections and Examinations at the SEC. Prior to the SEC, Mr. Wyatt was a principal and senior portfolio manager of a global multi-strategy hedge fund. Prior to that, he was a senior investment banker in the U.S. and U.K. Mr. Wyatt is a Chartered Financial Analyst. He graduated from the University of Delaware and holds an M.B.A. from Duke University's Fuqua School of Business.

Contents

CHAPTER 24: Conflicts of Interest
By Michael Koffler

CHAPTER 25: The Sides of "May": When Is "May" Deemed False and Misleading?
By Elizabeth M. Knoblock and Patricia Flynn

CHAPTER 26: Plain English Writing for Compliance Professionals
By Lois Yurow

CHAPTER 27: The Seven Deadly Sins: Common Ways Investment Advisers Violate their Fiduciary Duty
By David H. Lui and Jason K. Mitchell

CHAPTER 1

Introduction

By Lisa Crossley
National Society of Compliance Professionals

Compliance professionals do not ask for a lot. They need adequate tools (always a challenge in an age of fast moving technology), adequate staff (should they build for "normal" times, whatever they are, or for when multiple regulatory requests hit them at the same time), adequate support from senior management (tone at the top is not a slogan, it is a reality in the day-to-day work of compliance, in good times and bad), and adequate understanding from regulators (the recent spate of enforcement actions targeting compliance professionals has rightfully sent a wave of concern through the community). Every compliance professional has learned to stretch resources and prioritize risks. Anyone who claims that compliance is overfunded should spend a week walking in our shoes. Compliance professionals, those of us on the inside know, are able to make do because they are thoughtful, informed, and understand the real-world application of a rule, not just its words. It is in this spirit that I am delighted to provide a Forward for the second volume of *Modern Compliance.* First though, let me say a few words about the institution I am privileged to lead.

It is my honor to serve as the executive director of the National Society of Compliance Professionals (NSCP). NSCP is a nonprofit, membership organization dedicated to serving and supporting compliance in the financial services industry. NSCP is for compliance, by compliance. NSCP membership provides the financial services professional from the United States and Canada with a wide range of resources including a vast network of compliance peers, continuing education to further their knowledge and specialized skills, professional standards through our CSCP program and regulatory involvement through representation of compliance interests.

The history of NSCP reflects the recent history of compliance. NSCP was founded in 1986. In its early months it worked hard to attract a few hundred members. Today, membership has grown to more than 2,000. This tenfold increase mirrors the growth of the profession. From an afterthought it has become a central figure in the modern financial firm. In this regard, we should all recognize the work of Joan Hinchman. For several decades Joan served as NSCP's executive director. Under her leadership NSCP's membership and services grew, as did the profile of the compliance profession. I am honored to serve in the same position that Joan developed and made such an important part of the compliance community.

What is modern compliance? No simple answer will suffice. To paraphrase the words of the Securities and Exchange Commission, stated as it adopted compliance rules for funds and advisers, compliance seeks to prevent, detect, and promptly correct violations of applicable laws and rules. Anyone who has worked as a compliance professional would immediately recognize that these are important goals, but stating them is much easier than achieving them. How does one prevent violations? The answer covers a spectrum of behavior ranging from organizational culture, executive leadership, policies and procedures, self-monitoring, and self-testing to individual employees' own sense of ethics and acceptable behavior. In other words, prevention covers a vast range of ground, and its dynamic involves cultural, organizational, and even personal values. That, of course, is only prevention. Detection and prompt correction add additional levels of complexity and require additional expertise. A field like this is not amenable to simple or one-size-fits-all approaches. There is no comprehensive checklist. Instead, each aspect must be approached carefully and in depth. That is why I am pleased to welcome the second volume of Modern Compliance.

In Modern Compliance, each aspect of the practice of compliance receives the attention it requires. Chapters provide background, analysis, professional practices, as well as specific guidance regarding specific compliance topics. Some chapters are applicable to compliance wherever it is practiced, in whatever type of firm. Other chapters home in on the special problems of a particular type of firm or a particular regulator. Each chapter is thoughtful and informed. The book is helpful to established practitioners who want to deepen their understanding of compliance as a profession, as well as to aspiring practitioners who want to learn about the field.

The editors of Modern Compliance, David Lui and John Walsh, have both played active roles with NSCP. Both served on the board of directors, and David served a term as chairman. The contributors writing chapters are compliance thought leaders, and many are also active with NSCP. Reading the chapters one can hear the authenticity of practical experience. I am delighted to see the profession growing and developing through their work.

In addition to being helpful, this book is timely. Every time a compliance professional catches up with the current round of demands, someone moves the goal. It could be a new rule, a new interpretation, a new enforcement sweep, or new policy directions following a political election. Many people read about these developments in the news of the day. They might find them interesting, or not, depending on their personal taste. For compliance professionals these developments are more than interesting news. We live them, because our firms will be held to account for each change in course. In an environment of such uncertainty, bright line or check-the-box thinking will never suffice. Compliance professionals must understand the purpose for their work, the reasoning and policy behind the rules, and the deeper sources of knowledge—even science—supporting their endeavors. To face the ever-present risk of uncertainty, compliance professionals must do more than know. They must understand. From knowledge comes expertise. That is important, but not enough. From understanding comes judgment.

That is the key attribute we all need to successfully navigate changes in direction or nuance. That is why NSCP operates a deep program of training: to help professionals achieve the understanding needed for judgment. That is also why I welcome this book.

In sum, I am pleased to welcome the second volume of Modern Compliance. David, John, their contributors, and NSCP are working together to enhance the practice and professionalism of compliance. I look forward to a continuing relationship and wish them success with Modern Compliance.

ABOUT THE AUTHOR

Lisa Crossley is the Executive Director and for the NSCP. She is responsible for ensuring that the mission of NSCP is fulfilled through programs, strategic planning, and regulatory outreach. Ms. Crossley joined NSCP as its regulatory compliance liaison in 2010, being promoted to Deputy Executive Director in 2013. She has been a member of NSCP since 1993, serving on its board of directors from 2003 to 2006. Her prior professional positions include vice president and chief compliance officer for Spectrum Asset Management, a subsidiary of Principal Global InvesPors, vice president and director of compliance for Nuveen Investments, Inc. where she was responsible for the firm's investment adviser, broker-dealer, and mutual fund compliance programs and associate general counsel and chief compliance officer with Calvert Investments. Ms. Crossley received her bachelor of art degree from the University of Vermont and juris doctor degree from the Catholic University of America, Columbus School of Law.

CHAPTER 2

A History of Compliance

By John H. Walsh
Eversheds Sutherland

I. INTRODUCTION

Modern compliance has a short history. It first appeared in the 1960s, only half a century ago. Indeed, even 50 years seems over-long, because many of compliance's modern features began to emerge only in the 1990s. Given the brevity of its history, it is remarkable how much compliance has developed and changed from its point of origin. The speed of its growth suggests that compliance addresses important contemporary goals.

The historical foundations of compliance suggest several relevant goals. At the deepest level, there is an ancient and worldwide aspiration for voluntary compliance with the public interest. Examples of this type of thinking can be found in both European and Asian traditions. Closer to the surface, when modern financial regulation was first developed, early in the 20th century, two more specific aspirations took shape. The first was a vision of a simple code of ethics that would govern finance. The second was a vision of self-regulation, in which the financial community would regulate itself. Compliance provides a practical solution for achieving all of these goals.

The origins of modern compliance can be dated with precision. It first appeared in the early 1960s, when the securities markets were shaken by a terrible scandal. Regulators and political leadership leapt into action. Investigations, enforcement, a major study, and recommendations quickly followed. Congress enacted legislation imposing liability on broker-dealers when they fail reasonably to supervise persons who commit violations. In this setting, securities firms began to give attention to their own internal enforcement of governing laws and rules. Within a few years these internal processes had become sufficiently widespread among broker-dealers that the United States Securities and Exchange Commission (SEC) undertook to publish its expectations. The SEC organized an advisory committee that issued a *Model Guide for Broker-Dealer Compliance in 1974.* The guide was a seminal work that articulated many of the practical and continuing features of a compliance system. By the 1980s compliance was recognized as an established function within broker-dealers, but at this point, only as a "first line" of law enforcement for the regulators.

In the early 1990s compliance entered a period of intense development and growth. This took several forms:

- Contemporaries settled on certain essential institutional structures, including a designated compliance officer, policies and procedures, access to the highest levels in the organization, and periodic self-evaluations;
- They articulated a mission beyond local law enforcement that included the realization of affirmative values such as creating a preventive control environment and an effective code of ethics; and
- They extended compliance into multiple fields including global financial regulation, criminal law enforcement, bank regulation, corporate governance, health care, public company financial disclosure, and the regulation of asset managers.

Moreover, contemporaries began to debate the nature of compliance: was it inherently supervisory, inherently advisory, or something else? By the middle of the first decade of the twenty-first century compliance had grown into a highly articulated function that had been deployed across multiple sectors.

Recognition of compliance began to follow. This recognition took various forms: regulators stepped forward to protect compliance in the midst of the financial crisis; a global association of regulators recognized its value; and the United States Congress began to incorporate compliance into major legislation as a tool of public policy. Perhaps most importantly, regulators, industry groups, and others began to recognize that compliance is a unique field that must be endowed with certain key characteristics, including senior level governance, objectivity, and independence. There were missed opportunities. Nonetheless, the trend toward recognition has been unmistakable, including, most recently a multinational initiative to publish a global standard for compliance management.

After a half-century of accelerating development, compliance has become a dynamic and highly institutionalized field of endeavor with distinctive structures and characteristics. No longer simply a "first line" of enforcement for a single regulator, compliance provides a unique and independent service across multiple sectors. Compliance practitioners work every day with systems and practices that deliver compliance with the public interest and ethical standards. Through self-control of business, by itself and for itself, compliance is achieving true self-regulation.

Nonetheless, much work remains to be done. Compliance remains divided into multiple discrete areas defined by the rules or standards with which practitioners work. Many compliance practitioners and the firms they work for continue to see themselves as craftsmen, who apply specific tools to specific problems, instead of professionals, who share a common professionalism with other compliance practitioners around the globe. Perhaps the greatest challenge facing compliance today is to recognize that despite its multiple internal specializations, it is one field, one practice, and one profession. Perhaps the next major development in the ongoing history of compliance will be practitioners' recognition of their own shared professionalism across all of these specialized fields.

II. FOUNDATIONS

Modern compliance is built on deep foundations. Some stretch back thousands of years. From ancient times, voluntary compliance with the public interest has been seen as a positive and even inspiring value. These values reside at the roots of many contemporary ideas, including modern compliance.

The ancient Greeks believed the laws of the *polis* should be constructed to foster and enhance voluntary compliance, because it was through such compliance that citizens grew in virtue and reason. A modern commentator has described Aristotle's views:

> Voluntary compliance is essential to the law attaining its fundamental end of making citizens virtuous, or in other words of enabling them to fulfill their *telos* [or purpose] by helping them become rationally self-governing in their dealings with other people. If legislation does not take place in a way that encourages and permits voluntary compliance or consent, then it is inconsistent with the attainment of its citizens' ends, and is thus unjust.[1]

Hence, voluntary compliance is not simply submission to the dictates of the state. Rather, it is an essential element in the creation of a virtuous and rational society. Legislation should contemplate voluntary compliance, so that citizens can respond accordingly. Understood in this light, law creates a potential for reason and virtue, and voluntary compliance realizes and implements that potentiality among the citizens.

Ancient values regarding voluntary compliance were not limited to Europe. They can also be found in Asian thinking. Confucius taught that compliance obtained through the threat of punishment is insincere and unstable; those threatened with punishment will always find ways to circumvent such laws.[2] True social harmony—in Confucius's words, the harmonious oneness of heaven and humanity—comes from voluntary inner compliance with moral principles, known collectively as *li.* These principles are inculcated through training and education, establish moral expectations, and have a self-disciplinary effect on individuals. In ancient China most commercial relationships were regulated by *li*, not punitive law, and disputes were resolved through self-reflection, self-regulation, compromise, and the voluntary acceptance of decisions made by clans, guilds, and business associations. Again, rather than simple submission to the punishing power of the state, voluntary compliance with *li* was the expression of an individual's harmony with society. Modern scholars are reconsidering these Confucian ideals in the hope of creating commercial regulations in China that are suited to its culture and traditions.[3] The aspiration for voluntary compliance is so deeply seated in cultural and

---

1 Randall R. Curren, 22 *Reason Papers* 144, at 147 (Fall 1999) (emphasis in original) (review of Fred D. Miller, Jr., *Nature, Justice, and Rights in Aristotle's Politics*, Oxford University Press, 1995).

2 Angus Young, *Conceptualizing a Hybrid Approach in Enforcement and Compliance in China: Adopting Responsive Regulation and Confucian Doctrines to Regulate Commerce* (August 10, 2013), available online.

3 *Id.*

intellectual norms that any selection of examples seems invidious. Countless other instances could be cited from ethics, philosophy, theology, or political science. This general approbation of voluntariness gives compliance much intuitive appeal. But we need not limit ourselves to theoretical values. Compliance is ultimately a practical hands-on venture, and its inspiration should be found in practical values. With this in mind, perhaps the best example of the foundational goals animating the history of compliance will be found in a conversation between two consummate men of the world.

In the early 1930s, at the birth of national financial regulation in the United States, two senior executives met to discuss the financial crisis then gripping the country. Securities markets were crashing, banks were failing, and unemployment was surging. One of the executives, the newly elected president of the United States, proposed a solution to the other, the president of the New York Stock Exchange. Ethics—and what we would today call compliance—played a central role.

A Simple Code of Ethics

In April 1933, shortly after his inauguration as president of the United States, Franklin D. Roosevelt met with Richard Whitney, president of the New York Stock Exchange. The only record of the meeting is a follow-up letter Whitney sent to President Roosevelt.[4] Hence, our understanding of the conversation is entirely based on Whitney's description. Nonetheless, Roosevelt's policy vision for the financial sector can be heard in Whitney's words.

Roosevelt raised the possibility of the New York Stock Exchange adopting a code of ethics—simple enough, he said, for the public to understand. He also told Whitney that he hoped the code "might become a universal standard." The two presidents spent some time talking about how regulations adopted by the New York Stock Exchange could be made applicable to other exchanges. Whitney expressed some doubt about whether any code for the securities business could be made simple enough for the public to understand. But he assured Roosevelt that the vast majority of the exchange's members were "anxious to put the security business on a higher plane than it has ever been before."[5]

This conversation is remarkable on several levels. First, in the midst of the financial crisis of the early 1930s, the two presidents spoke of an ethical code and placing business on a higher plane. They explicitly considered ethics as a pragmatic policy solution. Second, they spoke of making the code a universal standard. To some extent this was a reflection of the power of the New York Stock Exchange. Given his position, Whitney could influence other market centers and actors. Beyond that, however, their discussion showed that the two presidents were reaching beyond the exchange and seeking to remake business at large into a new image. Third, although they did not use the term compliance, we can see it in their conception of the code as something so simple

[4] Letter of Richard Whitney to Hon. Franklin D. Roosevelt (April 14, 1933), unpublished letter available in the archives of the Franklin D. Roosevelt Presidential Library and Museum, Hyde Park, New York.

[5] For a more detailed discussion of the historical context in which this conversation occurred, *see* John H. Walsh, "A Simple Code of Ethics: A History of the Moral Purpose Inspiring Federal Regulation of the Securities Industry," 29 *Hofstra Law Review* 1015, 1039–40 (2001).

even a layperson would understand. Whitney questioned whether this was possible, and experienced compliance professionals may agree. Yet, the conception of the code as something simple suggests both voluntariness (it should be simple to understand and simple to follow) and visibility (onlookers should be able to appreciate that it is being followed). This is a powerful policy vision: ethical, universal, simple: and demonstrable.

Although Roosevelt's vision of a simple code of ethics played a role in the early development of financial regulation in the United States,[6] it did not lead immediately to modern compliance. Several more decades would pass before compliance appeared on the scene. Nonetheless, this vision reflects an aspiration that compliance could eventually fulfill. Could finance be governed by its own internal ethical code?

The conversation between the two presidents revealed another concept that has had a foundational role in modern compliance. Roosevelt asked Whitney whether the New York Stock Exchange could develop the simple code. In other words, at least in its initial expression, the code would be a creation of the private sector. This expressed the contemporary idea that finance should regulate itself.

Self-Regulation

In early 1933, during the same period in which he discussed the simple code of ethics with President Whitney of the New York Stock Exchange, President Roosevelt was embarking on a major initiative to bring self-regulation to the American economy. The National Industrial Recovery Act of 1933[7] established the National Recovery Administration (NRA). The NRA sought to eliminate unfair trade practices through mandatory codes of fair competition prepared by trade associations, subject to NRA approval.[8] The NRA applied to the entire economy, and hundreds of codes were adopted. As part of this adoption effort, an Investment Bankers Code Committee prepared a code of conduct for the securities business. This code contained provisions that continue to play a role in financial regulation, including broker-dealers' obligation to adhere to "just and equitable principles of trade," and their duty to consider the suitability of investments when making recommendations to customers. The NRA, however, did not survive. In 1935 the Supreme Court held that it was unconstitutional.[9] Roosevelt's expansive vision of an entire economy subject to self-regulation had failed.

The failure of the NRA did not end self-regulation in finance. During the heyday of the NRA, Congress had enacted the Securities Exchange Act of 1934, which provided for self-regulation by securities exchanges, such as the New York Stock Exchange.[10] Moreover, when the NRA was disbanded, the Investment Bankers Code Committee voluntarily remained in operation and worked to obtain legislation authorizing self-regulation that passed constitutional muster. In 1938 the Securities Exchange Act was

---

6 *Id.*

7 National Industrial Recovery Act, Ch. 90, 48 Stat. 195 (1933).

8 For a more detailed discussion of these events *see* Walsh, *A Simple Code of Ethics*.

9 *A.L.A. Schechter Poultry Corp. v. United States,* 295 U.S. 495, 550 (1935).

10 Securities Exchange Act of 1934, Ch. 404 § 6, 48 Stat. 881, 885–886 (1934).

amended to authorize securities associations, and the committee reorganized itself as the National Association of Securities Dealers (NASD),[11] which has since been reorganized into a successor organization known as the Financial Industry Regulatory Authority (FINRA). Roosevelt's vision lived on in finance.

Self-regulation had much in common with the simple code of ethics. Both sought to elevate business to a new level, higher, in Whitney's words, than it had ever been before. With a code, business people would adhere to a standard of conduct, and with self-regulation other business people would enforce that adherence. The legacy of this effort can be seen in modern standards of conduct, including those first developed by the Bankers Code Committee, and others since. Moreover, it was upon these foundations—ethics and self-regulation—that compliance would eventually be built.

III. ORIGINS

In the early days of national financial regulation in the United States, contemporaries seem to have divided the business community into two groups: people who were honest, and people who were not. The purpose of self-regulation was to muster the support of the former in controlling the latter. A 1938 statement by Senator Alben Barkley, who was later vice president of the United States, captures this understanding:

> While I know that most of the people in the banking business are honest and would need no regulation or supervision, I know as well that there are some who, because of incompetency or a careless regard of fair practices, need the influential guidance of government supervision...the 1938 self-regulatory law described in § 2.02[B] above is written upon the theory that regulation can best be achieved by the efforts of honest brokers and dealers themselves.[12]

In this environment, attention was focused on how honest business people could regulate others who were less so. The major breakthrough that led to modern compliance took place when honest people began to recognize that they needed to keep an eye on themselves. Self-regulation, they came to understand, should be internalized within each firm.

Special Study of the Securities Markets (1963)

In early 1960, serious violations of the securities laws came to light at the American Stock Exchange, then the second largest stock exchange in the country. A member firm, Re, Re and Sagarese, and the father and son who controlled it, Jerry and Gerard F. Re, were accused of wide-ranging misconduct. They had distributed securities in violation of the registration requirements, delivered prospectuses containing false and misleading

---

[11] Securities Exchange Act Amendments of 1938, Ch. 677, 52 Stat. 1070 (1938).

[12] Senator Barkley, Extension of Remarks, 83 Congressional Record 790 (1938) (capitalization conformed).

information, made purchases on the basis of undisclosed material information, engaged in inappropriate transactions as specialists on the exchange, failed to maintain required books and records, manipulated the prices of securities, and more.[13] The SEC initiated an enforcement action, expelled the two Res from the business, and revoked their firm's registration as a broker-dealer.[14]

As often happens in the aftermath of a scandal, regulatory attention quickly turned from the misconduct to the conditions that had allowed it to occur. In the spring of 1961 the SEC announced that it would conduct an inquiry of the American Exchange "to see why," in the words of a member of the SEC staff, "it was possible for something like this to happen."[15] At the time, the investigation was described as "the most extensive of its kind" since the 1930s.[16]

Congress, however, decided an even more comprehensive review of conditions in the securities industry was in order. On September 5, 1961, Congress enacted an amendment to the Securities Exchange Act authorizing and directing the SEC to make "a study and investigation of the adequacy, for the protection of investors, of the rules of national securities exchanges and national securities associations, including rules for the expulsion, suspension, or disciplining of a member for conduct inconsistent with just and equitable principles of trade."[17] The chairman of the SEC indicated that it would include a "new and comprehensive look" at exchange practices in a number of areas.[18] The study's director, Milton Cohen, later remembered that the scandal at the American Stock Exchange had been the principal thing Congress had in mind when it decided that the SEC should look at the total industry.[19]

A special staff of the SEC conducted the study, which was eventually known as the "Special Study of the Securities Markets." The SEC's chairman later indicated that the intent of the study had been to give special focus to the integrity of broker-dealers and their salesmen. "It is the broker-dealers," he said, "employing these salesmen, who must bear a responsibility of maintaining the necessary standards by adequate supervision. Responsible conduct on the part of broker-dealers and their salesmen can, and should be, our keystone."[20] The study was a priority for the agency. By the fall of 1962, the SEC indicated that it would curtail the expansion of other operations to fund the study's completion.[21]

---

[13] A summary of the case can be found at: *Securities and Exchange Commission News Digest* (Aug. 25, 1960).

[14] *See Securities and Exchange Commission News Digest* (May 5, 1961).

[15] *See* "SEC to Probe Am. Exchange; Rules, Policies, Practices to Be Scrutinized," *Chicago Daily Tribune*, page B5 (May 15, 1961).

[16] *Id.*

[17] SEC, *Report of the Special Study of the Securities Markets of the Securities and Exchange Commission*, Part 1, page 1 (Apr. 3, 1963) (hereinafter cited as "Special Study Report").

[18] *See* William L. Carey, Chairman, SEC, *Speech to the Investment Bankers Association of America*, page 12 (Nov. 28, 1961).

[19] Milton Cohen, statement at *The Roundtable of the 1963 SEC Special Study*, SEC Historical Society, transcript at pages 15–16 (Oct. 4, 2001).

[20] SEC, *Special Study Report* at 7.

[21] "SEC May Delay Enforcement Step-Ups to Obtain Funds for Stock Market Study," *Wall Street Journal*, page 8 (Oct. 16, 1962).

In the event, the study group issued its report in 1963. Contemporaries noted that the reaction of the securities industry was "amazingly quiet."[22] So quiet, in fact, that as the report was issued it was headline news that members of the investment community declined to comment.[23] They did, however, take it seriously. The New York Stock Exchange, for example, established five special committees to analyze the study's recommendations.[24] Indeed, the most noteworthy controversy was a public spat between the chairman of the SEC and the study's chief counsel. The chairman described the report as "mild," and the chief counsel took issue.[25] The controversy would be nothing more than a footnote, except it revealed the thinking of the study staff. The chief counsel was concerned that the mild characterization would have an adverse effect upon the prospects that the study's recommendations would be carried out, including, "one of the most important recommendations of the study…its suggestions for upgrading standards for securities salesmen."[26]

In fact, the study had paid careful attention to the standards applicable to securities salesmen. The starting point was the ethical standards they currently followed. The report found they used multiple inappropriate practices.[27] These abuses included "come-on" and "bait" advertising, "cold turkey" telephone calls, "boiler room" organizations, the use of special compensation to generate intense selling efforts, self-dealing, and more.

The problems documented by the study, the chairman of the SEC reported to Congress, resulted from "inadequacies in established enforcement machinery, both government and industry."[28] His language was significant. The problems arose because of inadequate "enforcement machinery." Moreover, the machinery was in "government and industry" alike. This revealed the study's fundamental vision of how to address abusive practices. Problems arose because of a lack of enforcement, which should include enforcement by the industry itself. This vision would characterize compliance for years to come.

Beyond the failures of enforcement, the study discussed existing methods of supervision and control within firms over selling practices. Broker-dealers, the study noted, had the ultimate responsibility for the conduct of their agents and employees.[29] The study went on to identify several of the controls used by the better firms to implement this responsibility, including through line managers, centralized oversight, review of transactions, oversight committees, internal audits, firm policies, approved lists, and even, at the largest firms, the use of "electronic data processing equipment (EDP)" to provide a daily "run" of information about transactions. In transmitting the Special

[22] David G. Mutch, "SEC Study Lauded," *Christian Science Monitor,* page 13 (Apr. 18, 1963).

[23] Robert E. Nichols, "SEC Study Evokes Icy 'No Comment,' Investment Community Cautious in Reacting to Lengthy Report," *Los Angeles Times,* page B8 (August 4, 1963).

[24] "Five Special Big Board Groups Reviewing Recommendations of SEC's Staff Report," *Wall Street Journal,* page 2 (Oct. 21, 1963).

[25] Arelo Sederberg, "Terming SEC Study 'Mild' Seen Unfair," *Los Angeles Times,* page C7 (Nov. 14, 1963).

[26] *Id.*

[27] *Special Study Report,* at 237 *et seq.*

[28] Letter of Transmittal of the Report of the Special Study of the Securities Markets, William L. Carey, Chairman SEC, to the President of the Senate and the Speaker of the House of Representatives (Apr. 3, 1963).

[29] *Special Study Report,* at 290 *et seq.*

Study Report to Congress, the chairman of the SEC said these voluntary efforts by responsible firms should be made generally applicable in regulations.[30]

In the immediate aftermath of the study, the SEC recommended to Congress that it enact new legislation requiring securities firms to internalize regulation through more effective supervision of their agents and employees.[31] Congress did so by authorizing the SEC to bring disciplinary actions against supervisors who failed to supervise reasonably persons who commit violations. These provisions, applicable to broker-dealers and investment advisers, have played a role in securities regulation ever since.[32]

Through the attention it gave to internalized responsibilities and controls, the Special Study of the Securities Markets played a critical role in the development of compliance. It shows an interesting trajectory. It began by investigating a failure by a traditional self-regulator: the American Stock Exchange. Then, as soon as the study staff began to examine the standards and practices of securities salesmen, their attention moved to a new type of self-regulation: the responsibilities and controls internalized within each securities firm. Years later, in a roundtable sponsored by the SEC Historical Society, study Associate Director Ralph S. Saul cited the development of compliance as one of the study's major accomplishments.[33] He said, "Setting up the whole supervisory compliance structure within firms, I think a lot of that is due to the Special Study. We emphasized that." Other observers have agreed that it was in the 1960s and 1970s that a small number of practitioners first began to create the compliance function within broker-dealers.[34]

Model Guide to Broker-Dealer Compliance (1974)

In the years after the Special Study of the Securities Markets, responsible broker-dealers worked to implement its recommendations. They began to draft compliance manuals, including, at one major firm, an "original 1971 manual" that served as the backbone of all that was to come.[35] As this work unfolded, the SEC decided that it had a role to play.

In early 1973, G. Bradford Cook, chairman-designee of the SEC, announced that an initiative to prepare a model compliance program for broker-dealers had begun in October 1972 as a cooperative venture with the regulated community.[36] In the near future, he said, an industry advisory group would submit its recommendations. The

---

30 *Special Study Report* at pages III–IV.

31 *See* House Report No. 1418, to accompany H.R. 6793 (May 19, 1964).

32 The provisions regarding firms are now codified at Securities and Exchange Act § 15(b)(4)(E) and Investment Advisers Act § 203(e)(6). The provisions regarding individual supervisors are now codified at Securities and Exchange Act §15(b)(6) and Investment Advisers Act § 203(f).

33 Ralph S. Saul, statement at *The Roundtable of the 1963 SEC Special Study*, SEC Historical Society, transcript at pages 55–56 (Oct. 4, 2001).

34 Edward H. Fleischman, Commissioner, SEC, *Perspectives from the Commission Table: Supervision; Address to the Compliance and Legal Division Seminar of the Securities Industry Association* (Apr. 5, 1989).

35 *Id.*

36 G. Bradford Cook, Chairman-Designee, SEC, *Keynote Address to PLI's "The SEC Speaks Again"* (Feb. 23, 1973).

goal was not to change the SEC's rules, but rather to conduct an educational project on existing requirements and day-to-day practices in the brokerage industry.

In early 1974 the advisory committee issued a public draft,[37] and in late 1974, it submitted its report to the SEC.[38] The report indicated that the objective of the advisory committee, as defined by the SEC, had been to provide an awareness of existing requirements and to suggest procedures by which the industry could comply with them. Participants in the effort had included securities firms, such as Merrill Lynch & Co., Inc., Goldman Sachs & Co., Baker, Weeks & Co., Inc., and First Southwest Company, as well as self-regulators, including the New York Stock Exchange, NASD, American Stock Exchange, and Midwest Stock Exchange. The committee had held 50 days of meetings to discuss the drafts and the report was 272 pages long. As the advisory committee noted, the size of the final report demonstrated the length and complexity of its undertaking.

The Guide to Broker-Dealer Compliance, or "Model Guide" that issued from the advisory committee's work bears a striking resemblance to countless compliance manuals since. It contained nineteen topical sections devoted to supervision, registration, financial and operational responsibility, customer accounts, oversight of branch offices, advertising and sales literature, investment advisory services, private placements, proprietary trading, research and recommendations, underwriting, as well as several more devoted to specific types of securities products. Each section had three parts: a statement of applicable laws or regulations, special problems arising in the area, and compliance procedures for addressing the problems.

Many of the procedures in the Model Guide would be familiar to compliance practitioners in the early 21st century. The guide contained checklists, outlines for interviews, specific controls, training, periodic inspection visits, forms to complete, due diligence information to collect and consider, regional compliance personnel, and similar procedures. Perhaps most suggestive of future developments, it contained a chapter on electronic data processing (EDP), with a discussion of compliance controls over manual input of data, review of printouts, consideration of "special computer codes to highlight certain types of accounts," and the possibility of using EDP for regulatory filings.

The SEC's Model Guide initiative demonstrates the energy and creativity of compliance. Within a decade of the Special Study, an array of compliance controls had been developed, deployed, debated by leading representatives of the business community, and included in the Model Guide. When viewed as indicative of what compliance practitioners did, and continue to do, the Model Guide was a landmark development. One could view much of compliance's later history as an elaboration on the controls first set out in the Model Guide.

---

37 "SEC Panel Issues Draft of Its Compliance Guide," *Wall Street Journal*, page 4 (Jan. 28, 1974).

38 *Guide to Broker-Dealer Compliance, Report of the Broker-Dealer Model Compliance Program Advisory Committee to the Securities and Exchange Commission*, Securities Exchange Act Release No. 11,098, 5 SEC Docket 472 (Nov. 13, 1974). A copy of the full report is available in the SEC Library.

On another level, though, the Model Guide also demonstrated contemporaries' perception of compliance. The Model Guide's treatment of the "compliance official" is revealing in this regard. The guide said:

> The Compliance Official of a broker-dealer is the person or persons vested by management with the ultimate authority and responsibility for supervisory controls and procedures designed to achieve compliance by the broker-dealer and associated persons with applicable securities laws, rules and regulations. The term "Compliance Official" does not denote a particular management or supervisory person, but rather it is used as a term of description to identify the person to whom authority and responsibility is delegated, regardless of the office he holds in the business entity involved.[39]

In other words, the compliance official was the manager responsible for achieving compliance. As the guide put it, the official must be "vested with sufficient authority and full support [of] senior management so that he is fully empowered to carry out his responsibilities successfully."[40]

The Model Guide appears to have intended the compliance official to be a member of senior management, because it stated that ultimate responsibility for compliance rested with senior management.[41] The guide also compared compliance to supervision, and the contrast is noteworthy. Supervisory responsibility could be delegated, and the term "supervisory person" meant those "subordinates" to whom such responsibilities had been delegated.[42] The perception this conveys identifies the compliance official as among the senior managers of the firm, and the supervisory person as among the subordinate officials, such as office manager, resident manager, sales manager, or administrative manager.[43] In short, in this sense, compliance described a function of senior line management: achieving regulatory compliance. It was not a specialized function within the firm dedicated to compliance. Indeed, the Model Guide expressly contemplated that this function would be assigned to persons holding other offices.

In the 1970s, when the Model Guide was created, compliance was seen primarily as a body of procedures for enforcing substantive rules or standards. One could summarize the overall approach of the guide as identifying rules and enforcing them. It was not a specialized function managed by specialized experts. Quite the contrary, it was assigned to senior managers of the firm who were often expected to hold other offices as well. Nonetheless, when viewed from the perspective of the shop floor, where specific procedures were applied to specific issues, broker-dealer compliance had taken a significant step forward.

---

39 *Guide to Broker-Dealer Compliance*, at 2–3.

40 *Guide to Broker-Dealer Compliance*, at 3.

41 *Guide to Broker-Dealer Compliance* at 2.

42 *Guide to Broker-Dealer Compliance*, at 2 and 49, note 1.

43 *Id.*

Compliance in the 1980s

By the 1980s, compliance had acquired several years of practical experience and had grown and flourished in many broker-dealer firms. Indeed, by the end of the 1980s, the work of the prior decades was already taking on something of the air of compliance's heroic period.

In a 1989 speech, Edward Fleischman, a commissioner of the SEC, spoke about the progress of compliance.[44] He noted the small number of practitioners in the 1960s and 1970s who had first begun to mold the compliance and legal functions within their firm and to draft the early compliance manuals. From those earliest days, he said, compliance had been working "to deploy new tools, to perform even more effectively, and to convey to line management (and to regulators) an articulate perspective on the profitability of compliance." The spirit penetrating a compliance conference, he said, should be pride: "pride in all that's been accomplished in the [last] quarter century."

These sentiments demonstrated the progress compliance had made since the publication of the Special Study of the Securities Markets. The original manuals had been developed and expanded until the earlier work served only as a backbone for larger and more sophisticated bodies of practice. Nonetheless, when we examine what contemporaries meant by compliance, we find that their understanding of compliance had hardly advanced beyond the days of the study and Model Guide. Compliance, in the contemporary understanding, remained an enforcement mechanism.

In the mid-1980s Aulana Peters, a commissioner of the SEC, articulated a vision of compliance that expressed the contemporary understanding. She was speaking about the SEC's enforcement program, and in doing so she described it to be like a pyramid. The SEC was at the top, she said, self-regulatory organizations for broker-dealers were in the middle, and finally, at the bottom, were the securities firms.[45] Because the SEC did not have the resources to pursue every violation, the commissioner said, the commission had to rely on brokerage firms as its "first line" of defense "to police their own ranks."

The commissioner's speech provided a powerful simile for the work of compliance. So powerful, in fact, that it would long outlive the 1980s. Even decades later, from time to time some of the images it expressed reemerge into public discourse. One must ask, however, what it means. As a simile for compliance, the pyramid communicates three propositions.

First, compliance is a police activity. The commissioner stated this two ways. Compliance was a substitute for SEC enforcement, and the SEC relied on broker-dealers to police their own ranks. In American terms, the police power has special meaning, because it is a power identified by the U.S. Constitution and conferred on the states to enforce

---

[44] Fleischman, *Perspectives from the Commission Table*.

[45] Aulana L. Peters, *Investor Protection: The First Line of Defense: Address to Brooklyn Law School's Securities Regulation Symposium* (Mar. 15, 1985).

their own laws and regulation.[46] Within any legal regime, however, the police power can readily be understood as a coercive exercise of public or governmental authority. In short, in this view, compliance did within the firm—coercive enforcement—what the government could do to the firm.

Second, compliance is at the bottom of a hierarchy. The image of a pyramid suggests both that compliance practitioners outnumbered regulators and self-regulators, and also that compliance was secondary, and even tertiary to them in regards to status. The commissioner heightened this imagery in her speech by calling compliance the "first line" of defense. Much like a Roman Legion of old, for which the first line was occupied by the youngest and least trained soldiers, with the better and more experienced soldiers in the second and third lines behind, the image of a first line continues to suggest lesser rank and skill.

Third and finally, the commissioner communicated that compliance's highest value was to serve as an agent of the regulators "higher-up" in the hierarchy. If, she suggested, the SEC had the resources to pursue every violation on its own, compliance would be unnecessary. It was only because the regulator lacked sufficient enforcement resources that compliance had a role.

The image of compliance expressed in Commissioner Peters' speech is unmistakable. Compliance was a police activity conducted by low-status personnel who served as local enforcement agents for the regulators. Indeed, one should emphasize, this was the image communicated by someone who was otherwise—at least judging by the remainder of her speech—a friend of compliance who rose to speak on its behalf. In this environment, one can understand why business managers and line personnel might view compliance as an outside imposition on their activities.

Many of the themes of Commissioner Peters' simile can be found in other contemporary statements regarding compliance. Public officials emphasized that firms' internal efforts were necessary to "stretch" the SEC's "thin resources."[47] SEC Chairman John Shad, who challenged the private sector to exercise more responsibility for its own ethics,[48] spoke of how compliance, specifically in regards to insider trading, could "continue to assist" the regulators, through a "joint assault of the securities industry and the Enforcement Division of the SEC."[49] Formal statements of the SEC, such as in an opinion issued by the full commission sitting as an adjudicative body, spoke of compliance as a form of enforcement: that is, as a responsibility of firms in which they must have the internal power and authority to compel compliance with applicable standards and requirements.[50]

---

46 United States Constitution, 10th Amendment.

47 Bevis Longstreth, commissioner SEC, *The Duty to Supervise: Self-Discipline Within the Securities Firm: Remarks to the Fifteenth Annual Rocky Mountain State-Federal-Provincial Cooperative Securities Conference* (Oct. 29, 1982).

48 In addition to serving as chairman of the SEC, John Shad was a leader in advocating business ethics.

49 John S.R. Shad, chairman SEC, *The SEC and the Securities Industry, Speech to the Securities Industry Association* (Dec. 2, 1981).

50 *In the Matter of Prudential-Bache Securities, Inc.,* 48 S.E.C. 372 (1986).

In the 1980s regulators also began to see opportunities to extend compliance to other areas. In 1985 the director of the SEC's division responsible for asset managers gave a speech in which she coined a phrase that would resonate for years: "Good compliance is good business."[51] Yet, when one looks behind the phrase, the speech itself mostly deals with the SEC's own regulatory actions such as its compliance inspections, its rulemaking and application processes, and a proposal then under consideration for a self-regulatory organization for investment advisers. The director only briefly mentioned firms' internal compliance. Firms must stress it, she said; they must keep their procedures up to date; and resources spent on new product development and marketing must be matched with more resources spent on compliance. Hence, the speaker suggests, even as good business, compliance remained secondary to regulatory activity.

Finally, in a hint of the development of compliance in following years, in the late 1980s Congress responded to a wave of insider trading scandals by enacting compliance requirements for broker-dealers and investment advisers. In 1988, the House Committee on Energy and Commerce noted that insider trading was a "serious problem in our securities markets."[52] The Committee went on to express concern about "the types of procedures Wall Street firms have in place to prevent insider trading violations given the great numbers of firm employees who have access to potentially invaluable confidential information and the apparent ease with which that information can be disseminated."

The time had come, the House Committee concluded, to require broker-dealers and investment advisers to design effective procedures to restrict and monitor access to highly sensitive materials, and prevent insider trading. The result was the Insider Trading and Securities Fraud Enforcement Act of 1988 (ITSFEA).[53] Codified at Section 15(f) of the Securities Exchange Act (now at Section 15(g)), and Section 204A of the Investment Advisers Act, the act required broker-dealers and investment advisers to "establish, maintain, and enforce written policies and procedures reasonably designed, taking into consideration the nature of such broker's [or adviser's] business, to prevent the misuse...of material, nonpublic information." In 1990, the SEC staff issued a report entitled "Broker-Dealer Policies and Procedures Designed to Segment the Flow and Prevent the Misuse of Material Nonpublic Information."[54] The report described the steps firms were taking to implement ITSFEA, including training, employee trading restrictions, physical barriers to separate departments, and surveillance procedures. The staff concluded that although firm procedures varied widely "in scope and comprehensiveness," certain minimum procedures were needed including: the maintenance of watch lists and restricted lists, review of employee and proprietary trading, documentation of procedures, and an active and responsible role for compliance.

---

[51] Kathryn McGrath, director Division of Investment Management SEC, *Good Compliance Is Good Business: Keynote Address to the 1985 ICI/SEC Procedures Conference* (Oct. 31, 1985).

[52] H.R. Rep. No. 100-910, at 13 (1988).

[53] P.L. No. 100-704, 102 Stat. 4677 (1988).

[54] SEC Division of Market Regulation, *Broker-Dealer Policies and Procedures Designed to Segment the Flow and Prevent the Misuse of Material Nonpublic Information.* (Mar. 1990).

By the late 1980s compliance had established itself in the broker-dealer community. Practitioners could look back with pride on all they had achieved, and ideas were already circulating about how compliance might apply in other areas, such as among asset managers. Moreover, Congress's response to the wave of insider trading cases in the 1980s hints at the future development of compliance. In ITSFEA Congress responded to a concern about a problem in the securities markets with requirements for better compliance. This response would be seen again, repeatedly, after 1990. Yet, at the same time, compliance was the bottom level of a regulatory pyramid. Nonetheless, despite this low starting position, in the coming years compliance would experience remarkable growth and development.

IV. DEVELOPMENT

In the early 1990s, compliance began to develop and grow with remarkable speed. It was an idea whose time had come. Perhaps like other ideas whose time suddenly arrives, compliance began to spring up in multiple locations, with multiple applications, and no apparent sense that individual efforts were part of a larger movement. Time and again, political leaders, task forces, prosecutors, commissions, regulators, courts, and others announced a newfound appreciation for compliance, as if no one had ever noticed it before. Only rarely, and only late in this period of ferment and growth, were efforts made to survey the movement as a comprehensive whole. It all began with a policy initiative directed from the highest level of global political leadership.

FATF Recommendation 20 (1990)

In July 1989, the heads of state or government of the seven leading industrial powers, known as the Group of Seven (G-7), held a summit in Paris. The conference was called the Summit of the Arch because it was held at the top of the newly constructed Grande Arche de la Defense. This was the fifteenth meeting of the G-7. Delegates in attendance included the president of host France, the presidents of the United States and the European Commission, the chancellor of West Germany, and the prime ministers of the United Kingdom, Canada, Italy, and Japan.

The summit addressed a variety of contemporary problems including: managing the debt of the world's poorest countries, the decline in rates of savings, the Uruguay round of trade negotiations, the environment, and drug issues.[55] In regards to the latter, the summit found that the "drug problem has reached devastating proportions." It stressed "the urgent need for decisive action, both on a national and an international basis." Among other initiatives, the summit decided to convene a financial action task force from summit participants and other interested countries to consider "additional preventive efforts" that could be taken "to prevent the utilization of the banking system and financial institutions for the purpose of money laundering."

---

[55] G-7 Paris Summit, *Economic Declaration* (Paris, July 16, 1989).

The task force, known as the Financial Action Task Force (FATF), was established in Paris under French presidency, and immediately began operations.[56] During the following months its membership was expanded to include additional countries. The task force also moved quickly to prepare recommendations for fighting money laundering. In April 1990, less than a year after its formation, the FATF issued a report containing forty recommendations.[57] A month later, in May 1990, the task force's member nations endorsed the report at the ministerial level.

Most importantly, in Recommendation 20, FATF endorsed the idea that financial institutions should develop internal programs to prevent money laundering. Moreover, FATF set out the minimum elements that each financial institution's program should contain. The recommendation stated:

> 20. Financial institutions should develop programs against money laundering. These programs should include, as a minimum:
>   a. The development of internal policies, procedures and controls, including the designation of compliance officers at management level, and adequate screening procedures to ensure high standards when hiring employees;
>   b. An ongoing employee training program; and
>   c. An audit function to test the system.

Although short and to the point, this recommendation was a powerful statement on the essential elements of a compliance program. Moreover, the institutional structure it described for compliance could be universally applied. It was inherently scalable and flexible. Every element could be adjusted depending on the size and nature of the firm. This provided an open-architecture for a compliance program that could be given any number of specific applications within specific firms.

After 1990, FATF has revised its recommendations several times. Nonetheless, each time it has preserved the statements in the original Recommendation 20 in one form or another. In 1996 and 2003 it renumbered the Recommendation, first to number 19 and then to number 15. Then, in 2012, FATF moved its text from the recommendations to the interpretative notes, where it now resides.[58] However, FATF's later treatment of this recommendation is less significant than its role in establishing a global model for compliance in the early 1990s.

FATF Recommendation 20 has played a significant role in the history of compliance. FATF's endorsement of internal programs with certain universal elements gave compliance credibility around the world. As a matter of prestige, FATF stood close to the

---

[56] A history of the origins of FATF can be found in *Financial Action Task Force on Money Laundering, Report 1990–1991* (Paris, May 13, 1991).

[57] *The Forty Recommendations of the Financial Task Force on Money Laundering 1990.*

[58] The current recommendations can be found in: *International Standards on Combatting Money Laundering and the Financing of Terrorism & Proliferation: The FATF Recommendations* (Paris, Feb. 2012). The relevant text appears in the interpretative notes to Recommendation 18.

pinnacle of global political leadership, and was supported by the leading economic nations of the world. As a matter of education, FATF worked actively in the years after 1990 to spread the implementation of its recommendations throughout the world economy. Finally, as a matter of enforcement, states that failed to cooperate were listed as "non-cooperative countries or territories," and every effort was made to treat them as pariahs in the global financial community. By 2014 only a handful of countries remained on the uncooperative list. Thanks to FATF, the desirability of internalized compliance—specifically in regards to antimoney laundering—has become a familiar concept around the world.

United States Sentencing Guidelines (1991)

The next major step in the development of compliance took place in the United States when a domestic commission issued guidelines on the appropriate sentences for business organizations convicted of criminal misconduct. The commission, known as the United States Sentencing Commission ("Sentencing Commission"), had been established by an act of the United States Congress in 1984. Over the next several years it held public hearings and issued public analyses of its goals. In 1987 it began issuing guidelines for sentencing individual defendants. Then, in November 1991, it issued guidelines for sentencing business organizations.

The guidelines for organizations were set out in Chapter 8 of the United States Sentencing Guidelines Manual (USSG Manual).[59] They operate by assigning points to a defendant's misconduct to create a culpability score, and then subtracting points known as mitigating credit to obtain a final score.[60] A source of mitigating credit was the business organization's compliance program. Moreover, the Sentencing Commission explained what a minimally effective program should contain. It did so by setting out seven key elements.

First, the organization must have standards and procedures to prevent and detect criminal conduct. As with FATF Recommendation 20, and indeed, the SEC's Model Guide for broker-dealers, policies and procedures were at the heart of the standards set out in the USSG Manual.

Second, the organization's governing authority must be knowledgeable about the content and operation of the compliance and ethics program, and must exercise reasonable oversight. A specific person within high-level personnel must be assigned overall responsibility for the compliance and ethics program, and day-to-day operational responsibility should be delegated to an individual who will report to higher-level personnel. The compliance program should be given adequate resources, appropriate authority, and direct access to the governing authority of the firm (or an appropriate

---

59 United States Sentencing Commission, *Federal Sentencing Guidelines Manual*, Chapter 8, "Sentencing of Organizations, Part B, Remedying Harm from Criminal Conduct, and Effective Compliance and Ethics Program" (1991).

60 A short summary of the guidelines can be found at Paula Desio, Deputy General Counsel, United States Sentencing Commission, *An Overview of the Organization Guidelines* (no date given).

subgroup thereof). This level of detail regarding compliance governance made the USSG Manual unique. Unlike prior guidance, the manual set out a specific chain of command, with a senior official, day-to-day manager, as well as resources, funding, authority, and reporting access.

Third, reasonable efforts should be made to not give substantial authority to an individual who has engaged in illegal activities or other conduct inconsistent with the compliance and ethics program. Of course, the screening of employees had played a role in both prior broker-dealer compliance and the FATF recommendation.

Fourth, the organization should take reasonable steps to communicate its standards and procedures, and conduct effective training programs appropriate to individuals' respective roles and responsibilities. Again, training was deeply engrained in prior compliance.

Fifth, the organization should conduct monitoring and auditing to ensure the compliance and ethics program is followed, and provide mechanisms for confidential or anonymous internal reporting or guidance. The organization will also periodically evaluate the program's effectiveness. Internal monitoring was inherent in compliance from its earliest days, and the idea of periodic evaluations had also been recommended by FATF.

Sixth, the compliance and ethics program should be consistently promoted and enforced through both incentives and discipline. This was an interesting aspect of compliance that had not received much prior attention. It would quickly come to be known as a "culture of compliance." The USSG Manual recognized that compliance includes both internal promotion and dealing with those who fall short.

Seventh, after criminal conduct has been detected, the organization should take appropriate steps to respond and prevent any similar conduct. One could expect this element to be given prominence in the USSG Manual because, as a source of sentencing guidelines, one can assume the manual would only be considered after some serious problem had occurred.

As can be seen, the USSG Manual reflected many previous developments in compliance. Nonetheless, it also presented new features that warrant special note. For example, the manual provided a much more detailed outline for compliance governance than previous sources. It also spoke to both compliance and ethics and included cultural concerns that could be overlooked if compliance is viewed solely as an enforcement mechanism. Finally, the manual focused on how a firm behaves after a problem is discovered, which highlighted compliance's role in crisis management.

The USSG Manual has played a role in many criminal proceedings. The Sentencing Commission reports that since the guidelines were implemented more than 1 million defendants—individual and organizational—have been sentenced under them.[61] The manual has also drawn litigation, including before the United States Supreme Court.

---

[61] *An Overview of the United States Sentencing Commission,* available online.

In 2005 the Court ruled that the detailed guidelines were voluntary for judges, that is, they could consider them but need not strictly follow them.[62] Finally, the manual's influence has spread beyond sentencing. Standards similar to those in the manual can be found in the principles federal prosecutors use to determine whether to bring charges against organizations.[63]

Beyond criminal proceedings, the guidelines have had a significant impact on compliance. The USSG Manual laid out a well-developed institutional structure for compliance, including policies and procedures, governance and management, employee screening, training, monitoring, a culture of compliance, and crisis management. In addition, the guidelines created incentives for adopting a compliance program. In the words of William W. Wilkins, Jr., chairman of the Sentencing Commission, the guidelines helped establish a "carrot and stick" approach.[64] The guidelines, he said, were intended to provide "incentives for organizations to establish meaningful compliance programs."

The USSG Manual played a crucial role in the development of compliance in the United States. It had an immediate impact. Press and commentators followed the progress of the Sentencing Commission and the guidelines, and emphasized how compliance programs could help companies avoid criminal prosecution, even when the programs were unsuccessful.[65] Twenty years after the guidelines were adopted an independent review of their application found that the guidelines had "achieved significant success in reducing workplace misconduct by nurturing a vast compliance and ethics movement and enlisting business organizations in a self-policing effort to deter law-breaking at every level of their business."[66] Much like FATF's promotion of the basic structure of compliance throughout the world, the USSG guidelines served to promote the fundamental structures and goals of compliance throughout the business community in the United States.

Arthur James Huff and the Nature of Compliance (1991)

In the early 1990s, an SEC enforcement case challenged the contemporary understanding of compliance. The legal question presented was whether a broker-dealer compliance official was a supervisor and responsible for the misconduct of an employee. As discussed above,[67] after the Special Study of the Securities Markets of the 1960s, the U.S. securities laws had been amended to make broker-dealers liable for the violations of supervised persons, if they had failed to supervise them reasonably. The enforcement case in the early 1990s addressed what this legal standard meant when applied to a

---

62 *U.S. v. Booker*, 543 U.S. 2200 (2005).

63 *See* Principles of Federal Prosecution of Business Organizations, Title 9, Chapter 9-28.800.

64 "Plan on Corporate Crime," *The New York Times*, page D2 (Oct. 29, 1990).

65 Daniel B. Moskowitz, "Compliance Programs Could Help Companies Avoid Criminal Prosecution," *Washington Post*, page 13 (Apr. 23, 1990).

66 Ethics Resource Center, *The Federal Sentencing Guidelines for Organizations at Twenty Years, A Call to Action for More Effective Promotion and Recognition of Effective Compliance and Ethics Programs: Report of the Ethics Resource Center's Independent Advisory Group on the 20th Anniversary of FSGO* (2012).

67 *See* § 2.03[A.].

compliance officer. As a matter of law, the case did little to resolve the issue, and the law of supervision remains unsettled to this day when applied to compliance professionals. Regardless, the case marked a turning point in the history of compliance.

Arthur James Huff worked in the Compliance Department of a major broker-dealer.[68] A securities salesman in the firm's Miami branch office engaged in a major fraud. The salesman conducted an investment scheme called either an "arbitrage" or a "short term trading" program and ran up millions of dollars in losses, mostly through trading options. He concealed these results from his customers by intercepting the broker-dealer's accurate account statements and sending customers fake versions of his own. The salesman was eventually caught, convicted of a criminal offense, and sentenced to ten years in federal prison.

Huff had been given certain responsibilities regarding options, including being named senior registered options principal (SROP), a position required by the broker-dealer's self-regulatory organization.[69] In various informal documents, such as an educational handbook, the SRO had suggested that an SROP had supervisory responsibility. When the salesman's misconduct came to light, the SEC staff charged the salesman's branch manager, regional manager, and Huff with a failure to supervise. The branch and regional managers settled the charges, leaving only Huff to contest them.

The SEC action against Huff was carried out in two steps. First, it was tried before an administrative law judge (ALJ); then the case was appealed to the commissioners who sat as a panel of adjudicators. Both the ALJ[70] and the commission[71] issued written decisions on the merits of the case. As the case made its slow progress—the commission ruled more than three years after the ALJ—it posed the question, what is compliance?

Before the ALJ, Huff described his duties as advisory in nature. He said he was responsible for developing and implementing policies, setting up compliance guidelines, reviewing activity in options accounts on a selective basis, preparing policies and procedures, following through on options situations when there were appearances of a concern or problem, investigating options problems and complaints, having in place supervisory procedures for the review of large or active options accounts, and assisting branch managers. This was a different activity, he said, than the "line supervision" provided by the firm's business managers, such as the branch manager in the Miami office. As a contested legal issue, within the enforcement action, Huff concluded from this that he was not a supervisor, and therefore not liable for the rogue salesman's violations.

The ALJ disagreed. The Compliance Department, he said, "As its very name suggests, is an integral part of the supervisory process, particularly in a large geographically dispersed" firm such as Huff's employer. Moreover, the ALJ said, Huff's employer

---

68 *In the Matter of Arthur James Huff,* Initial Decision of SEC Administrative Law Judge (Dec. 15, 1987) (hereinafter cited as "Huff, ALJ Decision").

69 In this case the self-regulator was the Chicago Board Options Exchange (CBOE), the primary U.S. market for trading options.

70 Huff, ALJ Decision.

71 *In the Matter of Arthur James Huff,* 50 S.E.C. 524 (Mar. 28, 1991)(hereinafter cited as "Huff, SEC Decision").

considered the Compliance Department an integral part "of the 'team' that shared responsibility for ensuring compliance by and supervision over" both the salesman and the branch manager. In short, the ALJ said, line officers and compliance personnel shared supervisory responsibilities. The ALJ also noted Huff's position as SROP, and said it "would be a travesty of the self-regulatory process" to ignore the self-regulatory organization's description of the position as supervisory. The ALJ found Huff liable for failure to supervise and suspended him from the brokerage business.

The sanction against Huff drew considerable attention, particularly because it was rare for the SEC to target compliance officials. In press coverage on the case, even the head of the SEC regional office that had prosecuted Huff admitted that it was "pretty unusual, in that there aren't that many cases against individual officers of compliance departments."[72] The enforcement action may have been rare, but within its historical context, the ALJ's analysis was highly conventional. One could see it as an echo of the SEC's Model Guide of the 1970s, which had described the compliance officer as the senior manager designated by the firm to provide supervision and ensure compliance. With this understanding of compliance, as the ALJ notes, its "very name" signifies supervisory responsibility. Moreover, the ALJ's decision revealed a deep commitment to the self-regulatory context in which compliance had emerged in the 1960s and had been understood through the 1980s. The broker-dealer's self-regulator had apparently intended this particular compliance position to have supervisory responsibility, and, in the ALJ's words, it would be a "travesty" to defeat that self-regulatory purpose.

If the Huff case had ended here, with the ALJ's decision, it would have marked a moment of continuity, even though the case itself had been rare. But Huff appealed the decision to the full commission. This gave all of the parties an opportunity to revisit their arguments. In addition, the Compliance and Legal Division of the Securities Industry Association (SIA), a broker-dealer industry group, submitted a friend-of-the-court brief.[73] The SIA questioned whether compliance officers should ever be deemed supervisors. Compliance practitioners, the SIA said, are advisors, not supervisors. They provide support, guidance, and systems to those charged with line management, but they do not have the power to hire, fire, reward or punish employees. In 1991 the commission issued its decision. The result can best be described as a muddle.

One of the commissioners recused himself from the decision, and the other four split evenly into two groups of two. All four agreed that the case should be dismissed, and it was. But each of the two groups had its own reasons and wrote its own opinion. As a result, as one of the four commissioners later said, "Huff is a difficult case to make much sense out of with these two somewhat disparate opinions."[74] The first opinion declined to decide whether Huff was a supervisor, and instead held that regardless of

---

[72] "Paine Weber Inc. Compliance Aide Suspended by SEC," *Wall Street Journal*, page 29 (Dec. 22, 1987).

[73] A 1988 statement by the head of the SIA's Legal and Compliance Division summarizing the argument was quoted in Fleischman, *Perspectives from the Commission Table*.

[74] Richard Y. Roberts, *Failure to Supervise Liability for Legal and Compliance Personnel: Remarks to the Securities Law Committee of the Federal Bar Association* (Dec. 7, 1992) (hereinafter cited as "Roberts, 1992 Speech").

his responsibilities, under the particular facts of the case, his actions were reasonable.[75] The second opinion, on the other hand, held that he was not a supervisor because he did not control the salesman, and therefore the commission need not consider whether his conduct was reasonable.[76] Despite the muddle, the decision marked a turning point for compliance for two reasons.

First, all four commissioners rejected the ALJ's reasoning that the self-regulatory process was a paramount consideration. With varying levels of analysis both opinions held that the views of the self-regulator did not control their assessment of whether Huff was a supervisor. Anne Flannery, a distinguished attorney who later served as the CCO of a major broker-dealer, helped represent Huff in his appeal to the commission. She indicates that a key part of the strategy on appeal was to focus on the statutory requirements for supervision.[77] In the early 1990s, Flannery indicated, compliance's regulatory and legal structure was relatively undeveloped. By focusing on the statutory requirements for supervision, Huff's legal team could argue that the self-regulator's position was relevant, but not binding in any respect. The commission agreed. The self-regulator's view, all four commissioners agreed, did not control their determination of the compliance position's legal responsibility. From a historical perspective—at least symbolically—one could see this as the moment when compliance began to emerge from the bottom layer of the enforcement pyramid. Compliance, the commissioners suggest, was not inherently below and subordinate to the traditional self-regulators.

Second, all four commissioners, again with varying levels of analysis, addressed the ALJ's reasoning that compliance was inherently supervisory. Three visions of compliance were before them. The ALJ reasoned that compliance's supervisory nature was suggested by its "very name." At the opposite extreme, the SIA argued that compliance was inherently advisory, and therefore necessarily never supervisory. In the middle was Huff's defense team. Flannery remembers that Huff's attorneys had "something of a difference of opinion" with the SIA over this point. Instead of arguing that compliance was inherently advisory, Huff's attorneys argued that although compliance was mostly advisory, there were circumstances under which it could be supervisory, but in the presenting case there was no evidence that the rogue broker had ever been subject to Huff's supervision. This more nuanced approach carried the day. Two of the commissioners opined that Huff was not a supervisor, which rejected the ALJ's view, and all four stated that their decisions were not based on the function Huff performed (i.e., "as a staff compliance officer"), which rejected the SIA's view. Instead, two of the commissioners opined, Huff's ability to control the salesman's behavior was the decisive question, irrespective of the department in which he worked. Again, from a historical perspective—here more than symbolically—one could see this as the moment when compliance began to emerge from its origins in the Special Study and the early compliance programs that had been designed to address the supervisory obligations

75 Huff, SEC Decision (opinion of Chairman Breeden and Commissioner Roberts).

76 Huff, SEC Decision (opinion of Commissioners Lochner and Schapiro).

77 Interview with Anne Flannery (Nov. 2014). Interviews will be cited only once. Absent further citation, all following quotations or references to the statements of the same individual are based on the interview.

that had resulted therefrom. Compliance, the commissioners found, was not simply another name for supervision.

The Huff case has an interesting historical legacy. One could say that the most important statements it made about the nature of compliance were purely negative. Unlike the views of the ALJ and the SIA, the SEC's opinion suggests that compliance has no special nature. Indeed, in the opinion of the two commissioners who most thoroughly considered these issues, the nature of compliance was irrelevant: The same supervisory "control" standard would apply to compliance practitioners as would apply to anyone else. Of course, in light of compliance's early history, this negative statement was a powerful message.

In the immediate aftermath of the Huff case, the SEC took up other cases involving legal and compliance personnel. Although those cases had important legal implications, they had less of a role in marking historical changes within compliance. However, the legacy of Huff lingered in public discourse. For example, in 1992, SEC Commissioner Roberts, who had joined the opinion finding that Huff had acted reasonably, gave a speech in which he continued to blast the SIA's view of the nature of compliance.[78] He said: "At a minimum the proposition that a…compliance officer could never be deemed a supervisor should be laid to rest." In 1993 SEC Commissioner Schapiro, who had joined the opinion holding that Huff was not a supervisor, also returned to the topic, and reiterated the view that legal responsibility should follow actual responsibility.[79] She said: "In the 1990s, compliance and legal personnel are part of the life blood of securities firms and have had to adjust to that reality….Increased actual responsibility in some cases may mean greater legal responsibility." From a historical perspective, her most noteworthy observation may have been that compliance had entered broker-dealers' "lifeblood."

Interagency Standards for Bank Safety and Soundness (1995)

In the mid-1990s compliance came to bank regulation. As with its arrival in broker-dealer regulation three decades before, the rise of compliance was born in an atmosphere of crisis. In this case, the crisis focused on retail banks and savings and loan associations (S&Ls), a type of retail bank in the United States that takes deposits and primarily provides home mortgage loans.

In the 1980s rising interest rates had posed a financial challenge to many retail banks and S&Ls. With most of their assets invested in fixed-rate, long-term mortgages, the S&Ls were unable to respond to customers' demand for higher interest rates for their deposits. This created a maturity mismatch: The banks were raising funds through demand deposits, which were vulnerable to fluctuations in short term interest rates; and they were investing those funds in long-term mortgages with fixed interest rates. Caught by sharply rising interest rates, numerous institutions failed. As they failed,

---

[78] Roberts, 1992 Speech.

[79] Mary Schapiro, commissioner, SEC, *Remarks at the National Association of Securities Dealers, Inc., Sixth Annual Education Seminar* (Oct. 5, 1993).

serious abuses were revealed across the sector, including fraud, accounting irregularities, self-dealing, extravagant compensation, poor lending decisions, and more. This led to multiple enforcement actions, criminal convictions, and widespread public disgust. This environment was quickly labeled the "S&L Crisis."

To respond, the U.S. Congress passed legislation requiring bank regulators to establish operational and managerial standards for a variety of relevant practices, including loan documentation, credit underwriting, asset growth, and compensation for bank and S&L insiders, such as directors, officers, and employees.[80] In the United States, bank regulation is conducted by a number of different agencies: the Board of Governors of the Federal Reserve System, the central bank; the Federal Deposit Insurance Corporation (FDIC), which administers the national deposit insurance program; the Office of the Comptroller of the Currency (OCC), which regulates national banks; and the Office of Thrift Supervision (OTS), which at that time regulated S&Ls. In July 1995, the agencies jointly released the new standards.[81]

The joint Standards for Safety and Soundness focused on the specific controls identified by Congress in the enabling legislation. These were the primary areas in which misconduct had occurred. However, the standards also addressed compliance on a more generalized level. Two aspects of this generalized statement warrant note.

First, the joint Standards addressed compliance with applicable laws and regulations. Initially, each of the substantive standards had recited that it included compliance with applicable laws and regulations. Then, in the final text, the regulators stated that repetition in each substantive standard was unnecessary. As a result, the regulators included a single statement requiring "compliance with applicable laws and regulations." The agencies explained, "The express requirement to ensure compliance with applicable laws and regulations is a necessary standard for internal controls and information systems."

Second, the joint standards addressed the bank regulators' practice of imposing compliance plans. The standards stated that if an institution failed to meet any of the standards, the relevant regulator could require it to submit an acceptable plan to achieve compliance. Such compliance plans would be required, the agencies said, when the failure to meet one of the standards was of such a severity that that it "could threaten the safe and sound operation of the institution." In addition, as the agencies noted, they would likely take additional supervisory actions until the deficiency had been corrected, including possible enforcement action.

The bank regulators' compliance plans illustrate an alternative path in the development of compliance. Unlike the sector-wide developments seen with broker-dealers, compliance plans were imposed on individual banks after an institution had otherwise

---

[80] Federal Deposit Insurance Corporation Improvement Act of 1991 (FDICIA) § 132, 105 Stat. 2236 (Dec. 19, 1991) (adding a new Section 39 to the Federal Deposit Insurance Act).

[81] Office of the Comptroller of the Currency, Board of Governors of the Federal Reserve System, Office of the Comptroller of the Currency, and the Office of Thrift Supervision, *Standards for Safety and Soundness*, 60 *Federal Register* 35674 (July 10, 1995).

failed to meet applicable standards. This individualized remedial approach would play a role in other sectors as well.

Development of the joint Standards for Safety and Soundness mimicked, to a remarkable degree, the historical process in which compliance had initially emerged. A crisis shakes existing institutions: in this case, retail banks and S&Ls. High-level public policy, again led by the U.S. Congress, requires action to prevent a recurrence. Then, specialized regulators take action both to address the specific issues that led to the crisis and to require more generalized compliance with applicable laws and regulations, hopefully to address future and yet unidentified problems. Compliance, at least at the regulatory level, was becoming an attractive policy response to crises.

In re Caremark International **(1996)**

By the mid-1990s, compliance was spreading far beyond its origins among broker-dealers. In 1996, a state court decision was handed down that introduced it into corporate governance. Specifically, the decision indicated that a board of directors, the most senior internal supervisory body for most large businesses in the United States, could escape private liability for corporate misconduct if it had exercised a good faith judgment that the corporation had a reasonable compliance system.

State courts in the United States play a critical role in corporate governance, because the laws of a corporation's state of domicile govern its practices. In this regard, the State of Delaware is especially important. It claims to be the home of 50 percent of all U.S. public corporations and 64 percent of the largest 500.[82] Caremark International, Inc., was a public company domiciled in the State of Delaware.[83] As a result of its domicile, claims by the company's shareholders against its board of directors were judged in the Delaware courts.

In 1994, a group of Caremark's shareholders claimed that the directors had breached their duty of care when they failed to exercise appropriate attention and had allowed the company to engage in a pattern of violations that eventually drew regulatory and criminal sanctions. Specifically, as a healthcare provider Caremark entered into contracts with doctors that were problematic under the Anti-Referral Payments Law. That law prohibits the payment of referral fees for patients whose medical bills are paid with government funds under the public health insurance programs known as Medicare and Medicaid. Instead of referral fees, Caremark paid referring doctors for other services, such as monitoring patients, consultations, and research. The Delaware court noted that these payments were not illegal in and of themselves, but they did raise the possibility of unlawful "kickbacks." The inspector general of the U.S. Department of Health and Human Services (HHS) conducted an investigation of the payments; federal criminal prosecutors eventually joined in; and Caremark pled guilty on a charge of mail fraud, paid a criminal fine, and made civil reimbursements, all of which totaled approximately $250 million. The shareholders did not claim that the board of directors knew about

[82] These statistics are made available by the Delaware Department of State, Division of Corporations.

[83] *In re Caremark, Inc.,* Derivative Litigation, 698 A. 2d 959 (Del. Ch. 1996).

the wrongful conduct. Instead the shareholders alleged that the directors were ignorant of the misconduct, and therefore, the shareholders said, liable for their inattention or negligence. Rather than contesting the claims, the directors entered into a proposed settlement with the shareholders, which under Delaware law had to be approved by the court.

This procedural background has some bearing, because the historical importance of the Caremark decision has dwarfed its legal authority. The judge decided only whether the proposed settlement was fair. But the reasoning by which he arrived at that conclusion had a dramatic impact on compliance.

The judge said that when a claim is made against directors predicated on the directors' ignorance of wrongful conduct, "in my opinion only a sustained or systematic failure of the board to exercise oversight—such as an utter failure to attempt to assure a reasonable information and reporting system exists—will establish the lack of good faith that is necessary to establish liability." In other words, the board will avoid liability if it exercises a good faith judgment that the corporation's "information and reporting system is in concept and design adequate to assure the board that appropriate information will come to its attention in a timely manner as a matter of ordinary operations, so that it may satisfy its obligations."

The judge then considered whether Caremark had such a system. In his decision the judge noted that Caremark had a "Guide to Contractual Relationships" that prohibited the misconduct under investigation; had issued an ethics manual; conducted internal training; had an internal audit plan designed to assure compliance with its business and ethics policies; established new policies requiring local branch managers to secure home office approval for certain transactions; and had appointed a compliance officer. In sum, the judge held, Caremark's information systems appear to have represented a good faith attempt to be informed of relevant facts. "If," he concluded, "the directors did not know the specifics of the activities" that led to liability, "they cannot be faulted." He approved the settlement ending the litigation.

Contemporaries viewed the *Caremark* opinion as creating "an incentive to create compliance systems to detect corporate wrongdoing."[84] One lawyer quoted in the press described the opinion to say: "Look, Mr. Director, you're going to have to take compliance seriously."[85] Moreover, the opinion had added weight because of Delaware's importance as a domicile for United States corporations. Much like the USSG Manual, the *Caremark* decision made compliance relevant to any type of business, especially, in this case, the largest corporations, many of which are incorporated in Delaware.

Open Letter to Health Care Providers (1997)

Caremark's problems with the Anti-Referral Payments Law illustrate the complexity of the legal regimes in which many businesses operate. From time to time particular

---

[84] Dean Starkman, "Compliance Ruling May Shield Directors," *Wall Street Journal*, page B5 (Dec. 24, 1996).

[85] Starkman, "Compliance Ruling," quoting Kirk S. Jordan.

lines of business draw heightened regulatory concern and enforcement. In the early 1990s, health care providers like Caremark found themselves under intense scrutiny. A series of investigations by the inspector general of HHS led to criminal actions against multiple providers. Violations included fraudulent claims on public medical insurance programs, kickbacks, violations of laws governing medical referrals, and others. In 1997 HHS addressed these problems with a compliance initiative.

In early 1997, HHS's inspector general was June Gibbs Brown. She had previously served in the Department of Justice, where she had worked with the Sentencing Guidelines, and with the mandatory compliance programs often required in the settlement of criminal actions against business organizations. In February, she issued *An Open Letter to Health Care Providers* that described a comprehensive regulatory compliance program.[86]

The 1997 letter was brief but to the point. It had three major elements. The first invited health care providers to join her in a national campaign to eliminate fraud and abuse from Medicare, Medicaid, and other health and human development programs. The second warned that her office had been given new resources to combat health care fraud, such as investigative and audit staff, and that it was pursuing "an intensified crackdown." She was committed, she said, to "vigorously pursue civil and criminal action against those who defraud this nation's health care programs." Finally, in the third element, she turned to compliance. Her office, she said, had been meeting with representatives of health care provider groups to draft model compliance programs. The effort had already led to the preparation of general guidelines containing the fundamental elements of any health care compliance program. Soon, she indicated, it would produce sector-specific models for each component of the health care community, such as clinical laboratories.

Although the letter did not recite the fundamental elements to which Inspector General Brown alluded, the first model was made available to the public the following month. In March 1997 HHS published model compliance guidance for clinical laboratories.[87] The model was notable for two reasons.

First, it stated that it was based on the inspector general's fraud investigations and the requirements imposed on clinical laboratories in corporate integrity agreements. These agreements were compliance obligations imposed on individual health care organizations following the inspector general's determination that they had violated the health care laws, such as, for example, by submitting false invoices for medical services, paying medical referral fees, and so on. The practice of entering into these agreements has continued, and in recent years more than 30 companies remain subject to them.[88] In practical terms, these agreements have created an ad hoc compliance structure for affected firms much like the Compliance Plans administered by bank regulators.

---

[86] June Gibbs Brown, *An Open Letter to Health Care Providers*, HHS Inspector General, Open Letter 02-1997 (Feb. 1997).

[87] Office of Inspector General HHS, *Publication of the OIG Model Compliance Plan for Clinical Laboratories*, 62 *Federal Register* 9435 (Mar. 3, 1997).

[88] Office of Inspector General HHS, *Focus on Compliance: The Next Generation of Corporate Integrity Agreements* (Aug. 27, 2012).

Second, the model described a compliance program with many familiar elements. They included written policies and procedures, in this setting including standards of conduct for lab employees and for limiting tests to those that are medically necessary; oversight of relations with physicians, including ongoing monitoring of those who direct both publically insured and other business to the same lab; controls over billing and marketing; record retention; naming a chief compliance officer; audits; corrective action; training; and more. The following year, HHS issued another model guide, this time for hospitals.[89] Since that time, several more have followed.

Beyond its specific messages, the Open Letter's tone and tenor were noteworthy. Inspector General Brown indicated that she and her staff were "committed to creating an atmosphere that encourages voluntary compliance and self-disclosure by health care providers." She admitted that "compliance programs are not a novel idea." Nonetheless, she indicated, "They are becoming increasingly popular as affirmative steps toward promoting a high level of ethical and lawful corporate conduct." Numerous providers had expressed an interest in them to protect their operations, and, she said, when her office or the Department of Justice investigate health care fraud, they would consider the entity's compliance efforts when considering the level of sanctions and the penalties that should be imposed.

Three years later, Inspector General Brown issued another open letter describing the progress of her compliance initiative. Her Open Letter of 2000[90] reported that the number of guidelines had risen to seven. In addition to clinical laboratories and the hospital industry; new guidelines had been issued for home health agencies; third-party billers; the durable medical equipment, prosthetics, orthotics, and supply industry; hospice providers; and Medicare+Choice organizations. Others were in store, such as one for the nursing home industry. Her successors in the position have continued the practice of issuing open letters, and they continue to discuss health care compliance and regulatory issues of interest to the health care community.

Inspector General Brown's Open Letter of 1997 and the following model guidance set out a complete regulatory program for health care compliance. It stated the regulator's policy of fostering compliance; described the regulator's specific expectations, in this case, through model compliance guidelines published in cooperation with the affected business segment; and revealed how the standards would be enforced, in this case through HHS's Corporate Integrity Program.

The introduction of compliance to the health care sector was a major development for compliance. At one level, it showed how compliance was reaching into new areas of human activity. A field initially developed to control the sales practices of securities salesmen had reached medical practitioners. At another level, the entry of

---

89 Office of Inspector General HHS, *Publication of the OIG Model Compliance Program Guidance for Hospitals*, 63 *Federal Register* 8987 (Feb. 23, 1998).

90 June Gibbs Brown, *An Open Letter to Health Care Providers*, HHS Inspector General, Open Letter 03-02-2000 (Mar. 9, 2000).

compliance into medicine showed how pervasive compliance was becoming in the modern economy. Health spending has been estimated to constitute approximately 17 percent of the gross domestic product of the United States, and significant percentages of other countries as well.[91] Entering this field was a major extension of compliance's reach.

The Sarbanes-Oxley Act (2002)

In the early years of the twenty-first century, financial markets were rocked by the failure of several leading businesses. Enron, a giant energy company, went bankrupt amid allegations of accounting and securities fraud. Leading executives would later be indicted, and some spent time in prison. At the time, it was the largest bankruptcy in history. Enron's collapse led to calls for regulatory reform. However, as Senator Paul Sarbanes, at the time chairman of the Senate Banking Committee later recalled, the pressure for reform quickly began to dissipate.[92] Then, WorldCom, an even larger communications company, went bankrupt and assumed the title of largest bankruptcy in history. Its CEO would eventually find himself in prison. After WorldCom failed, Senator Sarbanes recalled, everything changed in Washington, and everyone was in "full roar." Even the president demanded immediate action. The result was the Sarbanes-Oxley Act of 2002,[93] named for Senator Sarbanes and his colleague in the House of Representatives, Congressman Michael Oxley.

The act, often called "SOX," focused on financial accounting and internal controls. It contained a number of provisions, including a new self-regulatory organization for auditors, new grounds to sanction individuals who interfere with an audit, and many more. Most relevant to the history of compliance, it required senior executives to certify to the accuracy of their company's financial statements[94] and required companies to prepare an annual report on their internal controls, which would be audited by the company's outside auditors.[95]

As a result of the certification and internal control requirements, many companies established internal processes in which lower level employees certified the accuracy of information up to the executives, who were required to prepare the statutorily mandated certification. Special units, sometimes in the Compliance Department, were often created to manage the certification process and address any exceptions or problems that were uncovered. Many companies also undertook major initiatives to review their internal controls and prepare the reports that would be subject to audit. Risk control frameworks were highlighted. For example, the Committee of Sponsoring Organizations of the Treadway Commission (COSO) had promulgated risk control guidance

---

[91] The World Bank, *Health Expenditure, Total (% of GDP)* (2015).

[92] Joseph Nocerra, "For All Its Cost, Sarbanes Law Is Working," *The New York Times,* page C1 (Dec. 3, 2005).

[93] Sarbanes-Oxley Act of 2002, 116 Stat. 745 (July 30, 2002).

[94] Sarbanes-Oxley, § 302.

[95] Sarbanes-Oxley, § 404.

in the 1990s that drew renewed attention after SOX. COSO had described internal controls as having five interrelated components.[96] They were:

- The control environment, which set the tone for the organization and the foundation for other controls, including how employees are assigned and controlled, firm culture, and the attentiveness of the board of directors;
- A risk assessment, which was a mechanism for identifying the firm's objectives and associated risks;
- Control activities, which are policies and procedures to ensure that management directives are carried out;
- Information and communication, which includes both the flow of clear messages down from leadership and providing employees with a means to provide important information upward; and
- Monitoring, which includes both ongoing monitoring and separate evaluations, or audits.

In many firms, implementing SOX resulted in a chain of certifications and newly enhanced internal controls reaching from deep in the organization up to the senior executives and auditors.

SOX focused primarily on financial reporting, but it had a dramatic impact on compliance. Indeed, in its aftermath surveys reported 80 percent of participating companies planned to update their compliance initiatives because of SOX.[97] One observer, whose firm conducted annual compliance surveys, was *quoted* in the press saying: "It's like a newfound religion has formed around SOX compliance."[98] Many large public companies hired their first CCO.[99] SOX also had an impact on the tools used by compliance professionals. A variety of providers stepped forward with enhanced electronic monitoring tools, such as tools designed to detect expense account fraud.[100] Certification programs were developed to train company employees.[101] Boot camp ethics programs taught how to spot fraud.[102] In the aggregate, billions of dollars were spent, with one survey estimating the total at $3.5 billion[103] and another estimating that approximately $1 million was spent on compliance for every $1 billion in revenue.[104] As a professor at Stanford University Law School noted, "Compliance is becoming an industry unto itself."[105]

---

[96] COSO, *Internal Control—Integrated Framework* (1992 and 1994).

[97] Eve Tahmincioglu, "Profiting from Cures for the Sarbanes-Oxley Blues," *The New York Times*, page C5 (Dec. 29, 2005).

[98] Tahmincioglu, "Profiting from Cures" (quoting John Hagerty).

[99] Harry Hurt III, "Drop That Ledger! This Is the Compliance Officer," *The New York Times*, page B5 (May 15, 2005).

[100] Paul Burnham Finney, "Gotcha! Software, Tools Can Catch Expense-Account Padders (and Make Filing Easier)," *The New York Times*, page C8 (June 27, 2006).

[101] Tahmincioglu, "Profiting from Cures."

[102] Melinda Ligos, "Boot Camps on Ethics Ask the 'What Ifs'," *The New York Times*, page BU12 (Jan. 5, 2003).

[103] Tahmincioglu, "Profiting from Cures."

[104] Hurt, "Drop That Ledger!"

[105] Hurt "Drop That Ledger," quoting Joseph A. Grundfest.

SOX contained another requirement that warrants note: codes of ethics. Section 406 of the act directed the SEC to issue rules requiring public companies to disclose whether they had adopted a code of ethics that applies to its senior financial officers, and if the company had not adopted such a code, to explain why not. When the SEC adopted rules, it extended the code to cover the Chief Executive Officer (CEO) as well as the financial officers.[106] The SEC indicated that it seemed reasonable to do so, because the CEO is a superior official to the financial officers. It also defined a code of ethics and established standards for company to follow when disclosing it to the public.

The SEC defined a *code of ethics* as an assembly of written standards that are reasonably designed to deter wrongdoing and promote five goals. Those goals were:

- Honest and ethical conduct, including the ethical handling of actual or apparent conflicts of interest between personal and professional relationships;
- Full, fair, accurate, timely, and understandable disclosure in reports filed with the SEC as well as in other public statements;
- Compliance with applicable governmental laws, rules, and regulations;
- Prompt internal reporting of violations of the code; and
- Accountability for adherence to the code.

The SEC noted that it was not specifying every detail that a code of ethics must contain nor prescribing any specific language. Instead, it noted, it wished to "strongly encourage" companies to "adopt codes that are broader and more comprehensive than necessary to meet the new disclosure requirements."

The SEC also established disclosure requirements for the codes of ethics. The specific venues for disclosure chosen by the SEC are of less importance than its decision that codes must be disclosed. As a result, the specific ethical codes formulated by each issuer company would be revealed to the public. Moreover, Congress required, and the SEC implemented, rules requiring companies to disclose changes to or waivers from the code. Waivers of the code of ethics drew a great deal of attention at that time because it was believed that the problems at Enron had resulted, at least in part, from waivers to its code of ethics.[107] Going forward, early disclosure of such waivers could be a warning sign about potential trouble at a company.

SOX created a new focus on compliance in American business. The substance of SOX compliance was limited to financial reporting, with attendant internal controls and codes of ethics. But it introduced the concept, practice, and tools of compliance to large numbers of senior corporate executives. It was also a high-profile development. As one analyst said at the time, SOX became "the gold standard for governance, transparency and controls."[108] Moreover, because it involved major legislation and impacted the

---

[106] SEC, *Disclosure Required By Sections 406 and 407 of the Sarbanes-Oxley Act of 2002*, Release Nos. 33-8177, 34-47235 (Jan. 24, 2003).

[107] Frank Navran and Edward Pittman, "Corporate Ethics and Sarbanes Oxley," originally published in *Wall Street Lawyer* (July 2003), available from the Ethics Resource Center.

[108] David S. Joachim, "A New Law and Lots of Headaches," *The New York Times*, page G2 (Feb. 21, 2006).

highest levels of the business community, it drew extensive press attention, during both enactment and implementation. As one CCO said, SOX "helped create a new sense of urgency."[109] There were also complaints. Many business executives indicated that they supported the new law, although they were concerned about its cost.[110] Smaller firms in particular were challenged by the cost.[111] These issues would create considerable controversy. Nonetheless, as the debates and controversy continued, so did the enhanced attention to compliance. Perhaps more than any other single development in compliance's history, the Sarbanes-Oxley Act helped make compliance a household word, or at least, a word well known throughout the business community.

Compliance Rules for Asset Managers and Broker-Dealers (2003–2004)

In 2003 the SEC embarked on rulemaking to mandate compliance functions among asset managers—funds and investment advisers. The value of compliance for asset managers had been recognized as early as the 1980s, as discussed above.[112] Now, the SEC's rulemaking would establish a mandatory institutional structure for compliance including codes of ethics. Moreover, by the time the process had run its course, it had surveyed contemporary examples of compliance, restated compliance's goals, identified best practices, and added codes of ethics to the core compliance structure. While the SEC was engaged in this process, the NASD conducted its own rulemaking for broker-dealers. In many respects, this process could be viewed as a capstone to the development of compliance.

Before turning to the specifics of the rules, it would be helpful to briefly review the SEC's rulemaking process. When the SEC issues rules, it conducts a two-step process. First, it issues a document called a *proposing release* that sets out the rules it expects to issue, with the agency's commentary upon them, as well as a request for public comments. Within the administrative process of the United States government this is known as "notice and an opportunity for comment." After the public has had an opportunity to review the rules and provide comments, the SEC will make changes in the rules it believes appropriate to respond to the comments, and then issue a document called an *adopting release.* The adopting release finalizes the rules, that is, makes them binding and official, with updated commentary by the agency based on the public comments it had received. In addition, there is a third type of release, known as a *concept release.* A concept release does not propose specific rules. Instead it states ideas for possible future proposals and asks for public comments. Finally, when a self-regulatory organization wishes to issue new rules, it must submit them to the SEC for approval, which publishes the proposed rules for notice an opportunity for comment. All four of these types of releases—proposing, adopting, concept, and self-regulatory—played a role in the SEC's compliance rules.

---

109 *Id.*

110 Jonathan D. Glater, "Here It Comes: The Sarbanes-Oxley Backlash," *The New York Times,* page B5 (Apr. 17, 2005).

111 Joachim, "A New Law and Lots of Headaches."

112 *See* the discussion of compliance during the 1980s; *"Compliance in the 1980s*

Unlike many other compliance initiatives, the proposed rules for asset managers were not issued in the midst of a crisis. Robert Plaze, associate director and later deputy director of the SEC's Division of Investment Management, played a leading role in drafting the compliance rules. He remembers that although no crisis had shaken asset managers, the SEC's chairman, Harvey Pitt, called together his senior staff and highlighted the recent crisis in financial disclosure that had led to the Sarbanes-Oxley Act.[113] He instructed the staff to consider measures to avoid crises in other areas. In Plaze's words, the chairman said, "The next scandal may be yours, so you need to begin doing something to deal with it." As Plaze notes, in light of subsequent events: "He was prescient!"

In February 2003 the SEC issued a proposing release describing potential new compliance rules for asset managers.[114] Separate rules were proposed for investment advisers (Rule 206(4)-7) and investment companies (Rule 38a-1), but the two rules had many similarities. The release explained the SEC's views on why the rules were appropriate and should be considered. Four elements should be noted.

First, the release explained the role of compliance. In this regard, the SEC's proposing release took a traditional approach. SEC examiners, it said, "cannot be everywhere at all times." Moreover, the SEC said, it had learned to regard weak compliance controls as an indicator that undetected and uncorrected violations may have occurred. Accordingly, the SEC said, it could leverage its limited examination resources by focusing on firms with weaker compliance controls. The release continued, "Our ability to protect fund and advisory clients has in many respects come to rely upon the effectiveness of these compliance programs. They provide the first line of investor protection."

One could read this rationale for compliance as a throwback to the 1980s, when compliance was seen as nothing more than a "first-line" extension of the regulators. Certainly, the proposing release had much of that flavor. However, at the same time it also demonstrated a much more sophisticated appreciation of compliance. It said, "Funds and advisers with effective internal compliance programs administered by competent compliance personnel are much less likely to violate the federal securities laws." Also, when violations do occur, "they are much less likely to result in harm to investors." Finally, it added, "Many funds and advisers have established effective programs staffed with competent and trained professionals." In short, when discussing the role of compliance, the proposing release showed an interesting juxtaposition of thinking from the 1980s—compliance is a first line substituting for regulators who cannot be everywhere—with a more sophisticated appreciation for the field, including its practitioners' competence, training and professionalism.

---

113 Interview with Robert Plaze (Dec. 2014). As noted above, interviews will be cited only once. Absent further citation, all following quotations or references to the statements of the same individual are based on the interview.

114 SEC, *Compliance Programs of Investment Companies and Investment Advisers*, Proposed Rules, Release No. IC-25925, IA-2107 (Feb. 5, 2003) (hereinafter cited as "Compliance Rules Proposing Release").

Second, the proposing release surveyed contemporary examples of compliance systems. This survey of existing compliance systems, both domestic and foreign, was fairly unique. In prior cases, compliance initiatives were simply announced with no effort to trace the legacies that had informed them. Multiple parties, in multiple sectors, it appeared, had independently discovered the benefits of compliance, including a responsible compliance official, policies and procedures, and so on. There were a few exceptions. For example, in deciding the *Caremark* case, the Delaware court cited to the United States Sentencing Guidelines.[115] Then, some months later, when HHS issued its *Model Compliance Program Guidance for Hospitals* , it cited to the *Caremark* case when describing the duties of hospital directors.[116] However, this type of explicit line of descent was rare. Thus, the effort by the SEC to survey the field stands out. Plaze remembers that the staff conducted the survey because they "were looking to borrow good ideas."

The SEC's survey highlighted the chaotic state of contemporary compliance.[117] It cited to the Sarbanes-Oxley Act as an example of a system of internal controls used to ensure the integrity of financial reporting. Coming shortly after the highly publicized compliance initiatives triggered by SOX, this element of the survey is understandable, particularly in light of how Chairman Pitt had initiated the SEC's rulemaking process. The survey also pointed to bank regulators' safety and soundness standards, including compliance. As discussed above, bank regulators had adopted these standards after massive problems among S&Ls. The survey also pointed to a self-regulatory rule, specifically NASD Rule 3010(b) that required broker-dealers to adopt compliance procedures. The cited rule is interesting because it provided for the supervisory requirements of broker-dealers. Plaze has indicated that he recognized the NASD rule was narrower than the asset manager initiative, but many advisers are also registered as broker-dealers, and the SEC staff sought to anticipate objections that they should have taken account of existing requirements for broker-dealers.

The SEC's survey also identified several foreign compliance systems.[118] Plaze indicated that while travelling abroad on SEC business, he became aware that foreign regulators would cite to U.S. law as support for a regulatory change, "but we never did." The survey was intended to remedy this oversight. It cited to the Financial Services Authority of the United Kingdom, whose handbook said firms should take reasonable care to establish and maintain effective systems and controls for compliance with applicable requirements as well as to counter the risk that the firm may be used to further financial crime. The Fund Manager Code of Conduct of the Securities and Futures Commission of Hong Kong included provisions on appointing a designated compliance officer with a line of report directly to the firm's senior management; and sufficiently detailed compliance procedures to give senior management reasonable assurance that the firm complies with all applicable requirements at all times. In a harbinger of future

---

115 *In re Caremark, Inc.*

116 HHS, *Model Compliance Program Guidance for Hospitals*.

117 SEC, Compliance Rules Proposing Release.

118 The survey of foreign compliance systems, including citations to the relevant sources, can be found in note 25 of the Compliance Rules Proposing Release.

developments, the Hong Kong Code of Conduct also stated that compliance functions should be separated from operational functions. Finally, the SEC also pointed to the business governance standards promulgated by the French securities regulator, the Commission des Operations de Bourse. Although the governance standards, as such, do not appear directly relevant to compliance, governance and compliance had previously been linked in several settings.

Third, the SEC's proposing release set out the goals for a compliance system. Much of its discussion would be of interest only to compliance practitioners who work with asset managers; that was, after all, the point of the rulemaking. But in this context the SEC also made more general statements that had a bearing beyond any one particular sector. Most memorably, the SEC said that it would not enumerate specific elements that must be included in a firm's policies and procedures. Firms are too varied, the SEC said, to impose a single set of requirements. Rather, policies and procedures:

> ...should be designed to *prevent* violations (by, for example, separating operational functions such as trading and reporting), *detect* violations of securities laws (by, for example, requiring a supervisor to review employees' personal securities transactions), and *correct* promptly any material violations [emphasis in original].

Plaze recalls that these goals were drafted in consultation with the SEC's examination program, particularly with the help of Gene Gohlke, a long time examination manager. In formulating these goals—prevent, detect, and correct—the SEC gave compliance a mission statement.

Fourth and finally, the SEC's proposing release contained a discussion of the specific rules it was considering, Rule 206(4)-7 for advisers and 38a-1 for investment companies. In keeping with the development of compliance over the prior several years, the rules established certain key institutional structures: policies and procedures; a CCO; access for compliance to the senior levels of the organization, specifically funds' boards of directors; and an annual review. Perhaps most noteworthy in the proposed rules was the SEC's decision to require not just a designated compliance official but a specific position with a specific title: the CCO. The release stated that many funds and advisers had already designated a person to serve in this role, but it was not required, and some had not. Plaze indicated that "the most successful SEC rules are ones that obligate regulated entities to follow best practices," and that was the goal with the compliance rules. No matter how well-crafted policies and procedures might be, the SEC's proposing release said, they will be ineffective unless "well-trained, competent personnel administer them."

The SEC's proposing release provided a major statement on the purpose, status, and goals of compliance, as well as serving as an example of its development. It also contained some hints of the field's future. In a separate section of the release it indicated that it was exploring ways in which the SEC could make the best use of its own resources. One promising way, the release said, would be to rely more heavily on the private sector. It suggested four concepts for comment. Two of the concepts, a self-regulatory organization for asset managers and fidelity bonding, need not detain us. But the other two were more directly applicable to compliance. The first was to require firms to undergo a third-party compliance review. The release pointed to the use of independent reviews in fighting money laundering, which, as noted above, had been identified in FATF Recommendation 20. It also indicated that compliance consultants and others already performed "mock audits." The second was to require auditors reviewing the financial statements of investment companies to include a compliance review similar to their review of internal controls. The agency asked for comments on both.

Following publication of the SEC's proposing release and receipt of public comments, the SEC held an open meeting and adopted the final rules in December 2003.[119] On one level, the Compliance Rules Adopting Release was something of an anticlimax. The rules were adopted largely as proposed: policies and procedures, a CCO, access to fund boards of directors, and an annual review. More notable was the change in tone. Whereas the proposing release spoke of the need for a "first line" for the SEC, the adopting release focused instead on asset managers' own fiduciary duties and conflicts of interest. This change reflected the new conditions in which the adopting release was issued. In the months following the proposal events had taken a new and sudden turn.

In late 2003, Chairman Pitt's prescience about the danger of other crises bore fruit. A number of enforcement actions were developed against asset managers, by both state attorney-generals and the SEC, alleging that they had abused their fiduciary duties by allowing unfair special trading privileges to certain favored clients in return for various quid pro quo arrangements (a practice known as *market timing*). The adopting release highlighted these cases. Plaze remembers, "This was the first significant scandal in the mutual fund industry." There were anger and indignation about the scandals and the involvement of many fund advisers. For the staff drafting the compliance rules, in Plaze's words, "It was a challenge to find language that was forceful yet dignified and that the commissioners could all support." However, most remarkable about the SEC's response to the crisis was the speed of its response. Regulatory proposals often languish for years. In this case, the SEC adopted the compliance rules only ten months after they had been proposed.

The adopting release also reconsidered the concept items. The SEC announced that none would move forward at that time, except, it said, it may in the future reconsider requiring asset managers to obtain compliance reviews from third-party compliance experts. Plaze recalls that requiring third-party audits was viewed as a form of privatizing the SEC's examination function and could be considered analogous to the work of independent auditors. However, in his words, "The analogy was difficult." Compliance firms are not regulated and have no standards of review similar to those applied by financial auditors. Plaze also consulted with SEC enforcement attorneys who had been involved in administering enforcement settlements that required third party

[119] SEC, *Final Rule, Compliance Programs of Investment Companies and Investment Advisers*, Rel. Nos. IA-2204, IC-26299 (Dec. 17, 2003) (hereinafter cited as "Compliance Rules Adopting Release").

audits. They informed him that the settlements often worked only because the SEC staff could impose quality assurance, such as by requiring the firm to retain a highly qualified consultant instead of the least expensive and least competent available. This type of quality assurance, Plaze said, would be impossible across the entire industry. As a result, the concept item did not move forward at that time.

A few months after the SEC proposed Rules 206(4)-7 and 38a-1 for asset managers, the NASD proposed compliance rules for broker-dealers.[120] Although the NASD had long standing supervisory rules that included compliance policies and procedures—the SEC cited to these existing supervisory rules in its own proposing release—the NASD rules considered in 2003 focused on developing compliance's institutional structure. Much like the SEC's rules, the NASD required broker-dealers to designate one or more CCOs. They also gave the CCO access to the highest levels of the firm, in this case to the broker-dealer's CEO. Finally, they included an annual review and report, with the addition of a certification by the CEO that the firm has in place processes to establish, maintain, review, test, and modify policies and procedures that are reasonably designed to achieve compliance. The NASD had initially proposed a dual certification by both the CEO and the CCO, but eventually decided on the CEO alone, perhaps in the same spirit as the SEC's SOX code of ethics rulemaking, which had also focused on the CEO.

When the NASD proposed these rules, senior officials emphasized that their purpose was to support and enhance compliance. Robert R. Glauber, chairman of NASD, was quoted in the press saying:

> The purpose of this is to empower the brokerage firm compliance officer...We think it is absolutely crucial as part of the process of creating an environment in the firms that puts high standards of behavior first. We think this is a very important step to rebuilding investor confidence.[121]

This support was reiterated in the SEC's release publishing the NASD's rules for comment prior to SEC approval. The SEC recited the NASD's purpose for the rules as ensuring that compliance is given "the highest priority" by the firm's senior executive officers.[122]

The SEC's release also contained an interesting change in tone. Still describing the NASD's purpose, it said, "Comprehensive compliance and supervisory systems

[120] The NASD proposed the rules in June 2003, NASD, *NASD Requests Comment on Proposal to Amend Rule 3010 and Adopt Interpretative Material 3010-1*, Special Notice to Members 03-29 (June 2003); and issued them in final form, after SEC approval, in November 2004. NASD, *SEC Approves New Chief Executive Officer Compliance Certification and Chief Compliance Officer Designation Requirements*, Notice to Members 04-79 (Nov. 2004).

[121] Gretchen Morgenson, et al., "Accountability Is Focus of Rule Aimed at Chiefs of Wall Street," *The New York Times*, page C1 (June 4, 2003).

[122] SEC, *Self-Regulatory Organizations; Notice of Filing of Amendment No. 2 to a Proposed Rule Change by the National Association of Securities Dealers, Inc. Relating to Chief Executive Officer Certification and Designation of Chief Compliance Officer*, Release No. 34-50105 (July 28, 2004).

constitute the bedrock of effective securities industry self-regulation." This passage was notable because it recognized that compliance is a form of self-regulation. The release went on to describe compliance as "the primary strata of investor protection." This passage was notable because of its dramatic change in rhetoric. Indeed, it reversed the language in the SEC's proposing release for the asset manager rules. Now, instead of serving merely as a front line for the regulators, compliance was itself the "primary strata" of investor protection. In this new rhetorical environment, regulators and traditional self-regulators now occupied the secondary and tertiary strata. The compliance pyramid of the 1980s had been turned upside down.

In July 2004, a few months after adopting Rules 206(4)-7 and 38a-1 for asset managers, the SEC followed in the footsteps of SOX and required investment advisers to adopt codes of ethics. The regulatory vision sustaining this effort can be seen in a contemporary statement by William Donaldson, the SEC's chairman. Firms, he said, need a "company-wide environment that fosters ethical behavior and decision-making."[123] This environment, he continued, should be a "moral compass" guiding hiring decisions, operating practices, and internal policies and procedures. Moreover, when adopting the rule requiring advisers to adopt a code of ethics, the SEC said, "A good code of ethics should effectively convey to employees the value the advisory firm places on ethical conduct, and should challenge employees to live up to not only the letter of the law, but also the ideals of the organization."[124]

The rule adopted by the SEC was similar to an existing rule for funds that required them to establish codes of ethics to monitor employees' personal trading.[125] Plaze notes that extending similar requirement to advisers was another example of the SEC adopting a best practice in the industry.

The new code of ethics rule required advisers to include in their codes:

- A standard or standards of business conduct that the adviser requires of all of its supervised persons that must reflect the adviser's fiduciary duties;
- Provisions requiring the adviser's supervised persons to comply with applicable law;
- Provisions requiring certain advisory personnel to report their personal securities transactions and the adviser to review them;
- Provisions requiring supervised persons to promptly report any violations of the code of ethics; and
- Provisions requiring advisers to provide each of their supervised persons with a copy of the adviser's code of ethics and obtain from them a written acknowledgement of receipt.

As a result, codes of ethics under the new rule were far more extensive than reporting and monitoring personal securities trading.

---

[123] William Donaldson, *Remarks Before the Caux Roundtable* (Nov. 30, 2004).
[124] Investment Adviser Codes of Ethics, Release No's IA-2256 & ICA-26492 (July 9, 2004).
[125] SEC Rule 17(j)-1 under the Investment Company Act.

The SEC's Compliance Rules Adopting Release reflected the broad sweep of its goals for rule. A code of ethics, it said, should be more than a compliance manual. Rather, it said, a code of ethics should set out "ideals for ethical conduct," premised on fundamental principles of "openness, integrity, honesty, and trust." Indeed, after the SEC's rulemaking, the Investment Adviser Association issued guidance for a model code that covers a wide variety of topics, including gifts, entertainment, service on outside boards of directors, confidentiality, and numerous other issues that could implicate an adviser's ethics and fiduciary duty.[126]

One final aspect of the SEC's compliance rules drew considerable interest at the time. In the course of discussing a requirement that a fund's board of directors must approve the hiring or dismissal of the fund's chief compliance officer, the SEC said:

> The board, and the board alone can discharge the officer if she fails to live up to her position. Thus a chief compliance officer who fails to fully inform the board of a material compliance failure or who fails to aggressively pursue noncompliance within the service provider, would risk her position. She would also risk her career, because it would be unlikely for another board of directors to approve such a person as chief compliance officer.[127]

The SEC then stated in footnote 90, "If such a person were approved by another fund, our staff would enhance its scrutiny of the fund accordingly." This immediately triggered an outpouring of concern that the SEC would track CCOs of whom it disapproved from fund to fund. Plaze reports that he has "taken a lot of heat" for footnote 90. He also states, in light of later events, that he continues to stand by it. The goal of the 2003 rulemaking, he says, was to help upgrade compliance to a profession, and that includes professional obligations beyond those to a particular employer or client. The SEC does not have licensing authority over compliance practitioners, so footnote 90 was "what we came up with." He adds: it has worked. In his words, "Compliance professionals have really picked up their game and are playing a much more significant role in many asset management firms. There are really some impressive people who have been attracted to the profession."

Moreover, a few years later, the SEC clarified how it would deal with CCOs of whom it disapproved by beginning to issue compliance bars. In compliance bars the SEC resolves enforcement proceedings against compliance practitioners by barring them "from association in a compliance capacity with any broker, dealer, or investment adviser."[128]

---

[126] IAA, *Best Practices for Investment Adviser Codes of Ethics* (July 20, 2004).

[127] SEC, Compliance Rules Adopting Release.

[128] *See, e.g.*, *In the Matter of Consulting Services Group L.L.C., et al.*, Release Nos. 34-56612 and IA-2669 (Oct. 4, 2007).

One could view the SEC's and NASD's compliance rules as a capstone to the institutional development of compliance. Over the preceding decade and a half compliance had become increasingly institutionalized, with certain components consistently appearing in different setting: policies and procedures, compliance officers, access to the senior levels of the organization, and periodic assessments. All of these were codified in the SEC's and NASD's rules. Moreover, when considering the rules the SEC surveyed the field and adopted best practices. The concepts published by the SEC suggested possible routes forward in the field's future development, particularly third-party compliance audits, if the implementation issues identified by Plaze could be resolved. Finally, the SEC's decision to include codes of ethics in its compliance rulemaking demonstrates the continuing linkage between compliance and ethics. Compliance was more than a tool for building a control environment. Compliance carried in its "DNA"—to use a phrase made popular by then SEC Chairman William Donaldson[129]—an aspiration for creating ethical as well as law-abiding behavior. Through these rules compliance and ethics had become operational realities, with a defined institutional structure and a defined mission statement: to prevent, detect, and correct violations.

V. RECOGNITION

By the middle years of the first decade of the 21st century, compliance had reached an important moment in its history. From broker-dealers, sector of its origin, it had spread to global financial regulation, criminal law enforcement, bank regulation, corporate governance, health care, financial disclosure, asset managers, and ultimately back to broker-dealers in a new form. From a manual of control procedures it had grown into an institutional structure that embodied widely accepted forms: dedicated officials, policies and procedures, access to senior levels of the firm, and periodic assessments. From local law enforcement it had acquired the affirmative mission of creating a preventive control environment and codifying ethics. Nonetheless, despite this rich diversity of growth, recognition of compliance remained uneven.

In the years after 2004, the most noteworthy trend in the ongoing history of compliance was whether and how the development of the field would be recognized. This recognition took various forms, including: acknowledging compliance's new role, protecting it when threatened, and using it as an affirmative tool at the highest levels of public policy. However, a recurring theme came to dominate this period: compliance's role as a distinct control function that must be endowed with certain characteristics to fulfill its mission. Objectivity, in particular, would draw considerable attention, usually under the rubric of making compliance independent.

---

[129] *See*, e.g., William H. Donaldson, chairman, SEC, *Remarks Before the Economic Club of New York* (May 8, 2003) ("moral DNA" must be embedded within a company).

Board of Governors of the Federal Reserve System and Compliance Risk Management (2008)

In October 2008 the Board of Governors of the United States Federal Reserve System issued Supervisory Letter SR 08-8 that gave recognition to compliance.[130] This letter was a significant development in the history of compliance for several reasons:

- It identified compliance as a tool for public policy; it implemented global best practices;
- It recognized the unique characteristics of compliance risk;
- It articulated and elaborated a sophisticated vision of compliance; and
- It identified certain core features of a successful compliance regime.

In late 2008 the world financial system had entered a period of extreme crisis. On September 15, 2008, Lehman Brothers, a major financial services firm, filed for bankruptcy. Almost immediately, the Reserve Primary Fund, a major money market fund holding Lehman debt, experienced a run. That is, investors experienced a crisis of confidence in the entity and immediately sought to withdraw all of their funds. The run quickly spread to other money market funds. A few days later, on September 25, regulators shut down Washington Mutual, the largest S&L in the United States, after a massive run by its depositors. Central banks in the United States and Europe took extraordinary measures to address the crisis, including extending public insurance to nondepository money market accounts, buying newly issued stock to give banks more capital, and otherwise providing emergency liquidity to markets and institutions. This was in the environment in which the Federal Reserve issued SR 08-8.

SR 08-8 began with considerable understatement, given the crisis environment in which it was issued:

> In recent years, banking organizations have greatly expanded the scope, complexity, and global nature of their business activities. At the same time, compliance requirements associated with these activities have become more complex. As a result, organizations have confronted significant risk management and corporate governance challenges, particularly with respect to compliance risks that transcend business lines, legal entities, and jurisdictions of operation.[131]

The letter continued, "To address these challenges, many banking organizations have implemented or enhanced firm wide compliance risk management programs and program oversight."

---

[130] Board of Governors of the Federal Reserve System, *Compliance Risk Management Programs and Oversight at Large Banking Organizations with Complex Compliance Profiles*, SR 08-8 (Oct. 16, 2008) (hereinafter cited as "SR 08-8").

[131] SR 08-8.

The Federal Reserve indicated that it had previously emphasized the need for such firmwide compliance risk management through its examination program. The letter, however, was intended to clarify the Federal Reserve's views. For example, it said: "Organizations supervised by the Federal Reserve, regardless of size and complexity, should have effective compliance risk management programs that are appropriately tailored to the organization's risk profiles." Among banks, such a statement from the Federal Reserve could be expected to have the same effect as a rule issued by a nonbanking regulator.

The Federal Reserve also indicated that it believed its expectations, as set out in SR 08-8, were consistent with "global sound practices."[132] Specifically, it said, they were consistent with the global principles enunciated by the Basel Committee on Banking Supervision. The Basel Committee is a forum of bank regulators from around the world that has met since the 1970s in Basel, Switzerland. In April 2005 a task force of the committee had issued a high-level paper on compliance risk and the compliance function in banks.[133] Many of the propositions in SR 08-8 had been set out in the task force's paper. Several elements of the supervisory letter are worthy of note.

First, the letter recognized the unique nature of compliance risk. It said that although the guiding principles for sound risk management are the same for compliance and other types of risk, the former presents several unique challenges. Specifically, the letter noted that the quantitative analyses used for other risks, such as risk limits or aggregation and trend analysis, are less meaningful for compliance. These distinguishing characteristics, the letter said, underscored the need for large and complex organizations to establish firmwide compliance risk management programs and establish strong cultures of compliance.

Second, the SR 08-8 articulated a sophisticated vision of compliance governance. The board of directors, senior management, and the corporate compliance function are responsible for working together "to establish and implement a comprehensive and effective compliance risk management program and oversight framework that is reasonably designed to prevent and detect compliance breaches and issues." Boards, it continued, are responsible for setting an appropriate culture of compliance, establishing clear policies regarding the management of key risks, and ensuring that the policies are adhered to in practice. Senior management is responsible for communicating and reinforcing the culture established by the board, and implementing and enforcing the firm's compliance policies and compliance risk management standards. Finally, senior management of the corporate compliance function should report to the board, or a committee thereof, on significant compliance matters and the effectiveness of the compliance risk program.

Third, the letter identified certain core features of a successful compliance regime. Compliance, the Federal Reserve said, must be independent of the business lines for which it has compliance responsibility:

---

132 *Id.*

133 Basel Committee on Banking Supervision, *Compliance and the Compliance Function in Banks*, Bank for International Settlements (Apr. 2005).

> Federal Reserve supervisory findings at large, complex banking organizations consistently reinforce the need for compliance staff to be appropriately independent of the business lines for which they have compliance responsibilities. Compliance independence facilitates objectivity and avoids inherent conflicts of interest that may hinder the effective implementation of a compliance program.[134]

The letter went on to provide specific guidance on reporting lines for compliance, particularly in large banks, which the Federal Reserve defined as those with more than $50 billion in assets. For example, if compliance staff report to a business manager, the Federal Reserve said, they should also have a dual reporting line to a compliance official for their compliance functions.

SR 08-8 bears comparison to the prior joint Standards on Safety and Soundness. In 1995 the bank regulators simply issued a single statement—indeed, a single sentence—on compliance. Thirteen years later, based on its supervisory experience, in the midst of a major financial crisis, the Federal Reserve updated this guidance with a highly elaborated statement about its expectations for compliance. The contrast between the statement in 1995 and SR 08-8 highlighted how much compliance had developed and grown over the intervening period. The Federal Reserve recognized that compliance is a unique field that requires sophisticated governance as well as objectivity and independence. This was a mature vision of compliance as a unique control function.

Financial Crisis and Compliance Resources (2008)

The financial crisis of 2008 had a direct impact on compliance practitioners. Major financial firms declared bankruptcy, banks and money market funds suffered depositor or investor runs, and financial activity dramatically slowed around the world. Many financial firms took steps to save money such as reducing their payrolls. News of layoffs and reductions in staff were inescapable during those months. Estimates of financial sector layoffs were in the tens of thousands and growing. In early 2008, one estimate placed the total at 34,000 in New York City alone since the previous July.[135] By November the press was reporting that accelerating financial sector layoffs could reach 200,000 by the end of the year.[136] In this environment, concerns grew that layoffs and other reductions in resources would disproportionately fall on compliance.

On December 2, 2008, Lori A. Richards, director of the SEC's examination program, published the program's *Open Letter to CEOs of SEC-Registered Firms.*[137] The letter reviewed the importance of the compliance function. It was, she said, critical

---

[134] SR 08-8.

[135] "20,000 More Layoffs on Wall Street?" Deal Book, *The New York Times* (Mar. 28, 2008).

[136] Joel Bel Bruno, "Wall Street Layoffs Could Surge Past 200,000," *Huffington Post Business* (Nov. 23, 2008).

[137] Lori A. Richards, SEC Office of Compliance Inspections and Examinations, *Open Letter to CEOs of SEC-Registered Firms* (Dec. 2, 2008).

to ensure firms' operations compliance with the law and rules for industry participation and to ensure that the interests of "customers, clients, and shareholders are protected." She continued, "Compliance is a vital control function that helps to protect the firm from conduct that could negatively impact the firm's business and its reputation."

Having established the importance of compliance, Richards turned to the current circumstances in the financial sector. Many firms, she said were considering reductions and cost cutting measures. She wished to remind them, she continued, of their legal obligation "to maintain an adequate compliance program reasonably designed to achieve compliance with the law." She then quoted the chairman of the SEC, Christopher Cox, who had said:

Compliance programs have made huge strides in recent years in becoming more formalized and more robust...Now more than ever, companies need to take a long-term view on compliance and realize that their fiduciary responsibility requires a constant commitment to investors. That means sustaining their support for compliance during this market turmoil and beyond it as well.[138]The letter stated that firms' interactions with investors should meet high standards, and that by fulfilling their obligations, regulated firms in the financial services industry "can help restore and bolster public confidence in the fairness and integrity of our markets and market participants." It concluded: "Providing adequate resources to compliance programs and functions and ensuring that CCOs and compliance personnel are integrated into the activities of the firm are essential to that process."

A few months later, Richards returned to the topic. In a speech in March 2009, she indicated that firms should ask: Does the compliance program have adequate resources to do the job?[139]

"At the SEC," she said, "many of us have cautioned against making resource reductions to compliance programs that could undercut their effectiveness." CCOs, she continued, should consider whether their programs have sufficient resources, and include information about shortfalls in the annual compliance report. Finally, she said, firms should consider alternative ways to better target their resources, such as by having compliance leverage resources available elsewhere in the firm, or by investing in technology.

The crisis of 2008 impacted compliance practitioners, and Richards responded with support. Her efforts were in the nature of moral suasion—the CEOs who received her letter were under no obligation to respond. Nonetheless, in the midst of a crisis, Richard's letter demonstrated that regulators recognized compliance and that they were ready to protect it when necessary.

---

[138] *Id.*

[139] Lori A. Richards, SEC Office of Compliance Inspections and Examinations, *Compliance in Today's Environment: Step Up to the Challenge: Remarks Before the IA Compliance Best Practices Summit 2009* (Mar. 12, 2009).

IOSCO Principle 31 (2010)

In 2010, the world community returned its attention to compliance. In this instance, it did so through the International Organization of Securities Commissions (IOSCO), a global body composed of regulators from around the world. Currently, IOSCO reports that it has 120 member securities regulators, as well as 80 other participants, such as self-regulators and securities exchanges. The precise format for IOSCO's attention to compliance was its review and revision of existing guidance. This was not headline news. Yet, IOSCO's actions demonstrated the global community's recognition of compliance.

In the late 1990s IOSCO had undertaken to identify the essential elements of securities regulation. As a result of this effort, in 1998 it issued a set of thirty principles intended to guide securities regulators.[140]Most of the principles addressed issues of only indirect interest to compliance, such as information sharing among regulators. One principle, however, was directly relevant to compliance.

Among the principles applicable to the regulation of market intermediaries, that is, those in the business of managing individual portfolios, executing orders, dealing or distributing securities, and providing information relevant to the trading of securities, in 1998 IOSCO stated:

> 21. Market intermediaries should be required to comply with standards for internal organization and operational conduct that aim to protect the interests of clients, ensure proper management of risk, and under which management of the intermediary accepts primary responsibility for these matters [emphasis added].

In commentary, IOSCO articulated a number of potential regulatory actions to implement Principle 21, including: the observation of high standards of integrity, fair dealing, and diligence; terms of engagement with customers; information about customers; protection of customer assets; market practices; operational controls; conflicts of interest; and proprietary trading. Many of these comments are familiar elements of a compliance program. Nonetheless, the 1998 Principle 21 revealed an enforcement-centric world, in which regulators require and intermediaries comply. This would change in 2010.

Following the financial crisis of 2008, IOSCO undertook to bring its principles up-to-date. To do so, it issued new principles and revised several of the old.[141] Of greatest interest, Principle 21 was renumbered as Principle 31 and amended to read as follows:

> 31. Market intermediaries should be *required to establish an internal function that delivers compliance* with standards for internal organization and operational conduct, with the aim of protecting the interests of clients and their assets and ensuring proper management of risk, through which management of the intermediary accepts primary responsibility for these matters [emphasis added].

---

[140] IOSCO, *Objectives and Principles of Securities Regulation* (Sept. 1998).

[141] IOSCO, *Objectives and Principles of Securities Regulation* (June 2010).

One could view this 2010 statement of principle as marking the global triumph of compliance. Now, instead of regulators requiring and firms complying, IOSCO recognizes that intermediaries themselves should "establish an internal function that delivers compliance." Buried deep within the activity of a global association of securities regulators, the ground had moved.

After years of development for compliance, the IOSCO principle does not break new ground. Rather, it codifies in a globally sanctioned principle the development of compliance over the previous decades. The most important aspect of new Principle 31 is the recognition it conveys. Requiring an "internal function that delivers compliance" is now among the guiding principles of global securities regulation.

The 111th Congress of the United States (2010)

In 2010 the Congress of the United States recognized compliance. It was the 111th Congress elected since the beginning of the republic and hence is known by that designation. Within the space of a few months in 2010, the 111th Congress enacted high-profile and headline-grabbing legislation, including the Patient Protection and Affordable Care Act,[142] often called "Obamacare" after President Barack Obama, and the Dodd-Frank Wall Street Reform and Consumer Protection Act,[143] named for its sponsors Senator Christopher Dodd of Connecticut and Congressman Barney Frank of Massachusetts. These laws fundamentally revised how the United States government provides public insurance for health care, and how it regulates new financial products such as derivatives and swaps. The compliance provisions in these laws, on the other hand, were not high profile. Instead of grabbing headlines, they were obscure and deeply buried in legislative text. Nor did they produce any groundbreaking new compliance standards. Nonetheless, provisions in both laws showed that compliance had been recognized at the highest levels of policy making in the United States.

In the Patient Protection and Affordable Care Act, Subtitle E addressed integrity programs for Medicaid and Medicare, the leading programs through which the United States government provides health insurance. The act authorized HHS, in consultation with the HHS Office of the Inspector General, to establish core elements in compliance programs for medical providers and suppliers who wish to serve covered patients.[144] In other words, to be eligible to receive payments under the public insurance programs, a physician or supplier would need to establish a compliance program meeting the core requirements. A few months after enactment, the chief counsel of HHS's Office of the Inspector General indicated that the new provisions were consistent with his office's longstanding view that "well-designed compliance programs can be an effective tool for promoting compliance and preventing fraud and abuse."[145]

---

[142] Patient Protection and Affordable Care Act, 124 Stat. 119 (Mar. 23, 2010).

[143] Dodd-Frank Wall Street Reform and Consumer Protection Act, 124 Stat. 1376 (July 21, 2010).

[144] Patient Protection and Affordable Care Act § 6401.

[145] Lewis Morris, Testimony before the Committee on Ways and Means, Subcommittee on Health, Subcommittee on Oversight, United States House of Representatives (June 15, 2010).

In the Dodd-Frank Act, Title VII established a new regulatory regime for swaps and securities-based swaps (together referred to here as "swaps"), a common type of derivative financial instrument. The law established new requirements for derivative clearing organizations,[146] swap information processors,[147] swap dealers,[148] and major swap participants.[149] In each case, the newly registered entities were required to establish compliance programs in which a CCO would report directly to the entity's board of directors, review the organization's compliance, consult with the board of directors to resolve conflicts, administer policies and procedures, ensure compliance, and establish procedures for the remediation of noncompliance issues. The following year, while proposing rules to implement some of these provisions, the SEC indicated that it was explicitly basing its proposals on compliance rules already in place for self-regulatory organizations.[150]

The compliance legislation of the 111th U.S. Congress did not shake up compliance practices. Rather, it enacted fairly straightforward requirements that would have been familiar in concept to any experienced compliance practitioner. Moreover, the responsible agencies then responded to these enactments by stating that they understood them to be consistent with each agency's own longstanding practices. These were not radical provisions. Rather, the importance of these enactments can be seen in the recognition compliance had achieved in the public policy process. In reforming governmental health insurance and in creating a new regulatory regime for swaps, the United States Congress recognized compliance as a public policy tool.

Theodore W. Urban and the Nature of Compliance (2012)

In October 2009 the SEC instituted an enforcement action that revisited the nature of compliance. The case was brought against Theodore W. Urban, general counsel and head of compliance for a broker-dealer.[151] In many respects, this action resembled the case approximately twenty years earlier against Arthur James Huff. A salesman at the firm engaged in serious misconduct, and the SEC charged Urban with failure to supervise the rogue employee. Again, as with Huff, the case against Urban precipitated an outpouring of views about compliance with third parties filing friend-of-the-court briefs that raised arguments about the nature of compliance. However, as with Huff, the results were inconclusive.

Urban was the general counsel and head of compliance of a well-known regional broker-dealer headquartered in Baltimore, Maryland.[152] A salesman in an office in Beachwood, Ohio, and later in Baltimore, conducted a significant fraud, in which he manipulated

---

[146] Dodd-Frank Wall Street Reform and Consumer Protection Act §§ 725 & 763.

[147] Dodd-Frank Wall Street Reform and Consumer Protection Act § 728.

[148] Dodd-Frank Wall Street Reform and Consumer Protection Act §§ 731 & 764.

[149] *Id.*

[150] *Business Conduct Standards for Security-Based Swap Dealers and Major Security-Based Swap Participants*, SEC Release Number 34-64766, Proposed Rule, page 157, note 281 (June 29, 2011).

[151] Mr. Urban is a contributing author to this book.

[152] *In the Matter of Theodore W. Urban,* Initial Decision, Initial Decision Release No. 402 (Sept. 8, 2010).

the value of a company's stock by placing clients into highly concentrated positions, with significant margin debt, active trading of positions, and little client benefit. The salesman eventually pled guilty to a criminal charge and was sentenced to prison. When the misconduct came to light, the SEC charged Urban, the broker-dealer, and several line supervisors at the firm. The firm and all of the other individuals settled, leaving only Urban to contest the charges.

As with Huff, the SEC's enforcement action against Urban proceeded in two steps: first before an Administrative Law Judge, then before the five commissioners. As with Huff, the litigation focused on whether Urban was a supervisor within the meaning of the relevant legal standard, and if so, whether his supervision was reasonable. The ALJ found that Urban was a supervisor because other employees at the firm usually took his advice, but in the case of this salesman, it was reasonable for Urban to take no further action because his advice would have been futile. This legal formulation poses significant analytical difficulties that need not detain us here.[153] More interesting from an historical perspective is what this case said about the nature of compliance.

Many compliance practitioners believed the Urban case presented significant public policy issues. R. Gerald Baker, executive director of the Compliance and Legal Division of the Securities Industry and Financial Markets Association (SIFMA), a successor organization to the SIA, has indicated that the action against Urban was "the case we always hoped for."[154] SIFMA believed it presented an opportunity to obtain a clearer statement from the SEC about the nature of compliance. SIFMA filed a friend-of-the-court brief.[155] In addition, in a press release issued by the National Society of Compliance Professionals (NSCP), a professional organization for compliance officers, Charles Senatore, former chairman of the organization, said: "This matter raises public policy issues critical to the effectiveness of the role of a robust compliance program in a securities firm."[156] NSCP also filed a friend-of-the-court brief.[157]

SIFMA's brief was prepared jointly with the Association of Corporate Counsel, a group representing in-house attorneys. Regulators and the securities industry, they argued, have recognized the distinct role of legal and compliance professionals. These professionals advise and assist in developing policies and procedures, monitor business activity, investigate and report instances of misconduct, and offer recommendations

---

[153] For a discussion of the analytical difficulties raised by this approach as a matter of law, *see* John H. Walsh, "The Time Has Come to Reconsider the Gutfreund Standard," 45 *Review of Securities & Commodities Regulation* 177 (Sept. 2012).

[154] Interview with R. Gerald Baker (Dec. 2014). Mr. Baker is a contributing author to this book. As noted above, interviews will be cited only once. Absent further citation, all following quotations or references to the statements of the same individual are based on the interview.

[155] *In the Matter of Theodore W. Urban, Brief of Amici Curiae: The Securities Industry and Financial Markets Association, Including Its Compliance and Legal Society, and the Association of Corporate Counsel in Support of Appellee-Cross Appellant Theodore W. Urban*, Admin. Proceeding 3-13655 (Nov. 22, 2010).

[156] NSCP, *NSCP Files Amicus Brief in the Matter of Theodore W. Urban* (Nov. 23, 2010).

[157] *In the Matter of Theodore W. Urban, Amicus Brief of National Society of Compliance Professionals on Review of Initial Decision*, Admin. Proceeding 3-13655 (Nov. 22, 2010).

for remediation efforts. In short, these professionals play important advisory and monitoring roles. Moreover, the friends-of-the-court argued, the independence and objectivity of the legal and compliance departments is crucial when they assess and advise on legal and compliance matters. "Management," they said, "benefits greatly in its supervisory decisions by obtaining balanced, impartial, and informed advice from professionals who do not individually stand to gain or lose depending on the decision's outcome."

Baker believes this position reflected a significant change from the SIA's arguments in the Huff case. Instead of arguing that compliance is inherently advisory and therefore cannot supervise, SIFMA argued that as a control function compliance should be independent and objective, and therefore should not be supervisory. Anne Flannery who had, in her words, "something of a difference of opinion" with the SIA while litigating the Huff case, agrees that SIFMA is now taking a much more sophisticated position.

NSCP's brief also argued that independence is crucial to an effective compliance program. Compliance programs, the friend-of-the-court brief argued, were intended to supplement supervision "with independent observation and advice." Specifically, the NSCP said:

Vigorous compliance programs are a key aid to management's efforts to combat misconduct and malfeasance. In order to maintain the ability to root out misconduct, compliance personnel must have open communication with business personnel and advise feely on suspect behavior.

Moreover, in its brief, NSCP explicitly compared the work of a compliance official to an attorney's ability to provide "unbiased, independent legal advice." The SEC, the friend-of-the-court argued, should not interfere with the compliance officer's ability to deliver "unvarnished opinions" on problems faced by a firm.

In sum, both friend-of-the-court briefs emphasized that compliance should be independent and free to deliver objective or—in NSCP's words—"unvarnished" opinions. In the context of the pending litigation, the parties intended this analysis to bear on whether Urban was legally liable for the salesman's misconduct. More generally though, regardless of how it might have been applied to Urban's conduct,[158] this analysis reflected changing contemporary views on the nature of compliance. The Federal Reserve, for example, had already recognized that compliance must be independent to preserve its objectivity.

In January 2012 in an odd refrain from the result in Huff, three of the five commissioners recused themselves from the Urban matter, and the remaining two declared themselves

[158] The author wishes to note that while a member of the SEC staff, he played a small role in the prosecution of Mr. Urban. He also wishes to note that in commenting on the historical significance of the case, and particularly the policy arguments raised in the friend-of-the-court briefs, he states no view on the merits of the SEC staff's case, Mr. Urban's defense, or how the policies articulated in the friend-of-the-court briefs might have been applied to the specifics of Mr. Urban's conduct.

"evenly divided" as to whether the facts alleged by the staff had been established.[159] As a result, the proceeding was dismissed and, as the commission noted in its order of dismissal, the ALJ's initial decision had no effect. The SEC issued no opinions.

The Urban case was a missed opportunity to recognize the changes that were taking place in compliance. Flannery has reflected on the odd similarity between the commission's resolution of the Urban case and the earlier Huff case. In her words, the disposition of the Urban case "was either an elegant solution or very heavy handed." In either event, Flannery says, the SEC has failed to clarify its expectations for compliance and has created a "real muddle."

After compliance has spread to vast new fields and taken on new roles and new missions within firms, the SEC appears to remain deeply ambivalent about its own progeny. Did it create a mere first line of defense for itself, or did it set in motion a developmental process that has created a new and independent field of endeavor, with roles and values far beyond anything envisioned in the 1960s and 1970s? In 2010, the SEC missed an opportunity for leadership. As can be seen elsewhere in this chapter, others are stepping forward to fill the vacuum.

ESMA Guidelines on MiFID Compliance (2012)

In July 2012 the European Securities and Markets Authority (ESMA) issued guidelines on the compliance function in certain types of financial institutions.[160] The guidelines concluded a process that had begun in 2011 with a consultation paper[161] and had included public comments. The guidelines themselves are of interest, because they demonstrate the importance of compliance in one of the world's most significant economic areas. They are equally of interest because they reflect the global trend toward recognizing the essential features of a successful compliance regime.

ESMA is an independent authority of the European Union, located in Paris, France. It was created in 2011 to serve as the supervisory authority for securities, within the European System of Financial Supervisors. Michel Barnier, at that time European commissioner for the Internal Market and Services Directorate General, described the role of the supervisory authorities when they started their work.[162] The authorities do not replace national supervisors. Rather, Barnier said, although national regulators remain responsible for "daily surveillance," the European authorities are responsible for "coordination, monitoring, and if need be arbitration between national authorities, and will contribute to the harmonization of technical rules applicable to financial institutions."

---

159 *In the Matter of Theodore W. Urban,* Order Dismissing Proceeding, Release No. 34-66259 & IA-3366 (Jan. 26, 2012).

160 ESMA, *Final Report, Guidelines on Certain Aspects of the MiFID Compliance Function Requirements*, ESMA 2012/388 (July 6, 2012).

161 ESMA, *Consultation Paper, Guidelines on Certain Aspects of the MiFID Compliance Function Requirements*, ESMA 2011/446 (Dec. 2011).

162 Michel Bernier, "A Turning Point for the European Financial Sector, Declaration of Michel Barnier on the Start of the Three New Authorities for Supervision," European Commission Press Release Database Memo 11/1 (Jan. 1, 2011).

ESMA's guidelines on compliance were prepared to clarify the compliance requirements set out in a directive of the European Union that had harmonized members' regulation of investment services. The Directive on Markets in Financial Instruments (MiFID) regulates firms providing investment services and activities.[163] Among other things, MiFID required firms to establish effective risk management and compliance processes. In the words of ESMA's consultation paper, the compliance initiative was undertaken because the financial crisis had "highlighted the need for better and tighter monitoring and managing of risk (including reputational risk) by investment firms, and for a more comprehensive and proactive compliance strategy, especially in view of the plethora of evolving legislation and increasing levels of scrutiny from both regulators and investors."[164]

ESMA's guidelines were set out in a numbered series. They included several that addressed the compliance function. ESMA stated that the compliance officer must have "sufficiently broad knowledge and experience and a sufficiently high level of expertise so as to be able to assume responsibility for the compliance function as a whole and ensure that it is effective." Firms should ensure that compliance had sufficient resources, authority, and information. Also, much like the Federal Reserve a few years before, ESMA held that the compliance function should be independent. It said:

Investment firms should ensure that the compliance function holds a position in the organizational structure that ensures that the compliance officer and other compliance staff act independently when performing their tasks. The compliance officer should be appointed and replaced by senior management or the supervisory function.[165]

Again like the Federal Reserve, ESMA went on to address the combination of compliance management with other functions. ESMA noted that compliance management could be combined with other control functions, but not with internal audit.

ESMA's guidelines also addressed how a compliance program should operate. The guidance stated that firms should ensure that the compliance function:

- Takes a risk-based approach;
- Establishes a monitoring programme;
- Sends regular written compliance reports to senior management;
- Fulfills its advisory function through training, day-to-day assistance, and establishing new policies and procedures;
- Operates on a permanent basis (that is, by appropriately substituting for the compliance officer when he or she is absent); and
- Ensures that all applicable requirements are fulfilled when outsourcing some or all of the compliance function.

[163] European Union, Directive 2004/39/EC (Apr. 21, 2004).
[164] ESMA, *Consultation Paper*.
[165] ESMA, *Final Report*.

Like many of the other sources of recognition for compliance, ESMA's guidance was not headline news. Much of compliance's most important development has taken place in obscure settings, known only to specialized practitioners. In this case, even ESMA appears to have done little to publicize the guidelines. In the words of a consulting firm, published five months after issuance of the final guidance, ESMA had "hardly given any publicity to the guidelines."[166] This silence does not detract from the importance of the initiative. ESMA's guidance harmonized several key elements of a compliance regime across the European Union's financial sector. Just as important, the guidelines reflected several developments seen elsewhere, such as compliance's need for independence. Although the ESMA guidance differed in several details from the Federal Reserve's SR 08-8, a common spirit could be found animating them both.

SIFMA White Paper (2013)

In March 2013, SIFMA's Compliance and Legal Division released a document on the state of compliance, entitled *White Paper: The Evolving Role of Compliance.*[167] From time to time, SIFMA, or its predecessor the SIA, had issued white papers when the moment seemed opportune to review the current state of the field. R. Gerald Baker, executive director of SIFMA's Compliance and Legal Division reports that the paper was triggered by the "turmoil the industry experienced in the late 2000s." The aftermath of the financial crisis seemed opportune for a new white paper because compliance was being challenged by multiple new developments—globalization, new technology, new regulatory priorities, and even new regulators—as organizations entered new jurisdictions or new lines of work. For their part, regulators were enhancing their enforcement programs and establishing self-reporting mechanisms, which placed extra pressure on compliance. Finally, because of budgetary restraints, many firms were asking compliance to assume greater responsibilities with limited resources. As the white paper expressed it, because of these changes, compliance officers had come to inhabit an "increasingly complex world."

From the perspective of contemporary compliance, the white paper is a valuable source regarding many current issues and concerns. Moreover, from a historical perspective, the white paper provides a benchmark that allows for an assessment of the changes in the field. In this regard, the contrast between the white paper and the Model Guide of the 1970s is striking. In particular, three contrasts are worthy of note.

First, the white paper focused on the role of compliance as a risk and control function. To be effective in this role, compliance must have clearly defined duties, which distinguish its activities both from the business and other control functions. Beyond this, the white paper said, firms must protect compliance's independence. The paper set out three means of ensuring appropriate independence for compliance: its advice should not be subject to the approval of senior management; its personnel should be

[166] Charco & Dique, Risk Management & Compliance, *ESMA on Organization Compliance Function* (Jan. 13, 2013), available online.

[167] Securities Industry and Financial Markets Association, *White Paper: The Evolving Role of Compliance* (Mar. 2013).

solely responsible for performing compliance functions; and it should have sufficient tools and expertise to fulfill its responsibilities. Forty years before, in the Model Guide, there was no discussion of compliance's independence. Instead, the Model Guide had focused on the authority of the manager charged with the organization's compliance. The difference between these two documents marks the rise of compliance as a unique field of endeavor, distinct from day-to-day management.

Second, the paper discussed the complex responsibilities of compliance in its dealings with the firm's management, including the control group, firm committees, legal staff, internal audit, and risk management. The image of compliance that emerges from this discussion, particularly in regards to what the paper calls "front-office centered" activities, is a senior-level function that participates at the highest levels of firm governance. The Model Guide, on the other hand, focused on the operational controls that compliance could exercise. In other words, where the white paper discussed high-level strategic participation in firm leadership, the Model Guide had discussed specific operational control procedures. The difference between these two documents marks the rise of compliance out of an operational function on the shop floor—where, to this day, compliance operations remain in place—to an executive function that participates with the highest levels of the firm.

Third, the white paper discussed the importance of technology. Technology has facilitated and enhanced many compliance operations. At the same time, the paper notes, rapid changes in technology have posed significant challenges to compliance. New technology platforms allow employees to engage in both business and personal communications; business functions can use multiple data sets in real time to make decisions; accelerated business practices generate vast quantities of data; and algorithmic trading strategies challenge surveillance and monitoring. New technology has also given compliance new responsibilities, in areas such as data protection and privacy. The white paper notes that compliance is struggling to obtain the resources and expertise it needs to keep up. Forty years ago, at the time of the Model Guide, computer technology was just beginning to have an impact on business. The challenges discussed in the Model Guide were related to issues like controls over the manual entry of data, review of printouts, and consideration of special coding. The contrast between the white paper and the Model Guide marks the transformation of modern society as computational power has become cheap and widely distributed. It also marks how technology has changed from a tool that can assist compliance to a dynamic and fluid area that carries as many compliance challenges as opportunities. From a simple consumer of computer technology, compliance has become a player in addressing the challenges it raises.

The *White Paper: The Evolving Role of Compliance* discussed concerns and challenges facing compliance. The concerns are real and the challenges serious. Nonetheless, as a historical document, the document can help us understand the changes in compliance over its brief life. In it we can see how compliance had changed from its origins, only a few decades before. Compliance has become an independent field of endeavor, an executive function participating in the highest levels of firm governance, and a player in meeting the challenge of technological change.

ISO Standard 19600 (2014)

The most recent recognition of compliance was finalized in late 2014. An international group stepped forward to exercise global leadership for compliance, through the preparation of a global standard for compliance management. Just as the institutional development of modern compliance was first seen at the global level, with a recommendation from a task force established by the G-7, today another important development regarding compliance has taken place on the global stage. As the new standard is disseminated around the world, it can be expected to have an impact on every compliance practitioner.

The standard was developed under the auspices of the ISO. The ISO's name is an acronym translated variously, depending on one's language. In English it is taken to mean the "International Standards Organization." ISO is a global organization headquartered in Geneva, Switzerland, which claims to work with more than 160 countries. The ISO has issued standards in a wide variety of settings, including quality management, the ISO 9000 series; information security, the ISO 27000 series; and many others. The compliance management standard was issued as ISO Standard 19600.

Martin Tolar, chair of the International Committee developing ISO Standard 19600, has described its purpose and the process followed in its development.[168] The initiative began in 2012, he said, to provide "overarching guidelines" on what companies could and should do to respect their compliance obligations, irrespective of the source of the obligations. With such a standard, he continued, companies will be able to "benchmark their framework against international best practice." Australians stepped forward to lead the effort, and held the first meeting in Sydney in April 2013. A second meeting was held in Paris in October of the same year, and the standard was further discussed in a meeting in Vienna, Austria, in July 2014. The focus of participating nations, Tolar said, was to achieve a standard "that will serve the compliance profession in a practical way." Participating nations included Australia, Austria, Canada, China, France, Germany, Malaysia, Netherlands, Portugal, Singapore, Spain, and Switzerland. Several others, including Japan and the United Kingdom, had observer status.

The new standard was issued in its final firm on December 15, 2014.[169] The Standard begins by saying:

> Organizations that aim to be successful in the long term need to maintain a culture of integrity and compliance, and to consider the needs and expectations of stakeholders. Integrity and compliance are therefore not only the basis, but also an opportunity for a successful and sustainable organization.

---

[168] "What Are the Origins of the New ISO Standard on a Compliance Management System?" *Ethic Intelligence* (Nov. 2013).

[169] ISO, *Compliance Management Systems—Guidelines*, ISO 19600, First Edition (Dec. 15, 2014).

The standard states say that compliance is made sustainable by "embedding it in the culture of an organization and in the behavior and attitude of the people working for it." Policies and procedures must be integrated into all aspects of how the organization operates. In a refrain from the guidance provided by the Federal Reserve, ESMA, and the friend-of-the-court briefs in the Urban case, the standard also highlights compliance's independence, even as it is integrated into the organization's financial, risk, quality, environmental, and health and safety management processes, as well as its operational requirements and procedures.

The standard's discussion of integrity and the values provided by compliance is worth noting. Compliance has a role to play in safeguarding integrity, avoiding noncompliance, and enhancing socially responsible behavior. Specifically, the draft states:

> Organizations are increasingly convinced that by applying binding values and appropriate compliance management they can safeguard their integrity and avoid or minimize noncompliance with the law. Integrity and effective compliance are therefore key elements of good, diligent management. Compliance also contributes to the socially responsible behavior of organizations.

To implement these goals, the standard contains several elements, including: scope, context of the organization, leadership, policy, planning, support, operations, performance evaluation, and improvement. In regards to "scope," the standard is intended to apply to all types of organizations. In regards to the "context of the organization," the standard identifies the needs and expectations of interested parties, principles of good governance (including independence of the compliance function, its direct access to the governing body, and its authority and resources), as well as the identification, analysis, and evaluation of compliance risks. "Leadership" focuses on the organization's governing body and top management, and includes specifics on how they can demonstrate their commitment to compliance. "Policy" addresses the development of compliance policies for the organization, including the different roles of the governing body, the compliance function, and other managers and employees. "Planning" includes aligning compliance risks and objectives, and considering the steps that will be taken to achieve the objectives. "Support" includes the resources available to compliance, the competence of those responsible for compliance, internal awareness, communication, and documentation, as well as steps toward developing a supportive culture of compliance. "Operations" delves into operational planning and control of the compliance function, including in an outsourced environment. "Performance evaluation" includes monitoring, measurement analysis and evaluation of the compliance function. Finally, "Improvement" addresses how the organization should respond to nonconformity and noncompliance, including escalation of issues, with the goal of achieving continual improvement.

The development of a global standard for compliance management, with the active participation of several leading economies and observer status for several more, promises to be a major turning point in the recognition of compliance. Through an ISO standard, compliance management has achieved global recognition and a global benchmark. In addition, by writing a standard that is applicable to any regulatory regime, and any regulator, as well as any type of business—finance, manufacturing, or service—compliance is slipping free of its early constraints. One could view the ISO standard as final recognition for compliance. Compliance is ready to function in any organization, in any regulatory regime, in any country, and in any business sector. In sum, in the ISO standard integrity and effective compliance are being recognized on a global scale as key elements of, in the words of the ISO Standard: good, diligent business management.

VI. A HALF-CENTURY OF HISTORY

Over the last fifty years compliance has been transformed from an enforcement mechanism in one sector of one economy under the direction of one regulator, into a global phenomenon that is being applied in a wide variety of critical economic activities. To expand upon the words of SEC Commissioner Schapiro, spoken in the early 1990s about broker-dealers, by the early 21st century compliance was entering the lifeblood of the global economy.

Domestically, in the United States, compliance continues to spread and grow. Private entities are increasingly adopting compliance for their own purposes. Any number of examples could be highlighted. Two distinctively American activities are college athletics—particularly football—and charitable giving—with U.S. foundations leading the fight against diseases and other social ills. Many college athletic programs in the United States have established compliance systems to enhance their ethics and compliance with the rules of the National Collegiate Athletic Association (NCAA). In keeping with developments elsewhere in compliance, an electronic tool known as Compliance Assistant is now available to help college administrators, athletic departments, and student-athletes.[170] Also, the Council on Foundations, a private nonprofit group serving endowed grant-making organizations, offers compliance assistance to its members, and has published compliance guidance for their assistance.[171] Many other examples could be given. Public entities are also adopting compliance as a regulatory tool. A short list in the United States would include: the United States Equal Opportunity Commission (EEOC), a federal agency charged with enforcing laws against discrimination, which has been issuing a Compliance Manual, a section at a time, over several years;[172] the United States Department of Labor, which issued a Federal Contract Compliance Manual in July 2013;[173] the United States Federal Maritime Commission (FMC), which is promoting voluntary compliance with regulations governing international shipping;[174] and the Environmental Protection Agency (EPA), the agency responsible for enforcing the environmental protection laws which has, in its own words, "established programs to promote environmental compliance and correction of violations by offering incentives

---

170 NCAA, *Compliance Assistant*, available on the NCAA website.

171 Council on Foundations, *Check This: A Compliance Check List for Private Foundations* (2010).

172 EEOC, *Compliance Manual*, available on the EEOC website.

173 United States Department of Labor, *Federal Contract Compliance Manual*, available on the DOL website.

174 FMC, *Regulating the Nation's International Ocean Transportation for the Benefit of Exporters, Importers, and the American Consumer*, available on the FMC website.

to the regulated community in exchange for agreements to self-assess, disclose, correct and prevent future violations."[175] The list could go on.

As compliance has grown and spread, both continuity and change can be seen in its practice. In regards to continuity, on an operational level, a modern compliance practitioner would recognize the control procedures identified in the SEC's Model Guide of the 1970s. At the same time, over the last fifty years, compliance has been transformed by new developments. These have come in two waves. First, beginning in the early 1990s compliance was transformed into a distinctly institutionalized practice. Time and again, the core institutional structures essential for compliance management have been articulated: a designated compliance officer, policies and procedures, periodic assessments, and a special relationship with the highest levels of the organization. Repeatedly, these elements have been rediscovered, recognized, and applied in diverse settings, until now, pursuant to the draft ISO standard, they could be applied in any type of business anywhere in the world. Second, more recently, compliance has been transformed again, this time by the growing recognition that it is unique. It is not regulation or supervision, or a front line of defense for someone else. Compliance is a unique control function with its own goals and ethos. To achieve those goals, it must be independent and objective. Attention to establishing and protecting these characteristics, in an operational environment, has risen to the top of the agenda of many compliance practitioners. In many cases, the issue has been framed as a practical question: which institutional association—legal, risk, senior governance, or something else—best achieves both independence and effective integration into the firm?

Compliance is a new function, only fifty years old, yet it fulfills aspirations as old as civilization. Ancient philosophers, European and Asian, described voluntary compliance with the public interest as a path to reason and virtue. More recently, in the early 20th century, ethics and self-regulation were advanced as practical policy goals. Modern compliance practitioners continuously demonstrate how organizations can achieve these goals, even in the absence of compulsory or punitive state power. Compliance has transformed business ethics and self-regulation from aspirations into operational realities. Each firm, each business, each entity, organizes itself for its own self-control. The visionaries who first articulated these goals, early in the twentieth century or before, would likely be surprised by the operational forms their ideas have taken. Certainly, they would be amazed by the global nature of the current effort. But assuredly, they would have recognized and applauded modern compliance.

Although compliance has made great strides, a unique feature of its history has been its constant rediscovery. Viewing each development in isolation, it would appear that the benefits, structures, and implementing procedures of compliance have been rediscovered anew in each arena in which it has been applied. Much compliance literature continues to frame compliance solely in relation to the discrete requirements of a particular field of practice. Because of this, compliance remains highly balkanized, with compliance

[175] EPA, *Compliance Incentives Programs*, available in the EPA website.

practitioners in different areas working separately, with little communication and often less understanding of each other's work. Today, many compliance practitioners believe they are craftsmen who know how to apply specific compliance tools to specific local problems. Yet, when we look back on the last fifty years, we can imagine compliance as a building wave—rolling slowly at first, and then with more and more power—until it has swept through countless businesses, sectors, and countries. In the next half-century of compliance's history, perhaps compliance practitioners will come to recognize their participation in a common movement. When they do, they will see that despite their specializations, compliance is one field, one practice, and one profession.

ABOUT THE AUTHOR

A 23-year veteran of the Securities and Exchange Commission (SEC), **John H. Walsh** joined Eversheds Sutherland in October 2011. With his deep, insider's experience and perspective of the SEC, Mr. Walsh now represents broker-dealers, hedge funds, investment advisers, and other securities firms in compliance and regulatory issues involving the agency. He counsels clients on the full spectrum of securities issues from development and compliance to cooperation in examinations and defense in enforcement proceedings. In 2016 Mr. Walsh was elected to membership in the American Law Institute, the leading independent organization in the United States dedicated to the work of clarifying, modernizing, and improving the law.

At the SEC, Mr. Walsh played a key role in creating the Office of Compliance Inspections and Examinations (OCIE). He designed and implemented the SEC's securities compliance examination practices, first as a senior adviser for compliance policy and then, most recently, as associate director-chief counsel. In 2009, he served as OCIE's acting director and led a massive retraining of examination staff on antifraud techniques.

Prior to his tenure at OCIE, Mr. Walsh was special counsel to former SEC Chairman Arthur Levitt from 1993 to 1995. From 1990 to 1993, he worked in the SEC Division of Enforcement, serving first as senior counsel and then as chief of the branch of regional office assistance, where he regularly appeared before the SEC's closed meetings to present and discuss regional office enforcement cases. He also advised the commissioners and staff on securities laws and agency policy. Mr. Walsh began his career with the SEC in 1988 as an attorney in the Office of General Counsel.

CHAPTER 3

Core Requirements of a Compliance Program

By David H. Lui
Galliard Capital Management, Inc.

I. INTRODUCTION

This chapter will describe the basic framework presented by the Securities and Exchange Commission (SEC) compliance rules and give compliance professionals and others a sense of the common compliance requirements applicable to broker-dealers, investment advisers, and mutual funds.

Reliance in the securities compliance arena on the Federal Sentencing Guidelines, yielded in 2004 to the passage of the "compliance rules." The Federal Sentencing Guidelines set out a uniform sentencing policy for individuals and organizations convicted of felonies and serious misdemeanors in the United States federal court system, and set forth certain "mitigating factors" that would be considered in reducing the severity of sentencing, such as: training programs, well-developed control procedures and self-reporting.

The thought was that corporations that had implemented these safeguards voluntarily, even if those control structures had not prevented a violation, had proven their willingness to comply with legal requirements and therefore, they were deserving of a lessened sentence by virtue of their efforts to voluntarily implement control structures.

These general guidelines yielded in 2004 to the creation of three sets of rules, each set governing compliance in one of the separate areas of the securities industry: broker-dealers, investment advisers, and mutual funds. The enactment of this model created a formalized requirement for an internal control structure, transitioning "compliance" from the realm of sentencing mitigation to a legal requirement in the securities industry.

The compliance rule that governs the compliance activities of Investment Advisers is Rule 206(4)-7 under the Investment Advisers Act of 1940 ("Advisers Act").[1] It is a deceptively simple rule. It is less than a third of a page long and lays out the broad framework of the requirements of the compliance rule paradigm: (a) an annual review by (b) a chief compliance officer (CCO), who is (c) responsible for administering procedures of the Adviser that are adequate and effective in satisfying the requirements of the Advisers Act.

---

1 17 CFR 275.206(4)-7 (Rule 206(4)-7).

The Advisers Act model is elaborated upon and more detail is added for its application to registered investment companies (mutual funds) in Rule 38a-1 under the Investment Company Act of 1940.[2] Under Rule 38a-1, the model provided under Rule 206(4)-7 is extended from procedures reasonably designed to prevent, detect, and correct violations of the Advisers Act to procedures reasonably designed to prevent, detect, and correct violations of seven separate enumerated "federal securities laws." Although the coverage of the rule is limited to the activities of an investment adviser in the Advisers Act Rule, in Rule 38a-1, the CCO must report on the activities of many "service providers," including investment advisers and subadvisers, transfer agents, fund administrators and principal underwriters, in addition to the mutual fund itself.[3] Finally, the requirement of a "review" under Rule 206(4)-7 becomes the requirement to create a "written report" on material compliance matters and other compliance concerns. Although few advisers actually conduct a review that is unwritten, the Advisers Act standard, unlike Rule 38a-1, would allow for a review that remains undocumented.

The compliance rule that governs the activities of broker-dealers is Rule 3130 under the Securities Exchange Act of 1934. These rules are governed by the Financial Services Regulatory Agency (FINRA, the self-regulatory organization for broker-dealers) and essentially accomplish much the same objective of Rule 38a-1, but translates the Broker-dealer rule into the vernacular of the Broker-dealer world, referencing the role of registered principals and written supervisory procedures. Rule 3130(c) calls for the creation of a written compliance report (certification) mirroring the documentation requirements of Rule 38a-1.

The compliance rules represent a creative and innovative approach to the problem of how to address conflicts of interest within the securities industry. The compliance rules seek to create highly tailored processes, reflected by procedures that are individually crafted by each firm to cover the requirements of the federal securities laws in the innumerable situations where conflicts may arise between the need of the firm's client needs and firm structures. In that sense, the rules address a highly complex topic in a very simple framework.

It leaves the answer to the question of how to achieve compliance with the requirements of the federal securities laws within each firm's purview, as long as compliance is critically assessed and found to be both adequate and effective by an individual who is designated to make the review: the CCO. The rules might even be viewed as being fundamentally deregulatory in their effect, relying not on volumes and volumes of federal requirements, but leaving the design of ethical processes essentially in the hands of the industry that it seeks to regulate.

What could have otherwise required thousands and thousands of pages of regulation is elegantly disposed of with the requirement that a firm maintain procedures that are "reasonably designed to prevent, detect, and correct violations of federal securities laws"

---

[2] 17 CFR 270.38a-1, Compliance Procedures and Practices of Certain Investment Companies (Rule 38a-1).

[3] *See* Rule 38a-1(a)(1).

and that those procedures be "effective in their implementation"—as determined by a CCO who is made to care as a result of the imposition of his or her personal liability. This is the heart of securities law compliance, and once this fundamental principal is understood, the paradigm adopted by the SEC for compliance becomes perfectly clear.

II. CULTURE OF COMPLIANCE

In implementing the compliance rules, the SEC staff has often emphasized the key importance it assigns to establishing and maintaining a "culture of compliance." But what are the attributes of a culture of compliance?

Most compliance professionals would probably agree that the primary distinguishing element of firms that have a strong culture of compliance is that the rules that govern their activities are not read with an eye toward limiting these rules to their minimal applicability but are looked at in light of the purpose they are trying to achieve.

In this vein, many of the biggest compliance failures of our generation—including the failure of Enron—were executed by individuals who claimed to believe that they were operating within the letter of the law. However, judging by the collapse of the firm and the misconduct that later came to light, one could fairly suspect that these individuals had totally lost sight of the spirit of what the law intended to achieve. The requirements that had been lost in translation were often encapsulated by innocuous phrases like "disclosures that fairly represent," or references to "other material exposures" that allow certain discretion in interpretation but are very unforgiving if abused. A firm with a strong culture of compliance demands a response not just to the question asking, "What rule does this break?" but "Is this action fair to our clients and properly reflect our fiduciary obligation to put their interests before our own?"

Relationship of Ethics and a Culture of Compliance

A compliance function that elevates its mission from working to ensure that the staff is "following the rules" to working to build a culture that emphasizes its ethical duties to clients, shareholders and each other, is a firm that is more likely to have a strong culture of compliance.

An analogy in this regard may help make the point. On a ship, the role of compliance (in its narrowest sense), could be viewed as the role of the night watchman, who periodically checks whether the watertight doors are shut, the running lights are on, and the sound of the engine seems right as he makes his rounds, testing that everything is working as it should. Risk management mans the crow's nest, dutifully scanning the horizon for icebergs, ensuring the course is free of imminent danger, and ethics is the role of the captain, steering the ship to a point on the horizon. The engines could run just so, the lights all be blazing, no icebergs in sight—but if the captain lacks an ethical compass, the purpose of the business could be money laundering, facilitating the work of a drug cartel or identity theft—and no person attracted to the role of compliance could countenance his energies turned to that result.

Elevating the compliance function to have impact on the direction that the ship is steered is very important to each of us, and the challenge becomes how we gain the influence in the firm in which we work so that the role of compliance is not just that of the night watchman, but is that of the navigator, advising the captain how to steer the ship. In a firm with a strong culture of compliance, the CCO is not just the night watchman, but a "trusted adviser" to the captain. It is the single most important component of a successful compliance program.

Supervisory Buy-in

Another attribute of a firm with a strong culture of compliance is how deeply the supervisors within an organization, from the chief executive officer (CEO) downward, view the compliance mission as their own mission, as opposed to a series of requirements to be fulfilled by a Compliance Department or a CCO.

As will be discussed below, a strong supervisory structure is the first line of defense with respect to the implementation of compliance requirements. If the firm's supervisors don't grasp this duty and communicate the importance of compliance clearly, their direct reports will never value compliance because they will not be rewarded for the energy they take toward maintaining good compliance practices or punished if they fail in their efforts to achieve it. Supervisory "buy-in" to the mission of compliance is critical because the compliance professional, who has no direct supervisory responsibilities outside of a very limited sphere, must lead by influence. Without the buy-in of a firm's supervisory structure, he or she will not have the seniority and authority to fulfill the compliance function.

Attitudes Toward Controls

One of the most telling attributes of a culture of compliance is a firm's attitude toward controls.

When probed, very few people will hold themselves out as being unethical. The compliance professional who tries to distinguish him- or herself as having the "moral high ground" ethically will probably be disliked reasonably quickly. In a world where the people feel themselves to be acting ethically, a real question exists as to whether they will be accepting of the need for control structures that they might not view as being entirely necessary. That's to say that if "our people" would never cheat the system—frontrunning, acceptance of significant personal gifts from vendors, improper allocations—why implement "cumbersome" control practices? By and large, in that context, the controls can be viewed as just a "waste of time."

If, on the other hand, the firm accepts the notion that even if no one on its staff would ever knowingly abuse the process, the industry as a whole does need the controls, it is an important acknowledgment that supports a culture of compliance. Because it is impossible to call out where a problem may exist in the industry at any point in time, the controls must represent a communal standard that should exist across the board.

Thus, an attribute of a strong culture of compliance is the knowledge that the controls are necessary, not for any perceived problem within the firm, but as a reflection of the fact that the industry as a whole is subject to very real conflicts of interest, and even if employees know that they would not "cave in" to the pressures of a conflict of interest, that the industry needs these controls as a whole and that they exist for a larger good. Thus, the attitude toward controls itself is an important indicator of the firm's culture of compliance.

III. TONE AT THE TOP

Because achieving a culture of compliance depends on achieving buy-in from the various levels of management within a firm to maximize the compliance influence, that level of supervisory support is most effectively achieved when the message comes from the top of the firm. Thus, a strong message regarding the importance of compliance, when it comes from the highest level of the firm, is highly prized by all compliance professionals. But what is it that the CEO, chairman of the board or president of a company must do to set the right "tone at the top?"

Public Support of Compliance Goals

First and foremost, explicit public support of the goals and objectives of compliance by the highest level of management of the firm is essential. There must be no doubt in the minds of the leaders (or rank-and-file) of the firm that compliance is important to each level of management of the firm and that forwarding the firm's compliance program is equivalent to forwarding the CEO's own personal agenda for the firm.

There must be no doubt that as the ultimate manager of the firm, the CEO views the compliance program as the *firm's* compliance program. That is to say, that the program is not viewed as being the goal solely of the Compliance Department or, worse still, the goal solely of the CCO. Achieving the goal of the compliance program, as laid out by CCO, should be viewed as a goal of the firm—a goal that the success or failure of the firm might be measured by.

This type of support can take a fair amount of coordination to achieve. As will be discussed below, the compliance professional must create a clear vision and proposal for what the firm's compliance program should be. The compliance professional must present it to the leadership of the firm (not just the head of the firm) to assure all stakeholders that the plan is viable and deserves the support of management. They must create the opportunity for the firm's CEO to know that the plan has the support of the management team, and with that, give the CEO the comfort to support it whole-heartedly.

This type of management buy-in may take one or many rounds of back-and-forth negotiation to achieve, but it is well worth the effort, as it creates the environment necessary for the CEO to cautiously (at first) claim the compliance program as their own and go forward and endorse the importance of the compliance effort.

Public Support of Compliance Professionals

Like any of the people who directly or indirectly report to the CEO, he or she will not always agree with decisions of the firm's compliance professionals. However, a public disagreement with compliance can model a behavior that suggests that the CEO does not necessarily share the compliance goals being put forward.

Where a public rebuke is warranted, a strong tone at the top delivers a message that although a particular decision might have been executed poorly, the goal of promoting compliance should not suffer, and thus the compliance professional should redouble their efforts to achieve the plan and not allow a "poorly executed" decision to impact the need to continue to move forward. When a message delivered by the CEO impacts the firm's communal view of compliance, a strong compliance professional uses that as a teaching opportunity to help management understand how to reinforce the compliance mission.

Incorporating Compliance Goals Into the Firm's Mission Statement

One way for management to impact the way that a firm views compliance is the incorporation of compliance goals into the mission statement of the firm.

Reinforcement of the values of the firm relating to "strong ethical standards" and "integrity" or dealing with clients "fairly and honestly" can seem noncontroversial and innocent when added to the statement, but can be useful points of reference when passions become inflamed over particular issues that arise from time to time. It keeps in easy view those values that the compliance professional can leverage at important junctures.

If the opportunity presents itself to incorporate compliance goals into the mission statement of the firm, it should not be missed.

Compliance Goals and Compensation Incentives

One of the strongest statements of the importance of compliance within an organization is the inclusion among the goals and objectives of each person in his or her annual performance review process of a deliverable reflecting the employee's attitude toward fulfillment of compliance requirements.

Nothing speaks to working people as strongly as hitting them in the "pocketbook." Having an explicit goal that relates to procedures that employees must comply with, procedures that they must fulfill as supervisors, the attitude that they communicate to others regarding the importance of compliance and their ability to identify and properly respond to compliance exceptions, is a powerful statement of the firm's emphasis on having a strong culture of compliance.

Compliance goals cause supervisors to have conversations regarding compliance with their direct reports on an annual basis, and perhaps more importantly, it gives a compliance professional a reason to provide supervisors with useful input and feedback regarding their direct reports. Goal setting is a process vehicle that emphasizes the importance of compliance and where it can be had. It is a mark of an organization with a superior "tone at the top."

When you take a job as a CCO, probing management about the firm's attitude toward incorporating these compliance goals into the annual performance review process is desirable. It sends a strong message about how you feel compliance should be integrated into the management process of the firm, and is a moment when you may have significant leverage to make changes to a firm's processes.

Repetition

Repetition of the compliance message itself is a strong indicator of the strength of the firm's tone at the top.

Any propagandist knows that the more you say something, the more apt people are to believe that the opinion expressed is true. Compliance goals are not exempt from this truism. The more that management says that compliance with firm procedures is a priority for the firm, the more likely it is that the staff will "drink the Kool-Aid."

Repetition of the compliance message is also a useful tool when firm representatives answer SEC examination questions regarding the tone at the top. A file collecting the CEO's presentations, comments, emails, and other communications espousing the importance of compliance goals is strong evidence that the compliance message at a firm is heartfelt and real, not window dressing created for the needs of a moment.

Repeated messaging is also a form of protection that the compliance professional can offer the firm's CEO. It is his or her "insurance policy" that when executives were called to support compliance, they were right there and gave their Compliance Department the tools they needed to be successful. This repetition of the compliance message is not only for the firm's benefit, but for the personal benefit of the CEO. It protects executives from the charge that they were ambivalent toward the importance of the firm's control processes or that they did not understand the example they needed to portray. The compliance professional can use this self-interest to help the firm's leadership understand how this compliance goal can be important to them personally.

Tone at the top and culture of compliance are two of the basic underpinnings that help to create the right environment for the compliance message at a firm to be well-received and grow strong. It serves as fertile soil for the compliance message. With this ground prepared with the help of management, the compliance professional works to set the foundation of the framework of the three basic requirements of the compliance rules.

Basic Requirements of the Compliance Rules

Compliance rules are distinguished by certain core requirements that are fundamental to the creation of a compliance program whether you operate a broker-dealer, an investment adviser or a mutual fund. These fundamental elements are (a) written procedures that are adequate and effective; (b) a review or report on the firm's compliance program; and (c) a CCO who is personally liable for known but undisclosed issues.[4] Each of these fundamental elements will be discussed in turn.

IV. WRITTEN PROCEDURES

The most fundamental element of the compliance rules revolves around a requirement that a firm adopt procedures that are (1) adequate, or "reasonably designed to prevent, detect, and correct violations of the applicable federal securities laws;" and (2) are effective in their implementation.[5]

But what's the practical difference between "adequacy" and "effectiveness" from the standpoint of the work that a CCO needs to accomplish? Understanding the answer to this simple question is fundamental to fulfilling the compliance role, and may be most quickly and effectively answered by using a simple analogy.

Procedures are adequate if they are the right "tool for the job." Adequacy looks to whether the control process that you have put in place—scaled up or down to take into account the complexity of your firm—is up to the challenge presented to mitigate potential conflicts of interest, meet regulatory concerns and requirements, and provide supervisors with appropriate guidance regarding how to exercise their discretion. It reflects the needs of the task at hand: if you need a hammer, you can't do the job with a screwdriver.

The question of whether that tool is "effective," is a question that strikes a different chord. Issues of effectiveness emphasize the analysis of whether the tool (even assuming that it was the right tool for the job) is working as expected. Thus, an adequate and effective procedure is the right tool, and the knowledge that that tool is operating as it should makes you know it is adequate and effective.

How does developing effective procedures work? It really depends on the nature of the job you are trying to do. If, for example, you wanted to mow a lawn and that lawn really amounted to nothing more than a small patch of grass, an old-fashioned rotating blade push lawnmower might be all that was called for. If you had acres and acres of grass to

---

[4] *See* Rule 206(4)-7 under the Investment Advisers Act of 1940 for investment advisers (17 CFR 275.206(4)-7), Rule 38a-1 under the Investment Company Act of 1940 for mutual funds (17 CFR 270.38a-1), and FINRA Rule 3130 under the Securities Exchange Act of 1934 for broker-dealers.

[5] In Rule 38a-1(a)(1), the fund must adopt procedures that are "reasonably designed to prevent violations of enumerated federal securities Laws." These procedures are approved by the mutual fund's board in Rule 38a-1(a)(2), and in Rule 38a-1(a)(3), the annual report is designated as a review of the "effectiveness of implementation."

mow, a large tractor, with a seat, gas engine, and rotating blades might be the order of the day, and choosing the right tool is only the first step. That tool has to work. If the bearings have fallen out of the push mower, the blades won't turn. If you turn the key of the tractor, and nothing happens, you're sunk. It has to be the right tool, *and* it has to work. Adequacy and effectiveness: Those are what a CCO should seek in a firm's compliance procedures. Let's take each one of these concepts in turn.

Adequacy

In the parlance of the SEC, "adequate" procedures are procedures that are "reasonably designed to prevent, detect, and correct violations of applicable federal securities laws."[6] The procedure must work to accomplish this goal. But how does this work in operation?

Reasonably Designed. According to the compliance rules, a firm's procedures must be "reasonably designed to prevent, detect, and correct violations of the applicable federal securities laws." But why is the standard set to "reasonably designed" as opposed to "absolutely designed" or just "designed," and what significance does the standard of "reasonableness" in this context have?

These are very important questions, because they acknowledge that if a procedure is designed reasonably, even in the face of a violation, the compliance responsibility may have been adequately executed. Reasonableness is a key concept because compliance can't ever guarantee that people with free will who are employed by a securities firm won't intentionally or unintentionally cause violations of rules, no matter how well written those rules might be. So, the question of when, in light of a problem, a firm's compliance procedure still serves to protect the firm is a question of fundamental importance to a CCO.

SEC administrators will also generally acknowledge that there is no way for a CCO to stop business line managers and employees from breaking the rules applicable to their areas of concern. However, they would be quick to add that processes to prevent such violations can be put in place—even if you can't be sure that those processes will be 100 percent effective. Likewise, a CCO can design systems and various testing methodologies to test for and detect violations of law, and if found, correct them. But there is never a guarantee in life that all problems will be detected. But the SEC standard —reasonableness—is that our role requires that we should work hard to try.

Thus, the yardstick is not the absolute success of the procedures in preventing a violation (although this may be a piece of the puzzle), but whether they were thoughtfully designed. Part of an assessment of that design will be whether there were multiple

---

[6] Although Rule 38a-1 specifically references only the "prevention" of violations of federal securities laws, the Adopting Release of the rule broadens this mandate and calls for procedures that "prevent, detect, or correct" violations of those laws. *See* Release Nos. IA-2204; IC-26299; File No. S7-03-03 (the "Adopting Release"). Because the standard is that the procedures must be "reasonably designed," the lack of precision inherent to a standard based on "reasonableness" has preempted any discussion of whether the standard should be limited to "prevention."

checkpoints, safeguards, and other creative redundancies used within each procedure to prevent a violation, and, if a problem was still not prevented, whether it was detected quickly through thoughtfully created supervisory touch points or other separations of duties, and—after it was detected—whether there was a process employed by the firm that provoked a wholehearted effort to correct any damage that was caused. Thus, the issue is whether the prevention mechanism is robust and, if it does not prevent an issue, whether it can catch the issue quickly and resolve it. Reasonable design equals sound process.

This is a point of key importance and perhaps the greatest value a compliance person can bring to his or her firm. Even if a "bad actor" at a firm violates the federal securities laws, the procedures themselves should protect the firm from liability.

The impact of this construction of the compliance rules—seeking only that the procedures of a firm be "reasonably designed"—becomes clearest when a compliance officer assesses who may be liable for a violation. The natural progression of possible liability will be first to assess the liability of the individuals directly involved; secondly, look for failures to supervise those individuals and failures to supervise the levels of management above them; and then, to look for failures of the compliance program.

Even in the case of an intentional violation by an employee, if the procedures can be held out to be reasonably and effectively implemented, a claim of a failure of the firm's compliance program can be avoided, and as will be discussed below, so can the claims of failures to supervise. The creation of reasonably designed and effectively implemented procedures is the most effective way to prevent limited violations caused by individuals at a firm from growing into failures of the firm itself. It limits the scope of the violation to the "bad actor" and does not allow the liability to flow across the firm.

The challenge of the CCO in fulfilling this function is to effectively balance this emphasis on process on one hand while also having an eye to creativity on the other, so that the CCO is not simply a bureaucrat. The notion of how these "reasonable" redundancies, supervisory touch points, and separations of duties are put forward and incorporated in the procedures is all a matter of experience, insight, and intuition: It is a creative exercise, working with line management to understand the "art of the possible."

The successful CCO can point to the procedures in the face of a problem and fairly say, "Look, we thought about this risk—worked to avoid it—and even if someone stepped over the line, we found the damage quickly and made the injured party whole. Yes, someone may have gone 'off the ranch,' but as CCO, I can't prevent that. I can only work to see that processes that I believe to be reasonable are in place and that they have been effectively implemented."

If a CCO can say that, he or she should be able to avoid the firm's liability for the bad acts of an errant employee. This is when compliance adds the most value to the controls of a firm. It is compliance at its best.

Designating Desktop and Compliance Procedures. Although a firm has to satisfy the requirements of the compliance rules to be "adequate," are there processes in a firm that, although they need to be documented, are not necessary for compliance purposes, that is, their purpose is not to prevent, detect or correct violations of federal securities law. The question is which documents are actually "procedures" for the purposes of the compliance rules?

Clearly, there are many types of documents at a firm that are necessary to help employees understand how to do various tasks. There are manuals on how to operate systems, how to file expense reports, and even a sign over most coffee makers saying, "Turn off after 5 p.m." Which of these are the procedures that the compliance rules call on firms to maintain?

Many firms distinguish between "desktop procedures" and "compliance procedures." When designating whether a certain document is a compliance procedure, the CCO should ask whether the purpose of the procedure is to facilitate compliance with the applicable federal securities laws. In the broadest sense, all procedural documents support the goals of the federal securities laws. Even the sign over the coffee maker helps prevent fires and can be thought of (in the broadest sense) as supporting the firm's record retention requirements. Likewise, a document giving instructions on how to use the code of ethics system helps detect frontrunning, but does it help the employees running the system understand how to use their discretion or supervisory authority?

The most important practical distinction between compliance and desktop procedures is that compliance procedures:

- Will have to be tested and the results of that testing reported upward; and
- Will have to be monitored on an ongoing basis for the impact of changes in law, changes in business model, and other learnings that can be gleaned from patterns of compliance exceptions.

An incorrect designation of a procedure suggests that the Compliance Department did not think it worthy of testing, and if a problem emanates from that process, it will be a per se violation of the compliance rules.

Procedures that merely give instructions on how to use a system may have some value in maintaining smooth execution of operations, but they tend not to give much insight into whether the system (even if it is being competently used) is accomplishing its associated compliance objective. For example, the procedure regarding how to use a code of ethics system doesn't tell you much about what standards you should choose for monitoring the securities transactions of the access persons in your firm.

A key distinction between desktop procedures and compliance procedures is that any procedure that can be said to be used to mitigate conflicts of interest within a firm should be viewed as a compliance procedure that requires testing. To use any strategy that would relieve compliance from testing procedures that are used to address conflicts of interests should be fastidiously avoided because that strategy strikes at the heart of the SEC's vision in the creation of the compliance rules. Plus that strategy will almost certainly be flagged by regulators as a compliance failure if things go wrong.

Federal Securities Laws. In Rule 38a-1, procedures must be created to prevent, detect, and correct violations of the "federal securities laws," and the coverage of this term is clear because *federal securities laws* is defined in the rule. Because Rule 38a-1 is designed for mutual funds, the federal securities laws cover the various regulatory areas that may be applicable to a fund, including (1) the Investment Advisers Act of 1940; (2) the Investment Company Act of 1940; (3) the Securities Act of 1933; (4) the Securities Exchange Act of 1934; (5) the Bank Secrecy Act; (6) the Employee Retirement Income Act; (7) Title V of the Gramm-Leach-Bliley Act (regarding privacy of consumer information); and (8) the Sarbanes-Oxley Act of 2002.[7]

For investment advisers outside of the realm of managing mutual funds, the standard is a bit less clear. Although Rule 206(4)-7, on its face, relates only to the Investment Advisers Act of 1940 and not the six other acts that constitute the federal securities laws, the Advisers Act contains a code of ethics requirement under Rule 204A-1 that requires the reporting of violations of federal securities laws generally. Thus, a question may exist as to whether the broader code of ethics requirement subsumes the narrower compliance rule requirement. In other words, when an adviser's CCO tests for violations of the code of ethics requirement, must his or her review touch the broader array of federal securities laws?

Although the SEC has never availed itself of this "bootstrap" theory, a compliance officer should be mindful of the possible conflict between the two requirements, which could result in their extending their reviews beyond the confines of the Advisers Act to the other acts constituting the federal securities laws.

The Broker-dealer version of the rule seeks only that the CCO test and verify that the supervisory procedures are reasonably designed with respect to the activities of the FINRA member and its registered representatives and associated persons to achieve compliance with "applicable securities laws, regulations, and FINRA Rules." Arguably, this is the broadest provision of the three because it would touch any applicable securities law, which might be thought to go beyond the seven acts enumerated in the mutual fund version of the compliance rules. However, as a practical matter, the coverage is generally taken as being equivalent.

Use of Risk Inventories to Assess Adequacy. Developing adequate procedures as a matter of internal control processes presents unique challenges. How do you create a process to programmatically identify the procedures needed for your firm? How do you confirm that a certain set of procedures are the "right tools" to prevent, detect, and correct violations of the applicable laws? Generally speaking, the device that the industry has focused on to do this is a *gap analysis* or *risk inventory*.[8]

---

[7] *See* Rule 38a-1(e)(1).

[8] *See* Lori A. Richards, Working Towards a Culture of Compliance: Some Obstacles in the Path, National Society of Compliance Professionals 2007 Annual Meeting, Washington, DC (Oct. 18, 2007), www.sec.gov/news/speech/2007/spch101807lar.htm

A risk inventory addresses the issue of adequacy by assessing the risks and conflicts of interest confronting a particular firm, looking to which rule governs the issue and assessing whether a procedure of the firm actually exists to govern the issue. If there is no procedure to address the issue, a gap has been detected and the procedure needs to be created or enhanced.

Because the types of risks and conflicts affecting the firm can be wide ranging and difficult to identify, another best practice has developed among CCOs to take the processes of the firm and attempt to trace them through diagrams or checklists to see whether each portion of the process is covered by one of the firm's procedures. A diagram of this sort can be constructed as a type of flow chart, detailing the control points of each process of the firm: trading, custody, code of ethics reviews, reconciliations, marketing reviews, new product development, etc. Each such review seeks to identify conflicts of interest and as these conflicts are identified, the question becomes what controls exist to mitigate those conflicts? Once the risks of the firm are matched to governing procedures that are "reasonably designed to prevent, detect, and correct violations of federal securities laws," you have properly defined the scope of the firm's procedure base.

Conflicts of Interest: Follow the Money. Understanding the risks of loss and the conflicts of interest that may exist in your firm generally boils down into a familiar mantra that was made famous during the Watergate scandals of the Nixon Administration in the 1970s: "Follow the money."

The Watergate scandal, for anyone who was politically aware in the 1970s, will forever represent the granddaddy of all failure to supervise events. A scandal that ultimately caused a president to resign was broken wide open when a whistleblower from within the government approached two journalists at *The Washington Post* and told them some of the details surrounding the Republican-sponsored break in of the Democratic National Committee headquarters at the Watergate Apartments in Washington. The informer also gave details of the Nixon Administration's attempts to conceal the truth, leading to another famous mantra for compliance professionals: "The cover-up is worse than the crime."

The Nixon whistleblower (forever after known as "Deep Throat") wouldn't give *The Washington Post* journalists the complete story, but only told them to "follow the money," and eventually, the trail of money led back to President Nixon and his senior staff. Follow the money has since then stood for the notion that knowledge of financial incentives is a key element of understanding why things are structured the way they are. For a control person, such as a compliance professional, understanding when those incentives cause conflicts of interest or are otherwise at odds with a firm's stated values or ethical standards is a vital piece of the puzzle.

In the compliance context, following the money might mean fully understanding each team's bonus, salary, and other elements composing their compensation structure. It might mean understanding how vendors (and broker-dealers) are selected and what benefits might flow back to the firm by selecting one vendor over another. Soft dollar relationships can trigger this concern. It might mean understanding how the firm is compensated in various contexts and what elements of the relationship might represent a disclosable conflict between the interests of various clients.

Following the money is a time-tested prerequisite to understanding the conflicts that might exist in your firm. Without that knowledge, a compliance profession is ill-equipped to identify the issues that will govern whether the firm's procedures are adequate.

Another key learning from the Watergate scandal, "the cover-up is worse than crime," is worth a quick nod here as well. When a problem occurs, oftentimes it is an inadvertent issue or a bad choice made by a limited number of people. When a determination is made to hide something "under the carpet," invariably more people are involved; then it becomes a clearly intentional action and almost always represents a supervisory breakdown. For this reason, the Watergate cover-up, which ultimately included actions by the president of the United States, caused the downfall of the Nixon Administration and has since that time stood as a reminder of the dangers of a supervisory cover-up.

The Process of Creating a Procedure Draft. Once the process of identifying gaps is complete, there must be some form of programmatic involvement of business line managers, attorneys and compliance professionals to assess the nature of the reasonable controls required.

Generally speaking, it will be the role of the compliance professional to set out a strawman about what a reasonable control would be. The compliance officer will create the draft procedure. At times, this may instead be done by a proactive attorney or business line manager, but in the absence of such a draft, the creativity for the genesis of the document generally comes from compliance. In many ways, this is the best part of the job, because it lends itself to the greatest creativity: Should a committee be formed, or is a supervisory sign off enough? Does the task require a separation of duties among people or can it be done by a single person? Do multiple stakeholders need to formally sign off, and how and often should that sign-off be required and by whom should the output be reviewed? Addressing these needs in a creative way is what elevates the practice of compliance out of the realm of creating bureaucracy and into the creative realm necessary to truly add value to the firm.

Then these creative ideas must receive the buy-in of the other stakeholders. If the compliance person thinks a particular control is the right tool, but the attorney thinks it is more than what's necessary, and the business person thinks it's too cumbersome to implement, it's time to go back to the drawing board. It is the interplay of these three groups, working together under a management portraying a strong tone at the top that emphasizes the importance of compliance and creates the greatest likelihood that a firm's procedures will be deemed to be "adequate."

V. TESTING

The compliance rules call for a firm's procedures to be not only adequate (that is, as discussed above, reasonably designed to prevent, detect, and correct violations of federal securities laws) but also "effective in their implementation."[9] This requirement is the basis for the testing done by compliance that should be memorialized in an annual written compliance report.

There is no set requirement for how procedures should be tested, exactly what aspects of the procedures should be tested, or how often they should be tested. The fact that the written compliance report under Rule 38a-1 is required to be issued annually suggests that an ongoing recurring annual review is desirable, but even this is not required.

Types of Testing

Commonly, compliance officers recognize three types of testing: (1) transactional testing, (2) periodic testing, and (3) forensic testing.[10] Each of these will be discussed in turn.

Transactional Testing. Transactional testing (or monitoring) is testing that is done on a real-time, ongoing basis. The monitoring of trading on a daily basis would be an example of this testing type. With portfolio trading there is no tolerance for compliance violations because any purchase of securities outside of client guidelines is impermissible, and the damage caused made right generally by refunding the purchase price if the price of the security has decreased since the time of purchase. It essentially creates the potential for the creation of a put by the adviser in favor of the client. Code of ethics approvals are another example of providing ongoing, real-time approvals of permissible trading. This form of transactional testing is an effective mechanism for ensuring that individuals remain in compliance with applicable procedures and do not place their own interests in front of the interests of their clients.

Periodic Testing. For the items that don't require ongoing monitoring, some level of periodic review is still required to be able to assert—as the compliance rules require—that the firm's procedures are "effective in their implementation." The issue is what should be tested and how often those controls should be put through the discipline of testing.

Forensic Testing. Senior officials of the SEC staff have time and time again emphasized the need for firms to engage in a regimen of forensic testing to complement the monitoring and other forms of transactional and periodic testing that a firm might do. So what is forensic testing? How does it differ from other forms of testing?

Forensic testing is a form of testing that uses inferences and other indirect information to understand when a compliance program's controls are not acting as they should. For example, testing that identifies disparities in investment returns between clients

---

[9] Rule 38a-1(a)(3) and Rule 206(4)-7(b).

[10] *See* US Compliance Consultants, http://uscomplianceconsultants.com/3-types-of-compliance-testing/

may suggest improper allocation issues, and disparities between the personal accounts of portfolio traders and their clients allow a reviewer to infer that the trader may be misappropriating investment opportunities or front running. In either case, this type of forensic testing would point the compliance professional toward potential issues and allow him or her to make further inquiries to follow up on potential issues. Endless varieties of forensic testing can be designed, but they all share the attribute of testing indirectly for elements that the testers are seeking to assess.

What to Test

After going through the process of constructing a risk inventory that identifies the conflicts of interest in your firm, assesses the supervisory needs that call for documentation, and reviews other applicable regulatory requirements, a CCO should have a reasonably good idea about what procedures would be necessary to fulfill the requirement of adequacy. The next question is how to test them for effectiveness.

More than anything else, the question of whether a procedure is effective is one of whether the essential control points within that procedure are operating as anticipated. So how do you identify those essential control points that should be tested for effectiveness?

You first need a clear idea of what the procedure is attempting to accomplish. In this vein, many procedures are drafted to begin with a summary "purpose" section. As a preliminary matter, finding the controls that support this purpose can be as simple as going through each procedure document with a yellow highlighter to find the "testable" items. If after doing this, you find that some elements of the purpose have no controls, the exercise was a good one because it has helped you understand whether more is necessary to meet the standard of adequacy: prevention, detection, and correction of violations.

For example, a single procedure document might have three controls—or ten— that you deem to be "essential." A firm that has several dozen procedure documents constituting its "compliance manual" might be confronted with the need to test several hundred essential controls, or more, depending on the size and complexity of the firm. Once those controls are identified, the issue then turns to how often each control requires testing.

How Often to Test

The adopting release to the compliance rules calls upon the CCO to construct a compliance program that is nimble and responsive to events around him or her. Specifically, it emphasizes a program that reports annually regarding (1) changes in law, (2) changes in business model, and (3) patterns of compliance exceptions.[11] Let's take each one of these in turn, because understanding this requirement is key to knowing how often to subject your procedures to review.

---

[11] *See* the Adopting Release to Rule 38a-1 and Rule 206(4)-7, Rel. Nos. IA-2204; IC-26299; File No. S7-03-03, at Section II(B)(1).

Changes in Law. Changes in law, in this context, should be considered very broadly. It would include not only actual changes to the rules underlying the federal securities laws, but the guidance given in the proposing and adopting releases supporting those changes. It would include enforcement actions (hopefully always against other firms), whether successful or not, as they give insight into what types of activities the SEC might pursue and how regulators might view related, but slightly different, fact patterns. The notion of a change in law should take into consideration relevant SEC no action letters and exemption requests that might be applicable to a firm and the indications of how the staff might respond to related fact patterns. It should also respond to available reconnaissance regarding SEC examination requests and follow ups.

But perhaps most importantly, the notion of changes in law would apply to the changes that relate to your own firm: SEC deficiency letters and your responses, enforcement proceedings against your firm (if any), responses to whistleblower complaints, and any other communications in which your firm has made a factual undertaking to the commission staff suggesting how your policies and procedures are being implemented. Each of these items forms an important trigger in assessing how often to review the essential control contained in your firm's procedures.

Changes in Business Model. Changes in business models can arise from many different sources. They can result from the pressures that arise out of the growth of a firm or a firm's reduction in force. They can surface in the introduction of new products or the termination of product lines. They can develop even when a product line never changes but is marketed to new audiences. Changes can sprout with the employment of new mechanisms of marketing. In other words, a change in business model can emerge from any modification of product line, marketing techniques, or client base. They changes are a broad reading of the factors that may precipitate a requirement to modify the procedure's governing your firm's activities.

Changes in Patterns of Compliance Activity. The third element that the SEC recognizes as a spur to the need to revise compliance procedures arises out of results of the compliance program itself: the recognition of patterns of compliance exceptions that suggest that the monitoring regimen must be revised to tighten up the controls to change behaviors internally. Examples of this element might arise from testing that suggests that a certain supervisor needs to have more formalized guidance or information to be considered in his or her decision making, trading patterns that suggest that blackout windows on person trading need to be extended, or patterns of violations that need greater internal emphasis and sanctions to communicate the importance of avoiding such violations in the future. Even minor compliance violations should spur the question of whether a procedure needs to be changed.

The adopting release to the compliance rules suggested that the firm's response to these types of changes should be reported on annually in the CCO's compliance report.[12] Thus, the testing that looks at the firm's essential control points should at least mirror

12 *Id.*

this annual review requirement. However, as discussed above, although some forms of testing are transactional and should be done on an ongoing basis, others may warrant weekly, monthly, quarterly, or annual testing. The issue of how often to test for the changes referenced above and other violations ultimately is a reflection of the degree of risk each such matter presents to the firm. Thus the risk inventory, which is a key element of assessing the adequacy of the firm's procedures, can also be the touch point for assessing whether the risk profile of a particular process or essential control warrants testing more frequently than annually.

Updating Procedures

Understanding when the impact of these testing results reaches a critical mass requiring revisions to procedures is more of an art than a science. This understanding requires the input and integration of three different disciplines within a firm to accomplish: the legal staff, compliance, and the applicable business lines. The creation of a formalized (or, if you work in a small firm environment, informal) Procedure Review Committee or a Compliance Committee should periodically gather together to assess whether changes in the environment have created a need to revise individual procedures to respond to the changes.

Meetings for these constituencies to review each of the firm's procedures can be done on a rotating basis according to a procedure review calendar. All procedures should be scheduled for a periodic update, and industry best practices suggest that that update cycle should not extend beyond a year for any required procedure. The bottom line is as long as there is a process and methodology for how you have decided to address this issue, as long as you have reasonably designed a program that functions to respond to change and your program reviews each procedure's effectiveness of implementation, you have met professional standards. The selection of a reasonable methodology is left to the discretion of each firm: it is a form of self-regulation that is a fundamental premise of a compliance regimen.

However, that having been said, the closer a procedure gets to not having been reviewed for a full year, most compliance professionals would probably agree that the less likely it is that the procedure is still up-to-date. The passage of time itself at a certain point becomes a factor regarding whether it is reasonable to consider a procedure as being current. Even if no change is made, the procedure should still be reviewed and the review date recorded. If no such review is made, such a procedure is generally referred to within the industry is being "stale."

Leveraging the Testing of Other Control Groups

One of the issues faced by any compliance organization in a larger firm, and even some smaller firms, is that they are not the only entity in the organization that is responsible for "testing." For example, operations units will routinely engage in some degree of exception testing, audit functions will engage in "deep dive" reviews of particular issues, and the risk management area will often conduct stress testing of various types on portfolio holdings to ascertain how the portfolio might respond under certain scenarios.

The key factor here for compliance is to work carefully to see that none of the testing that they are doing is duplicative with the testing being done by other control groups. When the compliance rules were first issued, one of the most biting comments regarding the new testing regimen of the rules was that they duplicated the work that other internal organizations were doing. However, this perspective was quickly discredited. The compliance rules do not necessarily call on the Compliance Department to do all the testing required to assess the adequacy and effectiveness of a firm's procedures, only to conduct an annual review or create an annual report that includes an assessment of adequacy and effectiveness of implementation.

Thus, coordination is essential in determining who will test what and how the findings of that testing will be funneled into compliance to be reflected as part of the annual report (or review). For example, the Internal Audit Department may make an assessment of which areas that department will review at the beginning of the year. To the extent that the compliance group has no reason to believe that the audit team will execute their reviews in anything but a professional manner, compliance may rely on that review and turn its attention elsewhere rather than conducting a redundant review of the same areas.

Thus, it is important to ascertain early in the compliance review process which other control functions are "claiming" functional areas to review, and to steer clear of "doubling up" on the review of a single area in a single year. Not only would such a review yield little additional value, it would likely be destructive. The group targeted for multiple reviews would likely to balk at the added burden imposed by two uncoordinated reviews that might offer little marginal improvement to their internal processes. The broad-based compliance review of processes should therefore be molded around the "deeper dives" that may be conducted by other controls groups who may occupy the same regulatory space.

Three Lines of Defense

In the context of leveraging the other control functions that exist within a firm, it is often commonly said that securities firms have "three lines of defense." In the broadest sense, these are:

- The supervisory structure;
- The compliance structure; and
- The more specialized control functions, which tend to grow more and more robust as a firm grows larger.[13]

---

[13] Carlo V. di Florio, Director, Office of Compliance Inspections and Examinations, Address at the Private Equity International Private Fund Compliance Forum, New York, NY (May 2, 2012).

These more specialized control functions include internal audit, accounting, operations, legal staff, and "trade support." Understanding this model can be useful in helping the business lines understand the role of compliance and each of their own roles in a firm's control structure.

Supervision: The First Line of Defense. The first line of defense at any firm is the firm's supervisory structure. This is because, as a matter of Human Resource Department requirements, this supervisory structure is empowered with the responsibility to set goals and objectives for the employees reporting to them and to assess the quality of the work accomplished toward completing those goals. A necessary outgrowth of this authority is the "carrot and stick" of the power to hire, fire, and award or withhold compensation.

A strong supervisory structure, reinforced by compliance as a second line of defense (discussed below), offers other benefits as well. Supervisors who understand their obligations to maintain regulatory requirements can be the most important exponents of a strong compliance program within a firm. It is far more important that a supervisor be an advocate of measuring up to compliance standards than of merely looking to a Compliance Department to apply the procedures. This broader view of supervisory duties, one including a compliance call-to-action, diffuses compliance responsibilities throughout a firm and underlines the axiom of all firms that have a strong culture of compliance: "Compliance is everyone's responsibility." This disbursement of compliance duties within a firm is a far more effective way of communicating the compliance message than having the single voice of a Compliance Department stand behind the firm's compliance procedures.

This disbursed structure can be more intuitive to supervisors in the broker-dealer world, because the supervisory requirements in the world of Series 7 Registered Representatives and Series 24 Principals have a very explicit compliance component associated within the professionals' roles. Under the licensing regimen of FINRA, supervisors are trained to understand the compliance components of their role, and the maintenance of their license depends on it.

Failures to follow compliance practices by a supervisor will often trigger questions of "failures to supervise," and a regulatory examiner will quickly attempt to take a compliance failure at one level of a firm and move up the supervisory food chain. As discussed below, the only defense that the SEC recognizes in this vein also emphasizes the importance of the using of reasonably designed procedures under the supervisor's oversight to avoid the claim of a failure to supervise. Thus, the first stop for implementing compliance at any firm resides with this first line of defense: supervisory oversight.

The Compliance Department: The Second Line of Defense. The compliance emphasis on the administration of procedures is designed, as a regulatory matter, to support the supervisory function of a firm. By facilitating the creation of reasonably designed procedures, the compliance role works to protect line managers from claims that they have failed to supervise their staff.

The SEC in its panoply of rules has never defined "good" supervision. In fact, there is no rule even saying when a failure to supervise exists. The Investment Advisers Act does, however, in Section 203(e)(6), outline a defense to regulatory claims of a failure to supervise.[14]

Rule 203(e)(6) creates a safe harbor of sorts if: (a) a supervisor is acting pursuant to reasonable procedures, (b) has a system for applying them, and (c) knows of no red flags that exist that would otherwise spur the supervisor to action.

This standard is fully consistent with (and served as a model for) the requirements of the compliance rules. As such, it presents an important opportunity to show how the businessperson's supervisory needs mesh with compliance objectives. From a compliance standpoint, the development of procedures that are reasonably designed to prevent, detect and correct violations of federal securities law, are from a businessperson's standpoint, the same tools that he or she needs to avoid supervisory liability.

Using this common objective, the creation of these procedures can be presented as the fulfillment of a business need, and the businessperson can look at the support being provided by the compliance professional as being absolutely necessary for his or her own personal protection, as well as the protection of the firm. In this, compliance and the business are "sitting on the same side of the table," and share a common need.

The commonality of objectives between the supervisory line and compliance reinforces compliance as the firm's "second line of defense" (as discussed below) behind the firm's supervisors, and positions compliance as the best ally that the business line will ever have against a determination that they have failed in supervising the functions entrusted to them. With this assertion, most businesspeople will see the wisdom of supporting the compliance function, if only out of recognition of their own enlightened self-interest, to create a "shield" against claims of their failure to supervise a function.

A well-placed reminder that working to create reasonably designed procedures to personally protect the supervisor is a key element of the compliance mission can be just the argument needed to sway the business line toward working to keep the firm's procedures current. This is because the converse of this argument is also true. When a procedure doesn't track the supervisor's actions or isn't reasonably constructed, it stands as a dangling "sword," waiting at any moment to fall and injure the line manager it is supposed to support. A regulatory examiner could use the failure to follow or update a procedure (even if it somehow did not meet the business need) prior to claiming a failure to supervise by the line manager. The regulator will attempt to follow flawed procedures and supervisory practices "up the food chain" supervisor to supervisor as high in the supervisory structure of the firm as possible. In this sense, the procedures act much like the dividers that divide the oil tanks in an oil tank farm—preventing a fire in one from spilling out to the others and engulfing the whole facility in a conflagration.

---

[14] *See* 15 USC Section 80b-3(e)(6).

In one context, the procedure is the line managers' shield against claims that they failed to properly supervise their functions and in the other, a sword to be used against the managers to show that they have not properly fulfilled their role. This paradigm can be used to show the business professional that the help of the compliance professional is essential to the success of line management and compliance is operating at its best when the supervisors using a procedure understand that compliance does them a great service by facilitating the creation of procedures that can help the supervisors avoid a failure to supervise.

Internal Audit and Other Control Functions: The Third Line of Defense. If business line supervisors within a firm are the firm's first line of defense, and Compliance Department activities the second, are there other lines of defense? The answer is yes. Legal groups, accounting control groups, operations reconciliation groups and external counsel, auditors, trade control groups, and consultants can all fill specialized control functions. But at larger firms, the control group that stands out with a mission that is strikingly similar to the mission of compliance is the Internal Audit Department.

Like compliance, an internal audit team is tasked with testing the effectiveness of certain controls. Unlike compliance, there is generally no regulatory requirement that this review be undertaken. So the question becomes, with two groups occupying a similar space, how do they effectively coordinate and coexist?

The key here is a close reading of the regulatory requirement governing compliance. While the CCO is held to a standard of reviewing the adequacy of the firm's entire compliance control structure annually and testing the effectiveness of implementation, most audit groups annually determine the scope of their reach reasonably narrowly and schedule the particular reviews that they believe are necessary for them to conduct. Thus while compliance is charged with reviewing the entire control structure across a broad front, the auditors characteristically take deep dives into particular topics of concern. One is more shallow but far broader; the other is far more concentrated and deep.

The key element for compliance to successfully coexist with the Internal Audit Departments is close coordination. Best practices here would suggest periodic coordination meetings between the chief audit officer and CCO to share thinking on where control lapses might be. Whereas the Audit Department wishes to review certain topics that could also be reviewed by compliance, it is perfectly reasonable for the compliance person to use these meetings as due diligence to build comfort that the audit team will do a thorough job of testing that area and their tests prove reliable. There is nothing in the compliance rules that says that compliance must do all the testing itself. Only that the CCO must be satisfied that the procedures are effective, which can be determined on the basis of an audit report.

Likewise, the meetings with compliance can form an important feedback loop for internal auditors. A heads up from compliance about where issues seem to be developing can focus the auditor toward much more productive work in the coming cycle.

Similarly, calling on the resources of the audit team in this way is a way of leveraging existing control resources available to assist in the compliance mission.

This positive outcome, like many other facets of the business arena, depends on building trust. The Audit Department generally reports up through a separate supervisory line. To the extent that audit and compliance representatives become competitors in the same space, little coordination will be possible, and the win-win of leveraging resources will yield to a zero-sum game. Ongoing meetings and open conversations in periodic meetings help to avoid this result. With so many processes to test, there's little real need to fight over what to test; the goal should be to make space for all and leverage off of each other's successes.

Viewing the SEC as a Fourth Line of Defense. Avoiding preventable client/investor losses is the goal of all control structures. From time-to-time, it's important to remind ourselves that all internal control structures are aligned with the SEC in this result.

At times, however, the industry is less than graceful in achieving that result, and "bad apples" in our community can deceive their SEC examiners. At other times, the SEC is too strident in fulfilling its mission at the expense of an overwhelmingly honest industry. At the end of the day, most compliance professionals hope they never lose sight of the fact that they would far rather have an SEC examiner find an issue than endanger the investments of those who rely on us for the safety of their hard-won savings and investments. Occasionally, though, we have to be reminded of that just as the SEC may have to be reminded to tone down its rhetoric.

Each of the compliance rules has three common elements: adequate and effective procedures, an annual review, and a CCO. Now that we have reviewed the best practices surrounding the creation and maintenance of procedures, we'll turn our attention to the second requirement: an annual review or written report.

VI. ANNUAL REVIEW OR WRITTEN REPORT

The second of the three basic requirements of the compliance rules calls for an annual review or report that must be provided by the CCO and, at a minimum (in the mutual fund version of the rule) that must address the operation of the policies and procedures of each service provider and each material compliance matter that has occurred since the issuance of the previous annual report.[15] But although the mutual fund version of the rule calls for a written report, the investment adviser formulation of the rule calls only for an annual "review," without requiring that the review be actually written.[16] The broker-dealer standard is similar to the mutual fund formulation, seeking that the designated principal (the CCO) must submit to member's senior management no less than annually a report detailing the member's system of supervisory controls, the summary of the test results and significant identified exceptions, and any additional

[15] Rule 38a-1(a)(4)(iii).

[16] Rule 206(4)-7(b).

or amended supervisory procedures created in response to the test results.[17] Let's take each of these three different standards in turn.

Investment Company Act Standard

The Investment Company Act version of the compliance rules, Rule 38a-1, offers the clearest guidance regarding how the annual report should be documented and to whom it should be made. Rule 38a-1 calls for a written report to be delivered at least annually to the fund's Board of Directors.[18] The key elements are the fact that the report must be written and then distributed to the board, which then includes the board's counsel.

Service Providers and Other Similar Entities. The Investment Company Act standard demands that the activities of not only the mutual fund be reported to the fund's Board of Directors, but also certain enumerated "service providers" including the fund's: (a) investment advisers (including any subadvisers); (b) principal underwriters; (c) fund administrators; and (d) transfer agents.[19] In the Adopting Release to Rule 28a-1, the SEC took pains to note that although the term *service provider* refers only to a fund's advisers, principal underwriters, administrators, and transfer agents, the commission did not consider itself to be lessening a fund's obligation to consider compliance as part of its decision to employ other entities, such as pricing services, auditors, and custodians.[20] Thus, although inclusion of the activities of these other entities in the compliance report is discretionary, it is not beyond the scope of what an examiner, or a fund board, might find desirable.

This question often leads, especially in a post-Madoff regulatory environment, to whether the annual compliance report should include a review of the policies, procedures, and activities of the fund's custodian. Although an inclusion about the custodian is discretionary on the part of the fund's CCO, given the importance of the soundness of the controls offered by the custodian, going an extra distance to include an assessment of the custodian's controls carries certain logic. In most cases, this question will be settled by counsel for the independent trustees of the fund, who will make their own feeling known regarding whether they consider a Compliance review of the Custodian to be important. The board will almost universally follow their counsel's logic, and the CCO will find his or her hand all but forced to include it.

But regardless of which service providers are included, there is a bigger issue that exists with respect to the fund's service providers. The question is, especially when these service providers are unaffiliated to the advisers, how a compliance professional can have access to adequate information to give the same robust review to a service provider that the compliance person gives his or her own internal control structures? The answer to this question can be found in guidance known as the ICI Report issued by

[17] FINRA Rule 3130(b) and Rule 3130(c) .

[18] Rule 38a-1(a)(3).

[19] *Id.*

[20] Adopting Release of Rule 38a-1(2)(3), at note 7.

the SEC in response to an inquiry by the Investment Company Institute shortly after the compliance rules were adopted.[21]

The ICI Report gives important guidance regarding the level of review necessary for a service provider under Rule 38a-1. Specifically, it addresses the question of the degree of review required by a CCO of a service provider in the fund's annual compliance report by stating that a compliance professional looking at service providers may rely on "summaries" they provide in making the CCO's assessment of the service providers' policies and procedures.

Although the degree of detail provided to the recipient of the summary is generally in large part under the control of the service provider, these summaries must be robust enough to provide basic insights into:

- The adequacy and effectiveness of the service provider's procedures;
- Any material compliance matters that might have occurred at the service provider; and
- The resolution of any discovered issues.

Without these basic elements, additional information must be requested.

In addition to summaries provided by the service provider, most CCOs value the opportunity to actually visit a service provider and get a "feel" for its operations. It bears saying that if a firm relies on a summary, but could have easily seen that that elements of the summary were untrue by taking the time to visit the service provider's principal place of business, the CCO's review will likely have been considered to be inadequate.

Reasonable people will differ as to how often a service provider should be visited. Although some firms may hold out for periods of up to two years between visits (longer periods are unusual), others may seek to visit their service providers more frequently than annually, although this is unusual as well. Most CCOs attempt to maintain an annual schedule of visits to compliment the annual need to issue a revised compliance report.

It should also be recognized that not all service providers need be visited on the same schedule. For example, a mutual fund may wish to visit its transfer agent on a biennial basis, but visit subadvisers annually. A subadviser that has issues that, in the reviewer's opinion, need to be addressed may be visited more frequently for progress reports. Although there is no rule governing these activities, it is fair to say that any distinctions between service providers in the review process should be susceptible to a clear and cogent explanation to a regulatory examiner, mutual fund board member, or management.

Due Diligence Process. It is important that the service provider's reviewer develop an effective process when conducting due diligence. Commonly, the due diligence process should commence with a letter to the provider setting expectations for the coming review. A coordination call to kick off the review process is also much appreciated by the

[21] Investment Company Institute Report, Assessing the Adequacy and Effectiveness of a Fund's Compliance Policies and Procedures ("ICI Report") (Dec. 2005), at page 12.

target provider, and if this step is missed for any reason, the service provider should not be reluctant to initiate contact and work with the reviewer to outline a timetable and deliverables that will be sought in the review. Proactivity in this regard by the service provider will often be appreciated.

Prior to an on-site visit, the reviewer will often submit a written questionnaire to the service provider. A proactive reviewer will not only use a previous year's questionnaire (if available) as a starting point, but will solicit questions from other internal groups outside of the Compliance Department to seek input regarding service issues and conflicts that compliance professionals may not know.

Characteristically, the questionnaire will drill down on the service provider's compliance processes, key procedures, conflicts of interest, relationships to other firms, supervisory structures, and personnel issues. It will seek insight as to "how things work" at the service provider and who is responsible for what. It will also seek information as to how changes in law, changes in business model, and compliance concerns have been addressed since the last visit. In addition, a written questionnaire to a service provider will also generally ask that certain written materials be provided. These documents can include:

- *Annual compliance reports.* With the exception of the requirement that a broker-dealer, investment adviser, or mutual fund share its own annual report with management, a mutual fund's Board of Directors, and SEC examiners, there is no regulatory requirement that a service provider share its annual report with anyone else. However, such an obligation can be imposed by contract. For example, a mutual fund may incorporate terms into a contract with a subadviser that make the continued use of that entity conditional on an agreement to provide a copy of a subadviser's annual report. Thus,
  - When a service provider is unwilling to give a copy of its annual report (as is often the case), there are several common fallbacks that may serve as proxies to satisfy this request. Often, the service provider will be willing to give the due diligence reviewer a written summary of the annual report with a focus on any material compliance matters that are contained in the report and include a summary of the outcome of any deficiencies noted by the SEC in its most recent examination,
  - At times, if the service provider is not willing to provide this summary in writing, it can be presented orally, giving the reviewing CCO an opportunity to confirm the oral statements with their own written summary, which can be sent back to the service provider, and
  - Another work around can be had if a service provider is comfortable allowing the due diligence reviewer to review its annual report "on site" in a way that it cannot be reproduced. The idea in this context is that it is not objectionable that the report be read by the due diligence reviewer, as long as controls are in place to prevent its distribution to any third party;
- *Communications with regulatory examiners.* Generally speaking, on a periodic basis, every investment adviser, mutual fund, and broker-dealer is subject to regulatory examinations. These regulatory examinations may be conducted by any one of a

number of governmental agencies or self-regulatory organizations. A request for materials related to these regulatory contacts should be broad enough to take in examinations as well as other communications, and communications that go beyond discussions with the entity's primary regulator, to include any discussions with the SEC, FINRA, the Department of Labor (DOL), Office of the Comptroller of the Currency (OCC), Federal Reserve, Municipal Securities Rulemaking Board (MSRB), state regulators, and non-U.S. jurisdictions, just to name a few. An examination can be "for cause" or "routine." An examination generally concludes in one of three ways:

- No further action taken (often, this outcome is not documented), a deficiency letter, or a referral to the Enforcement Division of the SEC to assess whether legal action by the SEC is warranted as a follow-up to examination findings,
- The overwhelming percentage of examinations conclude with an exit interview that orally communicates the noted deficiencies, and then a more formal written "deficiency letter" is sent to the registrant. A SEC deficiency letter notes the examiner's observations and gives the registrant a certain amount of time to draft a deficiency response letter. A due diligence reviewer of a service provider will generally want to see any deficiency letter and any responses or follow-ups to ensure that no material issues were discovered and that all issues were resolved. Many registrants treat the confidentiality of their communications with examiners and other regulators with the same eye to confidentiality that they treat their annual compliance review, refusing to provide copies of these communications for due diligence purposes. As with access to annual reports, a reviewer can pursue some of the same strategies to gain insight into the existence of any findings, seeking to use summaries or viewing the deficiency response letter in a way that it cannot be reproduced, and
- If the service provider refuses to provide a copies of the actual regulatory correspondence, a report on the regulatory relationship to the due diligence reviewer is an essential part of the due diligence process. Were any material issues identified? Were all the issues that were discovered—material or not—addressed to the satisfaction of the examiners or other regulators? Were there any issues that touch the services that the service provider provides to the company doing the due diligence? Any questions that the target company is willing to answer regarding their regulatory relationships is of value to a due diligence reviewer, and should be memorialized in a memorandum back to the service provider from the person responsible for conducting the due diligence;

- *Key procedures.* A question often arises in the context of a due diligence review as to whether is a benefit to request all of the service provider's written procedures. The majority view on this question is that you should request only those documents that you intend to review and assess. Generally speaking, only "key" procedures should be requested. To have a cabinet full of documents that were never reviewed by the recipient is probably less desirable than never having requested them in the first place. But knowing what you need to see, asking to see those documents, reviewing them, assessing them and providing feedback is clearly the progression that represents the most proactive response. There will be many documents in the file of the service

provider that you won't request, to request many and never crack the cover probably starts to set out the facts of a review that is less than perfect. Which procedures you request and review depends totally dependent on the scope of the due diligence that you are conducting, but a good starting point might include:
  - Portfolio management processes, including allocation of investment opportunities among clients and consistency of portfolios with clients' investment objectives, disclosures by the adviser, and applicable regulatory restrictions,
  - Trading practices, including procedures by which the adviser satisfies its best execution obligation, uses client brokerage to obtain research and other services (e.g., soft dollar arrangements), and allocates aggregated trades among clients,
  - Proprietary trading of the adviser and personal trading activities of supervised persons,
  - The accuracy of disclosures made to investors, clients, and regulators, including account statements and advertisements,
  - Safeguarding of client assets from conversion or inappropriate use by advisory personnel,
  - The accurate creation of required records and their maintenance in a manner that secures them from unauthorized alteration or use and protects them from untimely destruction,
  - Marketing advisory services, including the use of solicitors,
  - Processes to value client holdings and assess fees based on those valuations,
  - Safeguards for the privacy protection of client records and information, and
  - Business continuity plans;
- *Disclosure documents.* Access to current disclosure documents is also an important part of any due diligence review. Ideally, these documents should be requested and reviewed prior to a due diligence visit because they should provide a preview for your understanding of how things work in the shop that you are visiting. If you read the documents before you arrive and still don't have a clear idea of the business model, operations, and potential risks or conflicts that may exist at the shop you are visiting, it is an indication that the disclosure is not fulfilling its function. Reviewing these documents should set the baseline for understanding the questions that you should ask in your questionnaire prior to your arrival. The types of disclosure documents that may be among your targets would include:
  - The Form ADV,
  - Any mutual fund prospectuses,
  - Any 408(b)(2) disclosure documents,
  - Representations and warranties contained in investment management or other contracts, and
  - Client advertising materials.

After analyzing the answers to their questionnaire, most due diligence reviewers will prepare an agenda for the meeting and a list of individuals who should be made available for interview. These people should represent the senior leadership of each area of the service provider as well as specific subject matter experts who are most familiar with the systems and processes that are the subject of the review. Prior to arrival, it is essential that the interview schedule be set, or the due diligence reviewer might find him- or herself with a wasted trip. In addition, the reviewer should prepare a list of questions to be asked on-site as a result of the review of disclosure documents, requested procedures, and the questionnaire. These questions may, or may not, be shared with the service provider prior to the visit.

The visit generally will take a single day or less; seldom does a due diligence reviewer stay for two days, unless there are particular issues requiring additional focus.

After the visit, it is imperative that the reviewer document the visit to preserve the information accumulated and the effort expended in the due diligence effort. A memorandum to management (or file) setting out the review process, dates of telephone contacts and visits, and the conclusions reached will be an essential backup to the conclusions contained in the annual report regarding the service provider. A memorandum to the service provider is a useful memorialization of the information provided, because if the information the memo contains is not contradicted, it can be assumed to be accurate.

Reviewers may also go through the exercise of preparing a "scorecard." A service provider scorecard, pioneered by Katie Kloster of Varde Partners in Minneapolis, takes a number of important issues, such as code of ethics violations, trading processes, and supervisory structures, and creates a heat map of red, yellow, orange, and green scores to summarize the adequacy of the service provider's controls in a format that can be quickly assessed by management.[22] It is a useful reference tool, as each of the reviewer's service providers can be assessed on a single sheet across a standardized group of important topics. Often, these heat maps (as they relate to the adequacy and effectiveness of service provider controls) can be incorporated into the due diligence reviewer's annual report as well as an important summary of the reviewer's due diligence program.

How Much Detail Is Appropriate for the Annual Report?

The question of how much detail to put forth in the annual report represents an important concern. On the one hand, creation of a thorough inventory of the issues that exist at an investment adviser, broker-dealer or mutual fund is a road map for a regulator or litigant who wishes to find fault with the adviser. On the other hand, a compliance professional's annual report is a legally required document that stands as proof of the CCO's reasonable diligence and satisfaction of his or her obligations because the CCO might otherwise be assessed with personal liability for a failure to appropriately execute due diligence.

In this sense, it is often thought (especially by attorneys) that the compliance obligation to report on violations of federal securities laws diverges from legal needs. This is especially true because the annual compliance report is required to include all material

[22] Katie Kloster, Service Provider Risk Evaluation Scorecard: A CCO's Tool, Mutual Fund Governance Consulting (Jan. 2007).

compliance matters and cannot be made subject to any legal privilege as a document legally required to be produced to SEC examiners (see below).

However, although the inclination of the legal staff may be to minimize the creation of a written record of compliance concerns, thereby creating less of a roadmap of the adviser's issues, its creation is exactly the mission of the compliance professional. But even having said this, an issue, even when discovered, cannot and should not be presented in anything but the best light possible, so long as information presented is completely truthful and not misleading. In this regard, the report should highlight (a) the process that uncovered the issue; (b) the issue itself; and (c) what has been done to resolve the issue. The documentation represented by the annual report offers an opportunity for the compliance officer to underscore the reasonableness of the process that they have created. As stated above, this underscores a fundamental goal of compliance.

The true role of the compliance professional is a person who can never "ensure" compliance with the federal securities laws. Instead, the call to action for compliance professionals is "to call it as they see it." The compliance formula runs as follows:

- I am the CCO;
- I am responsible for the administration of the firm's policies and procedures;
- As such, I have created a testing program to assess the adequacy of those procedures (that is, whether they are reasonably designed to prevent, detect, and correct violations of federal securities law) and whether
  - Those procedures are effective in their implementation,
  - This testing program has discovered the issues contained in the report (or "no material compliance matters," if that was the conclusion of the report), and
  - If any such issues have been uncovered, they have been resolved to the satisfaction of Compliance Department and management.

Whenever the CCO is called on to make an affirmation that speaks to their "assurances" that the firm is in compliance with federal securities laws—he or she should quickly recognize that this type of certification is a fact that, at any given moment, is unknowable to a moral certainty. The CCO is well served to use the formula referenced above to more precisely lay out his or her duties and the information possessed about the firm's compliance profile.

Although there is no set profile regarding how the report must be structured: to lay out (1) the CCO's responsibilities, (2) details of the testing program, (3) the findings, and (4) remedial actions taken. This formulation, in response to questions regarding compliance with the requirements of the firm's procedures, probably represents a best practice in the industry.

An annual compliance report should consist of the following elements described here.

Description of the Testing Process in the Report. The annual report should contain not only a discussion of the testing findings, but a reasonably thorough description of the testing process itself. It is an important statement of the due diligence that the CCO has conducted to be able to fairly assert, as most annual reports do, that "there were no material compliance violations" during the year.

There is no single formula that covers the endless permutations of how testing programs or their descriptions in an annual report can be structured. In fact, the allowance for this type of variety is a central theme of the compliance rules, which allows for any control structure to be reflected in a firm's policies and procedures so long as those policies and procedures are adequate and effective. However, when trying to look at the wide array of possible testing programs, it is fair to say that SEC guidance that a CCO work to make the success of the program "measurable" has special applicability here. Best practices in compliance testing require an expectation that a certain number of tests will be done in an annual review period and the results of each test retained, aggregated and reported annually.

For the methodology used to assess the adequacy of the firm's procedures, the report should discuss the process used to support the conclusion that a firm's procedures used are the right "tools," that is, whether they are reasonably designed to prevent, detect, and correct violations of law. This description of the process helps memorialize and support the "reasonableness" of the process and is thus an important element of the compliance program.

This work can take many forms. Most commonly, a discussion of a gap analysis or risk inventory will be created to discuss how the compliance reviewer looked for practices within the firm that should be covered by a procedure. Other times, discussion of the work that resulted in diagramming processes to look for lapses in the coverage offered by a firm's procedures will be used. No matter how the CCO achieved the outcome, it is a best practice for the annual report to describe the measures taken to assess the adequacy of the procedures and to recount any changes made in response to that assessment.

With respect to effectiveness, management and regulators will often respond to the notion that the annual report describes measurable "compliance deliverables"; that each procedure has a certain number of "essential control points" that serve to prevent, detect, or correct violations of law; and that each of these control points has been subjected to a recurring testing regimen over a period of time. In doing this, for example, a CCO might be able to say that a firm with 43 procedure documents in its "compliance manual" may have in each procedure an average of 8 essential control points, yielding an aggregate of 344 "essential control points."

A proactive compliance program may then feature creation of a testing calendar showing how often these items were scheduled to be tested. Other items may be added to the testing calendar on an ad hoc basis as new tests are developed or any other work that might be considered, for this purpose, a "test" is completed, and with this accomplished, a measurable and well-defined testing program can be described in this annual report.

However, although the structure just outlined is one way to approach this testing issue, it is not the only way. There are many. As long as a testing program is well defined and measurable, it is one of the areas where a CCO's creativity can shine through. The trick is, once this path has been discovered and paved, it should be clearly recounted in the annual report, so that the SEC and others who will assess "reasonableness" of the CCO's work have knowledge of why the compliance officer can feel comfortable in making affirmations regarding compliance to management, the government, or third parties regarding the adequacy and effectiveness of a firm's compliance program.

Discussion of Testing Findings. Once the process surrounding the assertion of the adequacy and effectiveness of the firm's procedures has been drafted, a separate section of the annual report should discuss the results of testing.

The mutual fund version of the Rule, Rule 38a-1, calls for the annual report to address (1) material changes to fund policies; and, more importantly, (2) material compliance matters. A great degree of judgment is required of the CCO in determining what constitutes a *material compliance matter,* basically distilling that definition to any matter about which the fund's Board of Directors would reasonably need to know to oversee fund compliance. The definition also goes on to specifically call out material compliance matters to be material weaknesses to process designs.

Assessing "Materiality." As a practical matter, only a small minority of annual reports will ever call out the existence of a material compliance matter. Most compliance professionals view this term, in practice, to be synonymous the type of matter that one would self-report to the SEC. This was almost certainly not the original vision for Rule 38a-1, but that is result as certainly reported by external counsel and others who have access to numerous reports.

However, many compliance professionals have developed a best practice that, if they have no issues that they would call out as material, still uses the annual report to disclose "high-priority, medium-priority, and even low-priority" nonmaterial issues to the board. This way, even if the SEC or a litigant were to disagree with the person who drafted the report about the characterization of an item as "material" or "nonmaterial," the fact that that item had been appropriately disclosed as part of the report would mitigate any damage that was incurred by the mischaracterization; the disclosure would have essentially fulfilled the necessary purpose of reporting the item.

In addition, this reporting strategy has the effect of implicitly securing the buy-in of the board to the imputed dividing line between material and nonmaterial issues. Presumably, if the board considered an item that the CCO had characterized as "nonmaterial" to be "material," board members would be under an obligation to suggest the change. How else, the compliance professional would rightly argue, could a compliance person know "what a board member would reasonably need to know to oversee fund compliance"? It is a useful mechanism to functionally share this burden of designating compliance issues as material with the board itself, and has thus become a best practice.

Following Up on Previously Reported Compliance Issues. In addition to functioning as the vehicle to recount the testing methodology and report on material compliance matters and other high priority nonmaterial items, the annual report is often used as a vehicle to report on the current disposition of items that were reported in the prior year.

Using the annual report in this manner makes sense because it closes the loop on the items previously reported and creates an official record of the resolution of those items. This is true even if quarterly "compliance reports" have been provided to a mutual fund board to show progress in the resolution of these items. If there are a large enough number of nonmaterial reportable items, using a heat map can quickly show which items have been resolved, are nearing resolution, have been started, or are not started.

Include Compliance Strategic Plan. A strategic plan for compliance, as the final section of the annual report, is not a required part of the annual report, but the moment of the issuance of the annual report is an opportune moment to set forth the resources that the Compliance Department needs to be successful and to build a consensus regarding the measures by which compliance should be judged in the coming year.

Having a strategic plan for compliance makes sense for several reasons. First, like any business unit, success is generally measured by the completion of agreed upon "deliverables." For the CCO to propose and achieve alignment on what these deliverables should be is an important milestone in determining an agreed-upon definition of the successful administration of a compliance function. Otherwise, the success of compliance is merely subject to the question of whether any issues were uncovered (easily viewed as an unsuccessful year for compliance) or the discovery of no issues (no news is good news, but still difficult to get excited about).

The execution of an agreed upon set of goals as set forth in a compliance strategic plan avoids the trap that exists if the best that compliance can achieve is "nothing to report." Instead, the use of the annual report to create a strategic plan takes the moment when the compliance reviewer has the greatest visibility in the organization, and uses it to assess personnel and system needs. The strategic plan, therefore, helps to successfully produce deliverables related to the creation of the tools required to assess adequacy and effectiveness.

Using the annual report to define the objectives of the Compliance Department also gives these objectives the communal visibility necessary in the organization to be able to hold them out universally as the firm's compliance program. Thus, the plan is enterprise wide rather than "the Compliance Department's plan," which other groups may or may not buy into, or, worse still, "the CCO's goals and objectives, "which may not be shared by anyone else. Progress on these goals and objectives can become a major focus of the activities of the firm's Compliance Committee, the vehicle created by most investment advisers (as discussed below) to be the recipient of the annual report.

The importance of creating a strategic plan for compliance is that it can be used to turn the perception of compliance into a group that, like other business line organizations, is essentially delivering a product—deliverables such as a defined number of different types of compliance tests through the year, or revising a certain number of procedures or emphasizing a particular type of gap analysis review. The underlying premise is that a strategic plan has made the completion of compliance goals measurable, and you can be proactive in completing a plan. No longer is success in compliance merely about the "luck of the draw" of finding a problem or not; it is about defining your success and being rewarded for creating a measurable and proactive compliance program. This goes to the heart of what the SEC called for in its creation of the compliance rules, and puts the compliance officer more squarely into the heart of controlling his or her own destiny.

The Advisers Act Standard

On its face, the Advisers Act standard for the annual review is very different from the Investment Company Act standard for the annual report. The Advisers Act standard allows for the possibility that the annual review not be memorialized in a written document, but that instead it merely be an unwritten "review." Presumably, the minimum requirement would be that a review of the adequacy and effectiveness of the procedures be done and "reported" orally. But even an oral report is not required. Because no report is required, it is not surprising that the Advisers Act also does not specify to whom any report would be made.

In a mutual fund context, the Advisers Act standard and the Investment Company Act standard work in tandem. For investment advisers to mutual funds who have no other clients, the overlap is complete, as the federal securities laws that the investment adviser must report on include the Investment Advisers Act, and there are no clients or regulatory needs that present issues that run beyond the requirements of what is anticipated in Rule 38a-1 for the firm's mutual fund clients.

However, most firms that serve as investment advisers to mutual funds also service nonmutual fund clients. In these cases, the side-by-side conflicts that may exist between these two types of clients demand a separate treatment of the Advisers Act issues that may exist for non-mutual fund clients. Likewise, These "Advisers Act only" clients may have distinct issues that do not arise in the context of the firm's management of mutual fund clients.

Thus, some advisers who service mutual fund and nonfund clients "side by side" will tend to write a report that separately analyzes the two groups or even write two separate annual reports—one under Rule 38a-1 with respect to mutual fund clients and the other with respect to Rule 206(4)-7 nonmutual fund clients.

Who Writes the Report? While Rule 38a-1 does say that a CCO must "provide" the annual report to the board, there is no requirement that a CCO must actually draft the annual report. However, given the fact that a CCO can have personal liability if he or she knows of material compliance matters that are not contained in the report, it is of central importance to the CCO to be given the authority to draft (or at least freely revise) the report. The ability of the CCO to do this, and the willingness of management to allow him or her to draft the report, can be fairly viewed as something of a litmus test of management's trust in compliance in one direction, and the ability and sensitivity of the CCO running in the other direction.

That's not to say, however, that other constituencies should not have the opportunity to comment on what the CCO has drafted before the report is issued, but it is clearly considered a best practice in the industry to have the CCO control the production of the annual report. This also serves to protect the firm from a claim that it has exercised "undue influence" on the CCO to avoid reporting on a particular item. The "undue influence" provision of the mutual fund version of the rule has been little used, but if the annual report is crafted in the CCO's own words, it is surely harder to make the case that the CCO was compelled not to disclose an item.

A Report to Whom? In the mutual fund context, Rule 38a-1 calls for the annual report to be delivered to the mutual fund's Board of Directors. But, in the adviser context, the question of who should receive the report is left unanswered. The reason for this is easy to understand because the Advisers Act does not even require that a report be written—it only calls for an "annual review."[23]

However, most investment advisory CCOs (as described above) take the review requirement to be best served when it is properly documented by an actual written report. Without a strict legal requirement to write a report, the question of to whom the report should be delivered is left to the discretion of the compliance professional.

As a supervisory matter, there would be little question that the report should be delivered to whoever supervises the compliance function. If the supervisor of the compliance function is not the CEO of the firm, as a matter of fulfilling the SEC emphasis on the importance of the firm's tone at the top, the CEO and other selected members of the management (if one exists) should also receive the annual report.

But most compliance professionals go a step further and use the standard in Rule 38a-1, which calls for the delivery of the report to "a board," as a guidepost. For advisers that have an Executive Committee, this standard is easy to fulfill because the report can be distributed to the members of that committee. If there is no such committee, the report can be distributed to the senior executive officer and his or her direct reports or group leaders.

But perhaps the best practice in this regard is to create a structure that mirrors the board delivery requirement called for by Rule 38a-1. This mirror structure is best accomplished through the creation of a Compliance Committee. A Compliance Committee, composed of members of the firm's management team, can serve many important compliance functions. Meeting on a periodic basis, it forms a body that can monitor the progress of the firm's compliance program or the implementation of a strategic plan, provide the compliance officer with an environment to receive feedback, discuss

---

[23] *See* Rule 206(4)-7(b).

resource needs, and generally heighten the profile of compliance concerns within the firm and emphasize the firm's culture of compliance. With the CCO as the chair of the committee, it also provides a forum in which the CCO can exert the influence necessary to administer a successful compliance function.

Broker-Dealer Annual Report Standard

Rule 3130 states that a designated principal (the CCO) must submit a report to member's senior management no less than annually detailing the member's system of supervisory controls, the summary of the test results and significant identified exceptions, and any additional or amended supervisory procedures created in response to the test results.

This standard for the production of an annual report is, of course, very similar to the standards set forth under the mutual fund and investment adviser versions of the rule. Here, as in the mutual fund version of the compliance rules, an actual report (rather than a review) is required. Like the mutual fund rule, the recipient of the report has been designated. Instead of the "material compliance matters" that are earmarked for reporting in the mutual fund rule, the notion of "significant identified exceptions" seems to suggest reporting that might theoretically be a little broader, but in practice, generally covers the same ground.

VII. REQUIREMENT TO DESIGNATE A CHIEF COMPLIANCE OFFICER

The third foundational requirement of the compliance rules is the requirement that the firm designate a CCO.[24] This compliments the other two requirements (the requirements of written procedures and an annual report) because it is the CCO who must administer the firm's procedures and provide the report to the board (in the case of a mutual fund) or senior management (in the case of a broker-dealer).

VIII. REPORTING STRUCTURE

Framing the reporting lines of the CCO can be difficult. On the one hand, the CCO is designed to serve as the leading control function to a firm, and that suggests that a separation of duties might be desirable, making the CCO independent of the firm's management to the extent possible. Outside of the mutual fund context, however, there is only one entity, and all functions generally flow up to a single CCO. An actual separation of that function from the advisory or brokerage firm itself would have been difficult (if not impossible) to orchestrate. In the mutual fund context, however, a mutual fund CCO could have reported to the fund board alone, without a connection to the investment adviser firm's management.

---

[24] Rule 38a-1(a)(4) for mutual funds, Rule 206(4)-7(c) for SEC-registered investment advisers, and Rule 3130(a) for broker-dealers.

The SEC rejected this approach however, and the rationale is instructive. The commission's thinking was that the CCO would ultimately have more access to information and greater influence in the organization if he or she were an "insider"—that is, if the CCO was a member of the investment adviser firm's senior management team.[25] This fundamental underpinning of the compliance rules, while taken for granted today, was for many, a reasonably close call. The issue was, at its base, whether a separation of duties in the compliance context was necessary to fulfill the control function. Was the CCO a "spy," the eyes and ears of the board—or even the eyes and ears of a regulator—or should the CCO be a "trusted adviser" of management sitting on the "same side of the table" as the executive team? The compliance rules opted for the approach that attempted to focus on the CCO as trusted adviser.

In the adopting release to the compliance rules, the SEC noted that a fund's CCO will often be employed by the fund's investment adviser or administrator.[26] The commission did not adopt a requirement that the CCO be employed by only the mutual fund (and not the adviser) because the SEC believed that such a provision would actually have weakened the CCO's effectiveness. Funds typically have no employees and delegate management and administrative functions, including the compliance function, to one or more service providers. If the SEC, in the rationale set forth in its adopting release, had precluded the CCO from being an employee of an adviser or any other service provider, the compliance officer would have to be divorced from all fund operations."[27]

If a separation of the fund CCO had been required by the SEC, the adviser's CCO would have continued to administer the adviser's compliance programs, and the role of the fund's CCO would have been limited to the oversight of service providers' compliance policies and providing advice to the board on their operation. As a result, the fund's CCO would have been almost entirely dependent on information filtered through the senior management of the fund's adviser rather than, for example, information received directly from a trading desk. Moreover, fund management would be unlikely to consult with an "outside" compliance officer on a prospective business decision to ascertain the compliance implications.

The SEC recognized, however, that a CCO who was an employee of the fund's investment adviser might be conflicted in his or her duties, and that the investment adviser's business interests might discourage the adviser from making forthright disclosure to fund directors of its compliance failures. The rule, as it was adopted, was designed to address these concerns by requiring a fund's CCO to report directly to the board. For many CCOs, this creates a dual reporting line.

The board, and the board alone, was then empowered to discharge the officer as fund CCO if he or she failed to live up to the position. Thus, the Adopting Release continued, "a Chief Compliance Officer who failed to fully inform the board of a material

---

[25] Adopting Release, Rule 38a-1, at note 89.

[26] *Id.*

[27] *Id.*

compliance failure, or who failed to aggressively pursue noncompliance within a service provider, would risk their position. The SEC noted that they would also risk their career, because it would be unlikely for another board of directors to approve such a person as Chief Compliance Officer."[28]

Although these provisions do not directly impact investment adviser or broker-dealer-only registrants, most mutual fund registrants are dual registrants, and the mutual fund standard has direct bearing on them. But the notions set forth in Rule 38a-1 also have "moral" applicability to the other versions of the compliance rules too. This is a relationship that many of the more detailed Rule 38a-1 standards have to the more abbreviated standards in the other rules, especially for investment advisers in Rule 206(4)-7. When SEC examiners and others look for how to interpret the skeletal version of the compliance rules offered to investment advisers, the joint adviser and fund guidance in the adopting release and the "buffed out" requirements for funds, although not directly applicable, cast a long shadow over the world of investment adviser compliance.

Seniority and Authority

The Adopting Release to Rule 38a-1 and 206(4)-7 makes a special point to affirm that a CCO should be competent and knowledgeable regarding the Advisers Act and should be empowered with full responsibility and authority to develop and enforce appropriate policies and procedures for the firm.[29] Thus, the CCO should have a position of "sufficient seniority and authority" within the organization to compel others to adhere to the compliance policies and procedures.[30]

The adopting release goes on to say in the fund context, that a fund's CCO should be "competent and knowledgeable" regarding the federal securities laws and should be empowered with full responsibility and authority to develop and enforce appropriate policies and procedures for the fund. The CCO of a fund, like the CCO of an investment adviser, should have sufficient seniority and authority to compel others to adhere to the compliance policies and procedures. Although this is the standard set forth in the adopting release, most CCOs know that it is not desirable to actually go so far in the power to "enforce" procedures and to actually usurp the position of business line management as the supervisor of the various functions of a firm. Doing that has significant implications for the CCOs personal liability if and when things go wrong.

But beyond this, there is no requirement for any particular educational background, certification, or license applicable to compliance as a discipline or compliance professionals as individuals. As a practical matter, however, many CCOs come to the position with a legal background. Either they are attorneys or have worked in a law firm in some capacity. Many others come to the profession from accounting and operations, and still others have worked strictly in compliance.

---

[28] Adopting Release, Rule 38a-1, at note 90.

[29] Adopting Release, Rule 38a-1, at note 73.

[30] Adopting Release, Rule 38a-1, at note 88.

At one time the New York Stock Exchange maintained a Series 14 certification for compliance professionals within a NYSE-Registered firm. That certification did not long survive the merger with the NASD into FINRA. Various other organizations offer a proprietary credential, such as the National Society of Compliance Professionals, which offers a credential known as the Certified Securities Compliance Professional (CSCP). National Regulatory Services, a prominent compliance consultant offers individuals a credential known as the Investment Adviser Certified Compliance Professional (IACCP). None of these credentials, while offering good insights into compliance duties and an individual's proficiency, is required to maintain any role in compliance.

Finally, many institutions of higher learning, such as the Wharton School of Business at the University of Pennsylvania, offer certificates focusing on compliance training, and these are generally very well regarded, but again, not required. The reality in this area is most of the background people have in compliance comes from doing the work rather than any form of formal training. Many other organizations and compliance consultants offer robust compliance training programs, both in person and online. It is generally considered desirable for each compliance professional within a group to attend at least one such training session in person annually, both for networking and training purposes.

However, in a more basic sense, the requirement that a CCO have the "seniority and authority" necessary for the role speaks to the CCO's stature and gravitas within the organization. It is a question of whether, without directly supervising the individuals within a firm, the CCO has the ability to affect conduct. Is the advice that they provide listened to or are they ignored? Is the person included in meetings or is compliance excluded? Are they given access to the information necessary to do the job? Are they viewed, not because of their role or title, but because of their bearing, as a trusted adviser and as being a necessary part of the decision-making process? In this vein, the stature of the CCO within the organization speaks to whether they have the seniority and authority necessary to do the job.

Competence Regarding Activities of Service Providers

This sense of gravitas extends to the CCO's relationships with service providers. The CCO, in exercising his or her responsibilities under Rule 38a-1, will also oversee the fund's service providers, which will have their own compliance officials. A CCO should diligently administer this oversight responsibility by taking steps to assure him- or herself that each service provider has implemented effective compliance policies and procedures administered by competent personnel.

The CCO should be familiar with each service provider's operations and understand those aspects of the operations that expose the fund to compliance risks. The CCO should maintain an active working relationship with each service provider's compliance personnel. Arrangements with the service provider should provide the fund's CCO with direct access to these personnel and should provide the CCO with periodic reports and special reports in the event of compliance problems. In addition, the fund's contracts with its service providers might also require service providers to certify periodically that they are in compliance with applicable federal securities laws, or could provide for third-party audits arranged by the fund to evaluate the effectiveness of the service provider's compliance controls. The CCO could conduct (or hire third parties to conduct) statistical analyses of a service provider's performance of its duties to detect potential compliance failures.

The CCO with Dual Roles

In many organizations, especially those investment advisers with a smaller number of employees, a single individual will tend to wear more than one hat. The chief financial officer (CFO) may be the head of marketing; the CEO may also be a portfolio manager and trader. The lead attorney may be the CCO (a special case discussed below); the CCO may be the head of operations. As the firm grows and becomes more complex, the roles tend to differentiate themselves so that individual roles coalesce around particular people. This is only natural. In a one-person firm, the owner is CEO—and everything else.

However, special issues arise when the compliance officer fills more than one role. For each "hat" that the compliance officer wears, a potential conflict arises. The supervisory duties of the noncompliance-related role (whether operations, trading, marketing, or legal) cannot be easily complemented by the control function that compliance would generally fulfill, which is to help ensure that the procedures under which that area operates are "reasonably designed to prevent, detect, and correct violations of federal securities law and are effective in their implementation." Simply put, when the CCO executes a supervisory, or "first line of defense" function, the role of compliance as a "second line of defense" is compromised, because the CCO is attempting to control his or her own activities.

This is a circumstance that calls for a significant degree of creativity, because the answer to the conflict lay in creating mitigating and compensating controls: finding creative ways where other mechanisms will backstop the conflict that the CCO has in controlling his or her own activities. This is more art than science, and thus the need for creativity.

For example, where the head of operations is also the CCO, a second level of business line sign-off may be required to approve "nonstandard" transactions to compensate for the fact that a review of those transactions by the same person (first as operations officer and then as compliance officer) may not produce an effective safeguard. The reason to introduce the additional level of control has nothing to do with any implication that the operations/compliance person is honest or dishonest, but just that if that particular person has missed an issue as the business line supervisor, there's no reason to believe he or she will spot it in the compliance role. The real purpose behind the need for a compliance review might be just to get a second set of eyes, with a different perspective, on the transactions.

If the CCO is in charge of marketing, similar "workarounds" should be sought. Perhaps the firm's attorney may be designated to review marketing materials for appropriate disclosures. The general theme is that when the CCO holds another role, the separation of control duties that the presence of a compliance function is designed to facilitate is compromised, and creativity must be used to design another way to achieve. It is in these types of contexts when a compliance person bringing creativity to bear on an issue is most valued.

The Attorney as CCO

A special issue exists with respect to the assertion of legal privilege when the firm's CCO is also working in a capacity as an attorney.

Courts have long recognized a common law privilege for attorneys to maintain certain information with a privilege against disclosing that information to the court. This is an outgrowth of an attorney's ethical obligation to maintain client confidences.[31] The attorney-client privilege exists because, an attorney must be able to possess full access to information about the client's circumstances in order to mount the most effective defense. The client has to be comfortable that he or she can tell this information to another person without fear of compelled disclosure. Not everyone can go to law school, but everyone in our system is due a zealous defense. This is only possible if the information given the attorney in anticipation of litigation, or the output of their work product, is shielded from discovery that could itself disadvantage the client.

Whereas others would have to answer a question in court, information given pursuant to an attorney/client privilege gives the attorney the right to respectfully decline to answer. From the attorney's perspective, this "right" is actually an ethical obligation, because the obligation to keep client confidences confidential is perhaps the highest ethical obligation of the legal profession.

However, where an attorney takes on a compliance role, compliance is not afforded a similar legal privilege. In fact, the essence of the compliance role is the reporting of all known material issues to management in a report that is designed to be reviewed by regulatory authorities as well. Thus, although the essence of the legal role emphasizes confidentiality and nondisclosure of work product, the essence of the Compliance role emphasizes reporting of any known material issues and disclosure of those issues in a required report.

As a result, it is very hard for an attorney working in a compliance role, such as a person who has accepted a role as "general counsel and CCO" to parse out when he or she is functioning as an attorney and when as a compliance professional. Clearly, the SEC will not recognize the annual compliance report as being subject to a legal privilege, but other communications, if impacting the compliance role, could be hard to shield as well.

---

[31] Geoffrey C. Hazard, Jr., "An Historical Perspective on the Lawyer-Client Privilege," Yale Law School Legal Scholarship Repository, Faculty Scholarship Series, http://digitalcommons.law.yale.edu/cgi/viewcontent.cgi?article=3288&context=fss_papers

If a privilege is claimed by an attorney who also works in a compliance role, regulators have made clear that the claim cannot be made as an afterthought. The regulators will look for a well-planned assertion of the privilege, including documents that are clearly marked "confidential-attorney client privilege" and a reference to the document entered into a "compliance log."

In this context, a privilege log is a list of documents for which the attorney is claiming privilege containing a description of the document (in a general sense), the date created and the distribution list. Documents that are distributed to a group that include others beyond those client representatives who have an absolute need-to-know can cause the document to lose its privilege, and thus narrow distribution lists are preferable to broad distributions. Documents produced in this way may also be marked "do not distribute," as the privilege may also be lost if the document is given to nonattorneys by any recipient.

Needless to say, working simultaneously as both an attorney and compliance officer can conflict—providing the key protections and ethical needs by the attorney can be compromised. Attorneys are well advised to carefully consider the legal requirements of the ethical obligation of confidentiality prior to accepting a compliance role.

This conflict, however, does not apply if an attorney is working strictly in a compliance role and not in a legal capacity. The fact that a person happens to be an attorney does not present an issue by itself so long as the attorney fulfilling the compliance role does not claim the role as the organization's legal adviser.

Serving as CCO of Multiple Entities

Other conflicts may arise where one individual serves as CCO for multiple related entities, especially if those entities are doing business together. Most commonly, these conflicts arise in two circumstances, serving as CCO for (1) a mutual fund and its investment adviser, or (2) an investment adviser and an affiliated broker dealer.

Serving as CCO of a Fund and Investment Adviser. Often, if an investment advisory firm is the sponsor of a mutual fund, a single CCO will serve both as the CCO for the fund under Rule 38a-1 and the adviser's CCO under Rule 206(4)-7. This type of structure is especially common if the fund is the adviser's sole client.

The issue here is that the adviser and the fund may have different interests and that given the adviser's almost complete control over the activities of the fund, a conflict between the two may be resolved in favor of the adviser. If the CCO of the fund is the same person as the CCO of the adviser, an important safeguard may have been lost.

The situation may became even more acute if the adviser services other separate account clients in addition to the mutual fund, as the interests of one group of clients may be favored over the interests of the other. Without separate CCOs, there would be no "independent watchdog" at each level exclusively tasked with looking out for the interests of their clients.

So what are the equities of resolving this potential conflict? In addressing this issue, one needs to turn back to the adopting release of the Rule 38a-1, which sought to make the CCO an "insider" rather than a type of independent examiner. As a result, the SEC chose to have the CCO report to management, to make the CCO be "part of the team" rather than an "outsider." It was thought that this would give the CCO better access to information, and in the long run, more influence to create compliant structures. And that decision was made with the full knowledge that a potential conflict existed.

When the fund is the adviser's sole client, if the CCO role for fund and adviser were separated and the fund CCO reported to the fund's board only, that would create the greatest possible separation of duties but would run counter to the "part of the team" approach that the SEC staff put forward in the adopting release. If the two were separate CCOs (one for the adviser, and one for the fund) with both reporting to the adviser's supervisory structure, although there might be a benefit to having a second person focus on the same issues from a distinct perspective, it's more an issue of having a second set of eyes. The second CCO would not have achieved a meaningful independence through a separate reporting chain.

The key element in the effectiveness of a fund CCO who is in the investment adviser's reporting chain is probably not the separation of duties, but the nature and quality of the confidentiality that the CCO shares with the board—specifically the board member who is the chair of the Compliance Committee or the chair of the board. Even if one person serves in both roles, to the extent the CCO can use the confidential relationship with the board to sound the validity of issues and the board can confidentially get comfort about the nature of the adviser's operations, in the long run, this will be far more effective than having a separate individual fill the fund CCO role. When the board doesn't have sufficient confidence in the adviser's culture of compliance, or lacks confidence in the individual designated as adviser's CCO, the board may demand the addition of a fund-only CCO.

When the adviser has other clients besides the mutual fund, side-by-side advisory issues may form another rationale for separating the role of adviser compliance from fund compliance. Side-by-side issues emerge when one class of advisory client is favored over another. This may occur as a result of differences in compensation structure to the adviser when, for example, separately managed accounts pay higher management fees than a fund client. The question that can arise in that context is whether the clients paying higher fees are being given the better investment opportunities to "keep them happy." Differences in the perceived importance of the client cause certain clients to be favored, causing side-by-side issues—the implication being that bigger, "more important" clients are receiving the best information and opportunities. In a third context, side-by-side issues can exist when one client funds the payment of expenses that benefit another client, such as when investment research is shared.

These situations call for additional sensitivity and care as the addition of the side-by-side issue adds complexity to the CCO's duties. It is a context in which the additional burden of focusing on controls to safeguard a separate population of clients might benefit from having a second professional involved who focuses on the adviser's issues from the point of view of a second group of clients. Although having a second CCO in this context might be more desirable to mitigate the perception of any potential conflicts, the adviser may also field a larger staff of compliance professionals, some of whom are tasked with reviewing procedures from the independent perspective of the different groups of clients within a firm. The question is the same one that the SEC originally grappled with. How can the fund CCO have an independent reporting line and still be an "insider?"

Like most compliance issues, where to deploy limited compliance resources most effectively becomes the heart of the issue.

Serving as CCO of an investment adviser and affiliated broker-dealer, dual broker-dealer and investment advisory registrants also often share a single CCO, and of course, with the differing interests of these two entities, each having a distinct purpose, may find their interests in conflict.

Potential conflicts in their regard may express themselves, from the adviser's perspective, in whether the use of the "captive" broker-dealer is in the best interest of the advisory client (especially if the broker-dealer is the exclusive broker executing the trades). This often distils itself into a discussion of "best execution."

To the extent that the brokerage services provided include fees for security selection, what is the benefit to the client of paying for that service again by selecting a separate investment adviser? To the extent that the fees are coordinated in a wrap arrangement of some type, why is selection of that particular adviser or broker in the best interest of the client as advisory client or brokerage client, respectively?

This question is made somewhat more complex by the fact that broker-dealers and investment advisers are legally subject to different standards of care with respect to their interactions with clients. Advisers must provide their advisory clients with a standard of care as a "fiduciary," but broker-dealers need only buy "suitable securities" for their clients. The fiduciary standard, which is often characterized as the "highest standard of care known to law," is generally not applicable to brokers.

It is generally conceded that these different standards arose out of unique historical reasons related to the passage of the Securities Exchange Act in 1934 for broker-dealers and the Investment Advisers Act in 1940 for advisers. The result has precipitated calls for "normalization" of the two standards of care in recent years, the existence of a different yardstick for the two types of financial intermediary does add a layer of complexity to the recognition of conflicts in dual registrants.

Clearly, given the nature of the relationships described above, serving as both a BD and IA CCO to a dual registrant or affiliated entities, the potential arises for conflicts that must be addressed in a way that is specific to the facts and circumstances of the entities.

Whether the result of this analysis is a desire to split the role or to create compensating controls is a determination that the CCO who holds the two roles that may conflict must continually validate throughout their tenure and they must stand ready to either defend or restructure.

CCOs Reporting to CCOs

In the largest securities conglomerates in the nation, CCOs for one entity may report to other CCOs. This may be true in the case of a large mutual fund complex in which a single family of mutual funds may be led by a worldwide fund CCO who then has the individual CCOs of the various investment advisers owned by that complex reporting to him or her.

On the one hand, a structure such as this complex may ameliorate the conflicts that might exist between the adviser and the fund. Having a separate adviser CCO reporting into the compliance chain would be desirable, just in the context of having a second set of eyes to look at an issue. On the other hand, when, for example, the mutual fund CCO is the investment adviser CCO's supervisor, one may well ask whether a true independence has been achieved.

Instead of truly creating an independent safeguard, one reason to create a structure such as this is to make a firebreak between the two CCOs, so that any material compliance issues that might be found to exist in the adviser can be said to be the responsibility of the lower-level CCO rather than actually flowing through to the global CCO. This structure has never been tested; however, whether a liability for failures can be avoided by the designation of two levels of CCOs probably depends on whether the superior CCO knew, or should have known, that the issue existed at the lower level—a standard that arises as a matter of the liability of a supervisor and probably exists for the supervisory CCO whether or not they designate their subordinate as a CCO.

Compensation Models

A lively discussion has surrounded the best way to compensate a CCO without creating a conflict of interest. As discussed above in the adopting release of the compliance rules, the SEC made the point that the commission had considered having the CCO reside outside of the organization that he or she serves. However, in seeking that a CCO be an insider to management, the question arises about whether it is appropriate for the CCO to participate in other types of incentive programs that the firm may allow its senior executives, such as stock option plans and incentive bonus plans.

The question is whether a CCO, if incentivized with a special bonus or in possession of a large number of stock options, will have a reason not to report or address important issues to enhance his or her own personal compensation package. The majority view on this issue is that when these forms of compensation are available to other key executives, they should be available to the CCO. Otherwise, the firm runs the alternative risk that the CCO will not be viewed as being in the "same league" as other key executives. He or she will not be viewed with the requisite seniority and authority afforded the other key executives.

Bonuses. The risk of the use of bonuses (single, lump-sum compensation payments that rely on the discretion of a supervisor for disbursement) as part of the compensation structure for a compliance professional is that they can be used to incentivize bad as well as good behaviors. Issuance of a bonus is often given broad discretion by a supervisor, and for a senior compliance professional reporting into the business line, the behavior rewarded may be minimizing the firm's regulatory risk exposure or approving otherwise "marginal" transactions.

A lump-sum payment can be an easy way to reward compliance people who avoided confronting issues that might be damaging to their supervisor. Even fair and honest businesspeople can fall prey to the notion that a compliance person is expressing opinions that "do not reflect the culture of the firm" and they should "loosen up." Whether this type of discussion is the primary feedback received by compliance after the first of the year, when bonuses are usually paid out, is often a concern in a room filled with senior compliance people.

Like most conflicts in the compliance arena, there are ways to mitigate this concern. A detailed annual strategic plan outlining deliverables to be provided by year end, or even goals and objectives outlined with an eye to measurable success factors, can serve to normalize expectations as to what constitutes a "successful" year, and thus what types of behaviors warrant the payment of a bonus. The key is to temper the otherwise absolute discretion of the supervisor to instead reflect the fulfillment of goals set at the beginning of the year.

The most important point here is that in the long run, denying a compliance person a bonus because of the risk that the bonus might be abused is generally viewed as having a long-term effect of separating the CCOs from the other executive-suite members of the firm. And it doesn't really solve the issue of abuse of compensation discretion either because merit increases in pay might be "held hostage" to the same type of concerns and are harder to regulate. Most firms have come to the conclusion that it is better to keep the CCO in the compensation structure shared by the other executives of the firm, and keep him or her as a "member of the team," as the SEC envisaged in the Adopting Release of Rule 38a-1. That way, when the CCO is successful in creating a strong compliance structure for the firm, the tools will exist to properly reward them for innovative and creative work.

Restricted Stock and Stock Options. The award of stock options raises concerns that seem, on their face, to be more difficult to address.

The concern in this regard is that by being given compensation that essentially represents the ownership of a piece of the company for which the compliance professional is structuring controls, the compliance professional is subject to an irreconcilable conflict of interest. If the CCO calls out a material compliance matter in a public way, if that issue is of significance, it may impair the value of the company and work against the economic interest of the compliance professional.

This is a concern, but it could also be just as forcefully argued that the compliance officer who has an ownership stake in the company would be more anxious to use his or her skills to protect the company and thus preserve or enhance personal ownership interest.

Another consideration in the mix is that these forms of compensation generally vest over four or five years and thus tend to facilitate the creation of an environment that involves less staff turnover and greater stability. Low turnover tends to create a stronger compliance environment. A more attractive compensation package also tends to attract better compliance talent, and participation in option programs generally attracts a more entrepreneurially minded compliance person. Both these attributes may be fairly looked upon by a firm as desirable from the standpoint of building a culture that is viewed as being more conducive to growth.

Use of options as also a "promise" of good things to come gives a small firm a shot at finding the best talent available and goes a distance toward equalizing the "playing field" between small and big firms in the search for talent.

Finally, if the use of options could prevent a compliance person from reporting issues, would this same rationale extend to the payment of normal salary? If an issue identified by compliance were of such great import as to affect the firm's viability, wouldn't that suggest that even the potential to disrupt normal payment of normal salary could weight the scale toward nonreporting, thereby making the mechanisms of the payment, be they stock, bonus or salary, inconsequential?

On balance, the majority view supports the notion that an award of stock does not represent a conflict so great as to guide the hand of the compliance professional to ignore their legal and ethical duty to report on issues discovered and to create the strongest control environment possible for the firm. In fact, many would argue that it enhances need to fulfill that role fully.

IX. CONCLUSION

The regulatory paradigm that governs the securities world places a strong emphasis on the development of internal controls through a discipline that has come to be known as compliance. A series of rules adopted in 2004 recognizes three pedestals on which the compliance structure in the securities arena stands:

- Designation of a CCO with the seniority and authority to execute the control functions assigned to him or her;

- Procedures adopted by the firm that are reasonably designed to prevent, detect and correct violations of applicable federal securities laws and are effective in their implementation; and
- An annual review, generally distilled into an a written report, that identifies all material compliance matters and discusses the firm's responses to changes in law, changes in business model and compliance matters during the past year.

Although the model is deceptively simple on its face, it conceals the underlying complexity of the firms it is designed to govern. Because no two securities firms share exactly the same business model, the SEC was confronted with the question of how to create standards to govern the innumerable potential conflicts of interest among the various elements of those business models are sliced together and torn apart by the dynamic processes of the American financial system. It is the compliance professional who is on the front line of finding the appropriate balance of creativity and process, control, and innovation that allows their firm to thrive while at the same time reducing regulatory risk to an acceptable minimum.

ABOUT THE AUTHOR

David H. Lui was chair of the industry's trade group, the National Society of Compliance Professionals, and has been a chief compliance officer for some of America's largest investment advisers, including Charles Schwab Investment Management, Franklin Advisers (Franklin Templeton), U.S. Bancorp Asset Management, and Galliard Capital Management, a $90 billion subsidiary of Wells Fargo. He is a graduate of Brown University with a bachelor of arts degree with Honors in History and a juris doctor degree from the University of California, Hastings College of the Law. He is admitted to practice in California and Minnesota.

CHAPTER 4

Overview of Compliance Considerations for Advisers to Registered Investment Companies

By Alan R. Gedrich and David F. Roeber
Stradley Ronon Stevens & Young, LLP

I. INTRODUCTION

The Investment Company Act of 1940 (1940 Act) is the key statute under which U.S. investment companies (i.e., mutual funds, exchange-traded funds, closed-end funds, and unit investment trusts) are regulated and governed.[1] Generally, all U.S. investment companies meeting the 1940 Act definition of investment company (and that cannot rely on an exception or exemption) must register with the U.S. Securities and Exchange Commission (SEC).[2] As of the end of 2015, U.S. investment companies held more than $18 trillion in assets, and approximately 44 percent of American households invested in such funds.[3] Investment companies are significant owners of corporate equity, commercial paper, government securities, and municipal securities. Such companies serve an important intermediary role in domestic and international financial markets.

The 1940 Act had its origins in the 1920s, when the idea of pooling funds to provide for diversification, economies of scale, and professional investment management began to gain some popularity with the investing public. However, the investment company industry was plagued with growing abuses and problems, and also was not immune to the devastating effects of the Stock Market Crash of 1929 and the Great Depression of the 1930s. In the mid-1930s, at the request of Congress, the SEC conducted a comprehensive analysis of the industry. Their results found that many investment companies were organized and operated to benefit the interests of their affiliates (such as sponsors), rather than the interests of their shareholders.[4] Following extensive hearings and testimony by

---

1 Unless otherwise indicated, all section and rule references herein are to the 1940 Act.

2 The Investment Advisers Act of 1940 (Advisers Act) is the primary law that regulates the activities of investment advisers, and all investment advisers (or subadvisers) to registered investment companies are also required to register with the SEC.

3 *See*, e.g., *2016 Investment Company Fact Book: A Review of Trends and Activities in the U.S. Investment Company Industry, 56th edition* (2016 IC Fact Book), Investment Company Institute (ICI), https://www.ici.org/pdf/2016_factbook.pdf

4 *Investment Trusts and Investment Companies: Investment Counsel, Investment Management, Investment Supervisory, and Investment Advisory Services*, Report of the SEC, H.R. Doc. No. 477, 76th Cong., 2d Sess. (1939).

regulators, government officials and financial industry leaders, as well as several preliminary bills, the 1940 Act was signed by President Franklin D. Roosevelt on August 22, 1940.

The 1940 Act established a comprehensive federal regulatory framework for the structure and operation of investment companies, and reflected congressional recognition that substantive shareholder protections beyond the disclosure requirements of the Securities Act of 1933 (1933 Act) and the Securities Exchange Act of 1934 (1934 Act) were necessary due to the unique character of investment companies and their role in the national economy.

The core regulatory provisions of the 1940 Act are designed to, among other things:

- Ensure disclosure of full and accurate information about the funds and their sponsors;
- Prevent changes in the character of funds without shareholder approval;
- Prevent unsound or misleading methods of computing earnings and asset values;
- Prevent insiders from managing funds to their benefit and to the detriment of investors;
- Prevent the issuance of securities having inequitable or discriminatory provisions; and
- Prevent excessive leveraging.[5]

Thus, the 1940 Act requires:

- Extensive registration and disclosure requirements;
- Declaration of fundamental investment policies;
- Daily valuation and liquidity requirements;
- Internal and external oversight (including fund governance requirements);
- Limitations on leverage;
- Strict custody requirements with respect to fund assets; and
- Restrictions on transactions with affiliates.

The purpose of this chapter is to briefly discuss the general framework for mutual fund compliance programs and then provide an introduction to certain core substantive compliance areas required by the 1940 Act for investment advisers who manage mutual funds (i.e., registered open-end management investment companies). This chapter focuses on mutual funds because they are the largest segment of the investment company market by far.[6] These core compliance areas can all be traced back to the original, underlying regulatory principles of the 1940 Act.[7]

---

[5] *See* Section 1(b), included in the appendix. *See also* SEC, *Protecting Investors: A Half Century of Investment Company Regulation, Division of Investment Management* (May 1992), https://www.sec.gov/divisions/investment/guidance/icreg50-92.pdf

[6] 2016 IC Fact Book.

[7] To be clear, this chapter is an introduction to certain 1940 Act compliance areas, but is not meant to provide an exhaustive list or overview of all required mutual fund compliance policies and procedures under the 1940 Act (or even meant to highlight all relevant subject areas generally). Furthermore, there are notable additional, or even alternative, compliance considerations for certain types of open-end investment company structures, the specifics of which are outside the scope of this chapter, such as for money market funds (most notably the requirements of Rule 2a-7), variable insurance funds, exchange-traded funds, index funds, or interval funds (which are technically closed-end funds but continuously offer their shares like open-end funds).

II. INVESTMENT COMPANY COMPLIANCE PROGRAMS (RULE 38a-1)

The SEC adopted rules establishing a mandatory institutional structure for mutual fund (and investment adviser) compliance functions in December 2003.[8] Rule 38a-1 requires each registered investment company to adopt and implement written policies and procedures that are "reasonably designed" to prevent violation of the "federal securities laws,"[9] including policies and procedures that provide for the oversight of compliance by each investment adviser (including subadvisers), principal underwriter, administrator, and transfer agent of the fund (the "primary service providers").[10]

The Compliance Rule Adopting Release outlines the minimum areas the SEC expects mutual funds (and advisers) to address in written policies and procedures.[11] Although such areas, together with the core substantive areas discussed below, may provide a starting point when developing a mutual fund compliance program, the 1940 Act, the other federal securities laws, and subsequent regulatory developments or SEC guidance since the adoption of Rule 38a-1, as mentioned earlier, require additional compliance policies and procedures.

Although not discussed in detail here, the 1940 Act and the other federal securities laws also impose significant obligations on mutual funds with respect to marketing and distribution of fund shares (including limitations on the use of fund assets for distribution), financial reporting and disclosure controls, codes of ethics/personal trading, recordkeeping, proxy voting, anti-money laundering (customer identification) programs, consumer privacy policies, and cybersecurity, to name a few. In addition, mutual funds are subject to the Internal Revenue Code of 1986 (tax code) with respect to their status as regulated investment companies. Mutual funds may also be subject to the Commodity Futures Trading Commission's (CFTC) regulatory requirements for commodity pool operators (CPOs).[12] Mutual fund compliance programs must be reasonably designed to prevent violation of the federal securities laws, and such programs are predominantly designed to facilitate compliance with all applicable legal and regulatory requirements.

In addition to requiring written policies and procedures, Rule 38a-1 also established a framework for board oversight, requiring that a mutual fund's policies and procedures, and those of each primary service provider, be approved by the fund board, including

8 *See Compliance Programs of Investment Companies and Investment Advisers,* 68 FR 74714 (Dec. 24, 2003) (adopting new Rule 38a-1 under the 1940 Act and new Rule 206(4)-7 under the Advisers Act) (Compliance Rule Adopting Release), https://www.gpo.gov/fdsys/pkg/FR-2003-12-24/pdf/03-31544.pdf

9 The scope of "federal securities laws" includes the 1933 Act, the 1934 Act, the Sarbanes-Oxley Act of 2002 (Sarbanes-Oxley), the 1940 Act, the Advisers Act, Title V of the Gramm-Leach-Bliley Act (1999), any rules adopted by the SEC under any of these statutes, the Bank Secrecy Act as it applies to funds, and any rules adopted thereunder by the SEC or the Department of the Treasury. Rule 38a-1(e)(1).

10 One notable omission from the service provider list in Rule 38a-1(a)(1) is the fund's custodian.

11 Such areas are included in Appendix A.

12 The CFTC's amendments to CFTC Rule 4.5 in early 2012 essentially subjected registered mutual funds to the CPO regulatory scheme. As a general matter, mutual funds that meet a *de minimis* trading test and a marketing test with respect to their transactions in "commodity interests," which includes certain derivatives, are excluded from the definition of CPO and the related regulatory requirements under the Commodity Exchange Act and CFTC rules.

by a majority of its "independent directors" (defined below).[13] Furthermore, each fund must also designate a chief compliance officer (CCO) responsible for administering the fund's compliance program, who is also subject to board approval. The adequacy and effectiveness of implementation of fund and primary service provider compliance programs must be reviewed annually, and the CCO must provide a written report to the board.

A word of caution applies to series trusts. Many investment advisers and subadvisers to mutual funds are increasingly taking advantage of the series trust structure, which generally provides multiple unaffiliated advisers with the ability to have their own proprietary mutual funds (structured as series of the same registered investment company corporate entity) while certain core services are outsourced to a third party as part of the arrangement. Such services generally include accounting, administration, distribution, fund governance, legal, and compliance. Although the series trust structure may allow advisers primarily to focus on managing portfolios and gathering assets and address other needed services in a cost-effective manner, such advisers are still responsible for ensuring that their funds comply with all 1940 Act regulations (plus the federal securities laws and other applicable regulations).

III. OVERVIEW OF CORE SUBSTANTIVE COMPLIANCE AREAS FOR INVESTMENT COMPANIES

This section will highlight and briefly address substantive core compliance areas for mutual funds in light of the core regulatory principles of the 1940 Act.

Registration and Disclosure

One of the primary policy goals of the 1940 Act is to protect investors from purchasing securities issued by investment companies without adequate information. Thus, mutual funds are subject to extensive disclosure requirements that are designed to help investors make informed investment decisions. Offering materials must be updated at least annually (and more frequently if necessary) to keep disclosure current and accurate.

Such information must be filed electronically with the SEC.[14] The SEC staff uses it in connection with its regulatory, disclosure review, inspection, and policy-making roles. Furthermore, most of the information is publicly available to the investing public, media, and other interested parties. Thus, important compliance functions are to ensure that adequate and accurate information about funds are provided in the relevant disclosures, as well as to ensure that the funds operate on an ongoing basis in compliance with such disclosures.

One of the key disclosure areas with respect to fund portfolio management is investment restrictions. The 1940 Act mandates a number of investment restrictions that must be

---

[13] All references to "directors" or "independent directors" herein also include "trustees" or "independent trustees," respectively.

[14] Via the SEC's Electronic Data Gathering, Analysis, and Retrieval (EDGAR) system.

disclosed and followed, and which generally cannot be changed without a shareholder vote. These limitations are designed to prevent funds from changing the character of their business without shareholder approval.

Registration Process and Disclosure Documents. The initial registration process for mutual funds is outlined in Section 8 of the 1940 Act. Section 8(a) provides that a fund may register under the 1940 Act by filing a notification of registration (Form N-8A) with the SEC. The fund is deemed registered when the notification is received by the SEC. Section 8(b) and rules thereunder generally require the (now registered) fund to file a registration statement on Form N-1A with the SEC to register the fund's securities under the 1940 Act and the 1933 Act.[15] This registration statement is required to be amended at least once a year to ensure that financial statements and other information do not become "stale," as well as amended throughout the year as necessary to reflect material disclosure changes.

The registration statement is composed of a prospectus (Part A), statement of additional information (Part B) (SAI), and certain other information (Part C). The core of the mutual fund disclosure regime is the prospectus. The prospectus includes the fund's investment objectives, principal investment strategies and risks, fees and expenses, performance, investment adviser(s), methods available to purchase and redeem shares, as well as certain financial highlights. The SAI expands on certain matters discussed in the prospectus, as well as provides additional information on matters such as fund history, fundamental investment policies, fund management, and pricing of fund shares. Part C provides other information regarding the fund and includes exhibits that are filed publicly with the SEC such as the fund's charter documents, service provider contracts, and other material agreements.

The other primary disclosure documents are annual and semiannual shareholder reports (Form N-CSR) (which include audited or unaudited financial statements, respectively, and management's discussion of fund performance), quarterly schedules of portfolio holdings (Form N-Q), and an annual proxy voting report (Form N-PX).[16]

These disclosure documents require input from numerous fund stakeholders and are an integral component of the fund compliance program. There are myriad requirements regarding the form and content of each document (as dictated by the applicable form, SEC rules, and SEC staff guidance from various sources), as well as with respect to the timing of required filings with the SEC and mailings (of certain documents) to shareholders. Taken together, these documents describe a significant portion of any given fund's operations.

---

[15] In practice, Form N-8A and Form N-1A are generally filed together. Also, although mutual funds are typically registered under both the 1940 Act and the 1933 Act, some mutual funds are registered under the 1940 Act but *not* the 1933 Act when the fund's shares are issued solely in private placement transactions (i.e., are not "public offerings" under Section 4(2) of the 1933 Act).

[16] Portable document format (PDF) versions of SEC Forms are at https://www.sec.gov/forms

Reporting Modernization. In October 2016 the SEC adopted rule and form amendments to modernize and enhance the reporting and disclosure of information by registered investment companies.[17] Such amendments include:

- A new monthly portfolio reporting form (Form N-PORT) requiring registered funds (other than money market funds) to provide portfolio-wide and position-level holdings data to the SEC on a monthly basis (rescinding the abovementioned Form N-Q);[18]
- A new reporting form (Form N-CEN) requiring registered funds to annually report certain census-type information in a structured data format (replacing the current semiannual reports made on Form N-SAR); and
- Enhanced and standardized disclosures in registered funds' financial statements.

For Form N-PORT, "larger entities" (i.e., funds in a fund group with $1 billion or more in aggregate net assets) have a compliance date of June 1, 2018, and smaller entities have a compliance date of June 1, 2019. Form N-CEN will have a compliance date of June 1, 2018, and the new financial statement requirements will have a compliance date of August 1, 2017.[19]

Investment Restrictions

The investment policies and restrictions addressed by the 1940 Act take a few different forms. Generally, Section 8(b)(1) requires a fund to include in its registration statement its policies regarding certain types of activities, including whether the fund reserves freedom of action to engage in such activities, and Section 13(a) prohibits the fund from changing certain of those policies without a shareholder vote (i.e., "fundamental" policies). As noted, these requirements are intended to prevent funds from substantially changing the nature and character of their businesses without shareholder approval. Certain investment limitations are also mandated by the 1940 Act (subject to related rulemakings or SEC exemptive relief).

Diversification. One required fundamental policy is a mutual fund's classification and operation as a diversified or nondiversified company. Diversification is a core regulatory principle of the 1940 Act and the tax code.[20] Under Section 5(b), management companies, which include open-end and closed-end investment companies, are divided or classified into "diversified companies" and "nondiversified companies" as declared in their registration statements. Section 5(b)(1) limits the amount that a diversified fund may invest in the securities of any one issuer (other than U.S. government securities).

---

[17] *See Investment Company Reporting Modernization,* 81 FR 81870 (Nov. 18, 2016), https://www.gpo.gov/fdsys/pkg/FR-2016-11-18/pdf/2016-25349.pdf

[18] Information contained on reports for the last month of each fund's fiscal quarter will be available to the public after 60 days, except for certain information that is excluded from public disclosure.

[19] For more information about reporting modernization, see Stradley Ronon Stevens & Young, LLP, *Investment Company Reporting Modernization Amendments—A Summary of an Extensive Overhaul* (Nov. 2016), http://www.stradley.com/~/media/Files/Publications/2016/Fund_Alert_November_7_2016.pdf

[20] Although briefly mentioned below, the tax code's diversification standards for investment companies are outside the scope of this chapter.

Specifically, 75 percent of the diversified fund's assets must be limited in respect of any one holding to an amount not greater than 5 percent of the fund's total assets and not more than 10 percent of the outstanding voting securities of such issuer. Any fund not meeting this test is deemed to be nondiversified and retains the freedom to operate on a nondiversified basis. Note that both diversified and nondiversified funds must meet the asset diversification requirements under Subchapter M of the tax code to qualify as a regulated investment company (RIC). As a general matter, the 1940 Act sets higher standards than does the tax code for funds that elect to be diversified. In practice, most funds that elect to be diversified are much more highly diversified than required by Section 5(b)(1).

As a fundamental policy, a fund cannot change its classification from diversified to nondiversified without a shareholder vote, but the reverse may occur (with certain limitations). Also, the SEC staff has stated that an investment company that registers as a nondiversified company but operates as a diversified company for three years is a de facto diversified company and cannot operate again as a nondiversified fund without a shareholder vote.[21]

Concentration. Section 8(b)(1) requires that a fund include a recital of its policy regarding industry concentration of its investments in its registration statement. This requirement generally reflects the view that such a policy is likely to be central to a fund's ability to achieve its investment objectives, and that a fund that concentrates its investments will be subject to greater risks than funds that do not follow such a policy. A fund is considered to concentrate its investments if it invests more than 25 percent of its net assets (exclusive of certain items such as cash, U.S. government securities, securities of other investment companies, and certain tax-exempt securities) in a particular industry or group of industries. With limited exceptions, a fund may not reserve freedom of action to concentrate or not concentrate in a particular industry at management's discretion and without shareholder approval. A registrant generally may select its own industry classifications, so long as the classifications are reasonable and the companies within a single industry have materially similar primary economic characteristics. In some instances, the SEC staff has taken certain positions regarding particular industry classifications.

Investments in Other Investment Companies. Section 12(d)(1) significantly limits the amount of a mutual fund portfolio that may be invested in other registered investment companies (i.e., fund of funds arrangements). Such limitations relate both to the portion of the mutual fund (the "acquired fund") that is owned by the purchasing fund (the "acquiring fund"), as well as the portion of the acquiring fund's assets that are invested in the acquired fund (and other mutual funds). These limitations are designed to prevent potentially abusive practices such as the "pyramiding" of control and undue influence, fee layering arrangements, and complex fund of funds structures that are difficult for investors to understand.[22]

---

21 *See*, e.g., SEC *Allied Capital Corp.* No-Action Letter (Jan. 3, 1989).

22 See, e.g., SEC *Northern Lights Fund Trust* No-Action Letter (June 29, 2015) (Northern Lights Letter), https://www.sec.gov/divisions/investment/noaction/2015/northern-lights-fund-trust-063015.htm

Section 12(d)(1)(A) generally prohibits an acquiring fund from:

- Purchasing more than 3 percent of the outstanding voting stock of the acquired fund;
- Purchasing securities issued by the acquired fund representing more than 5 percent of the value of the acquiring fund's total assets; and
- Purchasing securities issued by the acquired fund and all other mutual funds that, in the aggregate, represent more than 10 percent of the acquiring fund's total assets.

Section 12(d)(1)(B) generally prohibits the acquired fund from selling its securities to another mutual fund (i.e., the acquiring fund) if, immediately after the sale:

- More than 3 percent of the outstanding voting securities of the acquired fund is owned by the acquiring fund; or
- More than 10 percent of the total outstanding voting securities of the acquired fund is owned by the acquiring fund and other investment companies.[23]

Section 12(d)(1)(F) and Section 12(d)(1)(G) create statutory exceptions from the Section 12(d)(1) limits for funds that invest in unaffiliated and affiliated funds, respectively, subject to conditions that fund sponsors have found generally burdensome, if not unworkable. Over the years, the SEC has addressed the ability of funds to invest in other funds in the form of exemptive orders, rulemakings, and/or no-action relief. Such relief (collectively) has permitted funds greater freedom to invest in other funds and securities. Under Rule 12d1-1 for example, investments in shares of money market funds are not subject to the Section 12(d)(1) limits if certain conditions are met. Also, Rule 12d1-2 permits funds that rely on Section 12(d)(1)(G) to invest in unaffiliated funds, subject to the limits of Sections 12(d)(1)(A) and (F), as well as in any other types of securities that are consistent with the funds' investment objectives and policies.[24]

Fund registration forms require all funds that invest in other funds (and in particular funds of funds) to disclose the acquiring fund's pro rata portion of the cumulative net expenses charged by the acquired funds, along with related transaction fees, as a separate line item in the fee table (i.e., "acquired fund fees and expenses"). The SEC has adopted highly detailed instructions for calculating the amount of acquired fund fees and expenses and provides a disclosure exception when such fees and expenses are less than 0.01 percent (one basis point), in which case the fees and expenses should be reflected in general fund expenses.[25]

Investments in Securities-Related Issuers. Under Section 12(d)(3), a mutual fund generally may not purchase any securities of an issuer that is a broker or dealer, is engaged in the business of underwriting, or is a registered investment adviser (collectively, "securities-related issuers"). Rule 12d3-1 provides an exemption from Section 12(d)(3)

---

[23] The Section 12(d)(1)(A) and (B) restrictions are referred to herein as the "Section 12(d)(1) limits."

[24] The SEC's Division of Investment Management has also issued a no-action letter waiving the requirement that a fund of funds limit its investment portfolio to investments that qualify as securities under the 1940 Act. *See* Northern Lights Letter.

[25] *See* Item 3 of Form N-1A.

under certain circumstances. Under Rule 12d3-1, a fund may acquire securities of an issuer that derives 15 percent or less of its gross revenues from the business of being a broker-dealer, underwriter, or investment adviser ("securities-related activities"), unless the acquiring fund would then control the issuer. A fund may acquire securities of an issuer that derives more than 15 percent of its revenues from securities-related activities if:

- The acquiring fund will not own more than 5 percent of the outstanding securities of that class of the issuer's equity securities;
- The acquiring fund will not own more than 10 percent of the outstanding principal amount of the issuer's debt securities; and
- The acquiring fund has not invested more than 5 percent of its assets in the securities of the issuer.

Rule 12d3-1 does not exempt an acquiring fund's purchases of:

- Any securities issued by its investment advisers or distributors, or any affiliated persons of its advisers or distributors; or
- Any general partnership interest in a securities-related business.

Consequently, funds with significant positions in other mutual funds or securities-related businesses should implement policies to ensure that they regularly determine whether they are in compliance with the Section 12 limitations.[26]

Names Rule. Section 35(d) prohibits a mutual fund from using in its name any words that the SEC finds materially deceptive or misleading. Rule 35d-1 requires funds whose names suggest a particular type of investment or investment in a particular industry to have a policy that the fund will invest at least 80 percent of its assets in the type of investment suggested by the name (under normal circumstances). With respect to names suggesting investment in certain countries or geographic regions, funds must have an 80 percent policy regarding investments that are tied economically to the particular country or geographic region suggested by the name. Such 80 percent policies must be fundamental under Section 8(b)(3) (i.e., cannot be changed without a shareholder vote pursuant to Section 13(a)(3)), or the fund must adopt a policy to provide fund shareholders with at least 60 days prior notice of any change in the policy in the manner prescribed by Rule 35d-1.[27]

If a fund has a name that implies that its distributions will be exempt from federal income tax, or from both federal and state income tax (i.e., a tax-exempt fund), the fund must have a fundamental policy under normal market conditions to:

---

[26] *See also* Sections 12(d)(2) and 12(g) regarding limitations on investments in voting stock of insurance companies.

[27] Although fund names that include "global," "international" or "world" are excluded from the 80 percent requirement of the names rule, the SEC staff has informally taken the position that such funds must invest at least 40 percent of their net assets in a minimum of three countries (excluding the United States).

- Invest at least 80 percent of its assets in tax-exempt securities; or
- Invest its assets so that at least 80 percent of its income will be tax-exempt.

Daily Valuation and Liquidity

Certain regulatory provisions of the 1940 Act are designed to prevent funds from employing "unsound or misleading methods" in computing the asset value of their outstanding securities, as well as to subject funds to adequate independent scrutiny regarding such valuations.[28] In addition, one of the defining features of mutual funds is that their shares are required to be redeemable on a daily basis at their "current net asset value" (NAV) per share. Mutual fund shares are continuously offered for sale. Thus mutual funds price their shares at least once daily and must maintain liquidity adequate to convert a portion of their portfolio holdings into cash on a frequent basis.[29]

Under Section 22(e), mutual funds are required to pay redeeming shareholders within seven days of shares being tendered. In practice, mutual funds (or broker-dealers) typically pay proceeds within three business days of a redemption request.[30] The right of redemption can be suspended only in limited circumstances, such as when the New York Stock Exchange (NYSE) is closed (other than customary weekend and holiday closings), or when trading on that exchange is restricted.

Determining Valuation. With respect to valuation, the price of each portfolio security must be determined either by a market quotation, if a market quotation is "readily available," or by assigning a "fair value" as determined in good faith by the fund's board. This two-pronged approach has been in place since 1940, and there has been a multitude of SEC releases, staff letters, enforcement actions, and accounting publications since then providing guidance around fund valuation and associated board responsibilities, notably in the area of fair value.[31]

This daily valuation process results in the NAV per share of the fund. That is, the current market value of the fund's assets (minus any liabilities), divided by the number of shares outstanding. This NAV per share is the price used for mutual fund share transactions occurring that day, including new purchases, sales (redemptions), and exchanges between funds.[32] As required by Rule 22c-1, the specific time for pricing is set by the fund board (usually 4:00 p.m. Eastern time, when the NYSE closes). Such timing is disclosed in the fund's prospectus. Rule 22c-1 also requires "forward pricing," which

---

[28] *See* Section 1(b)(5).

[29] *See* Rule 22c-1 and Rule 2a-4. In order to meet a large redemption request, a redemption in-kind may also be permitted in certain circumstances.

[30] Due to the requirements of Rule 15c6-1 under the 1934 Act, broker-dealers must meet open-end fund redemption requests within three business days.

[31] The ICI has created an indexed and searchable compendium of valuation and liquidity guidance for mutual funds. *See SEC Valuation and Liquidity Guidance for Registered Investment Companies* (2015). *Volume 1*, https://www.ici.org/pdf/pub_15_valuation_update_vol1.pdf; *Volume 2*, https://www.ici.org/pdf/pub_15_valuation_update_vol2.pdf

[32] Investors may pay additional charges in connection with the purchase or sale of mutual fund shares (e.g., sales charges upon purchase or contingent deferred sales charges or redemption fees upon redemption).

means that shares are purchased or redeemed at the next-calculated NAV per share after the request is received by the fund (or financial intermediary).

As noted in the Compliance Rule Adopting Release, pricing of portfolio securities and fund shares is a critical fund (and service provider) compliance function. The fair valuation process in particular receives enhanced scrutiny from funds, boards, regulators, and independent auditors, because such good faith determinations are widely recognized to be more art than science, depending on the circumstances of each particular case.

Liquidity. Closely tied to the valuation of daily redeemable securities is liquidity (and liquidity risk management generally). If a mutual fund holds a material percentage of its assets in securities or other assets for which there is no established market, there may be a question concerning the ability of a fund to fairly establish daily NAV or pay proceeds to redeeming shareholders within the requisite time period after shares are tendered. Thus, mutual funds are required to maintain adequate liquidity.

Long-standing SEC guidelines generally limit an open-end fund's aggregate holdings of "illiquid assets" to 15 percent of the fund's net assets (interpreted to mean that a fund is limited from acquiring any illiquid asset if, immediately after such acquisition, the fund's holdings of illiquid assets would exceed 15 percent). A security is considered illiquid if it cannot be sold or disposed of in the ordinary course of business within seven days at approximately the value at which the fund has valued the investment.[33]

Liquidity Risk Management Rule. The SEC's historical emphasis on the importance of adequate liquidity in light of Section 22(e) was underscored in October 2016 when the SEC adopted a comprehensive, multilayered set of new and amended rules and forms designed to promote effective liquidity risk management throughout the open-end fund industry.[34] Such liquidity rules (including new Rule 22e-4 and related actions) are intended to reduce the risk that funds will be unable to meet shareholders' redemption requests or other legal obligations and mitigate dilution of the interests of fund shareholders. The liquidity rules are also intended to give investors better information to make investment decisions, and to give the SEC better information to conduct comprehensive monitoring and oversight of the fund industry.[35]

Rule 22e-4 will require all open-end funds (except money market funds) to adopt and implement a written liquidity risk management program that is reasonably designed

---

[33] *See, e.g.*, *Investment Company Liquidity Risk Management Programs, 81 FR* 82142 (Nov. 18, 2016) (Liquidity Risk Management Release), https://www.gpo.gov/fdsys/pkg/FR-2016-11-18/pdf/2016-25348.pdf. This 15 percent limit is essentially codified by the new liquidity risk management rules, discussed below, but the new standard is more demanding because funds must assess liquidity on an ongoing basis (not only upon acquisition of an illiquid investment).

[34] *See* Liquidity Risk Management Release. This action was taken in conjunction with the reporting modernization amendments discussed above, as well as amendments permitting open-end funds to use "swing pricing" to effectively pass on the costs stemming from shareholder purchase or redemption activity to the shareholders associated with that activity. *See Investment Company Swing Pricing*, 81 FR 82084 (Nov. 18, 2016), https://www.gpo.gov/fdsys/pkg/FR-2016-11-18/pdf/2016-25347.pdf

[35] *See* Liquidity Risk Management Release.

to assess and manage its liquidity risk, which is the risk that the fund could not meet requests to redeem shares without significant dilution of remaining investors' interests in the fund. Larger entities are required to comply with Rule 22e-4[36] and related amendments to Forms N-PORT and N-CEN by December 1, 2018 (smaller entities by June 1, 2019). The compliance date for amendments to Form N-1A under the liquidity rules is June 1, 2017.[37]

Oversight and Accountability

All mutual funds are subject to oversight from internal sources, such as boards of directors (including independent directors) and written compliance programs overseen by CCOs; and external sources, such as the SEC, the Financial Industry Regulatory Authority (FINRA), and external service providers, such as the independent auditor or independent legal counsel. This subsection will primarily focus on fund governance requirements and the role of the board.[38] As noted in the Compliance Rule Adopting Release, compliance with fund governance requirements is a critical compliance function.

As a general matter, fund directors play an important and active oversight role under the 1940 Act regulatory framework. Directors, particularly independent directors, act as "watchdogs" who perform the vital role of representing and guarding the interests of shareholders.[39] The external management of mutual funds presents inherent conflicts of interest (e.g., between fund managers and shareholders) and potential for abuses that the 1940 Act attempts to reduce. Fund boards are responsible for monitoring these potential conflicts of interest and have a fiduciary duty to represent the interests of fund shareholders. Thus, the 1940 Act establishes certain fund governance requirements and imposes significant responsibilities on fund directors, including specific responsibilities on independent directors.[40]

Independence Determination. Fund board members are considered "independent directors" (or "disinterested directors") if they are not an "interested persons" of the fund as defined in Section 2(a)(19).[41] This definition can be highly technical, but, as a general matter, independent directors are precluded from having (or recently having) any significant business relationships with the fund's adviser, principal underwriter

---

[36] Including new Rule 30b1-10 and new Form N-LIQUID, which generally require a fund to confidentially notify the SEC when the fund's level of illiquid investments exceeds 15 percent of its net assets or when its highly liquid investments fall below its stated minimum for more than a specified period of time.

[37] More information about the liquidity rules appears in Stradley Ronon, *What You Need to Know About the SEC's New Liquidity Risk Management Rule* (Nov. 2016), http://www.stradley.com/~/media/Files/Publications/2016/Fund_Alert_November_2_2016.pdf

[38] Funds affiliated with a bank may also be overseen by banking regulators and all funds are subject to the antifraud jurisdiction of each state in which the fund's shares are offered for sale or sold.

[39] *See, e.g., Role of Independent Directors of Investment Companies,* 66 FR 3734, 3736 (Jan. 16, 2001) (final rule) (Governance Rule Adopting Release), https://www.gpo.gov/fdsys/pkg/FR-2001-01-16/pdf/01-536.pdf; Correction, 66 FR 13234 (Mar. 5, 2001).

[40] Among other responsibilities and as discussed above, Rule 38a-1 established a framework for board oversight of mutual fund compliance programs and fund CCOs.

[41] Note that "interested person" of another person is a defined term in the 1940 Act; "independent director" and "disinterested director" are not (though the latter two terms are used in certain SEC rules and forms).

(i.e., distributor), or certain affiliates; and precluded from having any direct or indirect ownership of the adviser or certain related entities.[42]

Board Composition. Under Section 16, at all times 50 percent of fund directors must have been elected by shareholders and, to fill any board vacancies, at least two-thirds of directors must have been elected by shareholders (counting the new director(s)).

Section 10(a) generally provides that at least 40 percent of the members of an investment company's board of directors must be independent directors.[43] However, the SEC adopted a set of governance standards in 2001, including Rule 0-1(a)(7) that must be satisfied for funds to rely on certain exemptive rules (e.g., Rule 12b-1, permitting the use of fund assets to pay distribution expenses, and rules that permit funds to engage in certain types of transactions with affiliates).[44] Among other things, these governance standards require that a majority of a fund's board be made up of independent directors. Few funds can operate without relying on one or more of these exemptive rules. Thus, as a practical matter, a majority of the members of a board must be independent directors for most funds.[45] In practice, most fund boards have far higher percentages of independent directors (i.e., more than 75 percent).

Board Approval of Advisory Agreements and Distribution Agreements. Investment advisory agreements and distribution agreements establish the legal and contractual relationships between the fund and its investment adviser(s) and any principal underwriter(s) (i.e., the firm that serves as the distributor of the fund's shares), respectively. Under Section 15, these agreements must be approved by the fund's board and separately (in person) by a majority of the fund's independent directors. Advisory agreements must also be approved by a majority of the fund's outstanding voting securities.[46]

---

[42] *See also Interpretive Matters Concerning Independent Directors of Investment Companies*, 64 FR 59877 (Nov. 3, 1999) (statement of staff position) (discussing the SEC staff's views on the types of professional and business relationships that may be considered material for purposes of Section 2(a)(19)), https://www.gpo.gov/fdsys/pkg/FR-1999-11-03/pdf/99-27443.pdf. In addition, Item 3 of Form N-CSR imposes certain additional requirements for Audit Committee members who are determined to be audit committee financial experts to qualify as "independent."

[43] Also, Section 10(b)(2) requires, in effect, that independent directors comprise a majority of a fund's board if the fund's principal underwriter is an affiliate of the fund's adviser; and Section 15(f)(1) provides a safe harbor for the sale of an advisory business if directors who are not interested persons of the adviser constitute 75 percent or more of the fund's board for at least three years following the assignment of the advisory contract.

[44] *See* Governance Rule Adopting Release.

[45] The SEC adopted amendments to the governance standards in 2004 that would have required fund boards to have at least 75 percent independent directors (66 percent if there are only three board members) and for the board's chair to be an independent director. These two requirements were challenged and a federal appeals court ultimately invalidated them. The SEC sought additional comments on such governance standards in 2006 but has not taken further action. *See Investment Company Governance*, 69 FR 46378 (Aug. 2, 2004) (final rule), https://www.gpo.gov/fdsys/pkg/FR-2004-08-02/pdf/04-17460.pdf; 70 FR 39390 (July 7, 2005) (SEC response to remand by court of appeals), https://www.gpo.gov/fdsys/pkg/FR-2005-07-07/pdf/05-13314.pdf; 71 FR 35366 (June 19, 2006) (request for additional comment), https://www.gpo.gov/fdsys/pkg/FR-2006-06-19/pdf/06-5493.pdf

[46] In practice, the initial shareholder approval of an investment advisory agreement could be the vote or consent of the sole shareholder (e.g., fund sponsor) holding the initial seed capital shares.

Advisory and distribution agreements may only have initial terms of up to two years and may continue from year to year thereafter only if approved by a majority of the independent directors (in person), and must provide for their automatic termination in the event of an assignment.[47] Advisory agreements may be terminated, without penalty, by the board or by vote of a majority of the outstanding voting securities of the fund at any time (on not more than 60 days' written notice to the investment adviser). The advisory agreement must also describe the precise amount of the compensation to be paid to the investment adviser.[48]

In connection with the initial approval and the annual review of advisory agreements, Section 15(c) imposes on the board a duty to request and to review all information that may be necessary in order to evaluate the terms of the advisory agreements, and there is a corresponding duty of the investment adviser to provide the requested information. Each advisory agreement must be considered separately. Funds must provide reasonably detailed disclosure in shareholder reports and in certain proxy statements describing how their boards evaluate and approve their investment advisory arrangements.

Subadvisory agreements are treated the same as advisory agreements under the 1940 Act (i.e., required to meet the Section 15 requirements). However, the SEC has granted exemptive relief to a number of funds that permit the funds to implement a manager-of-managers structure. Such relief permits those funds, subject to a variety of conditions, to hire new subadvisers without obtaining shareholder approval (although board approval is still required).

Fund Audit Committees. A mutual fund must have an audit committee of its board of directors. Before an independent auditor is engaged by the fund to render audit or nonaudit services, the engagement must be approved by the audit committee.[49] Under Section 32(a), selection of the mutual fund's independent auditor must also be approved annual by the fund's independent directors. Section 32(a)(2) requires that such selection be submitted for ratification to shareholders, but Rule 32a-4 (relied on by most mutual funds) exempts funds from the shareholder ratification requirement when all of the members of the audit committee are independent directors and the board has adopted an audit committee charter.

Limits on Leverage

Two of the core policy concerns of the 1940 Act involve excessive borrowing by investment companies and the issuance of excessive amounts of senior securities (which

---

[47] *See* Section 15(a) and (b). *See also* Section 2(a)(4) (definition of "assignment").

[48] Section 36(b) imposes a fiduciary duty on the adviser with respect to the receipt of compensation for services, or of payments of a material nature, paid by the fund to the adviser or its affiliates. Section 36(b) also authorizes actions by shareholders and by the SEC against an adviser for breach of this duty. *See, e.g., Jones v. Harris Associates L.P.*, 130 S. Ct. 1418 (2010) (essentially upholding the longstanding "Gartenberg standard" that courts have consistently used to evaluate whether an adviser violated its fiduciary duty by receiving an excessive fee).

[49] Rule 2-01(c)(7) under Regulation S-X.

increase unduly the speculative character of the fund's junior securities).[50] Section 18 addresses the capital structure of mutual funds and generally limits the issuance of such "senior securities" and borrowing, subject to certain exceptions and further conditions. These restrictions are intended to prohibit complex capital structures, limit funds' use of leverage, and minimize the possibility that a fund's liabilities will exceed the value of its assets.

Mutual funds are generally prohibited from issuing senior securities by Section 18(f). Section 18(g) defines "senior security" to mean "any bond, debenture, note, or similar obligation or instrument constituting a security and evidencing indebtedness, and any stock of a class having priority over any other class as to distribution of assets or payment of dividends." This essentially includes any debt that takes priority over the fund's shares, such as a loan or preferred stock, but does not (by definition) include a borrowing from a bank which is for temporary purposes and which does not exceed 5 percent of the fund's assets at the time the loan was made.

Section 18(f) permits mutual funds to borrow from a bank (i.e., explicit leverage), provided the fund has "asset coverage" as defined in Section 18(h) of at least 300 percent for all borrowings. That is, the fund's total net assets are at least three times the total aggregate borrowings. Many funds voluntarily go beyond the 1940 Act prohibitions and adopt fundamental policies that further restrict their ability to issue senior securities or borrow. As noted above, such fundamental policies would require a shareholder vote to change. The SEC has as also issued exemptive orders permitting certain fund complexes to participate in an interfund lending facility (i.e., where funds lend to and borrow from each other for temporary purposes) subject to compliance with the conditions of the order.

Leverage can also be achieved implicitly through the use of certain types of portfolio investments. Although Section 18 on its face refers to explicit indebtedness, the SEC staff has taken the position that Section 18 covers certain other transactions, notably derivatives.[51] That is, such transactions may involve the issuance of a senior security subject to the prohibitions and asset coverage requirements of Sections 18(f)(1). However, the SEC and the staff have indicated that they will not object to mutual funds engaging in such transactions without complying with the asset coverage and other requirements of the Section 18(f)(1), provided that funds segregate assets or otherwise "cover" their obligations under the instruments, consistent with SEC and staff guidance.[52] A fund generally can cover an obligation by owning the instrument underlying that obligation. The fund also can generally cover a leveraged transaction by earmarking or segregating liquid securities equal in value to the fund's potential exposure from the transaction. The

---

[50] Section 1(b)(7).

[51] Specifically: reverse repurchase agreements, firm commitment agreements, standby commitment agreements, short sales, written options, forwards, futures, and certain other derivatives transactions.

[52] *See*, e.g., SEC Division of Investment Management, *Registered Investment Company Use of Senior Securities—Select Bibliography* (modified June 17, 2016), https://www.sec.gov/divisions/investment/seniorsecurities-bibliography.htm

assets set aside to cover the potential future obligation must be liquid, unencumbered, and marked-to-market daily. They may not be used to cover other obligations and, if disposed of, must be replaced.

Funds should have established detailed written policies and procedures in place that are designed to ensure compliance with Section 18, including policies to address coverage procedures with respect to derivatives and other transactions that have the effect of leveraging a fund's portfolio.[53]

Custody

Section 17(f) governs the custody of a mutual fund's assets, including its portfolio securities. A fund is required to maintain its securities and other investments with certain types of custodians (i.e., separate from the assets of the adviser) under conditions designed to assure the safety of the fund's assets. The strict rules on the custody (and reconciliation) of fund assets are designed to prevent theft and other fraud-based losses. Shareholders are further insulated from these types of losses by Section 17(g), which requires all mutual funds to have fidelity bonds designed to protect them against possible instances of employee larceny or embezzlement.

Custody of Fund Assets with Securities Depository. Section 17(f) permits a fund to maintain its securities in a system for the central handling of securities (commonly referred to as a "securities depository"). The SEC adopted Rule 17f-4 to establish conditions for the use of securities depositories or intermediary custodians (i.e., sub-custodians) by funds. Rule 17f-4 provides that a fund's custodian may place and maintain financial assets with a securities depository or intermediary custodian only if the custodian is obligated to exercise due care in accordance with reasonable commercial standards in acting as a securities intermediary to obtain and maintain financial assets. Rule 17f-4 also requires the custodian to provide, upon the fund's request, available reports concerning the custodian's internal accounting controls and financial strength. In addition, Rule 17f-4 holds any intermediary custodian to the same duty of care as required of the custodian.

Custody of Fund Assets Outside the United States. Rule 17f-5 governs the custody of fund assets located outside the United States. Under that rule, a fund's board has the authority to select, contract with, and monitor foreign custodian banks. However, Rule 17f-5(b) permits a board to delegate those responsibilities to a "foreign custody manager." Normally, the foreign custody manager selected for this purpose is the custodian for

---

[53] In December 2015 the SEC proposed rules designed to modernize the regulation of derivatives usage by mutual funds. If adopted, the rules would replace certain SEC and staff guidance developed over the years on mutual fund use of derivatives and impose new limits on fund use of derivatives. *See Use of Derivatives by Registered Investment Companies and Business Development Companies,* 80 FR 80884 (Dec. 28, 2015), https://www.gpo.gov/fdsys/pkg/FR-2015-12-28/pdf/2015-31704.pdf. *See also* Stradley Ronon, *What You Need to Know About the SEC's New Proposal on the Use of Derivatives by Registered Investment Companies and Business Development Companies* (Dec. 2015), http://www.stradley.com/~/media/Files/Publications/2015/IMG-Client-Alert-December-2015.pdf

the fund because fund custodians customarily maintain networks of foreign custodian banks and are best suited to select, contract with, and monitor foreign custodian banks.

In order to meet the conditions of this delegation, the board must find it reasonable to rely on the selected foreign custody manager to perform the delegated responsibilities.[54] Also, the foreign custody manager is required to provide written reports to the board giving notification of the placement of fund assets with a particular foreign custodian bank and of any material change in the status of a fund's foreign custody arrangements (at such times as the board deems reasonable and appropriate).[55] Finally, the foreign custody manager must agree to exercise reasonable care, prudence, and diligence appropriate to its safekeeping responsibilities or such higher standard as the board may require.

Rule 17f-5 requires the foreign custody manager to consider certain factors in selecting foreign custodian banks to be "eligible foreign custodians" for fund assets, and that the fund's foreign custody arrangements with a foreign custodian bank be governed by a written contract.[56] Rule 17f-5 also requires the foreign custody manager to establish a system for monitoring both the appropriateness of continuing to maintain the fund's assets with a particular foreign custodian bank and the terms of the foreign custody contract.[57] If an arrangement no longer meets the requirements of Rule 17f-5, the fund must withdraw its assets from the custodian as soon as reasonably practicable. The monitoring requirement is specifically designed to permit the fund to react promptly to negative developments.

Custody of Fund Assets with a Foreign Securities Depository. Rule 17f-7 governs a fund's use of foreign securities depositories. Each depository must qualify as an "eligible securities depository" under the rule. Rule 17f-7 allows a fund to arrange for its primary custodian to do preliminary and ongoing risk analysis regarding the use of particular foreign securities depositories.[58] The primary custodian must agree to exercise reasonable care in performing its duties under Rule 17f-7. If a custody arrangement with an eligible securities depository no longer meets the requirements of Rule 17f-7, a fund must withdraw its assets from the depository as soon as reasonably practicable. Although Rule 17f-7 does not assign a specific role to either the board of trustees or the investment

---

[54] Factors relevant to making this determination include: the expertise of the proposed delegate, its intended use of third party experts, the board's ability to monitor the proposed delegate's performance, and the proposed delegate's financial strength.

[55] The SEC has indicated that "material changes" would include changes in foreign custodians and could include events affecting a foreign custodian's financial status, such as a change in control. The SEC has also indicated that the foreign custody manager should include a discussion of its reasons for changing or maintaining a foreign custodian.

[56] Rules 17f-5(c)(1) and (2).

[57] Rule 17f-5(c)(3).

[58] Although Rule 17f-7 does not prescribe specific factors to assess risk, the adopting release provides that, generally, this analysis should cover: a depository's expertise and market reputation; the quality of its services; its financial strength; any insurance or indemnification arrangements; the extent and quality of regulation, and independent examination of the depository, its standing in published ratings, its internal controls, and other procedures for safeguarding investments; and any related legal protections. *See Custody of Investment Company Assets Outside the United States*, 65 FR 25630 (May 3, 2000), https://www.gpo.gov/fdsys/pkg/FR-2000-05-03/pdf/00-11000.pdf

adviser, the adopting release indicates that the decision to use a depository, based on the risk analysis information provided by the custodian, would likely be delegated by the board to the fund's investment adviser, subject to the board's general oversight.[59]

Fidelity Bond. Section 17(g) authorizes the SEC to require bonding of officers and employees of registered management investment companies who may singly, or jointly with others, have direct or indirect access to securities or funds of such investment companies by a reputable fidelity insurance company against larceny and embezzlement. Pursuant to this authority, the SEC adopted Rule 17g-1, which requires such coverage for investment companies in certain minimum amounts.

Rule 17g-1 provides that the coverage may be in the form of:

- An individual bond for each covered person or a schedule or blanket bond covering all such covered persons;
- A blanket bond that names the investment company as the only insured ("single insured bond"); or
- A bond that names the investment company and one or more other parties (the other parties that are permitted to be named as insureds under the bond are limited by Rule 17g-1 and include, among others, the investment adviser or distributor of the investment company) (a "joint insured bond").

Under Rule 17g-1, the board initially approves, and periodically reviews and considers renewal of such coverage. The rule requires a majority of the independent directors to review the coverage and determine that the fidelity bond is reasonable in form and amount, after considering all relevant factors including, but not limited to:

- The value of the aggregate assets of the investment company;
- The type and terms of the arrangements made for custody and safekeeping of assets; and
- The nature of the securities in the company's portfolio.

Rule 17g-1 contains certain required provisions for fidelity bonds and provides guidelines for the minimum fidelity bond coverage amounts that should be maintained based on the amount of aggregate assets of the investment company. The rule also requires certain SEC filings.

Prohibitions on Transactions with Affiliates

The 1940 Act contains a number of strong and detailed prohibitions on transactions with, and activities of, affiliated persons. Preventing the operation of a mutual fund for the benefit of affiliated persons is a core policy concern of the 1940 Act and funds should have established detailed written policies and procedures in place to address such transactions.

---

59 *Id.*

General Guidance for Affiliated Transactions. Under Section 17(a), an affiliated person of a mutual fund (i.e., first-tier affiliate), or any affiliated person of such person (i.e., second-tier affiliate), is generally prohibited from "knowingly" selling securities or other property to, or buying securities or other property from, the fund. Thus, a mutual fund cannot engage in principal transactions in securities with affiliated persons.[60] An affiliated person also generally cannot borrow money from the fund.[61] As an initial matter, properly identifying affiliated persons is a critical compliance function.

There are a number of statutory and regulatory exemptions from the Section 17(a) prohibitions. For example, Rules 17a-1 through 17a-6 exempt certain minor transactions between a mutual fund and its affiliates. Rule 17a-7 exempts a purchase or sale transaction between affiliated mutual funds, and between funds and other advisory accounts that affiliated solely by reason of having a common investment adviser, common directors, and/or officers, provided the transaction meets certain requirements. Among other provisions, Rule 17a-7 requires such transactions to be effected at the independent current market price of the security, without any brokerage commission or other remuneration (except for a customary transfer fee), and the directors of the investment company adopt procedures for such purchase and sale transactions.[62] Rule 17a-8 exempts certain mergers of affiliated funds.

Under Section 17(b), a person may file an application with the SEC for an order exempting a proposed transaction that is covered by Section 17(a) (and not covered by any of the exemptive rules) from the provisions of Section 17(a).

Joint Insurance Policies. Section 17(d) and Rule 17d-1 generally prohibit an affiliated person of a mutual fund (and affiliated persons of such persons) from participating in or effecting any transaction in connection with any joint enterprise or joint arrangement in which the mutual fund is a participant, unless an application for exemption from Section 17(d) has been approved by the SEC. The provisions are meant to minimize or prevent a fund from entering into a transaction on a basis that is different from, or less advantageous than, that of another participant. Rule 17d-1 includes certain exemptions for such joint arrangements as long as certain conditions are met; e.g., with respect to the investment advisory contract (subject to Section 15) between a fund and its investment adviser, and joint liability insurance policies.[63]

Affiliated Brokers. Section 17(e) generally prohibits a broker from effecting transactions for an affiliated fund on a securities exchange unless the broker's commission does not exceed the "usual and customary broker's commission." Rule 17e-1 is a safe harbor that establishes that an affiliated broker's commission, fee, or other remuneration will be deemed not to exceed the usual and customary commission if, among other things,

---

60 Section 17(a)(1) and (2).

61 Section 17(a)(3).

62 As discussed above, a fund's reliance on certain 1940 Act exemptive rules requires the board of directors of the investment company to satisfy the fund governance standards in Rule 0-1(a)(7). Such rules include Rule 17a-7.

63 Rule 17d-1(c) and (d)(7), respectively.

the commission is "reasonable and fair" compared to the commission received by other brokers in connection with comparable transactions involving similar securities being purchased or sold on a securities exchange during a comparable period of time.

Affiliated Underwritings. Section 10(f) prohibits a fund from purchasing any security during the existence of any underwriting or selling syndicate if the fund has certain relationships with a principal underwriter of such security. Prohibited syndicates generally include those in which an officer, director or trustee, investment adviser (including a subadviser), or employee of a fund or an affiliate of such persons is a member. Section 10(f) would prohibit a fund's purchase of such security from another member of the selling syndicate, absent compliance with the provisions of Rule 10f-3. Rule 10f-3 provides an exemption to this prohibition, subject to certain conditions, and permits a fund to enter into securities transactions that would otherwise be prohibited by Section 10(f).

IV. CONCLUSION

These core compliance areas have been supporting the underlying regulatory principles of the 1940 Act for more than 75 years. But, as noted above, these are only a starting point. The regulatory framework to which mutual funds are subject—both under the 1940 Act and other applicable regulations—is extensive and continues to evolve and adapt in order to protect the interests of mutual fund investors and mitigate risks to the broader financial system.

APPENDIX

Section 1(b) of the 1940 Act—Declarations of Policy

Upon the basis of facts disclosed by the record and reports of the Securities and Exchange Commission...and facts otherwise disclosed and ascertained, it is hereby declared that the national public interest and the interest of investors are adversely affected—

(1) When investors purchase, pay for, exchange, receive dividends upon, vote, refrain from voting, sell, or surrender securities issued by investment companies without adequate, accurate, and explicit information, fairly presented, concerning the character of such securities and the circumstances, policies, and financial responsibility of such companies and their management;

(2) When investment companies are organized, operated, managed, or their portfolio securities are selected, in the interest of directors, officers, investment advisers, depositors, or other affiliated persons thereof, in the interest of underwriters, brokers, or dealers, in the interest of special classes of their security holders, or in the interest of other investment companies or persons engaged in other lines of business, rather than in the interest of all classes of such companies' security holders;

APPENDIX

(3) When investment companies issue securities containing inequitable or discriminatory provisions, or fail to protect the preferences and privileges of the holders of their outstanding securities;

(4) When the control of investment companies is unduly concentrated through pyramiding or inequitable methods of control, or is inequitably distributed, or when investment companies are managed by irresponsible persons;

(5) When investment companies, in keeping their accounts, in maintaining reserves, and in computing their earnings and the asset value of their outstanding securities, employ unsound or misleading methods, or are not subjected to adequate independent scrutiny;

(6) When investment companies are reorganized, become inactive, or change the character of their business, or when the control or management thereof is transferred, without the consent of their security holders;

(7) When investment companies by excessive borrowing and the issuance of excessive amounts of senior securities increase unduly the speculative character of their junior securities; or

(8) When investment companies operate without adequate assets or reserves.

It is hereby declared that the policy and purposes of [the 1940 Act], in accordance with which the provisions of [the 1940 Act] shall be interpreted, are to mitigate and, so far as is feasible, to eliminate the conditions enumerated in this section which adversely affect the national public interest and the interest of investors.

Minimum Compliance Policies Outlined in Compliance Rule Adopting Release

The release notes that the fund's, or its adviser's, policies and procedures should address, at a minimum, the following issues identified for investment advisers:

- Portfolio management processes, including allocation of investment opportunities among clients and consistency of portfolios with clients' investment objectives, disclosures by the adviser, and applicable regulatory restrictions;
- Trading practices, including procedures by which the adviser satisfies its best execution obligation, uses client brokerage to obtain research and other services ("soft dollar arrangements"), and allocates aggregated trades among clients;

APPENDIX

- Proprietary trading of the adviser and personal trading activities of supervised persons;
- The accuracy of disclosures made to investors, clients, and regulators, including account statements and advertisements;
- Safeguarding of client assets from conversion or inappropriate use by advisory personnel;
- The accurate creation of required records and their maintenance in a manner that secures them from unauthorized alteration or use and protects them from untimely destruction;
- Marketing advisory services, including the use of solicitors;
- Processes to value client holdings and assess fees based on those valuations;
- Safeguards for the privacy protection of client records and information; and
- Business continuity plans.

The release also states that the SEC expects the fund's, or its service providers', policies and procedures to cover, at a minimum certain, other "critical" areas:

- Pricing of portfolio securities and fund shares;
- Processing of fund shares;
- Identification of affiliated persons;
- Protection of nonpublic information;
- Compliance with fund governance requirements; and
- Market timing.

ABOUT THE AUTHORS

Alan R. Gedrich is a partner in the Philadelphia, Pennsylvania, office of Stradley Ronon Stevens & Young, LLP, and a member of the firm's Investment Management Group. He represents investment companies, investment advisers, private funds, exchange-traded funds (ETFs) and fund sponsors on a wide range of matters, including all aspects of their organization, registration and operation, compliance matters, and acquisitions. In addition, he also serves as counsel to independent trustees of investment companies.

Mr. Gedrich graduated from the Pennsylvania State University and received his juris doctor degree from the University of Pittsburgh School of Law, where he served as managing editor of The Journal of Law and Commerce. Prior to attending law school, he worked for Coopers & Lybrand, CPA (presently, PricewaterhouseCoopers, LLP) and is a certified public accountant (inactive).

He is a frequent author and lecturer at investment management conferences on a variety of industry topics.

David F. Roeber is a senior associate in the Philadelphia, Pennsylvania, office of Stradley Ronon Stevens & Young, LLP and a member of the firm's Investment Management Group. He counsels investment companies, investments advisers, and independent directors/trustees to investment companies on a wide variety of regulatory, compliance, and corporate governance matters. In addition, he serves as the lead attorney for the UrbanPromise Legal Clinic in Camden, New Jersey.

Mr. Roeber graduated from Taylor University in Upland, Indiana, with degrees in Management/Systems and Political Science, and received his law degree from Rutgers School of Law in Camden, New Jersey.

CHAPTER 5

Chief Compliance Officers' Relationships with Fund Boards

By J. Christopher Jackson
Calamos Investments

> The substance and number of [SEC enforcement cases involving fund directors] show that the independent director community faces higher expectations, lower tolerance thresholds, and narrower scope for business judgment from regulators than ever before. Until recently, the [Securities and Exchange Commission] SEC had typically brought enforcement action against boards only in cases where the directors were alleged to be complicit in fraud. But now, it is using a rule initially heralded as a "tool" for directors—the fund compliance program rule—as a hammer against them, precisely what the industry had cautioned against. And because almost any problem can have roots in compliance failures, for those who wonder where director liability may exist, it is worrisome that the answer could be "anywhere."
>
> *Amy B. R. Lancellotta, Paulita A. Pike, and Paul Schott Stevens* [1]

I. INTRODUCTION

As the lead-in quote above sets forth, independent directors—the presumed SEC "watchdogs"—have been coming under greater scrutiny by the SEC and, in particular, the Division of Enforcement. More and more is expected of fund directors. As recent SEC rule proposals as well as Investment Management Guidance issued by the SEC's Division of Investment Management make clear, more and more is being expected of independent directors of fund boards. Concomitantly, a fund board's reliance, particularly that of its independent members, on the funds' chief compliance officer (CCO) has increased significantly. A confluence of events and factors is at work at this current time in the U.S. asset management and financial services industry, and fund CCOs are in the vortex of the advancing "storm." Events such as the market timing and late

1 Amy B. R. Lancellotta, Paulita A. Pike, and Paul Schott Stevens, "Fund Governance: A Successful, Evolving Model," *Virginia Law & Business Review*, Vol. 10 No. 3 (Spring 2016) (footnote references omitted).

trading scandals, the Sarbanes-Oxley Act of 2002, the compliance rule in late 2003, SEC fund governance reforms in 2001 and 2004, and the financial crisis of 2008 have had the effect of creating, allocating, and imposing on fund CCOs responsibilities that only have continued to increase over time. CCOs are the "eyes and ears" of the fund boards they serve. How the CCO goes about the task and the officer's relationship with the fund board are critical to the overall function of the fund industry. This chapter explores a modicum of the evolution of this relationship, but the majority of the remaining text focuses on suggested "key steps" a CCO can take to seek to enhance his or her "effectiveness" and ultimately, relationship with the fund board.

The focus of this chapter is to provide a view towards how CCOs relate and deal with fund boards from the CCOs' point of view. It assumes that the reader either is currently in that position or aspires to be a CCO to a fund board in the future. The chapter seeks to set forth in serial fashion a number of suggested practices—practices that, if followed, will produce positive results for both the compliance professional and the fund board for which the reader has the honor of serving as a CCO. These suggested practices, as noted, come from a CCO's perspective but would be deemed myopic if they did not place in the context of the rather large "watch" the SEC has placed in the reader's "pocket," as well as set forth some views from the fund board itself. It is important to start with the evolution of the "CCO" role, which has been in existence for some time, but came to prominence and a "defined role" in late 2003 in order for those in the industry to be reminded of the role that CCOs of funds are to play and what is expected of them. The focus of the text then quickly shifts to suggested practices, which are meant to be a corollary to this volume's other chapters and subjects.

This chapter will not focus on what happens if things go wrong in terms of the CCO's liability. Personal liability exists. It is not pleasant and it will almost certainly all but guarantee that those who are found liable will find it extremely tough sledding to ever work in a chief compliance role in the future.

II. EVOLUTION OF THE "FUND CCO"

Approximately 25 years ago the SEC issued its report, *Protecting Investors: A Half Century of Investment Company Regulation,* in which the SEC asked the Division of Investment Management to undertake a review of the Investment Company Act of 1940 (the "1940 Act").[2] As part of its report, the SEC reviewed the overall corporate governance of registered investment companies and found the governance model embodied in the

---

[2] *Protecting Investors: A Half Century of Investment Company Regulation* (May 1992), at https://www.sec.gov/divisions/investment/guidance/icreg50-92.pdf. Richard C. Breeden, then SEC chairman, stated: "While regulation to protect investors is vital to public confidence, overly broad regulation can limit the choices of investors, and unnecessary regulatory costs are ultimately passed through to investors. Therefore, two years ago I asked the Division of Investment Management to conduct a thorough study of our system. In particular, I asked them to look at areas where the law should be more flexible, or where regulatory costs could be reduced, without sacrificing the quality of investor protection. After a half century of market change, it is appropriate to consider where we can update and improve the overall system."

1940 Act was sound and recommended it be retained. Along with that assessment, the report recommended three limited modifications: namely:

- Increasing the minimum proportion of independent directors from 40 percent to a majority;
- Focusing the responsibilities of board members where they perform best, that is, exercising business judgment in conflict of interest situations, and eliminating certain rule-specific board requirements; and
- Eliminating or modifying a number of voting requirements that, in the SEC's view, do not comport with the realities of modern securities markets and can no longer be justified on an investor protection basis.[3] There was no mention of imposing a requirement for a CCO within the report. This would change a little more than 10 years later.

In December 2003, the SEC adopted the Final Compliance Rule going to investment adviser and investment company compliance programs: Final Rule: Compliance Programs of Investment Companies and Investment Advisers (the "Final Compliance Rule").[4] Vital to understanding the role of the CCO with respect to an investment company board of directors/trustees is a thorough understanding of the SEC's view of the role the CCO is to play as set forth in the adoption release of the Final Compliance Rule. The SEC noted:

Rule 38a-1 requires each fund to appoint a chief compliance officer who is responsible for administering the fund's policies and procedures approved by the board under the rule. A fund's chief compliance officer should be competent and knowledgeable regarding the federal securities laws and should be empowered with full responsibility and authority to develop and enforce appropriate policies and procedures for the fund. The chief compliance officer of a fund, like the chief compliance officer of an investment adviser, should have sufficient seniority and authority to compel others to adhere to the compliance policies and procedures"[Footnotes omitted].[5]

The SEC went on to emphasize the need for the independence of the CCO from the management of the fund. The SEC built into the Final Compliance Rule several elements to help ensure this independence. First, the rule requires that the CCO will serve at the pleasure of the fund's board of directors and that the fund board of directors (including a majority of the independent directors) can remove the CCO should he or she lose the board's confidence. (An important point to note here, it is critical that the fund board have every confidence in the fund's chief compliance officer. Too much is at stake for the board as a whole and in particular, its independent directors, to deal with a CCO in whom they lack confidence. More on this is discussed later in a list of suggested courses of action a CCO can take to obtain and maintain a board's confidence.) Second, the CCO must report directly to the fund's board of directors.

---

3 *Id.*

4 Final Compliance Rule, at 68 F.R. 74714 (Dec. 24, 2003), https://www.sec.gov/rules/final/ia-2204.htm

5 Final Compliance Rule, at 68 F.R. 74721.

Third, he or she must file an annual report with the board the directors that covers, at a minimum, the following:

- The operation of the policies and procedures of the fund and each service provider since the last annual report;
- Any material changes to the policies and procedures since the last annual report;
- Any recommendations for material changes to the policies and procedures as a result of the annual review; and
- Any material compliance matters since the date of the last report.[6]

Fourth, the Final Compliance Rule requires the CCO to meet in executive session with the independent directors at least once each year, without anyone else—such as fund management or interested directors—present at the meeting.[7] As the SEC noted, such meetings allow candor between CCOs and the independent directors. Such candor is indispensable.

The Final Compliance Rule was adopted against a backdrop of some key enforcement cases, not the least of which was market timing, a practice by which certain fund companies allowed investors to move in and out frequently in one or more of their funds notwithstanding fund procedures that limited purchases and redemptions within a fixed period of time. Compliance officers, according to the Final Compliance Rule release, were often advising management to curtail such practices, but were overruled. Direct access mandated in the Final Compliance Rule was believed an important step to help ensure the fund board and its independent directors were made aware of such issues. As noted by the SEC, "Under the new rule, the chief compliance officer will be responsible for keeping the board apprised of significant compliance events at the fund or its service providers and for advising the board of needed changes in the funds' compliance program."[8]

In order to support this aspect of the Final Compliance Rule, the SEC provided a "shield" to help protect a CCO in performing the functions envisioned by the Final Compliance Rule. Rule 38a-1(c) (adopting a similar concept from the Sarbanes Oxley Act of 2002 relating to influencing auditors) prohibits fund officers, directors, employees, and others from directly or indirectly taking "any action to coerce, manipulate, mislead, or fraudulently influence the fund's chief compliance officer in the performance of his or her duties under this section."[9]

From the Final Compliance Rule release, it is overtly clear that the SEC fully expects a CCO to perform his or her duties in managing the fund's compliance program. The SEC warns CCOs that failure to perform their duties under the Final Compliance Rule and "aggressively" pursuing noncompliance within a service provider could result in

---

6 Final Compliance Rule, at 38a-1(a)(4)(iii)(A) and (B).

7 Final Compliance Rule Rel., at 68 F.R. 74721 and Final Rule 38a-1(a)(4)9iv).

8 Final Compliance Rule Rel., at 68 F.R. 74722.

9 Final Compliance Rule Rel., at 68 F.R. 74729.

the loss of their jobs and, presumably, prevent them from being employed by another fund board or serving as CCOs to other funds' boards.[10]

III. AN APPROACH

As noted above, this chapter seeks to set forth in serial fashion a number of "suggested" practices that, if followed, will produce positive results for both the CCO and the fund's board. These suggested practices emanate from a CCO's perspective. As is true with most everything else about compliance, one size does not fit all. Each fund board has its own dynamic, its own history, and its own evolution. This adds to a CCO's challenge, because to be truly effective he or she must understand this context. Failure in this regard is not an option if the officer expects to succeed.

The suggestions that follow are in no particular order of priority. All are important and all will need to be drawn on at various points along the way. Although there is no substitute for "paying dues" and undergoing learning by "being in the arena," by following certain practices, an aspiring CCO may be able to make the path a bit straighter and a bit smoother.

What Model Does the CCO's Role Fit?

Depending upon the model that is put in place, potential advantages and potential challenges exist for the CCO. That role varies from one fund complex to another. As noted by the SEC in the Final Compliance Rule release, there is no one structure for the CCO role to assume.

> We expect that a fund's chief compliance officer will often be employed by the fund's investment adviser or administrator. We are not adopting a requirement that the chief compliance officer be employed by only the fund because we believe that such a provision would actually weaken her effectiveness. Funds today typically have no employees, and delegate management and administrative functions, including the compliance function, to one or more service providers. If we were to preclude the chief compliance officer from being an employee of an adviser or any other service provider, she would be divorced from all fund operations [footnotes omitted.][11]

The Mutual Fund Directors Forum in its report on the relationship that a board and CCO develop entitled *The Board/CCO Relationship* (the "MFDF Report") set forth a very useful grid depicting the various chief compliance officer models as well as the potential advantages and disadvantages of each.[12] Thus, the first suggested

---

[10] See Final Compliance Rule Rel., n. 90,"If such a person were approved by another fund, our staff would enhance its scrutiny of the fund accordingly," 68 F.R. 74722.

[11] Final Compliance Rule, at 68 F.R. 74722.

[12] Report of the Mutual Fund Directors Forum, *The Board/CCO Relationship*, http://www.mfdf.org/images/uploads/newsroom/Board-CCO_Relationship.FINAL.pdf

practice is for the CCO to ensure he or she knows which of these models, or variations on the same, the fund's role fits, and then to be cognizant of its potential pitfalls. Depending upon the model, the board and the adviser will need to adjust their roles and input to help ensure the CCO functions as envisioned by the Final Compliance Rule.

The MFDF Report describes fives models, each with attendant advantages and disadvantages.

Fund Only. In this model, the CCO works only for the funds or certain funds within the overall fund complex. The advantages to this model are:

- It allows the chief compliance officer independence from the adviser, and thus presumably lessens or does away with the potential for conflicts of interest between the adviser and the fund over compliance issues; and
- It leaves the CCO free to focus all of his or her time on the compliance matters affecting the fund and fund shareholders.

Disadvantages to this model include the potential lack of access the CCO has to the adviser and its personnel. The officer will be removed from the day-to-day activities of the adviser, and it may be difficult to influence decision making at the adviser level that has an impact on the fund. This model also may impede the flow of information the fund CCO needs to effectively carry out his or her duties vis-à-vis the funds.

A variation of the Fund Only model is a model in which the CCO is employed by the adviser with a direct reporting line to the fund board or chair of a committee (e.g., audit) and maintains a dotted line reporting relationship into the adviser (e.g., the adviser's CCO). In this type of relationship, the disadvantages associated with this model can be ameliorated to some degree.

Shared Fund/Adviser. In this model the CCO serves a dual compliance position for both the fund and the adviser. As noted in the MFDF Report, the advantage of this model is that the CCO is integrated into the adviser and the fund, and therefore is less dependent upon the adviser to provide information. That said, the model's disadvantage is that there are competing demands made on the CCO by both the fund and the adviser. As well, certain conflicts of interest that are not as present in the Fund Only model are present here in terms of compliance issues affecting the fund and the adviser.

Dual Function. This model, as described in the MFDF Report, positions the CCO to serve in another position at the adviser as well as serving as the CCO of the fund. In this model, the "other position" may be a chief risk officer role, the general counsel role, or an administration role, to name a few. The advantage here is that the fund's CCO is well integrated into the adviser's business and has a deep understanding of that business. The disadvantages include the competing nature of the positions on the time of the CCO as well as possible conflicts of interest as in the Shared Fund/Adviser model.

Another possible key disadvantage arises if the role in the adviser is that of general counsel and involves the attorney-client privilege. Here, an individual maintaining both a general counsel role at the adviser and the CCO position at the fund would be well advised to consider the prevailing state code of professional responsibility, as well as any relevant ethics opinions rendered by the state bar association.

Outsourced (Service Provider). This model envisions the CCO as employed by the fund service provider, such as the administrator. Advantages to this type of model include the familiarity the CCO would have with the service provider to the fund, the unique perspective the officer would have of the adviser, as well as the service to more than just one fund board. Disadvantages include the fact that the CCO is not situated on site at the adviser and thus is not fully integrated into the day-to-day activities of the adviser. Additionally, the officer experiences competing time demands between the service provider and the fund, and the potential for conflicts of interest between the interests of the fund on the one hand and the service provider on the other hand.[13]

Outsourced (Consultant). For this model, an outside third party serves as the CCO to the funds. This structure may be more prevalent with smaller funds/fund families and may provide the advantages of being cost effective and allowing the fund to have the benefit of the CCO's experience with other fund groups. Disadvantages mirror those found with the Outsourced (Service Provider) Model: lack of a physical presence at the adviser and competing time demands of the fund and the service provider's other clients. But it also adds a further disadvantage over all of the other models and that is its complete independence/isolation from the fund and service providers to the fund. Here, the CCO is more fully dependent on receiving information, particularly from the adviser and the key fund vendors, including the custodian and administrator.

The SEC's Office of Compliance Inspections and Examinations (OCIE) issued a National Exam Program Risk Alert in late 2015 dealing with outsourced CCOs that has bearing on the Outsourced Models set forth above.[14] The purpose of the alert was to share the SEC staff's observations from their examination of approximately 20 SEC-registered investment advisers and investment companies that outsourced their CCO function to unaffiliated third parties. Among other concerns, the SEC staff observed that certain outsourced CCOs were unable to clearly articulate the business or compliance risks of the registrant or, in cases where such risks were identified, whether compliance

[13] SEC OCIE, "Examinations of Advisers and Funds That Outsource Their Chief Compliance Officers, "National Exam Program Risk Alert, Vol. V, No. 1 (Nov. 9, 2015), https://www.sec.gov/ocie/announcement/ocie-2015-risk-alert-cco-outsourcing.pdf

[14] *Id.*

policies and procedures were in place to mitigate such risks.[15] In addition, the SEC staff noted that outsourced CCOs tend to rely on standardized checklists, noting that in certain instances the checklists were more generic in nature and lacked specificity with respect to key issues, practices, and strategies in place at the registrant. Moreover, responses received to the standardized questionnaires were not always consistent with the firm's business practices, and the outsourced CCO "did not appear sufficiently knowledgeable about the registrant to identify or follow-up with the registrant to resolve such discrepancies."[16]

The SEC found further problems with policies and procedures and the lack of consistency between what was in a registrant's compliance manual and actual practice. In certain instances, a registrant's compliance manual was a template provided by the outsourced CCO, and thus was not tailored to the registrant's business. With respect to the annual review process, the SEC staff noted in instances where the outsourced CCO was tasked with performing the annual review, which included the testing of the registrant's policies and procedures, there was a general lack of documentation evidencing the testing.[17]

OCIE concluded its alert by noting the following:

> Registrants, particularly those that use outsourced CCOs, may want to consider the issues identified in this Risk Alert to evaluate whether their business and compliance risks have been appropriately identified, that their policies and procedures are appropriately tailored in light of their business and associated risks, and that their CCO is sufficiently empowered within the organization to effectively perform his/her responsibilities. The staff observed fewer compliance-related issues at the registrants examined that had developed appropriate controls in each of the areas identified in this Risk Alert.

IV. KNOWING THE BOARD AND ITS EXPECTATIONS OF THE CCO

To be a truly effective CCO to a fund board, there is a lot that goes into the role, some of which is overt and made clear by such guidance as 1940 Act Rule 38(a)-1 and attendant policies and procedures, and some of which is "innate"—things that come from really knowing the board, the makeup of the board, and what board members expect. Like modern cars that incorporate complex navigation systems, the truly effective CCO comes to a board with a multitude of skills to navigate successfully. The MFDF Report said it as follows when advising its members on identifying an effective CCO:

---

[15] SEC OCIE, "Examinations of Advisers and Funds," at p. 4.

[16] SEC OCIE, "Examinations of Advisers and Funds," at p. 5.

[17] SEC OCIE, "Examinations of Advisers and Funds," at p. 6.

> In choosing a CCO, boards clearly look for an individual with the necessary technical expertise. However, boards often consider less tangible skills as well. A CCO's interpersonal skills and the ability to influence others typically prove as important as her technical qualifications.[18]

As a CCO, it is important from the start to gain the confidence of the board and its members. Key relationships and communication are vital. Board members—like any managers—hate surprises. Thus, communication is a key when the CCO deals with fund boards and can often make the difference in how the board receives key initiatives brought before it. Members who feel they have not been communicated with or dealt with in a manner that does not allow them to properly assess matters brought to the board will ultimately become much more resistant to the CCO's positions.

The interests of the independent members of the fund board and management/the adviser are not always aligned, but when there are differences or tension exists, good communication and a forum where these differences can be aired and explored typically leads to better results. The CCO has a difficult balance to strike in that in order to be effective, the he or she must be involved within the adviser and also have relationships with key vendors to the fund.

A CCO needs to understand that boards are typically not in the business of taking risks with compliance and adhering to the regulations that govern the funds they oversee. Increasingly, fund boards are looked to as, and are considered, the "watchdogs" of the shareholders of the funds on whose boards they sit. The CCO must keep in mind that funds do not typically have their own employees.

> A fund's board of directors oversees the operations of the fund and provides an independent check on fund management, particularly where the interests of the adviser or other service providers may conflict with the interests of the fund....Today, directors are critically important in overseeing what the fund is doing, by approving policies and procedures to prevent, detect, and stop violations of the federal securities laws, and by responding promptly and effectively to problems that do occur. We see you as partners in the effort to ensure that investors can invest in funds with confidence.[19]

To gain perspective on what board members expects from the CCO, it is critical to understand what the regulators expect of fund boards. The role of fund boards and independent directors generally is continuing to expand, whether it be in the areas of business continuity, sub-distribution payments and 12b-1 fees, liquidity, and reporting. The CCO who "gets this dynamic" can deal more effectively with these challenges.

---

[18] SEC OCIE, "Examinations of Advisers and Funds," at p. 2.

[19] Mary Jo White; "The Fund Director in 2016: Keynote Address at the Mutual Fund Directors Forum 2016 Policy Conference" (the "Forum Speech") (Mar. 29, 2016), https://www.sec.gov/news/speech/chair-white-mutual-fund-direcotrs-forum-3-29-16.html

V. BASE KNOWLEDGE OF THE TECHNICAL SIDE: "COMPETENT AND KNOWLEDGEABLE"

As noted earlier in OCIE National Exam Program Risk Alert,[20] Rule 206(4)-7 of the Advisers Act and Rule 38a-1 under the 1940 Act require registrants to:

- Adopt and implement written policies and procedures that are reasonable designed to prevent violations by the adviser and its supervised persons of the Advisers Act and its rules and violations by the fund of the federal securities laws and rules under those laws, respectively;
- Designate an individual as CCO to be responsible for administering the policies and procedures; and
- Review the policies and procedures at least annually for their adequacy and the effectiveness of their implementation. Fund CCOs must also prepare a written report to the fund's board of directors (footnotes omitted).[21]

The Final Compliance Rule expects that the fund CCO will be "competent and knowledgeable regarding the federal securities laws."[22] The dictionary defines the word *knowledgeable* as "possessing or exhibiting knowledge, insight, or understanding; intelligent; well-informed; discerning; perceptive."[23] The dictionary defines *competent* as "having suitable or sufficient skill, knowledge, experience for some purpose; properly qualified."[24] So just how "knowledgeable" and "competent" are CCO readers? Fund boards will and they will be concerned about their CCO's knowledge and competence, not just with respect to the federal securities laws and the funds' policies and procedures (each of which fund boards will expect the CCO to know well), but also with respect to the adviser, its business, and its products, as well as the various fund service providers such as the custodian, fund administrator, transfer agent, and middle office.

How to go about it? First, it goes without saying, but needs to be said in any event, that a CCO needs to know the funds his or her company offers, in detail: their strategies, key investment guidelines, objectives, and restrictions. The CCO also needs to know the policies and procedures of all key vendors and service providers: how they are implemented and interpreted and where the key issues lie. Certain models that funds and advisers use for CCO services may exacerbate the difficulty encountered with being very knowledgeable of the inner workings and key issues facing the adviser in particular.

---

20 SEC OCIE, "Examinations of Advisers and Funds," at n. 14.

21 SEC OCIE, "Examinations of Advisers and Funds," at p.2.

22 The "federal securities laws" are set forth in Rule 38a-1(e)(1)of the 1940 Act and are the following: (i) Securities Act of 1933, (ii) Securities and Exchange Act of 1934, (iii) Sarbanes-Oxley Act of 2002, (iv) Investment Company Act of 1940, (v) Title V of the Gramm-Leach-Bliley Act, (vi) the rules adopted by the SEC under any of the foregoing statutes, (vii) Bank Secrecy Act as it applies to funds, and any rules adopted thereunder by the SEC or the Department of Treasury.

23 *See* Dictionary.com at http://www.dictionary.com/browse/knowledgeable

24 From Dictionary.com, http://www.dictionary.com/browse/competent?s=t

Continuous learning is an absolute minimum requirement. Like all industries and businesses, change is occurring rapidly and in all substantive areas; the person standing still will be passed by very quickly. Key recent developments, such as the SEC's 2016 liquidity rule and 2016 reporting rule, illustrate the need to keep up.[25] These rules provide a degree of complexity, and impose on funds and fund boards additional and arguably extensive new requirements. As Chair White advised in her speech to the Mutual Fund Directors Forum in 2016, "The asset management industry and funds have been growing and evolving rapidly, and as we confront current risks in the industry, your [the directors'] role is even more important."[26]

In addition to various laws, regulations, policies and procedures, the CCO's role encompasses more, especially including risk. Although many asset manager firms have separate risk departments, as a CCO to funds, it is incumbent upon that officer to understand where the risks lie to the organization, if for no other reason than to asses such risks vis-à-vis the funds for which he or she serves as CCO. Good examples of such risks involve cyber security and business continuity. The SEC's Division of Investment Management has issued Guidance Updates with respect to each topic; the concerns extend to funds and their advisers.[27] In the Cybersecurity Guidance, the SEC staff made clear that funds and advisers should identify their respective compliance obligations under the federal securities laws in order take into account those obligations "when assessing their ability to prevent, detect, and respond to cyberattacks."[28] Similarly, in guidance entitled Business Continuity Planning for Registered Investment Companies, the SEC's Division of Investment Management stressed that fund complexes should consider how to mitigate exposures through compliance policies and procedures that address business continuity planning.[29]

When it comes to his or her role on a practical day-to-day basis, a CCO will be well served to read carefully a speech delivered for the SEC by Andrew Donohue, the SEC's former chief of staff, in May 2016. There Mr. Donohue set forth 14 insights on the approach to compliance, each born out of considerable experience he had gained both in the private and public sector.[30]

A core strength of the fund CCO is technical competence and knowledge. As noted, this is but one key to success as a fund CCO, but a critical one. It is a skill to be continuously and seriously undertaken; no excuses.

---

[25] SEC, Investment Company Liquidity Risk Management Programs; 81 FR 82142 (the "Liquidity Rule") and Investment Company Reporting Modernization; 81 FR 81870, https://www.sec.gov/rules/final/2016/33-10233.pdf

[26] SEC, Investment Company Liquidity Risk, at n. 21.

[27] SEC, IM Guidance Update No. 2015-02; "Cybersecurity Guidance" (Apr. 2015), https;//www.sec.gov/investment/im-guidance-2015-02.pdf; IM Guidance Update No. 2016-04; "Business Continuity Planning for Registered Investment Companies" (June 2016), https://www.sec.gov/investment/im-guidance-2016-04.pdf

[28] SEC, "Cybersecurity Guidance," at p. 2.

[29] SEC, "Business Continuity Planning," at p. 3.

[30] Andrew J. Donohue, "New Directions in Corporate Compliance: Keynote Luncheon Speech" (May 20, 2016), https://www.sec.gov/news/speech/donohue-rutgers-new-directions-corporate-compliance-keynote.html

Compliance Program Resources, Policies and Procedures, and the Annual Report

Any relationship with the fund board regarding the compliance function in general and the CCO specifically starts with the proposition that the fund and each service provider to the fund will have a comprehensive, well thought out and systematic compliance program. Such a compliance program must not only be in place, but it must function as seamlessly as is possible, and be constantly tested and kept up to date. Following are its key components, all of which need to be present.

The CCO

Rule 38a-1 of the 1940 Act mandates the appointment of a CCO and, as discussed throughout, this role is critical to the success of the entire compliance program. This chapter set forth the basic requirements and the fund board's expectations of the CCO and his or her role. It is from the CCO that the overall compliance program takes its direction.

The Resources

The CCO is a member of a team, and no one on the team can make it alone. CCOs need resources to carry on their role and functions, and those resources may come from the board itself, counsel to the independent board members or trustees, management of the adviser to the fund (tone at the top), the Compliance Department, in-house Legal Departments, Internal Audit Departments, and Information Technology Department. All boards are concerned with resources. There is not one board that will not ask a CCO in an executive session about resources. The response should be considered wisely. Being "under-resourced" is not a good option. A CCO with good experience and judgment should realize quickly whether more resources are needed and where on the scale from "nice to have" to "critical" they fall.

Policies and Procedures

The backbone of any compliance program is a good, effective set of policies and procedures. These must be developed in place, not just at the fund level, but at the adviser level and vendor level. There are a few "beware of" issues that every CCO must know. Beware of canned policies and procedures. One size does not fit all; funds' policies and procedures must be tailored accordingly by a CCO who is aware of the dangers in making assumptions. The prudent CCO can ill afford to assume. Constantly—at least annually—the Compliance Department should perform a "gap analysis" on the funds' policies and procedures, considering the investment strategies used by the funds. Any new funds and new strategies to take into account? This can be tied into the annual report process.

Certain fund groups will rotate review of policies and procedures such that at certain meetings during the year (e.g., at each quarterly board meeting) certain groupings of policies and procedures and any suggested updates and amendments to them will be considered. This allows the fund board and CCO to break up a large number of policies and procedures into logical groupings and provides the board members and independent legal counsel the opportunity to review those policies in more depth than if provided all at once on an annual basis.

The fund CCO cannot stop at the fund when it comes to policies and procedures, but must take into account each and every vendor and its overall compliance program and corresponding policies and procedures.

In addition to these actions, a comprehensive compliance calendar is essential to keeping an inventory of legal and regulatory requirements. Basic? Yes. Fundamental? Absolutely. A compliance calendar, done correctly, will take into account new and evolving requirements that can be picked up from new final rules, enforcement cases, Division of Investment Management Guidance Updates, and OCIE National Exam Risk Alerts, among other sources.

The Annual Report

The annual report is a very important document that allows the CCO to affirmatively demonstrate to a number of different constituencies that the overall compliance program is in place, robust, and affirmatively designed to seek to prevent, detect, and correct violations of the federal securities laws. There is no "one approach" to the design and substance of the annual report; at a minimum it should involve a comprehensive undertaking by the CCO and the compliance team.[31] Gene Gohlke, former associate director of OCIE, noted for the SEC some time ago that in assessing the annual review (which culminates in the annual report), examiners would look at nine areas. He said it this way:

> While the unique facts and circumstances of a firm will impact the work examiners do and the information they will request, examiners will typically ask questions in at least nine broad areas as they scrutinize a firm's annual review.
>
> These nine questions are:
>
> - Who conducted review?
> - What was reviewed?
> - When was review conducted?
> - How was review conducted?
> - What were findings from review work?
> - What recommendations were made?
> - What is current status of implementing recommendations?
> - What documentation was created/retained to reflect work done?
> - What was involvement of senior management in review?[32]

[31] The SEC in the Final Compliance Rule, stated as follows: "The [annual] report must address, at a minimum: (i) the operation of the policies and procedures of the fund and each service provider since the last report, (ii) any material changes to the policies and procedures since the last report,[81] (iii) any recommendations for material changes to the policies and procedures as a result of the annual review,[82] and (iv) any material compliance matters since the date of the last report" (footnotes omitted); 68 F.R. 74721.

[32] Gene A. Gohlke "Examiner Oversight of 'Annual' Reviews Conducted by Advisers and Funds" (Apr. 7, 2006), https://www.sec.gov/info/cco/ann_review_oversight.htm

Mr. Gohlke's speech provides the CCO with a comprehensive overview and a good checklist of what goes into an annual review and annual report.

VI. COMMUNICATION: BOARD AND BOARD COUNSEL

Critical to the fund board/CCO relationship is how each communicates with one another. In its MFDF Report, the Mutual Fund Directors Forum instructs the board, in part, as follows;

> The board should work with the CCO to establish a protocol for reporting material compliance matters, with a materiality trigger that favors reporting these types of issues to the board. An open discussion between the board and the CCO in executive session regarding materiality triggers can be helpful for both parties. The board can let the CCO know of its expectations regarding reporting —particularly in circumstances where the board fees that it is getting too much or too little information.[33]

In order to keep abreast of what the board expects, the following should be considered:

- Devising a communication plan with key board members, including the chair (if an independent board member) or the lead independent board member/trustee as designated by the board;
- Readying an agenda of key items to bring up with chair, whether it be a new regulation, new guidance from the SEC's Division of Investment Management, a new OCIE SEC National Examination Program Risk Alert, a new product initiative;
- Developing a give and take and a game plan to address with the chair;
- Considering additional dialogues with other key independent board members—particularly those who chair committees that deal with the oversight and approval of policies and procedures, such as the audit committee;
- Ensuring access to counsel to the independent board members because independent counsel plays a key role in the overall board governance, with
  - Key changes to policies and procedures run by independent counsel for review and comments ahead of when such policies and procedures will be presented to the board, helping to ensure counsel can advise the board on counsel's view of such policies and procedures and the adequacy thereof, and
  - Realizing different organizations will handle these relationships differently, but a good, healthy communication between the CCO and independent counsel will aid in the overall fund governance;
- Being forthright in all communications with the board, so that
  - Full and complete honesty is the *only* policy. The board must have complete confidence in its CCO,

---

[33] MFDF Report at p. 9.

  - Tensions exist. Disagreements will ensue. Judgment calls must and will be made. But through and above it all must be the unstated but total confidence by the board and its independent members in the CCO. Lose that trust and it is time to find a new job; and
- Recalling that no one can serve two masters. As CCO for the board and, by definition, having ready and good access to the adviser, it is incumbent upon that officer to be able to chart a course that takes into account the issues confronting each party and to help ensure a compliant result.

These caveats are easy to say, but real life teaches a different lesson.

VII. FUND SERVICE PROVIDERS: A CRITICAL KEY

A fund is simply that: a registered investment company. Its functions, overseen by the board of directors, are performed by service providers—investment advisers, custodian, transfer agent, administrator, pricing vendors, accountants, and independent counsel, to name a few. A CCO needs to understand and appreciate the need to seek to ensure that all service providers used by the funds he or she serves have adequate policies and procedures in place, as well as ongoing compliance programs to deal with the risks faced by the funds. SEC Chair Mary Jo White noted the following in a 2016 speech:

> Let me share what I think some appropriate questions may be for directors to ask. There are some obvious initial questions to ask fund management like how will my fund's and its service providers' compliance policies and procedures, business continuity plans and back-up-systems address these situations? If your funds and their service providers do not have robust plans and procedures, you have some urgent business to attend to. But even funds that have such plans and procedures in place cannot just declare victory. No continuity planning or compliance policies and procedures, however thoughtful, comprehensive and well-intentioned, will address every issue and prevent all potential harm. Directors of funds should also be thinking about and asking fund managers whether these events could happen at your fund, how to prevent them from happening, and how to respond promptly and effectively if they do occur....
>
> With respect to service provider issues that may arise, in addition to asking whether the funds and their service providers have back-up plans, boards should be asking more specifically: Has fund management considered the back-up systems and redundancies of the critical service providers that value the fund, keep track of fund holdings and transactions, and strike NAVs? Has fund management also considered specific alternate systems or work-arounds that may be necessary to continue operations

> or manage through potential business disruptions? Firms today rely on technology and third-party service providers for many key functions, and a failure of just one of those functions can have potentially very serious consequences for funds and their investors.[34]

As a fundamental matter, the Final Compliance Rule sets forth the basic requirement that funds' compliance policies and procedures must incorporate the oversight of their investment advisers, principal underwriters, administrators, and transfer agents.[35]

Recent incidents have increased the need to continue vigilance with respect to the fund's service providers. One such incident involved a well-known administrator that was unable to provide accurate net asset values (NAVs).[36] Concerns have also arisen regarding service providers to funds and how they specifically address business continuity and what business continuity plans they have in place; cybersecurity and the ability of the service provider to meet cyber threats; and pricing—particularly with respect to pricing vendors used by funds for prices for securities held by the fund and the methodology behind how prices are derived.

When it comes to creating a viable approach to vendors, the CCO should consider the factors examined here.

Service Provider Agreement

The CCO should start with the agreement in place with each service provider, understanding the relationship, the full nature of services to be provided, and the firm's rights and responsibilities under the agreement. It's advisable to seek assistance of the Legal Department or counsel to the funds when questions arise. It is important to know what the contract says.

Service Provider Policies and Procedures

The CCO needs a full understanding of the service provider's compliance program and its policies and procedures, particularly those with respect to the key services being provided to the fund. Larger vendors will make such policies and procedures or summaries thereof available electronically. A CCO must understand how and when updates, changes, and amendments to such policies are communicated. He or she

---

[34] Mary Jo White, "The Fund Director in 2016: Keynote Address at the Mutual Fund Directors Forum 2016 Policy Conference" (Mar. 29, 2016), https://www.sec.gov/news/speech/chair-white-mutual-fund-directors-forum-3-29-16.html

[35] Final Compliance Rule at 68 F.R. 74716. Footnote 28 of the Final Compliance Rule states as follows: "In this release, we use the term "service provider" to refer only to a fund's advisers, principal underwriters, administrators, and transfer agents. *By limiting the term in this manner, we are not lessening a fund's obligation to consider compliance as part of its decision to employ other entities, such as pricing services, auditors, and custodians*" (emphasis added).

[36] Kirsten Grind and Bradley Hope, "A New Computer Glitch Is Rocking the Mutual Fund Industry," *The Wall Street Journal* (Aug. 26, 2015), www.wsj.com/.../securities-pricing-problems-hit-u-s-mutual-funds-etfs-1440601913

will need to consider such changes in light of the fund and bring them to the fund board for review or approval.

Third-Party Reports on Service Providers

Certain service providers may provide, and the CCO should request, reports going to that service provider's Service Organization Control ("SOC1") report prepared in accordance with the Statement on Standards for Attestation Engagements No. 16 (SSAE 16), issued by the Auditing Standards Board of the American Institute of Certified Public Accountants. These reports, among other things, can provide the CCO and the board relative comfort over the control environment of the particular service provider.

Annual Onsite Visits

Annual onsite visits made by the CCO to each service provider are a good way to stay up-to-date with the various services, approaches, technologies, resources, and commitment to compliance at each service provider. The visits are vital to the overall compliance program and relationship with the CCO's board. Such visits also allow for detailed follow-up on newer SEC pronouncements or concerns, such as ones for cybersecurity and business continuity.

Rotational Service Provider Presentations to the Fund's Board

Service provider representatives should be asked to present to the board on a periodic basis. This serves a number of functions, including demonstrating systematic review and follow-up by board members regarding key service providers and key aspects of their services, allowing for a give-and-take by the board with the service provider, and providing an environment to raise key concerns and issues.

Service provider oversight, both by the board and the CCO, is becoming increasingly important as well as complex. Developing effective strategies to address same will enhance the CCO's relationship with the fund board.

VIII. THE SOFT SKILLS/INTANGIBLES

CCOs must possess a number of technical skills to perform their jobs effectively. Andrew Donohue, chief of staff at the SEC, noted same in a speech to compliance professionals, stating:

> Years ago, the skills and expertise required of the compliance area and its personnel were fairly straightforward. You had to develop a basic expertise in the laws and regulations that affect your business. Back then, compliance was comprised of lawyers, accountants and auditors, and some operational staff. In the future, I envision that the necessary expertise for

> compliance will consist of a far broader set of subjects, including expertise in technology, operations, market, risk, and auditing, to name a few. Even now, compliance personnel need to have a solid understanding of these areas, but I envision the role becoming even more demanding such that a CCO will truly need to be a jack of all trades with access to a wide array of skillsets.[37]

Compliance is evolving and ever changing. CCOs, in addition to the technical skills, must continually learn to deal effectively with myriad constituencies to do their job effectively. The ability to do so will be incrementally harder if the CCO role is an outsourced activity. CCOs must be able to deal with senior management and the various operational, trading, and distribution areas of the adviser and the distributor; develop and maintain good working relationships with the board and its independent counsel; effectively provide oversight with respect to each fund service provider; and address regulators and their concerns. CCOs who can effectively manage the range of relationships as well as competing interests of the funds, the adviser, and the distributor, staying abreast all the while with the changes in the regulatory landscape, will truly excel. It is to that level of excellence compliance professionals should all aspire.

IX. CONCLUSION

The subject of this chapter, CCOs and their relationship with fund boards, is a far-ranging topic. It involves effective dealings with a fund board. That relationship pulls in a variety of elements that include the basic regulatory requirements for the CCO role itself, what is expected of funds and their overall compliance programs, and the need to deal with multiple constituencies and to possess a number of skillsets, ranging from the technical to the intangible. The CCO role is constantly evolving and becoming more complex. At the same time, the industry continues to change, the amount of data provided to regulators has and is continuing to expand exponentially, the analytical capability of the SEC has increased significantly, and the specter of personal liability of the CCO is under the microscope.

Boards are under increasing pressure by the SEC in terms of their responsibilities and the breadth of matters to which they must attend. This pressure will continue to find its way to the fund CCO to partner with the board to help enable the board to fulfill its obligations and oversight activities. This relationship should be embraced by the CCO and it should be valued, relied upon and expanded. At the end of the day, the fund its shareholders will be the beneficiary.

---

[37] Andrew J. Donohue, *Remarks at the National Society of Compliance Professionals 2016 National Conference* (Oct. 19, 2016), https://www.sec.gov/news/speech/remarks-at-the-national-society-of-compliance-professionals-2016.html

ABOUT THE AUTHOR

J. Christopher Jackson is senior vice president and general counsel of Calamos Investments in Naperville, Illinois, where he has responsibility for the legal, compliance and internal audit functions of Calamos and its affiliated companies. He has been involved in the financial services industry since 1986. From 1986 to 1996, Mr. Jackson was associated with Van Kampen American Capital, Inc. (now known as Van Kampen Investments), in Oakbrook Terrace, Illinois as vice president and associate general counsel in charge of the investment advisory group. In 1996, Mr. Jackson joined Hansberger Global Investors, Inc. (HGI), a global asset management firm with offices in Fort Lauderdale, Moscow, Ontario, and Hong Kong and served as HGI's senior vice president, general counsel and assistant secretary from 1996 to 2006. Mr. Jackson was responsible for all investment advisory and general legal functions at HGI, as well as served on the board of trustees of the Hansberger Institutional Series open-end investment companies. Mr. Jackson joined Deutsche Asset Management in 2006 where he served as the director and head of U.S. retail legal for Deutsche Asset Management—Legal Division in New York. Mr. Jackson's primary responsibility at Deutsche Asset Management was overseeing the U.S. investment company business, which had approximately 130 open-end and closed-end investment companies. He joined Calamos in 2010.

Mr. Jackson is a member of the bars of the states of Illinois, Florida, and New York and also a member of the American Bar Association and Illinois State Bar Association (former chairman of the Corporate Law Departments Section Council). He is a member of the National Society of Compliance Professionals, served on the board of directors from 2002 to2005, and was the chairman of the board for two years. Mr. Jackson was reelected to the NSCP Board of Directors for a three-year term (2006–2008). Mr. Jackson was named the 2006 Compliance Leader of the Year by the Compliance Reporter in its Fourth Annual ARC Awards. Mr. Jackson is a frequent speaker on topics involving investment advisors and investment companies and has authored or coauthored numerous articles dealing with a wide range of investment advisory and investment company topics. Mr. Jackson received his bachelor of arts degree from Illinois Wesleyan University, his master of arts in Economics from Northern Illinois University, and his juris doctor degree from the University of Tulsa.

CHAPTER 6

Compliance in a Bank Investment Program Environment

By Karen M. Aavik
KeyBank, N.A.

I. INTRODUCTION

Broker-dealers and investment advisers have long been the subject of significant regulatory scrutiny, with the Securities and Exchange Commission (SEC), the Financial Industry Regulatory Authority (FINRA), the various states, and other regulatory bodies imposing requirements, prohibitions, and other boundaries and expectations on their day-to-day activities. The weight of these mandates is significant, and it requires compliance professionals[1] to employ a broad range of skills in order to ensure that their firms have implemented and maintain compliance and risk management programs designed to function—and evolve—with both industry and individual firm changes.

The compliance challenges are compounded when investment programs operate within a retail bank environment ("bank investment programs," BIPs). This complexity stems from the fact that banking regulators[2] impose additional requirements and expectations upon organizations that recommend or sell (directly or indirectly) retail nondeposit investment products (RNDIPs)[3] to their customers. The focus of the banking regulators is not primarily on the various securities laws/regulations that govern the investment industry,[4] but rather on the impact that the BIPs have on the safety and soundness of their respective larger

1 For purposes of this chapter, and unless otherwise noted, compliance professionals are the individuals charged with ensuring that the various compliance requirements set forth by the banking regulators with respect to BIPs are met.

2 Although different banking regulators may impact the obligations of certain banks with respect to their BIPs, this chapter will focus on the guidance and expectations set forth by the Office of the Comptroller of the Currency, which has jurisdiction over the BIP activities of national banks and federal savings associations. Although not directly subject to its mandates, state member and nonmember banks may nonetheless find the information contained herein useful in evaluating the strength of their respective compliance programs.

3 The Office of the Comptroller of the Currency defines an RNDIP as "any product with an investment component that, in most instances, is not an FDIC-insured deposit." United States. Office of the Comptroller of the Currency, *Comptroller's Handbook, Safety and Soundness: Retail Nondeposit Investment Products* (Jan. 14, 2015), at 4, http://www.occ.treas.gov/news-issuances/bulletins/2015/bulletin-2015-2.html

4 Although banking regulators do concern themselves with BIPs' adherence to securities laws/regulations, that focus is primarily on the impact of noncompliance on the safety and soundness of the banks rather than on the individual requirements of these mandates. The OCC Guidance, at 9, does, however, acknowledge the broad spectrum of obligations placed on BIPs, stating that "[a] bank's RNDIP sales program is subject to multiple laws, regulations, and regulatory policy requirements. Such sales programs must comply with the applicable federal and state banking, securities, and insurance regulatory requirements."

organizations. This concern manifests itself in additional requirements, which address issues ranging from the impact of the BIP on a bank's overall risk profile, to the effort that the organization puts forth to ensure that customers understand the nature and characteristics of the various RNDIPs made available through the retail channel of the bank. As such, BIPs that focus solely on the securities laws/regulations that govern their activities at the expense of those imposed by the banking regulators do so at their own peril.

This chapter discusses some of the most critical additional requirements and expectations imposed upon bank investment programs,[5] referencing the January 2015 Office of the Comptroller of the Currency (OCC) Retail Nondeposit Investment Products guidance ("OCC Guidance"),[6] which covers both securities- and insurance-related BIP activities, for the various topics covered. Although BIPs may offer products to a variety of different types of customers, this discussion focuses on retail sales, which generally include (but are not limited to) recommendations and sales to individuals[7] conducted on bank premises or from bank referrals to affiliated or unaffiliated broker-dealers.[8] The text addresses key issues at a higher level to help ensure the broadest applicability to the reader and his or her firm.

II. WHAT MAKES BANK INVESTMENT PROGRAMS DIFFERENT?

Bank investment programs are different from "standalone" broker-dealers and investment advisers in that the bank[9] must consider the impact of its BIP on the overall safety and soundness of the larger organization. In general, "safety and soundness" is a broad concept that encompasses the entire entity's activities; within the context of BIPs, it means

---

[5] Note that the topics covered within this chapter are not comprehensive (e.g., there are not detailed discussions regarding third-party provider management or product governance considerations). Readers wishing to obtain information regarding these matters—or additional, enhanced guidance regarding the subject matter covered—should consult the OCC Guidance and other relevant laws/regulations.

[6] The OCC Guidance, at 1, provides "comprehensive guidance...on activities involving the recommendation or sale of nondeposit investment products to retail customers" and "explains the risks inherent in banks' retail nondeposit investment product (RDNIP) sales programs and provides a framework for banks to manage those risks."

[7] OCC Guidance, at 3, defines individuals to include small businesses, partnerships and high net worth or other potentially sophisticated clients.

[8] OCC Guidance, at 2-3, states that specifically, retail sales include, but are not limited to, recommendations and sales to individuals: by bank personnel or employees of affiliated or unaffiliated third parties that are conducted in or adjacent to a bank's lobby area; from a referral of retail customers by a bank to an affiliated broker-dealer; from a referral of retail customers by a bank to an unaffiliated third party when the bank receives a benefit for the referral; from call centers conducted by bank employees or from a bank's premises; and initiated by mail from a bank's premises (including by electronic means, such as through a bank's website). They do not include: non-retail sales programs that target institutional customers; fiduciary accounts administered by the bank; sales of government and municipal securities conducted in the bank's dealer department located away from the lobby area; and affiliated broker-dealer activities that are a separate book of business not covered by a written brokerage arrangement with the bank." The OCC Guidance, at 6, also encompasses bank arrangements with registered investment advisers (RIAs) that enable those RIAs to offer advisory services to bank customers, noting that "the OCC treats these services as if they were the sale of RNDIPs if provided to bank customers outside of a bank's trust department."

[9] Responsibilities outlined by the banking regulators technically lie with the banks themselves; however, because of the complexity of securities requirements (as well as the investment subject matter expertise required in order to effectively identify risks and other relevant issues), bank-side compliance professionals often work in tandem with their securities counterparts and/or otherwise rely heavily on them in order to assist the bank in meeting its obligations.

that "banks should operate their RNDIP sales programs safely and soundly to *properly protect retail investors from harm* and to *control banks' risk exposures*"[10] [emphasis added]. Hence, to meet the expectations of the banking regulators, compliance professionals must incorporate additional measures designed to mitigate the added potential for harm to customers resulting from the fact that investment activities are occurring within a bank setting, and to the bank itself by virtue of the layers of risks that are inherent in the very existence of such a program. It is perhaps because of this additional responsibility that the OCC acknowledges that "starting and maintaining an RNDIP sales program requires a substantial commitment because the oversight process tends to be labor intensive, ensuring compliance with applicable law can be complex, and operating systems are costly."[11]

Safety and Soundness Considerations: Evaluating the Risks of a Bank Investment Program

A bank investment program with weak controls, poor risk management practices, and other similar deficiencies jeopardizes not only the strength and success of the BIP itself but also the health and stability of the larger organization. For this reason, banking regulators expect banks to identify, measure, monitor, and control the risks associated with BIPs by implementing effective risk management programs commensurate with the size and complexity of their respective programs.[12]

Identifying the Sources of BIP Risk

The first step in meeting this expectation is for compliance professionals—and the bank itself—to understand the sources of bank investment program risk. Broadly speaking, such risk is defined as "the potential that events, expected or unexpected, will have an adverse effect on a bank's earnings, capital, or franchise or enterprise value."[13] The OCC Guidance identifies five distinct sources of BIP risk:

Compliance Risk. Of the various risks identified, this is likely the one that compliance professionals are most comfortable managing because it is this type of threat that drives their day-to-day priorities and activities. As previously noted, organizations with BIPs are required to meet a wide variety of laws/regulations governing their securities-related activities, as well as certain additional mandates imposed by the banking regulators. Absent effective policies, procedures, and practices designed to ensure compliance with all of these mandates, banks may be subject to potential customer complaints, litigation, regulatory actions, and reputational damage.[14]

---

[10] OCC Guidance, at 1.

[11] OCC Guidance, at 27.

[12] See OCC Guidance, at 30. Specifically, the OCC states that each "bank should implement a risk management system commensurate with the associated risk exposures, size, and complexity of its RNDIP sales program... [and] tailor its risk management system to its needs and circumstances. A bank's risk management system should be dynamic in addressing changes to the bank's RNDIP sales program." This concept of a customized and evergreen risk management program thus mirrors the tone and intent of securities-specific obligations set forth by the SEC, FINRA, and other regulators having jurisdiction over broker-dealers and investment advisers.

[13] OCC Guidance, at 23.

[14] OCC Guidance, at 23-25.

Operational Risk. The OCC describes this threat as the risk that arises from insufficient bank oversight of RNDIP third parties and/or bank employees; sales practice misconduct; poor customer service; or adverse internal or external events that could affect transactions, business volumes, and efficient trade execution. It further notes that such risk can stem from a failure to meet obligations involving clients, products, and business practices; fraud; or securities transaction-based issues.[15] A subrisk within this category is what can be referred to as "contract risk," which applies when the bank uses a third-party provider (TPP) to offer RNDIPs to its retail customers. Contract risk arises when that provider neglects to meet its obligations under the agreement set forth between it and the bank, a failure that can jeopardize the bank's ability to meet its legal/regulatory obligations and thus adversely affect all of the other risks articulated by the OCC.

Strategic Risk. Strategic risk truly highlights the importance of effectively communicating information to the board of directors and senior management within the bank, because timely and accurate BIP (and industry) data enables those key parties to make educated resource decisions and meet the expectations of the banking regulators.[16] The OCC indicates that strategic risk can arise when business planning and implementation do not devote sufficient resources and risk management necessary to manage and control the risks associated with the BIP.[17]

Reputation Risk. According to the OCC, BIPs can expose banks to potential reputational damage via unsuitable sales practices,[18] customer misunderstanding regarding the risks associated with RNDIPs, and/or poor customer service.[19] As the nature of this description suggests, comprehensive training programs (incorporating discussions of both investment- and bank-related requirements and concerns) and an effective complaint management process[20] are essential to mitigating the threat of reputation risk.

Credit Risk. Credit risk comes into play when a BIP offers (through the bank) margin lending or securities lending to its customers. The OCC notes that this risk stems from the potential that a retail customer or a securities lending counterparty will fail to meet the obligations set forth within the lending agreement, thereby jeopardizing the bank's

---

15 OCC Guidance, at 25-27.

16 In addition to the emphasis placed on effective communication, the OCC Guidance, at 27, also notes the importance of "operating systems, delivery channels, managerial capacities and capabilities, third-party risk management, and product due diligence processes" when managing strategic risk.

17 OCC Guidance, at 27-28.

18 In considering the risk posed by unsuitable sales practices, it is important to remember that (within the context of BIPs) the view may be broader than traditional investment-focused "suitability concerns". For example, a licensed bank employee who fails to properly disclose during the sales presentation when he or she is switching from activities performed as a bank employee to those that are conducted as a registered representative would be subject to criticism because this omission increases the likelihood that the customer will not understand that the securities product purchased is not FDIC-insured. This concern does not apply to standalone broker-dealers and investment advisers.

19 OCC Guidance, at 28-29.

20 It is critically important that information regarding BIP-related customer complaints be provided to the larger bank organization because such data plays an important role in helping the bank to gauge the risks associated with the bank investment program (including, but not limited to, negative trends, emerging issues, potential problems associated with particular products/services, etc.).

current or anticipated earnings or capital. The OCC further notes that exposure exists for banks that engage directly in foreign exchange transactions with customers.[21]

Each of these risks represents its own separate and distinct threat to the safety and soundness of the bank; considered together, it is easy to see how a weak compliance and risk management program (without sufficient oversight by the bank) can perpetuate an environment within which the aggregate risk of the BIP exceeds the organization's articulated risk appetite.[22]

Implementing the Risk Management Program. Having identified and defined the primary sources of potential BIP risk, the compliance professional's next step is to use this knowledge to develop and implement a program to identify, measure, monitor, and control these risks.[23] Here the concept of a customized risk management program becomes even more critical, because compliance professionals must compare the structure, complexity, policies, procedures, and practices of their BIPs against these known risk categories in order to determine where real, definable threats exist—and how to manage them. The following sets forth steps for efficiently and effectively completing this process.

Identify Risk. This is the most critical phase of the risk management process because the failure to devote adequate time, attention, and expertise at the "ground level" virtually guarantees that all subsequent risk mitigation activity will be inadequate or otherwise flawed. The OCC provides a number of tips that serve as guidance to banks either creating or refreshing their respective programs, highlighting that the identification process should be:[24]

- **Comprehensive.**[25] To ensure that the identification process is truly comprehensive, compliance professionals must view their BIPs from a variety of angles and through various lenses.[26] To do this, they should consider creating a reference document that

---

[21] OCC Guidance, at 29-30. Note that this risk can be eliminated when, e.g., a bank has entered into an arrangement with a third-party provider whereby the extension of credit is facilitated by the latter and through an entity that is separate and distinct from the former. The potential to eliminate this one category of risk is significant; however, additional risks and obligations pertain to the use of third-party providers that must be addressed by the bank in order to meet regulatory expectations.

[22] The Committee of Sponsoring Organizations of the Treadway Commission (COSO) defines "risk appetite" as the "amount of risk, on a broad level, an entity is willing to accept in pursuit of value. It reflects the entity's risk management philosophy, and in turn influences the entity's culture and operating style." Rittenberg, Larry, PhD., and Frank Martens, The Committee of Sponsoring Organizations of the Treadway Commission (COSO). *Enterprise Risk Management: Understanding and Communicating Risk Appetite.* (Jan. 2012), http://www.coso.org/documents/ERM-Understanding%20%20Communicating%20Risk%20Appetite-WEB_FINAL_r9.pdf

[23] Although not set forth within the OCC Guidance, an additional underlying requirement to complete the risk evaluation cycle is for the bank to accept the residual risk associated with the various issues identified. This process (and the corresponding decisions made) should reflect the defined risk appetite of the organization.

[24] See generally, OCC Guidance, at 30-31.

[25] In addition to the author's recommendations, the OCC Guidance at 30-31 notes that the risk identification process should occur at the line of business level, and that compliance professionals should "identify interdependencies and correlations across business lines that may amplify risk exposures."

[26] For example, if the bank uses a third-party provider, the agreement setting forth the obligations and expectations of the parties should be a focal point, as it highlights areas that reflect opportunities for breakdowns—and thus risks to the organization. Also, the OCC Guidance, at 30, notes that risk identification "should be a continuous process that occurs at the individual transaction and aggregate business level."

identifies the five articulated sources of risk (as well as any additional threats based on the unique characteristics of the organization) and allows for recorded feedback from a variety of different relevant sources across the organization.[27] As each party shares his or her thoughts, new potential risks may be identified; these issues should be subsequently added to the master chart. When reviewing a specific activity or function, compliance professionals should follow the flow of the process, engaging key staff along the way to ensure that all risks and potential sources of breakdowns are identified and documented (with particular scrutiny applied to manual processes and other areas lending themselves to human error). All new issues identified through this process must be explored in order to ensure that the final product truly reflects the universe of potential BIP risks. Finally, although colleagues are critical resources for the risk identification process, it is also important to use audit reports, regulatory examination findings, risk assessments, and other objective data that reflect real or potential risks to the organization.

- **Ongoing.** The risk identification process should be ongoing, which requires compliance professionals to take certain steps in order to ensure that their core risk document remains relevant and accurate at all times.

  First, their understanding of changes in the securities and banking industries should be current to ensure that emerging threats are properly documented and addressed.[28] Once an issue/trend is identified, it should be added to the risk grid to not only begin the "measure, monitor, and control" phases of the process, but also to identify how the addition of that element impacts resource needs, other identified risks, the overall risk profile of the BIP, etc.

  Second, they must ensure that all key parties are aware that any changes in policies, procedures and/or practices that could impact the risk database should be reported to a central compliance source immediately.[29] In identifying these individuals, compliance professionals should be careful not to make their source list too narrow, but instead should include relevant parties from the Information Technology Department, the Privacy Office, etc. (as appropriate).[30]

Measure Risk. This phase of the risk management process is critical because it plays an important role both in the quality of the reporting up and across the organization, and in the subsequent allocation of resources by the bank's board of directors and senior

---

[27] These sources should include (where relevant) audit team members, compliance counterparts, inside counsel, operational risk personnel, and key BIP and other business unit staff who either play a role in, or have otherwise analyzed, the specific function being reviewed.

[28] This particular facet of the process highlights the importance of the relationship between the securities and banking compliance professionals because each can leverage the other in order to identify new laws/ regulations, emerging trends, and other developments that impact the BIP.

[29] An effective way to ensure that no significant changes "fall through the cracks" for an extended period of time is to set up a quarterly communication process that reminds individuals to share relevant changes with the compliance team (note that this process can also be leveraged to meet the various securities-related mandates as well).

[30] Compliance professionals should also ensure that their communications with these parties are consistent enough that they are in a position to be aware of critical personnel changes in a timely manner. When key identified parties leave or change their roles within the organization, compliance professionals should engage the new team member(s) immediately in order to advise them of their responsibilities with respect to the risk identification process.

management. In discussing the measurement of risk, the OCC notes that the sophistication of the tools used will vary across organizations depending on the complexity of their BIPs, and reminds banks that their measurement needs may change as their individual programs evolve. It further notes that assessment tools should be periodically tested to ensure their accuracy, and that tools should be used to assess the "risks of individual transactions and aggregate client portfolios, as well as interdependencies, correlations, and aggregate risks across lines of business."[31] This guidance reinforces the importance of the compliance professional's comprehensive understanding of his/her organization's BIP, while highlighting the need for measurement tools to be:

- **Meaningful.** Excessive risk measurement can ultimately be unhelpful at best (and detrimental at worst) because key issues can get lost amid a large volume of reporting. This loss can result in risk management program breakdowns in the monitoring and control phases of the process. To avoid this problem, compliance professionals should use their expertise (and that of their counterparts) to measure the more significant risks that the BIP poses to the bank. In evaluating risks to which resources should be devoted, areas to focus on include (but should not be limited to) manual processes, issues representing previous (and potentially significant) problems/breakdowns, and shifts in regulatory focus/requirements.[32] Also, it's important to remember that the areas that are the subject of ongoing scrutiny may evolve over time based on changes in the industry, the bank, and/or the BIP.[33]
- **Useful.** When evaluating the usefulness of a measuring tool, the compliance professional must keep in mind who the recipient of the information will be and what he or she needs to know. For example, the board of directors is generally charged with oversight of the organization and the various parts therein, as well as making strategic, resource allocation, and other similar decisions to ensure that aggregate and business unit-specific risk levels fall within the bank's established risk appetite. With that in mind, board members may require higher-level data (depending on the issue) that allows them to make appropriate, informed decisions. In contrast, a senior business leader (whose key function is, among other things, to make strategic decisions for his or her respective line(s) of business) should be made aware of circumstances that suggest that his or her focus, departmental resources, etc., should change. As such, the business leader will likely require more detail given his or her role in setting policy, approving changes in procedure, etc. As this suggests, the compliance professional must remain mindful of the fact that different tools may be more appropriate for different recipients.

[31] OCC Guidance, at 31.

[32] In conducting this analysis, it is also helpful to consider the potential impact (e.g., monetary, reputational) of the risk—i.e., what are the implications of the problem if the risk fully manifests itself—when evaluating its impact and recommending corresponding resource allocations.

[33] For example, during a previous risk identification exercise, a particular process/function may have been identified as a risky area in part because its success was dependent upon a manual process with no second review (i.e., there was no "second set of eyes" monitoring the activity to ensure that no costly manual errors were being made). That process may have been subsequently automated and "locked down" in terms of the ability of an individual(s) to intentionally or inadvertently modify the process. If that occurs, and in light of the other risks which have been identified within the BIP, it may become appropriate for the resources used to monitor that area to be repurposed to regularly review another emerging risk within the program.

- **Effective.** As a corollary to usefulness, to ensure effectiveness compliance professionals must ask whether the measurement tool effectively communicates important information. To truly measure risk and to subsequently gauge the need to devote more or less attention to a particular area, a tool should present data in a manner that is measurable/quantifiable, is easily understandable, and effectively communicates shifts/trends over time. To facilitate this, when faced with an option, compliance professionals should elect to present information quantitatively versus in narrative form (if appropriate), and the structure and format of the communication mechanism should allow for the highlighting of critical data.[34]

Monitor Risk. The monitoring component goes to the heart of the banking regulators' expectations with regards to BIPs, namely, that banks are expected to have their proverbial "finger on the pulse" of BIP-related risks at all times. The nature of this expectation reinforces—again—the concept of the risk management program being a living, breathing process that allows for adaptation in response to internal and external change. It also reflects the anticipated continuum between the identification, measurement, monitoring, and control phases of the risk management program, as the first two steps establish the issues/areas that represent the foundation for ongoing bank monitoring/oversight. In discussing this phase of the risk management process, the OCC highlights the need for frequent, ongoing reporting between the BIP and the bank, noting that such ongoing review enables bank management to make effective decisions across geographic, product, and division lines.[35] With this in mind, it is important to remember that:

- **Communication is Critical.** When considering communication within the context of risk monitoring, compliance professionals should do so broadly, bearing in mind that information flows in different directions and via a variety of channels. For example, a change in a bank's policies, procedures, and/or practices may have a direct or indirect impact on one or more identified risks;[36] as such, this key information should flow both to *and* from the bank. Mechanisms for ensuring the effectiveness of this communication must be established—and maintained. Similarly, tools such as key risk indicators (KRIs)[37] may be part of formal, periodic monitoring that is conducted within the BIP or by compliance professionals and subsequently provided to the bank, but more informal channels (e.g., working groups, a periodic verbal "touch base") can be very effective in terms of monitoring existing or emerging risks.[38] As these examples suggest, it is critical that

---

[34] For example, if a particular tool used to measure an issue does not readily display key information (such as longer-term trends that may suggest program modifications are necessary), the compliance professional should call out the meaningful data in some fashion (e.g., adding a summary grid which highlights critical information for the reader).

[35] OCC Guidance, at 31.

[36] For example, a change to the manner/mechanism by which annual privacy notices are delivered by the bank may impact the BIP's risk level as it pertains to Regulation S-P, as a process that may have been automated on the BIP side may be consequently changed to a manual process.

[37] A KRI is a tool that provides an early warning signal of increasing risk exposure. It can be leading (i.e., predictive) or lagging (based on historical data), depending on the nature of the issue being measured.

[38] This can be particularly helpful with respect to emerging risks, as an initial, informal "FYI" to a compliance professional by a business partner who is in a position to identify a new issue can get that potential risk in the queue for subsequent review/analysis.

compliance professionals have a broad understanding of the structure of the bank and the various compliance and other issues it is addressing at any given time,[39] and that the compliance professionals devote sufficient energy to cultivating key relationships with personnel across the organization.[40]

- **Third-Party Provider Relationships Pose Unique Monitoring Challenges.** The previous discussion regarding the importance of communication is clearly relevant within the context of a TPP relationship; however, there is an increased level of complexity within these scenarios because the third-party provider is separate and distinct from the bank and the BIP.[41] Because of this intricacy, the flow of information between the TPP and the bank/BIP can be less robust and/or consistent, and the volume, quality, and usefulness of the data diminished.

  To combat these challenges, compliance professionals should first review the terms of the agreement between the entities, which lay out the obligations of the TPP with respect to the BIP. By performing this exercise, the professionals will be able to identify areas representing potential breakdowns that may occur that are outside of the direct control of the bank—and thus to establish a foundation for the type of information that the TPP should be providing on a periodic basis.[42] In addition, compliance professionals should identify other areas meriting scrutiny (based on changes in the relationship, industry developments, regulatory guidance, etc.) and work with the TPP to implement meaningful formal monitoring that enables the bank to meet its regulatory oversight obligations. Finally, compliance professionals should establish formal meetings with key personnel within the TPP in order to ensure the effective, timely communication of critical risk data; notes should be taken, and identified risks should be communicated to appropriate personnel within the organization, with compliance professionals and other applicable parties following up on the identified issue(s).

Control Risk. This final phase emphasizes the important role that the board of directors and senior bank management play within the risk management continuum, and it relates to—and directly impacts—the organization's articulated risk appetite. The OCC notes the board's critical role in setting the bank's strategic direction and risk tolerances, and the importance of this information—and the corresponding limits

[39] This can be accomplished in a variety of different ways. For example, in addition to scheduled and impromptu meetings, investment compliance professionals can subscribe to e-communications that provide banking law/regulation updates, thereby giving them an independent and objective understanding of issues to supplement the information provided by colleagues.

[40] For example, investment compliance professionals should partner with their bank-side compliance colleagues, both formally (e.g., via monthly "update" meetings) and informally.

[41] The OCC Guidance, at 2, discusses at length the complexity of TPP relationships, as well as steps that should be implemented by banks to ensure that they are meeting their regulatory requirements. Of particular interest for purposes of this discussion is its statement that "a bank using third parties for its RNDIP sales program should implement effective risk management to safeguard its clients as well as the bank itself. The use of affiliated or unaffiliated parties does not relieve the bank from responsibility to take reasonable actions to ensure the third parties' activities meet regulatory requirements." Although important, this topic generally goes beyond the scope of this chapter, and compliance professionals who have BIPs that use third-party providers should consult the OCC Guidance for additional information.

[42] Note that the nature of the particular commitment will drive the need for, and frequency of, periodic exception or other reporting. For example, certain obligations imposed upon the third party provider may not represent significant risk to the bank, and thus may not warrant periodic monitoring.

on policies, procedures, and practices—being cascaded down throughout the bank.[43] These guardrails serve to give the identified risks context, and enable compliance professionals—and the bank as a whole—to identify when one or more risks exceeds those boundaries (and thus merits additional scrutiny). Given this, it is important to understand that:

- **Communication is Critical (Again).** With respect to controlling risk, it is essential that the risk appetite of the organization (established by the board of directors) be effectively—and regularly—communicated through management and to both BIP personnel and compliance professionals. If risk expectations are unclear, compliance professionals must seek clarification in order to ensure that they and their colleagues understand what is and isn't an acceptable risk level. Given that process owners and other individuals within the BIP may play more critical roles than others in terms of overseeing one or more identified risks, compliance professionals should make efforts to reinforce to those team members the risk appetite of the bank and the corresponding impact it has on the day-to-day activities of the BIP.

  When the risk management process reveals one or more risks that exceed these boundaries, and/or when the aggregate risk level of the BIP is elevated beyond acceptable levels, compliance professionals should initiate "off cycle reporting"[44] to key constituents, highlighting the nature and source of the risk, the steps that have been established to date to mitigate the threat, and what additional steps (if any) can/should be implemented to further reduce the risk. Feedback provided by these parties should then be analyzed and implemented in a timely fashion.

  Finally, compliance professionals should identify those risks that cannot (even with monitoring and controls in place) be reduced to a level that reflects the organization's defined risk appetite, and communicate them to senior bank management and the board of directors for their review and consideration. In doing so, the frequency and depth of ongoing monitoring and reporting should be discussed, and acceptable boundaries (unique to those concerns) should be established. Should the risk ultimately be accepted, evidence of that acceptance (and the justification behind it) should be documented.

Effectively Communicating Key BIP Risk Information

As the previous discussion illustrates, the effective communication of BIP risk information to key parties across the organization is critical to ensuring that banks are meeting their regulatory requirements. There are two primary considerations when a compliance professional is evaluating the most efficient and effective method for such delivery: who is receiving the feedback, and what the expectations are in terms of his or her overall role in BIP oversight—and within the organization as a whole. These separate and distinct expectations drive not only the type of data that each group should receive, but also the

---

43 OCC Guidance, at 31.

44 "Off cycle reporting" is communication that occurs prior to the next scheduled date for risk updates.

level of detail to which such reporting should go. Given this, compliance professionals should consider the following constituents and their unique needs.[45]

The Board of Directors. As previously noted, the board sets the bank's strategic direction and articulates its risk appetite; as such, it is essential that objective information that impacts its decision-making process be provided on a periodic (more often, if necessary[46]) basis. In establishing the framework for providing effective communication to board members, it is essential that compliance professionals remember that the board is not only evaluating risk information for the BIP; it is also considering the impact of that data on other business units and the organization as a whole.

The challenge in communicating with the board is that the information must highlight data critical to the performance of its duties in a clear and concise manner.[47] As such, information must be prominently displayed, with necessary explanatory data set forth to ensure that board members have the proper scope and context through which to evaluate the information.[48] Highlighted information may include (but need not be limited to):

- Data regarding new products/services and their potential risk impact on both the BIP and the bank;
- Positive and negative trends,[49] and what is being done about the latter;
- Internal audit and examination results and any lingering issues, associated ongoing risks, etc., that have not yet been addressed and/or cannot be fully mitigated;
- Significant changes in BIP senior management and other key roles and their potential impact on the program;
- Significant changes in risk assessments;
- Industry/enforcement trends; and
- BIP performance numbers.

New data should be highlighted and presented in a manner that enables the board members to compare current period information against statistics from previous timeframes; this will not only provide enhanced context, but it will also allow members to more effectively shift

[45] Note that the focus here is on the most obvious consumers of BIP information; however, there may be other key constituents that require data based on the structure, activities, etc., of the organization.

[46] Various factors might trigger the need for more frequent reporting of BIP data to the board of directors (e.g., a significant negative trend involving a core product offering, a sharp increase in the volume or impact of customer complaints). When an event/series of events occur that threaten to significantly impact the level of risk associated with the BIP and/or the overall safety and soundness of the bank itself, compliance professionals must ensure that this information is communicated to board members in a timely fashion so that any midcycle adjustments deemed necessary are made in a timely fashion.

[47] This requirement is particularly important given the volume and breadth of the data that is shared with board members on a regular basis. Compliance professionals should be cognizant of this potential roadblock to effective communication (and, subsequently, data consumption), and work to ensure that the most critical information is highlighted during live presentations, within printed materials, etc.

[48] This becomes particularly important when one or more board members do not have a strong BIP background and/or the knowledge necessary to fully evaluate the potential impact of the data.

[49] For example, an uptick in customer complaints in general and/or with respect to a particular product/service, region, and/or employee.

resources to meet both current challenges and the threat of emerging risks. To help ensure the effective communication of core data, material should present it in a manner that allows for easy and efficient interpretation; where possible, compliance professionals should use graphs and charts, and avoid long narratives that require board members to "search" for the information they need to do their jobs effectively. Finally, and perhaps most importantly, board members must have the ability to have their BIP questions answered in a timely manner so that they can respond efficiently and effectively to the changing landscape.

Bank Senior Management/Key Business Partners. These constituencies are responsible for (among other duties) executing on bank- and line of business-specific goals and objectives, while ensuring that activities conducted under their leadership are consistent with the bank's established risk appetite. Given the broad influence managers and business partners have over the larger organization, when a compliance professional establishes the communication framework with these individuals, it is essential that he or she cast a wide net, encompassing management from other lines of business, representatives from global/critical entity-wide control functions, etc. Absent such an expansive network, the BIP risks conducting its activities within a vacuum, thereby jeopardizing the quality of the information shared both across the organization and up to senior bank management and the board of directors, and inhibiting the bank's ability to meet the expectations of its regulators.

These constituencies represent not only one of the biggest challenges for compliance professionals, but also one of the key benefits to operating within a bank environment. On the one hand, their presence mandates a more complex communication structure, as core information must be collected, analyzed, and disseminated with the needs and goals of multiple different bank-side constituencies in mind. This increases the pressure faced by compliance professionals to ensure that the communication framework is both effective and dynamic in order to avoid critical data flow breakdowns. However, these additional parties can also (if properly understood and leveraged) aid the BIP in meeting its legal/regulatory obligations, enabling its compliance team to incorporate internal audit results into risk assessments, rely on global resources to aid in key functions (such as anti-money laundering and information security efforts), and more.

To take advantage of the opportunities they offer, however, compliance professionals must understand the structure of the larger bank organization, as well as the functions, activities, initiatives, and key players within the various parts. Compliance professionals should start by obtaining an accurate organization chart and considering each separate business unit contained therein. The focus should be not only on identifying opportunities for synergies (e.g., using the larger organization's BSA/AML program and activities), but also on what lines of business regularly engage with the BIP (through cross-selling activities, reviews/testing, etc.) and what corresponding information needs to be shared between the BIP and these various groups.[50] Compliance professionals should then

---

[50] For example, if a data breach involving the BIP occurs, it may be appropriate to communicate with the Privacy Office, the Information Security Office, the Information Technology Department, the Customer Service Department, and/or other areas across the organization, depending upon the nature and extent of the information compromised.

identify those within the various departments who are essential contacts—i.e., staff that manage key applicable functions, and thus are high enough within the organization to be impactful and make decisions, but close enough to the activity to understand how things work in practice and where potential issues/concerns exist. Depending upon the size and complexity of a particular line of business/function, compliance professionals may need to engage several individuals within the area in order to ensure that communication will truly be comprehensive and effective.

The goal here is threefold. First, it is to ensure that key bank-side areas know what is going on in the BIP and how it may impact the larger organization, and (conversely) for those individuals to think of—and engage in a timely fashion—investment compliance professionals when a new initiative is undertaken, an existing process is changed, etc., that may impact the BIP and the effectiveness of its compliance program. Second, it is to identify ways that each side can leverage and enhance the other's activities. For example, BIP compliance professionals can engage internal audit, operational risk, risk management, and other similar areas to coordinate/supplement monitoring and testing activities. Similarly, the bank-side control functions can evaluate and (if appropriate) use the work of the investment compliance professionals to produce more comprehensive reports and evaluations.[51] Third, a more subtle goal with respect to this communication is educating bank-side personnel at all levels on the nature and characteristics of the BIP, what its key business and compliance concerns are, where it focuses its resources, etc. The importance of this objective cannot be overstated, particularly given that the focus of the aggregate organization is generally on core banking activities.

Once an appreciation for the communication needs of the various constituencies has been established, the compliance professional must determine how targeted information will be delivered and how often that message should be received.[52] The former involves an evaluation of not only the type of data presentation that is most effective for each particular category of recipient (e.g., charts, graphs, KRIs), but also the format through which the information should be shared. The mechanisms available to compliance professionals mirror those currently used by independent broker-dealers and investment advisers (i.e., meetings, webexes, emails, and other communications/documentation), with one key (and very valuable) exception—the bank's established committee structure.[53]

---

[51] This is particularly beneficial when the parties coordinate (where appropriate) with respect to the focus of their individual reviews within the same area in order to encompass more aggregate subject matter, thereby increasing the comprehensiveness of oversight within those particular areas.

[52] The frequency of which key data is provided will be driven by factors such as the risk associated with the information, the fluidity of the data in question, etc. These are universal considerations that are not unique to BIPs and compliance professionals; as such, they will not be discussed at length within this chapter.

[53] Bank committees generally operate on preset schedules; this helps to ensure that information regarding existing or emerging risks is not be overlooked for long periods of time and/or goes unreported to one or more areas across the organization.

Banks generally have a committee structure (commensurate with their unique size, structure, and complexity) designed to ensure that critical risk and other information is disseminated to appropriate individuals in the organization, both within the same discipline (e.g., a bank-wide compliance committee) and across various lines of business and/or levels of authority. Using this structure to communicate important BIP information to a variety of constituents is beneficial for several reasons. First, it directly addresses the banking regulators' concerns with respect to securities activities taking place within the bank's retail network . By actively engaging, and sharing BIP information with, a variety of key bank-side constituents, compliance professionals are ensuring that those parties—and the bank in general—are aware of the activities, risks, emerging issues, etc., associated with the bank investment program. This allows for more effective (and documented) oversight, and gives the board of directors and bank senior management the data they need to make timely and effective modifications to resource allocations, strategic initiatives, policies, procedures, and practices. This helps ensure that the aggregate organization continues to operate within its stated risk appetite and corresponding tolerances, while contributing to a "no-surprises" compliance and risk environment. In addition, the BIP's participation on one or more of the bank's committees helps to keep it engaged and aware of the larger organization's activities, thereby positioning the BIP to effectively respond early on to issues and initiatives that may impact the strength of its compliance program (and thus to avoid last minute adjustments, preventable regulatory violations, etc.). Given the significant benefits of participation, compliance professionals should actively look for—and participate on—these valuable bank committees.

Once a process has been established to ensure that risks have been identified, measured, monitored, and controlled, and an effective, comprehensive communication framework has been built, it is essential that a mechanism be put in place to ensure that these elements are regularly revisited to validate their usefulness and effectiveness to both the BIP and the larger bank organization. Potential red flags that may indicate problems will vary based on the unique characteristics of the individual organization; however, triggers may include:

- Changes in products/services that introduce greater complexity and risk to both the BIP and the bank as a whole;
- The significant restructuring of one of more departments within the aggregate organization that were identified as critical during the initial evaluation process;
- The departure of one or more key business partners (which may result in a communication breakdown, the exodus of unique institutional and/or subject matter knowledge, etc.); and
- A change in the bank's stated risk appetite that results in a misalignment with the identified BIP risks, activities, etc.

When developments such as these occur, it is incumbent upon compliance professionals to reevaluate their programs, and to address any identified gaps and inconsistencies in a timely manner, communicating any lingering issues or concerns to appropriate BIP and bank personnel.

III. TARGETED COMPLIANCE ISSUES/CONSIDERATIONS FOR BANK INVESTMENT PROGRAMS

A key issue that distinguishes BIPs from standalone investment programs is the heightened potential for customer confusion. Although broker-dealers and investment advisers must always guard against customer misunderstanding regarding the nature and characteristics of investment products, the potential for confusion is even greater when an individual is purchasing securities within a bank branch (where FDIC-insured products are also made available to retail customers).[54] Customer confusion can stem from a variety of different sources, including (but not limited to):

- The location within which the sales are taking place (i.e., a bank branch);
- The primary products/services offered within that location (i.e., FDIC-insured products and other traditional bank offerings);
- The "dual hats" worn by licensed bank employees[55] (who may have facilitated the opening of an FDIC-insured bank account for the customer during his or her previous visit);
- A lack of clear disclosure with respect to the RNDIPs offered within the branch (either visual or verbal); and
- Overt and/or subtle messages with respect to the signage and advertising/marketing materials (collectively referred to as "marketing materials").

To minimize the likelihood of customer confusion, banks must ensure that customers are "clearly and fully informed of the nature and risks associated with RNDIPS."[56] With this standard in mind, various requirements have been established to minimize the potential for customer confusion, and thus to protect the investor, the bank, and the BIP. These obligations are among the most longstanding mandates for bank investment programs (dating back to the 1994 *Interagency Statement on the Retail Sale of Nondeposit Investment Products*);[57] thus, they represent the foundation upon which many subsequent bank BIP requirements have been built.

Advertising/Marketing Concerns

The rules and requirements[58] pertaining to marketing materials were designed to help ensure that clear distinctions are drawn between FDIC-insured and nondeposit

---

[54] This concern is clearly articulated within the OCC Guidance, at 1, which states (in part) that, "effective risk management is necessary to minimize the possibility of customer confusion associated with offering RNDIPs on bank premises...Of particular concern is the potential for customer confusion between insured bank deposits and uninsured RNDIPs."

[55] A "licensed bank employee" is an employee who is able to sell FDIC-insured and other similar bank products, while also maintaining the requisite FINRA and/or state insurance licenses needed to solicit and sell securities and/or insurance products.

[56] OCC Guidance, at 2.

[57] Federal Reserve Board, Federal Deposit Insurance Corporation, Office of the Comptroller of the Currency, Office of Thrift Supervision, Interagency Statement on Retail Sales of Nondeposit Investment Products (Feb. 15, 1994), https://www.fdic.gov/regulations/laws/rules/5000-4500.html

[58] Note that, where applicable, this discussion encompasses both print and website marketing requirements.

investment products and services. These expectations impact not only the content of the mandatory disclosure language,[59] but also how and where it is presented to the customer.

Mandatory Disclosures. One of the most important aspects of the marketing requirements are the core disclosures required for investment products sold through a BIP (be it via a proprietary broker-dealer or investment adviser, or through a third party provider). These requirements, originally set forth within the 1994 *Interagency Statement on the Retail Sale of Nondeposit Investment Products*[60] (and subsequently updated), mandate that investors be told, at a minimum, that investment and insurance products are not deposits, are not FDIC-insured, are not insured by any federal government agency, have no bank guarantee, and may lose value.[61] This information must be provided in a clear and conspicuous manner[62] orally during sales presentations and when investment advice is provided, orally and in writing prior to or at the time an investment account is opened, and within marketing materials.[63] By effectively communicating this information, banks are helping to ensure that customers are fully aware of the nature and characteristics of the RNDIPs they are purchasing prior to the execution of the investment transaction.

In addition to these mandatory disclosures, compliance professionals should also ensure that the relationship between the BIP, the bank and (if applicable) the TPP is fully and accurately explained to investors.[64] Such information not only further mitigates the likelihood of customer confusion based on the location at which his or her investments are being purchased, but also (in doing so) clarifies roles, relationships, and expectations with respect to the products and services being offered.

Mixed Marketing Concerns. Although the core disclosure requirements are fairly straightforward for investment-exclusive marketing materials, the obligations become more challenging when a marketing piece contains both FDIC-insured and RNDIP components.[65] This is because of the increased likelihood for customer confusion; as such, in conducting an advertising review containing mixed material, the compliance professional must focus equally on the *content* and the *placement* of the disclosure information.

---

59 OCC Guidance, Appendix A.

60 Note that the Interagency Statement establishes requirements that apply to, and are directed at, banks. FINRA-registered firms that operate on bank premises must comply with FINRA Rule 3160, "Networking Arrangements Between Members and Financial Institutions." Although this chapter focuses on BIP obligations from a bank perspective, compliance professionals should also consult FINRA Rule 3160.

61 Note that additional disclosures, if deemed necessary/appropriate, may be provided to further clarify the nature, characteristics, and/or risks associated with a particular type of RNDIP.

62 For written materials, "clear and conspicuous" generally means that the disclosures should be easy to see and find—i.e., the font size used should be similar to that of other parts of the marketing material, and the information should be highlighted (e.g., via a box, bolded lettering) to ensure that it stands out to the investor.

63 OCC Guidance, Appendix A.

64 For example, a BIP using the services of a TPP can state the following: "Securities and insurance products and services are offered at ABC Bank by DEF Securities, Inc., a registered broker-dealer and registered investment adviser, Member FINRA/SIPC. ABC Investments is the delivery channel for securities and insurance products and services offered by DEF Securities, Inc. ABC Bank and ABC Investments are not registered broker-dealers or investment advisers, nor are they affiliated with DEF Securities, Inc."

65 An example of this would be a customer brochure advertising both checking account offerings and RNDIPs.

To mitigate the potential for customer confusion, compliance professionals should ensure that the mandatory disclosure language for both product types is contained within the marketing material, and that it is clear to the reader which disclosure verbiage pertains to which products/services. To ensure such clarity, FDIC-insured product/service disclosures should be separate and distinct from RNDIP disclosures; in practice, this means that required verbiage should not be intermingled,[66] and disclosure language pertaining to specific products/services should be linked to them using asterisks, numbers or other mechanisms which clearly illustrate the information to which each product/service pertains. When possible, compliance professionals should ensure that disclosure language is on the same page (or in close, easily identifiable proximity) to the applicable product/service.

As this description suggests, it is critically important that BIP and bank-side compliance professionals maintain effective lines of communication with each other, and with their marketing business partners. All parties should have a working knowledge of FDIC-insured product and RNDIP disclosure requirements and mandates,[67] and a process[68] should be put in place to ensure that all applicable compliance constituents are required to provide formal sign-off for final marketing materials (with the policies and procedures surrounding mixed marketing reviews expressly prohibiting changes once these reviews have been completed). In getting to the final product, the process flow should require rereview by both compliance sides of the house when content changes are made by one or more parties; although onerous, this greatly mitigates the potential for a change correcting one side's compliance problem while creating a violation on the other. Finally, formal evidence of each individual review should be maintained, and marketing personnel must be made aware that any deviation from the preestablished process will result in a failure to move forward with the particular marketing piece. These combined steps will help ensure that the bank does not publish materials that violate RNDIP-related marketing requirements and expectations.

Setting and Circumstances Considerations

As the OCC Guidance notes, "The setting and circumstances surrounding the sale of RNDIPs is fundamental to ensuring that customers can readily distinguish between RNDIPs and FDIC-insured deposit products."[69] As such, BIP-related activities should:

---

66 For example, an FDIC-insured product/service disclosure should not be "broken up" by a RNDIP disclosure, and vice versa.

67 Given the complexity of the various disclosure requirements, it is often helpful to provide targeted training to the professionals charged with creating marketing materials. This training can include a discussion of both content and placement requirements, as well as the underlying motivation behind these mandates. Although initially time consuming, this effort will reduce both the amount of effort involved in future marketing reviews, and the frequency of having to finalize pieces after targeted deadlines due to multiple resubmissions aimed at correcting compliance-related errors.

68 To avoid problems pertaining to review turn-over times for BIP and bank-side compliance personnel, this process should incorporate service level agreements (SLAs) that outline expectations for business, marketing, and compliance personnel. These SLAs should incorporate timeframes that allow for the business lines and marketing team to move forward in a timely fashion, while not "tying the hands" of the compliance reviewers (e.g., the number of business days permitted for a compliance review may be made to correlate with the number of pages included in the marketing material).

69 OCC Guidance, at 52.

- Clearly identify the broker-dealer/investment adviser as the entity providing the investment services (versus the bank);
- Occur in a clearly marked area that is (to the extent practical) physically separate from the routine deposit-taking areas within the branch; and
- Limit unlicensed bank employees to performing only clerical or ministerial functions in connection with brokerage transactions.[70]

In practice this means that, in addition to the provision of the mandatory disclosures previously discussed, full-time investment personnel and licensed bank employees operating within branches should use (as appropriate) nametags, business cards,[71] and other similar mechanisms to reinforce the distinction between the two categories of products/services. To further highlight the difference, the locations within which BIP activities are being conducted should be designated by signage[72] clearly delineating those areas from deposit-taking locations. In addition, to accommodate their full range of acceptable solicitation and sales activities, licensed bank employees should conspicuously change their desk signage (in conjunction with providing the applicable business card) when shifting from an FDIC-insured to an RNDIP sales discussion (and vice versa).

One final consideration pertaining to setting and circumstances requirements is the limitations on unlicensed employees with respect to the BIP. The OCC Guidance reinforces the long-established prohibitions on unlicensed bank employees' activity; namely, that they can only perform, "clerical or ministerial functions, such as scheduling appointments with registered representatives, forwarding customer funds or securities, or describing in general terms the types of investment vehicles available from the bank's RNDIP sales program."[73] To ensure that unlicensed personnel do not exceed these limitations and inadvertently engage in prohibited solicitation and/or sales activities, a robust training program[74] should be established that clearly delineates the appropriate behavioral boundaries.

Key to effectively implementing this training program is identifying what area(s) within the bank are responsible for creating (to ensure proper content), implementing (to

---

[70] OCC Guidance, at 53.

[71] Licensed bank employees should be trained to explain the distinction between FDIC-insured products and RNDIPs—and their ability to solicit and sell both—at the time they are providing the "other" card and shifting the conversation from one type of product/service to the other.

[72] Desk signage should be used by full-time investment personnel and licensed bank employees (while operating within their investment capacity) in order to reinforce that their offices/desks are being utilized to conduct BIP solicitation/sales activities. In addition, signage can be suspended from the ceiling or placed on a wall to denote permanent investment sales locations and thus further distinguish those areas from those that accept bank deposits.

[73] OCC Guidance, at 53.

[74] Given the variety of circumstances that could result in violations of these restrictions, scenario-based training (with corresponding scenario-based tests to reinforce key concepts) should be used whenever possible. Training authors should work with both investment- and bank-side compliance professionals, as well as line of business employees, to identify likely situations in which otherwise compliant unlicensed personnel may inadvertently violate the rules. The goal is to get those parties thinking; as such, contact information should be provided at the end of the module so that employees know who to contact with additional questions.

ensure proper facilitation for newly hired and existing employees), and revising (based on identified issues, industry developments, etc.) the training. If the compliance professional has limited influence in one or more of these areas, it is critical that he or she actively engages the appropriate business partners to mitigate the likelihood of process breakdowns and/or implementation gaps. Because executing on the training initiative will likely be a shared responsibility (particularly within larger banks), it is critical that ownership for the various individual parts of the overall process is clearly assigned to the appropriate parties. In addition to taking steps to encourage full participation, compliance professionals should also ensure that an escalation procedure is in place to address scenarios where unlicensed employees have neglected to complete this critical requirement.[75] By facilitating this process, the compliance professional helps to ensure that all unlicensed bank employees are properly sensitized to the limitations of their roles with respect to the BIP,[76] and thus that the bank is meeting its regulatory requirements.

IV. TIPS/TAKEAWAYS FOR ESTABLISHING AND MAINTAINING AN EFFECTIVE BIP COMPLIANCE PROGRAM

The final section of this chapter sets forth some additional tips and takeaways for compliance professionals charged with ensuring that their organizations meet the BIP requirements set forth by the banking regulators. Although some points serve as reinforcement for previously discussed information, others enhance key points and/ or provide additional recommendations for meeting these obligations. Each point can—and should—be modified by compliance professionals to meet the unique needs of their respective organizations.

Tips for Engaging and Leveraging Bank-Side Functions and Personnel

In order to take full advantage of the resources made available through the larger bank organization, compliance professionals should apply the following.

Identify Global Programs That Can Help Meet BIP Compliance Requirements. Compliance professionals should use the bank's organizational chart—as well as their own understanding of financial institution compliance requirements—to identify global programs that can be leveraged to meet their BIP obligations. Opportunities for synergies across the organization can be identified via a variety of mechanisms, including the BIP's own risk assessment. These programs can ultimately be used to meet investment-related requirements (e.g., FINRA Rule 3310, "Anti-Money Laundering Compliance Program"), and as mechanisms for reporting BIP-specific initiatives, opportunities for

[75] As these mechanics suggest, the bank retail network must support this initiative; compliance personnel should ensure that key bank-side parties understand the importance of this training, and are willing to act in the event that there are one or more violations. If compliance personnel are unable to obtain this support, they should escalate this matter to more senior managers in a timely fashion.

[76] Although the focus of this training is clearly on unlicensed bank employees, compliance professionals may wish to encourage licensed BIP employees located within the branches to participate in the initiative as well; this would further sensitize them to the restrictions placed on their unlicensed colleagues and thus serve as additional reinforcement of the mandated limitations.

enhancement, etc., to the larger bank organization. Such engagement also offers the opportunity for BIP compliance professionals to stay connected to issues and initiatives being driven by the bank and/or their bank-side compliance counterparts. As such, if properly used, these functions can strengthen both the bank and the BIP-specific compliance programs.

Establish Effective Lines of Communication with Personnel Managing Those Programs. In order to ensure that the BIP continues to benefit from these global programs, it is critical that compliance professionals stay engaged with the bank-side personnel in charge of managing, revising, etc., those initiatives. Ideally, this engagement is both formal and informal. For example, periodic meetings (the frequency of which should be driven by the nature of the program, the likelihood of regulatory updates, etc.) should be established whereby each party has the opportunity to provide updates, share concerns, work through potential roadblocks, etc. Similarly, informal "off-cycle" communications (e.g., phone calls, emails) can be used to provide less critical information, request interim updates, and/or otherwise share data and ideas about potential initiatives and other developments. When important information is received, compliance professionals must ensure that they share the data with all relevant parties so that the benefit of the knowledge can be fully realized; if applicable, they should also ensure that working groups are formed, projects initiated, etc., in order to address key developments.

Ensure that BIP Compliance Professionals Are Aware—at All Times—of Key Bank-Side Initiatives (and Vice Versa). The strength of the bank's and the BIP's respective compliance programs are interdependent; as such, compliance personnel must ensure that they are aware of key initiatives within both the investment and bank areas, and that their knowledge is shared with applicable parties who might otherwise not be advised of critical developments. This knowledge should be gained both through open lines of communication with key personnel, and through participation on relevant bank-side and BIP-related committees. Such engagement will help to minimize the likelihood for process/procedure breakdowns across the organization (during both the implementation and maintenance phases of various initiatives), as well as to ensure that BIP-specific considerations are taken into account by bank counterparts (and vice versa). It will also serve to identify issues that should ultimately appear on—and be addressed through—the BIP's various risk assessments, priorities lists, etc.

Tips for Establishing an Effective Training Program

In order to ensure that BIP personnel are meeting relevant bank regulatory requirements (and thereby supporting and strengthening the organization's overall compliance program), compliance professionals should ensure the following.

They Have Identified—and Have Robust Training Around—Critical BIP Compliance Issues/Considerations. Although BIP personnel are very familiar with the various securities-related requirements that impact their roles, the banking regulator obligations that apply to the bank investment program are not as obvious to them. As a result, compliance professionals need to ensure that these employees are fully sensitized to the unique requirements and limitations imposed on BIPs, and how they impact their specific jobs on a day-to-day basis. To do this effectively, compliance professionals must understand the different functions performed within the bank investment program, how those roles can be used to support compliance requirements, and where activities (either deliberate or unintentional) can jeopardize adherence to these mandates. They must then create training (either broad-based or targeted) using delivery mechanisms that will effectively disseminate this critical information. As previously noted, scenario-based modules should be employed (where appropriate), and attendance must be mandatory (with disciplinary measures imposed upon those who neglect to meet their obligations). To accomplish this, compliance professionals should leverage their bank-side business partners, and encourage BIP managers to reinforce key issues through periodic meetings and other points of contact.

The Training Focuses Most on Potential Areas of Confusion and Those Compliance Elements That May Be Easily Overlooked. Again, scenario-based training is very effective in highlighting—and exploring—potential areas of confusion, as it is able to present critical guidance using common real-life examples. Sources for these examples can be industry developments, recent enforcement actions, institutional experience, etc. Training should be provided in accordance with a preestablished risk-based schedule that ensures that critical information is communicated without overwhelming personnel with training modules, emails, etc. This will increase the likelihood that key points are considered and absorbed by participants, and thus future compliance risks are mitigated. Compliance professionals should coordinate with their bank-side counterparts so that modules are released in a systematic manner and (to the extent possible) they support each other and the efforts of the various compliance areas. Finally, training should include all relevant parties and, at the conclusion of his or her respective module, each participant should clearly understand his/her role in supporting BIP compliance, and how that role fits into the larger organization's efforts.

Particular Attention Is Given to the Risks Associated with Licensed Bank Employees. As previously suggested, licensed bank employees pose unique risks to the bank's compliance program by virtue of their ability to offer both FDIC-insured products and RNDIPs to customers within a branch setting. Additional training should be developed for—and periodically assigned to—these individuals; modules should emphasize the importance of their role in achieving compliance and potential challenges and pitfalls associated with being able to solicit and sell both types of products and services. These discussions should highlight the acute potential for customer confusion that their unique roles generate and the various techniques that they should use to minimize that risk. They should also offer solutions to foreseeable scenarios that jeopardize compliance efforts. Finally, compliance professionals should ensure that key messages are reinforced to licensed bank employees through their BIP and bank-side management, and that each individual is made aware of the appropriate contact should he or she have questions, concerns, etc., pertaining to the guidance that is provided.

V. CONCLUSION

As this chapter has illustrated, compliance professionals working within a bank investment program have a variety of additional issues and concerns that they must address in order to ensure that their BIPs not only remain compliant, but also support the overall goals, initiatives and risk appetite of the larger bank organization. These obligations add significant complexity to an already challenging regulatory environment, requiring compliance professionals to incorporate banking regulator mandates into their BIP risk assessments and investment-related policies, procedures, and practices. To do this effectively, they must have deep technical knowledge of applicable laws and regulations, while also demonstrating an ability to actively engage both BIP and bank-side colleagues at all levels in order to facilitate the implementation of effective compliance and risk management programs. Although the challenges associated with this role are many, being able to successfully create, implement, and oversee a robust, multilevel compliance structure offers compliance professionals a unique opportunity to expand and enhance their compliance knowledge and proficiency, while simultaneously making significant contributions to the success of both their BIPs and their larger bank organizations.

ABOUT THE AUTHOR

Karen M. Aavik is a senior vice president and the director of corporate and wholesale practices for KeyBank, N.A., where she leads a compliance team that provides support for, and oversight of, numerous bank- and investment-side lines of business, functions, and disciplines across the organization. As a member of the Corporate Compliance Department leadership team, she frequently engages senior business leaders and business partners throughout KeyBank to facilitate the creation and implementation of effective policies, procedures, and practices in furtherance of the organization's compliance risk management program. In support of these efforts, Ms. Aavik analyzes laws, regulations, and guidance that impact her areas of responsibility, and performs third-party reviews, risk assessments, gap analyses, and other activities designed to ensure the timely and effective identification and mitigation of risk. Ms. Aavik previously served as the wealth management compliance officer, the ethics officer and the privacy officer for First Niagara Financial Group, and as an assistant general counsel in the First Niagara Legal Department. Prior to that, she held a number of embedded and oversight compliance risk roles in support of the Investment Group of M&T Bank.

Ms. Aavik holds a juris doctor (with concentrations in Finance Transactions, and Regulatory Law and Policy), a master of laws with honors (in Criminal Law, with a concentration in White Collar Crime), and a master of business administration (with a concentration in Finance) from the State University of New York at Buffalo, and is a member of the New York State Bar. She is FINRA Series 4, 7, 24, 53, and 63 licensed with KeyBank Capital Markets Inc.; is NYS Life, Accident and Health licensed; has her National Regulatory Services Investment Adviser Certified Compliance Professional (IACCP) designation; and earned the International Association of Privacy Professionals CIPP/US, CIPP/E, CIPT, and CIPM privacy credentials. Ms. Aavik has presented at numerous conferences, seminars and web-based training programs on topics pertaining to investment-specific laws and regulations, compliance program development and implementation issues, ethics matters and considerations, and the effective implementation and management of ethics reporting programs. She has contributed to articles regarding cybersecurity requirements within the investment industry, and currently serves as an editorial board member for *Modern Compliance* (volume 2) and the *Journal of Financial Compliance.*

CHAPTER 7

Independent Investment Firms Versus Bank-Owned Investment Firms: Differences and Similarities

By Diane P. Novak
DPN Consulting Services

I. INTRODUCTION

This chapter will focus on the differences and similarities between "independent" investment firms, which have no banks or bank holding companies as parent companies, and "bank-owned" investment firms, which are direct (or indirect) subsidiaries of a federally chartered depositary bank or bank holding companies.[1] Types of industry participants and ownership structures will be discussed and the bank-owned investment firm model will be covered in depth. Both the historical perspective on bank-owned investment firms and what is expected currently will be addressed.

After reading this chapter, you will have a better idea of how both independent investment firms and bank-owned investment firms are structured and how bank-owned investment firms currently address their unique compliance challenges and obligations.

II. BUILDING AN UNDERSTANDING OF INDUSTRY PARTICIPANTS AND OWNERSHIP

A number of different types of investment firms reside in the securities industry today. Many are considered quite small, having 10 or fewer employees. The Financial Industry Regulatory Authority (FINRA) defines "small firms" as those having 150 or less registered persons, and a large firm is defined as having 500 or more registered persons.

Investment firms may be broker-dealers, registered with FINRA or they may be investment advisers, registered with the Securities and Exchange Commission (SEC) (or a similar state securities commissioner). The term "dual registrant" refers to an investment firm that has registered as both a broker-dealer and an investment adviser.

---

1 This chapter does not address all investment limitations under the Bank Holding Company Act.

Business models vary widely depending upon the investment firm's customer base, products, services, and strategies. Some investment firms are exclusively retail based and accept only consumers as clients. Other investment firms are considered institutional, and these firms only work with nonconsumer clients such as corporations, pension funds, banks, endowments, insurance companies, and municipalities. Still other investment firms are more of a hybrid, with a mixture of both retail (consumer) and institutional (business) accounts.

Investment firms, through an approved product committee, may develop approved product lists. These lists are provided to sales personnel and outline the firm's specific product offerings. An approved product list further differentiates investment firms. Some investment firms offer "packaged products" such as mutual funds and annuities; others offer stocks and bonds; still others offer more specialized or complex products, such as private placements, REITs, derivatives, options, collateralized loan obligations (CLOs), and collateralized debt obligations (CDOs). Additionally, certain firms may offer all of these products.

Although broker-dealers make recommendations to clients regarding securities based on a commission schedule in a nonfiduciary capacity, investment advisers typically offer advice in a fiduciary capacity, are fee based, and may recommend a strategy vs a specific product.

For purposes of this chapter, two basic forms of ownership are discussed. The first is an independent investment firm; this type of investment firm may be a sole proprietorship, partnership or incorporated entity and may be publicly or privately held. Independent investment firms include Fidelity Investments or E*Trade. The second form of ownership, the bank-owned investment firm, will be the primary focus of this chapter. These bank-owned investment firms are subsidiaries of banks or bank holding companies. In other words, the bank is the parent company. Examples of bank-owned investment firms would include U.S. Bancorp Investments, JPMorgan Securities, and BancWest Investment Services.

III. HISTORICAL PERSPECTIVE

Shortly after the 1929 stock market crash, during a period of nationwide bank failures, and the Great Depression, two members of Congress proposed what is known as the Glass-Steagall Act (GSA). Passed in 1933, this act separated investment and commercial banking activities. The impetus for this mandated separation came from concerns about banks' overinvesting in the stock market and taking too much risk with depositors' money. Additionally, Congress was concerned about how this activity within banks may have contributed to the stock market crash.

In November of 1999, Congress repealed the GSA and established the Gramm-Leach-Bliley Act (GLBA). GLBA eliminated the GSA restrictions against affiliations between commercial and investment banks.

Deregulation began in the late 1980s and continued throughout the 1990s. As banks were allowed to broaden their business lines and their geographic presence, bank management quickly learned that having a broker-dealer or investment adviser subsidiary could be a profitable and complementary addition to their existing business model.

During this same time, the banking and securities regulators, who operated independently of each other, struggled to understand what this change would mean from a regulation, oversight, examination, and enforcement standpoint.

The former National Association of Securities Dealers (NASD), now the Financial Industry Regulatory Authority (FINRA), determined that bank-owned broker-dealers would follow their existing regulatory processes. The SEC followed suit regarding investment advisers. The federal banking regulators, however, were concerned about product suitability, consumer confusion regarding insured products and investment products under the Federal Deposit Insurance Corporation (FDIC), disclosures, setting and circumstances (selling investment products on bank premises), and more.

On February 15, 1994, the Office of the Comptroller of the Currency, the FDIC, the Federal Reserve Board, and the Office of Thrift Supervision (collectively, "bank regulators") issued an Interagency Statement on Retail Sales of Nondeposit Investment Products.[2] These new and very prescriptive requirements complicated most banks' approach to having broker-dealer or investment adviser subsidiaries or affiliates.

FINRA followed with Rule 3160 [3] in February of 1998, which requires that a broker-dealer that is a party to a networking arrangement with a financial institution provide certain written disclosures, at or prior to the opening of a customer account, including disclosures that securities products are:

- Not FDIC insured;
- Not deposits or other obligations of the bank and are not guaranteed by the bank; and
- Subject to investment risk, including possible loss of the principal invested.

FINRA Rule 3160 also requires that broker-dealers make these disclosures orally at or prior to the time that a customer account is opened if the account is opened on the premises of a financial institution. In addition, FINRA Rule 3160 expands the disclosure requirements with respect to an investment firm's advertisements and sales literature and requires that they include disclosures that:

- Announce the location of the bank where broker-dealer services are provided;
- Are distributed by the BD on the premises of a bank;

---

2 FDIC, Interagency Statement on Retail Sales of Nondeposit Investment Products (Apr. 20, 2014),https://www.fdic.gov/regulations/laws/rules/5000-4500.html

3 FINRA 3160, Networking Arrangements Between Members and Financial Institutions, http://finra.complinet.com/en/display/display_main.html?rbid=2403&element_id=9093

- Promote the name or services of the bank; or
- Are distributed by the BD at any other location where the bank is present or represented.

The Interagency Statement and FINRA Rule 3160 will be discussed throughout this chapter, because both requirements directly impact bank-owned investment firms' overall compliance programs.

IV. REGULATION AND REGULATOR IMPACTS

Securities Regulation and Law

It is important to understand that broker-dealers and investment advisers operate under securities laws and regulations separate from banking laws and regulations.

As previously mentioned, specific laws and regulations have been promulgated over the years to address bank-owned investment firms. The first of these is known as the Interagency Statement on Retail Sales of Nondeposit Investment Products.

The Interagency Statement was developed to address what the banking regulators viewed as potential conflicts or areas of confusion when nondeposit investment products were being offered to consumers in retail banking branches.

Key points within the Interagency Statement include:

- Adoption of a program management statement;
- Development of compliance related policies and procedures;
- The design and implementation of a risk management program;
- A compliance program designed to meet the size, scope, and complexity of the firm;
- An internal audit program;
- A formal product selection process, which typically includes a product committee;
- Defined guidelines for setting and circumstances under which nondeposit products are sold in retail bank branches;
- Standards for disclosure and advertising;
- Procedures regarding qualifications and training of sales personnel and bank personnel;
- Suitability and sales practices;
- A formalized compensation plan;
- Procedures outlining the acceptable location of securities and investment sales in bank branches versus deposit-taking activities;
- Guidance on dual employees of the bank and the investment firm(s); and
- Understanding bank regulatory oversight and internal governance.

As noted, FINRA followed with its own specific regulations focused on bank-owned investment firms selling on the premises of banks. These requirements are very similar to the Interagency Statement on Retail Sales of Nondeposit Investment Products and are covered in FINRA Rule 3160.

Regulatory Oversight: Impacts and Coordination

Independent investment firms will have fewer regulatory agencies interested in conducting oversight and examinations. On the other hand, bank-owned investment firms will be required to interact with the banking regulators periodically. The scope of activities of the regulators is summarized in Table 1.

TABLE 1. SECURITIES REGULATORS AND THEIR FOCUS

Regulator	Scope of Activities
FINRA	Examines and oversees all broker-dealers
SEC	Examines and oversees all investment advisers meeting the dollar threshold for SEC registration; oversees FINRA and less directly, broker-dealers
State securities regulators	Examine and oversee broker-dealers and investment advisers within their jurisdiction; regulated in each state through that state's securities commissioners' office
State insurance regulators	Examine and oversee investment firms that offer insurance products; regulated state by state through the individual insurance commissioner's office

All investment firms are concerned about overlapping or concurrent regulatory examinations by multiple regulatory agencies. Bank-owned investment firms have the additional burden of coordinating with both the securities regulators and the banking regulators, as shown in Table 2.

TABLE 2. FEDERAL AND STATE BANKING REGULATORS AND THEIR FOCUS

Regulator	Scope of Activities
Regulators include Office of the Comptroller of the Currency (OCC), the Consumer Financial Protection Bureau (CFPB), the Federal Reserve Board (FRB), the Federal Deposit Insurance Commission (FDIC), and state banking commissioners' offices	For bank-owned investment firms, banking regulators will defer to the securities regulators on securities related matters in most cases. Banking regulators are interested in compliance with the Interagency Statement and other matters not addressed in this chapter; state banking regulators also oversee state licensed banks that may have investment related affiliates

Specific Banking Regulations Impacting Bank-Owned Investment Firms

This analysis covers three significant banking regulations that can impact bank-owned investment firms. Regulation W addresses risks to banks who transact business with their affiliates. Regulation O governs any extension of credit to banks' executive officers, directors, and principal shareholders. Lastly, Regulation R is focused broadly on banks' securities activities.

This discussion summarizes these banking regulations and introduces potential impacts to a subsidiary or affiliate of the bank. Compliance officers should refer to the underlying requirements and as needed, consult legal counsel for further guidance.

Regulation W: Bank Affiliate Rules. In October 2002, the Federal Reserve Board published a final Regulation W, which implemented sections 23A and 23B of the Federal Reserve Act.[4] The FRB implemented Regulation W with an effective date of April 1, 2003. Sections 23A and 23B and Regulation W are designed to limit the risks to a bank from transactions between the bank and its "affiliates", and to limit the ability of a bank to transfer to its affiliates, the subsidy arising from the bank's access to the federal safety net (i.e., lower cost insured deposits, the payment system, and the discount window).[5] The statute and rule accomplish these purposes by imposing quantitative and qualitative limits on the ability of a bank to extend credit to, or engage in, certain other transactions with an affiliate. Transactions between a bank and a nonaffiliate that benefit an affiliate of the bank are covered by the statute and regulation as well, through the well-established "attribution" principle. However, certain transactions that generally do not expose a bank to undue risk or abuse of the safety net are exempted from coverage under Regulation W. [6]

Regulation W has proven challenging for some banks to implement fully. Best practices suggest that a holistic Regulation W program is the recommended approach and should include the following components:

- Program statement outlining the bank's enterprise-wide approach to managing and identifying Regulation W risks;
- Policies and procedures that address roles and responsibilities for compliance and other impacted business units;
- Regulation W risk assessment that clearly identifies where transactions may occur in the organization and their associated risk levels;
- Regulation W training for all bank and subsidiary employees;
- Testing and monitoring;
- Escalation and reporting; and
- Governance.

Program Statement. The Regulation W program statement is a foundational element that provides guidance and clarity to all stakeholders. The policy and the related procedures are linked to the program statement.

The program statement will vary based on the type of bank and the type of affiliates. Generally, when drafting a program statement, the compliance staff should consider:

---

[4] Affiliate Transactions (Regulation W), https://www.federalreserve.gov/bankinforeg/topics/regulation_w.htm

[5] Part 223—Transactions between Member Banks and their Affiliates (Regulation W), http://www.ecfr.gov/cgi-bin/text-idx?SID=e55dcafa8b8a8537e20484fa821dc83b&mc=true&node=pt12.3.223&rgn=div5#se12.3.223_12

[6] Adoption of Regulation W Implementing Sections 23A and 23B of the Federal Reserve Act, https://www.federalreserve.gov/boarddocs/srletters/2003/sr0302.htm

- An overview of the company and its affiliates, which define legal entity relationships;
- Objectives of the program, which typically include
  - Complying with the quantitative and qualitative limits on "covered transactions", as defined in the Federal Reserve Act and Regulation W,
  - Defining collateral related to affiliate credit,
  - Prohibiting the Bank from purchasing low quality assets,
  - Dealing with affiliates on terms and conditions, and under circumstances that are substantially the same, or at least as favorable to the bank as those prevailing at the time for comparable transactions with similar unaffiliated companies,
  - Documenting affiliate transactions and service relationships with agreement that include "arm's-length" terms,
  - Restricting the purchase of securities from an affiliate underwriter and any syndicate of which an affiliate is a member, and
  - Mitigating regulatory, legal, and reputation risk by ensuring that the bank has implemented effective Regulation W business practices throughout product lifecycles;
- The scope of the program, which includes roles and responsibilities, oversight, governance, and statutory restrictions;
- Key definitions help to build common understanding. Examples include the terms such as affiliate, common control affiliates, companies with interlinking directors, sponsored and advised companies, investment funds, financial subsidiaries (such as a broker-dealer or investment adviser), merchant banking affiliates, and bank entities.[7] Covered transactions should be defined and typically include:
  - Extensions of credit to an affiliate's purchase or investment in securities issued by an affiliate,
  - Purchases of assets by the bank from the affiliate,
  - Acceptance of a security issued by the affiliate as collateral for an extension of credit to any person or company,
  - The issuance of a letter of credit on behalf of the affiliate,
  - Bank transactions with third parties, the proceeds of which are used for the benefit of, or transferred to, the affiliate (the "attribution rule");[8]
- Specific roles and responsibilities for key stakeholders, which include the board of directors, the risk committee of the bank, the Regulation W compliance officer, compliance testing and monitoring, internal audit, finance, legal, and the business units; and
- Program elements, including risk assessment, policies and procedures, service agreements, monitoring and testing, control self-testing, training, governance, and oversight.

Policies and Procedures. Written policies and procedures are important aspects of a Regulation W program. These documents will guide the key stakeholders as they make day-to-day decisions regarding the applicability and impact of Regulation W.

---

7 §223.2 What Is an "Affiliate" for Purposes of Sections 23A and 23B? http://www.ecfr.gov/cgi-bin/text-idx?SID=e55dcafa8b8a8537e20484fa821dc83b&mc=true&node=pt12.3.223&rgn=div5#se12.3.223_12

8 §223.24 What Valuation Principles Apply to Extensions of Credit Secured by Affiliate Securities? http://www.ecfr.gov/cgi-bin/text-idx?SID=e55dcafa8b8a8537e20484fa821dc83b&mc=true&node=pt12.3.223&rgn=div5#se12.3.223_12

Policies and procedures should be reviewed at least annually and as material changes occur, to ensure that the bank continues to comply with Regulation W.

Risk Assessment. The individuals responsible for conducting the Regulation W risk assessment may vary based on the size, scope, and complexity of the bank. The Regulation W compliance officer or risk management may conduct the risk assessment. Internal audit staff may also be charged with conducting an independent risk assessment of the overall program. In more mature organizations, business units may have a role in conducting a risk assessment for their areas of responsibility. Ultimately, the risk assessment should help the bank to determine the inherent and residual risks, and in developing plans to manage and control those risks.

The Regulation W risk assessment is typically driven by the underlying regulations. With that said, there are operational risk components of Regulation W as well. The type and nature of the bank's transactions and the business units impacted will need to be considered.

Banks should consider conducting a risk assessment annually to ensure that material changes are captured and that the program keeps pace with the growth of the business.

Training. Best practices in Regulation W training extend beyond a basic understanding of the regulations. For training to truly be effective, the training program needs to include specific examples and situations that are applicable the bank's business model. Training also can be used to communicate roles and responsibilities. Additionally, banks can consider providing more extensive training to business groups that are key stakeholders in the process. As with any compliance training, Regulation W training should be refreshed annually.

Testing and Monitoring. Testing and monitoring may be performed by a corporate compliance testing team, by internal audit, and/or by impacted business units.

Best practices for an effective testing program include ongoing monitoring and escalation processes for Regulation W compliance. Testing should evaluate the regulatory requirements and the effectiveness of the bank's internal controls. Many banks have developed systems or databases that track and produce reports on affiliate organizational charts and ongoing affiliate transactions. These reports can be analyzed by the Compliance Department and will provide insight regarding the status of the Regulation W risk environment.

Escalation and Reporting. Banks should establish formal escalation and reporting processes to ensure that key stakeholders are receiving timely information. Typically, the Regulation O compliance officer or the bank's chief compliance officer (CCO) will provide the board of directors and relevant committees, with a quarterly Regulation W status report. This status report would include the past quarter's results from a testing and monitoring perspective, any exceptions identified, an assessment of the adequacy of the internal control environment, the status of training, recommendations for improvement, and other relevant updates on the Regulation W program.

Governance. Strong governance is a foundational element of a Regulation W compliance program. Much of what has been discussed related to Regulation W supports the idea of effective governance. Ensuring that stakeholders understand their roles and responsibilities is critical. The importance of ongoing collaboration and communication between Compliance, Internal Audit and the Business Units must be emphasized. Training plays a role in good governance.

The board of directors is typically charged with oversight of the program. In many banks, a compliance officer prepares and presents the progress and status of the Regulation W objectives, initiatives, and testing results. The Compliance Department may consult with finance, legal, business units and internal audit personnel in order to collect necessary data to prepare its status report.

Regulation O: Loans to Executive Officers, Directors, and Principal Shareholders of Member Banks (12 CFR Part 215). Banks and their boards of directors must recognize that credit related transactions between the banks and their directors, executive officers, significant shareholders, and certain other "related persons" present a higher risk of conflicts of interest.

Regulation O places restrictions on a bank lending to its "insiders," which are its principal shareholders, directors, executive officers, and their related interests. It's fairly easy, with the help of the Human Resources Department, to determine who is or is not a principal shareholder, director, or executive officer. Determining who or what a related interest is can be challenging. [9]

A bank's board of directors will frequently direct the establishment of a Regulation O related-person transaction policy. This policy is developed to assist the bank in avoiding actual or perceived conflicts of interest, and to guide the bank's business units and Compliance Department in the review, monitoring, and disclosure of such transactions in accordance applicable laws and regulations. [10]

Best practices for a related-party transaction policy include defining the scope of the policy, defining key terms and definitions, and documenting key roles and responsibilities, including the role of the board, board committees, and the corporate secretary. The policy should clearly describe transactions that are exempt from the policy, for example transactions arising in the ordinary course of business, transactions in which the related person does not have a material interest, or certain transactions that are subject to other approval processes.

---

9 Regulation O Federal Reserve Compliance Guide, https://www.federalreserve.gov/bankinforeg/regocg.htm

10 FDIC, Part 215—Loans to Executive Officer, Directors and Principal Shareholders of Member Banks (Regulation O), https://www.fdic.gov/regulations/laws/rules/7500-1300.html

Banks may have other policies and procedures that supplement the policy, such as processes for determining director selection and independence, and the bank's code of conduct and ethics policy.

The Compliance, the Lending, Finance, Legal, and the Human Resources Departments may all be engaged in a Regulation O transaction. The analysis of a proposed transaction typically takes place between the Regulation O compliance officer and Legal Department. The Credit and Finance Departments may have a role as well. Many banks develop tracking lists or a database to simplify the determination and to create documentation.

As noted earlier, the difficulty in analyzing transactions comes in reviewing who or what may be defined as a related interest. Here are some general guidelines:

- First, someone's relative is not automatically a related interest. If the spouse of an executive officer or director applies to the bank for a loan, that loan is not governed by Regulation O unless the executive officer or director is going to receive a direct financial benefit from the loan;
- Under the principal shareholder rules, the Compliance Department must attribute to a principal shareholder, all shares of the bank owned by the shareholder's spouse, minor children, or adult children living at home. This requirement is more complicated and means that if the borrower is the spouse of a principal shareholder or if the borrower is a shareholder and, if their shares, combined with the shares of their spouse and children equal or exceed 10 percent, the borrower is defined as a principal shareholder and subject to the principal shareholder restrictions.
- There may be other legal structures, such as executive officers, directors, or principal shareholders' trust accounts, that need to be considered as related interests as well.

In August 2006, and interrelated, the SEC published a final release that largely overhauled the prior rules and regulations for executive compensation disclosure. The release is titled Executive Compensation and Related Person Disclosure.[11]

As part of the release, the SEC requires disclosure of any transaction of more than $120,000 that has occurred since the last fiscal year or is currently proposed, in which the company is a participant and any related person has a direct or indirect material interest. "Transactions" include, but are not limited to, financial transactions, arrangements, or relationships. As under the prior regulations, the term clearly encompasses a company's compensation arrangements and employment relationships with related persons. Subsequent SEC staff interpretations have stated that all compensation, not just the employee's salary, must be counted toward determining whether the employment arrangement meets the $120,000 reporting threshold.[12] In response, banks generally disclose the employee's salary, cash bonus and any equity awards.

---

[11] SEC, Executive Compensation and Related Person Disclosure , Rel. Nos. 33-8732A and 34-54302A (Aug. 26, 2006), https://www.sec.gov/rules/final/2006/33-8765.pdf

[12] Item 404 of Regulation S-K, https://www.sec.gov/divisions/corpfin/guidance/execcomp404interp.htm

When a compliance practitioner deals with Regulation O analysis, he or she should proceed with caution within the firm. The Legal and Compliance Departments usually work very closely together on all related party transactions. Concurrence on the decisions reached and complete documentation is critical because this topic has been of interest to the banking regulators in recent examinations.

Regulation R: Securities Activities of Banks. The FRB and the SEC adopted Regulation R in October of 2009. Regulation R implements provisions of the Gramm-Leach-Bliley Act of 1999 (GLBA) regarding banks that are also involved in securities activities.[13] Regulation R details exceptions for banks from the definition of "broker" and "dealer." Activities that fall outside of these exceptions are required to be performed by a registered broker-dealer.

GLBA amended the Securities and Exchange Act of 1934 to align certain securities-related activities under the jurisdiction of the SEC, while leaving other securities activities conducted within banks with the federal banking regulators. GLBA's amendments are focused on "pushing out" all other securities transactions to a broker-dealer. Regulation R is primarily focused on four types of securities activity:

- Networking activities;
- Trust account activities;
- Sweep account activities; and
- Safekeeping account activities.

Networking Activities. Regulation R's amendments address two types of referral fees:

- Nominal one-time referral fee; and
- Institutional and high net worth client referral fees.

An amendment states that under a networking agreement, fees can be paid to bank employees who refer business to a registered broker-dealer; however, the fees must be nominal one-time fees. These fees must be fixed dollar amounts and not tied to the opening of a securities account or the sale of any securities product. Referral fees can be tied to appointment setting. The fees must be paid in cash.

Regulation R provided several calculations to assist banks in their determination. First, the fee is considered nominal if it is no greater than two times the average of the minimum and maximum hourly wages in the job family to which the referring employee belongs. Second, the fee also meets the nominal standard if it is less than or equal to 0.1 percent of the average of the minimum and maximum yearly base salaries in the job family to which the referring employee belongs. Lastly, a fee meets

---

[13] SEC, Regulation R: Exceptions for Banks from the Definition of Broker in the Securities Exchange Act of 1934—A Small Entity Compliance Guide, https://www.sec.gov/divisions/marketreg/tmcompliance/regulation_r_secg.htm

the nominal standard if it is no greater than 0.1 percent of the actual yearly base salary or twice the actual hourly wage of the bank employee making the referral. These calculations are operationally challenging in larger organizations. Most banks have taken a more pragmatic approach and have determined that $25 is a reasonable, nominal amount for referral fees.

The amendments allow for referral fees to exceed the nominal dollar amount for referrals of institutional or high net worth customers. Regulation R defines "institutional customers" to include companies, corporations, and partnerships with:

- At least $10 million in investments;
- $20 million in revenues; or
- $15 million in revenues if the customer is referred for investment banking services from a broker-dealer.

High-net-worth customers must have at least $5 million in net worth, excluding their residence and related liabilities. Disclosures related to the relationship between the banks and broker-dealer must be made and a suitability review must be conducted prior to any fee being paid. The Regulation R material provides further considerations for these nonconsumer accounts and their related referrals.

Trust Account Activities. The Exchange Act provides authority to banks to execute securities transactions in their role as fiduciary or trustee without registering as a broker-dealer. This authority is contingent on the transaction being handled in a Trust Department and the bank being "chiefly compensated" as a trustee or fiduciary, based on either an account-by-account or bankwide calculation. In both cases, "chiefly compensated" is based on a two-year average of "relationship compensation" divided by "total compensation." Relationship compensation includes fees charged to trust or fiduciary accounts, for example, administrative or annual fees, fees based on a percentage of assets under management, or capped or flat order processing fees.

Under Regulation R, a bank may only advertise that it provides fiduciary or trust securities services as part of advertisements related to its overall fiduciary or trust services. All advertisements must be balanced and not focus on one aspect of the business over another.

Regulation R provides further guidance on Trust Department activities.

Sweep Account Activities. Banks have been provided with an exception regarding sweep transactions. These transactions are defined as the investment of funds into registered no-load money market funds.

Regulation R allows banks to effect money market transactions for a customer without registering as a broker-dealer, if the bank also provides another service to the customer that does not require the bank to register as a BD, or money market transactions are provided to customers as part of a broader sweep account program.

Safekeeping Account Activities. Banks have been provided with an exemption related to conducting custody and safekeeping activities. Examples of these activities would include:

- Exercising warrants on behalf of customers;
- Settling customer securities transactions;
- Conducting securities lending for customers; and
- Holding securities that relate to a repurchase agreement.

Regulation R is expansive and includes significant detail on each of the four different types of activities that take place in banks. Regulation R also covers employee benefit accounts.

V. IMPACTS TO THE INVESTMENT FIRM'S COMPLIANCE PROGRAM

Compliance Process Impacts

This section will address foundational compliance elements of independent and bank-owned investment firms. All investment firms are required to designate a CCO. The CCO is typically approved by the investment firm's board of directors, and is charged with developing and implementing the investment firm's compliance program. Although compliance programs differ from firm to firm, the functions described here are usually managed in the Compliance Department or jointly between the business and that department.

The securities and banking regulators have been clear that investment firms must design and implement comprehensive compliance programs and consider their own size, scope, and complexity. Relevant regulations, product types, services provided to customers, the size of the firm, supervision and oversight, sales and delivery channels, and the governance structure must be factored in to a holistic approach to mitigate and manage compliance risk.

Policies and Procedures/Written Supervisory Procedures

Comprehensive policies and procedures are a critical element of the compliance program.

The FINRA website provides a helpful tool for broker-dealers, entitled the "WSP Checklist." Each investment firm can use this as a guideline when developing policies and procedures, but will need to pick and choose which categories on the checklist are relevant to the specific firm.

Major topics within the Written Supervisory Procedure (WSP) Checklist[14] include:

- Form filings;
- Business continuity planning;
- Hiring, registration and qualifications;
- Continuing education;
- General supervisory obligations;
- Supervisory system;
- Review of accounts and correspondence;
- Insider trading;
- Anti-money laundering;
- Communications with the public;
- Disclosures to customers;
- Customer information controls;
- Suitability;
- Fees charged to customers;
- Transaction review;
- Financial reporting;
- Recordkeeping;
- Internal controls;
- Investment company products;
- Options;
- Underwritings and private placements;
- Variable products;
- Trading and trading operations; and
- Handling of customer complaints.

The SEC has issued similar requirements for registered investment advisers. In 2003, the SEC issued new rules, effective February 5, 2004[15] The rules codified the SEC's expectations for these types of firms.

In its release, the SEC summarized the new rules by stating that firms registered with the SEC "must adopt and implement written policies and procedures reasonably designed to prevent violation of the federal securities laws, review those policies and procedures annually for their adequacy and the effectiveness of their implementation, and designate a chief compliance officer to be responsible for administering the policies and procedures." The SEC further commented that these new rules were specifically designed "to protect investors by ensuring that firms had internal programs in place to enhance compliance with the federal securities laws."

Additionally, the banking regulators have several expectations regarding policies and procedures. They expect investment firms to follow relevant FINRA and/or SEC

---

[14] FINRA, *WSP Checklist*, https://www.finra.org/industry/tools

[15] SEC, *Compliance Program for Investment Companies and Investment Advisers* (Dec. 17, 2003), https://www.sec.gov/rules/final/ia-2204.htm

regulations, but they also expect that the employees of the broker-dealer or investment adviser will follow certain bank policies and procedures. Examples of bank policies that may affect bank-owned investment firm employees include human resource policies, expense and vendor management policies, business continuity policies, technology and cybersecurity policies, ethics policies, and anti-money laundering policies.

The investment firm's Compliance Department is usually responsible for drafting and implementing compliance-related policies and procedures. The business units within an investment firm should also develop departmental policies and procedures that reflect their areas of operational responsibility. Compliance may be engaged in an advisory role in helping business units to develop their policies and procedures. Coordination between the Compliance Department and the investment firm's business units is critical to avoid contradictions or missing information.

Within bank-owned investment firms, the CCO must ensure that individuals responsible for drafting and implementing the bank's policies and procedures and those compliance staff responsible for the investment firm's policies and procedures develop a working relationship. Coordination and communication are critical to avoid conflicts between the two sets of policies and procedures.

Customer Complaints

The securities regulators have specific regulatory requirements regarding the handling, resolution, and reporting of customer complaints. FINRA defines complaint types by codes and has outlined timing requirements for reporting certain complaints to FINRA electronically.

Banking regulators appear to have raised the bar in recent years and expect banks to track, resolve, and report to the regulator, on banking related customer complaints.

Even though investment firms disclose whom to contact regarding a customer complaint (on websites and customer statements), unfortunately, as a bank-owned investment firm, customers may not always understand how or whom to contact when they decide to complain about their securities purchase or sale. A bank customer might send the investment firm a written complaint about their IRA account held at the bank. Investment firms and their related banks must have detailed procedures to ensure that personnel handling incoming complaints know how to handle the complaint. It is important for both the bank and the investment firm to receive complaint data timely. Specialized training of personnel handling complaints may be necessary to ensure that both the bank and the investment firm comply with their own prescriptive regulatory requirements.

As noted, the investment firm's Compliance Department handles securities-related customer complaints. Compliance staff coordinates with the bank, communicates with sales representatives, discusses the complaint with sales management and compliance management, and responds to the customer. Compliance is usually responsible for applicable regulatory filings on securities-related complaints as well. Supervisory oversight and a quality control process are helpful to ensure that complaints are coded properly and filed on a timely basis.

Investment firms should review customer complaints to determine whether trends exist, there are regulatory red flags, and/or a need to train or retrain personnel.

Lastly, bank management, and specifically the bank's Customer Complaint Department, may require that the bank-owned investment firm report on the details of complaints received by the investment firm and the ultimate resolution of those complaints. Many banks' Customer Complaint Departments track this data along with the bank's complaint data and look for trends or red flags in both data sets.

Advertising and Marketing

Over the years, the securities regulators have issued regulations and guidance related to general advertising and marketing, as well as some product specific requirements.[16] The focus of these requirements is full and fair disclosure. Misleading or inaccurate information is prohibited.

In many investment firms, the Compliance Department is responsible for working with the Marketing Department to develop compliant materials. Compliance also will work with FINRA's Advertising Department and determine whether any marketing collateral is required to be filed with the regulatory agency and determine the timing required for such reporting.

Knowledge of the related regulations, the timing triggers, and tracking of materials are all key elements within a compliance advertising and marketing program. For FINRA registered broker-dealers, a Series 24 Licensed Principal is required to approve advertising and marketing. Many broker-dealers have marketing principals in the Marketing Department as well as within the Compliance Department.

Additionally, the banking regulators are concerned about investment related advertisements or marketing materials. If you refer to the Interagency Statement, the spirit of this guidance is a well-informed client.

One of the unique challenges with a bank-owned investment firm is the idea of joint marketing. Joint marketing is when someone in the investment firm and the bank decide to discuss banking products and services and investment products and services in the same piece of marketing collateral. Compliance officers may handle this request by separating required text within the marketing piece and ensuring

---

16 *See* NASD Rule 2210, Communication with the Public; Notice 11-49, FINRA Provides Guidance on Advertising Regulation Issues; and Securities Act Rule 482.

full disclosure of the specific legal entities offering the various products or services. Details on specific products are usually not included in a joint marketing piece. Joint marketing should focus on high-level principles and encourage potential clients to meet with a licensed sales professional to discuss investment products and services based on their goals and risk tolerance. This is an important aspect of marketing oversight and it is critical that the CCO understands this process and ensures that the compliance marketing principal overseeing joint marketing has been adequately trained.

Testing, Monitoring, and Surveillance

Compliance programs should include a compliance testing policy and program. Within the program, the testing schedule and types of reviews should be documented. In bank-owned firms, coordination with the parent company's Internal Audit Department and corporate compliance testing teams may be necessary.

Investment firms' Compliance Department programs may be comprised of several types of testing, monitoring, or surveillance. In some cases, the process is centralized and compliance staff may use manual reports or automated systems to review transactions and accounts.

On-site branch reviews are another form of Compliance Department testing and monitoring. Compliance staff visit their registered branch locations and follow a standardized testing procedure based on the type, scope, and size of the branch and/or the investment firm. Branch reviews may be conducted on a full-scope routine basis, as targeted reviews (for example, related to one specific product), or for cause.

One consideration within bank-owned investment firms is the Results of Testing Report distribution. The compliance staff conducting the testing will issue a written report to the investment firm's responsible registered principal/senior manager. Additionally, there may be "setting and circumstances" issues that are identified during a branch review and these items may be communicated in a separate report to bank branch management for resolution.

Remediation and follow-up is critical to ensure that all issues identified by the Compliance Department are resolved within established time frames. Investment firms handle these processes differently, but the Compliance Department should track the individual findings (on a spreadsheet or in a tracking database) and ensure that any concerns are effectively remediated, regardless of whether the issue is owned by the investment firm or the bank branch management team.

Ultimately, the results of testing, monitoring and surveillance will be summarized and reported to the board of directors and/or other committees of the bank and the investment firm. This will be discussed further in this chapter's discussion of governance.

Monitoring for Personal Securities Transactions

All investment firms have an obligation to be aware of and monitor their employees' personal securities transactions. In some cases, this includes family member's transactions as well.

This subsection will cover options for monitoring and overseeing these types of accounts and transactions. Here is a list of considerations for building a program for monitoring:

- Size of firm;
- Scope of products and services;
- Parent company policy and equity;
- Personal accounts—held in-house or at a third-party firm;
- Control Room structure (in larger companies typically);
- Ethics policy for investment firm and the bank;
- Code of conduct for investment firm and the bank; and
- Insider trading policy and oversight.

The investment firm's policy should outline what the acceptable practices are within the firm regarding the purchase and sale of securities by employees and their family members. The manner in which these purchases and sales must take place should be determined when the policy is developed. Bank-owned investment firms may require one of the following:

- All purchases and sales must be made through the bank-owned investment firm that is a broker-dealer;
- No outside investment adviser accounts may be held for a bank-owned investment firm that is an investment adviser; or
- All purchases and sales must be made through an approved list of investment firms that have been vetted by the bank-owned investment firm.

The policy should also address any preclearance requirements or restricted securities. Particularly in investment firms with research analysts or portfolio managers, preclearance and restricted securities may be an ongoing factor.

In bank-owned investment firms, whose stock is registered and publicly traded, the policy should address how and when employees can purchase or sell the parent company's stock.

Larger bank-owned investment firms may develop a Control Room structure. The Control Room may include bank and investment firm compliance risk monitoring and mitigation strategies. Control Rooms are designed to bring together several key functions related to oversight and monitoring. Control Rooms are typically responsible for the monitoring of bank employee and investment firm employee securities transactions and accounts. These transactions and accounts are monitored for regulatory compliance and adherence to internal policies and procedures. Many Control Rooms use vendor or in-house electronic tools to help conduct this monitoring. A list of preclearance requirements and restrictions may be maintained and communicated by the control room. The ethics policy and ethics committee may be part of the Control Room structure. Insider trading policies and procedures, as well as related monitoring may be included within a control room. The investment firm's code of conduct monitoring and follow-up may be a function within the Control Room. Lastly, the Control Room may be responsible for developing training or attestations addressing specific Control Room functions and requirements.

Compliance Training

All investment firms are required to develop compliance training that is designed based on the needs of each firm. The banking regulators require that banks develop annual compliance training as well. Bank-owned investment firms should develop a training policy and related procedures. Annually, a needs assessment should be developed and executed. Training plans should be updated as regulatory expectations, products and services, or business needs change.

Needs Assessment. Within investment firms, the first step in designing the annual training plan is to conduct a needs assessment. This involves polling the investment firm's personnel and management to determine their needs. Other considerations, such as a pattern of problems that have been identified during branch reviews and/or as part of a series of customer complaints, should be addressed as training plans are updated. Regulatory "hot topics" and new product types should also be considered. The goal is to design a plan that is meaningful and provides educational material that is relevant to the investment firm and its employees.

Training Plan Development. Once the needs assessment information is analyzed, a training plan can be developed. For bank-owned investment firms, there may be bank required courses that the subsidiary employees will need to take as well. New courses should be reviewed for redundancy with existing training; existing training should be considered for archiving, if it is being replaced by a new course.

Training Plan Implementation. The next step is implementing the annual plan. The course selection may be broad and generic and/or include specialized course material for certain departments or groups of employees. The timely completion of assigned courses should be tracked by the Compliance Department. Communication to the participants should clearly state what is required and when.

Training Monitoring. During the fourth quarter of each year, most investment firms will evaluate where the employees are in terms of completing their annual training. Follow-up may be necessary to ensure that all training is completed within the prescribed time frames. In recent years, the securities regulators have filed enforcement actions against investment firms and their licensed personnel who do not complete their training on a timely basis, yet continue to perform regular duties, for example, in sales roles. If individuals do not complete their required annual training, this failure should be escalated to senior management. The investment firm's procedures should cover internal disciplinary actions, up to and including termination, if and as warranted.

Typically, someone in the bank's corporate Compliance Department will track and administer the annual bank compliance training. It will be important for the CCO and the compliance officer responsible for the investment firm's training plan to build a strong working relationship with the parent bank training team. Coordination, communication, and support will help to ensure that both plans are successful.

Registration and Licensing

Investment firms' registration and licensing requirements and processes are very similar across the various types, sizes, and scope of investment firms. FINRA and the SEC use an online registration portal, the Central Registration Depository (CRD), and make this tool available to the industry. Compliance is typically responsible for the administration, input, and maintenance of registration and licensing records.

The CCO and the registration and licensing manager work closely together to ensure that appropriate licensing is established and maintained with the SEC and FINRA. Compliance staff work closely with the business to ensure accurate licensing and registration of employees. The firm and staff may be registered with multiple entities, for example, both the SEC and FINRA, and those states where the individual is actively selling and/or has clients.

In bank-owned investment firms, many employees are considered "dual employees" of the investment firm and the bank. If this is the case, the individual's licensing records need to reflect the bank as a current employer, in addition to the investment firm. Independent investment firms do not usually have to worry about dual employee status unless they are comprised of multiple legal entities.

Individuals may be insurance licensed as well. The registration and licensing team within the Compliance Department usually handles the investment firm's agency licensing by state and the individual agents licensing within each state. The compliance staff responsible for this function must coordinate closely with the product team and each relevant insurance product company to ensure that any required agency and agent licenses are issued, appointed, and maintained appropriately.

Other Bank-Specific Considerations

The Secure and Fair Enforcement for Mortgage Licensing Act of 2008 (SAFE Act) was enacted on July 30, 2008, and mandates a nationwide licensing and tracking system, the Nationwide Mortgage Licensing System and Registry (NMLSR), for residential mortgage loan originators.[17] Some bank-owned investment firms also

[17] The Secure and Fair Enforcement for Mortgage Licensing Act of 2008 (SAFE Act), http://files.consumerfinance.gov/f/201203_cfpb_update_SAFE_Act_Exam_Procedures.pdf

have licensed banker programs. These individuals are bank employees who open checking and savings accounts and may periodically open a mortgage account as well. Licensed bankers work in the bank branches and are also part-time employees of the investment firm. Typically, the licensed banker candidate holds a limited securities license (Series 6) and an insurance license. These individuals must maintain licenses under the bank's SAFE Act requirements as well if they are loan officers (LOs) offering mortgage products.

Corporate compliance staff within the bank will typically be responsible for the oversight and monitoring of the SAFE Act requirements. Corporate compliance staff also develop and distribute the internal policy and procedures related to SAFE Act processes with the bank.

The SAFE Act policy usually covers the following areas:

- *Overview and purpose:* In January 2013, the Consumer Financial Protection Bureau (CFPB) issued final rules amending various mortgage-related regulations. These changes included amendments to the 2013 Mortgage Rules under the Equal Credit Opportunity Act (Regulation B), Real Estate Settlement Procedures Act (Regulation X), and the Truth in Lending Act (Regulation Z). Among these changes was the establishment of a broader definition of "loan originator," broader than that in the SAFE Act. This rule now requires that creditors that employ LOs ensure that they satisfy specific compensation, qualification, and identification standards before allowing LOs to perform their jobs;[18]
- *Effective dates:* After publishing the final rule in 2013, the CFPB issued additional clarification to help explain the LO requirements. Most provisions of this rule became effective on January 14, 2014; however, other provisions became effective on January 10, 2014;[19]
- *Scope of the policy:* To whom do the LO requirements apply?
- *Key definitions:* Definitions include the SAFE Act definition of a mortgage loan originator (MLO) and the Regulation Z definition, which is broader;
- Roles and responsibilities within the bank: Descriptions encompass, for example, the policy owner, mortgage loan officers, loan officers, SAFE Act administrator, business units impacted, compliance, legal, risk, internal audit, and the board of directors;
- *SAFE Act requirements:*
  - All employees designated as a MLO must register with the NMLSR and obtain a unique identification number (NMLSR ID),
  - Newly hired MLOs cannot originate loans until they are properly registered and licensed with NMLSR,

---

[18] 2013 CFPB, *Dodd-Frank Mortgage Rules Readiness Guide,* http://files.consumerfinance.gov/f/201307_cfpb_mortgage-implementation-readiness-guide.pdf

[19] Amendments to the 2013 Mortgage Rules Under the Equal Credit Opportunity Act (Regulation B), Real Estate Settlement Procedures Act (Regulation X), and the Truth in Lending Act (Regulation Z), https://www.consumerfinance.gov/policy-compliance/rulemaking/final-rules/amendments-2013-mortgage-rules-under-equal-credit-opportunity-act-regulation-b-real-estate-settlement-procedures-act-regulation-x-and-truth-lending-act-regulation-z/

  - Background checks will be performed prior to allowing an MLO to originate loans, and if a criminal history is identified, the MLO may not perform MLO duties,
  - MLOs must provide their NMLSR to consumers, as required by the rules;
- *Loan originator requirements pursuant to TILA (Regulation Z):*
  - If the LO is not already SAFE Act licensed, the Regulation Z requirements will apply and include a background check, a credit check, and specific training,
  - State legislation impacts, and
  - Approval requirements for the policy.

Lastly, in terms of licensed bankers, bank-owned investment firms need to identify who these dual employees are and ensure that their Securities Licensing Form U-4 is updated to reflect their role at the bank, in addition to their role within the broker-dealer and/or investment adviser as a securities sales person.

As referenced above, the Finance and Compensation Departments may engage periodically with the Compliance Department in matters of compensation. Compliance staff may coordinate with the Finance and Accounting Departments in an advisory role regarding regulatory requirements. Compliance staff may also support the departments during regulatory examinations. Certain investment firms may externally outsource aspects of finance and accounting to gain efficiency and expertise.

Although independent investment firms usually have their own dedicated financial and accounting staff, bank-owned investment firms may use bank staff who are dual employees or other Operations Department staff to help with these specialized functions.

VI. GOVERNANCE AND CHIEF COMPLIANCE OFFICER REPORTING

Governance

The securities regulators and banking regulators require that investment firms and banks establish governance and reporting to ensure that key management and executives stay apprised of the status of the compliance program and the risk profile of the investment firm.

Although governance varies from firm to firm, the following is a list of possible governance structures that may exist at either bank-owned investment firms or their affiliate banks:

- Board of directors—separate for the investment firm and the affiliated bank;
- The bank's nondeposit investment product committee—bank oversight;
- Product committee—separate for the bank and the investment firm;
- Ethics committee—may be enterprise-wide;
- Preclearance committee—may be enterprise-wide;
- Disciplinary committee—separate for the bank and the investment firm; and
- Compensation committee—separate for the bank and the investment firm.

Board of directors meetings will be held on a regular schedule as outlined in the investment firm's bylaws. Some boards meet quarterly, others, annually.

Independent investment firms and bank-owned investment firms have boards of directors that are frequently established when the firm is first registered. Independent investment firms' boards may be composed of internal and outside directors. Bank-owned investment firms have subsidiary boards of directors and may also be required to report periodically to the parent company, the bank's board of directors. Bank-owned investment firms usually have several senior managers within the bank who serve as members of the investment firm board of directors.

Per the interagency statement, banks that own investment firms will need to develop a nondeposit investment product committee. This committee meets as frequently as monthly and in some cases, quarterly. These meetings focus on consumer-based products that have been sold (by investment firms) in a bank branch and/or as a referral from the bank; their other area of focus is on new/changed products being offered to bank branch customers or through bank branch channels.

In addition to the nondeposit investment product committee required by bank regulators, most independent investment firms and bank-owned investment firms hold periodic product meetings to evaluate the performance of existing products and to conduct due diligence on potential new products. These meetings usually involve senior management with representatives of the Compliance, Legal, Finance, and Product Departments. The meetings relate to both securities and banking regulations.

The ethics committee provides oversight and decision making. As covered earlier, in larger investment firms this committee may be owned by the Control Room. The investment firm's code of conduct make be administered within the framework of the ethics committee. Breaches of policy or procedures are typically reported and discussed during the ethics committee.

Bank-owned investment firms may be integrated in to the bank's ethics committee. The preclearance committee reviews past issues/violations and may work to set new standards. This committee's members incorporate senior management and representatives from Human Resources, Legal, Compliance, Risk Departments.

The disciplinary committee is focused on action required after an internal violation has been identified by the compliance staff or other individual internally. Violations may also be identified through the review of customer complaints or the results of compliance monitoring, testing, or surveillance.

Lastly, the compensation committee is a structure usually seen in a medium or larger investment firm. Senior management typically participates with staff from the Compliance, Risk, Finance, Human Resources, and Legal Departments. The Compliance Department advises the committee of regulatory requirements and risks related to competition structures. Finance staff draft new compensation plans annually, after discussions that take place during the planning process. The committee reviews and approves the plan annually. Throughout the year, changes or adjustments should also require committee approval. Compliance staff may also be involved with the compensation committee as internal disciplinary actions are being considered.

Reporting by the Chief Compliance Officer

The investment firm's CCO is usually charged with consolidating relevant data regarding the firm's compliance status, analyzing that data, and reporting to the investment firm's board of directors during board meetings. When applicable, the CCO will also report to the bank's nondeposit investment product committee, or another bank oversight committee. Other reporting will be determined by each investment firm and may be event driven.

The CCO should consider best practices when reporting to executives and board members on the "state of compliance." Being well prepared and delivering a clear, concise, and transparent presentation is strongly encouraged. The CCO needs to determine who the audience is and adjust accordingly. Some audience participants may want details; others want only a summary of risk status. It's important to know the audience before the CCO finalizes and delivers the compliance risk report. Although narrative is interesting, defining and tracking metrics and key risk indicators will provide the audience with a better understanding of the current risk status of the investment firm over time.

VII. CONCLUSION

The goal of this chapter was to provide the reader with clarity on the differences and similarities between independent investment firms and bank-owned investment firms, and some of their overall compliance obligations.

The lessons learned in this chapter are designed to help broaden the reader's understanding of the compliance issues faced by bank-owned investment firms in the securities and financial services industry. Whether a practitioner is networking, attending a conference, organizing a seminar, or looking for a new job opportunity, this chapter should provide an appreciation for this unique and important market segment.

Note: This summary of regulations and requirements is for general information only and is not intended to render legal advice.

ABOUT THE AUTHOR

Diane P. Novak has more than 25 years of financial services compliance experience and is currently the owner and principal of DPN Consulting Services. Prior to her current position, Ms. Novak has worked in chief compliance officer and senior compliance management roles at Silicon Valley Bank, Citizens Securities, Toyota Financial Services, JPMorgan Chase, Washington Mutual, and U.S. Bank. Ms. Novak earned her bachelor of science degree cum laude in Business from Seattle University in Seattle, Washington, and her master of business administration from Regis University in Denver. She holds the FINRA Series 7, 24, and 63 licenses, as well as a trust compliance certification from Cannon Financial Institute. Ms. Novak currently resides in Boston.

CHAPTER 8

Constructing a Compliance System Across Multiple Distribution Channels

By Michele Hawkins, *Fort Washington Investment Advisors, Inc.*
Patrick Hayes, *Graydon Compliance Solutions, LLC*

I. INTRODUCTION

Challenges facing investment managers focusing on individual asset classes can be difficult enough, but there are particular, nuanced challenges facing those registered investment advisers (RIAs) and broker-dealers with multiple distribution channels and investment strategies. To complicate matters, firms have seen a myriad of regulatory changes over the last several years that affect investment advisers and other regulated entities.

This includes the enactment of Dodd-Frank Wall Street Reform and Consumer Protection Act ("Dodd-Frank"),[1] new and amended regulations from the Securities and Exchange Commission (SEC), the Commodities Futures Trading Commission (CFTC), the Financial Industry Regulatory Authority (FINRA), and now the Department of Labor (DOL) in the form of its Fiduciary Rule.[2] Compliance professionals have also seen that regulators are cracking down harder than ever, filing more than 850 enforcement actions in 2016 that resulted in orders and judgments totaling more than $4 billion in disgorgement and penalties.[3]

---

1 Dodd-Frank Wall Street Reform and Consumer Protection Act, P.L. 111-203, § 929-Z, 124 Stat. 1376, 1871 (2010) (codified at 15 U.S.C. § 78o).

2 On February 3, 2017, Donald Trump issued a presidential memorandum directing DOL "to examine the Fiduciary Duty Rule to determine whether it may adversely affect the ability of Americans to gain access to retirement information and financial advice," as well as review the negative consequences from the original applicability date of April 10, 2017. Subsequently, on March 10, 2017, DOL issued a memorandum, Field Assistance Bulletin No. 2017-01, clarifying the possible implementation of a 60-day delay to the Fiduciary Rule, and explaining the different possible enforcement policies should the rule still go in to effect on April 10, 2017. Given the constant change and confusion surrounding the DOL Fiduciary Rule, a legal or compliance professional should be consulted before a firm institutes any formal policies related to it.

3 SEC, "SEC Announces Enforcement Results for FY 2016," https://www.sec.gov/news/pressrelease/2016-212.html. These figures comprise asset managers of all types, including registered investment advisers, broker-dealers, and investment companies.

In order to meet these challenges, especially when there are multiple distribution channels, firms must establish clear boundaries and expectations for the management team, supervisors, employees, and compliance program. As a chief compliance officer (CCO), a key question to ask is, "What role does or should compliance play—is it the enforcer, the negotiator, the business partner?" History and recent events indicate that in order to have an effective and robust compliance program, the CCO and business partners must be aligned and working toward a common end. Much like building a house, creating an effective and robust compliance program starts with establishing the proper foundation, developing the right blueprints, and committing to action while using the right tools.

II. CONSTRUCTING AN EFFECTIVE COMPLIANCE FRAMEWORK

Building a Strategic Partnership as the Foundation

The first step in creating a sustainable and inclusive relationship with business partners is to build a solid foundation of understanding, openness, mutual respect, and defined core values. This foundation becomes particularly critical for development of strategic partnerships with business units that have competing priorities and interests, and in many instances, may represent differing strategic goals of a multifaceted firm. Before the CCO can provide the proper guidance on how a business decision will affect *all* areas of the firm and other business lines, he or she must foster credibility and rapport with the business units inside the organization. The CCO shouldn't always say "no" to new ideas but look for alternative ways to support the ideas of the various business units. The CCO should be someone that helps *drive* innovation rather than *stifle* it. The more business partners recognize the CCO's desire to work with them and help them get from "a to b," the greater traction he or she will have to implement the proper internal controls of the compliance program (i.e., the blueprint).

Create a Blueprint to Better Understand and Overcome the Challenges of a Multifaceted Firm

What can or should a CCO do to manage competing priorities, multiple business lines, and limited resources? A risk-based approach provides a great place to start. By focusing on the high-risk issues of each business unit that can cause the most harm to clients and to the firm, the CCO will be in the best position to apply the proper measures to help mitigate these issues (and likely protect his or her own career). An oft-employed technique is to use a risk matrix, highlighting from highest to lowest where the key risks are located within the firm. Developing the proper blueprint is essential for a multidimensional firm with multiple distribution channels. Before the CCO can start using tools and resources to build the proper internal compliance controls, he or she must draw up the right plans.

Implementing the Proper Compliance Structure Within a Multifaceted Firm

Implementation of compliance can often be considered as the hammer and nail, but not from hammering home compliance and regulatory requirements or nailing someone for a violation. Rather, the analogy of hammer and nail represents the ability to build the proper internal controls within all the business units of the firm. Key factors affecting the construction will typically include policies and procedures, business unit supervision, ongoing monitoring and maintenance, testing, and (of course) collaboration and engagement of the business units.

Much like a house, a compliance program is only as good as the sum of all its parts, and faulty construction or leaky pipes (no matter how small) can cause great headaches down the road. By using resources to identify the right tools for the job, committing those resources to action, and building a compliance program that helps mitigate against issues inside every business unit of a multifaceted firm, the CCO can feel good that loved ones—er, business units—are well protected from the regulatory storm and primed for continued growth and success. One of the best places to start in the construction of a compliance program within any multidimensional firm is through identifying and mitigating conflicts of interest.

III. CONFLICTS OF INTEREST

The term "conflict of interest" carries a heavy connotation. It generates strong feelings in the minds of many regulators, which in turn, resonate deep within the compliance community. This represents a direct extension of the notion that no matter how hard advisers may try to avoid conflicts, there is no escaping them fully—conflicts of interest are often inherently tied to a firm's business. However, when approached under the right framework, conflicts of interest can showcase to regulators that the firm takes its fiduciary duty very seriously, and can further highlight the compliance structure and robust internal controls that have been built to help mitigate these types of issues.

Working in a multifaceted or multidimensional firm with multiple distribution channels, the conflicts of interest that manifest are both numerous and complicated. As an example, Fort Washington Investment Advisors is a large RIA with strategies that include fixed income, public equity, private equity, and retail high-net-worth wealth management. With so many different business lines, client types, and internal needs, conflicts of interest can be found in almost every aspect of the business. And that's okay; that's to be expected. Compliance can add an extraordinary amount of value when these situations arise by providing insight into all the factors that the business units aren't thinking about when they are developing a new strategy or moving pieces with the organization. It's easy for someone solely focused on the continued growth and success of one particular business unit to not fully appreciate how that decision might affect other areas of the firm. That's where the role of compliance can add significant value—by providing wise counsel and illuminating how larger, strategic business decisions will impact all areas of the firm, including how potential conflicts may play a part. Described here are some of the more significant areas for potential conflicts of interest for multifaceted or multidimensional firms.

Material Nonpublic Information Barriers

At firms with numerous strategies, many advisers will often reference the investment horsepower or engine of the firm, and further discuss how they can better tap into that resource and use its full potential. At a high level, this type of initiative makes a lot of sense. If an RIA has 75 investment professionals, why wouldn't the adviser want to tap into the collective expertise of each pro and allow his or her knowledge to better inform the adviser's investment decisions and recommendations? As might be expected, it's never that simple. Many firms that find themselves in this position need to be very careful that they do not break down the regulatory-mandated physical and technological barriers designed to separate those investment professionals working in the public space versus those working with private placement debt or private equity. Section 204A of the Investment Advisers Act of 1940 (the "Advisers Act")[4] and 15(g) of the Securities Exchange Act of 1934 (the "Exchange Act")[5] for broker-dealers protect against the misuse of material nonpublic information (MNPI) by requiring firms to establish, maintain and enforce written policies and procedures reasonably designed to prevent its misuse by taking into consideration the nature of their business.

For firms with multiple strategies in the public and private space, these conflicts remain ever-present. There are, however, a number of barriers that compliance professionals and their respective firms can construct to help mitigate the risks inherent in the misuse of MNPI. At the outset, firms can employ physical barriers between those individuals working on the public and private side, from separation of cubicle or office spaces to placing the groups on different floors. In addition to physical barriers, firms can employ technological barriers for those employees on each side. By limiting access to electronic folders and other platforms, firms can effectively mitigate the flow of MNPI from the private to the public strategies.

The last, and often the most important barrier constructed is the information barrier. As articulated earlier, many firms wish to use the best resources available when engaging in the investment process, assessing market trends, and looking for strategic analysis of certain securities within the marketplace. In certain situations, this might require a public-side individual or group to receive access to MNPI. Should this occur, firms *must* establish the proper protocols to ensure an effective "over-the-wall" process. Often this process involves:

- Preapproval by the Compliance Department;
- Identifying the public-side employees who will be given access to MNPI of a specific company; and
- Prohibiting that over-the-wall employee from engaging in any personal or firm trading as it relates to any security of that company.

---

4 15 U.S.C. §80b-4a.

5 15 U.S.C. §78o(g). The Insider Trading and Securities Fraud Enforcement Act of 1988 (ITSFEA) added Section 15(f) to the Exchange Act, which was later renumbered as Section 15(g) by Dodd-Frank.

Whenever technological and information barriers are used, firms can employ a number of additional best practices to ensure the barriers are used effectively. These include:

- Establishing a formal, documented process to limit the spread of MNPI;
- Providing the proper training and reinforcing good habits among the employee base should MNPI be received;
- Ensuring information is categorized correctly once it's received by establishing independent checks and reviews of any confidentiality agreements, nondisclosure agreements, or any other similar legal agreements signed before any private debt or private equity strategy might receive MNPI; and
- Developing the appropriate systems and mechanisms for effective monitoring and ongoing surveillance.

Personal Trading and the Code of Ethics

As touched on for the over-the-wall process, personal trading of a firm's employees remains another conflict of interest for which every firm must establish the proper controls and put in place a firmwide code of ethics policy. Of all the unavoidable conflicts a firm must manage, the personal trading by its employees is one for which using the right technology can really become a distinct advantage and save the firm a lot of time, money, and resources.

For a multifaceted firm with a limited budget, finding the right technology to fit the business needs and to help supervise the personal trading by the firm's employees becomes an invaluable asset. The vendor landscape in this area is incredibly competitive, and many of these systems are very easily implemented into a firm's current compliance regime. In fact, many code of ethics compliance monitoring and software can automate a multitude of other necessary but tedious areas of compliance that go far beyond personal trading and include things like: quarterly affirmations, annual disclosures, gifts and entertainment, and pay-to-play political contributions reporting. In addition, some code of ethics monitoring systems include add-on capabilities that can be employed to monitor and analyze firm-level trading activity as well.

From complex trading systems to sophisticated products and investors, the growing trend in the industry appears to demonstrate that a technological solution is necessary for a firm to capture the entire universe of personal trading activity by its employees. Before making a final decision on the right technology vendor for a firm, some key factors to keep in mind are cost per user, additional resources gained (i.e., the number of compliance tasks that can be automated through the system), and time and resources saved. Certain technology programs can greatly enhance a CCO's ability focus on key issues and other areas of higher risk, rather than focused on the completion and documentation of menial tasks.

Soft Dollars

Given the competing interests of clients in different investment strategies, another conflict of interest augmented in multidimensional firms relates to the integration and management of "soft dollars."

Consistent with its obligation of seeking to obtain best execution for clients, firms may direct certain brokerage transactions to brokers who provide research and execution services to the firm. These soft dollars represent the benefits provided to an asset manager by a broker-dealer as a result of commissions generated from financial transactions executed by the broker-dealer for accounts or funds managed by the asset manager. Section 28(e) of the Exchange Act provides a safe harbor for persons who exercise investment discretion over client accounts to pay for research and brokerage services with commission dollars generated by financial transactions, as long as certain conditions are met.

The first of these conditions revolves around whether the product or service is eligible research or eligible brokerage (see Sections 28(e)(3)(A)-(C) of the Exchange Act). The second involves whether the product or service actually provides lawful and appropriate assistance in the performance of the adviser's investment decision-making responsibilities.[6] If the product or service has a mixed use,[7] the investment adviser must make a reasonable allocation of the costs of the product according to its use. Finally, the investment adviser must make a good faith determination that the amount of client commissions paid is reasonable in light of the value of the products or services provided by the broker-dealer.

In the financial services industry, soft dollars can represent an integral part of the research and analysis employed by many asset managers. But for those managers with multifaceted business lines, the use of soft dollars can present some very nuanced challenges, including the following:

- For those firms with public equity and fixed income strategies, firms need to be cognizant and specify (including in public filings like Form ADV) whether soft dollars are being used for both and, if they are, ensure that fees are being allocated appropriately to clients of both strategies;
- Certain clients (often larger, sophisticated institutional investors) will prohibit the firm from using brokerage fees related to transactions in its account to generate soft dollars. When this type of client is one of many in a strategy typically using soft dollars, the firm will be forced to balance the competing interests of the individual client restrictions versus the desire to share fees and expenses across all clients in the strategy. This expense shifting can occur not only between clients in the same strategy, but also between clients of the firm in different strategies (i.e., one fund may generate

---

6 SEC, Exchange Act Rel. No. 23170 (Apr. 28, 1986), https://www.sec.gov/rules/interp/34-23170.pdf

7 Id. The mixed use analytic approach discussed in the 1986 Release states that where a product or service obtained using client commissions performs functions that qualify as either research or brokerage under the safe harbor and performs functions that do not qualify as such, the money manager must make a reasonable allocation of the cost of the product or service according to its use.

all of a manager's soft dollars, but the manager uses those dollars to benefit other funds). Given the SEC's focus on transparency of fees, firms need to be cautious in this situation so as not to advantage certain clients at the expense of others; and

- Depending on the strategies employed, many firms with multiple business lines may be subject to multiple regulatory bodies. In this instance, firms should take notice to ensure the soft dollar approach taken complies with the rules and regulations of each applicable regulatory regime (e.g., what might pass for the SEC may be prohibited by the CTFC). This topic is explored at length later.

Regardless of the number of strategies employed, all firms must disclose and balance the benefits obtained via soft dollars with the duty of best execution. Because of the incentive to direct client brokerage to those brokers who provide research and services, firms should first disclose this conflict and then attempt to obtain "best execution" by considering many components of the trade including execution price, research obtained, and commissions charged, among other factors analyzed.

No matter what challenges a firm faces as a result of accepting soft dollars, developing an internal procedure for allocating transactions in a consistent manner and forming a soft dollar committee that regularly evaluates whether costs of the services are reasonable in light of the research and services provided, is a best practice universally recommended to mitigate potential conflicts. Such a committee structure is lauded by regulators.

Affiliations Between Registered Investment Advisers and Broker-Dealers

The conflicts of interest between affiliated investment advisers and broker-dealers are well established. At the outset, there are the recognizable conflicts associated with whether a client is placed in an adviser or broker-dealer account and the incentives associated with that placement, as well as the incentives of an adviser to use an affiliated broker-dealer for executing a client's trade despite substandard prices or other execution terms. Such items have been discussed at length and will not be examined in great detail here.

Instead, the current focus will demonstrate a particular challenge facing affiliated firms with multifaceted strategies. For example, advisers with sophisticated fixed income and public equity strategies may have within the same strategy both separately managed accounts and a publicly traded fund via the affiliated broker-dealer. In the course of its ongoing due diligence of the fund, the broker-dealer might conduct regular meetings and/or conference calls with the portfolio manager. When this occurs, the portfolio manager (and adviser firm) should be careful not to disadvantage its other clients by providing additional information to the affiliated broker-dealer that it wouldn't normally provide to its other clients in the strategy.

Disclosures

Broker-dealers and investment advisers employing nuanced strategies across multiple asset classes almost always require a robust set of accompanying disclosures to mitigate these ever-present conflicts of interest. Although keeping track of all these disclosures for each asset type and strategy can seem cumbersome and convoluted at times, it can often help frame the compliance program and provide an extra arrow in the CCO's quiver in defense of your program during a regulatory examination.

One best practice used by many firms to accomplish the difficult task of keeping disclosures up-to-date is the use of a working list. Throughout the year, as new regulations are passed or recommended, or as new enforcement cases shed light on an industry-best approach, these potential or upcoming changes are added to a working list established for each respective disclosure or regulatory filing (i.e., Form ADV or Form BD). Then, depending on the timeline for appropriate implementation, the working list serves as a top-of-mind reminder and confirmation that the necessary edits to documents are made in lock-step with the changes. The working list essentially functions as a conduit to implement mandated changes and institute best practices seen throughout the industry and with other firms. In this way, the most important disclosures and regulatory filings associated with the firm become part of living, breathing documents that change and grow as business changes and grows, a sentiment that carries a lot of weight with regulators.

Another way to keep disclosures up-to-date and ensure regulatory filings are amended appropriately is by engaging other business units in the completion of the project. As everyday practitioners of the rules and regulations affecting that area, these business units represent the front lines and can often provide additional valuable feedback on recent trends and practical application. Using Form ADV as an example, by engaging all business units on an annual basis (if not more frequently), they become invested in the regulatory filing as much as the Compliance Department is in coordinating it. Furthermore, the business units can use the engagement not only to make any necessary updates to their respective shares of the filing, but also as an opportunity to constructively review itself and focus on areas of improvement. The entire exercise further strengthens the relationship between the Compliance Department and the business units and highlights the positive role of compliance as strategic partner.

One final practice that firms with multifaceted business lines can use to enhance their disclosures and more effectively mitigate conflicts of interest is through repurposing disclosures across business units and using external reviews.

An example of repurposing can be seen when a firm applies new DOL regulations. For those asset managers that charge a level-fee, the disclosure statements provided to subject accounts and the analysis used under a level-fee fiduciary BICE can be employed whether the client is an institutional fixed-income investor plan or the 401(k) plan of a high-net-worth individual. In either case, the disclosures around the firm's status as fiduciary, compliance with the impartial conduct standards, and disclosure of all apparent conflicts must be properly distributed to the investor.

Regarding the use of external reviews, certain clients (typically sophisticated institutional investors) will mandate firms to undergo third-party compliance examinations every so often in order to manage their assets. In this situation, firms should look to repurpose the best practices and constructive feedback offered by the third party in order to bolster their own disclosures and filings, and in some instances, receive some free expert recommendations.

Conflicts as Opportunities

For any multifaceted firm with strategies across multiple asset classes, conflicts of interest are everywhere. But rather than focus on the inherent dangers those types of conflicts present, good compliance professionals can use conflicts as opportunities to showcase to regulators and clients the robust compliance system that has been set up at their respective firms. Fostering the right environment of always putting the client first inside the firm often becomes the biggest, and most vital approach to help mitigate any conflicts of interest that exist. One of the most effective ways to manage potential conflicts of interest and differing business interests within a multifaceted firm is through a robust governance and oversight structure.

IV. INTERNAL GOVERNANCE AND COMMITTEE STRUCTURES

A key component of an effective and robust governance structure is the establishment of oversight committees. The governance and oversight structure of an organization provides a solid fiduciary foundation and is often based on a two-tier supervisory structure. The first tier is composed of committees that include supervisory and functional roles such as compliance, operations, trading, and risk management. This working group provides daily oversight of business functions and client or contractual obligations. The second tier is made up of management, and may include boards of directors or trustees who provide the overall direction of the organization.

Compliance professionals have a duty to establish effective policies and procedures and to provide oversight and guidance to the business units that the Compliance Department supports. Compliance can play an integral role in establishing and maintaining an effective governance structure. However, the role of compliance can often be to balance having a seat at the table to provide strategic and regulatory guidance with not having any supervisory or decision-making authority. Compliance should serve in the role of adviser in the governance and committee structure. By doing so, compliance provides the business unit with the responsibility, freedom, and flexibility to manage itself, while providing support as required. One of the most important steps for a governance committee is ensuring that the committee is staying current and given the necessary tools and resources to maintain alignment with the overarching goals of the organization while meeting the needs of its clients and customers, adhering to regulatory requirements, and meeting its fiduciary duty.

An effective and robust governance process is good business. By implementing such a process, compliance professionals able to address the varied expectations of clients as well as those of regulatory agencies. A multifaceted firm can establish several committees to assist the firm in its overall governance process. This strategy includes having governance and oversight committees for investment-related decisions, due diligence of third parties (investment and operational), and risk management activities, as well as best execution, valuation, and proxy voting, to name a few. A multifaceted firm often has key stakeholders that represent the different areas of the firm and business units. These stakeholders participate in multiple governance committees; therefore, the governance process should be as similar as possible. This will allow the firm to have a repeatable and sustainable process while minimizing potential conflicts of interest.

One of the first steps in establishing a governance committee is in the formation of the committee charter. The committee charter documents key aspects, including the goals, frequency of meetings, reporting requirements, membership, and purpose of the committee. A good charter for any committee must be revisited periodically to ensure the information contained within continues to accurately represent the activities and purpose of the committee. Figure 1 outlines an example of a governance charter:

FIGURE 1. BEST EXECUTION COMMITTEE CHARTER

CHARTER/GOAL

To establish and implement policies and procedures to meet the firm's fiduciary and fundamental duties of seeking best execution for client transactions.

COMMITTEE MEETINGS

The committee will meet at least on a quarterly basis.

REPORTING REQUIREMENTS

Annual reports to board of directors.

MEMBERSHIP

Voting Members: Traders, portfolio managers, operations, etc.
Nonvoting Members: Compliance staff

COMPONENTS

The committee will establish and monitor the firm's trading practices, policies and procedures. This will include an initial evaluation and approval of new brokerage relationships and an annual evaluation of the approved broker list. The committee will also be responsible for reviewing transactions to assess the quality of such transactions and will conduct at least annually, or as required, a review of the firm's disclosure documents (Form ADV) to ensure that the disclosures are complete and accurate.

Another key aspect of the committee structure is maintaining documentation related to the reports reviewed and the discussions and decisions made during each meeting. Any committee secretary will tell you that memorializing the key discussions and decisions of a committee is more art than science. Documenting the key discussion points and decisions that will allow the committee members to reconstruct the conversation (at a high level) is vital when looking backwards to determine the reasoning behind key decisions and related discussions, as well as who participated, voted, or abstained from voting decisions. Once drafted, all members of the committee should have the opportunity to provide feedback on the meeting minutes before being finalized. Furthermore, as previously noted, compliance should serve in the role of adviser for compliance-related items, not as a voting committee member.

V. MANAGING THIRD-PARTY DUE DILIGENCE

General Background

The due diligence process can often serve as the best industry benchmarking. A robust due diligence and third-party oversight structure can provide your firm with the best practices it needs in light of new industry rules and regulations. Although firms should never rely on the compliance systems of third-party providers, the management of third parties—particularly through the ongoing monitoring and oversight performed—provides great opportunities to enhance the firm's compliance program and demonstrate the proper internal control structure to regulators.

For firms with multifaceted business lines, setting up the proper third-party due diligence and oversight structure can present difficult challenges. The external needs of an institutional fixed income and public equity money manager are very different from that of a private equity firm or a high-net-worth wealth management firm. Trying to juggle the competing interests of all three to find the right third parties to do business with can be complicated, but like many things in compliance, the best place to start is by developing the right process.

An effective way to jumpstart this process is by bringing together members of senior management across multiple business units to help identify the unique needs of the firm. This also includes developing the selection and approval process for third parties and setting up the proper committees (which can include the separation of investment-related committees from operational committees, when necessary). Once the basic process has been established, it really becomes a matter of execution. Initially, firms should target a small universe of top prospects within an identified subject area, and from there, move through the due diligence process to perform a comprehensive review of the firm. This will often include the completion of questionnaires, document request lists, and other discovery-laden items to better help the CCO and firm make an accurate and complete assessment.

Once this process is complete for each third party included in the universe of top prospects, not only will the CCO have arrived at the best entity for the business to partner with, he or she will also have obtained the best available ideas and industry practices on how to build out the compliance program and ensure the continued growth and success of the business.

Subadviser Due Diligence

As highlighted earlier, the oversight and due diligence process for third-party service providers is a great tool for not only growing the business, but also in documenting the robust nature of the compliance program. Due diligence requires thorough research and analysis, and when done properly, can also enhance a firm's ability to make quality decisions in choosing a particular subadviser.

As with most risk management and compliance practices, a useful first step in creating a subadviser due diligence process is to establish a policy that defines the scope, depth, and goals of the process, as well as the corresponding roles and responsibilities. There isn't one prescribed or preferred methodology; however, the steps outlined here are provided for consideration when establishing a subadviser due diligence program.

Once the goals have been established, the next step should be the fact-finding and discovery process, which could include either a request for information (RFI) or a due diligence questionnaire (DDQ). The production of the RFI or DDQ is a collaborative effort which should be done under the construct of an oversight and governance committee.

When evaluating managers for subadvisory purposes, the compliance portion of the review process should include an evaluation of the following items:

- Firm ownership structure;
- Management team;
- CCO and compliance team;
- Turnover within the organization;
- Legal or regulatory actions and/or fines;
- Regulatory filings (e.g., Form ADV and Form PF);
- Policies and procedures;
- Code of ethics;
- Political contribution policy;
- Insider trading policy;
- Evaluation of culture of compliance;
- Affiliated parties;
- Third-party service providers, including auditors, fund accounting, compliance consultants, etc.;
- Results of regulatory examinations;
- Conflicts of interest;
- Insurance coverage, including plans for errors and omissions and directors and officers;
- Compliance training;
- Annual compliance reviews;
- Risk management practices;
- Performance;
- Investment process; and
- Turnover rates.

The above list is not exhaustive. There is no one-size-fits-all approach to subadvisory due diligence. However, as with other aspects of compliance programs, there is an element of risk management when the CCO evaluates subadvisers. Conducting a risk-based approach will allow the organization to better evaluate potential business partners and understand their business practices, reputation, compliance, internal control structure, and capabilities. Due diligence information should be shared with the appropriate oversight committee and depending on the roles and responsibilities agreed upon by the committee, each group (e.g., compliance, operations, investments) should have a role in the due diligence process. In the end, the committee structure can help to enhance the overall process and provide an objective view of the overall best interest of the firm, while providing clients with the overall best service possible.

Compliance may often face challenges from the business when the CCO identifies and addresses certain concerns that manifest during the due diligence process. Compliance should seek buy-in from the business unit to provide legitimate business reasons why a certain third party (subadviser) is chosen over another when there are some concerns regarding compliance risks. By engaging the business unit and soliciting feedback on its findings, the compliance professional is able to more effectively present its concerns, as well as better understand the business unit's reasoning behind selecting one subadviser over another. All decisions should be formally documented and approved. Therefore, compliance staff should provide input while striking a balance between providing the business unit the flexibility to make decisions on its own, thus ensuring the firm isn't exposed to too much risk.

Upon hiring a subadviser, the firm should continue to monitor the relationship and activities of that subadvisor. This can and should include quarterly certifications, annual questionnaires and periodic onsite reviews, depending on the risk rating assigned to the firm. The quarterly certification process should capture information that will assist the advisor in determining whether there have been any violations or changes to the subadvisers' business or compliance programs. This can include questions related to:

- Trade errors;
- Changes in management;
- Inquiries or examinations by regulatory bodies;
- Litigation or pending lawsuits;
- Material violations to internal policies and procedures;
- Code of ethics violations;
- Changes to policies and procedures;
- Breaches to investment policy statements or subadvisory contract;
- Proxy voting;
- Soft dollar allocation;
- Best execution practices;
- Principal or agency transactions; and
- Commissions.

In the end, firms should prepare and condition themselves to mitigate risks for the organization and their clients by conducting robust due diligence, which includes the initial due diligence process as well as ongoing due diligence of their business partners. Due diligence is not for the faint of heart—the time and resource burn can be significant—but the results can be incredibly beneficial and, in the end, it's an excellent tool to further protect clients and the firm.

Private Equity and Private Fund Due Diligence

The increased focus on private fund due diligence by the SEC and other regulators only adds to the traditional challenges facing firms with multiple strategies across public and private asset types. Passed in 2010, Dodd-Frank brought with it increased regulatory scrutiny on private funds and forced over 1,500 previously exempt private fund advisers to register with the SEC.[8] In addition, the Office of Compliance Inspections and Examinations (OCIE) created the Private Funds Unit (PFU), which dedicates its time and resources to the examination of private fund advisers.

The PFU's mission is to apply industry and product knowledge to conduct focused, risk-based examinations, using OCIE's limited resources.[9] Furthermore, the PFU "plays a critical role in targeting and selecting exam candidates, scoping risk areas, executing examinations, and analyzing data" in coordination with the Division of Investment Management's Private Funds Group to influence policy and better detect areas of need within the industry.[10]

What does all this mean for advisers with exposure to private funds? It means the SEC considers private funds a high-risk area and top priority, and firms conducting business in the asset class would do well to construct a strong due diligence process, not just on the investment side, but also on the operational and compliance sides.

When performing this operational and compliance due diligence on underlying funds and GPs, firms should ask hard questions on key areas of private funds, including (but not limited to):

- Fees and expenses, accelerated monitoring fees, and expense allocation;[11]
- Proper disclosures and transparency in the fund's governing documents;[12]
- Transaction fees and the differentiation of brokerage versus advisory services;[13]

---

[8] Mary Jo White, Keynote Address at the Managed Fund Association: "Five Years On: Regulation of Private Fund Advisers After Dodd-Frank," MFA Outlook 2015 Conference, New York, New York (Oct. 16, 2015), https://www.sec.gov/news/speech/white-regulation-of-private-fund-advisers-after-dodd-frank.html

[9] Marc Wyatt, Private Equity: A Look Back and a Glimpse Ahead (May 13, 2015), www.sec.gov/news/speech/privateequity-look-back-and-glimpse-ahead.html

[10] *Id.*

[11] SEC, *In the Matter of Kohlberg Kravis Roberts & Co. L.P*, Rel. No. IA-4131 (Jun. 29, 2015), https://www.sec.gov/litigation/admin/2015/ia-4131.pdf).

[12] *In the Matter of Alpha Titans, LLC, et al.*, Rel. No. IA-4073 (Apr. 29, 2015),https://www.sec.gov/litigation/admin/2015/34-74828.pdf; In the Matter of Blackstone Management Partners L.L.C., et al., Rel. No. IA-4219 (Oct. 7, 2015), available at https://www.sec.gov/litigation/admin/2015/ia-4219.pdf

[13] SEC, *In the Matter of Blackstreet Capital Management, LLC and Murry N. Gunty*, Rel. Nos. 34-77959 and IA-4411 (June 1, 2016), https://www.sec.gov/litigation/admin/2016/34-77959.pdf

- Conflicts of interest;
- Use of advisory committees;
- Wind-down protocol;
- Valuation agents; and
- Fund extensions.

In addition to the risks inherent to these areas, firms with exposure to both private funds and public strategies must ensure the proper barriers (i.e., Chinese walls[14]) are in place to prevent the more traditional risks involved with the misuse of material nonpublic information. This will often require the creation and coordination of multiple barriers, including physical, technological, and informational walls between the relevant business units.

Given the increase in regulatory scrutiny over the private fund space, firms continuing to do business in this asset class must be sure to address the concerns of regulators and investors by creating a robust operational and compliance due diligence process to complement the investment due diligence performed. The efforts of the SEC in this area and specifically the PFU, however, should not be viewed unfavorably. The goal of the PFU, like the many compliance professionals reading this book, is to generate influence and impact in the industry and to bring compliance into focus. Its goals, like those of compliance professionals, demonstrate that having the right internal controls in an area like private fund due diligence can move compliance into the seat of value driver instead of cost center, helping private fund advisers identify the right investments that represent the best interests of their investors.

VI. UNDERSTANDING AND NAVIGATING MULTIPLE REGULATORY REGIMES

Firms with multiple distribution channels often face challenges unique from investment boutiques associated with one asset class because of exposure to multiple regulators. From the SEC, FINRA, CFTC, states and municipalities, and perhaps now (begrudgingly) the DOL, these firms attempt to navigate waters both foreign and tumultuous as they embark on investing in new and sophisticated asset strategies outside the traditional investment universe. For those firms brave enough to shoulder such regulatory scrutiny, this analysis will attempt to cover some of the current issues that must be addressed by multifaceted advisers while doing business under multiple regulatory regimes.

SEC

Without a doubt the most critical and well-established of the regulators covered in this chapter, the SEC continues to enhance the requirements it places on registered investment

---

[14] www.investopedia.com ("Chinese wall refers to an ethical barrier between different divisions of a financial or other institution to avoid conflicts of interest," Mar. 20, 2017).

advisers and other registered entities, and specifically on those RIAs with multifaceted business lines. A recent example of the enhanced requirements imposed by the SEC includes the 2016 amendments for Form ADV Part 1, primarily focused on increased reporting for all RIAs having separately managed accounts.[15] Among the amendments included additional reporting under Items 1 (Identifying Information), 4 (Successions), 7 (Private Fund Reporting), and 8 (Participation or Interest in Client Transactions), but the bulk of the additional requirements affected Item 5 (Your Advisory Business).

Beginning in October 2017 (or March 2018, for most firms that file annually), firms will now be forced to report specific numbers related to the quantities and types of clients at the firm (including whether they are U.S. or non-U.S. persons), wrap fee programs, and the data behind all of the firms' separately managed accounts. This includes essentially any client that is not a registered investment company (RIC), business development company (BDC), or pooled investment vehicle (including but not limited to private funds). Among the key information to be disclosed, firms will be required to:

- Identify separately managed account (SMA) clients and regulatory assets under management (RAUM) attributable to them;
- Identify asset types held by SMA clients;
- Calculate derivatives exposure and borrowing in aggregate across SMA clients; and
- Identify the custodians of SMA clients.

The level of reporting data that is required of the firm will depend on the RAUM size within three tiers of segmentation (less than $500 million, between $500 million and $10 billion, and greater than $10 billion).

The recent changes to Form ADV Part 1 demonstrate only a small piece of the continuing regulatory controls the SEC imposes on the financial services industry, and specifically, firms with strategies across multiple asset classes. For these firms, no topic is outside the scope of their compliance purview, from protecting retail investors from adverse fee arrangements to assessing the market-wide risks associated with cybersecurity.[16] To be successful, firms must remain vigilant in addressing any and all of the rules, regulations, and best practices espoused by the SEC.

FINRA

Another stalwart of the financial services regulatory landscape, FINRA most often affects multifaceted firms with various distribution channels when an adviser is dually registered as a broker-dealer or conducts business with affiliated broker-dealers. In either case, the situation is ripe with potential conflicts, including:

---

[15] SEC Release: https://www.sec.gov/rules/final/2016/ia-4509.pdf. SEC's redline of changes to Part 1A: https://www.sec.gov/rules/final/2016/ia-4509-form-adv-summary-of-changes.pdf

[16] SEC, Examination Priorities for 2016,https://www.sec.gov/about/offices/ocie/national-examination-program-priorities-2016.pdf

- Proper registration of dually employed sales and supervisory personnel;
- Distribution of proprietary products;
- Suitability of products and investors;
- Compensation and incentives; and
- Portfolio management and trading of affiliated accounts versus third-party accounts.

These conflicts are only exacerbated by the recent enforcement cases stressing firms' obligation to appropriately disclose fees to clients and differentiate between the advisory services of an RIA versus the transaction fees and brokerage expenses of a broker-dealer.[17] The SEC and FINRA, although similar in many ways and often seeking similar goals, are two different organizations that at times play very different roles in the regulatory landscape.

In order to protect against all these issues, multifaceted firms with multiple business lines should look to build consistency within a robust internal compliance structure that is solely focused on the golden rule of investment management: *always put the interests of the client first, and should those interests become compromised because of a conflict, disclose and explain it to the client.* Using this guiding principle as the standard lens by which compliance programs view any of the aforementioned issues will provide firms the proper framework to address and mitigate the issues associated with dual registration or the industry affiliations between RIAs and broker-dealers.

CFTC

The CFTC is the principal regulator of commodity pool operators (CPOs) and commodity trading advisers (CTAs). In charge of fostering market integrity in derivatives and similar-type products, the CFTC looks to protect the market and the public from fraud and abuse in relation to those securities subject to the Commodity Exchange Act[18] (i.e., the commodity futures markets). On the heels of the 2008 financial crisis, the U.S. government expanded the purview of the CFTC to include regulatory oversight of the swaps market, thus consolidating regulatory oversight of futures and swaps critical to the economy and how risk is effectively managed throughout the industry.

Many firms with strategies across multiple asset types will often find themselves subject to CFTC oversight and, at a minimum, need to file exemptions for various funds in order to avoid full registration and reporting requirements. For example, all entities supporting a commingled fund that trades in commodity interests must register with the CFTC or seek exemptive relief. Absent an exemption, CPOs and CTAs must register with the CFTC and join the National Futures Association (NFA), the self-regulatory organization overseeing the U.S. futures industry. The increased presence and use of derivatives in traditional and nontraditional securities and portfolios will only continue to strengthen the role the CFTC and NFA play in the financial marketplace.

---

17 SEC, *In the Matter of Blackstreet Capital Management, LLC and Murry N. Gunty,* Rel. Nos. 34-77959 and IA-4411 (June 1, 2016), https://www.sec.gov/litigation/admin/2016/34-77959.pdf

18 Sept. 21, 1922, ch. 369, § 1, 42 Stat. 998; June 15, 1936, ch. 545, § 1, 49 Stat. 1491; 17 CFR 1.

Therefore, multifaceted firms with exposure to derivatives, commodities, futures, and swaps via any pooled investment vehicle should first look to establish the level of their exposure by examining the:

- Number of pools the firm manages that deal in these security types;[19]
- Total gross capital contributions and total number of participants;[20]
- Total amount of futures traded;[21]
- Persons acting as director or trustee to the pool;[22] and
- Previous registrations with other regulatory bodies.[23]

Results from any of the above inquiries could provide exemptive relief and not require registration of the pool. For firms serving as both CPO and CTA to pooled investment vehicles, additional exemptive relief is attainable for advisers meeting certain requirements, namely:

- Only providing advice to pools currently operating under an exemption;[24] and
- Clients and pool participants meeting certain requirements.[25]

These exemptions are not comprehensive, and the CFTC published a reference guide to help firms understand whether they qualify for reduced reporting and disclosure requirements, and to ensure the firms make the proper filings.[26] For multidimensional firms with assets across asset classes, which often include various fund and pooled investment vehicles, avoiding full registration when possible and minimizing the required reporting to the CFTC is crucial to reducing the compliance burden, in addition to saving the firm precious time and money.

States and Municipalities

Whether or not a firm is large enough to be required to register with the SEC does not diminish many of the continued reporting and registration requirements at the state and municipal level. Even with $100 million of regulatory assets under management,[27] many multidimensional firms with strategies across asset types will need to register at the state and municipal level in a variety of different contexts:

---

19 17 CFR 4.13(a)(1) provides relief from CPO registration where one pool is operated at a time and the operator does not advertise, receive compensation, and is otherwise required to register with the CFTC.

20 17 CFR 4.13(a)(2) provides relief from CPO registration if gross capital contributions are less than $400K and none of the pools operated has more than 15 participants.

21 17 CFR 4.13(a)(3) provides relief from CPO registration when the pool trades minimal amount of futures.

22 17 CFR 4.13(a)(5) provides relief to a person acting as a director or trustee with respect to a pool whose operator is a registered CPO and is eligible for relief under 4.12(c).

23 17 CFR 4.5 provides relief from CPO registration to an investment company under the Investment Company Act of 1940; an insurance company subject to state regulations; a bank, trust, or any other such financial depository institution subject to U.S. regulation; or a trustee of a name fiduciary or an employer maintaining a pension plan that is subject to the Employee Retirement Income Security Act of 1974 (ERISA).

24 17 CFR 4.14(a)(8); CTA only provides advice to pools operating under 4.13(a)(3) exemption or provides advice as an RIA of 4.5 exempt pools, which is incidental to its securities advice and does not otherwise state it's a CTA.

25 17 CFR 4.7; CTA clients and pool participants must meet definition of "qualified eligible person," thereby receiving relief from certain financial, reporting and disclosure requirements.

26 "CFTC Part 4 Exemption Easy Reference Guide," https://www.nfa.futures.org/nfa-compliance/NFA-commodity-pool-operators/easy-reference-guide-part4.pdf

27 The Form ADV instructions indicate $100 million of AUM is the general threshold level to file as a registered investment adviser with the SEC. https://www.sec.gov/about/forms/formadv-instructions.pdf

- *Investment adviser representative filings*: Many firms (especially those with retail or wealth management divisions) will need to register selected investment professionals as investment adviser or broker-dealer representatives in the states where they look to conduct business. For most states, this occurs when the supervised person at the firm has more than 5 or 10 percent of clients that are natural persons, or serves in a sales or executive officer role;
- *State notice filings*: As part of their Form ADV filing with the SEC submitted through FINRA's Investment Adviser Registration Depository (IARD) system, firms must typically submit a notice filing and pay related fees in any state where it has a place of business or more than six nonexempt clients;[28]
- *Blue sky filings*: Each state has blue sky laws to regulate the offering and sale of securities within its borders. For any firm to sell securities, the blue sky laws of the state where the securities are sold often require registration and other obligations that must be met. On an annual basis, firms should review their blue sky filings for each state to make sure they meet any renewal requirements;
- *Lobbyist filings*: In order to receive investment mandates from certain public institutions, certain states (e.g., California) require firms to register as a lobbyist of the state and make periodic quarterly and annual filings; and
- *Municipal filings*: Certain municipal jurisdictions require disclosure of information before accepting the services of a contracting party. If that party has beneficial owners over a certain threshold (including, for example, a private fund), it is considered a controlling entity and can be required to file a disclosure statement and affidavit with the jurisdiction unless it means a certain exemption. An example of this type of municipal filing would be the Economic Disclosure Statement required by the City of Chicago.[29]

DOL

Much to the chagrin of investment advisers, broker-dealers, banks, and insurance companies everywhere, the DOL passed its Fiduciary Rule[30] in April 2016, which vastly increased who is considered a "fiduciary" of an employee benefit plan and other types of retirement accounts (e.g., IRAs) under ERISA as a result of giving investment advice or recommendations. The effect of this rule on industry participants is far too vast to cover in the scope of this chapter, so the focus here is on certain exemptions to the best interest contract (BIC) detailed in the rule that will have widespread application to multifaceted investment advisers and broker-dealers.[31]

---

[28] *North American Securities Administrators Association, Investment Adviser Guide,* http://www.nasaa.org/industry-resources/investment-advisers/investment-adviser-guide/. Exceptions to this general rule are Texas, Louisiana, New Hampshire, and Nebraska (where a single in-state client triggers a notice-filing obligation), and Colorado, which does not require notice filing unless the adviser has a place of business located with the state.

[29] City of Chicago, Economic Disclosure, Affidavit, Online EDS, https://www.cityofchicago.org/city/en/depts/dps/provdrs/comp/svcs/economic_disclosurestatementseds.html

[30] 29 CFR Parts 2509, 2510, and 2550. https://www.federalregister.gov/d/2016-07924

[31] On February 3, 2017, Donald Trump issued a presidential memorandum directing the DOL "to examine the Fiduciary Duty Rule to determine whether it may adversely affect the ability of Americans to gain access to retirement information and financial advice," as well as review the negative consequences from the original applicability date of April 10, 2017. Subsequently, the DOL issued its final rule on April 4, 2017, formally extending the final applicability date of the Fiduciary Rule for 60 days to June 9, 2017. Given the constant change and confusion surrounding the DOL Fiduciary Rule, the compliance professional should consult a legal or compliance professional before instituting any formal policies related to it.

As the CCO assesses the DOL Fiduciary Rule's effect on a business, Figure 2 represents a list of steps to determine the applicability and scope of associated obligations:

FIGURE 2.

1. Is the client account subject to ERISA?
   a. Examples of accounts subject to ERISA include pension plans, 401(k) plans, IRAs (traditional and Roth), or assets pulled from an IRA or 401(k) account to fund a new account.
2. Is the client considered "retail" qualified money?
   a. If a client has greater than $50M in AUM or is represented by an independent fiduciary (e.g. another investment adviser, broker-dealer, bank, or insurance company), a firm can likely rely on the financially sophisticated intermediary exception and thus avoid fiduciary status. As long as the firm (1) knows or reasonably believes that the independent fiduciary is capable of evaluating investment risks, and (2) has disclosed to the independent fiduciary its status and the existence of any financial interests (e.g., that it will be paid a percentage of assets if hired), the exception will apply.
      i. This exception is typically not available for private pension plans or 401(k) plans (i.e., nongovernment plans) involving less than $50 million in AUM, IRAs (Roth or traditional) without financially sophisticated intermediaries, and individuals who have pulled assets from an IRA or 401(k) to fund the account.
3. Does the firm qualify for the streamlined level-fee fiduciary BIC?
   a. If the firm receives payment solely on a fixed percentage of AUM or a set fee that does not vary based on investment recommendations, and neither the firm or its affiliates receives other fees or compensation in connection with the recommendation, then the streamlined BIC for level-fee fiduciaries may be available.
   b. This streamlined BIC requires a lower threshold of compliance against the full BICE standard and requires the following:
      i. Written statement of the firm's ERISA fiduciary status
      ii. Compliance with the impartial conduct standards
         1. Providing advice in the best interest of the client.
         2. Receiving reasonable compensation
         3. Avoid misleading statements to the investor
      iii. Disclosure of material conflicts of interest.
   c. The requirements listed can often be accomplished through the use of a signed disclosure statement or incorporated in the language of an investment management agreement during the process of onboarding a new client.

4. Are plan assets invested in proprietary mutual funds?
    a. A holdout from before the new Fiduciary Rule, the DOL maintained prohibited transaction exemption (PTE) 77-4 for advisers to proprietary mutual funds so long as certain requirements were met. These include disclosure, consent, and the avoidance of double fees.

All of the aforementioned exemptions and exceptions will help firms burn less time, money, and energy to comply with the requirements of the DOL Fiduciary Rule. For many registered investment advisers that previously served as ERISA fiduciaries for discretionary advice, compliance with the rule and any associated conduct standards will seem like second nature, and will generally entail little more than additional documentation of the activities already being performed.

For multifaceted firms that provide private fund advisory services, the risks and obligations associated with compliance to the DOL Fiduciary Rule are often greatly enhanced given the risky and illiquid nature of these private investments. Many firms engaged in this business line will need to make the strategic business decision to provide services to clients that don't meet one of the aforementioned exemptions (typically the financially sophisticated intermediary exception or $50M AUM) and the risk/reward associated with it.

Global Market Entity Identifier

The Global Market Entity Identifier Utility (GMEI), formerly known as the CICI Utility, is the Depository Trust & Clearing Corporation's (DTCC) Legal Entity Identifier (LEI) solution offered in collaboration with the Society for Worldwide Interbank Financial Telecommunication (SWIFT). GMEI is designed to create and apply a single, universal standard identifier to any organization or firm involved in a financial transaction internationally. It was developed in response to the financial crisis of 2008–2009 after governments and regulators called for new regulation of the financial markets.[32]

DTCC and SWIFT designed the GMEI solution with assistance from a consortium of 14 global financial services organizations led by the Global Financial Markets Association (GFMA) to meet global industry requirements across all asset classes. The solution went live in August 2012 and has since been endorsed by the Regulatory Oversight Committee (ROC), the group of global regulators established by the Group of 20 and the Financial Stability Board to oversee development of the Global LEI System (GLEIS). This endorsement means that GMEIs are recognized as pre-LEIs by all of the 55 global regulators who are members of the ROC and will be required by them on regulatory reporting as they upgrade reporting requirements. The GMEI utility operates as a Pre-Local Operating Unit within the GLEIS. On an annual basis, firms will need to review and (if necessary) update their GMEI filings.

---

[32] GMEI Utility, About the Global Markets Entity Identifier Utility, https://www.gmeiutility.org/aboutLEI.jsp

International Regimes

For those multifaceted firms participating in the international space, the regulatory demands rise to a much higher level than those investment managers that keep their operations domestic in nature. As a business continues to expand its borders, from the Alternative Investment Fund Managers Directive (AIFMD) regulations in Europe to The Securities and Futures Commission (SFC) in Hong Kong, firms should be mindful to hire the right outside legal counsel and compliance consultants to support their expansion. Vastly distinct from their U.S. counterparts, the demands and obligations of these regulatory regimes differ greatly by country. Before engaging in business in a new country, investment firms of all types would do well to bring in experts more familiar with the local systems and procedures.

VII. OTHER POTENTIAL CONSIDERATIONS FOR RIAS WITH MULTIPLE DISTRIBUTION CHANNELS

Compliance departments of a multifaceted firm with strategies across multiple asset strategies, public and private, are part engineer, architect, builder, and housekeeper. From identifying and laying the right foundation, formulating the right plan of construction, building the proper program, and consistently maintaining proper oversight, the Compliance Departments of these firms face many unique challenges not applicable to their single strategy counterparts.

Although certainly not exhaustive, this section represents a quick list of topics that firms providing advisory services for multiple strategies should take into consideration when building out their compliance programs.

Global Investment Performance Standards

In today's investment world, adherence to global investment performance standards (GIPS) is critically important for recognition with most institutional investors. But what about the retail and high-net-worth investors? What about private fund advisers? The differences in client base of many multifaceted firms with strategies across asset classes highlights the relevance (or lack thereof) of the GIPS standards to the continued growth and success of the business.

For those firms catering to institutional investors in the public markets, whether fixed income or public equities, being a GIPS-compliant firm will provide access to clients other firms just can't reach. In the retail and high-net-worth space, however, being GIPS-compliant presents some challenges. Many of these issues surround the timing of setting up a new account in order to make it open for trading, while concurrently placing it in the most accurate GIPS composite based on the client's investment objectives and risk tolerances. Sometimes it can take months to fully develop a client's investment policy statement and, in those situations, firms must balance the competing fiduciary duties of providing equal access to investment opportunities for similarly situated clients while safeguarding the client's investment objectives.

Unlike many public strategies, the presence of the GIPS standards in the private equity space has yet to take on material importance. In order for performance to be meaningful, the return calculations must be based on the fair value of the underlying securities. This becomes increasingly difficult in the private equity space, where objective valuations are very tough to come by. As a consequence, even sophisticated investors playing in the private equity space do not often mandate GIPS compliance of their investment managers.

Firms managing assets in all three of the examples above should carefully weigh the benefits of gaining GIPS compliance against the risks involved and the need to attract new clients.

Custody

Often a focus of regulators, custody of clients' assets is another area that presents nuanced challenges for multidimensional firms offering strategies across investment classes. Although not particularly important in the management of institutional money, custody is often a key part of doing business for advisers serving the retail high-net-worth space, as well as for private fund advisers. No matter how it affects the firm, it is critically important for the compliance program to establish the proper internal controls to appropriately identify and mitigate any conflicts involving custody of clients' assets.

At a high level, the four main ways investment managers will obtain custody of their clients' assets is through:

- Enhanced legal or fiduciary relationships (i.e., being a trustee or executor, having power of attorney, etc.);
- Possession of or access to client funds and securities (i.e., having customer usernames and passwords for trading and receiving checks);
- Third-party money movement and letters of authorization with which the firm affects the amount and timing of payment; and/or
- Deducting fees.

In other instances, investment managers may avoid having formal custody of their clients' assets if certain of their activities are limited in scope. Regarding the deduction of fees, firms should be aware that just this activity alone will not subject the firm to the annual surprise audit that comes with having custody over client funds. Also, regarding third-party money movement, firms should also note that typically like-to-like transfers will not qualify an account as subject to the annual surprise audit either.[33]

[33] For more information regarding recent changes to the Custody Rule, please see the SEC No-Action Letter from February 2017 (https://www.sec.gov/divisions/investment/noaction/2017/investment-adviser-association-022117-206-4.htm) and the associated FAQs (https://www.investmentadviser.org/eweb/docs/Publications_News/PublicDocs_UsefulWebsites/PubDoc/170221CustodyFAQs.pdf)

Legal Entity Name Changes

Multifaceted firms looking at a possible name change for one of their current strategies should be very careful to consider all ramifications in advance. What may seem like a relatively innocuous decision by the marketing team to attract new clients can often lead to an inordinate time, money, and resource burn for the other business units within a firm. To demonstrate, consider the following hypothetical: A publicly marketed fixed income strategy of a GIPS-compliant firm also has a pooled investment vehicle to provide access to the strategy for clients that can't meet the minimum for a separately managed account. In an effort to increase sales, the firm decides it needs to change the name of the strategy to something more recognizable by institutional clients.

That doesn't seem too difficult, right? Wrong. Start with marketing materials; if the firm would like to carry the performance of the strategy moving forward (and stay GIPS compliant), all marketing materials discussing that strategy will need additional disclosures discussing the name change. If there's an actual shift in any part of the investment objectives of the strategy to go along with the name change, a brand new GIPS composite will need to be created, which can often entail a significant amount of work.

Even if it is just the name, all of the legal fund formation documents (company or partnership agreements, private placement memorandums (PPMs), subscription packets, investor questionnaires) will need to be amended and updated. Additionally, regulatory filings with the SEC (Form ADV and Form PF), FINRA (for any securities sold through a broker-dealer), CFTC (if the strategy trades in futures and derivatives of any kind), DTCC (providing legal entity identifiers through the GMEI utility for private funds), and any state securities regulators (where applicable) will all need to be updated, and that's just naming a few.

VIII. CONCLUSION

The hidden yet onerous challenges just detailed for legal entity name changes are emblematic of many of the unique and nuanced difficulties facing multidimensional firms discussed throughout this chapter. Whether the firm is being regulated by multiple regulatory regimes or managing conflicts of interest between very distinct business units, creating an effective compliance program starts with establishing the proper foundation, developing the right blueprints, and committing to action while using the most suitable tools for the job.

Some of the topics discussed here may seem rather pedestrian, but being cognizant of them will save a CCO quite a few headaches down the road. A leaky faucet doesn't seem like a big deal until the pressure in the water pipes builds past its breaking point and, out of nowhere, the entire basement is flooded. At that point, the owner knows he or she can remedy the problem, but there is a significant time and resource burn that will be required in order to do it. Firms need to understand that business, marketing, investment, operations, and compliance practices don't exist in a vacuum.

For all compliance professionals, knowing that something like changing the name of an investment strategy with an associated pooled investment vehicle involves more than just a few edits to marketing collateral, will help provide the traction needed to have those challenging conversations with senior management regardless of the subject matter. Furthermore, by providing good counsel and revealing how these larger, strategic business decisions will impact all areas of the firm, the CCO's role in compliance will add significant value and further demonstrate his or her position as a trusted business partner.

ABOUT THE AUTHORS

Michele Hawkins is managing director and CCO for Fort Washington Investment Advisors, Inc. and its subsidiary Peppertree Partners, LLC. Fort Washington is headquartered in Cincinnati Ohio. Ms. Hawkins is responsible for all aspects of the firm's compliance program, including training, compliance monitoring, establishment of policies and procedures, auditing, risk management, due diligence, and all regulatory related initiatives.

Ms. Hawkins has more than 30 years of experience in the securities and financial services industry. Her duties have included investment adviser, private equity, mutual fund, broker-dealer, and transfer agent compliance, trading, operations, and management.

Ms. Hawkins joined the firm in 2000. Prior to joining Fort Washington she worked for Countrywide Financial Services, Inc., Leshner Financial Services, Inc., EF Hutton, and Paine Webber.

Ms. Hawkins has a bachelor of science in Business Management and has received the designation of certified regulatory compliance professional (CRCP) from FINRA/Wharton School of Business, as well as the NRS investment adviser certified compliance professional (IACCP) designation. She also serves on the advisory board for Xavier University Cintas Institute for Business Ethics and Social Responsibility, serves on the advisory committee and as audit chair for Bright New Leaders for Ohio Schools, served as chairperson of the Herbert R. Brown Society, and is a member of the National Society of Compliance Professionals (NSCP). In addition to her volunteer activities, Ms. Hawkins was named as a 2015 YWCA Career Woman of Achievement and in 2016 was honored by the United Way of Greater Cincinnati as a "Legend and Leader" in the community.

Patrick Hayes serves as CCO at Graydon Compliance Solutions, LLC. He brings years of legal, compliance, and financial services industry experience across a broad array of subject matter related to registered investment advisers, private equity and fixed income funds, broker-dealers, and insurance companies. Previously, Mr. Hayes served as private funds and regulatory compliance officer for Fort Washington Investment Advisors, Inc. In this role, he was responsible for coordinating all regulatory filings of the adviser and managed Fort Washington and its subsidiaries by providing compliance oversight, regulatory guidance, and by instituting effective governance and risk management practices. He directed the effective integration of the Securities Act, Exchange Act, Investment Company Act, and Advisers Act into the adviser's compliance program, and led all compliance efforts associated with the private equity division, private client group, financial planning, as well as its affiliated broker-dealer activities.

Prior to Fort Washington, Mr. Hayes worked as a litigation attorney at Vorys, Sater, Seymour & Pease LLP, where he practiced in general and complex civil litigation, with particular experience in corporate matters including *qui tam* False Claims Act cases. He received his juris doctor degree from the University of Cincinnati Law School and was inducted into the Order of the Barristers for outstanding ability in appellate advocacy. He received his bachelor of arts *magna cum laude* from the University of Notre Dame, where he majored in English.

Chapter 9

International Broker-Dealer and Investment Adviser Jurisdictional Considerations

By J. Keith Kessel
Nordea Bank

I. INTRODUCTION

The regulatory landscape in which foreign firms and U.S. firms with foreign affiliates conduct cross-border brokerage and investment advisory activities is largely viewed through the prism of a territorial approach to regulation. Many operational, marketing, and communication-related considerations affect a firm's ability to rely upon a registration exemption in the United States. Conversely, when conducting business outside the country, U.S. broker-dealers and investment advisers must consider the applicability of local securities law registration and regulation requirements, which as a general matter are not as permissive or codified in the United States. This article addresses those requirements for U.S. broker-dealers conducting business in the European Union, including differences between the U.S. and the EU approaches to various cross-border issues.

II. FOREIGN BROKER-DEALERS AND THEIR U.S. AFFILIATES OR U.S. INTERMEDIATING BROKER-DEALERS

The Securities and Exchange Commission (SEC) has promulgated Rule 15a-6 governing the circumstances in which foreign broker-dealers are subject to U.S. regulation, as well as the circumstances in which they are exempt from regulation. The appropriate approaches to navigating the regulatory exemptions have further evolved through a series of SEC no-action letters and some prevailing practices in the industry.

Rule 15a-6 carves out certain activities that do not subject a foreign broker-dealer to U.S. broker-dealer registration. Many interpretive questions remain regarding the activities and whether they fall within the exemption. Exempt behavior under Rule 15a-6 includes unsolicited transactions; distribution of certain research to institutional investors; trading between U.S. broker-dealers and foreign broker-dealers; and targeting certain identifiable groups of U.S. personnel overseas (e.g., military installations). The no-action letters address the availability of these exemptions in specific contexts such as order entry quotation systems, clearance and settlement, merger and acquisition (M&A) advisory firms based overseas, and employee stock option plans (ESOPs) serviced by an overseas broker-dealer for U.S.-based employees. This chapter analyzes the legal landscape for the brokerage business and suggests approaches to structuring the cross-border operations of U.S. firms and their foreign affiliates, as well as the activities of foreign broker-dealers in the United States, including the use of U.S. firms to "intermediate" their transactional business and interactions with U.S. investors.

U.S. Broker-Dealer Registration Requirements

The Securities Exchange Act of 1934, as amended ("Exchange Act"), requires that all brokers and their broker-dealer firms that are engaged in the securities business must be registered, unless otherwise exempted from the registration requirements.[1] Specifically, the Exchange Act provides in pertinent part as follows:

> §15(a)(1). It shall be unlawful for any broker or dealer which is either a person other than a natural person or a natural person not associated with a broker or dealer which is a person other than a natural person (other than such a broker or dealer whose business is exclusively intrastate and who does not make use of any facility of a national securities exchange) to make use of the mails or any means or instrumentality of interstate commerce to effect any transaction in, or to induce or attempt to induce the purchase or sale of, any security (other than an exempted security or commercial paper, bankers' acceptances, or commercial bills) *unless* such broker or dealer is registered in accordance with Section (b) of this section.[2]

---

[1] §15(a)(1) of the Securities Exchange Act of 1934, as amended.

[2] Before the pertinent exemptions are analyzed, a few other definitions from the Exchange Act are instructive in laying the regulatory groundwork.

§3(a). When used in [the Exchange Act], unless the context otherwise requires—...

(4) The term "broker" means any person engaged in the business of effecting transactions in securities for the account of others, but does not include...[certain specified activities contemplated for financial institutions/banks as a result of the Gramm-Leach-Bliley Act].

(5) The term "dealer" means any person engaged in the business of buying and selling securities for his/[her] own account, through a broker or otherwise, but does not include...[certain specified activities contemplated for financial institutions/banks as a result of the Gramm-Leach-Bliley Act]....

(9) The term "person" means a natural person, company, government, or political subdivision, agency, or instrumentality of a government....

(18) The term "person associated with a broker or dealer" or "associated person of a broker or dealer" means any partner, officer, director, or branch manager of such broker or dealer (or any person occupying a similar status of performing similar functions), any person directly or indirectly controlling, controlled by, or under common control with such broker or dealer, or any employee of such broker or dealer, except that any person associated with a broker or dealer whose functions are solely clerical or ministerial shall not be included in the meaning of such term for purposes of section 15(b) of [the Exchange Act other than certain persons with regulatory or disciplinary histories]....

(21) The term "person associated with a member" or "associated person of a member" when used with respect to a member of a national securities exchange or registered securities association means any partner, officer, director, or branch manager of such member (or any person occupying a similar status of performing similar functions), any person directly or indirectly controlling, controlled by, or under common control with such member, or any employee of such member.

Non-U.S. entities that fall within the definition of "broker" or "dealer" specified in §15(a)(1) must, absent an appropriate exemption, register with the SEC if they effect securities transactions or induce or attempt to induce the purchase or sale of any nonexempt security through U.S. jurisdictional means. This regulatory requirement is separate from the requirements governing registration of securities offerings under the Securities Act of 1933. Even though an issuance of securities may be exempt from the registration pursuant to Securities Act Regulation D, Regulation S, or Rule 144A, all sellers of these securities are subject to these broker-dealer registration requirements. The principal exemption from the broker-dealer registration requirement is codified in Rule 15a-6.

Exemptions from U.S. Broker-Dealer Registration

Pursuant to Exchange Act §15(a)(2) and Exchange Act Rule 15a-6, the SEC codified an exemption applicable from broker-dealer registration available to foreign broker-dealers that meet the requirements stated in the rule. The exemption became effective as of August 15, 1989. The exemption has been refined and modified over the years by no-action letters. The exemption pertains to federal registration with the SEC.[3]

Rule 15a-6 provides four broad subsections of exemptions. Two deal with institutional investors. Another deals with unsolicited transactions. The remaining subsection deals with several different types of transactions and solicitations that are deemed to be permissible for unregistered broker-dealers. See Appendix A to this chapter for the complete text of Rule 15a-6.

Analysis of Federal Registration Exemptions.[4] The importance for a broker-dealer to properly assess whether it needs to be registered with the SEC to conduct business in the United States cannot be emphasized enough. The consequences of a mistake can be severe, particularly because the SEC and the state regulators can initiate administrative legal proceedings and enforcement actions, or can simply deny a prospective registration application based upon the firm's compliance history. The enforcement actions against Credit Suisse and UBS are illustrative of the SEC's position regarding such matters. As a result, the industry has sought no-action letters in the same general timeframe, as the industry has become increasingly sensitized to the SEC's increased focus on this once "sleepy" rule.

The SEC has substantial discretion in enforcement. Both the registered, affiliated broker-dealer and unregistered broker-dealer should defer to the interpretation of the SEC, rather than taking the approach that the courts may view the application of U.S. jurisdiction more restrictively. The registered affiliate and unregistered broker-dealer would be well advised to pursue a conservative course of action insofar as it would

[3] Rule 15a-6 provides an exemption only from registration with the SEC. State regulators may impose separate registration requirements, despite the urging from the North American Securities Administrators Association to adopt uniform laws regarding registration.

[4] The SEC provided a good FAQ on this registration rule: https://www.sec.gov/divisions/marketreg/faq-15a-6-foreign-bd.htm

reduce the possibility of legal conflict with the SEC, which naturally bring significant costs, reputational damage, and distraction from conducting a firm's business.

The main registration exemptive provisions considered here involve:

- Executing unsolicited transactions;
- Providing research to major institutional investors;
- Having direct contacts with institutional investors under certain circumstances; and
- Some miscellaneous exemptions dealing with transactional business with registered broker-dealers, certain U.S. persons located abroad and persons temporarily present in the United States, broker-dealers serving as an administrator for employer-sponsored retirement plans, etc.

Unsolicited Transactions

The SEC views "solicitation" broadly and, consequently, so should firms with U.S. customers and U.S. resident customers. Because under Rule 15a-6 unsolicited transactions qualify for an exemption from registration for broker-dealers without a presence in the United States, this discussion examines what constitutes a solicitation.

The Fundamental Retail Client Relationship and Registration Requirement Is Based upon a Solicitation. Any of the following activities may be deemed by the SEC to be a "solicitation":[5]

- *Any* attempt by a broker-dealer to promote its business known in the United States, including through prospecting meetings or through advertisement;
- Telephone calls;
- A website that targets us investors, and a website that offers services generally, which does not specify the brokerage services are not available to U.S. persons;
- Instant messaging and emails;
- Social networking platforms such as LinkedIn, Facebook, etc., at which posts are made or their messaging platforms are used;
- Transmission of a market-maker's bid/ask quotations;
- The conducting of investment seminars;
- Recommendations likely to lead to a transaction with the recommending firm; and
- The provision by a broker-dealer of research to investors, even to investors who have activity sought out and requested the research.[6]

---

5 53 Federal Register 23645, 23650 (June 23, 1988) ("Proposing Release" of Rule 15a-6). *See also 54 Federal Register* 30013, 30021 (July 18, 1989) ("Adopting Release" of Rule 15a-6).

6 *U.S. Regulation of the International Securities and Derivatives Markets,* Fifth Ed., Vol. 2, Aspen Law & Business (citing Adopting Release at 30022 nn. 100-103 ("CREF also said that the communications between a foreign broker-dealer and a U.S. investor after the investor had opened its account with the foreign broker-dealer on the investor's own initiative should not be deemed solicitation. The [SEC] believes, however, that the existence of these communications could support the conclusion that the foreign broker-dealer was engaged in the securities business within the jurisdiction of the United States, by virtue of having regular customers, and thus was subject to U.S. broker-dealer registration requirements.")

Aside from the foregoing direct solicitations, several other activities may violate the unsolicited transaction exemption because they are "indirect solicitations:"

- Responding to a customer's unsolicited phone call in which the customer asks for ideas about whether to invest by providing several investing ideas;
- Providing contact information of the broker-dealer to the broker-dealer's corporate issuer client who employs the retail customer (e.g., in a warrant program), and otherwise; and
- Providing information to a third party when the unregistered broker-dealer knows or should know that it will reach U.S. customers or U.S. resident customers.

Online Services and Website Solicitations. A review of the SEC's analysis of research distribution indicates how expansively the SEC views promotional efforts. In summary, the SEC views "solicitation" as including any action by a broker-dealer intended to induce transactions, to develop customer goodwill or to make itself known.

A good illustration of the breadth of the SEC's view is its statement that a foreign broker-dealer could be deemed to have solicited a U.S. investor who on his own initiative opened an account with the foreign broker-dealer and became a "regular customer."

There have also been indications that the SEC would view a foreign broker-dealer granting access to an on-line trading facility to a U.S. customer as being inconsistent with the exemption. Based upon the foregoing, it would seem that the SEC would view a broker-dealer's website as one of the indicia of whether the broker-dealer is soliciting a client in the United States, and thus whether it would be required to register with the SEC.

In 1997, the SEC provided guidance *in dicta* regarding the effect of the providing access to quotation systems by institutional clients:

> The staff is confirming that providing U.S. investors with access to screen-based quotation systems that supply quotations, prices, and other trade-reporting information input directly by the foreign broker-dealers will not constitute an impermissible contact with a foreign broker-dealer, so long as any transactions between the U.S. investor and the foreign broker-dealer are intermediated in accordance with the requirements of Rule 15a-6. As you note, a foreign broker-dealer that directs quotations to U.S. investors through a proprietary system (as distinct from a third party system) would be viewed as having solicited any resulting transactions and thus could not rely on the exemption in paragraph (a)(1) and Rule 15a-6, although it would continue to be allowed to effect transactions in reliance on other available provisions of the rule.[7]

The intermediation requirement referenced above pertains exclusively to institutional investors and, to the extent that the SEC is considering liberalizing the rule, it would apply only to institutional investors.

---

[7] Cleary, Gottlieb, Steen & Hamilton, SEC No-Action Letter 1997 WL 177550, p. 12 (April 9, 1997).

The SEC views the provision of website services to retail investors very narrowly. The SEC prohibits foreign broker-dealers from making their trading and quotation system directly available to retail clients. In 1998, the SEC issued further guidance on these matters in the SEC's seminal interpretation on the use of Internet websites ("Internet Release").[8] The Internet Release unequivocally stated that:

> Broker-dealers must register with the [SEC] if they are *physically present* in the United States, or if, regardless of their location, they effect, induce, or attempt to induce securities transactions with investors in the United States. The issue, therefore, is whether the [SEC] would deem a broker-dealer's website to be an attempt to induce securities transactions with U.S. persons.

Websites can offer a variety of services that are deemed to be solicitations, including market information, real-time or delayed quote information, market summaries, research, portfolio modeling and tracking, contact information, fee schedules, and other analytic programs such as retirement and estate planning models, and college funding models. Essentially, "Websites advertise the broker-dealer's services to potential investors with the intent of attracting securities business."[9]

Because the SEC generally construes websites as solicitations, it stated in the Internet Release that broker-dealers may institute procedures designed to thwart the practical effect of a solicitation, thereby providing the broker-dealer with the assurance that the SEC would not regard the website as a *de facto* solicitation. The procedures must evidence that the broker-dealer has taken measures reasonably designed to ensure that it does not affect securities transactions with U.S. persons as a result of its Internet presence. The SEC has noted that the adequacy of the measures will depend upon the facts and circumstances. An essential component to demonstrating that communications are not targeted to the United States is the implementation of '"measures that are reasonably designed to guard against sales…to U.S. persons.' In general, the Web Site Release seems to suggest that U.S. issuers would likely have to resort to some means to limit U.S. investors' access to the Web site offering communications."

The Internet Release takes the position that a foreign broker-dealer generally would not be required to register as a result of its Internet presence if it takes the following measures:

- Posts a prominent disclaimer on the website affirmatively delineating the countries in which the broker-dealer's services are available, or stating that the services are not available to U.S. persons; and
- Refuses to provide *brokerage services* to any potential customer that the broker-dealer has reason to believe is, or that indicates that it is, a U.S. person, based on residence, mailing address, payment method, or other grounds.

---

8 SEC, *Interpretation: Re: Use of Internet Web Sites to Offer Securities, Solicit Securities Transaction, or Advertise Investment Services Offshore,* Rel. Nos. 33-7516, 34-39779, IA-1710, IC-23071(Mar. 23, 1998), https://www.sec.gov/rules/interp/33-7516.htm

9 *Id.*

The SEC generally expects all unregistered foreign broker-dealers to adopt procedures to ensure compliance with these safe harbor provisions. If unregistered broker-dealers have reason to believe that its customers are residents of the United States, the qualified safe harbor mentioned above could not be utilized if such U.S. residents used the firm's website for any of the available brokerage services.

The Internet Release underscores that the procedures suggested above are not exclusive. Broker-dealers are encouraged to institute other procedures designed to protect customers from becoming the recipient of their website's services. This theme is one that unregistered broker-dealers should note throughout the U.S. securities laws; specifically, the SEC will not commit itself to one position without adequate flexibility to initiate an enforcement action if it deems such an action would be appropriate or desirable in any particular case, as evidenced by its hedge language, "*generally* would not be required to register (emphasis added)" and by taking the position that broker-dealer can always "do more" in terms of being more conservative in their interpretation of the securities laws and their development of procedures designed to ensure compliance with inherently broad and ambiguous securities laws.

Notwithstanding the disclaimer and reasonable measures safe harbor contemplated above, if a particular U.S. customer has ever used an unregistered broker-dealer's website prior to relocating to the United States, then the unregistered firm could not rely on the unsolicited trade exemption with respect to that customer. Accordingly, the Internet Release stated:

> Foreign broker-dealers that have Internet Web sites and that intend to rely on Rule 15a-6's "unsolicited" exemption should ensure that the "unsolicited" customer's transactions are not in fact solicited, either directly or indirectly, through customers accessing their Web Sites. In particular, these broker-dealers could obtain, as a precaution reasonably designed to prevent that result, affirmative representations from potential U.S. customers that they deem unsolicited that those customers have not previously accessed their Web sites. Alternatively, a broker-dealer could maintain records that are sufficiently detailed and verifiable to reliably determine that such U.S. customers had not obtained access to its Web site.[10]

In response to the preceding footnote regarding websites being considered solicitations generally, Merrill Lynch wrote the SEC to request a clarification of that statement. Merrill Lynch stated that "[a] number of securities practitioners have read this statement as an expression by the [SEC] that any order routed through a broker-dealer's website cannot be considered unsolicited."[11] The SEC responded as follows:

---

[10] "Because of the nature and the operational practices associated with hosting foreign broker-dealers' Web sites, firms cannot in good faith consider an order routed to them via their Web sites as unsolicited."

[11] Letter from Kenneth S. Spirer, Merrill Lynch, to Robert L.D. Colby, SEC (Dec. 8, 1998).

The Internet Release was designed to clarify how the registration requirements of the U.S. securities laws apply to offshore Internet offers of securities and investment services. With respect to broker-dealer activities, it made clear that the content and nature of broker-dealer Web sites typically would cause them to be deemed advertisements of the broker-dealers' products and services. Because these Web sites may constitute the solicitation of a business relationship, they would subject the broker-dealers to registration obligations under the Exchange Act. The language contained in footnote 56 is intended to explain that a broker-dealer soliciting business relationships through its Web site cannot generally rely on Rule 15a-6's "unsolicited" transaction exemption. This footnote was intended to be read only in context and was not intended to address the question of whether a registered broker-dealer's Web site constitutes a "solicitation" for other purposes.[12]

Although the Adopting Release allowed for third-party systems, assuming that the customer could not receive an execution from the foreign broker-dealer, the practical effect of using such systems in light of the Internet Release would inevitably lead to the conclusion that within the context of offering brokerage services to employees of the corporate issuer that offers warrants through the unregistered firm to the issuer's employees, either a direct or indirect solicitation would occur if the third-party system was a domain of the employer of the foreign broker-dealer's customers. Because the employer of such customers will presumably communicate such functionality to its employees, regulators would probably construe such a relationship as having been solicited. Assuming that the issuer's U.S.-based employees have access to the quotation system, either for the warrant program or the entirety of website's applications, an indirect solicitation, at a minimum, would result.

Because the SEC views even indirect solicitations by unregistered foreign broker-dealers as a violation of the registration requirements, unregistered firms would be well advised to pursue a conservative approach. Unregistered firms should refrain from providing any services that could even remotely be considered an "indirect" solicitation. Understandably this view seems very expansive, but it is the view that practitioners should assume that the SEC takes. In fact, the Adopting Release stated:

The Commission generally believes that a narrow construction of solicitation would be inconsistent with the express language of section 15(a)(1), which refers to both inducing or attempting to induce the purchase or sale of securities...[13]

The SEC periodically offers additional guidance on the use of electronic media, but the Internet Release continues to be the seminal interpretation on Internet solicitation for international firms. Moreover, the SEC has stated that the operation of an ESOP would be exempt from broker-dealer registration in certain circumstances (described later). Succinctly stated, even though the broker-dealer may have solicited the issuer, if the broker-dealer does not solicit investors or transactions, even though it may operate

---

[12] Letter from Catherine McGuire, SEC, to Mr. Kenneth S. Spirer, Merrill Lynch (Jan. 13, 1999).

[13] 54 *Federal Register* 30013, 30018 (July 18, 1989).

a password protected website to facilitate plan-related transactions with ESOP participants, it would not trigger the broker-dealer registration requirement.

Employee Stock Ownership Plans

The SEC has taken the position that a foreign broker-dealer chosen by a foreign issuer to administer a global ESOP could rely on Rule 15a-6(a)(1) to transmit communications regarding the ESOP to, and effect transactions in the foreign issuer's securities for, U.S. employees of the foreign issuer or its U.S. subsidiary. Specifically, a foreign broker-dealer that administers or seeks to administer an ESOP or other plan that is an "employee benefit plan" as defined in 17 C.F.R. § 230.405, and that is established and administered in accordance with foreign law for a foreign issuer that is organized outside the United States and whose principal office and place of business are located outside of the United States would not, solely because of that activity, be considered to have solicited the U.S. employees or U.S. subsidiary, provided that the foreign broker-dealer:

- Deals exclusively with management and employee benefit representatives from the foreign issuer (so long as such persons are not located within the United States) in administering the plan; and
- Limits its activities with respect to U.S. persons to the following activities:

  1. Facilitating the transfer of the foreign issuer's securities to a U.S. person employed by the foreign issuer or its U.S. subsidiary,
  2. Sending required plan documents, account statements, confirmations, privacy notices, prospectuses, proxy statements or other legally required documents to the employee, and
  3. Selling, transferring, or otherwise disposing of the foreign issuer's securities, in each case so long as the activities described in (1) through (3) relate solely to foreign securities acquired by U.S. persons pursuant to the applicable employee benefit plan.

The SEC stated:

> The staff would not consider such conduct to involve the solicitation of a U.S. person even if the foreign broker-dealer actively solicits the foreign issuer as part of its efforts to become a plan administrator, so long as the foreign broker-dealer's active solicitation is performed entirely outside the U.S. and does not involve employees of the company who are located within the U.S.
>
> By contrast, the staff likely would consider a foreign broker-dealer that went beyond the circumstances described in this FAQ as having solicited a U.S. person. As the SEC explained when adopting Rule 15a-6, "the deliberate transmission of information, opinions, or recommendations to investors in the United States, whether directed at individuals or groups, could result in the conclusion that the foreign broker-dealer has solicited those investors."

> Finally, to the extent the foreign broker-dealer is unable to rely on Rule 15a-6(a)(1) for these purposes, it would not be precluded from relying on any other applicable exemption from broker-dealer registration, such as Rule 15a-6(a)(4)(iii), which permits foreign broker-dealers to effect transactions with a foreign person temporarily present in the U.S., with whom the foreign broker-dealer had a bona fide, pre-existing relationship before the foreign person entered the U.S.[14]

A foreign broker-dealer may engage in these activities in its capacity as administrator of a foreign issuer's employee benefit plan and in accordance with the terms and conditions of the plan.

For example, if a foreign issuer carries out a rights offering that is made available to all shareholders (including any employees holding shares pursuant to the terms and conditions of an employee benefit plan), the issuer (or its designee/service provider) would likely send all documents and instructions related to the rights offering to the foreign broker-dealer in its capacity as administrator, particularly if the foreign broker-dealer holds securities as nominee for the employees. In that situation, the administrator may forward those materials to a U.S. employee participating in the benefit plan, receive responses from the U.S. employee, and transmit those responses back to the issuer (or its designee/service provider).

Similarly, a foreign broker-dealer serving as administrator to a foreign issuer's employee benefit plan that involves options may receive and pass along requests from U.S. employees to exercise their options. In addition, a foreign broker-dealer, as administrator of the plan and/or holder of record of the applicable security, may transmit proxy materials, voting instruction forms, and any other similar documents and instructions to a U.S. plan participant. It also may receive instructions and responses back from the U.S. plan participant and act in accordance with those instructions.

It is important to emphasize, however, that under each of the examples described above (and any other scenarios that follow the same pattern), the foreign broker-dealer's actions must be passive in nature, involve no other indicia of solicitation, and be taken only in accordance with the terms and conditions of the foreign issuer's employee benefit plan or supplemental plan (e.g., the rights offering).

Websites

Although a transaction conducted over a foreign broker-dealer's website ordinarily would be considered a solicited transaction for purposes of Rule 15a-6(a)(1), the staff does not believe that it would be inconsistent with any prior SEC statement if, solely for the limited purpose of acting as the administrator of a foreign issuer's employee

---

[14] SEC, *Frequently Asked Questions Regarding Rule 15a-6 and Foreign Broker-Dealers* (Apr. 14, 2014), https://www.sec.gov/divisions/marketreg/faq-15a-6-foreign-bd.htm

benefit plan, a foreign broker-dealer made available to all participating employees (including U.S. persons) a password-protected website to manage their accounts. This position is conditioned on

- The foreign broker-dealer not otherwise using the website to solicit securities transactions from U.S. persons, or to effect transactions in any securities that were not received in connection with the U.S. employee's participation in the employee benefit plan;
- The employee benefit plan website being wholly-separate from, and not accessible via a link contained on, the foreign broker-dealer's primary website; and
- The plan website not linking or otherwise referring plan participants to the foreign broker-dealer's primary website.

Electronic Quotation System

The SEC has provided some guidance on the feasibility of an unregistered, foreign broker-dealer offering quotation services to U.S. investors. Specifically, the Adopting Release stated:

> The Commission generally would permit the U.S. distribution of foreign broker-dealers' quotations by third-party systems, e.g., systems operated by foreign marketplaces or by private vendors, that distributed these quotations primarily in foreign countries.... The Commission's position, however, would apply only to third-party systems that did not allow securities transactions to be executed between the foreign broker-dealer and persons in the United States through the systems. In addition, foreign broker-dealers whose quotes were distributed through the systems would not be allowed to initiate contacts with U.S. persons, beyond those exempted under the Rule, without registration or further rulemaking.[15]

The provision of a third party quotation system does not include the operation of a website for a broker-dealer. Except as noted below in a no-action letter, the SEC does not generally permit the use by U.S. investors of any electronic or Web-based services of unregistered broker-dealers.

By a way of no-action letter,[16] the SEC staff liberalized its traditional stance that third-party quotation systems that distribute foreign broker-dealers' quotations must do so "primarily in foreign countries" if they do not want to be viewed as engaged in a form of solicitation to U.S. investors.[17] In doing so, the SEC staff stated:

---

[15] 54 *Federal Register* 30013, 30018 (July 18, 1989) (the Release adopting Rule 15a-6). This position was liberalized somewhat with respect to institutional customers as a result of a Division of Market Regulation No Action Letter discussed later.

[16] Cleary Gottlieb No-Action Letter, 1997 WL 1777550 (Apr. 9, 1997).

[17] 54 *Federal Register* 30013, 30018 (July 18, 1989).

> The staff is confirming that providing U.S. investors with access to screen-based quotation systems that supply quotations, prices and other trade-reporting information input directly by the foreign broker-dealers will not constitute an impermissible contact with a foreign broker-dealer, so long as any transactions between the U.S. investor and the foreign broker-dealer are intermediated in accordance with the requirements of Rule 15a-6. As you note, a foreign broker-dealer that directs quotations to U.S. investors through a proprietary system (as distinct from a third party system) would be viewed as having solicited any resulting transactions and thus could not rely on the exemption in paragraph (a)(1) of Rule 15a-6, although it would continue to be allowed to effect transactions in reliance on other available provisions of the Rule.[18]

In light of the Cleary Gottlieb No-Action Letter, the SEC apparently now allows foreign broker-dealers to provide major U.S. institutional investors and institutional investors with assets of greater than $100 million with access to screen-based quotation systems that supply quotations, prices, and other trade-reporting information input directly by foreign broker-dealers. Furthermore, such contacts would not constitute an impermissible contact with the foreign broker-dealer, provided a SEC-registered broker-dealer intermediates the transactions between the U.S. investor and the foreign broker-dealer in compliance with Rule 15a-6. Thus, it logically follows that unregistered broker-dealers could provide U.S. institutional investors access to its quotations, prices and other trade reporting information as long as the registered broker-dealer intermediates the contacts in accordance with Rule 15a-6.[19]

In order to "intermediate" the quotation services, an affiliated broker-dealer may, therefore, provide such services through a "hot link" on its website that it supervises in accordance with FINRA Rule 2210, *Communications with the Public*, and Rule 3110, *Supervision*. Intermediated transactions may occur regardless of whether the foreign broker-dealer gives the U.S. investor direct access to a proprietary quotation system, although the SEC would regard a foreign broker-dealer that directs quotations to U.S. investors as having solicited any resulting transactions.[20]

Institutional Investors

The institutional investor exemptions are based upon the notion that such investors do not need the protections afforded under the U.S. broker-dealer regulations applicable to registered firms. Rule 15a-6 defines the various institutional investors. Furthermore, an SEC no-action letter expanded the definition of "major U.S. institutional investor" to encompass any entity, including an investment adviser,

---

[18] Cleary Gottlieb No-Action Letter, 1997 WL 177550 (Apr. 9, 1997), at 12.

[19] These accommodations do not, however, extend to noninstitutional investors because the context of the no-action letter only addressed matters relating to institutional investors.

[20] Cleary Gottlieb No-Action Letter, 1997 WL 177550 (Apr. 9, 1997), at 12.

that owns or controls in excess of $100 million in aggregate financial assets.[21] The expanded definition applies to both subsections (a)(2) and (a)(3) of Rule 15a-6.[22] This regulatory position now permits U.S.-affiliated foreign dealers to enter into transactions and have direct contacts on the same basis as allowed for those "major U.S. institutional investors" with:

- Business associations, partnerships and other entities that meet the minimum asset requirement; and
- Registered and unregistered investment advisers with assets under management in excess of the minimum threshold.[23]

The institutional investor exemptions are contained in Rule 15a-6(a)(2) and (3). These provisions are mutually exclusive.

Indirect Contacts

By way of summary, the first institutional investor exemption pertains *only* to major U.S. institutional investors and contains the following requirements:

- The research reports *do not* recommend the use of the foreign broker-dealer;
- The foreign broker-dealer *does not* initiate contact with those major U.S. institutional investors to follow up on the research reports, and *does not* induce or attempt to induce the purchase or sale of any security by those major U.S. institutional investors;
- If the foreign broker-dealer has a relationship with a U.S. registered broker-dealer in conformity with this rule provision (a)(3), any transactions in those securities contained in the research report must be effected *only* through that registered broker-dealer; and
- The foreign broker or dealer *does not* provide research to U.S. persons pursuant to any express or implied understanding that those U.S. persons will direct commissions to the foreign broker or dealer.[24]

In 2003, the SEC passed Regulation Analyst Certification ("Regulation AC") that requires that brokers, dealers, and their associated persons that are "covered persons" that publish, circulate, or provide research reports include in those research reports:

> (A) a statement by the research analyst (or analysts) certifying that the views expressed in the research report accurately reflect such research analyst's personal views about the subject securities and issuers; and

---

[21] Cleary Gottlieb No-Action Letter, 1997 WL 177550, p. 9 (Apr. 9, 1997), at 9.

[22] Cleary Gottlieb No-Action Letter, 1997 WL 219905 (Apr. 28, 1997).

[23] Cleary Gottlieb No-Action Letter , 1997 WL 177550, p. 9 (Apr. 9, 1997),at 9.

[24] This provision also prohibits any soft-dollar arrangement as defined in the Exchange Act. *See* 54 *Federal Register* 30013, 30023 (July 18, 1989). (The SEC "emphasize[d]" that even "implied" soft-dollar arrangements constitute solicitation.)

(B) a statement by the research analyst (or analysts) certifying either:

(1) that no part of his or her compensation was, is, or will be directly or indirectly related to the specific recommendations or views contained in the research report; or
(2) that part or all of his or her compensation was, is, or will be directly or indirectly related to the specific recommendations or views contained in the research report. If the analyst's compensation was, is, or will be directly or indirectly related to the specific recommendations or views contained in the research report, the statement must include the source, amount, and purpose of such compensation, and further disclose that it may influence the recommendation in the research report.

Rule 502 of Regulation AC would apply to public appearances made while the research analyst is physically present in the United States, if there is a corresponding research report that was published, circulated, or provided to a U.S. person in the United States.[25] Moreover, a U.S-registered broker-dealer may not distribute research prepared by its non-U.S.-registered broker-dealer without the certifications required by Regulation AC, unless an exemption to Regulation AC applies. Additionally, the website of the non-U.S. broker-dealer mus t have password protection features to limit who has access to the research report.[26]

In 2008, FINRA published in its Regulatory Notice 08-15, that foreign research analysts are exempt from the research analyst qualification examination per NASD Rule 1050.

NASD Rule 1050 states, in pertinent part:

(G) A member that distributes non-member foreign affiliate research reports that are clearly and prominently labeled as such must comply with the third-party research report requirements in FINRA 2241(h).

(H) For the purposes of the exemption in paragraph (f), the terms "affiliate," "globally branded research report," and "mixed-team research report" shall have the following meanings:

(i) "Affiliate" shall mean a person that directly or indirectly controls, is controlled by, or is under common control with, a member.
(ii) "Globally branded research report" refers to the use of a single marketing identity that encompasses the member and one or more of its affiliates.
(iii) "Mixed-team research report" refers to any member research report that is not globally branded and includes a contribution by a research analyst who is not an associated person of the member.

---

25 Division of Market Regulation, Responses to Frequently Asked Questions Concerning Regulation Analyst Certification (Apr. 26, 2005), Q&A 21.

26 Division of Market Regulation, Responses, Q&A 27.

The requirements of NASD Rule 1050(a) do not apply to an associated person who:

- Is an employee of a non-member foreign affiliate of a member firm ("foreign research analyst");
- Resides outside the United States; and
- Contributes, partially or entirely, to the preparation of "globally branded" or foreign affiliate research reports, but does not contribute to the preparation of a member's research, including a "mixed-team" report, that is not globally branded.

Broker-dealers that publish or otherwise distribute globally branded research reports partially or entirely prepared by a foreign research analyst must still have a registered principal or supervisory analyst review and approve such research prior to use and ensure that it complies with FINRA Rule 2241.

FINRA Rule 2241 codified in substantial part the principles of Regulation AC, which provides that the U.S. registered broker-dealer must develop written policies and procedures reasonably designed:

- To promote objective and reliable research that reflects the truly held opinions of research analysts; and
- To prevent the use of research reports or research analysts to manipulate or condition the market or favor the interests of the member or a current or prospective customer or class of customers.

U.S.-registered broker-dealers must treat third-party research reports as follows:

(h) Distribution of Third-Party Research Reports

(1) Subject to paragraph (h)(5), a registered principal or supervisory analyst approved pursuant to Incorporated NYSE Rule 344 must review for compliance with the applicable provisions of paragraph (h) and approve by signature or initial all third-party research reports distributed by a member.

(2) A member may not distribute third-party research if it knows or has reason to know such research is not objective or reliable.

(3) A member must establish, maintain and enforce written policies and procedures reasonably designed to ensure that any third-party research it distributes contains no untrue statement of material fact and is otherwise not false or misleading. For the purposes of this paragraph (h)(3) only, a member's obligation to review a third-party research report extends to any untrue statement of material fact or any false or misleading information that:

(A) should be known from reading the report; or

(B) is known based on information otherwise possessed by the member.

(4) A member must accompany any third-party research report it distributes with, or provide a web address that directs a recipient to, disclosure of any material conflict of interest that can reasonably be expected to have influenced the choice of a third-party research provider or the subject company of a third-party research report, including the disclosures required by paragraphs (c)(4)(C), (c)(4)(F), (c)(4)(G) and (c)(4)(I) of this Rule.

(5) A member shall not be required to review a third-party research report to determine compliance with paragraph (h)(3) if such research report is an independent third-party research report.

(6) A member shall not be considered to have distributed a third-party research report for the purposes of paragraph (h)(4) where the research is an independent third-party research report and is made available by a member (a) upon request; (b) through a member-maintained website; or (c) to a customer in connection with a solicited order in which the registered representative has informed the customer, during the solicitation, of the availability of independent research on the solicited equity security and the customer requests such independent research.

(7) A member must ensure that a third-party research report is clearly labeled as such and that there is no confusion on the part of the recipient as to the person or entity that prepared the research report. [Cite]

Miscellaneous Requirements/Regulations Regarding Research Reports

Some additional requirements apply to unregistered non-U.S. broker-dealers.

No Recommendations. Unregistered non-U.S. broker-dealers' research reports may not suggest that a U.S. institutional investor or U.S. customers generally use the unregistered broker-dealers for its securities services. The requirement is fact-sensitive and would require a review of the content of the research report. Aside from the absence of such suggestive language in a research report, another way to provide additional protection in this respect would be to place an appropriate disclosure to the effect that the research is complimentary and that the investor should use the services of a registered broker-dealer to purchase or sell the securities contemplated by the research. However, the registered broker-dealer can, in turn, trade with the unregistered broker-dealer pursuant to Rule 15a-6(a)(4)(i).

No Initiation of Contact. Second, unregistered non-U.S. broker-dealers may *not* initiate contact with major institutional investors who were the recipients of research reports *or* otherwise solicit those major institutional investors. This requirement warrants consideration of the solicitation analysis described above, specifically including the discussion of the website being presumably considered a solicitation absent a demonstration of "adequate measures" to protect against the use of the website by U.S. customers. Regardless of whether there is any direct follow-up contact with the recipients of the research reports, the website could be considered a solicitation/inducement. Once again, at a minimum, an unregistered broker-dealer would be required to have a prominent disclaimer on its website and should otherwise have adequate procedures designed to preclude the offering of its web-based brokerage services to major institutional investors that receive research reports.

Use of SEC-Registered Broker-Dealer. Third, any resulting transactions in U.S. securities stemming from the non-U.S. broker-dealer's research report should be placed through the SEC-registered broker-dealer.[27] The U.S. broker-dealer can trade directly with the non-U.S. broker-dealer, as permitted by Rule 15a-6. Depending upon whether such securities are U.S. or foreign securities, and depending upon the custodial relationship of the selling firm, several operational issues may affect the trading, delivery, clearance, and settlement processes.

The Adopting Release confirms that if an unregistered broker-dealer already has used the services of a broker-dealer registered with the SEC, then it must continue to use those services offered by the SEC registered broker-dealer:

> If, however, the foreign broker-dealer *already had* a relationship with a registered broker-dealer that facilitated compliance with the direct contact exemption in the Rule, the Rule would require all trades resulting from the provision of research to be effected through that registered broker-dealer pursuant to the provisions of that exemption [(a)(3)]. If the foreign broker-dealer had entered into this prior relationship, the procedures for identifying trades from major U.S. institutional investors and routing them through the registered broker-dealer largely would have been established. Thus, the benefits of a registered broker-dealer's intermediation in effecting trades would not be provided without imposing substantial additional costs.[28]

No Compensation Agreements. Fourth, unregistered broker-dealers may not receive brokerage compensation as a *quid pro quo* of its providing U.S. investors with research services. An unregistered broker-dealer cannot provide research services with the

[27] 54 *Federal Register* 30013, 30023, 3024 (July 18, 1989). ("The Rule as adopted allows a foreign broker-dealer to contact U.S. institutional investors if an associated person of a registered broker-dealer participates in each of these contacts. The Rule also allows a foreign broker-dealer to contact major U.S. institutional investors without participation of an associated person of a registered broker-dealer in any of these contacts. In each case, any resulting transactions must be effected through an intermediary registered broker-dealer, [footnote omitted] which need not be affiliated with the foreign broker-dealer through ownership or control....The Commission has determined to continue to require the intermediation of a registered broker-dealer, [footnote omitted] to address concerns regarding financial responsibility and effective enforcement of the U.S. securities laws. The Rule does not require, however, any affiliation between the foreign broker-dealer and the registered broker-dealer through ownership or control.")

[28] 54 *Federal Register,* 30022.

understanding that it will receive (transaction-based) compensation in exchange for the research services.[29]

Direct Contacts

By way of summary, the second institutional investor exemption, contained in Rule 15a-6(a)(3), pertains to U.S. institutional investors independent of the provision of research reports. It contains, *inter alia*, the following requirements:

- The foreign broker or dealer effects securities transactions through an SEC-registered broker-dealer and agrees to provide the SEC with required information, documents, testimony, and cooperation;
- The foreign associated person conducts *all* securities activities from outside the U.S., except for visits, provided that
  - The foreign associated person is accompanied by an associated person of a registered broker-dealer that accepts responsibility for all such communications (also known as the "chaperoning requirement"),
  - Transactions occurring as a result of such visits take place only through the SEC-registered broker-dealer, and
  - The broker-dealer is not subject to specified regulatory and criminal actions;
- The registered broker-dealer through which the transactions occur is exclusively responsible for, unless otherwise indicated
  - Securities executions,[30]
  - Issuing all required confirmations and statements,
  - Granting credit,
  - Maintaining the required books and records (in addition to the requirement pertaining to the foreign broker-dealer), and
  - Complying with the customer protection rules;
- The registered broker-dealer participates in all communications between the foreign broker-dealer and foreign associated person and the nonmajor U.S. institutional investor; and
- The registered broker-dealer otherwise complies with various recordkeeping, information-gathering, and service of process requirements.

---

[29] 54 *Federal Register,* 30023. ("The Commission wishes to emphasize, however, that neither the exemption nor this position regarding research [contained in section (a)(2)] is applicable with respect to "soft-dollar" arrangements between the foreign broker-dealer and U.S. persons (citing section paragraph (a)(2)(iv) of the exemption)....If a foreign broker-dealer provided research to a U.S. investor pursuant to an express or implied understanding that the investor would direct a given amount of Commission income to the foreign broker-dealer, the Commission would consider the foreign broker-dealer to have induced purchases and sales of securities, irrespective of whether the trades received from the investor related to the particular research that had been provided.")

[30] The SEC registered broker-dealer would be responsible for the compliance with the Exchange Act of the rules and regulations of its SRO, including the NASD Interpretative Material for the Suitability Rule for Institutional Customers, IM-2310—3. Notably, the NASD Institutional Suitability Rule has been renumbered and incorporated into the FINRA Rulebook, but still applies in this context.

An introducing broker-dealer cannot rely on the Rule 15c3–3(k)(2)(i) exception and maintain net capital of $100,000 while acting as a chaperone for a foreign broker-dealer under Rule 15a-6(a)(3) and relying on the Nine Firms Letter.[31] A registered broker-dealer that enters into a chaperoning arrangement with a foreign broker-dealer under Rule 15a-6(a)(3) is subject to a minimum net capital requirement of at least $250,000, unless the chaperoning broker-dealer has entered into a fully disclosed carrying agreement with another registered broker-dealer that has agreed, in writing, to comply with the SEC's broker-dealer financial responsibility rules with respect to the chaperoning arrangement. A broker-dealer that maintains minimum net capital of at least $250,000 and relies on the Rule 15c3-3(k)(2)(i) exception or a broker-dealer that is fully computing under Rule 15c3-3 may operate under the Nine Firms Letter. This net capital requirement is based on the chaperone's responsibilities under Rule 15a-6(a)(3)(iii).[32]

Firms that provide research into the United States, whether through websites or other media, should adopt effective internal controls designed to prevent transactions with U.S. persons.[33] Such sites should have disclosures that

- Affirmatively delineate the countries in which the broker-dealer's services are available or stating that the services are not available to U.S. persons; and
- Refuse to offer services to potential customers that the broker-dealer has reason to believe is a U.S. person.

Non-U.S. broker-dealers that are associated with a U.S.-registered broker-dealer must comply with Regulation AC, whereas non-U.S. broker-dealers that are not associated with a U.S.-registered broker-dealer must comply with Rule 15a-6(a)(2) in order to furnish research to major U.S. institutional investors. Firms without U.S.-registered affiliates may also rely on the exemption contained in Rule 503 of Regulation AC regarding the distribution of research reports covering non-U.S. securities.[34]

Use of an SEC-Registered Broker-Dealer

This discussion examines requirements for use of broker-dealers registered with the SEC.

Registered Broker-Dealer Responsible for Compliance. By the terms of the Rule 15a-6, unregistered non-U.S. broker-dealers must effect all institutional securities business through an affiliated or independent SEC-registered broker-dealer. The

---

[31] SEC letter to Giovanni P. Prezioso, Esq., Cleary, Gottlieb, Steen & Hamilton, 1752 N Street, N.W., Washington, D.C. 20036-2806 (Apr. 9, 1997). The Firms are Bear Stearns & Co. Inc.; Credit Suisse First Boston Corporation; CSFP Capital, Inc.; Goldman, Sachs & Co.; Lehman Brothers Inc.; Merrill Lynch, Pierce, Fenner & Smith, Incorporated; Morgan Stanley & Co. Incorporated; Salomon Brothers Inc; and Smith Barney Inc.

[32] SEC, Frequently Asked Questions Regarding Rule 15a-6 and Foreign Broker-Dealers, Q&A 13 (Apr. 14,2014), https://www.sec.gov/divisions/marketreg/faq-15a-6-foreign-bd.htm

[33] *See*, e.g., Division of Market Regulation, Responses to Frequently Asked Questions Concerning Regulation Analyst Certification (Apr. 26, 2005).

[34] Division of Market Regulation, Responses, at Q&A 20.

SEC-registered broker-dealer would be required to comply with certain operational requirements stipulated in the above excerpt from Rule 15a-6. Virtually all communications would have to be "chaperoned" by the SEC-registered broker-dealer. The registered principal of the SEC-registered broker-dealer must be familiar with the research reports, approve the material pursuant to FINRA rules, and ascertain whether the foreign associated person's statements are consistent with the foreign broker-dealer's current recommendations.[35] In essence, the registered broker-dealer is responsible for enforcing compliance with the federal and state securities laws by the foreign broker-dealer.[36]

With respect to establishing a relationship with a SEC registered broker-dealer, such a strategic arrangement can expand the very limited role that a foreign broker-dealer may take in the U.S. securities business. Any registered broker-dealer can serve as the registered broker-dealer that, if available, is a condition precedent to availing the foreign broker-dealer of the exemption contained in Rule 15a-6(a)(3). The foreign broker-dealer that seeks to rely on Rule 15a-6(a)(3) must enter into an arrangement with any existing SEC-registered broker-dealer or revitalize a previous arrangement, provided the respective participants have effectuated the necessary compliance procedures.[37] The associated SEC-registered broker-dealer may, but does *not* need to be, an affiliate of the foreign broker-dealer and may be located in the foreign broker-dealer's country.[38]

Clearance and Settlement Functions. The Cleary Gottlieb No-Action Letter also eliminated the operational duplication and complexity caused by interposing the U.S. broker-dealer in the clearance and settlement process for foreign and U.S. government securities.[39] The expanded clearance and settlement functions only apply to circumstances when the foreign broker-dealer agrees to make available to the intermediating U.S. broker-dealer clearance and settlement information relating to such transfers, and the foreign broker-dealer is not in default to any counterparty on any material financial transaction.[40] The no-action letter did not change the obligation of the foreign broker-dealer to ensure that each transaction or custodial arrangement qualifies in all other respects with Rule 15a-6.[41] The foreign broker-dealer may *not* serve as the custodian of funds or securities for U.S. However, the SEC may grant an exception to the custodian limitations placed upon such foreign broker-dealer through a no-action letter [42] or

---

[35] 54 *Federal Register* 30013, 30028, n. 179 (July 18, 1989). *See also* NASD Rules 2210 and 3010.

[36] 54 *Federal Register* 30013, 30025 (July 18, 1989). *See also,* e.g., NASD Rule 3010.

[37] 54 *Federal Register* at §9-29 (citing Adopting Release at text accompanying 54 *Federal Register* 30013, 3026 nn. 154-5 (July 128, 1989) and the requirement that the associated broker-dealer may not be a bank, even if the bank is acting in a broker-dealer capacity).

[38] See 54 *Federal Register* 30013, 30023, 30024 (July 18, 1989).

[39] Cleary Gottlieb No-Action Letter 1997 WL 17750, p. 10 (Apr. 9, 1997).

[40] *Id.*

[41] *Id.*

[42] *See,* e.g., Morgan Stanley India Securities Pvt. Ld., SEC No-Action Letter, 1996 WL 762988 (Dec. 20, 1996). (The SEC staff granted a broker-dealer the authority to effect the settlement of transactions in foreign securities for U.S. institutional customers through a foreign custodian affiliated with the broker-dealer, where the foreign law required that the securities be held in custody abroad. The letter also had application for record keeping and IT platform purposes.)

through the SEC's approval process for "satisfactory control locations" pursuant to SEC Rule 15c3-3. Some countries, for example, do not have omnibus account registration, requiring all securities registrations to be in the customer's name only. These difference can create challenges with the pledging and net capital issues related to establishing a "good control location."

Location of Business Must be Outside of United States. All securities activities must occur from outside of the United States., except for visits. The exemptive rule provisions summarized above indicate that, except for chaperoned visits, *all* securities activities of the foreign associated person must be performed from outside the country. It does not suggest that only some of the activities of a foreign broker-dealer with offices in the United States may be performed without having to register. The rule is fully encompassing. In addition, physical presence certainly constitutes something in excess of a "visit." Physical presence of a non-U.S. broker-dealer in the United States requires registration of the entire firm.[43]

In 1988, the Proposing Release stated:

> Sale of Securities to Foreign Persons...The staff's [of the Division of Market Regulation of the SEC] position regarding the application of the broker-dealer registration provisions to foreign broker-dealers trading with foreign customers is dependent on the trading taking place outside the United States. The staff believes that foreign persons resident in this country should receive the same broker-dealer protections as any other U.S. resident, and accordingly, the staff recommends that the Commission apply section 15(a) requirements to foreign broker-dealers trading with foreign persons in the United States.[44]

In 1989, the Adopting Release also briefly referenced that a territorial presence in the United States requires registration:

> In addition to requiring broker-dealer operations physically located within the United States to register, the Commission's territorial approach generally would require broker-dealer registration by foreign

---

[43] *See*, e.g., 54 *Federal Register* 30013, 30017 (July 18, 1989). ("[T]he Commission uses an entity approach with respect to registered broker-dealers. Under this approach, if a foreign broker-dealer physically operates a branch in the United States, and thus becomes subject to U.S. registration requirements, the registration requirements and the regulatory system governing U.S. broker-dealers would apply to the entire foreign broker-dealer entity. If the foreign broker-dealer establishes an affiliate in the United States, however, only the affiliate must be registered as a broker-dealer; the foreign broker-dealer parent would not be required to register [footnote omitted]. Under this arrangement, absent exemptions, only the registered U.S. affiliate would be authorized to trade with any person in the United States or perform securities functions on behalf of those customers, such as effecting trades, extending credit, maintaining records and issuing confirmations, and receiving, delivering, and safeguarding funds and securities [footnote omitted].")

[44] 53 *Federal Register* 23645, 23649 (June 23, 1988).

> broker-dealers that, from outside the United States, induce or attempt to induce trades by any person in the United States [footnote omitted].[45]

In light of the foregoing, regardless of which provision of Rule 15a-6 a broker-dealer seeks to use, it cannot have U.S.-based broker-dealer operations without being registered. Rule 15a-6 confirms this conclusion by virtue of its definition of a foreign broker-dealer. Specifically, the rule states:

> The term "foreign broker or dealer" shall mean any non-U.S. resident person (including any U.S. person engaged in business as a broker or dealer entirely outside the United States, except as otherwise permitted by this rule) that is not an office or branch of, or a natural person associated with, a registered broker or dealer, whose securities activities, if conducted in the United States, would be the definition of "broker" or "dealer" in sections 3(a)(4) and 3(a)(5) of the [Exchange Act].

Given the mutual exclusivity of the definition, unregistered broker-dealers must either be considered a U.S. broker-dealer or a foreign broker-dealer. If the broker-dealer is not a U.S. broker-dealer, then it must be a foreign broker-dealer. If the unregistered broker-dealer is a foreign broker-dealer, then Rule 15a-6 specifies some defining boundaries concerning how it must be structured. Specifically, it must be a "non-U.S. resident" person (which is defined to include various companies) that is not an office or branch of, or associated natural person of an SEC-registered broker-dealer, whose securities activities would fall with the Exchange Act definition of "broker" or "dealer" if conducted in the United States. Thus, unregistered broker-dealers may neither be a U.S. resident, nor may it be a branch of a SEC-registered broker-dealer.

The Internet Release affirmed this requirement:

> Broker-dealers must register with the [SEC] if they are physically present in the United States, or if, regardless of their location, they effect, induce, or attempt to induce securities transactions with investors in the United States. The issue, therefore, is whether the [SEC] would deem a broker-dealer's Web site to be an attempt to induce securities transactions with U.S. persons.

The Division of Market Regulation of the SEC published a compliance guide, wherein it stated:

> The SEC generally uses a territorial approach in applying registration requirements to the international operations of broker-dealers. Under this approach, all broker-dealers physically operating within the U.S. that induce or attempt to induce securities transactions must register, even if their activities are directed only to foreign investors outside the

[45] 54 *Federal Register* 30013, 30017 (July 18, 1989).

> U.S. In addition, foreign broker-dealers that, from outside the U.S., induce or attempt to induce trades by any person in the U.S. also must register. However, foreign broker-dealers may be exempt from U.S. broker-dealer registration if they meet the conditions of Rule 15a-6 under the [Exchange Act].[46]

An SEC no-action letter liberalized the extent to which foreign broker-dealers may have direct contacts with all U.S. institutional investors, by authorizing certain first time direct contacts between non-U.S. broker-dealers and "nonmajor" U.S. institutional investors.[47] The no-action letter also enabled foreign associated persons employed by U.S.-affiliated foreign dealers to engage in direct, "unchaperoned" oral communications from outside the United States with U.S. institutional investors when such communications take place outside of the trading hours of the New York Stock Exchange.[48] However, the foreign associated persons may not accept securities orders given during such contacts, except for those pertaining to certain foreign securities.

In addition to contacts originating from outside the U.S., the no-action letter also authorized foreign associated persons to have unchaperoned in-person contacts during visits to the United States with "major U.S. institutional investors," provided the number of days in which such in-person contacts occur does not exceed 30 per year and the respective foreign associated person engaged in such in-person contacts does not accept orders for securities transactions while in the United States.[49] The SEC also clarified the limitations associated with the foreign broker-dealer initiating certain follow up contacts with "major U.S. institutional investors" to which it has furnished research reports.[50]

Several international broker-dealer organizations have U.S. affiliates, which they either wholly own or own through an affiliated network or joint venture agreements with other international firms that need a U.S.-registered affiliated broker-dealer. In those cases, the foreign unregistered entities can use personnel that are employees both of the foreign broker-dealer and of the U.S. registered broker-dealer ("dual employees") in contacts with U.S. customers. The Rule 15a-6 Adopting Release contemplated and permitted this approach, provided the dual employees were "subject to the registered broker-dealer's supervision and control and satisfied all U.S. SRO qualification standards and were stationed outside the United States." Such persons would be subject to the supervision, books and records and market conducts rules of FINRA.

The SEC does not, however, permit such a dual employee approach where the foreign broker-dealer has its associated persons serving as U.S. resident dual employees.[51]

---

46 SEC Division of Market Regulation, Compliance Guide to the Registration and Regulation of Brokers and Dealers (Oct. 1998), at 6.

47 Cleary Gottlieb No-Action Letter, 1997 WL 177550, (Apr. 9, 1997), at 11.

48 *Id.*

49 *Id.*

50 *Id.*

51 54 *Federal Register* 30013, 30017, n 46 (regarding the suggestion for U.S. resident dual employees).

Accordingly, such a dual employee approach does not absolve the unregistered foreign broker-dealer from its registration obligations in instances where dually associated representatives are U.S. residents. The Adopting Release only endorsed dual employees being located outside of the United States:

> Assuming these persons were subject to the registered broker-dealer's supervision and control [footnote omitted] and satisfied all U.S. SRO qualification standards, [footnote omitted] the Commission believes that it is consistent with these principals for a registered broker-dealer's registered representatives stationed outside the United States with a foreign broker-dealer to contact persons in the United States from within or without this country on behalf of the registered broker-dealer.[52]

An older, but still relevant release is NASD Notice to Members 01-81, which expounded upon the treatment of Foreign Associates, as well as other matters related to conducting business abroad.

The SEC enforcement action against CentreInvest deals with the management and recordkeeping issues related to foreign firms and their U.S. affiliates. In this case, the SEC issued a cease and desist order to CentreInvest, Inc., a New York based registered broker-dealer and an unregistered Moscow based affiliate because the SEC maintained that the New York firm referred U.S. investors to its Moscow affiliate. According to the SEC, the Moscow affiliate did not qualify for the existing Rule 15a-6 exemption because it failed to adequately maintain records relating to customer transactions. Moreover, the SEC asserted that both firms knew their operations did not meet the requirements of Rule 15a-6. The SEC also asserted that employees of these firms solicited institutional investors in the United States to purchase thinly traded stocks of Russian companies without registering as a broker-dealer or complying with Rule 15a-6. The SEC also noted that the Moscow broker had an undisclosed control relationship with the New York affiliate.

Management from Abroad. Aside from the dual employee and geographical issues addressed above, the SEC has expressed concerns about dealing activities of foreign broker-dealers carried out by the U.S. affiliate that are essentially controlled by the foreign dealer.[53] As a result, the SEC stated in the Rule 15a-6 Adopting Release that it:

> does not intend this exemption to permit the foreign broker-dealer to act as a dealer in the United States through an affiliated registered broker-dealer. The…[SEC] recognizes that dealers in foreign markets may transmit securities positions to U.S. broker-dealer affiliates after the foreign markets close, so that the U.S. affiliates can continue trading those securities. If, however, the foreign broker-dealer controlled the

---

[52] 54 *Federal Register* 30017. *See also* NASD Notice to Members 01-81.

[53] *See*, e.g., Edward F. Greene, Edward J. Rosen, Leslie N. Silverman, et al., *U.S. Regulation of the International Securities and Derivatives Markets*, Fifth Ed., Vol. 2, New York: Aspen Law & Business (2004), §9-40.

> registered broker-dealer's day-to-day market making activities by explicit restrictions on the U.S. broker-dealer's ability to execute orders against a foreign broker-dealer's positions or to take independent positions, the foreign broker-dealer could be considered a dealer subject to U.S. broker-dealer registration requirements.[54]

The SEC has also apparently expressed concern about a U.S. broker-dealer that arranged trades in U.S. securities with U.S. institutional customers, which were reflected on the books and records of the foreign broker-dealer as having been executed.[55] The SEC stated that such transactions are foreign in name only and were essentially designed to evade U.S. registration requirements, exchange fees, and other regulations.[56]

The prohibition on managing the registered broker-dealer's operations does not apply to certain foreign securities transactions. Specifically, the requirement that the associated U.S. broker-dealer effects the transactions may be delegated to the qualifying foreign broker-dealer in the case of the physical execution of foreign securities traded in foreign markets on foreign exchanges.[57]

As previously stated, Rule 15a-6 permits registered U.S. broker-dealers and unregistered foreign broker-dealers, whether affiliated or not, to trade with each other. Furthermore, although the foreign broker-dealer is not permitted to control the day-to-day activities of the U.S. broker-dealer,[58] the foreign broker-dealer may have non-U.S.-resident dual employees. The dual employees would be associated with both the unregistered foreign broker-dealer and the U.S.-registered broker-dealer, provided the dual employees are subject to the supervision and control of the U.S. broker-dealer and otherwise are in compliance with the U.S. "qualification standards" and are "stationed outside the United States." [59]

Compensation Considerations. Unregistered broker-dealers may not receive transaction-based or fee-based compensation for securities activities requiring registration with the SEC. Compensation to dual employees for U.S. trades must be "trackable" to trades appearing on the "blotter" of the SEC-registered broker-dealer. Because trades appear on the blotter of the U.S broker-dealer, the U.S. broker-dealer will receive payment for the securities transactions. The registered broker-dealer may not pass those

---

[54] *U.S. Regulation,* Fifth Ed. (citing Rule 15a-6 Adopting Release at text accompanying 54 *Federal Register* 30013, 30030 n 205 (July 18, 1989).

[55] *U.S. Regulation,* Fifth Ed. (citing SEC Rel. No. 34-30920, Part III.B (July 14, 1992)). *See also* Vickers da Costa Rica Securities, Inc. citing in Adopting Release at 54 *Federal Register* 30013, 30030 n. 205.

[56] *Id.*

[57] 54 *Federal Register* 30013, 30025 n. 150 (July 18, 1989). In addition, pursuant to the Cleary Gottlieb No-Action Letter, transactions involving foreign securities or U.S. government securities effected in reliance of §15a-6(a)(3) may now be cleared and settled through the direct transfer of funds and securities between the U.S. investor and the foreign-broker, provided the foreign broker-dealer is not acting as the custodian of funds or securities.

[58] Vickers da Costa Securities, Inc. (citing in Adopting Release at 54 *Federal Register* 30013, 30030 n. 205 (July 18, 1989).

[59] *Adopting Release at text accompanying 54 Federal Register* 30013, 30017 nn.47-8 (July 18, 1989*). See* also NASD Notice to Members 01-81.

commissions or other forms of compensation through to the unregistered firm, but may pay the fees of the unregistered firm for broker-dealer services provided to the registered firm. Thus, in accordance with Rule 15a-6, an unregistered broker-dealer may trade with a registered broker-dealer, paying any commissions, mark ups or mark downs that the unregistered firm may charge the registered firm for buying or selling foreign securities.

FINRA Rule 2040 generally provides that a registered broker-dealer or its associated person may not, directly or indirectly, pay any compensation, fees, concessions, discounts, commissions or other allowances to any person that is not registered as a broker-dealer under Section 15(a) of the Securities Exchange Act of 1934, as amended. This prohibition provides an exemption from this restriction for certain foreign finders (as also contemplated in NASD NTM 01-81):

> (c) Nonregistered Foreign Finders
>
> A member may pay to a nonregistered foreign person (the "finder") transaction-related compensation based upon the business of customers the finder directs to the member if the following conditions are met:
>
> (1) the member has assured itself that the finder who will receive the compensation is not required to register in the United States as a broker-dealer nor is subject to a disqualification as defined in Article III, Section 4 of FINRA's By-Laws, and has further assured itself that the compensation arrangement does not violate applicable foreign law;
> (2) the finder is a foreign national (not a U.S. citizen) or foreign entity domiciled abroad;
> (3) the customers are foreign nationals (not U.S. citizens) or foreign entities domiciled abroad transacting business in either foreign or U.S. securities;
> (4) customers receive a descriptive document, similar to that required by Rule 206(4)-3(b) of the Investment Advisers Act, that discloses what compensation is being paid to finders;
> (5) customers provide written acknowledgment to the member of the existence of the compensation arrangement and such acknowledgment is retained and made available for inspection by FINRA;
> (6) records reflecting payments to finders are maintained on the member's books, and actual agreements between the member and the finder are available for inspection by FINRA; and
> (7) the confirmation of each transaction indicates that a referral or finder's fee is being paid pursuant to an agreement.

Additional Rule 15a-6 Regulatory Guidance

Rule 15a-6(a)(4) provides certain other exemptions. The only three exemptions that this discussion will cover include trading with an SEC-registered broker-dealer, trading with a U.S. person located abroad and trading with a foreign person temporarily present in the United States.

Trading by Unregistered Firms. Unregistered firms may trade with registered broker-dealers without triggering registration of the unregistered firm. NASD Rule 2420 prohibits unregistered broker-dealers from providing any commissions or selling concessions received from a NASD member firm to a non-NASD member firm. Thus, as discussed previously, the registered firm may not pass through commissions that the registered firm receives from a U.S. customer. The registered firm may pay the fees assessed by the unregistered firm for transactional services provided to the registered firm, provided the unregistered firm complies with Rule 15a-6 and does not use U.S. jurisdictional means.

Also, the unregistered firm may not manage the activities of the unregistered firm. In other words, the unregistered firm should defer to the judgment of the registered firm as it relates to conducting business with U.S. customers and ensuring compliance with applicable rules and regulations. NASD Notice to Members 01-81 provided guidance on conducting business abroad, which has relevance to dually associated registered representatives located abroad, on the premises of the Rule 15a-6 broker-dealer.

Trading with a U.S. Person Located Abroad. The language of the U.S. resident-abroad exemption pertains to "U.S. citizens resident outside the United States, provided the transactions occur outside the United States, and that the foreign broker or dealer does not direct its selling efforts to identifiable groups of U.S. citizens resident abroad." Thus, unregistered broker-dealers could conduct business with U.S. persons located abroad, provided unregistered broker-dealers do not solicit various identifiable groups of such investors residing abroad, such as U.S. military personnel. Additionally, if any individual with whom the foreign broker-dealer was able to permissibly provide broker-dealer services moved back to the United States, then the restrictions and parameters contemplated in Rule 15a-6 would presumably apply. Moreover, if any such "identifiable groups of U.S. citizens," or any of the individuals in that group, moved back to the United States, then logically the SEC would consider any resulting transactions as solicited (because the overseas contact to identified groups of U.S. citizens contemplated "selling efforts" being made) and also subject to the restrictions and parameters otherwise contemplated in Rule 15a-6.

Trading with Foreign Person Temporarily Present. The language of the temporarily present exemption pertains to "a foreign person temporarily present in the United States, with whom the foreign broker or dealer had a *bona fide* preexisting relationship before the foreign person entered the United States." This exemption is the classic "vacationers" or "business travelers" exemption. Notably, it refers to people being "temporarily present," not "temporary residents." Suffice it to say that once a foreign person has established his or her primarily residence in the United States, where that person spends the majority of his or her annual residential time, then this exemption would be probably be inappropriate and inapplicable.[60] The establishment of a U.S. taxable status also suggests that the presence is something other than temporary.

Notable Enforcement Actions that Effectively Demonstrate the Requirements of Rule 15a-6

This discussion summarizes Rule 15a-6 enforcement actions of note.

SEC Charges Against Credit Suisse for Unregistered Services for U.S. Clients. In February 2014 Credit Suisse agreed to wrongdoing and a $196 million settlement for administrative proceedings. The firm had provided cross-border securities services to thousands of U.S. clients. The SEC issued a press release, noting in part:

> According to the SEC's order, it was not until after a much-publicized civil and criminal investigation into similar conduct by Swiss-based UBS that Credit Suisse began to take steps in October 2008 to exit the business of providing cross-border advisory and brokerage services to U.S. clients. Although the number of U.S. client accounts decreased beginning in 2009 and the majority were closed or transferred by 2010, it took Credit Suisse until mid-2013 to completely exit the cross-border business as the firm continued to collect broker-dealer and investment adviser fees on some accounts.

The SEC's order finds that Credit Suisse willfully violated Section 15(a) of the Securities Exchange Act of 1934 and Section 203(a) of the Investment Advisers Act of 1940. Credit Suisse admitted the facts in the SEC's order, acknowledged that its conduct violated the federal securities laws, accepted a censure and a cease-and-desist

---

[60] 54 *Federal Register* 30013, 30030 (July 18, 1989). ("The Commission does not believe that it would be appropriate to establish a separate standard of residency for the purpose of claiming this exemption different from those generally established under state or federal law. [footnote omitted] As stated in [the Proposing Release], questions regarding the temporary nature of a person's presence in this country would be fact-specific. [footnote omitted]. The Commission would take the position, however, that a foreign person not otherwise deemed a resident of the United States under applicable law would be presumed to be temporarily present in this country for purposes of paragraph (a)(3) of the Rule.") *See also* 53 *Federal Register* 23645, 23649 (June 23, 1988). ("Foreign persons domiciled abroad, but who are temporarily present in this country, pose a different question. The staff is of the view that a foreign broker-dealer that solicits or engages in securities transactions with or for such persons while they are temporarily present in this country need not register with the Commission, provided that the foreign broker-dealer had a bona fide preexisting relationship with such persons before they entered the United States (footnote omitted). The status of a foreign national as a temporary visitor or a U.S. resident, of course, would be subject to factual analysis on a case-by-case basis. [Apart from concerns about broker-dealer registration, foreign broker-dealers should be careful that any offers or sales of securities made within the United States comply with the registration provisions of the Securities Act.] Nevertheless, where the foreign investors are not merely temporary visitors, the staff believes that U.S. broker-dealer registration requirements should apply to foreign entities effecting securities transactions.")

order, and agreed to retain an independent consultant. Credit Suisse agreed to pay $82,170,990 in disgorgement, $64,340,024 in prejudgment interest, and a $50 million penalty.[61]

Some of the material facts of the case and excerpts from the SEC order include:[62]

> From at least 2002 until its exit from its business of providing broker-dealer and investment adviser services to certain U.S. clients (the "U.S. cross-border securities business"), which Credit Suisse Group AG (CSAG) began in 2008, CSAG, through actions of certain of its relationship managers (RMs) violated the federal securities laws by providing certain cross-border brokerage and investment advisory services to U.S. clients. During that time, CSAG had as many as 8,500 client accounts that held securities and were beneficially owned by U.S. residents. CSAG RMs solicited and provided broker-dealer and advisory services to some of these clients. CSAG was aware that in certain instances, if its representatives provided such services in the United States or by use of the mails or through interstate commerce, this would have required U.S. broker-dealer and investment adviser registration and that CSAG was not registered. CSAG realized approximately $82 million in pre-tax income through the unlawful aspects of the U.S. cross-border securities business.
>
> Certain CSAG representatives, among other things, traveled to the United States to solicit new clients and service existing clients by providing investment advice and by inducing and attempting to induce securities transactions. In connection with these activities, certain CSAG representatives met with existing and prospective clients and communicated with them through email and the mails. CSAG received transaction-based compensation and advisory fees for these services. These activities required registration.
>
> CSAG understood that there was risk of violating the federal securities laws by providing broker-dealer and investment adviser services to U.S. clients. To manage and mitigate the risk that prohibited broker-dealer and investment adviser services might be provided to U.S. clients, beginning in 2002, CSAG enacted directives and policies which prohibited its representatives from engaging in the improper conduct described in the Order. These directives and policies were designed to allow the U.S. clients to be serviced in a manner consistent with the federal securities laws. Beginning in 2002, CSAG also arranged for certain of its legal and compliance staff and RMs in Switzerland with at least one U.S. client

---

61 Credit Suisse Agrees to Pay $196 Million and Admits Wrongdoing in Providing Unregistered Services to U.S. Clients, SEC Press Release 2014-39 (Feb. 21, 2014), https://www.sec.gov/news/press-release/2014-39

62 *Securities Exchange Act of 1934,* Rel. No. 71593 (Feb. 21, 2014); *Investment Advisers Act of 1940,* Rel. No. 3782 (Feb. 21, 2014), https://www.sec.gov/litigation/admin/2014/34-71593.pdf

> to be trained on the directives and policies. CSAG did not expand this training to all RMs worldwide with U.S. clients until 2008. CSAG did not effectively implement these policies and did not sufficiently monitor the U.S. cross-border securities business. As a result, violations of CSAG's policies and the federal securities laws occurred.
>
> Nonetheless, it took CSAG almost five years—from 2009 to mid-2013—to decrease the average securities assets under management in U.S. client accounts from, in the aggregate, approximately $5.75 billion in 2008 to approximately $34 million by mid-2013. CSAG continued to collect some broker-dealer and investment adviser fees on certain accounts of U.S. clients that held securities until the relevant account was terminated.

Other Notable Cases. An earlier case involved UBS, another Swiss broker-dealer. It ostensibly arose from the UBS's settlement with the IRS efforts to pursue U.S. investors that may be using offshore accounts to avid U.S. taxes. The SEC has alleged that various UBS affiliates that were not registered as broker-dealers provided brokerage and advisory services to certain of UBS's U.S. clients. These unregistered broker-dealers did not report transactions and accounts and allegedly assisted helped to structure transactions to assist investors in their illegal tax avoidance. The SEC alleged that UBS as a whole knew about these arrangements, knew that they were illegal, and covered them up.[63]

In 2012, another SEC press release noted the settlement by four India-based financial services firms—Ambit Capital Private Limited, Edelweiss Financial Services Limited, JM Financial Institutional Securities Private Limited, and Motilal Oswal Securities Limited—for their violations of the registration requirements. Those firms agreed to pay more than $1.8 million combined to settle the SEC's charges.

According to the SEC's orders against the firms, the four engaged with U.S. investors in some of the following ways despite being unregistered broker-dealers:

- Sponsored conferences in the United States;
- Had employees travel regularly to the United States to meet with investors;
- Traded securities of India-based issuers on behalf of U.S. investors; and
- Participated in securities offerings from India-based issuers to U.S. investors.[64]

III. FOREIGN ADVISERS

The regulatory landscape for foreign private investment advisers is relatively simpler because the registration threshold pertains to assets under management, the number

---

[63] *SEC v. UBS AG* Case 1:09-cv-00316 (Feb. 19, 2009), https://www.sec.gov/litigation/complaints/2009/comp20905.pdf

[64] SEC Charges Four India-Based Brokerage Firms with Violating U.S. Registration Requirements, SEC Press Release 2012-241 (Nov. 27, 2012), https://www.sec.gov/news/press-release/2012-2012-241htm

of accounts, and indications of the firm's market presence. However, the SEC may also take into consideration the firm's marketing and its operational segregation from U.S.-affiliated firms. Moreover, private fund advisers are subject to a different set of criteria. In both cases, U.S. firms with foreign adviser affiliates should be aware of how to structure and segregate operations in order to not run afoul of the investment adviser registration laws. Moreover, the SEC has provided important guidance regarding special purpose vehicles (SPVs) and the ability of a general partner or managing member to rely upon a "filing adviser," enabling the foreign adviser not to register with the SEC as an investment adviser ("relying adviser"). Those dynamics naturally introduce other operational, structural, and planning considerations in order to maintain compliance with the U.S. federal securities law.

Non-U.S. Adviser Registration Exemptions

As a result of changes established by the Dodd-Frank Act, the Investment Advisers Act of 1940, as amended,[65] provides three primary exemptions from SEC registration available to non-U.S. advisers:

- The foreign private adviser exemption;
- The private fund adviser exemption; and
- The venture capital fund exemption.

Foreign Private Adviser Exemption. Section 202(a)(30) of the Advisers Act defines a *"foreign private adviser"* as any investment adviser who—

A. Has no place of business in the United States;
B. Has, in total, fewer than 15 clients and investors in the United States in private funds advised by the investment adviser;
C. Has aggregate assets under management attributable to clients in the U.S. and investors in the U.S. in private funds advised by the investment adviser of less than $25,000,000; and
D. Neither—
    i. Holds itself out generally to the public in the United States as an investment adviser; nor
    ii. Acts as—
        I. An investment adviser to any investment company registered under the Investment Company Act of 1940; or
        II. A company that has elected to be a business development company pursuant to section 54 of the Investment Company Act of 1940 (15 U.S.C. 80a–53), and has not withdrawn its election.

---

[65] Investment Advisers Act of 1940 [As Amended Through P.L. 112-90, Approved January 3, 2012], https://www.sec.gov/about/laws/iaa40.pdf

The Advisers Act defines a "private fund" as an issuer of securities that would be an investment company but for the following exceptions:

- A fund that does not publicly offer its securities and has 100 or fewer beneficial owners of its outstanding securities (referring to Investment Company Act Section 3(c)(1));[66] and
- A fund that does not publicly offer its securities and limits its owners to qualified purchasers (referring to Investment Company Act 3(c)(7)).

"Qualified purchasers" are defined in the Investment Company Act[67] as natural persons with at least $5 million in investments (more than just securities); certain grantor trusts; and any legal person, including discretionary asset managers, who have $25 million or more in asset under management. A private fund includes a private fund that invests in other private funds. A fund organized outside the U.S. that does not market to U.S. persons (does not "use U.S. jurisdictional means") its offering generally would not be considered a "private fund" for purposes of Investment Company Act of 1940.

A "place of business" naturally includes any office where an investment adviser provides investment advisory services, solicits, meets with, or otherwise communicates with clients, but also includes any other location that an adviser holds itself out to the general public as a place where it provides these services. Offices from which an adviser conducts solely administrative and back office activities generally do not fall under this definition, assuming these activities are not intrinsic to providing investment advisory services and the adviser does not communicate with clients from such location. However, temporary offices such as a hotel or even an auditorium *may be included,* depending on the activities conducted there. The SEC explained that whether a temporary office or location is a place of business "will turn on whether the adviser representative has let it generally be known that he or she will conduct advisory business at the location, rather than on the frequency with which the adviser representative conducts advisory business there." The SEC also stated that any office from which an adviser regularly communicates with its U.S. and non-U.S. clients would be a place of business. In addition, an office or other location where an adviser regularly conducts research would be a place of business because research is intrinsic to the provision of investment advisory services.

A place of business is treated as being "in the United States" if it is treated as located in the United States as defined in Regulation S promulgated under the U.S. Securities Act of 1933, as amended (Regulation S).[68] An investor or client generally is treated as being in the United States if that investor or client is a "U.S. person" for purposes of Regulation S, except with respect to certain discretionary or similar accounts that are held for the benefit of U.S. persons by certain non-U.S. dealers or other non-U.S. professional fiduciaries.

---

66 There are look-through rules applicable to Section 3(c)(1) funds and such 100 owner threshold requires aggregating of all beneficial owners of 10 percent or more investors.

67 Investment Company Act of 1940 [As Amended Through P.L. 112-90, Approved January 3, 2012], https://www.sec.gov/about/laws/ica40.pdf

68 SEC, *Final Rule: Offshore Offers and Sales (Regulation S),* https://www.sec.gov/rules/final/33-7505.htm

However, if a person was not actually in the United States at the time the person became an investor or client (including each time that an investor in a private fund acquires securities in such fund), that person may be treated for purposes of this rule as not being in the United States. Under this exception, if subscriptions for private fund interests were submitted and accepted such that these interests were acquired when the applicable investors were outside the country, those investors (and the related subscription amounts) would be excluded from the adviser's assets and investors attributable to the United States. This exception applies even if, for example, the investors subsequently relocated to the country (although future subscriptions or future acquisitions of securities would be analyzed by reference to the location of the investors at the time such subscriptions were submitted and accepted).

There is a similar analysis under Rule 15a-6 brokerage business when overseas investors subsequently relocate to the United States. If an adviser reasonably believes that an investor or client is not "in the United States" at the time that they became an investor or client, then the adviser can reasonably treat such investor or client as *not* being in the United States

"U.S. persons" are defined in Regulation S to mean persons who reside in the U.S. (regardless of their citizenship), not persons who are U.S. citizens. Therefore, for these purposes citizenship is generally irrelevant. However, similar to Rule 15a-6, one possible issue that may become evident with future regulatory guidance that is citizenship related is whether investment advisers should treat identifiably groups of U.S. citizens as U.S. residents for purposes of the private fund adviser exemption.

The SEC takes a broad view as to what activities by an investment adviser/manager constitute "holding itself out to the public." Essentially, any marketing activities, including letting it be known by word of mouth that the adviser is available to be retained, constitutes holding itself out for purposes of the Advisers Act. Using letterhead indicating activity as an investment adviser, or maintaining a telephone listing or otherwise that the firm will accept new advisory clients is sufficient to be considered as holding itself out. Moreover, hiring a third party to solicit clients on his behalf would be considered as holding itself out.

The SEC staff has also provided guidance about what advice about securities entails. Any person providing advice to others about specific securities, such as stocks, bonds, mutual funds, limited partnerships, and commodity pools, for a fee, would fall within the investment adviser definition. Other examples of advice that may trigger a registration requirement include:

- Advice about market trends;
- Advice about the selection and retention of other advisers;
- Providing a selective list of securities even if no advice is provided as to any one security; and
- Asset allocation advice.

The foreign private adviser exemption is significantly narrower that the private fund adviser exemption in that, along with the very limited asset threshold, it requires the adviser to look through private funds and count any U.S. investors in the fund towards the fewer than 15 U.S. clients and investors limit of the test, although the adviser does not have to double-count the private investment fund as a client for this purpose. An adviser may be required to also look through persons who are nominal holders of a security issued by a private fund to count the investors in the nominal holder when determining if the adviser qualifies for the exemption. For example, holders of the securities of any feeder fund in a master-feeder arrangement may be deemed to be the investors of the master fund. However, an adviser may treat as a single investor any person who is an investor in two or more of the adviser's private funds.

An adviser relying on the foreign private adviser exemption is not required to make any filing with the SEC.

Private Fund Adviser Exemption. For foreign private advisers who do not qualify for the foreign private adviser exemption and who manage only private funds with U.S. investors (no separate accounts with U.S. investors), the private fund adviser exemption may be available.

This exemption is available to an adviser *solely* to private funds, even with a place of business in the United States, provided it has less than $150 million in assets under management in the United States. For a non-U.S. adviser, thereby enabling it to rely upon a registration exemption if:

- All of its clients that are U.S. persons are qualifying private funds; and
- All assets it manages at any place of business in the United States are solely attributable to qualifying private funds and have a total value of less than $150 million. "Private fund," "U.S. person," and "place of business" have the same definitions as for a foreign private adviser exemption.

Non-U.S. advisers can use the private fund exemption without regard to the type or number of non-U.S. clients or the amount of assets managed outside the country. Non-U.S. advisers are only required to count their U.S. clients and only private fund assets that are managed from a place of business within the United States.

Accordingly, a non-U.S. adviser is permitted to manage an unlimited amount of qualifying private fund assets provided its principal office and place of business is outside the United States and it does not manage any assets for U.S. persons other than qualifying private funds. Because this exemption pertains to private funds, non-U.S. advisers may not rely on the private fund exemption if it has U.S. clients in separately managed accounts.

Venture Capital Fund Exemption. Finally, investment advisers to solely venture capital funds, regardless of the amount of assets managed, are exempt from the registration requirements of the Advisers Act as well. Thus, a single adviser that manages both venture capital funds and other types of funds cannot qualify for the venture capital exemption. Unlike the private fund exemption, to benefit from the venture capital fund exemption, non-U.S. advisers may not disregard their non-U.S. advisory activities and *all* of their clients, including their non-U.S. clients, must be venture capital funds.

A "venture capital fund" is defined as a private fund that satisfies the following conditions:

- Represents to investors that the fund pursues a venture capital strategy;
- Does not provide investors with redemption rights;
- Holds no more than 20 percent of the fund's assets in "nonqualifying investments" (excluding cash and certain short-term holdings) (qualifying investments generally consist of equity securities of qualifying portfolio companies that are directly acquired by the fund);
- Does not borrow (or otherwise incur leverage) more than 15 percent of the fund's assets, and then only on a short-term basis (i.e., for no more than 120-days); and
- Is not registered under the Investment Company Act of 1940 and has not elected to be treated as a business development company.

An investment adviser to a venture capital fund that is otherwise relying on the exemption could not identify the fund as a hedge fund or multi-strategy fund (i.e., venture capital is one of several strategies used to manage the fund) or include the fund in a hedge fund database or hedge fund index. A venture capital fund is a private fund that represents itself as being a venture capital fund to its investors and potential investors, which implies that the fund invests primarily in operating companies and not, for example, in entities that hold oil and gas leases. Whether or not a fund represents itself as pursuing a venture capital strategy, however, will depend on the particular facts and circumstances. Statements made by a fund to its investors and prospective investors, not just what the fund calls itself, are important to an investor's understanding of the fund and its investment strategy.

What if a non-U.S. adviser does not qualify for an exemption?

Non-U.S. advisers conducting advisory business in or impacting the United States that do not qualify for any of these exemptions will have to register with the SEC as described below. However, before registering with the SEC, non-U.S. advisers might consider structuring their U.S. operations to minimize the U.S. regulatory impact by establishing a separate U.S. advisory affiliate and registering such affiliate with the SEC under the Advisers Act. Organizational separation of the U.S. advisory activities provides a greater degree of insulation between the activities if the U.S. registrant and the non-U.S. adviser. It also provides greater flexibility in addressing different or conflicting regulatory requirements that the U.S. may impose. The registration and other substantive provisions of the Advisers Act ordinarily should not apply beyond the separately organized U.S. registrant; registering the non-U.S. adviser for its U.S. advisory business would subject the entirety of its global operations to U.S. regulatory requirements under the Advisers Act.

The SEC paved the way for a similar approach for affiliated business to share the customer and regulatory responsibilities as contemplated in Rule 15a-6 with the intermediation requirement for affiliated broker-dealers when one broker-dealer is registered and the other one is not. That approach relates to the notion of relying advisers, as contemplated below. Based upon whether the foreign financial institution managing the money has a U.S.-affiliated or -unaffiliated adviser that manages money on its behalf, the following procedures have been used in reliance upon an SEC no-action letter:[69]

Pursuant to the SEC no-action letter, the procedures governing such advisers are generally expected to operate as follows.

For relying advisers and SPVs, U.S. investment advisers may have a number of employees, related entities or other related persons providing investment advisory services to clients. The following, despite their investment advisory activities, will not have to separately register with the SEC as an investment adviser:

- Any natural person associated with U.S. RIA will not have to register as an adviser solely as a result of their activities as associated persons of U.S. RIA;
- An entity (special purpose vehicle or SPV) set up to provide certain services to a private fund advised by U.S. RIA will not have to separately register as investment adviser with the SEC provided
  - U.S. RIA establishes the SPV to act as the private fund's general partner or managing member,
  - The SPV's formation documents designate the investment adviser to manage the private fund's assets,
  - All of the investment advisory activities of the SPV are subject to the Advisers Act and the rules thereunder, and the SPV is subject to examination by the SEC, and
  - U.S. RIA subjects the SPV, its employees, and persons acting on its behalf to U.S. RIA's supervision and control and, therefore, the SPV, all of its employees and the persons acting on its behalf are "persons associated with" the registered adviser (as defined in Section 202(a)(17) of the Advisers Act).

For relying advisers, the firm may register itself and each other adviser that is controlled by or under common control with U.S. RIA through a single registration statement.[70] Such other advisers are designated "relying advisers" and U.S. RIA, which files the registration statement, is designated as the "filing adviser." Such a registration is permitted if the following conditions are met:

---

[69] SEC, Response of the Office of Investment Adviser Regulation Division of Investment Management (Jan. 18, 2012) **https://www.sec.gov/divisions/investment/noaction/2012/aba011812.htm**. See also the Unibanco line of no-action letter, which the SEC may still honor to the extent that such requests are consistent with the foreign private adviser exemption and the regulatory themes underlying this Dodd-Frank-created exemption. See Gary L Granik, Janna Manes, Nicole M. Runyan, Lauren Connolly and Linda Y. Kim, "Unibanco After Dodd-Frank: The Extraterritorial Reach of the Investment Advisers Act," *Investment Lawyer,* Vol. 20, No 2 (Feb. 2013).

[70] Response of the Office of Investment Adviser Regulation Division of Investment Management, SEC No-Action Letter (Jan. 18, 2012), https://www.sec.gov/divisions/investment/noaction/2012/aba011812.htm

- The filing adviser and each relying adviser advise only private funds and separate account clients that are qualified clients (as defined in Rule 205-3 under the Advisers Act) and are otherwise eligible to invest in the private funds advised by the filing adviser or a relying adviser and whose accounts pursue investment objectives and strategies that are substantially similar or otherwise related to those private funds;
- Each relying adviser, its employees and the persons acting on its behalf are subject to the filing adviser's supervision and control and, therefore, each relying adviser, its employees and the persons acting on its behalf are "persons associated with" the filing adviser (as defined in section 202(a)(17) of the Advisers Act);
- The filing adviser has its principal office and place of business in the United States and, therefore, all of the substantive provisions of the Advisers Act and the rules thereunder apply to the filing adviser's and each relying adviser's dealings with each of its clients, regardless of whether any client or the filing adviser or relying adviser providing the advice is a United States person;
- The advisory activities of each relying adviser are subject to the Advisers Act and the rules thereunder, and each relying adviser is subject to examination by the SEC;
- The filing adviser and each relying adviser operate under a single code of ethics adopted in accordance with Advisers Act Rule 204A-1 and a single set of written policies and procedures adopted and implemented in accordance with Advisers Act Rule 206(4)-(7) and administered by a single chief compliance officer in accordance with that rule; and
- The filing adviser discloses in its Form ADV (Miscellaneous Section of Schedule D) that it and its relying advisers are together filing a single Form ADV in reliance on the position expressed in this letter and identifies each relying adviser by completing a separate Section 1.B., Schedule D, of Form ADV for each relying adviser and identifying it as such by including the notation "(relying adviser)."

For relying advisers an umbrella registration applies (effective when 5.20.2015 proposed amendments are adopted) U.S. RIA may register itself and each other adviser that is controlled by or under common control with U.S. RIA through a single registration statement. Such other advisers are designated "relying advisers" and U.S. RIA, which files the registration statement, is designated as the "filing adviser." Such a registration is permitted if the following conditions are met:

- The U.S. RIA (filing adviser) and one or more relying advisers conduct a single private fund advisory business and each relying adviser is controlled by or under common control with U.S. RIA (the filing adviser);
- The U.S. RIA (filing adviser) and each relying adviser advise only private funds and clients in separately managed accounts that are qualified clients (as defined in Rule 205-3 under the Advisers Act) and are otherwise eligible to invest in the private funds advised by the filing adviser or a relying adviser and whose accounts pursue investment objectives and strategies that are substantially similar or otherwise related to those private funds;

- The U.S. RIA (filing adviser) has its principal office and place of business in the United States and, therefore, all of the substantive provisions of the Advisers Act and the rules thereunder apply to the filing adviser's and each relying adviser's dealings with each of its clients, regardless of whether any client or the filing adviser or relying adviser providing the advice is a United States person;
- Each relying adviser, its employees, and the persons acting on its behalf are subject to U.S. RIA's filing adviser's supervision and control and, therefore, each relying adviser, its employees and the persons acting on its behalf are "persons associated with" U.S. RIA (filing adviser) (as defined in Section 202(a)(17) of the Advisers Act);
- The advisory activities of each relying adviser will be subject to the Advisers Act and the rules thereunder, and each relying adviser is subject to examination by the SEC;
- The U.S. RIA (filing adviser) and each relying adviser will operate under a single code of ethics adopted in accordance with Rule 204A-1 under the Advisers Act and a single set of written policies and procedures adopted and implemented in accordance with Rule 206(4)-(7) under the Advisers Act and administered by a single chief compliance officer in accordance with that Rule; and
- The U.S. RIA (filing adviser) will file and keep up-to-date, as required, Schedule R to its Form ADV, which contains certain identifying information.

IV. U.S. BROKER-DEALERS ENGAGING IN BUSINESS IN THE EUROPEAN UNION

This section briefly addresses U.S. firms that have business in the European Union, including what types of behavior trigger a registration requirement and how the substantive provision of European legislation affects such U.S. firms. This discussion examines the U.S. compliance issues associated with foreign broker-dealers, some of which have U.S. affiliates. However, firms should also have some appreciation for certain international opportunities and practices that they may encounter. These include the EU jurisdictional regulations that affect U.S. broker-dealers and investment advisers. In the process, such firms should be also aware of some of the substantial regulatory difference that would impact their operations if they fall within the jurisdiction of the EU and one or more of its member states.

U.S. Broker-Dealers Conducting Business in the EU

MiFID. The Markets in Financial Instruments Directive ("MiFID") establishes the legal parameters by which EU financial services may provide investment services. Furthermore, MiFID establishes a licensing requirement across the EU and sets forth organizational and conduct standards for how investment services may be provided.

MiFID, covering securities markets, investment firms, and intermediaries, was created in response to the financial crisis to help forge a more competitive and integrated EU financial market. However, recent events and market developments have demonstrated weaknesses in some of its underlying principles, and highlighted areas in need of re-inforcement or revision.

Regarding non-EU firms ("third-country firms") being able to access EU markets, the regulatory parameters are not harmonized under MiFID. Each member state may deal with this issue in its own way, subject to the general principles of the European Union.

A third-country firm that establishes a branch in an EU member state and obtains authorization to provide investment services from it cannot make use of a "passport" to provide those services elsewhere in the EU. AAA new authorization will potentially be required in each member state. The only way to obtain a passport is by establishing and obtaining authorization for a separate legal entity in a member state.

MiFID II. The EU has sought to amend MiFID through legislation known as "MiFID II," which reinforces and replaces portion of MiFID by:

- Ensuring that trading takes place on regulated platforms;
- Introducing rules on high frequency trading;
- Improving the transparency and oversight of financial markets—including derivatives markets;
- Improving conditions for competition in the trading and clearing of financial instruments; and
- Strengthening the protection of investors by introducing robust organizational and conduct requirements.

The MiFID II effective date was set as January 2018. MiFID refers to firms located outside of the EU and third-country firms. In other words, "third country" refers to jurisdictions outside the EU and "third-country firms" are entities incorporated outside the EU, whether they do, or seek to do, business by way of a branch established in the EU, or on a cross-border basis i.e., providing services to persons in one jurisdiction from a place of business in another jurisdiction without any establishment in the client's jurisdiction.

With the review of MiFID, the European Securities and Markets Authority (ESMA) and the European Commission have attempted to create a harmonized regime for granting access to EU markets for firms in third countries. However, this regime is limited in scope to the cross-border provision of investment services and activities provided to professional clients and eligible counterparties.

MiFID has three main client categories:

- "Eligible counterparties" include MiFID investment firms and Banking Consolidation Directive (BCD) credit institutions as examples, as well as those who are "opted up" on the basis of their experience and expertise. A firm may only treat a client as an eligible counterparty in relation to eligible counterparty business, e.g., dealing/ arranging activities;
- "Professional clients" include credit institutions, investment firms, and collective investment schemes as examples, as well as "opted up" retail clients; and
- "Retail clients" are all other clients.

Professional clients should have the experience, knowledge, and expertise to make their own investment decisions and properly assess the risks incurred. As a point of comparison, this part of the professional client requirement resembles the requirements of FINRA's institutional suitability rule when it defines certain institutions as institutions that are afforded less protection that the retail clients under the general suitability rule but operate in such a way that they specifies that they need a certain level of sophistication to evaluate the risks of the investment. In particular, FINRA Rule 2111(b) (Institutional Suitability Rule) requires that certain institutions specified in Rule 4512(c), in the belief of the broker-dealer, have a reasonable basis to believe that the institutional customer is capable of evaluating investment risks independently, both in general and with regard to particular transactions and investment strategies involving a security or securities. Qualified institutional buyers, as contemplated in Rule 144A, are also considered eligible for such institutional suitability treatment

Full EU agreement ("harmonization") has not been achieved for third-country firms for retail clients and opted-up professional clients and, as a result, member states are free to continue to apply national rules. However, when member states choose not to maintain their respective national regime, MiFID II provides for a detailed set of rules that are designed to harmonize the requirements with which the branch of the third-country firm will have to comply in order to be authorized by the national competent authority of the EU member state. Third-country firms dealing with professional clients or eligible counterparties will, on the other hand, be permitted to operate on a cross-border basis either from outside the EU or from a branch in a member state, subject to various conditions.

A third country firm may provide investment services to eligible counterparties and per se professional clients on a cross border basis where such firm is registered with ESMA.

ESMA will only register such third-country firms when:

- the European Commission has adopted a decision that the prudential and business conduct requirements in the firm's home third country have equivalent effect to MiFID II and Capital Requirements Directive IV;[71]
- The European Commission's decision also concludes that such third country also has an effective and equivalent system for the recognition of investment firms authorized under the respective third-country legal regime;
- The firm is authorized and effectively supervised in its home third country in respect of the provision of the relevant services (as with the requirements for branch authorization, this would restrict the scope of cross-border services that a regulated

[71] The Capital Requirements Regulation (CRR) and Directive (CRD IV) introduced a supervisory framework in the European Union that reflects the Basel III rules on capital measurement and capital standards. *See* Regulation (EU) No 575/2013 on prudential requirements for credit institutions and investment firms (CRR)) and a directive (Directive 2013/36/EU on access to the activity of credit institutions and the prudential supervision of credit institutions and investment firms)—the global standards on bank capital (the Basel III agreement) into EU law.

third country firm can perform to the extent that any such services are not regulated in the home third country); and

- Cooperation arrangements exist between ESMA and the firm's third-country national competent authority which, among other provisions, relate to the exchange of information and co-ordination of supervisory activities.

Different Types of Clients. MiFID II applies to firms providing services specifically to retail clients and professional clients that elect to be treated as a retail client for suitability purposes. However, the Regulation on Markets in Financial Instruments ("MiFIR"), which is the implementing regulation of MiFID, provides that branches authorized pursuant to MiFID II may provide investment services to eligible counterparties and per se professional clients across the EU, provided their third-country legal and supervisory framework has been recognized by the European Commission as equivalent. However, when such a third-country firm wishes to provide services to retail clients and opted-up professional clients in other member states, it would either need to:

- Apply for a separate authorization in each member state in which it wishes to provide services and establish a branch in each one (where the member state's regime provides for this possibility); or
- Comply with the local regime governing market access in case of retail or opted-up professional clients.

When a member state has implemented the MiFID II provisions on the establishment of third-country branches, a third-country firm that has not established a branch in that member state will generally not be able to provide investment services with or without any ancillary services to retail clients or opted-up professional clients. When a member state's regime does not require the establishment of a branch, the provision of services to retail clients and opted-up professional clients will be subject to the respective national requirements.

Services to Retail and Elective Professional Clients. MiFID II Article 39 allows (but does not require) member states to require third-country firms wishing to provide investment services or perform investment activities with or without ancillary activities to retail or elective professional clients to set up a branch in the relevant member state. When this is the case, the branch can be authorized in that member state only if it meets certain conditions:

- The firm requires, and has, authorization to provide the services in the country of its establishment, and it is supervised in its performance of them, and the relevant regulator pays regard to Financial Action Task Force (FATF) recommendations on the prevention of money laundering and terrorist financing;
- There are appropriate cooperation agreements between the home country regulator and the relevant member state;
- The branch has sufficient freely available initial capital;

- The branch appoints one or more persons to manage it, and each relevant person complies with the provisions of CRD4 on governance and the management body in the same way that all firms covered by MiFID II must;
- The third-country "home" country has in place an agreement with the relevant European Economic Area (EEA) member state that fully complies with the OECD Model Tax Convention on Income and Capital; and
- The firm belongs to a compensation scheme authorized or regulated in accordance with the Investor Compensation Directive.

Under MiFID II Article 40, the applicant firm must also provide the relevant member state regulator with information about itself, its supervisor, its domestic management and compliance arrangement and details of its initial free capital.

Under MiFID II Article 41, once authorized, the firm must comply with the requirements of MiFID II on organization, trading, conflicts of interest, investor protection (including the rules on disclosure, suitability and appropriateness, best execution, client order handling and dealing with ECPs). It must also comply with relevant rules on trading venues, and MiFIR's requirements on transparency and transaction reporting.

MiFID II Article 42 provides that when a client initiates services, however, there is no requirement for the third-country firm to set up a branch specifically to perform those services. However, if the firm is required to have a branch, it cannot market new categories of product or service to the client other than through the branch.

Services to per se Professional Clients and ECPs. MiFIR Article 46 provides that a different regime applies under MiFIR to a third-country firm wishing to provide investment services or carry out investment activities with or without ancillary activities to or with per se professional clients and eligible counterparties within the EU with or without setting up a branch. These firms may do so based on registration with ESMA. ESMA will do this based on an application when:

- There is an equivalence decision in place (see Article 47);
- The firm is authorized in the jurisdiction where its head office is established to provide the services and activities it wishes to provide in the EU, and is subject to effective supervision and enforcement; and
- ESMA has established cooperation agreements with the third-country regulator in line with Article 47.

Member states may, however, allow these services and activities on the basis of national regimes where there is no equivalence decision in place.

A registration with ESMA will cover the entire EU. No member state can impose any requirements on the third-country firm additional to those set out in MiFID II and MiFIR, or treat these firms more favorably than other firms. However, they may at their discretion allow third-country firms to provide services and activities to ECPs and per se professionals if there is no equivalence decision in effect.

Registered third-country firms must tell customers before providing any investment service that they are not allowed to provide services to anyone other than an ECP or per se professional and that they are not supervised in the EU, and must disclose the name of their home country supervisor.

As with MiFID II, third-country firms may provide services without registration to clients who have approached the firm on their own initiative, but may not market any new products or investment services to those clients. These third-country firms must offer to submit any disputes to dispute resolution mechanisms in a member state before they provide any service.

Under MiFIR Article 47, the European Commission's equivalence decision about the firm's home regulator will be made only if:

- The firm's activities require authorization and are subject to ongoing supervision and enforcement;
- There are sufficient and appropriate capital requirements and requirements on shareholders and members of the management body;
- There are adequate organizational requirements around internal controls;
- There are appropriate conduct of business rules; and
- There are rules preventing market abuse.

ESMA will also have to have in place cooperation agreements with the relevant authorities.

If a third-country firm is already authorized under Article 39 of MiFID II, it can provide services to ECPs and per se professional clients without setting up any more branches, but must comply with the information requirements in Article 34 of MiFID II that apply to EU firms wishing to passport on a services basis and will be subject to the supervision of the EU home state of the branch.

Under MiFIR Article 48, ESMA will keep a publicly available register of registered third-country firms, setting out which services the firms can provide and who is responsible for their supervision.

MiFID II Direct Access to EU Eligible Counterparties and Certain Professional Clients. A third-country firm is permitted to provide investment services or perform activities directly to eligible counterparties and to those categories of clients considered to be professionals (under Section 1 of Annex 2, MiFID II) in the EU without the requirement to establish an EU branch only if the European Commission has first determined that the third country's legal and supervisory regime is broadly equivalent to the EU's in certain respects.

A firm based in a third country deemed equivalent will need to apply to ESMA to be included in a register of permitted third-country firms, and ESMA will duly register it provided that (i) the firm is authorized to provide the relevant investment services or activities in the jurisdiction of its head office and (ii) appropriate cooperation arrangements are in place with the relevant third country.

An EU member state may require that a third-country firm establishes a branch in that state and obtains authorization from the member state's competent authorities in order to be permitted to provide services to retail clients or to those retail clients who request to be considered professionals (under Section II to Annex II, MiFID II). Because each member state may require the establishment of a branch, there is no European passport available for a firm wishing to provide services to retail and certain professional clients. The legislation is silent about whether a third-country firm may provide services to a retail client in a member state where that member state does not require the establishment of a branch and the position is therefore unclear.

Passporting from an EU Branch to Eligible Counterparties and Certain Professional Clients. Once a third-country firm has established an authorized branch in an EU member state (if required to do so to access retail clients) and that firm is established in a country whose legal and supervisory framework is recognized as broadly equivalent by the European Commission, the firm will be permitted to provide its investment services and to perform activities throughout the EU to eligible counterparties and professional clients (within Section I of Annex II) without the need to establish further branches. The branch would need to comply with the information requirements for the cross-border provision of services and activities under MiFID 2. In these circumstances, there is no requirement for the branch to register with ESMA as a permitted third-country firm.

Regulatory Technical Standards of ESMA for Third-Country Firms. RTS 5 in Article 46(7) of MiFIR provides for Regulatory Technical Standards (RTS)[72] to set out the information a third-country firm applying for authorization must submit to ESMA. The standards also say how these firms must notify clients of the limitations on their activities that MiFIR mandates.

The information ESMA requires is:

- Full name of the firm, including its legal and relevant trading names;
- Head office address;
- Contact details of the firm – address, phone number and email addresses;
- Contact details of the person in charge of the application;
- If available, details of the firm's website, national identification number, legal entity identifier and bank identifier code;
- Name and address of home country competent authority (with details of areas of competence if more than one) and links to appropriate registers if available;
- Information on which investment services, activities and ancillary services it is authorized to provide in its home jurisdiction, which must take the form of a written declaration by the home country regulator; and
- Investment services and activities to be provided or performed in the EU, and any ancillary services.

---

[72] Regulatory Technical Standards are additional guidance that ESMA can create financial services firm about how to implement various regulations. *See*, e.g., https://www.esma.europa.eu/convergence/guidelines-and-technical-standards

Practicalities for Third-Country Firms

Third-country firms do not need to wait for the European Commission's approval of the RTS to plan how they wish to conduct business in the EU once MiFID II is implemented. The key decision must be which services a third-country firm wishes to provide, to which types of customer, and in which jurisdictions within the EU. From this flows the fundamental decisions on whether:

- It will be necessary to set up a branch in one or more EU member states and apply for authorization there—noting that MiFID II does not allow any form of passport for branches authorized in one member state to provide services into another or set up a branch in any other. This assumes, of course, that the home country regulation and regulator meet the required conditions if the relevant member state imposes them. This decision will also involve an assessment of the financial requirements and the organizational and conduct of business rules with which the firm will have to comply (and prove its readiness to do so in its application);
- The firm will wish to provide services only to per se professionals and ECPs, in which case it will wish to consider the benefits of applying for ESMA registration—again, assuming the home country regimes are adequate to allow this;
- It may wish to combine the two regimes, as MiFIR allows; or
- None of these options will work, and the firm will be faced with the need to assess whether it should establish an EU-based subsidiary for its EU business, and whether that subsidiary would meet the authorization conditions.

So, the position for third-country firms is still not completely harmonized, especially where they may wish to provide services to retail clients, or services that are not regulated in their home countries. MiFID II may present opportunities, but it also presents challenges. Third-country firms with an interest in acting for EU clients should consider the impact of both.

V. U.S. INVESTMENT ADVISERS ENGAGING IN BUSINESS IN THE EUROPEAN UNION

Investment advisory firms that want to conduct business in the EU, they are governed by MiFID II and by ESMA. As with broker-dealers seeking authorization in the EU, the firms would need to seek clearance from the local financial service authority (FSA) in the respective country where they want to designate an office location for their EU business. The prevailing wisdom still seems to be that subadvisers to a EU-authorized firm do not need to seek such clearance, but if an investment adviser establishes the direct customer relationship of an EU client, including a mutual fund (known as UCITS in the EU) or unregistered funds (including private equity funds, hedge funds, and other private funds), collectively known as "alternative funds," then such firms should become authorized/registered in the EU to conduct investment business.

ESMA regulates the fund management industry in accordance with the two main pieces of EU legislation in this area known as Directive on Undertakings for Collective Investment in Transferable Securities (UCITS) and the Alternative Investment Fund Managers Directive (AIFMD).

UCITS

As described by ESMA, the UCITS Directive is a framework for investment funds to be sold to retail investors throughout the EU. This means that funds authorized in one member state can be marketed in another member state using the passporting or reciprocity mechanism. Notably, ESMA has a form of whistleblowing by which people can notify EMSA if a market participant is violating the registration/passporting provisions governing such UCITS funds.

AIFMD

The AIFMD applies to managers of hedge funds, private equity funds, real estate funds, among other non-UCITS funds. Alternative investment funds can be sold to professional investors throughout the EU on the basis of a passport. The AIFMD is notable for the detailed regulatory reporting regime that it introduced, which requires managers to submit an extensive set of information to their national authorities on aspects such as their investment portfolios, leverage, collateral, risk, volatility, and management. The FSA ordinarily requests to file the organizational and offering documents of the alternative fund.

Although it is not presently the case, ESMA has been involved in prompting the discussion on the possibility of non-EU funds and managers to be able to expand their business throughout via the EU passport concept.

Investor Protection Approach

As with in the United States, the legislative and regulatory approach is to afford greater protection to retail investors and less to parties deemed to be more sophisticated and professionally involved in the marketplace. Specifically, professional investors and eligible counterparties are afforded less protection. Packaged retail investment products (PRIPs), including the more recent focus insurance-based investment products, have sought to build upon earlier work of PRIPs. Investor disclosure regulations, such as those known as the Key Information Document Regulation (KID Regulation), are required to provide investors a succinct and plainly written disclosure about the main issues that investors should consider when evaluating an investment. Succinctly and clearly disclosing the risks is an important aspect of providing meaningful customer disclosure. The KID Regulation seeks to provide a basis for investors across the EU to efficiently compare the features of investment products. The product manufacturer is responsible for developing the KID and the investment firm is responsible for distributing it.

Broker-dealers and investment advisers should verify where they have the obligation to provide the KID, that the product providers have KIDs available for them, and that any hyperlinks to KID websites work. If broker-dealers or investment advisers conclude that they are not responsible for providing the KID because they act as agent for the product provider, then the distribution agreements should clearly articulate the responsibilities of the respective firms.

Miscellaneous EU Regulation Pivotal in the Financial Services Regulatory Landscape

In addition to the foregoing, no dance through the EU investment regulatory journey would be satisfactory unless it mentioned the Market Abuse Directive and its July 3, 2016, Market Abuse Regulation (MAR). For larger U.S. firms, the requirements of MAR will not be surprising, but, nevertheless, MAR introduced requirements on EU firms to establish compliance and market surveillance procedures to address the maintenance of company official insider lists, case-based insider lists, insider trading, front running, market sounding, etc.

MAR also set in place a requirement to report suspicious activities when firms suspect potential violations of the foregoing prohibitions. Company officials' insider lists require financial services firms to maintain lists of any senior official of a company, as well as their closely associated persons (CAPs) who are presumed to have nonpublic information about their companies. CAPs are generally defined as a variety of family members and people who are under the guardianship of the senior official, as well as companies owned and/or controlled by those covered individuals to the point of exceeding the definitional thresholds contemplated in MAR's CAP definition. The FSAs of the various EU countries enforce/interpret MAR in different ways regarding the CAP definition. In any case, once one has ascertained that a senior official of a public company has reportable holdings, then he or she is required to make certain public disclosures (generally via the company's financial statements and press release to the market center) of their holdings.

Case-based insider lists apply to any circumstances that the financial services firm wants to designate, such as to certain mergers and acquisitions, corporate financing activities, private equity into public equity (PIPE) offerings, legal actions, etc. in which one could take advantage of nonpublic information are subject to MAR and the firm's compliance procedures.

MAR defines "market sounding" as a communication of information, prior to the announcement of a transaction, in order to gauge the interest of potential investors in a possible transaction and the conditions relating to it such as its potential size or pricing, to one or more potential investors. MAR imposes certain recordkeeping requirements, information protection procedures, and disclosure procedures for those person who possess market sounding information. In the case of activities under the scope of MAR, investor consent may be required for market soundings.

MAR requires firms to establish and maintain "effective arrangements, systems and procedures to be able to detect suspicious orders and transactions." Firms must maintain sufficient detail in the information being reported to effectively fulfill their obligations under MAR, and ESMA expects firms to have its surveillance system at least partially structured such that automated controls, system alerts, and associated monitoring functionality that supplements any manual procedures that may also be appropriate. Firms must have systems capable supporting the analysis of every transaction and order, individually and comparatively. Thus, firms should consider what sorts of metrics and surveillance systems parameters would provide meaningful information in order to trigger a firm's need to investigate at a deeper level whether insider trading or other forms or market abuse may have occurred, warranting a suspicious transaction report to the regulatory authorities. Such systems, within the context of an international financial services firm, should provide appropriate insight to the enterprise-wide corporate financing, wholesale banking, and wealth management operations for clients who possess information, resources, connections, and insight to take advantage of market. When such systems are not integrated into the enterprise-wide control framework, the justification for the restrictions or compartmentalization of information and controls should be well-documented, including for reasons of conflicts of interest, "Chinese walls," differing privacy regulations in various jurisdictions of the affiliated firm's network of companies, etc.

VI. CONCLUSION

In light of jurisdictional issues addressed in this chapter, one can appreciate the importance of effectively structuring the operations, disclosures, customer interaction, websites, offering documents, and multiple other facets of a firm's business model. Effective planning can help avoid compliance problems and the significant costs associated with violating the securities laws.

APPENDIX A. EXEMPTION OF CERTAIN FOREIGN BROKERS OF DEALERS

§15a-6. (a) A foreign broker or dealer shall be exempt from the registration requirements of Sections 15(a)(1) or 15B(a)(1) of the [Exchange Act] to the extent that a foreign broker or dealer:

(1) effects transactions in securities with or for persons that have not been solicited by the foreign broker or dealer; or

(2) furnishes research reports to major U.S. institutional investors, and effects transactions in the securities discussed in the research reports with for those major U.S. institutional investors, provided that:

  (i) the research reports do not recommend the use of the foreign broker or dealer to effect trades in any security;

  (ii) the foreign broker or dealer does not initiate contact with those major U.S. institutional investors to follow up on the research reports, and does not otherwise induce or attempt to induce the purchase or sale of any security by those major U.S. institutional investors;

APPENDIX A. EXEMPTION OF CERTAIN FOREIGN BROKERS OF DEALERS

- (iii) if the foreign broker or dealer has a relationship with a registered broker or dealer that satisfies the requirements of paragraph (a)(3) of this rule, any transactions with the foreign broker or dealer in securities discussed in the research reports are effected only through that registered broker or dealer, pursuant to the provisions of paragraph (a)(3); and
- (iv) the foreign broker or dealer does not provide research to U.S. persons pursuant to any express or implied understanding that those U.S. persons will direct commission income to the foreign broker or dealer; or

(3) induces or attempts to induce the purchase or sale of any security by a U.S. institutional investor or a major U.S. institutional investor, provided that:
- (i) the foreign broker or dealer:
  - (A) effects any resulting transactions with or for the U.S. institutional investor or the major U.S. institutional investor through a registered broker or dealer in the manner described in paragraph (a)(3)(iii) of this rule; and
  - (B) provides the [SEC]...with information or documents within the possession, custody, or control of the foreign broker or dealer, any testimony of foreign associated persons, and any assistance in taking evidence of other persons, wherever located, ...
- (ii) the foreign associated person of the foreign broker or dealer effecting transactions with the U.S. institutional investor or the major U.S. institutional investor:
  - (A) conducts all securities activities from outside the U.S., except that the foreign associated persons may conduct visits to the U.S. institutional investors and major U.S. institutional investors within the United States, provided that:
    - (1) the foreign associated person is accompanied on these visits by an associated person of a registered broker or dealer that accepts responsibility for the foreign associated person's communications with the U.S. institutional investor or the major U.S. institutional investor; and
    - (2) transactions in any securities discussed during the visit by the foreign associated person are effected only through the registered broker or dealer, pursuant to (a)(3) of this rule; and
  - (B) is determined by the registered broker or dealer to:
    - (1) not be subject to statutory disqualification specified in section 3(a)(39) of the [Exchange Act], or any substantially equivalent foreign
      - (i) expulsion or suspension from membership,
      - (ii) bar or suspension from association,
      - (iii) denial of trading privileges,
      - (iv) order denying, suspending, or revoking registration or barring or suspending association, or
      - (v) finding with respect to causing any such effective foreign suspension, expulsion, or order;
    - (2) not to have been convicted of any foreign offense, enjoined from any foreign act, conduct, or practice, or found to have committed any foreign act substantially equivalent to any of those listed in [various the Exchange Act provisions]; and
    - (3) not to have been found to have made or caused to be made any false foreign statement or omission substantially equivalent to any of those listed in [the statutory disqualification provision of the Exchange Act]; and

APPENDIX A. EXEMPTION OF CERTAIN FOREIGN BROKERS OF DEALERS

(iii) the registered broker or dealer through which the transaction with the U.S. institutional investor or the major institutional investor is effected:
(A) is responsible for:
(1) effecting the transactions conducted under paragraph (a)(3) of this rule, other than negotiating their terms;
(2) issuing all required confirmations and statements to the U.S. institutional investor or the major U.S. institutional investor;
(3) as between the foreign broker or dealer and the registered broker or dealer, extending or arranging for the extension of any credit to the U.S. institutional investor or the major U.S. institutional investor in connection with the transactions;
(4) maintaining the required books and records ...
(5) complying with Rule 15c3-1 under the [Exchange Act] with respect to the transactions; and
(6) receiving, delivering, and safeguarding funds and securities in connection with transactions on behalf of the U.S. institutional investor or the major U.S. institutional investor in compliance with the [Customer Protection Rule];
(B) participates through an associated person in all oral communications between the foreign associated person and the U.S. institutional investor, other than a major U.S. institutional investor;
(C) has obtained from the foreign broker or dealer, with respect to each foreign associated person, [certain types of information specified in the SEC record keeping rule, including foreign sanctions];
(D) has obtained from the foreign broker or dealer and each foreign associated person written consent of service of process for...; and
(E) maintains a written record of the information and consent required [in the two previous sections of this rule], and all records in connection with trading activities...

(4) effects transactions in securities with or for, or induces or attempts to induce the purchase or sale of any security by:
(i) a registered broker or dealer...;
(ii) the African Development Bank,...;
(iii) a foreign person temporarily present in the United States, with whom the foreign broker or dealer had a bona fide, pre-existing relationship before the foreign person entered the United States;
(iv) any agency or branch of a U.S. person permanently located outside the United States, provided that the transactions occur outside the United States; or
(v) U.S. citizens resident outside the United States, provided that the transactions occur outside the United States, and that the foreign broker or dealer does not direct the selling efforts toward identifiable groups of U.S. citizens resident abroad.

(b) When used in this rule,
(1) the term "family of investment companies" shall mean...
(2) the term "foreign associated person" shall mean any natural person domiciled outside the United States who is an associated person, as defined in section 3(a)(18) of the [Exchange Act], of the foreign broker or dealer, and who participates in the solicitation of a U.S. institutional investor or a major U.S. institutional investor under paragraph (a)(3) of this rule.

APPENDIX A. EXEMPTION OF CERTAIN FOREIGN BROKERS OF DEALERS

(3) the term "foreign broker or dealer" shall mean any non-U.S. resident person (including any U.S. person engaged in business as a broker or dealer entirely outside the United States, except as otherwise permitted by this rule) that is not an office or branch of, or a natural person associated with, a registered broker or dealer, whose securities activities, if conducted in the United States, would be the definition of "broker" or "dealer" in sections 3(a)(4) or 3(a)(5) of the [Exchange Act].

(4) the term "major U.S. institutional investor" shall mean a person that is:
   (i) a U.S. institutional investor that has, or has under management, total assets in excess of $100 million, provided ...
   (ii) an investment adviser registered with the [SEC] under section 203 of the Investment Advisers Act of 1940 that has total assets under management in excess of $100 million....

(7) the term "U.S. institutional investor" shall mean a person that is :
   (i) an investment company registered with the [SEC] under section 8 of the Investment Company Act of 1940; or
   (ii) a bank, savings and loan association, insurance company, business development company, shall business investment company, or employee benefit plan defined in [Regulation D of the Securities Act of 1933] ...; a private business development company defined in Rule 501(a)(2) ...; an organization defined in section 501(c)(3) of the Internal Revenue Code ...; or a trust defined in Rule 501(a)(7) ...

(c) The [SEC], by order after notice and opportunity for hearing, may withdraw the exemption provided in paragraph (a)(3) of this rule with respect to subsequent activities of a foreign broker or dealer or class of foreign brokers or dealers conducted from a foreign country, if the [SEC] finds that the laws or regulations of that foreign country have prohibited the foreign broker or dealer, or one of a class of foreign brokers or dealers, from providing,... information or documents,...testimony...,or assistance...,related to activities exempted by paragraph (a)(3) of this rule.

ABOUT THE AUTHOR

J. Keith Kessel specializes in the business advisory services from a legal strategy perspective and is involved in structuring transactions involving private equity, venture capital, corporate finance, licensing/supply/distribution, regulatory compliance and other securities industry matters. Mr. Kessel has been a corporate, securities and transactional lawyer, and compliance professional in the financial services industry for the past 23 years (as of this writing). During that time, Mr. Kessel has served in various executive, legal, and compliance roles, as well as other advisory roles through strategic partners, for a multitude of corporations and trust companies, including investment advisers, investment companies, broker-dealers, banks, investment banks, private equity firms, insurance agencies, stock exchanges and securities clearing and depository institutions, as well as other financial service providers. He has worked in law firms for approximately 8 years and worked in the industry/corporations for the balance of his career. He has also provided compliance and business law services for securities industry firms for his entire career.

Mr. Kessel has spoken at legal and compliance conferences, as well as for company sponsors, regarding private equity, banking, financing strategies, risk management, investment management and broker-dealers' activities. He has lectured in Europe, the United States and the Middle East on topics such as Cross Border Investment Advisory Compliance Matters, International Broker-Dealer Legal, Compliance and Operational Matters, International Company Restructuring, Dispute Resolution Strategies, International Banking Risk Management Programs, Anti-Money Laundering, etc.

Mr. Kessel has published articles and blogs on matters such as "Market Conduct & Registration Considerations Governing International Distribution—an EU & U.S. Perspective;" "International Retail Compliance Concerns;" "International Broker-Dealer and Investment Banking Strategies," "Essential Considerations for International, Unregistered Broker-Dealers, Investment Companies, Investment Advisers and Investment Banks," "Raising Capital and/or Doing Business in the U.S." "How Do I Judge Our Risk Controls," "Financing Business with U.S. Capital," "Legal and Deal Considerations for U.S. Private Investment Funds and Investment Management."

Mr. Kessel has practical experience in analyzing issues, providing legal and business solutions and implementing those solutions both domestically and internationally. Mr. Kessel has a bachelor of science degree from the University of Maryland, College Park, Maryland, and the juris doctor degree from Temple University School of Law, Philadelphia. He has also attended the London School of Economics and Political Science, Drexel University in Philadelphia, and the University of Helsinki.

Chapter 10

State Securities Regulators: Forgotten, But Not Gone

By Mark W. Bell
Tirador Compliance LLC

I. INTRODUCTION

On a warm late summer day, two examiners from the Colorado Division of Securities walked down Denver's 16th Street to the local office of a national investment advisory firm. The state examiners presented the office manager with a document request letter and informed him that they were conducting an examination. The manager, knowing that the Securities and Exchange Commission (SEC) regulated his firm, questioned whether he was required to comply with the request. The examiners suggested he contact his firm's compliance office for instructions. In short order, all met in a conference room with compliance staff from New York on speakerphone.

In May of that year, the firm had hired an experienced investment adviser representative (IAR), submitted a Form U4 application for his registration, and promptly put the representative to work. At the time of the U4 submission, the representative was a defendant in securities-related litigation alleging damages in millions of dollars, and the U4 properly disclosed the litigation. The representative had been going about his work, meeting with clients and gathering assets, while the firm collected fees for his services. Neither the office manager nor the firm's compliance staff could understand why the state had a concern.

The representative's U4 had hit the registration queue at the Colorado Division of Securities, and three older disclosure items plus the then-current litigation raised questions. Staff at the division had sent two separate requests for further information to the advisory firm but had not received a response. During the entire time that the representative had been working for the firm, his registration status with the State of Colorado displayed "Pending" in the Investment Adviser Registration Depository (IARD).

What had happened to the state's letters requesting information remained a mystery. The examiners believed and prevailed, that:

- The representative's registration with the state was incomplete;
- He therefore was engaging in unlicensed advisory activity; and
- He and the firm were collecting advisory fees from that unlicensed activity.

No one at the firm had confirmed successful registration. It would prove an expensive gap in procedure. The firm submitted a Letter of Acceptance, Waiver, and Consent (AW) and paid the state a fine in excess of $20,000.

II. A CAUTIONARY TALE

This anecdote illustrates why investment advisory firms for whom states are not the primary regulator need to remain aware of state regulation.

This chapter seeks to highlight the distinction between advisers and representatives, then sketch out state regulatory jurisdictions for investment advisers and broker-dealers, and lastly, to identify some likely interactions that firms may have with state regulators in the day-to-day course of business.

III. WHO (OR WHAT) IS AN ADVISER?

In most people's minds, the term "investment adviser" conjures an image of a serious but approachable professional in a suit, meeting with clients to plan for their newborn's college education, their savings for retirement, and/or managing their investment portfolio.

Here, it is important to highlight the distinction between common use of a term and its regulatory meaning.

In securities regulation, both at the federal or state level, "investment adviser" (or often, "advisor") usually refers to a legal entity, *not* an individual. An investment adviser registers with the Securities and Exchange Commission (SEC) or state securities regulator using Form ADV. The individual is an IAR or "supervised person," and registers via a Form U4. In the increasingly rare case of sole proprietorship, the sole proprietor registers with both Forms ADV and U4.

In small shops, this indeed seems like a distinction without a difference.

For example, Estelle Peterson runs a one-woman boutique investment firm, "Stellar Advisors, LLC." Estelle meets with clients, manages portfolios, writes newsletters, takes out the trash, and files Form ADV annual amendments. For all practical purposes, Estelle is Stellar Advisors, and in her customers' eyes, Estelle is an investment adviser. But to a regulator, Estelle is an IAR, and she is not a registered investment adviser (RIA). Stellar Advisors, the firm, is the adviser.

The Investment Advisers Act of 1940, as amended ("40 Act"), defines an adviser as "any person who, for compensation, engages in the business of advising others...as to the value of securities or as to the advisability of investing in, purchasing, or selling securities, or who, for compensation and as part of a regular business, issues or promulgates analyses or reports concerning securities."[1]

Under the 40 Act, the individual, or IAR, is a supervised person: "any partner, officer, director (or other person occupying a similar status or performing similar functions), or employee of an investment adviser, or other person who provides investment advice on behalf of the investment adviser and is subject to the supervision and control of the investment adviser."[2]

This sometimes minute distinction is key, because regardless of whether the SEC or a state regulates a firm, most state securities regulators retain regulatory jurisdiction over licensing, registration, and qualification of the individuals providing advisory services on behalf of the investment adviser. (Note that actions of an individual on behalf of the firm are considered acts of the firm itself.)

The office manager in the opening anecdote was correct, but only partially. Indeed, the SEC, not the State of Colorado, carried regulatory jurisdiction over his firm. What he had overlooked is that Colorado still regulated the licensing of both the new representative and the supervisor himself.

IV. STATE JURISDICTION OF INVESTMENT ADVISERS AND THEIR REPRESENTATIVES

Investment Advisory Firms

The 40 Act established federal regulation of RIAs by the SEC. Most states did not regulate RIAs until implementation of the National Securities Market Improvement Act (NSMIA) of 1996, and subsequent states' passages of their own adviser statutes. NSMIA divided regulatory authority over RIAs, and preempted state regulation of SEC-regulated or statutorily exempt RIAs. Under NSMIA, advisors with less than $25 million in assets under management came under the purview of state securities regulators beginning in 1999.

The Dodd-Frank Wall Street Reform and Consumer Protection Act, enacted in 2010 (and fortunately known just as "Dodd-Frank") created the category of "midsized" advisers—those with between $25 million and $100 million in assets under management. Most of these midsized advisers moved to state jurisdiction in 2012.

RIAs therefore fall under regulation by either the SEC or the state(s), but not both. SEC-regulated advisers may also be referred to as "federal covered advisers" (FCAs).

---

1 §202(a)(11).
2 §202(a)(25).

In order to avoid requiring RIAs to switch back and forth between state and SEC regulation due to market or client asset fluctuation, a state-regulated adviser may choose to remain under state regulation up to $110 million assets under management (AUM), and an SEC-regulated adviser may remain under SEC jurisdiction until its AUM drops below $90 million.[3]

In addition to the $90 million to $110 million "buffer," there are other exceptions to the $100 million boundary between SEC and state jurisdiction:

- An adviser controlling, controlled by, or under common control with an investment adviser registered with the SEC will register with the SEC;[4]
- An adviser that is *not* registered with a state securities regulator at the time of application to the SEC, who expects to be eligible for SEC registration within 120 days may register with the SEC;[5]
- An adviser required to register in 15 or more states due to client geographies (a "multistate" adviser) may register with the SEC.[6] No state can require an out-of-state adviser to register until it has more than five clients who reside in that state (the federal *de minimis* standard[7]);
- An adviser who provides investment advice exclusively over the internet may register with the SEC. An internet adviser may provide investment advice through other means (e.g., in person) to fewer than 15 clients during a 12-month period;[8]
- Until July 1, 2017, firms with their principal place of business in Wyoming were required to register with the SEC. The SEC has taken action against several firms that attempted to use this exception fraudulently, without their principal place of business in fact being in Wyoming.[9]
- The State of New York does not examine firms with between $25 million and $100 million AUM. The SEC therefore regulates these midsized firms in New York.
- Firms with AUM between $25 million and $100 million that are exempt from registration with their home state must either elect to register with their home state, register with the SEC (in this situation, they may register with the SEC even though their AUM is below $100 million), or qualify for an exemption from federal registration as well (e.g., the private fund adviser exemption, which requires an "exempt reporting adviser" filing but not a full-blown registration).

Summaries of each state's registration requirements, fees, *de minimis* thresholds, and links to the state's regulatory agency are available from the North American Securities Administrators Association (NASAA).[10]

---

[3] 17 CFR §275.203A-1.

[4] 17 CFR §275.203A-2(b).

[5] 17 CFR §275.203A-2(c).

[6] 17 CFR §275.203A-2(d).

[7] §222(d).

[8] 17 CFR §275.203A-2(e).

[9] SEC Administrative Proceedings 3-16371, 3-16368, and 3-16369.

[10] North American Securities Administration Association, State Investment Adviser Registration Information, http://www.nasaa.org/industry-resources/investment-advisers/ia-switch-resources/state-investment-adviser-registration-information/

Although NSMIA preempted state regulatory authority over federal covered advisers, state regulators retain the following jurisdictions that pertain to FCAs:

- *Fraud:* States may specifically investigate and bring enforcement actions against an FCA (or an entity exempt from registration) for "fraud or deceit;"[11]
- *Representative licensing:* State securities regulators retain the prerogative to license, register, or qualify IARs of FCAs.[12] Inherent in this authority, as illustrated in the introduction to this chapter, is the authority to investigate and bring enforcement in the case of unlicensed advisory activity; and
- *Unregistered, nonexempt securities:* Although securities registration is a topic outside the scope of this chapter, compliance officers should be wary of unregistered securities. The 40 Act defines a security as "any note, stock, treasury stock, security future, bond, debenture…"[13] and goes on with a lengthy list from there. A more accessible pocket definition, and one that most state regulators use, is the Howey Test. Under the Howey Test, a security involves four elements[14]
  - An investment of money,
  - In a common enterprise,
  - With the expectation of profits, and
  - Relying solely or substantially on the efforts of others.

If a firm is offering or recommending an unregistered investment with these characteristics, compliance personnel should ensure that the offering is exempt from registration; both the SEC and the states will take a keen interest if it is not! Specific circumstances and questions in this area are best addressed by an experienced, competent securities attorney.

Investment Adviser Representatives

The SEC does not qualify or license IARs; that is the prerogative of the states. Whether the advisory firm is registered with the SEC or state regulators, the applicable state regulator will issue qualification requirements for IARs and regulate licensure.

Exceptions apply to these states:

- The State of Wyoming began regulating IARs on July 1, 2017.
- The State of New York does not license IARs of either state or federal-registered advisers. For individuals who represent state-registered investment advisers, New York does require either the Series 65 exam or the combination of the Series 7 and 66 examinations.

---

[11] 17 CFR §275.203A(3)(b)(2).
[12] 17 CFR §275.203A(3)(b)(1)(A).
[13] §202(a)(18).
[14] *SEC v. W.J. Howey Co.*, 328 U.S. 293 (1946).

V. STATE JURISDICTION OF BROKER-DEALERS AND THEIR REPRESENTATIVES

Broker-Dealers

State regulation of securities brokers predates federal regulation by two decades. Kansas passed the first securities laws in 1911.[15] Other states followed, and state securities laws became known collectively as "blue sky" laws. The federal Securities Act of 1933 and the Securities Exchange Act of 1934 did not supplant these state securities laws. The 1934 Act created the Securities and Exchange Commission with authority to regulate broker-dealers through various self-regulatory organizations (SROs) like the New York Stock Exchange (NYSE) and National Association of Securities Dealers (NASD)—later merged into the Financial Industry Regulatory Authority (FINRA).

State securities regulators retain jurisdiction over broker-dealers alongside the SROs. Hence, a broker-dealer firm may undergo separate examinations by both FINRA and state regulators. Because of limited state resources and the existence of FINRA's regulatory regimen, many states conduct, but do not emphasize, routine examinations of FINRA member broker-dealers.

Registered Representatives

In parallel with FINRA, states license registered representatives (RRs) of broker-dealers. State requirements for RR licensure are not completely uniform. Not all states require the Series 63. A representative whose resident license is in a non-Series 63 state will need to successfully pass the 63 (or an equivalent, like the Series 66 Combined Examination) to receive a license in other states.

State licensure is not automatic for an RR, particularly if the representative has a disciplinary history. For example, an out-of-state broker-dealer firm may request licensure so that one of their existing representatives may call prospects in the state to offer securities. If that RR has a "checkered" Form U4, the regulator in the new state may request additional information about representative's disciplinary history, and might request that the broker-dealer withdraw the application or deny it outright, although the representative is actively licensed with FINRA and in other states.

VI. LIKELY INTERACTIONS WITH STATE REGULATORS

Federal Covered Advisors

For federal covered advisors, the jurisdiction of state securities regulators is limited by NSMIA and Dodd-Frank revisions. As outlined earlier in this chapter, state regulators retain jurisdiction over:

---

[15] North American Securities Administrators Association, Our Role, http://www.nasaa.org/about-us/our-role/

- Qualification and licensing of individual IARs;
- Conduct of both IARs and RIAs in cases of suspected fraud or deceit; and
- The sale of unregistered, nonexempt securities by FCAs.

If a state securities regulator contacts an FCA, it is likely related to one of these three areas.

Broker-Dealers

Any broker-dealer doing business in a state is subject to routine examinations by state securities regulators. These are relatively infrequent in some states because:

- State regulators often view FINRA-regulated broker-dealers as lower-risk entities than RIAs whose only regulatory oversight is that state itself; and
- States with smaller regulatory staff may not have resources to conduct thorough examinations of large broker-dealers.

State regulators also conduct examinations of broker-dealers "for cause," when there is suspicion of regulatory infraction. Compliance staff should be aware that a regulator does not have to, and in many cases does not, provide prior notice of an examination and does not disclose whether an examination is routine or for cause.

Broker-dealers will also receive information requests in connection with examinations of an independent RIA for whom the broker-dealer provides custody for client assets or whose IARs are also RRs of the broker-dealer's firm.

In the case where the broker-dealer is the custodian for an RIA's clients' assets, the examiner will want to confirm the amount of assets under management claimed by the RIA and may request client lists, trade blotters, fee billing ledgers, information about any complaints received by the custodian, frequency of trading errors, and/or any other patterns that may raise concern about the RIA's operations.

In addition, many RIAs function as branch offices of broker-dealers for securities transactions outside of the advisory role. When examining a dually registered independent RIA, securities regulators typically request that the broker-dealer provide client lists, trade blotters, trading errors, copies of IAR personnel files, and other information needed to review branch office compliance with broker-dealer procedures, and the effectiveness of the broker-dealer's supervision of the branch.

In practice, state securities regulators can request a very wide range of information from a broker-dealer because of regulatory jurisdiction.

VII. NORTH AMERICAN SECURITIES ADMINISTRATORS ASSOCIATION

The NASAA comprises securities regulators from U.S. states, Canadian provinces, and Mexico. NASAA itself is not a regulatory organization but writes model rules and regulations which states may adopt, advocates state regulatory concerns nationally, provides resources to member regulators, and offers investor education.

Nearly all broker-dealer representatives or IARs have contributed to the NASAA's coffer, whether they know it or not. NASAA writes the FINRA-administered 60-Series state law qualification examinations, and the fees for these examinations provide operating funds for NASAA.

VIII. CONCLUSION

Humorist Will Rogers quipped, "Be thankful we're not getting all the government we're paying for." The compliance professional, considering an alphabet soup of FINRA, SEC, FinCEN, DOL, CFPB, SIPC, and *ad nauseum*, may not share Mr. Rogers' sentiments! State securities regulators add some "local flavor" to that alphabet soup, even for firms not under direct state regulation.

The essential takeaways are that for regulatory purposes, firms are investment advisers; individuals are not. There are exceptions to the $100 million AUM line between state and federal regulation. State regulators retain jurisdiction regarding federal covered advisory firms, including fraud, representative licensing, and unlicensed nonexempt securities. State securities regulators have full jurisdiction regarding broker-dealer firms. A firm primarily regulated by the SEC or FINRA should be prepared to be contacted by state securities regulators from time to time.

ABOUT THE AUTHOR

Mark W. Bell founded Tirador Compliance LLC in 2015 to provide local, in-person compliance services and consulting to small and medium-sized Colorado investment firms. Mark is principal consultant and managing member for Tirador.

Mr. Bell served as securities examiner with the Colorado Division of Securities for two years, examining more than two dozen state-registered advisers. He also developed desktop software solutions to streamline examination processes.

He was subsequently senior compliance analyst for CoBiz Financial, a regional financial holding company. At CoBiz, Mr. Bell provided internal compliance consulting to the holding company's broker/dealer, RIA, insurance and bank affiliates. He began his financial services career in 2005, managing an existing Edward Jones branch office, substantially increasing revenues and assets under management.

Mr. Bell's compliance training includes: North American Securities Administrators Association (NASAA) 2012 national conference; National Society of Compliance Professionals (NSCP) national conferences; SEC Denver Region "In-Reach" meetings; and FINRA Compliance Boot Camp.

Previously, Mr. Bell was a technical account manager and technical support analyst for Software AG, managing key relationships with some of the largest and most demanding Fortune 100 database clients in the country.

Early in his career, Mr. Bell served as a social insurance specialist for the Social Security Administration (SSA). At the SSA, he developed a ground-breaking public information campaign, training more than 120 disability advocates, vocational professionals, and attorneys. He created a new workflow model that he helped SSA implement regionally and nationally, leading a group of specialists to establish a regional adjudication team.

Mr. Bell earned his master of business administration from the University of Colorado at Denver in 2005, regularly making the dean's list.

CHAPTER 11

Privilege Issues Relating to SEC Inspections: A Primer

By Christopher S. Petito
Willkie Farr & Gallagher LLP

I. INTRODUCTION

Attorney-client privilege[1] performs a valuable service for clients. It creates a protected space where clients can consult with their counsel without fearing that their discussions could subsequently be compelled to be disclosed to others, including the government and adversaries in litigation.[2]

Regulatory inspections by the staff of the Securities and Exchange Commission (SEC) can present difficult privilege issues for registrants. On the one hand, as a legal matter, attorney-client privilege and attorney work product privilege can be relied upon in an SEC inspection to protect privileged materials and information from production to the SEC staff. As a practical matter, however, declining to provide privileged material to the SEC staff may lead them to draw adverse inferences as to the contents of the withheld materials. Moreover, privilege may not be available with respect to some types of records, given the SEC's position that, as a general matter, privilege cannot be claimed with respect to annual compliance reports and records of routine compliance monitoring. And, further complicating the calculus, while disclosure of privileged materials to the SEC inspection staff may satisfy their immediate needs, it may result in a waiver of the privilege, with undesirable consequences in subsequent SEC inspections or collateral criminal cases or civil litigation. What's a chief compliance officer (CCO) to do in order to maintain the confidentiality of privileged communications and still satisfy the requests of regulatory inspection staff?

There are no clear-cut rules as to whether to disclose privileged information. Each situation must be addressed on its own merits. The purpose of this chapter is to provide an overview of the doctrines of attorney-client privilege and attorney work-product privilege,

---

[1] This chapter was published substantially in this form as an article in the July-August 2016 issue of Practical Compliance & Risk Management for the Securities Industry, a Wolters Kluwer publication.

[2] *See*, e.g., *Upjohn Co. v. United States*, 449 U.S. 383, 389-91 (1981) (citing Trammell v. United States, 445 U.S. 40, 51 (1980); Fisher v. United States, 425 U.S. 391, 403 (1976); and Hunt v. Blackburn, 128 U.S. 464, 470 (1888)).

including the concepts of waiver and selective waiver, and to discuss certain circumstances in which they arise in the context of compliance programs and SEC inspections.

II. THE LEGAL DOCTRINES OF ATTORNEY-CLIENT PRIVILEGE AND ATTORNEY WORK PRODUCT PRIVILEGE

The attorney-client privilege protects confidential communications between clients and attorneys for the purpose of obtaining or rendering legal advice. The attorney-client privilege can be invoked if the following requirements are met:

- The holder of the privilege is, or sought to become, a client;
- The person to whom the communication was made is a member of the bar or a subordinate of a member of the bar and was acting as a lawyer in connection with the communication;
- The communication relates to a fact of which the attorney was informed by the client, outside the presence of strangers, for the purpose of obtaining primarily either an opinion of law, legal services or assistance in a legal proceeding, and not for the purpose of committing a crime or tort; and
- The privilege has been claimed and not waived by the client. Attorney-client privilege can be waived by disclosure to a third party.[3]

The work product doctrine applies to notes, memoranda, briefs, and similar documents prepared by or at the direction of counsel in preparation for litigation.[4] The work product doctrine provides a qualified privilege; an opposing party may obtain information for which work product privilege has been claimed if it can show that it needs the information and cannot obtain it in any other way.[5] This protection also is unavailable where the information has been disclosed to an adverse party or the advice pertains primarily to business rather than legal concerns.[6]

The statutory provisions that grant inspection power to the SEC do not expressly recognize privilege claims. However, as a general matter the SEC recognizes privilege claims as legitimate grounds for refusing to produce documents or provide information in an inspection.[7] One exception is records of routine compliance monitoring and

---

[3] *United States v. United Shoe Machinery Corp.,* 89 F. Supp. 357, 358-59 (D. Mass. 1950). *See also* Upjohn Co., 449 U.S. 383 (1981).

[4] *Hickman v. Taylor,* 329 U.S. 495, 511 (1947) ("This work is reflected, of course, in interviews, statements, memoranda, correspondence, briefs, mental impressions, personal beliefs, and countless other tangible and intangible ways—aptly though roughly termed by the Circuit Court of Appeals in this case as the 'work product of the lawyer.'").

[5] *Id.* ("Where relevant and nonprivileged facts remain hidden in an attorney's file and where production of those facts is essential to the preparation of one's case, discovery may properly be had.")

[6] *In re Kidder Peabody Securities Litigation,* 168 F.R.D. 459 (S.D.N.Y. 1996).

[7] *See,* e.g., Letter from Jane E. Jarcho, National Associate Director IAIC Examinations, OCIE, to Senior Executive or Principal of a Registered Investment Adviser, dated Feb. 20, 2014, at n.6, available at https://www.sec.gov/about/offices/ocie/nbe-final-letter-022014.pdf ("under certain circumstances, documents may remain private under attorney-client privilege"); *see also* SEC, Division of Enforcement, Enforcement Manual, §4.3, at 75 (June 4, 2015), available at https://www.sec.gov/divisions/enforce/enforcementmanual.pdf ("The staff must respect legitimate assertions of the attorney-client privilege and attorney work product protection").

reports required under the federal securities laws, such as reports of the annual compliance reviews required under the SEC's compliance rules for investment companies and investment advisers.[8] The SEC's position is that, as a general matter, privilege cannot be claimed with respect to these records because they were "meant to be available to the SEC staff for examination."[9]

III. PRACTICAL PRIVILEGE ISSUES

Ongoing Business and Compliance Activities

As a general matter, registrants should plan ahead for SEC inspections. Depending on the nature of the registrant and its business, inspections may occur more or less frequently; but all registrants should be prepared to be inspected at some point, particularly if the SEC adopts an inspection program using third-party inspectors. Once the inspection request arrives, the registrant may have little time to prepare for the inspection or correct any problems.

Advance planning should include how to address privilege issues. Recordkeeping systems and policies should be designed so that privileged documents and other materials can be readily identified. For example, privileged documents should be clearly labeled as such, to make it easy to segregate privileged from nonprivileged documents in response to an inspection request. The registrant's personnel also should be sensitized to avoid actions that might risk inadvertently waiving privilege, such as mixing business advice and legal advice in the same document or failing to recognize that drafts of documents containing attorney comments may be privileged.

Personnel should also be cautioned against inadvertently disclosing privileged documents to third parties. Attorneys are frequently copied on communications among business clients to keep them informed as to the progress of transactions and other matters on which they are working and to provide them with the opportunity to provide legal advice when and as appropriate. Particularly with e-mail, which may comprise long chains of messages and replies on a particular subject, it may be all too easy to overlook that a chain of messages forwarded outside the firm includes a privileged message from counsel.

Compliance Reviews and Reports

Privilege issues may frequently arise regarding reports to or by a registrant's CCO. The SEC staff is interested in these reports because they can provide a roadmap to compliance issues. For this reason, registrants may wish to withhold these reports to the extent possible from both the SEC staff and third parties. In some circumstances, a registrant might also

---

[8] Lori A. Richards, director, OCIE, *The New Compliance Rule: An Opportunity for Change,* presented at Investment Company Institute/Independent Directors Council Mutual Funds Compliance Programs Conference (June 28, 2004), https://www.sec.gov/news/speech/spch063004lar.htm, citing *Compliance Programs of Investment Companies and Investment Advisers,* 1940 Act Rel. No. 26,299, n. 94 (Dec. 17, 2003), https://www.sec.gov/rules/final/ia-2204.htm ("Rule 38a-1 Adopting Release").

[9] *Id.*

want to provide these reports to the SEC staff to demonstrate its good faith and diligence in addressing compliance issues. Also, production of the report may provide the most efficient means of educating the SEC staff about a possible issue and demonstrate that it was resolved appropriately. Registrants, however, might hesitate to provide these reports to the SEC staff out of concern that disclosure to the SEC would waive the privilege as to private litigants as well. Accordingly, registrants should seek to structure the CCO's responsibilities and his or her participation in particular compliance matters so as to preserve the registrant's ability to claim attorney-client privilege where otherwise appropriate.

It is clear that a CCO can obtain confidential legal advice and should be able to participate in a business entity's consultations with its counsel to obtain legal advice. However, as a result of the special status, under the applicable SEC rules, of both the CCO and certain reports prepared or provided to him, those reports might not be privileged.

Annual Compliance Review and Report. The SEC has indicated that a CCO's annual reports and the underlying compliance reports cannot be protected from disclosure to the SEC staff by privilege.[10] Accordingly, registrants should expect to provide copies of the annual reports to the SEC staff as part of an inspection.[11]

The staff also has stated that if the CCO reports to the legal department, "counsel will have to clearly articulate instances of client privilege and show great effort to segregate any dual responsibilities."[12] However, the staff also has stated that it will honor claims of attorney-client privilege, provided that these claims are specific and are not used as a stalling effort.[13]

As a result, inclusion of privileged matters in the CCO's annual report would waive privilege and make the information available not only to regulators but also to private litigants. The consequences of this waiver could be particularly severe in jurisdictions that follow the doctrine of subject matter waiver. Production of these reports to the SEC staff raises selective waiver issues similar to those attending the production of internal investigative reports. As discussed below, all circuit courts but one that have addressed the issue have concluded that disclosure of such a report to a third party waives privilege as to everyone, not just to the party to which it was provided.

To be clear, disclosure of facts that were the subject of a privileged communication with counsel, without disclosing that those were communicated to counsel, should not waive attorney-client privilege.[14] Inclusion in an annual compliance report of a description of

---

[10] Rule 38a-1 Adopting Release, at n.94; Richards, *The New Compliance Rule*.

[11] Rule 206(4)-7 does not require investment advisers to prepare a written report on the annual compliance review required under the rule. However, many advisers prepare them as a means of memorializing the procedures and the results of the review.

[12] Richards, *The New Compliance Rule*.

[13] *See, e.g.*, "Attorney-Client Privilege Can Be Asserted If Not Too Broad, Official Says," *BD Week* (Dec. 1, 2008).

[14] *See, e.g.*, *Fisher*, 425 U.S. at 403 (1976) ("preexisting documents which could have been obtained by court process from the client when he was in possession may also be obtained from the attorney by similar process following transfer by the client in order to obtain more informed legal advice"); *SEC v. Gulf & Western Indus. Inc.*, 518 F. Supp. 675, 681-2 (D.DC. 1981) (noting *in dicta* that a fact does not become privileged through disclosure to counsel).

the facts of a particular compliance situation would not by itself waive privilege as to communications with counsel concerning that situation. However, careful consideration should be given as to whether to include counsel's advice in the report, as that might result in a waiver of privilege.

A question sometimes asked is whether work papers generated in annual review procedures are protected by privilege if the review procedures were conducted by counsel or by an outside consultant at the direction of counsel, either internal or external. As a general matter, the SEC takes the position that records of annual review procedures are not privileged to the extent that they are required to be maintained under the applicable recordkeeping rules.[15]

Accordingly, it may be difficult to maintain a claim of privilege with respect to at least some of the work papers of an annual compliance review conducted by counsel. The SEC might take the position that those records were not privileged because they were required to be maintained under the applicable recordkeeping rule. In addition, in practice the registrant may need to demonstrate to the SEC staff the adequacy of the design of the annual review and the conduct of the review procedures, so as to be able to demonstrate that it had satisfied the annual review requirements under the applicable compliance rule. The registrant as a practical matter may not be able to establish this if all of the documentation forming the basis for the report is withheld on grounds of privilege. Accordingly, from a practical perspective registrants should expect and plan to make sufficient underlying review documentation available to the SEC staff, or create specific nonprivileged documentation, sufficient to reflect the review and support the annual report.

As noted above, however, CCOs may consult with and obtain privileged legal advice from counsel, including advice concerning compliance procedures and the annual compliance review. In practice, therefore, legal counsel can be involved in the annual review process without waiving privilege, provided that counsel's participation is for the purpose of giving the CCO legal advice on the scope of the review, adequacy of review procedures, or specific matters uncovered during the conduct of the review. In order to preserve the privilege with respect to these communications, communications with counsel for the purpose of obtaining legal advice should be documented separately from the work papers or underlying reports expected to be made available to the SEC staff to document the annual review process.

Mock Audits. A question frequently asked is whether and in what circumstances "mock audits" are covered by attorney-client privilege. Mock audits are inspections of a registrant's compliance procedures intended to simulate SEC inspections and to

---

[15] *See* Rule 38a-1(d)(3) under the Investment Company Act of 1940 (the "1940 Act") ("The fund must maintain...any records documenting the fund's annual review pursuant to paragraph (a)(3) of this section..."); *see also* Rule 204-2(a)(17)(ii) under the Investment Advisers Act of 1940 ("Advisers Act") ("Any records documenting the investment adviser's annual review of those policies and procedures conducted pursuant to [Rule 206-4(7) under the Advisers Act]").

evaluate the adequacy of the registrant's compliance program or specific aspects of the compliance program. Mock audits generally are conducted by three types of firms:

- Compliance consulting firms;
- Law firms; and
- Accounting firms.

Other types of firms may also conduct mock audits.

If a firm other than a law firm is engaged to perform the mock audit, attorney-client privilege generally would not apply to the mock audit procedures. However, if a law firm is engaged to conduct the mock audit and it in turn engages another, nonlegal firm specialist to assist in conducting audit procedures, attorney-client privilege generally should apply. Under case law, the argument is that the communications with the law firm concerning the audit are privileged because they are for the purpose of obtaining legal advice as to the adequacy of the registrant's compliance program, and communications with the nonlegal firm specialist would fall under the umbrella of that privilege because they should be treated as communications to the law firm.[16] Accordingly, to protect against arguments that attorney-client privilege does not apply because the law firm is performing a nonlegal function, the retainer agreement should clearly indicate that the law firm is being retained to give legal advice as to the adequacy of the compliance program. Information gathering by the registrant's internal compliance personnel at the direction of outside counsel arguably should likewise be privileged on similar grounds. As noted earlier, if a mock audit is conducted as part of the registrant's annual review procedures, a claim of privilege as to the mock audit report or underlying documentation may be subject to challenge on the grounds that they comprise records relating to the annual audit that are required to be maintained.

In some circumstances, a registrant may decide to conduct a mock audit with its internal compliance personnel or a nonlegal consulting firm. In these circumstances, attorney-client privilege would still apply to communications with counsel for the purpose of obtaining legal advice with respect to the specific issues. For example, if the mock audit found indications of a compliance issue, counsel could be consulted at that point for advice concerning that specific issue, and subsequent communications with counsel, or information gathering at the direction of counsel, regarding that issue would be covered by attorney-client privilege or possibly attorney work product privilege, depending on the circumstances.

---

[16] *In re Kellogg Brown & Root, Inc.*, 756 F.3d 754, 758 (D.C. Cir. June 27, 2014) ("[C]ommunications made by and to nonattorneys serving as agents of attorneys in internal investigations are routinely protected by the attorney-client privilege."). In *Kellogg*, the internal investigation was conducted by in-house counsel and outside counsel was not involved, and the court noted that the involvement of outside counsel was not necessary to invoke attorney-client privilege. *See also Geller v. North Shore Long Island Jewish Health System*, 2011 WL 5507572, at 3 (E.D.N.Y. Nov. 9, 2011) (holding that interviews conducted by the corporate compliance officer and documents she created regarding those interviews were privileged, because she created them while acting as agent of litigation counsel).

Finally, registrants should be aware that, even if a mock audit is conducted under the direction of legal counsel, the privilege claim may be waived by disclosure of the existence of the mock audit or the audit results to third parties, including third parties other than the SEC. Whereas as a general matter relations with investors are beyond the scope of this chapter, note that investment advisers for business reasons may want to disclose the results of a mock audit (particularly if they are favorable) to clients and prospective clients, and that this disclosure may result in waiver of the privilege in a subsequent SEC inspection.

Consequences of Disclosing Privileged Materials to the SEC

General Circumstances. There is no set way to respond to requests by the SEC staff for privileged documents. Each case presents its own particular facts and circumstances, affecting both the degree to which the SEC staff will pursue access to the documents and the registrant's evaluation of the consequences of compliance or noncompliance with the request. In many cases, the SEC staff will be sensitive to the registrant's concerns. However, where the SEC staff believes it has a real need to review a privileged document, it may persist in its request.

Whether to disclose privileged materials or information may present the registrant with hard choices. The consequences may be unclear, and either alternative may present a mixture of favorable and unfavorable consequences of uncertain magnitude. While disclosing the privileged communication or a subsequent enforcement action (if the inspection has found an actionable problem), waiving the privilege may increase the registrant's exposure to collateral private litigation or other cases. Conversely, asserting the privilege may protect the registrant from the collateral consequences of waiver, but it may prejudice the registrant in its dealings with the SEC inspection staff or in subsequent enforcement actions by providing grounds for the SEC staff to deny cooperation credit.

When the SEC staff suspects that particular practices or violations may be improper or illegal, disclosing the privileged communications may resolve the issue in the registrant's favor. The privileged communications may establish the propriety of the conduct in question. The privileged communication also may corroborate nonprivileged information provided to the SEC staff. Even if the communication does not fully explain the questioned conduct, it can show that the registrant was acting in good faith by consulting with counsel and following counsel's advice. Providing the privileged communication may also strengthen the SEC staff's perception that the registrant is cooperating fully, which may help ensure a favorable outcome of the inspection and avoid, or at least favorably influence, any subsequent enforcement action. Being labeled as "uncooperative" may also damage the registrant's reputation with shareholders, customers, and suppliers, with resulting harm to its business. Moreover, if the contents of the privileged communication are innocuous or are readily available from other, nonprivileged sources, a waiver may be deemed justifiable on the grounds of "no harm, no foul."

Yet registrants may also have legitimate reasons for not disclosing privileged communications. The privileged communication might not be exculpatory, or it may be subject to varying interpretations, either in or out of context, some of which might be unfavorable. Waiving privilege as to innocuous or beneficial privileged communications might be construed to imply that privileged communications as to which privilege is not waived are harmful to the registrant. Finally, because disclosure of privileged communications to one third party usually waives the privilege as to other parties—even where registrants want to disclose privileged information to the SEC—registrants may be reluctant to forego the ability to assert privilege in collateral private litigation.

In many cases, the effect on subsequent SEC enforcement actions may not be a significant consideration, because it may be deemed unlikely in light of the types of issues uncovered in the inspection. However, in cases when subsequent enforcement action is a real possibility, the impression created by the registrant in the inspection stage may carry over to the enforcement proceeding. It may prove extremely difficult to recover if the inspection staff forms the impression that a registrant is frustrating the inspection process through privilege claims. Accordingly, in those circumstances, the potential impact of a waiver or assertion of the privilege on the subsequent enforcement proceedings should weigh heavily in the registrant's decision whether to waive privilege in the inspection.

Selective Waiver

As a general matter, intentional disclosure of privileged communications or information to one person results in a waiver of the privilege to others with respect to undisclosed communications or information concerning the same subject matter.[17] Efforts to establish an exception to this rule for disclosure to the SEC or criminal authorities for the most part have been unsuccessful. This issue has been addressed in many cases involving disclosure of investigative reports or parts of investigative reports to the SEC. All circuit courts but one that have addressed this issue have concluded that disclosure of privileged documents or information to the SEC also waived privilege as to third parties.[18] The rationale of the cases declining to permit "selective waiver" is that it would enable parties to manipulate the privilege by selectively asserting it against only some adversaries.

---

[17] *See Fed. R. Evid. 502(a)* ("...the waiver extends to an undisclosed communication or information in a federal or state proceeding only if: (1) the waiver is intentional; (2) the disclosed and undisclosed communications or information concern the same subject matter; and (3) they ought in fairness to be considered together").

[18] Compare *Diversified Industries, Inc. v. Meredith*, 572 F.2d 596, 611 (8th Cir. 1978) (en banc) (holding that disclosure of protected materials to the SEC during a formal investigation did not waive privilege in subsequent civil litigation), with *In re Steinhardt Partners, LP*, 9 F.3d 230, 235 (2d Cir. 1993) (voluntary submission to the SEC of a memorandum prepared at the SEC's request constituted a waiver of privilege as to third parties). *See also In re Qwest Communications International Inc.*, 450 F.3d 1179 (10th Cir.), cert. denied, 127 S.Ct. 584 (2006); *In re Initial Pub. Offering Sec. Litig.*, No. 21 MC (SAS), 2008 WL 40093 (S.D.N.Y. Feb. 14, 2008), at 6 (declining to allow selective waiver, but suggesting that *In re Steinhardt* "counseled a case by case approach to selective waiver" and noting that there is a strong presumption against a finding of selective waiver, and it should not be permitted absent special circumstances").

A leading case in this area, *In re Steinhardt Partners, LP*, stated that selective waiver might be permitted when the SEC and the disclosing party have entered into an express agreement that the SEC will maintain the confidentiality of the disclosed information.[19] However, the *Steinhardt* case—which held that the disclosure of a Wells submission to the SEC waived work product privilege—did not involve a confidentiality agreement, and few other courts have accepted the *Steinhardt* court's invitation. Some subsequent district court cases in the Second Circuit involving confidentiality agreements have recognized selective waiver, but others have not.

An example of a case in which "selective waiver" was permitted is *Cardinal Health, Inc. Securities Litigation*.[20] There, the court quashed a subpoena for documents that a public company's counsel had collected and provided to the SEC enforcement staff and a U.S. Attorney's Office subject to a confidentiality agreement. The documents included work papers, analyses, and case files of counsel to the company's audit committee relating to an investigation by the audit committee into allegedly improper accounting practices. The court concluded that work product privilege had not been waived because the company's audit committee and the government shared a common interest in eliminating financial irregularities and ensuring that the company's accounting practices were legitimate.

On the other hand, in a subsequent case, *Gruss v. Zwirn*,[21] the court declined to permit "selective waiver" and cast doubt on whether a confidentiality agreement with the SEC could ever enable a party to maintain a privilege claim as to documents provided to the SEC. There, counsel for hedge funds gave an oral presentation to the SEC concerning the results of an internal investigation regarding "financial irregularities" at the funds, subject to an agreement that the SEC would "maintain the confidentiality of the protected materials…except to the extent that the staff determines that disclosure is required by law or would be in furtherance of the commission's discharge of its duties and responsibilities." PowerPoint slides used by counsel in this presentation purported to set forth summaries of what witnesses told the hedge funds' counsel in the investigation. In subsequent civil litigation, the plaintiff sought access to the factual portions of counsel's notes and summaries of the witness interviews. The court concluded that the disclosure to the SEC had waived privilege as to the requested portions of those notes and summaries.[22] The court acknowledged that the *Steinhardt* case indicated that in some circumstances a confidentiality agreement could affect the waiver analysis. However, the court concluded that on the facts presented the SEC's commitment to maintain the confidentiality of the disclosed materials was "illusory" because the confidentiality agreement gave the SEC "unfettered discretion" to provide the disclosed materials to others.

---

19 9 F.3d 230 (2d Cir. 1993).

20 2007 WL 495150 (S.D.N.Y. Jan. 26, 2007).

21 296 F.R.D. 224 (S.D.N.Y. 2013); see also *Gruss v. Zwirn*, 2013 WL 3481350 (S.D.N.Y. 2013).

22 Plaintiff had not sought access to the "opinion work product" portions of those notes and interviews, so the court did not address whether work product privilege had been waived as to them as well.

More recently, in *In re Symbol Technologies, Inc. Sec. Lit.,*[23] the court permitted selective waiver in denying a motion to compel production of documents that had been disclosed to the SEC enforcement staff subject to a confidentiality agreement. The documents at issue related to an internal investigation of revenue misstatements in the company's financial statements in violation of federal securities law and a consent order entered against the company in a prior enforcement case. The court found that the work product privilege had not been waived because, as a factual matter, the company and the SEC shared a common interest in ensuring that the company complied with the prior consent judgement and had sound accounting practices, and the confidentiality agreement demonstrated that the company intended to safeguard these documents from further disclosure, notwithstanding that the relevant terms of the confidentiality agreement were identical to the terms of the agreement in *Gruss* (quoted earlier). The court distinguished *Gruss* on the grounds that the court in *Gruss* had determined that the parties were adversarial, whereas in *Symbol Technologies* the court had found that the company and the SEC had a common interest that "overshadowed any possible adversarial relationship." The court further stated that in any event it disagreed with the *Gruss* court's conclusion that the confidentiality agreement with the SEC was either unenforceable or provided no meaningful protection, on the grounds that the *Gruss* court cited no binding precedent for its conclusion and, in the *Symbol Technologies* court's view, that conclusion appeared to be inconsistent with *In re Steinhardt.*

Because of the substantial weight of contrary authority, registrants should recognize that a confidentiality agreement with respect to the disclosure of privileged documents to the SEC inspection staff might not protect the disclosed documents from production to third parties. However, *Cardinal Health* does indicate that in appropriate factual circumstances, a party may be able to limit the waiver consequences of disclosure to the SEC. Accordingly, as a matter of best practice, if a registrant decides to waive privilege, it should enter into an appropriate confidentiality agreement with the SEC staff in order to place itself in the best position to argue that a "selective waiver" should apply to its disclosed material.

Protecting Privilege During the Inspection

Registrants also should take steps to protect the privilege during the inspection. Upon receiving the inspection notice, the registrant should evaluate the requests to determine whether they call for the production of privileged documents. It may be appropriate at this stage to consult with counsel to help evaluate whether a valid privilege applies and to determine the best course in responding to the staff's request.

Logs. Prior to producing documents for review by the SEC inspection staff, the registrant should review the documents for privileged materials. If the registrant decides not to produce requested records on privilege grounds, the privileged documents should be segregated and preserved at least until the conclusion of the inspection and any resulting

---

[23] 2016 BL 334855 (E.D.N.Y. Sept. 30. 2016).

enforcement proceeding, regardless of any other document retention requirements that may apply. The registrant also should maintain a log of the documents being withheld on privilege grounds. The SEC staff will expect to review the log, which should include information such as the author, date, subject matter, name of the current custodian of the document, names of people who have had access to the document, and the grounds for nonproduction. The SEC staff also should be notified in writing of the assertion of privilege.

In addition, the registrant should seek to mitigate any adverse impression that might be caused by the assertion of privilege. The SEC staff will not necessarily draw an adverse inference from a privilege claim. However, as a practical matter the SEC staff may view privilege claims unfavorably if they think these claims are being used to prevent the SEC staff from obtaining the information necessary to complete the inspection. When possible, the registrant should suggest alternative means of providing the desired information without compromising the privilege. The registrant also should explain to the SEC staff the concerns that are causing it to maintain the privilege claim.

If the registrant decides to produce privileged documents, the registrant should keep a record of the documents produced. This record usually may be included in the log that registrants should keep listing all of the SEC's inspection requests and the registrant's responses.

Restricting Distribution. The registrant should takes steps to limit further distribution of the documents to third parties. As a general matter, the SEC may use documents that it obtains through its inspection powers in its own enforcement cases and may share them with other regulators and prosecutors. The SEC will not give up its rights to make use of documents for these purposes. However, registrants can take steps as a practical matter to prevent further distribution if (as is most often the case) the inspection does not result in any enforcement action.

First, the confidential treatment under the SEC's Freedom of Information Act (FOIA) rules should be requested, and the documents should be marked as "FOIA confidential" in accordance with those rules. Following these procedures will give the registrant notice of any attempt by private parties to obtain the documents and an opportunity to oppose the request.

Second, the SEC should be asked for a confidentiality agreement. The purpose of the confidentiality agreement is to establish that the registrant did not intend to waive the privilege as to any parties other than the SEC (and the parties to whom the SEC properly may disclose the privileged materials). As discussed earlier, this may prove helpful in defending against efforts by third parties to obtain these materials on grounds of waiver.

Finally, the SEC should be asked to return the documents (and destroy any copies) at the conclusion of the inspection. The SEC inspection staff is not required to keep copies of all of the documents that they have reviewed in an inspection. If the privileged documents are not relevant to any of the findings in the deficiency letter or any subsequent proceeding, the SEC staff may return the documents, which then cannot be disclosed by the SEC to third parties.

IV. CONCLUSION

Attorney-client privilege and the attorney work product doctrine play important roles in the U.S. legal system. Not all communications with attorneys, however, are privileged. As noted earlier, the privilege might not apply to some communications with attorneys because they involve business advice rather than legal advice. The SEC staff takes the position that some compliance program materials, such as annual compliance review reports, are not subject to privilege. And, in addition, an otherwise privileged document may lose its privileged status through inadvertent waiver.

When these privileges apply, registrants can rely on them to decline to provide information and documents to the SEC inspection staff. In some cases, however, production of privileged information may provide the most direct way of defusing staff concerns and resolving an SEC inspection without further action. Deciding whether to disclose privileged materials to the SEC inspection staff may present registrants with difficult questions as to the consequences in other related proceedings, and registrants should carefully weigh the potential short- and long-term benefits against the potential drawbacks.

ABOUT THE AUTHOR

Christopher S. Petito is counsel in the Washington office of Willkie Farr & Gallagher LLP. Mr. Petito practices corporate and securities regulatory law involving investment company, investment adviser, and broker-dealer matters, including advising on all aspects of the design, organization, and registration of investment companies and related insurance products, as well as providing regulatory and compliance counseling.

Chapter 12

Compliance and Internal Audit: The Fraternal Twins

By Jerry C. Danielson
Lincoln Financial Network

I. INTRODUCTION

The purpose of this chapter is to explore the similarities and differences between two corporate functions in the financial services industry: compliance and internal audit. More importantly, it also examines techniques that compliance officers can and should learn from internal audit, and how they can work together to complement the firm's compliance effectiveness and efficiency.

II. ORIGINS

Internal Audit

Internal audit is the older of the two professions. The term "audit" has its roots in Latin from the Roman era word *auditus*[1] meaning "a hearing." Official examination of accounts was originally an oral procedure.

In more current days, the audit function has been shaped and governed by the Institute of Internal Auditors (IIA), which is a worldwide professional body of auditors. The IIA promulgates the International Standards for the Professional Practice of Internal Auditing ("standards") which are part of the Mandatory Guidance, which also includes a Code of Ethics, Core Principles, and the Definition of Internal Auditing. Supplementing the standards are the Implementation Guidance (practice advisories) and Supplemental Guidance (recommended guidance). Together, these form the rules for the practice of internal auditing, not unlike the Code of Professional Responsibility used by attorneys in the practice of law.

[1] Online Entomology Dictionary.

One of the most critical of the standards is Standard 1100, Independence and Objectivity:

> The internal audit activity must be independent and internal auditors must be objective in performing their work.

Further, Standard 1130 makes clear that objectivity is impaired if the auditor is auditing work for which they were responsible within the previous year, and for which the chief audit executive (CAE) has responsibility.

Culturally, the entire basis for internal audit is independence and objectivity. Any compromise of either of those imperatives diminishes the creditability and hence the effectiveness of the internal audit organization.

Compliance

"Compliance" as used in this chapter and more generally in the volume of which this chapter is a part, means in essence "compliance with federal, state, and self-regulatory organizations securities laws and regulations." As used here, the term is fairly narrowly defined as "securities compliance," i.e., compliance with the aforementioned laws and regulations. As such, compliance is a much younger profession than auditing, dating back essentially to the enactment of the various federal securities laws in the 1930s.

With the increasing dependence on financial institutions to fund and preserve modern societies, legislation increasingly regulates securities issued and traded by those institutions. With each new financial crisis, new laws and regulations have been enacted to ensure that "this will never happen again." Within the working life of many experienced compliance professionals, there was the junk bond crisis of the early 80's, the savings and loan crisis of the late '80s and early '90s; the dot com bubble of the late 90s; the Enron scandal of the early 2000s; and the real estate financial crisis (Great Recession) of '07 to '09. Each in turn builds on regulations that were enacted in earlier crises to tighten the regulatory framework in an effort to prevent the new crisis from recurring.

Beyond that, various indiscretions within the financial industry create new and more vigorous regulation. One need look no further than the Madoff case.[2] Again, the intent of the regulations is to generally protect consumers and the financial integrity of the financial industry.

As each new layer of regulation is placed on the financial services industry, there is a need for the industry to set aside resources and people to create, implement and comply with the regulations on an ongoing basis. Typically this involves a growth in the compliance staff of the organization. These compliance people are charged with knowing and understanding the regulations, assisting management in crafting policies

---

[2] See for example, Diana B. Henriques, *The Wizard of Lies: Bernie Madoff and the Death of Trust*, The New York: Times Books/Henry Holt (2011).

and procedures to comply with applicable regulations, and overseeing the effectiveness and efficiency of those procedures.

Currently, the compliance profession has a membership organization similar in some senses to the Institute of Internal Auditors, which is the National Society of Compliance Professionals (NSCP). NSCP has developed a code of ethics, but as yet, does not have standards or guidance like the IIA does. However, conformance to the regulations enforces a certain form of standards on the profession. Further, informal practices have grown by various means, including gatherings of compliance professionals at seminars and conferences, addresses by regulators to such gatherings, and actual guidance from regulators via documentation such as no-action letters, notices to members, etc. All of these have given some uniformity to the profession. Certification programs such as the certified securities compliance professional (CSCP) and the required passage of various tests by FINRA such as the Series 7 and Series 24, add to establishing quality standards for compliance professionals.

So although the compliance profession is not as prescribed in its function as the internal audit profession, there are distinct similarities that will continue to grow.

III. DISSIMILARITIES BETWEEN AUDIT AND COMPLIANCE

The single greatest point of dissimilarity between audit and compliance is that alluded to above: independence and objectivity. Compliance, to be effective, needs a degree of independence and objectivity, but it is qualitatively different from the manner in which audit must function. For audit to fulfill its role as an impartial force delivering objective assurance, advice, and insight, it cannot have the function that it is testing to be under the control of audit. Put another way, audit should not have control functions that it then is supposed to audit. As an exaggerated example, if audit were responsible for the approval of sales material, it could not then turn around and audit the sales material approval process with any degree of credibility. Further, audit should not be the decision maker on specific policies or procedures because, again, if the auditor audits those policies or procedures, he or she is not impartial.[3] Audit's strength is its lack of conflicts of interest and impartiality. Putting audit in a position of control and policy making creates inherent conflicts of interest and the appearance, if not actuality, of partiality.

Compliance on the other hand, is intricately bound up with policy and procedures. Frequently, the compliance staff is both the author and the implementer of various policies and procedures. In the previous example, a compliance officer will frequently define the policy on sales material, build the procedure for approval, and staff the unit that processes approvals. It would be impossible for compliance staff to self-audit its sales material approval unit to the same standard of independence and objectivity as used

[3] The standards make clear that audit may *consult* on policies and procedures, but the auditor must not be the decision maker. Various other safeguards built into the standards around this issue attempt to maintain the auditor's independence and objectivity. An interesting case that delves into these issues is the Enron–Arthur Andersen scandal, which focused on Enron's relationship with its external auditor on both an audit and consulting basis.

by an internal auditor. Management relies on compliance professionals to be expert in the laws and regulations, to interpret those laws and regulations, and to create policies and procedures to abide with those laws and regulations. Management relies on audit professionals to verify that that compliance process is working effectively and efficiently.

For this reason, audit and compliance would never be merged into a single unit or profession absent a major shift in the conceptual basis for the two professions.

Building on these different strengths, there is a common doctrine of three lines of compliance defense for a firm's business. In today's business environment, management is the first line of defense against lack of effectiveness and efficiency. Compliance, as part of management, is the second line of defense, devising strategies and assisting in carrying out procedures for the defense of the firm. Audit is the third line of defense, independently verifying that the first two lines of defense are functioning well.[4]

There is another substantive difference between audit and compliance: the scope of their respective mandates. Audit is charged with the effectiveness and efficiency of the entire firm. This extends far beyond the realm of securities compliance with which compliance typically deals. Audit's purview can include anything from assuring cash receipts in the cafeteria, to upkeep on the company plane, to human resource issues such as the Americans with Disabilities Act or the various Equal Employment Opportunity Commission (EEOC) pronouncements, and many, many issues beyond in the wider firm. Although auditors tend to specialize in functional areas such as information technology audit, or departmental audits, e.g. Treasury functions, they are by necessity, generalists. As a result, they are focused on procedures. What is in writing that they can test becomes the easiest path for them to follow, if not always the most productive. Compliance, on the other hand, requires minute understanding of highly nuanced laws and regulations. Sometimes this results in judgment calls that are not necessarily in writing. This fundamental difference can lead to strife between the two units.

IV. SOME FURTHER SIMILARITIES

Despite the philosophical and functional differences between audit and compliance, there are similarities. Just as auditors must be independent for philosophical reasons, the Compliance Department needs to be outside the chain of actual supervisory control for a very practical reason, i.e. the possibility of liability for failure to supervise in cases where the compliance officer has no actual hire/fire or other reasonable supervisory powers. Putting a compliance officer in that position is very unfair and should be avoided if at all possible. As a result, the Compliance Department stands somewhat outside of the business lines, in an advisory role, exerting influence without actual authority. Auditors are in the same position. Whatever their reports may say, the audit client may choose to disregard the opinion and findings.

---

4 For an excellent discussion of audit as the third line of defense and the need for independence and objectivity, see the IIA's International Professional Practices Framework, *Internal Audit and the Second Line of Defense Practice Guide* (Jan. 2016), https://chapters.theiia.org/montreal/ChapterDocuments/Guide%20pratique%20_%20Audit%20interne%20et%202%C3%A8me%20ligne%20de%20ma%C3%AEtrise.pdf

There is a more important similarity that is of growing importance. Auditors specialize in measuring effectiveness and efficiency. They have numerous tools designed to that end. As compliance has evolved over the last 30 years, professionals have moved from an early position of simply requiring procedures being in place, to reporting to senior management that the procedures are in place (e.g., FINRA Rule 3130), to a sense that in order for certification to take place, some modicum of underlying testing needs to validate that the procedures are indeed effective. This brings the discussion directly into the territory staked out by internal audit, i.e., testing the effectiveness of compliance procedures. And from a business entity standpoint, compliance officers are not only interested in whether the procedure is effective but also whether it gets the job done at the least cost to the firm while remaining effective. In other words, is it "efficient?"

This process in which compliance measures effectiveness and efficiency represents a real opportunity to learn from the auditing profession. Chief compliance officers (CCOs) do not need to reinvent wheels that are fully functional and serve the purpose. Although it is true that some audit tools need to be tweaked to fully suit the CCO's purposes, there is no need to create those tools from scratch.

V. AUDITING—THE PROCESS

The profession of auditing stands independent of the specific type of firm or process within which it is housed. An auditor in a bank, an insurance company, a broker-dealer or an investment adviser is going to follow the same essential process in the practice of his or her trade. Arguably, the same process would be followed in manufacturing, medical, transportation, or any other industry, with only the specific tools being adjusted for the locale. Similarly, compliance as a profession should operate in very similar fashions regardless of the particular type of legal entity within which the profession is housed. This section discusses certain audit practices that may be of use to compliance officers.

Risk Assessments

Risk assessment exists on two levels for the compliance officer, as it does for the internal auditor. First, what are the risks to the firm? Second, what are the risks of a particular policy or procedure that is being examined by the auditor or compliance officer?

The risks to the firm should be examined periodically. This may take the form of long-range planning, such as three to five years out, looking at overall trends and issues of importance in the firm's space. Usually it involves at least a one-year look ahead in most firms. The results of this risk assessment then form the basis for the audit plan for the next year.

The risk assessment may be performed through a variety of means. A common method is described here. Assuming the firm is on a calendar year basis, toward August or

September a risk assessment questionnaire would be developed. It would cover various risks such as the following:

- Strategic exposure, including new products, potential extreme markets, etc.;
- Organization and operational changes, including outsourcing, operational reorganizations, personnel changes;
- Service and marketplace exposure, including customers, agents, media risk, product design changes, etc.;
- Financial loss risk;
- Information technological risk, such as new systems, upgrades, cybersecurity, or the risk of remaining on obsolete platforms;
- Regulatory and legal risk;
- Fraud risk; and
- Other (the "what keeps the CCO up at night" question).

For each risk identified, questionnaire items would examine mitigating controls. The risk would then be ranked in terms of its potential to actually occur (high, medium, low) and then what its impact would be if it did come to pass (high, medium, low). This would be counterbalanced by the control environment (well controlled, moderately controlled, uncontrolled).

Sample Scenario. Working through an example, suppose the Sales Material Review Department has thousands of pieces to review annually. From the factors above, the CCO learns that that department has had high personnel turnover and are staffed by new hires. Further, a new system is being installed. Compounding the situation is that the firm is rolling out a new product in an area highlighted by regulators. For that department, the change of personnel would be ranked a high risk. The likelihood of errors stemming from the change would be high. Assuming new systems and personnel, the control environment is probably low. And because it is all happening in the context of a highly visible product to the regulators, this would constitute a high-risk area to the firm that must be closely monitored.

In September/October, the various audit managers would contact their major clients and conduct these risk interviews, usually with the senior leader of the business area, but also including middle managers who actually live with the day to day risks. At the end of the process, the risks with the rankings would be combined in a spreadsheet or database with ratings. Each risk would also be rated for the degree to which it was effectively controlled.[5] The resulting numeric scores would give a risk ranking which could be used as the jumping off point for planning the next succeeding audit year.

---

5 Note that for any given process, there is "inherent risk," which is the uncontrolled risk if things go badly. It is essentially the "total loss" scenario where the process melts down. However, there are usually controls in place that mitigate the risk. The risk remaining after taking into account the controls is the "residual risk"—what is likely to happen given that controls are in place. If the controls are strong and effective, the residual risk is minimal. If the controls are sloppy or poorly applied, there is substantial residual risk. The point of the risk assessment process is to gain information about controls in place in order to pinpoint where the highest residual risk resides.

Note that this is a "jumping off point," not "the plan." Risk assessment is an inherently judgmental process. As the CCO interviews managers, he or she faces two potential problems:

- The manager may untruthfully deny any risk exists in his or her business area;[6]
- The manager may simply not recognize that risk exists, which could stem from a variety of reasons such as inexperience or incomplete information.[7]

The audit manager must use his or her experience, knowledge of the industry gained through seminars, trade publications, etc., and, for lack of a better word, instinct, to look at the numeric results and determine whether they truly represent the risk status of the enterprise. If the numeric results don't match what the auditor "knows," the plan must be adjusted.

The result is a catalogue of risks to the firm, ranked in a priority order. The chief audit executive (CAE) must then look at the CAE's resources and make a determination of which risks will be audited during the next calendar year.[8] The CAE builds the plan around these numbers and presents it to the audit committee of the board of directors (or whatever executive governs the internal audit function which could be the chief executive officer, general counsel, chief financial officer, etc.). The plan may be tweaked at that point for the differing views of top executives and is then issued. That is the blueprint for the following year.

This process must be applied in a rational fashion. One extreme application of the foregoing principle is an attempt to list *every* risk, e.g., a meteor strike on the firm's data center. Although listing every possible contingency that might knock out a data center could be an endless task, the important point that should be considered is what happens if, for whatever reason, the data center is disabled? The trick in this process is focusing on real risks at a level low enough to identify them, but not so low as to get into an obsessive-compulsive round of trivia. The opposite extreme is to take such a high-level look that specifics cannot be identified, e.g., the firm could have a regulatory problem. Stating the kind of problem, procedure, department, etc., are all critical information to have to develop a plan of action.

---

6 Note that doing these interviews with a number of managers frequently had the effect of "triangulating" a risk, i.e., even if Manager A denies risk, Manager B and Manager C may point out risk in Manager A's area due to the potential impact in their own areas.

7 Consider the financial crisis, during which many financial models at sophisticated firms would work from incremental change in financial affairs. For example, if the market historically never went more than X percent from a particular point, the model would assume safety if the firm hedged to that point. However, in the financial crisis that began in 2007, "black swan" events occurred,—catastrophic changes in market conditions that the models could not take into account. These types of events remain a wildcard in any risk assessment.

8 Audits are typically scaled in hours. A routine audit may take 400 hours. If the firm has 20 auditors working 40 hours per week, the total available hours would be 41,600 hours (40 × 52 × 20), but the estimate must be reduced by a factor for vacations, training, etc., so if the estimate calculates figure 80 percent effectiveness, that means 33,200 hours available, or 83 audits. That means the Audit Department will be capable of performing 83 audits in a year, assuming no other duties such as Sarbanes-Oxley (SOX) oversight. In a major financial institution, that is a proverbial drop in a bucket. The auditors must work hard to concentrate their efforts on the highest risk areas, because there are probably hundreds if not thousands of identifiable risks.

Understanding the audit risk assessment process is important to the compliance officer for two reasons. First, if a compliance function is on the audit schedule, it probably didn't get there by chance. Trying to get the auditor to back off, postpone, or basically just go away, is not going to happen because commitments have been made to senior personnel, probably much higher than the CCO, that the audit will take place.

Second, it provides a methodology for annual risk assessments in the CCO's own area. What are the key procedures/departments in the enterprise from a compliance standpoint? What risks are compliance officers facing? What controls do they have in place? How much residual risk exists after controls are considered? Have officers talked to the people in charge of those procedures to determine whether risks have evolved or new risks have appeared? Have officers reported in a coherent, logical fashion, to the CCO or president what risks exist to compliance in the enterprise?

Working with Auditors. The annual risk assessment process is a prime opportunity to steer internal auditors in a direction that will be useful to the compliance function—a chance not to be missed. If the CCO is not being contacted by the Internal Audit Department regarding compliance risk, he or she should probably proactively go to that department and request the opportunity for input. The CCO may use the opportunity to educate auditors on where compliance risk resides within the enterprise and what controls are in place. This will probably be a fairly high-level discussion. Then, if the CCO has areas of concern, he or she can let the auditors know what they are and why. There are probably multiple operational areas that are critical to overall compliance, such as cashiering and marketing, over which compliance officers have no control but which may concern them. This is an opportunity to have an ally go in and look under the hood to see what is really going on. The result should be better compliance for the entire organization. If the CCO doesn't do this proactively, compliance personnel run the risk that the Internal Audit Department could select some process that is well controlled and presents a mild risk for audit. Such a detour is a waste of time for both departments. But the Internal Audit people "don't know what they don't know," and a compliance officer's silence only allows that sort of decision making to go on.

Risk Assessment: Tactical

The actual audit that will be assigned to the auditors to accomplish will be "generally specific," i.e., the auditor will know he or she has a specific topic, procedure, or department to audit, but have no guidance on what actually goes on in that area (barring previous audit work the auditor may have done there) or how to go about auditing the subject area. Fortunately, audit standards provide a prescribed methodology for dealing with this, called the "general audit program" (the name varies by company but the concept is the same). The general audit program lays out a series of steps for dealing with an audit, which applies regardless of the specific subject matter. This approach will vary depending on the firm, its culture, and traditions, but auditors usually follow these basic steps.

1. Open the audit internally by a review of the annual risk assessment in which the audit was identified, or other documentation requesting the audit. Review any work previously done in the area. Consult with external auditors for any input if a publicly audited firm. Consult with information technology (IT) audit staff for input.
2. Contact the audit client and inform it of the audit, usually by an initial phone call, then followed with a formal written notification.
3. Meet with the audit client management to define the scope of the audit. Auditors will ask about the business objectives of the unit/process, business risk and concerns, and what automated systems are involved. This is a critical point for the compliance manager.
4. Gain an understanding of the unit/process. Remember, the auditors' general direction has come from above and may be very high level. This is the stage where the auditors drill down to understand the specifics of how the department/ process is put together. They will interview key personnel. They may perform a "walkthrough."[9] They will put together a flow chart or a narrative of how the process works. They will ask for any procedural documentation that is used by people performing the function.
5. Evaluate the controls around the process. This is known as the control evaluation (CE). This is the first point where an audit can "bite" the compliance officer. The auditor will look at a particular risk, the control that is designed to mitigate that risk, and evaluate whether it appears, on paper, to be effective. If the control, even on paper, appears to be ineffective, that issue will then go to the report.[10] If the control appears that it may be or is effective, that control may be one slated to be tested during the audit. Note that during any audit, IIA standards require that the possibility of fraud be included in the planning. Once the key controls are identified, the auditor moves on to planning the test program.[11]
6. Creation of the test program. The test program may look something like that in Figure 1. The test program will identify the objective of the step, the sample and its source that is being tested, the attributes that are being tested for, and who completed the test step and when. A copy of the work paper will be attached to the relevant step.

---

[9] A "walkthrough" is a step by step demonstration, possibly using several sample transactions of the entire process being audited.

[10] For example, if during the audit process of the outside brokerage accounts of staff, it is found that the 407 letters are sent to the employee's broker-dealer, but no method exists to track whether statements are received from that broker-dealer, that fact constitutes a control weakness that would go to the report.

[11] Some audit departments will pause at this point to consult with the client and discuss the key controls and weaknesses. This is the ideal opportunity to clear up any misunderstandings that the auditors may have about how the process is put together. Correcting bad information here will save hours of the auditors' time and will make the final result much more useful to both parties.

FIGURE 1. TEST PROGRAM

Step #	Test Step	Work Paper	Person Completing Test and Date:
1.	**Objective:** To ensure the accurate completion of trade tickets.		
	Sample: Select 300 trade tickets from XYZ report. Verify the following:		
1.a.	Was the trade ticket time stamped?	Attachment col. A.	Jcd 1/1/17
1.b.	Did the trade ticket accurately reflect if it was solicited or unsolicited?		

7. Testing then begins. Ideally, the compliance officer should have a relationship with the audit team that ensures that as the auditors find issues, they will tell him or her about it. Sometimes this is very informal through a phone call, sometimes it is more formal, via an audit comment sheet.[12] The degree of formality will tell him or her much about how serious the auditors view the finding, although this is not always a sure guide. This is another step in the process where the compliance officer's input is critical. If there is a reasonable basis to believe that the finding is in error, now is the time to provide evidence that that is the case. Provide the evidence in writing.
8. Exceptions noted from the testing will be taken to an exception master list, sometimes called the summary of audit findings (SAF). The SAF will note each finding, the work paper where it is located, and how it was disposed of (e.g., further information was received and it turned out not to be an exception, it was a minor matter and verbally discussed with management, or it was taken to the report).
9. Draft report. As testing is concluded, a draft report is prepared. If time permits, the draft report will be circulated to management prior to an exit conference.
10. Exit conference. If a draft report has not been previously prepared, it will be delivered at this conference. Either way, if the draft came to the compliance officer before or during this conference, the auditors will go over their findings and their rationale. This is pretty much the officer's final chance to mitigate any findings on the report. A CCO can certainly request some time to review the draft and get back to the auditors with corrections or further information that wasn't previously made known to them. Modifications at this point are still possible.
11. The report is issued. At this point, the report is set in stone and will be distributed to all relevant players. This typically includes the immediate manager of the area, his or her manager above the area, the audit committee, and possibly external auditors if the firm uses them. The report may or may not have an opinion. The IIA does not mandate that opinions be issued, so some firms just list findings. Many other firms do have their auditors issue opinions and the terminology varies greatly.

[12] The audit comment sheet goes by various names in various firms. Its purpose is to document that something the auditor has found is indeed a problem. Frequently this sheet is used when the auditors believe they are treading on uncertain or controversial ground, and they desire to nail down exactly what is transpiring. A compliance officer ignores the audit comment sheet at his or her peril.

Satisfactory, needs improvement, and unsatisfactory are fairly common terms. Similarly, practice varies over whether remediation steps are included. In many firms, the report simply states the finding. In others, the Internal Audit Department will insert remediation steps. Still others will ask the business area to come up with reasonable remediation steps and will consult with the business area on what those might be. In the latter case, that would occur between the draft report and final report, because the remediation would be included in the final report.

12. Follow up. The audit team will continue to follow up on the remediation plan, requiring actual documentation of the corrective steps until all remediation is completed. In some cases, if the issue was severe enough, the auditors will return to retest the issue that was the problem to assure that remediation has taken place.

The foregoing can seem like a lengthy and complex process, and indeed it can be. Of what use is it to a compliance officer? Whereas compliance people may not choose to execute each and every step or even the majority of steps, the following concepts from the audit are very useful.

Annual risk assessments are absolutely vital to demonstrate to the regulators a commitment to compliance. Having a methodology to follow, a way to document and evaluate risk, and a mechanism to translate that evaluation into action is important.

Having a methodology ("audit process") around the assessment of individual procedures and processes, identifying the process, spotting key controls, and locating the critical controls gives the compliance officer in-depth knowledge of where the firm's compliance strengths and weaknesses lie. Doing such evaluations on an ad hoc basis, especially when a number of compliance officers are involved in a large department, risks gaps in levels of understanding and control.

If a compliance officer is charged with creating the annual CCO report, be it for a broker-dealer, investment adviser, or investment company, he or she should be especially interested in standardized testing procedures. Documenting what is being tested, why (the objective), how the sample was drawn, and what the results of the specific tests were, give credence that the testing was thorough and detailed. The ability of regulators, external examiners, or auditors or others to go in and repeat the tests based on the tests' documentation, so that the testers can come to the same conclusions, is a matter of comfort to those who rely on the officer's work.[13]

Finally, without doubt, the tracking of issues and the remediation of those issues via documented corrective action is critical. The ability to state that process XYZ was reviewed, issues 1, 2, and 3 were uncovered, and the firm can evidence their correction in these documents is a powerful tool to demonstrate reasonable compliance efforts.

---

[13] There are disagreements as to the proper level of documentation. Some auditors, out of an abundance of caution, like to keep copies of every sample tested, which can lead to enormous amounts of even electronic data, e.g. a copy of every customer file reviewed. A more reasonable approach is keeping copies of the actual exception noted and a list of the other files reviewed that had no exception, e.g. a list of client files. Those lists could later be pulled if it was actually necessary to go in and reverify the test itself.

VI. ADDITIONAL TIPS FOR WORKING WITH AUDITORS

Subject Matter Expert

The compliance professional is the subject matter expert in his or her sphere of responsibility. The auditor is the "visitor," but one with a specific task to do, and frequently has specialized training in the compliance professional's subject matter, although probably not the technical knowledge of the exact process. Sharing knowledge openly and frequently can make that task much more productive for both parties involved. Remember that the compliance officer has several entry points where knowledge of compliance issues can make a big difference. The first is the annual risk assessment, in which the compliance officer can help steer the audit staff in the direction of the highest risk to the firm. Sandbagging the auditor by saying there is no risk in the firm's area is disingenuous. The auditors know better. All they have to do is read the FINRA or SEC disciplinary releases or cases (and they do). Besides which, other areas in the firm may "rat the officer out," a fact the auditors are well aware of and put to use. Building credibility by being frank will build trust that can shortcut the audit process so that instead of demanding to see every jot and tittle of a process, the auditor may take a small sample and the officer's word.

Note that this does not mean that whether the auditors trust the officer or not, he or she will get a free pass on processes that are well controlled. Although most of the emphasis in the last few years has been on "risk-based" auditing and controls, there must still be a certain amount of verification that processes believed to be well controlled actually are well controlled. By way of example, suppose a highly controlled process has been automated for some time. There is no reason to believe it is broken. However, in a routine audit of this vital process, it was discovered that a minor manager, in an effort to save the firm, shut off mail notifications for transactions at a minimal amount by simply adjusting the settings on the automated program. Unless an audit periodically reexamines even well-controlled processes, the possibility exists that risk can rise without anyone being cognitively aware of it. This is why auditors will sometimes examine processes that apparently are not broken.

Another entry point for the compliance officer's knowledge is during the audit itself. He or she can achieve this by first, steering the audit staff in the direction of the most important controls and their current status, and second, by explaining to the auditor why something that appears to be an issue actually isn't due to the technical language of the law or its interpretations that the auditor might not know.

Finally, a compliance professional's knowledge is absolutely critical to the audit in crafting workable, compliant solutions. Because the compliance officer is far closer to the process, he or she will be much more aware of what is possible in terms of remediation. Having an audit report that requires an unworkable remediation is dangerous if regulators obtain the report and question why the remediation has not taken place.

Timing

As noted above, many Audit Departments plan out their entire subsequent year at the end of the current fiscal or calendar year. They have committed to the audit committee of the board of directors or other senior level personnel that the plan will be accomplished. For a compliance officer to indicate that the timing of the audit is not convenient really does not carry a lot of weight. That is an extremely common plea which, if heeded by auditors, would essentially put them out of business.

That is not to say that if there are truly exigent circumstances, that the audit will not be postponed or perhaps cancelled outright. For example, if a major reorganization is about to take place, or due to a new system an existing process is about to be completely revamped, the auditor may decide that auditing an activity that will no longer exist in a few months makes little sense and move on to other audits. (There is always a backlog of potential audit candidates that can be moved up in priority.) Similarly, if key personnel are going to be unavailable for a finite time, or there has been an unexpected crush of business, it may be possible to convince the audit staff to postpone the audit. Just be assured that they will be back, and an excuse such as this will not grant immunity in perpetuity.

Type of Audit

Not all "audits" are the same. The process described above was what would normally be a "full" audit—meaning prework, extensive testing, report, opinion, remediation, and follow up. However, there are lesser degrees of audits that may make sense. They go by various names, depending on the firm.

Review. One version might be called a "review." A review essentially goes to the control evaluation stage but does not progress to testing. In essence, the audit staff is looking at the paper procedures, perhaps does some walk-throughs, and evaluates the controls without testing.

Report. Another version is the "report," which may consist of a description of the strengths and weaknesses of the system. This sort of examination may make sense when management is trying diligently to come into compliance but knows that there are gaps that are likely to make the ultimate results of a full audit "unsatisfactory." This type of review can assist management in crafting solutions without unduly burdening either side with extensive work to arrive at a foregone conclusion.

Consulting. Another version of this would be a "consulting" engagement. In a consulting engagement, the audit staff is brought in at the request of management to review a particular problem or issue, and to assist management in crafting solutions for the issue. This can be quite valuable to management because the auditor may have worked with similar problems in different parts of the enterprise to which this particular management does not have access, and be able to suggest solutions that weren't immediately obvious. Similarly, the audit staff has the time and resource to dig into a problem to find root causes that management may not have time or resources to do. This can be very valuable in finding solutions.

Investigation. A final variation is the "investigation." As the word implies, this is a serious look into a specific problem that may entail malfeasance. The Internal Audit Department is ideally situated with personnel and resources to do in-depth, detailed investigations into particular situations that line management does not have the scope to do. This may be appropriate in some situations.

Communication

Practicing auditors may consider it a failure if they make it all the way to the exit conference and surprise the audit client with a finding. In a reciprocal relationship, communication should flow continually through the audit process. The exit interview should be a recap of what is already known. Granted, sometimes due to time constraints or simple human forgetfulness, issues might slip, but that outcome should be the exception, not the rule. If this is not happening, the compliance officer should reach out to the auditors involved to build the relationship.

Synergy

The audit/compliance relationship is not a one way street. Auditors have valuable skills and resources. Their chief strength is doing in-depth dives on specific subjects. They frequently have IT tools that can assist them in this type of work which are not available to compliance due their limited use in the general business environment and the learning curve to understand how to use them. For this reason, it is a mistake to never pick up the phone and call the firm's auditor.

One of the most obvious times to contact an auditor is in special investigations. All compliance officers will have occasions when a particular individual or individuals are suspect for a variety of reasons. The first call should, of course, be to your counsel to get the case under attorney-client privilege. But if the case involves data crunching and/or review of large amounts of documentation or interviews, the second call may well be to the Internal Audit Department to line up the resources necessary to get the job done. Law or your in-house investigators will seldom have the resources necessary to do a large, thorough examination. The Audit Department provides an excellent source of manpower and skill to accomplish these deep dives.

The other area where auditors can be extremely beneficial is when the Compliance Department has questions about the effectiveness or efficiency of a particular compliance procedure. Compliance officers may lack the jurisdiction to go into a particular business area to run tests. Or they simply don't have the skillset or hours available to dive into this sort of endeavor. Jurisdiction is not a problem for internal auditors, and they do have the skillset to thoroughly examine any given process. If the audit/compliance working relationship is decent, auditors will squeeze the time in to help the Compliance Department. As an example, does the compliance staff have confidence that all emails are being properly archived? Are there parts of the business entity that are not required to archive and others that must? How does the compliance officer know everyone is in the right bucket? How do compliance officers know which sets of emails are being reviewed and which aren't? This is a project that the Internal Audit Department can pursue with vigor while compliance officers simply lack the time or knowledge to do so. Yet such an activity is critical in the regulatory environment to attain a high degree of confidence in this process.

Simply put, if there are aspects of the firm's operation, inside or outside of the compliance officer's control, that keeps him or her up at night, the CCO should consider inviting auditors in to thoroughly examine the area and report back.

VII. CONCLUSION

It is natural for a person to resent being criticized, and compliance officers are no exception. And, face it, the auditor's job can be viewed as criticism. That can be an uncomfortable relationship.

But if compliance officers can put that aside, and consider the function that the Audit and Compliance Departments fulfill for the firm, it is obvious that both are necessary. It is further evident that compliance professionals can and should learn from audit professionals. Compliance staff can, particularly in procedural methodologies, and should use audit staff to further compliance's mission. The Audit Department has the staff, expertise, time and resources to help verify compliance in areas within and outside of the Compliance Department's jurisdictional reach. Teamwork between the areas makes the firm better.

ABOUT THE AUTHOR

Jerry C. Danielson is currently assistant vice president-field assurance with the Lincoln Financial Network. His current duties encompass managing field inspections for Lincoln Financial Group's retail distribution. Formerly, Mr. Danielson was AVP-LFG internal audit compliance with duties that included overseeing audits of compliance on an enterprise-wide basis for topics within insurance, anti-money laundering, privacy, securities laws and regulations, as well as other subjects. Previous to that, Mr. Danielson was the CCO for Lincoln National Corp. from 1989 to 1996. Prior to that, he was employed in various legal and compliance roles with Lincoln National Life Insurance Company (1987 to 1989) and Mutual Security Life Insurance Company (1978 to 1987), including associate general counsel.

Mr. Danielson has been active in the insurance and securities industry. He has been on the board of directors of the National Society of Compliance Professionals (1991 to1994, 2001 to 2004, and 2014 to 2017), and various committees of the NSCP. He has also served on various subcommittees of the American Council of Life Insurers. He is a past president and board member of the Fort Wayne Chapter of the IIA. Mr. Danielson is on the editorial board of *Practical Compliance & Risk Management for the Securities Industry.* He was also a member of the audit committee for the City of Fort Wayne, Indiana, 2010 to 2014). Mr. Danielson is a frequent panelist for seminars dealing with audit, compliance and anti-money laundering matters, including sessions for NSCP, American Council of Life Insurers (ACLI), and the American Conference Institute, as well as being a former lecturer on audit and investigation topics for National Association of Securities Dealers (now known as FINRA).

Chapter 13

Performing Due Diligence and Oversight of Third-Party Service Providers

By Michelle L. Jacko, *Jacko Law Group, PC*
Robert R. Boeche II, *Jacko Law Group, PC*
Tina Mitchell, *Core Compliance & Legal Services, Inc.*
Craig Watanabe, *Core Compliance & Legal Services, Inc.*

I. INTRODUCTION

For various reasons, a financial firm may choose to partner with external third-party service providers (TPSPs) for the performance of essential tasks, rather than performing such tasks internally. Working with TPSPs opens a financial firm up to various types of risks—operational, legal, and regulatory. Costs associated with failing to properly address and monitor such risks not only include monetary losses plus loss of reputation and/or market share, but can also lead to injunctions, sanctions, suspensions, or permanent disbarments by regulators. Nevertheless, there are numerous reasons to use TSPSs whose synergies and benefits often outweigh such risks, especially if risks are properly mitigated. Financial firms often engage a TPSP because of the vendor's experience in performing certain tasks, cost and time considerations, and common industry practice.

Regardless of the impetus for these relationships, regulators require financial firms to conduct initial and ongoing due diligence on TPSPs. This chapter will discuss the regulatory requirements of financial institutions for performing due diligence on TPSPs; the types of due diligence reviews available; common challenges for evaluating service providers; and how to best structure, document and maintain a thorough due diligence program.

II. REGULATORY EXPECTATIONS FOR INITIAL DUE DILIGENCE AND ONGOING MONITORING OF TPSPS

"Due diligence" is the level of prudence, judgment, activity and care a reasonable person exercises under particular circumstances in order to avoid harm.[1] For the past

[1] From http://definitions.uslegal.com/d/due-diligence/

several years, regulators such as the U.S. Securities and Exchange Commission (SEC) and the Financial Industry Regulatory Authority (FINRA) have placed a high priority on ensuring that financial institutions have strong due diligence programs in place covering their use of external TPSPs.[2]

SEC and FINRA Requirements and Interpretations

The practice of performing due diligence on and ongoing oversight of TPSPs is not viewed as a "best practice" by regulators. Rather, such practices are viewed by regulators to be mandatory, as stated by regulators in written interpretations and guidance regarding compliance rules and regulations. When enforcing this requirement, regulators, among other sources, typically rely upon guidance described here.

Rule 206 and Rule 206(4)-7 under the Investment Advisers Act of 1940. Section 206[3] and Rule 206(4)-7 thereunder of the Investment Advisers Act of 1940, as amended (the "Advisers Act"), require investment advisers to adopt written policies and procedures reasonably designed to prevent violations of federal securities laws. Part of this requirement is for investment advisers to conduct due diligence on TPSPs to ensure any tasks outsourced by the adviser to such third-parties are being conducted pursuant to federal law. Although the SEC's formal guidance does not give a great amount of detail as to the extent and scope of such due diligence requirements, the SEC generally looks for due diligence "reasonably designed" to detect and prevent violations of federal securities laws.

Rule 38a-1 Under the Investment Company Act of 1940. Similar to the rules imposed on investment advisers by the Advisers Act, Rule 38a-1 under the Investment Company Act of 1940 requires investment companies to adopt written policies and procedures reasonably designed to prevent violations of federal securities laws. Stipulations of this rule include implementing procedures governing the performance of due diligence on TPSPs. In April 2016, the SEC emphasized this requirement as part of a *Guidance Update* and stated therein, "because funds...outsource critical functions to third parties, the [SEC] staff believes that they should consider conducting thorough initial and ongoing due diligence of those third parties."[4]

FINRA Notice to Members 05-48.[5] FINRA Rule 3010 requires members to design a supervisory system and corresponding written supervisory procedures that are appropriately tailored to each member's business structure.[6] In its Notice to Members 05-48 (NTM 05-48), FINRA[7] established that "outsourcing an activity or function to a third party does not

---

[2] FINRA's 2016 Regulatory and Examination Priorities Letter (Jan. 6, 2016), http://www.finra.org/sites/default/files/2016-regulatory-and-examination-priorities-letter.pdf

[3] Section 206 outlines those prohibited transactions of investment advisers, which include, among other provisions, antifraud provisions that generally prohibit an adviser from engaging in any practice that is fraudulent, deceptive or manipulative.

[4] SEC, *IM Guidance Update* No. 2016-04 (June 2016), https://www.sec.gov/investment/im-guidance-2016-04.pdf

[5] National Association of Securities Dealers, *Notice to Members, Outsourcing* (July 2005), http://www.finra.org/sites/default/files/NoticeDocument/p014735.pdf

[6] *See FINRA Rule 3010(a) and (b)*; and *Notice to Members (NTM) 99-45 (June 1999)*.

[7] The Notice to Members was actually promulgated by NASD in 2005. The NASD would later consolidate with the member regulation, enforcement, and arbitration operations of the New York Stock Exchange to form FINRA in 2007.

relieve members of their ultimate responsibility for compliance with all applicable federal securities laws and regulations."[8] As a result, for those members who outsource parts of their business, Rule 3010 supervisory procedures must also include procedures regarding such outsourcing practices to ensure compliance with applicable laws and rules. NTM 05-48 states that these supervisory procedures must be structured to ensure such arrangements are monitored, including "conducting a due diligence analysis of the third-party service provider."[9] NTM goes on to remind members that such due diligence should not only occur at the time a service provider is selected, but that members have "a continuing responsibility to oversee, supervise, and monitor the service provider's performance of covered activities."[10]

Notably, more recent guidance appears in Notice to Members 11-14, and Letters to Members March 9, 2009, and March 1, 2010.[11]

Regulatory Guidance and Considerations for Features of a Due Diligence Program

Codified regulations and written guidance are not the only sources financial professionals should review when developing a robust due diligence program ensuring TPSPs are performing services compliantly. SEC speeches and past precedent of enforcement actions also provide valuable insight into other topics a due diligence program should cover. The following highlights provide a sampling of such guidance.

SEC Comments and Guidance Statements. For the past several years, the SEC has continued to stress the importance of conducting thorough due diligence on TPSPs. As part of the SEC's 2009 "CCOutreach Regional Seminars,"[12] the SEC noted that "advisers should review each service provider's overall compliance program for compliance with the federal securities laws and should ensure that service providers are complying with the firm's specific policies and procedures." The SEC stated examiners will assess the adviser's "disclosures, contracts with clients, and contracts with service providers to determine whether the services and reporting obligations are consistent with disclosures and that all obligations are adequately addressed and overseen by the adviser." The SEC noted specific risk factors to be examined including, but not limited to:

- An adviser relying too heavily on a TPSP;
- An adviser changing TPSPs; and
- Whether an adviser is a "related person"[13] to the TPSP.

8 FINRA, *Notice to Members, Outsourcing* (July 2005), http://www.finra.org/sites/default/files/NoticeDocument/p014735.pdf

9 *Id.*

10 *Id.*

11 The complete text of the Notice to Members and Letters to Members referenced may be found at http://www.finra.org/sites/default/files/NoticeDocument/p123398.pdf, https://www.finra.org/sites/default/files/Industry/p118113.pdf, and http://www.finra.org/sites/default/files/Industry/p121004.pdf, respectively.

12 SEC CCOutreach Regional Seminars, *The Evolving Compliance Environment: Examination Focus Areas* (Apr. 2009), https://www.sec.gov/info/iaiccco/iaiccco-focusareas.pdf?inf_contact_key=07351db9b4125acf3f4299fd40614c744fbfea546bef99d0fa64a529ed41d25f

13 As part of its Form ADV Glossary, the SEC has defined "related persons" as any person that is under common control with an adviser.

More recently, as part of the SEC's September 2015 National Examination Program Risk Alert, the Office of Compliance Inspections and Examinations (OCIE) launched a cybersecurity effort, wherein vendor management was specifically called out. The staff specified:

> Some of the largest data breaches over the last few years may have resulted from the hacking of third-party vendor platforms. As a result, examiners may focus on firm practices and controls related to vendor management, such as due diligence with regard to vendor selection, monitoring and oversight of vendors, and contract terms. Examiners may assess how vendor relationships are considered as part of the firm's ongoing risk assessment process as well as how the firm determines the appropriate level of due diligence to conduct on a vendor.[14]

This emphasis alone is a call to action for the industry to focus risk management programs on due diligence of TPSPs.

Further, the SEC has proposed rules for transition planning, which among other emphases, stresses the importance of ensuring TPSPs understand their role within an advisory firm's business continuity plan,[15] particularly if they are a critical service provider to the adviser. This further emphasizes that due diligence of TPSPs must be a critical component of a financial institution's compliance program.

Enforcement Actions. The SEC has taken a number of financial institutions to enforcement over failure to conduct adequate due diligence of its TPSPs. More recent cases include the following.

- *In the Matter of Cantella & Co.*, IA Rel. No. 4338 (Feb. 23, 2016): The SEC found[16] that Cantella, a registered investment adviser, took insufficient steps to confirm the accuracy of F-Squared Investments, Inc.'s historical data and other information contained in advertising materials distributed by Cantella. Adequate due diligence on F-Squared's proposed data and calculation methodologies, such inaccuracies would have been identified. Because Cantella failed to perform due diligence, the advertisements showed results that were inflated substantially over F-Squared's actual performance. Cantella consented to the entry of the order finding that it violated, among other infringements, Section 206(4) of the Advisers Act, and, without admitting or denying the findings, agreed to pay a $100,000 penalty. Subsequently the SEC sanctioned 13 additional advisers in a series of SEC orders[17] who had also relied upon F-Squared for marketing purposes without properly performing due

[14] OCIE's 2015 Cybersecurity Examination Initiative, *National Exam Program Risk Alert*, Volume IV, No. 8 (Sept. 15, 2015), https://www.sec.gov/ocie/announcement/ocie-2015-cybersecurity-examination-initiative.pdf

[15] *Adviser Business Continuity and Transition Plans*, Rel. No. IA-4439, File No. 87-13-16, https://www.sec.gov/rules/proposed/2016/ia-4439.pdf

[16] Per the SEC, the findings in this matter were pursuant to Cantella & Co.'s offer and not binding on any other person or entity in the referenced proceeding or any other proceeding.

[17] For a list of the related orders, *see* https://www.sec.gov/news/pressrelease/2016-167.html

diligence on F-Squared, its calculation methodologies and/or obtaining proper documentation to verify such calculations. The penalties assessed against the firms ranged from $100,000 to a half-million dollars based upon the fees each firm earned from the related strategies. As stated by Andrew J. Ceresney, director of the SEC Enforcement Division, "when an investment adviser echoes another firm's performance claims in its own advertisements, it must verify the information first rather than merely accept it as fact."[18] This message clearly illustrates the SEC's position that due diligence of third-parties is the responsibility of the adviser;

- *In the Matter of Calhoun Asset Management, LLC, and Krista Lynn Ward,* IA Rel. No. 3428 (Jul. 9, 2012): The SEC alleged that materially false and misleading statements were made by Calhoun, the investment adviser to two funds of funds, and Ward, its principal and sole employee, about the firm's due diligence process. Calhoun touted due diligence process in marketing materials and the firm's website, particularly on the selection of investment managers, but failed to conduct such due diligence. Instead, Calhoun outsourced the services to a third-party vendor, on whom Calhoun did not perform due diligence or monitor in any capacity. As a result, Calhoun received a $50,000 penalty (joint and several basis with Ward), and Ward was barred from brokerage and advisory business with right to reapply in five years;
- *In re Merrill Lynch, Pierce, Fenner & Smith Incorporated,* FINRA Letter of Acceptance, Waiver and Consent No. 2008014187701 (Jun. 24, 2012): Merrill Lynch outsourced some of its proxy functions for certain accounts of its adviser programs to a TPSP. The TPSP misdirected proxy ballots, used outdated proxy delivery designations, and conducted clerical errors. FINRA alleged that Merrill Lynch had, among other infringements, failed to establish a supervisory system to reasonably supervise the delivery of proxies to certain customers. FINRA argued that had such due diligence processes been in place, Merrill Lynch would have been detected such errors. Merrill Lynch consented to the imposition of various sanctions, censure, and a $2.8 million fine.

III. TYPES OF DUE DILIGENCE REVIEWS

A firm can conduct a TPSP due diligence review in various ways. This section explores:

- Considerations for using internal versus external resources for conducting TPSP due diligence;
- How to effectively use checklists and questionnaires; and
- Tips for conducting onsite evaluations.

Internal Versus External (Third-Party) Due Diligence

Options for Performing Due Diligence. Due diligence requires knowledge and understanding of the type of product and service a firm seeks to evaluate. In some cases, a firm may not have the internal resources to conduct the due diligence because of lack of time or knowledge. In other instances, an external due diligence provider may not

[18] *Id.*

understand the intricate details of what needs to be performed and what circumstances apply. Thus, before a firm commences any type of due diligence, it is important to determine whether the party selected (in the form of an internal staff person or an external provider) has sufficient knowledge and experience to know the right questions to ask and the right red flag areas to explore prior to beginning the due diligence process.

Notably, many external resources are available to conduct *product* due diligence (particularly in direct participation programs). However, fewer providers offer due diligence on TPSPs. Consequently, many financial firms likely turn to a compliance consultant or attorney to provide such services.

From a practical standpoint, outsourcing due diligence can be costly. It can also be a more complex process than internal investigations. It is often difficult to assess the quality of due diligence performed by an external source and to evaluate whether the external source "got it right." Furthermore, the work required is highly dependent on the nature of the services provided. For example, information technology (IT) consultants, fund accountants, and custodians are critical service providers; the services they offer are complex, requiring a significant amount of effort by a firm to perform due diligence. On the other hand, due diligence of other TPSPs, such as a compliance consultant or attorney, will focus on different areas and may not be as complex to perform. Later, this chapter explores how due diligence checklists and questionnaires can direct inquiries to relevant areas pertaining to that particular TPSP.

For these and other reasons, firms often opt to perform their own due diligence on third-party service providers. It is imperative to understand that performing due diligence is complex and requires skill. Firms that handle the due diligence internally must have personnel with the requisite knowledge and skill to perform effective reviews. Such staff needs to know what documents to request, what questions to ask, and how to detect potential problems. Performing effective due diligence requires recognition skills. Issues must be vetted and identified as potential red flags requiring follow-up. Firms that have less experienced staff may need to invest in training staff members who will perform due diligence. Although due diligence is addressed at industry conferences, most often these skills are acquired through experience. Therefore, it is essential to have a knowledgeable, experienced professional oversee the process.

Table 1 compares the major advantages and disadvantages of the two paths due diligence may take.

TABLE 1. ADVANTAGES AND DISADVANTAGES OF THE TWO AVENUES FOR TPSP DUE DILIGENCE

	Advantages	Disadvantages
Internal	Lower cost and more control	Firm may not have expertise or experience
External	Convenient and generally performed by knowledgeable and experienced individuals	High cost and quality of the review may be difficult to independently assess

SOC Reports. In many cases when performing due diligence, a firm will receive and rely upon externally derived reviews such as service organization control (SOC) reports. A service auditor develops a SOC report to report on the controls at an organization that provides services to and is relied upon by other user entities. For the financial industry, the most commonly seen is the Statement on Standards for Attestation Engagements No. 16(SSAE 16) report as required under the American Institute of Certified Public Accountants (AICPA) for practitioners at service organizations.[19]

Some due diligence officers rely heavily on SOC reports, almost treating them as external due diligence reviews. SOC reports can be extremely helpful in providing valuable insight into the TPSP's controls, but like most tools, there are certain limitations as to what the report covers. For example, the SOC report is based on accounting standards that measure the financial controls at an organization. For SSAE 16, there are two types of SOC reports: Type 1 (SOC 1) and Type 2 (SOC 2). In a SOC 1 engagement the auditor reviews the controls in the subject organization as of a particular date, and thus is a snapshot of the control environment. In a SOC 2 engagement the auditor examines how the controls were designed, implemented, and managed over a period of time (typically six months.) Auditors performing a SSAE 16 engagement must examine the financial, operational, and compliance controls using the five Trust Services Principles and Criteria, which include:

- *Privacy:* examination of the collection, use, retention, disclosure, and disposal of personal information;
- *Availability:* examination of controls to ensure the subject is available for operation and use as agreed or committed to customers;
- *Processing integrity:* examination of whether system processing is complete, accurate, timely, and authorized;
- *Confidentiality:* examination of whether information designated as confidential is protected; and
- *Security:* examination of whether the system is protected against unauthorized access, use, or modification.[20]

SOC reports vary greatly in length.[21] A typical report is technical and not easy for a layperson to understand. When a firm reviews a SOC report, it is important to focus on the independent service auditor's report and any assertions made by the company. If the auditor's opinion is qualified, the TPSP could prove to be a nonstarter.

Although a SOC report provides useful information for conducting due diligence, it may not be all-encompassing, particularly for the unique services that a TPSP could provide for the organization. Therefore, thoughtful consideration must be made as to

---

[19] SSAE 16 is the accounting standard that became effective in June 2011 and superseded the Statement on Auditing Standards 70 (SAS 70).

[20] The Security principle was updated in 2014 to reflect today's greater awareness of cybersecurity and includes seven categories of review: organization and management, communications, risk management and design and implementation of controls, monitoring of controls, logical and physical access controls, system operations, and change management.

[21] A typical size SOC report is 100 pages.

what the next steps should be in the assessment. Because SSAE 16 reports are costly, only the larger TPSP will likely be able to provide them.

Using Checklists and Questionnaires

As with so many areas within a compliance program, checklists provide a valuable tool in standardizing what information the firm should collect and consider in assessing any TPSP. A due diligence checklist is designed for use by the due diligence officer for overseeing what areas must be reviewed. On the other hand, a due diligence questionnaire (DDQ) is designed to be sent to the subject company for a response to a request for information. Both serve separate and distinct, yet complementary purposes.

Typical types of information sought during a due diligence review include the following:

- Background information on the service provider;
- Services provided;
- Qualifications of the firm and firm personnel;
- Recent changes at the firm;
- Disclosure of litigation, regulatory inquiries, or customer complaints;
- Disclosure of material conflicts of interest;
- References;
- Privacy policy;
- Data security policy;
- Business continuity plan;
- Information relevant to applicable regulatory requirements (e.g., requisite licensing);
- Proof of insurance;
- Financial records;
- Sample contract; and
- SOC reports.

Figure 4 at the end of this chapter provides a sample due diligence checklist.

In some instances, the TPSP may have updates to these topics completed in a due diligence report that the provider will automatically forward to the user firm. In other instances, the user firm must create its own DDQ to seek these responses. A due diligence officer should periodically review the DDQ to update records based on changes in regulation, servicing needs, and risk profiling of the TPSP.

Onsite Evaluations

Purely documentary reviews have their limitations, so a comprehensive review will include an onsite visit. The qualitative information obtained during an onsite interview can be a valuable complement to the quantitative information gleaned from a documentary review. For example, consider *Moneyball: The Art of Winning an Unfair Game,* a novel by Michael Lewis.[22] This story was based on Billy Beane, the general manager of the

[22] In 2011, this real-life story was made into a movie featuring Brad Pitt, Jonah Hill, and Philip Seymour Hoffman.

Oakland Athletics, who for a time revolutionized baseball scouting by relying solely on statistics (such as on-base percentage) to evaluate players. Traditional scouting combined both statistical (quantitative) analyses and an experienced scout's subjective evaluation of seeing the player in action (qualitative) to evaluate the talent. Billy Beane's contribution to baseball undeniably proved the worth of quantitative analytics, but most successful teams still augment their scouting with qualitative judgments from scouts. Likewise, with vendor due diligence, an onsite visit can provide valuable insights that augment the evaluation of a vendor and the responses the TPSP provides on paper.

Five primary objectives for the onsite visit enable the due diligence officer to:

- Observe business operations;
- Validate information provided;
- Review documents and systems;
- Develop relationships; and
- Detect red flags.

Although an officer may not be able to assess the quality of the services provided by the vendor until the TPSP is engaged, he or she can discern a lot by observing how the provider works with other clients. What is the environment of the workplace? Is it organized? Do employees seem engaged, enthusiastic, and knowledgeable? Does the vendor have well-thought out responses on how it would service the firm's needs and handle any issues that might arise?

Importantly, an onsite visit provides an opportunity to validate information provided. Does the documentation align with the due diligence officers' understanding of the vendor's business practices? Are key employees able to articulate more than a sales pitch? Do their responses give the officers confidence in the services the TPSP will be providing? How much experience and expertise does the firm have in handling clients similar to this firm?

In some instances, the vendor may be unwilling to share certain information in response to a due diligence questionnaire but will allow visitors to review such information onsite. In other instances, IT and other systems would require demonstrations, which are best viewed while onsite.

Developing a good working relationship with critical service providers is important. In most cases, firms have few opportunities to meet face-to-face with their TPSP; and telephone calls and emails are no substitute for direct human interaction in developing good working relationships. Understanding the firm, its needs, and the people that the TPSP will interact with will help establish a strong foundation for good service by that vendor.

As indicated earlier, performing due diligence is complex. Specifically, it requires a set of skills—one of which is the ability to spot potential red flags. It is the due diligence officers' job to probe, dig deep, and get the requisite information to make a determination of the match of the firm with the TPSP. Some skills in detecting red flags are familiarity with the types of issues that may be encountered and open-mindedness to issues that may be atypical. For example, customer service may be a high priority for a clearing firm or custodian. What are the TSPS's response times? What is the ratio of customer service agents to clients? Some red flags can be detected from documentary reviews, but others only become apparent at the provider's site. The officers should know the difference and during the onsite visit focus on those that can only be detected onsite, such as observations of workflow issues or vague/evasive responses to pointed questions.

Key to a good outcome for the onsite review is proper preparation. The due diligence officers should have performed a thorough documentary review so they have a good understanding of the service provider and can ask intelligent, probing questions. Moreover, the documentary review may reveal clues about potential red flags, for example, ones signaled by vague responses in a DDQ. The due diligence officers should arrive onsite prepared with an agenda and a list of questions. They should interview key personnel independently, if possible. Independent interviews may uncover contradictions or additional information that may not come out in a group interview.

Onsite visits are time-consuming and costly, so they are typically reserved for critical service providers such as clearing firms and custodians. However, when performed skillfully, onsite reviews are an invaluable component of a comprehensive due diligence review.

IV. COMMON CHALLENGES FOR EVALUATING SERVICE PROVIDERS

Risk Profile for the TPSP

Each TPSP should be assigned a risk level for monitoring purposes. The factors considered when officers assign a risk level to a TPSP will vary, but the significance of the risk level should be commensurate with each service provider's applicable overall risks and conflicts. For example, all else being equal, a subadviser that has regulatory disciplinary history should be assigned a higher risk level than a subadviser that doesn't have disciplinary history. The example provided here is simple to understand, but in other cases, evaluation and acceptance of risk varies greatly dependent upon facts and circumstances and therefore requires careful analysis and consideration.

How to Begin Risk Profiling. Risk profiling should begin at the enterprise level of the TPSP and take into consideration the following areas:

- Financial risk;
- Operational and resource risk;
- Key personnel turnover risk;
- Privacy/information security risk;
- Legal/compliance risk;
- Business continuity/succession plan risk; and
- Affiliate risk.

Next, officers should consider whether the services performed by the TPSP are critical to the firm and providing services to clients (dubbed the critical provider risk). The officers consider whether the TPSP has direct contact/relationship with the firm's clients, such as a custodian, subadviser, solicitor, or associated broker-dealer. Then the profilers consider whether any TPSP is providing more than one type of service to the firm and/or the firm's clients. For example, an investment adviser that uses a custodian with a broker-dealer affiliate that provides trade execution for the adviser's clients would be a more "critical" service provider due to the multiple services provided.

Thereafter, the profilers consider the services provided (service risk), looking at the strengths and weaknesses attributable to that service provider in performing the services. Profilers ask:

- Does the service provider have extensive expertise in providing the services?
- What is the level of customer satisfaction achieved?
- Is the service one that is currently under regulatory scrutiny (e.g., independence of third-party auditors)?

The final step is identifying conflicts of interest that are specific to each service provider and the services they provide (conflict risk), which is discussed in detail later in this chapter.

For each of these areas, the profilers assign a risk level (such as high, medium, and low). The risk level assigned to each factor in many cases could be subjective and within a firm's discretion of its risk appetite. The profile should document the analysis, and determine the probability or likelihood of whether any of the identified risks will occur and the damaging effects it would have if not handled properly.

Conflicts Surrounding Use of Service Providers

Outsourcing services to a TPSP is very common in the financial services industry, and in some cases, is mandatory in order to adhere to applicable federal and/or state regulations.[23] However, whether a provider is required or not, certain material conflict areas need to be considered and addressed as part of a firm's service provider evaluation process. This discussion describes some higher risk areas, with examples of conflicts for each.

Compensation Flow/Revenue Sharing. Compensation arrangements tied to services can often lead to finding conflicts. One common example is when a firm uses an affiliated service provider, wherein the owner(s) of both companies are the same or under common control. This arrangement creates a conflict of interest because the owner(s) receive a benefit when the affiliated firm receives the service fee. Another example is an advisory firm using a broker-dealer to execute client transactions and certain employees of the advisory firm also serve as registered representatives of

[23] For example, Rule 206(4)-2 under the Advisers Act requires investment advisers that are considered to have custody (other than for fee debiting authority) to obtain annual surprise audits from an independent accounting firm.

the broker-dealer who receive transaction and/or trailing commissions (e.g., 12b-1 fees) based on those transactions. As further discussed later, such conflicts necessitate action steps by the financial institution to disclose and mitigate or eliminate the conflict.

Direct and Indirect Benefits. A conflict also presents itself when the firm hiring the TPSP receives direct or indirect benefits as a result of the service provider arrangement. This comes into play, for example, when smaller advisory firms enter into arrangements with certain custodian/brokers to provide custody and trading services to its clients (e.g., Charles Schwab, Fidelity, Pershing, or TD Ameritrade). Under these bundled arrangements, in addition to the services and benefits received by the firm's clients, the firm also receives benefits and services, but at no additional cost. These services and benefits generally include access to client data via an online portfolio accounting system, a dedicated trading desk, access to real time market data, investment research, recordkeeping services, facilitation of the payment of advisory fees, and other business and management support. Although these arrangements are permissible, advisers must address the applicable conflicts.

Relationships with Key Personnel. Nepotism is not necessarily a bad thing, but it is a conflict that must be identified and addressed when a firm hires a family member as a TPSP directly or engages a company that employs a family member as a service provider. The term "family member" should be applied in a very broad sense and not only include immediate blood relatives, but also certain nonrelated persons, including but not limited to long-term friends, adult children of close friends or clients, and domestic partners. This approach was driven home in two 2016 SEC enforcement actions.[24] London-based public accounting firm Ernst & Young (E&Y), along with a senior partner and an auditor, agreed to pay approximately $9.3 million in settlement charges. SEC investigations determined that there had been violations of auditor independence rules due to undisclosed close personal relationships between the E&Y auditors and personnel at the E&Y clients being audited.

Affiliations. Compensation arrangements, and use of firm affiliates and/or close family members as TPSPs present inherent conflicts. Moreover, conflicts also may exist with certain TPSP affiliations (such as ownership affiliations as well as strategic partnerships within the financial industry) that should be reviewed and disclosed. An example of such a strategic partnership would be a situation in which an advisory firm enters into a solicitation arrangement with an individual who is employed at an unaffiliated investment advisory firm or a broker-dealer.

When a firm handles conflicts, the best practice is to eliminate the conflict. However, in some cases, elimination only switches one conflict for another. For example, hiring an unaffiliated service provider would eliminate the compensation conflict that arises

---

[24] *In the Matter of Ernst & Young LLP and Gregory S. Bednar, CPA,* Rel. No. 3802 & 78872 (Sept. 19, 2016) and *In the Matter of Ernst & Young LLP and Robert J. Brehl, CPA, Pamela J. Hartford, CPA, and Michael T. Kamienski, CPA,* Rel. No. 3803 & 788783 (Sept. 19, 2016).

from hiring an affiliated service provider, but if the unaffiliated service provider were owned by the son of the firm's largest client, there would still be a relationship conflict that would need to be addressed.

Numerous mitigation steps can be taken; many revolve around the type and materiality of each conflict. Although there are too many to list in this chapter, some core mitigation steps can be applied to all service provider conflicts:

1. Provide clients with detailed disclosures in relevant documents (e.g., client agreements, marketing collateral, Forms ADV, and offering documents) that include information outlining the conflict(s), along with a summary of how the firm addresses the conflict(s).
2. Maintain documentation outlining the reason(s) why elimination of the conflict was not a viable solution (i.e., why it was believed to *not* be in the best interest of clients).
3. Assign a higher risk level to service providers that have one or more material conflicts.
4. Implement heightened oversight (e.g., more frequent reviews) for service providers with higher risk levels.
5. Implement conflict of interest policies and procedures, identifying material conflicts and how the firm addresses the conflicts.

Contract Language Considerations

Each service provider arrangement should be memorialized in a written contract and include, at a minimum, an outline of the services being provided and the role of each party. Importantly, a contract is a legal document that should be drafted and/or reviewed by legal counsel that is well versed in federal and state securities laws. Even so, there are a few topics that should be considered for inclusion in a contract with a service provider that may not be standard in all contracts. These include:

- Disclosure of applicable conflicts of interest and how addressed;
- Authorization of performing periodic due diligence reviews and access to relevant records;
- Requirement for notification of material changes to firm and key personnel;
- Limits on authority to act on behalf of firm and marketing activities for the firm;
- Outline of books and records to be maintained (including time period and method of retention);
- Certifications of compliance/legal/financial viability;
- Confirmation of E&O insurance;
- Required disclosures to be provided to ERISA clients under ERISA Rule 408(b)(2);
- Cybersecurity and safeguarding controls (if the TPSP will be receiving or transmitting data related to a client account);
- Responsibility and limitation regarding sub-contractors used by service provider; and
- Return of records upon termination of relationship and destruction of confidential information in the TPSP's possession.

Service Provider's Industry Experience

Engaging an experienced and knowledgeable TPSP is critical. This is especially true when a financial institution is required by regulation to hire a TPSP. Such is the case when an investment adviser must have annual surprise audits performed by an accounting firm because it has custody of client assets. The challenge, of course, is finding a service provider that has the necessary depth of experience in the specialized area needed.

There is a never-ending list of TPSPs in the financial industry. In fact, there are a number of TPSPs that specialize in niche areas. Given this fact, where does one start when there are a plethora of service providers to choose from?

The following resources are helpful consider for gathering information about the service provider's experience:

- *Industry referrals:* ask the TPSP for a list of clients to contact;
- *Internet searches:* Google the name of the service provider to see what shows up;
- *Website review:* review the TPSP's website to gather information on firm history;
- *Referral services:* research service provider referral services for a list of applicable TPSPs to consider;
- *Staff interviews:* talk with service provider staff members that perform the specific services and also determine employee turnover rate; and
- *Industry networks:* check with industry peers to obtain recommendations.

V. HOW TO STRUCTURE A DUE DILIGENCE PROGRAM

What to Review

During the due diligence process, a variety of documents and information will need to be gathered from each TPSP. Initially, requests should be made covering core areas, such as:

- Corporate structure and company history;
- Affiliates;
- Products and services;
- Operational structure;
- Financials and corporate accounting;
- Insurance coverage;
- Key employees (new and terminated); and
- Legal and compliance (including regulatory exams, as applicable).

Next, the information requested should focus on the type of TPSP and the specific services that will be used by the firm. Following are some examples (this list is not all-inclusive):

- Custodians (custody of client assets)
  - Classification and holding of client assets,
  - Use of subcustodians,
  - Process for securing safety of assets,
  - Securities lending practices,
  - Settlement processes, and
  - Reporting on account holdings and transactions;
- Accounting firms (annual financial audits and surprise exams)
  - Status of registration with the Public Company Accounting Oversight Board (PCAOB),
  - Process for monitoring adherence to auditor independence requirements,
  - Types of clients, and
  - Experience in performing acquired services;
- Subadvisers (investment management services)
  - Regulatory registration status,
  - Compliance program structure,
  - Biographies of investment personnel,
  - Firm/strategy performance,
  - Other services offered,
  - Brokerage practices,
  - Proxy voting practices, and
  - Service providers used;
- Solicitors (client/investor referrals)
  - Industry licenses and state registration status,
  - Process for finding potential clients,
  - Employment history, and
  - Other solicitation arrangements;
- Broker-dealers (brokerage and trade execution services)
  - Regulatory registration and FINRA membership status,
  - Compliance program structure,
  - Other services offered,
  - Securities investor protection corporation (SIPC) coverage,
  - Best execution assessments, and
  - Market making practices.

It's also extremely important to determine and review the procedures and controls each TPSP has in place covering:

- Risk and conflict identification and management;
- Confidentiality and safeguarding of nonpublic information (including identity theft);
- Cybersecurity;
- Anti-money laundering;
- Business continuity; and
- Prevention of violations of applicable regulatory and/or firm requirements.

Gathering and reviewing certain information regarding competitors also should be included in the process, during both initial and subsequent reviews.

How to Conduct a Due Diligence Review

The method for gathering the information can vary, but the most common ways include:

- Performing onsite visits;
- Interviewing key personnel (in person and via teleconferences);
- Using questionnaires (both internal and external);
- Reviewing websites, social media, blogs;
- Perform internet searches;
- Requesting copies of various documents; and
- Obtaining industry/client reference letters.

A due diligence process should begin by ranking each TPSP by risk and conflict level, and the same approach can be used when reviewing all the information and documentation gathered. In other words, commence with reviewing the materials covering the highest risk and conflicts areas for the service provider ranked with the highest risk level.

Also, when gathering information from a TPSP, the reviewer(s) should verify the accuracy of verbal assertions made. The reviewer shouldn't be reluctant to ask pointed questions when interviewing senior managers and always ask for clarification when needed. The reviewer should consider the reliability of the source of information, especially when it appears too good to be true or when it's from an unknown third party.

Once the review process is over, the reviewer(s) should have a clear understanding of the TPSP's business practices, along with risk and mitigation controls, and be able to make an informed recommendation to senior management on whether to continue using the service provider.

Who Should Perform the Review. A strong due diligence program takes time and effort, and requires involvement from more than just the firm's compliance personnel. A number of factors are considered when the reviewer makes a determination, including:

- The size of the firm;
- The number of service providers used;
- The person(s) or department managing the arrangements; and
- The frequency of reviews needed.

Larger firms should opt for having a due diligence committee in charge of performing reviews. For smaller firms, it's usually best to have the reviewer(s) be the personnel responsible for managing the TPSP relationship, with oversight by the firm's chief compliance officer (CCO) or equivalent.

When a reviewer assigns responsibility, the roles, required steps, and expectations should be clearly outlined. A committee can accomplish this by having a written charter that provides the framework for the reviews. Individual reviewers can develop standard operating desktop procedures and review them periodically with senior management.

Frequency of Reviews. Once the compliance professional performs an initial due diligence review, the frequency of subsequent reviews should not be a "one size fits all" approach. It's always a good rule of thumb to perform formal due diligence reviews on an annual basis, but a firm should have a review process in place that appropriately corresponds with each TPSP. Timing depends on a number of factors that will affect the frequency of reviews. These factors include, but are not limited to:

- The risk level assigned to the service provider during the initial or most recent due diligence;
- The extent of identified conflicts surrounding the relationship;
- Amount of client facing involvement;
- Changes to regulations affecting the service provider or the firm;
- The type of service/product being provided;
- The terms of the contract;
- Changes to the firm's business and/or services being provided; and
- Legal and/or disciplinary history.

The service providers with high risk levels, material conflicts, and historical legal and/or disciplinary events should be reviewed more frequently and before those with a lower risk level (as was discussed for assigning risk profiles for service providers).

There also are certain factors that may mandate an ad hoc review, such as:

- Departure of key employee(s);
- Regulatory action;
- Widespread disaster (e.g., earthquake, hurricane); and
- Cybercrime.

Depending on the issue warranting the impromptu review, the reviewer may want to consider whether a surprise onsite visit is justified.

Notably, a firm's risk ranking for service providers will most likely change over time, which may prompt a change to the frequency of reviews. For example, a core TPSP was recently the subject of a regulatory proceeding for law violations directly resulting from a lack of adequate procedures and controls. In this scenario, the service provider should be ranked as "high risk" and an ad hoc review performed to determine the steps the TPSP is taking to correct the violation and ensure the same (or similar) violation does not happen again. Also, because this is a core TPSP some form of due diligence (e.g., questionnaires or telephone interviews with senior management) should be performed periodically in between and in addition to an annual review. This will enable the reviewer to confirm that updated controls and procedures are being followed and that no other violation has occurred. Then, after a couple of years if the service provider has shown that the additional procedures and controls are adequate and appear to be effectively preventing another violation, the risk level can be lowered to "medium" and less frequent reviews performed, unless other high-risk factors are associated with the service provider.

The person(s) performing due diligence reviews should implement an ongoing monitoring process. This not only helps determine when routine reviews are necessary but also helps track events that trigger unscheduled reviews.

Developing a Standardized Flow and Monitoring System

In developing an ongoing monitoring program, the best place to start is with a list of all current TPSPs used by the firm, listing the name and type of service provider, the date of the service contract, a brief summary of the services provided, and—last but not least—the assigned risk level. From there, the reviewer should set up electronic files for maintaining all documents, correspondence, and reports. This can be done by using data-storing software or by creating files on the firm's network system. Whichever method is used, it is imperative that security measures be implemented to help preserve the integrity of the information and to limit the sharing to only personnel required or allowed to have access. Also, the data should be segregated by TPSP and stored in a manner that enables easy retrieval of specific documents. When it comes to data storage, organization is key.

A systematic process for reviews is the next essential step. Wherever possible, the reviewer should automate reminders. For example, smaller firms can set up a due diligence calendar using Microsoft Outlook or equivalent program, which allows for electronic tracking of both past and future due diligence activity and will provide automated alerts on upcoming reviews for to enable due diligence team members to adequately prepare. For large firms with numinous service providers, software is available that has a multitude of capabilities, including but not limited to notification of upcoming reviews, the provision of due diligence reports, and retention of data.

Importantly, as noted above, service providers with high risk levels should be scheduled for more frequent reviews.

Lastly, a tracking system that captures the firm's completed due diligence reviews should be put into place. This system should capture the following information:

- The date each review was performed;
- The type of reviews performed (e.g., initial, quarterly, annual onsite, etc.);
- The method of each review (e.g., questionnaire, internet search, third-party provider, telephonic Q&A, or offsite versus onsite);
- The date and type of report provided to senior management; and
- The location of documents and data collected related to the review.

Although there are a few choices on how best to structure a tracking system, using technology will create many efficiencies (including time and money), particularly if the firm has a large number of service providers. This a technologic approach enables the firm to most easily run specific reports based on the information maintained in the software, which can further help to identify gaps or potential areas of concern that require follow-up.

Perform Periodic Assessments of Your Due Diligence Program

Due diligence programs should be dynamic and evaluated from time to time to evaluate their effectiveness. Firms need to ensure that they are asking the right questions, assessing high-risk areas and gathering meaningful data in order to ascertain the strength of a service provider. When a reviewer performs this assessment, he or she should consider the following:

- Is the current due diligence process efficiently generating appropriate and timely responses from service providers?
- Are reviews being performed in accordance with firm written policies and procedures?
- Does it appear that information related to risk and conflicts of interest is being effectively solicited and obtained from service providers?
- Are reviewers spending sufficient time on each review?
- Are the correct employees performing the reviews?
- Does the report and documentation maintained reflect the full process? A due diligence report should include
  - The amount of time spent to conduct the due diligence review,
  - A description/summary of what was reviewed,
  - The identity of the reviewer(s),
  - Whether any additional requests for information were made, and
  - The findings and recommendations from the due diligence team.

Firms also should consider having an evaluation of their due diligence program performed by a third party from time to time, because this assists senior management in confirming whether the program aligns with the firm's needs and is structured effectively.

Employee Training

The first consideration is who should be trained and how frequently. Depending on the size of the organization and the sharing of responsibilities for gathering and assessing due diligence information, it could be prudent to provide general training to all employees. For those employees intimately involved in the due diligence process, more frequent training is required to review overall firm protocols, regulatory requirements (as applicable), and detection of red flags.

Training can be delivered using a variety of methods. Webinars from reputable providers, desktop training (using case examples), classroom instruction, and one-on-one mentoring are just a few commonly used methods. To document that such training occurred, the trainer should use and maintain a sign-in sheet and agenda to help demonstrate what was discussed and when. This will be particularly helpful during a regulatory examination.

The trick to good training is to engage the audience. This can be accomplished in a few different ways. A first consideration is using a roundtable type setting so attendees can ask questions at any time. Next, real life examples help to "personalize" the experience. The trainer can conduct an advance survey for attendees about the firm's current due diligence practices by using a survey system. Having a survey's results may help to inspire a more dynamic discussion. In turn, results also may alert the trainer to any potential gaps to address real-time during the training.

VI. BEST PRACTICES FOR DOCUMENTING A DUE DILIGENCE REVIEW

Information to Capture

There is a saying in compliance: "If you didn't document it, it didn't happen," which stresses the importance of documenting reviews; and this certainly applies to due diligence of service providers.

When formulating a typical computer folder structure, the reviewer may use the sample in Figure 1.

FIGURE 1. SAMPLE FOLDER STRUCTURE

<Compliance>
    <Due Diligence>
        <Product Due Diligence>
        <Investment Manager Due Diligence>
        <Service Provider Due Diligence>
            <Name1>
                <Name1 2016 Due Diligence Review>
                <Name1 2017 Due Diligence Review>
            <Name2>
                <Name2 2017 Due Diligence Review>

Within this folder configuration, there should be certain subfolders. For example, within the 2017 Due Diligence Review folder, a best practice is to include the following types of data and information:

- Due diligence questionnaire;
- Due diligence report (summarizing the review and results);
- Completed due diligence checklist;
- Service Organization Control (SOC) report;
- Policies and procedures manual;
- Business continuity and cybersecurity plan(s);
- Marketing collateral;
- Website screenshots;
- Internet search screenshots;
- Internal notes from discussions and interviews; and
- Reports and other collateral provided by the TPSP.

A sample due diligence checklist is given later in this chapter; it provides the structure for the review and ensures that reviews are comprehensive and consistent. The other items, with the exception of the due diligence report, are incorporated into the checklist as the procedure for performing due diligence. Finally, the report written by the due diligence officer will highlight any findings, make a recommendation, and provide the rationale for the recommendation. The reports are often relatively brief: one page or less.

Two factors differentiate a thorough due diligence effort: a well-annotated checklist and copious notes from discussions and interviews. Notes can also be appended to Adobe Acrobat files such as SOC reports or internet search results. These notes all demonstrate that the documents were reviewed and not just collected and filed.

Identifying Red Flags

The ability to identify red flags is a critical skill for due diligence best practices. Because red flags come in all shapes and sizes, recognition can be challenging. To make this point, here are some examples.

Example 1: Damaged Reputation. Alan Thackery is performing due diligence on Shareset, a file-sharing vendor under consideration for his firm's client portal. The due diligence seems to be going well when Alan discovers that an internet search reveals Shareset changed names recently. Drilling down in the search pages he discovers the firm has suffered a recent catastrophic failure that resulted in several client lawsuits. The name change was to mitigate reputational damage from the incident. Had Alan not conducted this type of search, this red flag could have been undetected.

Example 2: Omitted Contract Term. As part of an initial due diligence review of a CRM vendor, Marie Padella reviews the contract. Per her due diligence checklist, the two key provisions are the confidentiality and data ownership provisions. The contract is silent with regard to data ownership. This is an invisible red flag; most omissions are not apparent and can be very difficult to detect. Some firms have lost all of their CRM data when changing vendors because of data ownership issues. Thus, for Marie the data ownership clause is a critical part of the due diligence review for this vendor.

Example 3: Decreased Customer Service. Pete Labuda's firm has been using the same order management system, SalesTracker, for the past several years. As part of his ongoing due diligence, Pete reviews the vendor's sales literature and skims the biographies of "Our Team." He notices many new team members and is curious about the level of service SalesTracker is providing. When Pete interviews his firm's traders, he discovers that they believe SalesTracker's customer service has dramatically declined. This is a red flag that requires further investigation in order for Pete to determine whether to continue using this TPSP.

These illustrations are just a sampling of the breadth of issues a due diligence officer may encounter in performing due diligence. Spotting red flags is a recognition skill and, like most skills, it is generally developed through experience. If the firm does not have someone experienced in performing due diligence, the officer should consider external resources that can offer mentoring and other assistance, such as attorneys and compliance consultants.

Developing Firm Protocols for Initial and Ongoing Due Diligence

Due diligence is an important duty of financial institutions, which should be addressed in the firm's policies and procedures manual. Figure 2 offers a template for developing protocols.

FIGURE 2. SAMPLE DUE DILIGENCE POLICY

[Firm name] uses unaffiliated TPSPs to assist it in providing certain services to the firm for the servicing of our clients. Upon entering into agreements with such TPSPs, [firm name] will oversee that these TPSPs are completing those services for which they are contracted. Failure by the TPSPs to meet their obligations could not only subject [firm name] to a situation wherein we are not fulfilling our obligations, but moreover, could subject our clients to unnecessary risks associated with the inadequate or failed completion of the contracted services.

In conducting due diligence and evaluating the soundness of a TPSP, [firm name] considers the material risks associated with its reliance on those services provided by the TPSP. The firm will analyze and consider, among other things, the following:

- The TPSP's ability to adequately meet their contractual servicing obligations;
- Any material changes to the TPSP's business or services;
- The continued satisfaction of our team with the TPSP's product or services (including response times and communications); and
- Overall specific performance.

Figure 3. shows a sample procedure useful for the first-time and continued evaluation.

FIGURE 3. SAMPLE EVALUATION PROCEDURE

[Firm name] will conduct due diligence of our TPSPs and oversee those services outsourced to the TPSP, particularly for those which assist in the furnishing of advisory services to our clients.

[Firm name] will evaluate such TPSPs by conducting the following.

Initial Due Diligence

- Request the TPSP to complete [firm name's] Due Diligence Checklist [Questionnaire]; the firm will thereafter evaluate the responses and consider the TPSP's proposed services and any risks posed by outsourcing services to the vendor.
- [Firm name] will determine the exact services to be provided by the TPSP and will ensure that clear descriptions of these services appear in the TPSP's contract.
- Designated [firm name] employees to write a report summarizing the due diligence review, which will include a recommendation about whether or not the TPSP appears to meet XYZ's due diligence standards. The firm will include any recommendation for the frequency of ongoing due diligence to be performed on the TPSP based on its risk profile.

Ongoing Due Diligence

- Employees that use the TPSP's product or service should be kept apprised of the required components of the service and [firm name's] expectations of the service. Should the TPSP not meet this servicing standard, employees should escalate this information to the designated person overseeing the vendor relationship.
- The designated person overseeing the TPSP is responsible for working with the due diligence team to pinpoint areas requiring review. Should the designated person learn of an issue with the TPSP, that person should report the issue to the [designee].
- [Firm name] should conduct due diligence on all TPSP on a systematic basis utilizing the firm's due diligence checklist [questionnaire]. The frequency of the review will be determined at the inception of the relationship (based on the TPSP's risk profile), which shall be reviewed no less than annually.
- To evidence our due diligence efforts, [firm name] will author and maintain a written report summarizing the type of due diligence review conducted and include any recommendation(s) in terms of further reviews or investigations needed and whether the firm should or should not use the services of the vendor.

Depending on the type of TPSP and their risk profile, due diligence can be very time-consuming. Therefore, it is important to develop a protocol for determining how often each vendor should be reviewed, and the methodology to use for such review (e.g., through reports, onsite visits, telephonic interviews, or all three). Consequently, the due diligence officer should develop a due diligence calendar to ensure that critical TPSPs are being reviewed as needed.

VII. DUE DILIGENCE QUESTIONNAIRES

One of the primary ways to capture and maintain pertinent information concerning TPSPs is through the use of DDQs. They bring efficiency to the due diligence process by standardizing the diligence questions posed to TPSPs most frequently. They questionnaires also give insight into the specific TPSP's services, risk processes, management, and performance. With it, an adviser can better determine whether a particular TPSP can effectively support the adviser's business activities.

Considerations for Drafting Due Diligence Questionnaires

An adviser must recognize and take into consideration applicable securities laws and its responsibilities under those laws when creating its standard DDQ template. The DDQ should be sufficiently customized and detailed to cover areas related to the TPSP's services and operations that may create risks, conflicts, or other effects on the firm's business.

Understand the Role of the TPSP. Prior to drafting a DDQ, the adviser should understand the role the TPSP will (or does) occupy on behalf of the adviser. For instance, if using the services of a subadviser to manage some or all of an adviser's assets, the adviser should carefully evaluate the TPSP's performance, adherence to guidelines and its portfolio model, reputation, management team, business continuity plan, succession plan, compliance program, and marketing, to just name a few.

Identify Risks. The types of risks inherent to a given TPSP differ greatly depending upon the services provided. For instance, when dealing with TPSPs that have access to nonpublic client information, the firm will want to ensure the TPSP has taken measures to safeguard such information. In furtherance of this, as part of the DDQ, advisory firms will want the TPSP to provide responses to such questions as:

- What personnel of the TPSP will have access to the client information?
- What types of safeguards are currently in place to protect client information?
- Does the TPSP employ a cybersecurity program, and if so, what does it entail?
- What, if any, breaches have occurred in the past that resulted in client information being shared?

Some additional risks may include: geographic location, industry experience, background of TPSP owners, the TPSP's lack of internal policies and procedures, type of reports/documentations/services provided, and compensation structure. The DDQ should ask questions that address these risks and the steps taken by the TPSP to address such risks.

Ongoing Reviews. Typically, the information collected in response to a DDQ represents a snapshot of the activities of a TPSP at a certain point in time and is current only as of the date the DDQ is completed. No due diligence program is perfect. Each due diligence process undertaken for a potential or active TPSP will reveal strengths and weaknesses of the due diligence program. That discovery is why it is important for advisers to continuously monitor TPSPs to ensure they are sufficiently performing the services for which they were contracted, and that no new risks to the advisers have become evident since the prior DDQ. This ongoing review is expected by regulators[25] and is an important piece of the due diligence program.

Reviewing DDQ Responses

As mentioned above, DDQs are designed to provide a basis for advisers to commence their due diligence reviews of TPSPs, but are neither designed to be an exhaustive list of questions that may be relevant to a given TPSP, nor the sole tool used in performing due diligence. Once the DDQ has been created and customized to fit the services provided by a given TPSP, an advisory firm must effectively distribute and review responses to the DDQ. This can be a robust process that entails multiple facets beyond simple delivery and receipt of the DDQ. It is recommended that firms design internal policies and procedures (or "standard operating procedures) governing such activities. For example, consider the following review processes.

Designating a Point Person. The due diligence officer should designate a single point of contact or a small dedicated group to oversee the distribution, collection and review of DDQs. Channeling information can often simplify the process. Having someone familiar with such aspects as the timing, plus the manner and means of delivering a DDQ can reduce inefficiencies. Additionally, having a single point of contact also promotes consistent recordkeeping practices and establishes a liaison for TPSPs to contact should they have any questions when completing the DDQ.

Trust But Verify. This should be the mantra for any compliance program, but it is especially true for firms when conducting due diligence on any TPSP. DDQs are a great way to gather lots of information about a TPSP in an expeditious fashion. However, simply relying upon the answers to the DDQ itself is not always sufficient. Firms need to take additional steps to be sure that the information provided by the TPSP in the DDQ is accurate and verifiable. Such sentiments were articulated by Andrew J.

---

[25] As discussed as part of FINRA Regulatory Notice 11-14, a firm's supervisory procedures should include "an ongoing due diligence analysis of each current or prospective third-party service provider to determine, at a minimum, whether: (1) the third-party service provider is capable of performing the activities being outsourced; and (2) with respect to any activities being outsourced, the member firm can achieve compliance with applicable securities laws and regulations and applicable FINRA and MSRB rules."

Ceresney, former director of the SEC's Enforcement Division, when he stated, "When an investment adviser echoes another firm's…claims…, it must verify the information first rather than merely accept it as fact." [26] With this in mind, firms should be proactive and wherever possible, investigate whether the responses provided by the TPSP in a DDQ are truly accurate.

Onsite Due Diligence. Going hand-in-hand with the "trust but verify" mantra is the recommendation to perform onsite due diligence of TPSPs when possible. The purpose of onsite due diligence, described previously, is to verify and cross-check the information that has been collected and analyzed as part of the DDQ and other means. Additionally, this personal interaction gives the firm an opportunity to interview TPSP personnel to clarify any questions the firm may have regarding TPSP's responses given as part of the DDQ and to allow the TPSP to demonstrate that the services contracted are being effectively performed. Firms should be thorough and structured in their approach to onsite due diligence in order to prevent wasted energies. Such preparation should include, but is not limited to: understanding processes of the TPSP, knowing who serves in management roles for the TPSP, and having an agenda set beforehand. It is important to remember that even though the firm's due diligence team is a visitor in these meetings, they are also the agenda-setters and should be the ones leading the onsite review.

Going Beyond the TPSP. Just as advisers use TPSPs to perform certain services on behalf of their firm, so too, do TPSPs use certain vendors to assist in their business operations. Well-drafted DDQs should ask questions not only in regard to the TPSP itself, but also as to whom, when, and how that TPSP may make use of the services of other vendors. Depending on the responses received, the due diligence reviewer may need to take additional steps to perform due diligence on the TPSP's critical vendors. This is especially true when the firm is dealing with third-parties responsible for the safeguarding of client information. The level of due diligence to be performed will vary depending on the due diligence program of the TPSP itself, and whether it is viewed as sufficient to identify and address risks associated with such third parties.

Drafting a Due Diligence Report. A firm must document its internal controls to demonstrate the dynamics of the protocol. This is particularly true when it comes to due diligence. A due diligence report should summarize the process used to conduct due diligence as well as all findings related to the examination of the TPSP. Generally, the report includes a profile of the TPSP highlighting the description of its services, business model, operations, compliance program, and management. The report should also include an overview of the industry in which the TPSP operates and how the adviser plans to use its services. It is important to include within the findings any outside vendors the TPSP materially relies upon in performing its services on behalf of the

---

[26] SEC, Investment Advisers Paying Penalties for Advertising False Performance Claims (Aug. 25, 2016), https://www.sec.gov/news/pressrelease/2016-167.html

adviser. Included as attachments to the report should be those documents collected throughout the due diligence process, including but not limited to:

- Any and all contracts between the adviser and the TPSP;
- The business continuity and cybersecurity plans;
- Succession plan;
- Confidentiality terms and conditions;
- Most recent audited financial and regulatory filings of the TPSP (if applicable); and
- All other pertinent documents demonstrating the TPSP's ability to effectively perform services on behalf of the adviser.

Red Flags and Requests for Additional Information

Once the DDQ responses and supporting documentation have been properly vetted and analyzed, the due diligence team will need to decide whether to either move forward, continue with, or terminate the TPSP relationship. An important factor in reaching this determination is to assess whether the information collected shows any potential "red flags" relating to the TPSP. Red flags refer to circumstances suggesting conflicts of interest, corruption risk, or other factor that should be properly identified and mitigated through adequate safeguards.

If red flags have been identified, it is critical that further inquiry be undertaken prior to engaging or continuing with the TPSP. Any red flags identified need to be considered in the context of the industry and jurisdiction in which the TPSP operates. An effective due diligence program allocates resources by ranking risks. Higher risk TPSPs should be evaluated more frequently and scrupulously than a lower-risk profiled vendor. Based upon the level of risk associated with a given TPSP, the firm should assign monitoring tools congruent with addressing such risks (e.g. audits, unannounced visits or meetings, and annual training).

Although all red flags should be carefully considered by the firm, not all will lead to a termination of relationship. For example, a TPSP's failure to respond to a particular question on a DDQ should be deemed a red flag. However, the TPSP may have not understood the question or intentionally omitted its response due to trade secret or confidentiality concerns. If a red flag is discovered, the due diligence reviewer must be sure to escalate this issue to the appropriate designated person for further action.

For TPSP relationships that require more in-depth due diligence, the firm should consider using outside counsel for investigation and/or resolution of red flags. Such actions are typically reserved for critical third-party partners that present a higher degree of risk or for situations when numerous red flags are discovered.

In addition to the identification of red flags, firms also need to consider whether the information collected throughout the due diligence process provides enough information to effectively determine whether or not to engage or continue retaining the TPSP.

Often, additional information is required to help fill any gaps that may exist. To that end, it is imperative to establish due diligence procedures and then review them often to address gaps within the process.

VIII. OTHER DUE DILIGENCE CONSIDERATIONS

A situation may arise that leads the firm to determine that it is best to terminate the relationship with the TPSP. This outcome typically arises when:

- The due diligence responses are incomplete, inadequate, or not truthful;
- The servicing needs of the firm have changed and the TPSP can no longer satisfy the current requirements of the firm;
- The management team or financial condition of the TPSP has materially changed; or
- The services provided by the TPSP are unsatisfactory and are insufficient or substandard.

If it is the firm terminating the relationship, the due diligence officer should follow the notification provisions for termination as set forth in the TPSP servicing agreement (e.g., such as providing a written 30-day notice). If, on the other hand, the TPSP is terminating the relationship with the firm, the officer must be sure to do the following:

- Get all books and records the TPSP maintained on the firm's behalf for the duration of the relationship, particularly if there are regulatory requirements to maintain said records;
- Attempt to download or obtain all critical data that the firm owns;
- Determine whether notification is required to clients (e.g., custodian or broker-dealer changes); and
- To the extent the TPSP had access to confidential client information and/or trade secrets of the firm, review how they will be returning or destroying such information; be sure to review the terms of the TPSP and comply with them accordingly.

IX. DUE DILIGENCE CHECKLIST

Due diligence is a dynamic process that involves careful deliberation. Recent enforcement actions highlight that firms must take reasonable steps to ask intelligent, customized questions designed to delve into whether anything is suspect or awry.[27] Failure to conduct an adequate investigation, particularly when red flags are present, is a compliance program failure that will likely lead to formal actions being taken—by the regulators and/or the firm's clients. Figure 4 provides a sample checklist.

---

[27] See, for example, *In the Matter of Neal R. Greenberg,* https://www.sec.gov/litigation/admin/2010/33-9139.pdf and *In the Matter of Paul H. Heckler and Yosemite Capital Management,* https://www.sec.gov/litigation/admin/2010/ia-3005.pdf

FIGURE 4. SAMPLE CHECKLIST TO USE IN SERVICE PROVIDER DUE DILIGENCE PROCESS

[Name of firm]

SERVICE PROVIDER DUE DILIGENCE FORM

The following form should be used for reviewing service providers that will provide services to [insert name of firm] (the "firm"). This form should be retained in a file that includes copies of all documents used to conduct due diligence on the service provider.

SERVICE TO BE OUTSOURCED

1. **Type of service to be outsourced:**

☐ Accounting/Finance: ______________ ☐ Compliance Consulting: ______________

☐ Legal Services: ___________________ ☐ Administrative Functions: ______________

☐ Information Technology: ___________ ☐ Operations/Support Functions: __________

☐ Other: ________________________________

2. **Is this service essential to the operation of the firm (i.e. transaction order entry; custody and prime brokerage; service designed to promote rapid recovery of operations etc.)?**

☐ Yes ☐ No

APPROPRIATENESS OF OUTSOURCING

1. **Potential impact on firm if service provider fails to perform:**

Financial Impact:	☐ High	☐ Medium	☐ Low	☐ N/A
Reputational Impact:	☐ High	☐ Medium	☐ Low	☐ N/A
Operational Impact:	☐ High	☐ Medium	☐ Low	☐ N/A
Customer Service Impact:	☐ High	☐ Medium	☐ Low	☐ N/A
Potential Losses to Customers:	☐ High	☐ Medium	☐ Low	☐ N/A
Comply with Regulatory Requirements:	☐ High	☐ Medium	☐ Low	☐ N/A
Costs to firm:	☐ High	☐ Medium	☐ Low	☐ N/A
Degree of Difficulty Replacing Service Provider:	☐ High	☐ Medium	☐ Low	☐ N/A

Comments:

____

____

____

2. **Is there an affiliation or other relationship between the firm and the service provider?**

☐ Yes ☐ No

If yes, please describe the relationship and any potential conflicts of interest:

____

____

____

3. Is the service provider a regulated entity subject to independent supervision?

☐ Yes ☐ No

If yes, name of regulator: ______________________________

SERVICE PROVIDER INFORMATION

1. General Information

Firm Name: ______________________________

Firm Address: ______________________________

____

Contact Name(s): ______________________________

CRD # (if applicable): ______________________________

Phone: ______________ Fax: ____________ Website: ____________

2. Is the service provider owned/controlled by a Parent Co.?

☐ Yes ☐ No

If yes, name: ______________________________

3. Personnel:

Approximate number of employees: ______

Does the service provide hire independent contractors? ☐ Yes ☐ No

4. Background Information:

How many years has the service provider been in business? ______

How many years has the service provider provided the outsourced function? ________

Is the service provider known to the firm or employees of the firm? ☐ Yes ☐ No

If yes, please name the individual(s) and describe any prior experience each had with the service provider:

____

____

DUE DILIGENCE

1. What methods did the firm use to verify the service provider's information? (Choose all that apply; attach relevant documents to this report.)

☐ FINRA Public Disclosure
☐ Entity Formation Documents
☐ Credit/Background Check
☐ Form BD/ADV
☐ Personal Referral
☐ 10K
☐ Policies and Procedures Manual(s)
☐ Marketing Materials
☐ Onsite Inspection
☐ Internet Research
☐ SEC Public Disclosure
☐ Independent Research
☐ Media/News Reports
☐ Business Plan
☐ RFP
☐ Personal Interviews
☐ Financials
☐ Sales Materials
☐ Confidentiality Procedures and Contracts for Not Sharing Information

Other ______________________________

2. **If the service is outsourced, does that represent any special risks to the firm if the vendor does not perform as contracted (e.g., loss of data, etc.)?**

____

____

____

3. **Should the vendor's office be visited?** ☐ Yes ☐ No

4. **Please describe the background and experience of individuals who will be performing the services:**

____

____

____

5. **Based on your review of the information, has the service provider and/or its principals been subject to any regulatory, criminal or civil disciplinary issues?**

   ☐ Yes ☐ No

   If yes, please describe:

____

____

____

6. **Based on your review of the information, please describe the service provider's ability and capacity to perform the outsourced activities effectively, reliably, and to a high standard (include in your description relevant technical, financial, human resources, and/or other assets of the service provider):**

____

____

____

7. **Does the service provider have a business continuity plan?**

   ☐ Yes ☐ No

   If yes, please describe:

____

____

____

8. **Is privacy and protection of non-public information a factor in outsourcing?**

   ☐ Yes ☐ No

   If yes, comment on the adequacy of the service provider's for safeguarding non-public information:

____

____

____

Does the firm maintain notes from personal interviews and onsite inspections; printouts from public disclosure sites, etc.)? ☐ Yes ☐ No

If yes, please identify where this evidence is maintained: ____________________

____

9. **After reviewing the information, are there any questionable issues or potential conflicts of interest?**

   ☐ Yes ☐ No

   If yes, please describe:

   ____

   ____

   ____

CONTRACTS AND AGREEMENTS

1. **Has (or will) the firm entered into a written agreement with the service provider?**

   ☐ Yes ☐ No

   If yes, please identify the relevant provisions and disclosures in the contract (choose all that apply).

   ☐ Provides for firm and regulator access to records
   ☐ Defines responsibilities of all parties subject to contract
   ☐ Provide quality services measures
   ☐ Defines how responsibilities will be monitored
   ☐ Disclosure of breaches in security
   ☐ Requirement to maintain a disaster recovery plan
   ☐ Firm and client confidentiality
   ☐ Liabilities of the parties
   ☐ Payment arrangements
   ☐ Guarantees and indemnities
   ☐ Term and termination date
   ☐ Information security provisions (i.e., data to remain uncorrupted and secure)

   Other relevant provision(s): ______________________________

2. **Was the written agreement reviewed by legal counsel?**

   ☐ Yes ☐ No ☐ N/A

   If yes, name of legal counsel: ______________________________

   Date of Review: ______________

3. **Was the written agreement reviewed by the manager responsible for outsourcing functions?**

   ☐ Yes ☐ No

   If yes, name of manager: ______________________________

   Date of Review: ______________

OVERSIGHT AND PERIODIC REVIEW

1. **Who is responsible for the periodic oversight and review of the outsourced service?**

   ____

2. **Identify the individual(s) who will monitor the outsourced service.**

   ____

3. Identify the tools that will be used to monitor the outsourced service:

☐ Service delivery reports prepared internally
☐ Service delivery reports supplied by the service provider
☐ Publicly available resources
☐ Performance levels established in written agreement
☐ Internal auditor
☐ Onsite inspection
☐ External auditor
☐ Attestations by service provider
☐ Other: ______________________________

____

4. Frequency of monitoring:

☐ Daily ☐ Weekly ☐ Monthly ☐ Quarterly ☐ Annually

Other: ______________________________

5. If deficiencies are found, are procedures in place to respond to such deficiencies (i.e., communicate with the service provider; terminate the contract)?

☐ Yes ☐ No

DOCUMENTATION REVIEW AND APPROVAL

1. Individual(s) responsible for completing this due diligence review:

____

☐ The firm has elected to use the service provider above.
☐ The firm will not use the service provider above.

______________________________ ______________
Signature Date

X. CONCLUSION

It is essential to keep improving and evolving the due diligence process. To that end, the firm should establish a due diligence committee, identify what is working, and what requires improvement. The firm should conduct periodic risk assessments on due diligence processes and assess whether the firm is doing enough, asking the "right" questions, and collecting meaningful data. Management should review which employees are best suited to analyze due diligence data and assess periodically if they continue to be the most qualified to do so. For new products, a due diligence officer should ensure that the product is understood, that training and surveillance systems are established, and that suitability considerations are evaluated as necessary. For new services, the officer should check the terms of servicing agreements with the TPSP to ensure it is fulfilling its obligations—from a servicing, contractual, and legal perspective. Importantly, the firm must remember to train. Training is the key to success for any effective due diligence program. The due diligence team members must understand why due diligence is being conducted and identify how it can continuously improve. They should review DDQs frequently and not allow them to go static. By keeping this process continuous, the firm will be in a position to advance its due diligence of TPSPs as the financial industry and its regulations continue to progress.

ABOUT THE AUTHORS

Michelle L. Jacko, Esq.,. is the managing partner and CEO of Jacko Law Group, PC, which offers corporate and securities legal services to broker-dealers, investment advisers, investment companies, hedge/private funds and financial professionals. In addition, Ms. Jacko is the Founder and CEO of Core Compliance & Legal Services, Inc., a compliance consultation firm.

Ms. Jacko specializes in investment advisory and broker-dealer firm formation, hedge and private fund development, mergers and acquisitions, transition risks, and investment counsel on regulatory compliance and securities law. Her practice is focused on the areas of corporate and compliance risk management, contracts, policies and procedures, testing of compliance programs (including evaluation of internal controls and supervision), performance advertising, soft dollar arrangements, best execution, separation agreements, and much more.

Previously, Ms. Jacko served as of counsel at Shustak & Partners, PC. Prior to that, she was vice president of compliance and branch manager of the Home Office Supervision team at LPL Financial Services, Corporation (Linsco/Private Ledger). Ms. Jacko also served as legal counsel of investments and CCO at First American Trust, FSB and held the position of compliance manager at Nicholas-Applegate Capital Management. In addition, Ms. Jacko was with PIM Financial Services, Inc., and Speiser, Krause, Madole & Mendelsohn, Jackson.

Ms. Jacko regularly presents at conferences throughout the nation, and is a frequent contributor to various industry journals. In 2013, Ms. Jacko was appointed to the Editorial Advisory Board for the Wolters Kluwer publication *Practical Compliance and Risk Management for the Securities Industry*. She is cofounder of the Southern California Compliance Group and is involved in the American Bar Association (Business Law Section), State Bar of California (Corporations Committee, where she serves as vice-chair of education), and San Diego County Bar Association. She also is a FINRA arbitrator. Ms. Jacko was named as a Top 20 Rising Star for "Who's Who" in Upcoming Compliance Professionals by *Compliance Reporter* magazine in 2006. In 2014, Ms. Jacko was named as a finalist for San Diego Magazine's 2014 Woman of the Year Award. She was also recognized as a finalist for San Diego Business Journal's 2014 Women Who Mean Business Awards.

Ms. Jacko received her juris doctor degree from St. Mary's University School of Law and bachelor of arts in International Relations from the University of San Diego. She is admitted to the State Bar of California and United States District Court, Southern District of California. Ms. Jacko is a past two-term board member for the National Society of Compliance Professionals (NSCP), holds NSCP's certified securities compliance professional (CSCP) designation, and is an active member and presenter.

Robert R. Boeche II provides strategic legal counsel at the Jacko Law Group to investment advisers, broker-dealers, private funds, and other financial professionals. Mr. Boeche advises clients on all aspects of formation, registration, and ongoing operations. He regularly counsels clients regarding the legal issues surrounding all matters of business entity formation, including state filings, document preparation, and general corporate governance matters, as well as succession planning. Mr. Boeche is responsible for drafting contracts, sales agreements, and client disclosure documents, as well as reviewing/preparing regulatory responses. He has extensive experience in all matters of investment adviser registration and compliance, including advising clients on solicitation and marketing activities.

Mr. Boeche regularly presents at conferences throughout the nation, and is a frequent contributor to various industry journals such as those of Schwab and Wolters Kluwer and others. He is involved in the State Bar of California (Corporations Committee) and the San Diego County Bar Association (where he serves on the Business and Corporate Law's Advisory Board). Mr. Boeche also was named as one of San Diego Transcript's 2014 Top Attorneys for corporate transactional law in 2014.

Mr. Boeche received his juris doctor degree from the University of San Diego School of Law, where he was involved as a member of the school's "National Mock Trial Team" and was the recipient of such awards as "Best Oral Advocate" and "Cali Award." Prior to his joining JLG, Mr. Boeche worked at the law firm of Wilson, Sonsini, Goodrich and Rosati in their Corporate Division, where he focused on transactional law related to corporate finance, corporate governance, debt and equity financing, and mergers and acquisitions. Mr. Boeche is admitted to the State Bar of California.

Tina Mitchell, practicing at Core Compliance & Legal Services, has more than 30 years of securities experience providing practical compliance solutions for clients. Her practice focuses on investment adviser compliance risk management, including performing marketing and advertising reviews, annual reviews and focused risk assessments, SEC mock audits, authoring/assessing policy and procedure manuals, drafting codes of ethics and evaluating trading and portfolio management operations. Ms. Mitchell also specializes in mentoring and training CCOs and other compliance personnel and assists them with maintaining their firm's compliance programs.

In addition, Ms. Mitchell frequently authors articles and periodically presents in webinars and at conferences.

Prior to joining CCLS, Ms. Mitchell was the senior vice president and CCO for Engemann Asset Management, a federally registered investment adviser owned by the Phoenix Companies. Engemann managed assets for registered investment companies, wrap programs, and high-net-worth clients. During most of her 14-year employment at Engemann, Ms. Mitchell was responsible for the firm's continued compliance with federal and state securities laws. She also served as the secretary of the Phoenix Engemann Funds (part of the Phoenix Family of Funds) and compliance liaison between Engemann and the Phoenix Engemann Funds board of trustees.

Ms. Mitchell has served as a FINRA arbitrator for the past 20 years and served as president of the Southern California Compliance Group for three years. She also is a member of the California 40' Act Group.

Craig Watanabe serves as a senior compliance consultant for Core Compliance & Legal Services, with particular focus on practical, risk-based compliance solutions. Mr. Watanabe is also a financial advisor at Penniall & Associates, Inc., bringing extensive experience in investments and wealth planning. With more than 30 years of industry experience as a financial planner, branch manager, operations manager, CCO and chief operating officer (COO), Mr. Watanabe provides our clients with a high level of compliance consulting support in areas of broker-dealer and investment adviser compliance, investment banking, insurance, commodities, retail investment advisory, and ERISA plans.

Prior to his joining CCLS, Mr. Watanabe worked at Advisor Solutions Group as a senior compliance consultant. In this capacity, Mr. Watanabe provided comprehensive compliance consulting and outsourcing to retail RIAs. Prior to that, Mr. Watanabe served as the COO and CCO at Penniall & Associates. During his six-year tenure, Mr. Watanabe implemented an outcomes-oriented approach to protect investors, advisers, and the firm.

Mr. Watanabe served on the FINRA District 2 Committee from 2008-11 and was chairman of the Committee in 2011. Mr. Watanabe served six years on the NSCP board of directors and was chairman of the board in 2013. Mr. Watanabe is a frequent speaker at compliance conferences and has authored numerous articles and training modules for compliance professionals.

Chapter 14

The Ins and Outs of Outsourcing Compliance

By Mark Alcaide
NCS Regulatory Compliance

I. INTRODUCTION

In John Lanchester's article in *The New York Times Magazine* on December 18, 2016, he discussed the deep personal investment that people make in their work in Japan. The word *shokunin*, which has no direct translation in English, means a "master or mastery of one's profession." According to Lanchester, the word captures the way Japanese workers approach their jobs.[1]

Most investment advisers and brokers might use the word *shokunin* to describe how they approach their profession. The vast majority are confident that they have mastered the skills required to excel at their jobs. Unfortunately, compliance is one extremely important element of operating a registered investment adviser (RIA) or broker-dealer, and many financial services professionals fall short in this area. For that reason, firms should decide whether outsourcing compliance is worthy of consideration. As they make this decision, firms should recognize that there are many options available, not just outsourcing the chief compliance officer (CCO) position. Although this chapter focuses on RIAs, outsourcing can also benefit broker-dealers.

II. REGULATORS HAVE HIGH EXPECTATIONS

The word *outsourcing* is viewed negatively by many people and is often associated with workers losing their jobs. In fact, many people outsource certain tasks every day, such as hiring someone to cut the lawn or paying an accountant to prepare tax returns. In most cases, people could do the job themselves, but it is often a more efficient use of people's time to delegate these tasks to someone else, or they're confident that the person hired can do a better job.

When the word "outsourcing" is applied to RIAs and broker-dealers, firms may not fully understand what it means for them. Essentially, by strategically outsourcing some

[1] John Lanchester, *The New York Times Magazine* (Dec. 18, 2016), p. 20.

compliance tasks, RIAs and investment adviser representatives (IARs) may have the opportunity to spend more time doing what they do best: providing advisory services to clients and marketing their firms. Broker-dealers may also benefit by outsourcing elements of their compliance program to a third-party service provider in order to maximize the efficiency of their personnel.

Many firms equate outsourcing compliance with outsourcing the CCO position, which is only one of numerous options available. In general, outsourcing enables firms to tap compliance resources and expertise, which are not necessarily available in-house. Just as investment advisers sometimes hire third-party money managers to enhance their advisory services, firms can outsource compliance tasks to a third-party service provider specializing in this area. Similarly, firms can simultaneously improve their compliance ecosystems and growth prospects by delegating compliance tasks to a service provider.

Whether or not RIAs or broker-dealers outsource compliance, regulators have high expectations of their compliance programs. Without experienced and capable people dedicated to compliance functions, firms will have difficulty meeting those expectations. When RIAs fail to meet regulators' expectations, they are likely to receive a deficiency letter from the examination team—or worse. Certain compliance deficiencies, especially repeat violations, can result in an enforcement action against the RIA, as well as members of the firm who are responsible for the misconduct.

In a recent enforcement action, the administrative assistant for an RIA in Lexington, Kentucky, was chosen as the firm's CCO along with her other duties. The RIA put her in charge of compliance, even though she had no formal training in that field. The firm did not appoint a new CCO until several years later. The new CCO did have education and training regarding the Investment Advisers Act and its rules. The RIA also engaged an experienced outside consulting firm to help the new CCO revise the firm's policies and procedures manual. By then, however, the damage had been done.[2]

The Kentucky case is not an isolated instance. At many firms, principals must juggle a number of responsibilities and cannot devote the time needed to run the compliance function. Compliance responsibilities are too often ignored as the firm's day-to-day operations take precedence. The inevitable mistakes—even innocent ones—can have long-term consequences.

III. POLICIES AND PROCEDURES MUST LIVE UP TO REGULATORS' EXPECTATIONS

Policies and procedures can help prevent those mistakes. Policies and procedures are the equivalent of a pilot's flight manual. An RIA's policies and procedures should address routine and extraordinary situations that an adviser will deal with when operating an advisory firm. These policies and procedures are often referred to as the RIA's compliance manual.

---

[2] *In re: Dupree Financial Group, LLC*, SEC Administrative Proceeding File No. 3-17616 (Oct. 5, 2016).

Meeting regulators' high expectations begins with policies and procedures, because they are the lynchpin of firms' compliance programs. Rule 206(4)-7 under the Investment Advisers Act of 1940, better known as the Compliance Rule, requires advisers registered with the SEC to adopt and implement written compliance policies and procedures. Most states impose similar requirements on advisers registered in their jurisdiction. These compliance policies and procedures should be designed to protect the interests of investors and prevent violations of federal securities laws. In addition, Rule 206(4)-7 requires each RIA to designate a CCO to develop and enforce its compliance policies and procedures.

The intent of the Compliance Rule is to prevent harm to clients and investors. Section 206 of the Investment Advisers Act, as implemented in Rule 206(4)-7 thereunder, requires advisers to adopt thorough and complete compliance policies and procedures. The failure to do so can be a violation, even if no one was harmed.

Many CCOs don't know where to begin when drafting policies and procedures. Although policies and procedures templates abound, the devil is in the details. RIAs should identify all of the specific compliance risks they face, as well as their conflicts of interest. There should be written policies and procedures implemented by the firm to address each of them. Every compliance risk should be matched with a control.

RIAs should implement compliance policies and procedures intended to prevent deficiencies from occurring, detect deficiencies that have already occurred, and correct those violations. Although the Compliance Rule affords RIAs with flexibility in designing policies and procedures, firms must address the following areas at a minimum:

- Accuracy of disclosures made to clients, investors, and regulators, including account statements and advertisements;
- Portfolio management processes;
- Trading practices;
- Proprietary trading and personal trading activities of supervised persons;
- Safeguarding of clients' assets from conversion or inappropriate use;
- Books and records, including steps taken to prevent unauthorized alteration or use and unwarranted destruction;
- Marketing practices including the use of solicitors;
- Valuation processes and how fees are calculated based on those valuations;
- Safeguards to protect clients' privacy and confidential information; and
- Business continuity plans.

Just about every RIA will need policies and procedures that go beyond the minimum requirements.

An RIA's policies and procedures should incorporate the firm's business continuity and disaster recovery plan ("BCP"). RIAs should implement a comprehensive BCP that addresses a wide range of contingencies, such as where the firm will conduct business if the primary location is no longer available.

All federally registered RIAs, as well as some state-registered firms, must conduct an annual review of their policies and procedures to measure whether they are effective. Even if an annual review is not required, state-registered advisers will benefit by conducting one. The process is simplified by conducting interim reviews when significant compliance events, changes in business arrangements, and regulatory developments occur. An RIA should also measure how effective its policies and procedures are.

Conducting these annual reviews may require a skill set that is not available at the firm. Compliance personnel might conduct a cursory review of the firm's policies and procedures with no insight about what improvements are necessary. For example, in a 2015 enforcement action, the CCO for an RIA informed the firm's president on several occasions that he needed help to fulfill his compliance responsibilities, which included the annual review.[3]

Rule 204-2 under the Investment Advisers Act, better known as the Books and Records Rule, mandates that RIAs must keep copies of all compliance policies and procedures in effect during the last five years. The RIA must also retain its inventory of compliance risks, as well as copies of the firm's annual reviews of its policies and procedures.

In almost every deficiency letter issued by securities regulators, the examination team points to inadequate policies and procedures as a contributing factor that led to the misconduct. In many cases, the deficiency letter will urge the RIA to implement stronger policies and procedures to correct the problems observed. These revisions will help the firm to avoid repeating the same mistakes that got it into trouble. Recidivist violations increase the likelihood that an enforcement action will be brought against the firm and the individuals involved.

It should not take an examiner to recognize that a firm's compliance program is inadequate. There are several obvious signs that the firm is likely to have problems:

- The firm has not implemented policies and procedures to address critical areas, such as cybersecurity measures and safeguarding of clients' personally identifiable information;
- The firm is relying on a template and policies and procedures that have not been customized and do not fit its business model;
- The firm's actual practices differ from its policies and procedures;
- Compliance personnel are not in the loop on major decisions impacting the firm; and
- The firm is not adhering to its policies and procedures.

Policies and procedures should address the very real problems that are faced by investment advisers. For example, there should be procedures in place specifying the steps that should be taken when a client appears to be cognitively impaired.

---

3 *In re: Pekin Singer Strauss Asset Management Inc., Ronald L. Strauss, William A. Pekin, and Joshua D. Strauss,* SEC Administrative Proceeding File No. 3-16646 (June 23, 2015).

IV. USING STRATEGIC OUTSOURCING TO MEET REGULATORS' EXPECTATIONS

Firms need much more than well-drafted policies and procedures to operate an effective compliance program. They may reap benefits by strategically outsourcing specific compliance tasks. As an example, RIAs can seek assistance in areas such as:

- Annual risk assessments and compilation of a risk inventory;
- Identifying weaknesses in the firm's policies and procedures;
- Revising the firm's compliance manual and enhancing its policies and procedures;
- Acting as a service bureau administrator for the RIA's Investment Adviser Registration Depository (IARD) account;
- Drafting thorough and accurate brochures and brochure supplements;
- Preparing and filing annual renewal documents, amendments, and state notice filings;
- Conducting mock audits;
- Creating and maintaining compliance calendars;
- Compliance education and training;
- Interaction with regulators;
- Email reviews;
- Privacy notice, privacy policies, and cybersecurity;
- Form 13F filings with the SEC;
- Review of advertisements, including websites and social media; and
- Records retention and destruction.

Outsourced service providers can provide a knowledgeable and objective perspective on the firm's operations.

Strategic outsourcing may also benefit broker-dealers. For years, broker-dealers have successfully used outsourced financial and operations principals ("FinOps"). The same cost-benefit analysis that applies when hiring outsourced FinOps can be applied to decisions regarding whether to outsource compliance. An outsourced service provider can offer assistance with the following tasks:

- Creation and maintenance of a through compliance program;
- Testing of compliance policies and procedures;
- Surveillance of trades;
- Suitability analysis;
- Email review;
- Review of marketing and advertisements;
- Books and records;
- FINRA Rule 3120 Annual Compliance Report;
- FINRA Rule 3130 Annual Certification Report;
- Regulatory filings;
- Interaction with regulators; and
- Employee training.

As they decide whether strategic outsourcing makes sense, firms should consider factors such as:

- Cost of hiring someone to handle compliance versus the expense incurred by engaging a service provider;
- Complexity of the firm's business model;
- Expertise to handle compliance responsibilities in-house; and
- Availability of additional resources or personnel to comply fully with the applicable rules and regulations.

At most busy broker-dealers and RIAs, it is unusual to find employees with time on their hands to take on compliance-related duties.

In this age of specialization, it is often prudent for firms to call in experts. In many cases, this recourse makes more sense than hiring an extra person. It is also another way to show regulators that the firm is allocating sufficient resources to compliance.

When deciding whether strategic outsourcing makes sense, firms should not make their decision on the basis of cost alone. RIAs and broker-dealers owe it to themselves to conduct due diligence of service providers offering these services and should ask for references. Many providers offer consulting packages that include a number of services that might otherwise be billed separately. Compliance consulting packages often prove to be a more cost-effective approach.

When firms engage in strategic outsourcing, they are still responsible for fulfilling their compliance obligations. Firms cannot plead ignorance as an excuse for deficiencies in the compliance programs.

V. REGULATORS' EXPECTATIONS OF CCOS

A firm's CCO is often the point person in dealings with examiners. Examiners expect CCOs to be willing to stand up to senior management and to possess a wealth of knowledge that goes well beyond an understanding of rules and regulations.

Andrew J. Donahue, former chief of staff for the SEC, offered guidance regarding the knowledge CCOs need to have or develop to be effective. CCOs should know and understand the following:

- Laws, regulations, and compliance requirements pertaining to their firms in view of their business model and jurisdiction;
- The firm's supervisory structure and internal operations;
- The firm's conflicts of interest and how they are identified and resolved;
- The types of products and services that are offered to clients, including their profit margin, so the CCO can conduct a robust analysis of the potential conflicts;
- The firm's compliance and other technology platforms;

- The firm's existing policies and procedures and how they are administered;
- The markets in which the firm operates, including any specific practices that raise compliance concerns;
- The firm's culture and whether it has allocated sufficient resources to compliance; and
- What expertise is lacking at the firm, so the CCO can recognize situations in which additional assistance is needed.[4]

If firms lack compliance expertise in a particular area, they should consider hiring a service provider to plug the gaps. Nevertheless, even if firms engage a service provider, they still need a strong, knowledgeable, and competent CCO.

Compliance personnel, as well as principals, should take advantage of opportunities to learn more about their obligations and responsibilities. The SEC's Compliance Outreach Program is designed to help RIAs and broker-dealers stay compliant. These programs provide a forum to discuss current regulatory issues and to exchange ideas for developing effective compliance programs. State securities regulators also sponsor educational conferences on compliance issues. In addition, FINRA holds many conferences and educational events to keep securities professionals informed about regulatory developments and rule changes, as well as offering practical guidance on compliance issues.

NSCP, the National Society of Compliance Professionals, offers education, resources, and support to compliance professionals. In addition, RIA publications like *IA Watch*, law firms, and compliance consulting firms offer conferences that address timely and important issues impacting CCOs.

In short, firms need strong, knowledgeable and competent CCOs. In addition, to meet regulators' expectations, firms should provide CCOs with all of the resources and educational opportunities they need in order to succeed. The question arises: as part of an outsourcing program, should the CCO position be outsourced as well?

VI. OFFICE OF COMPLIANCE INSPECTIONS AND EXAMINATIONS OUTSOURCING RISK ALERT

When deciding whether to outsource the CCO position, firms should consider SEC staff's observations regarding examinations of investment advisers and investment companies that have already taken this approach. On November 9, 2015, the Office of Compliance Inspections and Examinations (OCIE) published a risk alert that dealt with the growing trend of outsourcing compliance activities to external parties, such as consultants or law firms.[5] OCIE staff conducted almost 20 examinations as part

---

4 Andrew J. Donahue,, *Remarks at NRS 30th Annual Fall Investment Adviser and Broker-Dealer Compliance Conference* (Oct. 14, 2015), https://www.sec.gov/news/speech/donohue-nrs-30th-annual.html

5 National Exam Program Risk Alert , *Examinations of Advisers and Funds That Outsource Their Chief Compliance Officers*, Vol. V, No. 1(Nov. 9, 2015) (Risk Alert), https://www.sec.gov/ocie/announcement/ocie-2015-risk-alert-cco-outsourcing.pdf

of its Outsourced CCO Initiative, which focused on investment advisers and investment companies. The risk alert stressed that "advisers with outsourced CCOs retain the responsibility for adopting and implementing an effective compliance program."

As part of the initiative, OCIE staff evaluated the effectiveness of the examined firm's compliance programs and outsourced CCOs by considering whether:

- The CCO was administering a compliance environment that addressed and supported the goals of the applicable laws and rules;
- Compliance risks were appropriately identified, mitigated, and managed;
- The compliance program was reasonably designed to prevent, detect, and address violations of the rules and regulations governing the firm's activities;
- The compliance program supported open communication between service providers and those persons with compliance oversight responsibilities;
- The compliance program was proactive, not reactive;
- CCOs appeared to have sufficient authority to compel adherence to compliance policies and procedures and received adequate resources to perform their responsibilities; and
- Compliance seemed to be an integral component of the RIA's culture.

Staff members observed that certain outsourced CCOs rarely visited the RIA's offices and conducted only limited reviews while on-site. In addition, staff members found that some outsourced CCOs did not fully understand the RIA's business practices and did not communicate regularly with the firm's principals. They did not always have full access to the firm's documents. Some of these CCOs had limited visibility and prominence within the registrants' organization, which meant they had little authority to ensure compliance with the firm's policies and procedures.

Staff members also found that firms' compliance manuals often contained superfluous or inapplicable policies and procedures. As an example, a firm might have implemented performance advertising policies and procedures, even though it never advertised performance. Similarly, some compliance manuals included policies and procedures for collecting management fees in advance, even though the RIA billed in arrears.

Form ADV was recently amended to make it easier for the regulators to keep tabs on outsourced CCOs. On August 25, 2016, the SEC released a Final Rule amending Item 1.J. of Form ADV to require an RIA to report whether its CCO is compensated or employed by any person other than the adviser. Before that change, Item 1.J. of Form ADV only required each RIA to provide the name and contact information for the firm's CCO. The release explained the SEC's rationale for the change:

> As discussed in the Proposing Release, our examination staff has observed a wide spectrum of both quality and effectiveness of outsourced chief compliance officers and firms. Identifying information for these

> third-party service providers, like others on Form ADV, will allow us to identify all advisers relying on a particular service provider and could be used to improve our ability to assess potential risks.[6]

If a particular outsourced CCO or provider is found to be ineffective, the SEC may decide to look at other firms making use of those services.

VII. FIRMS MUST PROVE TO REGULATORS THAT THEY'RE SERIOUS ABOUT COMPLIANCE

RIAs and broker-dealers should be able to demonstrate to examiners that compliance is a priority, not an afterthought. This is illustrated in two recent SEC enforcement actions.

On June 23, 2015, a Chicago-based RIA settled an SEC enforcement proceeding against the RIA, as well as three of its senior officers.[7] The RIA's officers did not make its compliance program a priority, as evidenced by the following actions:

- The president promoted an individual with minimal compliance experience and training to serve as CCO;
- The CCO only had a limited amount of time to spend on compliance;
- The president did not provide the CCO with adequate guidance regarding his duties and responsibilities nor was he given sufficient staff to assist him; and
- The president required the CCO to seek his approval before making compliance expenditures.

The president had insisted that the CCO give a higher priority to his other—noncompliance—responsibilities. Because of his research duties and other responsibilities, the CCO could only devote 10 to 20 percent of time to compliance-related matters. The SEC determined that the president's failure to devote sufficient resources to compliance contributed substantially to the RIA's compliance failures.

In another example, on January 21, 2015, the SEC alleged that a firm in New York City had failed to implement an effective compliance program.[8] From at least 2008 to 2012, the firm's CCO carried out few if any of her compliance obligations and spent most of her time managing individual accounts. From 2008 until 2011, one of the firm's two principals handled the compliance responsibilities for the firm's advisory business, even though he had minimal training and knowledge regarding the Investment Advisers Act.

---

6 *See Amendments to Form ADV and Investment Advisers Act Rules*, Investment Advisers Act Rel. No. IA-4509 (Aug. 25, 2016) (the "Release"), https://www.sec.gov/rules/final/2016/ia-4509.pdf

7 *In re: Pekin Singer Strauss Asset Management Inc., Ronald L. Strauss, William A. Pekin, and Joshua D. Strauss*, SEC Administrative Proceeding File No. 3-16646 (June 23, 2015).

8 *In re: du Pasquier & Co., Inc.*, SEC Administrative Proceeding File No. 3-16350 (Jan. 21, 2015).

The SEC noted that when the firm finally engaged someone to be its designated compliance officer—a separate position from the CCO—that person possessed inadequate training and knew little about the Investment Advisers Act. In addition, the SEC determined that the firm failed to provide adequate training to employees regarding the RIA's policies and procedures.

Cutting corners on compliance sends the message that compliance is not a priority for the firm. When firms allot only a small percentage of their budget to the compliance function, it might be an indication that they are not seriously committed to operating an effective compliance program.

VIII. POTENTIAL BENEFITS TO BE GAINED FROM STRATEGIC OUTSOURCING

In view of OCIE's outsourcing risk alert and these recent enforcement actions, firms that outsource their CCO position can expect skeptical questions from examiners. Examiners are likely to test whether an outsourced CCO fully understands the RIA's operation, which is vital to administrating a compliance program. Sadly, some in-house CCOs do not understand their own firm's business model.

Although there can be pitfalls when the CCO position is outsourced improperly, it may be beneficial for firms to outsource specific tasks to a service provider. These providers can help firms to implement and manage compliance calendars. For example, a calendar makes it less likely that an RIA will overlook important compliance obligations such as the Rule 206(4)-7 requirement that SEC-registered investment advisers conduct annual reviews of their policies and procedures. Attorney Rita Dew of Delray Beach, Florida, offered this guidance in a white paper published by National Compliance Services, Inc., the predecessor of NCS Regulatory Compliance:

> Selective outsourcing can give CCOs an independent and fresh set of eyes for compliance reviews conducted by experts who deal on a regular basis with securities regulators. Compliance outsourcers also have access to state and SEC deficiency letters. These letters are issued by a firm's regulator following an examination, and pinpoint areas in which a firm's compliance is weak. A compliance consultant can use these letters, without identifying the recipient, to guide their clients on what examiners' priorities are, and how they will be scrutinized, in real time.[9]

Compliance service providers become aware of regulatory trends and concerns before risk alerts are published. These providers see the deficiency letters advisers are receiving, which signals what issues examiners are focusing on during examinations.

---

[9] Rita Dew, "Weighing the Benefits of Outsourcing Compliance" (Dec. 2, 2014), http://www.ncsregcomp.com/whitepapers/.

Advisers would be naïve if they were to think they can avoid responsibility for compliance problems through outsourcing. Nevertheless, strategic outsourcing can add value to a firm's operation in the following ways:

- Compliance questions can be answered quickly with a phone call or email;
- Existing resources can be used more efficiently and cost-effectively;
- Additional hiring may be avoided; and
- Potential compliance pitfalls can be identified and avoided.

Compliance service providers can even add value to hiring decisions. They can provide insight as to whether an applicant's disciplinary history will adversely impact the firm.

When compliance tasks are outsourced to a third party, that individual is not influenced by the firm's incentive structure. In many cases, supervised persons are more willing to accept advice from an outsider. Service providers might be able to suggest ways for the firm to streamline its operations.

Firms may also benefit from the expertise offered by most providers. Even if a member of the firm is willing to take time away from clients to become well-versed on compliance matters, it is doubtful that he or she will know as much as service providers dealing with these matters on a daily basis. Service providers are likely to be more current regarding regulatory developments, especially if they interact on a regular basis with the SEC, FINRA, and state securities regulators. Service providers can also help RIAs develop and implement policies and procedures to address regulators' priorities.

An outsourced service provider should do more than just supply boilerplate policies and procedures. In a risk alert published on February 7, 2017, OCIE published a list of the five compliance topics most frequently identified in deficiency letters sent to SEC-registered investment advisers.[10] One of those deficiencies was a failure to tailor policies and procedures to the firm's business model.

Relying on boilerplate policies and procedures may undermine a firm's compliance program. There is no one-size-fits-all compliance manual. Examiners may question why a firm has policies and procedures that do not apply to its business model. The compliance manual may contain policies and procedures that are being ignored by advisory personnel. A customized manual is a better alternative than one replete with generic policies and procedures that are totally irrelevant to the firm's day-to-day business activities. Firms with simpler business models usually don't need overly complex policies and procedures.

Finally, outsourced service providers should offer checklists, so RIAs can evaluate their policies and procedures on an interim and annual basis. A few firms offer online tools to ensure that the evaluation process is meaningful.

---

[10] National Exam Program Risk Alert, *The Five Most Frequent Compliance Topics Identified in OCIE Examinations of Investment Advisers*, Vol. VI, No. 3 (Feb. 7, 2017), https://www.sec.gov/ocie/Article/risk-alert-5-most-frequent-ia-compliance-topics.pdf

IX. NEWLY REGISTERED ADVISERS MAY BENEFIT MOST FROM STRATEGIC OUTSOURCING

Although newly registered advisers often have limited budgets, they may benefit most by strategically outsourcing certain compliance tasks such as creating policies and procedures. One of the SEC's recent initiatives has been to examine newly registered advisers. The newly registered adviser may have no idea what policies and procedures are necessary. Many new RIAs possess little or no knowledge regarding how to become registered, how to market their services, or what fees to charge. Knowledgeable service providers can give novice advisers an overview of the prevailing practices in the area, as well as specific advice on how to stay within the lines.

Whether an RIA is newly registered or has been in business for years, building a relationship with a service provider can pay dividends. The provider will become familiar with the RIA's business model and can offer guidance regarding approaches taken by other advisory firms. The RIA's policies and procedures should be far more professional and thorough than if the adviser had drafted them alone. If questions are raised about the RIA's compliance decisions or books and records, the service provider can help the adviser explain why certain steps were taken. Conversely, if an adviser has ignored a service provider's advice and examiners find out, the consequences for the RIA are likely to be more severe.

Securities regulators expect CCOs to be knowledgeable and well versed on compliance matters. Service providers should provide educational materials and training to CCOs, as well as other members of the firm. Customer-oriented service providers offer newsletters and webinars on compliance topics, and should also be proactive in notifying and explaining new rules and regulations affecting the RIA. In addition, a service provider's technology can help an RIA's compliance program to run more smoothly and efficiently.

X. FINRA AND BROKER-DEALERS' CONCERNS ABOUT OUTSOURCING

The outsourcing issue is not limited to the RIA space. FINRA's *2016 Regulatory and Examination Priorities Letter* gave this advice:

> Firms continue to look for opportunities to reduce costs by outsourcing key operational functions. FINRA will review firms' due diligence and risk assessment of providers of outsourced services and their supervision of those services. FINRA reminds firms that while certain tasks can be performed by a third-party provider, the responsibility to supervise covered activities for compliance with applicable federal securities laws and regulations, as well as self-regulatory organization rules, remains with the broker-dealer. Moreover, firms must avoid outsourcing functions that are required to be performed by qualified registered persons. It is essential that broker-dealers appropriately supervise outsourced activities and that

> firms conduct adequate initial and ongoing due diligence of outsourced providers. This concern is also applicable to employees of affiliates conducting certain functions on behalf of the broker-dealer.[11]

Firms should create books and records to prove they conducted due diligence of each and every service provider before deciding whether to engage them.

XI. CONCLUSION

Although firms should consider looking for a hand to help them with their compliance obligations, they cannot hand off their responsibilities entirely. They should not view third-party service providers as a crutch. Ideally, a service provider can do the heavy lifting for a firm and provide valuable insight.

In working with compliance service providers, CCOs should provide direction. For example, some CCOs barely look at an advertising piece before sending it to an outside firm for review. The better approach is for the CCO to review the piece first in view of the firm's business model, strategy, and investment philosophy. It is helpful to identify statements that are inconsistent with how the firm transacts business. Aside from identifying those problem areas, the CCO might point out issues with a particular service or product that have generated complaints in the past. The outside compliance firm can then use its expertise to conduct a more in-depth review.

At some firms, the managing partner is a dominating force, which is why they are so successful. It can also explain why some CCOs are afraid to buck horns with that individual. Weak CCOs are sometimes reluctant to push back on a principal who wants to plow forward without regard for compliance. Those CCOs want an outside firm to be the bad guy. It is one thing to call upon an outside party to back up the CCO's position. It is another to seek outside help because of an unwillingness to stand up to the firm's principals. When this happens, it is clear that the firm has appointed the wrong person to be CCO.

Even if a firm's compliance staff members are experienced, professional, and knowledgeable, the firm may not have the expertise in-house to resolve all of the issues that arise. In those instances, it may be necessary for a firm to outsource certain tasks to a service provider. This might only require a one-time engagement if the CCO receives guidance on how to resolve those issues going forward. Outsourcing can give firms increased capacity and bandwidth.

Smaller firms usually rely on a principal to serve as CCO. Hiring a service provider can ease that person's work load. A firm with a simple business model may have less need to outsource compliance tasks to a service provider.

---

[11] FINRA, *2016 Regulatory and Examination Priorities Letter* (Jan. 5, 2016), http://www.finra.org/industry/2016-regulatory-and-examination-priorities-letter

No matter how big or small a firm is, it might make sense to have a service provider conduct a mock audit to measure whether its compliance program is in good shape. As part of their due diligence, firms should make certain that the service provider does not have a vested interest in selling additional services and will denigrate the current compliance program as part of its marketing strategy.

The decision whether to hire a service provider is usually more clear-cut when principals and compliance personnel know what they don't know. If principals and compliance personnel are willing to recognize and admit their weaknesses, they know when it's time to ask for help. And if they choose to go it alone, they will need to master all of the rules and regulations that go hand-in-hand with compliance. If they meet that extremely high standard, principals and CCOs can proudly say that the word *shokunin* accurately describes their approach to compliance.

ABOUT THE AUTHOR

Mark Alcaide is NCS Regulatory Compliance's chief operating officer (COO) and chief financial officer (CFO). Mr. Alcaide leads the firm's management team in developing and delivering all elements of Regulatory Compliance's services, its strategic plan, and all policy and management initiatives. His role centers on business and client relationship development, and on overseeing all financial and administrative operations.

Mr. Alcaide spent the previous 20 years working for Ropes & Gray, a leading national and global law firm, the Clinton Foundation, Fidelity, Gillette, and Price Waterhouse Coopers, where he in various roles performed CFO and COO responsibilities. In each of these roles, his focus was on building world-class functions across all support areas, designing cost-effective client solutions, and engaging directly with clients to fashion innovative service and pricing offerings.

Mr. Alcaide also serves on several boards, including as vice president and executive committee member of the Kents Hill School, as well as treasurer and executive committee member of Acton Boxborough Youth Soccer/Strikers United, one of the largest youth soccer organizations in Massachusetts.

Chapter 15

Exchange-Traded Products Compliance

By Victor Frye, J.D.

I. INTRODUCTION

Exchange-traded products (ETPs) assets have been growing at an unprecedented pace in both the United States and global markets. The number and types of exchange-traded products are also increasing quickly, and the regulatory environment surrounding these products has garnered much attention from Congress and the press. Understanding these products and designing effective compliance programs around them are not simple tasks.

There are many advantages to ETPs. They generally have lower expense ratios and lower transaction and related costs. Their structure adds the liquidity of an exchange-traded instrument, a defense against market timing with the ability to buy and sell shares throughout the trading day, and trade price transparency via the "tape" or exchange ticker. They are also more accurate at tracking their underlying indexes. Of course, with these advantages come some disadvantages. ETP purchases and redemptions generally require paying a broker commission, have a divergence between the exchange-traded fund's (ETF) share price and net asset value (NAV), and sometimes have a longer delay receiving sales proceeds (generally one day longer than mutual funds).

ETPs are generally organized as either unit investment trusts (UITs) or open-ended management companies. The UITs operate ETPs that are passively managed funds that contain a fixed portfolio. Open-ended management companies have the ability to manage assets with more flexible portfolios and may employ sampling techniques, holding a representative sample of the securities held in the ETF's benchmark index. ETPs follow a variety of strategies and may be either benchmarked to equity, commodity, fixed income and other hybrid indices, or commodities or actively managed to accomplish certain financial or other goals.

This chapter will explain the various types of exchange-traded products in the market, the legal parameters around offering such products, and the operational and compliance mechanics that need to be in place for an exchange-traded product sponsor.

II. LEGAL STRUCTURE FOR EXCHANGE-TRADED PRODUCTS

How Exchange-Traded Products Operate

ETPs are designed to continuously offer shares on a national securities exchange such as NYSE Arca, BATS, or NASDAQ. Shares are sold in the primary market in large blocks called creation units (CUs) to institutional broker-dealers called authorized participants (APs) that sell the shares to brokers and market makers and their respective customers. In the simplest analogy, exchange-traded shares are similar to a corporate stock and may be purchased, sold, or even shorted by retail investors through a broker dealer at a market price somewhere between the current bid/ask spread listed on the securities exchange. Unlike a corporate stock, shares of the exchange-traded product often represent an interest in an underlying pool of assets valued or guaranteed in value by the sponsor supporting the value of the shares.

Generally ETPs issue and redeem directly from the fund by receiving or delivering "basket" shares in-kind to or from its APs. In some instances, certain types of ETPs, such as exchange-traded notes (ETNs), or ETFs that contain securities of issuers in certain countries, may have redemption restrictions and/or those products create and redeem shares exclusively for cash. Generally, an AP may purchase the ETP units in either cash or with an in-kind basket of assets that reflects the composition of the fund's holdings. The sponsor makes public the requirements for the deposit or creation basket and will also indicate whether transactions are limited to cash on a daily basis.

An AP purchasing or redeeming using an in-kind deposit basket will also include a balancing cash deposit to ensure the exact value of the basket assets matches the value of fund shares. These in-kind transactions generally result in lower transaction costs and may provide tax efficiencies. It is important for an ETP's compliance program to have written procedures for the creation and redemption process and to test for compliance with such procedures. Once the AP sells the creation unit shares to the secondary market or a market maker, the shares will trade at a spread above or below the NAV on a listed exchange.

When one buys or sells an ETP in the secondary market, ETP shares typically trade at a price between the highest price an ETP purchaser is willing to buy the shares (the "bid") and the lowest price a seller is willing to part with the ETP shares (the "ask"). As a result, investors often purchase ETP shares at slightly over market prices and sell for slightly lower. This bid/ask spread is lower when there is a high volume of trading in an ETP. It is important to remember that newly issued and other ETPs may not have large trading volumes, so when retail investors execute large purchases in the secondary market, it is prudent to use a limit order or other strategy to ensure intended execution.

Exchange-Traded Investment Companies and Products

Typical legal structures for exchange-traded products include ones described here.

Open-Ended Investment Companies. Open-end investment companies, which are subject to the Investment Company Act of 1940 (the "1940 Act") unless provided exemptive relief, are the most popular vehicle used to sponsor an ETF. Many of the operational features of mutual funds that are only registered under the 1940 Act are similar to ETFs except that accounts of the beneficial owners in the secondary market ETF shares are held in accounts at a broker-dealer and no transfer agent functions are performed by the fund for retail investors.

Investment company ETFs are offered and sold by a prospectus that is delivered no later than at the time of confirmation for any transaction similar to stocks or nonexchange-traded mutual funds. The registration statement for an ETF will be filed with the SEC on Form N-1A and must be updated no less frequently than annually. Annual and semiannual financial statements generally must be made available via the sponsor's website as well as mailed to existing shareowners. In many respects, the compliance challenges for these ETPs are similar to those for conventional mutual funds. It is also important to remember that other investment companies that invest in ETFs will be subject to the investment restrictions of Section 12(d)(1) of the 1940 Act.[1]

Exchange-Traded Commodity Pools. Another type of structure for ETPs is a commodity trust or partnership. These ETPs are typically not regulated under the 1940 Act because they do not meet the 1940 Act asset type or income restrictions. For example, commodities do not produce sufficient "good" income under Subchapter M of the Internal Revenue Code to qualify for investment company tax treatment.[2] ETPs structured as partnerships for tax purposes may have special income tax considerations when reporting income to retail investors on form K-1, similar to operating limited partnership income distributions. Commodity pools are primarily regulated by the Commodity Futures Trading Commission (CFTC) and are also subject to both CFTC rules and rules adopted by the National Futures Association (NFA).

Commodity ETPs are also generally sold by prospectus and are filed with the SEC on Form S-1 (or S-3 for seasoned issuers). Unlike investment company securities, a specific number of shares are registered and, once sold, additional shares must be registered for the offering. The sponsor must track the number of shares that have been sold and may not credit redemptions back to the number of shares registered. Financial statements also must be made available on the sponsor's website and will appear on the annual report Form 10-K. Quarterly financials are filed on Form 10-Q. These must be either mailed or otherwise made available to existing shareowners. From time to time amendments to a commodity trust's registration statement must be filed to update the prospectus

---

1 Generally, under Section 12(d)(1) the investing investment company or acquiring fund may not own more than 3 percent of the ETF's shares, commit more than 5 percent of the acquiring fund's assets to the ETF's shares, and may not commit more than 10 percent of the acquiring funds shares in investment company ETF shares as a whole. The SEC has provided exemptive orders and no action relief to investment companies, but specified conditions of those orders must be followed. The ETF or the acquiring fund's prospectus will indicate whether an exemptive order is being relied upon. To prevent pyramiding, if the ETF is relying on an exemptive order to exceed the limits, then an acquiring fund will not be permitted to exceed the limits when purchasing that ETF's shares.

2 26 CFR 1.852-1, Taxation of Regulated Investment Companies.

or to register additional shares. Like an operating company, a commodity ETP would also file Form 8-K to disclose material events.

Exchange-Traded Notes. ETNs are generally unsecured debt products subject to the credit quality of the ETN issuer. Unlike the products mentioned above, there may or may not be a pool of assets earmarked to cover the investments. Typically, ETN returns are tied to the performance of a market index and backed by the assets of the issuer, who may hedge the obligations owed under the ETN. ETNs are generally subject to both the rules of the exchange on which they list and laws applicable to debt/bond instruments. Sponsors of ETNs issue and redeem notes as a means to keep the ETN's price in line with a calculated value. The decision to issue additional notes is at the sponsor's sole discretion. ETN offerings typically are made though takedowns from an existing registration statement, most typically a shelf registration on Form S-3. Table 1 summarizes asset types of exchange-traded companies or products.

TABLE 1. ETPS BY UNDERLYING OR REFERENCE ASSET TYPE, AS OF YEAR END 2014[1]

Underlying or Reference Asset or Strategy	Number	Total Market Cap ($ Millions)	Total Traded Value ($ Millions)
Asset Allocation	**36**	**$7,435**	**$14,380**
ETF	24	$7,402	$14,344
ETN	2	$33	$36
Alternative Strategies	**330**	**$42,985**	**$1,952,802**
ETF	209	$31,865	$1,296,485
Non-1940 Act pooled investment vehicles	25	$4,727	$142,465
ETN	96	$6,392	$513,852
Commodities	**118**	**$55,336**	**$406,728**
ETF	7	$213	$810
Non-1940 Act pooled investment vehicles	38	$50,880	$390,213
ETN	73	$4,273	$15,705
International Equities	**367**	**$380,023**	**$2,497,521**
ETF	361	$376,941	$2,495,865
ETN	6	$3,082	$1,657
Municipal Bond	**32**	**$14,273**	**$20,186**
ETF	32	$14,273	$20,186
Sector Equity	**297**	**$304,588**	**$2,782,522**
ETF	281	$290,219	$1,000,037
ETN	16	$10,915	$18,137
Taxable Bond	**217**	**$290,219**	**$1,000,037**
ETF	214	$290,219	$1,000,037
ETN	3	$26	$49
U.S. Equity	**267**	**$909,677**	**$8,581,038**
ETF	252	$907,557	$8,579,330
ETN	15	$2,119	$1,707
Grand Total	**1,664**	**$2,004,591**	**$17,255,263**

1 These figures reflect an analysis by SEC staff of market data obtained through subscriptions to Morningstar Direct and Bloomberg Professional Services. Figures are as of the last trading day of 2014. SEC, *Request for Comment on Exchange-Traded Products,* Rel. No. 34-75165; File No. S7-11-15.

III. INITIAL COMPLIANCE STRUCTURE

Framework: Applicable Policies and Procedures

All 1940 Act registered ETFs as well as other ETPs should start with a core of compliance procedures to safeguard against violations. Assuming the more restrictive structure of the 1940 Act, typically the fund would have a core set of procedures such as:

- A code of ethics for the ETP, the adviser or sponsor, and the distributor;
- Policies and procedures to prevent insider trading;
- Anti-money laundering policies;
- Pricing and valuation procedures;
- Best execution and directed brokerage policies;
- Policies for affiliated transactions;
- Proxy voting procedures;
- Liquidity review and determination policies;
- Joint transaction procedures;
- Borrowing or leverage guidelines;
- Name test procedures;
- Whistleblower policy—required by the exchanges;
- Attorney conduct guidelines for registration statements and other documents filed with the SEC;
- Advertising procedures—for the distributor or sponsor;
- Safeguarding procedures for client information or assets;
- Business continuity plan; and
- Other policies outlining conditions of specific no action or exemptive relief being relied upon.

A robust compliance program has both a front-end and back-end testing element for compliance investment restrictions and prospectus and tax guidelines, as applicable. The front-end system should be built into the advisor or sponsor's trading system or model. The back-end testing typically is done on a post-trade basis and monitored through the fund's accounting or administration system. The compliance staff should also perform periodic and random testing based on regulatory risk assessments.

Rule 38a-1 under the 1940 Act requires investment company ETPs to adopt a comprehensive compliance program and appoint a chief compliance officer (CCO). The CCO is required to report to the board, at least annually, that the compliance programs including the programs of the service providers (the fund advisor or sponsor, the distributor, and/or administrator or transfer agent) have been reviewed and continue to be effective. Any material changes to these programs must be reported.

Whistleblower Procedures

Section 301[3] of the Sarbanes-Oxley Act of 2002 ("SOX) requires that the audit committee establish "whistleblower" policies and procedures. The procedures should cover the receipt and handling of complaints of questionable accounting practices; internal controls or auditing matters; and the anonymous and confidential submission by employees, the public company's subsidiaries, or other affiliates whose financial information is part of the company's public financial statements.

SOX Section 806[4] details the antiretaliation guidelines for the company. A company is prohibited from discharging, demoting, or otherwise discriminating against any employee or affiliated person who provides whistleblowing information about that company's financial statements or processes when the employee or affiliate believes there is a violation of securities rules or federal financial laws. The employee or affiliate may alert any governmental authority, in any proceeding pending or about to be commenced concerning such a violation or to any person with supervisory authority over the employee or affiliate authorized by the company to investigate the violation or conduct. Section 922(a)[5] of the Dodd-Frank Wall Street Reform and Consumer Protection Act mandated the inclusion of a "whistleblower bounty" and antiretaliation programs. The SEC adopted Regulation 21f[6] to implement these programs effective August 12, 2011.

The audit committee in conjunction with company management should create relevant whistleblower policies and procedures. A review of current corporate structures, policies, and procedures should precede the writing. Existing processes may be applicable to some or all of the potential whistleblower policies and procedures. The laws do not stipulate how complaints should be received and handled, but the employees or affiliate filing complaints should feel comfortable with the methods implemented by the company.

The whistleblower policy should include procedures for the registration and disposition of complaints, including the availability of a hotline or other anonymous disclosure methods. There should be procedures designed to manage how complaints are received, documented, delegated, investigated, and forwarded to the audit committee for review and action. According to Section 806 of SOX, there must be a policy established to safeguard employees, as this section also makes it illegal to retaliate against whistleblowers. All aspects of the filing of a complaint to its disposition should be documented and part of the company's regular recordkeeping procedure.

Certification Requirements

Because ETPs are listed on a securities exchange, they are subject to certain certification requirements for published financial reports. ETPs must maintain disclosure controls

---

3 Sarbanes-Oxley Act of 2002, § 301. Public Company Audit Committees.

4 Sarbanes-Oxley Act of 2002, § 801: Corporate and Criminal Fraud Accountability Act of 2002.

5 Dodd-Frank Wall Street Reform and Consumer Protection Act (P. L. 111-203) ; § 922: Whistleblower Protection.

6 17 CFR 240.21F-2, Whistleblower Status and Retaliation Protection.

and procedures. Generally, disclosure controls and procedures apply to financial and nonfinancial information that is material, and required to be provided in public reports. Although "internal controls" are generally focused on financial reporting, disclosure controls are broader, often include internal controls, and also apply to all material information to be included in public reports, both within and outside of financial statements.

Disclosure controls and procedures should manage the required release of material information through their creation, accumulation, and submission to management to ensure discussion about the information is taking place on a timely basis. They should be comparable to financial reporting systems, but should be designed to capture nonfinancial information as well.

Effectively designed disclosure controls and procedures should include the following:

- *Disclosure controls committee:* The committee should review the materiality of the information gathered, determine the disclosure requirements, identify issues with disclosure requirements and information, as well as develop and coordinate the structure and procedures to ensure material information is handled in a timely manner and delegated to management;
- *Standard reporting package/process:* This process should engage the appropriate people and direct the required information to appropriate users;
- *Inventory the reporting requirements and keep inventory current:* The committee should keep a list of up-to-date requirements from the SEC as well as generally accepted accounting principles (GAAP) as they pertain to disclosure controls.
- *Clarify roles and responsibilities for generating required disclosures:* As part of the procedures, roles should be well defined and provide accountability for disclosures that need to be generated. Specific individuals or corporate roles (i.e., the CCO) should be identified with explicit timing defined and monitored for disclosing material information;
- *Align the disclosure controls and procedures appropriately:* The procedures should align with the fair reporting of material information. When appropriate consider corporate performance expectations, compensation or incentive programs, and other positive behavior practices that encourage fair reporting; and
- *Document and communicate disclosure controls:* The company's disclosure controls and procedures should be documented and approved by management. Those that are responsible for the disclosures should be well aware of the controls and procedures by receiving a written copy, appropriate training, and certifying its receipt in writing.

Regulation FD Policies and Procedures

Fair disclosure rules under Regulation FD[7] prohibit funds from selectively disclosing material nonpublic information to analysts, investors, and others without concurrently making widespread public disclosure. All investors should have the same information

[7] 17 CFR 243.100-243.103, General Rules Regarding Selective Disclosure.

and equal access to a company's material disclosures at the same time, according to the rule. Regulation FD requires that if someone acting on behalf of the fund discloses certain material, nonpublic information, then the fund must disclose the information to the general public. The material, nonpublic information could include such items as earnings information; new products; mergers, acquisitions, litigation or tender offers; and other material information regarding a fund's business strategies.

A fund can implement a number of policies and procedures to mitigate the risk of violating fair disclosure regulations. A Regulation FD program generally should include:

- A written investor relations policy that includes a section addressing the requirements of Regulation FD;
- Periodic Regulation FD compliance training by the general counsel;
- An earnings guidance policy that addresses when and how earnings are to be released;
- Periodic review by counsel of proposed written communications to advisers and clients;
- A procedure for prompt corrective disclosure upon learning of a Regulation FD violation and self-reporting of the violation to the SEC using SEC Form 8-K; and
- Adoption of remedial measures to address violations and to prevent a reoccurrence.

A specific program of policies and procedures will need to be created specific to the individual circumstances of each organization. All ETFs should use the most recent release of Regulation FD as guidance for building a program.

IV. REGULATORY REVIEW PROCESS AND EXEMPTIVE RELIEF

Perhaps the most important compliance considerations are those associated with the exemptive relief conditions. The SEC has stated that one of its primary targets during examination inspections will be to ensure that conditions of a sponsor's exemptive relief order are being observed. These conditions may be unique to the sponsor, so it is important to review the conditions of the order and make a checklist for compliance inspection. This section discusses some of the primary exemptive relief provisions, but each issuer will be subject to an even more extensive list detailed in the exemptive application.

Before an ETP may be traded on a national exchange, it must first be registered under the Securities Act of 1933 ("the Securities Act"). In addition, if the ETP is an investment company subject to the 1940 Act, the ETP must obtain an order from the SEC to relax limitations on redemption, offer, sale, and pricing of redeemable securities under Section 6(c) of the 1940 Act to be exempt from Sections 2(a)(32), 22(d), 22(e) and from Rule 22c-1. Also, these funds must seek an SEC order (under Sections 6(c) and 17(b) to be exempt from Sections 17(a)(1) and 17(a)(2) of the 1940 Act) to permit the purchase and sale of fund property inherent to in-kind creation and redemption. These exemptions allow the investment companies to offer shares exclusively in CUs and then allow those shares to trade at secondary market prices.

ETPs must also request exemption from Rules 101 and 102 of Regulation M under the Securities and Exchange Act of 1934 ("the Exchange Act"). The SEC will request the issuer to attest to the existence of an effective and efficient arbitrage mechanism in the secondary market to ensure the market price of the ETP does not vary substantially from its NAV. Some ETPs may be able to rely on class exemptions, but in order to do so, the SEC has stated specific conditions required for the relief to be effective. Compliance staff should verify that the conditions of any class relief relied upon is continuously met by the ETP.

Investment Restrictions (Generic Relief for Equity Index-Based ETPs)

The SEC has issued generic no-action relief that allows equity index based ETPs to operate without a specific exemptive order from many of the legal investment restrictions imposed by the federal securities laws.[8] If an ETP is relying on any no-action relief letter, the compliance staff must monitor to ensure the conditions listed in the no action position exist, including:

- The ETP must contain at least twenty or more different component stocks with no one position representing more than 25 percent of the total value of the ETP;
- At least 70 percent of the component ETP stock must have a minimum float value of at least $150 million and a specified minimum average daily trading volume;
- If the ETP has 200 or more component securities, then 50 percent of the component securities must meet the trading and volume standards; and
- The ETP must track a publicly available equity index composed of securities that have publicly available last sale information.

The SEC has also outlined similar relief standards for fixed income index-based ETPs.

Nongeneric Exemptive Relief Required

Trading ETPs on an exchange may require the issuer to obtain certain specific exemptive or no-action relief from provisions or rules of the Exchange Act, most notably certain trading related rules and Rule 19b-4.[9] Regular business operations of ETPs often violate these provisions and rules without relief. The SEC regularly grants such relief, sometimes by blanket exemptions. In general, funds must request relief from the SEC in these areas: limited direct redeemability, secondary market trading, and in-kind purchase and redemptions by large shareowners.

Standard Conditions for Exemptive Relief

Because APs can buy and sell CUs at NAV, and buy and sell related ETF shares at intraday market prices, arbitrage opportunities are created. The arbitrage system is a vital component to the functioning of an ETF. Arbitrage opportunities are created when the

---

8 SEC Division of Market Regulation, Exemptive Relief for Exchange-Traded Index Funds letter to American Stock Exchange (Aug. 17, 2001), https://www.sec.gov/divisions/marketreg/mr-noaction/etifclassrelief081701-msr.pdf

9 17 CFR § 240.19b-4, Filings with Respect to Proposed Rule Changes by Self-Regulatory Organizations.

market price of an ETF share differs from its daily NAV. The buying and selling activity of the APs helps to keep the market price at or near NAV. Under most actively traded ETF market conditions, the deviation of the market price from NAV stays within 2 percent. The SEC has recognized that deviations are a necessary part of market activity and has stated certain conditions in its standard ETF exemptive order. They include:

- Shares of an ETF must be listed on a national exchange;
- The listing exchange will publish daily the current value of the ETF's basket of securities on an interval basis (usually 15 second intervals)(such value the "intraday indicative value," or IIV);
- An ETF must publish on its website what securities will be included in the purchase and redemption baskets as well as the prior days' NAV, closing price, and any premiums or discounts against the NAV;
- The ETF must not market itself as an open-ended mutual fund; and
- Marketing materials for the ETF must highlight the limited redeemability of the fund's shares and are subject to Section 12(d)(1) fund-of-fund limitations contained in the 1940 Act.

Standard Exemptions by Statute/Regulation

Most ETFs are organized as open-end investment companies. As such, they are regulated by federal restrictions including the 1940 Act and the Securities Act, among others. These two acts allow ETFs to operate like mutual funds. ETFs, like mutual funds, must publish to shareholders annual and semiannual reports and an annual prospectus. Unlike mutual funds, ETFs can be sold like stocks on an exchange. This difference requires ETFs to be exempt from various rules and regulations to allow them to function as designed. Without them, the funds will be in violation, as described here.

Investment Company Act of 1940 Exemptions. The 1940 Act, through its rules, places many restrictions on how funds conduct business. Funds must file an application for exemptive relief from the SEC, including those in the standard conditions for exemptive relief. The 1940 Act permits ETFs to register as open-end investment companies or UITs.

To act as an ETF and to comply with federal regulations under the 1940 Act, relief from the following sections must be requested:

- Section 2(a)(32) to allow for the purchase and redemption of CUs;
- Section 22(d) and Rule 22c-1 to allow exchange trading of ETF shares at prices other than NAV;
- Section 22(e) to allow redemptions proceeds to be tendered in excess of the seven-day requirement;
- Section 12(d)(1) to allow ETF shares to be sold to investment companies above the 1940 Act's fund-of-funds limitations;

- Section 26(a)(2)(c) when ETFs organized as UITs are granted additional relief for certain marketing requirements and other expenses occurred by the sponsor;
- Section 17(a)(1) and Section 17(a)(2) to allow in-kind purchases and redemptions of CUs by affiliates with the ETP; and
- Section 2(a)(3) to allow ownership of 5 percent or more of outstanding securities.

The SEC provides a partial exemption from section 17(a) to the extent necessary to permit in-kind purchases and redemptions of ETF CUs by way of section 17(b): Application for exemption of proposed transaction from certain restrictions. The SEC provides that the following shall be granted such application and issue such order of exemption if evidence establishes that:

- The terms of the proposed transaction, including the consideration to be paid or received, are reasonable and fair and do not involve overreaching on the part of any person concerned;
- The proposed transaction is consistent with the policy of each registered investment company concerned, as recited in its registration statements and reports filed under this subchapter; and
- The proposed transaction is consistent with the general purposes of this subchapter.[10]

Exchange Act "Trading Rules" Relief. Funds must meet the listing rules for the exchange upon which they are listed. They must apply for and receive relief from certain Exchange Act provisions and rules from the SEC governing broker-dealers and activities related to distribution of ETF shares. Because ETF shares are continuously offered and are also traded in the secondary market, various issues with ETF trading also arise under the Exchange Act. For the benefit of broker-dealers that trade ETF shares, the staff of SEC Division of Trading and Markets has granted certain no-action and interpretive relief under several provisions of the Exchange Act and the rules and regulations thereunder.

This relief has been published in letters, some giving "generic class relief" and are made available to all ETFs sharing stated characteristics and meeting stated conditions, and others addressing identified ETFs that, in light of particular structural or operational features, fall outside the scope of the generic letters (e.g., actively managed ETFs).

In order not to violate federal regulations for the Exchange Act, relief from the following sections must be requested:

- Section 11(d)(1) to allow broker-dealers to extend credit to customers in certain situations;
- Rule 10b-10 to allow customer confirmations to exclude certain information on individual trades in a purchase or redemption, but make that information available on demand in a timely manner;

10 Investment Company Act of 1940; 15 U.S.C. §§ 80a- 17(a), (b), Transactions of Certain Affiliated Persons and Underwriters.

- Rule 10b-17 to waive the delivery notice of certain actions (i.e., dividend distribution, stock splits, rights offerings, etc.);
- Rule 14e-5 to allow the redemption of fund shares by a dealer-manager of a tender offer for a component security of the fund under certain circumstances; and
- Rule 15c1-5 and 15c-6 to allow the waiver of required disclosure of control by a broker or dealer with respect to certain transactions involving Fund shares.

Margin: Section 11(d)(1). Section 11(d)(1) of the Exchange Act in general places limits on the ability of broker-dealers to extend credit to purchasers of shares offered by that broker-dealer. Extending or maintaining credit, or arranging for the extension or maintenance of credit, on shares of new-issue securities is limited if the broker-dealer was involved in the distribution of the new-issue securities within the previous 30 days. Due to continued issuance, the SEC believes that broker-dealers that sell ETP new-issue securities are participating in the distribution of a new issue for purposes of Section 11(d)(1). If an ETP holds a portfolio composed solely or largely of newly issued securities, there is a risk that APs could also use the ETP structure to avoid the new-issue lending restrictions.

The SEC has granted no-action relief allowing the use of margin credit in connection with the purchase of ETF shares by broker-dealers *only on the secondary market*. The SEC has also offered no-action relief to permit broker-dealers to extend credit to ETP customers purchasing through broker-dealers that are authorized participants with the following conditions:

- No one involved in the purchase of the ETP shares receives a payment or other economic incentive from the issuer (other than noncash compensation permitted under FINRA rules); and
- The broker-dealer does not extend credit to a customer on a share of an ETP before 30 days have passed from the date that the ETP's shares were initially traded.

Content of Confirmations: Rules 10b-10 and 10b-17. Rule 10b-10 requires a broker-dealer that completes a transaction on the behalf of a client to provide the customer with written confirmation of the completion of the transaction regarding each security in the shares. Because compliance with Rule 10b-10 would burden brokers transacting in ETFs if confirmations were required for all securities in the basket of securities tendered or redeemed in a primary market ETF transaction, relief is necessary. The SEC has granted relief allowing broker-dealers to omit information in creation/redemption transactions. The identity of each security, and the price and number of shares of each individual portfolio security being tendered or received are subject to the following conditions:

- That confirmation to the client containing all the information required by the rule be furnished upon request; and
- Those requests will be fulfilled in a timely manner.

Tender and Exchange Offers: Rule 14e-5. Rule 14e-5 prohibits a person who makes a cash tender or exchange offer for an equity security from purchasing the security other than under the terms of that offer. The rule could be seen as limiting the ability of the dealer manager of that offer for a particular security included in the ETF's portfolio from purchasing and redeeming ETF shares during the offer period. The SEC has offered exemptive relief for this rule to permit dealer-managers to purchase and redeem ETF shares during the timeframe of the pending tender or exchange offer.

Disclosure of Control Relationships: Rules 15c1-5 and 15c-6. A broker-dealer under Rule 15c1-5 are required to disclose any control relationship between itself and the issuer of a security being purchased or sold. If that broker-dealer has any connection with any distribution of securities being purchased, it is required to disclose that relationship to the customer under Rule 15c1-6.

Regulation M. Regulation M bans certain business activities that "may increase a security's offering price (and so increase the offering proceeds); stabilize the market price of an offered security in order to avoid a price decline during the sales period or in the immediate aftermarket; or induce or attempt to induce prospective investors to buy in the aftermarket."[11] Rules 101 and 102 of Regulation M generally prohibit distribution participants, issuers, selling security holders, and their underwriters and/or APs from purchasing, bidding for, or attempting to induce others to purchase or bid for covered securities during the restricted period of a distribution of securities. ETPs are continually creating and distributing new securities; therefore, the restricted period would rarely end. Without relief from the rules, ETP securities purchases by APs (a distribution partner) or by the issuer during redemption would violate Rules 101 and 102 of Regulation M.

Rule 101 prohibits a distribution participant, in connection with a distribution of securities, from bidding for or purchasing from or attempting to purchase or induce any person to bid for or purchase such security.[12] Rule 102 prohibits issuers, selling security holders, or any affiliated purchaser of such person from bidding for, purchasing, or attempting to induce any person to bid for or purchase a covered security during the applicable restricted period in connection with a distribution of securities effected by or on behalf of an issuer or security holder.[13]

Categories of Exemptions by Fund Type

Self-Indexing Funds. Index-based funds are the predominant form of ETFs. These funds in some way duplicate the index's component securities by fully replicating or sampling. In a full replication, the ETF invests in every component of the specified index in similar proportions. In a sampling strategy, the ETF only invests in certain

---

[11] 17 CFR Part 242, Regulation M, SHO, ATS, AC, and NMS and Customer Margin Requirements for Security Futures.

[12] *Id.*

[13] *Id.*

components of the chosen index due to costs involved in holding every security. The securities in which a sampling occurs are intended to mirror the index fund's capitalization, industry, and fundamental investment characteristics to perform in a similar economic manner as the index itself. Components that are not chosen for the ETF fund may be substituted by other instruments that are similar and expected to perform as such. ETFs are indexed to equity, fixed income, broad-based, narrow (such as industries or sector-based), international, or other customized indices.

Actively Managed Funds. Actively managed ETFs, which appeared for the first time in 2008, exist due to exemptive orders granted by the SEC. Unlike index-based ETFs, these funds do not track an index and are actively managed by a portfolio advisor much like actively managed mutual funds. Under SEC exemptions, these funds are required to publish their securities holdings and other portfolio assets daily.

Inverse and Leveraged Funds. A leveraged fund seeks a specified multiple of the performance of an underlying securities index without being limited to multiples of 125 percent, 150 percent, or 200 percent, up to a multiple of 300 percent. An inverse fund is a fund that seeks daily investment results that correspond to the inverse of an underlying securities index. An inverse leveraged fund is a fund that seeks a specified multiple of the inverse performance of an underlying securities index without being limited to multiples of 125 percent, 150 percent, or 200 percent, up to a multiple of 300 percent. Inverse and leveraged ETPs require specialized exemptive relief because of higher risks associated with the products. Currently, the SEC is no longer providing this relief to new entrants.

Use of Derivatives

Since the financial crisis of 2008, the use of derivatives has come under heightened scrutiny within the financial community. As such, ETFs that employ the use of derivatives have faced tougher examinations. Derivatives are useful but can pose greater risk to the fund's assets, as well as increasing leverage and counterparty risks. ETFs that use derivatives have not escaped this closer look and must comply under the regulations of the 1940 Act.

Derivative use by investment companies has encouraged the SEC to develop a regulatory framework through the release of no-action letters. The 1940 Act requires derivative investments to comply its provisions, including the limitations of Section 18, which also governs the issuance of senior securities, diversification requirements, concentration limitations, valuation, and more. A general statement of policy[14] was issued in 1979 to categorize certain derivatives, firm commitment agreements and standby commitment agreements in relation to Section 18. The SEC stated that the use of derivatives can be equivalent to issuing senior securities. The SEC found that a mutual fund could comply with Section if 18 it covered its payment obligations on senior securities by

---

14 SEC, *Securities Trading Practices of Registered Investment Companies,* Rel. No. 10666 (Apr. 27, 1979), https://www.sec.gov/divisions/investment/imseniorsecurities/ic-10666.pdf

maintaining separate accounts or earmarking cash or cash equivalents to meet those obligations. There are currently more than 20 SEC no-action relief letters that expand on Release 10666.

In March 2010, the SEC posted a release titled "SEC Staff Evaluating the Use of Derivatives,"[15] (the "March 2010 Release")and in August 2011, the SEC also released the "Use of Derivatives by Investment Companies under the Investment Act of 1940,"[16] which was intended to be an extension of the prior release. The SEC gathered information on how ETFs and other financial companies used derivatives. The intent was to review what additional protections ETFs using derivatives would need under the 1940 Act. The March 2010 Release placed a moratorium on allowing new derivative use in registered investment companies.

The outcome, stated in 2012 by Norm Champ (director, SEC Division of Investment Management), was that:

- The ETF's board will periodically review and approve the ETF's use of derivatives and how the ETF's investment adviser assesses and manages risk with respect to ETF's use of derivatives; and
- The ETF's disclosure of its use of derivatives in its offering documents and periodic reports is consistent with relevant SEC and staff guidance.

The SEC granted no-action relief to companies, including active ETFs that had been relying on exemptive relief for their use of derivatives. This relief was granted on the condition that no actively managed ETF previously relying on the relief would invest in options contracts, futures contracts, or swap agreements. The no-action relief states that the SEC will not recommend enforcement action if these actively managed ETFs invest in such instruments, provided that they comply with the conditions above.[17] The moratorium from the March 2010 Release effectively remains in place for new relief applications for inverse and leveraged ETFs.

Advertising and Marketing Restrictions

Generally, advertisements for ETFs by a broker-dealer or its direct affiliate are subject to the FINRA public communication advertising rules and must be filed following the same standards as other investment company materials. For ETFs that are subject to both commodity pool regulations by the NFA and FINRA rules, the Investment Company Institute (ICI), in a letter dated December 28, 2012, confirmed with the NFA that compliance with applicable SEC requirements will be deemed to constitute compliance with the NFA Compliance Rule 2-29 for most purposes. However, compliance with the

---

[15] SEC Press Release 2010-45, "SEC Staff Evaluating the Use of Derivatives" (Mar. 25,2010), https://www.sec.gov/news/press/2010/2010-45.htm

[16] SEC, "*Use of Derivatives by Investment Companies Under the Investment Company Act* of *1940,* SEC Rel. No. IC-29776; File No. S7-33-11 (Aug. 31, 2011), https://www.sec.gov/rules/concept/2011/ic-29776.pdf

[17] Derivatives Use by Actively Managed ETFs, SEC No-Action Letter (Dec. 6, 2012), https://www.sec.gov/divisions/investment/noaction/2012/ moratorium-lift-120612-etf.pdf

more general antifraud provisions of NFA Compliance Rule 2-29 still applies. The ICI letter also confirmed that, compliance with FINRA's rules for filing, review, approval, recordkeeping, and supervision will satisfy obligations under NFA Compliance Rules 2-9 and 2-29 and related interpretive notices.

In looking at compliance systems for ETF advertising materials, each sponsor should have a written manual describing the general content standards mandated by the regulators. Materials must be classified based on their content and use, and all advertising materials should be provided to a compliance professional for sign-off and review. Typically firms institute a central database that logs in each type of communication, such as correspondence, institutional sales material, or retail advertising.

Firms include many considerations when marketing these products. ETFs must not confuse the public by referring to themselves as mutual funds. Offering materials must state that the shares may only be purchased in the secondary market and may not necessarily be bought at NAV.

With the advent and exponential growth of social media such as Facebook and Twitter, firms can be one tweet or post away from mistaken marketing. FINRA guidance on the subject can be found in the January 2010 FINRA Regulatory Notice 10-06,[18] which discusses recordkeeping, social media website supervision, and what factors firms should consider when developing social media policy.

Exchange Listing Compliance Considerations

Exchanges typically require each ETP provider to send a daily holdings file to the exchange and the values for the holdings will be displayed as the intraday indicative value (IIV) by major market data vendors at a specified frequency based on the underlying asset class. For example, for equities, NYSE Archipelago Exchange (Arca) will display the values once every 15 seconds. If the exchange-traded sponsor becomes aware that the information is not being displayed correctly, they must promptly notify the exchange. Also, most sponsors will be required to publish a daily NAV and make it available to all market participants.

It is therefore important to design a compliance system that regularly checks to make sure the data is regularly transmitted to the relevant exchange and, if required, made available on the sponsor's website. The sponsor's business continuity plan should address what will happen in the event the website goes down or the data feeds become unavailable. In any event, major disruptions of this nature must be reported to the exchange and will likely result in a trading halt if they are not promptly addressed.

If the ETP's index is maintained by an affiliate of the sponsor, the sponsor or fund adviser is required to maintain information barrier requirements, or a "firewall," around

---

[18] FINRA Regulatory Notice 10-06 , Social Media Web Sites: Guidance on Blogs and Social Networking Web Sites (Jan. 2010), https://www.finra.org/sites/default/files/NoticeDocument/p120779.pdf

the personnel that have access to information concerning changes and adjustments to the index composition. These firewalls may follow similar compliance procedures used by broker-dealers that segregate research and trading business units that are controlled by the same complex. Typical compliance procedures would be physical separation of staff units, electronic segregation and password protection of business unit information-based job functions, training, and acknowledgments showing these standards have been frequently communicated to staff.

Because the shares of ETPs are traded intraday, it is important for firms to have information dissemination procedures about any material events that could impact a fund's share price. For example, NYSE Arca's Rule 5.3(i)(2) requires a sponsor to immediately disclose information when the information is likely to significantly affect the price of fund shares or is likely to be considered important by a reasonable investor in determining whether to buy or sell fund shares. Most firms adopt formal policies, including a Regulation FD policy, describing the restrictions and affirmative duties of where and when to disclose information that could materially impact the price of fund shares.

Certain administrative actions must also be promptly disclosed to the exchange, including changes in officers, audit committee members or directors, corporate actions, suspension of creations or redemptions, and dividend payments.[19] Depending on the type of action, the exchange may require preapproval from the exchange after a firm files a supplemental listing application. For example a supplemental application would be required if the ETP changed its name, altered its underlying index or reference asset, changed its ticker symbol, or declared a stock split.

Firms grapple with important considerations about continued listing standards for ETPs. After its first year of operations, an ETP must have at least 50 beneficial owners to meet the continued listing standards. Also a sponsor must monitor the shares outstanding for each ETP to ensure there are enough shares outstanding for the creation and redemption process.

Effective Testing Programs

In 2003, the SEC began requiring all investment advisers, and subsequently all investment companies, to conduct annual review of their compliance program, including policies and procedures.[20] Records of these reviews are to be kept for no fewer than five years.[21] In November 2007 the SEC's Office of Compliance Inspections and Exemptions (OCIE) a document detailing forensic testing measures for investment companies and advisers. It was intended to provide investment companies, investment advisers, and CCOs with examples of forensic testing measures that may be used to assess compliance, addressing risk areas that are often the focus of examinations.[22]

---

[19] NYSE Arca Rule 5.3(i)(1)(i)(H) requires notice of dividend payments to be made at least 10 days prior to the record date.

[20] Investment Advisers Act of 1940, Rule 206(4)-7(b), Investment Company Act of 1940, Rule 38(1)1.

[21] Investment Advisers Act of 1940, Rule 204-2(a)(17)(ii).

[22] SEC, *Forensic Measures for Funds and Advisers* (Nov. 14, 2007), https://www.sec.gov/info/cco/forensictesting.pdf

There are many different types of programs that are used by SEC examiners. In most tests, the focus on strategic risk assessment and the necessary data are already available in company records. For other tests, additional data may need to be collected.

The various tests listed by the SEC in its forensic testing guidance may include:

- Portfolio management and trade allocation;
- Brokerage arrangements and execution;
- Valuation;
- Personal trading;
- Safety of client assets; and
- Marketing and performance advertisements.

Portfolio Management and Trade Allocation. Forensic testing may identify performance disparities among client accounts by comparing performance among accounts managed under similar styles (large cap growth, large cap core, etc.). For example, the test may entail a review of trades in each account over a specified period to identify clients with a higher percentage of profitable trades or a lower proportion of unprofitable trades. Forensic testing may also look at turnover at the end of several performance periods to search for activity that may show "portfolio pumping" or those transactions that appear to "window dress" the performance of accounts. Such testing may also identify accounts managed under similar strategies whose performance is higher than average over a testing period.

Brokerage Arrangements and Execution. An execution examination reviews fees and commissions paid to broker-dealers by clients. It may also compute the average commission paid *to broker-dealers* during the identified time period. In contrast it will compute the average commission paid *by advisory clients* during the identified time period. Lastly, it may compute the total commission paid to broker-dealers and identify accounts with any patterns of trade and commission errors.

Valuation. Valuation examinations review the pricing of securities and the differences between the selling prices and fair values. Such tests also evaluate fund shareholder turnover rates to determine the accuracy of a fund's portfolio pricing policies. Lastly, the examinations will identify any large percentage changes in the fund's NAV to review the accuracy of the process used to determine the daily NAV while looking for intentional misvaluation and NAV errors.

Personal Trading. Because insider trading could become a compliance nightmare, this examination focuses on the personal trading among clients and accounts of insiders. Reviewing access persons' trades, analyzing trading patterns that may indicate abuse, and reviewing client accounts for unreported brokerage accounts compose a large portion of the examination. Personal trading tests also look into disparities between clients and accounts of insiders as well as the overall percentage of profitable trades in those accounts.

Safety of Client Assets. A review of the fund's third-party statements and reconciliations is the focus of this type of examination. It looks for patterns and differences between those and the adviser's books. Items that appear inconsistently could indicate misappropriation of client assets or sloppy recordkeeping.

Marketing and Performance Advertisement. Marketing materials, like financial records, must adhere to strict standards. Tests periodically examine recordkeeping practices to ensure that documents are being retained and are easily accessible. Even today, according to FINRA, some records must be kept in hard copy and be accessible immediately.[23]

Annual Review of Internal Financial Controls. On December 31, 2016, The Public Company Accounting Oversight Board's (PCAOB's) update of Auditing Standard No. 5 became effective as AS 2201: *An Audit of Internal Control over Financial Reporting That Is Integrated with an Audit of Financial Statements.*[24] Reviews are to be conducted no less frequently than annually and records of the tests must be kept for a minimum of five years.[25] The standard requires that an annual written report be delivered to the fund's board.

Paragraph .75 of Auditing Standard 2201 requires that in an audit of internal control over financial reporting, the auditor should obtain written representations from management:

- Acknowledging management's responsibility for establishing and maintaining effective internal control over financial reporting;[26]
- Stating that management has performed an evaluation and made an assessment of the effectiveness of the company's internal control over financial reporting and specifying the control area;[27]
- Stating that management did not use the auditor's procedures performed during the audits of internal control over financial reporting or the financial statements as part of the basis for management's assessment of the effectiveness of internal control over financial reporting;[28]
- Stating management's conclusion, as set forth in its assessment, about the effectiveness of the company's internal control over financial reporting based on the control criteria as of a specified date;[29]
- Stating that management has disclosed to the auditor all deficiencies in the design or operation of internal control over financial reporting identified as part of

---

[23] Exchange Act rules mandate record retention requirements. Interestingly, broker-dealers must keep for a shorter period (three years) than investment advisers (five years) and registered funds (six years). It is best to retain records for the longest period applicable.

[24] PCAOB, *Auditing Standard AS 2201: An Audit of Internal Control Over Financial Reporting That Is Integrated with an Audit of Financial Statements,* https://pcaobus.org/Standards/Auditing/Pages/AS2201.aspx

[25] PCAOB, *Auditing Standard No.5, An Audit of Internal Control Over Financial Reporting That Is Integrated with an Audit of Financial Statements, https://pcaobus.org/Standards/Auditing/Pages/Auditing_Standard_5.aspx*

[26] PCAOB, *Auditing Standard AS 2201: An Audit of Internal Control Over Financial Reporting That Is Integrated with an Audit of Financial Statements,* https://pcaobus.org/Standards/Auditing/Pages/AS2201.aspx

[27] *Id.*

[28] *Id.*

[29] *Id.*

management's evaluation, including separately disclosing to the auditor all such deficiencies that it believes to be significant deficiencies or material weaknesses in internal control over financial reporting;[30]

- Describing any fraud resulting in a material misstatement to the company's financial statements and any other fraud that does not result in a material misstatement to the company's financial statements but involves senior management or management or other employees who have a significant role in the company's internal control over financial reporting;[31]
- Stating whether control deficiencies identified and communicated to the audit committee during previous engagements pursuant to paragraphs .78 and .80 have been resolved, and specifically identifying any that have not; and[32]
- Stating whether there were, subsequent to the date being reported on, any changes in internal control over financial reporting or other factors that might significantly affect internal control over financial reporting, including any corrective actions taken by management with regard to significant deficiencies and material weaknesses.[33]

Compliance Programs

Rule 38a-1 of the 1940 Act[34] imposes ongoing requirements for ETPs registered under the 1940 Act, their advisers, and their service providers to maintain, review, test, and modify the written compliance policies and procedures that have been adopted and found by the entity to be reasonably designed to prevent violations of the federal securities laws. It also requires funds to appoint a CCO. The rules contain four major components: adoption and implementation of written policies and procedures; approval of the compliance program by the fund's board or other governance structure; annual review of the program; and the appointment of a CCO to administer the compliance program. Although complying with this rule is the desired result, the first step to developing a compliance program is to conduct a risk assessment.

Risk Assessment. The purpose of a risk assessment is to identify risk, evaluate the its threat, and develop the means to mitigate it. The process will help to prioritize risks based on their threat level and to develop programs, policies, or procedures that will help alleviate or remove them. Some risks may be easily addressed; other, ongoing risks will need continual monitoring and assessment. The simplest way to view a risk assessment plan is to divide it into its three steps: identify the risks, assess the risk, and respond to the risks.

Identifying the Risks. At the beginning of the process, the firm will want to review all business functions (financial, administrative, strategic, marketing, etc.) to understand the breadth of compliance risks faced. The firm employs strategies such as these:

---

30 *Id.*

31 *Id.*

32 *Id.*

33 *Id.*

34 17 CFR 270.38a-1, Compliance Procedures and Practices of Certain Investment Companies.

- *Develop assessment criteria:* Develop a set of criteria to organize risk by impact and likelihood of occurrence or other criteria based on the business. The criteria for identifying compliance risk should allow for significant differentiation for ranking and prioritization. A rating scale that incorporates characteristics of the level of impact, likelihood, vulnerability, and speed of onset is an important part of future steps. Ensure that all involved in the assessment understand the criteria developed;
- *Assess risks:* Using the defined criteria, identify potential and actual risks within the organization. Risks are generally first tested qualitatively, then quantitatively. Qualitative assessment assesses each risk according to the scale developed and provides information on impact, likelihood, vulnerability, etc. Quantitative assessment, which is generally more costly and time consuming, assigns a numerical value to risks, and takes into account risk interactions;
- *Assess risk interactions:* Some risks stand alone; some may interact with other identified risks. This interaction can cause the potential for greater damage and may be identified as material risks by OCIE. A holistic approach to risk assessment evaluates individual risks and how all identified risks interact with each other;
- *Prioritize risks.* Once the assessment is complete, prioritize the risks in order of magnitude, importance, timeliness, or risk level or threat. Some organizations find it helpful to create a risk profile that outlines all the risks an enterprise faces. Risks can be prioritized not only on their financial impact but also in categories such as advertising or marketing compliance, reputational risk, or the health and wellbeing of the organization.

Respond to Risks. The results of the risk assessment and prioritization provide the framework for responding to and mitigating the identified risks. Developing policies and procedures, identifying key staff to monitor and address ongoing risk, and creating a quickly accessible recordkeeping system are all potential risk mitigation strategies. The findings of the risk assessment should be regularly reviewed to incorporate new activities, products, or findings in subsequent assessments.

V. DEVELOP POLICIES AND PROCEDURES

To prevent the fund from violating federal security laws, Rule 38a-1 under the 1940 Act requires a reasonably designed set of written policies and procedures to be put in place as part of a compliance program.[35] This program and the compliance programs of the fund's service providers—including the fund's adviser, principal underwriter, administrator, and transfer agent—are to be approved by the fund boards. The fund board must find that the compliance program is reasonably designed to prevent violations of federal laws by the fund and its service providers.

Fund policies and procedures should cover the unique compliance needs of the organization. They should address how risks are identified, managed, and mitigated. They should also include procedures for testing, reviewing, and assessing the policies and

---

[35] 17 CFR 270.38a-1, Compliance Procedures and Practices of Certain Investment Companies.

procedures themselves. Compliance program policies and procedures should cover the pricing of portfolio securities and fund shares; processing of fund shares; identification of affiliated persons; protection of nonpublic information; compliance with fund governance requirements; and market timing.[36]

At a minimum, a fund's policies and procedures, under Rule 38a-1, must attend to the topics addressed in this section.

Pricing of Portfolio Securities and Fund Shares

Funds are required to develop policies and procedures to

> [M]onitor for circumstances that may necessitate the use of fair value prices; establish criteria for determining when market quotations are no longer reliable for a particular portfolio security; provide a methodology or methodologies by which the fund determines the current fair value of the portfolio security;[37] and regularly review the appropriateness and accuracy of the method used in valuing securities, and make any necessary adjustments.[38]

Processing of Fund Shares

The rule requires that a fund have in place procedures that segregate orders received before the fund prices its shares and that the fund should not only approve and periodically review the policies and procedures of transfer agents, as required by the rule, but should also take affirmative steps to protect themselves and their shareholders against late trading by obtaining assurances that those policies and procedures are effectively administered.

Identification of Affiliates

Funds should have policies and procedures in place to identify affiliates and to prevent unlawful transactions with them.

Protection of Nonpublic Information

The rule[39] requires funds to establish, maintain, and enforce written policies and procedures reasonably designed to prevent the adviser or any of its associated persons from misusing material, nonpublic information. It should also address other potential misuses of nonpublic information, including the disclosure to third parties of material information about the fund's portfolio, its trading strategies, or pending transactions,

---

[36] *Id.*

[37] In determining fair value, some funds use correlations between the exchange prices of foreign securities and other appropriate instruments or indicators, such as relevant indices, American Depository Receipts, and futures contracts. Software developed by vendors is today available to assist funds to determine the fair value of portfolio securities.

[38] 17 CFR 270.38a-1.

[39] Although Rule 38a-1 does this implicitly, Rule 17j-1(b) under the 1940 Act, Section 204A under the Advisers Act and Rule 10b-5 under the 1934 Act do this explicitly.

and the purchase or sale of fund shares by advisory personnel based on material, non-public information about the fund's portfolio.

Compliance with Fund Governance Requirements[40]

The fund's boards of directors should be elected by the fund's shareholders, and a certain percentage should be independent directors. To rely on many of the exemptive rules, independent directors must constitute a majority of the board, must be selected and nominated by other independent directors, and if they hire legal counsel, that counsel must be an independent legal counsel. A fund's policies and procedures should be designed to guard against, among other things, an improperly constituted board, the failure of the board to properly consider matters entrusted to it, and the failure of the board to request and consider information required by the 1940 Act from the fund adviser and other service providers.

Although these required areas need to be addressed, they do not cover all that may need policies and procedures. Some other topics that could be included are portfolio management trading activities and practices (failure to obtain best execution, interpositioning of an affiliated broker-dealer, failure to periodically and systematically review execution quality); propriety trading of the adviser and personal trading by employees; accuracy of disclosures made to investors, clients, and regulators; and safeguarding client assets from conversion or misuse.[41]

Development of a Recordkeeping System

Firms generally are required to maintain copies of all current policies and procedures. They are to be retained for a minimum of five years by an adviser registered with the SEC under the Investment Advisers Act of 1940 as amended (P.L. 112-90) and six years for fund records under the 1940 Act.[42] Materials provided to the board of directors in connection with their approval of the funds and its service providers' policies and procedures and the annual written reports by the fund's CCO should also be retained. Funds are to maintain all annual review records. Typically, records will be maintained electronically, which will assist in the SEC examination process.

Section 31 of the 1940 Act identifies particular records that are to be maintained by firms. The fund and its underwriters, brokers, dealers or investment advisers must maintain and preserve the books and other documents that constitute the basis of the financial statements. In addition, investment advisers that are not majority-owned subsidiaries, depositors, and principal underwriters must maintain records of their transactions with the fund. These books and records are subject to examination by the SEC.

---

[40] SEC, *Final Rule: Compliance Programs of Investment Companies and Investment Advisers,* Rel. No. IA-2204; File No. S7-03-03.

[41] Several of these are required under the Advisers Act.

[42] 17 CFR 270.38a-1.

Rule 31a-1 requires an investment company to maintain and keep current the following:

- Original entry journals containing an itemized and detailed record of all securities purchases and sales, all receipts and deliveries of securities, and all receipts and disbursements of cash and all other debit and credits;
- General and auxiliary ledgers reflecting all asset, liability, reserve, capital, and income and expense accounts, including separate ledger accounts for specific activities as set forth in the rule;
- Corporate charters, certificates of incorporation or trust agreements, by-laws, and minute books of meetings;
- Specific records of each transaction and investment as set forth in the rule;
- A record identifying their person or persons, committees, or groups authorizing the purchase or sale of portfolio securities;
- Files of all advisory material received from the investment adviser or any persons from whom the fund accepts investment advice; and
- Any other records as appropriate.

Rule 31a-2 requires an investment company to maintain and keep current the following:

- Journals, ledgers, and corporate documents must be preserved permanently, the first two years in an easily accessible place
- The other records described above must be preserved for six years, the first two years in an easily accessible place
- The following records must also be preserved for six years, the first two years in an easily accessible place:
  - Any advertisements, pamphlets, circulars, form letters, or other sales literature addressed to or intended for distribution to prospective investors;
  - Any record of the initial determination that a director is not an interested person and each subsequent determination (including any questionnaire used to make such determination);
  - Any materials used by the disinterested directors to determine that a person who is acting as their legal counsel is an independent legal counsel; and
  - Any documents or other written information considered by the directors pursuant to Section 15(c) of the 1940 Act in approving the terms or renewal of a contract or agreement between the company and an investment adviser.

Finally, Rule 38a-1 contains additional recordkeeping requirements with respect to fund compliance programs.

Reporting Policies

The 1940 Act has several reporting components for investment companies. Periodic reporting to the SEC and shareowners is required.

Periodic Reporting to the SEC Investment Companies. Section 30(a) of the 1940 Act requires the annual filing of certain documents, information, and reports. Investment companies that have securities listed on a national exchange must file annually under Section 13(a) of the Exchange Act. However, pursuant to Rule 30d-1, a registered investment company that is required to file annual and quarterly reports pursuant to Section 13(a) of the Exchange Act shall satisfy its requirements by filing reports on Form N-CSR and Form N-Q.

Other rules that need to be addressed include the following:

- Rule 30b1-1 requires a registered management company to file a semiannual report on Form N-SAR within 60 days after the close of each fiscal semiannual period;
- Rule 30b1-4 requires a registered management investment company to file an annual report on Form N-PX not later than August 31 of each year, containing the fund's proxy voting record for the most recent 12-month period ended June 30;
- Rule 30b1-5 requires a registered management investment company to file quarterly reports on Form N-Q not more than 60 days after the close of the first and third fiscal quarters;
- Rule 30b1-7 requires a money market fund to file a monthly report on Form N-MFP not later than the fifth business day of each month;
- Rule 30b2-1(a) requires a registered management investment company to file a report on Form N-CSR not later than 10 days after the transmission to shareholders of any report required pursuant to Rule 30e-1(a); and
- Rule 30b2-1(b) requires a registered management investment company to file a copy of any periodic or interim report or similar communication containing financial statements that is transmitted to shareholders but is not required to be filed under Rule 30b2-1(a) not later than 10 days after the transmission to shareholders.

Periodic Reporting to Shareowners. Section 30(a) of the 1940 Act requires the annual filing of certain documents, information, and reports to shareowners at least semiannually. Some of the reports listed only required in the *annual report* are so noted. The reports must include the following:

- Financial statements (in the case of the annual report, they must be audited), which include
  - Statement of net assets (or assets and liabilities),
  - Schedule of investments,
  - Statement of operations,
  - Statement of changes in net assets,
  - Statement of aggregate dollars amounts of purchase and sales of investment securities, and
  - Financial highlights;
- Statement of aggregate remuneration paid to directors, officers, and others;
- The report of the accountants *(annual reports only)*. Section 30(g) requires the audit report to state that the independent public accountants have verified securities owned either by actual examination or by confirmation from the custodian;
- Information concerning changes in and disagreements with accountants;

- Biographical information for each director and officer required by Item 12(a)(1) of Form N-1A *(annual reports only)*;
- Statement of availability of additional information about fund directors *(annual reports only)*;
- If any matter was submitted to a shareholder vote during the period covered by the report, or if shareholder consents were solicited, the date and type of meeting and a summary of the matter(s) and the results of the vote. For an election of directors, the report should contain the names of the directors who were elected and the names of any directors whose term is continuing;
- Management's discussion of fund performance *(annual reports only)*. The presentation must include
  - A discussion of the factors that materially affected fund performance during the most recently completed fiscal year, including the relevant market conditions and the investment strategies and techniques used by the fund's adviser. Particular attention must be paid to text accompanying the financial statements, because it may be viewed as advertising or sales literature,
  - A line graph showing the growth of $10,000 invested over the last 10 fiscal years (or period since the fund was first registered, if shorter), and the growth of $10,000 invested in "an appropriate broad-based securities market index" for the same period, and
  - A table showing the fund's average annual return for the 1-, 5-, and 10-year periods ending at the end of the most recently completed fiscal year, and a statement that past performance does not predict future performance and that the graph and table do not reflect the deduction of taxes that a shareholder would pay on fund distributions or the redemption of fund shares. Rule 34b-1, which governs the timeliness of performance information in sales literature, provides an exemption;
- An expense example;
- Graphical representation of holdings;
- Statement regarding availability of quarterly portfolio schedule;
- Statement regarding availability of proxy voting policies and procedures;
- Statement regarding availability of proxy voting record; and
- Statement regarding basis for approval of investment advisory contract.

The reports must be transmitted to shareowners within 60 days of the end of the fiscal period to which the report refers. Reports must be filed with the SEC on From N-CSR no later than 10 days after they are first transmitted to shareowners. Rule 30-1(d) allows open-end investment companies to transmit current a prospectus in lieu of the annual or semiannual report if all the information required is contained therein. The 60-day transmittal rule applies with this exception. Also note that reporting obligations for investment companies were changed in 2016 and new Forms N PORT and N CEN will be required.

VI. REPORTING REQUIREMENTS FOR COMMODITY POOLS

The forms listed in Table 2 must be filed with the SEC and NYSE if the ETP is registered as a commodity pool. Those listed in Table 3 must be filed with the CFTC.

TABLE 2. SEC AND NYSE REQUIRED FILINGS FOR COMMODITY POOLS

Form Name/Filing	Reporting Period	SEC Filing Requirement	NYSE Filing Requirement
Form S-1	Registration of common units of beneficial interest	Required to file registration statement to register securities under the Securities Act	Deemed filed with the NYSE Arca when filed on the EDGAR system
Form S-3	Registration of common units of beneficial interest	Required to file registration statement to register securities under the Securities Act	Deemed filed with the NYSE Arca when filed on the EDGAR system
Prospectus Form 424(b)(3)	Updated as necessary		Deemed filed with the NYSE Arca when filed on the EDGAR system
Certification & Notice of Termination of Registration or suspension of duty to file reports under Sections 13 and 15(d) of the 1934 Exchange Act (Form 15)	To be filed as necessary	Required to terminate or suspend the duty to file reports under Rule 12h-3(b)(1)(i)	Deemed filed with the NYSE Arca when filed on the EDGAR system
Registration for Certain Classes of Securities Pursuant to Section 12(b) or 12(g) of the Exchange Act (Form 8-A)	Upon effectiveness of registration statement	Required to register under the 1934 Exchange Act	Deemed filed with the NYSE Arca when filed on the EDGAR system
Initial Statement of Beneficial Ownership of Securities (Form 3)	Upon becoming and officer of the Trust or a beneficial owner of more than 10% of the securities of the trust (reporting person)	Within 10 days of the event by which the person becomes a reporting person. In the case of the trust, the reporting persons must file no later than the effective date of the registration statement	Not Applicable
Statement of Changes of Beneficial Ownership of Securities (Form 4)	Acquisition or disposition date of securities	Before the end of the second business day following the day on which a transaction resulting in a change of ownership of a reporting person has been executed	Not Applicable
Annual Statement of Beneficial Ownership of Securities (Form 5)		By or on the 45th day after the trust's fiscal year end	Not Applicable

TABLE 2. SEC AND NYSE REQUIRED FILINGS FOR COMMODITY POOLS			
Form Name/Filing	**Reporting Period**	**SEC Filing Requirement**	**NYSE Filing Requirement**
Information to be included in statements filed pursuant to Rule 13d-1(a) and amendments thereto filed pursuant to 13d-2(a) (Schedule 13D Rule 13d-101)	Unitholders (including the trust's officers) who beneficially own 5% or more of the trust's units	All officers of the trust or investors who acquire 5% or more of the trust's units. Must be amended "promptly" to show any change of 1% or more in ownership	Not Applicable
Schedule 13G (Rule 13d-102)	Within 10 days after acquisition	Passive investors who acquire 5% or more of the trust's units (and own less than 20% of the trust's units). Must be amended "promptly" if the passive investor acquired greater than 10% of the trust's shares	Not Applicable
Form 10-K	Annual	Due 60 days after FYE	Deemed filed with the NYSE Arca when filed on the EDGAR system
Form 10-Q	Quarterly	Due 40 days after fiscal quarter end	Deemed filed with the NYSE Arca when filed on the EDGAR system

TABLE 3. CFTC REQUIRED FILINGS FOR COMMODITY POOLS			
Filing	**Form Name**	**CFTC[2] Filing Requirement**	**File Date**
Account statement delivered to pool participants	Account Statement	Each CPO must periodically distribute to each participant in each pool that it operates, within 30 calendar days after month end, an account statement, which shall be presented in the form of a statement of income (loss) and a statement of changes in net asset value. The account statement must contain an oath or affirmation that, to the best of the knowledge of the individual making the oath or affirmation, the information contained in the document is accurate and complete. This oath or affirmation must be made by a representative duly authorized to bind the CPO. *See* 17 C.F.R. §4.22.	Within 30 days following the end of the pool's required monthly reporting period

TABLE 3. CFTC REQUIRED FILINGS FOR COMMODITY POOLS

Filing	Form Name	CFTC[2] Filing Requirement	File Date
Annual report delivered to pool participants and the National Futures Association (NFA)	Annual report/Form PFs	Each CPO must distribute an annual report to each participant in each pool that it operates, and must electronically submit a copy of the report and key financial balances from the Report to the NFA pursuant to the electronic filing procedures of the NFA, within 90 calendar days after the end of the pool's fiscal year or the permanent cessation of trading. *See* 17 C.F.R. §4.22.	Within 90 days after fiscal year end
Quarterly report to NFA	Form CPO-PQR	Each CPO must report on a quarterly basis to NFA specific information on certain pools that it operates within 60 days after the end of each quarterly reporting period. *See* 17 C.F.R. §4.22.	Within 60 days after quarterly reporting period

[1] Commodity Futures Trading Commission Regulation 40.2, 17 CFR 4.20.

SEC Examination

Over the past few years, the regulatory landscape has shifted greatly. The SEC has made many changes to the way it expects firms to prepare and manage their testing programs and is being more aggressive in enforcement actions. OCIE has stated that it will "examine ETFs for compliance with applicable exemptive relief granted under the Securities Exchange Act of 1934 and the Investment Company Act of 1940 and with other regulatory requirements, as well as review the ETFs' unit creation and redemption process."[43] The office will focus on sales strategy, trading practices, disclosures involving ETFs (including excessive portfolio concentration), primary and secondary market trading risks, adequacy of risk disclosure, and suitability (particularly in niche or leveraged/inverse ETFs).[44]

OCIE's focus on market-wide risks should also be taken into consideration when a firm develops an effective testing program. Although regulation system compliance and integrity and cybersecurity are a concern for all financial firms, the SEC has stated that examining liquidity controls will be a focus going forward by examining

[43] National Exam Program, OCIE, "Examination Priorities for 2016, https://www.sec.gov/about/offices/ocie/national-examination-program-priorities-2016.pdf

[44] *Id.*

advisers to ETFs that have exposure to potentially illiquid fixed income securities. The examinations will include a review of the various controls a firm has surrounding market risk management, valuation, liquidity management, trading activity, and regulatory capital.[45]

It is more important than ever for firms and advisers to be prepared to manage examinations; infractions can have serious consequences. The majority of enforcement actions originate from OCIE examinations. Clients and other business partners are increasingly asking to review deficiency letters. A comprehensive testing program can alleviate many findings before an examination begins.

Preparing for an Exam. There are several steps to preparing for an exam. The first, and probably most important, is identifying a point of contact for OCIE. The CCO is the most logical choice. The firm should review previous examination records and letters of deficiency to familiarize itself with previous issues. The CCO should arrange for work areas and resources for the examiners, including compiling an organized set of files required for the exam. Lastly, the CCO should prepare one or more opening presentations to be given upon the examiners' arrival.

The Exam. Once the meetings with appropriate individuals are scheduled, documents are organized and collected, and the initial presentation is complete, the examiners will review the firm's files. Examiners are not to take or make copies for themselves. The CCO should be present during all interviews that are conducted by OCIE. During the exam, the firm may address any deficiencies identified.

SEC examiners are looking to find whether efficient and effective controls are in place. The firm should be able to produce evidence that problems are being addressed as they occur and are resolved promptly. The SEC staff want to see that risks have been identified, managed, and mitigated.

Examination Results. There are three results to an examination: no finding or violations, a deficiency letter, and an enforcement referral. If no findings or violations are found, no action will be required of the firm. Should any be found, OCIE will issue a letter of deficiency. Any findings that need immediate attention require a written response to OCIE. Possible corrective actions can include, but are not limited to, revising compliance policies or procedures; implementing new exception or surveillance reports; and changing the level or frequency of review.

VII. SIGNIFICANT SEC NO-ACTION LETTERS APPLICABLE TO ETFS

The following is a list of some no-action letters that are applicable to exchange-traded funds. A no-action letter is written by the staff of a government agency in reply to a request by an organization that is subject to regulation by that agency. The letter indicates

---

45 *Id.*

that the government agency will not recommend that legal action be taken against the requesting organization should the entity engage in a course of action proposed by the organization through its request for a no-action letter.

The following no-action letters are applicable to all ETFs:[46]

- *iShares Trust, et al.* October 22, 2008;
- *Barclays Global Fund Advisers, et al.* March 12, 2009;
- *FQF Trust, et al.* December 13, 2011;
- *Derivatives Use by Actively-Managed ETFs.* December 6, 2012; and
- *SPDR Series Trust, et al.* June 24, 2015.

The following no-action letters are applicable to all ETPs:[47]

- *Select Sector SPDR Fund and Diamonds Trust.* July 6, 2000;
- *Market Vectors ETF Trust, et al.* March 26, 2012; and
- *SPDR S&P Dividend ETF,* March 28, 2016.

VIII. CONCLUSION

Designing a compliance system for ETPs is a complex task that should be undertaken during the product development phase. Depending on the structure of the product, the SEC could take several months before granting an exemptive order. If a firm is a mutual fund sponsor, the CCO should not assume that the compliance system for ETPs can merely duplicate that which is used for mutual funds—especially if the product is not an investment company registered under the Investment Company Act of 1940.

As one example, unlike with mutual funds, the transfer agent will not know the identity of beneficial owners in the secondary market. To monitor for affiliates and potential conflicts of interest, the CCO may choose to run regular ownership reports from a shareowner servicing agent that routinely fulfills the ETP's disclosure delivery requirements. These reports may also be used to monitor the number of beneficial owners and their ownership in the funds. Authorized participants may also hold large inventories of shares and it is common for the distributor of an ETP to use an irrevocable proxy agreement so that the AP does not have a voting interest in an ETP, which could create unintended affiliation or control issues.

Compliance staff should work closely with legal and accounting staff to ensure all federal securities law requirements and valuation issues are being addressed in the compliance program. A detailed checklist for each requirement showing who is accountable should be reviewed and signed off by management, especially prior to any new ETP launch.

---

[46] https://www.sec.gov/divisions/investment/im-noaction.shtml#etfs

[47] SEC Division of Investment Management, Staff No-Action and Interpretive Letters (Apr. 7, 2017), https://www.sec.gov/divisions/investment/im-noaction.shtml#etp

Do not hesitate to use additional resources that may be of additional help, such as the compliance staff at the exchanges or compliance personnel at any service providers. The CCO should stay alert to current regulatory developments such as the SEC's recent derivatives proposal. Compliance professionals should attend industry seminars and trade association conferences to develop a network of qualified individuals who can assist with the firm's compliance goals. The Compliance Department also should conduct regular testing and mock examinations of its compliance program to ensure it remains robust and effective.

ABOUT THE AUTHOR

Victor Frye joined ProShares in 2002 as CCO and has more than 30 years of experience working in the financial services industry. Mr. Frye is responsible for a team of professionals who oversee all regulatory and compliance matters for both ProShares ETFs and ProFunds mutual fund trusts; as well as for ProShares and ProFunds investment advisers. Before joining ProShares and ProFunds, Mr. Frye was assistant vice president and compliance officer for the Calvert Group of mutual funds and its operating companies. He also served previously as a member of NASD District Committee No. 9. Mr. Frye received a bachelor of arts degree with honors from Denison University, and he earned his juris doctor degree from the Washington College of Law at American University. He is a member of both the Pennsylvania and District of Columbia Bar Associations.

CHAPTER 16

Private Fund Specific Regulatory Requirements

By Jeff Blumberg
Faegre Baker Daniels, LLP

I. INTRODUCTION

This chapter addresses the additional compliance obligations to which managers of private funds (as that term is defined in Section 202(a)(29) of the Advisers Act[1]) are subject due to the management of such private funds.

II. INVESTMENT COMPANY ACT

Pooled investment vehicles that invest in securities would generally (absent the exceptions discussed below) fall within the definition of an "investment company" as provided Section 3(a)(1) of the Investment Company Act of 1940, as amended ("40 Act").[2] The common exceptions to this status are commodity pools (discussed below) and real estate funds. Absent an exemption from registration or an exception to the definition of an investment company, an investment company is required to register as such under Section 8 of the 40 Act. The most common exceptions relied upon by registered investment advisers for the pooled investment vehicles that they manage are Sections 3(c)(1) and 3(c)(7).

Section 3(c)(1)

Section 3(c)(1) of the 40 Act provides that notwithstanding the definition of an investment company provided in Section 3(a), "any issuer whose outstanding securities (other than short-term paper) are beneficially owned by not more than 100 persons

---

1 A "private fund" is an issuer that would be an investment company, as defined in Investment Company Act of 1940, as amended (15 U.S.C. 80a-3), but for Section 3(c)(1) or 3(c)(7) of that act.

2 An "investment company" is any issuer that(1) Is or holds itself out as being engaged primarily, or proposes to engage primarily, in the business of investing, reinvesting, or trading in securities; (2) Is engaged or proposes to engage in the business of issuing face-amount certificates of the installment type, or has been engaged in such business and has any such certificate outstanding; or (3) Is engaged or proposes to engage in the business of investing, reinvesting, owning, holding, or trading in securities, and owns or proposes to acquire investment securities having a value exceeding 40 per centum of the value of such issuer's total assets (exclusive of government securities and cash items) on an unconsolidated basis.

and which is not making and does not presently propose to make a public offering of its securities" is not an investment company required to register. Notwithstanding this exception from the definition of an investment company, an issuer relying on Section 3(c)(1) is a still deemed to be an investment company for purposes of the purchase or other acquisition by such issuer of any security issued by any registered investment company and the sale of any security issued by any registered open-end investment company to any such issuer.[3]

It is important to note that Section 3(c)(1) itself does not require any specific investor suitability requirements in order to rely on this exception. However, one of the requirements to rely on Section 3(c)(1) is that the issuer not make a public offering of its securities. Most funds that rely on Section 3(c)(1) to avoid registration as an investment company also rely on Rule 506 adopted under Regulation D of the Securities Act of 1933, as amended (the "Securities Act") to ensure that the offering of the fund's securities do not constitute a public offering.

100 Beneficial Owner Limit. The primary limitation for a private fund relying on Section 3(c)(1) is that it limit the beneficial owners of its securities (other than short-term paper) to no more than 100 persons. Many industry participants cite a "99 investor limit" for Section 3(c)(1), but from a technical perspective, the interest a general partner or managing member has in a private fund is arguably not a "security" for this purpose since that entity has an active role in managing the private fund, so many firms take the position that you can have a full 100 beneficial owners in a 3(c)(1) fund at any particular moment. In addition, the 100 beneficial owner limit is a "real time" test in that one looks at the private fund at the relevant moment to determine the number of beneficial owners (i.e., former beneficial owners are not included).

In addition to the 100 beneficial owners described above, a 3(c)(1) fund may accept investments from an unlimited number of "knowledgeable employees."[4] Knowledgeable employees are described more in the Section 3(c)(7) discussion.

Look-through rules. Counting the number of beneficial owners for a 3(c)(1) fund is not always as straightforward as it might seem. There are a number of specific situations in which a single capital account in a 3(c)(1) fund could be counted as multiple beneficial owners and, conversely, when multiple capital accounts can be collapsed into a single beneficial owner.

When an entity invests in a fund that relies on 3(c)(1), it is generally treated as a single beneficial owner except under certain circumstances. When the investing entity itself relies on 3(c)(1) or 3(c)(7) and that entity owns 10 percent or more of the *voting* securities of the target fund, the target fund must look through the investing fund for purposes of determining the number of its beneficial owners.[5] For this reason, many

[3] Sections 12(d)(1)(A)(i) and 12(d)(1)(B)(i) of the 40 Act.

[4] SEC Rule 3c-5 adopted under the Investment Company Act of 1940, as amended.

[5] SEC Rule 3c-1 adopted under the Investment Company Act of 1940, as amended.

private funds structure their governance provisions to allow them to take the position that the private fund is issuing *nonvoting* securities. A no-action letter of the Securities and Exchange Commission (SEC) addresses when an entity that is organized as a limited partnership is issuing nonvoting securities. Generally, the SEC takes the position that a limited partner owns a voting security if it may do any of the following:

- Remove or replace the limited partnership's general partner;
- Vote on the election or removal of the limited partner's general partner in the event of the general partner's death, insanity or retirement;
- Terminate the limited partnership if one of the initial general partners ceases to serve in that role; or
- Take part in the conduct or control of the limited partnership's business.[6]

In addition, the SEC has taken the position that even if a limited partnership interest is nonvoting under the analysis above, a limited partnership interest is still a voting security if the limited partner has an economic interest that gives it the power to exercise a controlling influence over the partnership (the general accepted standard here is a 25 percent ownership stake in the limited partnership[7]).

Integration. Because the exception provided for under Section 3(c)(1) is based primarily on the number of beneficial owners, the SEC has developed an additional doctrine to address the fact that it would be simple for the investment manager of a private fund that relies on Section 3(c)(1) to simply set up a new private fund as the first fund approaches the 100 beneficial owner limit. This doctrine, called *integration*, states that the SEC may collapse (or integrate) multiple private funds managed by a single investment manager that rely on the exception provided under Section 3(c)(1) unless a reasonable investor would see the two funds as materially different. Consequently, if the two funds have more than 100 beneficial owners in the aggregate, the exception provided for under Section 3(c)(1) would no longer be available to either fund. The types of differences that are generally accepted as being "material" may include investment strategies, fee structures, tax status of the fund or its investors, and liquidity profiles, among others.

One significant caveat to the integration doctrine is that the SEC has expressly stated that it would not integrate a fund that relies on Section 3(c)(1) with a fund that relies on 3(c)(7) as long as the two funds are not commingling their portfolios. In other words, an investment manager can manage a 3(c)(1) fund and a 3(c)(7) one side-by-side with identical fees, liquidity, and investment strategies and the SEC will never collapse the 3(c)(7) fund into the 3(c)(1) fund and take the position that the 3(c)(1) fund has exceeded the limit on beneficial owners as long as the two funds do not have shared ownership of a brokerage account.

---

6 Standish Equity Investments, Inc. SEC No-Action Letter (Dec. 15, 1993).

7 The 25 percent threshold is based on the SEC definition of "control," which presumes control with a 25 percent ownership interest.

Section 3(c)(7)

Section 3(c)(7) of the 40 Act provides that notwithstanding the definition of an investment company provided in Section 3(a), "any issuer, the outstanding securities of which are owned exclusively by persons who, at the time of acquisition of such securities, are qualified purchasers, and which is not making and does not at that time propose to make a public offering of such securities" is not an investment company required to register. Similarly to private funds that rely on Section 3(c)(1), notwithstanding this exception from the definition of an investment company, an issuer relying on Section 3(c)(7) is a still deemed to be an investment company for purposes of the purchase or other acquisition by such issuer of any security issued by any registered investment company and the sale of any security issued by any registered open-end investment company to any such issuer.[8]

In addition to qualified purchasers, a private fund that relies on the exception provided under Section 3(c)(7) can allow investors who are "knowledgeable employees." A knowledgeable employee is generally:

- An executive officer (defined below), director, trustee, general partner, advisory board member, or person serving in a similar capacity of the relevant private fund or that private fund's investment manager; or
- An employee of the relevant private fund or the private fund's investment manager (other than an employee performing solely clerical, secretarial, or administrative functions with regard to such company or its investments) who, in connection with his or her regular functions or duties, participates in the investment activities of such private fund, other private funds, or investment companies, the investment activities of which are managed by such investment manager, provided that such employee has been performing such functions and duties for or on behalf of the private fund or its investment manager, or substantially similar functions or duties for or on behalf of another company for at least 12 months.

An "executive officer" is the president; any vice president in charge of a principal business unit, division, or function (such as sales, administration or finance); an officer who performs a policymaking function, or any other person who performs similar policymaking functions for the private fund or for its investment manager. In the context of the investment management industry, private funds rarely have employees of their own, so this definition is effectively referencing the relevant personnel of the private fund's investment manager.

For purposes of the requirement that the securities of a private fund relying on Section 3(c)(7) are purchased by a qualified purchaser or a knowledgeable employee, transfers of such securities by gift or bequest (more generally, transfers that are not for "value") or where the transfer was caused by legal separation, divorce, death, or other involuntary event, are still deemed to have been purchased by a qualified purchaser.

---

[8] Sections 12(d)(1)(A)(i) and 12(d)(1)(B)(i) of the 40 Act.

Again, similarly to the Section 3(c)(1) requirements, one of the requirements to rely on Section 3(c)(7) is that the issuer not make a public offering of its securities. Most funds that rely on Section 3(c)(7) to avoid registration as an investment company also rely on Rule 506 adopted under Regulation D of the Securities Act to ensure that the offering of the fund's securities does not constitute a public offering.

Qualified Purchaser Requirement. One of the requirements under Section 3(c)(7) is the investor suitability/sophistication standard (unlike the requirements under Section 3(c)(1)). In order to purchase an interest in a private fund that relies on the exception provided under Section 3(c)(7), an investor must be a "qualified purchaser" as that term is defined in Section 2(a)(51) of the 40 Act.

A "qualified purchaser" is one of the following:

1. Any natural person (including any person who holds a joint, community property, or other similar shared ownership interest in an issuer that is excepted under Section 3(c)(7) with that person's qualified purchaser spouse) who owns not less than $5,000,000 in net investments;
2. Any company that owns not less than $5,000,000 in Net Investments and that is owned directly or indirectly by or for two or more natural persons who are related as siblings or spouse (including former spouses), or direct lineal descendants by birth or adoption, spouses of such persons, the estates of such persons, or foundations, charitable organizations, or trusts established by or for the benefit of such persons;
3. Any trust that is not covered by clause 2 and that was not formed for the specific purpose of acquiring the securities offered, as to which the trustee or other person authorized to make decisions with respect to the trust, and each settlor or other person who has contributed assets to the trust, is a person described in clause 1, 2, or 4 ; or
4. Any person, acting for its own account or the accounts of other qualified purchasers, who in the aggregate owns and invests on a discretionary basis, not less than $25,000,000 in net investments.

"Net investments" means the value of the investor's Investments (defined below) less the aggregate amount of any outstanding indebtedness incurred to acquire (or for the purpose of acquiring) such Investments.

"Investments" means:

- Securities;
- Real estate, *but only if held for investment purposes*;
- Commodity interests, *but only if held for investment purposes*;
- Physical commodities, *but only if held for investment purposes*;
- Financial contracts, *but only if entered into for investment purposes*; and
- Cash and cash equivalents (as each of these terms is defined below), *but only if held for investment purposes.*

Investments do not include collectibles such as jewelry, artwork or antiques, even though such collectibles may be held for investment purposes.

"Securities" carries the meaning of the term as defined in Section 2(a)(1) of the Securities Act, such as stocks, bonds, and notes. However, securities issued by an issuer that controls, is controlled by, or is under common control with the individual (e.g., an interest in a family-owned or closely held business) are *not* investments *unless* the issuer of the securities is:

- A "public" company;[9]
- An "investment company" within the meaning of the 40 Act, including a registered investment company and a foreign investment company;
- A company that would be an "investment company" within the meaning of the 40 Act but for one or more of the "exclusions";[10]
- A commodity pool; or
- E company with shareholders' equity of not less than $50 million.[11]

For purposes of the term "securities," a person is deemed to "control" a company if such person has the power to exercise a controlling influence over the management or policies of such company, unless such power is solely the result of such person's official position with such company (e.g., as a director or officer of such company. A person who beneficially owns, either directly or through one or more "controlled" companies, more than 25 percent of the voting securities of a company, is presumed to "control" such company.)

"Real estate" means real estate within the common sense meaning of that term. Residential real estate may be considered to be held for investment purposes if deductions with respect to such real estate are not disallowed by Section 280A of the Internal Revenue Code. Real estate is not considered to be held for investment purposes if it is used by the investor or a "related person" for personal purposes or as a place of business, or in connection with the conduct of the trade or business of the investor or a "related person," provided that if the investor is engaged primarily in the business of investing, trading or developing real estate, any real estate owned by the investor in connection with such business may be considered to be held for investment purposes. (For purposes of the term "real estate," a person is a "related person" of the investor if such person is a sibling, spouse or former spouse of the investor, a direct lineal descendant or ancestor of the investor by birth or adoption, or a spouse of any such descendant or ancestor.)

"Commodity interests" means commodity futures contracts, options on commodity futures contracts, and options on physical commodities traded on or subject to the rules of:

---

[9] A public company is one that files reports with the SEC pursuant to Section 13 or Section 15(d) of the Exchange Act, or that has a class of securities listed on a "designated offshore securities market" (as that term is defined in Regulation S under the Securities Act).

[10] Section 3(c)(1) through Section 3(c)(9) or Rules 3a-6 or 3a-7 of the 40 Act.

[11] Calculation must be determined in accordance with generally accepted accounting principles (GAAP) as reflected on the company's most recent financial statements, provided such financial statements present the information as of a date within 16 months preceding the date of the subscription agreement.

- Any contract market designated for trading such instruments under the Commodity Exchange Act and the rules and regulations thereunder; or
- Any board of trade or exchange outside the United States, as contemplated by Part 30 of the rules and regulations under the Commodity Exchange Act.

If the investor is engaged primarily in the business of investing, reinvesting, or trading in commodity interests, any commodity interest owned by the investor in connection with such business may be considered to be held for investment purposes.

"Physical commodities" means physical commodities (e.g., gold and silver) with respect to which commodity interests are traded on a contract market, board of trade, or exchange described earlier in for commodity interests. If the investor is engaged primarily in the business of investing, reinvesting or trading in physical commodities, any physical commodity owned by the investor in connection with such business may be considered to be held for investment purposes.

"Financial contracts" means financial contracts as defined in Section 3(c)(2)(B)(ii) of the 40 Act, such as swaps and similar individually-negotiated financial agreements. If the investor is engaged primarily in the business of investing, reinvesting or trading in financial contracts, any financial contract entered into by the investor in connection with such business may be considered to be held for investment purposes.

"Cash and cash equivalents" include foreign currencies, bank deposits, certificates of deposit, bankers acceptances, similar bank instruments, and the net cash surrender value of insurance policies. Neither cash used by an individual to meet everyday expenses nor working capital used by a business is considered to be held for investment purposes.

III. PRIVATE PLACEMENTS: RULE 506

A public offering of securities generally requires registration of the securities under Section 5 of the Securities Act, but an offering of securities that does not constitute a public offering is exempt from that registration requirement. Specifically, Section 4(2) of the Securities Act provides that the registration requirements of Section 5 do not apply to "transactions by an issuer not involving any public offering."

As noted above, one of the requirements under both Sections 3(c)(1) and 3(c)(7) is that the fund is not offering its securities in a public offering. But relying on Section 4(2) can be problematic because the Securities Act does not clearly establish what constitutes a "public offering." So, funds that rely on Section 3(c)(1) or 3(c)(7), as well as most other pooled investment vehicles, rely on the "private placement" approach provided for under Regulation D. Regulation D is a safe harbor adopted under Section 4(2) that provides more concrete guidelines for conducting a nonpublic offering (commonly referred to as a "private placement").

Under Regulation D, there are three general offering approaches that fall within the "safe harbor" provided by the regulation.

Rules 503 and 504 are not commonly used in the private fund world because they have limits on the aggregate amount of securities that may be offered under those rules.[12]

In contrast, Rule 506 has no limit on the amount of securities sold and instead focuses on the method of offering and the character of the investors. The basic requirements for a traditional Rule 506 offering are that:

- The securities are not offered or sold "by any form of general solicitation or general advertising;" and
- The securities are sold to no more than 35 "nonaccredited" investors (thus excluding "accredited investors."

A relatively recent amendment to Rule 506 allows the issuer to offer or sell its securities in a manner that constitutes general solicitation or advertising if certain additional investor suitability criteria are met (discussed later as one of the methods for offering distinctions).

Accredited Investor Requirement

The exception from the definition of an investment company under Section 3(c)(1) of the 40 Act does not include any requirements relating to investor suitability, so there would no prohibition under the 40 Act from having a 3(c)(1) fund that had 100 nonaccredited investors. But the vast majority of 3(c)(1) funds in the industry do not follow that framework. The rationale behind this practice is that a 3(c)(1) fund cannot offer its securities in a "public offering," and the simplest way to ensure that an offering is not a public offering is to rely on Regulation D, and most commonly on Rule 506 because most private funds would not be interested in limiting their capital raises to $1 million or $5 million.

So, for a Rule 506 offering, the securities of the issuer making a private placement can be sold to no more than 35 nonaccredited investors. For this reason, most 3(c)(1) funds sell their securities only to individuals and entities that the fund reasonably believes are accredited investors to stay under the 35 person limit.

Under Section 3(c)(1), an "accredited investor is

1. An individual whose net worth (excluding the value of the primary residence of such natural person), or joint net worth with spouse, exceeds $1,000,000 as of the date of this agreement;
2. An individual whose gross income exceeded $200,000 in each of the two most recent calendar years, or whose joint gross income with the individual's spouse exceeded $300,000 in each of the two most recent calendar years and, in either case, the individual has a reasonable expectation of his or her ingle or joint gross income reaching the same level in the current year;

---

[12] Rule 504 allows no more than $1,000,000 in sales; Rule 505 allows no more than $5,000,000 in sales.

3. A partnership, corporation, limited liability company (LLC) or business trust that either
   a. Is 100 percent owned by individuals who are accredited investors under (1) or (2) above, or
   b. Was not formed for the specific purpose of investing in a particular issuer and whose total assets exceed $5,000,000;
4. An employee benefit plan:
   a. Whose investment decision is made by a plan fiduciary (as defined in Section 3(21) of the Employee Retirement Income and Security Act of 1974, as amended) that is a bank, savings and loan association, insurance company or registered investment adviser,
   b. Whose total assets exceed $5,000,000 as of the date of the representation; or
   c. If a self-directed plan, whose investment decisions are made solely by persons who are accredited investors;
5. A U.S. bank, U.S. savings and loan association or other similar U.S. institution acting in its individual or fiduciary capacity;
6. A broker-dealer registered pursuant to Section 15 of the Securities Exchange Act of 1934, as amended;
7. An organization described in Section 501(c)(3) of the Internal Revenue Code of 1984, as amended, with total assets exceeding $5,000,000 and not formed for the specific purpose of investing in the relevant issuer;
8. Any trust with total assets exceeding $5,000,000, not formed for the specific purpose of investing in the relevant issuer, and whose purchase is directed by a person with such knowledge and experience in financial and business matters that he or she is capable of evaluating the merits and risks of the prospective investment;
9. A plan established and maintained by a state or its political subdivisions, or any agency or instrumentality thereof, for the benefit of its employees, and which has total assets in excess of $5,000,000; or
10. An insurance company as defined in Section 2(13) of the Securities Act of 1933, as amended, or a registered investment company.

"Net worth" means the excess of total assets at fair market value over total liabilities, excluding:

- The value of the individual's primary residence; and
- Any indebtedness that is secured by such primary residence, up to the estimated fair market value of such primary residence at the time of the representation.[13]

[13] Note that if the amount of the indebtedness outstanding at the time of the representation exceeds the amount outstanding 60 calendar days prior to the date of the representation, other than as a result of the acquisition of the investor's primary residence, the amount of such excess must be included as a liability, and indebtedness that is secured by the investor's primary residence in excess of the estimated fair market value of such residence on the date of the representation must also be included as a liability.

Method of Offering Distinctions

Historically, offerings that relied on Regulation D and Rule 506 had to be made without any general solicitation or advertising, which explicitly included any advertisement, article, notice, or other communication published in any newspaper, magazine, any media or broadcast over television or radio, and any seminar or meeting whose attendees had been invited by any general solicitation or general advertising. In practice, this meant that issuers relying on Rule 506 had to be very careful about any "public" exposure about the issuer. For instance, many successful private fund managers are considered experts in the investment industry, so the media outlets like to interview them for various purposes. In connection with those interviews, if the manager discusses the private fund that he or she manages, there is a significant risk that the SEC would consider that a "general solicitation or advertisement" that would invalidate the issuer's Rule 506 private offering.

For an offering that does successfully avoid "general solicitation and advertising," the accredited investor requirement to keep to the 35 investor limit may be met provided the issuer has a reasonable basis to believe that the investor is, in fact, an accredited investor. The industry standard for this reasonable basis is a written representation from the investor that the investor meets one of the accredited investor criteria discussed above. That written representation is usually included in the subscription materials that an investor is required to submit to an issuer during the purchase of an interest in the issuer. So, unless the issuer has reason to believe that the investor is not being truthful in that written representation, the issuer can accept that representation at face value and treat the investor as an accredited investor.

However, with the passage of the Jumpstart Our Business Startups Act of 2012 (the "JOBS Act"), there is an alternative to the prohibition on general solicitation and advertising. Under Rule 506(c), an issuer may offer its securities using general solicitation or advertising and still maintain its "private placement" character by limiting the investors to accredited investors only and by verifying the accredited investor status of those investors.

As noted above, for an offering that does not involve general solicitation or advertising, a written representation from the investor is sufficient for purposes of treating that investor as an accredited investor. But for a Rule 506(c) offering that does involve general solicitation or advertising, that representation from the investor is insufficient. The issuer must verify the accredited investor status of the investor to be able to accept the investor into the private fund. Verification can take many forms, and the SEC has been careful to avoid any specific requirements about what that verification must look like, and has made clear that the determination of whether any particular verification method is sufficient is a facts and circumstances determination. However, the SEC provided a number of examples in the adopting release for Rule 506(c) that it would generally accept in this regard:

- With respect to whether an investor is an accredited investor on the basis of income, reviewing any IRS form that reports the investor's income for the two most recent years (including, but not limited to, Form W-2, Form 1099, Schedule K-1 to Form 1065, and Form 1040) and obtaining a written representation from the investor that he or she has a reasonable expectation of reaching the income level necessary to qualify as an accredited investor during the current year;
- With respect to whether the investor is an accredited investor on the basis of net worth, reviewing one or more of the following types of documentation dated within the prior three months and obtaining a written representation from the investor that all liabilities necessary to make a determination of net worth have been disclosed:
  - With respect to assets, bank statements, brokerage statements and other statements of securities holdings, certificates of deposit, tax assessments, and appraisal reports issued by independent third parties; and
  - With respect to liabilities, a consumer report from at least one of the nationwide consumer reporting agencies;
- Obtaining a written confirmation from one of the following persons or entities that such person or entity has taken reasonable steps to verify that the investor is an accredited investor within the prior three months and has determined that such investor is an accredited investor:
  - A registered broker-dealer;
  - An investment adviser registered with the SEC;
  - A licensed attorney who is in good standing under the laws of the jurisdictions in which he or she is admitted to practice law; or
  - A certified public accountant who is duly registered and in good standing under the laws of the place of his or her residence or principal office.

Form D Requirements

An issuer that is relying on Rule 506 of Regulation D to conduct a private placement has a filing obligation on Form D with respect to that offering. The Form D must be filed with both the SEC and, potentially, with one or more state securities regulators depending the specific state requirements.

SEC. The SEC Form D filing is generally due within fifteen days of the first sale of an issuer's securities. In addition, the SEC Form D filing must be amended or updated under the following circumstances:

- To correct a material mistake of fact or error in the previously filed notice of sales on Form D, as soon as practicable after discovery of the mistake or error;
- To reflect a change in the information provided in the previously filed notice of sales on Form D, as soon as practicable after the change; and
- Annually, on or before the first anniversary of the filing of the notice of sales on Form D or the filing of the most recent amendment to the notice of sales on Form D, if the offering is continuing at that time.

Notwithstanding the second bullet above, no amendment is required for Form D to reflect a change that occurs after the offering terminates or a change that occurs solely in the following information:

- The address or relationship to the issuer of a related person identified in response to Item 3 of the notice of sales on Form D;
- An issuer's revenues or aggregate net asset value (NAV);
- The minimum investment amount, if the change is an increase, or if the change, together with all other changes in that amount since the previously filed notice of sales on Form D, does not result in a decrease of more than 10 percent;
- Any address or state(s) of solicitation shown in response to Item 12 of the notice of sales on Form D;
- The total offering amount, if the change is a decrease, or if the change, together with all other changes in that amount since the previously filed notice of sales on Form D, does not result in an increase of more than 10 percent;
- The amount of securities sold in the offering or the amount remaining to be sold;
- The number of nonaccredited investors who have invested in the offering, as long as the change does not increase the number of investors to more than 35;
- The total number of investors who have invested in the offering; or
- The amount of sales commissions, finders' fees, or use of proceeds for payments to executive officers, directors, or promoters, if the change is a decrease, or if the change, together with all other changes in that amount since the previously filed notice of sales on Form D, does not result in an increase of more than 10 percent.

State Filings. In addition to the federal Form D filing, an issuer that is relying on Rule 506 for a sale of its securities in a particular state may be required to file Form D with that state's securities regulator and to pay a filing fee.

Prior to the National Securities Markets Improvement Act of 1996 (NSMIA), an issuer that was relying on Rule 506 for private placements had to conduct state-by-state reviews of the applicable requirements for each state in which it sold its securities. In fact, many law firms that practiced in this area had one or more associates who spent all of their time assisting the firms' clients with this analysis and filing process. However, as part of NSMIA, the federal government provided for federal preemption for Rule 506; the only requirements any state could impose on a Rule 506 offering were filing a copy of the federal Form D (on the same filing schedule as the federal standard), payment of a filing fee, and consent to service of process from the relevant state. Many states have exemptions from their Form D filing requirements for limited offerings in their state (determined by either number of investors or investor suitability), but a full review of each state's Form D obligations is beyond the scope of this review.

One significant outlier in this regard is the State of New York. New York does not currently have any rules relating to the submission of Form D with respect to Rule 506 offerings in the state. Instead, New York has a requirement for the registration of the issuer of securities in a private placement rather that any registration or filings requirements for the securities themselves. Most industry participants (including the New York State Bar Association) believe that New York's requirements under state law are inconsistent with the provisions of NSMIA and are, therefore, invalid. However, many private fund managers, in an abundance of caution, make the filings and pay the fees called for under New York state law.

Bad Actor Certifications

One additional new provision of Rule 506 that came out of the JOBS Act was the addition of certain disqualifiers with respect to reliance on Rule 506 for issuers of securities. These "bad actor" disqualifiers prevent certain issuers from relying on Rule 506 for private placements. One significant factor with respect to the bad actor disqualifiers is that it is not just the issuer and its personnel that may trigger a disqualification under Rule 506. In addition to the issuer itself, a bad actor disqualification with respect to any of the following will prevent the issuer from relying on Rule 506:

- Predecessor of the issuer;
- Affiliated issuer;
- Director,
- Executive officer or other officer participating in the offering;
- General partner or managing member of the issuer;
- any beneficial owner of 20 percent or more of the issuer's outstanding voting equity securities, calculated on the basis of voting power;
- Any promoter connected with the issuer in any capacity at the time of such sale;
- Any investment manager of an issuer that is a pooled investment fund;
- Any person that has been or will be paid (directly or indirectly) remuneration for solicitation of purchasers in connection with such sale of securities;
- Any general partner or managing member of any such investment manager or solicitor; or
- Any director, executive officer, or other officer participating in the offering of any such investment manager or solicitor or general partner or managing member of such investment manager or solicitor.

Specifically, the exemption from registration of a privately placed security under Rule 506 is not available if the issuer or any of the persons described under Section 506(d).

IV. COMMODITY EXCHANGE ACT

Although the majority of the compliance obligations for investment managers of private funds originate from the federal securities acts, if a private fund includes commodity futures in its portfolio, it is considered to be a commodity pool and its operations are governed by the Commodity Exchange Act (CEA) and the rules adopted thereunder as well. This section summarizes some of the more common futures-related compliance obligations for private funds that trade futures contracts.

For funds that trade solely commodity futures (and certain funds that trade predominantly commodity futures with limited securities in their portfolios), the provisions of the 40 Act relating to the registration of investment companies may not apply because these private funds would not meet the definition of an "investment company" under the 40 Act.

CPO Requirement

A private fund that trades even a single commodity futures contract meets the definition of a commodity pool, and under the CEA rules the investment manager of a commodity pool must be registered as a commodity pool operator (CPO) unless it can meet an exemption from such registration.

The CEA requires every CPO to register as such with the U.S. Commodity Futures Trading Commission (CFTC) unless such CPO is:

- "Excluded" or "excepted" from the definition of "commodity pool operator;"
- Exempt from registration as a commodity pool operator; or
- Not subject to registration because such commodity pool operator
  - Is located outside the United States and its territories and possessions,
  - Does not operate any onshore commodity pool, and
  - Does not operate any offshore commodity pool that has or solicits investors (domestic or foreign) located in the United States or its territories or possessions.[14]

"Commodity pool operator" means any person engaged in a business that is of the nature of an investment trust, syndicate, or similar form of enterprise. This person, in connection therewith, solicits, accepts, or receives funds, securities, or property, from other persons, either directly or through capital contributions, the sale of stock or other forms of securities, or otherwise. The purpose of receiving the funds is trading in any commodity for future delivery or commodity option on or subject to the rules of any U.S. "contract market" or foreign futures exchange.[15] An investment trust, syndicate, or similar form of enterprise of this type is a "commodity pool."

Some private funds are clearly commodity pools because their portfolios are primarily invested in commodity futures contracts or other investments that are clearly subject to futures regulations. Other private funds may invest primarily in securities and use commodity futures only to a limited extent (e.g., to hedge market exposures). The CFTC, however, interprets the term *commodity pool* in the broadest possible sense and takes the position that if a private fund uses futures *to any extent* (i.e., even a single futures contract) and *for any purpose* (i.e., hedging or speculative), the private fund is considered a commodity pool, with the result that the operator of the fund must register as a CPO under the CEA—unless an "exclusion" or "exception" from the definition of CPO, or an exemption from registration, is available. Thus, a commodity pool encompasses not

---

[14] Sections 3(a)(1) of the 40 Act.

[15] Section 1a(11) of the Commodity Exchange Act, as amended.

only those private funds that are outside the scope of the 40 Act because they focus on trading in commodity futures, but also private funds that rely on Section 3(c)(1) or 3(c)(7) to avoid registration as investment companies and that use commodity futures to any extent and for any purpose.

Further, under the CFTC's interpretation, a fund-of-funds that does not directly use commodity futures is nevertheless a commodity pool if it invests in underlying funds that use commodity futures to any extent and for any purpose, with the result that the operator of a fund-of-funds must register as a CPO under the CEA—unless an "exclusion" or "exception" from the definition of "commodity pool operator," or an exemption from registration, is available. On the opposite side of this analysis, there is a no-action letter issued by the SEC to the Managed Funds Association that makes clear that a fund-of-funds that invests *only* in underlying funds that trade commodity futures (and are, therefore, not within the definition of an investment company) is not an investment company notwithstanding the fact that the fund-of-funds technically invests in the securities of the underlying funds.[16]

Regardless of a CPO's registration status, each person who comes within the definition of a CPO is subject to certain operational requirements (see CFTC Rule 4.20) and advertising requirements (see CFTC Rule 4.41), to all provisions of the CEA and the CFTC's rules prohibiting fraud by CPOs, and to all other provisions of the CEA and the CFTC's rules that apply to all commodity market participants, such as the prohibitions against manipulation and the trade reporting requirements.

Registration as a CPO

In order to register with the CFTC as a CPO, a firm must file with the National Futures Association (NFA):

- A completed online Form 7-R, together with certain financial statements (note, however, that CPOs, in their capacities as such, are not subject to any net capital requirement).
- A completed online Form 8-R, fingerprint card and a fee of $85 for each "principal" of the firm. A "principal" of the firm means any of the following:
  - Any person, including but not limited to a sole proprietor, general partner, managing member, officer, director, designated supervisor, or person occupying a similar status or performing similar functions, who has the direct or indirect power, through agreement or otherwise, to exercise a controlling influence over any activity of the CPO that is subject to CFTC regulation (except that directors who are not also officers or employees and who do not engage in certain specified activities may be excused from the fingerprinting requirement pursuant to CFTC Regulation §3.21(c)),

[16] Managed Futures Association, SEC No-Action Letter (July 11, 1996), https://www.sec.gov/divisions/investment/noaction/1996/mfa071196.pdf

- Any holder or beneficial owner of ten percent or more of the outstanding shares of any class of stock of the CPO, and
- Persons who have contributed 10 percent or more of the CPO's capital (with certain limited exceptions).

Special requirements apply to "principals" that are not natural persons. In that case, not only must the "principal" file a Form 8-R, but each of the following natural persons must file a Form 8-R and a fingerprint card:

- Each holder or beneficial owner of 10 percent or more of the outstanding shares of any class of stock of the "principal;" and
- Each person who has contributed 10 percent or more of the "principal's" capital (with certain limited exceptions).

This process is subject to being repeated where all the "principals" of a nonnatural person "principal" are themselves nonnatural persons (with certain exceptions).

The registration process typically takes approximately seven to eight weeks, unless each person who is required to file a Form 8-R and fingerprint card and each "associated person" (discussed below) of the CPO, already has a Form 8-R and fingerprint card on file with the NFA, in which case the process typically takes around 2-3 weeks.

It is unlawful for a CPO to operate a commodity pool (including the solicitation of investors for the pool) or to represent that it is registered as a commodity pool operator, unless and until its registration is effective.

Filing Deadline. A registered CPO must refile its Form 7-R annually within 30 days following the date designated to such CPO for such filing by the NFA.

"Associated Person" (AP) Registration Process. In addition to the registration of the CPO itself, each AP of a registered CPO must register as such with the CFTC. An AP is an individual who solicits orders, customers, or customer funds (or who supervises persons so engaged) on behalf of the CPO. In effect, an AP is anyone who is a salesperson or who supervises salespersons for a CPO. The registration requirements apply to any person in the supervisory chain-of-command and not only to persons who directly solicit or supervise the solicitation of customer funds.

Registration as an AP is generally required unless:

- The individual is already registered as a CPO in his or her own capacity; or
- The individual is already registered with the Financial Industry Regulatory Authority (FINRA) as a representative of a registered broker-dealer and will only act in the capacity of an associated person associated with a CPO.

In addition, in instances where a CPO's commodity interest activity accounts for no more than 10 percent of its annual revenue, the chief operating officer, general partner, or other principal in the supervisory chain-of-command may be eligible for exemption from associated person registration.

In order to register with the CFTC as an AP, an individual must file with the NFA:

- A completed online Form 8-R, fingerprint card, and a fee of $85;
- Evidence from FINRA that the individual has passed the National Commodity Futures Exam (Series 3) within the past two years (if, however, the private fund for which the AP solicits investors—or supervises such solicitation—uses commodity futures solely to hedge or manage the risk of the private fund's securities positions, it may be possible to obtain a waiver of the examination requirement); and
- Verification of the Form 8-R pursuant to CFTC Rule 3.12(c).

A fingerprint card and fee are not required for a particular AP if the AP is currently registered with the CFTC in another capacity or is listed as an AP or principal of another CFTC registrant.

It is unlawful for a person to engage in the type of activities that require his or her registration as an AP, or to represent that he or she is registered with the CFTC or is an AP of a particular CPO, before the time when his or her registration as an AP of such CPO is effective.

Exception from Definition as a CPO. CFTC Rule 4.5 excludes certain regulated persons (each, a "qualified regulated person") from the definition of a CPO in connection with their operation of specified types of investment vehicles (each, a "qualified regulated vehicle").

Specifically, subject to the requirements discussed later for Rule 4.5(c) requirements, the following exclusions from being defined as a commodity pool operator apply:

- Under Rule 4.5(b)(1), the principals and employees of any investment company registered under the Investment Company Act;
- Under Rule 4.5(b)(2), any insurance company subject to regulation by any state (together with its principals and employees), to the extent such insurance company manages the assets of one or more "separate accounts" established and maintained or offered by such insurance company pursuant to the laws of any state, under which income gains and losses, whether or not realized, from assets allocated to such separate accounts are, in accordance with the applicable contracts, credited to or charged against such accounts, without regard to other income, gains or losses of such insurance company;
- Under Rule 4.5(b)(3) any bank, trust company, or financial depository institution subject to regulation by the United States or any state (together with its principals and employees), to the extent such bank, trust company or other financial depository institution manages the assets of one or more trusts, custodial accounts, or other separate investment vehicles for which it is acting as a fiduciary and with respect to which it is vested with investment authority and

- Under Rule 4.5(b)(4) any trustee or named fiduciary of (or any person designated or acting as a fiduciary pursuant to a written delegation from or other written agreement with the named fiduciary), and any employer maintaining, a pension plan that is subject to Title I of the Employee Retirement Income Security Act of 1974 (ERISA).

Note, however, that none of the following pension plans is considered to be a commodity pool, with the result that persons having authority over such plans are not considered to be commodity pool operators with respect to such plans and therefore are not required to comply with the requirements described below with respect to such plans:

- A noncontributory plan covered under Title I of ERISA;
- contributory "defined benefit plan" covered under Title IV of ERISA (provided that, to the extent an employee has the voluntary right to contribute to the plan, no part of such voluntary contribution is committed as margin or premiums for futures positions);
- A plan defined as a "governmental plan" under Section 3(32) of Title I of ERISA;
- An "employee welfare benefit plan" that is subject to the fiduciary responsibility provisions of ERISA; or
- A plan defined as a "church plan" in Section 3(33) of Title I of ERISA with respect to which no election has been made under 26 U.S.C. 410(d).

Rule 4.5 Requirements

In order to take advantage of the Rule 4.5 exclusion, the qualified regulated person that operates a particular qualified regulated vehicle must:

- Disclose in writing to each existing and prospective participant in such vehicle that such vehicle is being operated by a person who has claimed an exclusion from the definition of the term "commodity pool operator" under the Commodity Exchange Act and, therefore, is not subject to registration or regulation as a commodity pool operator under that act;
- File a notice of eligibility with the CFTC and the NFA containing specified information and representations, prior to the time it commences management of such vehicle; and
- Respond to certain CFTC inquiries ("special calls") regarding compliance with the provisions of Rule 4.5.

If any of the information contained or any representation made in the notice of eligibility becomes inaccurate or incomplete, the entity or person that filed such notice must file a corrected notice within 15 days after the occurrence of the event which requires the correction. The exclusion provided by Rule 4.5 is effective only so long as all of the qualified regulated person complies with requirements of the rule.

At present, Rule 4.5 is the only CFTC rule that excepts or excludes persons from the *definition* of "commodity pool operator." However, there are additional CFTC rules that exempt certain persons from *registration* for that designation.

Exemptions from Registration as a CPO. Unlike the provisions of Rule 4.5, which excepts certain regulated entities from being considered CPOs, Rule 4.13 provides for exemptions from registration as a CPO.

Rules 4.13(a)(1) and (a)(2) provide exemptions from CPO registration for the operators of essentially "family, club, or small pools." Specifically, under these rules, a person is not required to register as a CPO in *either* of the following situations:

- Such person
  - Operates only one commodity pool at any given time,
  - does not receive any compensation or other payment, directly or indirectly, for operating such pool (except reimbursement for the ordinary administrative expenses of operating the pool),
  - Does not use any advertising in connection with such pool (which includes the systematic solicitation of prospective participants by telephone or seminar presentation), and
  - Is not otherwise required to register with the CFTC and is not a business affiliate of any person required to register with the CFTC; *or*
- The total gross capital contributions such person receives for units of participation in *all* of the pools that it operates or that it intends to operate do not exceed $400,000 in the aggregate, and none of such pools has more than 15 participants at any given time (not counting such person and certain related persons enumerated in Rule 4.13(a)(2)(iii)).

In order to rely on CFTC Rule 4.13(a)(1) or (a)(2), a CPO must comply with the various requirements described for the rule and must:

- Promptly furnish to each pool participant of each pool that it operates a copy of the monthly statement the CPO receives from the futures commission merchant for such pool; and
- Clearly show on such statement, or on an accompanying supplemental statement, the net profit or loss on all commodity interests closed since the date of the previous statement.

Rule 4.13(d) provides that if a CPO relies on the exemption from CPO registration provided by Rule 4.13(a)(1) or (a)(2) but subsequently registers as a CPO, the CPO must include with its registration application the financial statements and other information required by CFTC Rules 4.22(c)(1) through (5) for each pool that it has operated as an operator exempt from registration. Such information must be presented in accordance with generally accepted accounting principles (GAAP) consistently applied. If such CPO is granted registration, it must comply the CFTC's rules with respect to each such pool it operates.

CFTC Rule 4.13(a)(3) enables a CPO to avoid registration if, for *each* pool the CPO operates pursuant to Rule 4.13(a)(3), it complies with *all* of the following requirements:

- Such pool offers and sells its interests in an offering exempt from registration under the Securities Act;
- Such pool does not market its interests to the public in the United States (i.e., the pool must "privately place" its interests to the extent it markets them in the United States);
- Such pool does not market itself as a vehicle for trading futures;
- Such pool limits sales of its interests to persons who are (or whom the CPO reasonably believes to be), at the time of investment (or at the time of conversion of such pool to Rule 4.13(a)(3) status)
  - Accredited investors,
  - Trusts that are not accredited investors but that were formed by accredited investors for the benefit of family members,
  - Knowledgeable employee, or
  - Certain types of qualified eligible persons under CFTC Rule 4.7(a)(2)(viii)(A);
- Such pool meets one of the following tests with respect to its futures positions (including security futures), whether entered into for hedging or speculative purposes, at all times:
  - The aggregate initial margin and premiums required to establish such positions, determined at the time the most recent position was established, does not exceed 5 percent of the liquidation value of the pool's portfolio (after taking into account unrealized profits and unrealized losses on any such positions it has entered into), or
  - The aggregate net notional value of such positions, determined at the time the most recent position was established, does not exceed 100 percent of the liquidation value of the pool's portfolio (after taking into account unrealized profits and unrealized losses on any such positions it has entered into); and
- The operator of the pool complies with the additional requirements described later in the chapter.

The "notional value" is calculated for each futures position by multiplying the number of contracts by the size of the contract, in contract units (taking into account any multiplier specified in the contract), by the current market price per unit, and for each option position by multiplying the number of contracts by the size of the contract, adjusted by its delta, in contract units (taking into account any multiplier specified in the contract), by the strike price per unit.[17] The pool operator may net contracts with the same underlying commodity across designated contract markets, registered derivatives transaction execution facilities, and foreign boards of trade.

---

[17] For example, a single CBOT wheat futures contract is for 5,000 bushels of wheat, so the notional value of that contract is equal to the spot price of a bushel of wheat (at the time of such determination) multiplied by 5,000.

A pool operator that relies on Rule 4.13(a)(3) to avoid CPO registration may also operate pools in reliance on Rule 4.5 without subjecting itself to registration (provided, of course, that it complies with the conditions of that rule in relation to such pools).

The application of Rule 4.13(a)(3) to a fund-of-funds presents a challenging analysis, so the CFTC included, in Appendix A to its final rule release, several examples of how the rule applies to a fund-of-funds. Three examples are provided.

- The most pertinent provides that if the operator of a fund-of-funds allocates no more than 50 percent of the fund-of-fund's assets to "investee funds" that trade futures (without regard to the extent of such trading) and does not trade any futures directly on behalf of such fund-of-funds, the operator may rely on Rule 4.13(a)(3) in connection with operating such fund-of-funds;
- If the operator of a fund-of-funds allocates assets to one or more "investee funds," each of which has a CPO that is either claiming relief from registration under Rule 4.13(a)(3) or registered as a CPO but that represents in writing to the operator of the fund-of-funds that the "investee pool" operated by such registered CPO will be managed in accordance with the limitations of Rule 4.13(a)(3), the operator of the fund-of-funds may rely on Rule 4.13(a)(3) in connection with operating such fund-of-funds; and
- If a fund-of-funds both allocates assets to one or more investee funds and directly trades futures interests, the operator of that fund-of-funds must treat each pool of assets (investee funds, on the one hand, and direct-traded assets, on the other) as separate pools of assets that must each independently meet the requirements of Rule 4.13(a)(3).

The examples provided by the CFTC responded to specific comments letters submitted by the public, so they are not intended to provide an exhaustive overview of the application of the Rule 4.13(a)(3) to a fund-of-funds situation. Based on a reasonable reading of the proposed rule, the comment letters submitted to the CFTC and the final rule, the relief provided by Rule 4.13(a)(3) in the context of a fund-of-funds is potentially much broader than the relief illustrated in the examples. However, the only way to ensure that a specific set of circumstances allows for a claim of exemption is to request clarification directly from the CFTC staff. Appendix A was officially rescinded by the CFTC, but the CFTC has said managers can rely on it until additional guidance has been issued (that statement was made more than five years ago).

Additional Rule 4.13 Requirements

In addition to the items already described, for a CPO to claim the relief provided by CFTC Rule 4.13(a)(1), (a)(2), or (a)(3), the operator must comply with the following requirements in addition to those previously summarized.

Notice to Investors. A CPO that wishes to rely on CFTC Rule 4.13(a)(1), (a)(2), or (a)(3) with respect to a particular pool in order to avoid registration as a CPO must furnish to each prospective pool participant a written statement that:

- Discloses that the operator is exempt from registration with the CFTC as a CPO and, therefore, unlike a registered CPO, is not required to deliver a disclosure document or a certified annual report to participants in such pool; and
- Describes the basis on which the operator qualifies for exemption from registration.

The operator is required to provide this written statement to a prospective pool participant no later than the time it delivers a subscription agreement for the pool to such prospective participant. The recommendation here is to include the written statement as part of the offering memorandum for the pool (usually on the cover) or, if the pool will not have an offering memorandum, as part of the subscription agreement itself (generally on the execution page of the agreement).

Notice of Exemption. A CPO that wishes to rely on CFTC Rule 4.13(a)(1), (a)(2), (a)(3),or (a)(4) with respect to a particular pool in order to avoid CPO registration must file a notice of exemption with the NFA. The notice of exemption must include:

- The name, main business address, main business telephone number, main facsimile number, and main email address of the CPO and the name of the pool for which it is claiming the exemption;
- The specific rule pursuant to which the CPO is claiming the exemption (i.e., Rule 4.13(a)(1), (a)(2), (a)(3), or (a)(4));
- A representation that the CPO will operate the pool in accordance with the provisions of the applicable rule; and
- The manual signature of a representative duly authorized to bind the operator.

The notice of exemption with respect to a particular pool must be filed with the NFA prior to the delivery of a subscription agreement for such pool to a prospective investor. If a CPO currently registered as such with the CFTC wishes to withdraw its registration and take advantage of the registration relief provided by Rule 4.13, the CPO must first:

- Notify all of the current investors in the pool(s) that it operates that it intends to withdraw its CPO registration and claim this relief; and
- Provide the investors with an opportunity to withdraw from such pool(s) prior to implementing such change.

A notice of exemption is effective immediately upon filing with the NFA provided that it is materially complete. Each operator that files a notice of exemption must, within 15 days of the operator becoming aware of any facts or circumstances that make such notice inaccurate or incomplete, file a supplemental notice with the NFA to that effect that includes such amendments as may be necessary to render the notice accurate and complete.

A notice of exemption is not "blanket" in nature (i.e., it does not cover all funds that a CPO operates pursuant to Rule 4.13). Instead, an operator that wishes to avoid registration as a CPO in reliance on Rule 4.13 must file a notice of exemption for *each* pool that it operates pursuant to the rule.

Books and Records. The books and records obligations for the manager of a pool that relies on Rule 4.13 are essentially the same as the requirements under SEC rules. All such books and records must be available for inspection upon the request of any representative of the CFTC or other U.S. regulatory agency with jurisdiction. The manager must also submit to any requests from the CFTC to demonstrate its eligibility to rely on, and its compliance with, the exemption under Rule 4.13.

Audited Financial Statements. If a pool for which the operator has filed a notice of exemption under Rule 4.13 distributes an annual report to its participants, that annual report must be presented and computed in accordance with GAAP consistently applied and, if certified by an independent public accountant, must be certified in accordance with the provisions of CFTC Rule 1.16.

Interplay Between Exempt and Nonexempt Pools. A CPO may operate pools under Rule 4.13(a)(3) even though the CPO is registered with the CFTC as such. Although the principal purpose behind Rule 4.13(a)(3) is to provide an exemption from CPO registration, these rules also greatly reduce the regulation that would otherwise apply to a CPO in connection with operating pools. Thus, a CPO that is registered as such because, for example, it operates public commodity pools, may nevertheless operate other pools pursuant to Rule 4.13(a)(3) in order to reduce the regulation that would otherwise apply to it in connection with operating such pools. In this case, however, the CPO must:

- Furnish to each prospective participant in any pool that such CPO operates pursuant to Rule 4.13(a)(3) or (a)(4) a written statement that such CPO will operate such pool as if such CPO were exempt from registration as a CPO, containing a description of the basis on which such CPO will operate such pool; and
- Otherwise comply with the requirements of Rule 4.13(a)(3) or (a)(4), as the case may be.

Exemptions from Part 4 Requirements. Commodity pools that offer their securities to accredited investors must generally comply with various disclosure and reporting rules under applicable CFTC rules (the Part 4 Rules) and must file the disclosure document with the NFA for review and comment. However, a registered CPO that operates its private fund in accordance with CFTC Rule 4.7 avoids all of the disclosure requirements of CFTC Rules 4.21, 4.24, 4.25, and 4.26 with respect to such fund and is subject to reduced reporting obligations under CFTC Rule 4.22, as well as reduced recordkeeping requirements under CFTC Rule 4.23, with respect to such private fund. The CPO otherwise remains subject to all applicable requirements of Part 4 of the CFTC's regulations with respect to such private fund, including general antifraud rules.

The primary limitation for a private fund operating under Rule 4.7 is that the private fund may admit only investors that meet the requirements to be "qualified eligible persons." Additional obligations include the items detailed next.

Disclosure Requirements

The offering document for a 4.7-exempt private fund must "prominently disclose," on the cover page, the following statement:

> Pursuant to an exemption from the commodity futures trading commission in connection with pools whose participants are limited to qualified eligible persons, an offering memorandum for this pool is not required to be, and has not been, filed with the commission. The commodity futures trading commission does not pass upon the merits of participating in a pool or upon the adequacy or accuracy of an offering memorandum. Consequently, the commodity futures trading commission has not reviewed or approved this offering or any offering memorandum for this pool.

The statement will be deemed to be "prominently disclosed" if it is displayed in capital letters and in boldface type (at least 10 point in size).

The cover page of the private fund's annual audited financial statements must contain a legend to the effect that the CPO has filed a "notice of claim for exemption" for the fund under CFTC Rule 4.7.

One item to note regarding past performance, CFTC Rule 4.7 also provides that a CPO may claim relief from disclosing the past performance of such CPO's Rule 4.7 pools in the disclosure documents for such CPO's nonexempt pools, except to the extent that such past performance is material to a particular nonexempt pool. However, a CPO that claims this relief and that determines not to include the past performance of its Rule 4.7 pools in the disclosure documents for its nonexempt pools must state, in a footnote to the past performance information contained in the disclosure document for any such nonexempt pool, that such CPO is operating or has operated pools whose performance is not disclosed in such disclosure document.

Offering Restrictions

The private fund must generally offer and sell its securities exclusively by way of:

- The "private placement" exemption provided by Section 4(2) of the Securities Act (and/or Rule 506 of Regulation D thereunder); and/or
- Regulation S under the Securities Act (for offerings outside of the United States).

Filing Requirements

The CPO for the private fund must file a "notice of claim for exemption" for the fund with the CFTC and the NFA through the NFA's website. This notice must be filed *prior* to any offer or sale of the fund's securities, if the CPO wishes to avoid the full-blown disclosure requirements to which it otherwise would be subject. (Under Rule 4.7(d)(ix)(A)(2), special provisions apply when the CPO of an already existing fund wishes to convert the fund to Rule 4.7 status.)

Reporting Requirements

Quarterly Reports. The CPO must distribute to participants in the pool, no less frequently than quarterly within 30 days after the end of each reporting period, a statement setting forth:

- The net asset value of the pool as of the end of the reporting period;
- The change in net asset value from the end of the previous reporting period; and
- The net asset value per outstanding unit of participation in the pool as of the end of the reporting period.

"Net asset value" means total assets minus total liabilities, determined in accordance with GAAP, with each position in a commodity interest accounted for at fair market value.

Annual Reports. The CPO must distribute to participants in the pool, within 90 days after the end of each fiscal year, an audited annual report for such fiscal year (elected in accordance with CFTC Rule 4.22(g)) setting forth:

- A statement of financial condition (balance sheet) as of the end of such fiscal year;
- A statement of income (cost) for such fiscal year; and
- Appropriate footnote disclosure and any other material information.

The financial statements in the annual report must be presented and computed in accordance with GAAP consistently applied and must be certified in accordance with CFTC Rule 1.16.

The CPO must file the annual reports with the CFTC and the NFA as well as distributing them to pool participants. Extensions of the filing deadline may be obtained in the limited circumstances described in CFTC Rule 4.22(f).

Oath or Affirmation Required. Each quarterly and annual report must contain a signed oath or affirmation that, to the best of the knowledge and belief of the individual making the oath or affirmation, the information contained in the report is accurate and complete. It is unlawful for such individual to make such oath or affirmation if he or she knows or should know that any of the information in the report is not accurate and complete.

The following information must appear immediately following the signed oath or affirmation:

- The name of the individual making the oath or affirmation and the capacity in which such individual is signing;
- The name of the CPO on whose behalf such individual is making such oath or affirmation; and
- The name of the pool to which the report relates.

Books and Records. The CPO of a 4.7-exempt private fund must maintain books and records relating to the fund with the same obligations as discussed above for 4.13 exempt funds.

Annual Affirmation of Eligibility. Each of the CPO-related exemptions requires an annual reaffirmation of the CPO's eligibility of the exemption—whether as an exemption from registration or an exemption from the pool disclosure obligations under Part 4.

V. PRIVATE FUND ADVISER EXEMPTION

For private funds that invest in and trade securities in more than a *de minimis* amount, the investment manager of that private fund will generally meet the definition of an investment adviser under both federal and state law. There are a number of potential exemptions from registration as an investment adviser at both the state and federal levels, but this section will address the state exemptions only on a cursory level.

Prior to the JOBS Act, most private fund managers were able to avoid registration as an investment adviser if they so desired. At the federal level, there was an exemption from registration for investment advisers that:

- Had fewer than 15 clients in any 12 month period (and a private fund is generally considered to be a single client for this purpose); and
- Did not hold itself out to the public as an investment adviser (and most private funds were offered on a "private placement" basis, so it was relatively easy to meet this requirement as well).

Many states also had exemptions based on either the number of clients or the character of those clients.

With the adoption of the JOBS Act, the allocation of responsibility for oversight of investment advisers between the states and the SEC was adjusted with, as a general rule, investment advisers with less than $100 million in assets under management (AUM) being subject to the states as their primary regulator and advisers with $100 million or more in AUM being subject to the SEC as their primary regulator. In addition, the federal "fewer than 15" exemption was revoked and was replaced by the "private fund adviser exemption."

Investment advisers in the $25 million to $100 million range are primarily subject to state regulation, but if the state in which the adviser maintains its primary place of business does not require the investment adviser to register, a potential federal registration obligation must be addressed.

SEC Exemption Requirements

The federal exemption under Rule 203(m)-1 provides for an exemption from full registration but does require an annual notice filing—an exempt reporting adviser

(ERA) filing that is essentially, an abbreviated Form ADV. An investment adviser whose principal place of business is *within* the United States is not required to register with the SEC (subject to the ERA filing), if the investment adviser :

- Provides investment advisory services solely to one or more qualifying private funds; and
- The regulatory AUM for such private funds is less than $150 million.

An investment adviser whose principal place of business is *outside* the United States is not required to register with the SEC (subject to the ERA filing), if the investment adviser:

- Has no client that is a United States person except for one or more qualifying private funds; and
- All assets managed by the investment adviser at a place of business in the United States are solely attributable to private fund assets, the total value of which is less than $150 million.

State-Level Exemptions

As described earlier, many states had and still offer exemptions from registration as an investment adviser based on the number and/or character of the investment adviser's clients. For instance, some states have de minimis exemptions for investment advisers with fewer than 6 or fewer than 15 clients in any 12 month period. In addition, some states do not count clients that are either "accredited investors" or "qualified clients" in that client count. So, for investment advisers to private funds holding less than $25 million in AUM, it is not uncommon to be able to avoid both registration and notice filing. However, once an investment adviser to private funds hits $25 million in AUM, it will generally either have to register with the state in which it maintains its principal place of business (and potentially other states as well), or make an ERA filing with either the local state (if it requires such filing to claim an exemption) or with the SEC.

VI. FIDUCIARY STATUS OF PRIVATE FUND MANAGERS

Managers of private funds are generally considered fiduciaries to the funds they manage, as well as for certain purposes, to the investors in those funds. The basic fiduciary duty to the private fund itself is established both under the Advisers Act as well as under state law governing the structures that are commonly used for private funds, i.e., limited partnerships (LPs) and LLCs.

SEC Rule-Based Status

Although there is a common law basis for an investment adviser's fiduciary duty to its clients (generally emanating from principal/agent concepts and trust law), that duty may vary from state to state. At the federal level, Section 206 of the Advisers Act is a general antifraud provision (it prohibits any practice that is fraudulent, deceptive or manipulative) that the courts have generally interpreted to create a fiduciary duty to an investment adviser's clients.[18] However, it has become clear through both industry practice and a failed attempt by the SEC to change the definition of "client" that the client to whom an investment adviser owes this fiduciary duty in the context of an investment adviser to a private fund is the private fund itself, rather than the investors in the private fund. This is a rather technical distinction, but one should consider the following situation: a private fund manager manages a single private fund with $20 million in AUM of which a single investor represents 50 percent of the assets. The fund's governing documents include a gate that allows the investment adviser to defer withdrawals that exceed 20 percent of the fund's aggregate AUM. The large investor decides to withdraw all of the capital account. In deciding whether to invoke the contractual gating provision, the investment adviser has to address the conflict between the individual investor and the fund as a whole. If the investment adviser owed a true fiduciary duty to both the individual investors and the fund itself, it would find itself in an impossible position because either decision on the gate could have material adverse effects on one or the other.

Notwithstanding that the investment adviser's primary duty runs to its client (i.e., the private fund), after losing its bid to change the definition of "client," the SEC adopted Rule 206(4)-8, which provides that it shall constitute a fraudulent, deceptive or manipulative act, practice, or course of business within the meaning of the Advisers Act for any investment adviser (whether registered or not) to a pooled investment vehicle to:

- Make any untrue statement of a material fact or to omit to state a material fact necessary to make the statements made, in the light of the circumstances under which they were made, not misleading, to any investor or prospective investor in the pooled investment vehicle; or
- Otherwise engage in any act, practice, or course of business that is fraudulent, deceptive, or manipulative with respect to any investor or prospective investor in the pooled investment vehicle.

Rule 20-6(4)-8 established a heightened duty to investors in private funds without establishing a full-blown fiduciary duty directly to such investors. In other words, an investment adviser must treat investors in a private fund that it manages fairly, but it does not create a duty to put the interests of any particular investor over the interests of any other investor or the private fund as a whole.

State Law-Based Status

In addition to the fiduciary status as an investment adviser, a general partner of a limited partnership or the managing member of an LLC l generally has a fiduciary duty to both the entity it manages and the owners of that entity's securities. However; when the duty to the entity conflicts with a duty to an owner of the entity, the duty to the entity generally trumps the duty to the owner. State law may allow variations to

[18] *SEC v. Capital Gains Research Bureau*, 375 U.S. 180 (1963).

that duty by contract—either a complete waiver or as a reduction in obligations—but such ability depends on state law. Delaware law (most private funds are organized under Delaware law) generally allows the governing agreement of a private fund to establish whatever level of duty a general partner or managing member of a private fund, provided that the agreement cannot remove the implied contractual covenant of good faith and fair dealing.

Custody Rule

The Custody Rule (Rule 206(4)-2) applies whenever a registered investment adviser has, or is deemed to have, custody of a client's assets. In the context of most onshore private funds, the entity that acts as the general partner of an LP or the managing member of an LLC would be deemed to have custody of the entity's assets under the terms of the Custody Rule. Thus, if the general partner or managing member is a registered investment adviser (or is an affiliate of a registered investment adviser), the investment adviser will be required to comply with the Custody Rule with respect to the private fund's assets.

The most common approach for a manager of a private fund to comply with the Custody Rule is to have the private fund audited on an annual basis by an independent public accountant that is registered with, and subject to regular inspection by, the Public Company Accounting Oversight Board (PCAOB) in accordance with its rules, with the resulting report delivered to investors within 120 calendar days of the end of the private fund's fiscal year (or within 180 calendar days for a fund-of-funds).

If a private fund cannot comply with the annual audit approach, the requirements for compliance with the Custody Rule are the same as for a traditional separately managed account:

- Assets are held by a qualified custodian;
- At least quarterly statements are sent to investors (or their independent representatives) by the qualified custodian; and
- Annually, there is independent verification of the private fund's assets.

VII. DISCLOSURE ISSUES

The federal securities laws are, to a large extent, a mandatory disclosure regime—especially the Advisers Act. For purposes of marketing and selling interests in private funds, the primary securities laws that are generally implicated are the Securities Act and the Advisers Act.

Although both of these acts do have certain prohibited activities, to a large extent a private fund can be operated in whatever manner the manager of the fund wishes provided that full and fair disclosure of such activities and the conflicts of interest they entail is provided to prospective investors prior to an investment (and ongoing disclosure is provided to investors as necessary).

The most common approach to providing this disclosure is by a confidential private placement memorandum (also called an offering memorandum or a disclosure document). In point of fact, for a private offering made only to accredited investors, the Securities Act does not actually require delivery of an offering memorandum. However, as a practice point, experts would never recommend marketing a private fund without an offering memorandum – that document is the manager's first line of defense in a lawsuit alleging fraudulent marketing. It is difficult for a disgruntled investor to argue that he or she was unaware of a particular practice of a private fund if that practice is fully described in the relevant offering memorandum and the investor signed a subscription agreement representing that he or she received and understood the offering memorandum.

Offering Document Issues

Many of the recent SEC enforcement cases and settlements have centered around the sufficiency of the disclosure provided to prospective investors in the offering memorandum. This risk is heightened for private equity style funds in which an investor could be in the fund for upward of 10 years without an opportunity to withdraw. As the industry matures, certain modes of operation may evolve, thus creating potential gaps between the practice that was described in the offering memorandum and the actual practice 10 years later.

Liquidity Disclosures. Liquidity of an investor's capital account is a primary disclosure item that should be included in the offering memorandum. Unlike in a separately managed account, in which the owner of the account can, at any time, fire the investment adviser and take control of the account to liquidate holdings, in a private fund an investor's access to his or her capital is limited. An investor needs to know how frequently capital can be withdrawn, how far in advance the fund must be notified of a desired withdrawal, and how quickly money will be distributed after the effective date of the withdrawal. Even more importantly, investors need to be made aware of any limitations on the ability to withdraw capital: suspensions of withdrawals, gating provisions, side pockets, etc.

The SEC has also been very clear that it does not like preferential liquidity in pooled investment vehicles (e.g., when one investor has a right by side letter to withdraw more frequently or on shorter notice) due to the potential for the investor with preferential liquidity to withdraw prior to the full realization of a market move, thereby leaving the other investors bearing a larger portion of those losses. Although the SEC generally does not have the authority to determine that a particular preferential liquidity arrangement is not acceptable, it does have the authority to determine that the disclosure provided to other investors about that preferential liquidity was insufficient.

Valuation Policies. Valuation is an issue for traditional investment management because fees are generally based on the value placed on the assets in a client's account. But in a private fund context, valuation takes on an even more significant role in determining relative ownership of the private fund's investment account when cash is contributed or withdrawn. If assets are overvalued, a new investor gets a smaller portion of the account than he or she should receive and a withdrawing investor gets overpaid.

The SEC has brought several recent actions addressing valuation policies of pooled investment vehicles, both in the private fund sector as well as the registered investment company sector. The SEC's approach to these actions has not been to take the position that the firm determined an inaccurate value for a particular position in the portfolio. Rather, the argument has been that the firm did not have reasonable valuations procedures and internal controls for determining those positions and did not accurately disclose to investors how positions would be valued. This approach is a common theme for the SEC when it comes to regulatory assessments. Rarely does the SEC take the position that a registered investment adviser got an incorrect result for a particular procedure. Instead, the SEC takes the position that the process or internal controls the investment adviser has established are not reasonable or sufficient for the situation.

Best practice for valuation is to establish a valuation committee composed of personnel from the various functional areas within a firm: operations, trading, portfolio management, compliance, etc. For each determination of value, any member of the committee whose compensation is affected by the value determination should be recused from that vote (at a minimum, and conservatively, from the discussion). In addition, although a representative from compliance should be present in every committee meeting for the firm, if the individual in question has no actual expertise that contributes to the valuation determination, that person could be made an ex officio member.

Expense Allocations. Expense allocations are another recent area of activity for the SEC, especially in the private equity fund sector. Expense allocations are generally not a primary concern in the traditional separately managed account sector, if for no other reason than expenses charged to a separately managed account will appear on the brokerage statement for the account, giving the client timely notice of expenses that have been borne by the account. For a private fund, those expenses are not as obvious and are generally reported only in the fund's annual audit.

The reason expense allocations have been such a significant issue in the private equity sector was mentioned earlier: the disclosure documents for a private equity fund are drafted at the beginning of the fund's lifecycle and cannot be easily adjusted as the fund matures. Thus, if there are expenses that were not fully considered or expected at the launch, it may be difficult for the manager of a private equity fund to justify charging certain expenses to the fund. For open-ended private funds, it more a matter of adjusting the offering memorandum to reflect the adjusted expense treatment and getting consent from the investors (usually by giving prior notice of the change enough in advance to allow investors to withdraw before the change becomes effective).

Conflicts of Interests. Conflicts of interest are a perennial issue for the SEC; as noted earlier, full and fair disclosure of a conflict of interest generally cures claims of breach of fiduciary duty or other violations under the Advisers Act (with a few exceptions). So, fully disclosing all of the conflicts an investment adviser has in managing and trading for a private fund is of primary importance.

The hardest part about disclosing conflicts of interest is not in drafting the language to provide disclosure but rather in identifying them. The simplest of mantras can usually help in finding the vast majority of conflicts: "follow the money." However, the money trail does not always identify all of the material conflicts, especially in the context of a private fund. In addition to following the money, the manager of a private fund needs to pay attention to its various counterparty relationships and determine whether anything in that relationship creates a conflict.

For instance, in a recent SEC settlement, the manager of a private fund was sanctioned by the SEC for accepting reduced legal fees for legal work done for the management entity by the firm that also did work for the manager relating to the private fund it managed without giving the private fund the benefit of any reduction in legal fees.[19] So, a reduction in expenses can create just as much a conflict of interest as an increase in income.

VIII. MARKETING AND ADVERTISING

Marketing a private fund is qualitatively different than marketing a general investment adviser's fund. This difference is perhaps best illustrated between marketing a security and marketing a service. Marketing of a security must be done in compliance with the 33 Act and the 34 Act as well as the Advisers Act, whereas marketing of an investment adviser's services is generally subject only to the requirements of the Advisers Act.

General Prohibitions

Under the 33 Act, there is a general prohibition against offering unregistered securities unless the security or offering is exempt under Sections 3 and 4. The securities of a private fund are not exempt under Section 3, so unless the manager of a private fund wants to go through the process of registering the securities of the fund, it has to rely on the exempt offering transaction under Section 4.

Section 4(a)(2) of the 33 Act exempts from the registration requirements any offering that does not involve a public offering (the "private placement" exemption). Unfortunately, Section 4(a)(2) is somewhat lacking on detail as to what makes an offering "public," so the SEC adopted Regulation D as a safe harbor. Rules 501 and 502 lay out the basic constructs for private placements under Regulation D, and Rules 504, 505, and 506 establish three different levels of Regulation D private placements. As articulated earlier, 504 has a $1 million limit, 505 has a $5 million limit, and 506 is for unlimited offerings. Because very few private funds want to limit the capital they raise, most private funds conduct Rule 506 offerings.

---

[19] *In the matter of First Reserve Management, L.P.*, Investment Adviser Rel. No. 4529 (Sept. 14, 2016).

Rule 506 Limitations

As touched on previously, there is no limit to the amount of capital that can be raised in a Rule 506 offering, but there are certain limitations on how that capital can be raised and who can purchase those securities. There are two primary limitations for 506 offerings:

- The securities may not be offered by any form of general solicitation or general advertising; and
- The securities may be sold to accredited investors and 35 nonaccredited investors. In addition, to the extent a nonaccredited investor is solicited for a Rule 506 offering, that investor must receive certain mandated disclosures that are described in Rule 502.[20]

This 506 limitation to no more than 35 nonaccredited investors with the mandatory disclosure is the basis for why most private funds that rely on Section 3(c)(1) of the 40 Act require their investors to be accredited.

Use of Placement Agents

In today's environment, one of the most challenging aspects of managing a private fund is raising capital for the fund, which is why many private fund managers retain placements agents to assist in that process. A placement agent is comparable to a "solicitor" in the context of a traditional investment management business.

Some firms that provide placement agent services to private funds try to characterize themselves as "finders" rather than as placement agents to avoid the SEC's stance that acting as a placement agent requires broker-dealer affiliation. In a no-action letter issued to Paul Anka in 1991,[21] the SEC agreed that the activities contemplated by that letter would not require Mr. Anka to register as a broker-dealer or be affiliated with a broker-dealer. However, the SEC staff has noted since then informally that the same letter today would likely receive a different answer.

Regardless of the status of a placement agent as a finder or as a broker, there is an issue with disclosure of the conflict of interest that such a referral creates where the referrer is receiving compensation for making that referral. The SEC has conceded that the Cash Solicitation Fee Rule (Rule 206(4)-3) does not directly apply to this situation because a placement agent is not referring a client, but is instead soliciting the sale of a security. But in the same publication in which the SEC acknowledged that the rule does not directly apply, the staff did make clear that it did think full disclosure of the conflict to the prospective investor is appropriate and necessary.

---

[20] Note that there is no mandatory disclosure for sales to accredited investors, so a private fund that offers its securities only to accredited investors could make that offer without providing an offering memorandum. However, that approach would be dangerous given that without some level of written disclosure, it is difficult to prove what information was provided to a prospective investor that leaves the private fund vulnerable to lawsuits from disgruntled investors.

[21] Paul Anka, SEC No-Action Letter (July 24, 1991).

Given this basic disclosure requirement, many private fund managers opt to provide the same model disclosure for private fund solicitations as for managed account solicitations to keep their procedures as simple as possible (rather than establishing two different model disclosures, they use the cash solicitation fee language for private fund solicitations as well).

IX. PERFORMANCE COMPENSATION ISSUES

The stereotypical fee structure for a private fund is 2/20: a 2 percent annual asset-based management (typically charged monthly or quarterly) and a 20 percent incentive allocation on net new profits (typically charged quarterly or annually). For a private fund that is managed by a registered investment adviser, that 20 percent incentive allocation creates a potentially higher investor suitability standard (depending on which 40 Act exemption the manager's private fund uses).

In order for a federally registered investment adviser to charge a "performance fee" (a percentage of the investment gains realized by account the adviser manages), the client must be a "qualified client," which generally means:

- A natural person who, or a company that, immediately after entering into the contract has at least $1 million under the management of the investment adviser;
- A natural person who, or a company that, the investment adviser entering into the contract (and any person acting on his behalf) reasonably believes, immediately prior to entering into the contract, either:
  - Has a net worth (together, in the case of a natural person, with assets held jointly with a spouse) of more than $2.1 million (excluding any positive value of the person's primary residence), or
  - Is a qualified purchaser as defined in section 2(a)(51)(A) of the Investment Company Act of 1940 at the time the contract is entered into.

In the case of a company that is:

- A private fund that relies on Section 3(c)(1) of the 40 Act to avoid registration as an investment company;
- An investment company registered under the 40 Act; or
- A business development company, as defined in Section 202(a)(22) of the Advisers Act, each equity owner of any such company (except for the investment adviser entering into the contract and any other equity owners not charged a fee on the basis of a share of capital gains or capital appreciation) must meet the definition of a qualified client.

For a private fund that relies on Section 3(c)(7) of the 40 Act, each of its investors must be a qualified purchaser and, therefore, meets the definition of an qualified client.

X. ERISA/BENEFIT PLAN ASSET ISSUES

One of the largest pools of assets available to investment advisers as potential clients in the United States is retirement plan assets. But managing retirement plan assets exposes the investment adviser to an additional layer of regulatory rulemaking. Assets held in traditional multiemployee corporate pension plans are subject to the Employee Retirement Income Security Act of 1974, as amended (ERISA). In addition, assets held in other types of retirement plans that are themselves not subject to ERISA are subject to similar rules under the Internal Revenue Code of 1986, as amended (tax code).

25 Percent Threshold Test

As noted above, investors in a private fund are not, for most purposes, considered to be clients of the investment adviser of the fund. So merely having an investor in a private fund that is a "benefit plan investor" (basically, an investor subject to ERISA or the analogous provisions of the tax code) does not mean that the investment adviser to the fund is managing assets of a benefit plan investor and subject to those rules. But both ERISA and the tax code include statutory language that establishes that if the benefit plan investor's ownership (in the aggregate) of a pooled investment vehicle (like a private fund) is "substantial," then the rules that apply to directly managing a benefit plan investor's assets apply to managing the assets of that pooled investment vehicle.

The threshold for "substantial" ownership is 25 percent or more of the equity of any class of security issued by the pooled investment vehicle. However, in calculating that percentage, any nonbenefit plan investor assets that are owned or controlled by the investment adviser or its affiliates must be excluded. If benefit plan investor ownership hits the 25 percent threshold, then the assets of the private fund are deemed to be "plan assets," and the regulatory requirements must be addressed.

A common misconception in determining the 25 percent threshold is that if a private fund hits the 25 percent threshold due solely to non-ERISA assets (e.g., IRAs), then there are no regulatory ramifications. This is only partially correct. In this circumstance (where the private hits the 25 percent threshold but has no true ERISA assets), the purely ERISA requirements are not triggered (so, for instance, the investment adviser is not obligated to purchase an ERISA fidelity bond). But the provisions under Section 4975 of the tax code would still apply to managing the private fund's assets.

Managing "Plan Assets"

The most onerous operational limitations that arise from managing private funds deemed to be plan assets are the "prohibited transaction" rules. There are two types of prohibited transactions: self-dealing and party-in-interest.

Self-dealing prohibited transactions are fairly straightforward and are relatively easy to police. A self-dealing transaction is any transaction in which the investment adviser uses its position of authority to provide a benefit to itself. The most obvious self-dealing transaction would be in the case of an investment adviser of a fund-of-funds that receives a rebate of management fees or incentive compensation from the manager of one of the underlying funds in its portfolio (as opposed to having that rebate flow to the fund-of-funds itself). An analogous situation for a direct trading fund would be the use of soft dollar benefits to offset expenses that would otherwise be expenses of the investment adviser.

There is, however, a useful safe harbor for certain uses of soft dollar benefits under Section 28(e) of the Exchange Act. The 28(e) safe harbor provides that no investment adviser:

> Shall be deemed to have acted unlawfully or to have breached a fiduciary duty under state or federal law...solely by reason of his having caused the account to pay a member of an exchange, broker, or dealer an amount of commission for effecting a securities transaction in excess of the amount of commission another member of an exchange, broker, or dealer would have charged for effecting that transaction, if such person determined in good faith that such amount of commission was reasonable in relation to the value of the brokerage and research services provided by such member, broker, or dealer, viewed in terms of either that particular transaction or his overall responsibilities with respect to the accounts as to which he exercises investment discretion.

Party-in-interest prohibited transactions are more involved and can be much more difficult to police. A party-in-interest transaction is any transaction in which the counterparty to the investment adviser is a party-in-interest to a benefit plan investor and comprises any portion of the plan assets that the investment adviser manages. The difficulty in policing party-in-interest transactions is identifying all of the parties-in-interest to the benefit plan investors in a private fund and then ensuring that none of those parties-in-interest are selected to provide services to the fund.

There is, however, a class exemption issued by the Department of Labor that allows certain otherwise prohibited party-in-interest transactions when the investment adviser meets certain criteria. Under Prohibited Transaction Class Exemption PTCE 84-14, an investment may transact with a party-in-interest in all but one limited set of circumstances if the investment adviser is a qualified professional asset manager (QPAM), which means it:

- Is registered as an investment adviser;
- Has at least $1 million in book value; and
- Has at least $85 million in assets under management.

The one set of circumstances that being a QPAM does not address is where the party-in-interest was responsible for selecting the investment adviser to provide services to the benefit plan investor.

XI. FINRA RESTRICTED PERSON RULES

Most FINRA rules have limited applicability to private funds (generally, only those private funds with a broker-dealer affiliate), but two significant exceptions to this are FINRA Rules 5130 and 5131, which address how FINRA members can allocate shares of initial public offerings (IPOs).

FINRA members are limited by Rule 5130 and 5131 in how they allocate shares of IPOs to their clients. The rules are designed to address the conflicts of interest that having certain types of clients can create for broker-dealers.

Rule 5130 restricts FINRA members from allocating shares of IPOs to other brokerage industry participants, such as registered representatives and owners of broker-dealers and portfolio managers or other individuals responsible for directing brokerage business.

Rule 5131 restricts FINRA members from allocating shares of IPOs to officers and directors of companies that are likely to need the services of an investment banker.

De Minimis Treatment of Restricted Persons

In the context of pooled investment accounts like private funds, the FINRA restrictions on allocations of IPOs still apply, but in a slightly adjusted way. Rather than a single restricted person tainting the entire private fund, if ownership in the fund by restricted persons is less than the applicable percentage (depending on the rule), the private fund can ignore the restricted person ownership and purchase IPO securities without concern. If restricted person ownership exceeds the relevant percentage and the private fund's governing agreements allow, the fund can specially allocate purchases of IPO securities in excess of the appropriate percentage away from the restricted person(s).

For Rule 5130, the relevant percentage is ten percent (10 percent). If restricted persons under Rule 5130 own 10 percent or less of the fund's outstanding equity, the private fund can ignore the restricted person ownership.

For Rule 5131, the relevant percentage is 25 percent. If restricted persons under Rule 5131 affiliated with a particular company own 25 percent or less of the fund's outstanding equity, the private fund can ignore the restricted person ownership.

XII. ANTI-MONEY LAUNDERING REQUIREMENTS

Under current law and regulations, private funds and their investment advisers have limited statutory obligations relating to the prevention of money laundering. The Uniting and Strengthening America by Providing Appropriate Tools Required to Intercept and Obstruct Terrorism Act of 2001("USA PATRIOT Act") established a framework for anti-money laundering (AML) regulations in the financial services industry, but currently only the custodial side of the investment management industry has regulations that are in force.

Current Obligations

Under the current state of law and regulation, the only affirmative obligation a private fund has under statute or regulation is to ensure that investors in the fund do not appear on the List of Specially Designated Nationals and Blocked Persons published by the Office of Foreign Asset Control (OFAC), which is part of the U.S. Treasury.

Notwithstanding the limited obligations under current statute and regulations, most private funds take additional steps in connection with verifying the identity and source of funds of their investors.[22] In addition, many private funds agree to take on additional AML responsibilities at the bequest of their trading partners (e.g., their prime brokers).

USA PATRIOT Act Obligations

When the PATRIOT Act was enacted, there were proposed regulations for investment advisers and managers of private funds, but the original regulations were never adopted. The Treasury reproposed regulations in September 2015 that would implement AML requirements for registered investment advisers. As of the date of this publication,, that proposal has not been acted upon, but the industry expects that at some point these rules (or rules substantially similar) will be adopted.

Under the currently proposed rule, registered investment advisers will be required to develop and implement a written anti-money laundering program that is reasonably designed to prevent the investment adviser from being involved in money laundering or the financing of terrorist activities. At a minimum, an adviser's AML program should:

- Establish and implement policies, procedures and internal controls reasonably designed to this end;
- Provide for independent testing of the program (either by internal personnel not involved with managing the program or by third party consultants);
- Designate a person or persons responsible for the implementation of the AML program; and
- Provide for ongoing training of firm personnel.

Obviously, the AML rule is formulated very similarly to SEC rules for registered investment advisers: a principles-based statement of obligations with little in the way of specific requirements. This means that a registered investment adviser will need to conduct a risk assessment of its clients and services as they relate to anti-money laundering and financing of terrorist activities to determine how robust a firm's policies and procedures will need to be. Most investment advisers should be able to leverage their brokerage and custodial relationships to assist them in developing their own internal policies and procedures once the rule becomes effective.

---

[22] For example, many private funds require copies of drivers' licenses or passports to be provided by individual investors or copies of organizational documents and corporate authorizations from entity investors.

XIII. MATERIAL NONPUBLIC INFORMATION AND EXPERT NETWORKS

MNPI and Expert Networks

The SEC has identified a number of areas of enhanced concern for the private fund industry, and at the very top of that list is insider trading. Given the insular nature of the alternative investment industry and the amount of money that the industry both controls and generates, the SEC considers the likelihood of opportunities to make investment decisions based on material, nonpublic information more prevalent in the alternative investment industry.

Material Nonpublic Information

Material nonpublic information (MNPI) in the context of private funds arises in two contexts in the alternative investment industry. First, the traditional conception where a portfolio manager of a private fund has an inside source for information about an issuer that the portfolio manager is able to access to take advantage of information before it becomes public. Second, the concept of the private fund industry as an "old boys' network" in which they all help each other and act in concert to exert pressure on issuers to take certain actions. This second construct is less an insider trading claim (because the private fund managers do not generally have any duty to the issuers they are pressuring) than a market manipulation claim (they are using their aggregate influence to impact corporate actions without following the usual requirements for activist shareholders.

Knowing that the SEC has the private fund industry squarely in its crosshairs for these risks, advisers would do well to build the proper internal controls to mitigate against them and remain vigilant for trading irregularities demonstrating a misuse of MNPI.

Use of Expert Networks

An additional potential source of material, nonpublic information that is commonly seen in the private fund industry is the use of "expert networks." While expert networks certainly have a valid role in the private funds industry, there was a period of time when certain players in this space were actively marketing themselves to private funds as sources of material, nonpublic information.

The legitimate role for an expert network service is to provide broad, industry-specific knowledge and expertise to a portfolio manager or analyst who is trying to build a better understanding of a particular investment sector. For instance, if a portfolio manager decides he or she wants to build an investment thesis in the semiconductor industry but has no existing knowledge base from which to start, that manager could retain an expert network to make an introduction to an industry expert (usually someone who has spent several years working in that industry) who can help build that basic understanding.

Using the same basic scenario but in an illegitimate role, the portfolio manager would retain the expert network to identify a recent employee of the particular company in which the portfolio manager is looking to make an investment with the expectation that the former employee would provide inside information about the company. In 2010, the SEC conducted a sweeping exam of registered investment advisers regarding their use of expert networks and discovered a number of expert network firms that provided this service exactly.[23]

Most of the expert network services that currently service our industry either survived that sweep because they provided only legitimate assistance or because they came into being since that sweep occurred. Regardless of inception, all of them have developed their own internal compliance policies and procedures to address this issue. Any investment adviser that is considering using an expert network should conduct due diligence on the potential service provider to ensure that it has reasonable policies and procedures and adheres to them consistently. In addition, many investment advisers layer their own compliance program on top of the expert network's program, including aspects such as compliance chaperoning, introductory disclosure scripts, and limited access to a select list of firms.

XIV. ADDITIONAL REGULATORY FILINGS

A final area to touch on for private fund compliance is the various regulatory filings that can be contemplated when a firm operates a private fund. This section will not go into significant detail on each potential filing but merely summarize the circumstances that could create an obligation for the filing.

Form D

Form D was addressed briefly above, but given the frequency with which these filings are not made, it bears repeating. Form D is the filing necessary to claim the "private placement" safe harbor under Regulation D. The filing must be made with the SEC within 15 calendar days of the first sale of an interest in the private fund. In addition, filing a copy of Form D is one of three requirements a state may impose on an issuer that is relying on Rule 506 (the other two being a filing fee and an appointment of agent for service of process), and the state level filing (if required) must also be made within 15 calendar days of the first sale in the relevant state (some states require amendments on an annual basis or whether the information for the state changes).

Form 13D and Form 13G

Forms 13D and 13G are used to report ownership of 5 percent or more of a publicly traded equity security. Form 13D is used primarily for investors who are taking an activist position with respect to the issuer. Form 13D must be filed within 10 calendar days of crossing the 5 percent threshold. Form 13G is the short-form disclosure for

[23] *SEC Brings Expert Network Insider Trading Charges*, Rel. No. 2011-38 (Feb. 3, 2011).

the 5 percent ownership threshold that may be used only if the investor is holding the equity securities as a passive investor (i.e., is not attempting to influence the operations of the issuer in any way). In addition, Form 13G may not be used once the ownership hits a 20 percent threshold (when it must convert to a Form 13D). Depending on the character of the investor, Form 13G is due either within 10 calendar days of the transaction that breaches the 5 percent threshold or within 45 calendar days of the end of the year in which the threshold was crossed.

Form 13F

Form 13F is the "institutional investment manager" disclosure. If an institutional investment manager (and a registered investment adviser is almost always an institutional investment manager) manages client portfolios holding at least $100 million in Schedule 13(f) securities as of the end of any calendar month during a year, that institutional investment manager must file Form 13F within 45 calendar days of the end of that calendar year. Once the adviser is required to file Form 13F, the filings are required quarterly until and unless the adviser completes an entire calendar year when the month-end values are all below the $100 million threshold.

Form 13H

Form 13H is the large trader filing. A "large trader" is any person that directly or indirectly exercises investment discretion over transactions in NMS securities in an aggregate amount in excess of:

- 2 million shares or $20 million in fair market value in a single day; or
- 20 million shares or $200 million in fair market value in a calendar month.

A large trader has an obligation to file Form 13H and to be assigned a large trader identification number (which must be provided to all of the large trader's brokerage counterparties). The filing obligation is "promptly" after crossing one of the above thresholds. After the initial filing, a large trader must make an annual filing with the SEC within 45 calendar days of the end of the year. If during the prior year, the large trader has not conducted trades in excess of the threshold levels, it can file for inactive status on its annual amendment, in which case there are no further filings required until and unless the trader exceeds the thresholds again in the future.

In addition to the initial and annual filings, amended filings must be filed "promptly" following the end of the calendar quarter in which any of the information contained in a Form 13H filing becomes inaccurate for any reason. For example, if a large trader changes its name, business address, organization type (e.g., the large trader partnership reincorporates as a limited liability company), or regulatory status (e.g., a hedge fund registers under the Investment Company Act), or when its organizational chart changes in a manner relevant under Item 4(a) (e.g., it adds or removes a securities affiliate), it must file an amended 13H promptly (typically within 15 days) after quarter-end.

Form PF

Form PF must be filed by registered investment advisers that manage private funds that have $150 million or more in assets (including assets in parallel strategies held in separately managed accounts). The timing on the filing of the form depends on the private fund assets under management for the investment adviser. For small advisers (any adviser that is not a large adviser which means $1.5 billion in "hedge fund" assets, $1 billion in "liquidity fund" assets, or $2 billion in "private equity fund" assets[24]), Form PF must be filed annually within 120 calendar days of the end of their fiscal year. For large hedge fund managers, Form PF must be filed quarterly within 60 calendar days of the end of their fiscal quarter. For large liquidity fund managers, Form PF must be filed quarterly within 15 calendar days of the end of their fiscal quarter. And for large private equity fund managers, Form PF must be filed annually within 120 calendar days of the end of their fiscal year. In addition to the timing differences, small advisers are required to complete an abbreviated Form PF.

Form CPO-PQR (CFTC) and PQR (NFA)

Unlike Form PF, which has asset-level triggers for filing obligations, Form CPO-PQR must be filed by any CPO that operated a pool for which it was required to be registered during the relevant reporting period (the scope of the filing does change as the assets in the funds become larger). Note that if the manager of a private fund is registered as a CPO (either for historical or strategic reasons) but currently does not have any private fund that would require it to be registered (for instance, a private fund that relied on CFTC Rule 4.13(a)(3) does not require its manager to be registered as a CPO), there is no Form CPO-PQR filing obligation.

For an investment adviser that is required to file both Form PF and Form CPO-PQR, the CFTC has determined to accept a copy of Form PF and an abbreviated Form CPO-PQR as compliant. Bear in mind that this treatment for CFTC filings does not carry over to NFA Form PQR filings as well.

The filing deadlines for the CFTC and NFA filings do depend on asset size, similarly to the Form PF filings. For small CPOs (with less than $150 million in aggregate gross assets under management in the pools), the obligation is to file Schedule A of Form CPO-PQR within 90 calendar days of the calendar yearend. For midsized CPOs ($150 million to less than $1.5 billion in aggregate gross assets under management in the pools), the obligation is to file Schedules A and B of Form CPO-PQR within 90 calendar days of the calendar yearend. For large CPOs ($1.5 billion or more in aggregate gross assets under management in the pools), the obligation is to file Schedules A, B, and C of Form CPO-PQR within 60 calendar days of the end of each calendar quarter. For NFA Form PQR, there is a quarterly filing obligation within 60 calendar days of the end of the calendar quarter regardless of the aggregate assets under management in the pools.

---

[24] The terms "hedge fund," "liquidity fund" and "private equity fund" are used here as they are defined in Form PF.

XV. CONCLUSION

This chapter addressed the additional compliance obligations to which managers of private funds as the term is defined in Section 202(a)(29) of the Advisers Act are subject due to the management of such private funds. The chapter summarized requirements for private funds provided in the 40 Act, Rule 506, Commodity Exchange Act, and Securities Act.

ABOUT THE AUTHOR

Jeff Blumberg is an experienced investment management lawyer with Faegre Baker Daniels who regularly advises clients on regulatory, corporate governance, business, and structural matters. He counsels registered and unregistered money managers—including hedge fund managers, investment advisers, broker-dealers, commodity trading advisers, and commodity pool operators.

Mr. Blumberg advises the managers of both U.S. and offshore investment funds on daily operations and planning, funding, and structuring strategies that comply with regulatory requirements. He drafts and reviews fund documentation and agreements. Mr. Blumberg also counsels investment advisers, commodity trading advisers, and commodity pool operators on operations and other key business matters, including mergers and acquisitions, regulatory investigations and examinations, compliance policies and procedures, contracts, advertising, and securities valuation.

In addition to advising many independent money management firms, Mr. Blumberg advises investment managers that are affiliates of larger financial institutions, including banks and insurance companies.

Prior to practicing law, Mr. Blumberg spent seven years working in the financial services industry with one of the largest independent financial services firms in the Chicagoland area, where he provided advanced marketing support for the firm's sales force, was a registered principal for the firm's broker-dealer office and acted as the internal compliance officer for the firm.

CHAPTER 17

Select Issues in Trading Compliance for Investment Advisers

By Matthew J. Fitzgerald
PGIM Fixed Income

I. INTRODUCTION

Investment advisers registered with the U.S. Securities and Exchange Commission (SEC) increasingly face regulatory scrutiny with respect to their trading and investment practices. As a result, investment advisers' compliance staff and chief compliance officers (CCOs) can struggle to keep abreast of increasingly complex markets, instruments, and investment strategies. The SEC, via Rule 206(4)-7,[1] issued under the Investment Advisers Act of 1940, as amended (the "Advisers Act"),[2] compels registered investment advisers and their CCOs to maintain policies and procedures reasonably designed to ensure compliance with law.

Nonetheless, determining what is both good practice and reasonable process in the context of trading can be highly factual, even subjective. The SEC provides little guidance on certain trading topics and no guidance on others. In the current enforcement environment, published settlements and cases underscore prohibited themes and behaviors but rarely elaborate on permitted, encouraged, or even reasonable practices. Faced with grayness or uncertainty, one must revert to first principles. This chapter intends first to touch on a few relevant trading and trading related investment adviser compliance themes, and second, to attach some practical thoughts to the dynamic and inherently complex areas of antifraud and best execution. Investment advisers share some characteristics, including a common U.S. regulator, with broker-dealers and may be dual registered as broker-dealers, so the chapter will draw on some themes common to both broker-dealers and investment advisers. Intentionally, this chapter sticks to matters of SEC jurisdiction and precedent.

---

1 17 CFR 206(4)-7.

2 15 U.S.C. 80b-1 *et seq*. Throughout this chapter, the term "investment adviser" shall mean a corporate investment adviser registered under the Advisers Act.

II. FRONT AND CENTER: COMPLIANCE AND INSIDER TRADING

Long before CCOs became mandatory,[3] there was insider trading.[4] In the 1980s, SEC Rule 10b-5 gained celebrity, with some highly publicized and audacious wrongs leading to civil and criminal penalties.[5] More recently, the proliferation of hedge funds, the use of expert networks by investment advisers and some egregious activity contributed to a wave of criminal prosecutions and some high-profile civil and criminal trials and settlements under Rule 10b-5.[6] Jail sentences for insider trading appear to be growing longer,[7] whereas misdeeds increasingly cross borders and involve multiple parties, markets, issuers, or instruments.[8] The United States is not alone in prosecuting insider trading. For example, the UK Financial Conduct Authority (FCA) announced recently a criminal action against a former BlackRock employee who ultimately pled guilty to insider dealing.[9] Between March of 2009 and March of 2016 alone, the FCA won 28 criminal convictions related to insider dealing.[10]

Trading Related Fraud Is an SEC Enforcement and Audit Priority

Preventing improper conduct by key market participants and illegal practices by broker-dealers and investment advisers is central to the SEC's role. Former SEC Chairman White, for example, cited among the SEC's significant accomplishments charging more than 240 individuals with insider trading between April 2013 and May 2016, including actions against those trading on information misappropriated from others.[11]

In addition, the SEC's Office of Compliance Investigations and Examinations (OCIE) has, since at least 2008, included among its items for examination focus the Trading of

---

3 Rule 206(4)-7 under the Advisers Act was amended to require a CCO to be appointed by registered advisers effective February 5, 2004. *See Compliance Programs of Investment Companies and Investment Advisers*, 68 Fed. Reg. 74714 (Dec. 24, 2003).

4 Section 10(b) of the Securities Exchange Act of 1934, as amended (15 U.S.C. Section 78j(b)) became effective on October 1, 1934; Rule 10b-5 was first adopted on May 21, 1942. *See* 15 U.S.C. Section 78hh; Exchange Act Release No 3230 (May 21, 1942).

5 *See*, e.g., "Highlights of the Wall Street Scandal; From Levine Arrest to Drexel Settlement," *The New York Times* (Dec. 22, 1988).

6 Indeed, Martha Stewart's case turned insider trading into tabloid fodder, while Preet Bharara's 85 insider trading convictions obtained by using wiretaps and aggressive prosecutions increased the stakes for insider trading. *See S.E.C. v. Martha Stewart and Peter Bacanovic,* 88 S.E.C. Docket 2121, 2006 WL 2252393 (August 7, 2006); Statement of Manhattan U.S. Attorney on the Acquittal of Rengan Rajaratnam, U.S. Justice Department Press Release (Tuesday July 8, 2014).

7 Compare "Boesky Sentenced to 3 Years In Jail in Insider Scandal," *The New York Times* (Dec. 19, 1987) and *U.S. v. Rajaratnam,* 09 Cr. 1184, 2010 WL 4867402 (S.D.N.Y. Nov. 24, 2010), *aff'd, United States v. Rajaratnam*, 719 F.3d 139 (2d Cir. 2013) (upholding an 11-year sentence for 14 counts of trading on material nonpublic information).

8 *See U.S. v. Rajaratnam.*

9 *Former Investment Manager Charged with Insider Dealing,* FCA Press Release (Sept. 29, 2016); "Mark Lyttleton Pleads Guilty to Insider Dealing," FCA Press Release (Nov. 2, 2016).

10 *Insider Dealers Sentenced In Operation Tabernula Trial,* FCA Press Release (May 5, 2016).

11 *SEC Accomplishments*, SEC website (last modified September 19, 2016).

Investment Advisers.[12] More specific topics for OCIE scrutiny include: trade blotters, brokerage arrangements and conflicts of interest/insider trading.[13] So compliance professionals know that the SEC is likely to focus on these topics in an examination, but how does one prepare?

The First Commandment: Rule 10b-5

For all its fame, Rule 10b-5 is nuanced, with decades of common law interpretations. The rule states:

> It shall be unlawful for any person…
>
> a) To employ any device, scheme, or artifice to defraud,
> b) To make any untrue statement of a material fact or to omit to state a material fact necessary in order to make the statements made, in the light of the circumstances under which they were made, not misleading, or
> c) To engage in any act, practice, or course of business which operates or would operate as a fraud or deceit upon any person, in connection with the purchase or sale of any security.[14]

Notably, neither Section 10(b) of the Securities Exchange Act of 1934, as amended[15] (Exchange Act), nor Rule 10b-5 state that it is illegal or unlawful to trade while in possession of material nonpublic information (MNPI).[16] To the courts, "classical" insider trading prohibits officers or directors of public companies from trading on information unavailable to the market.[17] This looks more explicit when one rereads paragraphs (b) and (c) of Rule 10b-5. "Misappropriation theory" applies Rule 10b-5 to individuals outside of the company, or "tippees," that obtain MNPI.[18] The misappropriation theory can create tippee liability if:

- The tipper had a fiduciary duty not to disclose the MNPI he or she passed; and
- The tippee knows that the tipper breached his or her duty by disclosing MNPI to obtain a personal benefit, directly or indirectly (generally because trading is expected to follow the disclosure).[19]

---

[12] Office of Compliance Inspections and Examination, "Investment Adviser Examinations: Core Initial Request for Information" (Nov. 2008).

[13] *Id.*

[14] 17 CFR 240.10b-5.

[15] 15 U.S.C. Section 78j. ("It shall be unlawful for any person…(b) To use or employ, in connection with the purchase or sale of any security registered on a national securities exchange or any security not so registered, or any securities-based swap agreement any manipulative or deceptive device or contrivance in contravention of such rules and regulations as the Commission may prescribe as necessary or appropriate in the public interest or for the protection of investors").

[16] *U.S. v. Newman*, 773 F.3d 438, 445 (2d Cir. 2014).

[17] *Id., citing Chiarella v. U.S.* 222, 226-230 (1980).

[18] *Newman*, 773 F.3d at 445; *Chiarella*, 222 U.S. at 232.

[19] Salman v. United States, No. 15-628 at pages 2,5, 7-8 (U.S. Dec. 6, 2016)(a jury can infer a personal benefit where the tipper receives something of value or makes a gift of the confidential information to a family member or friend), citing *Dirks v. SEC*, 463 U.S 646, 664 (1983).

Misappropriation theory was codified at least partially by SEC Rule 10b5-1 in 2000.[20] Rule 10b5-1 prohibits as "manipulative and deceptive devices":

> *The purchase or sale of a security of any issuer, on the basis of material non-public information* about that security or issuer, *in breach of a duty of trust or confidence* that is owed directly, *indirectly, or derivatively*, to the issuer of that security or the shareholders of that issuer, or to any other person who is the source of the material nonpublic information.[21]

"Indirect" or "derivative" obligations may be passed from tipper to tippee. Rule 10b5-2(b) separately enumerates "duties of trust or confidence" that include "whenever a person agrees to act in confidence, which expressly includes the execution of a non-disclosure agreement.[22]

Rule 10b5-1(c) also recognizes and codifies certain affirmative defenses. These affirmative defenses provide both challenges and opportunities for compliance officers. Importantly, the investment adviser may demonstrate that a purchase or sale of securities is not "on the basis of" material nonpublic information by demonstrating that:

- The individual making the investment decision to purchase or sell the securities was not aware of the information; and
- The investment adviser had implemented reasonable policies and procedures to ensure that individuals making investment decisions would not violate the laws prohibiting trading on the basis of material nonpublic information. These policies and procedures may include those that restrict any purchase, sale, and/or causing any purchase or sale of any security as to which the person has MNPI, or policies and procedures that prevent individuals from becoming aware of MNPI.[23]

What Does This Mean to Me?

Takeaways from this quick review of the Section 10(b) antifraud rules are:

- If an investment adviser possesses MNPI regarding an issuer when the investment adviser trades, then any trade it makes in related securities and or derivatives presumptively breaches Rule 10b-5 and 10b5-1;
- Investment advisers frequently execute nondisclosure agreements with investee companies and so may owe independent duties of confidence to such issuers under Rule 10b5-2(b). This exacerbates 10b-5 risks if the issuer supplies MNPI to the investment adviser;

---

[20] *Final Rule: Selective Disclosure and Insider Trading*, SEC Release No. 34-43154, 65 Fed Reg. 51716 (Aug. 15, 2000); 17 CFR 240.10b5-1.

[21] 17 CFR 240.10b5-1 (emphasis supplied).

[22] 17 CFR 240.10b5-2(b)(1).

[23] This defense is only available to "persons other than natural persons." 17 CFR 240.10b5-1(c)(2). Thus, investment advisers or their corporate affiliates may assert the defense, but individual officers, traders and portfolio managers cannot. Under Rule 10b5-1(c), effective policies and procedures can therefore shift insider trading risk to individual wrongdoers from the investment adviser.

- Investment advisers likely owe contractual duties of confidence to their clients, whose securities they may be trading. This can also exacerbate 10b-5 risks if the client similarly tips, taints, or merely supplies MNPI to the investment adviser;
- Investment advisers themselves may have information about trade flows, issuers, or clients that regulators may consider to be MNPI;
- Training is important because it makes people stop and think. Traders, portfolio managers, and investment adviser employees need to understand that if they have MNPI for an issuer they should minimally refrain from trading and seek guidance from their legal or compliance officers; and
- By establishing information barriers, restricted lists and insider trading policies and procedures investment advisers can create affirmative defenses to potential Rule 10b-5 violations and may substantially reduce insider trading risk to the advisory entity. Such defenses are addressed at more length later.

Section 204A of the Investment Advisers Act of 1940 "Commands" More

Investment advisers and control persons of investment advisers are also covered by Section 204A of the Advisers Act, which amplifies the basic antifraud provisions of Exchange Act Section 10b and Rule 10b-5. Although Rule 10b-5 prohibits trading while in possession of MNPI, Section 204A affirmatively obliges every investment adviser to:

> Maintain, and enforce written policies and procedures reasonably designed, taking into consideration the nature of such investment adviser's business, to prevent the misuse…of material, nonpublic information by such investment adviser or any person associated with such investment adviser.[24]

Recently, the SEC fined a broker-dealer/investment adviser because it had "no written policies and procedures in place to prevent the misuse of [MNPI]" by its affiliated hedge fund and fund management employees.[25]

Section 204A v. Rule 204A-1: Personal Trading Only?

Rule 204A-1 under the Advisers Act lists the requirements for an investment adviser's code of ethics but explicitly addresses only the misuse of material nonpublic information by access persons of investment advisers in their *personal* trading.[26] The rule implicitly addresses other forms of misuse of inside information beyond personal trading, such as front-running or tailgating customer orders, or misusing market knowledge or MNPI for the benefit of clients rather than oneself.[27] What policies must be maintained under Section 204A and

[24] 15 U.S.C. Section 80b-4a; substantially similar obligations attach to broker-dealers under Section 15(g) (formerly Section 15f) of the Exchange Act and Related Rules. *See* 15 U.S.C. 78o(g).

[25] *See In the Matter of Sidoti & Company, LLC*, SEC Release No. 80027 (Feb. 13, 2017).

[26] 17 CFR 204A-1.

[27] 17 CFR 204A-1(a)(1) and (2). The *Sidoti &Company* order underlines the potential peril of trading either personally *or* for clients absent sufficient policy and procedural safeguards from affiliate-possessed MNPI. *See Sidoti & Company*, at 4.

how does a compliance officer "enforce" them? The answer cannot be uniform, because the reasonableness of both design and implementation depend on the facts and circumstances of each business and the extent and nature of the risks in each investment adviser's business model. Nonetheless, SEC examinations are likely to scrutinize the investment adviser's code of ethics and the express and implied requirements of Rule 204A-1. Recent enforcement actions under Section 204A apply the code of ethics to certain consultants[28] but otherwise offer limited assistance in outlining issues other than personal trading.[29]

Codes of Ethics Under Rule 204A-1: Principles for "Reasonable" Investment Adviser Trading Policies

Certain prohibitions appear critical to a reasonable policy under Section 204A and Rule 10b-5. For example, the policy should restrict trading in any securities while in possession of MNPI generally. This may seem obvious.[30] For investment advisers, Rule 204A-1(a) mandates and sets forth five minimal requirements for a code of ethics:

- A standard of business conduct required of persons supervised that reflects the adviser's and advisory fiduciary obligations;
- Provisions requiring supervised persons to comply with the federal securities laws (including Rules 10b-5 and 10b5-1);
- Provisions requiring the initial and periodic (not less than quarterly) reporting and review of personal securities transactions and holdings;
- An obligation to report violations of the code of ethics to the CCO or other designee; and
- Provisions requiring delivery of the code to each relevant employee and written acknowledgment of its receipt.

An investment adviser with a public company affiliate should consider adding to the code of ethics specific provisions:

- Prohibiting trading one's own company securities while in possession of company-related MNPI; and
- Employing blackout periods leading up to the release of quarterly earnings and for a sufficient time thereafter to permit the public dissemination of such information.

---

28 *Federated Global Investment Management Corp.*, Investment Advisers Act of 1940 Release No. 4401 (May 27, 2016) ($1.5 million fine imposed for failing to prevent the misuse of MNPI under Section 204A of the Advisers Act by an outside consultant who was an "access person" under the Investment Adviser's Code of Ethics).

29 *See*, e.g. *Merrill Lynch, Pierce, Fenner & Smith Incorporated*, Investment Advisers Act of 1940 Release No. 2851 (Mar. 11, 2009) (Broker-dealer/investment adviser fined $7 million for permitting day traders and favored customers to trade ahead of prospective trades of institutional clients in violation of Section 15g (formerly 15f) of the Securities Exchange Act and Section 204A of the Advisers Act); *Morgan Stanley Incorporated and Morgan Stanley DW Inc.*, Investment Advisers Act of 1940 Release No.2526 (June 27, 2006) (Broker-dealer/investment adviser fined $10 million for willfully violating Section 15g (formerly 15f) of the Securities Exchange Act and Section 204A of the Advisers Act in which the adviser's "watch list" monitoring procedures were not followed on a "massive" number of securities and accounts).

30 Although many high-profile cases involve public securities, Rule 10b-5 applies to "any" securities, including private securities. 17 CFR 240.10b-5(c). For private securities transactions, MNPI can be problematic when one party has superior information to its counterparty and does not disclose the information.

The policy should expressly prohibit trading in either of the following:

- Employees' accounts if the employee has MNPI; or
- Client accounts when the account or portfolio manager has access to, or its business unit may have access to, MNPI.

Procedures may be employed to implement a restricted list of securities for which MNPI was received or expected and/or to block relevant company and individual trades in restricted list securities. Policies may also clarify that if the investment adviser has MNPI, then all securities and related derivatives like options or total return swaps are prohibited from trading until the investment adviser is "cleansed" either through public disclosure of the MNPI, or the expiration of its materiality. Although Rule 204A-1 requires preapproval of participation in an initial offering or private or limited offering only, the preapproval of all personal trades is a control commonly employed to prevent transactions in securities for which investment advisers or their employees hold MNPI. Many firms will not preclear any personal trade in a name on the applicable restricted list.

Similar, Slightly Broader Requirements for Advisers of 1940 Act Funds

Investment advisers of funds registered under the Investment Company Act of 1940, as amended (the "Investment Company Act") must adopt a code of ethics compliant with Investment Company Act Rule 17j-1.[31] Rule 17j-1 itself includes an antifraud provision that closely resembles Rule 10b-5, and tailors Rule 10b-5 to registered funds. Rule 17j-1 makes it unlawful, in connection with the purchase or sale, by certain enumerated persons:

> (1) To employ any device, scheme or artifice to defraud *the Fund*; (2) To make any untrue statement of a material fact *to the Fund* or omit to state a material fact necessary in order to make the statements made *to the Fund*, in light of the circumstances under which they are made, not misleading; (3) To engage in any act, practice or course of business that operates or would operate as a fraud or deceit on *the Fund*; or (4) *To engage in any manipulative practice with respect to the Fund.*

Emphasized text in the previous paragraph highlight the only differences between Rule 17j-1(b) and Rule 10b-5.

Rule 17j-1 is otherwise very similar to Rule 204A-1, requiring quarterly and annual holdings reports and preclearance.[32] Unlike Rule 204A-1, the 17j-1 fund code of ethics must be adopted by the fund board *and* the fund's investment adviser, who must report at least annually to the board regarding issues under the code.[33] In addition, the 17j-1 code applies broadly to the "access persons" of the fund. Access persons may

[31] 17 CFR 270.17j-1.
[32] *Id.*
[33] 17 CFR 270.17j-1(c)(2).

include directors, officers, and general partners of the fund, its investment adviser, and even its principal underwriter in addition to employees.[34] Employees of the fund or its adviser are access persons if they make, participate in or obtain information regarding the purchase or sale of any securities by the fund.[35]

Okay, the Firm Has a Code of Ethics; Can It Protect the Business from MNPI?

Public Side and Private Side Businesses. Most diversified financial institutions and many investment advisers include divisions, subsidiaries, or entities that conduct "public side" business and other divisions, subsidiaries, or businesses that are considered "private side" businesses. A single investment adviser may also have both public side and private side businesses and divisions within it. Private side investment advisory activities vary considerably, but most often include either:

- Participating in private securities offerings, financings or other nonregistered transactions; or
- Receiving confidential information or MNPI that is released by the issuer on a selective basis, most often pursuant to a nondisclosure agreement.

Examples of private side investments or business lines in which an investment adviser may participate include: private equity, real estate (direct purchases and/or finance), leveraged finance (including loans, mezzanine debt deals and private or semiprivate debt offerings, mergers and acquisitions, or merger and acquisitions (M&A) financings, hedge fund offerings), and other similar transactions. Although information passed from private issuers about these transactions may or may not be material with respect to the deal and/or issuer in question, the fact of a deal or financing itself can be MNPI.

Public side businesses of investment advisers may include managing listed equity, publicly traded debt or investments into any fund or security registered with the SEC.

Operating private side businesses freely and flexibly without impairing or restricting public side businesses is a goal shared by professional investors and their compliance officers. The compliance officer for an investment adviser that operates both public side and private side Businesses may be called upon to:

- Build information barriers between investment teams;
- Advise with respect to whether information received is in fact MNPI;
- Restrict trading;
- Limit information flow; or
- Prevent unintended disclosure of MNPI to any of the public, public side businesses, other private side businesses, or unauthorized personnel.

---

[34] 17 CFR 270.17j-1(a).

[35] 17 CFR 270.17j-1(a)(2).

The private side compliance officer may assist with processes to:

- Contain such information within the firm or division;
- Monitor access to private data; and/or
- Comply with confidentiality agreements.

The public side compliance officer for an investment adviser or financial institution may seek to:

- Enhance controls to inhibit, limit, or direct the flow of any private side information into the public side; and
- Create processes to restrict public side trading or otherwise reduce risk of legal or regulatory violation if the public side receives MNPI.

The public side compliance officer may also conduct surveillance on both personal and firm trading in securities for which the private side has received MNPI. Both public and private side investment advisers with MNPI frequently enforce the code of ethics restrictions on personal and firm trading.

MNPI containment is especially vital to an investment adviser that receives the information under an obligation of confidence. As discussed earlier, anyone who discloses MNPI when they have a duty to maintain the confidence of such information risks liability under Section 10b and Rules 10b-5 and 10b5-2.

Managing Material and Nonpublic Information. A dramatist might consider MNPI to be analogous to kryptonite, that powerful comic book element from Superman's home planet that is capable of paralyzing even the greatest superhero. Mishandled MNPI or the allegation of MNPI mishandling can destroy the reputation and stability of the mightiest of organizations.[36] Thus, it makes sense that financial service organizations, including investment advisers, devote substantial resources to create and manage sophisticated information barriers. Few recipes exist, but the SEC does provide some guidance regarding the components of an information barrier.[37]

Preventing Access: Physical Separation. Physically separating public side and private side businesses seems simple. Public side businesses and private side businesses that have MNPI about an issuer or security must be physically separated from each other if the public side business wishes to continue to trade that issuer or security. Compliance officers may be asked to opine on the adequacy of physical barriers, but reasonable minds can differ on what facts and circumstances create sufficient physical

---

[36] *See* e.g., Kurt Eichenwald, "The Collapse of Drexel, Burnham Lambert; Drexel, Symbol of Wall St. Era, Is Dismantling: Bankruptcy Filed," *The New York Times* (Feb. 14, 1990), http://www.nytimes.com/1990/02/14/business/collapse-drexel-burnham-lambert-drexel-symbol-wall-st-era-dismantling-bankruptcy.html

[37] *Staff Summary Report on Examinations of Information Barriers: Broker Dealer Practices Under Section 15g of the Securities Exchange Act of 1934* (Sept. 27, 2012); and *Amendments to Beneficial Ownership Reporting Requirements*, SEC Release No. 34-39538, 63 Fed. Reg. 2854 at 2857-58 (Jan. 12, 1998). *Sidoti & Company, LLC* (as described in SEC Administrative Proceeding 3-17843, Feb. 13, 2017) demonstrates that an effective barrier not only restricts employee trading but also restricts affiliated fund managers' trading for the fund if the managers have access to MNPI.

separation to constitute a physical barrier. Analyzing some physical separations are easy. For example, if an investment adviser's asset management group is in a separate building from its broker-dealer affiliate's M&A team, then there is little worry that the mergers and acquisitions (M&A) team's MNPI is too physically proximate to the investment adviser's traders or portfolio managers. It is equally easy to conclude that a parent company's European investment banking business is physically separate from the parent's U.S. investment advisory business. For most investment advisers, separate floors may provide adequate physical separation between public side and private side investors. Groups on the same floor might also be physically separated by a soundproof wall. But closer calls may arise. Is key card access and locked door restriction required? Certainly, key card restrictions are advisable, especially between high-risk groups like fundamental equity (public side) and a private equity (private side) team that evaluates leveraged buyouts (LBOs). Can two physically separated businesses share a lobby, receptionist, cafeteria, or stairwell and remain physically separate? Can two groups of investors maintain a barrier if they are separated only by four rows of non-investing employees? Does the answer change if a compliance officer sits on the desks? "Perhaps" or "it depends" may be the correct answer. Physical layout and other mitigants will differ in every locale. There are few per se rules in barriers, which carry both intrinsic risk and the opportunity for creative controls and solutions.

Preventing Access: Technological Separation. An effective information barrier also must include technological separation. Physical separation is very likely inadequate if employees on either side of an information barrier can access each other's MNPI via their laptops or PCs. Again, the facts and circumstances of each company's technology will dictate both the adequacy of a technological barrier and the tools available to segregate one business unit's information from another's. Minimally, MNPI access should be limited to those within an information barrier by drive access, password controls, or other technological security. Generally, more conservative access controls are appropriate for more sensitive information.

Separate networks or systems, like separate buildings and floors, are the easiest technological barriers to establish (and to plead and prove), especially when no users overlap across systems or networks. Separate servers may also provide sufficient technological barriers when business units are entirely discrete. But shared employees, functions, and technologies can muddy the technological barrier's effectiveness—even where public side and private side businesses share only one information technology (IT) support person. Shared servers, vendors or networks also create challenges. The sophistication of today's technology and related access controls provide the opportunity to build bespoke access based on each business unit's needs. Compliance and technological control personnel must stay coordinated with human resources (HR) and the IT and information security departments, as applicable, to provide secure access to new employees and to remove access to secured drives when employees leave. Similarly, if employees move internally within the organization or its barrier components, technological access and the timing of access need to be carefully considered to minimize related barrier risks.

Other Barrier Factors. The SEC staff notes other factors that may prove persuasive in establishing information barriers. For example, when seeking to establish a two-way information barrier under Sections 13 and 16 of the Exchange Act of 1934 the staff endorsed:

- A compensation scheme that decoupled the rewards of persons on one side of the barrier from the performance of those on the other side, and
- Written policies and procedures reasonably designed to prevent the flow of information to and from the other business units.[38]

The frequency with which a barrier is crossed may also impact its efficacy.[39] Physical separation, technological separation, and the entirety of other facts and circumstances in *each case* will ultimately determine the adequacy of any MNPI information barrier.

III. THE FIDUCIARY RIDDLE OF BEST EXECUTION

Few trading topics are as murky and paradoxical as the investment adviser's duty of best execution, which at times more resembles an "I know it when I see it" definition than an objective standard of fiduciary trade execution. Many practitioners think of best execution as merely the lowest or best price that can be paid for a security. This may be because subjective factors fade with time, but an objective, "best" price remains constant, even in hindsight. A perfectly rational buyer may pay more for a higher quality item in certain circumstances, however, and not rely solely on paying the lowest price. For example, one would not criticize the investment adviser that paid more to avoid executing a trade with Lehman Brothers, Inc., on the day (perhaps the month?) before Lehman Brothers, Inc., failed. Using only price to determine best execution can be short-sighted, because the fiduciary's duty of care requires it to examine the facts, circumstances and risks intrinsic to its counterparties, markets and execution venues in the context of each trade. All over-the-counter, electronic communication network (ECN), and market maker prices have disparate risks and rewards, so nonprice, subjective factors may ultimately determine best execution.

SEC Perspective on Best Execution

A common law fiduciary owes a duty of loyalty to its clients[40] and a duty of care.[41] The duty of loyalty effectively prevents fiduciaries like investment advisers from putting

[38] *Amendments to Beneficial Ownership Reporting Requirements*, SEC Release No. 34-39538 at Page 17; 63 Fed. Reg. at 2858 (Jan. 12, 1998). *See also, Sidoti & Company*.

[39] *Amendments to Beneficial Ownership*, at 18.

[40] *See*, e.g., *Meinhard vs. Salmon*, 249 N.Y. 458 at 464 (Dec. 31, 1928) ("Many forms of conduct permissible in a workaday world for those acting at arm's length, are forbidden to those bound by fiduciary ties. A trustee is held to something stricter than the morals of the market place. Not honesty alone, but the punctilio of an honor the most sensitive, is then the standard of behavior").

[41] See, e.g., *Smith vs. Van Gorkum*, 488 A.2d 858 (Del. 1985) (fiduciaries have a duty to exercise informed judgment and care in assessing business transactions and related pricing).

their interests ahead of their clients' when trading. For example, an investment adviser might breach its duty of loyalty by choosing to trade with an affiliate at a price greater than the price available elsewhere. Similarly, the duty of care requires the fiduciary to execute trades skillfully, carefully and expertly but *not* always perfectly. Duties of loyalty and care have been read into Section 206 of the Advisers Act, which states:

> It shall be unlawful for any investment adviser...(1) to employ any device, scheme, or artifice to defraud any Client;...(2) to engage in any transaction, practice, or course of business which operates as a fraud or deceit upon any client;...(3) acting as principal for his own account, knowingly to sell any security to or purchase any security from a client, or acting as broker for a person other than such client, knowingly to effect any sale or purchase of any security for the account of such client, without disclosing to such client in writing before the completion of such transaction the capacity in which he is acting and obtaining the consent of the client to such transaction;... or (4) to engage in any act, practice, or course of business which is fraudulent, deceptive, or manipulative....[42]

Section 206 more resembles an antifraud provision than a statement of fiduciary duty. But for an investment adviser who must disclose its trading practice in Form ADV,[43] the antifraud and fiduciary trading obligations may closely intertwine. There is little specific SEC guidance with respect to how the fiduciary duty of best execution is defined within the Advisers Act or related regulations, especially when viewed against the broad business models and the broad product and service offerings of the investment adviser.

In a 1986 interpretive release relating to soft dollars the SEC provided a concise but imprecise standard for best execution, stating that "money managers must...execute securities transactions for clients in such a manner that the *client's total cost or proceeds in each* transaction is the *most favorable under the circumstances*."[44] By emphasizing costs and proceeds, the SEC suggests a quantitative, objective bias in defining best execution. The interpretive release paradoxically follows by saying:

> A money manager should consider the full range and quality of a broker's services in placing brokerage, including among other things, the value of research provided as well as execution capability, commission rate, financial responsibility, and responsiveness...the determinative factor is not the lowest possible commission cost, but whether the transaction represent the best *qualitative* execution for the managed account...[45]

---

42 15 U.S.C. Section 80b-6.

43 Form ADV Part 1A and Item 8 (Participation or Interest in Client Transactions) and Part 2A and Items 6 (Performance-Based Fees and Side-by-Side Management, 12 (Brokerage Practices) and 16 (Investment Discretion).

44 *Interpretive Release Concerning the Scope of Section 28(e) of the Securities Exchange Act and Related Matters*, SEC Release No. 23170 (Apr. 28, 1986).

45 *Id.* (Emphasis supplied.)

The 1986 interpretive release emphasized and recent enforcement matters reinforced that an investment adviser's best execution duties include periodic evaluation of best execution[46] and an evaluation of trade performance against the broader market.[47]

FINRA Rule Informs "Best Ex"

Given sparse guidance and SEC enforcement cases that typically involve either exceptional or egregious behavior, FINRA Rule 5310, governing broker-dealer best execution, is highly instructive for investment advisers. Rule 5310 imposes an obligation on broker-dealers to "*use reasonable diligence* to ascertain *the best market* for the subject security and buy or sell in such market so that the resultant *price to the customer is as favorable as possible under prevailing market conditions*."[48] Notably, the FINRA duties apply to broker-dealers even though they less frequently act in a fiduciary capacity than do investment advisers.

Rule 5310 cites transactional factors and market or venue factors that influence both the reasonableness of trading diligence and what is best execution under the circumstances. Transactional factors include: the size and type of the transaction or instrument being traded, and the terms and conditions of the order.[49] Best execution for a trade of 100 shares of a highly liquid US equity security might look very different than best execution when purchasing a USD100 million position in a thinly traded emerging market convertible note, or a related derivative. Market or venue factors influencing what is reasonable diligence for best execution include: the character of the market for the security (e.g., price, volatility, relative liquidity, and available communications), the number of markets available, the number of markets checked, and accessibility to quotes.[50]

FINRA Rule 5130 commentary adds that when reviewing their execution quality, broker-dealers should attend to the following factors, which are equally relevant to investment advisers that trade:

- Price improvement (i.e., even better execution than quoted/expected);
- Price disimprovement, including differences between prices quoted and execution prices (i.e. worse execution);
- The likelihood of execution of limit orders;
- Speed of execution;
- Size of execution; and
- Transaction costs.

---

[46] *In the Matter of A.R. Schmeidler & Co.*, Investment Advisers Act of 1940 Release No 3637 (July 31, 2013) (Dual registered investment adviser and broker-dealer's increased revenue share with a clearing broker violated best execution, absent new services or responsibilities and benchmarking against other providers).

[47] *In the Matter of Goelzer Investment Management,* Investment Advisers Act of 1940 Release No 3638 (July 31, 2013) (disregard of best execution policies, including requirement for self-assessment of dual registered broker dealer's execution quality breached both best execution duty and disclosures).

[48] *Best Execution and Interpositioning*, FINRA Manual, Rule 5310 (emphasis supplied).

[49] *Id.*

[50] *Id.*

When considering costs, a fiduciary should consider explicit costs such as commissions, and implicit costs, like market impact and price movement resulting from large trades, which can vary with the skill and inventory of any broker-dealer. At times, transaction costs can be minimized through off-exchange trades, dealer commitment of capital, or trading algorithms, any of which may assist the investment adviser to remain anonymous and/or reduce implicit and explicit costs of trading. Specialized services provided by a broker-dealer may justify payment of higher commissions consistent with best execution. Subjective execution factors such as a broker-dealer's market knowledge and reliability of execution and clearing may equally justify its use. Such subjective factors are less quantifiable than price, but arguably no less important.

What Is *Not* "Best" Is Also Very Important...

What is *not* best execution is also worth discussing, not only because it helps to define best execution in practice but also because best execution failures further an understanding of how best execution can become a problem for an investment adviser. For example, when an investment adviser chooses a broker-dealer or trading venue based on gifts and entertainment received, that adviser may:

- Fail to provide best execution;
- Breach the fiduciary duty of loyalty, and
- Breach compensation rules under the Investment Company Act.[51]

Similarly, increasing order flow to brokers-dealers based on family or romantic relationships generally constitute undisclosed conflicts of interest for both the investment adviser and the fund.[52] Arguably, undisclosed personal or affiliate relationships can breach fiduciary loyalty and candor obligations, even where best execution is obtained.[53] Similarly, 1940 Act Rules prohibit rewarding dealers with brokerage as a quid pro quo for that dealer's sales of fund shares.[54]

FINRA Rule 5310 excludes interpositioning from best execution. "Interpositioning" is the practice of adding a broker-dealer to the trade execution chain that either does not add value but receives compensation or receives disproportionately more payment for the service provided than can be justified by the value provided. Both the interpositioned broker-dealer and the investment adviser that facilitates or permits payments from interpositioning face potential enforcement.[55]

---

[51] *In the Matter of Scott E. De Sano, et al.*, Investment Company Act of 1940 Release No. 28534 (Dec. 11, 2008) (directing order flow based on gifts and entertainment violates Section 17(e)(1) of the Investment Company Act).

[52] *De Sano*, at 10.

[53] The U.S. Supreme Court has held that investment advisers acting in a fiduciary capacity must disclose conflicts regardless of the outcome of the investment adviser's trades or recommendations. *See SEC v. Capital Gains Research Bureau, Inc. et al.*, 375 U.S. 180 (1963).

[54] 17 CFR 270.12b-1(h).

[55] FINRA Rule 5310; *Goelzer Investment Management*.

What Does This Mean to Me?

Takeaways for compliance personnel from this quick review of best execution authority include:

- An investment adviser has a fiduciary duty to seek best execution;
- Experts can help to establish best execution. The investment adviser may tap its traders' expertise to help establish oversight and evidence of best execution. Senior experts may also review the other experts' trades;
- Benchmarking traders' performance against public data can evidence best execution when such data is available. Investment advisers may compare execution prices against
  - Time and price data (e.g., for U.S. listed equities and NMS securities),
  - Trading ranges,
  - Closing prices, and
  - Fixing or other price data as available and applicable;
- A trading committee or other oversight body can assist in meeting the duty of care with respect to trading and best execution. A trading committee can review available metrics, serve as an escalation point for execution related issues, and provide an efficient source of senior trading oversight; and
- Investment advisers should maintain policies and procedures that accurately reflect their trading practices, and are consistent with their public disclosures regarding trading.

Client Direction: An Exception to Best Execution

If a client "directs" an investment adviser to trade through a specified broker-dealer, regardless of other considerations, then the investment adviser is generally relieved of its trading discretion and ability to choose brokers and its obligation to seek or obtain best execution.[56] The client may logically use the payment of brokerage commission to further its own interest—for example, in lieu of paying management fees to the broker-dealer's affiliate or to obtain research or other services using some or all of the brokerage commissions as soft dollars.[57]

Client Direction: A Caveat

Before an investment adviser accepts a direction from its client to trade only with a specified broker-dealer, the investment adviser should obtain an express written waiver of best execution along with the direction, either in the investment management agreement for that client or in a separate letter of direction from the client to the investment

[56] "Best Execution and Interpositioning," *FINRA Manual,* Rule 5310, Supplementary material .09. ("If a member receives an unsolicited instruction from a customer to route that customer's order to a particular market for execution, the member is not required to make a best execution determination beyond the customer's specific instruction.")

[57] Unlike client commission arrangements that raise conflict of interest concerns addressed by Section 28(e), directed brokerage arrangements do not raise the same concerns because they typically involve use of a client's commission dollars to obtain services that benefit the client directly.

adviser. Failure to do so may put the investment adviser on the defensive for exclusively funneling orders to the dealer the client selected, especially if the client's memory lapses. The client may direct brokerage to obtain benefits that more than outweigh the additional costs of directed execution, but since the investment adviser is not always privy to the benefits experienced by the client, the directed investment adviser must protect itself from what otherwise could appear to be a breach of the duty of care and/or loyalty. In addition, investment advisers are required to disclose directed brokerage arrangements in Part 2A of Form ADV.

Soft Dollars: Is This Just a Complicated Exception to Best Execution?

Section 28(e) of the Securities Exchange Act provides a safe harbor to the investment adviser that actually and intentionally "pays up" and does *not* get the best price for its client. This paradox recognizes that all broker-dealers are not equal and that some provide research or other services that more than justify a higher commission. In fact, Section 28(e) of the Securities Exchange Act states:

> No person...shall be deemed to have acted unlawfully or to have breached a fiduciary duty under state or federal law...solely by reason of his having caused the account to pay a member of an exchange, broker or dealer an amount of commission...in excess of the amount of commission another member...would have charged, *if such person determined in good faith that such amount of commission was reasonable in relation to the value of the brokerage and research services provided by such member, broker, or dealer, viewed in terms of either that particular transaction or his overall responsibilities with respect to the account* as to which he exercises investment discretion.[58]

When the smoke clears, it appears that Section 28(e) is saying that for the right reasons, the client can pay extra brokerage commissions as long as he or she receives value for the money and uses that value for the right reasons, which does not sound like an exception to best execution at all!

Agency trades with an identifiable commission provide an investment adviser with a soft dollar opportunity for both equity and fixed income trading.[59] Eligible Research or brokerage services provided directly to an investment adviser by the broker-dealer that executes the investment adviser's trades are considered "first party" soft dollar services. Payments by an executing broker to a third party (sometimes called "third party" soft dollars) are also permitted under Section 28(e), for qualifying services, but only to the extent that the service is used for the benefit of the investment adviser's clients or customers. Investment advisers may contract with their broker-dealers to accumulate soft

[58] 15 U.S.C Section 78bb(e) (emphasis supplied).

[59] *Carolina Capital Markets, Inc.*, SEC No Action Letter (July 30, 2013)(SEC Staff blesses soft dollar arrangements for fixed income brokerage commissions). It bears mention that nonagency markups have not been approved by the SEC staff for soft dollar arrangements.

dollar credits for payment by the broker-dealer to any number of third parties providing research, trade ideas or other permitted services. Certain "mixed use" services, or services used in part to benefit the investment adviser and in part to benefit the clients or accounts, must be equitably allocated and supported by adequate records.[60] Investment adviser overheads (like rent or office space) may not be paid with soft dollars.[61] Of course, the investment advisers' soft dollar arrangements must also be disclosed to the clients in Form ADV as well as in relevant offering materials.

IV. CONCLUSION

In the absence of abundant SEC guidance with respect to standards for investment advisers' trading compliance, the compliance professional must remain flexible, creative, and close to his or her business. By considering the topics addressed in this chapter, compliance personnel may be able to enhance antifraud measures and better evidence compliance with fiduciary obligations regarding trading.

ABOUT THE AUTHOR

Matthew J. Fitzgerald is the CCO for PGIM Fixed Income, the public fixed income business unit of PGIM, Inc., a Prudential Financial, Inc. company. Mr. Fitzgerald has been a securities lawyer and compliance officer for more than 25 years, working with global banks, broker-dealers, funds, and investment advisers in both finance and asset management. He has extensive background in capital markets, derivative products and fund formation, including his time as a managing director at BlackRock and nine years of private legal practice. Mr. Fitzgerald began his career in futures and options trading. He has a bachelor's degree in psychology from Yale University and a juris doctor degree from The Emory University School of Law.

[60] *Commission Guidance Regarding Client Commission Practices Under Section 28(e) of the Securities Exchange Act of 1934*, SEC Release No. 34-52635 (Oct. 19, 2005).

[61] *Id.*

CHAPTER 18

Investment Advisers and the Best Execution Obligation

By Mederic ("Med") Daigneault
National Regulatory Services

> We expect that an adviser's policies and procedures, at a minimum, should address the following...to the extent that they are relevant to that adviser:...Trading practices, including procedures by which the adviser satisfies its best execution obligation....
>
> *Adopting Release, Compliance Programs Rule*

I. INTRODUCTION[1]

If one were to hire a personal shopper to update her wardrobe, and she had sufficient faith (or foolishness) to turn over a personal credit card for the undertaking, that client might expect that the new fashion consultant would take reasonable measures to avoid overpaying for the articles acquired on the client's behalf. A professional, the client might presume, would search for bargains, avoid excessive fees, and, of course, never run up costs by choosing to purchase the clothing at a higher-priced vendor simply to receive some personal benefit, such as "door-buster" prizes or frequent shopper rewards. In many ways, the concept as held by the Securities and Exchange Commission (SEC) of an adviser's best execution obligation is similar to this scenario. Much like a personal shopper can choose *both* a client's new duds *and* where to buy them, through a discretionary investment management agreement (or similar understanding), the adviser is typically granted *both* the authority to determine which securities or other investments to buy and sell on behalf of the client, *and* which broker dealer (or other counterparty) to use when entering those trades. The crucial difference, of course, is that a personal shopper is *not* a fiduciary and has no legal compulsion to put the client's interests ahead of the shopper's own.

For the adviser, this grant of discretionary authority comes with genuine responsibility: an obligation to thoughtfully select the broker dealer for any particular trade so that the client's total cost or proceeds in the transaction is the most favorable *under the circumstances.* Though referred to as "*best* execution," this standard does not oblige the

---

[1] This chapter was first published in Mr. Daigneault's book entitled *The Core: Practical Advisers Act Compliance for the Private Fund Adviser,* 2015.

adviser to obtain the lowest possible price when buying a security or the highest possible price when selling, nor does it require that the adviser obtain the lowest possible transaction costs. Instead, the best execution benchmark is a mix of both these quantitative factors and the qualitative factors that make a particular broker's services more valuable than another's, all else being equal, such as superior service, valuable research or insight, financial solvency, and discretion, among others. As articulated by the SEC:

> "As a fiduciary, a money manager has an obligation to obtain "best execution" of clients' transactions under the circumstances of the particular transaction. The money manager must:... *execute securities transactions for clients in such a manner that the client's total cost or proceeds in each transaction is the most favorable under the circumstances.* A money manager should consider the full range and quality of a broker's services in placing brokerage...."[2]

Best execution is a totality test.

II. PRACTICAL APPLICATION

When it comes to best execution, the SEC has merely articulated a broad concept, not a process. To apply this concept on a daily basis, an adviser must do more than simply recite the obligation in a written policy. The firm must know what it is looking for and then look for it. In other words, an adviser must define "best execution" in the context of its trading practices in discernible, measurable terms, and then periodically and systematically measure the brokerage services received on behalf of clients against these criteria.

As mentioned above, best execution includes a balance of both quantitative and qualitative factors. By definition, quantitative factors are readily calculated and compared, one against another. These include the price at which the security was bought or sold relative to the price received by others trading in the same security, as well as the commission and/or other transaction costs (or markups/markdowns) charged by the broker dealer for executing the trade.

Quantitative Factors

Price. Markets do not have unlimited liquidity. Should an adviser enter an order that is simply too large to promptly execute in full because adequate supply (for buys) or demand (for sales) simply isn't available, the broker will generally "work the trade" over time, buying or selling blocks of securities as they can. Done correctly, a skilled broker can often minimize the market impact of a large order without running up the price of the security on purchases or dropping it on sells. If a broker frequently executes the adviser's buy instructions well above, and sell instructions well below, that which it

---

2 *Interpretive Release Concerning the Scope of Section 28(e) of the Securities Exchange Act of 1934 and Related Matters*, Exchange Act Rel. No. 23170 (Apr. 23, 1986).

might have received, then the client's total cost or proceeds in transactions executed by that broker would clearly not be the most favorable under the circumstances. Strictly speaking, price can be a measure of a broker's skill and finesse.

In evaluating brokerage services, then, the adviser should periodically compare, on at least a sample basis, the execution prices received for trades executed by each broker against the price it might have received during roughly the same period. Of course, the obvious question is, how does a firm measure the price it *might* have received? To what can the firm compare the price received? How can an adviser know whether it could have done any better? For best execution purposes, there are two relatively common methodologies for measuring price: volume-weighted average price (VWAP) and opportunity cost surveys.

VWAP is calculated by dividing the dollar value of all transactions in a security over a particular period of time by the total volume (or total shares traded) for the period. In other words, VWAP provides the average price the firm would have received if it had participated in every transaction in the security over the measurement period by the same percentage that its trade made up of the total trade volume for the period. By comparing the execution price received by the firm against VWAP for the same period (which can be one or more days or part of a day), the adviser can evaluate how the trade ranks relative to the average.

Opportunity cost surveys or reviews are another means of measuring the price received against the price that might have been received had the adviser chosen another path. Opportunity cost represents the risk of delay between the time a trade decision is made and the broker's execution of that trade.[3] Opportunity cost surveys, then, measure the price the firm received relative to the price the firm would have received assuming that its trade could have been executed immediately and in its entirety—without market friction or liquidity problems, delays or transaction costs—once the decision to trade was made.

Although not used nearly as often by advisers to measure price for best execution purposes as VWAP is, opportunity cost reviews are typically a far better comparative measure of price for transactions placed in certain illiquid securities in which the adviser's trade or trades make up the majority of the trading volume in the security over the measured period. Under those circumstances, the price received by the adviser largely *is* the average and VWAP is meaningless.

Commissions. If seeking best execution meant seeking the lowest possible transaction costs, then clearly a broker charging two cents per share to execute a trade is preferred to a broker charging four cents per share to execute the same trade. Although transaction costs can hardly be evaluated apart from the level of service provided by the broker dealer or other counterparty, transaction costs, whether in the form of commissions,

---

[3] Jean-René Giraud, *Best Execution for Buy Side Firms: A Challenging Issue, a Promising Debate, a Regulatory Challenge* (June 2004), http://www.edhec-risk.com/features/Best%20Execution%20Survey/attachments/Best%20Execution%20-%20A%20challenging%20issue,%20a%20promising%20debate,%20a%20regulatory%20challenge.pdf

ticket charges, or other transaction fees or charges, should be isolated, considered, and compared when evaluating the execution received on behalf of clients, as applicable.

By systematically evaluating these criteria, the adviser is in a good position to begin comparing brokers and to plan future trading activity accordingly. And there are service providers that can provide this information to advisers for a fee. As mentioned above, however, these measures don't tell the whole story. Qualitative factors, although subjective and significantly harder to gauge than quantitative factors, are often of even greater import.

Qualitative Factors

Qualitative factors are service-related characteristics of the brokers selected to execute trades on behalf of clients, the relative value of which may be weighted differently by advisers depending upon the significance assigned to them. The appeal of these attributes will necessarily depend on the types of securities traded by the adviser, including the general liquidity of the markets in which the adviser trades, the scarcity of quality research, and the level of trading activity, among other things. The adviser must determine for itself which broker qualities are most critical, based on its investment strategies and trading patterns, and determine how it will assess these characteristics on a regular basis. Notwithstanding, there are certain common qualitative criteria critical to evaluating brokerage services that most advisers should consider, depending on its investment program and needs, including the broker's financial stability and reputation, confidentiality; willingness to commit capital; research; responsiveness; market reach; and knowledge or expertise in a particular industry, geography, or issuer.

Financial Stability. As a general rule, advisers should seek to place trades with brokerage firms that are financially sound and should refuse to place client assets at risk unnecessarily by trading through brokers with material, known (or knowable) financial difficulties or through foreign brokers that do not segregate customer assets from the assets of the broker. This is particularly important when entering into certain over-the-counter derivative contracts and assuming counterparty risk with respect to such a firm.

Confidentiality. As discussed above, a skilled broker can minimize the market impact of a large order without running up the price of the security on purchases or dropping it on sells. If the broker does not use discretion, however, or worse, broadcasts the order to the street, the price of the security can be run up or down, because other market participants are tipped off to the large order before the adviser's desired quantity can be bought or sold and the adviser's aim is thwarted.

Willingness to Commit Capital. Depending on the order, some brokers may be able to "create" liquidity for the adviser. If the adviser is selling a large position, for example, certain brokers, acting as principal rather than agent, may purchase the securities for their own accounts, thereby placing their own capital at the mercy of the market for the security and the corresponding fluctuations in its price.

Research and Expertise. Information is important, and well-timed insight imperative for many advisers. Sell-side analysts know this. They work diligently to gather intel, combing through company financials, announcements, and reports, and speaking with executives, customers, suppliers, competitors, and industry experts, all to provide the kind of insight that will entice investors, including advisers, to direct their trades to the broker's trade desk. And if the research is beneficial, why not? Though the commissions charged may be higher than those charged by others, the goodwill established by the order flow may result in additional, actionable information down the line.

Responsiveness. Truly superior execution often begins when the adviser reaches a representative on the phone rather than an answering machine; when the representative gets the order right the first time; and when, should a problem arise, the representative resolves it promptly and fairly. These traits should not be overlooked by the adviser when evaluating the quality of the execution received.

Market Reach: When it comes to quality of execution, a broker's expertise and ability to find and tap liquidity in the particular markets in which the adviser is trading cannot be underestimated.

III. A BROKER IS A BROKER, IS A BROKER...NOT

To a certain extent, where the adviser chooses to direct a transaction will turn on its needs for the particular trade or, in some cases, future anticipated needs, such as market access, research, and information. The adviser, therefore, may seek to link these needs with brokers best equipped to meet them. This correlation then will naturally depend on the category the broker falls into, such as "traditional," "execution only," or electronic communication networks ("ECNs").

Traditional brokers bundle trade execution capability with proprietary or third-party research and other valuable services into their commission charges or other trading costs. These costs tend to be significantly higher than execution-only brokers and ECNs. Traditional brokers may have substantial expertise with respect to particular companies, industries, markets, countries, or regions. They may also sponsor insightful conferences or set up meetings with issuer executives. Traditional brokers can execute trades on either an agency or principal basis, the latter sometimes requiring that they risk their firm's own capital in order to complete a trade.

Execution-only brokers, as the name suggests, do not typically provide research or ancillary services. Nor do these brokers typically trade on a principal basis for their own accounts. As a result, they cannot "create" liquidity for the adviser and must rely on natural market flow to fill adviser trades. Importantly, execution-only brokers will charge significantly lower commissions and transaction charges than traditional brokers in most cases. Consequently, as compared to traditional brokers, they are often the better choice for executing trades in highly liquid securities.

ECNs are electronic systems matching buyers and sellers of securities. Transacting through an ECN typically costs considerably less than ordering the same trade through a traditional or execution-only broker. However, ECNs are not active in all markets, and often there is insufficient liquidity for the adviser to fill orders for all securities through an ECN.

Of course, under certain circumstances, and in the best interests of clients, the adviser may also decide to internally cross transactions among two or more clients to eliminate trading costs. For example, when rebalancing the portfolios of two clients whose accounts are managed in parallel, as is often the case when accounts are managed per a model portfolio, the adviser may decide to "journal" certain trades among the accounts rather than going through a broker dealer, thereby eliminating commissions and other transaction costs. Under these circumstances, the adviser transfers cash from one account and securities from the other until the accounts are back in the proper balance. Although saving on transaction costs, internal cross trades can also give rise to certain regulatory concerns, including valuation issues and, when the client accounts include one or more private funds, the possibility that the cross trade may be regarded by regulators as a "principal transaction" requiring special notice and consent prior to settlement of the trade.[4]

IV. EVALUATING BROKERAGE—"WHO, WHEN, WHAT, AND HOW?"

To be clear, the adviser's obligation is not necessarily to *obtain* best execution, but to *seek* it. In practice, this means that SEC examiners typically don't find a firm deficient for failing to meet this standard from time to time if it has, nevertheless, faithfully reviewed and refined its processes, as disclosed. The reverse is also true.

Again, the SEC has not mandated any particular process for seeking best execution. As a result, firms have adopted many different methodologies, some effective, and some woefully unproductive exercises. (Of course, there are also those that neglect the responsibility altogether.) Set forth here is one means by which an adviser may evaluate brokerage executions. It is not, however, the only acceptable method of doing so.

Who

In general, responsibility for brokerage reviews should be clearly set forth in the firm's written procedures, along with the criteria that should be reviewed. In all but the smallest of firms, this responsibility should fall to a governing body, or "Best Execution Committee," composed of persons with worthwhile insight concerning the criteria to be reviewed. In determining which staff should participate on the committee, therefore, the adviser should consider the best execution criteria to be evaluated. Depending on the firm, the committee will typically include portfolio managers, the head trader, analysts, and the chief compliance officer (CCO), among others. Portfolio managers

---

4 *Gardner Russo & Gardner*, SEC Staff No-Action Letter (June 7, 2006).

and analysts will typically have the best read on the value of research received when seeking to develop investment theses or trading decisions, whereas the head trader will have the most valuable insight regarding each broker's market reach, confidentiality, willingness, and ability to commit capital and overall responsiveness. The CCO, among his or her other responsibilities, should seek to ensure that the criteria reviewed by the committee are, in fact, those set forth in the firm's best execution procedures and disclosed to clients in Form ADV, Part 2A at Item 12.

When

The Best Execution Committee should meet regularly to review the brokerage services received over the immediately preceding period. The regularity of these reviews will necessarily depend on the level of trading activity undertaken by the adviser, with more frequent reviews for firms with high-volume trading. In any event, reviews should be undertaken at least annually and, for many firms, at least quarterly.

What

In advance of each committee meeting, relevant information relating to the quantitative and qualitative factors selected by the firm should be gathered or prepared and provided to each member of the committee. These may include, for example:

- A random sampling of execution prices received as compared to VWAP, opportunity cost, or some other relevant measure for the same trading period;
- Commission reports showing the amount charged by each broker per security, as well as the total amount of commission dollars spent with each executing broker over the preceding period; and
- The firm's trade error log, as applicable.

To capture relevant qualitative contributions, many advisers will also create a spreadsheet listing each broker dealer through which trades were entered down the far left column, and each qualitative criterion to be assessed across the top row. The firm will then request that each portfolio manager, analyst, and trader assign each broker dealer a score of 1 to 10 for each measure listed. Naturally, there are many variations on this approach. Some advisers will assign a limited number of points to each person permitted to vote, for example, 50. Then they are permitted to vote their points however they wish. If a trader feels strongly about a particular broker, he or she can vote all 50s points on that one broker. Other advisers give greater deference to the input of certain individuals or groups within the firm. For example, an adviser that assigns a premium to research may give greater weight to the input of portfolio managers and analysts than to traders. Regardless of the approach taken, each has a similar aim: to make qualitative considerations quantifiable and susceptible to comparison.

Finally, the committee should also be mindful of conflicts of interest and consider whether trade order flow to any particular broker dealer is unexpected or suspicious.

To assist in this evaluation, the committee should consider personal or family relationships between staff and broker dealer representatives and review the firm's gifts and entertainment logs, as well as outside business activity and affiliations reports submitted by firm staff, among other considerations. (Conflicts of interest are discussed later.)

How

Based on its assessment of this information, the committee can compare and rate the services of each broker-dealer the adviser has done business with over the prior period and create, maintain, and suggest changes to an approved broker list, and/or the brokerage "budget." In addition to its review of brokerage, the committee should, from time to time, reexamine the firm's best execution policies, procedures, disclosures, and evaluation processes to determine whether these continue to be accurate and effective and whether they could be improved in any way.

The substance of each Best Execution Committee meeting should be documented through a written agenda and/or minutes, and this documentation should be retained along with all relevant reports prepared and reviewed as part of the evaluation. These records will be requested during the firm's next SEC examination and will be critical to demonstrating that the adviser has met its fiduciary obligations in this regard.

V. BEST EXECUTION AND FIXED INCOME SECURITIES

Although the best execution standard springs from fiduciary principles and therefore applies to an adviser's trading activity, regardless of the nature of the securities or other investments transacted on behalf of clients, it's plainly easier to apply when trading in equities than in fixed income instruments. Among other things, this situation is due to inherent differences in the way these securities are bought and sold. Moreover, due to the innumerable types of investment products that fall into the "fixed income" category and the amount and type of relevant information available, the same review criteria cannot be applied to an evaluation of trade executions in all such investments.

"Fixed income securities" refers to a wide variety of investment products that generally provide fixed, periodic payments over time and the return of principal upon maturity. These securities include, among many others, a broad assortment of bonds, notes, mortgage-backed securities, asset-backed securities, and collateralized debt obligations. For the sake of clarity and conciseness, the following discussion will focus primarily on the best execution complications and considerations of transacting in bonds.

Complications

In the first place, there are generally no commissions charged when a dealer buys or sells bonds. Instead, the dealer charges a markup or markdown (depending on whether it is buying or selling the bonds). Because this markup/markdown is incorporated into the price of the security, often in addition to other hidden costs borne by the client, it is generally difficult to discern the dealer's total compensation for the trade. Furthermore, fixed income securities are typically bought and sold from a dealer's own inventory, on a principal basis, rather than on a centralized exchange. Consequently, unlike the price of common stock traded over an exchange, the price of the same bond can vary significantly from dealer to dealer at any given time. The result: the fixed income "market" is decentralized and provides very little transparency on a pretrade basis.

"Pretrade transparency" refers to the pertinent information regarding the bond available prior to placing a trade, such as trade interest and dealer quotations. Many in the field maintain that access to relevant pretrade information can lower a client's overall transaction costs by increasing an adviser's bargaining power with the dealer. For example, a dealer may be less likely to hold to its price if the adviser recognizes that it would receive a much better price by taking its trade elsewhere. Of course, in lieu of pretrade transparency, a review of post-trade information regarding recent transactions in a particular bond or comparable bonds can also provide some leverage when negotiating with a dealer, even if it is somewhat less influential.

Depending on the security, advisers may be able to obtain some useful pretrade information, including publicly posted bid/ask spreads and indications of interest. Some insight might also be obtained through electronic services provided by Bloomberg, Reuters, TradeWeb, and MarketAxess, among others, though this information is provided for relatively few bonds—including bonds participating dealers would prefer to sell—and it is only relevant for a limited period of time.

Depending on the types of fixed income securities traded, then, firms are more often compelled to rely on post-trade data regarding the particular bond or comparable bonds to evaluate the quality of executions received. For example, the Financial Industry Regulatory Authority (FINRA) has established the Trade Reporting and Compliance Engine (TRACE) to gather and disseminate pricing and transaction information regarding certain corporate bonds, U.S. agency debentures, and asset-backed and mortgage-backed securities.[5] A similar system, the Electronic Municipal Market Access website (EMMA), established to increase transparency in the municipal securities market, was developed by the Municipal Securities Regulatory Board (MSRB).

Whereas TRACE and EMMA provide post-trade transparency with respect to some of the more frequently traded fixed income securities, traders in other fixed income products often must gather what information they can from their network of industry contacts or by deducing pricing information from macroeconomic data as it relates to the securities under consideration, such as interest rates, benchmark securities, credit ratings, and currency values. This information can be used to gauge, generally, at what the securities *should* be valued.

With these thoughts in mind, one might assume that shopping the trade among multiple dealers would provide the best chance of receiving the most favorable price. Yet

---

[5] TRACE rules require virtually all transaction information in TRACE-eligible securities to be reported by FINRA member dealers within minutes of the trade.

other practical realities can limit an adviser's ability to do so. For example, in the time it takes to obtain and compare quotes, the initial dealer's price may have changed. If it changes significantly, the adviser will have just lost out on an opportunity and increased its client's overall costs by trying to do the right thing. Furthermore, a fixed income security with the desired characteristics may be traded by only a single dealer, or no other dealer may have the ability to execute the trade in the sought-after size.

Considerations

All told, depending on the fixed income securities an adviser seeks to trade, the amount and type of relevant pricing information can vary greatly. This fact will have a huge impact on whether the firm relies primarily on pretrade evaluation processes made by the trader in seeking best execution, or post-trade reviews coupled with prospective determinations of where future order flow should be directed based on these reviews—or (more likely) both.

These and other considerations were deliberated in a cogent white paper released in 2008 by the Asset Management Group of the Securities Industry and Financial Markets Association (SIFMA) with input from SIFMA-member firms and outside legal counsel.[6] Following an explanation of the critical difficulties in seeking best execution in the context of fixed income trading, the white paper provides several guidelines to assist firms in developing processes to evaluate fixed income securities executions. In addition to many of the suggested practices discussed in this chapter, having applicability to both equities and fixed income securities, the white paper suggests the following, among others:

- Consider the types of fixed income products traded on behalf of clients and determine the most relevant information available for each type of security. With this information in hand, the adviser can determine its best execution review strategy—for each type of security, the extent to which it will rely on a pretrade evaluation of data and/or a post-trade review of transactions. Note that the guidelines do *not* suggest that one method should be used to the exclusion of the other;
- Leverage technology for monitoring and compliance when practical and consider these resources when developing a best execution review process. Some SIFMA-member firms had developed proprietary systems to gather information in otherwise nontransparent securities. Others rely on systems tapping into available data and adapted their best execution approach accordingly; and
- If, for transactions in any particular securities, the adviser will rely primarily on the trader's evaluation of pretrade information in deciding which dealer will provide best execution for the trade, the firm's policies and procedures should set forth the criteria that may be used when making that choice and, perhaps more importantly, those criteria that may not (e.g., those that give rise to conflicts of interests).

---

6 Securities Industry and Financial Markets Association, *SIGMA AMG White Paper: Best Execution Guidelines for Fixed-Income Securities* (Sept. 2008), http://www.sifma.org/issues/item.aspx?id=21333

It also is important to recognize that the regulatory obligations of fixed income dealers and the amount of transparency provided are evolving. In July 2012, for example, the SEC issued its *Report on the Municipal Securities Market*, which contained a number of recommendations for improving the municipal securities market, including steps to enhance pretrade and post-trade transparency and reinforce existing dealer obligations, possible legislative reforms, and voluntary actions of market participants, among others. In April 2013, the SEC hosted a roundtable on fixed income markets that sharpened several concepts for improving the transparency and efficiency of certain fixed income markets. And on December 5, 2014, the MSRB's first explicit best execution rule for transactions in municipal securities, MSRB Rule G-18, was approved by the SEC. FINRA Rule 2232, effective May 2018, and amendments made by the MSRB to Rule G-15, effective September 2017, both seek to enhance bond market price transparency (i.e., the dealer's markup/markdown) under certain circumstances. Advisers that regularly trade in fixed income securities for their clients should monitor these and related developments to determine how best to exploit any increase in available information and consider adapting its best execution approach accordingly.

VI. PRIVATE EQUITY AND REAL ESTATE FUNDS

Best execution guidance, such as it is, predates the requirement that most private equity and private real estate fund advisers register under the Investment Advisers Act of 1940 ("Advisers Act"). And at first blush, the standard seems to be entirely inapplicable to the business models of these advisers. After all, most private equity funds will typically trade the securities of private—not public—companies, including privately issued stock, limited partnership interests, limited liability company interests, or debt with attached warrants, preferred stock, or some other equity-like instruments, among other things. No broker needed. Often, these deals may be brought to the adviser's attention by, and are only available through, a particular investment bank or other intermediary acting as lead to an investment group. How could the adviser have any discretion or ability to apply best execution principles under these circumstances? Similarly, many private real estate funds may invest solely in real property...square footage, bricks, mortar...dirt. Others invest in mortgage notes, the private securities of real estate holding companies, property management companies, or developers, among other real estate-related investments. Surely, the concept of best execution does not—could not—apply to these business models. Could it?

It's true, both private equity and private real estate fund deals are often discreetly negotiated transactions that do not involve a broker dealer intermediary. Nevertheless, both can and do use their negotiation power to seek the most favorable terms reasonably available under the circumstances of a particular transaction, consistent with the adviser's fiduciary duty. In fact, often the adviser or its affiliated person acting as general partner to the fund has the discretionary authority to select numerous different professionals that will be involved in facilitating a deal, including, depending on the type of fund and the particular deal: attorneys, accountants, consultants, appraisers, real estate agents, and information technology and due diligence professionals, among others—just as an adviser trading in public securities has the discretion to select the broker dealer used to facilitate a trade. Therefore, even if advisers don't call it best execution, similar standards should apply to the firm's engagement of these professionals. For example, if the adviser will engage an affiliated entity, such as a parent company or subsidiary, to facilitate the transaction in one capacity or another, and the adviser or its related general partner will cause the fund to compensate that affiliate for these services, this creates an inherent conflict of interest that must be addressed through appropriate disclosure, policies, and procedures.

The best execution standard similarly has parallel significance under other common circumstances arising in the businesses of these advisers. For example, although private equity and private real estate fund advisers will generally make investments on behalf of their funds with capital raised solely from the funds' limited partners or investors, some may also finance these investments, partially and sometimes substantially, with debt obtained from a bank or other financial institution. Under these circumstances, the criteria used to select the financial institution to provide financing are analogous to those used to seek best execution when trading publicly traded securities, including the total costs and terms of the transaction (or financing) and the service level provided.

Moreover, some private equity fund advisers or their affiliates may be compensated a "transaction fee" payable by each portfolio company or the fund for its services in structuring and negotiating transactions and to cover expenses incurred in the acquisition or sale of portfolio companies as well as add-on and other investments made on behalf of the fund. Such fees are akin to commission costs charged by broker dealers, and engaging an affiliate under these circumstances creates an inherent conflict of interest requiring appropriate disclosure, policies, and procedures.

Based on careful assessment of its own business model and practices, private equity and private real estate fund advisers should consider adopting policies that set forth standards, comparable to best execution, by which it will select third parties, such as professionals, intermediaries, and banks, among others; and the procedures the firm will employ to ensure that these standards are met; and that pertinent conflicts of interest are fully disclosed to clients and investors in a timely and meaningful way.

Finally, it is important to recognize that for a private equity fund, exiting a position may sometimes involve taking a company public or disposing of securities acquired after exercising warrants or similar instruments after the company has been taken public. Under these circumstances, it will be incumbent upon the adviser to seek best execution when selecting a broker-dealer to execute the trade. The time to adopt a best execution policy and procedures is before such a circumstance arises.

VII. CONFLICTS OF INTEREST

Conflicts have tendrils reaching into all aspects of a firm's business. It is easy to understand why the topic has made the list of the SEC's National Examination Program (NEP) priorities in one form or another each year since the Office of Compliance Inspections and Examination (OCIE) began publishing the program's prime focus areas. As explained in the NEP's 2013 publication:

> Conflicts of interest, when not eliminated or properly mitigated and managed, are a leading indicator and cause of significant regulatory issues for individuals, firms, and sometimes the entire market. Over the past several years, the NEP has identified conflicts of interest as a key focus of its risk-based strategy, and an integral part of our assessment of which firms to examine, what issues to focus on, and how to examine those areas.[7]

When one discovers a conflict of interest, it is not uncommon to explain it away by saying, "Well, but everyone does that," as if that excuse would work any better with an SEC examiner than it does with a traffic cop.

In theory, all things being equal, the adviser should want to obtain the best possible execution for its trades. This is because obtaining the optimal balance of the best price, at the lowest transaction cost, while receiving the highest quality service under the circumstances, should improve performance—at least modestly— thereby increasing the adviser's overall compensation and making it easier to raise assets. However, advisers often receive benefits beyond execution services from broker dealers. For example, as already mentioned, certain brokers may provide valuable information or research. They may also refer potential new clients or investors for pooled investment vehicles managed by the adviser. Advisers may also have affiliated broker dealers. When an adviser must decide between executing a transaction with a broker with which the adviser has such an arrangement and one without, all things are clearly not equal. If the adviser can maintain a valuable referral arrangement with a broker, for example, by directing a certain level of trades or commission dollars to the broker, it might decide to do so even though the commission rates charged to its clients for those trades are higher than might be charged by another broker, or the overall quality of execution is poorer than might be attained elsewhere.

Perhaps surprisingly, the best execution obligation does not prohibit the adviser from obtaining a benefit from the executing broker that does not add any value to the particular transaction or the client for which it is entered, so long as the benefit is fully and fairly disclosed in advance. Undeniably, however, receiving a direct benefit from a broker that does (or seeks to do) business with the adviser can influence the adviser's decisions regarding with which broker dealer to enter a particular trade. It creates a conflict between the adviser's interest in receiving the perk and the client's interest in

---

7 Securities and Exchange Commission National Examination Program, *NEP's Examination Priorities for 2013*, p. 2.

receiving the most favorable trade execution under the circumstances. And, among the most common arrangements that can conflict with an adviser's obligation to seek best execution are those involving soft dollars.

Soft Dollars

No, the term does not speak to cuddly currency. Soft dollars are, essentially, credits earned from commissions paid to broker dealers. These credits can be used by an adviser to pay for research or other perks. For example, an execution-only broker may be willing to execute a particular trade at one cent per share. Another broker might execute the same trade at three cents per share, but it offers the adviser a credit of two cents per share that can be used to "purchase" research or other benefits prepared by the executing broker or a third party. Such arrangements may be treated like revolving credit lines whereby the broker may advance payment for research or other benefits in exchange for an explicit or implicit promise from the adviser that the broker will receive additional commission dollars in the future to reimburse it for the expense.

Strictly speaking, the adviser is the one who benefits from the research provided by brokers, even though the firm's clients are the ones who foot the bill. Sure, one could argue that clients are the ultimate beneficiaries, because the research empowers the adviser to make better investment decisions. But that is the adviser's job and responsibility in the first place. After all, that's why clients pay advisory fees. Moreover, in theory, the adviser could use the soft dollar credits earned from one client's commission dollars to benefit another client altogether. This would not be unusual when the adviser manages accounts pursuing different strategies. Under these circumstances, the adviser is not making its brokerage decisions strictly based on best execution principles or its client's best interests.

Notably, the SEC highlighted soft dollar usage by hedge fund advisers in particular (among other issues) as a perennial compliance risk and focus area for examiners during its 2014 National Compliance Outreach Seminar. And in its 2015 Examination Priorities, the SEC cautioned that staff will scrutinize and evaluate whether firms prioritize trading venues based on payments or credits for order flow in contradiction of their best execution duties.

Without some specific regulatory license, soft dollar practices would leave firms vulnerable to a charge of breach of their fiduciary duty...or worse.

Fortunately, the Securities Exchange Act of 1934 offers a lifeline, a "safe harbor," in Section 28(e). Any investment adviser that meets the requirements of this safe harbor is protected from liability for breaching its fiduciary duty under state and federal securities laws, including Section 206 of the Advisers Act, for causing its clients to pay more than the lowest possible commission rates to a broker dealer for "*effecting* a trade" so long as the adviser determines "in good faith" that the commissions paid were "reasonable in relation to the value of the *brokerage* and *research* services *provided by* such...broker or dealer" (emphasis added). The safe harbor also provides protection from liability for using soft dollar credits earned from one client's trades to benefit another client. Through several interpretive releases issued by the SEC over many years, the commission has clarified and reclarified its interpretation of the applicability of 28(e) culminating with the 2006, *Commission Guidance Regarding Client Commission Practices Under Section 28(e) of the Securities Exchange Act of 1934.*

Under this guidance, in order to rely on the safe harbor provided by 28(e), the adviser must meet each element of a three-step test:

1. The product or service received from the broker must be "research" or "brokerage," as defined;
2. The product or service must actually provide lawful and appropriate assistance in the performance of the adviser's investment decision-making activities; and
3. The adviser must make a good faith determination that the amount of the client commissions paid is reasonable in light of the value of products or services provided.

No SEC examiner will accept an adviser's claim of reliance on the safe harbor if it fails to establish each of the law's requirements. All three points must be met.

Safe Harbor Step One: "Research" and "Brokerage"

The first step requires that the adviser determine whether the product or service provided in exchange for client commissions falls within specific statutory parameters, that is, it is eligible research or brokerage.

1.A. Research. The criteria provided in the statute define research as advice, analyses, and reports pertaining to specified subject matter that may plausibly enlighten the adviser with respect to its investment decision-making process. With respect to "advice," the safe harbor requires that the research relate to:

- The value of securities;
- The advisability of investing in, purchasing, or selling securities; or
- The availability of securities or purchasers or sellers of securities.

Critically, the form the advice takes is irrelevant to the inquiry. It may be provided in hard copy or electronic format—even verbally as a "hot tip" offered to the adviser's analyst over the phone (as long as the tip does not convey, and was not otherwise formulated on the basis of, material nonpublic information, of course).

In order for analyses or reports to be eligible research under the safe harbor, they must concern:

- Issuers;
- Industries;
- Securities;
- Economic factors and trends;
- Portfolio strategy; and
- The performance of accounts.

1.A.1. Reasoning or Knowledge. The common element of the research subject-matter requirements, regardless of the form the research takes, is that it reflects substantive content, an expression of reasoning or knowledge. For example, meetings with corporate executives for the purpose of receiving a verbal account of the performance of a company would constitute eligible research, because such reports impart knowledge regarding an issuer. A seminar or conference relating advice or analysis as to the advisability of investing in securities or pertaining to economic trends, for example, would also be eligible research under the statute, though a conference pertaining to the adviser's compliance with Advisers Act requirements would not. Of course, even with respect to an eligible conference or seminar, only the conference or seminar expense is entitled to protection, not the travel expenses, meals, or lodging costs incurred by the adviser's staff in order to attend. Similarly, software that provides analyses of securities portfolios is eligible as an expression of reasoning or knowledge.

1.A.2. Mass-Marketed Publications Ineligible. Although they may also include an expression of reasoning and knowledge from time to time relating to the subject matter of Section 28(e)(3)(A) and (B), mass-marketed publications are not eligible for safe harbor protection and should be differentiated from research. Mass-marketed publications consist of periodicals intended for and marketed to a broad, public audience and generally have a low cost. As the name suggests, when one seeks to categorize a publication, the assessment should focus on how it is marketed, not the means of its distribution. Trade magazines and technical journals concerning specific industries, for example, may be eligible if intended to serve the interests of a narrow readership rather than the public at large, even if available via the internet. By definition, mass-marketed publications are not intended to cater to a small, specialized readership.

1.A.3. Inherent Tangibility. Unlike products or services that reflect the expression of reasoning or knowledge, tangible items, including those with innately physical characteristics, are not eligible as "research" under the safe harbor. These include, among others, office equipment, furniture, business supplies, and computer hardware and accessories, as well as basic overhead expenses such as salaries (including those of analysts conducting research on behalf of the adviser), rent, legal fees, accounting fees, and accounting software. Inherently tangible items are not eligible as research services because they do not reflect substantive content, reasoning, or knowledge.

1.A.4. Third Party Research and Commission Sharing. Section 28(e)(1) provides in relevant part that:

> [N]o person...shall be deemed to have acted unlawfully or to have breached a fiduciary duty under state or federal law,...solely by reason of his having caused (an) account to pay a broker...an amount of commission for *effecting* a securities transaction in excess of the amount of commission another...broker...would have charged for effecting that transaction, if such person determined in good faith that such amount of commission was reasonable in relation to the value of the brokerage and research services *provided by* such...broker... (emphasis added).

On its face, the text clearly seems to restrict eligibility under the statute to the receipt of proprietary research of the broker-dealer executing the trade. What else could "provided by" and "effecting" the transaction mean?

But what about third-party research? It does seem that allowing an adviser to select the broker most likely to provide the best possible execution for a trade, while remaining free to seek the most insightful research from whatever source, would be in the best interests of clients. Could the law really be written to disallow such an approach?

The rationale for the statutory language linking research "provided" to the broker dealer "effecting" the trade as it does, is rooted in a congressional intent to eliminate the custom of "give-ups." Give-ups were a common practice before adoption of the safe harbor in which a portion of the standard commission paid to one broker for executing a trade was required to be "given up" to another broker by the executing adviser. Often these outlays were paid by the executing broker to another broker having no role in the trade for which the commission was paid. Instead it was offered in exchange for having provided some benefit *to the adviser*, such as client or investor referrals.

Having considered this history and congressional concern in the context of arrangements common in "modern day" 2006, the SEC distinguished the functional allocation between providers of brokerage and research from the practice of give-ups. The SEC reasoned that "provided by" as used in the statute does not mean that the research was necessarily *prepared by* the broker "effecting" the trade, if the broker-dealer effecting the trade was *legally obligated to pay* for the research, whether by contract or otherwise. Alternatively, the safe harbor is also available when the broker dealer effecting the trade is not legally obligated to pay for the research but instead *pays* the preparer of the research directly, takes steps to assure itself that the client commissions are used only to pay for *eligible* research, and develops and maintains procedures so that research payments are documented and paid for promptly.

This construal, then, would permit brokers effecting transactions to provide advisers with access to research prepared by others and to pay for that research using commission dollars paid by the adviser's clients. It does not necessarily address how two brokers might share commissions when one facilitates the execution of the trade and the other facilitates access to research. For example, in some arrangements, one broker may execute trades and provide research while another sharing in the commission clears and settles the trade. In other arrangements, an introducing broker may enable access to research but have no role in effecting the trade. Clearly, a broker-dealer "effects" a trade under the safe harbor if it executes, settles, or clears the trade. However, the SEC has clarified that a broker also "effects" a trade within the meaning of the safe harbor—and therefore could share commissions with another broker—if it performs any one of four functions, including:

- Taking financial responsibility for customer trades until the clearing broker dealer has received payment or securities (i.e., one of the broker dealers must be at risk for the customer's failure to pay);

- Making and/or maintaining records relating to customer trades required by the commission or SRO rules, including blotters and memoranda of orders;
- Monitoring and responding to customer comments concerning the trading process; and
- Generally monitoring trades and settlements.

1.B. Brokerage. A securities transaction is a process. Each trade has a definite beginning and an end. The trick is defining those boundaries. Section 28(e)(3)(C) affirms that a person "provides brokerage…services" insofar as he or she "effects securities transactions and performs functions incidental thereto (such as clearance, settlement, and custody) or required in connection therewith by rules of the SEC or a self-regulatory organization of which such person is a member or person associated with a member or in which such person is a participant." The SEC has dubbed the chronological characteristic of the trading process the "temporal standard" and concluded that effecting a securities transaction begins when the order is transmitted to the broker and ends when it is cleared and settled.

Although broker-dealers provide advisers with many services and benefits beyond the execution of securities transactions, for purposes of the safe harbor, only brokerage services that relate to the execution of securities transactions qualify for protection. The temporal standard is a tool to distinguish among eligible and ineligible brokerage services. And yet the plain wording of the statute indicates that eligible brokerage includes not only those actions necessary to effect a securities transaction but also functions incidental to the process. Explicitly included in this category are clearance, settlement, and custody. The SEC also interprets certain post-trade actions to be incidental to the execution of securities transactions and, therefore, eligible brokerage, including:

- Post-trade matching of transaction information;
- Electronic communication of allocation instructions between institutions and broker dealers;
- The exchange of other messages among brokers, custodians, and institutions related to the trade; and
- Routing of settlement instructions.

With respect to the reference to "custody" in the statute, only short-term custody as it relates to effecting, clearing, and settling the particular transaction is entitled to protection.

Perhaps paradoxically, communication products or services related (or incidental) to execution, clearance, and settlement, including dedicated lines between the broker and the adviser's OMS and trading software used to route orders (including algorithmic trading strategies software), *are* eligible as "brokerage" under the temporal standard. However, advisers should clearly distinguish these from ineligible hardware, such as telephones and computer terminals (including those used in connection with OMS and trading software). Nor does software used for recordkeeping or administrative purposes, such as managing portfolios or quantitative analytical software used to test hypothetical scenarios, fit the bill. These are unequivocally "overhead" of the adviser.

Safe Harbor Step Two: Lawful and Appropriate Assistance

If an adviser determines that a product or service received from a broker-dealer constitutes "brokerage" or services incidental to the execution of securities transactions under the statute, the inquiry generally ends there. If the adviser seeking to rely on the safe harbor determines that the benefit received qualifies as "research," however, it must take the additional step of inquiring whether the research provides lawful and appropriate assistance to the adviser with respect to its investment decision making. The key to this assessment is ascertaining how the adviser uses the eligible research. For example, an adviser might seek to use client commissions to pay for analysis of account performance. Analysis of account performance could constitute eligible research under the safe harbor as it reflects an expression of reasoning or knowledge regarding subject matter included in Section 28(e)(3)(B). However, if the adviser will use the analysis for the purpose of marketing its services, or the interests of a fund managed by the adviser, then the fact that it may qualify as eligible "research" under the statute is inconsequential. Its use will not qualify for protection under the safe harbor. When used in connection with the adviser's marketing efforts, the research manifestly, does not provide lawful and appropriate assistance with respect to the firm's *investment decision-making responsibilities*.

2.A. Mixed-Use. Then again, this analysis is not an all-or-nothing proposition. Some products or services hold both eligible and ineligible uses. A proxy voting service, for example, might receive proxy ballots on behalf of an investment adviser, vote, and submit those ballots to the issuer, then provide reporting regarding votes cast. These services are plainly not "research" under the safe harbor because they do not involve an expression of reasoning or knowledge related to any of the topics listed at Section 28(e)(3)(A) or (B), nor is it likely that it could provide lawful and appropriate assistance in the adviser's investment decision-making responsibilities. And yet a proxy voting service may also provide information and analysis regarding issuers that the adviser could use to determine the prudence of retaining a position in a security or of adding to or trimming that position. That portion of the service should be eligible under the safe harbor, not merely because it qualifies as research but also because it is used in a manner that provides lawful and appropriate assistance with respect to the adviser's investment decision making.

The same product or service can therefore serve dual purposes, even several purposes, some of which are eligible under the safe harbor and therefore may be paid for with client commissions (i.e., soft dollars) and others are ineligible, and therefore a firm expense (i.e., hard dollars). These are referred to as "mixed-use" products or services, and an adviser is required to make a good faith allocation of the cost of the product or service per its use.

This situation gives rise to yet another conflict for the adviser. Why? Because the more of the cost of a product or service the adviser allocates to eligible uses, the further it can reduce its out-of-pocket expenses. Recognizing this inherent conflict, the SEC has emphasized that an adviser must keep adequate records concerning its mixed-use allocations to be able to make a good faith showing of its determination of the soft dollar cost for any mixed-use product or service. It is also important to note that advisers using client commissions to pay for products or services with mixed uses must plainly disclose the inherent conflict of interest related to making allocations among hard and soft dollars.

Safe Harbor Step Three: Reasonableness

The final step requires that the adviser make a good faith and *documented* determination that the amount of client commissions paid is reasonable in light of the value of products or services provided by the broker dealer. The burden of proving reasonableness lies with the adviser. Thus, the opening *assumption*, for all intents and purposes, is that *the adviser has overpaid* using client commissions and must stand ready to establish otherwise.

Accordingly, to evaluate the appropriateness of the amount paid, the adviser must ascertain or estimate the value of research or brokerage services received. Of course, in the "real world," the value of research is determined by what one will pay for it, right? Well...yes and no. Yes, if paying with one's own money. If, however, Adviser A were purchasing research (or any other thing for that matter) using *Client B's* money, and that client had little or no way to monitor what the adviser was buying or whether it was worth what Client B was paying, the adviser might be less concerned with the cost.

From time to time, an officer at a firm receiving third party research on a soft dollar basis may explain that because the research provider issued an invoice, the amount of the invoice must be what the research is worth and no review is necessary. Although avoiding the review process is not lacking in appeal, this rationale misses the point. If the adviser claims reliance on the safe harbor but has failed to make any effort at an independent assessment of the value of the product or service received—whether in terms of the potential return for clients, avoidance of losses or otherwise—the "good faith" standard will not have been met. The adviser must, at minimum, review the invoices received and document whether the cost appears exorbitant. Without appropriate, documented review, the adviser will be unable to meet its burden of proof. And the invoice alone is insufficient.

Advisers receiving proprietary research from an executing broker (and therefore, no separate invoice for the research is provided), should ask the broker to provide its unbundled price for the same research when offered to others.

Documentation is particularly critical for any adviser that receives both eligible research and other, ineligible benefits from a broker, such as shelf space or investor or client referrals. (Note that this scenario is distinct from one in which the adviser receives a product or service having both eligible and ineligible uses.) Should such an adviser fail to record its conclusion that the amount of commission dollars paid was reasonable in light of the value of the research received, an SEC examiner may assume that the adviser overpaid to retain the benefit.

Important Limits and Considerations

Note that advisers may *not* rely on the safe harbor for brokerage or research services that are paid for with commissions earned on trades placed in client accounts managed on a nondiscretionary basis. Nor is it available when clients have directed the use of a particular broker. In the 2001 release interpreting 28(e), the SEC also explained that fees charged on principal trades were not quantifiable or fully disclosed in a manner that would permit an adviser to evaluate their reasonableness in relation to the value of brokerage or research services received. As a result, an adviser may not rely on the safe harbor in connection with trades in fixed income securities that are not executed on an agency basis, though the SEC was later persuaded by NASDAQ to allow certain "riskless principal transactions" that are reported and confirmed under NASD rules.

Finally, should an adviser, through its action or inaction, make a trade error, correction of that error is entirely the responsibility of the adviser. In an open letter to Charles Lerner, then director of enforcement, Department of Labor, dated October 25, 1988, the SEC stated:

> The division believes that an investment manager has an obligation to place orders correctly for its advised and nonadvised accounts. Accordingly, if an investment manager makes an error while placing a trade for an account, then the investment manager, in order to comply with its obligation to the customer, must bear any costs of correcting such trade. Because an investment manager itself is responsible for any losses resulting from an inaccurate or erroneous order placed for an advised account, a broker provides no value to that advised account by offsetting the trade and carrying the loss. Instead, this conduct solely benefits the investment manager.

Soft dollars may not be used to pay for the adviser's trade errors.

Disclosure

As a fiduciary, an investment adviser is required to mitigate conflicts of interest through full and fair disclosure so that the client or investor can make up his or her own mind and protect his or her own interests. In addition, the adviser must adopt written policies and procedures reasonably designed to address the conflict and ensure that the client's interests are placed ahead of the adviser's. Not surprisingly, then, Section 28(e)(2) obliges any person exercising investment discretion with respect to an account to "make such disclosure of his policies and practices with respect to commissions that will be paid for effecting securities transactions, at such times and in such manner, as the appropriate regulatory agency, by rule, may prescribe as necessary or appropriate in the public interest or for the protection of investors." Although not a rule per se, the instructions to Form ADV, Part 2, require that advisers disclose, at Item 12, the factors considered by the adviser when selecting or recommending broker dealers and for determining the reasonableness of their compensation. Regarding research and soft dollar benefits, in particular, the instructions provide, in part:

> If you receive research or other products or services other than execution from a broker dealer or a third-party in connection with client securities transactions ("soft dollar benefits"), disclose your practices and discuss the conflicts of interest they create...
>
> a. Explain that when you use client brokerage commissions (or markups or markdowns) to obtain research or other products or services, you receive a benefit because you do not have to produce or pay for the research, products, or services.
> b. Disclose that you may have an incentive to select or recommend a broker-dealer based on your interest in receiving the research or other products or services, rather than on your clients' interest in receiving most favorable execution.
> c. If you may cause clients to pay commissions (or markups or markdowns) higher than those charged by other broker dealers in return for soft dollar benefits (known as paying-up), disclose this fact.
> d. Disclose whether you use soft dollar benefits to service all of your clients' accounts or only those that paid for the benefits. Disclose whether you seek to allocate soft dollar benefits to client accounts proportionately to the soft dollar credits the accounts generate.
> e. Describe the types of products and services you or any of your related persons acquired with client brokerage commissions (or markups or markdowns) within your last fiscal year...
> f. Explain the procedures you used during your last fiscal year to direct client transactions to a particular broker dealer in return for soft dollar benefits you received.

Although these instructions are quite thorough, advisers should also be sure to include, as applicable, disclosure regarding the incentive created by soft dollar arrangements to unnecessarily and excessively trade client accounts merely to generate soft dollar credits that can be used to benefit the adviser. Also, as discussed above, for advisers receiving mixed use items, further disclosure regarding the inherent conflict of interest when making an allocation among hard- and soft-dollar-eligible uses of such products or services should also be explained.

Naturally, advisers must carefully assess their own circumstances to determine what other disclosures may be required to satisfy their fiduciary obligations. On a recent visit to a foreign, SEC-registered adviser to assist with the firm's annual review, for example, a consultant learned that the firm had been engaged by two large clients to manage separate accounts in parallel with a private fund also managed by the adviser. As the review progressed, the consultant discovered that each of these separate account clients had prohibited the firm—by contract—from earning soft dollar credits in trades placed in their accounts. Yet these clients received the benefit of research paid for by the fund without having shouldered their fair share of the costs, thereby creating a conflict among these clients and the fund—a conflict that should have been but never was disclosed to investors or prospective investors in the private fund.

To be clear, if an adviser prefers to live life on the edge, it *can* enter into soft dollar arrangements that fall beyond the bright line and relative safety of Section 28(e). Although cautioning advisers to be specific enough in their disclosure to ensure that clients understand the types of products or services received using soft dollars so that clients can fully evaluate possible conflicts, the instructions to Form ADV, Part 2, further require that the description of products and services received by the adviser:

> Must be more detailed for products or services that do not qualify for the safe harbor in Section 28(e) of the Securities Exchange Act of 1934, such as those services that do not aid in investment decision-making or trade execution. Merely disclosing that you obtain various research reports and products is not specific enough (emphasis added).

Of course, detailed disclosures regarding outlandish soft dollar practices engaged in by some firms are rarely provided in the adviser's Form ADV or elsewhere, thereby compounding the charges against them when these practices are uncovered by the SEC. For example, in an action brought in 2013 against a hedge fund manager and its founder and president for soft dollar abuses, among other things, the SEC specifically cited the firm for *failing to disclose* that client commissions would be used to pay "grossly inflated" rent to a company owned by the adviser's president, and for his divorce settlement and personal timeshare in New York![8]

Other Interests That Conflict with Best Execution Obligation

When an adviser formulates a process for seeking best execution, including a determination of evaluation criteria, how those criteria will be evaluated and how often, the adviser must seek to identify and eliminate, or mitigate and disclose, conflicts of interests that may interfere with this obligation. In addition to soft dollar arrangements, common conflicts that may interfere with an adviser's fiduciary duty to seek best execution include, among others:

- Using a related broker to execute advisory client trades, or executing trades on behalf of advisory clients as a dually registered entity and receiving both advisory fees and brokerage commissions;
- Formal or informal client or investor referral arrangements with a broker dealer;
- The receipt of gifts or entertainment from broker dealers,
- Portfolio managers or traders with a personal or family connection to a broker dealer representative,

---

8 *In the Matter of J.S. Oliver Capital Management, L.P. and Ian O. Mausner,* Investment Advisers Act Rel. No. 4431 (June 17, 2016).

- Principals, portfolio managers or traders, who frequently trade their personal accounts, seeking to lower their personal brokerage costs by promising to direct the adviser's client order flow to the broker, and;
- The practice of engaging in cross trades, agency cross trades or principal transactions.

Importantly, conflicts identified should be periodically (at least annually) reevaluated by the firm's best execution committee, conflicts committee or another designated governing body or person to determine whether, over time, relevant circumstances have changed and whether, as a result, controls established to address the conflict continue to be sufficient and the firm's disclosures continue to be accurate and adequate.

VIII. CONCLUSION

Consider the following tale: Lost in thought on a drive to work, a young woman realized, too late, that she was speeding—shaken from her reverie by flashing red and blue lights. When the officer told her how fast she was going, she was incredulous. She decided to contest the fine. Arriving at the courthouse weeks later, the woman was informed that she would have to wait to present her case. She quietly slipped into the back of the courtroom to observe the proceedings until called.

On the bench sat an elderly judge who had clearly presided over too many disputed traffic violations. He was irritable and bored. (This was not looking good for the young woman.) Before him paced a former state trooper who had found himself on the other end of the citation pad. He was questioning on the stand the issuing officer, who, contrary to custom, had actually shown up to the courthouse that morning to testify. The cited former trooper was prattling on about the unreliability of radar technology and denying that he had been traveling as fast as the citing officer claimed.

The judge had heard enough. He had a full docket. Lifting his sagging mug out of his hands, he asked, "If you please, just tell the court how fast *were* you going?"

"Well, I'm not exactly sure, your honor, maybe 55, 57, miles per hour," came the reply.

"Maybe?" the judge countered, sitting up a bit straighter now and reaching for his gavel. "Did you look at your speedometer?"

"Well, no, but..." the former trooper began but was promptly interrupted by a "WHACK!" as the judge brought down the gavel.

"Guilty! Pay the fine. Next case."

The lesson for every investment adviser that must one day demonstrate to an SEC examiner that it has sought to meet its best execution obligation is this: if the firm didn't look, it won't have a leg to stand on. Simply relying on the size, stature, and name recognition of the broker-dealers commonly used to execute client trades won't carry the day. Instead, the adviser must periodically and systematically *evaluate* the brokerage received on behalf of clients, based on relevant criteria, and identify and address conflicts of interest that may interfere with its fiduciary obligation to seek best execution.

ABOUT THE AUTHOR

Mederic ("Med") Daigneault is the director of consulting operations and senior director of private fund services at National Regulatory Services (NRS). He works closely with compliance officers to identify their firms' regulatory obligations, conflicts of interest, and other risks in the development and implementation of comprehensive compliance programs. Mr. Daigneault practiced law as a corporate and securities lawyer before joining NRS in 2004.

During the last decade and a half, he has aided hundreds of investment advisers to understand and meet their regulatory obligations. He is a frequent speaker at industry conferences and topical seminars sponsored by a wide variety of financial industry associations, vendors, and regulators. He has contributed to and has been sought for comment by leading industry publications regarding complex compliance issues.

Chapter 19

Sound Practice Guidelines for Quantitative Investment Managers

By The Writing Committee of the Chicago Quantitative Alliance

I. INTRODUCTION[1]

Quantitative investing dates as far back as the first hedge fund founded by Alfred Winslow Jones in 1949. Today, quantitative investing and "quants" are mainstream, and quant products may be found among the investments of major pension plans, foundations, endowments, family offices, fund of funds, and institutional investors. Quants grew quickly because of their sharply lower cost of computing, and the proliferation of electronic databases, and superior investment performance (Ruhl and Timig, 2011). Quants also could offer lower fees than fundamental approaches, offer less risk relative to benchmarks and be less dependent on a handful of star portfolio managers.

However, with growth in assets and longer exposures to varying market conditions, problems arose. In August 2007, some equity quant portfolios suffered highly unusual sharp losses for a few days, followed a few days later by equally sharp gains (Lo and Khandani, 2008). This "quant meltdown" did not seem to affect the broad market or more fundamentally managed portfolios. Both quants and their clients were surprised by this event, because it seemed to imply that there was some sort of previously unknown common risk factor that ran through diverse equity quantitative strategies.

Then, during the financial crisis and its aftermath, some quant processes (along with many fundamental portfolios) performed significantly worse than their long-term track records. Some firms faced major client losses and upheaval as a result. Later, the May 6, 2010, "flash crash" intensified concerns about computer-driven investing and trading. Afterward, in February of 2011, one of the titans of quantitative investing and research

[1] This chapter was created by a writing committee developed by the Chicago Quantitative Alliance (CQA). It has been designed as a work-in-progress. It is being made available to allow all interested parties to provide ideas, criticisms, and feedback or otherwise engage with the working group and to further develop the ideas contained herein. It should not be taken as representative of an industry consensus, the opinion of the CQA members or individual members of the writing committee on the covered topics, as particular guidelines may be added, removed, strengthened, softened, or otherwise modified in the future. It should not, in its current form, be used by any party as basis for any production development, be it internal, regulatory, due diligence, legal, or in any other capacity that may have actual material consequences, and neither the CQA nor the writing committee bear any responsibility for such use.

and his firm were hit with significant fines and penalties for allegedly mishandling a material coding error in a quantitative model (CQA, Rel. 33-9181).

Substantial focus has been placed on warning signs and protective procedures and ways to rectify errors through thorough and timely monitoring. A groundbreaking 2012 conference organized in New York by the Society of Quantitative Analysts (SQA) brought regulators and quants together to discuss quant investing. Afterward, the board of directors and many of the members of CQA concluded that CQA, in its role as a global, not-for-profit professional organization dedicated to the needs of quants, was ideally suited to draft a sound practices document for quant investing. Founded in Chicago in 1993, CQA has more than 500 members across the United States, Europe, and Asia. CQA and other quant organizations like SQA and the Q-Group, among others, have small, part-time staffs, mostly depending on volunteers for their activities.

Although the increased spotlight on quant investing initially motivated this effort, the drafting group and commenters quickly evolved to focus on a broader set of questions:

- How can we make quantitative investing better?
- How can we increase public trust and understanding of our efforts? How can we ensure that we are always deserving of that trust?
- How can we continue the innovation that has long been part of quant, while fostering new entrants with new ideas, ensuring that innovation truly serves the needs of clients and the efficiency and fairness of financial markets?

"Sound practice" documents have been published to help investors select and monitor numerous types and aspects of traditional and alternative investing, including topics such as equities, fixed income, private equity, due diligence, risk management, valuation, operational risk, and liquidity, to name a few. This chapter is CQA's response to the questions above and supplements existing ones by focusing on aspects that particularly concern quantitative investment managers.

The nature of quantitative investing encompasses a broad group of financial market participants and creates a diverse audience for this chapter. Therefore, the most difficult task was to define the scope and framework. The next section defines some of the principles that guided this approach realizing that "one size does not fit all."

II. METHODOLOGY AND GUIDING PRINCIPLES

This covers a broad spectrum of topics and stakeholders, applying the following guidelines:

- Uses a "principles-based" approach, and avoid being "prescriptive," without being too generic. To balance these competing requirements, this generally:
  - Introduced each section with fairly high-level principles that are likely to apply to all firms,

  - Provides appropriate caveats where we believe that more concrete guidelines would be useful to a substantial majority of our audience, and
  - Provides examples how the principles could be adapted to different situations;
- Avoids opining on particular strategies, techniques, algorithms, risk methodologies, or any other "investment" decision, and focus on sound business principles;
- Considers that different types and sizes of quantitative firms face different issues, require different types of approaches and controls, and provide differing recommendations;
- Builds and focuses on quant-specific issues while acknowledging existing "sound practices" documents and regulatory guidance; and
- Understands that the term "sound practices" can be ambiguous and where possible
  - Provide a common language and bridge cultural differences that often exists between quants and nonquants, and
  - Improve processes and communications with clients, investors, regulators, service providers, and other stakeholders.

The aim is not to provide a "checklist" for passing regulatory audits, but assume that the good-faith adoption of these principles, combined with appropriate levels of transparency and documentation, will generally satisfy the requirement to have "reasonable controls in place to prevent breaches of fiduciary duty."

III. SCOPE AND AUDIENCE

While avoiding defining the term "quantitative," the chapter nonetheless needs to specify its target audience.

Target Firms

The committee decided to focus on "quantitative investment managers"—that is, those firms that use quantitative models to manage capital for investors, have a "fiduciary duty" toward such investors, carry investment risk at least overnight, and, if registered, are subject to the Investment Company Act of 1940 ("1940 Act"). Excluded from the definition are "trading firms," most notably high-frequency trading (HFT) firms, whose primary business model involves rapid trading, generating returns from short, small market moves, and holding very limited net positions, capital, and principal risk at any given time, and none overnight.

In making these choices:

- The distinction is arbitrary with plenty of examples of firms that fall in-between those categories;
- Both groups fully qualify as "quantitative"; and
- The majority of recommendations outlined herein are applicable to both groups.

Nevertheless, the committee felt that some narrowing of the scope was warranted and that the large number of caveats present throughout the chapter to account for the diversity of the firms would be unmanageable without this distinction.

Other Target Audiences

In addition to the managers, this chapter should be useful to other groups such as regulators, investors, auditors (external/internal), compliance and risk officers, fund boards of directors, and service providers.

IV. STRUCTURE OF THE CHAPTER

The chapter is composed of three primary sections, which deal with risk management, compliance, and governance. The division is more along primary responsibility lines:

- Guidelines in the risk management section are primarily for quants, business users (traders, portfolio managers, etc.), risk managers, board of directors risk committees and/or auditors (where such functions exist in a standalone fashion);
- Topics in the compliance section primarily for compliance and legal personnel; and
- Governance issues mostly concerning senior management and board of directors.

V. RISK MANAGEMENT

This section is quant-specific, and in particular, relates to issues around model risk, validation, and testing.

Strategy Context

The committee's recommendations will vary due to the diversity of quant strategies. The spectrum of quantitative managers ranges from the "pure quant" strategies, where human judgment goes into design of models, calibration, and setting of parameters, however, the production "model" operates (and often executes trades) with little or no human intervention. At the other end of the spectrum is "traditional" investors, who use, among other tools, quantitative models (such as stock screens or pricing calculators), but are free to use or disregard any results from such models.

The majority of quantitative investors fall somewhere in-between the "pure quant" and "traditional" types, where investment activity is primarily determined by model outputs, but also subject to some degree of validation or oversight by investment professionals (generically referred to as "portfolio managers"). These investment processes are not strictly tied to any underlying investment strategy, whether it is an active program trading or "fundamental quant."[2]

---

[2] This categorization of different approaches to quantitative investments is similar to the more carefully laid out hierarchy in Darnell, 2007.

The following sections reflect this middle-ground approach to some extent and follow the "model creation" ⟶ "model usage" ⟶ "investment action" sequence.

1. The first discussion on model development and lifecycle management focuses on issues around research, model development and implementation, and the management of model risk from both a control and an intrinsic perspective.
2. Following that, the discussion explains models, including portfolio management and the interaction of "human judgment" and model outputs. To the extent there are quant-specific issues, the next steps (trading and execution) are covered. This particular section may have less applicability to "pure quant" investors.
3. The next discussion covers additional controls around data quality and governance.

Model Development and Lifecycle Management

Although this chapter has not attempted to define "quantitative strategies," the primary activity of quants is to develop financial models. A generally accepted definition of a model is an approximate representation of some aspect of the real world. We refer to a definition provided in financial regulation, which, although geared at a different class of institutions, introduces most of the modeling aspects covered in the following sections. According to the Office of the Comptroller of the Currency (OCC) (2011-12):

> The term model refers to a quantitative method, system, or approach that applies statistical, economic, financial, or mathematical theories, techniques, and assumptions to process input data into quantitative estimates. A model consists of three components: an information input component, which delivers assumptions and data to the model; a processing component, which transforms inputs into estimates; and a reporting component, which translates the estimates into useful business information. Models meeting this definition might be used for analyzing business strategies, informing business decisions, identifying and measuring risks, valuing exposures, instruments or positions, conducting stress testing, assessing adequacy of capital, managing client assets, measuring compliance with internal limits, maintaining the formal control apparatus of the bank, or meeting financial or regulatory reporting requirements and issuing public disclosures. The definition of model also covers quantitative approaches whose inputs are partially or wholly qualitative or based on expert judgment, provided that the output is quantitative in nature.

This discussion's use of a regulatory definition does not imply that the practices addressed are designed to satisfy the requirements of any regulatory directive. This popular definition provides many of the ingredients a model management and governance framework should consider.

The high-level components of a framework for model development and lifecycle management are defined as follows:

- *Model Catalog:* A complete inventory of all models, with each model tagged with at least the attributes of
  - Category—most models within a particular firm will fall within a finite group of categories, facilitating the establishment of appropriate governance. Typical examples may include:
    - Individual asset pricing models (a.k.a. "calculators"), which may be stochastic, fundamental, closed-form, structured, etc.,
    - Statistical/factor based models,
    - Portfolio and trading optimizers,
    - Signal and pattern recognition (and response) algorithms, and
    - Risk and capital models (VaR, counterparty and CVA, economic and regulatory capital);
  - Criticality—because most firms have dozens to hundreds of models, it is not feasible (or desirable) to impose the same level of controls around all of them. The level of criticality assigned to a particular model will broadly correlate to the amount of risk exposure associated with it. This will generally be a function of
    - Category: A firm's stock selection model is usually the most critical,
    - The amount of "exposure" (assets, portfolio strategy allocations, etc.) that rely on this particular model. For example, a volatility surface model is more critical for an equity derivatives firm than the foreign exchange curves used for occasional hedging,
    - The intrinsic uncertainty of the model, even when used within appropriate parameters (for example, correlation models for structured products are intrinsically more uncertain than interest rate swaps),
  - Ownership—to ensure proper model governance and accountability, each model should have a formally assigned owner (an individual or a group). Additionally, a "business" owner, or sponsor, may also be assigned.
- *Model Management Protocols:* Policies and procedures around the controls that should be applied to each of the models (or groups thereof) with the primary purpose of mitigating model risk arising from "operational deficiencies" (as opposed to model risk generated by intrinsic uncertainties). These protocols—model validation, change control, documentation, and testing—are covered in the remainder of this section. The primary types deficiencies they are designed to address fall under three main categories:
  - Improper model design: Faulty economic or financial logic, market or data assumptions, relationships, correlations, and incorrect translation of business logic into an algorithm, etc. Corresponding controls include proper model validation and testing programs need to be in place to manage and monitor these types of risk,
  - Faulty model implementation: Coding errors, improper calibration or data usage, unauthorized access or code releases, hidden relationships within the code, etc.

with corresponding controls of proper change control and testing protocols need to be in place to manage these types of risks, and
  - Inappropriate model usage: Incorrect economic interpretation of model outputs, use of the model outside the environment for which it was designed, running the model with faulty data or parameters, failing to identify the assumptions under which the model is valid, etc. Corresponding controls include risk from improper usage can be mitigated by a combination of robust model documentation, testing, and an effective governance and accountability regime.
- *Model Usage Protocols:* The OCC definition touches on the issues already introduced, namely, that models do not exist in a vacuum and that the investment process always involves some form of human judgment and intervention. The various degrees to which "discretion" is applied to a model-driven strategy, the feedback into the models, and controls around interventions and overrides are addressed shortly.
- *Model Governance*: The operational framework, including individual roles and responsibilities, to develop the specific terms and ensure consistent implementation of all the guidelines described herein. The nature of the governance structure will vary widely by institution type and size and this chapter will not attempt to define a "right" one. However, in broader terms, it should be managed by a committee that
  - Includes (senior) personnel, whether dedicated or not, from all relevant areas—research, modeling, validation, audit, investment, trading, risk, compliance, etc.,
  - Is responsible for developing, validating, and enforcing the control processes and protocols described in this section, as well as the supervisory, cultural, regulatory, and external-facing aspects of the firm's business that are directly related to its modeling activities,
  - Facilitates the communication among different groups involved in the development and use of models (important at large, geographically dispersed organizations), and
  - Is empowered to challenge model developers and users, including restricting or preventing business activities, if necessary, and to escalate potential issues to the next management level.

Change Control

The models used here in the broad sense of the entire code base that underlies a firm's investment decisions are constantly changing, with new models or components being developed, and existing ones being corrected, modified, or retired. Change control defines a set of processes and controls to mitigate the risks associated with changes to the models in the production environment.

The extent of the required controls increases rapidly with the size and complexity of the code base and of the institution. However, even smaller firms with a modest number of models should carefully define these processes because:

- They have to be tailored to the unique nature of the firm's modeling and investment framework;

- Developing robust practices early in this area creates a solid foundation for subsequent development. The accumulation of a poorly developed or managed code base without it inevitably leads to increasing maintenance costs and eventually to a very expensive "overhaul"; and
- A lack of reasonable change controls is an obvious shortcoming that regulators and investors will notice, which can cause irreparable damage in the event of a code-related problem.

The following guidelines developed by the Futures Industry Association in 2012 outline the typical components of a robust change control framework:

- *Authorization:* Changes to the production environment should be subject to review and approval by a responsible party. The extent of the review performed should be commensurate with the magnitude of the proposed changes; and
- *Auditability:* Establish procedures for communicating requirements, changes, and functionality related to their proprietary software and technical infrastructure, as well as maintain an audit trail of such changes, allowing them (or a third party) to accurately determine
  - When a change was made and by whom, and
  - The person approving the change, checks performed in the approval process, and reason and nature of the change.

The following items represent the typical steps in a well-managed software release process and should be clearly documented (on their own or within a broader model validation policy):

1. *Initiation:* The initiator of the change should define the rationale, requirement(s), and/or nature of the change and, when applicable, its criticality and potential impact(s);
2. *Approval requirements:* Requirements should be specified for the change to be approved. These should be predefined in a policy, but may be determined or adjusted case-by-case, and would typically include review levels, testing, or documentation requirements, etc.;
3. *Approval:* Prior to deployment, a responsible party should review if the approval requirements have been satisfied and either provide sign-off for release or request additional checks. This review may occur prior to development or after development is completed;
4. *Scheduling:* Prior to deployment, a planned change should be scheduled for release into the production environment, and considered along with any other planned changes for potential impact; and
5. *Deployment:* Depending on change, it may be appropriate to deploy to the entire production environment at once or in phases to mitigate risk and ease the reversion of the change, if necessary.

Deployment contains four phases:

1. *Preparation:* the change is prepared for release and the current production environment is backed up to allow for change reversion.
2. *Execution:* the change is released to the production environment.
3. *Validation:* the change and the state of the production environment should be verified for accuracy. The scope of a firm's validation process should be proportionate to the change being made.
4. *Completion/reversion:* a successful validation should result in completion of the change. If the change cannot be validated, the environment should be reverted.

In *post-deployment,* the consideration is how certain changes may affect trading in the production environment. Where possible, substantive changes should be activated initially with appropriately restricted risk limits and access to markets.

In *glass breaking,*[3] modelers and developers are regularly faced with emergencies where a delay in code changes may have a deleterious effect on clients, the firm, or markets. The response is to push such changes into production as quickly as possible and not wait for the approval process. In glass breaking, change control policies should include provisions for such situations:

- Specify who is allowed to make (or fast track approve) such changes;
- Reversion processes should still be deployable;
- The same approval conditions that would have been requested under the normal process should be followed after the fact (generally in an accelerated fashion); and
- The changes should be fully auditable, carefully reviewed, and subject to additional controls such as error management, escalation policies, or supervisory matters.

In addition to the FIA recommendations above, quant managers should consider the following general guidelines:

- Maintain a development environment that is isolated from the production environment. This will help to determine whether the code has been updated appropriately before moving it into a production environment;
- Developers should follow good programming practices. In particular, large-scale systems software has its own professional standards and set of best practices, including modularity, error-tracking systems, release planning, automated builds, and code reviews;
- Access/ability to change code should be restricted to authorized individuals; and
- To avoid unnecessary maintenance complexities, usage of specific models (or components thereof) should be tracked, and procedures for decommissioning obsolete ones should be implemented.

[3] Glass breaking has been included here but it is not part of the FIA guidelines.

Model Validation

Model validation is the set of processes and activities intended to verify that models are performing as expected. Effective model validation requires an assessment of the unique risk exposures faced by each quant manager, along with an alignment with relevant industry guidelines.

As with any investment process, there is no guarantee that models will deliver the intended investment results. The purpose of model validation is to ensure that the model generates investment portfolios consistent with the ideas underlying the process. For example, if the process is intended to favor value stocks, portfolios generated by the process will usually tilt towards typical value metrics.

Model Validation Process. Organizational considerations such as fund size, structure, investment strategies, operational complexity, staffing, and governance all contribute to make any quant manager's Model Validation framework fairly unique, and these governance issues are discussed later in the chapter. However, the same suggestions made for setting and documenting robust processes for change control, even in smaller firms, apply to model validation policies, namely:

- They must be carefully tailored to each firm's requirements;
- It is beneficial over the long term to initially establish good practices;
- It is an effective way to demonstrate to regulators and investors that "reasonable controls" are in place to "prevent breaches of fiduciary duty"; and
- There is an expectation that firms should have an independent model validation process, which does *not* imply a requirement of an entirely separate, dedicated group of people, but may be appropriate for large institutions.

The remaining section focuses on the relevant components of a model validation process regardless of organizational structures. The OCC defines a model in terms of three components:

- An input component that delivers data and assumptions to the model;
- A processing component that contains the theoretical model and transforms the input component into estimates via the computer code; and
- An output component, which translates the processed estimates into financial and economic information.

Although model validation will incorporate an analysis of all three components, the process should optimally begin during the model creation process to ensure that all significant sources of model risk are appropriately identified and addressed. Additionally, any changes to a model's design or enhancements to accommodate new products, behavioral elements, or reports should be considered in light of existing assumptions and limitations around use and any updates that are needed in the model validation process.

Model validation can be an iterative process and requires the participation of all the parties involved in the design, development, testing, documentation, and use of models. Although models may need to be periodically revalidated, this discussion primarily addresses the initial "validation" exercise for the development of a new model.

Depending on the firm's structure, the process can be:

- *Subsequent to development:* The model is designed, developed, implemented, documented, and sometimes tested. This information is passed on to the validators, who may then require additional documentation or testing, etc. This typically occurs at large institutions with separate validation teams; or
- *Concurrent with development:* The validation of each component is performed as each component is finished (e.g., when the initial algorithm is developed from theory, its validity is verified before it moves into the implementation stage, etc.). This approach is more typical at smaller firms, where validation is handled primarily by peers and/or personnel who are closely embedded within the development teams.

Model Validation Components. It is impossible to generally define all aspects of model development and usage that may need to be validated. This discussion describes the broad categories of checks and provides common examples. The applicability of specific items and the extent of the validation will depend on the nature of the model and its criticality within the overall strategy.

Validating the Theory, Logic, and Algorithm. The degree of validation at this stage will vary greatly depending on whether the models in question are:

- Brand-new or modifications to existing ones (generalizations/specializations, adaptations to new or changing markets or products, etc.);
- The typical steps involved are:

    1. Review of the theory and logic used to construct the model, including all of the supporting documentation. This is particularly relevant for new models.
    2. Verification that the algorithm accurately represents the theory. This may often include the construction of a simplified, nonproduction prototype.
    3. When the model is a modification of an existing one, verify that they converge in the expected manner.
    4. Verification or definition of the limits of applicability of the model in relation to market regimes, data inputs, parameters space, time horizons, etc. These can be defined either as:
        - Point limits (e.g., model is applicable only in low volatility regimes where a particular indicator is less than some threshold), or
        - Tolerance thresholds or confidence intervals (e.g., model uncertainty is an increasing function of a particular volatility indictor). Limit definitions in these terms provide the basic blocks for the quantification and mitigation of model risk.

Validating the Input Component. Models typically require inputs from various sources:

- External data (market, fundamental, macroeconomic, historical, etc.); or
- Internal data (model parameters, outputs from other models, "modified external data," etc.)

Valid data ranges (of values or variability) may be more restrictive than those specified by general controls.

Later the chapter addresses the issues around (external) data governance and quality controls. However, the validation process of each individual model requires additional specifications that *may* need to be addressed. The following nonexhaustive list provides some common examples:

- Exception handling/correction mechanisms may need to be model-specific; and
- Most firms perform some preprocessing of raw data (aggregation, standardization, etc.) before it is fed to a model. This initial manipulation is, in some sense, a model itself. In some situations, the assumptions made may correlate with or affect the assumptions of the consuming model, and may need to be remedied.

Internal inputs, whether free parameters or outputs from other models, need to be similarly evaluated for appropriate ranges and other suitability conditions.

There are two additional considerations regarding the validation of inputs (either internal or external):

- The ideal "output" of this validation step should be provided as extension of the limits of applicability described above; and
- Because most models depend on several types of data and parameters, it is essential to perform this analysis so they can be correlated. For example, a forecast model for commodity prices may be valid only within a given range of volatility of U.S. dollars against a currency basket. However, the range may depend on some parameters such as the weights of the basket, and the window used to measure the volatility. These are the most difficult validation steps, but also the most important to uncover inconsistencies that can otherwise go undetected.

Validating the Processing Component: Translating Algorithm to Code. The final stage in model development is the translation of the algorithm into computer code. The steps of this component will vary among organizations. The following represents a generic list of guidelines:

- A line-by-line code review (by peers or dedicated validation staff) is generally needed (model validation or change control);
- If quant modelers write the final production code, the validation process should include checks on coding standards. Otherwise, that may be the domain of the technology and systems development life cycle (SDLC) specialists;
- Outputs should be compared with the following, as applicable

- Theoretical predictions (especially when closed-form solutions are known),
- Outputs from an independently produced simplified prototype,
- Outputs from comparable or related models that have been validated, and
- Third-party models.

Model Validation Reports

The results of the model validation exercise should be summarized in a written report and reside with the model documentation. The report should include:

- A description of the methods used to validate the underlying theoretical assumptions and whether the documentation used to support them is sufficient;
- A description of the steps taken to verify the algorithm, assumption, and checks on inputs, and whether the documentation and testing requirements around them are sufficient;
- The results of all checks on outputs against any of the possible benchmarks and in what scenarios;
- Determinations of the limits of applicability inferred from the three items above. To the extent possible they should
  - Provide recommendations for controls and/or restrictions around model usage, and specify the costs/risks of using the models outside those limits,
  - Be specific with respect to particular inputs and any correlations among them, and
  - Ensure that the documentation is sufficient and understandable by model users and other users who may not have deep technical expertise;
- An overall assessment of the potential risks associated with the model
  - Recommendations for follow up revalidation schedule, extent, and conditions,
  - Triggered by changes in the model, changes in market conditions, failures of some tests, etc., and
  - Routine periodic reviews usually reserved for critical and/or high-risk models.

Documentation (for Modelers and Developers)

Robust documentation is particularly critical in a quantitative context. The general benefits of documentation are:

- Preservation of institutional knowledge (reduces key person risk);
- Easier on boarding and training of new staff; and
- Supportive evidence for the management of internal/external audits and regulatory examinations.

Model documentation can be delineated into three categories:

- *Code documentation:* This topic is part of coding standards and is not addressed in this chapter;
- *Technical documentation:* Written primarily by the modelers, validators, and model users; and
- *External documentation:* Written primarily for investors and regulators.

Model documentation is typically written during the model development phase and finalized in the iterative process of validation and deployment. The primary components that need to be included are:

Investment Objective, Theory, and Logic. This forms the basis for the first step in the model validation process. Depending on the nature of the model, this section may typically include:

- High-level business and/or financial theory underlying the model, including, when available, academic literature and an assessment of industry standards for similar models;
- Model assumptions (e.g., particular market environments, time horizons) and, to the extent known, the limitations on such assumptions and/or constraints on model use arising from these limitations;
- Comparison to a related model. This is relevant when a model is a modification, extension, generalization, or simplification of an existing model. Specifications of the relative behavior and convergence regimes provide a strong basis for validation and testing.

Algorithm Description. Detailed logic for the construction of the algorithm, including:

- The math, numerical methods, and any other details needed for implementation (e.g., use of grids, interpolation methods, specific correlation techniques, etc.);
- Specific assumptions about inputs (external data, free parameters, and outputs of other models), and, to the extent known, the risk sensitivities to such inputs;
- Implementation issues that consider the particular environment of the firm. Care should be taken to avoid excessive details and quick obsolescence, but could include items such as:
  - Reuse of existing libraries or components (and conversely any foreseeable effects the new model may have on the existing environment).
  - Specification of output formats (if these are feeds to other models or processes).
  - Specification of any APIs (to other models, libraries, user interfaces, etc.).
  - Special data feeds, quality controls, cleansing, or exception management requirements that differ from standard processes.

Special requirements on systems architecture, hardware, database management, etc. These types of issues will generally arise only for major models such as VaR where performance may become a relevant factor.

Testing Specifications. Detailed specifications for pre- and post- release testing requirements as described elsewhere in the chapter.

Usage Guidelines: This section should be written for business owners, users, and other stakeholders that are directly involved (e.g., operations, risk managers). The contents depend on the type of model but would generally contain:

- A summary of the technical issues.
- Detailed descriptions of the assumptions used, the limits of applicability (as described for model validation) and the risks of using the models outside these valid ranges.
- Any additional information about key risk areas (and potential mitigations), alternative models, pricing considerations, etc.
- Regulatory, compliance, internal policy, or client driven constraints on the usage of the model or setting of parameters and overrides.
- Potential reporting requirements (internal, management, regulatory, investor, etc.).

Finally, it is a good practice to attach model validation reports and any change control documentation to the technical package.

Testing

Of all controls, practices, and recommendations addressed in this chapter, probably none is as critical as testing the models thoroughly. This discussion covers some high-level practices around the testing of models.

General Principles for Testing. The type and extent of testing will vary with the purpose and the stage at which it is being performed:

- *Purpose:* Although the distinction is not always clear, it is nevertheless helpful to delineate separate categories of tests, such as
  - Business logic performed during model validation to ensure that the algorithm accurately reflects the theory (and its mathematical formulation) that the model is intended to represent,
  - Coding/development extensively performed as part of change control as well as ongoing testing. This involves testing the implementation of the algorithm to ensure it does not contain coding errors or affect other models within the environment, and
  - Usage can often be a "brute force" exercise by running models using as many different combinations of inputs, parameters, and market scenarios as feasible to test the accuracy of the limits of applicability and measure the effects of the usage of models outside such limits, which is the primary mechanism for quantifying model risk;
- *Stages:* The three distinct stages of testing include
  - Prerelease—the extensive testing performed during model validation and change control processes,
  - Post-release—routine or ongoing testing of all models in production. This ensures that unchanged models have not been inadvertently affected by other changes in the system, as well as tests large number of scenarios, and
  - Forensic—comprehensive testing after a negative event (e.g., the discovery of an error) to find the cause, assess materiality, etc.;

- *Scope:* The scope of testing will typically be at least as broad as the model validation, but often will have additional components included. In particular, testing can be done on:
  - Individual models—most types of tests mentioned are for a particular model (e.g., a pricing calculator) or a well-defined component of a wider model (e.g., the correlation model used to compute a particular weight of a portfolio optimizer), and
  - Holistic—periodic tests on the entire system,
    - Even under best coding standards as code is added, complexity increases and unintended effects may manifest in seemingly unrelated modules (e.g., changes to shared libraries),
    - When the overall size of the code base reaches certain thresholds, management of cyclomatic complexity, logging of usage of particular components, and removal of obsolete code become very important issues. Lack of these controls leads to escalating costs of "support and management,"
    - Some components that do not by themselves fall under the definition of "models." Thus, they may not go through validation and change management, or at least not to the same extent, but nevertheless impact the modeling systems to which they are somehow coupled (e.g., user interfaces, data cleansing processes, internal and external messaging and communication protocols, etc.), and
    - In many "modular" or multicomponent models, the most common source of errors is during the "handover" from one component to another. This is especially common where different teams are responsible for the different components.

Testing Specifications

"Testing specifications" was listed as one of the required components of robust model documentation. The nature of these specifications will be model-dependent, but some common items that should be detailed are:

- Market regimes/datasets the tests should be run against;
- Stressing grids for all inputs and parameters;
- Specification of expected behavior under these stresses (e.g., monotonicity or inflection points, asymptotic cases, convergence, etc.);
- Convergence at limiting cases when a model is a special or generalized case of another;
- Appropriate tolerance thresholds (which can themselves be variable); and
- Frequency of testing (which can be also be multitiered).

In addition to the business-specific requirements of each type of model, there are practical considerations in the setup of testing environments. For many quantitative firms, this is a complex business decision, because there is the need to balance the obvious benefits of more and more sophisticated testing with the increasing costs associated with it. Some of the components of the testing framework that need to be defined/created are:

- At least one stable testing environment, insulated from the production environment;
- Multiple, complete and statistically representative "market states" against which tests can be repeated without variation;

- Mirror testing platforms if there are multiple production platforms - automatic monitoring procedures that would catch results outside established thresholds and provide some sort of alerts to the appropriate personnel;
- Reporting; and
- For prerelease testing, sign-off protocols indicating that testing has been successfully completed (part of the change control process).

The Investment Process

The previous discussion primarily addressed issues related to the design, development, and maintenance of models. This discussion focuses on the use of models, a function that may or may not be executed by the same group of people that develop them, with the understanding that the separation of the two processes may not apply to all firms. As previously mentioned, the examination focuses on the functional aspects of the processes, with the assumption that many need to be thoroughly documented, and discuss specific policies and procedures and other compliance, supervisory, and governance issues.

The selected topics covered are those that most commonly introduce operational risk and potential for compliance violations in the steps leading from "model outputs" to "business actions." Some examples of such output-to-action process chains are:

- Portfolio optimization or trade recommendations ⟶ Trades ;
- Asset valuation ⟶ Pricing ; and
- VaR/capital models ⟶ Capital allocation and Corporate actions.

Because the chapter has defined quantitative investment managers as the *primary* target audience, the current discussion will use the first of these examples as a referential framework. However, the issues addressed are equally applicable to a wider spectrum of contexts.

The discussion looks at the various controls employed by model developers to ensure that models are constructed and maintained to represent the underlying investment strategy. The look here focuses on the protocols available for the model users, who are ultimately responsible for ensuring that the outputs of the models are consistent with assumptions and expectations.

- First, the text addresses checks performed on a routine basis *before* any investment actions are taken;
- The next discussion focuses on a very quant-specific problem of determining what actions can be taken (still prior to execution) when model outputs cannot (or should not) be used as they are; and
- Finally, the text looks at recommended practices for monitoring of the overall process to ensure that the models and the results remain in line with the investment strategy and goals.

Use of Model Outputs for Portfolio Construction

The strategy context briefly touched upon the continuous spectrum of investment approaches, from a "pure quant" black-box type, with no human input, to a more "traditional," discretionary approach supported by some quantitative tools. This model uses the middle-of-the-road type as a typical firm, where models generate optimized portfolios or trade recommendations are reviewed by an investment team (portfolio construction) before execution (trading).

The extent, type, and frequency of "output validation" performed at this stage, the tools used, and the actions taken by the investment team will vary greatly as a function of size, approach philosophy, investment strategy, asset classes, etc., but generally involves:

- An initial, usually automated, "sanity check" that detects outliers based on strategy-specific parameters, such as
  - Values outside reasonable ranges,
  - Variability that is excessive from previous periods or directionally opposite from what would be expected given some changes in market or other variables, and
  - Poor correlation with comparable assets;
- A form of "manual" reviews will be in place, and depending on the investment strategy (and in particular on the frequency and volume of trading), will be applied to
  - Only "outliers" noted through automated processes, because this is appropriate for firms whose strategy involves large amounts of daily trades,
  - All values that are outside some pre-defined thresholds as defined in the checks above. Under these conditions, the entire market could be an "outlier" on certain days, and
  - All recommendations that are typical of firms with low trading volume that are at the fundamental end of the strategy spectrum;
- Less common, but critical for certain types of strategies are checks on recommendations that were expected, but were not produced by the model. Such expectation criteria can be driven by, for example:
  - New information about individual securities, and
  - Expected behavior given overall market moves.

Depending on the level of type of review that is performed, the possible outcomes are:

- The reason(s) for the anomaly are understood, the outputs are deemed acceptable, and the next steps can be taken with no further action;
- The outputs are deemed unacceptable and may trigger any or all of the following corrective actions
  - An intervention in the investment process,
  - Feedback to the modeling, data, or other teams if the origin of the anomaly is understood and stems from a problem with the model, data, or other component of the modeling process,

- Further review (typically in a joint effort of all groups involved) if the origin of the problem cannot be determined, and
- Internal escalation to the appropriate levels if the issue appears to be caused by "other" problems (e.g., an individual's error or intentional misconduct, process failure, breach of any internal, risk or compliance controls or guidelines, etc.).

It is worth emphasizing that the number and diversity of activities, checks, and actions performed at this stage is typically very high. Without well-established and documented processes and controls, these activities become error-prone and expose the firm to a considerable amount of investment, operational, regulatory, and reputational risk.

Investment Actions (Interventions)

One principal way in which quantitative investors with different strategies and approaches differ is in the amount and types of human "interventions" in the quantitative process. The term itself is somewhat value laden because it implies a "fix" to what should be an automated process. This is the opposite investment philosophy of the types of manager CQA chose to use as archetype, and for whom model outputs are a tool that guides decisions made by the investment team. Interventions are typically driven by the following factors:

- Particular output values that are flagged in the validation processes;
- Information that becomes available after the models have been run and not considered; and
- Client instructions such as new or changes to existing constraints on their portfolios, fund inflows, and fund outflows.

Although it is difficult to list the possible types of causes for and responses to such issues, there are two classifications that will typically guide the decisions, controls, and policies around interventions. The first classification is based on the type and/or materiality of the intervention. This can be a single categorization or a matrix. A typical classification scheme may look like this:

> Routine issues that are expected to occur on a regular basis, have well-established responses, and typically do not require escalation or pre-approval beyond the professionals responsible for the day-today management of the portfolio. Note, however, that frequent and regular recurrence of the same type of problem may signal a model, process, or other deficiency. Some examples of routine issues and responses are listed in Table 1.

TABLE 1. TYPES OF RESPONSES TO INTERVENTIONS	
Issue Requiring a Routine Intervention	**Typical Responses**
A suspicious trade recommendation is flagged and traced back to bad input data.	Remove security from trading universe until the problem is corrected. Correct the data or use an approximation.
News about a company, data release, or analyst recommendations or forecasts becomes available.	Remove security from trading universe until the news data is incorporated into the model
Client requests additional limits on a particular name, sector, or other category.	Manually change the list of recommended trades for the client's portfolio (restrict purchases or force a sale). Change the model parameters and rerun model for the client's portfolio.
Particular constraints, preset or dynamic, cannot be captured or handled properly by the models.	Actions will be taken on a daily basis to address the issues.

Nonroutine types cover several subcategories of issues and will typically require preapproval or sign-off from a more senior officer before action may be taken. Examples of these types of issues are:

- *Unusual:* may raise potential for a more severe problem or have no "standard" approach.
- *Material:* may cause large impact on clients or firm.
- *Broad or systemic:* appear to affect an unusually large number of assets/portfolios.

Systematic issues appear to increase in frequency and/or severity and are usually symptomatic of some shift that requires a review of the models, assumptions, or parameter settings. These are typically not handled on a daily basis, are subject to a more rigorous evaluation, and typically approved by a senior investment officer or committee.

A second classification scheme is based on the intervention method and goes to the core of the issues of whether it is a "correction" or "normal part of business as usual."

Override Model Inputs. In response to any of the types of aforementioned situations, an investment professional may make corrections to inputs (e.g., fix bad data), change model parameters (e.g., concentration thresholds or factor weights), change the universe (e.g., remove certain assets), or tweak the model by some other means. This is a common approach for routine interventions because it requires a good understanding of the cause of the unsatisfactory result and the knowledge of which "knobs" on the model can be turned to produce the desired changes.

Override Model Outputs. An alternative is to manually change the outputs directly (e.g., remove a security from a list of recommended trades). These actions are more clearly identified as an "override." Examples of common situations when they are used are:

- The origin of the unacceptable outcome is not understood;
- The changes to the settings that would be required to "force" the desired output changes are not viable (e.g., they cause the model to fail or not converge, violate an internal or client guideline, cannot be captured properly by the model, etc.);
- The effect that would result from re-running the model with different settings is deterministic (or can be computed in closed form), and there is no reason to rerun; and
- Parameter changes require a large-scale rerun (e.g., recalibration against historical data), which cannot be performed timely.

Execution Time Overrides. Referred to as off-model trades, these are typically decisions made by traders during execution and can be driven by any number of reasons:

- Inability to execute the trade, lack of liquidity, or unavailability of the asset in the market;
- Prices, bid-offer spreads, or other relevant market parameters have moved materially between the recommendation signoff and time of trade;
- Flagging by pre-trade compliance and guidelines checks that the trade would be in violation of some control not caught during portfolio construction phase; and
- Client instructions.

Depending on the organizational structure, traders may or may not have the authority to make these and related decisions (e.g., to make a trade in a comparable security instead).

Regardless of the nature of and the philosophical stance on such investment action, all of the following are critical controls needed to minimize exposure to potentially serious breaches of compliance, regulatory, or client constraints:

- Policies and procedures categorizing intervention types, actions to be taken, (pre) approval requirements, authority and escalation levels, etc. ;
- Regular reviews at an appropriate senior level of investment actions that have been taken (including routine ones);
- Recordkeeping of all such actions, approvals, and reviews; and
- Clear disclosures to investors about how the process works, even when it is presented as an integral part of the investment process. Such distinctions can be lost on nonquants who often view any "intervention" in the context of a model-driven strategy as a "correction to something that went wrong."

Feedback Loop. An earlier discussion concerned model validation at the construction and initial testing phases. However, it is the ongoing risk and performance monitoring by the investment team that provides the real world testing and validation of model results.

In firms where investment personnel and model developers are separate, it is important to have good communication channels. The more separate the groups are (by function, location, reporting lines, etc.), the more formalized the protocols. Examples of information that should be routinely provided to the modeling groups are:

- Discrepancies between actual and expected performance/results. These signals are often aggregated and can be indicators of any number of issues, including incorrect model assumptions, coding errors, etc.;
- Performance trends, which may be indicative of shifts in market regimes, are not captured by the models, or take them outside their limits of applicability;
- Types of interventions that are required more often than expected. This can be caused by a model's inability to capture particular variables or constraints and may require functional enhancements; and
- Unusual behavior that may have been resolved through an intervention, but may signal a problem in the code that manifests under certain combinations of inputs.

While the control functions (risk and compliance in particular) should not intermediate this feedback mechanism, they should be fully involved in the process, because deficiencies in the models may also indicate other control breaches.

Execution

This subsection covers the final step in the investment sequence of the typical quantitative manager, executing trades after the recommendation list or "optimized portfolio" has been validated by the investment team. The nature of this function, the amount of discretion traders have in deviating from the model recommendations, and the extent to which it has any quant-specific concerns vary considerably, even among firms with an overall similar approach. It ranges from a third, fully integrated component of the investment decision-making team (in addition to model developers and model users) to a nearly automated function, more connected to operations than the front office. In different types of quantitative firms, where execution related to something other than trading of public equities, such as fixed income, structured products, or other illiquid assets, the separation between portfolio construction and execution may not exist altogether.

Consequently, this discussion will only cover a few of the controls commonly employed by trading desks at typical quantitative managers:

- *Pretrade checking:* Many firms employ one last "line of defense" before trades are executed, by using some form of rules-based engine to detect potential violations of internal policy, compliance, regulatory, or client guidelines that may slip through the portfolio construction process;

- *Segregation of duties:* Later there is a discussion of the general issues of corporate governance, conflicts of interest and separation of duties. In the context of quantitative investment managers, there are often additional levels of separation that are put in place as a risk control measure, although there is no regulatory requirement to do so; and
- *Execution time overrides:* These have been addressed already, but the levels of controls around such "off-model trades" should be equivalent to those previously described.

Appendix A summarizes the numerous additional standard practices, guidelines, and regulatory requirements that need to be followed by anyone executing trades on clients' behalf.

Data Governance and Integrity

Accurate data is one of the most critical components of any quantitative process, and its careful management is paramount to long-term success.[4] Failure along any portion of the data custody chain (setup, loading, verification, validation, cleansing, standardization, usage) can lead to incremental degradation in performance and/or increase in risk, increased regulatory scrutiny (even if there is no detected problem) and can occasionally be the cause of catastrophic failures. Conversely, superior data management structures provide firms with a competitive advantage by decreasing the noise in performance signals, which can lead to model enhancements.

Data Catalog and Ownership. As with models, the initial step is to define what constitutes data. Examples of categories of data at a typical firm are market, macroeconomic, fundamental company, relative value/sentiment, and portfolio data.

The vast amount and diversity of data used in quant models points to the first important principle of data governance: All data should have clearly defined business owners who understand its meaning, criticality, and usage, and who are ultimately responsible for its management (and accountable for failures). Depending on the size and complexity of the institution and the volume and diversity of its data requirements, there may be several layers of ownership:

- *Business owner:* typically a (senior) member of the modeling, research, portfolio management, or trading team.
- *Chief data officer:* although not found at all institutions, it will typically be a senior management person (chief technology, investment, or operations officer).
- *Technology manager:* Usually a member of the information technology (IT) team who handles daily activities associated with a specific set of data feeds.
- *Data steward:* Larger companies may have an additional intermediary between the business owner, who, for example, may be responsible for equity data, and the IT team. Data stewards will usually ensure that the quality control processes defined

[4] There are many adages on this topic, such as "garbage in, garbage out," "no integrity, no independent testing," "no history, no back-testing," and so on.

for particular feeds/sources are implemented (and improved). At many firms, data stewards may be members of the same team as the business owner, while at larger institutions there may be a dedicated team.

The data team is responsible for all of the data management protocols discussed in the following sections:

- Identification of new data requirements and changes to existing requirements;
- Setup of new market data, including licensing requirements and vendor management, as applicable.;
- Daily oversight of data loading, processing, and storage activities;
- Establishment and ongoing review of data integrity checks, including modifications that may be required due to changes in vendor feeds such as when a vendor incorporates a validation or processing step previously performed by the firm;
- Daily oversight of data quality, including exception review and resolution activities; and
- Define, implement, and monitor data access controls. Typical factors that determine access to production data are:
  - Write access—most, if not all, write operations should be executed through production interfaces and any manual write access should be as narrowly restricted as possible, carefully logged, and monitored, and
  - Read access—restrictions are typically based on a need-to-know principle and include considerations of client confidentiality, material nonpublic information, separation of duties/conflicts of interest, vendor licensing restrictions, etc.

Setup of New Market Data

Data Requirements. Prior to establishing a new market data feed, the data owner should clearly define the data requirements. Requirements may include frequency of obtaining the data, date/time when the data should be obtained, specific data fields that are needed, format of data (flat files, spreadsheets, etc.), and data transmission mechanism (file transfer protocol or FTP, web download, etc.).

Data Licensing. Licensing agreements should be in place when market data is obtained from an external vendor/service provider to outline the service levels for delivery and exception handling/escalation procedures for data errors and delays.

Data Load Completeness. The firm should establish checks to verify that raw data is loaded in its entirety from the source. When a vendor provides feed-level information (e.g., headers, trailers), checks should be performed to ensure that the information loaded into the internal systems matches source files. When data is obtained from a nonsystematic process, appropriate verification procedures (e.g., spot checks) should be implemented.

Data Load Timeliness. Systematic alerts should be established to notify appropriate personnel of data delays. Estimated times of arrival should exist for each data feed, and procedures established to handle delays in data transmission, including vendor escalation and resolution protocols, thresholds for data outage/unavailability, among others. Where data is obtained in a nonsystematic manner, alerts should trigger the required personnel to conduct data retrieval processes. Similarly, alerts should prevent downstream-automated processes from proceeding without proper data quality controls.

Data Storage. A copy of the raw data should be stored, where possible, in its original form as received from the source. Subsequent data computations/adjustments may be made as long as the source copy is available. Judgment should be used to determine the period of time necessary for retaining source files and in light of regulatory retention requirements

Data Standardization/Normalization. For large volumes of market data, it is a good practice to normalize the data storage, which involves organizing data fields and layouts to reduce data redundancies/dependencies and facilitates future data retrieval.

Data Logging/Auditability/Sign-offs. Source data records should be stored with date/time stamps for auditability purposes and investigating future data-related issues. Where subsequent computations/changes to data occur, the appropriate level of logging should be turned on for key data items. If the data processing workflow involves reviewing and signing-off on verified data, evidence of sign-offs for accountability should be retained.

Integrity Checks on Market Data

The type of integrity checks and the extent to which they are performed is driven by various factors, including the nature of the data and the manner in which it is used. For example, data that varies or moves quickly (such as stock prices) requires checks that are more frequent, compared to static data (such as earnings). Data that is used as a primary input across a large number of models/quantitative factors may require more exhaustive checks than data that is one of many inputs to a model/factor. Materiality considerations and judgment in determining the number and types of checks should be implemented for data integrity:

- Checks for missing and stale data are the procedures for determining the time ranges for stale or missing data may vary, and be revisited periodically;
- Threshold checks on data are checks for large swings/changes in market data such as where data is erroneous or erroneously appended, can be a useful check that can be applied to cleansed or raw data;
- Checks against multiple sources is a check for data integrity involves obtaining the same market data item from more than one source and comparing the same data among multiple sources; and
- Other checks for consideration are that data owners should determine the appropriate types of checks. Other checks are constituent checks (the sum of weights of

benchmark constituents should equal 100), directionality checks (changes in bond prices should be in line with changes in yields), or sampling-based checks (material changes in a sample of data points in a population). Receiving proper notification from vendors for changes in data format may also be a relevant check.

Exception Processing and Resolution

Procedures should address the daily workflow for reviewing and resolving data exceptions. The procedures should outline the data owners responsible for performing these activities, a timeline for conducting the activities, resolution tasks for different types of exceptions (for example, required action for missing data items), escalation protocol if the resolution steps are unclear or unknown, vendor/service provider contact information, and data sign-off procedures.

The procedures should be reviewed with the chief information officer or senior portfolio managers before implementation, and revisited and updated periodically, as needed. In addition, a log can be maintained of recurring data exceptions and their resolution. Any subsequent changes to the data (both raw and derived data), and data sign-offs may be logged for audit-ability purposes.

VI. COMPLIANCE

Compliance is responsible for ensuring that a firm's practices conform to its obligations. This process includes determining what those obligations are, designing corresponding internal policies and procedures, and ensuring that those policies and procedures are followed. Obligations come from many sources, such as regulatory, legal, and internal and external constituents' requirements and expectations and vary among firms. Registered investment advisers are subject to more SEC rules than proprietary trading groups. A firm's contracts with investors, brokers, and others can yield additional, specific duties as well as operation in particular jurisdictions or trading specific instruments. In addition, firms may voluntarily take on extra duties such as maintaining enhanced controls on operational or investment risk beyond those strictly required by regulations and contracts.

Once these mandatory and voluntary restrictions are identified, a firm must develop and enforce appropriate policies and procedures. This might involve creating teams and committees, empowering officers, documenting processes, arranging for internal and external audits, providing training, designing compensation and advancement incentives, and other such activities. Several of the obligations faced by quant firms, both mandatory and voluntary, relate specifically to the quantitative nature of their investment processes. This chapter addresses those quant-specific compliance concerns. The constraints discussed below do not relate to all quant firms. They enumerate the potential approaches for those firms that must or choose to deal with these issues:

- First, what documents and other files describing the investment process must a quant firm generate and maintain? Legal guidance in this area is limited, and there is much debate over how to apply rules from other areas to the quantitative trading industry;

- Second, how should firms respond when things go wrong, meaning when they encounter undesired or unanticipated events?
- Finally, how should a firm's compliance procedures change when some of the activities it ordinarily monitors are outsourced to separate entities, potentially limiting the firm's ability to manage individual steps that lead to the agreed deliverable?

VII. DOCUMENTATION

Comprehensive documentation provides firms with the ability to quickly detect and remediate problems of all types, demonstrate compliance with regulatory requirements, and gain the confidence of clients and investors. Documentation is described here in terms of these broad categories:

- *Technical:* intended primarily for teams running the various parts of the business. From a quant standpoint, this is code and model documentation.
- *External (disclosures):* intended for investors and regulators. Policies and procedures covers both internal mandates and external aspects such as regulatory matters; and
- *Recordkeeping:* required for effective ongoing management, ad-hoc analysis of problems, and regulatory audits.

Model Documentation (for Investors and Regulators)

An earlier discussion covered the documentation of a trading firm's investment process for use by its modelers and developers. This documentation can also be useful to external parties such as clients and regulators. Client demands and regulatory requirements help to shape which descriptions of the investment process will be disclosed or documented. At the same time, concerns over unwanted dissemination of trade secrets and legal risk from misrepresentations commonly limit the amount of detail trading firms are willing to share with clients and regulators.

Documentation of an investment process can be used in various ways, with different levels of specificity for each:

- Quant managers will generally develop documentation for internal purposes;
- Quant mangers will likely disclose some information about their investment processes to clients, either as a matter of course during the process of acquiring new investors, or in special circumstances, such as after the discovery of an error; and
- Regulators may request more detailed information about a firm's investment process in a quant audit or other contexts, to verify conformity with representations in marketing materials, and requirements of applicable law.

Internal Documentation. There are benefits to having model documentation that is both broad and deep. Capturing how automated processes interact with manual risk-control procedures and other nonautomated portions of the investment process can help to drive continual improvement, ensure uniform practices across the firm, and optimize the division of labor between human- and computer-driven procedures. At the same time, a thorough understanding of the details of the investment process, including a model's assumptions, intended scope of use, and history of modifications, is necessary if the firm is to diagnose errors quickly and effect improvements.

External Documentation. By contrast, a less detailed summary document will generally be sufficient for external parties. Some level of detail will likely need to be shared with potential investors (at least orally) as part of the sales process, but this would generally not include revelation of source code or even specific details of a firm's financial model. Similarly, regulators have a justifiable interest in verifying that a firm's investment process conforms to the disclosures made to investors, but this does not imply a need to review every detail of a firm's quantitative models.

As a fiduciary, an investment management firm has a duty and obligation to implement and follow appropriate procedures, and checks and balances across various aspects of its investment processes. A summarized version of the model documentation that includes descriptions of procedures for validation and documentation along with broad-stroke outlines of the general investment strategies, will establish satisfaction of this duty while preserving the intellectual capital of the firm. Specifically, as long as the purpose or intent of the model is stated in the form of a summary document, it will assist to identify and address the firm's governance framework in reference to the model and its validation, scope, and history.

The form and content of such summary is less easily defined and varies among firms. Quant managers are faced with a delicate balance when developing appropriate language to describe their investment process and models. In particular, they need to ensure that sensitive proprietary intellectual property is not compromised, while providing a plain-English explanation of their investment processes without providing a roadmap to the model.

SEC-registered quant managers can use Form ADV Part 2A to summarize disclosures surrounding the risks associated with computerized or modeled investment strategies. Some potential risks to consider disclosing include model design risk, model implementation risk (including coding errors, input errors, etc.), hardware/technology disruption risk, human judgment decision risk, and data input/quality errors.

More generally, details of the investment process to potential investors can occur in a variety of contexts, including promotional materials, road shows, and informal discussions. Quant managers need to ensure that no such communication contains language that could potentially mislead clients and investors, such as implicit guarantees that the system will always perform as intended and that no coding errors will occur.

Unambiguous disclosures present their own difficulties, however. First, a firm must abide by the policies disclosed to investors that it will follow, which imposes additional burdens on the investment manager beyond the legal baseline. Second, and conversely, in the event of significant changes to the investment process, the firm must update all of its disclosures to remain consistent with actual practice. Thus, as discussed for policies and procedures, the firm should have procedures to ensure that disclosure documents remain current and are updated whenever a significant change is made to the model/investment process and that clients are informed.

A quant manager should be prepared to provide regulators with further documentation about its investment process and models. This might include drafting regulator-ready summaries even before inquiries arrive. One challenge faced by investment managers is determining how much detail to include in such summaries. Regulatory organizations such as the Securities and Exchange Commission (SEC), Financial Industry Regulatory Authority (FINRA), or Financial Accounting Standards Board (FASB) may mandate certain disclosures, and firms in turn may volunteer to disclose additional details in order to provide insight into their culture and provide a better understanding of the controls surrounding their investment processes.

A quant manager should also be sensitive to any publicly available information regarding its models and strategies that, when combined with disclosures that the firm has made to clients, prospects, or regulators, might enable someone to "reverse-engineer" the firm's processes and compromise its intellectual property. It is also recommended that individuals who have access to key data points sign non-disclosure agreements.

Policies and Procedures

Rule 206(4)-7 of the Investment Advisers Act of 1940 ("Advisers Act") requires all investment advisers including quantitative firms to "[a]dopt and implement written policies and procedures reasonably designed to prevent violation" of the Advisers Act and the rules thereunder by their supervised persons. The SEC has stated that an adviser's failure to have adequate compliance policies and procedures in place will constitute a violation of its rules independent of any other securities law violation.[5] The rule's adopting release also states, "each adviser, in designing its policies and procedures, should first identify conflicts and other compliance factors creating risk exposure for the firm and its clients in light of the firm's particular operations, and then design policies and procedures that address those risks."

Although Rule 206(4)-7 does not specify the areas to be covered by an adviser's compliance program, the rule's adopting release made clear that an "adviser's policies and procedures, at a minimum, should address certain areas to the extent that they are relevant to that adviser."[6]

Many quantitative investment advisers use complex computer programs to implement their strategies. As previously discussed, quantitative firms should identify and mitigate

---

[5] U.S. Securities and Exchange Commission (2003), SEC Rel. No. IA-2204 (2004), https://www.sec.gov/rules/final/ia-2204.htm

[6] *Id.*

the risks associated with model development, testing, and change control procedures in any policies. In 2011, the SEC suggested that "quant managers need to ensure that their compliance policies and procedures are tailored to the risks of their model's strategies, and that compliance personnel are integrated into the development and maintenance of their investment models" (SEC Press Release 2011-37).

This statement perplexed compliance professionals about what skills were necessary to integrate themselves into the involvement of the complex functions and processes. Many people in the industry believed this was possibly an expansion of the compliance responsibilities beyond the role intended by the adopting release of Rule 206(4)-7.[7] Although there is broad consensus that there is no requirement to involve compliance personnel in the day-to-day operations or oversight of business or other noncompliance functions (such as model development and enhancements), U.S. regulators have consistently emphasized a heightened attention towards the *role* of compliance to oversee the firm's risk identification process and ensure that appropriate policies and procedures are adopted, implemented, and followed.[8]

An adviser should organize its written compliance policies and procedures in the form of a compliance manual, which should be revised, as needed, and distributed to all employees initially and when material changes occur. An adviser does not necessarily have to memorialize all of its practices and procedures. In some instances, it may be sufficient for the policy to allocate responsibility within an organization for the timely performance of various obligations, such as who is responsible for quality control when computer models are updated. Thus, a firm might decide to memorialize more of its practices than regulatorily required. Whenever a firm decides that particular documentation is beneficial, the compliance team should confirm that the investment or risk management team has adequately documented its processes in its procedure and for lifecycle management.

The formulation and implementation of a robust model policy should have sufficient details that state the expectations of, and provide transparency, clarity, and accountability regarding, model risk management processes. It should cover all aspects of the model risk management steps, including type of models covered, model ranking rationale, roles and responsibilities of all affected groups, due-diligence requirements for various stages of model life-cycle processes, development, implementation, model usage and change management processes. The model policy should also provide details on governance and validation aspects, including model incident management and resolution procedures, and provide guidance on model documentation requirements, model output record retention standards, version control procedures, and documentation of model output usage in the investment processes.

---

7 See, e.g., Barrentine, Lofchie, and Bondi (2011).

8 The following is a typical and consistently repeated speech excerpt (Carlo di Florio, 2011): "The business is the first line of defense responsible for taking, managing, and supervising risk effectively and in accordance with the risk appetite and tolerances set by the board and senior management of the whole organization. Key support functions, such as compliance and ethics or risk management, is the second line of defense. They need to have adequate resources, independence, standing, and authority to implement effective programs and objectively monitor and escalate risk issues."

Recordkeeping

Advisers Act Section 204 requires advisers to retain certain materials and keep records of their activities. Quant investment firms should be prepared to share these records, if requested. This requirement is complicated by the fact that for a quant firm, the precise definition of a "record" is not clear. For instance, records could include past versions of prototype and production code, past versions of databases, fully restorable production environments and databases, data inputs and logs, intermediate stored results, final outputs, and nonquant-specific material such as trade tickets, approval records, and client communications.

A quant shop may elect to retain records of its activities that it is not legally obligated to record. Additional recordkeeping can lead to quality improvement, recognition of errors, and help to demonstrate due diligence in the event of lawsuits. Moreover, the possibility exists that additional records will need to be shared with the SEC, in which case the firm would not be immune to Freedom of Information Act (FOIA) requests. Some firms may wish to retain these additional records but resist sharing the full complement of their materials with the SEC. Other firms might want not to record certain information, if such recordkeeping is not legally mandatory, but retain material that the firm believes would benefit its operations. In either case, it is not advisable for firms to bear any regulatory duties beyond what is prescribed by the Advisers Act.

Advisers Act Section 204 permits the SEC to require *by rule* that investment advisers retain and produce such records as deemed "necessary or appropriate in the public interest or for the protection of investors." To achieve this goal, the SEC created Rule 204-2, which lists the categories of records that all investment advisers are required to maintain.

The challenges faced by quant firms is that the records surrounding intellectual property, such as investment models and computer code, generally do not fall within any of the categories of records listed in Rule 204-2. Currently, Rule 204-2 does not envision the production or retention of a trade secret like computer models or code.[9] Quant firms should retain and produce all required books and records related to the business and transactions generated by the code.

For many quantitative investment advisers, there is substantial value in the intellectual property of its computer code and other quantitative proprietary formulas. For this reason, most quant firms limit their own employees' access to the code and make a tremendous effort to preserve the confidentiality of their most valuable trade secrets. Further, many firms require nondisclosure agreements when using the services of third parties.

9 Over the last 20 years, the few changes to the books and records rule have been limited to recordkeeping requirements in conjunction with new rules such as Rule 206(4)-7 ("Compliance Rule"), Rule 204A-1 ("Code of Ethics"), Rule 204-3 (amendments to Form ADV), Rule 206(4)-2 (Custody), Rule 206(4)-5 (Political Contributions), and Rule 206(4)-6 (Proxy Voting).

Revealing computer code and other proprietary information provided to the SEC creates a significant business risk for quant firms in that their most valuable trade secrets could be exposed to others, through for example, a FOIA request or through private litigation discovery requests. As outlined below, the SEC cannot guarantee that any information obtained during regulatory examinations will remain confidential.

Senior SEC examination officials at various industry conferences have recognized that the SEC is sensitive to the proprietary trade secrets associated with quant firms' formulas and code, and will attempt to identify the critical information that will provide the examiners the necessary insights on the investment process without requesting access to the code (e.g., white papers prepared by the firm that detail the purpose and strategy of the model). SEC officials have also mentioned that firms need proper documentation of models and firms that lack such documentation will have longer visits by the SEC as they may have to review source code.

In light of these comments, quant firms should be able to identify records that can help demonstrate a robust control structure around its investment model or code, such as a list of employees with access rights, and how changes to the code are performed. Trading records, performance reports, client statements, custodian statements—all of which show the results of the investment process—are helpful. The challenge with creating any records, such as a white paper, is to ensure the documents remain current and relevant to the firm's business practices.

One key point for quant firms to consider is that under the current regulatory regime, the SEC cannot guarantee that any records provided during an examination will remain confidential. On September 16, 2010, former Chairman Mary Schapiro testified before the U.S. House of Representatives Committee on Financial Services to defend Section 929*I* of the Dodd-Frank Act.[10] Among its provisions, Section 929*I* amended the Advisers Act to include the provision that "the commission shall not be compelled to disclose any records or information provided to the commission under Section 204, or records or information based upon or derived from such records or information, if such records or information have been obtained by the commission for use in furtherance of the purposes of this title."

In her testimony, Schapiro stated that the existing FOIA exemptions alone were insufficient to protect sensitive and proprietary information obtained during examinations. Schapiro also noted that the FOIA exemptions are unavailable to the SEC when responding to a subpoena served in private litigation. Schapiro concluded by noting that Section 929*I* "will provide certainty to registrants by clarifying that the sensitive information the commission receives in its examination or surveillance efforts can be protected from compelled disclosure." Unfortunately, Section 929*I* was *repealed* on October 5, 2010.

---

[10] Mary L. Schapiro, "Legislative Proposals to Address Concerns Over the SEC's New Confidentiality Provision" (Sept. 16, 2010), http://www.sec.gov/news/testimony/2010/ts091610mls.htm

As Schapiro's testimony makes clear, the current confidentiality protections available to registered entities cannot guarantee that a quant firm's trade secrets will remain confidential. If a firm provides this information to the SEC, there a number of different circumstances by which the information may be disclosed to others.

When Things Go Wrong

Quant shops often operate investment models that are complex and implemented with sizeable computer code that uses data feeds from multiple sources. Inevitably, errors creep into their operations. It is important for firms to have policies and procedures in place before these errors occur. In particular, a firm should have clear guidelines for error definition and management; for escalation and reporting of errors to senior management, the board, or regulators; for ramifications on employee compensation, especially when the client must be made whole following the error; and for improvements to operations following the discovery of an error.

Error Management. Errors range from those that strictly pertain to the quant investment process to other types, such as compliance or code of ethics breaches, and trading errors.

One difficult and sensitive decision for quant managers is how to determine the materiality of an error. Materiality is a subjective concept, what a reasonable person believes is material in one situation may not necessarily be material in another situation. Materiality will usually determine whether the error needs to be escalated or self-reported. This is difficult to define because the firm's size, culture, and investment approach will determine the kinds of events that will need to be reviewed by the firm's chain of command.

Materiality thresholds based on impact amounts, which are adequate in other areas of the firm, are not very useful for modelers because it is virtually impossible to gauge the impact on performance of a particular coding feature or error. Accordingly, alternatives to monetary thresholds should be considered, such as risk-based perspectives or a focus on qualitative matters, including compliance, reputational, and regulatory risk. Although there will always be an element of judgment involved, there should be an effort made to best define materiality in terms of investment performance impact and other important criteria. Irrespective of the way materiality is established, it should be documented and approved prior to applying it in an escalation.

From an oversight perspective, a sound practice would be to establish an independent function, or at least an error management committee, in direct control of all aspects of error monitoring, escalation, remediation, and impact assessment, which in turn would draw from other parts of the quant firm as needed for specific expertise or resource availability.

In the event that a material error has occurred, quant managers should inform the clients that were impacted as soon as reasonably possible. It is helpful to memorialize the protocol for when an error occurs. In some instances, it may take some time to determine the full impact of an error, but quant managers should not delay informing affected clients. Generally, clients understand that errors do occasionally occur, and they will appreciate a timely notification and periodic updates as the firm is working to resolve the matter. It may be appropriate for the client relationship manager to have the initial conversation with clients about the error. Once the error analysis is completed, the firm can follow up with a more formal communication from a senior level executive explaining the nature of the error, the corrective steps taken to ensure it does not recur, and any necessary monetary remedies. If the error is significant and affects many client accounts, quant firms should work closely with their legal counsel to determine if the error should be reported to regulators.

There are benefits to having documented policies and procedures for how to recognize and respond to errors. At the very least, however, these policies will reduce uncertainty when significant errors occur. Policies also reduce the risk that a firm will be accused of designing ad hoc or ambiguous error response practices and help with internal audits, continual improvement, and consistency of practice.

Finally, the disclosure of these written policies before errors actually occur can undercut claims of fraud. The SEC has brought enforcement actions against companies without written error policies, when ambiguity in errors is used perpetrate fraud on clients. One example is the case of M & I Investment Management Corporation.[11]

On the other hand, written policies and procedures cannot be too precise or prescriptive, or they would not apply to all circumstances. Moreover, they cannot demand too much information on the error, because precise estimates of impact are commonly available only after significant time and expense. Overly prescriptive error polices could also introduce a risk that a firm did not follow its policies. Policies that commit to fixed periods for correcting errors could be too restrictive for serious errors.

An effective error policy should address:

- The person(s) informed when an error is discovered;
- The triggers for escalation to senior management;
- The triggers for disclosure of errors to clients;
- The triggers for disclosure to insurers, including errors and omission insurance;
- The actions undertaken when sanctioning employees;
- The testing and checks to be performed to uncover unnoticed errors. This would include pre-rollout testing and ongoing testing of production systems.
- The classification of errors into a category, of which there are at least three
  - Agent exceeds scope of authority—voidable at strict liability,
  - Illegal act—void at *mens rea* set by statute, and
  - Breach of fiduciary duty, especially negligence—voidable given lack of due care. This follows from Restatement (Second) of Agency § 416 and Restatement (Second) of Trusts § 218;
- Fire drills to prepare for the discovery of significant errors; and
- Internal audit of error frequency for the purposes of continual improvement, for spotting unexplained changes, and for verifying compliance with error policies.

[11] IAA Rel. No. 1318, 51 SEC Docket (CCH) 1375 (June 30, 1992).

Intentional or reckless acts are not defined as errors, despite the fact that such acts might result in legal liability. In addition, trading errors do not include good faith errors in judgment in making investment decisions for clients. Compensation is discussed subsequently in the chapter. The SEC will often ask for lists of trade errors during examinations so it is wise for firms to keep a record of these errors.

Firms should respond differently to errors that occur during development and prototyping, which are expected as part of the development process, and those that occur in a production environment, which are unwarranted and subject to escalation and disclosure, and which may affect employee compensation.

Ongoing forensic testing and monitoring should be performed by quant firms to ensure that their investment models continue to operate as intended. Rule 206(4)-7 of the Investment Advisers Act requires firms to perform an annual compliance review, which should involve different kinds of forensic testing.

When used as a monitoring activity, forensic testing can identify issues that were not caught during initial testing or that have developed due to changing environments and data. Day-to-day processing might not identify these issues, and it is critical to include forensic testing as part of a quant firm's internal controls. Firms should focus on gaining insight from existing data to determine whether undiscovered or unexpected circumstances exist that contradict the initial intentions of the investment model. Issues and problems identified through forensic testing, validation, and monitoring should be proactively communicated to all relevant individuals in the firm with a plan for corrective action and follow-up.

Escalation Policies. Quant firms have the responsibility and obligation to appropriately escalate issues or errors identified through investment model validation or other forms of oversight. Examples of what may constitute an issue that needs to be escalated are trade errors, coding errors, compliance breaches, and control failures. Findings from both internal and external audits related to investment models should be communicated, escalated, and addressed as required as well.

Escalation should be timely and include senior staff or board members as necessary. After issues are escalated and discussed, appropriate remediation plans for corrective action should be developed and implemented. Assessments should consider how the error affected investment performance and be communicated appropriately. This includes reaching out to clients if the error was deemed material and had affected their portfolios. Transparency is a key piece in developing effective escalation policies.

This escalation process should be defined, documented, and shared with necessary staff. A sound practice would be to ensure these escalation policies are reviewed by individuals with appropriate seniority before being finalized. In addition, quant firms should consider whether it is necessary to have different escalation policy and procedures for models in the development stage and models that are in live production. In addition, employees should be trained on how to follow these policies and handle an issue when it occurs. The process should be vetted with required control groups (e.g., compliance, legal, audit) before being implemented. Control groups such as compliance personnel should consider these escalation policies and procedures when developing their audit review plans.

A difficult and sensitive decision for quant firms is how to determine the materiality of what needs to be escalated or perhaps self-reported to the appropriate regulator. This situation is hard to define in that size, culture, and nature of investment approach will have an impact on what should be considered a serious event that needs to be reviewed by the "chain of command." There will always be an element of judgment involved, but there should be an effort made to best define materiality in terms of investment performance impact and other important criteria. This materiality calculation should be documented and approved prior to applying it in a true escalation situation. Quant firms should consult with their appropriate legal counsel when they encounter a potential materiality discussion.

The key is to have a clearly defined process in place so that issues can be remedied immediately. Controls need to have been established so that the decision-making process is efficient, well thought out, and well documented.

Disclosures. Similar to other asset managers or investment shops, quant firms may be faced with a legal obligation to disclose errors, as stipulated in regulations and fiduciary duties. Notwithstanding legal responsibility, there may also be marketing benefits of voluntary disclosure, as this would reflect a culture of honesty and transparency within the firm. These benefits, however, would need to be weighed against the negative publicity and reputational costs of disclosing errors. It is wise for quant firms to have policies and procedures established in advance for such voluntary disclosures. In the case of M & I Investment Management Corporation referred to earlier, the SEC chided the adviser for not including a policy of disclosing "the nature and extent of the error and of the proposed method of rectifying it" to affected clients.

Other issues that affect the disclosure decision are whether errors should be disclosed to all clients, to affected clients only, or to negatively affected clients only, and the timing of disclosure: during the discovery of the error, during its diagnosis and correction, or during reimbursement of lost funds to the client caused by the error, if any.

Compensation. The considerations that can affect compensation, with respect to errors causing monetary losses to investors, and to model validation, should be mentioned in the firm's compensation policies. For simple "fat-finger" or trading errors, the standard is to make clients whole, but what does that mean for quant firms, and where should the funds to compensate the clients come from? As noted for error management, there exist at least three categories of errors:

- *Agent exceeds scope of authority:* per Restatement (Second) of Agency § 401 the firm must pay for investor losses (but maybe not forgone profits?) that (happen to) result from a violation of the principal's instructions even if the violation reduced the risk of such an outcome. However, shouldn't the lack of causation at least be a defense?
- *Illegal act:* damages are set by statute, but this generally leads to rescission.
- *Breach of fiduciary duty, especially negligence:* probably leads to rescission, but less clear. Note that Restatement (Second) of Trusts § 213 bars netting between unrelated errors.

In each case, the firm will suffer monetary losses because the client will need to be made whole. There is wide agreement on making the client whole, but there are differences over where the funds should be drawn. If firms wish to draw funds from the agent who committed the error, by clawing back bonuses or by cutting compensation, or if they wish to terminate the agent's employment, this should be clearly stated in the firm's compensation policies. Note that, as stated earlier for error management, trading errors do include good faith errors in judgment in making investment decisions for clients. For traditional funds, however, this results in a clear line: some errors result in rescission; other events that might resemble errors are in fact errors done in good faith and result in no loss of compensation. For quant funds, however, an error in a single line of code could have two independent effects, each of which falls on opposite sides of the line. That makes the decision to repeal compensation more complicated.

Firms that have the resources to conduct model validation in-house should be aware of the OCC regulatory guidance on compensation for members of the validation team. Specifically, the regulation states that the compensation of these members cannot be tied to profits generated by the model. For smaller firms that derive all of their operational revenue from a single model or a single line of business, this limit might be difficult to enforce. Still, firms should try to ensure that compensation and bonuses of model validation staff are not directly tied to model performance, but tied to other metrics that measure firm performance, such as sales, for example.

Improvement. Learning from errors can prove valuable, although sometimes it can be costly. Many firms keep an error log and incidents, and it is helpful to periodically review past errors and incidents to identify any potential weaknesses in a firm's compliance structure. It may be useful to memorialize what changes or improvements to processes were made to ensure that the error or incident does not recur. Finally, it may be helpful to have a cross-departmental committee review each error or incident and discuss any other potential weaknesses or risks that may have not been identified.

Outsourcing Policies and Monitoring

Many quant firms leverage third-party service providers to help build and maintain their investment models. Alternatively, they may decide to purchase models from third parties and host the software internally. Either way, there needs to be a risk and control framework in place to monitor the risk associated with these relationships. This framework should be a modified version from the version used when the firm develops models internally; however, in general, the same checks should be performed.

It is sound practice for quant firms to have a vendor management program in place. Vendor management programs should require performing appropriate due diligence over key service providers before signing a contract, and continuing throughout the relationship. Typically, these due diligence reviews can include assessing a firm's business continuity/disaster recovery plans (shown in Appendix B), information security policies, control infrastructure, financial standing, client service, and any legal concerns. These programs become more important when the firm is dealing with key vendors that will be providing primary business processes such as investment model development and support. Building strong communication channels with these vendors is essential.

If a firm makes a decision to leverage third-party models, but not fully outsource them, a standard model risk and control framework should be applied. This includes all controls in change management, validation, testing, and monitoring processes. Advisers are generally not at fault for errors caused by other participants, such as vendors. Accord Restatement (Second) of Trusts, Section 204 states that "the trustee is not liable to the beneficiary for a loss or depreciation in value of the trust property, or for a failure to make a profit, not resulting from a breach of trust." However, advisers might bear a duty to choose reputable vendors and monitor the activities of their vendors diligently. If a company bears contractual or regulatory duties, it generally cannot escape those simply by delegating its tasks to a vendor. This observation drives many of the recommendations that companies test and evaluate products from vendors before relying on them.

If a firm makes the decision to outsource part of its operations to third-party models, it should:[12]

- Ensure there are appropriate internal processes in place for selecting vendors;
- Require vendors to provide an explanation of the products' components, design, and intended use prior to purchase;
- Fully evaluate whether the model is appropriate for the firm's needs based on information gathered from the vendor;
- Require vendors to provide appropriate testing results that show their products work as expected;
- Require that vendors outline models' limitations and assumptions; and
- Require vendors to conduct ongoing performance testing and disclose results to their clients, and to make appropriate updates when needed.

It is critical to develop as much in-house understanding of the third-party product as possible. Strategically, if a firm decides to rely fully on an external party for a process so

---

[12] Board of Governors of the Federal Reserve System, Office of the Comptroller of the Currency, *Supervisory Guidance on Model Risk Management* (Apr. 4, 2011), http://occ.gov/news-issuances/bulletins/2011/bulletin-2011-12a.pdf

important to the firm's success, it is essential to build a sufficient internal understanding of the process and product. If the third party ceases business, or its product is no longer supported, it is crucial that internal resources can either take over management of the models or have the insight and understanding to move the firm in another direction as seamlessly as possible. For example, the Futures Industry Association (FIA) recommends that parties agree in advance that the client will have access to the vendor's source code if that vendor goes bankrupt.

VIII. GOVERNANCE

"Governance" means the overall structure used to oversee and manage one or more particular risks, whether financial, legal, compliance, operational, or reputational. As the focus of this chapter is on the process of managing the risk of quantitative investments, in particular, the discussion of governance will be focused on quantitative investment risk. Done properly, the governance process serves to tie together and reinforce the supervisory, compliance, risk management, and validation functions discussed throughout this chapter. A strong governance function is essential to the effectiveness of quantitative investment management and helps ensure that the risk management framework aligns with disclosures, implied or actual, made to clients as well as the broader risk management approach and tolerance of the firm and its regulators.

The Role of the Senior Executives and the Board

An effective governance process requires that a firm's senior executive officer and board of directors or other governance body embrace responsibly for good governance. Their focus should be on creating a positive firm culture by setting a tone at the top that demonstrates the firm's commitment to its quantitative risk process, and this tone is reflected in decisions involving budgets, compensation, discipline, hiring, promotions and by setting an example by their own behavior.

Some might think that quantitative investment processes can create special governance challenges because senior managers might not have the technical background to fully understand the details of quantitative models or quantitative investment processes. However, in almost any business there are technical issues that are outside the scope of direct knowledge of the chief executive officer (CEO).

The Role of Senior Management. Senior management can take practical steps to support that culture by ensuring that adequate development, testing, validation, and implementation policies and procedures are established and followed consistently. Senior management can ensure that resources are sufficient, that risk management staff is competent and properly compensated, and that this staff has sufficient authority in the organization to play an effective role. It is also crucial that senior management from the firm's control, operational, and business functions work together seamlessly to design and implement the firm's general processes and procedures. This means that control and operational functions that are fully involved in the planning process are kept informed of new or unexpected developments, and that support or sign-off of the relevant control and operational functions are necessary before business functions can move forward.

Collectively, the senior representatives involved in this process should have the expertise, authority, and independence to manage the firm's quantitative risk processes. In a larger firm, this might include senior representatives from each of the model risk management areas as well as senior business leaders (e.g., research, trading, and portfolio management, as well as senior members of control and operational functions such as compliance, risk management, audit, finance, and IT).

Larger firms may formalize the process by which senior management works together by creating a committee that operates pursuant to a formal charter and written procedures. Other firms may adopt an informal process such as a working group. What is important is that senior management from both the control and business functions work together as one and that specific responsibilities and decisions be documented. This relationship will also further set the tone for a culture of compliance and create a forum for escalating and vetting issues when they arise.

The primary responsibility to ensure that models are designed, implemented, and used appropriately resides with the investment team. Although validation and compliance functions can provide additional oversight and controls, the investment team is the first line of defense in model risk management.

In addition to the independent risk management and compliance functions discussed in this document, the investment team should implement a robust set of policies and procedures to ensure appropriate model supervision and use. This discussion offers a recommended framework for investment teams, and is intended to provide an outline of the key attributes that can be implemented by any sized firm.

Day-to Day Management and Control. This chapter has previously discussed sound practices to support a robust and proper quantitative investment practices. These topics are likely to include those discussed here.

Policies and Procedures Governing Day-to-Day Operations and Supervision. Policy guidelines are not static and need to be reevaluated relative to changes in the firm's business policies, practices, products and markets, industry or economy, and external regulations. The governance function should have a means of staying abreast of industry developments and evaluating them relative to current policies and business goals. Compliance staff can provide guidance on developing appropriate procedures, but each business unit's senior manager is ultimately responsible for his respective team.

It is important that there is clarity across teams of who is accountable for each component of the risk management framework. It is helpful if these responsibilities are well documented and effectively communicated. It is also important that everyone in the firm recognize that compliance and ethical behavior are part of everyone's job description. Quantitative investment strategies require specialized expertise in development, testing, implementation, and production support. As a result, it is important that the required expertise, relative to roles and responsibilities, and staff requirements are adequately estimated and in line with budget expectations.

Addressing Conflicts of Interest. Broadly defined, a "conflict of interest" exists when two or more activities or relationships are incompatible to some extent. In the investment management industry, a conflict of interest may arise from any activity or business relationship in which an adviser's interest competes with the interest of its clients. Conflicts may involve divided loyalty (client/client conflict) as well as self-dealing (client/adviser conflict or client/adviser affiliate conflict).

As in other areas in investing, conflicts of interest might arise in quant processes. What might seem to be in the best interests of an individual or a team might not be in the best interests of clients or other constituencies. It might not be possible to eliminate all possible conflicts of interest, but there are some practical steps that can help manage and mitigate potential consequences of conflicts. As mentioned in describing execution, a potential conflict of interest could exist when the portfolio management and trading functions are performed by the same individuals. The segregation of these duties is one way to mitigate this potential conflict.

Error management poses another potential conflict of interest between advisers and its clients. An established error management and escalation policy helps mitigate this potential conflict.

Compensation structures should be carefully designed to be aligned with the interests of clients and other constituencies. In particular, associates should not expect extraordinary compensation because of taking inappropriate risks or shortcuts within the investment process.

Controls to Monitor That Supervisory Reviews Are Being Performed. Those monitors include:

- Controls to monitor that supervisory reviews are in fact happening; and
- Controls to monitor for unexpected outcomes.

Escalation. Escalation policies were discussed earlier. From a governance perspective it is important that there is a process for upstream reporting on periodic basis and as material concerns arise. In addition, investment returns should largely be achieved by bearing reasonable risks. The governance function should seek to ensure that the risks borne are reasonable, well understood, and consistent with risks communicated to clients and other critical constituents. This might be thought of as having three levels:

- *Portfolio risk:* at the individual model/strategy/portfolio level, the risks of the portfolio should be reasonably consistent with the established risk metrics of the strategy, like beta and leverage, and the types of instruments held in the portfolio should be reasonably disclosed and consistent with the risk profile of the strategy. Stress testing might be appropriate to anticipate how risk might change under reasonably foreseeable scenarios;

- *Model risk:* should be well understood and consistent with the risk parameters of the firm. Sensitivity testing can be carried out to determine how the model will perform given different parameter inputs. Constraints can be used to mitigate model risk; and
- *Overall:* the quantitative risk management framework should fit into the broader risk management of the firm. The governance function should do its best to ensure that the level of risk is within overall firm tolerance.

Periodic Testing, Auditing, and Review. The firmwide governance function should meet periodically to review exceptions, overrides, audit results (internal and external, if applicable), and performance and risk levels relative to benchmarks.

Training and Periodic Attestations

Training on a firm's governance structure, reporting, and escalation expectations should be performed on a continual basis as a reminder of the established procedures and protocols. Periodic attestations that the procedures have been followed and the reporting of any exceptions are good governance tools.

Investment Team

Similar to other investment managers, quant firms will have a chief investment officer (CIO) who will oversee the management of the investment portfolios and will also be responsible for formulating the firm's investment strategy and managing the investment team. For smaller firms the CIO may also act as the CEO, president, or managing director. Other members of the investment team will generally include fund managers, investment managers, research directors/analysts, and traders.

Generally, the primary responsibility to ensure that models are designed, implemented, and used appropriately resides with the investment team. Although validation and compliance functions can provide additional oversight and controls, the investment team is the first line of defense in model risk management.

In addition to the independent risk management and compliance functions discussed in this chapter, the investment team should implement a robust set of policies and procedures to ensure appropriate model supervision and use. This subsection discusses a recommended framework for investment teams, and is intended to outline the key attributes that can be implemented by a firm of any size.

Supervision and Oversight. Investment team supervisors need to set the tone for the importance of a robust risk management framework, a culture of communication, and incentives for all functions involved with the models to address and/or escalate significant issues or concerns. Supervisors are responsible for ensuring that developers and users have the appropriate expertise to perform their functions and have the resources to support their processes.

Model Approval. Supervisors and/or their delegates (e.g., risk managers) should approve models prior to implementation. A robust approval process includes a review and discussion of the risk management processes, including if possible, a review by a peer that did not develop the model but has the skills and expertise to have done so. The specific review materials will vary by firm, but can be expected to provide supervisors and risk managers enough detail to conclude on the following:

- Developers and users have the appropriate expertise to execute their responsibilities;
- Adequate resources or planned spending and development are in place to support the process;
- Operational risks have appropriate mitigation procedures and the amount of risk is acceptable;
- The model is theoretically sound and adequately benchmarked to other approaches;
- Developers and users understand the limitations and assumptions of the model enough to avoid misuse and misapplication;
- The judgmental and qualitative aspects of the model are sound, and users are applying them in systematic, unambiguous, and reproducible manner; and
- Expected risk analytics and performance outcomes are well defined, and appropriate reporting is in place.

Periodic Review. In addition to the initial approval process, supervisors and their delegates should perform periodic reviews and have appropriate supporting management reporting. Reports should be clear and comprehensible and consider that supervisors may have varying levels of quantitative expertise. Ideally, management reporting should highlight potential exceptions to risk and performance expectations, providing supervisors with a tool to assess model accuracy and stability and asking developers and users constructive questions. Examples include examining confidence intervals in statistical models, assessing stress tests and scenario analysis, calculating performance and risk relative to expectations, and providing feedback from compliance and validation functions.

IX. CONCLUSION

Quantitative processes are complex and quantitative firms vary in size and diversity. The term "quant" can refer to "black box" processes tied directly to trading or largely traditional managers that use quantitative tools. In light of these factors, this chapter has attempted to provide you with ideas that can be applied across a wide spectrum of firms.

Quantitative processes are not perfect. Anyone who has worked with computers knows they are not infallible, and the humans who code, operate, and use computer output can and do make mistakes. Although errors cannot be eliminated, steps can be taken to reduce the probability of error, and perhaps more importantly, to address errors when they occur.

Perhaps the most important attribute of a successful quantitative investment organization is the hardest to quantify. A sound quantitative process has an open, honest, and intellectually rigorous environment and an absolute commitment to integrity. Based on the tone established at the top, all members of the organization should feel comfortable questioning issues that they legitimately believe might be detrimental to the interests of clients or other key constituents.

By taking into consideration the information discussed within this chapter, the hope is that compliance professionals working with quant firms acquired valuable insight and tools that can be applied to establish a sound quantitative investment process.

APPENDIX A. TRADING CONTROLS

Best Execution

As investment advisers, quant managers have a fiduciary duty to seek best execution for client transactions. Factors used by quant managers to determine best execution for a particular transaction may include, among others:

- The broker's effectiveness in executing and settling trades;
- The reliability, integrity, confidentiality, promptness, reputation, and financial condition of the broker (including past execution history with the broker);
- The size of the trade, its relative difficulty, and the security's trading characteristics and liquidity;
- The quality and breadth of products and services offered by the broker; and
- The broker's willingness to accept the quant manager's standardized commission rates.

To properly manage a best execution program, a quant manager should have the following processes in place:

Due diligence review: Broker-dealers that wish to trade with the quant manager, including new client directed brokers, should be subjected to a due diligence process consisting of three parts: (1) review of the broker's Form BD for disciplinary history, stability of the business, and potential conflicts of interest, etc.; (2) review the broker's financial stability and net capital requirements; and (3) a qualitative determination of the broker-dealer's reputation within the industry.

APPENDIX A. TRADING CONTROLS *(cont'd)*

Best execution review: Traders should monitor the trading practices, gather relevant information, and periodically review and evaluate the services provided by broker-dealers such as the quality of executions, research, commission rates, and overall brokerage relationships, among other things. A best execution committee, along with traders, compliance, and investment team should meet periodically to discuss the traders' evaluations and determinations of best execution, using internal and third party analyses.

Broker-dealer approval: After a broker-dealer is approved, it becomes subject to the best execution review process. The best execution committee may reduce the volume of trades executed with a broker-dealer if the quality of its execution begins to decline. Trading with the broker-dealer should cease if execution does not improve. Furthermore, a quant manager should cease trading with a broker-dealer if an event arises where the broker-dealer cannot achieve best execution (i.e., will not agree to a lower commission rate).

Recordkeeping: Documentation and materials related to broker-dealer due diligence and best execution reviews should be maintained by compliance and trading teams and a summary of the quant manager's brokerage and best execution practices should be disclosed on an adviser's Form ADV Part 2A.

Trade Allocation

In principle, all executions carried out on an aggregated order basis must be allocated to participating investors in a fair and equitable manner. No investor should receive preferential treatment over another.

Therefore, quant managers should consider the following guidelines.

Preexecution assessment: All participating clients and accounts and the desired initial investment amounts in a purchase or sale should be determined and documented prior to the placing of the order and the subsequent execution.

Trades directly booked to client accounts following execution—as soon after trade execution as practical, the trade allocations should be filled, booked, and processed as per the initial determination of participants and volume. If the order was not completed in its entirety, then the volume that was transacted should be allocated on a pro-rata basis across all participating clients and accounts. Under no circumstances should there be any "warehousing" of trades, where they are allocated or held in any form of suspense account for allocation to a client account or fund at a later date. Note: This does not include presettlement reallocation of trades due to an error. In this situation, reallocation can occur subject to compliance approval.

APPENDIX A. TRADING CONTROLS *(cont'd)*

Post-trade reallocation to accounts: Once a trade has been booked according to predetermined allocations, it may not be reallocated to another account. Any changes to holdings must be made through market priced and executed sales and purchases. For IPOs, allocation should occur once the quantity purchased has been confirmed by the broker.

Non-pro-rata allocation by exception only: If a pro-rata allocation is not practical due to an "uneconomic" or "inefficient" fill from a client perspective or because of account liquidity, strategy, or investment guideline constraints, the trader may refer to the relevant fund manager for a decision to allocate on a non-pro-rata or manual allocation basis.

Monitoring and control: Traders should keep the details and records of the participating accounts and allocation and volume amounts, such as trade blotters. Quant managers should undertake a post-trade monitoring and review process in order to validate and analyze the allocation of trades. This process could occur on a regular or periodic basis, as applicable, to each fund in order to validate that the above requirements have been followed.

APPENDIX B. DISASTER RECOVERY (BUSINESS CONTINUITY PLAN)

A temporary interruption or long-term loss of infrastructure or key personnel could adversely affect quant managers' operations and ability to service their clients. To help minimize the impact of such events, quant managers should develop and document comprehensive business continuity plans in the context of their business. The purpose of the plan is to help ensure rapid recovery and resume critical operations on a timely basis. These plans should consider the availability and continuity of their investment models and the security of their intellectual property, and be communicated to all employees.

The SEC takes the position that an adviser's fiduciary obligation to its clients includes the obligation to take steps to protect its clients' interest from being placed at risk as a result of the adviser's inability to provide services after a disaster, death of key personnel, or other interruption of the business.[14] Also, the recordkeeping Rule 201-2(g)(3) requires advisers that maintain records in electronic formats to establish and maintain procedures to safeguard the records from destruction or loss.

[14] *See*, e.g., SEC Rel. No 2204 2003, n. 22.

APPENDIX B. DISASTER RECOVERY (BUSINESS CONTINUITY PLAN) *(cont'd)*

Quant managers should develop procedures the firm will follow in the event of a disruption to normal business operations. These procedures should be developed after performing a risk assessment of the firm's operations and business, as well as identifying various possible scenarios and how they will be addressed.

To help minimize the impact of certain types of disruptions, quant managers should consider the use of backup failover infrastructure, such as servers and network hardware that can support key services, including investment models, trading applications, and supporting services such as back office and even email. A focus should be placed on protecting against the loss of data or significant down time. Some controls and procedures quant managers should consider are as follows:

- *Committees:* Disaster recovery and crisis management teams are essential in addressing business interruptions promptly;
- *Distribution of plan/training:* Employees should be trained and how to perform business functions during a disaster;
- *Communications with employees:* Establish methods for contacting personnel, and require retention of the contingency plan at their homes;
- *Workplace recovery (alternative physical facilities)*: If appropriate, identify and contract with predesignated possible locations for employees (including each essential business group) to report in the event the offices are displaced. Determine whether it is appropriate to identify a different geographical zone for recovery facilities. Ensure that critical functions can be performed either in a secondary location or remotely;
- *Backup communication:* Create a redundant and diversified network of carriers. Arrange to contact utilities (voice and data communications, Internet, etc.) for use and call forwarding;
- *Backup and access to records storage:* Regular back up of all file servers, electronic systems, software, documents, and electronic correspondence ensures immediate accessibility;
- *Internet access :* Ensure employees' access to crucial information through the Internet;
- *Communications with clients and others:* Establish methods for communicating to clients, brokers, custodians, and other service providers to make them aware of status and any alternative work flows;
- *Pricing:* If necessary, outline fair-value pricing policies and procedures that will be used if catastrophes or other events call into question the market quotations of securities.
- *Loss of Key Personnel:* Consider designating backup personnel to handle a key person's duties as well as the methods by which the adviser will handle clients' accounts in the event of a loss of key personnel. Sole proprietors should consider designating an individual to promptly notify clients of his or her death or incapacity, and answer any questions regarding how to contact the custodian or brokerage firm regarding the status of their accounts.

APPENDIX B. DISASTER RECOVERY (BUSINESS CONTINUITY PLAN) *(cont'd)*

Testing

Business continuity plans should be tested regularly and should demonstrate that systems and controls are resilient to the loss of critical infrastructure or key individuals. The SEC staff has indicated that business continuity objectives should include a high level of confidence, through ongoing use or robust testing, that critical internal and external continuity arrangements are effective and compatible (Gadziala, 2003). Quant managers should consider routinely testing and assessing recovery and resumption arrangements to ensure connectivity, capacity, and the integrity of data transmission, as well as functionality and volume capacity. This includes testing the primary site and backup arrangements. Test scenarios could include wide-scale disruptions that affect the accessibility of key staff, and demonstrate the ability to recover and resume within target recovery times.

Quant managers should document and maintain test results and update procedures in their business continuity plans as appropriate. Also, if possible and appropriate, include third-party service providers in the disaster testing. Issues that are identified during testing should be resolved, as needed.

WORKS CITED

1. Alternative Investment Management Association. "Guide to Sound Practices for European Hedge Fund Managers." 2007.
2. Angel Oak Advisory, LLC, Prepared by David J. Green, Managing Director. "Model Risk Management Framework and Related Regulatory Guidance." April 2012. http://www.angeloakadvisory.com/resources/Risk%20Model%20Validation%20Framework.pdf
3. Barrentine, Glen, Steven D. Lofchie, and Bradley J. Bondi. "Quantitative Investment Models and Compliance Policies and Procedures: the Securities and Exchange Commission Order Involving the AXA Rosenberg Entities." *Cadwalader.* Feb. 17, 2011. http://www.cadwalader.com/resources/clients-friendsmemos/quantitative-investment-models-and-compliance-policies-and-procedures-the-securities-andexchange-commission-order-involving-the-axa-rosenberg-entities
4. Bernstein, Peter. *Capital Ideas: The Improbable Origins of Modern Wall Street.* Hoboken, NJ: Wiley, 1991.
5. Board of Governors of the Federal Reserve System and Office of the Comptroller of the Currency (OCC). "Supervisory Guidance on Model Risk Management (OCC 2011-12)." April 2011.
6. Capital Markets Risk Advisors and Buy-Side Risk Managers Forum. "Risk Principles for Asset Managers." 2008.

7. Darnell, Max. "Piloting Quantitative Investment Strategies." *First Quadrant LP-FQ Perspective*, September 2007.
8. Derman, Emmanuel. "Model Risk." *Goldman, Sachs & Co. Equity Product Strategy*, April 1996. di Florio, Carlo V., Director, Office of Compliance Inspections and Examinations, U.S. Securities and Exchange Commission. "The Role of Compliance and Ethics in Risk Management." *Speech by SEC Staff: NSCP National Meeting.* October 17, 2011. http://www.sec.gov/news/speech/2011/spch101711cvd.htm
9. Futures Industry Association. "Software Development and Change Management Recommendations." March 2012. http://www.futuresindustry.org/downloads/Software_Change_Management.pdf
10. Gadziala, Mary Ann, Associate Director, U.S. Securities and Exchange Commission. "Speech by SEC Staff: Disaster Recovery and Business Continuity Planning." May 1, 2003.http://www.sec.gov/news/speech/spch050103mag.htm.
11. Grinold, Richard C. "The Fundamental Law of Active Management." *Journal of Portfolio Management* 15 (1989): 30-37.
12. Lo, Andrew, and Amir Khandani. "What Happened to the Quants in August 2007?: Evidence from Factors and Transactions Data." *Journal of Financial Markets* 14 (October 2008).
13. Meyer, Christian, and Peter Quell. *Risk Model Validation.* London, Risk Books, 2011.
14. Risk Standards Working Group. "Risk Standards for Institutional Investment Managers and Institutional Investors." 1996.
15. Ruhl, Dennis, and Theodore Timig. "Re-quantifying your Portfolio: Is Now the Time?" *Insights, JP Morgan Asset Management.* March 2011.
16. Schapiro, Mary L. "Speech by SEC Chairman: Remarks at SIFMA's Compliance and Legal Society Annual Seminar." March 23, 2011. http://www.sec.gov/news/speech/2011/spch032311mls.htm
17. Sirri, Erik, Director, Division of Trading and Markets, U.S. Securities and Exchange Commission. "Testimony Concerning Lessons Learned in Risk Management Oversight at Federal Financial Regulators." March 18, 2009. http://www.sec.gov/news/testimony/2009/ts031809es.htm
18. Society of Quantitative Analysts. *Model Risk, Quants and the Law.* April 26, 2012. https://m360.sqaus.org/ViewEvent.aspx?id=46036&instance=0
19. U.S. Securities and Exchange Commission. "Investment Advisers Act Release No 2204." *Final Rule: Compliance Programs of Investment Companies and Investment Advisers.* December 17, 2003. http://www.sec.gov/rules/final/ia-2204.htm
20. "Press Release 2011-37." *SEC Charges AXA Rosenberg Entities for Concealing Error in Quantitative Investment Model.* February 3, 2011. http://www.sec.gov/news/press/2011/2011-37.htm
21. U.S. Securities and Exchange Commission, Enforcement Division. "Release No. 9181 - Administrative and Cease-and-Desist Proceedings *In the Matter of AXA Rosenberg Group LLC, AXA Rosenberg Investment Management LLC, and Barr Rosenberg Research Center LLC.*" Feb 3, 2011. http://www.sec.gov/litigation/admin/2011/33-9181.pdf

ABOUT THE AUTHOR

This chapter is the product of a paper drafted by the writing committee of the Chicago Quantitative Alliance (CQA), as revised to meet the requirements of republication in *Modern Compliance.* The CQA is a nonprofit organization formed under Section 501(c)(6) of the U.S. tax code. The organization is guided by a board of directors who are all volunteers. CQA has no paid employees and exists solely for the benefit of its members and to promote the interests of the quantitative investment community. The primary goal of the group is to facilitate the interchange of ideas between leading quantitative professionals. The discussion is focused on practitioner issues and involves active participation by all members.

Chapter 20

Adviser Custody, Part 2: Managing Private Funds

By Elizabeth M. Knoblock
Elizabeth M. Knoblock, PLLC

I. INTRODUCTION

In Volume 1 of *Modern Compliance,* the general parameters of Rule 206(4)-2 under the Investment Advisers Act of 1940 ("Advisers Act"), also known as the Custody Rule, were examined and discussed.[1] However, the elements of the Custody Rule applicable to pooled investment vehicles (PIVs) were expressly excluded from in-depth discussion at that time.[2] This chapter picks up where that chapter ended to analyze the unique aspects of the rule that may be relied upon by advisers managing PIVs. Coverage includes regulatory, compliance, and enforcement issues relating to PIVs or "private funds." This chapter excludes custody issues related to registered investment companies, or "mutual funds," which are regulated by the Investment Company Act of 1940 and related Rule 17f-5.[3] This chapter also excludes custody of any commodity interests held in any PIV, because commodities are regulated exclusively under the Commodity Exchange Act.[4] Finally, this chapter does not address state custody rules, which may vary significantly from the Custody Rule.

II. REGULATORY SCHEME FOR PRIVATE FUND CUSTODY

As a refresher, the Custody Rule comes into play for all advisers registered, or required to be registered, under the Advisers Act if they have, or are deemed to have, "custody." The rule defines "custody" as "holding, directly or indirectly, client funds or securities, or having any authority to obtain possession of them" and provides examples of when an adviser is deemed to have custody, which are:

---

1 Elizabeth M. Knoblock, "Adviser Custody: What You Need to Know," in *Modern Compliance: Best Practices for Securities & Finance,* Vol. 1, David H. Lui and John H. Walsh, eds. (Wolters Kluwer Financial Services, 2015), at 423.

2 Knoblock, "Adviser Custody."

3 Mutual funds are exempted from the Advisers Act. *See* ¶ 206(4)-2(b)(5).

4 Commodity Exchange Act, 7 U.S.C. §2(a)(1)(A).

- Possession of client funds or securities, unless received inadvertently and returned within three business days of receipt or checks made payable to a third party (except that, adviser has five business days from receipt to forward tax refunds inadvertently received from tax authorities, or proceeds received connection with various class action lawsuits or other legal actions, or stock certificates, dividends, or evidence of new debt from issuers in connection with class action);[5]
- Any arrangement that authorizes or permits adviser to withdraw client funds or securities (e.g., check signing authority, general power of attorney, direct debiting of advisory fees, access to client's accounts); and
- Acting in any capacity that gives adviser, or any supervised person, legal ownership or access to client funds or securities (e.g., general partner, managing member, trustee).[6]

Generally, PIV managers have custody based on the capacity in which they act. Serving as the general partner of a limited partnership, the managing member of a limited liability company, the trustee of a trust, or any comparable position for another type of PIV, constitutes custody under the rule. Because private funds are often structured so that the manager or a related entity serves as the funds' general partner, managing member, or trustee in order to control all aspects of the funds, the investment adviser or a related person is generally deemed to have custody. Custody by a related person is imputed to the adviser unless the related person and the adviser are "operationally independent" of each other.[7]

PIV managers who also manage separate accounts may have custody of the separate accounts they manage, depending on whether their activities involve some other form of custody. If PIV managers have custody of nonfund client accounts, they must rely on surprise examinations for the nonfund accounts, even if those clients coinvest alongside a PIV.[8]

III. PRIVATE FUND CUSTODY COMPLIANCE OPTIONS

Like other advisers with custody, PIV managers who are deemed to have custody may comply with the audit requirements of the Custody Rule by undergoing an annual surprise audit. If this option is chosen, PIV managers must comply with all of the rule's standard provisions,[9] including:

---

5 SEC, Response of the Office of Chief Counsel Division of Investment Management, Investment Adviser No-Action Letter (Sept. 20, 2007), http://www.sec.gov/divisions/investment/noaction/ 2007/iaa092007.pdf

6 Custody Rule ¶206(4)-2(d)(2). *See also* "Staff Responses to Questions About the Custody Rule" (updated Dec. 13, 2013) ("Custody FAQ") Question II.1 on inadvertent custody by the SEC staff, https://www.sec.gov/divisions/investment/custody_faq_030510.htm

7 For a discussion of operational independence, *see Final Rule: Custody of Funds or Securities of Clients by Investment Advisers*, Rel. No. IA-2968 (Dec. 30, 2009) ("Adopting Release"), text at nn. 110-113.

8 Custody FAQ X.1. ("audit approach is not available if the client is not a [PIV]").

9 *See*, e.g., Custody FAQ VI.1 ("adviser, among other things, must have a reasonable basis, after due inquiry, for believing that the qualified custodian sends quarterly account statements to each investor in the pool and must obtain an annual surprise examination with respect to the pool's assets....Adviser must maintain privately offered securities owned by the pool with a qualified custodian.").

- Maintaining fund assets with a qualified custodian;[10]
- Instructing the fund's qualified custodian to send quarterly account statements directly to each fund investor;[11]
- Engaging an "independent public accountant"[12] to conduct an annual "surprise" examination of the PIV's funds and securities[13] "pursuant to a written agreement;"[14]
- Providing the PIV's accountant with a Form ADV-E; and
- Ensuring that the accountant files the ADV-E electronically within 120 days of the time chosen by the accountant for the surprise examination.[15]

Advisers are only required to maintain "funds and securities" with a qualified custodian.[16] However, PIV managers often face difficult decisions regarding whether or not fund assets are securities. For example, real estate funds may hold various instruments evidencing property ownership, some of which are considered securities under federal and state securities laws. In addition to property interests that are clearly securities, such as units in real estate investment trusts and mortgage-backed securities, the SEC has opined that "notes representing...mortgages and other interest in real estate are investment securities for purposes of the [Investment Company] Act [of 1940]."[17] Any instrument considered a security is subject to the qualified custodian requirement. Advisers who are unclear about the legal nature of their investments should consult qualified legal counsel for advice.

Managers who rely on annual surprise audits and also invest private fund assets in privately offered securities cannot rely on the exemption from the qualified custodian requirement for privately offered securities.[18] In addition, the staff has addressed the issue of when an adviser has custody of privately offered uncertificated securities.[19] The staff focused on whether the adviser directly or indirectly holds the securities, or has any authority to possess them; concluding that, "an adviser that is a general partner of a limited partnership or a trustee of a trust would always have custody of such securities held by the partnership or the trust."[20] If a PIV manager holds such securities in a private fund that does not undergo an annual audit, the manager can satisfy the requirements

---

[10] Custody Rule ¶206(4)-2(b)(2). "Qualified custodian" is defined in ¶206(4)-2(d)(6).

[11] Clients may designate an "independent representative" to receive notices and account statements required by the Custody Rule on their behalf. *See* Custody Rule ¶206(4)-2(a)(7). "Independent representative" is defined in Custody Rule ¶206(4)-2(d)(4).

[12] Custody Rule ¶206(4)-2(a)(4). "Independent public accountant" is defined in ¶206(4)-2(d)(3).

[13] Instructions to Form ADV-E give details on the surprise audit.

[14] Custody Rule ¶206(4)-2(a)(4). For private funds, the written agreement "may be evidenced in a partnership agreement, disclosure statement, or engagement letter with the auditor," when arranging for PIV audits. Custody FAQ I.5., citing footnote 47 in *Custody of Funds or Securities of Clients by Investment Advisers; Final Rule*, Rel. No. IA-2176 (Oct. 1, 2003).

[15] Custody FAQ IV.6.A. (Form ADV-E and surprise examination report must be filed electronically through IARD by independent public accountant performing surprise examination).

[16] *See*, e.g., Custody FAQ II.3.

[17] SEC Division of Investment Management Protecting Investors: A Half Century of Investment Company Regulation, (1992), Ch. 1, p. 67, n. 251, citing SEC, *Report On The Public Policy Implications Of Investment Company Growth,* H.R. REP. No. 2337,89th Cong., 2d Sess. 328 (1966).

[18] See Custody Rule ¶206(4)-2(b)(2)(ii) and Custody FAQ VII.1.

[19] *See* Custody FAQ VII.3.

[20] *Id.*

of the Custody Rule with respect to these securities "by keeping the originally signed subscription agreement (instead of the security itself) with a qualified custodian or having the custodian act as nominee for the" fund.[21]

PIV managers also have the option of complying with the Custody Rule by obtaining audited fund financials instead of surprise audits.[22] PIVs are exempt from the notice and account statement delivery requirements,[23] and are deemed to be in compliance with the annual surprise audit requirement if the fund audit approach is followed.[24] The staff has clarified that no minimum number of fund investors is required for a PIV manager to rely on the audit exemption; even a PIV formed by the general partner with only a nominal capital account and a single limited partner may rely on the audit approach to custody compliance.[25]

Private fund audits exempt the manager from the annual surprise examination requirement if the necessary conditions are met. First, PIV funds and securities, other than certain privately offered securities, must be maintained with a qualified custodian.[26] The requirement to maintain privately placed securities with a qualified custodian is waived if, among other conditions, the private securities are uncertificated and transferable "only with prior consent of the issuer or holders of the outstanding securities of the issuer."[27]

Second, the funds must undergo an annual financial statement audit prepared by an independent public accountant in accordance with generally accepted accounting principles (GAAP). The staff has provided some exceptions to the GAAP requirement for non-U.S. funds and non-U.S. advisers. First:

> Pooled vehicles organized outside of the United States, or having a general partner or other manager with a principal place of business outside the United States, may have their financial statements prepared in accordance with accounting standards other than U.S. GAAP so long as they contain information substantially similar to statements prepared in accordance with U.S. GAAP. Any material differences with U.S. GAAP must be reconciled.[28]

However, the audits must still be "made by an independent public accountant and meet with requirements of U.S. generally accepted auditing standards (U.S. GAAS)."[29] In fact, the staff has put all PIV managers on notice that if an audit "does not meet U.S. GAAS requirements, the adviser cannot rely upon the audit provision."[30] The staff also

---

[21] Custody FAQ VII.2.

[22] Custody Rule ¶206(4)-2(b)(4).

[23] Custody Rule, at sub¶¶(a)(2) and (a)(3).

[24] Custody Rule, at sub¶(a)(4).

[25] See Custody FAQ VI.11.

[26] PIV managers generally use a prime broker or other broker-dealer as their funds' qualified custodian.

[27] Custody Rule ¶206(4)-2(b)(2).

[28] Custody FAQ VI.5, citing Goodwin, Proctor & Hoar, No Action Letter (Feb. 28, 1997).

[29] *Id.*

[30] Custody FAQ VI.6.

confirmed an earlier PIV no-action position, stating that "offshore advisers registered with the SEC are not subject to the custody rule, with respect to offshore funds.[31]

Third, PIV annual financial statements must be distributed to fund investors within the required time frame (generally, 120 days of the end of the fund's fiscal year;[32] 180 days for funds-of-funds[33]). A "fund-of-funds" is a PIV that "invests 10 percent or more of its total assets in other pooled investment vehicles that are not, and are not advised by, a related person of the pool, its general partner, or its adviser."[34] A "related person" of an adviser "includes officers, partners, directors, most employees, and anyone controlled by, controlling, or under common control with the adviser."[35]

The staff has also answered questions concerning distribution time limits for certain top tier funds-of-funds. In one example, the time was extended to 260 days.[36] Audited fund financial statements satisfy the examination requirement only if performed by an independent accountant registered with, and subject to inspection by, the Public Company Accounting Oversight Board (PCAOB)[37] annually and upon any PIV's liquidation.

IV. UNIQUE DISCLOSURE REQUIREMENTS FOR PRIVATE FUND CUSTODY

Form ADV, the adviser registration statement, requires all advisers to disclose whether they or their related persons have custody of client cash, bank accounts, or securities.[38] This information is considered material and must be updated promptly for changes. Similarly, all managers and their related persons must disclose the approximate dollar amount custodied and number of clients whose assets are custodied, but these items are only required to be updated annually.[39] However, private fund managers have additional custody disclosure requirements. For example, they must disclose whether an independent public accountant conducts an annual audit of their PIVs and distributes the audited financial statements to fund investors.[40] If so, the accountant's name and contact information must be provided on Schedule D, Section 9.C., unless they have provided this information in response to Section 7.B.(1)B., Question 23 of Schedule D. PIV managers must also disclose the prime brokers and/or custodians who handle their private funds' assets.[41]

---

[31] Custody FAQ VI.5, citing ABA Subcommittee on Private Investment Entities, No-Action Letter (Aug. 10, 2006) ("ABA Letter"). The ABA letter defines "offshore adviser" and "offshore fund."

[32] *See* Custody Rule ¶206(4)-2(b)(4)(i). However, enforcement action will not be recommended against an adviser that "reasonably believed that the pool's audited financial statements would be distributed within the 120-day deadline, but failed to have them distributed in time under certain unforeseeable circumstances." Custody FAQ VI.9.

[33] *See* Custody FAQ VI.7.

[34] *Id.*

[35] *Id.*

[36] *See* Custody FAQs VI.8A and VI.8B. *See, also,* Adopting Release and the ABA Letter.

[37] *See,* e.g., Custody FAQ II.8. *Cf.* Robert Van Grover, Esq., Seward & Kissel LLP, No-Action Letter (Oct. 4, 2016) (extending relief from PCAOB inspection requirement through earlier of date SEC approves permanent PCAOB program for inspection of broker and dealer auditors or Dec. 31, 2019).

[38] *See* Form ADV, Part 1, Item 9.A.(1) and 9.B.(1).

[39] *See* Form ADV, Part 1, Items 9.A.(2) and 9.B.(2).

[40] *See* Form ADV, Part 1, Item 9.C.

[41] *See* Form ADV, Part 1, Schedule D, Item 7.B.(1)B., Questions 24 and 25.

Advisers should also take note of the staff's most recent pronouncement with respect to inadvertent custody. Even managers who primarily advise PIVs may be affected by the guidance if they simultaneously manage private accounts. In response to a request by the Investment Advisers Association (IAA) for clarification of the impact of standing letters of instruction or other similar asset transfer authorization arrangements (SLOA) established by a client with a qualified custodian, the staff responded that an adviser whose clients use SLOAs has custody of client assets under the Custody Rule.[42]

However, the request for no-action relief was granted to the extent that the IAA sought permission for such advisers to avoid a surprise audit if they implement a list of compliance policies and procedures by October 1, 2017. Permissible SLOAs can only involve unrelated third-party transfer instructions and be subject to change only by clients. Another required procedure demands that clients' custodians send an initial and annual notice to the clients confirming and reconfirming the SLOA—a responsibility that custodians may or may not be willing to undertake. In addition, advisers with SLOA custody must include client assets subject to SLOAs in their responses to Form ADV, Item 9, in the next annual ADV amendment after October 1, 2017.

In a guidance issued by the staff on the same day as the IAA no-action letter update, the staff stated: "The custodial agreement between a client and custodian may grant an adviser broader access to client funds or securities than the adviser's own agreement with the client contemplates. Depending on the wording of or rights conferred by these custodial agreements, an adviser may have custody, and may also be subject to the surprise examination requirement, even though it did not otherwise intend to have such access."[43] The staff noted, however, that advisers could avoid this inadvertent custody by sending a written letter or similar notice to custodians and clients with such arrangements stating that the adviser has only "delivery versus payment" authority over its clients' assets and obtaining written consent from both clients and custodians to this limitation on their authority.

V. RELEVANT PRIVATE FUND CUSTODY ENFORCEMENT ACTIONS

The Custody Rule has presented challenges to all types of advisers, including PIV managers. In 2013, the SEC's National Examination Program (NEP) published a risk alert on the most commonly observed Custody Rule violations, which identified PIV managers' failure to comply with the audit approach as one of the top four categories of custody-related deficiencies.[44] The risk alert concluded that PIV managers who opted to rely on the audit approach failed to comply for several different reasons, including: failure to engage an "independent" accountant or an accountant registered with, and subject to inspection by, PCAOB; failure to prepare audited financial statements in

---

[42] Investment Adviser Association, SEC No-Action Letter (Feb. 21, 2017), https://www.sec.gov/divisions/investment/noaction/2017/investment-adviser-association-022117-206-4.htm. *See also* updated Custody Rule FAQ II.4.

[43] "*Inadvertent Custody: Advisory Contract Versus Custodial Contract Authority*," IM Guidance Update 2017-01 (Feb. 21, 2017), https://www.sec.gov/investment/im-guidance-2017-01.pdf

[44] NEP Risk Alert, "Significant Deficiencies Involving Adviser Custody and Safety of Client Assets" (Mar. 4, 2013), http://www.sec.gov/about/offices/ocie/custody-risk-alert.pdf

accordance with GAAP; failure to distribute statements timely or distributing audited financial statements only "upon request," rather than to all fund investors; and failure to perform a final audit on liquidated pooled investment vehicles. Subsequently, the NEP reported that custody is considered a "core risk" for advisers, defined as "those risk areas that are common to the business model utilized by a particular category of registrant and that have existed for a sustained period and are likely to continue for the foreseeable future."[45]

In addition to prosecuting a number of garden-variety fraud cases against PIV managers involving misappropriation of client assets, the SEC has brought and resolved a number of administrative proceedings addressing the kinds of private fund custody violations identified in the risk alert. Some provide useful information to PIV managers seeking to comply with the Custody Rule.

From a compliance perspective, the most instructive PIV custody case involves an adviser that, among other things, apparently misunderstood the terms of the fund audit exemption and wrote the requirements of the exemption incorrectly in its compliance policies. In *Clean Energy Capital*,[46] the adviser and its principal failed to use a qualified custodian, segregate fund assets, or otherwise comply with the fund audit exemption, in part, because the adviser's written custody policy incorrectly described the audit exemption as a three-pronged "or" test rather than a three-pronged "and" test. As a result, the adviser and its principal did not prepare or distribute audited financial statements for the funds. Understanding and correctly capturing the contents of the Custody Rule in written policies and procedures is critical to compliance.

PIV managers have also struggled with the concept of maintaining all fund assets with a qualified custodian. For example, In *Lakeside*,[47] a PIV manager routinely held cash belonging to its various private fund clients in three bank accounts established in the names of law firms employed by the adviser. The adviser claimed reliance on the audit approach, but frequently failed to deliver audited financial statements timely. Even if the statements had been timely delivered, however, there is no exemption from the requirement to use a qualified custodian for client cash; only privately offered securities are exempt from the qualified custodian requirement when PIV managers satisfy the audit exemption. To settle the proceeding, the adviser undertook not to solicit or accept any new clients, new investments, or capital contributions to its private funds.

Similarly, in *Reid S. Johnson*,[48] the adviser's owner kept paper stock certificates owned by the funds in a locked file cabinet on the firm's premises, in a storage facility to which he

---

[45] OCIE National Exam Program, "Examination Priorities For 2014" (Jan. 9, 2014) at 3; http://www.sec.gov/about/offices/ocie/national-examination-program-priorities-2014.pdf

[46] *In the Matter of Clean Energy Capital, LLC and Scott A. Brittenham*, SEC Rel. Nos. 33-9667, 34-73386, IA-3955 (Oct. 17, 2014), http://www.sec.gov/litigation/admin/2014/33-9667.pdf

[47] *In the Matter of Lakeside Capital Management, LLC And Dennis H. Daugs, Jr.*, SEC Rel. Nos. 34-72635, IA-3877 and IC-31159 (July 17, 2013), https://www.sec.gov/litigation/admin/2014/34-72635.pdf

[48] *In the Matter of Reid S. Johnson*, Rel. Nos. 34-77625, IA-4368 and IC-32073 (Apr. 14, 2016), https://www.sec.gov/litigation/admin/2016/34-77625.pdf

owned the only key, or in his personal residence, instead of with a qualified custodian. However, this case also involved a veritable smorgasbord of private fund and other custody violations, including the adviser's failure to accurately determine the securities over which it had custody; failure to ensure that client securities were maintained by a qualified custodian; failure to obtain surprise examinations in lieu of audited fund financials; failure to adopt adequate written custody procedures; and falsely stating in the firm's ADV that it did not have custody, even though the firm and its members managed and controlled various PIVs. As a result, the firm's owner was subjected to numerous penalties, including an industry bar coupled with a requirement to complete 30 hours of compliance training before seeking permission to reassociate in the industry.

PIV managers who fail to obtain annual audits from an independent public accountant subject to regular inspection by the PCAOB should consider the *Total Wealth* case.[49] In that proceeding, a PIV manager engaged in a fraudulent scheme involving undisclosed revenue-sharing fees in its family of private funds that resulted in severe penalties. The SEC also found that the adviser's violation of the Custody Rule made it nearly impossible for fund investors to discover the scheme on their own.

Untimely distribution of audited financial statements is at the heart of several PIV custody violations. For example, in *Gerasimowicz*,[50] the owner of a registered adviser and its affiliated unregistered adviser aided and abetted the advisers' misappropriation of approximately $2.65 million from the PIV they managed by, among other things, failing to distribute annual audited financial statements to fund investors timely. As a result, in addition to penalties and fines assessed against the advisers, the principal was barred from any securities industry activities or associations. Again, the custody violations helped blind investors to the advisers' fraud.

One case of untimely distribution stands out due to the number of times the adviser repeated the violation. In *Sands Brothers*,[51] the manager and its cofounders—who had previously settled an SEC enforcement action for failure to obtain independent verification of client assets over which they had custody—were charged with repeatedly providing their private fund investors with late audited financial statements—another violation of the Custody Rule. Over a three-year period, the audited financials for ten funds were delivered to investors anywhere from 40 days to eight months late. This

---

[49] *In the Matter of Total Wealth Management, Inc., Jacob Keith Cooper, Nathan McNamee, and Douglas David Shoemaker*, Rel. Nos. 33-9989, 34-76642, IA-4291 and IC-31935 (Dec. 14, 2015) (adviser settlement),https://www.sec.gov/litigation/admin/2015/33-9989.pdf; *In the Matter of Total Wealth Management, Inc., et al.*, Rel. Nos. 33-9990, 34-76643, IA-4292 and IC-31936 (Dec. 14, 2015) (McNamee and Cooper, adviser representatives, settlement),https://www.sec.gov/litigation/admin/2015/33-9990.pdf; and *In the Matter of Total Wealth Management, Inc., et al.*, Initial Dec. Rel. No. 860 (Aug. 17, 2015) (principal, Cooper, violated Custody Rule),https://www.sec.gov/alj/aljdec/2015/id860bpm.pdf

[50] *In the Matter of Walter V. Gerasimowicz, Meditron Asset Management, LLC and Meditron Management Group, LLC*, Initial Decision, Rel. No. 33-9401 (May 3, 2013), https://www.sec.gov/alj/aljdec/2013/id496cff.pdf. *See also In the Matter of Walter V. Gerasimowicz, Meditron Asset Management, LLC, et al.*, Rel. No. 33-9451 (Sept. 17, 2013) (Notice That Initial Decision Has Become Final).

[51] *In the Matter of Sands Brothers Asset Management, LLC, Steven Sands, Martin Sands, and Christopher Kelly*, Rel. Nos. IA-4273 and IA-4274 (November 19, 2015), https://www.sec.gov/litigation/admin/2015/ia-4273.pdf and https://www.sec.gov/litigation/admin/2015/ia-4274.pdf

resulted in a $1 million penalty for the adviser and its cofounders, plus a one-year suspension from raising money from new or existing investors and a three-year obligation to retain a compliance monitor. This case also came down heavily on the firm's former chief compliance officer (CCO), who, in addition to being slapped with a personal monetary penalty, was suspended for one year from acting as a CCO or appearing or practicing before the SEC as an attorney.

In reporting on the settlement of *Sands Brothers*, Andrew M. Calamari, director of the SEC New York Regional Office, remarked:

> The custody rule is not a technicality. It is a critical investor protection provision designed to help ensure that investor assets are safe...Sands Brothers and its senior-most officers have persistently disregarded their obligations under the law and left their clients waiting for months at a time to have the materials they need to verify the existence and value of fund assets.[52]

Failure to prepare audited financial statements in accordance with GAAP is exemplified by *Alpha Titans*,[53] a case that included willful violations of the Custody Rule by both the adviser and its accountant. After improperly allocating fund assets to pay undisclosed operating expenses, including rent, salaries and benefits, the adviser, two executives, and the fund accountant knew the financial statements were misleading, but distributed them to fund investors anyway. The statements included an unqualified audit opinion by the accountant that the financials were stated fairly. All parties, including the accountant, were subjected to SEC penalties. Accounting professionals who aid and abet PIV managers by providing unqualified opinions they know to be misleading are not beyond the reach of the SEC.

Another group of custody cases involve PIV managers who failed to satisfy either the surprise examination requirement or the fund audit exemption. For example, in *Parallax*,[54] a PIV adviser failed to satisfy either the annual surprise exam requirement or the fund audit exemption, because the private fund was audited by an accountant that was not PCAOB-registered and the adviser failed to deliver the financial statements to fund investors on time. Both the adviser's owner and the CCO knew that the accountant was not PCAOB-registered, but retained him anyway. In addition, the CCO was aware of the 120-day delivery deadline, but failed to take any steps to ensure compliance. In *Envision*,[55] a PIV adviser and its owner failed to satisfy either

---

[52] SEC Announces Charges Against Investment Advisory Firm and Top Officials for Custody Rule Violations, SEC Press Release 2014-242, https://www.sec.gov/News/PressRelease/Detail/PressRelease/1370543316114

[53] *In re Alpha Titans, LLC, Timothy P. McCormack, and Kelly D. Kaeser, Esq.*, Rel. Nos. 34-74828, IA-4073 and IC-31586 (Apr. 29, 2015), *available at* https://www.sec.gov/litigation/admin/2015/34-74828.pdf; and *In the Matter of Simon Lesser, CPA, CA*, Rel. Nos. 34-74827, IA-4072 and IC-31585 (Apr. 29, 2015), https://www.sec.gov/litigation/admin/2015/34-74827.pdf

[54] *In the Matter of Parallax Investments, LLC, John P. Bott, II, and F. Robert Falkenberg*, Rel. Nos. 34 75625, IA-4159, IC-31741 (August 6, 2015); *available at* https://www.sec.gov/litigation/admin/2015/34-75625.pdf

[55] *In the Matter of Envision Capital Management, Ltd. and Michael M. Druckman,* Rel. Nos. 33-9187; IA-3160 (Feb. 16, 2011),https://www.sec.gov/litigation/admin/2011/33-9187.pdf

the annual surprise exam requirement or the fund audit exemption, and sent account statements directly to fund investors in violation of the Custody Rule. In *Further Lane Asset Management,*[56] the adviser and its affiliated adviser not only engaged in fraud related to a fund-of-funds under their control, the adviser and its CEO failed to arrange an annual surprise examination or fund audits despite maintaining custody of assets of hedge funds they managed, and failed to ensure that fund investors received quarterly account statements from a qualified custodian. Finally, in *Knelman,*[57] the adviser to a fund of private equity funds had custody of the fund's assets, but the fund of funds was not subject to annual surprise examinations or fund audits and investors did not receive quarterly account statements from a qualified custodian. The settlements in all of these cases were costly to both the adviser and the individuals held responsible for causing them.

Vector Wealth Management[58] provides a particularly painful example of the potential consequences of failure to undergo either an annual surprise examination or comply with the fund audit exemption. In *Vector*, an employee was able to forge checks and misappropriate dividends owed to certain investors in PIVs managed by the adviser without detection for three years. Even though the adviser had custody of the funds' assets throughout the time period, it neither underwent annual surprise exams nor delivered audited annual financial statements to pooled fund investors and failed to ensure delivery of quarterly account statements by an independent custodian. In addition, the adviser failed reasonably to supervise its employee, lacked policies and procedures reasonably designed to prevent violations of the Custody Rule, and failed to conduct an annual review of its policies and procedures. Upon finding the violations, the adviser promptly terminated the employee, restricted his account and system access, initiated an internal investigation, self-reported to the SEC, and notified and repaid all affected clients with interest. Despite these remedial acts, the SEC still undertook the administrative proceeding. The adviser did, however, receive credit for its actions, including cooperation with SEC staff. In lieu of any monetary penalty, the SEC imposed a censure and cease and desist order and the adviser undertook to retain an independent compliance consultant to conduct annual reviews of its internal controls, policies, and procedures for two years.

Finally, *Barclays*[59] illustrates the special custody pitfalls that can trap large firm asset managers who undergo mergers or acquisitions. After acquiring the advisory business of another firm, a dual registrant adviser/broker-dealer failed to enhance its compliance infrastructure sufficiently to integrate and support the rapid growth of its advisory business. This resulted in improper practices and inadequate disclosures, including Custody

---

[56] *In the Matter of Further Lane Asset Management, LLC, Osprey Group, Inc., and Jose Miguel Araiz a/k/a Joseph Michael Araiz*, SEC Rel. Nos. IA-3707, 34-70759 and IC-30767 (Oct. 28, 2013), https://www.sec.gov/litigation/admin/2013/34-70759.pdf

[57] *In the Matter of Knelman Asset Management Group, LLC and Irving P. Knelman*, SEC Rel. Nos. IA-3705 and IC-30766 (Oct.28, 2013);https://www.sec.gov/litigation/admin/2013/ia-3705.pdf

[58] *In the Matter of Vector Wealth Management, LLC*, Rel. No. IA-3587 (Apr. 18, 2013), https://www.sec.gov/litigation/admin/2013/ia-3587.pdf

[59] *In the Matter of Barclays Capital Inc.*, Rel. Nos. 34-73183 and IA-3929 (Sept. 23, 2014), http://www.sec.gov/litigation/admin/2014/34-73183.pdf

Rule violations. The adviser had custody, because it was contractually permitted under certain circumstances to withdraw client funds maintained with a qualified custodian with respect to limited partnerships and limited liability companies on its private fund platform. Thus, the adviser was required either to comply with the audit exemption or have a reasonable basis, after due inquiry, for believing that the qualified custodian sent account statements, at least quarterly, to each client for which the qualified custodian maintained funds or securities, identifying the funds and securities in the account at the end of the period and setting forth all transactions in the account during that period. However, the adviser neither had a reasonable basis to believe that account statements were sent, nor did it qualify for the audit exemption, because it failed to timely distribute the funds' audited financial statements. In addition, even though a related person also had custody of client funds and securities, the adviser failed to obtain a written internal control report prepared by an independent public accountant from its related person. These failures resulted in, among other things, a $15 million penalty and an undertaking to engage an independent compliance consultant to conduct an internal review.

VI. GUIDELINES FOR PRIVATE FUND ADVISERS' CUSTODY POLICY AND PROCEDURES

As discussed in Part 1 of the Custody Rule review, advisers with custody must adopt and implement written policies and procedures reasonably designed to prevent Custody Rule violations. Determining whether custody exists is still step one, and the general procedures outlined in Volume 1 of *Modern Compliance* are as relevant to PIV managers as they are to other advisers. For PIV managers who choose to rely on the surprise examination approach to compliance rather than the fund audit exemption, a review of those procedures is advisable. However, PIV managers should also be aware of the nuances applicable to their situation. For example, when a qualified custodian sends quarterly account statements directly to separate account clients, the statement shows only the clients' funds and securities held and transactions entered into on the clients' behalf. However, when a private fund's qualified custodian is required to send account statements directly to investors in a PIV, the statement sent "should be a statement of funds and securities held by the pool and transactions entered into by the pool," not just a statement of the investor's ownership interest in the pool.[60] Similarly, when confirming a surprise examination of a PIV, the accountant's confirmation procedures should include confirmation with the PIV's investors of:

> (i) [F]unds and securities held by the pooled investment vehicle as of the date of the examination and (ii) contributions and withdrawals of funds and securities to and from the pooled investment vehicle by the investor since the date of the last examination. The quarterly account statements required to be sent by the qualified custodian[s]...should provide investors with the information necessary to respond to the confirmation.[61]

[60] Custody FAQ VI.2.
[61] Custody FAQ VI.3.

In addition, the SEC staff has stated that, with respect to private funds, a PIV manager can accept a single independent representative to serve for all limited partners rather than a separate independent representative for each, "so long as the representative is, in fact, independent and satisfies the [Custody Rule's] definition."[62]

Because the majority of PIV managers represent their intention to comply with the fund audit exemption, the lessons provided by custody-related enforcement actions against advisers who claimed reliance on the audit exemption, but failed to satisfy the applicable conditions, are valuable. Also, as with surprise examinations, there are important staff responses in the Custody FAQ, which are important for PIV managers to understand. Several of these are discussed in this chapter, but PIV managers should review the Custody FAQ at least annually to ensure awareness of the most current staff responses.

VII. CONCLUSION

There is little doubt that compliance with the Custody Rule is a key element of compliance with the Advisers Act for all advisers. However, PIV managers' face heightened compliance concerns, because it is usually impossible to claim the absence of custody. A thorough understanding of the alternative means and methods of custody compliance is, therefore, especially critical when managing private funds. Whether the surprise examination or fund audit approach is adopted, adherence to *all* requirements is essential.

---

[62] Custody FAQ VI.4.

ABOUT THE AUTHOR

Elizabeth M. Knoblock is the managing member and sole owner of Elizabeth M. Knoblock, PLLC, a private law firm. She is a securities lawyer with more than 35 years of legal practice and business experience. As first noted in the 2007 edition of Chambers USA, Ms. Knoblock has the "... ability to see the business viewpoint and to interact with management on difficult issues...." Over the course of her career, she has focused on the laws governing investment advisers, registered investment companies, hedge funds and private accounts, including institutional, retail, and wrap fee clientele. Ms. Knoblock has significant experience with securities-related policies and procedures, disclosure, compliance and regulatory issues. Ms. Knoblock began her regulatory career with the Office of General Counsel of the Commodity Futures Trading Commission, followed by a stint with the Division of Investment Management of the Securities and Exchange Commission, before moving to Wall Street, where she spent five years in various legal positions with dual registrant brokerage firms, including Kidder Peabody, Gruntal, and Shearson Lehman Hutton. She subsequently served for a decade as general counsel of Templeton Investment Counsel, Inc., in Florida and for more than a decade as a partner with two separate international law firms. In addition to managing her firm, Ms. Knoblock serves on the advisory board of *Practical Compliance & Risk Management* for the Securities Industry, a Wolters Kluwer publication, is a past board member of the National Society of Compliance Professionals and a much sought after speaker at industry conferences. She was honored by National Regulatory Services, an industry compliance service provider, as the only speaker to have been invited to speak, and to have spoken, for 29 consecutive years at its national compliance conferences and has continued to speak for them for more than 30 consecutive years at this time.

Ms. Knoblock is a member of the state bars of New York, Florida, Alabama, and the District of Columbia. Her educational degrees include a magna cum laude dean's list bachelor of arts from Stetson University in Deland, Florida; a dean's list juris doctor degree from Georgetown University Law Center in Washington, DC; and an LLM/ master in Securities Regulation, also from Georgetown, plus a dean's list master of business administration from NOVA University, both of which were obtained while working full-time as a securities lawyer.

Chapter 21

Compliance in the Age of Connectivity

By John H. Walsh
Eversheds Sutherland

I. INTRODUCTION[1]

Cultures of compliance have received considerable attention over the years from regulators, compliance professionals, and academics. Regulators have persistently advocated for the development of strong cultures of compliance within regulated firms.[2] For example, in his excellent and thought-provoking remarks, Andrew ("Buddy") Donohue, regulator and former compliance professional, described how he could become comfortable in a compliance role; the culture of the firm in which he functioned evidently played an important role. In addition, academics have studied organizational culture and its impact on compliance.[3]

Despite all of this attention, compliance professionals have reached an apt moment to reconsider cultures of compliance. Looking to the future, one can see significant challenges taking shape. Developments in the wider world could eventually—strike that, *will* eventually—pose fundamental challenges to the culture of compliance as it is understood today. In his 2016 book, *The Industries of the Future*, Alec Ross subtitles a chapter, "World leaders Take Notice: The 21st Century Is a Terrible Time to Be a Control Freak."[4] In his conversations with foreign heads-of-state—Ross served for several years as senior adviser for innovation to the United States secretary of state—he encountered a recurring theme: when he asked what one thing had most changed over the previous 15 years, the heads-of-state almost always cited a perceived loss of control. Through connection technologies, including the internet and social media, citizens and networks of citizens have obtained information and power previously reserved

---

1 This chapter is taken from John Walsh's comments at Rutgers Law School symposium, New Directions in Corporate Compliance. See the Rutgers Law Review: Address at Rutgers Law School Center for Corporate Law and Governance Symposium: New Directions in Corporate Compliance (May 20, 2016)

2 *See*, e.g., Aulana L. Peters, *Investor Protection: The First Line of Defense* (Mar. 15, 1985), https://www.sec.gov/news/speech/1985/031585peters.pdf

3 *See*, generally, Milton C. Regan, Jr., Moral Intuitions and Organizational Culture, 51 St. Louis *U. L.J.* 941 (2006-2007), http://scholarship.law.georgetwn.edu/facpub/457

4 Alec Ross, *The Industries of the Future*, Simon & Schuster (2016), at 186.

to large hierarchies, such as media companies and governments.[5] As Ross suggests, a key question going forward, which will greatly affect each state's economic character and performance, will be how the state responds to this systemic loss of control and diffusion of power.[6] Will a state be able to handle the open access, globalization, and constant innovation of the new century? One could ask the same questions about corporate compliance.

Compliance, as it is understood today, developed in an age of hierarchical power and control. Compliance professionals have spent decades developing and refining the command-and-control methodologies possible within hierarchical structures.[7] When the electronics revolution arrived, it ended up reinforcing compliance (after an initial period of uncertainty) as more transactional information and communications flowed through controlled channels where they could be captured and monitored.[8] Even today, this process of enhancement continues, as bigger data sets and more powerful analytics promise even better compliance.[9] Nonetheless, looking ahead, connectivity is approaching a looming inflection point, and compliance will be challenged by the same loss of control and diffusion of power faced by heads-of-state.[10] How will compliance respond in the looming Age of Connectivity? What will compliance oversight be like when employees feel a loose connection with their employer (not least because many of them will be independent contractors) and yet carry in their hands mobile computers—often called smartphones—that keep them in constant and private contact with dense personal networks transcending any operational controls imposed by the firm? These are not theoretical questions. The future has already arrived.

II. RIVER ROUGE AND THE ORIGINS OF COMPLIANCE

When the compliance field was created in the 1960s and 1970s, the world economy was based on large-scale manufacturing.[11] The height of economic prowess was embodied in the assembly plant.[12] If one wanted to form a visual image of what this meant, there would be none better than the River Rouge assembly plant outside of Detroit.[13] The factory was huge, measuring a mile-and-a-half long and a mile wide.[14] Its core structure had won architectural awards as a humane facility, mostly because of the glass that al-

---

5 Ross, *Industries of the Future,* at 199-202 (discussing Pakistani woman who used the internet to start a business).

6 Ross, *Industries of the Future,* at 215.

7 Russ, Industries of the Future, at 965.

8 *See,* e.g., John H. Walsh, "Big Data and Regulation, Part I: The Regulators; Regarding Regulation," *Corp. Couns.* (May 6, 2014) [hereinafter Walsh, *Part 1*], http://www.corpcounsel.com/id=1202653950093/Big-Data-and-Regulation-Part-1-The-Regulators?slreturn=20170216230801

9 *Id.*

10 *See* Ross, *Industries of the Future,* at 215.

11 Stephen Meyer, "The Degradation of Work Revisited: Workers and Technology in the American Auto Industry, 1900-2000," *Automobile Am. Life & Soc'y,* http://www.autolife.umd.umich.edu/Labor/L_Overview/L_Overview.htm (last visited Mar. 1, 2017).

12 *Id.*

13 The Henry Ford, Ford Rouge Factory Tour: History & Timeline," https://www.thehenryford.org/visit/ford-rouge-factory-tour/history-and-timeline/ (last visited Mar. 1, 2017).

14 *Id.*

lowed natural lighting to enter the workspace.[15] Schoolchildren studied the facility as emblematic of modern society's progress and economic development. Most important, though, was what the facility contained—a vast and powerful assembly line.[16] Machines and assembly line employees worked in tandem—in such rapid action that the human eye would have difficulty distinguishing between the two—and turned out vast numbers of precisely manufactured goods.[17] In the River Rouge's case, the final products were high-end automobiles.[18]

Within the factory, the shop floor was only the bottom layer of a vast organizational structure that made the assembly plant possible.[19] Standing behind the workers were supervisors, and behind the supervisors—in an organizational, if not literal, sense—were managers, and behind the managers were executives, in a command-and-control structure reaching from the shop floor to the executive suites.[20] Viewed as a pyramid, information flowed up the structure from the vast shop floor, and commands and controls flowed down from the executive suite through increasingly expansive ranks of middle management.[21] The result was a precise and highly structured pyramidal organization that ensured consistent and optimal output on the shop floor.[22]

Not surprisingly, when the compliance movement was created it was made in this image. The Securities and Exchange Commission (SEC) first established compliance as a discipline in the 1960s as the result of a special study of the securities markets,[23] and first gave it concrete shape in the 1970s, through the work of an advisory committee that the agency organized and sponsored.[24] By the 1980s, robust compliance systems could be found throughout the securities business and had begun to spread to other sectors of the economy. Many of the compliance controls developed in those early days are still in use today.[25] Moreover, contemporaries visualized this compliance regime in the same pyramidal shape that characterized the structure of corporate control.[26] In 1985 a commissioner of the SEC likened compliance to a pyramid in which the federal regulator was at the top, self-regulators were in the middle, and compliance practitioners were on the bottom.[27] In such a hierarchy, the commissioner said, compliance served as the front-line for the higher-ups, including,

---

15 *Id.*

16 Lindsay-Jean Hard, "The Rouge: Yesterday, Today, & Tomorrow," University of Michigan Taubman College of Architecture and Urban Planning (Dec. 4, 2005), http://www.umich.edu/~econdev/riverrouge/

17 *Id.*

18 *Id.*

19 *Id.*

20 *Id.*

21 *Id.*

22 *Id.*

23 SEC, *Report of the Special Study of the Securities Markets of the Securities and Exchange Commission,* H.R. Doc. No. 95, Pt. 1 (1963), at 4.

24 *Guide to Broker-Dealer Compliance: Report of the Broker-Dealer Model Compliance Program Advisory Committee to the Securities and Exchange Commission,* Exchange Act Rel. No. 11,098, 5 SEC Docket 472 (Nov. 13, 1974). A copy of the full report is available in the SEC Library.

25 Miriam Hechter Baer, "Governing Corporate Compliance", 50 B.C. L. Rev. 949, 962–63 (2009), http://lawdigitalcommons.bc.edu/bclr/vol50/iss4/2

26 SEC, *Annual Report, 41st, of the SEC for the Fiscal Year Ended June 30, 1976,* (1974), at iv [hereinafter Annual Report].

27 Peters, *Investor Protection*, at 7.

presumably, SEC commissioners at the very top.[28] The image is striking: the lowest level is the front line for the top, suggesting all are part of the same command-and-control structure. Regulators, self-regulators, and compliance practitioners were all part of the same hierarchical pyramid.

In retrospect, it can be seen that certain unstated assumptions played an important role in the River Rouge approach to compliance. Five in particular warrant note. First, perhaps most importantly, there was a defined shop floor. Whether it was a sales office, trading desk, or some other setting, the work to be controlled took place within a physically bounded location.[29] Someone working in compliance could point to the controlled location and the boundary line where the zone of control ended.[30]

Second, supervisors could observe operations within that location.[31] In the early days, much of this was in-person: a supervisor stood or sat in close proximity to the operations being supervised, much as a supervisor in the River Rouge plant actually watched the work being done.[32] In time, it became less personal but always subject to the assumption that the supervisor continued to enjoy an equivalent power of observation. In many cases a concern of the modern supervisor focused on with preserving his or her power of observation across increasingly complex and diffuse organizational structures.

Third, relevant business operations, such as communications with customers, could be captured and assessed for conformity to defined standards.[33] Regulatory standards, still in effect today, reflect this heritage when they require firms to preserve copies of written communications sent and originals of communications received.[34] The words used in the regulation—"copies" and "originals"—have a diminished meaning in the increasingly electronic world. Nonetheless, the regulations' unstated assumption—that relevant communications should be captured, retained, and monitored—remains in place.

Fourth, firms had the power to sanction defective output, up to and including the most devastating measure of control: termination from employment and possibly from a line of business (pursuant to a regulatory bar).[35]

Fifth, and finally, contained within these assumptions, usually unstated, perhaps even unrecognized, lurked a vision of the business organization as another River Rouge. Operations, according to this view, proceed along a linear route, much like an assembly line, with inputs added in an orderly fashion at discreet points along the

---

28 Peters, *Investor Protections*, at 8-9.

29 SEC Annual Report, at 5-8.

30 *Id.*

31 *Id.*

32 Hard, "The Rouge."

33 Hard, "The Rouge," at 49–68.

34 *See*, e.g., 17 C.F.R § 240.17a-4(b)(4) (2016).

35 SEC, Annual Report, at 19–20.

critical path. To this day, one often hears the word "industry" used as a synonym for business, even when the business in question has nothing to do with the assembly of physical goods.[36]

What was the point of this model of compliance? In a word, it could be called "conformity." This is not intended as an insult. In French, "compliance" is *conformité,* or, conformity. The word may summon images of identical teenagers submitting to peer pressure, but seen from the perspective of the River Rouge it makes sense. The fundamental purpose of the controls imposed on the shop floor was to avoid nonconforming output.[37] Here again, the experience of compliance has been similar.

To understand the relationship between conformity and compliance, it would help to consider another term used by Alec Ross cited earlier: "control freaks."[38] A control freak is someone who "attempts to dictate how everything is done around them. Being a control freak seems to be associated with some unpleasant psychological conditions, such as a tendency to micromanagement and feelings of inner vulnerability.[39] The name is not flattering, but the meaning is appropriate. For the River Rouge plant to work the way it did, precise micromanaged conformity was necessary.[40] If one piece was the wrong size or mounted incorrectly, the next piece wouldn't fit, with cascading implications down the assembly line. Inner vulnerabilities among production workers (inattention, boredom, a hangover, distraction by the operator of the next machine) must be controlled.

Similarly, if a business function subject to compliance (say, for example, selling securities), produces defective output (say, to follow the example, selling securities that are unsuitable for a buyer), cascading negative consequences could be expected in the buyer's financial life and, ultimately, in the legal and regulatory repercussions visited on the selling firm.[41] Here again, inner vulnerabilities in the sales force (greed, unwarranted enthusiasm, lack of diligence, lack of curiosity about the buyer) must be controlled. Perhaps control freaks created River Rouge, but their efforts allowed massively complex industries and businesses to flourish.[42] Indeed, the control freaks of the 20 century made it possible to deliver precise and conforming outputs, including compliance outputs, over vast scales, new technologies, widespread operations, and sophisticated designs.[43] This achievement should not be forgotten. Nonetheless, one must wonder: how will this organizational culture fare in the 21 century?

---

36 An assumption in John H. Walsh's early essays, "Right the First Time: Regulation, Quality and Preventive Compliance in the Securities Industry," *1997 Colum. Bus. L. Rev.* (1997), at 165.

37 Meyer, "The Degradation of Work Revisited."

38 Ross, *Industries of the Future,* at 217.

39 *Id.*

40 Meyer, "The Degradation of Work Revisited."

41 *See,* e.g., Financial Industry Regulatory Authority *FINRA Manual,* § 2111 (2014), http://finra.complinet.com/en/display/display.html?rbid=2403&element_id=9859; Norman S. Posner, "Liability of Broker-Dealers for Unsuitable Recommendations to Institutional Investors," *2001 B.Y.U. L. Rev.* 1 (2001), at 1493, 1494–150.

42 Morris Tanenbaum and William K. Holstein, "Mass Production," *Encyclopædia Britannica,* https://www.britannica.com/technology/mass-production

43 *Id.*

III. THE ELECTRONICS REVOLUTION

Over the last several decades the world has experienced a revolutionary transformation driven by electronics. Records have been moved from paper to electronic media, access to records has been automated ("access" is understood as any means of searching and retrieving data), and communications have increasingly migrated from paper to electronic devices. Different approaches for measuring the stunning growth in electronics abound. In one approach, electronic data usage is compared to the data contained within the pages housed within the Library of Congress.[44] Because the paper-based Library of Congress occupies several buildings in Washington D.C., (including the Madison Building, one of the largest in the city), this reference can be understood to mean a lot of data. Yet, data sets of this size have entered business and regulation. In a recent enforcement case brought by the SEC, the staff compiled an investigative record of 11 terabytes, equal in size to the amount of data stored on paper-based records in the Library of Congress.[45] In another approach, the computational power available to NASA during the Apollo program—landing astronauts on the moon was a triumph of 1960s-era manufacturing—is compared to a modern smartphone.[46] The conclusion: each handheld smartphone has millions of times the computational power available to NASA (in total, not just on the spacecraft) at the time of the moon landings.[47] Finally, an electronic service firm recently estimated that as of 2009, e-mail usage outnumbered paper mail usage by a factor of 89 to 1.[48]

Regulations citing to "copies" and "originals" are not completely obsolete, but the trend is clear.[49] However one chooses to illustrate the growth of electronics in our society, the reality of the transformation is inescapable.

The electronics revolution has also had a dramatic impact on compliance. As early as the 1970s, in the revolution's earliest days, the compliance field was an early adopter. The report of the 1970s-era advisory committee, sponsored by the SEC, indicated that Compliance Departments were already using automated data processing, with runs of trades and other outputs being used to help monitor firms' activities.[50] Since then compliance professionals have used electronics to achieve levels of collection and monitoring undreamed of in the paper-based world of the past. By way of illustration,

---

[44] *See* e.g., Stewart Bishop, "'Big Short' Money Manager Lobs New Claims over SEC Courts," *Law 360* (Apr. 2, 2015) https://www.law360.com/articles/638793/big-short-money-manager-lobs-new-claims-over-sec-courts (discussing the money manager's complaint that the Division of Enforcement's file is "the size of the entire Library of Congress").

[45] As of this writing, the matter is on appeal from the SEC to the Court of Appeals for the D.C. Circuit. *Harding Advisory LLC and Wing F. Chau v. S.E.C.*, U.S.C.A Case 17-1070, Document 1664841, Order Governing Submission of Documents (D.C. Cir. March 7, 2017)(noting Petition for Review was filed Mar. 6, 2017).

[46] Nick T., "A Modern Smartphone or a Vintage Supercomputer: Which is More Powerful?" phoneArena.com (Jun. 14, 2014), http://www.phonearena.com/news/A-modern-smartphone-or-a-vintage-supercomputer-which-is-more-powerful_id57149

[47] *Id.*

[48] Pingdom, "Email vs. Snail Mail" (Infographic) (Sept. 29, 2010), http://royal.pingdom.com/2010/09/email-vs-snail-mail-infographic/

[49] *See*, e.g., 17 C.F.R. §§ 240.17a-4(b), 270.31a-2(f) (2016).

[50] *Guide to Broker-Dealer Compliance,* at 3-5.

regulators reviewed the method by which the SEC had recorded examinations in the 1960s. Examiners used index cards with preprinted boxes in which examiners could enter information such as the name of the firm, date of the examination, and key findings.[51] Available space on the card was so limited that findings could be expressed only in summary entries such as citations to rules. Several examinations were recorded on the same card.[52] Today, electronic records have allowed large volumes of detailed information about a firm to be collected, stored, and searched by examiners.[53] As the cost of data collection and storage has come down, similar capabilities have spread to compliance professionals and, increasingly, to everyone.[54] Moreover, the electronics revolution is far from over. It remains an area of significant growth and development for regulation and compliance.[55] A quick review of some of its applications highlights the point.

At the most basic level, the ability to screen large data sets allows regulators and compliance professionals to search for misconduct that would otherwise be buried in the noise produced by a firm's day-to-day operations. In September 2014, for example, the SEC brought an enforcement action based on a single nonconforming trade, worth about $27,000, net, against an adviser managing a portfolio worth more than $1 billion.[56] The ability to ferret out such one-off instances of nonconformity radically transforms compliance and regulatory oversight. In the past, presumably, a pattern of misconduct or some degree of intentionality (the SEC noted in its order that intent was not a relevant consideration) would have been necessary before such a problem rose to a level triggering regulatory and compliance notice and correction.[57]

At a more sophisticated level, analysis of multiple data sets may enable regulators and compliance professionals to search for predictive signals that reveal misconduct as it takes shape. The chair of the SEC, Mary Jo White, spoke to this issue in 2014.[58] She said the agency is using "powerful new data analytics and technology tools" to "aggregate and analyze a broad band of data to identify potentially problematic behavior,"[59]including, she added, "exciting new technologies—text analytics, visualization, search, and predictive analytics—to cull additional red flags from internal

---

[51] John H. Walsh, "Big Data and Regulation, Part 2: Legal and Compliance," *Corp. Couns.* (June 20, 2014), http://www.corpcounsel.com/id=1202660050197/big-data-and-regulation-part-2-legal-and-compliance/

[52] *Id.*

[53] Walsh, "Big Data and Regulation, Part I."

[54] Quentin Hardy, "The Era of Cloud Computing," *The New York Times* Bits (June 11, 2014), http://bits.blogs.nytimes.com/2014/06/11/the-era-of-cloud-computing/?r=0.or "The Era of the Cloud," *The New York Times* (June 12,2014), p. F1.

[55] Walsh, "Big Data and Regulation, Part I."

[56] *Antipodean Advisors LLC,* Exchange Act Rel. No. 34-73115 (Sept. 16, 2014), https://www.sec.gov/litigation/admin/2014/34-73115.pdf. This case was one of several announced on the same day alleging similar violations. *See* SEC Sanctions 19 Firms and Individual Trader for Short Selling Violations in Advance of Stock Offerings, SEC Press Release (Sept. 16, 2014), https://www.sec.gov/news/press-release/2014-195

[57] *Id.*

[58] Mary Jo White, *Chairman's Address at SEC Speaks 2014* (Feb. 21, 2014), https://www.sec.gov/News/Speech/Detail/Speech/1370540822127

[59] *Id.*

and external data and information sources."[60] The use of predictive analytics is incredibly exciting from a compliance perspective. Indeed, compliance will be fundamentally transformed when its resources can be directed at areas where problems are predicted to occur, instead of areas where red flags suggest problems have already occurred.[61] Certainly, the SEC seems to be making a big regulatory commitment to quantitative tools for its examination program,[62] enforcement program,[63] and in its risk assessment and oversight operations.[64]

Finally, the use of e-mails and other electronic communications has enabled regulatory and compliance investigators to enjoy new power. With e-mails, investigators have become accustomed to the ability to obtain in-depth forensic knowledge of the actual operations of various departments and executives.[65] Anyone who has conducted targeted forensic reviews both before and after the widespread use of electronic communications appreciates the new investigative power they allow.[66] Investigators no longer must rely on witnesses' recollections of past events.[67] Raw contemporaneous communications provide much more powerful evidence.[68]

In light of these developments, the electronics revolution has been a major enhancement to compliance. One could easily look to the future and see a golden age of compliance emerging with the continued use of electronics. To place these developments in the context of the organizational culture of the River Rouge facility, electronics have replaced the shop floor, but the result remains the same.[69] Instead of ranks of supervisors, from the shop floor to the executive suite, looking over each other's shoulders, electronic monitoring tools scan data sets for nonconforming output, predict potential problem areas, or provide in-depth forensic evidence of operations.[70] The River Rouge plant model has survived, although in a new form.[71] More recently, however, new developments suggest a new inflection point may be developing, with new challenges. Perhaps this time the River Rouge model of organizational culture really is at risk.

---

60 *Id.*

61 *Id.*

62 Walsh, "Big Data and Regulation, Part I."

63 SEC Announces Cherry-Picking Charges Against Investment Manager, SEC Press Release (June 29, 2015), http://www.sec.gov/news/pressrelease/2015-132.html

64 *See,* e.g., SEC Announces Creation of Office of Risk and Strategy for its National Exam Program, SEC Press Release (Mar. 8, 2016), http://www.sec.gov/news/pressrelease/2016-38.html

65 Frederik Armknecht and Andreas Dewald, "Privacy-Preserving Email Forensics," 14 *Digital Investigation* (2015), at S127, S127–28.

66 Zachary G. Newman and Anthony Ellis, "Reliability, Admissibility, and Power of Electronic Evidence," Am. Bar Ass'n (Jan. 25, 2011), https://apps.americanbar.org/litigation/committees/trialevidence/articles/012511-electronic-evidence.html

67 *Id.*

68 *Id.*

69 *See* Meyer, "The Degradation of Work Revisited"; Sameh Shamroukh, "Extending JIT Value Beyond Enterprise Boundaries," *Manufacturing Bus. Tech.* (Oct. 5, 2016), http://www.mbtmag.com/article/2016/10/extending-jit-value-beyond-enterprise-boundaries.

70 Shamroukh, "Extending JIT Value."

71 *Id.*

IV. THE LOOMING CHALLENGE OF CONNECTIVITY

In recent years, the electronics revolution has entered new territory. Powerful handheld computers—recall those smartphones with millions of times the computational power of NASA's Apollo program[72]—have enabled new patterns of communication, known generically as social networks.[73] Individuals with similar interests self-select themselves into communication groups to share news, pictures, personal or business information, and whatever else moves them.[74] Adopters cover a wide spectrum, from social "friends" posting minute-by-minute accounts of their lives,[75] to like-minded ideologues posting commentary on the news of the day,[76] to activists (and even terrorists) posting minute-by-minute action-reports to guide compatriots away from riot police (or toward softer targets).[77] In every case the result is a dense personal network of electronic communications—often called "connectivity"—that provides each participant with extraordinary levels of detailed and real-time information.[78]

Clay Shirky, a commentator on the development of social media, has described its impact on organizational structures.[79] In his view, the major effect of connectivity has been to reduce the overhead or embedded cost of forming an organizational group.[80] As Shirky describes it, in the past, formal management was required to integrate the multiple disparate actions required for complex activities.[81] As a result, "for most of modern life, our strong talents and desires for group effort have been filtered through relatively rigid institutional structures because of the complexity of managing groups."[82] This proposition is familiar to anyone who has studied the River Rouge organizational model.[83] Now, though, through connectivity, "most of the barriers to group action have collapsed, and without those barriers, we are free to explore new ways of gathering together and getting things done."[84] The old limits on the "size, sophistication, and scope of unsupervised effort" have disappeared.[85] Shirky calls the resulting infor-

---

[72] Tibi Puiu, "Your Smartphone Is Millions of Times More Powerful That All of NASA's Combined Computing in 1969," *ZMI Science* (Oct. 13, 2015), http://www.zmescience.com/research/technology/smartphone-power-compared-to-apollo-432/.

[73] *See* Michael Ray, *Social Network*, *Encyclopedia Britannica*, https://www.britannica.com/topic/social-network (last visited Mar. 1, 2017).

[74] *Id.*

[75] Sue Scheff, "Facebook Is Not a Diary," *Huffington Post* (July 3, 2013), http://www.huffingtonpost.com/sue-scheff/facebook-is-not-a-diary_b_3537300.html

[76] Caitlin Dewey, "The Most Compelling Reason to Never Talk Politics on Facebook," *The Washington Post* (Aug. 4, 2016), https://www.washingtonpost.com/news/the-intersect/wp/2016/08/04/the-most-compelling-reason-to-never-talk-politics-on-facebook

[77] *See*, e.g., Tim Lister & Emily Smith, "Social Media @ the Front Line in Egypt," CNN (Jan. 28, 2011), http://www.cnn.com/2011/WORLD/africa/01/27/egypt.protests.social.media/

[78] *See* José van Dijck, "Social Media and the Culture of Connectivity," OUP: Blog (Feb. 25, 2015), http://blog.oup.com/2013/02/social-media-culture-connectivity

[79] Clay Shirky, *Here Comes Everybody: The Power of Organizing Without Organizations,* Penguin Press(2008), at 18-21.

[80] Shirky, *Here Comes Everybody,* at 21.

[81] *Id.*

[82] *Id.*

[83] Meyer, "The Degradation of Work Revisited."

[84] Shirky, *Here Comes Everybody,* at 82.

[85] Shirky, *Here Comes Everybody,* at 21.

mational bonus "cognitive surplus."[86] Individuals enjoying this level of connectivity, within their chosen networks, are able to tap into the observational and cognitive powers of the entire group, using time and resources previously expended on overhead managerial activities.[87] Instead of the 20century model of communications, in which a small number of people created content and distributed it via one-way media, such as print or television, information exchanges have become multidirectional, with each participant in the network both producer and consumer.[88] Raw information in the form of text or image flows more rapidly and with more immediate consequences, with the benefit of more widespread commentary and other inputs and with greater ability to trigger real-time action.[89] Moreover, the world has only begun to explore the full potential of this new organizational form. As it takes shape, the world will fully enter the Age of Connectivity.

One must always be careful about the hype that surrounds each new technological development, and connectivity has attracted its share.[90] Nonetheless, scholars have begun to consider the implications of connectivity in the workplace and have drawn positive conclusions.[91] For example, Paul Leonardi of the University of California, Santa Barbara, created an interesting experimental protocol in which he had the opportunity to study patterns of communication and productivity in a large financial services firm both before and after it rolled out a pilot enterprise social networking site.[92] The internal nature of the site allowed him to isolate relevant behaviors, and the fact that it was a pilot allowed him to use another, similar department in the same firm as a control.[93] At the end of the study, Leonardi concluded that the networking allowed an "awareness of ambient communication," (and "vicarious learning") that increased "metaknowledge" about the organization, such as by informing coworkers of who knew what (thus reducing the need for duplicative work effort).[94] Beyond simple efficiency (although, one must note, in a large organization reducing duplication is a worthy goal), Leonardi found that employees who changed their behaviors to take advantage of the new platform (many did not) acquired a "vision advantage" over their colleagues.[95] In essence, adopters shifted their behavior from responding reactively to problems to "proactively aggregating knowledge by observing coworkers' visible communications," which helped

---

[86] Clay Shirky, *Cognitive Surplus. How Technology Makes Consumers into Collaborators* 9–12 (2010), at 9-12 [hereinafter Shirky, Cognitive Surplus]. Shirky also pointed to the role of leisure time in creating this surplus.

[87] Greg Urban and Kyung-Nan Koh, "The Semiotic Corporation: An Introduction to the Supplement Issue," 3 *Signs & Soc'y* (2015), at S1, S4-S5.

[88] Shirky, *Cognitive Surplus*, at 14-15.

[89] Shirky, *Cognitive Surplus,* at 14-17.

[90] Rhys Maliphant, "What 4 Recent Deals Tell Us About the Future of Connectivity," *Pivotl* (Sept. 8, 2015), http://www.pivotl.com/2015/09/08/what-4-recent-deals-tell-us-about-the-future-of-connectivity/

[91] *See*, e.g., Paul M. Leonardi, "Social Media, Knowledge Sharing, and Innovation: Toward a Theory of Communication Visibility," 25 *Info. Sys. Res.* (2014), at 796, 796–97.

[92] *Id.*

[93] Leonardi, "Social Media, Knowledge Sharing, and Innovation," at 799-803.

[94] Leonardi, "Social Media, Knowledge Sharing, and Innovation," at 812-813.

[95] Leonardi, "Social Media, Knowledge Sharing, and Innovation," at 809, 812. Leonardi draws on the work of R.S. Burt in regards to the concept of a "vision advantage," and notes that with enterprise social networking all employees could share in that advantage, regardless of network position.

them "bring new levels of innovation to [the firm's] products and services."[96] Leonardi concluded that the vicarious learning and proactive knowledge aggregation enabled by networking constituted "new ways of working" that were quite positive.[97]

This is neither the time nor the place to discuss the new ways of working that could arise in the Age of Connectivity. Its full power remains unknown but is certainly promising. The purpose of this chapter is to consider not its promise but rather how it may challenge compliance. Given the origins of compliance, in what here is called the River Rouge approach to organizational culture, the starting point should be to ask: Will connectivity pose a significant challenge to the hierarchical form of organization?[98] The short answer is: Yes.

Connectivity has already challenged hierarchical organization structures, with deadly results. In this less-than-perfect world, the critical challenges posed by new social realities often first manifest themselves on the battlefield.[99] The world is currently celebrating (if that is the right word) the centennial of the First World War, where the overwhelming power of manufacturing (like the assembly line inside the River Rouge plant) first unmistakably manifested itself.[100] Connectivity has had a similar introduction to the world. While fighting the War in Iraq, the U.S. military, and especially the Special Forces, found that Al Qaeda in Iraq could exploit real time networked information to strike autonomous blows against U.S. allies and then evade the U.S. military's slower moving hierarchical response.[101] The enemy used real-time connectivity to strike and disappear as information flowed more slowly up the U.S. military's command and control pyramid, and responsive orders flowed back down.[102] The operational advantages of the connected approach became so pronounced that U.S. field commanders began to realize that despite their advantages in training, efficiency, and material, they were unable to defeat an under-resourced insurgency.[103] In the words of General Stanley McChrystal, they started asking: "Why were we losing?"[104] The answer, General McChrystal and his team concluded, was that networked solutions, such as the strategy Al Qaeda in Iraq was using against them, thrive in chaotic and fast-moving environments.[105] Connected solutions present themselves as a "chaotic mess."[106] Nonetheless, General McChrystal suggests that networking permits solutions that are "capable of doing things that no single designer, however masterful, could envision—things far beyond an individual planner's capacity to comprehend and control."[107]

---

96 *Id.*

97 *Id.*

98 Henry Ford, Ford Rouge Factory Tour.

99 *See*, e.g., Stanley McChrystal, Tantum Collins, David Silverman, *Team of Teams: New Rules of Engagement for a Complex World*, Portfolio (2015), at 226, 251.

100 Meyer, "The Degradation of Work Revisited.".

101 McChrystal, Collins, Silverman, et al., *Team of Teams*, at 16-19.

102 McChrystal, Collins, Silverman, et al., *Team of Teams*, at 17-19.

103 McChrystal, Collins, Silverman, et al., *Team of Teams*, at 18-19.

104 McChrystal, Collins, Silverman, et al., *Team of Teams*, at 19.

105 McChrystal, Collins, Silverman, et al., *Team of Teams*, at 248-249.

106 *See*, e.g., McChrystal, Collins, Silverman, et al., *Team of Teams*, at 248.

107 *Id.*

Luckily, in most cases, the failure to understand and respond to the new connected reality will not lead to combat deaths and civic destruction. Nonetheless, many people seem to misunderstand its transformative nature.[108] They believe connectivity is nothing more than a lot of information. To date, most legal commentators seem to be thinking along these lines and are primarily concerned about protecting the personal information people share with their networks.[109] For example, commentators ask whether employees have a reasonable expectation of privacy in their social media records,[110] whether "cyber-vetting" is appropriate when assessing candidates for jobs,[111] and whether surveillance is an appropriate work-force management tool.[112]

Compliance, on the other hand, has different concerns. In some respects, compliance professionals approach connectivity from much of the same perspective as the military.[113] How, they ask, will they devise control systems for the chaotic mess in a networked environment? Again, much like the military, compliance professionals ask: how can they identify and control rogue actors who will have all of the advantages of operating autonomously within dense networks of real-time information? Fraud, like warfare, is a fact of human life. Moreover, as General McChrystal observed, when a rogue network is freed from the obligation to achieve something constructive, it can dispense with precision and coordination and become even more dangerous.[114] These are not theoretical questions. An example of connectivity, already common in many firms, highlights the looming challenge.

Many firms have established bring your own device or "BYOD" policies.[115] When a firm permits BYOD, employees carry a personal smartphone with the firm's controlled communications system as well as their own uncontrolled personal systems.[116] BYOD enhances employee satisfaction by allowing them ready access to their personal communications and networks, and efficiency, as they can use their favorite tools and search engines throughout the day.[117] On the other hand, BYOD policies have generated numerous difficult legal and administrative issues encompassing e-discovery,[118]

---

[108] *See,* e.g., McChrystal, Collins, Silverman, et al., *Team of Teams,* at 19.

[109] *See* Saby Ghoshray, "The Emerging Reality of Social Media: Erosion of Individual Privacy Through Cyber-Vetting and the Law's Inability to Catch Up," 12 *J. Marshall Rev. Intell. Prop. L.* (2013), at 551, 552-553; Patricia Sánchez Abril, et al., "Blurred Boundaries: Social Media Privacy and the Twenty-First-Century Employee," 40 *Am. Bus. L.J.* (2012), at 63, 64-65.

[110] Sánchez Abril, et al., "Blurred Boundaries," at 64-65.

[111] Ghoshray, "The Emerging Reality of Social Media," at 573-577.

[112] Saby Ghoshray, "Employer Surveillance Versus Employee Privacy: The New Reality of Social Media and Workplace Privacy," 40 *N. Ky. L. Rev.* (2013), at 593, 594.

[113] Miriam Hechler Baer, *Governing Corporate Compliance*, 50 B.C. L. Rev. 949, 979-980 (2009).

[114] McChrystal, Collins, Silverman, et al., *Team of Teams,*, at 244–45 (comparing a rogue network like Al Qaeda in Iraq to a network with constructive goals, like supply chain management, aid distribution, marketing, and national governance).

[115] Melinda McLellan, James A. Sherer, and Emily R. Fedeles, "Wherever You Go, There You Are (With Your Mobile Device): Privacy Risks and Legal Complexities Associated with International "Bring Your Own Device' Programs," 21: 3 *Rich. J.L. & Tech.* (2014), at 11, 1-3.

[116] McLellan, Sherer, and Fedeles, "Wherever You Go, There You Are," at 1-2.

[117] McLellan, Sherer, and Fedeles, "Wherever You Go, There You Are," at 2-3.

[118] *Id.*

cybersecurity, privacy, employment issues arising from an "always reachable"[119] workplace dynamic, books and records retention,[120] litigation over remote wipes of the BYOD device (a security measure required by many firms that allow BYOD),[121] and even international complications, because BYOD users carry their devices across international borders and through differing foreign privacy regimes.[122] Indeed, the issues are so difficult that some commentators have suggested "BYOD" could stand for "bring your own disaster" to work.[123] Without detracting from these issues, compliance professionals have yet another concern with BYOD. At any given moment in the workplace, deep inside the alleged control perimeter around the firm, even in the presence of supervisors exercising their alleged power of observation, a BYOD employee has private access to the connected world, for good or ill.

Ongoing developments threaten more of the same. New communication and networking applications are constantly emerging, some of them expressly designed to be transitory, elusive, and difficult to control.[124] Parents of minor children worry about these applications, and compliance professionals should, too.[125] Moreover, one hears a great deal of discussion in the news about the deployment of unbreakable encryption on smartphones and its impact on law enforcement.[126] Compliance professionals, when they hear this, must wonder what the impact of encryption will be when employees know their private communications, even those sent on a BYOD from deep within the firm during the workday, are unbreakably protected.[127] Moreover, legal trends seem to be moving in the direction of giving employees even greater privacy.[128] Several states have moved to restrict employers' ability to monitor employees' social media accounts by restricting their ability to demand the employees' usernames or passwords.[129] Some states allow employer investigations to ensure compliance with applicable laws and

[119] McLellan, Sherer, and Fedeles, "Wherever You Go, There You Are," at 3.

[120] McLellan, Sherer, and Fedeles, "Wherever You Go, There You Are," at 17.

[121] McLellan, Sherer, and Fedeles, "Wherever You Go, There You Are," at 28.

[122] McLellan, Sherer, and Fedeles, "Wherever You Go, There You Are," at 6-7 (surveying the field).

[123] Hope A. Comisky and Tracey E. Diamond, "The Risks and Rewards of a BYOD Program: Ensuring Corporate Compliance Without Causing "Bring Your Own Disaster" at Work," 8 *Charleston L. Rev.* (2014), at 385, 410.

[124] Brett Nuckles, "5 Best Secure Messaging Apps," *Bus. News Daily* (Oct. 24, 2016), http://www.businessnewsdaily.com/6981-secure-messaging-apps-business.html

[125] *See* "New Snapchat App Worrying Parents," NBC-2 (Dec. 4, 2012), http://www.nbc-2.com/story/20259970/new-snapchat-app-worrying-parents. The tension between rogue actors and privacy on social media can be seen in an easy experiment. Google "Snapchat," a social application designed to be transitory, and responsive hits will cover the gamut from FBI warnings that criminals are exploiting the application to take advantage of children, to other warnings (presumably intended for a different audience) that police may be able to retrieve the transitory messages after all.

[126] See, e.g., Carrie Cordero and Marc Zwillinger, "Should Law Enforcement Have the Ability to Access Encrypted Communications?" *The Wall Street Journal* (Apr. 19, 2015), http://www.wsj.com/articles/should-law-enforcement-have-the-ability-to-access-encrypted-communications-1429499474

[127] Michael Cobb, "How Will Android Encryption by Default Affect Enterprise BYOD?" *SearchSecurity*, http://searchsecurity.techtarget.com/answer/How-will-Android-encryption-by-default-affect-enterprise-BYOD (last visited Mar. 1, 2017).

[128] "State Social Media Privacy Laws," *Nat'l Conf. of State Legislatures* (Jan. 11, 2017), http://www.ncsl.org/research/telecommunications-and-information-technology/state-laws-prohibiting-access-to-social-media-usernames-and-passwords.aspx#stat (surveying relevant state statutes).

[129] *Id.*

regulations,[130] but others, such as New Jersey, do not.[131] How, then, will compliance ensure that employees are not using personal networks for business-related communications or even exploiting the apparent authority of the firm for the employee's own purposes? Indeed, some regulators, such as the National Labor Relations Board (NLRB) are not just creating no-compliance zones; they are affirmatively protecting employees' ability to discuss the employer, in negative detail, on social media, as a form of protected speech.[132] As these developments begin to add up, the BYOD in an employee's hand will become an increasingly powerful symbol of the growing ascendance of connectivity over compliance.

Are employees using BYODs to send secret messages—in real time—about the nonpublic information they have just learned? Are they leveraging their latest work assignment to enhance their negotiations for a new job? Are they posting social commentary about the supervisor sitting across the conference room table? Or are they—as one would hope—using the power of connectivity to enhance their own productivity and value to the firm? Who knows? Compliance professionals accustomed to the hierarchical model shudder at their loss of control. They should. Connectivity is challenging many of the operational assumptions upon which compliance professionals have based their work. They are losing their bounded space; connected cyberspace stretches out around the world. They are losing their power of observation; with unbreakable encryption they will lose it completely. They are losing their ability to capture and assess work-related activities; how does one capture and control a widely shared "cognitive surplus"? They are losing their ability to sanction nonconforming conduct; how will they even know?[133] Finally, they are losing their vision of their workplace as a River Rouge-style assembly line;[134] dense multipoint webs will fill the future just as linear critical paths filled the past.[135]

BYOD policies are only one example and are only illustrative. The critical issue is *not* whether employers should allow BYODs inside the firm. Trying to prohibit them outside of highly defined and secured areas, such as a trading desk, is probably futile and even counterproductive: the promise of vicarious learning and cognitive surplus is just as alluring to employers as it is to workers.[136] No business wants its workforce locked into the technology and mind frame of the last century.[137] Rather, the critical issue is how to respond to connectivity, not how to prevent it.

---

[130] *See, e.g., Md. Code Ann., Lab. & Empl.* § 3-712(e) (LexisNexis 2016).

[131] N.J. Stat. Ann. § 34:6B-6 (West 2016).

[132] *See, e.g.,* Office of Public Affairs, Acting General Counsel Releases Report on Employer Social Media Policies, NLRB (May 30, 2012), https://www.nlrb.gov/news-outreach/news-story/acting-general-counsel-releases-report-employer-social-media-policies. The NLRB's general counsel has issued a series of reports describing cases brought against employers for social media policies that are deemed overbroad and chilling to employees' organizational rights.

[133] McLellan, Sherer, and Fedeles, "Wherever You Go, There You Are, at 2.

[134] The Henry Ford, Ford Rouge Factory Tour.

[135] Meyer, "The Degradation of Work Revisited."

[136] "Cognitive Surplus-Heard of It? Every Finance Department Should Tap into It!" *Adra: Blog* (Nov. 14, 2012), http://www.adra.com/blog/2012/11/14/cognitive-surplus-heard-of-it-every-finance-department-should-tap-into-it/

[137] *Id.*

Moreover, another development, not directly relevant to the rise of connectivity, should also be mentioned. This is the ongoing atomization of the hierarchical firm separate and apart from the impact of technology.[138] One economist has estimated that approximately 1 out of 10 U.S. workers is already engaged in an "alternative employment arrangement," and most prove to be independent contractors.[139] Compliance professionals today must deal with large numbers of independent contractors, temporary employees, outsourced activities, interns, externs, and other human resource practices that have the effect of decomposing the firm into semiautonomous actors with low levels of connection with the institution.[140] Why, these workers already ask, must they be subjected to the training, monitoring, and culture experienced by full-time employees? Building a culture of compliance in such an environment already poses significant challenges. At the same time, as connectivity grows, these autonomous workers will bring their own networks with them into the workplace.[141] Compliance professionals who consider the future must look forward to a world in which many workers view their relationship with the firm as purely contractual and at arm's-length, whereas their relationships with their personal networks are dense, in real time, and completely private.[142] At some point these workers will escape from the culture of the firm and even from its command-and-control hierarchy. Indeed, many of them probably already have.

When Alec Ross met with heads-of-state, he asked how would they deal with the systemic loss of control and diffusion of power resulting from the open access, globalization, and constant innovation of the new century?[143] These are challenges for more than heads-of-state. They are also challenges for corporate compliance. How compliance professionals address them will play an important role in the future of compliance. Moreover, today's workforce does not live in a binary world where the hierarchy is intact and all-powerful, or connectivity has completely broken it down. More likely, compliance professionals will struggle with situations in which enhanced connectivity challenges their controls, but the regulatory requirements and legal concepts developed for the hierarchical world remain in place. As connectivity grows, so will the challenge to compliance.

V. INHERENT COMPLIANCE

As the world shifts from the society and economy of the 20 century, in which information and productive relationships were controlled by hierarchical organizations, into the 21 century, in which networks will increasingly challenge hierarchies, perspectives on cultures of compliance must change as well. River Rouge-style external

---

[138] *See,* generally, Jeffrey A. Eisenach, Navigant Econ. L.L.C., "The Role of Independent Contractors in the U.S. Economy" (2010), https://www.aei.org/wp-content/uploads/2012/08/-the-role-of-independent-contractors-in-the-us-economy_123302207143.pdf

[139] *Id.*

[140] Eisenach, Navigant Econ. L.L.C., "The Role of Independent Contractors, at 16-17.

[141] Eisenach, Navigant Econ. L.L.C., "The Role of Independent Contractors," at 21-28 (noting several areas where employers hire independent contractors to use their networks and resources for the employer's benefit).

[142] Brendon Schrader, "Here's Why the Freelancer Economy Is on the Rise," *FastCompany* (Aug. 10, 2015), https://www.fastcompany.com/3049532/the-future-of-work/hereswhy-the-freelancer-economy-is-on-the-rise

[143] Ross, *Industries of the Future,* at 215.

controls will become increasingly difficult to impose. Instead of information flowing up a pyramid and commands and controls flowing back down, the connected social dynamic will become increasingly networked and autonomous. How should compliance respond?

Compliance professionals need to focus more attention on what—for want of a better term—could be called "inherent compliance." Compliance is inherent when compliance-fostering structures or practices are inherent in the organization of a firm or function.[144] In other words, inherent compliance is not imposed from the outside. It is not based on external commands and controls.[145] To return again, for a moment, to the River Rouge structure, inherent compliance is not based on a supervisor standing behind the assembly line, watching every move in a defined and structured sequence.[146] Rather, inherent compliance is embedded in the organizational culture of the firm and its operations and will operate even when external controls are unavailable among the multipoint webs and nodes of a network.[147]

Stating what is needed—inherent compliance—is a lot easier than describing what it is or how to deliver it. Don Langevoort and Greg Urban's scholarship is more than simply interesting and thought provoking, although it is that as well. Rather, their work helps illustrate how compliance professionals can begin to respond to the looming challenge of connectivity. Langevoort's work with behavioral ethics shows the many ways in which a human actor can become more or less ethical.[148] Professor Urban's work with anthropology shows how human groups use symbols to replicate cultural norms.[149] Their scholarship should play an important role in helping compliance personnel to think about the future of compliance policy. In essence, their work is beginning to demonstrate a possible path to inherent compliance.

Behavioral Ethics

First, from Don, is the study of behavioral ethics, including the many ways in which human actors fool themselves into believing they are more ethical than they really are.[150] Langevoort has stated that people generally cheat more than they should, but

---

[144] Charles H. Le Grand, "Building a Culture of Compliance," IBS America 3 (2005), http://www.qualitymag.com/ext/resources/files/white_papers/BuildingaCultureofCompliance-IBS.pdf

[145] *Id.*

[146] Le Grand, "Building a Culture of Compliance;" Meyer, "The Degradation of Work Revisited.

[147] Le Grand, "Building a Culture of Compliance,", at 3-4.

[148] Donald C. Langevoort, *Selling Hope, Selling Risk: Corporations, Wall Street, and the Dilemmas of Investor Protection,* Oxford University Press (2016); Donald C. Langevoort, "Behavioral Ethics, Behavioral Compliance," in Jennifer Arlen, ed., *Research Handbook on Corporate Crime and Financial Misdealing*, http://scholarship.law.georgetown.edu/cgi/viewcontent.cgi?article=2519&context=facpub; Donald C. Langevoort, "Cultures of Compliance," *Am. Crim. L. Rev.* (forthcoming); Hillary A. Sale and Donald C. Langevoort, "'We Believe:'" Omnicare, Legal Risk Disclosure and Corporate Governance," 66, No. 3 *Duke L.J.* (2016) at 763-795, http://scholarship.law.duke.edu/dlj/vol66/iss3/10

[149] Greg Urban, "Corporations in the Flow of Culture," 39 *Seattle U. L. Rev.* 321, 349-51 (2016); Greg Urban, "Symbolic Force: A Corporate Revitalization Video and Its Effects," 3 *Signs & Soc'y* (2015), at S95, S95–S96; Urban and Koh, "The Semiotic Corporation, at S4-S5.

[150] Langevoort, "Behavioral Ethics, Behavioral Compliance."

less than they could.[151] He also discussed the compliance implications of this insight in more detail in his contribution to Arlen's *Research Handbook*.[152] It appears, he said, that people have cognitive buffers that enable them to delay awareness of the ethical nature of an act until they are committed to it and its rationalization.[153] This allows everyone to cheat a little, and when his or her ethical consciousness catches up, to engage in after-the-fact rationalization.[154] In short, cheating (at least to some degree) is a universal practice, and it is fed by a temporal mismatch between act and ethical awareness.[155]

Langevoort's scholarship is interesting in its consideration of the challenges to compliance in the looming Age of Connectivity. If human cognition interferes with ethical behavior, such as by buffering and delaying ethical awareness, what will happen when employees have free reign, during the workday, on their own fully encrypted personal networks? With no external controls to restrain them, will workers slowly slide down the slippery slope into ever more pernicious cheating and ever more self-serving rationalization? New and responsive forms of compliance must be developed.

Langevoort makes an observation that may be helpful in this regard: in many organizations, he says, "ethics is a potentially uncomfortable subject."[156] Given the traditional organizational culture of advisory firms, this makes sense. Ethics can seem like a personal matter and, in any event, why worry about it when the externally imposed command-and-control structure will catch nonconforming output? Now though, as individuals shake free of the hierarchy, the ethics with which they represent the firm takes on new meaning. Perhaps the time has come to challenge the reluctance to discuss ethics in the workplace.

How can compliance professionals translate Langevoort's insights into a culture of compliance? Making ethics an affirmative element in the workplace may focus attention upon it in ways that will help overcome businesspeople's inherent cognitive buffering and delay.[157] Indeed, when people in a workplace push ethics and compliance into the foreground of decision making, freely discuss the ethical considerations in business questions, and are free to remark on the business ethics of competitors and others, it will (hopefully) become increasingly difficult for ethical realization to be left lurking in the unaware shadows of cognition.[158] This is called "framing."[159] When an issue is framed as ethical, people tend to produce more ethical choices.[160] By making ethics and compliance explicit and affirmative (rather than negative and reactive), one can hope people will better frame their work—both in the office and on their networks.

---

[151] Donald Langevoort, *Address at Rutgers Law School Center for Corporate Law and Governance Symposium: New Directions in Corporate Compliance* (May 20, 2016).

[152] *Id.; see also* Langevoort, "Behavioral Ethics, Behavioral Compliance."

[153] Langevoort, "Behavioral Ethics, Behavioral Compliance."

[154] *Id.*

[155] *Id.*

[156] *Id.*

[157] Dori Meinert, "Creating an Ethical Workplace," *Soc'y for Hum. Resource Mgmt.* (Apr. 1, 2014), https://www.shrm.org/hr-today/news-hr-magazine/pages/0414-ethical-workplace-culture.aspx

[158] *Id.*

[159] Langevoort, *Address at Rutgers Law School.*

[160] *Id.*

An example of this approach as a regulatory or compliance strategy can be found in the SEC's rulemaking for the code of ethics rule for investment advisers.[161] A code should be more than a compliance manual, the SEC said:

> Rather, a code of ethics should set out ideals for ethical conduct premised on fundamental principals [sic] of openness, integrity, honesty, and trust. A good code of ethics should effectively convey to employees the value the advisory firm places on ethical conduct, and should challenge employees to live up not only to the letter of the law, but also to the ideals of the organization.[162]

In any event, most codes of ethics ended up looking like codes of law by listing prohibited conduct of greater or lesser length and detail.[163] Nonetheless, as an aspirational statement, the SEC's vision for advisory codes of ethics is very suggestive of how framing can support inherent compliance.

Anthropology

Second from Professor Urban is the study of anthropological culture, including the use of symbols and rituals to define and replicate cultural norms within an organization.[164] As an example, Professor Urban referred to a corporate video made by Harley-Davidson, Inc., and he explored the effects of the video more thoroughly in an article published in 2015.[165] The video had a high aesthetic quality, showed a positive image of the company and the people who worked there, and played on themes such as certain social settings (small towns and rural America), deeper national images (flags), and motivational goals (underdogs winning in the end).[166] In interviews, Professor Urban determined that some viewers were attracted by the video, others repulsed.[167] The effect, he concluded, was to make the symbolism contained in the video a gatekeeper in which the video caused a "transference of affectual quality" that oriented individuals' attitudes to the collective; in this case, the Harley-Davidson company.[168] In short, as Professor Urban explained that, the video represents the corporation to itself, thus "helping to create and maintain group boundaries."[169]

This type of self-symbolism is very interesting when considering the challenge to compliance in the looming Age of Connectivity. In essence, it suggests a new source of workplace boundaries, defined not by a shop floor and a supervisor's physical power of

---

[161] 17 C.F.R. § 275.204A-1 (2016).

[162] Investment Adviser Codes of Ethics, 69 Fed. Reg. 41696, 41697 (July 9, 2004).

[163] *See,* e.g., "Investment Advisor Code of Ethics," Charles Schwab, http://www.schwab.com/public/schwab/nn/legal_compliance/important_notices/iacoe.html (last visited Mar. 1, 2017).

[164] See, e.g., Urban, "Corporations in the Flow of Culture," at 321-322.

[165] Urban, "Symbolic Force," at S95; Greg Urban, *Address at Rutgers Law School Center for Corporate Law and Governance Symposium: New Directions in Corporate Compliance* (May 20, 2016).

[166] Urban, *Symbolic Force,* at S105-S107.

[167] Urban, *Symbolic Force,* at S97.

[168] Urban, *Symbolic Force,* at S100.

[169] Urban and Koh, "The Semiotic Corporation," at S5 (internal quotations omitted).

observation but by the affectual qualities that inspire and motivate employees. Indeed, in a 2016 work Professor Urban distinguishes between the "anthropological corporation," which is a productive group characterized by an "at least somewhat distinctive culture," and the "legal corporation," which is a creature of state recognition.[170] One can imagine applying the same terms to the networks that spring up so easily in a connected environment. The legal corporation may inhabit the controlled side of a BYOD smartphone, but a successful anthropological corporation will have an impact on the BYOD's personal side as well.

How can compliance professionals translate Urban's insights into a culture of compliance? Making ethics an affirmative element in the firm's symbolism of itself, to itself, may help invigorate the compliance of the anthropological corporation. This type of people-centered symbolism may, at first glance, appear to belong in the Human Resources Department. Nonetheless, from a compliance perspective, one could ask, what core compliance attributes belong in the images within which the company represents itself, to itself? One that springs readily to mind is honesty. A symbolic focus on honesty serves several goals in that it:

- Provides an affectual sense of identity for the group ("we are honest people");
- Provides core compliance priorities that can guide decision making (ask: was this a dishonest act or an honest person making an honest mistake?);
- Helps provide legitimacy to the compliance program (both for those who make a decision and those in the anthropological group who assess a decision's cultural legitimacy); and
- Provides opportunities for ritualized maintenance of the relationship between the anthropological and the legal corporation (dishonest people will be shown the door).

An example of how this approach might work in a regulatory or compliance context can be seen in the facts of a fairly notorious enforcement case. The SEC brought an action against Theodore Urban, general counsel and head of compliance of a broker-dealer, alleging that he had failed to supervise a particular salesman effectively.[171] The salesman had engaged in various forms of misconduct, eventually pleaded guilty to securities fraud and making a false and fictitious statement; he was sentenced to time in prison.[172] The case against Theodore Urban for failure to supervise the salesman had a long history, with a decision by an administrative law judge that was eventually overturned in 2012 by an evenly divided SEC decision.[173] The interest in the case today is not with the broker's misconduct or with the history of the case, or even, for that matter, with the allegations against Urban. Rather, it is with an apparently small anecdote buried within the administrative law judge's lengthy

---

[170] Urban, "Corporations in the Flow of Culture," at 350.

[171] *Urban,* Exchange Act Rel. No. 402, 99 SEC Docket 994, 2010 WL 3500928, at *1 (Sept. 8, 2010), *Dismissed by an evenly divided Commission*, Exchange Act Rel. No. 3366, 102 SEC Docket 3284, 2012 WL 1024025 (Jan. 26, 2012). Greg Urban stated that although they share the same last name, he and Theodore Urban are not relatives, at least insofar as Greg knows.

[172] *Urban,* Exchange Act Rel. No. 3366 (Sept. 2010), at *31.

[173] *Urban,* Exchange Act Rel. No. 3366 (Sept. 2010), at *49; *Urban,* Exchange Act Release No. 3366, 102 SEC Docket 3284, 2012 WL 1024025, at *1 (Jan. 26, 2012).

initial decision. Apparently, in January 2003, as soon as the problematic salesman arrived at the firm, he lied to compliance.[174] He signed his wife's name to an option agreement for a joint account, claiming he had a power of attorney for her.[175] In fact, none was on file with the firm.[176] Moreover, that same day, the firm received a temporary restraining order that the salesman's wife had obtained against him.[177] A compliance professional said the salesman had lied, and was "going to be trouble."[178] Indeed, he was. By the time he was finished, the SEC had sanctioned the firm[179] and most of his supervisors.[180]

Why is this recounting important? At the beginning of a very long and unfortunate series of events, a compliance professional had already decided that the salesman was untruthful and would be trouble. In the traditional view of compliance, based on the command-and-control search for nonconforming outputs, the salesman had not yet produced any defective goods. Indeed, he had barely arrived at the firm. Yet, from a people-centered perspective, the salesman had already demonstrated the key necessary information: he was a liar. The salesman had already demonstrated that he did not belong at a firm that defined itself, to itself, in its own self-symbolism, as inherently honest. Such a firm would have had an opportunity to act out a ritual of self-definition, as in the example, by asking the liar to leave as soon as he had arrived and before any damage was done.

Resiliency

Third, and finally, is the study of networks and their resilience. A recurring theme, among those who study today's increasingly networked world, is that the Age of Connectivity will be chaotic and messy.[181] In the past, organizations were modeled on the physical sciences with reductionist behaviors and explicit causation.[182] Frederick Winslow Taylor made this approach famous, and the Taylor System, as his ideas became known, led to the emergence of independent Inspection Departments[183] that can be viewed as the intellectual, if not organizational progenitors of the independent Compliance Department. The precisely controlled environment of the River Rouge structure owed much to his insights.[184] Increasingly, however, the life sciences are becoming the model for organizations, and much else in society, through the intellectual organiz-

---

[174] *Urban*, Exchange Act Release No. 402, at *8.

[175] *Id.*

[176] *Id.*

[177] *Id.*

[178] *Id.*

[179] *Ferris Baker Watts, Inc.*, Exchange Act Rel. No. 34-59372, 95 SEC. Docket 498, 2009 WL 321327, at *1 (Feb. 10, 2009).

[180] *See*, e.g., Exchange Act Rel. No. 34-60628, 96 SEC Docket 2246, 2009 WL 2857622, at *1 (Sept. 4, 2009).

[181] *See* e.g., Andrew Zolli and Anne Marie Healy, *Resilience: Why Things Bounce Back*, Simon & Schuster (2012), at 17-20. General McChrystal was previously cited for the same proposition. *See* McChrystal, Tantum Collins, David Silverman, *Team of Teams*, at 248-249.

[182] J.M. Juran, A History of Managing for Quality in the United States of America, in *A History of Managing for Quality* (1995), 554-557; Frederick Taylor Winslow, PBS: "Who Made America," https://www.pbs.org/wgbh/theymadeamerica/whomade/taylor_hi.html

[183] Juran, A History of Managing for Quality.

[184] Juran, A History of Managing for Quality, at 556–57 (commenting on relationship between Taylor and American productivity gains).

ing principle known as a network.[185] The concept of a network provides an analytical framework for understanding complex systems, many of which are biological, and has been applied to multiple manifestations in a wide range of fields.[186] For example, viewed as networks, similarities can be seen in the behaviors of tuberculosis infections and terrorist organizations or, somewhat differently, in the sustainability of coral reefs and financial institutions.[187] Moreover, beyond an analytical framework, networked operations provide tactical advantages, as General McChrystal discovered.[188] Based on his combat experiences with Al Qaeda in Iraq, he concluded that it takes a network to fight a network.[189] As adversaries (military and business) network themselves to remain competitive in the Age of Connectivity, how will compliance function in that environment? Luckily, the health of networks has received much recent attention, and there are lessons for compliance in this work.

In their 2012 book, *Resilience: Why Things Bounce Back,* Andrew Zolli and Anne Marie Healy consider why some networks can respond to threats and overcome crises, while others, faced with apparently smaller problems, collapse into newer and less optimal states.[190] Many networks, the authors suggest, are robust yet fragile.[191] However effective those structures may have been at addressing historic problems, they are vulnerable to the unexpected, mostly because they have somehow lost the diversity and flexibility necessary to respond to new and different challenges.[192] From monocultures to group think, when networks lose diversity and flexibility, they acquire fragility. The response, the authors suggest, is something called "strategic looseness."[193] This approach has two parts: "fixedness" of values and purpose, including, in an organizational context, significant levels of trust; and "fluidity" of strategies, structures, and actions, including creative responses to unexpected events.[194] Remarkably enough, this is very similar to the two-step prescription offered by General McChrystal: "shared consciousness" and "empowered execution."[195] In General McChrystal's terms:

> Shared consciousness is a carefully maintained set of centralized forums for bringing people together. Empowered execution is a radically decentralized system for pushing authority out to the edges of the organization.[196]

---

[185] *See,* e.g., Zolli and Healy *Resilience*, at 19.

[186] *Id.* (describing the term as "a universal, abstract reference system for describing how information, resources, and behaviors flow through many complex systems").

[187] *Id.*

[188] McChrystal, Tantum Collins, David Silverman, *Team of Teams,* at 248–49.

[189] McChrystal, Tantum Collins, David Silverman, *Team of Teams,* at 251.

[190] Zolli and Healy *Resilience*, at 19.

[191] Zolli and Healy *Resilience*, at 16-17.

[192] Zolli and Healy *Resilience*, at 19.

[193] Zolli and Healy *Resilience*, at 259.

[194] Zolli and Healy *Resilience*, at 259-260. For a discussion of the role of trust, *see* Zolli and Healy *Resilience*, at 144-190, which describes how "resilience is predicated on trust in a system, allowing potential adversaries to move seamlessly into cooperative mode" and giving examples.

[195] McChrystal, Tantum Collins, David Silverman, *Team of Teams,* at 244.

[196] McChrystal, Tantum Collins, David Silverman, *Team of Teams,* at 245.

Whichever terms are used—fixedness of values or shared consciousness—the result is much the same. Organizational resilience is primarily subjective and based upon the values and knowledge shared by networked individuals. General McChrystal calls creating this subjective state the "heavy lifting" that must precede decentralized decision-making.[197]

How can compliance professionals translate Zolli and McChrystal's insights into a culture of compliance? Making ethics explicit and establishing a shared expectation of honesty as a basis for mutual trust would—one hopes—prime an organization for resilient responses to ethical or compliance challenges.

The next step would be to develop shared consciousness by providing transparent information to everyone on the network. Once compliance transparency can be achieved, vicarious ethics learning and recombinant compliance innovation will be possible. The electronics revolution makes this kind of transparency possible in large groups, really, for the first time in history.[198]

The final step would be to push authority out to the edges of the organization. Zolli and Healy call this "adhocracy."[199] Instead of seeking precise and predetermined actions, as in hierarchical organizations, adhocracies respond to new challenges with creative trial and error.[200] Importantly, creative responses may not always be the best, and feedback loops play an important role in deciding what does and does not work.[201] Again, the availability of massive data flows will allow a level of feedback not even imagined in the past. Through ongoing trial and error, and active feedback, it will be possible to identify both emerging systemic weaknesses and the efficacy of different responses. This is the essence of a self-healing network. As General McChrystal put it, somewhat differently, in a connected environment, leadership becomes a form of gardening in which the goal is no longer to control individual outputs, but to shape the ecosystem.[202]

An example of how this approach might work in a regulatory or compliance context can be seen in its application to enforcement or disciplinary policy. What should be done when a worker who is deeply engaged in a firm's shared values, who has been provided up-to-the-minute relevant information, somehow generates nonconforming output? In the command-and-control world of the River Rouge structure, the answer is simple: the failure should be sanctioned.[203] Today, regulators' enforcement dockets are full of cases sanctioning people and firms for good-faith nonconforming output, even when the problem arose in highly complex environments and no one was hurt.[204]

---

[197] McChrystal, Tantum Collins, David Silverman, *Team of Teams*, at 244.

[198] Identifying compliance transparency as a goal also shows some of the challenges facing compliance in the Age of Connectivity. Current human resources and privacy law can be expected to make achieving such transparency very difficult.

[199] Zolli and Healy *Resilience*, at 264-270.

[200] Zolli and Healy *Resilience*, at 264-266.

[201] Zolli and Healy *Resilience*, at 260-264.

[202] McChrystal, Tantum Collins, David Silverman, *Team of Teams*, at 226.

[203] *See* "Part II, River Rouge and the Origins of Compliance."

[204] *See*, e.g., Urska Velikonja, "Reporting Agency Performance: Behind the SEC's Enforcement Statistics," 101 *Cornell L. Rev.* (2016), at 901, 929-930.

Resilience theory, on the other hand, suggests that greater emphasis should be placed on the self-healing characteristics of the network.[205] Has an honest person made a good faith mistake, chosen a less than optimal response, or overlooked some latent potential failure in a complex system? In a self-healing network, the questions become: what is the scope of the situation, what can be done to rectify it, and what can be learned about the nature of the challenge going forward? Adhocracies must expect some level of breakage, and compliance professionals must insist that the network focus on healing itself, including healing any harm to customers impacted by a failure. On the other hand, external controls, such as those imposed by regulators, would be most effective when targeting situations that fundamentally threaten the network as a whole, such as instances of intentional dishonesty. The more a network can respond on its own and heal its own ethical and compliance challenges through its own inherent processes, the more resilient it will become.

VI. CONCLUSION

These are the earliest days of the Age of Connectivity, and only the passage of time will reveal its full impact on compliance. As a famous philosopher of our times is alleged to have said(that would be Yogi Berra), "It's hard to make predictions, especially about the future."[206] This chapter is not offered as a roadmap but only to provide a few suggestions about what connectivity may mean to compliance and how compliance professionals might respond. Much like the heads-of-state interviewed by Alec Ross and cited at the beginning of the chapter, compliance professionals must get ready for a loss of control and diffusion of power.[207] Moreover, as General McChrystal learned in Iraq, rogue networks are capable of terrible harm, and River Rouge-style hierarchies are not very effective against them.[208] It takes a network to fight a network. How will an effective culture of compliance operate in a connected environment? Perhaps, instead of fearing their loss of control in the chaotic mess, successful compliance professionals of the future will use tools like behavioral ethics, anthropology, and resilience theory to help develop self-healing cultures of compliance. The challenge will be to make compliance work in the looming Age of Connectivity. The future is upon those in the compliance field. It is time to get ready.

---

[205] Zolli and Healy *Resilience*, at 80-81.

[206] Beatrice Santorini, "Yogi Berra: Sayings and Ripostes," *Linguistic Humor*, http://www.ling.upenn.edu/~beatrice/humor/yogi-berra.html

[207] Ross, Industries of the Future, at 215.

[208] McChrystal, Tantum Collins, David Silverman, *Team of Teams*, at 17-19.

ABOUT THE AUTHOR

A 23-year veteran of the Securities and Exchange Commission (SEC), **John H. Walsh** joined Eversheds Sutherland in October 2011. With his deep, insider's experience and perspective of the SEC, Mr. Walsh now represents broker-dealers, hedge funds, investment advisers, and other securities firms in compliance and regulatory issues involving the agency. He counsels clients on the full spectrum of securities issues from development and compliance to cooperation in examinations and defense in enforcement proceedings. In 2016 Mr. Walsh was elected to membership in the American Law Institute, the leading independent organization in the United States dedicated to the work of clarifying, modernizing, and improving the law.

At the SEC, Mr. Walsh played a key role in creating the Office of Compliance Inspections and Examinations (OCIE). He designed and implemented the SEC's securities compliance examination practices, first as a senior adviser for compliance policy and then, most recently, as associate director-chief counsel. In 2009, he served as OCIE's acting director and led a massive retraining of examination staff on antifraud techniques.

Prior to his tenure at OCIE, Mr. Walsh was special counsel to former SEC Chairman Arthur Levitt from 1993 to 1995. From 1990 to 1993, he worked in the SEC Division of Enforcement, serving first as senior counsel and then as chief of the branch of regional office assistance, where he regularly appeared before the SEC's closed meetings to present and discuss regional office enforcement cases. He also advised the commissioners and staff on securities laws and agency policy. Mr. Walsh began his career with the SEC in 1988 as an attorney in the Office of General Counsel.

CHAPTER 22

The Future of Compliance

By Andrew Bowden
Jackson National Life Insurance Company

I. INTRODUCTION

Humility is the first, and most important, ingredient in making predictions. As Phillip Tetlock established in "Expert Political Judgment," even "experts" have a woeful record of predicting future events.[1]

Looking back on 2016, the record of failed predictions lengthened in memorable ways...Brexit, President Trump, and one lesser mistaken assessment of future events that may have been missed: the odds given before the start of the 2015-16 English Premier Soccer League season that Leicester City would win the title. The league consists of 20 teams, suggesting that if the teams were evenly matched, the preseason odds of any team winning the league would be 1 in 20. Historically, however, the teams have not been evenly matched, or anything close to it. In fact, since the league's inception in 1992, only 5 different teams had won the league before the 2015-16 season. At the start of that season, Leicester City, a recent bottom dweller that had never won the league, was given a 1 in 5,000 chance of winning the league according to odds posted by William Hill, a British bookmaker.

Of course, Leicester City, a 5,000 to 1 shot, won the Premier Soccer League title in 2016, proving lots of bettors wrong,[2] costing British bookmakers in the neighborhood of $15 to $25 million (depending on whom can be believed), and serving as a recent reminder not only of so-called experts' penchant for getting the future wrong, but for getting it wildly wrong.[3]

---

[1] Tetlock collected and analyzed more than 82,000 predictions made over two decades by 284 people whose professions included commenting or offering advice on political and economic trends. He concluded that so-called experts are generally no better than nonexperts at making predictions and that neither group is better at making predictions than simple rules and models. Philip E. Tetlock, *Expert Political Judgment* (Princeton: Princeton University Press, 2005).

[2] If more bettors had correctly assessed the likelihood of Leicester City winning the title, the odds would have been posted at something less than 5,000 to 1.

[3] By quick comparison, the 1969 World Champion New York Mets—the so-called "Miracle Mets"—were generally given preseason odds of 1 in 100 of winning the Fall Classic. The 1980 gold medal winning U.S. Hockey team—the "Miracle on Ice"—was given a 1 in 1,000 chance of beating the Soviet Union in the Olympic tournament. And, for those betting persons who may be tempted to wager on future events, during 2016, William Hill was offering 5,000 to 1 odds that Barack Obama will play cricket for the English national team as a second act following his presidency...and that Kim Kardashian will be elected president of the United States in 2024.

So...chastened by recent events and cognizant that the predictions in this chapter will likely prove inaccurate, I nevertheless offer two predictions on the future of compliance. Over the next decade, the most effective compliance teams will allocate significantly more capital than they do today, and employ much more sophisticated techniques, to analyze their organization's culture and data. The former seeks to analyze an organization from the top down, whereas the latter approaches the organization from the bottom up.

II. CULTURE

On October 20, 2014, the Federal Reserve Bank (the "Fed") hosted a workshop entitled "Reforming Culture and Behavior in the Financial Services Industry."[4] Speeches made by senior Fed officers generally addressed the perceived problems with culture, the responsibility of senior leaders to correct perceived problems, and the roles of incentives and penalties.

In his closing, William Dudley, the president and chief executive officer (CEO) of the New York Fed, said:

> [I]f those of you here today as stewards of these large financial institutions do not do your parts in pushing forcefully for change across the industry, then bad behavior will undoubtedly persist. If that were to occur, the inevitable conclusion will be reached that your firms are too big and complex to manage effectively. In that case, financial stability concerns would dictate that your firms need to be dramatically downsized and simplified so they can be managed effectively. It is up to you to address this cultural and ethical challenge.[5]

This is strong stuff: get culture right or be dismantled.

The Fed's late 2014 pronouncements have been followed more recently in the United States by the Financial Industry Regulatory Authority (FINRA) and in the United Kingdom by the Prudential Regulatory Authority (PRA).

---

[4] U.S. securities regulators have been particularly focused on culture since the beginning of the decade. In April 2003, Lori Richards (then director of the Office of Compliance Inspections and Examinations (OCIE) at the Securities and Exchange Commission (SEC)) gave a seminal speech, "The Culture of Compliance," in which she articulated her view of the characteristics of an organization with a compliant culture. *The Culture of Compliance, Remarks at the Spring Compliance Conference of the National Regulatory Services* (Apr. 23, 2003), https://www.sec.gov/news/speech/spch042303lar.htm). Richards' speech was shortly followed by another from Stephen Cutler (the director of the Division of Enforcement at the SEC), *Tone at the Top: Getting it Right,* in which Cutler stated, "Violations of the securities laws are very frequently the product of both individual failings and a deficient corporate culture....[W]e're trying to induce companies to address matters of tone and culture." Stephen M Cutler, *Tone at the Top: Getting it Right, Remarks at the Second Annual General Counsel Roundtable* (Dec. 3, 2004) https://www.sec.gov/news/speech/spch120304smc.htm

[5] William C. Dudley, *Enhancing Financial Stability by Improving Culture in the Financial Services Industry, Remarks at the Workshop on Reforming Culture and Behavior in the Financial Services Industry* (Oct. 20, 2014), https://www.newyorkfed.org/newsevents/speeches/2014/dud141020a.html

The first item in FINRA's 2016 examination priorities letter is a declaration to formalize its assessment of firm culture.[6] In a related letter sent to a number of broker-dealers, FINRA opined that cultural failures "impose significant harm on investors and the markets as well as the firms themselves."[7]

In his speech given in early 2016, then outgoing CEO of the PRA and the incoming CEO of the U.K.'s Financial Conduct Authority, Andrew Bailey said, "Culture has a major influence on the outcomes that matter to us as regulators. My assessment of recent history is that there has not been a case of a major prudential or conduct failing in a firm which did not have among its root causes a failure of culture...."[8]

All of these warnings, pronouncements, and regulatory focus make it clear that the stakes are incredibly high for organizations and their compliance teams. But what is culture? How can it be measured? How can it be regulated? Where are compliance professionals headed?

In the past, most conversations about, and assessments of, culture have focused on process, policies, and procedures, including things like:

- "Tone at the top;"
- Corporate values and how they are articulated;
- Internal complaint and investigation programs;
- Compensation incentives;
- Training;
- Budgets and staffing; and
- Governance structures.

These kinds of cultural assessment are crude and not very probative ... more akin to phrenology (the debunked 19th century belief that one's character and mental ability were determined by shape and size of one's skull) than a science sufficiently evolved to justify breaking up international banks or identifying the root causes of compliance failures. Nevertheless, experts in studying and understanding culture are moving from simplistic assessments of culture that focus on the indicia and apparatus of culture to more precise measurements that will help compliance and risk professionals to better understand culture and to quantify the extent to which it mitigates or exacerbates risk.

An invaluable work on analyzing corporate culture comes from Macquarie University in Australia. For a few years, two professors there (Elizabeth Sheedy and Barbara Griffin)

---

6 *2016 Regulatory and Examination Priorities, FINRA,(* Jan. 5, 2016), http://www.finra.org/industry/2016-regulatory-and-examination-priorities-letter

7 FINRA, *"Establishing, Communicating and Implementing Cultural Values, (*Feb. 2016), http://www.finra.org/industry/establishing-communicating-and-implementing-cultural-values

8 Andrew Bailey, *Culture in Financial Services—A Regulator's Perspective, Remarks at the City Week 2016 Conference(* May 9, 2016).

have been conducting assessments of culture across large financial institutions.[9] At least three of the distinctions and observations they make are very important to understanding where we are headed.

Prioritizing Compliance and Risk Management

First, the professors define and measure compliance and risk culture not by what management does or doesn't say or do, but as the shared perceptions of employees of the relative priority given to compliance and risk management by the organization. The key point here is their distinction between the indicia of culture (e.g., tone at the top, articulated values, incentive structures, staffing, standing) and how those cultural indicators are perceived by employees.

This makes sense. People are not dumb. They are observant, and they know lip service when they see it. Recall that Enron had a beautiful code of conduct.[10]

Thus, the only way to accurately assess culture is to survey employees' perceptions of the importance that the company places on compliance, risk management, escalation, fair treatment of customers, etc.

Scoring the Culture

Second, the professors of Macquarie found that if employees across an entire organization are surveyed, perceptions vary in statistically significant ways among business units within the organization. The professors identified significant variations in the culture scores within large organizations at the business unit level. Culture is a local construct and very much dependent on interactions with close colleagues and the immediate management. Thus, tone at the top is less important in shaping perceptions of a business unit than tone in the middle.

Perceptions as Predictors

Third, while the academic or systematic study of culture within financial institutions is still evolving, earlier and more evolved research into industrial accidents and safety suggest that perceptions of culture can be predictive. Early efforts to mitigate the risk of industrial accidents focused on technology or engineering solutions, such as, "Put a safety shield here. Do this before you do that. Don't ever do that." The focus was on governance, rules, and process.

---

[9] Elizabeth Sheedy and Barbara Griffin, *Empirical Analysis of Risk Culture in Financial Institutions: Interim Report*, Macquarie University (Nov. 2014), https://www.lse.ac.uk/accounting/CARR/events/Sheedy-Risk-Culture-Paper-Nov-14.pdf; Elizabeth Sheedy and Barbara Griffin, "*Risk Governance, Structures, Culture, and Behavior: A View from the Inside*," Macquarie University (May 12, 2016), https://papers.ssrn.com/sol3/papers.cfm?abstract_id=2529803

[10] Lee Augsburger, "How Compliance Can Teach Ethics," in *Modern Compliance: Best Practices for Securities & Finance* (Wolters Kluwer, 2015), p. 185.

According to the professors at Macquarie, breakthroughs in industrial safety began to occur in the early 1980s with the identification and emphasis on organizational climate (or "safety culture") and attempts to shape employee perceptions of the priority that the organization and each supervisor placed on safety. They found that employees' perception of the priority placed on safety predicted the likelihood of accidents.

Impact on Problem Prevention

So, one may predict that compliance teams will be spending more time on the culture within their organizations and that the tools they use for assessing culture will become more sophisticated and useful. They will do this for two reasons.

First, if culture is perceptions, and those perceptions are predictive, compliance officers will conclude that they can materially increase the effectiveness of their compliance program and their firm's efforts to instill a "culture of compliance" by regularly surveying employees; analyzing perceptions of distinct business units (or subcultures); and allocating relatively greater training, surveillance, and compliance resources to those business units that do not perceive a high value placed on compliance and risk management. Culture survey tools will help compliance teams evolve from "reactors" to "predictors."

Second, although it is beyond the current means and jurisdiction of regulators to conduct firmwide employee surveys on their own, regulators will evolve from their simple assessments of the indicia of culture and become more active and aggressive in attempting to predict where problems may occur. For example, in the previously referenced examination request letter that FINRA sent to a number of broker-dealers at the beginning of 2016, FINRA asked (among more customary inquiries regarding culture) for information about how firms assess and measure the impact of their cultural values and the policies and procedures the firms have adopted to identify and address subcultures that may depart from or undermine the cultural values articulated by senior management.

III. ADVANCED DATA ANALYTICS

In his book, *The Quants*, Scott Patterson traces the origin of the application of advanced mathematics and quantitative theory to the business of making money in financial markets.[11] According to Patterson, "quants" first began to apply their unique skills to the financial services industry in 1965, when Ed Thorp applied his Ph.D. in mathematics to figuring out how to make money trading stock warrants.

Since then, quants have played a leading role in financial services, almost always to the purpose of making money for themselves or the firms that employ them. Quants have built order-routing algorithms, market models that aggregate and analyze data in real time from a vast array of diverse sources, and tools that analyze the text of a 10-K

[11] Scott Patterson, *The Quants*, Crown Business (2010).

in milliseconds. After five decades, however, the role of quants in financial services is expanding, and the change is not being led by the industry. Rather, the Securities and Exchange Commission (SEC) is leading a revolution, born of necessity, in the use of advanced data analytics to identify and address compliance issues.

In the early 2010s, the SEC staff observed that although they had less human capital than they desired, they had superabundant information at their disposal, including data that the SEC compelled firms to file directly with it—data that firms voluntarily posted on their websites and to industry repositories, and data that was otherwise publicly available in the media or in public records.

The SEC began to hire and deploy individuals highly educated, trained, and experienced in computer science, mathematics, and financial engineering to help make better use of the data that was available. These were not people with an interest in, and facility with, Excel or Access. Rather, the SEC began to hire people with Ph.D.'s who had previously worked at hedge funds, for NASA, or in advanced medical research.

The SEC deployed these computer and data scientists not to make money but to help the SEC evaluate where to best allocate its scarce resources, and how to identify and prove securities law violations. The application of advanced data analytics to compliance and enforcement questions and issues worked so well that the SEC now possesses tools to examine potential compliance issues that, in almost all instances, the industry does not possess.

The SEC now regularly uses quants and advanced data analytics in three ways: predictively, tactically, and in the field. If it hasn't already, each of these developments, which continue to evolve, will materially change the way compliance professionals do their job.

IV. PREDICTIVE ANALYTICS

Development

The first and most important question in the Office of Compliance Inspections and Examinations (OCIE) is: who should be examined? This used to be determined in a rotation, where every investment advisory firm was examined within some time-based cycle. As the industry grew in relation to SEC resources, cycle exams became impracticable. The SEC therefore moved to a risk-based examination program in the early 2000s.[12] Examiners who had an interest in data and some aptitude with Excel—usually accountants or lawyers by training—led early efforts to analyze data to identify investment advisers that exhibited signals of higher risk. They made some assumptions about

[12] As of late 2016, the SEC had allocated approximately 1,000 staff to examine roughly 28,000 registrants. Marc Wyatt, Inside the National Exam Program in 2016, Remarks at the National Society of Compliance Professionals 2016 National Conference (Oct. 17, 2016), https://www.sec.gov/news/speech/inside-the-national-exam-program-in-2016.html). Approximately 500 OCIE examiners are allocated to investment adviser examinations.

the types of events that might be indicative of heightened risk—explosive growth or diminution in assets under management, departure of key individuals, or sheer size—and developed a basic set of metrics and rankings that regional offices could consider when selecting exam candidates.

Although this was a valiant effort that made intuitive sense, it was not very scientific or precise. As OCIE began to hire quants in the early 2010s, it began work on tools that used machine learning to analyze years' worth of enforcement and examination information. The SEC performed regression analyses that more accurately identified not only the factors or combination of factors that had been indicative of heightened risk in the past, but also the predictive weight of those factors. The SEC also regularly tested the accuracy of the tool's predictions as real-world experience was gained to sharpen the models and their predictive ability.

By 2015, the data used in OCIE's predictive process for advisers was principally drawn from past exams and enforcement actions, regulatory filings, and third-party data. In addition, the staff had plans to add textual analysis of brochures and a wealth of other SEC and publicly available information which would further develop the tool and its predictive ability.

In the broker-dealer space, FINRA is improving tools that analyze data on all registered individuals over time, including their employment history, complaint and disciplinary history, and credit and judicial history. These tools help FINRA predict the firms, branch offices, and individuals who present the highest risk to investors and the integrity of the markets.

Uses for Allocating Resources

Even though a compliance team working at a particular firm does not have access to industry-wide data like the SEC and FINRA, there are important implications in the development of compliance tools built by quants that can assess the risk profile of a firm or an individual over time. For starters, it is a highly effective aid in deciding where to allocate precious compliance resources. A compliance team that can use a quantitatively sound process to identify in real time business units or individuals whose activities pose relatively higher risks to the organization has a decided edge in getting ahead of, or more promptly detecting, compliance problems. Some organizations have already developed sophisticated tools to collect and analyze the voluminous "digital exhaust" that all employees emit to assess internal cybersecurity threats. By monitoring patterns (and changes in patterns) in the programs and equipment an employee uses (e.g., e-mail, scanners, copiers, phones, access badges) and where the employee goes with those programs and equipment (e.g., computer drives, websites, servers), an organization has an improved probability of detecting promptly an employee who poses an internal cyber threat.

Such tools can also enable a compliance team to adjust controls in ways that help the business. For example, a compliance team that is highly effective at consistently detecting in real time potentially problematic patterns of behavior, or compliance violations, may have the flexibility to loosen certain overly restrictive front-end compliance controls that are often designed to discourage or thwart a disreputable employee, but with which all employees are required to comply. Many compliance officers have heard the lament of employees frustrated by perceived growth and intrusion of compliance policies and procedures on their daily work.

Risk Assessment

At the same time, a compliance team that possesses an effective risk prediction tool could work with the business to develop customized controls for certain units or individuals. For example, a compliance team at a broker-dealer might work with the business to design calibrated payouts for registered representatives based upon the risk profile of that representative's business practices. Arguably, a representative with a lower risk profile warrants a higher payout than an equally productive representative with a higher risk profile. Such tools and techniques would have the additional virtuous benefits of encouraging the behavior that the firm wants and enabling the firm to better compensate and retain productive and compliant talent.

Finally, it is becoming increasingly important for compliance officers and businesses to understand the tools that regulators are using and how the actions and disclosures of their firm raise or lower its risk profile in the eyes of the regulator. For example, the business and compliance personnel at a broker-dealer should understand whether, and the extent to which, they are increasing or decreasing the risk of regulatory scrutiny by FINRA with every hiring decision they make. The business and compliance personnel at an investment adviser should understand whether, and the extent to which, they are increasing or decreasing the risk of regulatory scrutiny by the SEC with every change they make to their investment programs and, in turn, to their disclosures and regulatory filings.

V. TACTICAL DATA ANALYTICS

The SEC is also developing tactical data analytic tools that aid in examination and enforcement where there is a particular issue of concern. For example, a risk alert published by OCIE in August 2015 has not received the attention it deserves.[13] The alert explains that the SEC wanted to examine how structured products were sold by broker-dealers, including to whom structured notes were sold (and resold) and how the sales were supervised. Before the development of advanced data analytics, such an inquiry would have been exceptionally labor intensive, limited in scope, and heavily reliant on sampling. All of these challenges, in turn, would have adversely affected the SEC's ability to rely on the findings to make recommendations or to take other regulatory action.

---

[13] "Broker-Dealer Controls Regarding Retail Sales of Structured Securities Products," *SEC National Exam Program Risk Alert* (Aug. 24, 2015), https://www.sec.gov/ocie/announcement/risk-alert-aug-24-2015.html

Reading the alert, one gets a sense of just how much times have changed. In it, OCIE reports that it examined over 26,600 sales of structured products that occurred over a two-year period in 10 branch offices from several different firms, totaling more than $1.25 billion in aggregate value. As part of its analysis, for each transaction, OCIE analyzed the customer's age, investment objectives, risk tolerance, and approval for options trading. OCIE also analyzed resales to assess the frequency and price at which structured products were sold before maturity, as well as the frequency with which transactions at each firm exceeded the firm's internal policies and limits. (For example, if the firm had a policy that the purchase price of a structured note should not exceed more than 10 percent of the value of the account, how often was this policy overridden?)

Although it may not be immediately apparent, and OCIE did not mention it in the report, the vast quantities of information that the office examined often came from different systems and sources within the firms examined. OCIE was often comparing information across customer information, trading, pricing, portfolio accounting, e-mail, and/or compliance systems. The staff and the quants at the SEC were knitting together and analyzing information from different systems within the firms examined that those firms themselves had never aggregated or analyzed.

This is not uncommon. Most firms have data stored across multiple systems in different formats that they do not aggregate or analyze for any purpose, much less to conduct testing or surveillance. In the future, effective compliance teams will employ the advanced data analytic skills and tools necessary to use this far flung information to gain insights about a particular activity or their firm's compliance with applicable regulations.

VI. IN THE FIELD

Finally, advanced data analytics are being used in the field to transform the examination process. In the past, regulatory examinations often started with a request for and review of policies and procedures. In the event that trading information was reviewed, it was generally drawn from a short time period (a few days or weeks), and the quality of the analysis was dependent on the exam team's ability to sort the data into columns in Excel and to discern signals of potentially problematic activity. This is not a knock on the examiners. They made the best use of the tools available to them at the time.

When OCIE put quants into the field with examiners with the imperative to help the examiners become better, faster problem solvers, the quants quickly identified an opportunity for significant improvement. They built the National Exam Analytics Tool (NEAT), which enables every examiner to quickly run scores of tests against years' worth of trading data as part of any or every examination.[14]

The implications are significant.

[14] Mary Jo White, *The SEC in 2014, Remarks at the 41st Annual Securities Regulation* Institute, Coronado, California, (Jan. 27, 2014), https://www.sec.gov/News/Speech/Detail/Speech/1370540677500

Most examinations no longer begin with a focus on policies and procedures. They begin with requests for information and lots of it. The information provided to the regulator is not sampled. Rather, up to hundreds of thousands of transactions are routinely tagged and systematically analyzed. In a 2014 speech, SEC Chair Mary Jo White claimed that NEAT had recently been used to analyze 17 million transactions in 36 hours.[15] Scores of tests are run quickly to identify, for example, instances when trades happened shortly before news announcements or significant price moves, whether allocations that were made over time tended to benefit systematically one or more clients over others, or whether there is evidence of excessive mark-ups or mark-downs.

Formerly at the SEC, compliance officers were all too often on the periphery during the critical data collection and analysis stage of the examination process, as the staff dealt directly with firm's data architects and storage experts to collect the information the staff wanted. Such information, in most instances, had never previously been analyzed by the compliance team and certainly not with the sophisticated tools available to the SEC examiners. In the future, effective compliance teams will be staffed with individuals who can interact directly with regulators on data issues, and, just as importantly, those compliance teams will have the tools and talents to analyze the data with the same proficiency as the regulators.

VII. CONCLUSION

I claim no special experience or insight that enables me to make predictions about the future of compliance with any greater accuracy than other so-called experts, whose record is poor. Over the last 30 years, however, I have come to know and admire many compliance professionals and their business colleagues. In my experience, they are curious and resourceful and, more than anything else, dedicated to getting it right for their clients, colleagues, and owners. If regular surveys of employee perceptions about the relative importance placed on compliance and risk management by business units and firms, and the application of advanced data analytics to large data sets, can help not only to detect, but also to predict, where harm to clients and other compliance violations may be occurring, then I believe their compliance teams will continue to evolve by using these tools and techniques to enhance their effectiveness.

---

[15] *Id.*

ABOUT THE AUTHOR

Andrew Bowden is senior vice president and general counsel for Jackson National Life Insurance Company. Mr. Bowden oversees the company's legal and compliance departments and serves on the executive forum. He also serves as the chair for the Michigan Life & Health Insurance Guaranty Association and as an adjunct professor at the Michigan State University College of Law.

Mr. Bowden joined Jackson National in May 2015. Previously, he worked for three and a half years at the SEC, serving as the director of the SEC's OCIE from June 2013 through April 2015. Prior to his work at the SEC, he served in a variety of legal and business roles over 17 years at Legg Mason, including executive director, chief operating officer, and general counsel at Legg Mason Capital Management. Prior to joining Legg Mason, Mr. Bowden was a trial attorney and partner at a Baltimore law firm, where he handled securities related litigation and arbitrations.

Mr. Bowden holds a bachelor's degree from Loyola University in Maryland (*summa cum laude*) and a juris doctorate from the University of Pennsylvania (*cum laude*).

CHAPTER 23

Big Data: Using Data Analytics

By Keith Marks, E. J. Yerzak, Brian DeDonato, and Jackie Hallihan
Ascendant Compliance Management, Inc.

> For hundreds of years, physical paper documents and human beings dominated our securities operations. Today, data dominates. Digital data is part of every aspect of our markets. And this new reality is challenging all of us. The proliferation and reliance on data has disrupted our markets—oversight and regulation need to evolve to keep pace. In this new world, we need new tools.
>
> —Commissioner Kara M. Stein, April 14, 2015[1]

I. INTRODUCTION

In February 2014, Assistant Regional Director Erozan Kurtas unveiled the Securities and Exchange Commission's (SEC) newest big data project, the National Exam Analytics Tool (NEAT). Kurtas, who is now the head of Advanced Data Analytics at FINRA, began his speech discussing the tremendous amount of data produced every 60 seconds, citing:

- 11 million instant messages;
- 698,445 Google searches;
- 168 million+ e-mails; and
- 1,820 terabytes (TB) of data.

Kurtas was sending a clear message: the world has changed significantly, and the way firms approach market regulation must also change. Through NEAT and other advanced big data projects, the SEC has sought to close the proverbial technology gap between Wall Street and regulators. It is no secret that the SEC has been eager to crack down on fraud and insider trading, and now they are looking to big data to level the playing field.

Although a complete technology overhaul at the SEC is far from finished, it has clearly used data-driven rulemaking for more than a decade. Registered investment advisers

[1] Kara M. Stein, "The Dominance of Data and the Need for New Tools," SIFMA Operations Conference (Apr. 14, 2015), https://www.sec.gov/news/speech/2015-spch041415kms.html.

must adhere to stringent regulatory filing requirements for Form ADV, Form PF, Form 13F, Form 13H, and Forms 13D and 13G, each of which provides data. The potential of increased surveillance capabilities with databases containing information obtained from websites, e-mails, and electronic communications, as well as the surveillance of social media use and electronic communications by investment advisory supervised persons, including what they search on the internet and whom they contact, remains in the future.

Securities markets have evolved markedly from their origins as in-person transactions and face-to-face dealings in one room. Today's markets are vastly different, with paper-based trading by humans largely replaced by the bits and bytes of multiple electronic trading venues, with buyers and sellers in many cases matched automatically and with transactions measured in nanoseconds. People are creating data at incredible rates—with 2.5 quintillion bytes of data being generated every single day and 90 percent of the data in existence today having been created in just the past two years.[2] According to market intelligence and information technology firm International Data Corporation (IDC), 18 percent of the digital data in the United States would have discernible value if it were classified with relevant tags and analyzed, with this number expected to grow to 40 percent by 2020. Yet IDC estimates that less than 0.5 percent of such data is actually being analyzed.[3]

Perhaps recognizing that vast amounts of trading data are out there, and that such data may prove useful in the early detection of fraudulent activity or market manipulation, the SEC has begun requesting a greater quantity of information from investment advisers during regulatory examinations, then populating the data into proprietary databases and applications it has developed. Processing this volume of transactional data and searching for meaningful information would be nearly impossible without the power of computers and technology. The SEC is searching for that indicator, or combination of indicators, to identify heightened risk or noncompliant activity. The SEC appears poised to search for those red flags—such as indicators of front-running, insider trades, and fund performance that seem too good to be true—and is devoting a greater allocation of its resources and budget to this big data priority.

This chapter focuses particularly on the use of trade data analytics in the regulation and examination of registered investment advisers and broker-dealers, and primarily concerning SEC-registered investment advisers.

II. SEC PRIORITIES

On January 11, 2016, the SEC's Office of Inspections and Examinations (OCIE) released its Examination Priorities for 2016,[4] reiterating that its top three priorities

---

2 IBM, "What Is Big Data?" https://www-01.ibm.com/software/data/bigdata/what-is-big-data.html

3 John Gantz and David Reinsel, "The Digital Universe in 2020: Big Data, Bigger Digital Shadows, and Biggest Growth in the Far East" (Dec. 2012), https://www.emc.com/collateral/analyst-reports/idc-the-digital-universe-in-2020.pdf

4 National Exam Program, OCIE, "Examination Priorities for 2016" (Jan. 11, 2016), https://www.sec.gov/about/offices/ocie/national-examination-program-priorities-2016.pdf

remained consistent with those from 2015, including "using our evolving ability to analyze data to identify and examine registrants that may be engaged in illegal activity."

In January 2017, the introduction of the SEC's National Examination Priorities for 2017 letter concluded:

> With the objectives of being data-driven and risk-based, we have incorporated data analytics into the vast majority of our examination initiatives to identify industry practices and/or registrants that appear to have elevated risk profiles.[5]

Examination priorities letters from the SEC reveal that the SEC's capabilities in this area have indeed evolved, even as the focus has held steady.

In the Examination Priorities for 2015 letter,[6] the SEC named as one of its top three priorities the development of data analytics to identify signals of potential illegal market activity. Further glimpses into the regulator's data analytics capabilities through the SEC's issuance of examination priorities emerged from prior years. The Examination Priorities for 2014 letter states that the National Exam Program uses a "risk-based approach to targeting registrants and business practices" by using and improving its "quantitative and qualitative tools," which includes the formation of the Quantitative Analytics Unit within the SEC. The Examination Priorities for 2014 contains an informative footnote that describes these tools that the SEC enhanced throughout 2013:

> The resources that the NEP has expanded in 2013 include its Quantitative Analytics Unit, a team of specialists with postgraduate degrees in fields such as computer science and mathematics that is able to evaluate risks in the algorithms, models, and software of the most sophisticated investment firms, as well as the NEP's Risk Analysis Examination initiative, which examines clearing firms and large broker-dealers by downloading and analyzing all transactions cleared by a firm over a period of several years.[7]

Going back further, compliance professionals were put on alert in OCIE's Examination Priorities for 2013 letter that the SEC was using data analytics to prioritize its examination resources. In that release, the SEC stated the examination priorities were selected using several components of information and risk analytics that were derived from sources including the following:

---

[5] National Exam Program, OCIE, "Examination Priorities for 2017" (Jan. 2017), https://www.sec.gov/about/offices/ocie/national-examination-program-priorities-2017.pdf

[6] National Exam Program, OCIE, "Examination Priorities for 2015" (Jan. 2015), https://www.sec.gov/about/offices/ocie/national-examination-program-priorities-2015.pdf

[7] National Exam Program, OCIE, "Examination Priorities for 2014" (Jan. 9, 2014), https://www.sec.gov/about/offices/ocie/national-examination-program-priorities-2014.pdf

- Information reported by registrants in required filings with the Commission;
- Information gathered through examinations conducted by the NEP and other regulators;
- Communications with other U.S. and international regulators and agencies;
- Industry and media publications;
- Comments and tips received directly from investors and registrants;
- Data maintained in third-party databases; and
- Interactions with registrants, industry groups, and service providers (outside of examinations).[8]

Fast forward to today, and it is clear that the SEC continues to expand its leverage of data analytics to inform examination priorities. The regulator is increasingly relying upon technology to maximize its ability to use its limited examination and enforcement resources effectively. In its FY 2016 Budget Request by Program, the SEC highlighted the growing burden of assessing compliance risk amidst a proliferation of sophisticated trading tools by requesting additional resources, stating, "to effectively identify misconduct, the Division [of Enforcement] needs sophisticated technology tools to collect and analyze market data" and "sufficient analytical tools, as well as staff to analyze data from these tools, to ensure it keeps pace with [the] constantly evolving environment."[9]

Additional key areas of focus from the SEC's 2015 and 2016 Examination Priorities include using data analytics to identify recidivism, microcap fraud, excessive trading, and broker-dealers that have not filed a suspicious activity report (SAR) as part of their anti-money laundering (AML) programs. Furthermore, a new focus is on registered entities' supervision of branch offices. Examiners are now using data analytics to drive the selection of branch offices for examinations, with data indicators providing for a risk-based focus on those branch offices that appear to demonstrate deviations from the compliance data points provided by the firm's home office.

III. WHAT IS BIG DATA?

In a nutshell, "big data" is the term used to refer to the storage, processing and analysis of large quantities of data. Gartner defines the term as "high-volume, high-velocity and high-variety information assets that demand cost-effective, innovative forms of information processing for enhanced insight and decision making."[10] Big data is made possible by advances in both storage and computing technology. Essentially, as the cost of data storage has decreased, data users are able to store more information in a

---

8 National Exam Program, OCIE, "Examination Priorities for 2013" (Feb. 21, 2013), https://www.sec.gov/about/offices/ocie/national-examination-program-priorities-2013.pdf

9 SEC, *FY 2016 Budget Request by Program,* https://www.sec.gov/about/reports/sec-fy2016-budget-request-by-program.pdf

10 Gartner, "Gartner IT Glossary," www.gartner.com/it-glossary

cost-effective manner. Deriving actionable, meaningful intelligence from the mountains of data requires more than simply saving every message, e-mail, voicemail, instant message, video, social media post, transaction, trade, signal, filing, report, document, and other relevant structured and unstructured data. Rather, to gain meaning from the underlying data, users also need well-designed applications capable of querying the vast data sets quickly and efficiently. Big data applications therefore require scalability and must be able to handle larger and larger volumes of data without compromising speed to an unworkable level.

Why is big data important to both financial regulators and the financial institutions themselves? The use of powerful analytics tools on market-wide and firm-specific data feeds, when combined with publicly available data on events such as mergers, acquisitions, pricing, and performance data from other examined firms, allows the SEC to detect potential patterns of improperly disclosed or unlawful trading activity.

Today's interconnected digital economy is one in which information is global and parties to securities transactions may be located anywhere. Risk may be introduced by any entity handling that transactional data at any stage in the process. In addition, market-wide or systemic risks in the financial sector may be discernible only from an analysis of thousands of data feeds from numerous sources across the world. Such an analysis is only made possible when the entity conducting the analysis has access to the necessary data, and even then, only when such data points have been appropriately tagged or consistently categorized.

Big data and privacy are increasingly seen as competing interests. For instance, in their personal lives, many shoppers willingly use store loyalty cards to attain discounts at the grocery store or retail establishments. An entire generation is growing up in a culture in which personal information is posted freely on social media sites. These are the inputs that enable big data analytics about people's personal lives. All of this data is being stored in various databases to enable companies and marketers to crunch the numbers and to create a profile of each customer, his or her brand preferences, spending habits, and connections.

This same big data concept is at work in the regulatory context as well. With the advent of legal entity identifiers (LEIs), disclosures on Form ADV, Form PF, other regulatory filings including Forms 13F and 13H, and information requested during regulatory examinations, all of a firm's transactions, counterparties, and securities pricing are now, or soon may be, sitting in giant regulatory databases—sortable, searchable, and reviewable in comparison to other firms and the broader financial markets.

Welcome to the age of big data, when everything is tracked from end to end. Data analytics professionals see how regulators are using big data (as explored next). These professionals also see the ways in which advisers can leverage available information to more effectively monitor and manage risk within their firms.

IV. HOW THE REGULATORS USE BIG DATA

In a speech on March 20, 2015, then-Commissioner Luis Aguilar described the SEC's current use of big data as providing transparency to the industry. Former associate director and chief counsel of OCIE John Walsh wrote that this transparency is essential to the compliance industry, particularly to understand compliance program responsibilities under Rule 206(4)-7 of the Investment Advisers Act.[11] He noted that regulators have come to understand that big data must be timely, accurate, and complete. In the Examination Priorities for 2016, OCIE states:

> We will continue to use our analytic capabilities to identify individuals with a track record of misconduct and examine the firms that employ them. For example, we will assess the compliance oversight and controls of investment advisers that have employed such individuals after they have been disciplined or barred from a broker-dealer; AML; microcap fraud, and excessive trading. We will continue to analyze data, including data obtained from clearing brokers, to identify and examine firms and their registered representatives that appear to be engaged in excessive or otherwise potentially inappropriate trading.[12]

Compliance professionals face the same challenge to meet regulatory demands to ensure data can be delivered in the format required by regulations and in regulatory examinations. In many forms, the data is required in a manner specifically designed to categorize the information such as Forms 13F and PF. Advisers, however, needed to create certain data sets for the regulators to meet Form PF requirements. Form ADV Part 2 is not as easily categorized, especially when compared to trade blotters that are highly structured and easily categorized.

The most critical big data is transactional data. The SEC now requests 27 separate trade blotter data fields from advisers for an SEC exam and can increasingly cross-reference that data to other market data sources. This transactional data is in addition to the request for 15 separate client data fields and, for advisers to private funds, 21 separate private fund data fields. In addition, the SEC continues to mandate the collection of more data points through an expansion of Form ADV filing requirements, including the adoption of amendments to Form ADV Part 1A on August 25, 2016.[13] The adopting release for the Form ADV Amendments in August 2016 readily acknowledges that certain amendments "are designed to improve the depth and quality of information that we collect on investment advisers, facilitate our risk monitoring initiatives and assist our staff in its risk-based examination program."[14] In its Fiscal Year 2016 Budget

---

11 Sutherland Asbill & Brennan LLP Corporate Counsel, "Big Data and Regulation, Part II: Legal and Compliance" (June 20, 2014), Sutherland.com

12 National Exam Program, OCIE, "Examination Priorities for 2016."

13 *Form ADV and Investment Advisers Act Rules,* SEC Rel. No. IA-4509, SEC File No. S7-09-15 (Aug. 25, 2016), https://www.sec.gov/rules/final/2016/ia-4509.pdf

14 *Id.*

Request by Program, the SEC noted that in 2014, the Division of Enforcement used data analytics to identify and bring charges against 34 individuals for reporting violations. The 2016 budget request devotes an entire section to the importance of big data in facilitating its enforcement efforts:

> Using Big Data to Detect and Investigate Violations: The Division is increasingly leveraging big data to detect and investigate misconduct. As an example, the staff has developed new analytical tools to detect suspicious trading patterns to assist in building insider trading cases. In addition, the Financial Reporting and Audit Task Force is partnering with the Division of Economic and Risk Analysis to refine a tool that will enable the staff to detect anomalous results (and thus potential case leads) in large amounts of public company filing data. Moreover, the recently established Center for Risk and Quantitative Analytics coordinates risk identification, risk assessment, and data analytic activities, with the goals of proactively identifying threats to investors and bringing cutting-edge analysis to bear on the Division's work. The Division expects that these improved information processing and analysis capabilities will yield a steady stream of additional case leads. The Division accordingly needs commensurate technology tools and staff to review and analyze those leads.

As the above excerpt suggests, big data is quickly becoming the new normal for the Division of Enforcement. In its fiscal year 2017 budget request, the SEC reinforced this by notion by stating as follows:

> The SEC has made substantial progress in modernizing its technology systems, streamlining operations, increasing our use of data analytics, and increasing the effectiveness of its programs. The SEC's FY 2017 budget request…seeks to build on this progress by supporting a number of key information technology (IT) initiatives, including: expanding data analytics tools that assist in the integration and analysis of huge volumes of financial market data, employing algorithms and quantitative models that can lead to earlier detection of fraud or suspicious behavior and ultimately enabling the agency to allocate its resources more effectively.…The Division has filed a number of cases during the past fiscal year where data tools and analysis played a significant role in their origin or investigation, a trend that Enforcement sees continuing into the following fiscal year and beyond.[15]

It is a new era of enforcement in which the stakes are high, and the SEC has brought its most advanced weapons to the battlefield to combat fraud, with code names like MIDAS (the Market Information Data Analytics System) and NEAT (National Data Analytics Tool), described next.

---

[15] SEC, *FY 2017 Congressional Budget Justification* (Feb. 2016), at 5, 60, https://www.sec.gov/about/reports/secfy17congbudgjust.pdf

Market Information Data Analytics System

The impetus for a market analytics tool can be traced back to the "flash crash" that occurred on May 6, 2010. What happened on that fateful day? According to a joint report, nicknamed the "Flash Crash Report," issued by both the SEC and the Commodity Futures Trading Commission (CFTC) in response to a request by the U.S. Senate Committee on Banking, Housing, and Urban Affairs, the U.S. Senate Committee on Agriculture, Nutrition and Forestry, and the House Committee on Financial Services:

> On May 6, 2010, the prices of many U.S.-based equity products experienced an extraordinarily rapid decline and recovery. That afternoon, major equity indices in both the futures and securities markets, each already down over 4% from their prior-day close, suddenly plummeted a further 5–6% in a matter of minutes before rebounding almost as quickly.
>
> Many of the almost 8,000 individual equity securities and exchange traded funds (ETFs) traded that day suffered similar price declines and reversals within a short period of time, falling 5%, 10%, or even 15% before recovering most, if not all, of their losses. However, some equities experienced even more severe price moves, both up and down. Over 20,000 trades across more than 300 securities were executed at prices more than 60% away from their values just moments before. Moreover, many of these trades were executed at prices of a penny or less, or as high as $100,000, before prices of those securities returned to their "pre-crash" levels. By the end of the day, major futures and equities indices "recovered" to close at losses of about 3% from the prior day.[16]

The Flash Crash Report alleges that the event was caused by a single trader placing a sell order using an automated algorithm designed to place orders at 9 percent of the trading volume for the preceding minute. The algorithm did not take into account other factors such as price or time, and managed to execute a volume of trades over the span of 20 minutes that in the past had taken several hours to complete. The amassed trades caused the price of E-mini S&P 500 futures contracts to fall by more than 5 percent over the course of four-and-a-half minutes.[17]

Although prices eventually stabilized after trading was temporarily halted, the Flash Crash Report identified several factors as having contributed to the market failures on May 6, 2010:

---

[16] CFTC and SEC, *Findings Regarding the Market Events of May 6, 2010: Report of the Staffs of the CFTC and SEC to the Joint Advisory Committee on Emerging Regulatory Issues"* (Sept. 30, 2010), https://www.sec.gov/news/studies/2010/marketevents-report.pdf

[17] CFTC and SEC, *Findings Regarding the Market Events,* at 3.

- At a time of market stress, a large sell order executed via automated algorithm can cause sharp price movements, because a high trading volume may become an unreliable metric for actual liquidity;
- The derivatives and securities markets are interconnected; and
- Trading pauses and circuit breakers can be effective stabilizing measures, but may be limited in their effectiveness if they are effected via proprietary halts imposed by particular market participants inconsistently.

Essentially, as the SEC worked with the CFTC to piece together the events that led to the Flash Crash, and to enable them to assess market trends and anticipate such activity in the future, the SEC came to realize that it needed a big data solution to a big data problem: how does the oversight body make sense of an interconnected market that trades significant volumes in the blink of an eye and that can cause significant disruption just as quickly? MIDAS was the golden idea of the two commissions.

The Division of Risk, Strategy, and Financial Innovation (Risk Fin) and the Division of Trading and Markets of the SEC issued a request for information (RFI) on September 20, 2010 in which they sought information on data analysis software that could help them collect, aggregate, and monitor the financial markets in real time, using real-time data feeds measured in milliseconds. The divisions wanted this application to help the SEC access the market data in such a way that would permit it to perform meaningful and efficient analysis of the transaction data.

The RFI specifically sought information on the ability to:

- Store transactions and orders from the various equity exchanges with the time of occurrence measured to the millisecond;
- Aggregate these transactions and orders with identifiers that preserve the original trading venue where the order occurred and any supplemental information related to the trade or order, such as order type, when available;
- Provide a data structure that allows these data to be accessed quickly and efficiently for analysis, and
- Allow this to be done in specified intervals, such as in by-the-millisecond, by-the-second and by-the-minute snapshots.

The SEC issued its request for proposal for such a tool on November 30, 2011, formally announcing its desire for "an equity and equity option market data collection and analysis solution that combines access to data services, applications, and related databases and provides SEC staff with the same speed, ease, and reliability of data collection and analysis that is available to sophisticated market participants." A little more than six months later, the SEC selected Tradeworx as the vendor to implement its big data market analysis solution, and in January 2013, MIDAS was officially released to SEC staff.

MIDAS is a cloud-based tool implemented by the SEC to facilitate the tracking of bids and offers for equities, equity options, and futures contracts from multiple data sources. The MIDAS platform enables regulators to develop a complete picture of the overall market stability for a security at any point in time. The data inputs to MIDAS include the consolidated tapes and a proprietary data feed from each of 13 national equity exchanges, in addition to a proprietary data feed from Thesys Technologies, an affiliate of Tradeworx that provides colocation services and low-latency market data.

The proprietary data feeds track information such as the action (e.g., posted orders, quotes, modifications, cancellations, and trade executions), the type of order, the size of the order, price, duration, order identifier, and a timestamp. These are the same proprietary data feeds that many high-frequency trading firms use, but because there are volumes of records every microsecond (one millionth of a second), it is far too much information for the average investor to be able to digest and use effectively.

The underlying data is therefore a mix of both public and proprietary data feeds that are aggregated and stored in the cloud where the data is accessible to the SEC. These various data feeds inform the ability of MIDAS to monitor the financial markets, to home in on a snapshot of the markets to piece together market events, and to view market trends over the long term. Figure 1 illustrates the particular inputs to MIDAS.

FIGURE 1. DATA FEEDS THROUGH MIDAS TO THE SEC

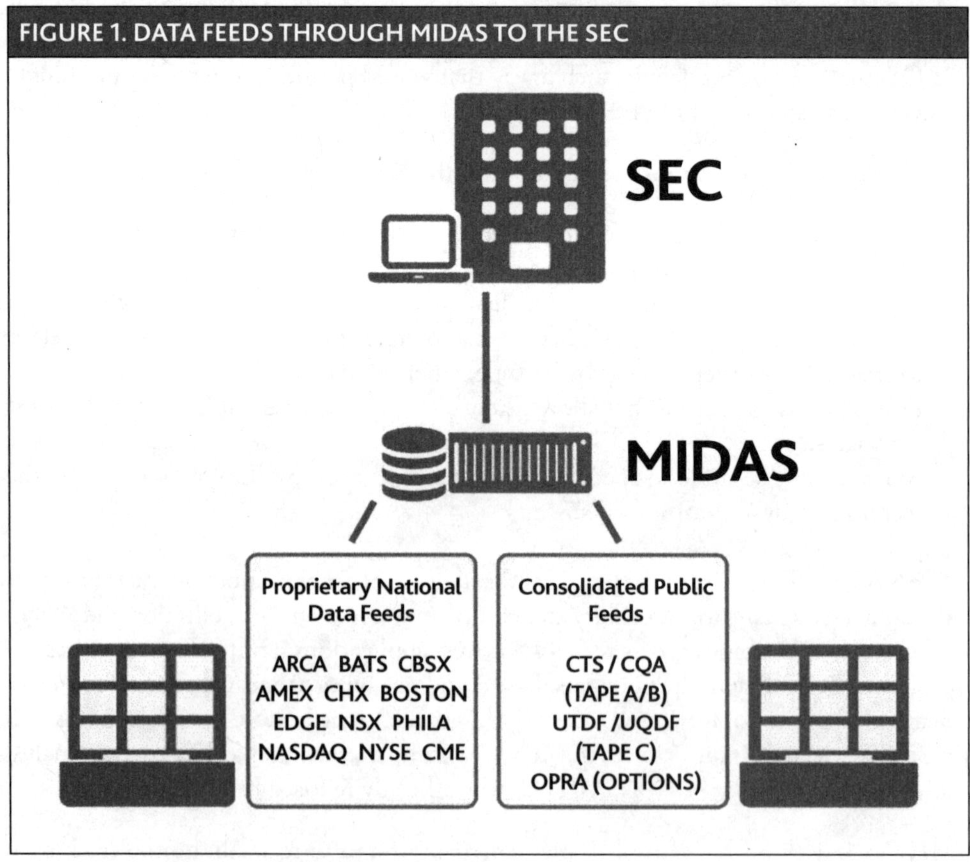

According to the SEC, MIDAS gathers about 1 billion records every day from the proprietary feeds, and these records bear timestamps down to the microsecond. This vast collection of data enables the SEC to efficiently analyze 100 billion records comprising thousands of securities at once and to perform the analysis over various time periods up to one year. MIDAS appears to have begun paying dividends quickly, enabling the SEC's Division of Economic and Risk Analysis (DERA) to create detailed reports dissecting trading pauses, volume spikes, and market volatility, including an analysis of ETF trading pauses in U.S. equity markets on August 24, 2015.[18] MIDAS makes this type of statistical analysis not only possible, but practical.

National Exam Analytics Tool

As noted in the Introduction, in February 2014, Erozan Kurtas introduced NEAT at SEC Speaks as an initiative to allow examination teams to review trade blotters more successfully. Mr. Kurtas introduced NEAT as offering a solution to examiners to address the complexity of attempting to analyze trading data through older, insufficient tools such as Excel and Access.

Mr. Kurtas described the issues as: volume, variety of data, and velocity. He wrote that "any single characteristic is manageable and not big data. Only when [the characteristics] interact and do conditions fundamentally change, and what was once just data becomes big data." Mr. Kurtas' data also reflected his further interest in tying social media information to the trade data but did not indicate resources allocated to that yet.

NEAT is now used in every investment adviser examination conducted by the SEC's Boston Regional Office, according to the office's associate director of exams, Kevin Kelcourse. SEC examiners can now perform more efficient analyses of commissions, cross trades and principal trades, Regulation M, fair allocation of investment opportunities, and other trading patterns—including those that may indicate insider trading.

SEC Commissioner Kara Stein noted, "I believe that this kind of data-driven risk assessment is necessary to operate effectively in increasingly sophisticated financial markets."[19] At the National Society of Compliance Professionals (NSCP) Conference in November 2014, then OCIE Director Andrew Bowden told attendees that the SEC now had a tool, NEAT, that provided the type of testing that compliance professionals should consider. Director Bowden noted the SEC has often been at least perceived as being behind the industry in fast-computing. The flash crash demonstrated this. However, he told the audience that the SEC had now created a tool ahead of the industry's technology and suggested that compliance professionals review whether their trade analytics are sufficient.

---

[18] Austin Gerig and Keegan Murphy, "The Determinants of ETF Trading Pauses on August 24th, 2015," SEC White Papers (Feb. 23, 2016), https://www.sec.gov/dera/staff-papers/white-papers/feb2016-dera-white-paper-etf-volatility.html

[19] Kara M. Stein, The Dominance of Data and the Need for New Tools: Remarks at the SIFMA Operations Conference (Apr. 14, 2015), https://www.sec.gov/news/speech/2015-spch041415kms.html

Feeding the SEC's growing appetite for data analytics, examiners now generally request larger volumes of data from investment advisers as part of regulatory examinations. Nowhere is this more readily apparent than in requests for firms' trade blotter data, with some exams requesting trading data for a span of five years. Trade blotter data obtained from firms is run through NEAT by the SEC, enabling the regulator to efficiently review the trading activity for anomalies, aberrations, potential trade errors, front-running, and other patterns of activity.

Examination findings now include reports about transaction allocations, Regulation M, fair pricing, and other possible market misconduct. According to the SEC, the agency charged more than 230 individuals in insider trading cases over a three-year period (April 2013 to May 2016), noting that it brought these actions "while developing analytical tools to help identify patterns of suspicious trading."[20] Compliance professionals do not want to be left holding the bag when one of these reports turns up a real violation. Director Bowden's message means that having a reasonable compliance program and meeting the requirements of Rule 206(4)-7 in the future may mean conducting trade analytics and monitoring for market manipulation. That's not possible without a big data solution.

Aberrational Performance Inquiry

In 2011, the SEC cited return persistence as an indicator of hedge fund fraud in the Enforcement Division of Asset Management Unit's Aberrational Performance Inquiry (API) initiative. "Return persistence" refers to the level of correlation between a fund's monthly returns, or simply, the level of influence the returns in the prior periods have on the current period's returns. The idea is not to target firms with a strong performance track record, but rather to create a sample of firms exhibiting return persistence and use data analytics to identify fund returns that appear inconsistent with a fund's investment strategy, peer composite, or other benchmark. As Robert Khuzami, then-director of the SEC's Division of Enforcement, stated in the inquiry, "We're using risk analytics and unconventional methods to help achieve the holy grail of securities law enforcement—earlier detection and prevention."[21]

The API cited two cases where performance attribution and risk analytics helped bring enforcement actions against investment advisers to private funds. In *SEC vs. Chetan Kapur; Lilaboc, LLC, d/b/a ThinkStrategy Capital Management, LLC*, the SEC found that from at least 2003 through mid-2009, Kapur and ThinkStrategy disseminated false and materially misleading information to investors concerning the performance, longevity, and assets of two private funds. The same complaint also alleges that Kapur used false performance records to raise capital for Fund A and Multi-Strategy Fund B, launched in 2006 and 2007, respectively, and would also later be found to have misstated assets and performance to investors.

---

20 Gerig and Keegan Murphy, "The Determinants of ETF Trading Pauses."

21 SEC, "SEC Charges Multiple Hedge Fund Managers with Fraud in Inquiry Targeting Suspicious Investment Returns" (Dec. 1, 2011), https://www.sec.gov/news/press/2011/2011-252.htm

In the second complaint, *SEC vs. Michael R. Balboa and Gilles T. De Charsonville*, the SEC alleged that Balboa, a portfolio manager to the now-defunct hedge fund Millennium Global Emerging Credit Fund, conspired with a broker to provide false mark-to-market quotes for illiquid and nonexchange-traded securities. The fund's valuation procedures required two prices from outside dealers be reported to the fund's independent valuation agent, GlobeOp Financial Services, Ltd., and outside auditor, Deloitte & Touche (Bermuda), Ltd. The case states that Balboa provided GlobeOp with false marks for two different securities on 17 different occasions, conveying to GlobeOp that the marks were independent market quotes in each instance. "I believe that this kind of data-driven risk assessment is necessary to operate effectively in increasingly sophisticated financial markets," said then-SEC Chief Economist and Director of DERA Mark J. Flannery in regard to the API model.

Robert Kaplan and Bruce Karpati, then co-chiefs of the SEC Enforcement Division's Asset Management Unit, added, "The extraordinary returns reported by these advisers and portfolio managers were, in most cases, too good to be true. In other cases, outlier returns were a telltale sign that something else was amiss. We are applying analytics across the investment adviser space—beyond performance and beyond hedge funds."[22]

Many advisers rely on annual private fund audits or GIPS verification to prevent fraudulent performance. It is clear that valuation policies and practices to ensure accurate data, and procedures to control calculations will remain high SEC priorities.

Regulatory Examinations of Investment Advisers

In fiscal year 2015, OCIE conducted approximately 2,000 registrant examinations, recovering about $120 million for investors.[23] This demonstrated an increase from 2014, when OCIE conducted more than 1,850 registrant examinations—which itself was a 15 percent increase from 2013. Then-SEC Chair Mary Jo White commented that the SEC's success was largely the result of "continued integration of technology into its program." NEAT has been rolled out to examiners across the country to enable them to broadly canvas registrants' trading activities and then strategically narrow the scope of their examinations to areas that pose the greatest risks. But NEAT is now one of many new data analytics platforms available to examiners. In order to address the increase in data reported to the SEC through regulatory filings by corporate registrants, the SEC has developed new technologies to parse, examine, and display data. For example, the Corporate Issuer Risk Assessment (CIRA) program uses a dashboard that simplifies the quantitative modeling required in the staff's review of issuer filing.

---

[22] *Id.*

[23] SEC, *Agency Financial Report, Fiscal Year 2015* (Nov. 2015), https://www.sec.gov/about/secpar/secafr2015.pdf

Another technology developed to facilitate regulatory examinations is the Broker-Dealer Risk Assessment (BDRA) program.[24] The BDRA was created in conjunction with OCIE in order to better prioritize areas of risk inspections:

> The process works as follows. BDs are first classified by their type of dealing activity — for instance whether or not they carry customer securities on their books (i.e., a "carrying broker"). This allows staff to analyze how a firm's behavior compares to its peers. We then look for predictors of potentially anomalous or concerning behavior, which include potential risks related to, for example, its operations, financing, workforce, or firm structure. Risk factors in each of these areas are created from information collected in mandatory disclosure by BDs, such as from the FOCUS, BD, BR, and U4-5 filings. A score card rates how each firm's activity in each of these areas compares to its peer firms, and results from these score cards are used to help prioritize the sequence of BD inspections as well as areas for examiners to focus on.[25]

With an arsenal of new technologies, the SEC is hoping to strengthen its risk-monitoring capabilities, taking a preventive approach to providing regulatory safeguards for the asset management industry. Going forward, OCIE is expected to continue to develop its data analytics technologies to better identify risks, including the considerations for new rules and regulations that would require additional data directly from advisers regarding funds' investments in derivatives, the liquidity and valuations of holdings, and securities lending purchases.

V. REGULATORY BIG DATA SYSTEMS

Table 1 summarizes the data analytics tools used by U.S. regulators.

TABLE 1. COMPILATION OF SEC AND FINRA DATA ANALYTICS TOOLS

Technology	Regulator	Overview
National Exam Analytics Tool (NEAT)	SEC	With NEAT, SEC examiners are able to access and systematically analyze massive amounts of trading data from firms in a fraction of the time it has taken in years past. Among its many uses, NEAT can search for evidence of potential insider trading by comparing a database of significant corporate activity like mergers against the companies in which a registrant is trading and analyze how the registrant traded at the time of those significant events. NEAT can review all the securities the registrant traded and quickly identify the trading patterns of the registrant for suspicious activity.[1]

[24] SEC, *Broker-Dealer Risk Assessment Program* (Aug. 13, 2002), https://www.sec.gov/oig/reportspubs/aboutoigaudit354finhtm.html

[25] Mark J. Flannery, "Insights into the SEC's Risk Assessment Programs," Global Association of Risk Professionals 16th Annual Risk Assessment Convention (Feb. 25, 2015), https://www.sec.gov/news/speech/insights-into-sec-risk-assessment-programs.html

TABLE 1. COMPILATION OF SEC AND FINRA DATA ANALYTICS TOOLS		
Technology	**Regulator**	**Overview**
Market Information Data Analytics System (MIDAS)	SEC	MIDAS is the SEC's implementation of a system that combines advanced technologies with empirical data to promote better understanding of markets. Every day MIDAS collects about 1 billion records from the proprietary feeds of each of the 13 national equity exchanges timestamped to the microsecond. MIDAS allows the SEC to readily perform analyses of thousands of stocks over periods of six months or even a year, involving 100 billion records at a time.[2]
Office of Risk Assessment and Surveillance	SEC	OCIE's Office of Risk Assessment and Surveillance aggregates and analyzes a broad band of data to identify potentially problematic behavior. In addition to scouring the data [it] collect[s] directly from registrants, [OCIE] look[s] at data from outside the SEC, including information from public records, data collected by other regulators, SROs and exchanges, and information that our registrants provide to data vendors. This expanded data collection and analysis not only enhances OCIE's ability to identify risks more efficiently, but it also helps...examiners better understand the contours of a firm's business activities prior to conducting an examination. The Office of Risk Assessment and Surveillance is developing exciting new technologies—text analytics, visualization, search, and predictive analytics—to cull additional red flags from internal and external data and information sources. These tools will help...examiners be even more efficient and effective in analyzing massive amounts of data to more quickly and accurately home in on areas that pose the greatest risks and warrant further investigation. In an era of limited resources and expanding responsibilities, it is essential to identify and target these risks more systematically.[3]
Aberrational Performance: Performance Analytics	SEC	An initiative by the Enforcement Division's Asset Management Unit that uses proprietary risk analytics to identify hedge funds with suspicious returns. Performance that is flagged as inconsistent with a fund's investment strategy or other benchmarks forms a basis for further investigation and scrutiny. The SEC's Aberrational Performance Inquiry is a joint effort among staff in its Division of Enforcement, OCIE, and Division of Risk, Strategy, and Financial Innovation.[4]
Comprehensive Automated Risk Data System (CARDS)	FINRA	CARDS will involve account reporting requirements that would allow FINRA to collect, on a standardized, automated, and regular basis, account information, as well as account activity and security identification information that a firm maintains as part of its books and records.[5]
Fund Analyzer	FINRA	The Fund Analyzer offers information and analysis on more than 18,000 mutual funds, exchange traded funds (ETFs) and exchange traded notes (ETNs). This tool estimates the value of the funds and impact of fees and expenses on an investment and also allows the investor the ability to look up applicable fees and available discounts for funds.[6]

TABLE 1. COMPILATION OF SEC AND FINRA DATA ANALYTICS TOOLS		
Technology	**Regulator**	**Overview**
Order Audit Trail System (OATS)	FINRA	FINRA has established the OATS, as an integrated audit trail of order, quote, and trade information for all National Market System (NMS) stocks and OTC equity securities. FINRA uses this audit trail system to recreate events in the life cycle of orders and more completely monitor the trading practices of member firms. Under FINRA Rules 7410- 7470, FINRA member firms are required to develop a means for electronically capturing and reporting to OATS specific data elements related to the handling or execution of orders, including recording all times of these events in hours, minutes, and seconds, and to synchronize their business clocks. These rules were approved by the SEC on March 6, 1998.[7]
Trade Reporting and Compliance Engine (TRACE)	FINRA	TRACE is the FINRA-developed vehicle that facilitates the mandatory reporting of over-the-counter secondary market transactions in eligible fixed-income securities. All broker-dealers who are FINRA member firms have an obligation to report transactions in corporate bonds to TRACE under an SEC approved set of rules.[8]

ENDNOTES

1 Mary Jo White, "The SEC in 2014" (Jan. 27, 2014), https://www.sec.gov/news/speech/2014-spch012714mjw

2 SEC, "MIDAS: Market Information Data Analytics System" (Oct. 13, 2013), https://www.sec.gov/marketstructure/midas.html#.WPfkwNIrKUk

3 Mary Jo White, "Chairman's Address at SEC Speaks 2014" (Feb. 21, 2014), https://www.sec.gov/news/speech/2014-spch022114mjw

4 "SEC Charges Hedge Fund Adviser and Two Executives with Fraud in Continuing Probe of Suspicious Fund Performance," SEC Press Release(Oct. 17, 2012), https://www.sec.gov/news/press-release/2012-2012-209htm

5 Joyce Hanson, "SIFMA warns investors will pay for FINFRA CARDS plan," Investment News.com (June 18, 2014), http://www.investmentnews.com/article/20140618/FREE/140619920

6 FINRA, "Fund Analyzer," http://apps.finra.org/fundanalyzer/1/fa.aspx

7 FINRA, "OATS" (Mar. 1998), http://www.finra.org/industry/oats

8 FINRA, "Trade Reporting and Compliance Engine (TRACE)," http://www.finra.org/industry/trace

Enforcement Actions: Data Analytics Drives Targeted Examinations and Trading Reviews

Presently, information is taken from every single registrant and data mined, including data on individuals associated with firms (civil cases, criminal cases, etc.). Certain data will be flagged, such as significant growth or decrease in assets under management (AUM), the identity of fund auditors, or auditor or CCO resignations, for example. They continually look for other sources of information to help mine data. By filtering information at the top, they can see where firms give signs of risks!

Previous SEC Director Carlo V. di Florio has described the "Wash, rinse, repeat" process of data analytics, which is that the SEC has certain hypotheses of what causes risk and tests these hypotheses to determine accuracy and then repeat the process again.

2014 marked the first year in which the SEC's big data seeds began to bear fruit, as evidenced by a then-record number of 755 enforcement actions filed during the fiscal year ending September 2014 and a number of "first-ever" cases brought. Mary Jo White expressed at the time that, "The innovative use of technology—enhanced use of data and quantitative analysis—was instrumental in detecting misconduct and contributed to the Enforcement Division's success in bringing quality actions that resulted in stiff monetary sanctions."[26] The enforcement trend appears to be the new normal, as the SEC brought more than 2,400 enforcement actions between April 2013 and May 2016.

Among the enforcement actions, the SEC charged a man living in Ontario, Canada, with coordinating a market manipulation scheme involving "layering"; Aleksandr Milrud recruited online traders, primarily from China and Korea, to place orders for the purpose of tricking others into buying or selling U.S. publicly traded stocks at artificially inflated or depressed prices. Milrud wired funds to an offshore bank account and had cash delivered to him in a suitcase in an attempt to distance himself from certain manipulative transactions.[27]

Success with Data and Regulation M

In September 2013, the SEC brought enforcement against 23 firms for rule violations and issued a risk alert highlighting Rule 105 compliance. One year later, the SEC announced enforcement actions against 19 firms and an individual trader for short sales in violation of Rule 105 of Regulation M:

- A crackdown on short-selling violations in advance of stock offerings; and
- A result imposing cease-and-desist orders and more than $9 million in civil penalties.

In March 2014, the SEC closed on the largest-ever monetary sanction for Rule 105 short-selling violations: $7.2 million.

On October 16, 2014, the SEC announced its first high-frequency trading manipulation case brought under Section 10(b) and Rule 10b-5 of the Exchange Act. The SEC alleged that a New York-based high-frequency trading firm engaged in fraudulent conduct in connection with the purchase and sale of securities through a practice known as "marking the close." Using a sophisticated algorithm, the firm manipulated the closing prices of thousands of publicly traded securities in its favor by placing a large volume of rapid-fire trades near the close of trading almost every trading day during a six-month period in 2009.

In addition, the high-frequency trading firm allegedly implemented additional algorithms to ensure that its orders received priority over other orders when trading imbalances existed between buy and sell orders. The algorithm was ironically called "Gravy."

The SEC has indicated that it is conducting a number of other investigations targeting manipulative activities by computer-driven trading firms.

---

[26] "SEC's FY 2014 Enforcement Actions Span Securities Industry and Include First-Ever Cases " SEC Press Release 2014-230 (Oct. 16, 2014), https://www.sec.gov/news/press-release/2014-230

[27] "SEC Charges Canadian Man with Conducting Fraudulent Trading Scheme," SEC Press Release 2015-4 (Jan. 13,2015), https://www.sec.gov/news/pressrelease/2015-4.html

Data Analytics Drives Targeted Examinations and Trading Reviews

Erozan Kurtas' statistics involving social media data offer a glimpse into where SEC staff is looking for new sources of information and how to harness all of that big data. By filtering information, they can see where firms indicate signs of risks.

With respect to data analytics in the field, incredible strides have been made, according to Bowden. A unit of the SEC located in Salt Lake City that reviews information from clearing firms began to look at transactions to identify churning, cherry picking, and other areas of concern without an adviser even knowing that the review was occurring. The unit provides regional offices with the results and specific names of firms to research/investigate (which Bowden referred to as "hot leads"). In 2014, this Risk Analysis and Examination Group (RAE) analyzed more than a billion transactions from approximately 350 firms and used these analyses for referrals to enforcement.[28]

Together, the RAE unit and the NEAT tool provide the tools to analyze information more completely. OCIE is using the NEAT tool in the field and including data from the Bloomberg system and news events to help run analysis. The utility of the tool has significantly helped OCIE to perform more efficient exams, according to Bowden.

Predictions

There will be more instances of data unveiling fraud. The ability to review all transactions for certain rule violations is a revolutionary breakthrough the SEC needs. For registered investment advisers, this means more transparency of trading violations and patterns that signify outliers and anomalies that require further review.

There Will Be More Trading Violations. Following are the types of rule violations predicted to continue to arise that the use of big data tools may detect:

- Undisclosed principal and agency cross transactions;
- Lack of best execution;
- Marking the close;
- Portfolio pumping;
- Insider trading;
- Regulation M violations;
- Unreported trade errors;
- Improper allocation of investment opportunities;
- Systemic pricing biases and account favoritism;
- Front running;
- Account churning; and
- Suitability of investments.

28

There Will Be More Inaccurate Regulatory Reporting Violations. Here are some types of reporting inaccuracies predicted to continue:

- Forms 13D and 13G;
- Form 13F;
- Form PF;
- Form 13H;
- Form ADV; and
- Investment Company Act reporting.

The ability of data systems to measure variables and produce visual and predictive analytics will further change the required skill set of compliance professionals. Although some large businesses may have versions of these tools, it will not be practical for smaller firms to build these solutions themselves. The SEC essentially has thrown out the challenge: join the big data revolution.

VI. LEVERAGING TECHNOLOGY TO MANAGE COMPLIANCE RISK

Regulators are generally concerned with two primary risk categories: those that are derived from various forms of market misconduct (e.g., securities fraud), and market-wide systemic risks, or threats created from the "correlated activities of many market participants" (e.g., bank failures).[29] The SEC relies on the market risk assessments performed by the Division of Economic and Risk Analysis (DERA) to protect investors, and ensure stability and order for our financial markets.

To detect market misconduct, DERA has implemented risk management frameworks and technologies such as CIRA, the Corporate Issuer Risk Assessment. Through this tool the SEC seeks to detect anomalous patterns in the financial reports such as 8-K and 10-K filings. At the 16th Annual Risk Assessment Convention, Mark Flannery, then the chief economist and director of DERA, described how the system works, stating. He stated "We can look at how inventory at a manufacturing company is moving relative to sales, because an unusual inventory buildup might lead managers to be aggressive in their accounting. When combined with other risk indicators, SEC staff may decide to focus more attention on the reporting firm. Members of the SEC's cross-agency Fraud Task Force are frequent users of the CIRA system."[30]

DERA is also actively involved in the development of technologies to detect when a hedge fund manager misvalues assets to inflate or smooth its returns. DERA can examine when brokers treat some investors with preference over others when allocating trades.

---

[29] It is important to note that market misconduct can also be a market-wide systemic risk, as one could certainly argue the events of 2008 are a clear example of market misconduct leading to significant market dislocations and instability. However, how the SEC has chosen to assess risk is predominately based upon the derivation of such risk factors, and how to best mitigate them.

[30] SEC, "FY 2017 Congressional Budget Justification" (Feb. 2016), at 5, https://www.sec.gov/about/reports/secfy17congbudgjust.pdf

DERA has also developed a broker-dealer risk assessment tool that helps SEC examiners allocate resources by assessing a broker-dealer's comparative riskiness relative to its peer group. It's also working closely with the Enforcement Division's Financial Reporting and Audit Task Force and the Division of Corporation Finance on developing a tool to assist in identifying financial reporting irregularities that may indicate financial fraud and help assess corporate issuer risk.

Using Automated Analysis and Monitoring Tools

Automation can be used in many ways to manage operational risk, although not all risk management controls are capable of being automated. For the most part, investment advisers attempt to implement viable automated risk controls while keeping in place certain manual controls in order to ensure the automated processes are indeed working effectively or need to be adjusted. Advisers leverage technology to manage compliance risk through online compliance attestation portals, automated brokerage feeds for tracking the holdings and transactions of supervised persons, performing pretrade and post-trade blotter analysis, and for using programmed rules to prevent certain types of transactions of security types, position limits, or prevent traders from effecting short sales in these that would cause a violation of Regulation M. Compliance professionals have a lot of obligations on their plates. Automated tools, software, and applications can ease some of the reporting and data collection burden and enable compliance staff to focus on high-risk areas for their firms or on tasks which cannot be easily automated.

Technology cannot completely replace the compliance function at advisers because technology is only as good as its programming. It may flag potential issues from a rules-based or pattern-matching standpoint that a human could easily identify as irrelevant nonissues. Large numbers of false positives in automated systems provide opportunities for human input to adjust settings and parameters.

Nonetheless, regulatory expectations reveal that the SEC increasingly expects to see firms leveraging technology—to the extent feasible—to manage compliance risk, as evidenced by examination document request letters including years of email, trade blotter data, and forensic testing. A completely manual process is likely to be a red flag for the SEC, for several reasons:

- A paper-based process arguably provides an easier opportunity to fabricate or falsify records, for example, by back-dating compliance logs to evidence testing that may not have been performed on the date listed;
- completely manual processes are prone to human error; and
- Manual processes generally take significantly more time than automated processes, meaning time-starved compliance professionals may be spending too much time on certain functions and leaving certain aspects of their compliance programs unmonitored.

Leveraging Operational Risk Management Technology

Given the SEC's trend of processing volumes of trade blotter data from examined firms through NEAT, investment advisers are well advised to perform their own data analytics and trade surveillance—in essence, to see what the SEC sees when it looks at the same data. Although spreadsheet applications such as Microsoft Excel can be used for limited sorting, finding any meaningful patterns over time requires the use of more sophisticated database tools and technology that allows advisers to run queries and generate reports regarding their trade blotter activity over a given period of time.

The use of automated risk management and surveillance tools by investment advisers should not be surprising. Heightened regulatory scrutiny, when combined with limited compliance resources and personnel, and an ever-expanding set of regulatory requirements with which to comply, has left many firms struggling to do more with less. Many firms are implementing operational and compliance risk frameworks to track risk factors and monitor compliance controls more efficiently. The implementation of such frameworks enables compliance professionals to spend their time on tasks that are less susceptible to automation. Outlined in Figure 2 are operational frameworks that advisory firms can implement to track operational risks and controls.

FIGURE 2. OPERATIONAL FRAMEWORKS FOR OPERATIONAL RISKS AND CONTROLS

Risk Matrices and Scoring Systems

- A risk matrix is an operational risk management framework that defines and categorizes risk factors.
- Risk factors are identified through either a top-down or bottom-up approach.
- Risk factors assigned a risk score (e.g., Low, Medium, High).
- Risk factors assigned a probability (e.g., Not Applicable (<10%), Not Likely (<25%), Possible (~50%), Probable (>50%), Highly Anticipated (>90%)).
- Primary and optional secondary controls are assigned to each risk factor (optional manual, technical, automated).
- Risk factors/scores monitored in real-time. Controls reviewed and updated periodically.

Example of a Top-Down Approach

An operational risk model that uses a top-down approach begins with the broad evaluation of high-level operational categories:

- Legal/Regulatory/Compliance
- Trading/Valuation
- Technology/Business Continuity/Disaster Recovery
- Assets Under Management/Financial and Organizational Suitability
- Quality of Service Providers Used
- Reputational Risk

Example of a Bottom-Up Approach

An operational risk model that uses a bottom-up approach begins with the evaluation of specific operational processes and internal documents to identify high-risk areas:

- Changes to registrations or filings with regulators
- Compliance memos to the management committee
- Types of reviews conducted to validate best execution
- Documentation of trade errors
- Recent marketing materials and compliance sign-offs
- Testing frequency of business continuity and disaster recovery plans
- Appropriateness of information security policies and procedures

Regardless of whether a firm chooses to implement a top-down risk management framework or a bottom-up approach, risk factors must be addressed with specific controls. Often there is an automated control that can be implemented through the use of technology, such as pretrade compliance controls for trading violations that are programmatically enforced through order management and execution technologies. Figure 3 outlines various technology products capable of serving as primary or secondary controls as a firm builds an internal risk management framework.

FIGURE 3. TYPES OF PRODUCTS SERVING AS CONTROLS

Leveraging Tech for Trading Compliance

- Performance Measurement and Investor Reporting Systems
  - Performance measurement and return attribution systems
  - Customized benchmarks and composite management
  - GIPS performance reporting standards
- Understanding the entire trade lifecycle.
  - Pretrade versus post-trade compliance (OMS) and in-trade risk management (OMS/PMS)
  - Post-trade statistical testing and post-trade blotter analytics
  - Gathering volume medians and measuring deviations
- Examples of Post-Trade Blotter Testing:
  - Fund/account, strategy, and asset class volume profiles
  - Window-dressing
  - Wash trading
  - Style drift
  - Excessive trading
  - Market manipulation
- Approved Brokers Testing and Commissions Reports
- Best Execution (EMS)
  - Total cost analysis
  - Implementation shortfall analysis
  - Market impact analysis
- Cross Trades and Principal Transactions
- Short-Term Trades and Trade Errors
- Trade Sequencing, Allocation, & Pricing
- Return Persistence and Aberrational Performance

Leveraging Tech for Legal and Compliance Functions

Compliance functions and records management that can be automated or facilitated by technology:

- Email, Instant Messaging, and Social Media Surveillance, Retention, and Review
- Order Management Systems, Pretrade and Post-Trade Compliance
- Post-Trade Blotter Testing
- Monitoring for Sales Practice Abuses
- Insider Trading Prevention
- Pay to Play
- Personal Securities Transactions—Preclearance for Restricted Securities/Industries, and Transaction Review
- Gifts and Entertainment
- Proxy Voting
- Regulation S-P
  - Encrypted file transfer (e.g., Email, Dropbox, Box)
  - Access controls (file, folder, active directory permissions, password controls)
  - Secure remote access (e.g., VPN, restrictions on flash drives and printing)
  - Wireless access
  - Centrally managed anti-virus, operating system (OS), and application patches
  - Intrusion Detection Systems (IDS) and Intrusion Prevention Systems (IPS)
- Managing Compliance Program Rule and COE Rule Records
  - Policy and procedure acknowledgments
  - COE acknowledgements
  - Access person PST reports
  - Calendaring daily, weekly, monthly, and annual forensic testing
  - Organization of records in preparation for examination

Leveraging Tech for Valuation

"Return persistence" refers to the level of serial correlation between a fund's monthly and quarterly returns:

- First-order auto-correlation: correlation between the return in time period t and the return in the previous period, $t - 1$
- Tracking the first-order autocorrelation coefficient
- Durbin-Watson test for autocorrelation
- High risk area for private equity, private real-estate and hedge funds that hold illiquid assets. Concerns over disclosure of smoothed returns series.

"Aberrational performance" refers to returns that are inconsistent with the fund's investment strategy or other benchmark. In 2011, the SEC cited return persistence as an indicator of hedge fund fraud in its Aberrational Performance Inquiry (API). The SEC stated consistent monthly returns in excess of 3 percent of a benchmark led examiners to uncover improper valuation practices for illiquid securities and inflated monthly returns at two hedge funds.

VII. BEYOND BIG DATA: WHAT'S NEXT?

Consolidated Audit Trail (CAT)

The SEC adopted Rule 613[31] in July of 2012 to require SROs and national securities exchanges to jointly submit a national market system plan detailing how they would develop, implement, and maintain a consolidated audit trail (CAT) to collect and accurately identify orders, cancellations, modifications, and trade executions for Reg NMS securities.[32] The initial proposal was submitted to the SEC in September of 2014, amended in February of 2015, and published for comment in April of 2016.

Although there are certainly many critics of the proposed plan and the timeline for its implementation, the SEC expects the first data submissions to the central repository to occur within one year after the plan is approved. The SEC will have access to all CAT data through an online targeted query tool, in addition to user-defined extracts and bulk queries.

CAT Data Submissions and Requirements. Following are the types of proposed consolidated audit trail requirements for SROs, national securities exchanges, and members:

- Requires national securities exchanges, SROs, and its members to submit detailed information to the central repository concerning the receipt and origination of orders; information about how the order was routed including all broker-dealers, national securities exchanges or foreign exchanges; the audit trail of internal routing of orders between desks or departments within a broker-dealer; and all modifications, cancellations, executions, and customer identifications;
- Requires, in addition to a customer ID, information about the customer including the account number, account type, customer type, date account opened, and large trader identification number (LTID) to be submitted to the central repository;
- Requires certain data to be reported to the central repository by 8 a.m. Eastern time the following trading day, and be subsequently available to regulators for their analysis;
- Requires all reportable events to be reported to the central repository in a way that allows the central repository to efficiently and accurately link them to an order through its entire life cycle from generation through routing, modification, cancellation, or execution;
- Requires each broker-dealer and national securities exchange to be assigned a code that uniquely and consistently identifies such broker-dealer or national securities exchange that will be reported to the central repository along with every reportable event;
- Requires each account holder, as well as any person who has trading discretion over an account holder's account, to be assigned a code that uniquely and consistently

---

[31] SEC, "Rule 613 (Consolidated Audit Trail)" Aug. 2016), https://www.sec.gov/divisions/marketreg/rule613-info.htm

[32] FINRA, "Consolidated Audit Trail (CAT)," http://www.finra.org/industry/consolidated-audit-trail-cat

identifies such account holder or person with trading discretion over the account, that will be reported to the central repository for every order originated; and

- Requires SROs and their members to synchronize the business clocks they use to record the date and time of any reportable event, and requires timestamps for each reportable event to the central repository to be in millisecond or finer increments.

The rule allows the SROs to determine the specifics of how market participants would report data to the central repository. Although this might allow for multiple electronic formats, the data must be reported in a way that enables the central repository to send it to regulators in a uniform electronic format.

Cybersecurity: The Risks Associated with Safeguarding Big Data

The proliferation of big data maintained by financial institutions has contributed to a corresponding rise in the cybersecurity risks associated with that data. Particularly as significant quantities of sensitive or confidential personal information and trading data are stored in one or more databases at firms, and as the regulators increasingly request and use that information, the need to adequately protect those records becomes paramount.

There is a regulatory basis for maintaining cybersecurity controls around big data. Rule 204-2(g) under the Advisers Act requires that several conditions must be met when records are maintained electronically by investment advisers:

- The records are indexed in a manner capable of "easy location, access, and retrieval";
- A "legible, true, and complete copy of the record on the medium on which it was stored" or a "legible, true, and complete printout of the record" can be provided promptly to the Securities and Exchange Commission upon request;
- If requested, the adviser can provide "means to access, view, and print the records"; and
- The adviser separately keeps another copy of the records in any format permitted by the rule.[33]

Advisers Act Rule 204-2(g) imposes further requirements for the safekeeping of such records. Investment advisers storing records electronically are required to establish procedures designed to:

1. "[R]easonably safeguard [the records] from loss, alteration, or destruction";
2. "Limit access to the records only to the parties with the proper authorization"; and
3. "[r]easonably ensure that any reproduction of a nonelectronic original record on electronic storage media is complete, true, and legible when retrieved."[34]

---

[33] E. J. Yerzak, "Demystifying the Cloud: Electronic Storage of Records by Investment Advisers in the Cloud Computing Era" , *Practical Compliance and Risk Management for the Securities Industry,* Wolters Kluwer Financial Services (May-June 2012), at 6-7.

[34] *Id.*

These electronic safeguards are important because they serve not only to protect the records from unauthorized use but also to maintain the integrity of the underlying data. Analyses derived from big data are entirely without value if the data sets on which they are based are inaccurate or have been compromised. Essentially, the number crunching and utility of big data analysis starts with the assumption that the data is valid; otherwise, the data is likely to skew any results stemming from the use of the information in calculations. Why is this significant? The SEC's use of big data to inform its understanding of the financial markets will result in flawed understanding and conclusions if the underlying data is inaccurate or incomplete. In addition, and more concerning for advisers, is that the use of big data to detect insider trading or improper trading activity that could lead to an enforcement action potentially can be based upon erroneous recognition of trading patterns that might not be present had the data been clean.

Consequently, with big data comes big responsibility. Investment advisers providing data to the SEC in response to requests for such information must be able to attest to the accuracy of such data. Likewise, regulators requesting big data from regulated entities should be entitled to rely upon the accuracy of the information presented to them, yet cannot always take firms at their word because data may have been intentionally altered to mask illicit activity, may have been inadvertently entered or changed, or may have been unknowingly compromised by a third party. However, the SEC does have the benefit of not viewing big data in a vacuum. When one firm's data appears inconsistent with similar data provided by other firms, that occurrence can serve as a warning flag to the examination staff that something may be amiss at the firm where the data anomaly is present. Similarly, a firm's own data, when known to be verified or correct, could be used to pinpoint inaccuracies or inconsistencies in other portions of the firm's own data.[35] Therefore, the regulatory focus on cybersecurity has the dual benefit of driving firms not only to bolster their defenses to protect their crown jewels from external hackers and malicious insiders, but also to provide assurances to some extent as to the reliability and accuracy of the data maintained by the adviser.

Standardizing and Safeguarding Electronic Information

As the SEC moves toward implementing a consolidated audit trail, it should also set up an in-house office with the main function of helping the regulator develop a comprehensive approach to collecting, standardizing, and overseeing data. In an April 2015 speech, Commissioner Kara Stein said that the growing amount of increasingly complex data coming into the agency shows that the SEC is in need of an Office of Data Strategy, led by a chief data officer.[36]

---

[35] *See,* e.g., D. Che, M. Safran, and Z. Peng, "Database Systems for Advanced Applications" *Proceedings of the 18th International Conference, DASFAA 2013, International Workshops,* Wuhan, China (Apr. 22-25, 2013), Springer (Aug. 17, 2013), at 9-10. ("In the past, data mining systems were fed with relatively accurate data from well-known and quite limited sources, so the mining results tend to be accurate too; thus accuracy and trust have never been a serious issue for concern....In the case of big data, the copious data sources and gigantic volumes provide rich sources to extract additional evidences for verifying accuracy and building trust on the selected data and the produced mining results.")

[36] Kara M. Stein, "The Dominance of Data and the Need for New Tools: Remarks at the SIFMA Operations Conference" (Apr. 14, 2015), https://www.sec.gov/news/speech/2015-spch041415kms.html

Looking Ahead

OCIE will continue to focus on current and emerging high-priority areas and will further enhance its use of data analytics to identify risks.

SEC Priorities. Its highest priority being conflicts of interest, the SEC's asset management unit talks about the following being the overarching concern across all types of advisers:

- *For private funds generally:* conflicts of interest, valuation, controls, undisclosed fees, undisclosed conflicts, related parties transactions;
- *For private equity:* undisclosed and misallocated fees and expenses;
- *For hedge funds:* suspicious returns, principle transactions without prior written disclosure; and
- *For separately managed accounts:* conflicts of interest, fee arrangements, compliance.

Need for New Tools: Dominance of Data. Commissioner Stein summed up the two sides of the data question, "How do we promote innovation and the use of technology and data analytics while understanding that there are limitations and risks?"[37]

And she answered, "It is vital that everyone works together to develop best practices in detecting and dealing with data breaches. Boards, senior management, and line employees should constantly be asking questions about how to prevent and detect such breaches. I also believe that knowledge sharing is critical to creating resiliency."[38]

VIII. CONCLUSION

On March 20, 2015, Commissioner Aguilar spoke to the Georgia Law Review Annual Symposium. In his well-crafted remarks, he reflected on the financial crisis of 2008-2009, the 2010 enactment of the Dodd-Frank Wall Street Reform and Consumer Protection Act, and the more than 250 new rules the SEC has voted on since then. As a result, he wanted to speak on two "fundamental challenges that will cut across several important regulatory responsibilities": big data and globalization.[39]

Every time investment advisers turn around, either the news is describing new big data applications or another SEC official is discussing big data. Commissioner Aguilar stated he will be focused on "how the SEC should prioritize its use of data and technology to become a more effective regulator."

The regulation of investment advisers is driven by advisers' fiduciary responsibility and numerous rules and regulations, including the requirement to have written policies and procedures designed to detect and prevent violations of securities laws. Big data is a tool that can be—and is being—harnessed by both regulators and private industry. Big data represents a new challenge and loads of opportunity!

---

[37] *Id.*

[38] *Id.*

[39] Luis A. Aguilar, "Preparing for the Regulatory Challenges of the 21st Century" (Mar. 20, 2015), https://www.sec.gov/news/speech/preparing-for-regulatory-challenges-of-21st-century.html

ABOUT THE AUTHORS

Keith Marks is the senior vice president and general counsel of Ascendant Compliance Management, Inc., providing consulting, annual compliance program reviews, risk assessments, onsite mock examinations, and registration services to clients including hedge fund managers, private equity managers, institutional advisers, wrap fee managers, Internet-based advisers, wealth managers, and financial planners. He regularly speaks to compliance professionals and advisory firm staff at in-house training programs and at various industry association conferences. Mr. Marks produced Ascendant's Form ADV Part 2 Template, of which the firm provided more than 6,000 free copies in 2010-2011, to assist the industry transition. He has been published seven times in the *Schwab Compliance Review.*

Before joining Ascendant, Mr. Marks helped create and deliver the IACCP designation as director of investment adviser services at National Regulatory Services (1999-2007). He practiced law as an associate with Day, Berry & Howard LLP (now Day Pitney LLP) (1997-99). He also served as law clerk for the Honorable Francis M. McDonald in Connecticut's Supreme Court (1996–1997) and the Honorable Barry R. Schaller in Connecticut's Appellate Court (1995–1996).

Mr. Marks earned his juris doctor degree *magna cum laude* from Western New England College School of Law (1995), and his bachelor of arts degree *magna cum laude* from the University of Connecticut (1992) with majors in Political Science and English.

Mr. Marks also serves as president of the New England Broker Dealer Investment Adviser Association (NEBDIAA) (2012-2017), a nonprofit organization, incorporated in 1997. The purpose of NEBDIAA is to provide a forum to help NEBDIAA's members meet the increased regulatory demands placed on investment advisers, broker dealers, and persons who provide services to investment advisers and broker dealers.

E. J. Yerzak is vice president of technology at Ascendant Compliance Management. He assists advisers to hedge funds, private equity funds, funds of funds, and other investment advisers in bridging the gap between compliance and cybersecurity risk management. In addition to conducting compliance program annual reviews, risk assessments, and acquisition due diligence reviews, Mr. Yerzak is vice president of Ascendant's technology team, which provides cybersecurity consulting services to Ascendant's clients—ranging from network vulnerability scanning to onsite cybersecurity risk assessments to assistance in implementing the NIST cybersecurity framework. He has authored articles and alerts on emerging regulatory and technology issues, and is regularly requested to speak as a cybersecurity expert at industry conferences and events throughout the country. He is a certified information systems auditor (CISA), certified information security manager (CISM), and certified in risk and information systems control (CRISC).

Mr. Yerzak holds a bachelor of arts in both English and Computer Science *magna cum laude* from Colgate University, a master of science degree in Computer Information Technology from Central Connecticut State University, as well as a juris doctor degree *magna cum laude* from Quinnipiac University School of Law. He is a member of the State Bar of Connecticut.

Brian DeDonato is the CAIA consultant and director ACM Trading Analytics at Ascendant Compliance Management. He joined the Ascendant team in April of 2014. Assisting in compliance reviews, risk assessments, and operational due diligence for Ascendant's investment adviser, hedge fund, and private equity clients, Mr. DeDonato spends the majority of his time on trade surveillance and trade blotter analysis, reporting to senior executives, risk managers, and traders at top-tier asset managers across the United States.

Mr. DeDonato graduated *cum laude* from the University of Massachusetts with a bachelor of science degree in Business Administration with a concentration in Finance. He is a chartered alternative investment analyst and a member of the CAIA Association. In December of 2014, Mr. DeDonato passed the certified information systems auditor exam.

Jackie Hallihan is the director of business strategy of Ascendant Compliance Management, and has more than 25 years of regulatory and risk management experience. She was the founder of National Regulatory Services in 1983, where she started the compliance resource business and served as its president for almost 20 years. Ms. Hallihan also founded the National Society of Compliance Professionals, a nonprofit organization for compliance officers, staff, and lawyers serving the compliance industry, which now boasts more than 2,000 memberships. She has been a leading speaker to compliance professionals, including in-house training programs and various other industry association conferences, and has received numerous industry awards.

Ms. Hallihan also served as a director and the clerk of the New England Broker-Dealer Investment Adviser Association (NEBDIAA), a nonprofit organization, incorporated in 1997 (2012-2017). The purpose of NEBDIAA is to provide a forum to help NEBDIAA's members meet the increased regulatory demands placed on investment advisers, broker-dealers, and persons who provide services to investment advisers and broker-dealers.

CHAPTER 24

Conflicts of Interest

By Michael Koffler
Eversheds Sutherland

I. INTRODUCTION

The former director of the Office of Compliance Inspections and Examinations (OCIE) of the Securities and Exchange Commission (SEC) once famously compared conflicts of interest to "viruses that threaten the organization's wellbeing."[1] Recently, the Department of Labor (DOL) adopted rules that would greatly expand the number and scope of financial advisers that would be fiduciaries under the Employee Retirement Income Securities Act of 1974, as amended (ERISA) as a result of its conclusion that such advisers' conflicts of interest harm retirement plan participants and owners of individual retirement accounts (IRAs) and threaten their retirement income. In the past few years the SEC has brought numerous enforcement actions against investment advisers for failing to mitigate their conflicts of interest, and the Financial Industry Regulatory Authority (FINRA) has likewise focused on conflicts of interest in its examinations of broker-dealers. For their part banking regulators have long focused on the conflicts of interest faced by bank trust departments and have issued comprehensive guidance as to how banks should mitigate their conflicts.

Conflicts of interest in the financial services industry can present substantial compliance risks. To begin with, conflicts are highly regulated, and in certain cases, prohibited, by laws, regulations, and interpretive guidance. Improper conflicts of interest may result in regulatory sanctions such as fines, judgments or settlements, or costly litigation. Conflicts of interest at financial institutions[2] also can pose various operational risks, including the potential for misconduct by directors, officers, and employees.

Firms' reputations can be negatively affected if they engage in, or appear to engage in, improper conflicts of interest or self-dealing. Actual or apparent conflicts of interest can jeopardize clients' confidence that a firm will treat them fairly. There are numerous examples in which a loss of client trust because of questionable loyalty has led to a firm's undoing. For this reason, and to effectively manage reputation risk, many firms are careful

[1] Carlo V. di Florio, "Conflicts of Interest and Risk Governance" (Oct. 22, 2012), https://www.sec.gov/News/Speech/Detail/Speech/1365171491600

[2] In this chapter, the terms "financial institution" and "firm" are used synonymously to collectively refer to investment advisers, broker-dealers, national banks, and federal savings associations.

to avoid not only activities that could result in regulatory sanctions or litigation, but also those that raise even the appearance of improper conflicts of interest or self-dealing. These firms recognize that their ability to thrive in the marketplace depends, in large part, on their success in cultivating and maintaining a satisfied, loyal client base, which can be adversely affected by improper conflicts of interest.

Regulatory Approaches to Conflicts

As the level of assets managed and advised by financial institutions has grown in recent years, so has regulators' focus on conflicts of interest. By some measures, such as the DOL's recent fiduciary rule, the SEC's record number of enforcement actions and level of fines targeting investment advisers' conflicts of interest, and FINRA's targeted reviews focusing on conflicts of interest, financial industry regulators have never been as focused on financial institutions' conflicts of interest. The approaches to conflicts of interest taken by these regulators share certain common traits but also vary in some very important respects. These differences are attributable, in part, to differences in the statutory schemes administered by the regulators and the different roles, responsibilities, and duties owed by the various kinds of financial institutions.

For instance, and as discussed subsequently, the DOL's approach to conflicts of interest can be clearly discerned from its recent rulemaking expanding the definition of fiduciary under ERISA and a related prohibited transaction exemption it crafted, which focuses on mitigating conflicts of interest of financial services firms when providing investment advice to ERISA plans and IRAs. The heart of this exemption focuses on ensuring that the investment advice is in the retirement investor's best interest, notwithstanding that the person providing the advice has material conflicts of interest. The DOL's approach is to prescribe certain elements that must be satisfied in order for the conflict to have been satisfactorily mitigated.

In contrast, the SEC and FINRA have taken a more principled approach to conflicts of interest. The securities regulators' approach has been to encourage broker-dealers and investment advisers to review their compensation systems, sales practices, and operations to identify, document, and inventory their conflicts and to design appropriate policies, procedures, and controls to manage and disclose their conflicts. This process typically entails creating a risk matrix outlining a firm's conflicts; mapping policies, procedures, and controls to the conflicts; and disclosing the conflicts fully and fairly to clients. A firm might, for instance, manage conflicts by enhancing the supervision and review of the advice provided, having a department or unit not tied to the advice review the advice, revising compensation practices to reduce or eliminate conflicts created by the payment of cash or noncash compensation tied to the advice provided, and/or designing and implementing standards and criteria that are designed to ensure the advice is of high quality and is in the client's best interests. For its part, the Office of the Comptroller of the Currency (OCC), in turn, has taken a different approach to identifying and mitigating conflicts that is grounded in trust law and the regulations it administers. This chapter reviews the approaches taken by the DOL, the OCC, the SEC, and FINRA to conflicts of interest under the regulatory regimes they implement and summarizes the key guidance and principles of these regulators regarding conflicts.

Types of Conflicts

The chapter then discusses a number of types of conflicts common to financial institutions that provide investment advice to clients. First, the chapter discusses conflicts arising from the role(s) played by different types of financial institutions and the receipt of certain types of compensation that varies depending on the advice provided to clients. These conflicts can, in turn, be broken down into two main categories:

- Those that arise as a result of arrangements with third parties, such as the receipt of different levels of compensation from sales of different securities and investment products, revenue sharing payments, and the receipt of marketing allowances; and
- Those that result from the internal compensation practices adopted by financial institutions, such as differential compensation payouts, "commission specials," and internal sales contests.

Wrap fee programs involve unique conflicts that arise from the fact that the sponsor receives the same amount of compensation regardless of the level of trading in the account (which creates an incentive to have a modest amount of trading in the account). Other investment advisory programs, including SMA and UMA programs, involve conflicts of interest created by different economics that a sponsor may have with different subadvisers or the different economics that a subadviser may have in one program as opposed to another. Similarly, a model manager with its own set of direct clients often will have different economics with these clients as compared to the economic arrangements it enters into with third party platform providers that have their own client base and receive models and trading signals from the model manager. These different client economics put pressure on such managers concerning their allocation of investment opportunities and their decision on how to implement their investment ideas.

Second, the chapter focuses on conflicts associated with the decision of how to implement portfolio management decisions in the context of exchange-traded securities. These conflicts typically involve the receipt of some economic benefit for placing trades with one particular broker-dealer or other trading venue as opposed to another. Such conflicts include the receipt by an asset manager of: soft dollars; client referrals from executing broker-dealers; payment for order flow; or other economic other benefits associated with placing trades with particular executing broker-dealers, custodians, or trading venues. Principal trades, agency cross trades, and cross trades involve a unique set of conflicts of interest that arise when portfolio management decisions are implemented through buying securities from clients, selling securities to clients, executing transactions between client accounts, or acting as a broker both for the advisory client and a party on the other side of the transaction.

Third, financial institutions face conflicts whenever they have different economic relationships with different clients. Such conflicts may arise, for instance, because of the use of different fee schedules with different clients or entering into performance-based fee arrangements with some clients, but not others (so-called "side-by-side management"). Receiving different fees for managing different types of assets (e.g., equity versus fixed income, or domestic securities versus international securities) also creates asset allocation recommendation conflicts because the adviser receives different levels of compensation depending on a client's asset allocation. Conflicts are also present with the decision of how to allocate expenses associated with managing pooled investment vehicles.

Fourth, financial institutions may have conflicts arise as a result of outside business activities engaged in by their personnel, such as when an employee is a director of, or the financial institution provides services to, a company that the manager is considering buying or selling. Private equity managers can have conflicts when their personnel are involved in the management of portfolio companies and any manager may have a conflict if an employee has an economic stake or interest in a company the manager may buy or sell.

Mitigating Conflicts

After describing many of the common conflicts that financial institutions face in providing investment advice to clients, the chapter finally discusses how financial institutions can effectively identify, document, and mitigate their conflicts and design a system for monitoring the effectiveness of their mitigation efforts.

II. REGULATORY APPROACHES TO CONFLICTS

Conflicts of interest are defined similarly by financial industry regulators as essentially entailing situations in which a financial institution has a relationship or activity that causes its interests to compete with the interests of its clients. Typically, conflicts arise in circumstances that cause a financial institution to provide self-interested advice or take other actions for pecuniary reasons. As the Supreme Court observed, they arise when circumstances "incline an investment adviser—consciously or unconsciously—to render advice which was not disinterested"[3] and thus further its own financial interests. This might mean serving the interest of the firm over that of a client, or it could mean serving the interest of one client over other clients. It could also mean an employee serving his or her own interests over those of the firm or its clients.[4] If conflicts are not carefully managed, the result can be a failure to protect clients' interests, with the attendant regulatory and reputational risks already mentioned.

For these reasons, financial industry regulators have placed a high priority in reviewing firms' conflict management practices. This section summarizes the views and regulatory approaches taken by the DOL, the OCC, the SEC, and FINRA to conflict management.

---

3 *SEC v. Capital Gains Research Bureau, Inc.*, 375 U.S. 180, 194 (1963) ("*Capital Gains*").

4 *di Florio, "Conflicts of Interest and Risk Governance."*

Department of Labor Regulation of Conflicts

ERISA and Its Statutory Mandates. ERISA is a comprehensive statute designed to protect the rights and interests of employee benefit plan participants and beneficiaries. Under ERISA and the Internal Revenue Code of 1986, as amended (tax code), a person is a fiduciary to an employee benefit plan or IRA to the extent the person engages in specified activities, including rendering investment advice for a fee or other compensation, direct or indirect, with respect to any moneys or other property of the plan. ERISA safeguards plan participants by imposing trust law standards of care and undivided loyalty on plan fiduciaries, and by holding fiduciaries accountable when they breach these obligations. Under this regulatory structure, fiduciary status and responsibilities are central to protecting the public interest in the integrity of retirement benefits.

The broad public interest in ERISA-covered plans is reflected in the statute's imposition of stringent fiduciary responsibilities on parties engaging in important plan activities. One of the ways in which ERISA protects employee benefit plans is by requiring that plan fiduciaries comply with fundamental obligations rooted in the law of trusts. In particular, investment advice plan fiduciaries must manage plan assets prudently and with undivided loyalty to the plans, their participants, and beneficiaries.[5] In addition, such fiduciaries to plans and IRAs must refrain from engaging in "prohibited transactions," which the statute does not permit, absent an applicable statutory or administrative exemption, because of the dangers posed by the associated conflicts of interest.[6]

ERISA and the tax code impose on investment advice fiduciaries of plans and IRAs a duty not to act on conflicts of interest that may affect the fiduciary's best judgment on behalf of the plan or IRA. The prohibitions extend to a fiduciary causing a plan or IRA to pay an additional fee to the fiduciary, or to a person in which such fiduciary has an interest, that may affect the exercise of the fiduciary's best judgment. Likewise, an investment advice fiduciary is prohibited from receiving compensation from third parties in connection with a transaction involving the plan or IRA.

When fiduciaries violate ERISA's fiduciary duties or the prohibited transaction rules, they may be held personally liable for any investor losses resulting from the breach.[7] Violations of the prohibited transaction rules are subject to excise taxes under the tax code or civil penalties under ERISA.[8]

The DOL amended its definition of "fiduciary" to better reflect the scope of the statutory text and its purposes and to better protect plans, participants, beneficiaries, and IRA owners from conflicts of interest. The DOL's philosophy toward conflicts of interest

---

[5] ERISA Section 404(a).

[6] ERISA Section 406 and Code Sec. 4975. Prohibited transactions include sales and exchanges between plans and parties with certain connections to the plan, including fiduciaries. These provisions also prohibit self-dealing and other conflicted transactions involving plan fiduciaries.

[7] ERISA Section 409; *see also* ERISA Section 405.

[8] Code Sec. 4975 and ERISA Section 502(i).

can be seen in its justification for its recent rulemaking. In the release adopting the revised definition of fiduciary,[9] the DOL noted that:

> Plan participants and IRA owners often lack investment expertise and must rely on experts—but are unable to assess the quality of the expert's advice or guard against conflicts of interest. Most have no idea how advisers are compensated for selling them products. Many are bewildered by complex choices that require substantial financial expertise and welcome advice that appears to be free, without knowing that the adviser is compensated through indirect third party payments creating conflicts of interest or that opaque fees over the life of the investment will reduce their returns....Timely regulatory action to redress advisers' conflicts is warranted to avert such losses.[10]

From the DOL's perspective, traditional broker-dealer compensation practices, such as brokerage commissions, revenue sharing payments received from mutual funds and their managers, and mark-ups on bonds sold from their own inventory involve acute conflicts of interest that must be properly managed to ensure the conflicts do not impact the advice provided to retirement investors. In the DOL's words, "[w]hat is presented to an IRA owner as trusted advice is often paid for by a financial product vendor in the form of a sales commission or shelf-space fee, without adequate counter-balancing consumer protections to ensure that the advice is in the investor's best interest."[11]

The DOL's regulatory impact analysis of its final rulemaking concluded that conflicted advice is widespread and causes serious harm to retirement plan and IRA investors. In addition to concluding that the impact of financial institutions' conflicts of interest on retirement investment outcomes is large and negative, the DOL pointed to the asymmetries of information and expertise between ordinary retirement investors and financial institutions as support for its revised rules.

By extending the definition of fiduciary the DOL has sought to mitigate conflicts, including conflicts created by increased profits to financial institutions when investors select certain investment products rather than others or engage in larger or more frequent transactions. The DOL also noted that financial institutions capture price spreads from principal transactions and asserted that compensation arrangements often are calibrated to align their interests with those of their affiliates and product suppliers and thus introduce serious conflicts of interest between firms and retirement investors. In this respect, the DOL asserted that personnel of financial institutions often are paid substantially more if they recommend investments and transactions that are highly

---

[9] Employee Benefits Security Administration, Department of Labor, Definition of the Term "Fiduciary"; Conflict of Interest Rule—Retirement Investment Advice, 81 *Federal Register* 20946 (Apr. 8, 2016).

[10] *Id.* Similarly, the DOL stated that "[m]ost retail investors and many small plan sponsors are not financial experts, are unaware of the magnitude and impact of conflicts of interest, and are unable effectively to assess the quality of the advice they receive."

[11] *Id.*

profitable to their employer, even if they are not in investors' best interests. According to the DOL, these financial incentives sometimes bias the recommendations provided to retirement investors.

The DOL believes that disclosing conflicts alone does not adequately mitigate the conflicts faced by financial institutions. In contrast to the regulatory philosophy espoused by the SEC and FINRA, the DOL believes that:

> Disclosure alone has proven ineffective to mitigate conflicts in advice. Extensive research has demonstrated that most investors have little understanding of their advisers' conflicts of interest and little awareness of what they are paying via indirect channels for the conflicted advice. Even if they understand the scope of the advisers' conflicts, many consumers are not financial experts and, therefore, cannot distinguish good advice or investments from bad. The same gap in expertise that makes investment advice necessary and important frequently also prevents investors from recognizing bad advice or understanding advisers' disclosures. Some research suggests that even if disclosure about conflicts could be made simple and clear, it could be ineffective—or even harmful.[12]

Given the foregoing, and the trust law standards of care and undivided loyalty imposed by ERISA, it is not surprising that the DOL's approach is to "ensure that advice is in consumers' best interest, thereby rooting out excessive fees and substandard performance otherwise attributable to advisers' conflicts."[13] In contrast to the approach under other regulatory schemes, the DOL's approach seeks to "include strong protections calibrated to ensure that adviser conflicts are fully mitigated such that advice is impartial."[14] From the DOL's perspective:

> The statutory definition and associated fiduciary responsibilities were enacted to ensure that plans can depend on persons who provide investment advice for a fee to make recommendations that are prudent, loyal, and untainted by conflicts of interest....When Congress enacted ERISA in 1974, it made a judgment that plan advisers should be subject to ERISA's fiduciary regime and that plan participants, beneficiaries, and IRA owners should be protected from conflicted transactions by the prohibited transaction rules.[15]

---

[12] *Id*. The DOL went on to say that "In addition to problems with the effectiveness of such disclosures, the possibility of inconsistent oral representations raises questions about whether any boilerplate written disclosure could ensure that the person's financial interest in the transaction is effectively communicated as being in conflict with the interests of the advice recipient....A disclosure regime, standing alone, would not obviate conflicts of interest in investment advice even if it were possible to flawlessly disclose complex fee and investment structures."

[13] *Id*.

[14] *Id*.

[15] *Id*. The DOL added that "ERISA and the Code place special emphasis on the elimination or mitigation of conflicts of interest and adherence to substantive standards of conduct, as reflected in the prohibited transaction rules and ERISA's standards of fiduciary conduct."

In sum, ERISA and the tax code are skeptical of the dangers posed by conflicts of interest and generally prohibit conflicted advice.

The Best Interest Contract Exemption. Simultaneous with the DOL's expanded definition of "fiduciary" it also published a new exemption—the "best interest contract exemption" (BICE)[16]—which permits, subject to appropriate safeguards, broker-dealers, insurance agents, and others that act as investment advice fiduciaries to receive a variety of forms of compensation that would otherwise violate prohibited transaction rules and trigger excise taxes.[17] The BICE is designed to address conflicts of interest associated with a wide variety of payments broker-dealers, insurance agents and others receive in connection with retail transactions involving plans and IRAs. The DOL's approach to conflicts of interest is perhaps best illustrated through its design of this prohibited transaction exemption. In order to protect the interests of the plan participants and beneficiaries, and IRA owners, the exemption requires financial institutions to take a number of steps, including:

- Acknowledging fiduciary status for itself and its personnel with respect to the investment advice to the retirement investor.
- Adhering to enforceable "impartial conduct standards" of fiduciary conduct and fair dealing with respect to such advice, including:[18]
  - Providing advice that is in the customer's "best interest" (i.e., investment advice that reflects the care, skill, prudence, and diligence under the circumstances then prevailing that a prudent person acting in a like capacity and familiar with such matters would use in the conduct of an enterprise of a like character and with like aims, based on the investment objectives, risk tolerance, financial circumstances, and needs of the retirement investor, *without regard to* the financial or other interests of the financial institution, its personnel, or any affiliate, related entity, or other party),

---

[16] Employee Benefits Security Administration, Department of Labor, Best Interest Contract Exemption, 81 *Federal Register* 21002 (Apr. 8, 2016) ("BICE Release").

[17] A fiduciary's receipt of commissions, sales loads, 12b-1 fees, revenue sharing and other payments from third parties that offer investment products would generally violate the prohibited transaction provisions of ERISA Section 406(b) and Code Sec. 4975(c)(1)(E) and (F) because the amount of the fiduciary's compensation is affected by its investment advice.

[18] In the case of IRAs and non-ERISA plans (e.g., Keogh plans) the exemption requires that the standards be set forth in a contract with the retirement investor. The contract with retirement investors regarding IRAs and non-ERISA plans must include, among other things: the financial institution's acknowledgment of its fiduciary status and that of its personnel; the financial institution's agreement that it and its personnel will adhere to the impartial conduct standards, including a best interest standard; the financial institution's warranty that it has adopted and will comply with anticonflict policies and procedures reasonably and prudently designed to ensure that personnel adhere to the impartial conduct standards; and the financial institution's disclosure of information about its services and applicable fees and compensation. The written contract requirement does not apply to advice to retirement investors regarding investments in plans that are covered by ERISA plans in light of the existing statutory framework, which provides a preexisting enforcement mechanism for these investors.

- – Avoiding misleading statements,[19]
- – Receiving no more than reasonable compensation;[20]

- Implementing policies and procedures reasonably and prudently designed to prevent violation of the impartial conduct standards and to mitigate any harmful impact of conflicts of interest;
- Refraining from giving or using incentives for financial institutions personnel to act contrary to the customer's best interest; and
- Fairly disclosing the fees, compensation, and material conflicts of interest (defined later) associated with the recommendations.

By complying with the relevant conditions, the BICE permits financial institutions and their personnel to receive commissions and other common forms of compensation, provided appropriate safeguards against the harmful impact of conflicts of interest on investment advice are implemented. The exemption strives to ensure that financial institutions' recommendations reflect the best interest of their retirement investor customers,[21] rather than the conflicting financial interests of the financial institutions and their personnel.

"Without Regard to." The phrase "without regard to" on the prior page is an expression of ERISA's duty of loyalty and is based on longstanding concepts derived from ERISA and the law of trusts. This standard is meant to express the concept, set forth in ERISA Section 404, that a fiduciary is required to act "solely in the interest of the participants…with the care, skill, prudence, and diligence under the circumstances then prevailing that a prudent man acting in a like capacity and familiar with such matters would use in the conduct of an enterprise of a like character and with like aims." ERISA Section 404(a)(1)(A) requires fiduciaries to put the interests of beneficiaries first, without regard to the fiduciaries' own self-interest. The phrase "without regard to" is intended to incorporate the objective standards of care and undivided loyalty that have been applied under this statutory provision.

Under these objective standards, financial institutions must adhere to a professional standard of care in making investment recommendations that are in the retirement

---

[19] In particular, the rule provides that statements by the financial institution and its personnel about the recommended transactions, fees and compensation, material conflicts of interest, and any other matters relevant to a retirement investor's investment decisions, may not be materially misleading at the time they are made.

[20] This standard requires that compensation not be excessive, as measured by the market value of the particular services, rights, and benefits the financial institution is delivering to the retirement investor. The DOL noted in the adopting release for the BICE that the reasonableness of the fees depends on the particular facts and circumstances at the time of the recommendation. Several factors inform whether compensation is reasonable including, *inter alia,* the market pricing of services provided and the underlying assets, the scope of monitoring, and the complexity of the product. No single factor is dispositive in determining whether compensation is reasonable; the essential question is whether the charges are reasonable in relation to what the investor receives.

[21] Protected retirement investors include plan participants and beneficiaries, IRA owners, and "retail" fiduciaries of plans or IRAs (generally persons who hold or manage less than $50 million in assets, or are not banks, insurance carriers, registered investment advisers, or broker-dealers), including small plan sponsors.

investor's best interest. The financial institution and its personnel may not base recommendations on their own financial interest in the transaction. Nor may they recommend an investment that does not meet the objective prudent person standard of care. Importantly, and unlike the regulatory regimes administered by the SEC or FINRA, full disclosure of a conflict of interest is insufficient.[22]

Anticonflict Policies and Procedures. One BICE condition requires a financial institution to adopt and comply with anticonflict policies and procedures and to insulate the institution's personnel from incentives to violate the best interest standard. To be within the exemption, the financial institution must oversee the recommendations made by its personnel and prepare a written document describing its policies and procedures.[23] The document must accurately describe or summarize key components of its policies and procedures relating to conflict-mitigation and incentive practices in a manner that permits retirement investors to make an informed judgment about the stringency of the financial institution's protections against conflicts of interest.

The required policies and procedures have several components:

- The financial institution must adopt and comply with written policies and procedures reasonably and prudently designed to ensure that its personnel adhere to the impartial conduct standards;
- In formulating its policies and procedures, the financial institution must specifically identify and document its "material conflicts of interest" and adopt measures reasonably and prudently designed to prevent the material conflicts of interest from causing violations of the impartial conduct standards[24]; and
- The financial institution must designate one or more people (by name, title or function) responsible for addressing material conflicts of interest and monitoring its personnel's adherence to the impartial conduct standards.

A "material conflict of interest" exists when a financial institution or its personnel have a financial interest that a reasonable person would conclude could affect the exercise of its best judgment as a fiduciary in rendering advice to a retirement investor.

The financial institution's policies and procedures also must require that neither the institution nor (to the best of its knowledge) its affiliates or related entities use or rely on quotas, appraisals; performance or personnel actions, bonuses, contests, special

---

[22] *Donovan v. Bierwirth,* 680 F.2d 263, 271 (2d Cir. 1982) ("the decisions [of the fiduciary] must be made with an eye single to the interests of the participants and beneficiaries") *see also Bussian v. RJR Nabisco, Inc.,* 223 F.3d 286, 298 (5th Cir. 2000); *Leigh v. Engle,* 727 F.2d 113, 126 (7th Cir. 1984).

[23] The financial institution also must make copies of the document available to retirement investors, free of charge, upon request, and put a copy of the document on the financial institution's website.

[24] The DOL noted in the adopting release for the BICE that the aim of the policies and procedures requirement is to require financial institutions to take prophylactic measures to ensure that their personnel adhere to the impartial conduct standards. The exemption does not specify the precise content of the anticonflict policies and procedures, but rather sets out overarching standards for assessing their adequacy. This flexibility is intended to allow financial institutions to develop policies and procedures that are effective for their particular business models.

awards, differential compensation, or other actions or incentives that are intended, or would reasonably be expected, to cause its personnel to make recommendations that are not in the best interest of a retirement investor. This requirement does not prevent a financial institution from providing its personnel with differential compensation based on the investments purchased if the financial institution's policies and procedures and incentive practices, when viewed as a whole, are reasonably and prudently designed to avoid a misalignment of the interests of its personnel with the interests of the retirement investors.[25]

The DOL noted that the exemption's goal is not to wring out every potential conflict, no matter how slight, but rather to ensure that financial institutions and their personnel "put retirement investors' interests first, take care to minimize incentives to act contrary to investors' interests, and carefully police those conflicts that remain."[26]

The DOL believes that the anticonflict policies and procedures safeguard the interests of retirement investors by requiring financial institutions to consider the conflicts of interest affecting the advice provided to such investors, take concrete steps to mitigate the impact of the conflicts, and ensure financial institutions' personnel adhere to the impartial conduct standards. The DOL expects financial institutions to identify material conflicts of interest applicable to their provision of investment advice and to reasonably and prudently design policies and procedures to prevent those particular conflicts from causing violations of the impartial conduct standards. The extent and contours of the policies and procedures will depend on the types of and pervasiveness of the conflicts in a financial institution's business. In the adopting release for the BICE the DOL advised financial institutions to carefully focus on the particular aspects of their business model that potentially create misaligned incentives.[27]

Types of Required Disclosures. Although the exemption does not primarily rely on disclosure as a means of protection, the DOL notes that "disclosure can serve a salutary purpose in the right circumstances and is critical to obtaining the

[25] The BICE permits differential compensation based on neutral factors tied to differences in the services delivered to an investor with respect to the different types of investments. However, differential compensation based on the differences in the amounts of third party payments paid to the financial institution in connection with investment recommendations is not permitted. Thus, differential compensation is permitted only if (1) it is subject to policies and procedures "reasonably and prudently designed to prevent material conflicts of interest from causing violations of the impartial conduct standards" and (2) differentials are not intended and would not reasonably be expected to cause personnel to make recommendations that are not in the best interest of the retirement investor. Differential compensation between categories of investments could be permissible if the compensation structure and lines between categories were drawn based on neutral factors that were not tied to the financial institution's conflicts of interest, such as the time or complexity of the advisory work.

[26] BICE Release.

[27] With respect to retirement investors in IRAs and non-ERISA plans, the financial institution must warrant in its contract with such investors that it has adopted and will comply with the anticonflict policies and procedures (including the obligation to avoid misaligned incentives). The warranty, and the potential liability associated with that warranty, impose the obligation on financial institutions and give them an incentive to prevent harmful conflicts of interest and to protect retirement investors from misaligned incentives that encourage violations of the Best Interest standard. The warranty also ensures that there is a means to redress any failure to do so.

[r]etirement [i]nvestor's knowing assent to the conflicted advisory relationship."[28] The BICE requires extensive disclosure of material conflicts of interest and the advisory relationship in the form of contract disclosures, point-of-sale disclosures and web-based disclosures. These disclosures are intended to ensure that the retirement investor is fairly informed of the financial institution's conflicts of interest and those of its personnel.

With respect to the disclosure required in the contract,[29] the financial institution must clearly and prominently, in a single written disclosure:

- State the best interest standard of care owed by the financial institution and its personnel to the retirement investor; inform the retirement investor of the services provided by the financial institution and its personnel; and describe how the retirement investor will pay for services (e.g., that the retirement investor will pay commissions or other forms of transaction-based payments);
- Describe material conflicts of interest, disclose any fees or charges the financial institution, its affiliates, or its personnel imposes and state the types of compensation that the financial institution, its affiliates, and its personnel expect to receive from third parties in connection with investments recommended to retirement investors;
- Inform the retirement investor that the investor has the right to obtain copies of the financial institution's written description of its conflicts policies and procedures adopted in accordance with the requirements previously described, as well as specific disclosure of costs, fees, and compensation, including third-party payments regarding recommended transactions, in dollar amounts, percentages, formulas, or other means reasonably designed to present materially accurate disclosure of their scope, magnitude, and nature in sufficient detail to permit the retirement investor to make an informed judgment about the costs of the transaction and about the significance and severity of the material conflicts of interest, and describe how the retirement investor can get the information, free of charge;
- Include a link to the financial institution's website containing more detailed disclosures and inform the retirement investor that
  - The model contract disclosures are updated and are maintained on the website, and
  - The financial institution's written description of its conflict policies and procedures (described above) are available free of charge on the website; and
- Disclose to the retirement investor whether the financial institution offers proprietary products or receives third-party payments with respect to any recommended transaction. If the financial institution limits investment recommendations, in whole or part, to proprietary products or investments that generate third-party payments, it must disclose the limitations placed on the universe of investments that it may offer. The institution also must provide specific disclosure of the extent to which recommendations are, in fact, limited on that basis.

---

[28] BICE Release.

[29] *See* the earlier explanation of when a contract with retirement investors is required.

A subset of the foregoing information is required to be provided to retirement investors prior to or at the same time as the execution of a recommended transaction. The BICE also requires financial institutions to disclose on their websites other information including:

- A description of the financial institution's business model and the material conflicts of interest associated with that business model;
- A schedule of typical account or contract fees and service charges; and
- A model contract with the disclosures described above; a description or summary of the key components of the institution's policies and procedures relating to conflict-mitigation and incentive practices in enough detail that permits retirement investors to make an informed judgment about the stringency of the institution's protections against conflicts of interest.

To the extent applicable, each financial institution must also:

- List all product manufacturers and other parties with whom the financial institution maintains arrangements that provide third party payments to the financial institution or its personnel;
- Describe the arrangements, including a statement on whether and how these arrangements impact personnel compensation; and
- Provide a statement on any benefits the financial institution provides to the product manufacturers or other parties in exchange for the third party payments.

In addition, all financial institutions must disclose their compensation and incentive arrangements with their personnel including, if applicable, any incentives (including both cash and noncash compensation or awards) to such personnel for recommending particular product manufacturers, investments or categories of investments to retirement investors, or for personnel to move to the financial institution from another firm or to stay at the financial institution, and a full and fair description of any payout or compensation grids.

Importantly, the DOL makes clear that the website must fairly disclose the scope, magnitude, and nature of compensation arrangements and material conflicts of interest in sufficient detail to permit visitors to the website to make an informed judgment about the significance of the institution's compensation practices and material conflicts of interest associated with its recommendations.

Proprietary Products and Third-Party Payments. If a financial institution restricts its investment recommendations, in whole or in part, to investments that are proprietary products (products that are managed, issued, or sponsored by the financial institution or an affiliate) or that generate third-party payments[30] it must meet additional conditions in order to fall within the BICE. In particular, the financial institution must:

[30] Third-party payments include sales charges that are not paid directly by the plan, participant or beneficiary account, or IRA; gross dealer concessions; revenue sharing payments; 12b-1 fees, distribution, solicitation, or referral fees; volume-based fees; fees for seminars and educational programs; and any other compensation, consideration, or financial benefit provided to the financial institution or an affiliate or related entity by a third party as a result of a transaction involving a plan, participant or beneficiary account, or IRA.

- Document in writing its limitations on the universe of recommended investments;
- Document in writing the material conflicts of interest associated with an arrangement where it receives third-party payments or involving the offer or sale of proprietary products;
- Document any services it will provide to retirement investors in exchange for third-party payments, as well as any services or consideration it will furnish to any other party, including the payor, in exchange for the third-party payments;
- Reasonably conclude that the limitations on the universe of recommended investments and material conflicts of interest will not cause the financial institution or its personnel to receive compensation in excess of reasonable compensation;
- Reasonably determine, after consideration of its policies and procedures, that these limitations and material conflicts of interest will not cause the financial institution or its personnel to recommend imprudent investments; and
- Document the bases for its conclusions.

In addition to the foregoing, all recommendations by personnel of a financial institution involving the sale of proprietary products or the receipt of third-party payments:

- Must reflect the care, skill, prudence, and diligence under the circumstances then prevailing that a prudent person acting in a like capacity and familiar with such matters would use in the conduct of an enterprise of a like character and with like aims, based on the investment objectives, risk tolerance, financial circumstances, and needs of the retirement investor; and
- May *not* be based on their financial or other interests or on their consideration of any factors or interests other than the investment objectives, risk tolerance, financial circumstances, and needs of the retirement investor. In describing this requirement, the DOL stated that it requires "insulation of the [personnel of the financial institution] from conflicts of interest when making recommendations from the restricted menu."[31]

These conditions reflect the DOL's "deep and continuing concern regarding the [f]inancial [i]nstitutions' own conflicts of interest in limiting products available for investment recommendations. The purpose…is to require [f]inancial [i]nstitutions to carefully consider their business models and form a reasonable conclusion about the impact of conflicts of interest associated with these particular limitations on [the personnel's] advice. The exemption will be available only if the [f]inancial [i]nstitution reasonably concludes that these limitations, in conjunction with the anticonflict policies and procedures, will not result in advice that violates the standards set forth in the exemption."

DOL's Conclusion. The DOL's approach to conflicts of interest is illustrated by its view that the impartial conduct standards represent baseline standards of fundamental fair dealing that must be met when fiduciaries make conflicted investment recommendations

---

[31] BICE Release.

to retirement investors. The DOL concluded that broad relief from ERISA's and the tax code's prohibited transaction provisions should be provided to investment advice fiduciaries receiving conflicted compensation *only if* such fiduciaries provide advice in accordance with the impartial conduct standards. In the view of the DOL, the impartial conduct standards are necessary to ensure that financial institutions' recommendations reflect the best interest of their retirement investor customers, rather than the conflicting financial interests of the financial institutions and their personnel. Financial institutions bear the burden of demonstrating compliance with the exemption and face liability for engaging in a nonexempt prohibited transaction if they fail to provide advice that is prudent or otherwise in violation of the exemption's conditions. The DOL views the threat of liability as an important deterrent to violations of important conditions under an exemption that accommodates a wide variety of what it believes are dangerous compensation practices.[32]

The fiduciary duties under ERISA and the tax code are different from those applicable under the securities laws. In this respect, the DOL notes that ERISA and the tax code prohibit fiduciaries from engaging in transactions involving self-dealing and conflicts of interest unless an exemption applies. It therefore crafted the BICE in accordance with standards that ensure that retirement investors can uniformly expect to receive advice that is in their best interest with respect to their retirement investments. From its perspective, the DOL fashioned an exemption that mitigates conflicts of interest and ensures that financial institutions and their personnel adhere to fundamental fiduciary standards, regardless of their business models and compensation practices.

OCC Regulation of Bank Conflicts

The OCC's *Comptroller's Handbook, Conflicts of Interest*,[33] was prepared for OCC examiners in connection with their examination and supervision of national banks and federal savings associations (FSAs). The handbook explains the risks inherent in conflicts, provides a framework for managing those risks and serves as a useful resource for banks engaged in asset management activities. Banks can use the handbook as a guidepost in evaluating their risk management systems to avoid and manage conflicts of interest[34] that arise from their fiduciary or other asset management activities. In this respect, the Handbook provides a broad overview of the types of conflicts of interest that may occur in banks' asset management activities, the risks associated with such conflicts of interest, and the OCC's expectations for banks' management of these risks. Appendix A of this chapter, which is taken from the handbook, provides a sample OCC conflicts of interest request letter.

---

[32] *Id.*.

[33] OCC, *Comptroller's Handbook, Conflicts of Interest*, https://www.occ.gov/publications/publications-by-type/comptrollers-handbook/conflictofinterest.pdf

[34] The handbook states that conflicts of interest arise whenever a bank engages in self-dealing and in any situation where a bank's ability to act in the best interests of its account beneficiaries or clients is impaired. Self-dealing occurs when a bank, as fiduciary, engages in a transaction with itself or related parties and interests.

Banks must deal with clients fairly and must require ethical behavior from their officers, directors, and employees. Bank fiduciaries have a heightened responsibility to avoid impermissible conflicts of interest and to ensure that they are acting in the best interests of fiduciary accounts. These fiduciaries have a duty of loyalty to account beneficiaries that is rooted in the common law for trusts. The duty of loyalty, which is a fundamental duty owed by a fiduciary to the beneficiaries of a fiduciary account, is the duty of a trustee "to administer the trust solely in the interest of the beneficiaries...[and to not engage] in transactions that involve self-dealing or that otherwise involve or create a conflict between the trustee's fiduciary duties and personal interests...[and] to deal fairly and to communicate to the beneficiary all material facts the trustee knows or should know in connection with the matter."[35]

Bank regulations set forth requirements related to fiduciary activities that might involve conflicts of interest. More specifically, 12 CFR 9.12 (Self-Dealing and Conflicts of Interest) and 12 CFR 150.330-150.370 (Restrictions on Self-Dealing), which govern the fiduciary activities of national banks and FSAs, respectively,[36] specify certain investments and transactions that are not generally permissible for bank fiduciaries that exercise investment discretion. 12 CFR 9.5 (Policies and Procedures) and 12 CFR 150.140 (Exercising Fiduciary Powers) require that national banks and FSAs, respectively, adopt and follow policies and procedures adequate to maintain their fiduciary activities in compliance with applicable law, including, where appropriate:

- Brokerage placement practices (12 CFR 9.5(a) and 12 CFR 150.140(a));
- Methods for ensuring that fiduciary officers and employees do not use material inside information in connection with any decision or recommendation to purchase or sell any security (12 CFR 9.5(b) and 12 CFR 150.140(b)); and
- Methods for preventing self-dealing and conflicts of interest (12 CFR 9.5(c) and 12 CFR 150.140(c)).

In addition, 12 CFR 12.7 and 12 CFR 151.140 (Securities Trading Policies and Procedures) also require that national banks and FSAs, respectively, adopt certain securities trading policies and procedures, including several relating to potential conflicts of interest between accounts or between bank employees and accounts. The objective of these required policies is to prevent banks and related parties from engaging in impermissible conflicts of interest.

Self-Dealing Between Related Parties and Interests and Fiduciary Accounts. Certain bank conflicts of interest are prohibited under all circumstances; others are permitted subject to certain conditions and proper oversight by bank management. Transactions

[35] *Comptroller's Handbook,* citing Restatement (Third) of Trusts section 78.

[36] *See also* 12 CFR 150.380-150.400 (Compensation, Gifts, and Bequests).

between related parties and interests[37] of a bank fiduciary and its fiduciary accounts represent self-dealing and are prohibited except under very limited circumstances. In particular, the following generally are not permitted in fiduciary accounts for which a bank has investment discretion:

- Investing in stocks or obligations of companies owned or controlled by related parties and interests;
- Investing in assets of, or acquired from, related parties and interests; and
- Lending, selling, or otherwise transferring assets to related parties and interests.

In addition, 12 USC 92a(h) and 12 USC 1464(n)(7) generally prohibit national banks and FSAs, respectively, from lending funds held in trust to any officer, director, or employee. Penalties against the individuals making or receiving such loans may include fines, imprisonment, and removal from banking. The bank may also be subject to OCC administrative sanctions, including civil money penalties.

Under 12 CFR 9.5(c) and 12 CFR 150.140(c), national banks and FSAs, respectively, must adopt and follow policies and procedures to ensure that dealings between related parties and interests and fiduciary accounts are identified, monitored, and appropriately restricted. Appropriate internal controls and risk management practices must be in place to identify, in advance, transactions that would pose a conflict of interest, and to prevent those that would not comply with applicable laws, regulations, or internal policies. Banks are also expected to have appropriate risk management processes in place that include an initial analysis to ensure that such activities are properly authorized and consistent with the bank's fiduciary obligations. The handbook comments that such processes should include ongoing monitoring to ensure that the bank identifies, analyzes, and appropriately reacts to relevant changes in circumstances. It also observes that a bank's risk management processes should require that exceptions to bank policy are identified and escalated to a designated committee of the board of directors responsible for fiduciary oversight or a designated senior manager for resolution or approval.

Using Affiliated Service Providers. A bank is permitted to use affiliates' personnel and facilities to perform services related to the exercise of its fiduciary powers, such as investment management, unless prohibited by applicable law. Such delegated activities remain subject to oversight by the bank's board of directors, and to oversight responsibilities in accordance with OCC guidance on service provider oversight.[38] The handbook notes that the level of oversight must be sufficient to ensure that the bank is properly fulfilling its fiduciary responsibilities. Among other things, compensation to affiliates

---

[37] "Related parties and interests" refers to persons and organizations covered by the self-dealing restrictions contained in 12 CFR 9.12 and 12 CFR 150.330, applicable to national banks and FSAs, respectively. Related parties and interests include the bank or any of the bank's directors, officers, or employees, affiliates of the bank or any of the affiliates' directors, officers, or employees, and any individual or organization with whom or which there exists an interest that might affect the exercise of a bank fiduciary's best judgment. The term "affiliate" would include firm subsidiaries in which the firm has more than a 50 percent ownership interest. *See* 12 CFR 9.2(a) and 12 CFR 150.60; *see also* 12 USC 221a(b).

[38] *See* OCC Bulletin 2013-29, "Third-Party Relationships: Risk Management Guidance." *See also* Frequently Asked Questions to Supplement OCC Bulletin 2013-29, located at https://www.occ.treas.gov/news-issuances/bulletins/2017/bulletin-2017-21.html.

for services they provide must be based on market terms in accordance with the Board of Governors of the Federal Reserve System's Regulation W.[39]

Importantly, bank fiduciaries are not permitted to receive financial benefits from related parties and interests in exchange for delegating fiduciary activities or purchasing products to support the servicing of fiduciary accounts, unless the financial benefit is authorized by applicable law, the financial benefit is disclosed in accordance with applicable law, and the decision to delegate to such parties is based on the best interests of the account.

More generally, banks that purchase services from, or engage in business transactions with, related parties and interests on behalf of fiduciary accounts are engaging in self-dealing and have a conflict of interest. Such conflicts of interest are permissible only if:

- They are explicitly authorized by applicable law;
- They are properly disclosed in accordance with applicable law;
- Fees charged for the services are reasonable; and
- Service provider selection is based on the best interest of the account.

Bank fiduciaries may allocate brokerage business to affiliated broker-dealers if not prohibited by applicable law. Unless the use of the affiliated broker-dealer is explicitly authorized under applicable law, however, the brokerage services must be provided on a not-for-profit basis. In either case, a bank is required to obtain best execution for its fiduciary clients.

Investment in Proprietary Products. Bank fiduciaries with investment discretion are required to make decisions concerning the investment of fiduciary assets based exclusively on the best interests of the fiduciary account. The selection of investment products offered or sponsored by a bank fiduciary or an affiliate for which the bank or affiliate receives compensation represents a conflict of interest because the revenue generated by such products may affect the fiduciary's judgment when deciding how to invest fiduciary funds. The handbook provides that bank fiduciaries with investment discretion should have processes in place to:

- Identify potential conflicts of interest related to proprietary investment products;
- Ensure that the use of proprietary investment products is authorized by applicable law and disclosed in accordance with applicable law; and
- Ensure that such products are prudent investments for each account.

Dealings with Third Parties That Result in Financial Benefits to Related Parties and Interests. Under the principles of 12 CFR 9.12(a) and 12 CFR 150.330, applicable to national banks and FSAs, respectively, the OCC takes the position in the handbook that a bank generally is not permitted to accept any financial benefits directly or indirectly conditioned on the investment of discretionary assets in a particular investment. This prohibition includes arrangements in which a bank fiduciary receives direct or indirect

[39] 12 CFR 223, "Transactions Between Member Banks and Their Affiliates (Regulation W)."

compensation from parties to whom the bank has delegated fiduciary activities, such as investment management, or to whom the bank has allocated fiduciary brokerage business. Such arrangements could affect the bank's exercise of judgment and therefore are permitted only if:

- Authorized by applicable law;
- Disclosed in accordance with applicable law;
- Consistent with safe and sound banking practices;
- Subject to appropriate initial and ongoing due diligence and oversight; and
- The resulting investments are appropriate for each account and consistent with applicable law.

The handbook cautions that such arrangements should be reviewed by legal counsel and approved by the committee of the board of directors responsible for fiduciary oversight before entering into such arrangements. It also provides that these arrangements should be reviewed periodically to ensure that they are properly authorized under applicable law, disclosed in accordance with applicable law, and do not impair the bank's ability to properly exercise its fiduciary duties.

If permitted by applicable state law, a bank fiduciary may enter into a transaction presenting an otherwise impermissible conflict of interest based on the proper and informed consent of all beneficiaries if the transaction is fair and executed in the beneficiaries' best interest. State law may require that, to obtain proper consent, a bank must fully and completely disclose to the beneficiaries the facts about the conflict. The handbook counsels obtaining an opinion of counsel regarding the permissibility of, and requirements for, such consent under applicable law before relying on beneficiary consent to authorize an otherwise impermissible conflict of interest.[40]

OCC fiduciary regulations permit sales between fiduciary accounts and loans between fiduciary accounts if the transactions are fair to both accounts and not prohibited by applicable law.[41] For securities transactions in fiduciary, agency, and custody accounts, OCC regulations[42] require that banks maintain and adhere to policies and procedures that provide for the crossing of buy and sell transactions on a fair and equitable basis for the parties to the transaction, provided such transactions are permissible under applicable law. OCC regulations[43] also require that a bank maintain and adhere to policies and procedures that provide for the fair and equitable allocation of securities and prices to accounts when the bank receives orders for the same security at approximately the same time. These policies and procedures should provide for fair and equitable allocation, whether the bank places the orders for execution individually or in combination (for block trades).

---

[40] The handbook also notes that in some cases, the best course of action may be to obtain a court order authorizing the conflict of interest in question. The OCC further recommends that where there is an ambiguity, the bank should evaluate the risks involved, and management should obtain approval for the transaction in question from the committee of the bank's board of directors responsible for fiduciary oversight.

[41] 12 CFR 9.12(d)-(e) and 12 CFR 150.370 (national banks and FSAs, respectively).

[42] 12 CFR 12.7(a)(3) and 12 CFR 151.140(c) (national banks and FSAs, respectively).

[43] 12 CFR 12.7(a)(2) and 12 CFR 151.140(b) (national banks and FSAs, respectively).

Employee Conduct. The handbook affirms that banks engaged in fiduciary and other asset management activities should implement policies, procedures, and corresponding internal controls to prevent employees from improperly benefiting from their association with the bank's fiduciary and other asset management activities. In this respect:

- Transactions between fiduciary accounts and related parties and interests are prohibited by OCC regulations except in limited situations, as noted above;
- Under 12 CFR 9.15(b) and 12 CFR 150.390, for national banks and FSAs, respectively, both types of institutions are prohibited from allowing officers and employees to retain compensation for acting as a cofiduciary with the bank in the administration of a fiduciary account, unless specifically approved by the board of directors;
- It is impermissible in most circumstances for a fiduciary officer or employee to accept gifts or bequests of fiduciary assets. For instance, 12 CFR 150.400 prohibits FSAs from allowing such gifts unless the bequest or gift is directed or made by a relative of the officer or employee, or is specifically approved by the bank's board of directors. The handbook states that it expects national banks to also adhere to this fiduciary standard; and
- When national banks and FSAs evaluate compensation plans for employees, they should consider the potential impact on employee behavior and avoid provisions that might cause employees to act other than in the best interest of clients.

The handbook provides that a bank's corporate governance processes should comprehensively address conflicts of interest with respect to its administration of fiduciary and other asset management accounts. Among other provisions, the handbook states that the board of directors should adopt strong written policies that closely govern the relationship between related parties and interests and fiduciary accounts, and should ensure that management implements a process to monitor and validate compliance with these policies. In addition, the handbook counsels that a bank's policies and procedures establish management's expectations for employee behavior and observes that effective processes and controls should be in place to alert management to improper employee conduct.

SEC Regulation of Investment Adviser Conflicts

The Supreme Court has construed the antifraud provisions of Sections 206(1) and (2) of the Advisers Act as establishing a federal fiduciary standard governing the conduct of investment advisers.[44] Accordingly, under the Advisers Act, investment advisers are fiduciaries.[45] Fundamental to the federal fiduciary standard are the duties of loyalty and care.[46] The duty of loyalty requires an adviser to serve the best interests of its clients. This includes an obligation to provide investment advice that

---

[44] *Capital Gains. See also Transamerica Mortgage Advisors, Inc.*, 444 U.S. 11, 17 (1979) ("[T]he Act's legislative history leaves no doubt that Congress intended to impose enforceable fiduciary obligations.").

[45] *See* Capital Gains, at 191-192.

[46] *See, e.g., Proxy Voting by Investment Advisers,* Investment Advisers Act Rel. No. 2106 (Jan. 31, 2003).

is in clients' best interests and not to subordinate clients' interests to its own.[47] An adviser's duty of care requires it to "make a reasonable investigation to determine that it is not basing its recommendations on materially inaccurate or incomplete information."[48] The SEC, its staff, and the courts have provided guidance on these duties over time through rules, interpretive statements, and orders issued in enforcement actions. This guidance has addressed, among other topics, disclosure of conflicts of interest, suitability, having a reasonable basis for investment advice, and principal trading and cross trading.

The SEC staff has stated that as a fiduciary, an adviser must avoid conflicts of interest with clients and is prohibited from overreaching or taking unfair advantage of a client's trust. A fiduciary owes its clients more than mere honesty and good faith. A fiduciary must be sensitive to the conscious and unconscious possibility of providing less than disinterested advice, and it may be faulted even when it does not intend to injure a client and even if the client does not suffer a monetary loss.[49] The fiduciary duty is imposed by operation of law because of the nature of the relationship between the two parties[50] and is made enforceable by the antifraud provisions in Section 206 of the Advisers Act.

Disclosure of Conflicts of Interest. The fiduciary standard applies to the investment adviser's entire relationship with its clients and prospective clients, imposes upon investment advisers an "affirmative duty of 'utmost good faith, and full and fair disclosure of all material facts,' as well as an affirmative obligation to 'employ reasonable care to avoid misleading'" clients and prospective clients.[51] Accordingly, the duty of an investment adviser to refrain from fraudulent conduct includes an obligation to disclose material facts to its clients when failure to do so would defraud or operate as a fraud or deceit upon a client.[52] As a general matter, the SEC has stated that an adviser must disclose all material facts regarding each conflict so that the client can make an informed decision whether to enter into or continue an advisory relationship with the adviser, or take some action to protect himself or herself against the conflict.[53]

As part of its fiduciary duty, an investment adviser must fully disclose to its clients all material information that is intended "to eliminate, or at least expose, all conflicts of interest which might incline an investment adviser—consciously or unconsciously—to render advice which was not disinterested."[54] Over the years, the SEC has brought

---

[47] *Id. See also Amendments to Form ADV,* Investment Advisers Act Rel. No. 3060 (July 28, 2010) ("Release IA-3060").

[48] *See Concept Release on the U.S. Proxy System,* Investment Advisers Act Rel. No. 3052 at 119 (July 14, 2010).

[49] *Regulation of Investment Advisers by the U.S. Securities and Exchange Commission* (March 2013), https://www.sec.gov/about/offices/oia/oia_investman/rplaze-042012.pdf (citing *Capital Gains*).

[50] *See In the Matter of Arlene W. Hughes,* Exchange Act Rel. No. 4048 (Feb. 18, 1948).

[51] *Id; See also Capital Gains.*

[52] *Id.*

[53] Release IA-3060 ("the disclosure clients and prospective clients receive is critical to their ability to make an informed decision about whether to engage an adviser and, having engaged the adviser, to manage that relationship").

[54] *Capital Gains.*

many enforcement actions against advisers that failed to disclose or failed to adequately disclose conflicts of interest. Many advisers may not realize that an adviser's fiduciary duty of disclosure is broad and that delivery of the adviser's Form ADV brochure may not fully satisfy the adviser's disclosure obligations. In this respect, General Instruction 3 to Part 2 of Form ADV provides as follows:

> Under federal and state law, you are a fiduciary and must make full disclosure to your clients of all material facts relating to the advisory relationship. As a fiduciary, you also must seek to avoid conflicts of interest with your clients, and, at a minimum, make full disclosure of all material conflicts of interest between you and your clients that could affect the advisory relationship. This obligation requires that you provide the client with sufficiently specific facts so that the client is able to understand the conflicts of interest you have and the business practices in which you engage, and can give informed consent to such conflicts or practices or reject them. To satisfy this obligation, you therefore may have to disclose to clients information not specifically required by Part 2 of Form ADV or in more detail than the brochure items might otherwise require.

The duty to disclose material facts applies to conflicts of interest—or potential conflicts of interest—that arise during an adviser's relationship with a client. The type of required disclosure will depend on the facts and circumstances but, as noted, an adviser must disclose all material facts regarding a conflict so that the client can make an informed decision whether to enter into or continue an advisory relationship with the adviser. For example, if an adviser selects or recommends other advisers for clients, it must disclose any compensation arrangements or other business relationships between the advisers, along with the conflicts created, and explain how it addresses these conflicts.[55] The SEC has brought many enforcement actions against investment advisers in connection with their failure to disclose such practices as inequitably allocating profitable trades to clients, failing to seek best execution when placing orders with a broker-dealer that provides economic benefits to the adviser, and investing in securities of companies in which the adviser or an affiliate has a financial interest.

In summarizing an adviser's fiduciary obligations, the SEC staff has said that an adviser's fiduciary duty means that:

> You owe your clients a duty of undivided loyalty and utmost good faith. You should not engage in any activity in conflict with the interest of any client, and you should take steps reasonably necessary to fulfill your obligations. You must employ reasonable care to avoid misleading clients and you must provide full and fair disclosure of all material facts to your clients and prospective clients. Generally, facts are "material" if a reasonable

---

[55] *See* Item 10 of Form ADV, Part 2A.

> investor would consider them to be important.[56] You must eliminate, or at least disclose, all conflicts of interest that might incline you…to render advice that is not disinterested. If you do not avoid a conflict of interest that could impact the impartiality of your advice, you must make full and frank disclosure of the conflict. You cannot use your clients' assets for your own benefit or the benefit of other clients, at least without client consent. Departure from this fiduciary standard may constitute "fraud" upon your clients (under Section 206 of the Advisers Act).[57]

Principal and Cross Trades. Investment advisers registered with the SEC are restricted by Advisers Act Section 206(3) when entering into principal and agency-cross trades with their clients. Section 206(3) addresses the potential for self-dealing that could arise when an investment adviser acts as principal in transactions with clients, such as through price manipulation or the dumping of unwanted securities into client accounts.[58] Section 206(3) makes it unlawful for an adviser, acting as principal for its own account, knowingly to sell any security to or purchase any security from a client, or acting as broker for a person other than such client, knowingly to effect any sale or purchase of any security for the account of such client, without disclosing to such client in writing before the completion of such transaction the capacity in which he is acting and obtaining the consent of the client to the transaction.[59]

The SEC staff has taken the position that the adviser must disclose the capacity in which the adviser is acting and any compensation the adviser receives for its role in such a transaction.[60] The adviser must provide sufficient disclosure for a client to make an informed decision and provide the opportunity for the client to withhold consent. Written disclosure must be provided and consent must be obtained separately for each principal transaction, i.e., blanket consent for principal transactions is insufficient.[61]

Compliance with the disclosure and consent provisions of Section 206(3) does not, by itself, satisfy an adviser's fiduciary obligations with respect to a principal trade. The

---

[56] Economic conflicts of interest, such as undisclosed compensation, are material facts that must be disclosed by investment advisers. *IMS/CPAs & Assocs.*, Exchange Act Rel. No. 45019, at 8 (Nov. 5, 2001)) (recognizing that a "fact is material if there is a substantial likelihood that a reasonable investor would consider it important in making an investment decision"), aff'd sub nom., *Vernazza v. SEC*, 327 F.3d 851 (9th Cir. 2003); accord Capital Gains Research Bureau, Inc., 375 U.S. at 200-201.

[57] "Information for Newly-Registered Investment Advisers," https://www.sec.gov/divisions/investment/advoverview.htm

[58] *See* Investment Trusts and Investment Companies: Hearings on S. 3580 Before the Subcomm. of the Comm. on Banking and Currency, 76th Cong., 3d Sess. 320-22 (1940).

[59] The SEC has applied Section 206(3) not only to principal transactions engaged in or effected by an adviser, but also when an adviser causes a client to enter into a principal transaction that is effected by a broker-dealer that controls, is controlled by, or is under common control with, the adviser. *See Interpretation of Section 206(3) of the Advisers Act of 1940*, Investment Advisers Act Rel. No. 1732, at n.3 (July 17, 1998) ("Release 1732").

[60] *Id.; see also Opinion of Director of Trading and Exchange Division,* Investment Advisers Act Rel. No. 40 (Feb. 5, 1945).

[61] *Id.*

SEC has stated that Section 206(3) must be read together with Advisers Act Sections 206(1) and (2) to require that the adviser disclose additional facts necessary to alert the client to the adviser's potential conflict of interest in the principal trade. In addition, the adviser's fiduciary duties are not discharged by such disclosure and consent. The adviser also must have a reasonable belief that the entry of the client into the transaction is in the client's interest.[62]

The SEC has adopted less rigorous requirements for engaging in agency-cross trades (i.e., where the adviser is also a broker-dealer and executes the client's orders by crossing such orders with orders of nonadvisory clients) by relaxing the prior disclosure and consent requirement for each such trade.[63] Rule 206(3)-2 under the Advisers Act permits agency-cross transactions without requiring the adviser to provide transaction-by-transaction disclosure to the client if, among other requirements:

- The client has executed a written consent after receiving full disclosure of the conflicts involved, which must be renewed each year;
- The adviser provides a written confirmation to the client at or before the completion of each transaction providing, among other things, the source and amount of any remuneration it received;
- The adviser provides the client with an annual summary of all agency cross transactions; and
- The disclosure document and each confirmation conspicuously disclose that consent may be revoked at any time.

The rule does not relieve advisers from the duty to act in the best interests of their clients, including the duty to seek to obtain best price and execution for any transaction.

Effecting cross trades between clients (when a third party broker is used) is not specifically addressed by the Advisers Act, but the SEC has brought enforcement actions against investment advisers alleging that the advisers failed to seek best execution in securities transactions for certain advisory clients because of an undisclosed trading practice involving cross trades between client accounts. Cross trades involve potential conflicts of interest because the adviser could have an incentive to favor one client over another. The adviser's duty of loyalty requires it to act in the best interests of each client. The SEC has brought enforcement actions alleging an adviser's failure to fulfill this obligation.

Code of Ethics and Personal Securities Transactions. Each investment adviser registered with the SEC must adopt a written code of ethics.[64] At a minimum, the adviser's code of ethics must address the following areas:

---

[62] Release 1732. *See also* Rocky Mountain Financial Planning, Inc., SEC No-Action Letter (pub. avail. Feb. 24, 1983).

[63] Release 1732.

[64] Advisers Act Section 204A, and Rule 204A-1 thereunder.

- *Standards of conduct.* The code must set forth a minimum standard of conduct for all supervised persons, which must reflect the adviser's and its supervised persons' fiduciary obligations;
- *Compliance with federal securities laws.* The code must require supervised persons to comply with the federal securities laws;
- *Personal securities transactions.* The code must require each "access person"[65] to report his or her securities holdings at the time that the person becomes an access person and at least once annually thereafter and to make a report at least quarterly of all personal securities transactions in reportable securities to the adviser's chief compliance officer (CCO) or other designated person;
- *Preapproval of certain securities transactions.* The code must require the CCO or other designated person(s) to preapprove investments by access persons in IPOs or limited offerings;
- *Reporting violations.* The code must require all supervised persons to promptly report any violations of the code to the adviser's CCO or other designated person(s); and
- *Distribution and acknowledgment.* The code must require the adviser to provide each supervised person with a copy of the code, and any amendments, and to obtain a written acknowledgment from each supervised person of his or her receipt of a copy of, and any amendments to, the code.

Compliance Programs. Investment advisers registered with the SEC are required by Rule 206(4)-7 under the Advisers Act to adopt and implement written policies and procedures that are reasonably designed to prevent violations of the statute. The SEC has said that it expects these policies and procedures to be designed to prevent, detect, and correct violations of the Advisers Act. Advisers must review those policies and procedures at least annually for their adequacy and the effectiveness of their implementation, and designate a CCO to be responsible for administering the policies and procedures. These policies and procedures are not required to contain designated elements. Rather, investment advisers are expected to analyze their particular individual operations, identify conflicts and other compliance factors that create risks, and then design policies and procedures that address those risks. These policies and procedures should provide for the effective control of the various conflicts created by an adviser's operations.[66]

The Regulation of Broker-Dealer Conflicts

Antifraud Provisions. Broker-dealers that do business with the public generally must become members of FINRA. Under the antifraud provisions of the federal securities laws and FINRA rules relating to just and equitable principles of trade and high standards

---

[65] Rule 204A-1(e)(1) under the Advisers Act defines "access person" generally as a supervised person who has access to nonpublic information regarding clients' securities purchases or sales of securities. If an investment adviser's primary business is providing investment advice, all of the adviser's directors, officers, and partners are presumed to be access persons.

[66] *Compliance Programs of Investment Companies and Investment Advisers,* SEC Rel. No. IA-2204 (Dec. 17, 2003).

of commercial honor, broker-dealers are required to deal fairly with their customers.[67] This fundamental obligation proscribes certain conduct and has been articulated by the SEC, FINRA, and the courts over time through rules, interpretive statements, opinions, and orders issued in enforcement actions.

Broker-dealers are subject to a comprehensive set of statutory, SEC, and FINRA requirements that are designed to promote business conduct that, among other things, protects investors from abusive practices. Section 15(c) of the Securities Exchange Act of 1934, as amended (the Exchange Act) prohibits a broker from effecting any transaction in or inducing or attempting to induce the purchase or sale of any security by means of any manipulative, deceptive, or other fraudulent device or contrivance. Moreover, the federal securities laws and FINRA rules require broker-dealer mark-ups, commissions, and fees for services to be fair and reasonable.[68] The SEC and the courts have held that the antifraud provisions of the federal securities laws require broker-dealers to sell securities at prices reasonably related to the market price.

Generally, under the antifraud provisions, a broker-dealer's duty to disclose material information to its customer is based upon the scope of the relationship with the customer, which depends on the facts and circumstances. When a broker-dealer merely processes a customer's order, but does not recommend securities or solicit customers, the information that the broker-dealer is required to disclose to its customer is narrow, encompassing only the information related to the consummation of the transaction. In such circumstances, the broker-dealer generally does not have to provide information regarding the security or the broker-dealer's economic self-interest in the security.[69]

However, when recommending a security, a broker-dealer may be liable if it does not give honest and complete information. A broker-dealer also may be liable if it does not disclose material adverse facts of which it is aware.[70] For example, in making recommendations, courts have found broker-dealers should have disclosed: acting as a market maker for the recommended security, trading as principal with respect to the recommended security, and revenue sharing with respect to a recommended mutual fund.[71] In addition, Rule 10b-10 under the Exchange Act generally requires a broker-dealer effecting customer transactions in securities to provide written confirmation

---

[67] FINRA Rule 2010 (Standards of Commercial Honor and Principles of Trade) states that a firm "in the conduct of its business, shall observe high standards of commercial honor and just and equitable principles of trade." In addition, FINRA Rule 2020 (Use of Manipulative, Deceptive or Other Fraudulent Devices) provides that no firm "shall effect any transaction in, or induce the purchase or sale of, any security by means of any manipulative, deceptive, or other fraudulent device or contrivance."

[68] A number of FINRA rules address compensation, including: NASD Rule 2440 (Fair Price and Commissions), IM-2440-1 (Mark-Up Policy), IM-2440-2 (Additional Mark-Up Policy For Transactions in Debt Securities, Except Municipal Securities), FINRA Rule 5110 (Underwriting Compensation), FINRA Rule 5250 (Payments for Market-Making), NASD Rule 2830 (Investment Company Securities), FINRA Rules 2310 (Direct Participation Programs), 2320 (Variable Contracts of an Insurance Company) and 5110 (Corporate Financing Rule—Underwriting Terms and Arrangements), and NASD Rule 2830 (Non-Cash Compensation).

[69] *See* SEC, *Commission Staff Study on Investment Advisers and Broker-Dealers,* at 55 (Jan. 2011), https://www.sec.gov/news/studies/2011/913studyfinal.pdf

[70] *Id.*

[71] *Id.*

to the customer of the execution of the transaction, at or before completion of the transaction. The confirmation must disclose, among other requirements, whether the broker-dealer is acting as agent or principal and its compensation, as well as any third party remuneration it received or will receive. This information allows customers to verify the terms of their transactions and provides disclosure on potential conflicts of interest. Exchange Act Rules 15c1-5 and 15c1-6 require a broker-dealer to disclose in writing to the customer if it has any control, affiliation, or interest in a security it is offering or the issuer of such security.[72]

Supervision Obligations. To address conflicts more broadly, the federal securities laws and FINRA rules require broker-dealers to have comprehensive supervisory structures. Under Section 15(b) of the Exchange Act, a broker-dealer and its supervisory personnel may be held liable for failing to supervise an individual who engages in bad behavior unless the broker-dealer has established supervisory procedures and a system for applying the procedures, and individuals reasonably discharged their supervisory responsibilities.[73] FINRA also requires its members to maintain a comprehensive supervision system. FINRA Rule 3110 requires each broker-dealer to establish, maintain, and enforce a written supervisory system; designate supervisory personnel; and conduct an annual internal inspection.

In particular:

- FINRA Rule 3110(a) requires each broker-dealer to have a supervisory system for the activities of its associated persons that is reasonably designed to achieve compliance with applicable securities laws and regulations and FINRA rules, and sets forth the minimum requirements for the broker-dealer's supervisory system;
- FINRA Rule 3110(b) requires broker-dealers to establish, maintain, and enforce written procedures to supervise the types of business in which they engage and the activities of their associated persons that are reasonably designed to achieve compliance with applicable securities laws and regulations and FINRA rules; and
- FINRA Rule 3110(b)(6) requires each broker-dealer to have procedures reasonably designed to prevent the standards of supervision in FINRA Rule 3110(a) from being compromised due to the conflicts of interest that may be present with respect to the associated person being supervised, such as the supervised person's position, the amount of revenue such person generates for the broker-dealer, or any compensation that the supervisor may derive from the associated person being supervised.

Similarly, FINRA Rule 3110(c)(3) generally prohibits an associated person from conducting a location's inspection if the person either is assigned to that location or is

---

[72] With respect to Rule 15c1-5, the disclosure of control or affiliation must be made before entering into any contract for the purchase or sale of the security, and if this disclosure is not in writing, it must be supplemented by giving or sending a written disclosure before completion of the transaction (i.e., no later than three business days after the date of the contract to purchase or sell a security). Similarly, Rule 15c1-6 requires written disclosure of the broker-dealer's interest in a security it is offering at or before the completion of the transaction. FINRA requires similar disclosures. *See*, e.g., FINRA Rules 2262 and 2269.

[73] A parallel provision appears in Section 203(e)(6) of the Advisers Act and applies to investment advisers.

directly or indirectly supervised by, or otherwise reports to, someone assigned to that location. This rule also requires broker-dealers to have procedures reasonably designed to prevent the effectiveness of the inspections from being compromised due to the conflicts of interest that may be present with respect to the location being inspected. Those conflicts include but are not limited to, economic, commercial, or financial interests in the associated persons and businesses being inspected. Under this standard, a broker-dealer's review of its businesses must be reasonably designed to assist it in detecting and preventing violations of, and achieving compliance with, applicable securities laws and regulations and FINRA rules. To that end, broker-dealers are expected to be diligent in identifying potential conflicts of interest and the manner in which they will be addressed to prevent a location's inspection from being compromised.[74]

Rules Addressing Conflicts. Certain SEC and FINRA rules require broker-dealers to disclose or otherwise address certain conflicts of interest commonly faced by broker-dealers. For instance, the SEC and FINRA have adopted rules to address conflicts of interest that can arise when security analysts recommend equity securities in research reports and public appearances.[75] By requiring certain certifications and disclosures, these rules are intended to promote the integrity of research reports and investor confidence in those reports and analyst public appearances.

The federal securities laws and FINRA rules also restrict broker-dealers from participating in certain transactions that may present acute potential conflicts of interest. For example, FINRA rules generally prohibit a member with certain conflicts of interest from participating in a public offering, unless certain requirements are met.[76] FINRA members also may not provide gifts or gratuities to an employee of another person to influence the award of the employer's securities business.[77] FINRA rules also generally prohibit a member's registered representatives from borrowing money from or lending money to any customer, unless the broker-dealer has written procedures allowing such borrowing or lending arrangements and certain other conditions are met.[78] In addition to these broad obligations, FINRA and the SEC have adopted rules that mandate disclosures or outright prohibitions on certain activities. Appendix B of this chapter lists certain FINRA and SEC rules that mandate disclosures or prohibit certain activities involving conflicts.

Moreover, the SEC's Regulation M generally precludes persons having an interest in an offering (such as an underwriter or broker-dealer and other distribution participants) from engaging in specified market activities during a securities distribution. These rules

---

[74] *See* FINRA Regulatory Notice 14-10, http://finra.complinet.com/net_file_store/new_rulebooks/f/i/FINRANotice_14_10.pdf. *See also* FINRA Rule 3120, which details the requirements for a broker-dealer's supervisory control system.

[75] *See* e.g., FINRA Rule 2241.

[76] FINRA Rule 5121. The rule requires prominent disclosure of the nature of the conflict in the prospectus, offering circular or similar document for the public offering, and in certain circumstances, the participation of a qualified independent underwriter.

[77] FINRA Rule 3220.

[78] FINRA Rule 3240.

are intended to prevent such persons from artificially influencing or manipulating the market price for the offered security in order to facilitate a distribution.

FINRA's Outreach Efforts on Conflicts of Interest. In 2012, FINRA reviewed how its broker-dealer members identify and manage conflicts of interest. As part of this review, the self-regulatory organization met with executive business and compliance staff of its members to discuss their approaches to conflict identification and mitigation. At these meetings, the broker-dealers discussed the conflicts they manage and the processes in place to identify and assess whether business practices put the broker-dealers' or their employees' interests ahead of those of their customers. In preparation for its meetings, FINRA requested that broker-dealers submit certain information, including a summary of the most significant conflicts they manage, the names of the departments and persons responsible for conducting conflicts reviews, a summary of the types of reports or other documents prepared at the conclusion of a conflicts review, and the names of the departments and persons who receive reports or other documentation summarizing a conflicts review.

In August of 2015, FINRA announced a conflicts of interest review concerning broker-dealers' compensation practices and their oversight of their retail brokerage business. FINRA noted that conflicts of interests represent a recurring challenge that contributes to compliance and supervisory breakdowns. The intent of FINRA's review was to assess the efforts broker-dealers make to identify, mitigate and manage conflicts of interest relating to compensation practices. In connection with its review, FINRA requested written responses to 19 questions, which appear in Appendix C.

In February 2016, FINRA announced a review of member firms' culture noting that firm culture has a profound influence on how a broker-dealer conducts business, including how it manages conflicts of interest.[79] FINRA set out to assess how broker-dealers establish, communicate, and implement cultural values, and whether cultural values are guiding business conduct. In announcing the review FINRA noted that one estimate places fines and litigation costs to broker-dealers, or their parent companies, related to cultural failures at more than $300 billion since 2010. FINRA commented that this underscores the critical importance of broker-dealers establishing and implementing strong cultural values.

As part of its review, FINRA met with executive business, compliance, legal, and risk management staff of broker-dealers to discuss cultural values and how members communicate and reinforce these values. FINRA noted that it was particularly interested in how its members measure compliance with their cultural values, what metrics, if any, are used, and how members monitor for implementation and consistent application of these values. FINRA's goal was to better understand industry practices and determine whether its members are taking reasonable steps to properly establish and implement their cultural values within their companies. In preparation for its

---

[79] The announcement is available at http://www.finra.org/industry/establishing-communicating-and-implementing-cultural-values.

meetings, FINRA requested that broker-dealers submit certain information, which is listed in Appendix D.

FINRA Conflicts Report. Following FINRA's 2012 review of broker-dealers' approaches to conflicts management, FINRA published a report on its findings of industry practices.[80] FINRA used broker-dealers' responses to its conflicts review letter, in-person meetings and a follow-up compensation questionnaire to develop the observations detailed in this report. As discussed in a later section, the report describes best practices used by broker-dealers to identify and manage conflicts of interest. FINRA stated in the report that it expects broker-dealers to consider the practices presented in the report, and to implement a strong conflict management framework.

III. TYPES OF CONFLICTS

The type or nature of conflicts of interest that financial institutions providing investment advice may have is limitless, and, as the financial industry regulators have recognized, providing investment advice does, on some level, invariably involve having to manage conflicts of interest.[81] Conflicts of interest are present whenever the interests of a financial institution, its affiliates, or its personnel differ from the interests of a client.

Conflicts can be very difficult to identify, particularly when they unconsciously impact behavior. They can require deep introspection to uncover and require objective analysis. As a former director of the SEC's OCIE stated, "[w]hile some conflicts of interest stand out, others can be very subtle, so an adviser must look, with more than a casual glance, at every aspect of its business, and its relationship with clients, and carefully consider whether it has a conflict of interest."[82] Given the myriad situations in which conflicts arise and the varied types of conflicts, there is no single or "right" way to categorize them. And certain conflicts fit more than one category regardless of what lines are drawn.

This section contains a brief discussion of some common types of conflicts in the asset management, financial wealth, and brokerage industries.

Conflicts Created by Roles

Many conflicts facing financial institutions arise from the role(s) they play and the compensation they receive and/or pay to their personnel in connection with the advice they provide to clients. Take broker-dealers as an example. In the context of making recommendations and providing advice to customers, a large number of broker-dealers participate in primary offerings of securities. These broker-dealers enter into agreements with issuers, principal underwriters, syndicate members, or wholesalers in

---

[80] *FINRA Report on Conflicts of Interest* (Oct. 2013), http://www.finra.org/sites/default/files/Industry/p359971.pdf ("*FINRA Conflicts Report*").

[81] *Id.*

[82] Lori Richards, "Fiduciary Duty: Return to First Principles," (Feb. 27, 2006), https://www.sec.gov/news/speech/spch022706lar.htm

order to obtain rights to distribute and participate in the securities offerings (and the right to be compensated for their distribution efforts). For offerings of securities, these broker-dealers serve as principals for their own accounts or as agents of those for whom they engage in distribution efforts. This structure is mandated by applicable FINRA rules[83] and is the way securities offerings have long been distributed to the public. Thus, in the context of securities offerings, broker-dealers act for their own account or as agents of the issuer, principal underwriter, syndicate members, or wholesaler at the same time they provide advice and recommend the purchase of securities to customers. These broker-dealers are contractually obligated (generally on a firm commitment or best efforts basis) to distribute the very securities that they advise on and recommend to investors. The contractual arrangements underlying the distribution of securities offerings means that such broker-dealers have competing loyalties (on one hand to sell as much as possible and on the other hand to provide suitable investment advice) whenever they recommend and sell securities in offerings.

Broker-dealers thus face an inherent tension in serving as an agent in the chain of distribution in a securities offering and recommending these securities to customers. Retail broker-dealers participating in securities offerings are hired by issuers, underwriters, dealer-managers, or syndicate members to offer securities to the public. These broker-dealers thus serve as agents of these parties and not as agents solely of the customer. And these broker-dealers are paid by the issuers, underwriters, dealer-managers or syndicate members only if they are successful in distributing the securities to their customers. In other words, in the context of securities offerings, their primary role is to distribute and sell securities to the public.[84] Given the foregoing, broker-dealers participating in offerings have conflicts of interest because:

- Their primary purpose is to sell securities to customers, which means that their allegiance primarily is to the issuer, underwriter, dealer-manager, or syndicate member and not the customer; and
- They get compensated only if there is a sale of the security they are offering.

Similar conflicts arise if a financial institution sells securities to a client or buys securities from a client. These "principal transactions" are subject to heightened regulatory scrutiny under the law. For instance, Section 206(3) of the Advisers Act prohibits an investment adviser from directly or indirectly entering into a principal transaction with a client unless the adviser has notified the client in writing and obtained the client's informed consent to the transaction. In particular, Section 206(3) requires an investment adviser wishing to engage in a principal transaction to disclose to such client in writing before the completion of the transaction the capacity in which the adviser is acting and obtaining the consent of the client to such transaction.

---

[83] *See*, e.g., FINRA Rule 5160 applicable to selling syndicate agreements; FINRA Rule 2320 ("No member who is a principal underwriter as defined in the Investment Company Act may sell variable contracts through another broker-dealer unless ...(2) there is a sales agreement in effect between the parties"); *see also* FINRA Rule 3280, which prohibits "selling away" by associated persons of a broker-dealer.

[84] Under Section 202(a)(11)(C) of the Advisers Act, in order to avoid having to register as investment advisers any advice provided by these broker-dealers to their customers must be solely incidental to their sales efforts.

Other conflicts that may be impacted by the role played by a financial institution include the following:

- Participating in customer transactions;
- Purchasing goods and services from clients;
- Charitable contributions made by a financial institution to an organization the financial institution is seeking to acquire as a client;
- Interests in securities (affiliate stock, client stock, managed mutual fund);
- Providing research on issuers of securities underwritten or distributed by the firm;[85]
- Trading ahead of research reports or trading ahead of customers;
- Participating in IPO allocations;
- Private securities transactions;
- Transactions by or for associated persons;
- Sharing in customer accounts;
- Political contributions to a government official by a municipal securities underwriter;
- Market making activities;
- Performing multiple roles with respect to a client or a transaction (e.g., adviser, underwriter, lender, principal counterparty, or derivative counterparty);[86]
- Possessing material, nonpublic information; and
- Transactions with affiliates.

Conflicts Created by Compensation Arrangements

Conflicts often arise from compensation arrangements entered into by a financial institution, which cause the institution to receive different amounts of compensation depending on the advice provided to the client. Some of these arrangements arise through agreements with third parties that can cause the financial institution to receive different levels of compensation in connection with the sale of different securities and investment products. Revenue sharing payments and the receipt of marketing allowances fall into this category. Other conflicts result from the internal compensation practices adopted by financial institutions, such as differential compensation payouts and internal sales contests that create incentives for employees to recommend certain securities or investment products over others.

Broker-Dealers. It is common for broker-dealers to receive more compensation and to pay their employees more in connection with the offer and sale of certain products as compared to other products. Examples include:

---

[85] In addition, research may be disseminated to clients at different times, thereby potentially favoring some clients over others. Similarly, a firm may provide preferential access to strategists' market commentary and trading ideas. Within broker-dealers, research personnel may be subject to pressure from investment bankers to issue reports or change existing ratings to help win or sustain investment banking business. Likewise, issuers may pressure research personnel to issue favorable reports in return for investment banking or other business. In addition, research may be biased to support the broker-dealer's sales and trading activities.

[86] In the context of advising on mergers and transactions, broker-dealers face conflicts to the extent they advise one bidder for a company while financing another, advise on both sides of the same deal, advise a seller while financing a buyer, finance multiple bidders, or advise on a deal while having an interest in one or more involved parties.

- Different levels of gross dealer concessions received by a broker-dealer on the sale of certain securities as compared to others;
- Broker-dealers paying a higher percentage of gross dealer concessions for the sale of certain securities as compared to others;
- Sales contests and cash bonuses;
- "Commission specials" paid to registered representatives of a broker-dealer on the sale of specified securities over a specified time;
- Selling proprietary products;
- Selling products that result in economic benefits to affiliates;
- Noncash compensation arrangements that result in trips and awards to registered representatives;
- Underwriting or other relationships with issuers;
- Revenue sharing payments and other compensation received from issuers of certain securities or investment products or different amounts of such payments received on different securities or investment products;
- Marketing allowances received from issuers of certain securities or investment products or different amounts of such allowances received on different securities or investment products;
- Training, support, or infrastructure integration received from issuers of certain securities or investment products or different amounts of such services received on different securities or investment products;
- Gifts, gratuities, and business entertainment practices;
- Receiving multiple sources of revenue on certain products;
- Mutual fund breakpoints; and
- Commissions, mark-ups, and charges.

Dual Registrants. Dual registrants face a conflict in recommending that a client open up or allocate additional funds to an investment advisory account as opposed to a brokerage account given the different economics and payment streams associated with this recommendation. The SEC recognizes that both investment advisers and broker-dealers can inappropriately receive compensation tied to trading in a client's account. For instance, the SEC staff has noted in its annual publication of examination priorities that it will "continue to examine investment advisers and dually registered investment adviser/broker-dealers that offer retail investors a variety of fee arrangements (e.g., asset-based fees, hourly fees, wrap fees, or commissions). The focus here is on recommendations of account types and whether the recommendations are in the best interest of the retail investor at the inception of the arrangement and thereafter, including fees charged, services provided, and disclosures made about such arrangements."[87] This

[87] Office of Compliance, Inspections and Examinations National Exam Program, 2016 Examination Priorities, https://www.sec.gov/about/offices/ocie/national-examination-program-priorities-2016.pdf. *See also* Office of Compliance, Inspections and Examinations National Exam Program, 2015 Examination Priorities, https://www.sec.gov/about/offices/ocie/national-examination-program-priorities-2015.pdf ("Where an adviser offers a variety of fee arrangements, we will focus on recommendations of account types and whether they are in the best interest of the client at the inception of the arrangement and thereafter, including fees charged, services provided, and disclosures made about such relationships.")

focus by the SEC staff reflects that just as broker-dealers can churn investor accounts to generate inappropriate levels of commissions investment advisers can inappropriately charge ongoing investment advisory fees on an assets-under-management basis without providing commensurate ongoing investment advisory services (often referred to as "reverse churning").

Investment Advisers. Investment advisory programs can involve a variety of compensation-related conflicts of interest. For instance, wrap fee programs involve unique conflicts that arise from the fact that the sponsor receives the same amount of compensation regardless of the level of trading and customization in the account. This economic paradigm creates an incentive for program sponsors to restrict clients' ability to impose reasonable restrictions because managing clients' accounts on a customized basis increases the costs and burdens of operating their wrap programs. In this regard there is a potential conflict between the interests of sponsors, who want to achieve efficiency and scale in their programs, and the interests of clients. This infuses a significant amount of risk into the adviser's conclusion that a client's restriction(s) are unreasonable. As a result, some advisers use committees to articulate restrictions deemed to be reasonable and unreasonable, ensure that acceptable restrictions are accommodated, review client restriction requests, and determine whether the list of acceptable restrictions should be modified. Whether or not a committee is used, a wrap sponsor should have procedures to ensure that its wrap program is operated to accommodate reasonable client restrictions if the adviser wishes to fall within the safe harbor provided by Rule 3a-4 under the Investment Company Act of 1940, as amended.

The economics underpinning wrap fee programs also may lead sponsors to favor portfolio managers that:

- Accept a larger haircut (i.e., are willing to accept a smaller portfolio manager fee) to be in the sponsor's program than comparable portfolio managers; or
- Trade less than comparable portfolio managers.

In addition, sponsors and portfolio managers may have affiliations or financial relationships that could cause a sponsor to want to select a given portfolio manager over others. It is important for sponsors to review their procedures and criteria for selecting portfolio managers to ensure that any conflicts of interest inherent in the selection process are properly managed and that the portfolio managers recommended or selected are in clients' best interests.

Investment advisers may have conflicts of interest in other investment advisory programs they sponsor, including separately managed account programs and unified managed account programs, as a result of negotiating different economics with different sub-advisers or because of different economics that they may have in one program versus another. Similarly, a model manager with its own set of direct clients often will have different economics with these clients compared to the economic arrangements it is able to negotiate with third-party platform providers that have their own client base and receive models and trading signals from the model manager. These different client economics put pressure on such managers concerning their allocation of investment opportunities and their decision on how to implement their investment ideas.

One of the more common types of conflicts facing asset managers is the need to value "Level 3" securities whose fair value cannot be determined by using observable measures, such as market prices. Level 3 assets are typically illiquid, and fair values can only be calculated using estimates or risk-adjusted value ranges. Managers have conflicts in valuing such assets if their advisory fees are based on the value of the assets being managed, including the value of unrealized gains or losses in the portfolio; in such instances, the values attributed to such assets will impact the investment advisory fees received by the adviser. Even when a manager's fees are not based on the value of the assets (such as when the fees are based on the amount of committed capital) the manager has a conflict in the value ascribed to such assets if such values will impact the performance record reported or advertised by the adviser.

Trading Conflicts

In addition to conflicts of interest associated with the advice provided to clients, financial institutions have conflicts in deciding how to implement their portfolio management decisions in the context of exchange-traded securities. These conflicts typically involve receiving an economic benefit in consideration of placing trades through a particular broker-dealer or other trading venue or different economics associated with the manner in which orders are allocated or with whom they are traded. Such conflicts include:[88]

- The receipt of soft dollars (e.g., research) in consideration of the commission dollars directed to a particular broker-dealer;
- The receipt of payments for order flow in consideration of directing trades to certain trading venues;
- The receipt of client referrals from broker-dealers selected to execute client trades;
- Allocations of investment opportunities among clients;
- The affiliate of the manager having a banking or investment relationship with issuers of securities purchased by the manager;
- Investing in companies that are also firm clients;
- The receipt of payments, reduced fees, or other economic benefits in consideration of using particular custodians;
- Placing client orders with an affiliated broker-dealer;
- Acting as a broker-dealer in connection with a transaction for which a financial institution also serves as the investment adviser;

[88] Other conflicts may also arise as a result of trading activity. For example, an adviser that buys securities of an issuer in which it has a financial interest has a conflict in purchasing the security and also has a conflict if it votes proxies of that issuer. Similar trading and proxy voting conflicts can also occur if the issuer of a security purchased by an adviser also is a client of the adviser or if the adviser buys securities of an issuer for which a spouse (or other family member) of an officer of the adviser is an executive of the issuer.

- Engaging in agency cross transactions, in which an adviser acts as broker for both its advisory client and the party on the other side of the transaction;[89]
- Effecting cross-trades between clients, which involves a potential conflict of interest (because the manager may be inclined to favor one client over another for economic reasons);
- Aggregating client orders and bunching trades. Advisers that aggregate orders of securities face conflicts when they disaggregate the orders to client accounts because, for example, not all securities may have been acquired at the same price. Advisers should implement procedures designed to ensure that the trades are allocated in such a manner that all clients are treated fairly and equitably (e.g., at the average price). As an additional example, when orders are not completely filled, advisers can allocate on a pro rata, rotational, or random basis;
- Selective dissemination of portfolio holding information;
- Allocating orders for IPOs or other securities that are scarce and attractive investment opportunities. In these situations, advisers may be prone to favor accounts that provide the adviser with greater revenue, at the expense of accounts that are less favored by the adviser;
- Allocating the cost of a mixed-use product under the SEC's soft dollar guidance. When a product or service obtained using client commissions performs functions that qualify as either "eligible research" or "brokerage" under the safe harbor in Section 28(e) of the Exchange Act *and* also performs functions that do not, the money manager must make a reasonable allocation of the cost of the product or service between eligible and ineligible uses. Only the portion of the product that assists with the adviser's investment decision-making processes may be paid for with soft dollars;
- Trading ahead of customer orders;
- Resolving trade errors;
- Personal securities trading;
- Trading for proprietary or affiliated accounts;
- Directed brokerage;
- Solicitation arrangements;
- Determining valuation for Level 3 securities;
- Financial stakes in market makers or trading venues;
- Placing clients in an obligation of the firm or an affiliate;
- Placing clients in an affiliated investment product;
- Placing clients in investment products sponsored by companies from which the firm receives financial benefits;
- Investing clients in different parts of an issuer's capital stack; and
- Giving different advice to different clients.

---

[89] As noted earlier, Rule 206(3)-2 under the Advisers Act permits "agency cross transactions" without transaction-by-transaction disclosure if certain conditions are satisfied.

Client Conflicts

Investment managers have conflicts if they have negotiated different levels of advisory fees with different clients or charge certain clients performance-based fees and other clients only asset-based fees. The risk is that the manager will favor certain clients by, for example, giving them the benefit of their best investment ideas before implementing those ideas for other clients that are not as profitable. Advisers that agree to manage certain accounts for free or at reduced rates need to carefully review their allocation decisions and be mindful of their best execution obligations to ensure such clients are not systematically disadvantaged.

Investment managers face conflicts in allocating client assets if they charge clients more for managing certain asset classes or types of securities (e.g., equities) as compared to others (e.g., fixed income or cash). These economic differences create a risk that managers will skew allocation recommendations towards the assets that result in the greatest amount of advisory fees. Relationships with certain clients can also create conflicts for managers if the relationship results in some direct or indirect benefit to the adviser. For example, an adviser may be inclined to act favorably toward accounts managed for service providers that provide services to the manager or accounts that may refer clients or offer other benefits to the manager.

Conflicts may also arise as a result of investment restrictions or limitations that clients may place on the management of their assets, which could impact the adviser's costs of managing such accounts or prevent the adviser from being able to aggregate trades for such clients with the orders for other clients. Similarly, certain clients may demand more reporting or different kinds of reporting than the adviser typically offers. Some clients may require advisers to provide certifications, copies of internal policies, or other information, all of which could lower the profitability of such clients vis-à-vis other clients of the adviser.[90]

Conflicts are also present with the decision of how to allocate expenses associated with private funds, because the manager is essentially deciding what costs and charges it will pay for and which costs and expenses will be charged to the private fund and paid for by the limited partners or other investors in the fund. Managers have conflicts if they advise clients to invest in different parts of a company's capital structure, particularly if the company experiences economic difficulty in the future. In situations involving workouts or bankruptcies, recommendations or decisions that may be good for one client may be harmful to the interests of the other client(s).

---

[90] In the private fund context, it is common for institutional investors to demand that the general partner or managing member enter into side letter agreements that provide certain rights, information or protections to these investors as compared to other investors in the fund. Side letters may create special obligations on the part of the general partner or managing member with respect to such investors and could thus result in conflicts of interest.

Conflicts Created by Outside Business Activities

Financial institutions may face conflicts as a result of outside business activities of the institution or its personnel, such as when an officer is a director of, or has an ownership stake in, a company which the institution is considering buying or selling. Similarly, conflicts can arise because of business relationships a financial institution or an employee has with a company the manager is considering buying. Conflicts can also arise if an employee engages in a business activity that competes with the financial institution for purchasing assets or provides a service that may be used by the manager. Even in the absence of a direct conflict, outside business activities vie for an employee's attention and energy and thereby impede the employee's performance on behalf of the financial institution.

Sometimes employees will participate in an endeavor, such as acting as a director or advisory board member of a company, which will cause them to learn material, nonpublic information about an issuer. Such information may prevent the employee's financial institution from being able to buy securities of the issuer or exiting an existing position in the issuer. At other times, an employee of a financial institution may befriend or develop a relationship with an executive of a company that results in a conflict, such as when the company seeks support for its position on a proxy matter that runs contrary to the financial institution's voting policies.

IV. MANAGING CONFLICTS

There is no limit on the types or number of conflicts. They can take virtually any form and present themselves in myriad circumstances. As Gene Gohlke, former associate director of OCIE, once quipped, "they are everywhere."[91] Accordingly, clashes of interests do not lend themselves to easy analysis and management. And, as is the case with many aspects of a business, they often do not remain fixed in form or effect but may evolve over time as the business grows and develops. What is a minor conflict today can become a threat to the business tomorrow. Likewise, even if a conflict is well understood and mitigated today, changes in the firm's business can significantly alter the frequency, likelihood, or impact of a conflict or the firm's ability to measure or manage the conflict in the future. Accordingly, managing conflicts is a never-ending process. As a firm's business evolves so will its conflicts—and so should the firm's internal controls, policies, and procedures in response.

Conflicts Framework

A financial institution's conflicts framework is the combination of its ethics culture, organizational structures, policies, processes, incentive structures, and internal controls

[91] Gene Gohlke, *Remarks before the Fund of Funds Forum* (Nov. 14, 2005), https://www.sec.gov/news/speech/spch111405gag.htm

that, in their totality, shape a firm's management of conflicts of interest.[92] The OCC, DOL, SEC, and FINRA have, at various times and using similar nomenclature, indicated that they expect financial institutions to design and implement a firmwide framework to identify and manage conflicts of interest.

"Tone from the Top" and Firm Culture. One key to developing an effective conflicts framework is the tone from the top—the attitudes and practices exhibited by the firm's executives. To be effective, firm leadership must require not only adherence to the letter of the law, but a commitment to high ethical standards and to putting clients' interests first. An essential practice for financial institutions is to establish a tone from the top that stresses ethical decision making and fair treatment of clients. Executives set the tone in their day-to-day actions and decisions. It is important that management consistently communicate and demonstrate the values expected of employees and monitor employees' behavior to ensure that it aligns with the firm's stated values. As FINRA has observed,[93] conflict management frameworks cannot be expected to succeed without strong support from a firm's leaders. The board of directors can also play an important role in setting the tone. By playing an active role in understanding the significant conflicts a firm faces and setting the firm's overall approach to conflicts management, the board can signal the importance the highest levels of the firm attach to addressing conflicts issues.

Although communicating a firm's values to its personnel is important, it is not nearly as vital as ensuring that the firm's practices are consistent with the values that are communicated. Firms should review their practices to see whether there is daylight between what they say they do and what they actually do. Firms are well advised to review such areas as their hiring practices; the vetting of potential new employees; incentive compensation arrangements; the review and approval of new clients, products, services, and business arrangements; the thoroughness of their supervisory reviews and audits; the handling of internal whistleblowers; the visibility provided to the legal and compliance departments into the activities of the firm's business units and whether these departments have a "seat at the table;" the activities of the board; and the response to violations of the firm's policies or procedures. All of these practices should be consistent with the values articulated by management to firm personnel. There may be no greater mistake that some firms make than to speak with one voice but to act with another. As is the case with many matters, the actions taken by senior management speak much louder than their words and provide a strong indication of a firm's "real" culture.

In addition to the foregoing considerations, financial institutions should consider the following questions:

- Do the Compliance Department, the Conflicts Committee, and others responsible for conflicts have sufficient resources to identify, monitor, track and manage conflicts?

---

92 *FINRA Conflicts Report.*

93 *Id.*

- Does the Compliance Department receive support from senior management? Is the department regularly asked to counsel on business decisions before they are made?
- Are senior managers participating in "public" compliance/training meetings on conflicts?
- Are top revenue producers and senior executives treated differently than others with respect to conflicts and other compliance issues?
- Are employees free to express concerns about conflicts without fear of negative repercussions?
- Is the efficacy of the firm's conflicts of interest controls and processes evaluated on an ongoing basis, and are changes made to reflect changes to the firm's business operations?
- Are issues and concerns about conflicts of interest promptly addressed?
- Are exceptions to the firm's conflicts policies or processes frequently granted in order to reach business goals (e.g., revenue targets)?

Conflicts Management Structure. A good tone from the top and corresponding culture form just the first step to managing conflicts of interest. To protect financial institutions and clients from the negative consequences of conflicts supporting policies, processes, controls, and training are critical. Financial institutions should establish carefully designed and articulated structures to manage the conflicts that arise in their business. These structures include clearly defining and communicating the expectations, roles, and responsibilities of the committees, individuals, and other bodies that play key roles in managing and mitigating conflicts.

In reviewing the conflicts structures developed and used by broker-dealers, FINRA observed two main approaches that firms have taken in developing a structure to manage conflicts. Although these approaches reflect practices engaged in by broker-dealers, FINRA's observations are applicable to investment advisers, national banks, and FSAs as well.

Distributed Model. One common approach to conflicts management is a distributed model, in which responsibility for identification and oversight of conflicts is spread out within a firm with no single office or department having overall "ownership." In this model, the business units have front-line responsibility for identifying and managing conflicts. Committees address conflicts that are specific to their scope of responsibilities and control functions support the business units and the committees in varying degrees. Policy "ownership" for conflicts issues is thus diffused among the business units.[94]

As FINRA notes, one benefit of this approach is that it places responsibility for identifying and managing conflicts upon the individuals most familiar with the details of a particular business and who are in a position to take measures to mitigate those conflicts. In addition, a firm with this model usually does not need to create new reporting lines to manage conflicts. One potential downside to the distributed model is that

[94] *Id.*

individuals within a business unit may be unaware of conflicts in their business that arise due to activities in other business units. In addition, individual business units may handle similar types of conflicts in different ways without making a conscious decision that those differences are appropriate. Furthermore, management teams devoted to the business units may not be focused on conflicts issues because many other issues jockey for their time and attention. As a result, there may be varying degrees of commitment and resources devoted to identifying and mitigating conflicts across the firm.[95]

Centralized Model. The second main approach to managing a firm's conflicts framework uses a centralized conflicts office or committee.[96] This dedicated conflicts office or committee can be part of firm management or can be integrated into an existing, compliance-related group. The office or committee oversees the firm's conflict management framework and works with business units to manage significant conflicts within, and across, business units. The office or committee also works with business units to review and assess conflicts on an ongoing basis, coordinates business unit conflicts officers, and works with business units to identify and manage unique conflict situations.[97]

Firms with a dedicated, centralized conflicts office or committee may still (and often do) place primary responsibility for identifying conflicts with the business units. In this respect, such firms often instill "conflicts officers" in the various business units to help address conflicts that arise in the normal course of business. The conflicts officers act as a resource to the business unit in managing conflicts, are a point of contact for individuals who wish to raise potential conflicts concerns, and can escalate conflicts as warranted to the centralized conflicts office or committee. These individuals often are part of the firm's risk or compliance functions.[98]

There are several potential benefits of a centralized, enterprise-level approach to conflicts management. The office or committee creates a platform to maintain a sustained, firmwide focus on conflicts. FINRA notes that a similar focus may be difficult to achieve when responsibility for conflicts is diffused among business units and/or various firm-level management committees. Creating a dedicated office or committee can send a strong message to firm employees about the importance of conflicts to executive management. In addition, the office or committee can provide visibility on conflicts issues to executive management and, as appropriate, the board. Finally, a centralized office or committee can help ensure a consistent approach to conflicts management across business units and the entire firm.[99]

FINRA observes that the centralized model is not without potential downsides. First, it may diminish the sense of responsibility for conflicts in the business units. To mitigate this risk, certain firms adopt measures specifically designed to prevent this from happening by, for example, explicitly placing front-line responsibility for identifying conflicts

---

[95] *Id.*
[96] *Id.*
[97] *Id.*
[98] *Id.*
[99] *Id.*

with the business units. A second drawback is that establishing a centralized model can be a significant undertaking. Firms may need to create new reporting structures, policies, and processes as well as implement technology programs to support the operation of the conflicts office. Such efforts may be required because the conflicts office or committee needs a broad array of information about the firm's business activities to evaluate the conflicts the firm may face.[100]

The Need for a Tailored Approach. Regardless of which general approach to designing a conflicts management structure a financial institution selects, the various financial regulators have long emphasized that a firm's approach to conflict management must be tailored to its business model, types of conflicts, size, office structure, supervisory systems, reporting chain, technology capabilities, and culture. Otherwise, the policies and procedures that are adopted to manage conflicts of interest will be ineffective. Accordingly, financial institutions should review and consider the considerations cited in light of their operations, structure, systems, culture, and personnel, designing a conflicts management structure that is tailored for, and will be effective in overseeing, the conflicts their business activities generate.

If that results, for example, in an enterprise-level set of content standards for conflicts policies and a requirement that each business unit create its own conflict policy in line with the enterprise standard, so be it. If such an approach is consistent with the financial institution's business operations and structure and will help ensure firmwide consistency while allowing business units to tailor their policies to their specific requirements, then that is a good approach for that particular financial institution to take. But such an approach may be a very poor choice for another financial institution. There is no "one size fits all" approach that every financial institution should follow, and there may be more than one approach that could prove to be effective in mitigating and managing conflicts for a given firm. There is thus no "right" or "best" approach and what works well for one institution may be ineffective or worse for another institution. What matters is that the conflicts management structure a firm adopts is effective in identifying and mitigating the conflicts that firm faces.

Conflicts of Interest Structures and Internal Controls. Financial institutions need to adopt and implement structures, policies, procedures, and processes to identify and manage conflicts of interest. To this end, an effective compliance program for managing conflicts of interest typically includes the following elements:

- A firmwide definition of conflicts of interest that enables employees to understand and identify conflicts of interest that may arise in a firm's business;
- Adoption of a best interests of the client standard in the firm's code of ethics;
- A clear delineation of employees' responsibilities with respect to identifying and managing conflicts of interest;
- Defined escalation procedures for handling conflict situations;

---

[100] *Id.*

- Proactive and systematic identification of conflicts of interest in a firm's business on an ongoing and periodic basis;
- Appropriate reporting of material conflicts to executive management and the board;
- Periodic review and testing of the firm's conflicts management framework to ensure adherence to applicable laws and regulations and firm policies;
- Identification of all laws and regulations relating to conflicts of interest applicable to the products and services the firm offers; and
- Periodic self-assessments to determine actual and potential conflicts of interest, their respective risks, and the quality and effectiveness of current controls.

Certain of these elements are discussed in more detail next.

Board and Management Supervision. Among other factors, an effective conflicts management structure is characterized by an active board of directors, senior management supervision, and sound processes for risk assessment, control, and monitoring. In establishing and promoting an appropriate culture and tone from the top, the board and senior management should adopt a code of ethics that, among other topics, sets forth general expectations for ethical behavior and compliance with applicable law. Firms' codes typically establish the broad context within which employees make decisions about how to handle conflicts. The code may be required by the regulatory framework in which the firm operates,[101] and generally contains a broad commitment to the fair treatment of clients and requirements to avoid or manage conflicts. For instance, a firm's code may articulate (and may be required by applicable regulation to articulate) a best-interests-of-the-client standard and require all conflicts to be resolved so that the client's interests never are subjugated to the interests of the firm or its affiliates. A firm's code establishes a yardstick against which the behavior of employees may be measured.

Many financial institutions use standing committees or ad hoc groups on an as-needed basis to address conflicts issues as they arise. FINRA has observed that these may include senior firm management committees, such as a risk management committee or similar body, or a cross-divisional conflicts forum for compliance personnel. Such bodies are particularly useful for financial institutions that employ a distributed model for conflict management because they facilitate the sharing of information about business and regulatory developments and the management of conflicts in different parts of the firm. Having a forum in which to share effective practices and lessons learned as well as business activities that impact multiple divisions or groups is helpful for identifying and mitigating conflicts of interest.[102]

Policies and Procedures. To properly manage the compliance, operational, reputation, and strategic risks associated with conflicts of interest, financial institutions need to adopt and implement policies, procedures, and processes designed to:

---

[101] For instance, SEC-registered investment advisers are required to adopt a code of ethics under Rule 204A-1 under the Advisers Act.

[102] *FINRA Conflicts Report.*

- Identify actual and potential conflicts of interest in the firm's activities and the risks associated with such conflicts;
- Identify transactions or activities that pose a conflict of interest, and prevent those that would not comply with laws, regulations, or internal policies in advance;
- Measure and assess risks associated with each type of conflict of interest;
- Provide timely, accurate, and pertinent reports that monitor conflicts on an ongoing basis and identify exceptions, enabling appropriate individuals and committees to take appropriate actions;
- Prevent or eliminate impermissible conflicts of interest;
- Establish limits for permissible conflicts of interest; and
- Prevent and identify unethical or improper employee behavior.

Many financial institutions use (and may be required to maintain) an enterprise-level conflict of interest policy. These policies often contain the following elements:[103]

- *A statement on objectives, policy or rationale:* The policy typically summarizes the institution's business activities, its common conflicts and notes that a failure to manage these conflicts effectively may result in sanctions, loss and/or reputational damage.
- *A discussion of the types of conflicts the financial institution may face:* The policy typically provides general guidance on the factors that can lead to a conflict of interest and often contains examples of specific conflicts relevant to the institution's business.
- *A description of roles and responsibilities:* The policy should articulate the role of management and employees in managing conflicts and note who has responsibility for identifying and addressing conflicts.[104]

A firm's processes and systems should be sufficient to identify and to monitor on an ongoing basis the various conflicts of interest that result from the firm's business activities. To be effective, the institution's conflicts policies and procedures should be tailored to address the risks associated with the firm's particular conflicts. They also need to be clear and precise and should specify:

- Who is responsible for taking action;
- What action is required to be taken;
- When are such actions to be taken;
- How to document the actions that are taken;
- What records should be created and how and where should they be maintained;
- What should be done if problems arise; and
- What is the review procedure to assess the efficacy of the policies and procedures and when should such review be conducted.

---

[103] *Id.*

[104] Firms' enterprise-level conflict of interest policies may contain additional elements, such as a description of conflict escalation procedures, which are discussed below.

Conflicts Inventory Reviews. It is common practice for financial institutions to implement ongoing processes and periodic reviews, to identify, create, and maintain an inventory of conflicts raised by their business. An ongoing review helps financial institutions identify conflicts in near real-time and to address them quickly. A periodic review permits financial institutions to consider the conflicts raised by their business in a structured, comprehensive way. That could be particularly valuable for firms that use a decentralized approach to conflicts management where there may be a less consistent focus on conflicts issues.[105]

Recording conflicts in a central inventory serves several purposes. It enables financial institutions to track their conflicts, determine whether they are increasing or decreasing, and to assess whether they are being properly managed. Firms should craft policies, procedures and controls around each conflict identified. The inventory enables firms to quickly determine if there are any gaps in their controls. It also makes it easier for firms to audit their processes to determine if the conflicts are being managed effectively. Finally, it may allow the firm to categorize or group conflicts in ways that facilitate reporting and analysis of types of conflicts.[106]

Conflict Escalation Procedures. To be effective, financial institutions' policies should contain an escalation process for managing conflicts of interest that cannot be handled through day-to-day firm processes and include a description of individuals' roles and responsibilities and organizational contact points for escalation. Having clear processes for escalating conflicts of interest is an important element. Firms may have a single process for escalating conflicts or processes that vary by business unit or the type of conflict (as well as an enterprise-level "catch-all" escalation process that captures conflicts that do not fit into a firm's existing escalation procedures). The goal is to clearly articulate employees' roles and responsibilities as well as the circumstances and manner in which they should invoke the escalation processes.[107]

Conflict Questionnaires, Checklists, and Interviews. Many financial institutions use conflicts questionnaires disseminated to various departments and employees to help identify conflicts of interest in their line of business. Senior personnel are often asked to classify and prioritize conflicts of interests in their operations. To achieve this goal, it often is helpful to periodically review a company's organizational charts of its personnel and affiliates to identify conflicts. Similarly, conflicts often are unearthed by:

- Reviewing a company's product lines and analyzing how different parts of the organization intersect in bringing products to market; and
- Overlaying a review of the products' target markets, profitability, and resource needs for the organization.

---

[105] *FINRA Conflicts Report.*
[106] *Id.*
[107] *Id.*

Many firms create conflicts checklists and conduct interviews of key personnel that are tasked with managing conflicts to help understand whether the firm's conflicts are being managed appropriately. The checklists often review, among other items:[108]

- Relationships and transactions among affiliates;
- Products and services;
- Changes in the nature, type, or number of clients;
- Sources of revenue and expenses (which can include a review of financial statements and business credit card statements and employee expense reports);
- Distribution practices;
- Processes (portfolio management, trading, operations, marketing, etc.);
- Money flows into and out of the financial institution;
- How clients are obtained;
- What services are outsourced;
- Compensation practices;
- The trading activity, performance, and portfolio turnover of accounts;
- Changes in the selection of executing broker-dealers and market centers;
- The level of commissions paid;
- Changes in the profitability of business lines; and
- The number and types of operational issues (e.g., trade errors, valuation problems).

The results are entered into the firm's conflicts inventory and are categorized and memorialized. These various data points are often summarized in a report that is then sent to and analyzed by the firm's Conflicts Committee, which often is responsible for ensuring that the various conflicts in the inventory are appropriately mapped to policies, procedures, processes, and internal controls. As a final control mechanism, the Conflicts Committee may require personnel responsible for overseeing certain conflicts to certify in writing that certain conflict reviews or other tasks have been completed.[109]

Management Information Systems. Financial industry regulators have stated that a firm's management information system and related processes should provide adequate information to alert firm personnel to conflicts and ensure that exceptions to firm policies are reported to the appropriate officers, employees, and supervisory committees. The firm's management information system should provide management with timely, accurate, and pertinent information about the nature and scope of conflicts. This system should highlight exceptions that represent potential violations of the firm's policies. Such systems and related processes should enable management and board to effectively:

- Determine whether specific conflicts are permissible under applicable law and consistent with the firm's policies;
- Monitor and help ensure appropriate resolution of conflicts that are impermissible or inconsistent with the firm's policies;
- Monitor potential conflicts of interest;

---

[108] *Id.*

[109] *Id.*

- Evaluate the level of risk to the firm presented by conflicts of interest; and
- Determine the firm's aggregate risk from conflicts of interest.[110]

Surveillance and Monitoring. Financial industry regulators have made clear that financial institutions should develop surveillance programs to determine whether certain products or services are causing employees to act contrary to clients' interests due to conflicts of interest. Processes should include ongoing monitoring to ensure that firms identify, analyze, and appropriately react to relevant changes in circumstances. As one example, financial institutions can design reports that identify spikes in the offer or sale of products or services that involve conflicts of interest, unusual spikes in revenue attributable to certain products or services, significant changes in the recommendation of particular products or services by certain employees or groups of personnel (such as those in a particular office or region), or other patterns indicative of inappropriate conduct.

Periodic Self-Assessments and Audits. Financial institutions are expected to have appropriate control systems in place to assess the effectiveness of the processes they have implemented to manage conflicts. This involves implementing processes through which the institutions periodically self-assess and audit the effectiveness of their conflicts framework. Often, these processes are part of firms' risk management programs. An effective audit program is essential to ensuring that the controls and processes implemented to manage conflicts of interest are working properly. An audit program can also determine whether conflicts of interest are managed in accordance with applicable law and with a firm's policies and procedures.

Conflicts Disclosure. For disclosure to be effective, financial institutions should seek to ensure clients make informed decisions. The goal is to ensure that conflicts of interest are fully and fairly disclosed so that the client's decision can fairly be said to be the result of an informed decision. This means taking steps to ensure that the financial institution discloses and that the client understands: the nature of the financial institution's conflicts of interest, what factors give rise to and create the conflict, the scope of the conflict, and the potential impact and ramifications of the conflict on both the financial institution and the client.

One result of the foregoing considerations is that conflicts of interest must be disclosed at a point in time when the client can make a meaningful choice about how to proceed. If a conflict of interest is not disclosed until after there could be adverse consequences to the client from a decision, then the disclosure is inadequate and should not be relied on to help cure the conflict. In such circumstances, the duress to the client caused by the untimely disclosure taints the consent and renders it ineffective.

One action financial institutions should consider doing, particularly for acute conflicts, is not only to provide written disclosure of a conflict but also to obtain the client's written consent. The process of obtaining such consent signals to the client that consent is

---

[110] Handbook. *See* supra at note 33.

an important decision that should be made only after due consideration of the material facts. The consent also memorializes the disclosures made to the client and demonstrates that the client's decision was informed.

Hiring Practices. Employing ethical individuals is an integral part of maintaining a culture of compliance in which conflicts of interest are properly addressed. Many clients have been told, "You are what you recruit and hire." From a cost-benefit perspective, no other practice may provide more value to a financial institution than to be rigorous and thorough in its hiring process. So many consequences flow from the hiring process. Financial institutions will gain significant benefits by being more thoughtful in the criteria they use to vet potential employees. These institutions should look beyond revenue considerations when making hiring decisions and also consider the "risk costs" that accompany hiring certain employees. Firms' due diligence processes need to move beyond looking at obvious black marks that show up on an individual's background check (such as on a Form U4 or U5).

Financial institutions would be well-served to dig into the business and regulatory background of a candidate, review and understand the composition and mix of the candidate's business, review and analyze the sources and types of revenue, the number and nature of clients, and the conflicts of interests associated with the candidate's business practices. Firms should also consider whether the nature of the candidate's business practices and clientele are a good fit for the firm and its culture. Do the candidate's business practices, clientele, products, or services vary from the way the firm conducts business? Would the firm be able to supervise the individual under its existing supervisory structure and management information systems? How good of a fit is the candidate for the firm? Would integrating the candidate into the firm require a large amount of resources? What kind of new conflicts of interest would be presented if the candidate were hired? Does the firm have experience in managing the types of conflicts of interest that would come with the candidate? If not, what processes and internal controls would need to be built to detect, monitor, and manage these conflicts of interest?

To mitigate against the pressure to hire individuals who may have problematic backgrounds, some financial institutions give their Compliance Department veto rights over hires. Some financial institutions also have begun to create "risk scores" that attempt to provide a balanced overview of the risks associated with hiring candidates.[111] Conflicts of interest are among the data points that are considered in arriving at a candidate's risk score (together with such items as the level of compliance behavior, client complaints, regulatory sanctions, terminations for cause, frequent changes in employment, internal disciplinary action, violations of law, employment history, financial standing, and credit history).

Training. Training on ethics and conflict of interest policies is an important component of financial institutions' conflicts management framework. Training prepares employees to recognize when a potential conflict exists and to make appropriate decisions about

---

[111] *FINRA Report on Conflicts of Interest* (Oct. 2013), http://www.finra.org/sites/default/files/Industry/p359971.pdf ("*FINRA Conflicts Report*").

handling conflicts consistent with the institution's policies, procedures and ethical standards. Training is also an important vehicle to communicate firm culture, specific requirements of a firm's code of ethics and its conflicts management framework. In addition to general conflicts management and ethics training, it is important to also provide targeted conflicts training to address conflicts that may frequently arise or that present unique challenges. If a financial institution tracks the existence and management of conflicts it may be able to provide targeted training on a prospective basis that helps mitigate the impact of conflicts and the risks they present.[112]

Other Tools to Address Conflicts

Compensation is a major source of conflicts of interest. The financial incentives and rewards that firms offer staff may influence their behavior in ways that affect clients. In order to mitigate compensation-related conflicts effectively, firms could implement a number of measures, including the following:

- *Compensation practices:* Financial institutions can review their compensation systems and avoid structures that create incentives for staff to provide advice or make recommendations of products or services that are not in the best interests of clients. As an example, broker-dealers can periodically review their compensation practices to see whether they create incentives for personnel to favor one type of product over another.[113] They also can avoid compensation arrangements that enable registered representative to increase their compensation disproportionately through an incremental increase in sales. More broadly speaking, all financial institutions can adjust employees' compensation practices so that they are consistent with clients' interests. For instance, financial institutions can base compensation and bonuses, in part, on how well the products they recommend perform, plus employees' degree of compliance with the institution's policies and procedures and/or the management of conflicts. In recent years, firms have begun to adjust their compensation and performance evaluation processes by including factors tied to clients' experiences and outcomes, and compliance with firm policies and procedures, in an effort to promote good conduct by their employees.

---

[112] *Id.*

[113] It is fairly common for broker-dealers' compensation grids to have different payouts that vary by product type—for example, equities, bonds, mutual funds, and variable annuities. This structure encourages registered representatives to recommend certain products over others. To mitigate the conflicts of interest created by such a compensation structure, broker-dealers can institute "product neutral" compensation grids that pay a flat percentage of the revenue a registered representative generates, regardless of the products recommended. Although this eliminates one variable that may influence recommendations, registered representatives will still have an incentive to favor products that pay higher commissions because these produce larger payouts. Thus, a customer purchase may result in different amounts credited to a representative's revenues, even though the percentage payout from the amount of the credit is the same. In addition, a conflict is created if a representative's desire to move to a higher payout level influences the number or type of recommendations he or she makes to customers. As FINRA observed in its *Conflicts Report,* this conflict is heightened when there is a large increase in the percentage payout between revenue tranches, when there is a high probability that a few, incremental sales will move a registered representative to a new payout level, or when increased payout percentages are applied retroactively once a threshold is satisfied.

- *Monitoring advice provided by personnel:* Firms' supervisory programs can include measures to assess whether employees' recommendations are in fact influenced by thresholds in a firm's compensation structure. As one example, FINRA observed in its *Conflicts Report* that some broker-dealers perform enhanced surveillance and supervision as registered representatives approach thresholds that:
  - Move the registered representative to a higher payout percentage in a firm's compensation grid;
  - Qualify a representative to receive a back-end bonus; or
  - Qualify a representative to participate in a recognition club.
- *Compensation penalties:* Some financial institutions adjust the compensation paid to employees who do not properly manage conflicts of interest in accordance with the firm's policies and procedures. Such actions demonstrate a dedication to conflict management and signal to employees that the financial institution takes its ethical values seriously. Ensuring that employees act in accordance with the institution's policies, procedures, and values shows the importance management places on conflicts management and the institution's culture. For these reasons, some firms impose compensation penalties on employees who do not properly manage conflicts of interest or otherwise engage in conduct detrimental to clients or the firm.
- *Segregating responsibilities and checks and balances:* Certain conflicts can be mitigated by segregating responsibility for different business activities. For example, many financial institutions separate the portfolio management function from the trading function to ensure that portfolio managers cannot place trades. This type of "checks and balances" can reduce the opportunity for conflicts. By focusing on the functions performed by personnel, financial institutions can avoid situations in which assigned job responsibilities may create conflicts if the same individual were tasked with multiple job duties.

V. CONCLUSION

Conflict identification and mitigation is a never-ending process. In order to avoid the adverse impacts that may be caused by conflicts of interest, firms need to seek to continuously improve their procedures for identifying and mitigating conflicts and assess the effectiveness of their internal controls and processes. Strict attention is required to manage conflicts because it only takes a single oversight for an unmitigated conflict to cause client harm and destroy a firm. Accordingly, constant vigilance against the impacts of conflicts is a price that needs to be paid for the privilege of being a financial institution and managing clients' assets or providing investment advice. No less stringent a standard can be accepted when so much is at stake and the financial repercussions of the investment advice provided to clients is so significant and long-lasting.

APPENDIX A. SAMPLE OCC CONFLICTS OF INTEREST REQUEST LETTER [112]

Note: This request letter is only a sample. Actual information requested must be specifically tailored to the firm under review and should be commensurate with the firm's size, risk, and complexity of operations.

Review: *OCC Examination of [X Firm] Conflicts of Interest—Asset Management*

Request Items:

1. Policies and procedures related to conflicts of interest. Include those required under
   - 12 CFR 9.5 and 12 CFR 12.7(a) (national firms) or 12 CFR 150.140 and
   - 12 CFR 151.140 (FSAs) for all applicable asset management business units.
2. The firm's code of ethics and any related policies.
3. A summary of any circumstances that resulted in termination or other disciplinary action of an asset management employee for violation of the code of conduct or ethics policies, or other engagement in improper conflicts of interest.
4. If not addressed in policies and procedures, briefly describe the firm's practices related to avoiding impermissible self-dealing and conflicts of interest. Include the following, as applicable:
   - Investment of fiduciary accounts in obligations of or assets acquired from related parties and interests (both investment and retention).
   - Investment in proprietary investment products or investment products from which the firm receives a fee.
   - Crediting client accounts for 12b-1 and administrative fees received when the firm is not authorized to retain such fees.
   - Proxy voting for firm and firm holding company stock and for obligations of other related parties and interests.
   - Market timing and late trading in mutual funds and collective investment funds (CIF).
   - SEC restrictions applicable to affiliated mutual funds.
   - Loans, sales, or transfers from related parties and interests.
   - Loans to fiduciary accounts.
   - Loans between fiduciary accounts.
   - Brokerage placement, including use of affiliates.
   - Soft dollar policies.

[112] Office of the Comptroller of the Currency, Comptroller's Handbook, https://www.occ.gov/publications/publications-by-type/comptrollers-handbook/conflictofinterest.pdf

APPENDIX A. SAMPLE OCC CONFLICTS OF INTEREST REQUEST LETTER *(cont'd)*

- Payments for order flow to related parties and interests.
- Allocation of block trades.
- Cross trading between accounts.
- Reporting of personal securities trading by firm employees and related oversight.
- If applicable, oversight of conflicts of interest when the firm serves as indenture trustee.
- Purchase of securities underwritten by the firm or affiliate for fiduciary accounts.
- Business referral arrangements (if applicable).
- Fee discounts and concessions.
- Incentive compensation for fiduciary employees.

5. A summary of audit and compliance review plans related to conflicts of interest in the firm's asset management area.
6. Reports of any audit, compliance, or other reviews and any self-assessment related to conflicts of interest in the firm's asset management areas conducted since the last examination. Include management's response to and action plans resulting from any concerns raised in these reports.
7. A brief description of any complaints or litigation involving real or alleged conflicts of interest outstanding or resolved since the last examination.
8. A copy of the approved securities list for managed accounts.
9. A summary of any new products approved since the last examination and the firm's analysis of potential conflicts of interest related to such products.
10. A list of proprietary cash management vehicles used for fiduciary funds awaiting investment or distribution and a summary of accounts that hold such assets. Include firm and affiliate deposit accounts, firm or affiliate money market mutual funds, and short- term CIFs.
11. If own-firm or firm-affiliate deposit products are used in fiduciary accounts, provide the methodology for determining the interest rate paid for such deposits. Include documentation related to the firm's periodic analysis of interest rates paid, including any comparison of rates paid with those available from third parties.
12. A list of any obligations of the firm or its affiliates or related parties held in fiduciary accounts and a summary of accounts that hold such assets. Include
    - Firm or affiliate certificates of deposits and time deposits.
    - Firm or holding company stock and debt instruments.
    - Direct obligations of related parties and interests, including affiliates.

APPENDIX A. SAMPLE OCC CONFLICTS OF INTEREST REQUEST LETTER *(cont'd)*

13. A list of any third-party investment products for which the firm receives a fee, such as mutual fund 12b-1 or administrative fees, and the accounts that hold such assets. Include
    - A summary of such fees retained by the firm and a list of accounts for which the firm retains the fees.
    - A summary of such fees credited to owning accounts and a list of accounts that receive such credits.
14. A list of any mutual funds for which the firm is deemed an affiliate under Section 17 of the Investment Company Act of 1940, including funds for which the firm exercises discretion or has voting authority over 5 percent or more of the outstanding shares.
15. A list of any other investment products sponsored, managed, or underwritten by the firm or an affiliate or for which the firm provides any service for which the firm is paid a fee, such as an ETF, structured product, hedge fund, or private equity fund.
16. A summary of any financial benefits the firm receives from third-party service providers and parties to whom the firm delegates fiduciary activities.
17. A summary of applicable incentive compensation arrangements in place at third parties to whom the firm delegates fiduciary activities, such as investment management.
18. A summary of any business referral arrangements between the firm and third parties, including any direct or indirect compensation between the parties.
19. A list of approved brokers and the policy and basis for selecting those brokers.
20. A summary of any affiliated brokerage arrangements, including whether trades executed under such arrangements for discretionary accounts are executed on a for-profit or not- for-profit basis.
21. A summary of any soft dollar arrangements in place. Include applicable commission rates, conversion ratios, and the research and brokerage services provided under the arrangement. Include a summary of the firm's practices for disclosing such arrangements to fiduciary accounts.
22. A summary of any cross trades between accounts since the last examination.
23. A list of any loans made between fiduciary accounts since the last examination and a list of any loans between fiduciary accounts that are past due.
24. A list of any loans from fiduciary accounts to related parties and interests.
25. A list of any securities held in fiduciary accounts that were underwritten by the firm, an affiliate, or a subsidiary of the firm.

APPENDIX A. SAMPLE OCC CONFLICTS OF INTEREST REQUEST LETTER *(cont'd)*

26. A list of any closely held corporations, partnerships, or other assets held in fiduciary accounts for which insiders—such as directors, officers, or employees—act as general partner or have a controlling interest or the ability to influence decisions.
27. A summary of employee incentive compensation plans with respect to fiduciary accounts.
28. A list of insider accounts for which a director, officer, or employee is a grantor or beneficiary and any fee concessions in place for such accounts.
29. A list of any loans from the firm to fiduciary accounts or secured by fiduciary assets.
30. A list of any securities for which the firm is trustee that are in default.
31. A summary of any financial support provided by the firm or an affiliate to a fiduciary account or CIF.
32. A summary of any purchase made by the firm since the last examination of an asset from a fiduciary account. Include
    - Purchases made based on the written advice of legal counsel in order to cure a contingent or potential liability.
    - Purchases made at the direction of the OCC.
    - Purchases of defaulted assets from CIFs the firm administers.
33. A list of any fiduciary accounts for which a firm director, officer, or employee is cofiduciary.
34. A list of any gifts or bequests received by any fiduciary officer or employee from a fiduciary account.
35. A list of any other significant (potential or actual) fiduciary conflicts of interest and self- dealing of which firm management is aware. Include
    - Summary of potential conflicts identified through the firm's annual review of accounts for which the firm has investment discretion.
    - Summary of potential conflicts identified through the firm's annual review of accounts for which the firm is indenture trustee.
36. A summary of any instances where a fiduciary account owns an asset controlled by, or has engaged in transactions with, individuals or organizations with whom the firm has determined that there is a related interest that might affect the exercise of the firm's best judgment.

APPENDIX B. SELECTED FINRA AND SEC RULES ADDRESSING CONFLICTS [113]

- Exchange Act Rules 15c1-5 and 15c1-6 generally require written disclosure to a customer if a broker-dealer has any control, affiliation, or interest in a security it is offering or in the issuer of the security.
- FINRA Rule 5130 generally prohibits firms and their associated persons from purchasing a new issue for any account in which the firm or an associated person has an interest, except in accordance with the rule's conditions.
- FINRA Rule 2124 requires transaction-by-transaction disclosure and written consent for net trades involving noninstitutional customers. Net trades with institutional customers are subject to different consent requirements. For these purposes, a net trade is a principal transaction in which, for example, a market maker, after having received an order to buy a security, purchases the security from another broker-dealer or customer and then sells it to the customer at a different price.
- Regulation M generally prohibits, broker-dealers participating in a distribution from bidding for or purchasing the offered security during a certain restricted period, or inducing another person to do so. Regulation M also regulates various market activities in connection with an offering and requires that firms notify FINRA or the market where certain bids are to be posted. FINRA Rule 5190 sets forth Regulation M notification requirements for firms.
- If a firm controls, is controlled by, or under common control with an issuer of a security, FINRA Rule 2262 requires disclosure to the customer prior to commencing a transaction in the security.
- FINRA Rule 5280 prohibits firms from using nonpublic advance knowledge of a research report to change its inventory position in a security or derivative of the security.
- FINRA Rule 2269 generally requires written disclosure to customers for trades in any security in which the firm is participating in the distribution or is otherwise financially interested.
- FINRA Rule 2241 restricts the activities of and the relationships between a firm's research analysts and its investment bankers and personal trading by research analysts in the stocks that they cover.
- FINRA Rule 3220 prohibits firms from giving anything worth more than $100 annually to employees of other firms where the payment is made because of the employer's business.
- FINRA Rule 5121 prohibits firms with a conflict of interest from participating in a public offering unless certain conditions are met, including prominent prospectus disclosure of the conflict.
- NASD Rule 2341(k) prohibits a firm from favoring the sale of a fund because of brokerage business that has been or may be directed to the firm
- FINRA Rule 3240 prohibits borrowing from or lending to customers unless strict conditions are met.
- FINRA Rule 5320 generally prohibits firms from trading ahead of a customer order for the firm's own account

[113] *FINRA Conflicts Report,* http://www.finra.org/sites/default/files/Industry/p359971.pdf, Appendix I.

APPENDIX C. FINRA CONFLICTS OF INTEREST REVIEW—COMPENSATION AND OVERSIGHT [114]

August 2015

As referenced in FINRA's Annual Priorities Letter, conflicts of interest represent a recurring challenge that contribute to compliance and supervisory breakdowns which can lead to firms and registered representatives, at times, compromising the quality of service they provide to clients. While we have observed instances of positive change since we issued the Report on Conflicts of Interest in October 2013, the intent of this review it to continue our assessment of the efforts employed by firms to identify, mitigate, and manage conflicts of interest, specifically with respect to compensation practices.

In connection with this review, which will cover the time period August 2014 through July 2015, we request that responses to the questions and requests below be provided in writing by no later than Friday, September 18, 2015. The scope of our review is limited to your firm's retail accounts,[115] and therefore all responses should be limited to that aspect of your business.

1. Identify and describe the composition of the departments or committees that are responsible for reviewing and approving compensation policies for the firm's registered persons, including supervisory personnel, involved in retail brokerage.
   a. Describe the role of the board in reviewing and approving individuals' compensation packages as well as compensation policies as a whole.
   b. What role do corporate functions—such as finance, human resources, compliance, or risk—play in the review and approval of business line remuneration policies?
2. Identify and describe the controls utilized to *identify* compensation-related conflicts of interest.
   a. Identify the team(s) or individual(s) that are responsible for developing and implementing the identified controls.
   b. Describe the initial review and approval process that occurred for the identified controls.
3. Identify and describe the controls (e.g., neutral grid, fee-capping, compensation penalties) utilized to *manage* compensation-related conflicts of interest.
   a. Identify the team(s) or individual(s) that are responsible for developing and implementing the identified controls.
   b. Describe the initial review and approval process that occurred for the identified controls.

[114] Conflicts of Interest Review—Compensation and Oversight, http://www.finra.org/industry/conflicts-interest-review-compensation-and-oversight

[115] Accounts that do not meet the definition of "institutional account" contained in FINRA Rule 4512(c) are deemed retail accounts for this request.

APPENDIX C. FINRA CONFLICTS OF INTEREST REVIEW—COMPENSATION AND OVERSIGHT *(cont'd)*

4. Identify and describe surveillance efforts or supervisory processes that have been implemented to assess whether potential compensation-related conflicts of interest are materializing in your firm's retail brokerage business.
   a. Describe specific underlying surveillance/supervision efforts that have been implemented. Include the identity of the department(s) responsible for the surveillance or supervision.
   b. Describe whether surveillance/supervision efforts are performed on a routine basis and, if so, how often.
   c. Describe escalation procedures in place for situations that suggest a compensation-related conflict of interest is materializing.
   d. Indicate how many compensation-related conflict of interest escalations occurred during the period of August 2014 through July 2015.
5. Describe how current compensation structures balance short-term incentives for registered representatives and clients' long-term interests. Include a description of any components of compensation structures designed mitigate compensation-related conflicts of interest.
6. If changes to compensation structures were made during the period of August 2014 through July 2015, summarize each change and identify the strategic goal of each change.
7. Identify and describe the terms and conditions of each standardized enhanced and deferred compensation package[116] your firm offers to recruit or retain registered representatives including who is authorized to provide such packages and who must approve such packages. Indicate the degree to which these compensation packages are contingent upon a registered persons' production derived from particular product types or product families. Identify the number of registered representatives currently receiving compensation from each standardized enhanced or deferred compensation package.
8. Describe the use of nonstandard (i.e., negotiated) enhanced and deferred compensation packages by your firm to recruit or retain registered representatives. Indicate the degree to which these compensation packages are contingent upon a registered persons' production derived from particular product types or product families. Identify who is authorized to provide such packages and who must approve such packages. Further, identify the number of registered representatives currently receiving non-standard enhanced and deferred compensation packages.
9. Identify production thresholds that entitle any registered representative to higher compensation whether paid in the form of higher commission payout, higher base salary or higher discretionary bonus. Indicate whether these thresholds are communicated to registered representatives.

[116] "Standardized enhanced or deferred compensation package" is defined as a compensation package that is available for offer based upon set parameters established by your firm. Illustrative Example: A registered person who manages assets of more than $xxx,xxx can be offered a compensation package with ABC terms.

APPENDIX C. FINRA CONFLICTS OF INTEREST REVIEW—COMPENSATION AND OVERSIGHT *(cont'd)*

10. Describe the terms and conditions of any direct production penalties in place which, based upon events occurring, can result in a decrease in compensation paid to registered representatives.
11. Describe the approach to compensating direct and indirect managers of registered representatives involved in sales to retail accounts, including sales managers (or similar function), business supervisors, and compliance personnel. Indicate whether compensation packages are tied to production either through direct commission payout, higher base salary, or discretionary bonus. Indicate if thresholds for higher compensation are communicated to managers.
12. Describe broadly how products approved for sale are displayed or otherwise communicated to registered representatives. For example, are products presented by product category (e.g., mutual fund or annuity)? Is an internal search feature available?
13. For each method used by your firm to display approved product to registered representatives, describe how the display order of products is determined and identify the group or department that makes the decision.
14. Describe any methods employed or processes in place to promote the sale of specific products or categories of products. (Example: preferred product list, enhanced commission payouts, etc.)
15. Using the table in attachment A, identify the products offered to retail accounts and describe all types of income received for each product (e.g., commission/concession, 12b-1 fee, income from other revenue sharing arrangements, payment for shelf space, etc.) For each type of income, state whether the income is split with registered representatives on a per transaction basis pursuant to a payout schedule or other terms.
16. Describe your firm's policy for permitting third-party product or sponsor representatives to meet with registered representatives. Include details about requirements, if any, for supervisors or managers to attend.
17. Describe your firm's policy for permitting registered representatives to attend off-site, overnight educational session that are sponsored by issuers or product sponsors.
18. Identify by name the Top 10 proprietary or affiliated products as well as the Top 10 independent products sold to retail accounts during the period of August 2014 through July 2015. Total revenue to your firm for each product should be the measurement used in identifying products identified on each list.
19. Identify any flat fee or annual payments that your firm has received to make a product available for sale by its registered representatives.

APPENDIX D. FINRA REVIEW—ESTABLISHING, COMMUNICATING, AND IMPLEMENTING CULTURAL VALUES[117]

February 2016

Firm culture has a profound influence on how a broker-dealer conducts its business, including how it manages conflicts of interest. A culture that consistently places ethical considerations and client interests at the center of business decisions helps protect investors and the integrity of the markets. Conversely, failures in these areas can impose significant harm on investors and the markets as well as firms themselves. One estimate places fines and litigation costs to firms, or their parent companies, related to cultural failures at over $300 billion since 2010. This underscores the critical importance of firms establishing and implementing strong cultural values.

FINRA is reviewing how firms establish, communicate, and implement cultural values, and whether cultural values are guiding business conduct. As part of this review, we plan to meet with executive business, compliance, legal, and risk management staff of your firm to discuss cultural values. We would also like to discuss how your firm communicates and reinforces those values directly, implicitly and through its reward system. We are particularly interested in how your firm measures compliance with its cultural values, what metrics, if any, are used, and how you monitor for implementation and consistent application of those values throughout your organization.

One definition of "firm culture" is the set of explicit and implicit norms, practices and expected behaviors that influence how employees make and carry out decisions in the course of conducting the firm's business. Your firm may have its own definition of "firm culture" that it can use to prepare for our meeting and respond to this letter.

This inquiry is not an indication that FINRA has concerns about your firm's culture or has determined that your firm violated any rules or regulations. Rather, our goal is to better understand industry practices and determine whether firms are taking reasonable steps to properly establish and implement their own cultural values within the firm. Knowing firms' practices in this area, and the challenges they face, will help FINRA develop potential guidance for the industry and determine other steps that could be taken.

In preparation for our meeting, we request that your firm submit the following information (or indicate instances where the requested information is not available) to FINRA by March 21, 2016:

[117] FINRA, Establishing, Communicating, and Implementing Cultural Values, http://www.finra.org/industry/establishing-communicating-and-implementing-cultural-values

APPENDIX D. FINRA REVIEW—ESTABLISHING, COMMUNICATING, AND IMPLEMENTING CULTURAL VALUES *(cont'd)*

1. A summary of the key policies and processes by which the firm establishes cultural values. In the summary, include whether this is a board-level function at your broker-dealer or at the corporate parent of the firm. If it is a board-level function, describe the board's involvement. Also, provide a description of any steps you have initiated or completed in the past 24 months to promote, strengthen or change your firm's culture.

2. A description of the processes employed by executive management, business unit leaders, and control functions in establishing, communicating and implementing your firm's cultural values. Include a description of how executive management communicates, promotes and establishes a "tone from the top" as it relates to cultural values (to the extent not covered by the previous question). Include a description of the firm's approach to ensure that its cultural values are adopted and applied by middle management.

3. A description of how your firm assesses and measures the impact of cultural values (to the extent assessments and measures exist) and whether they have made a difference at your firm in achieving desired behaviors. Provide a summary of the policy statements, procedures, mission statements or other related documents that reflect your firm's assessments and measures.

4. A summary of the processes your firm uses to identify policy breaches, including the types of reports or other documents your firm relies on, in determining whether a breach of its cultural values has occurred.

5. A description of how your firm addresses cultural value policy or process breaches once discovered. What efforts are used to promptly address these policy or process breaches? What is the escalation process to surface and resolve such breaches?

6. A description of your firm's policies and processes, if any, to identify and address subcultures within the firm that may depart from or undermine the cultural values articulated by your board and senior management.

7. A description of your firm's compensation practices and how they reinforce your firm's cultural values.

8. A description of the cultural value criteria used to determine promotions, compensation, or other rewards.

ABOUT THE AUTHOR

Michael Koffler helps U.S. and foreign investment advisers and broker-dealers design, distribute, and operate advisory programs, private funds, and investment products offered to institutional and individual clients. The author of multiple compliance-related chapters and articles, Mr. Koffler represents many of the best-known U.S. investment advisers and broker-dealers that manage or distribute unified managed accounts, wrap accounts, managed accounts, private funds, and other pooled investment vehicles. He has extensive experience in the day-to-day regulatory, operational, and compliance issues facing investment advisers and broker-dealers in the retail, institutional, and retirement markets.

Mr. Koffler frequently counsels investment advisers, broker-dealers, and banks on investment management issues, including: conflicts; trading; disclosure; brokerage allocation and aggregation issues; soft dollar arrangements; compliance with the Department of Labor's Fiduciary Rule; privacy and cybersecurity; anti-money laundering; advertising; and other regulatory compliance matters. He regularly advises clients on business operations, financial and operational issues, regulatory reporting, performance advertising and global investment performance standards (GIPS) compliance, internal controls, compliance programs, and the use of algorithms and automated tools. He also counsels banks and insurance companies on securities issues associated with the management and distribution of investment products and helps them develop innovative products and services and to distribute them through new channels.

Mr. Koffler regularly guides clients through SEC, FINRA, and state examinations and investigations, helping the clients to respond to deficiencies cited by securities regulators. Additionally, he counsels clients on mergers, acquisitions, and joint ventures involving broker-dealers and investment advisers. Mr. Koffler is recognized as a leading authority on distribution issues arising in connection with 529 plans.

He began his career at the SEC, serving in the Division of Investment Management. That unique perspective and knowledge continues to inform Mr. Koffler's work today.

Chapter 25

The Sides of "May": When Is "May" Deemed False and Misleading?

By Elizabeth M. Knoblock, *Elizabeth M. Knoblock, PLLC*
Patricia Flynn, *INTECH Investment Management, LLC*

I. INTRODUCTION

For years, the word "may" has been used in financial industry disclosure documents to describe any number of things that a firm registered with the Securities and Exchange Commission (SEC) might, could, or would do, or had done upon occasion. Yet, in a handful of recent SEC enforcement actions, the regulator has taken issue with investment advisers use of the word when making disclosures in their Forms ADV. This chapter examines the circumstances in which the SEC has objected to the use of "may" by investment advisers and the consequences associated with using it in a manner deemed false and misleading.

II. SEC SETTLEMENT ORDERS INVOLVING "MAY"

As a grammarian might explain the issue, the words "can," "may," and "will" are auxiliary, or helping, verbs. "Can" is commonly used to denote the ability to do a thing; "may" denotes possibility or permission; and "will" denotes the certainty of something occurring. However, through various enforcement actions, the SEC has now indicated that investment advisers must be especially careful when using "may" in Form ADV disclosures. In fact, the SEC has concluded that advisers' use of the word "may" in their disclosure is misleading when it suggests that an action is only a possibility if the facts demonstrate that the action has already occurred.

For example, in a settled matter, the principals[1] of Belvedere Asset Management were found to have violated Section 206(2) of the Investment Advisers Act of 1940 ("Advisers Act") by disclosing only that a conflict of interest may occur when, in fact, the conflict actually existed. According to the settlement order, the adviser initially failed to disclose to its clients any conflict of interest relating to its relationship with an affiliated mutual

---

[1] SEC, *In the Matter of Jan Gleisner and Keith D. Pagan*, Rel. No. IA-4537 (Sept. 28, 2016); https://www.sec.gov/litigation/admin/2016/ia-4537.pdf

fund. Later, the Form ADV was amended to state that the adviser "may invest clients in registered funds advised by it, which would create conflicts of interest to the extent that Belvedere receives fees on both account and fund assets." However, the amended ADV was not offered or provided to clients even though the ADV described the change as material and an outside compliance consultant had advised the principals to make delivery of the disclosure to clients.

Subsequently, the adviser provided at least some clients with a separate disclosure related to the conflict, but the document stated only that it "'may' invest clients' assets in one or more of its registered funds and charge additional fees for those fund investments, which 'may' create a conflict of interest."[2] However, the SEC found this disclosure inadequate, because the clients' assets had already been invested in an affiliated mutual fund when the disclosure was made. The SEC concluded that this meant the conflict was actual, not potential. To settle the proceedings, the principals agreed to provide a copy of the SEC order to any prospective clients for one year following the issuance of the order and were ordered to cease and desist, make disgorgement plus interest and pay a penalty.

Similarly, principals[3] of Concord Equity Group Advisors were found by settlement order to have violated the Advisers Act by failing to disclose commission-sharing arrangements and the conflicts of interest associated with such arrangements. The respondents had entered into an undisclosed arrangement with an unaffiliated broker-dealer to provide trade execution for their clients at a commission rate of $0.01 per share executed, while charging clients between $0.04 and $0.06 per share and paying the excess commission to the adviser's affiliated broker-dealer as a "referral fee," even though no referrals were made by the adviser or its affiliated broker-dealer to the executing broker-dealer. The adviser's initial Form ADV, which was not amended for several years, "contained no discussion concerning the affiliated broker-dealer or the commission-sharing arrangement."[4]

Moreover, even after amending the Form ADV years later, the disclosure stated only that an affiliated entity:

- "May receive referral fees for referring prospective institutions to other broker dealers including customers of registrants [sic] related entities;"
- That an affiliated broker-dealer "can process unsolicited transactions for institutional customers which may include a client" of the adviser; and
- That the affiliate "has yet to commence or transact any such trading," even though it had already received more than $1 million worth of "referral fees" that clients were unaware had been paid from their commissions.[5]

---

2 *Gleisner and Pagan,* at 5, ¶18.

3 SEC, *In the Matter of Alan Gavornik, Nicholas Mariniello, and Lee Argush,* Rel. No. 34-73678 (Nov. 24, 2014), https://www.sec.gov/litigation/admin/2014/34-73678.pdf

4 *Gavornik, Mariniello, and Argush,* at 7, ¶19.

5 *Gavornik, Mariniello, and Argush,* at 7-8, ¶¶20, 21, and 22.

In addition, the Form ADV stated that the adviser received "no products, research, or services in turn [sic]" for suggesting brokers to its clients, even though its affiliate was regularly receiving the excess commissions from the unaffiliated broker-dealer.[6]

According to the order, the use of the prospective "may" in the various Form ADV disclosures "is misleading because it suggested the mere possibility that Tore [the affiliated broker-dealer] would make a referral and/or be paid 'referral fees' at a later point, when in fact a commission sharing arrangement was already in place and generating income" to the affiliated entities and principals.[7] The SEC found that use of the prospective term "may" was misleading, because it suggested the mere possibility of referral arrangements at a later point even though the arrangement was already in place. This conclusion was not changed by a subsequent Form ADV revision, because even then, the disclosure continued to state only that the adviser "may have a conflict of interest regarding the recommendation of an executing broker dealer in that it may receive compensation," without disclosing that the commission-sharing arrangement already existed and that payments had already been made.[8]

As a result, the principals were censured, ordered to cease and desist, make disgorgement with interest, and pay penalties. In addition, the chief compliance officer (CCO), who was primarily responsible for drafting and revising the ADV disclosure, was suspended from all aspects of participating in the financial industry for 12 months.

Similarly, Advantage Investment Management[9] settled SEC charges that it failed to disclose the existence of, and conflicts associated with, a five-year, forgivable $3 million loan from a dual-registrant broker-dealer and investment adviser that provided execution, custody, and reporting services to 90 percent of its client assets under management. At the time the loan agreement was entered into, the adviser made no disclosure of its existence. Four years later, the adviser added a disclosure regarding the possibility that certain of its advisory representatives may have received forgivable loans from the dual registrant if they had recently joined the adviser from another financial services firm and also disclosed that receipt of such loans "presents a potential conflict of interest in that an IAR has a financial incentive to recommend that a client engage with the…[adviser and the representative] for advisory services in order for the loan to be forgiven."[10] However, the Form ADV failed to affirmatively disclose the existence of the loan agreement funding these loans or that the conflict actually existed given that all of the adviser's representatives had already received loans and the loans were still outstanding.

As with the other cases, the adviser was found to have willfully violated Advisers Act Section 206(2). The adviser was censured, ordered to cease and desist, and charged a $60,000 penalty for the false and misleading disclosure.

---

6 *Id.*

7 *Gavornik, Mariniello, and Argush,* at 8, ¶22.

8 *Gavornik, Mariniello, and Argush,* at 8, ¶23.

9 SEC, *In the Matter of Advantage Investment Management, LLC,* Rel. No. IA-4455 (July 18, 2016); https://www.sec.gov/litigation/admin/2016/ia-4455.pdf

10 *Advantage Investment Management,* at 4, ¶11.

III. SEC ADMINISTRATIVE PROCEEDINGS

In addition to the settled enforcement actions discussed above, SEC administrative law judges (ALJs) have decided three other cases involving advisers using the "may" disclosure, among other factors. Two of the three actions discussed below held that the disclosure was false and misleading. Although the third case was decided in favor of the adviser, it was reversed by the SEC in a final decision.

In the first instance, a principal[11] of an investment adviser was found to have violated the Advisers Act for, among other reasons, having inaccurate Form ADV and contract disclosures regarding receipt of various forms of compensation. Initially, the ADV failed to make any disclosure of performance-based compensation and referral and advisory fees paid by offshore hedge funds. Following an SEC examination, the ADV was amended to state that the adviser "may receive incentive or subscription fees from certain investment companies" and "may receive performance-based compensation from certain investment companies."[12] The principal testified that he believed "that 'may' is accurate and not misleading because [the adviser] did not always receive compensation and whether [the adviser] received these fees depended on the client."[13]

The ALJ was not convinced and concluded that the adviser's "disclosure that it may receive incentive, subscription, and performance-based compensation from certain investment companies was inaccurate and misleading because it actually *was* receiving this compensation"[14] [emphasis in original]. Quoting from the *Merriam-Webster Dictionary,* the ALJ stated further: "'May' is used to 'indicate possibility or probability.'"[15] Because the payments had already been received, the existence of compensation was a fact, not merely a possibility. Given the ALJ's conclusions, a better way to disclose the payments subject to a contingency would be to state that the adviser receives incentive, subscription, and performance-based compensation depending on the arrangement entered into with the client.

Another ALJ decision, *Total Wealth Management,*[16] held, among other rulings, that it is "grossly inaccurate and misleading for an investment adviser to represent that revenue sharing agreements 'may' happen, when they had in fact already happened and governed a substantial portion of client investments."[17] The adviser primarily had invested client assets in private funds and had entered into revenue sharing agreements involving sharing a portion of fund advisory fees or receiving incentive, referral, or consulting fees from many of the funds or fund managers based on fees charged by the funds to

---

[11] *In the Matter of Larry C. Grossman and Gregory Adams,* Init. Dec. Rel. No. 727 (Dec. 23, 2014); https://www.sec.gov/alj/aljdec/2014/id727bpm.pdf

[12] *Grossman and Adams,* at 19.

[13] *Grossman and Adams,* at 20.

[14] *Grossman and Adams,* at 36.

[15] *Grossman and Adams,* at 38.

[16] *In the Matter of Total Wealth Management, Inc., et al.,* Init. Dec. Rel. No. 860 (Aug. 17, 2015); https://www.sec.gov/alj/aljdec/2015/id860bpm.pdf

[17] Total Wealth Management, at 32.

adviser's clients. As in previous cases, initially the adviser made no disclosure of the arrangements. After undergoing a review performed by an independent compliance consultant, the firm was advised to amend the ADV to disclose that the adviser had a conflict of interest associated with receiving fees from firms offering securities to its clients. However the consultant was fired and the recommended amendment was not implemented. Instead, the adviser amended its Form ADV to state that it "may have arrangements with certain independent managers whereby the adviser receives a percentage of the fees charged by such independent managers" without mentioning any related conflicts of interest.[18]

The ALJ noted that these "disclosures were made after Total Wealth had already entered into revenue sharing agreements with numerous entities and had invested enormous amounts of client funds in these entities."[19] In addition, the adviser's argument that using the word "may" to disclose the revenue sharing and consulting agreements was appropriate, "because an investor could potentially have a portfolio consisting entirely of funds without revenue sharing agreements" was rejected by the ALJ.[20] The ALJ concluded that "this argument mischaracterizes the purpose of the disclosure. The disclosure is not intended to address whether a client's portfolio may include funds with revenue sharing agreements, but whether such revenue sharing agreements were in place at all. Because such agreements were in place, disclosing that such agreements may be in place was false and misleading; the disclosures failed to make clear there were actual, present conflicts of interest at play."[21]

Finally, in contrast to the preceding cases, the ALJ decision in *The Robare Group*[22] resulted in support for the adviser's use of "may." As in the case against Total Wealth Management, the SEC had charged that the firm's use of "may" in connection with its disclosure of certain commission sharing arrangements with another firm was false and misleading. The adviser's ADV used "may" in several instances to explain compensation it received under a revenue sharing arrangement with an unaffiliated custodian. Fees could be paid to the adviser for client assets placed in various no-load mutual funds offered by, but not affiliated with, the custodian.

The adviser's president testified that the word "may" was used, "because the original program agreement provided that the underlying mutual funds could stop payments at any time."[23] The ALJ sided with the adviser, contending that the agreement between the adviser and the custodian informed the adviser "that the underlying mutual funds could change or suspend payments at any time," and he concluded that "[u]se of the word "may" thus accounts for the possible cessation of payments."[24]

---

18 Total Wealth Management, at 15.
19 Total Wealth Management, at 32.
20 *Id.*
21 Total Wealth Management, at 32-33.
22 *In the Matter of The Robare Group, Ltd., et al.,* Init. Dec. Rel. No. 806 (June 4, 2015); https://www.sec.gov/alj/aljdec/2015/id806jeg.pdf
23 *The Robare Group,* Init. Dec. Rel. No. 806, at 13.
24 *The Robare Group,* Init. Dec. Rel. No. 806, at 38.

However, the ALJ's initial decision was reversed by the SEC on November 7, 2016.[25] Contrary to the conclusion reached by the ALJ, the SEC determined that the adviser and its principals violated Advisers Act Section 206(2) by negligently failing to fully and fairly disclose the revenue sharing agreement with the unaffiliated custodian for several years and by failing to disclose adequately and completely the conflict of interest arising from the agreement even after disclosing the arrangement. According to the final decision, the initial disclosure made by the firm that the principals testified was intended to refer to the arrangement was wholly inadequate, because "disclosure that it *may* receive selling compensation in the form of 12b-1 fees in no way revealed that TRG actually had an arrangement with [custodian], that it received fees pursuant to the arrangement, and that the arrangement presented at least a potential conflict of interest"[26] [emphasis in original]. Moreover, the SEC concluded that even disclosure added later to clarify the existence of the arrangement was inadequate, because it failed to mention that not all of the unaffiliated no-load mutual fund assets on the custodian's platform" resulted in fees; therefore, the "disclosure failed to reveal that [adviser] had an economic incentive to put client assets into eligible...funds over other funds on the...platform," and without that information, clients would be unable to "properly assess the relevant conflicts."[27] As a result, respondents were ordered to cease and desist, and a $50,000 penalty was imposed on each principal.

As compliance officers approach the Form ADV annual amendment season, the wisest course is to proactively scrub disclosure documents for any potentially misleading uses of the word. Firms should consider avoiding words like "may," "might" or "could," when it is clear that the situation being disclosed already exists. Firms should describe related conflicts of interest in a way that makes clear that the conflicts will or do exist—if not for all clients, at least for affected clients—and explain what the firm is doing to avoid or mitigate the conflicts.

As CCOs review their firm's existing Forms ADV, they can do a search for the word "may" and, whenever possible, modify the sentence to eliminate the word or provide more detailed factual information. This exercise has been performed by at least one

---

[25] SEC, *In the Matter of the Robare Group, Ltd, et al., Opinion of the Commission,* Rel. No. IA-4566 (November 7, 2016); https://www.sec.gov/litigation/opinions/2016/ia-4566.pdf

[26] *The Robare Group Opinion,* at 10.

[27] *The Robare Group Opinion,* at 10-11. *See also In the Matter of Royal Alliance Associates, Inc., SagePoint Financial, Inc. and FSC Securities Corporation,* SEC Rel. Nos. IA-4351 and 34-77362 (March 14, 2016) (dual registrant adviser /broker-dealer affiliates found to have violated Advisers Act Section 206(2) by disclosing in their Forms ADV that they "may receive 12b-1 fees from mutual fund investments in fee-based advisory accounts" but failing to disclose anywhere that they had a conflict of interest when selecting mutual fund share classes "due to a financial incentive to place non-qualified advisory clients in higher-fee share classes over lower-fee share classes of the same mutual fund," resulting in censure, disgorgement, and interest of more than $2 million and a penalty of $7.5 million).

advisory firm. That firm concluded that the word "may" was still appropriate in about two dozen instances. However, more than 50 uses of the word were eliminated from its ADV. Appendix A of this chapter provides some examples from those ADV revisions to help compliance officers when reviewing their firms' Forms ADV.

IV. CONCLUSION

Although this chapter reviewed "may" cases brought against investment advisers, other financial industry participants, including mutual funds, hedge funds, and even broker-dealers, should consider reviewing their disclosures, because "false and misleading" could apply to any mandatory disclosure. Firms seeking to avoid being the next poster child for "may"-related enforcement actions would be wise to reconsider how they are using this term in existing disclosure documents.

APPENDIX A. EXAMPLES FOR EXAMINING FORM ADV REVISIONS

The following are examples of ADV-related revisions:

Clients ~~may~~ *will* incur certain charges imposed by custodians, brokers, and other third parties, such as custodial fees, deferred sales charges, odd-lot differentials, transfer taxes, foreign exchange transaction fees, wire transfer and electronic fund fees, as well as other fees, taxes, and governmental charges.

The adviser ~~may invest~~ *invests* in shares of investment companies that charge asset management fees and other fees, which are in addition to the advisory fees charged by the adviser.

Performance-fee arrangements ~~may~~ create an incentive for an adviser to take risks in managing assets that would not otherwise be taken in the absence of such arrangements. Similarly, ~~adviser may have an incentive to favor~~ larger or higher fee-paying accounts *could be favored* because they ~~may~~ generate more revenue for *an adviser*.

Depending on the client's country of domicile, *sometimes* there ~~may be~~ *are* government or regulatory limitations on investments in certain securities, which ~~may affect~~ *affects* the adviser's ability to invest in such securities.

The trading techniques used by the adviser ~~may~~ result in a higher portfolio turnover rate and/or related trading expenses that ~~may adversely~~ affect performance.

APPENDIX A. EXAMPLES FOR EXAMINING FORM ADV REVISIONS *(Cont'd)*

Global securities ~~may~~ *tend to* be volatile and ~~may~~ involve greater risks, including currency risk, adverse political or economic developments in certain countries, the relative lack of information, relatively low market liquidity, and the potential lack of strict financial and accounting controls and standards.

Potential conflicts of interest ~~may~~ exist when an investment adviser manages more than one client account. The adviser ~~may buy~~ *buys* and ~~sell~~ *sells* securities of issuers, or ~~engage~~ *engages* in other investments on behalf of more than one of its clients, including affiliated accounts. *As a result*, advisers ~~may give~~ advice and/or actions in the performance of their duties with respect to clients in any given strategy that ~~may~~ *can* differ from the advice given, or the timing or nature of actions taken, with respect to other clients that ~~may~~ invest in some of the same securities or strategy.

The adviser will not effect any principal or agency cross securities transactions for client accounts. The adviser will also not intentionally cross trades between client accounts. However, the adviser's investment process ~~may result~~ *results* in situations in which some of its accounts ~~may~~ sell securities when other accounts purchase the same securities at or about the same time. All such transactions are executed through unaffiliated brokerage firms.

The selection of broker-dealers used to execute orders depends on type-of-trade and past-execution performance. The adviser gives primary consideration to obtaining the most-favorable price and efficient execution. ~~The adviser may, however, pay~~ *Paying* a higher commission than would otherwise be necessary for a particular transaction *is possible* when, in the adviser's opinion, to do so would further the goal of obtaining the most-favorable available execution and ensuring the transaction as a whole represents the best qualitative and quantitative execution.

The adviser has a limited number of arrangements whereby from time to time it ~~may compensate~~ *compensates*, either directly or indirectly, affiliated and/or unaffiliated persons for client referrals and/or service. Under such arrangements, the adviser generally pays a ~~percentage~~ *portion* of the investment advisory fee payable to the adviser by the client. This fee ~~may vary~~ *usually varies* according to each agreement. Clients referred to the adviser will not be charged more than similarly situated clients who were not referred to the adviser. Referral arrangements are entered into in accordance with Advisers Act Rule 206(4)-3.

APPENDIX A. EXAMPLES FOR EXAMINING FORM ADV REVISIONS *(Cont'd)*

The adviser's discretionary authority ~~may~~ *can* be subject to restrictions imposed by certain federal securities laws. Depending on the client's country of domicile, there ~~may be~~ *are* government or regulatory limitations on investments in certain securities, which ~~may affect~~ *affect* the adviser's ability to invest in such securities. In addition to investment limitations imposed by applicable regulations, certain investment companies, commingled funds, and separately managed accounts ~~may~~ have established certain restrictions on the types and quantities of securities that ~~may~~ *can* be purchased.

The following are examples of when "may" could be appropriate:

The adviser *may* allow an existing client with multiple accounts above the minimum to open another account below the minimum account size.

Laws, regulations, or contracts restrict how much of a particular security in which the adviser *may* invest on behalf of a client, and affect the timing of a purchase or sale.

The adviser does not have custody or possession of client assets. The adviser encourages all clients to carefully review the statements received from their qualified custodian and compare custodial records to the account statements provided by the adviser. The adviser's statements *may* differ from custodial statements due to accounting procedures, reporting dates, or valuation differences for certain securities.

ABOUT THE AUTHORS

Elizabeth M. Knoblock is the managing member and sole owner of Elizabeth M. Knoblock, PLLC, a private law firm. She is a securities lawyer with more than 35 years of legal practice and business experience. As first noted in the 2007 edition of Chambers USA, Ms. Knoblock has the "...ability to see the business viewpoint and to interact with management on difficult issues...." Over the course of her career, she has focused on the laws governing investment advisers, registered investment companies, hedge funds and private accounts, including institutional, retail, and wrap fee clientele. Ms. Knoblock has significant experience with securities-related policies and procedures, disclosure, compliance and regulatory issues. Ms. Knoblock began her regulatory career with the Office of General Counsel of the Commodity Futures Trading Commission, followed by a stint with the Division of Investment Management of the Securities and Exchange

Commission, before moving to Wall Street, where she spent five years in various legal positions with dual registrant brokerage firms, including Kidder Peabody, Gruntal, and Shearson Lehman Hutton. She subsequently served for a decade as general counsel of Templeton Investment Counsel, Inc., in Florida and for more than a decade as a partner with two separate international law firms. In addition to managing her firm, Ms. Knoblock serves on the advisory board of *Practical Compliance & Risk Management* for the Securities Industry, a Wolters Kluwer publication, is a past board member of the National Society of Compliance Professionals and a much sought after speaker at industry conferences. She was honored by National Regulatory Services, an industry compliance service provider, as the only speaker to have been invited to speak, and to have spoken, for 29 consecutive years at its national compliance conferences and has continued to speak for them for more than 30 consecutive years at this time.

Ms. Knoblock is a member of the state bars of New York, Florida, Alabama, and the District of Columbia. Her educational degrees include a *magna cum laude* dean's list bachelor of arts from Stetson University in Deland, Florida; a dean's list juris doctor degree from Georgetown University Law Center in Washington, DC; and an LLM/masters in Securities Regulation, also from Georgetown, plus a dean's list master of business administration from NOVA University, both of which were obtained while working full-time as a securities lawyer.

Patricia ("Trish") Flynn is senior vice president and CCO for INTECH Investment Management, LLC. Ms. Flynn has more than 20 years of compliance and regulatory experience. She is a certified public accountant and has a bachelor of science degree in Accounting from the University of South Florida. Ms. Flynn completed the NASD Institute-Wharton Certificate Program in 2002 and is a certified regulatory and compliance professional (CRCP). She is a former board member of the National Society of Compliance Professionals and holds the CSCP designation.

CHAPTER 26

Plain English Writing for Compliance Professionals

By Lois Yurow
Investor Communications Services, LLC

I. INTRODUCTION

Businesses and government agencies that use plain language save money. Public companies that communicate with the markets in plain language attract investors. Those two advantages should be appealing to any organization. This chapter aims to convince you that plain language is also a compliance imperative.

This chapter has three main sections. The first explains plain language and summarizes its many benefits (and a few potential drawbacks). The second discusses why compliance officers should devote time to instilling plain language across their organizations, and where that effort might start. The final section introduces some techniques for converting key existing documents into plain language and ensuring that new documents are clearly expressed from the start. I hope you are inspired to create a priority list of documents to change and changes to make, and gain confidence that the effort is worth your time.

II. PLAIN LANGUAGE AND ITS BENEFITS

What is Plain Language?

Definitions of plain language (or its counterpart, "plain English") abound, as do strategies for achieving it. This chapter explores some of the details later, but there are a few common threads that run through every definition. Generally speaking, a plain language document:

- Uses words that are familiar to the target audience;
- Explains the specialized words that are unavoidable;
- Is laid out and organized so the target audience can easily find information;
- Looks like material the target audience was meant to read; and
- Addresses the topics it needs to address but is no longer than necessary.

As one government agency put it, plain language "pays special attention to the person who is reading the document or filling out the form. It considers what the reader needs to know as well as what the writer wants to say."[1]

The prevailing theme is respect for your audience. When you draft a document that gives your readers information they need in language they can understand, and doesn't make them sift through unnecessary verbiage or deploy a search tool to find key points, you demonstrate respect for their intelligence and their time.

Some readers may recall Christopher Cox, who was chairman of the Securities and Exchange Commission (SEC) for several years beginning in 2005. Once discussing why retail investors may ignore things like annual reports and proxy statements, Cox explained, "The most obvious [reason] is that investors are busy people. Wading through dense legalese isn't their day job, and they ordinarily just don't have time for it. If time is money, then poorly written disclosure documents are wasting one of the investor's most important assets."[2]

What's In It for Me (or My Firm)?

On any given day, there may be a dozen challenges that compete for your attention at work. Why add plain language to the list? Can rewriting existing disclosures, contracts, and policies, and introducing plain language into the firm's drafting practices going forward, possibly be worth the time? Absolutely.

Using plain language ultimately may reduce your list of challenges. That isn't just my opinion. In his 2012 book, *Writing for Dollars, Writing to Please*,[3] law professor Joseph Kimble summarized the findings of 50 (!) plain language case studies in business, government, and law. Over and over he cites instances in which plain language saved time and money, produced better results, and enhanced the drafter's credibility. Other studies show that plain language reduces errors and their related effects (such as litigation), fosters a more loyal clientele, and improves staff morale—probably because employees understand what they need to do and aren't dealing with confused and frustrated customers.[4]

I can attest to the error-reduction claim from my own experience. In more than 20 years of editing 10-Ks and proxy statements—documents that demand precision—I have found dozens of inconsistencies and inaccuracies. I am confident that none of my clients set out to confuse or mislead anyone. Instead, I think these mistakes occur because the initial drafter did not completely understand the issue, and perhaps started with an outdated template or inapt language copied from another company's document. The

---

[1] Ontario Dept. of Education, *Implementing Plain Language: A Manager's Guide*, ERIC ED382984 (June 1992), at 5.

[2] Christopher Cox, "Plain Language—The Benefits to Small Business" (Feb. 26, 2008), https://www.sec.gov/news/testimony/2008/ts022608cc.htm

[3] Joseph Kimble, *Writing for Dollars, Writing to Please: The Case for Plain Language in Business, Government, and Law*, Durham, NC: Carolina Academic Press (2012).

[4] Ontario Department of Education, *Implementing Plain Language*, at 1-4.

problem is, once an error is committed to the page, subsequent reviewers may be too rushed, too unfamiliar with the subject matter, or too polite to challenge it. Even when documents get updated periodically and reviewed by legal counsel, there is a tendency to skim the content that has "always been there" rather than reading it with a critical eye.

With all of these possible benefits—and particularly in light of the risk that your firm may be using a document that is flat-out wrong—there's no question that attention to plain language is a worthwhile use of compliance resources. As you will see below, you need not plan a full-scale assault; even a few carefully chosen skirmishes can pay off.

Are There Any Drawbacks to Plain Language?

When plain language is shown to have so many benefits, it is only fair to ask whether there are any downsides. I will admit to two.

I hinted at one burden a few paragraphs ago: anyone writing a document in plain language needs to understand the content thoroughly. That may involve asking a lot of questions to suss out the facts, and reading the pertinent regulations. It always requires thinking of the best way to present information, in context, to the intended audience. This process is laborious and occasionally awkward, especially the first time. Updating a plain language document is considerably less painful, and to a certain extent so is drafting a document from scratch.

Second, plain language documents often are shorter than the original (reducing printing, duplicating, and mailing costs for anything committed to paper), but not always. You may need to add an illustrative chart, paragraph breaks to avoid intimidating blocks of text, or a glossary to explain technical terms. Those revisions, which contribute to reader comprehension, justify the real estate they require. I give "before" and "after" word counts in many of my examples later in this chapter so you can see how different types of revisions might affect the overall length of your document.

There are other alleged drawbacks to plain language—such as lack of precision and sophistication—that Professor Kimble ably dispatches in his book.[5]

III. PLAIN LANGUAGE AND COMPLIANCE

> Under federal and state law, you are a fiduciary and must make full disclosure to your clients of all material facts relating to the advisory relationship.....This obligation requires that you provide the client with sufficiently specific facts so that the client is able to understand the conflicts of interest you have and the business practices in which you engage, and can give informed consent to such conflicts or practices or reject them.[6]

---

[5] Kimball, *Writing for Dollars, Writing to Please,* at 11-43.

[6] General Instructions for Part 2 of Form ADV, Item 3.

The previous section showed why plain language is a good idea as a business matter. But compliance is different—or maybe not. At the risk of vastly oversimplifying things, your job is to make sure that everyone in your firm follows applicable laws and regulations, and that all of your policies, procedures, and systems contribute to that mission. That means you all have to understand each other and the firm's key documents. In addition, as the above instruction to Form ADV emphasizes, you need to make it possible for your clients to understand what you do and generally how you do it.

Start with You

In a May 2016 speech, then-SEC Chief of Staff Andrew Donahue cautioned listeners in compliance functions to be wary of colleagues who resort to technical language:

> If someone can't explain something to you in plain English, either they don't understand it well themselves or you need to do more homework on it. My experience has been that really competent people can explain something in their area in a very simple manner. When people resort to buzz words or the use of highly technical terms, I am always suspicious.[7]

The SEC's former associate director of enforcement gave a similar warning three years earlier: "Be skeptical of explanations that don't add up regardless of who provides them. If someone explains something to you in a way that you don't understand, don't accept it."[8]

Fundamentally, this is the flip side of the argument that plain language engenders trust. When people don't communicate plainly, it tells us one of these things:

- They don't want us to understand, so they are deliberately obfuscating;
- They don't care whether we understand, so they are inattentive to their language;
- They think we already do (or should, or maybe can't) understand, so they are cavalier about their language; or
- They don't understand, and they are hoping we won't notice.

All of these possibilities are potential compliance problems. If the person responsible for how your firm does something—allocates trades or assesses fees, perhaps—cannot explain it to you, it's entirely possible that person's subordinates aren't doing what your policies require. This is not a farfetched idea. In a recent Risk Alert,[9] the SEC's Office of Compliance Inspections and Examinations (OCIE) identified the top five compliance issues cited in deficiency letters to advisers in 2015 and 2016. One of

---

7 Andrew Donohue, "New Directions in Corporate Compliance," Rutgers Law School Center for Corporate Law and Governance (May 20, 2016), https://www.sec.gov/news/speech/donohue-rutgers-new-directions-corporate-compliance-keynote.html

8 Stephen Cohen, "Remarks at SCCE's Annual Compliance and Ethics Institute" (Oct. 7, 2013), https://www.sec.gov/News/Speech/Detail/Speech/1370539872783

9 Office of Compliance Inspections and Examinations, "The Five Most Frequent Compliance Topics Identified in OCIE Examinations of Investment Advisers" (Feb. 7, 2017), https://www.sec.gov/ocie/Article/risk-alert-5-most-frequent-ia-compliance-topics.pdf

OCIE's chief concerns was "advisers [that] appeared to not be following their compliance policies and procedures."

Moreover, if managers and employees don't have a clear understanding of what they should be doing, what are the chances that your Form ADV and advisory contracts properly describe how things work? It doesn't bode well for your duty to provide "full and fair disclosure of all material facts." And as aptly stated by Lori Richards, former head of OCIE, "Whether intentional, inattentive or inept, the result [of deficient disclosure] is the same—advisory clients are not being provided with accurate information about the adviser."[10]

Plain language cannot occur in a vacuum; it works best when straightforward communication is the norm firmwide. Consider my point above: converting even a single key document into plain language will require at least one person to commit time and focused attention. Nobody will have the incentive (or permission) to make that investment unless management agrees it is a worthwhile endeavor. You are in the best position to cultivate that buy-in and support.

Similarly, plain language is more than a matter of style, and it cannot be accomplished unless it is consistent with "company culture and policy."[11] A good editor can clean up your words, but that doesn't necessarily mean you are providing complete and accurate information to your clients or enforcing thorough and rigorous internal policies. To achieve plain language, management must be comfortable putting the firm's practices under a microscope so they can be examined and described. Again, you are in the best position to pitch that undertaking.

Customer-Facing Employees

OCIE has considered deficient disclosure a "top five" problem for over a decade.[12] These concerns have not abated,[13] despite the SEC's more recent requirement that advisers produce plain English brochures that give "clients and prospective clients . . . clear disclosure that they are likely to read and understand."[14] Firm representatives who work directly with clients should be armed with a Form ADV, an advisory agreement, policies, and other administrative disclosures and forms—all drafted in plain language. Consider the advantages that would confer:

- If the disclosures and agreements that prospective clients read are clear and comprehensive, they can decide whether to retain the firm without puzzling over who you are and what you do.

---

[10] Lori A. Richards, "Fiduciary Duty: Return to First Principles," Eighth Annual Investment Adviser Compliance Summit, Washington, D.C. (Feb. 27, 2006), https://www.sec.gov/news/speech/spch022706lar.htm

[11] Peter Crow, "Plain English: What Counts Besides Readability?" *The Journal of Business Communication,* Vol. 25, No. 1 (Winter 1988), at 87-95, 88-89.

[12] Richards, "Fiduciary Duty: Return to First Principles."

[13] Office of Compliance Inspections and Examinations, "Examination Priorities for 2016," https://www.sec.gov/about/offices/ocie/national-examination-program-priorities-2016.pdf

[14] SEC, Amendments to Form ADV (adopting release) (July 28, 2010), at 3.

- When clients have questions, it will be easier for advisers and other customer service employees to respond accurately because they will have a firm grasp on what your documents say.
- If all the terms of your relationship are spelled out with unmistakable clarity, clients are less likely to initiate disputes, and disputes that do arise should be easier to resolve.
- If a client relationship sours, lawyers will be able to counsel the firm more effectively because *they* will have a clear understanding of the obligations you did and did not assume.
- When courts and regulators can efficiently read your disclosures and agreements, they can more easily determine whether your communications are adequate and whether you have met your obligations. (They also will appreciate the fact that you did not waste their time.)

Administrative and Technology-Focused Employees

Even the people at your firm who don't advise clients or analyze portfolios can benefit when your key internal documents are written in plain language. To quote Mr. Donahue again: "[T]he policies and procedures you expect the firm and its personnel to follow…will be most effective if they are as simple as possible, are explained in plain English and are intuitive to those that have to comply with them."[15]

Consider, for example, policies that are implemented through computer programs. The employees or service providers who write the code need to understand what the policies are meant to accomplish. Suppose you have an internal rule that says, "The fund will invest a maximum of 5 percent in the holdings of any single, nondomestic issuer." I concede that is nothing if not plainly stated. However, this simple rule raises many questions, and part of plain language is avoiding obvious questions by providing ready answers. Here are just some of the things the person coding a 5-percent limit rule needs to know:

- Is the mandate only prospective, or does it require the fund to divest securities if an existing holding appreciates and surpasses the 5-percent mark?
- How is 5 percent calculated? Do you just look at equities, or are all securities and cash included?
- Who is an issuer? Can the fund invest 5 percent in a subsidiary and 5 percent in the parent company, or are those investments combined?[16]

These are great questions, and not everyone would anticipate them. To ensure that your policies, procedures, and disclosures "reflect actual practice,"[17] someone who understands the administrative and technological side of the firm should be involved in periodically reviewing your written materials to raise questions like these.

15 Donahue, "New Directions in Corporate Compliance."

16 Kerri Marinek, "The 'Plain English' Myth of Coding a Compliance Rule Library" (Jan. 26, 2016), http://www.impconsults.com/news/2016/1/26/the-plain-english-myth-of-coding-a-compliance-rule-library

17 Richards, "Fiduciary Duty: Return to First Principles."

Dealing with Regulators (and Potentially Courts)

As you well know, your work and the work of others in your firm have implications for your regulatory posture. The SEC has championed plain English for two decades, beginning with rules adopted (and *A Plain English Handbook*[18] published) in 1998. Among other things, this mindset affects how OCIE conducts exams. As Ms. Richards once explained:

> At the start of every exam, SEC examiners review the information that the adviser disseminates...to see how an adviser describes its business....Throughout the exam, the examiners will continue seeking information about how an adviser's business works and what services are provided to clients. When discrepancies or omissions between the firm's written disclosures and its actual practice are identified, this will trigger heightened scrutiny by the exam staff. As a fiduciary, it is fundamental that what you tell your clients is, in fact, how you conduct your business.[19]

OCIE's 2017 risk alert expanded on that point. A "top five" compliance problem is that "certain compliance programs [do] not take into account important individualized business practices such as the adviser's particular investment strategies, types of clients, trading practices, valuation procedures and advisory fees....[S]ome advisers use 'off-the-shelf' compliance manuals that have not been tailored to the adviser's individual business practices."[20] As explained above, this is not just a matter of cleaning up language. Making sure that public disclosures and internal documents reflect "the firm's actual business operations"[21] is a substantive compliance imperative.

The SEC is looking for consistency, consistent accuracy, and clarity. And it isn't just regulators that expect market participants to use plain language. Recently, law professor J. Scott Colesanti demonstrated that, through its advocacy, the SEC has "raised expectations concerning the efforts devoted to customer communications."[22] Professor Colesanti cites court cases dealing with securities matters, as well as insurance and bankruptcy, to support his view that "plain English has seeped into the prosecutorial and judicial consciences and become a concrete factor in cases alleging shortcomings by company management."[23] (He acknowledges but does not approve of the trend.)

---

[18] SEC, Office of Investor Education and Assistance, "*A Plain English Handbook: How to Create Clear SEC Disclosure Documents*" (Aug. 1998), https://www.sec.gov/pdf/handbook.pdf

[19] Richards, "Fiduciary Duty: Return to First Principles."

[20] OCIE, "Five Most Frequent Compliance Topics."

[21] Richards, "Fiduciary Duty: Return to First Principles."

[22] J. Scott Colesanti, "Demanding Substance or Form? The SEC's Plain English Handbook as a Basis for Securities Violations," *Fordham Journal of Corporate & Financial Law,* Vol. XVIII (2012), at 95-122, 118.

[23] Colesanti, "Demanding Substance or Form?," 117.

IV. PLAIN LANGUAGE TECHNIQUES

Now, the Well-Chosen Skirmishes

I hope the foregoing has converted the skeptics into believers and motivated the believers to take action. Again, you need not (and it would be unproductive to) tackle every document at once. Instead, be strategic and start with the document that will have the greatest impact. That may be the form that everyone in the office complains about or the one that clients always complete incorrectly. It could be the policy you find yourself explaining over and over. If there is no obvious contender, turn to the document that should be in plain English anyway: your ADV. This is the tool the firm uses to present itself to the world; it must simultaneously communicate to clients with limited investing experience and satisfy SEC rules. Moreover, since ADVs are public, clients and potential clients can easily compare yours to ADVs from other firms and favor the adviser that seems most committed to being understood.

I promised that you can convert your documents over time rather than all at once. Similarly, even when you revise a document, you don't need to do absolutely everything right away. I will present several possible types of revisions, starting with the changes likely to have the most noticeable effect and progressing to more subtle refinements. Choose the ones that make the most sense for your document and your schedule.

Because Form ADV is fundamental to the industry, I drew from several to find the examples that appear below. (For the record, all of the "before" examples are real.) Nevertheless, the techniques I discuss are not specific to disclosure. You can use them to improve any written document.

There are three rules that apply no matter what kinds of revisions you decide to make.

1. Read carefully. Very, very carefully. Do not skim anything. You need to know exactly what content you are working with, and you may find a spelling error or a missed word along the way.
2. Think about whether the document reflects reality. If it has an outdated description of a policy the firm changed six months ago, the clarity of that description is irrelevant.
3. Think about whether something is missing. Recall the 5-percent limit example above. Does the document raise questions that it fails to answer? Does it contain acronyms, industry terms, or internal slang that should be spelled out or defined?

And now, to revise!

Organize the Content

Organizing your content involves two steps: group like information together, and then make sure that information appears in a logical progression. This is a sensible starting place because good organization will confer several benefits.

Among other things, if your document discusses Topic X in three different places, there probably is some repetition. The drafter couldn't assume that someone reading about Topic X on page 13 would remember the details back on page 4, so those details get repeated. (Alternatively, pages 4 and 13 were written by different people and the two sections were never reconciled.) The solution is to cover Topic X thoroughly once in the most logical section of the document. In all the other places that Topic X comes up, add a cross reference: "For more information about X, please see '*Name of Section*' on page #." Eliminating needless repetition is laudable on its own, but you also just made your document shorter.

Once all of your information is chunked together by topic, think about how to order those chunks. For example, maybe you can't describe the firm's investment strategy without referring to a fundamental economic concept or using a few technical terms. If so, you need to explain those things before the strategy section. Don't force the reader to use a search tool to find critical definitions or flip pages to find helpful background information.

Figure 1 demonstrates what you can accomplish by reorganizing.

FIGURE 1. REORGANIZING CONTENT

Before

OTHER FINANCIAL INDUSTRY ACTIVITIES OR AFFILIATIONS

White Brokerage, a wholly-owned subsidiary of Brown Advisers, is a FINRA limited securities broker-dealer and an insurance agency. As such, the subsidiary and its representatives make available products for non-qualified deferred compensation plans, company retirement plans (such as 401(k) plans) as well as life, disability and long-term care insurance. Brown Advisers does not transact any investment purchases or sales through White Brokerage on behalf of its clients. However, if Brown Advisers' clients wish to hire a broker for a company retirement plan or deferred compensation plan, they will be referred to White Brokerage by Brown Adviser's affiliated persons. Should the clients referred by Brown Advisers purchase these products through the subsidiary, those of Brown Advisers associated persons who are also employees of the subsidiary may be eligible to receive a percentage of the commissions generated by these sales. However, no client is obligated to use the subsidiary to purchase these products. When appropriate to the needs of the client, White Brokerage will refer clients in need of insurance services to one or more affiliated and/or non-affiliated insurance agencies. Should insurance products be purchased as a result of these referrals, White Brokerage will receive a percentage of the commissions generated by these sales. Brown Advisers' associated persons who are also employees of White Brokerage may also be eligible to receive a percentage of the compensation paid to White Brokerage. However, no client is obligated to purchase insurance products from these individuals.

The Blue Financial Group, Inc. (Blue), Brown Advisers' parent company, is a New York holding company. It has numerous subsidiary corporations which are engaged in retail and wholesale insurance operations. When appropriate to the needs of the client, Brown Advisers will refer clients in need of insurance to Blue and its subsidiaries. Should insurance products be purchased as a result of these referrals, Brown Advisers' associated persons may also be eligible to receive a percentage of the commissions generated by these sales. However, no client is obligated to purchase insurance products from these individuals.

[340 words]

After

OTHER FINANCIAL INDUSTRY ACTIVITIES OR AFFILIATIONS

White Brokerage, a wholly-owned subsidiary of Brown Advisers, is a FINRA limited securities broker-dealer and an insurance agency. White and its representatives offer products for nonqualified deferred compensation plans and company retirement plans, as well as life, disability, and long-term care insurance. Brown Advisers' parent company, the Blue Financial Group, Inc., is a New York holding company. Blue has many subsidiaries that are engaged in retail and wholesale insurance operations. White, Brown, and Blue share many employees.

Brown Advisers does not transact any investment purchases or sales through White Brokerage on behalf of its clients. However, it is not unusual for employees of White, Brown, and Blue to refer clients to each other when appropriate to the needs of the client. For example:

- If a client of Brown Advisers needs a broker for a company retirement plan or deferred compensation plan, Brown Advisers will suggest White Brokerage.
- White Brokerage and Brown Advisers may refer clients in need of insurance services to one or more agencies affiliated with Blue.

Clients are never obligated to act upon these referrals. Should a client of White or Brown choose to purchase products or services from a related party based on a referral, the entity making the referral and some of that entity's employees may receive a percentage of the commissions generated by that sale.

[227 words]

Doesn't the "after" version look friendlier? It's also 113 words shorter, with no loss of content. The original disclosure said three times in two paragraphs that related persons can receive commissions by recommending affiliates, but clients are not obligated to accept those recommendations. By grouping the information more efficiently, the reorganized text makes that point just once.

Announce the Structure

This one is easy! You now have groups of information. Generally speaking, each group should have a distinct header. Suppose a prospective client wants to know how your firm calculates fees. It would be great if there was a header that said something like "How we calculate fees." That would be considerably better than an eight-paragraph section called "Administrative matters," in which fee calculations are explained in paragraph five.

Let's assume you have eight paragraphs discussing eight different administrative details that govern your client relationships. Insert a header ("Administrative Matters" if you must, but you can probably think of something more descriptive) at the beginning of that section in bold, maybe using a slightly larger font than the body of the document. Then give each paragraph an appropriate subhead ("How we calculate fees," and so on), in a size and font that shows it is subordinate to "Administrative Matters."

If you apply this logic throughout the document, the design of your headers will show the hierarchy—which things are categories of other things, and which things are entirely new topics. More important, when each topic is isolated under a descriptive header or subhead, readers can easily find what they are looking for. If your document is long, consider using the headers and subheads to create a table of contents, which essentially is an outline that shows how all the sections fit together.

Think Visually

A plain language document uses white space, decent margins, and short focused paragraphs. Our eyes and our brains need visual interest and regular breaks.

Print out a copy of whatever you are revising and flip through the pages. Does it look like something you would want to read, or is it unapproachable? Here are some things to consider.

- If you have blocks of right-justified text, convert your document to "align left," which will give you a solid left margin but a jagged right margin. Right-justified text has odd spacing to force all the words into the prescribed format. It's harder to read and visually less welcoming. (And yes, I realize the book you're holding has a justified right margin.)
- If you have a paragraph that runs more than half a page, think about whether it covers too much ground. Can you break it into two smaller paragraphs, each addressing a distinct point? Is there text that can be converted into a bullet list? Compare the "before" and "after" examples under "Organize the content" above. The first paragraph of the "before" version looks too dense to wade into.
- If your content has a lot of numbers or "if x, then y" language, it may work better as a chart or table. (Look at Figure 3 for a good example.)
- If the descriptive headers you wrote are not jumping off the page, play with the font (make it larger or darker) and the placement (center them, or increase the white space above and below).
- If you consistently have more than 15 or 20 words across a single line of text, consider enlarging your font or your side margins.

Figure 2 provides an example of disclosure that lends itself to a bulleted list.

FIGURE 2. CONVERTING TEXT TO A LIST

Before

Except to the extent the client directs otherwise, the Adviser will use its discretion in recommending the broker-dealer and therefore the commissions charged. In selecting or recommending a broker-dealer, the Adviser will comply with its fiduciary duty to obtain best execution and with the Securities Exchange Act of 1934. Client directed brokerage may: 1) limit the Adviser's ability to negotiate commissions and to obtain volume discounts; 2) create a conflict of interest arising from brokerage firm referrals; and 3) create a disparity in commission charges among clients. When selecting or recommending a broker, the Adviser will take into account such relevant factors as (a) price, (b) the broker-dealer's facilities, reliability and financial responsibility, (c) the ability of the broker-dealer to effect transactions, particularly with regard to such aspects as timing, order size and execution of order, (d) the research and related brokerage services provided by such broker-dealer to the Adviser, notwithstanding that the account may not be the direct or exclusive beneficiary of such services and (e) any other factors the Adviser considers to be relevant. The payment of brokerage compensation to the adviser will also be considered as a factor in the Adviser's recommendation of a broker-dealer. The Adviser may choose brokers who charge an increased commission in exchange for providing commission revenue known as "soft dollars." The Adviser uses "soft dollars" to purchase research in the form of services, software, and a proxy voting service. The Adviser may also allocate trades to certain broker-dealers in order to obtain research for which a dollar value cannot be determined. The research obtained through soft dollar payments and trade allocations benefit many clients, not just those participating in commission generating trades and may, therefore, represent a conflict of interest. Clients may pay higher commissions than may be obtained through other firms due to the Adviser's soft-dollar and trading arrangements.

The Soft Dollar and Best Execution Committee, comprised of the trader, a member of the investment team, and the chief compliance officer, monitors and evaluates execution quality and the selection of executing broker/dealers. The Committee also approves and reviews all soft dollar credits and purchases and oversees client-directed brokerage requirements.

[359 words]

After

You are entitled to select a broker-dealer to execute transactions for your account. This is known as "directed brokerage." However, if you designate a particular broker-dealer, you may not get the benefit of our ability to negotiate commissions and to obtain volume discounts. As a result, the commission you pay may differ from commissions paid by our other clients for similar transactions. Moreover, directed brokerage may create a conflict of interest arising from brokerage firm referrals.*

Unless you instruct us otherwise, we will use our discretion to select a broker-dealer to execute transactions for your account. When we select or recommend a broker-dealer, we will comply with our fiduciary duty to obtain best execution. In particular, we will consider things like:

- price;
- the broker-dealer's facilities, reliability, and financial responsibility;
- the ability of the broker-dealer to effect transactions, particularly with regard to such; aspects as timing, order size, and execution; and
- the research and related brokerage services the broker-dealer provides to us.

We also will consider whether the broker-dealer compensates us for the referral.

We may choose brokers that charge an increased commission that incorporates "soft dollars." We use soft dollars to purchase services like research, software, and a proxy voting service from broker-dealers. The research we obtain through soft dollar payments may benefit many of our clients—not just those who participate in commission-generating trades. This may represent a conflict of interest.

Our soft dollar and trading arrangements may cause you to pay higher commissions than would have been available from another broker-dealer.

Our Soft Dollar and Best Execution Committee—made up of the trader, a member of the investment team, and the chief compliance officer—monitors and evaluates execution quality and the selection of executing broker-dealers. The committee also approves and reviews all soft dollar credits and purchases and oversees client-directed brokerage requirements.

[303 words]

---

* I don't understand why this is true, which means the disclosure raises a question it doesn't answer.

Editorial commentary: My goal here was to break up the long paragraph, which was easily done by shifting one of the lists within the text to bullet points. I also pulled out the explanation of soft dollars—a technical term that may be unfamiliar to the reader—and moved it to a separate paragraph. My rewrite provides an example of personalized disclosure (using "we" and "us" rather than "Adviser," and "you" rather than "the client"). In an effort to eliminate extraneous detail, I removed the references to complying with the Securities Exchange Act and to considering "any other factors the Adviser considers to be relevant" because they are both too broad to be helpful. Finally, please don't ever say "comprised of"! See below under "Attend to Grammar and Other Annoyances" for more on that.

Figure 3 is an example of disclosure that is perfect for a chart, which looks better and is immeasurably easier to understand.

FIGURE 3. CONVERTING COMPLICATED TEXT TO A GRAPHIC DISPLAY

Before

Fees for investment supervisory services are billed in advance at the beginning of each quarter, calculated on the value of the assets under management the last day of the previous calendar quarter. In situations when a client may transfer assets and execute a management agreement between billing periods, IA Company may assess a one-time pro-rata fee, in arrears, for that interim period. Clients pay their own trading cost (see section 12(B) below). Fees are based on the following schedule for the following asset management services:

"A" Model (minimum account is $500,000), "B" Model (minimum account is $250,000), "C" Model (minimum household account is $250,000 combined), "D" Model (minimum account is $500,000), "E" Model (maximum account is $250,000), and accounts not assigned a specific model.

Account Value	Annual Fee
On the first $500,000	1.375%
On the next $500,000	1.250%
Over $1,000,000	1.000%

"F" Model (minimum account is $750,000)

1.00% of account value in addition to 20% performance fee (see "Performance Based Fees" below).

Custom Portfolio Managed Accounts (minimum account is $250,000)

Account Value	Annual Fee
On the first $1,000,000	1.500%
On amounts over $1,000,000	1.000%

401K (employee directed version)
The fee schedule for advisory services related to the 401K (employee directed version) is 1.00% of the first $1,000,000 of plan assets and 0.65% of plan assets over $1,000,000. Minimum plan size is $250,000.

Fixed Income Account (minimum account is $500,000)
0.50% of account value

After

Fees for investment supervisory services are billed in advance at the beginning of each calendar quarter, based on the value of the assets under management on the last day of the previous quarter. If you first retain IA Company, or transfer additional assets to an existing IA Company account, at any time other than the first day of a calendar quarter, we may assess a one-time pro rata fee, in arrears, for that interim period. In addition to fees for advisory services, you are responsible for your own trading costs. (See section 12(B) below for information about trading costs.)

Annual advisory fees for IA Company's various asset management services are as follows:

Model	Account minimum, if any	Account maximum, if any	Fee on first $500,000	Fee on next $500,000	Fee on amounts over $1,000,000
*A	$500,000	N/A	1.375%	1.25%	1.00%
B	$250,000	N/A	1.375%	1.25%	1.00%
C	$250,000	N/A	1.375%	1.25%	1.00%
D	$500,000	N/A	1.375%	1.25%	1.00%
E	N/A	$250,000	1.375%	N/A	N/A
Accounts not assigned a specific model	N/A	N/A	1.375%	1.25%	1.00%
F	$750,000	N/A	1.00% plus 20% performance fee (1)	1.00% plus 20% performance fee (1)	1.00% plus 20% performance fee (1)
Custom Portfolio Managed Accounts	$250,000	N/A	1.50%	1.50%	1.00%
Fixed Income Account	$500,000	n/a	0.50%	0.50%	0.50%
Employee Directed 401K plans	$250,000	n/a	1.00%	1.00%	0.65%

(1) See the discussion under the heading Performance Based Fees below.

* I assume that somewhere else in the brochure the adviser explains the difference between the A Model and the D Model.

Streamline the Content

Now we are getting into some serious editing, but you can approach it in two phases. In this phase you will ensure your document makes sense, and eliminate unnecessary details and superfluous words.

First, consider whether your language is straightforward or convoluted. Is there anything the average person would need to read more than once? Figure 4 shows fee descriptions from two different ADVs that could have been written with more concern for the reader.

FIGURE 4. STREAMLINING UNDULY COMPLICATED CONTENT

Before

Client fees are generally billed quarterly, in advance, based on the prior quarter-end market value (adjusted for any credit or debit balance) of the client's account. Any initial or subsequent deposit of cash and/or securities made on a day other than the first day of a calendar quarter will be subject to a management fee charge for the prorated remainder of the calendar quarter, provided both of the following conditions are met: (1) the market value of the amount deposited is at least $100,000; and (2) the calculated prorated management fee charge is at least $250.00. If either condition is not met, no partial-quarter management fee will be charged.

[109 words]

After

Fees generally are billed quarterly, in advance, based on the prior quarter-end market value (adjusted for any credit or debit balance) of your account. Typically, when you deposit cash or securities on a day other than the first day of a calendar quarter, we will charge a prorated management fee. However, if your deposit is less than $100,000 or the prorated fee would be less than $250.00, we will waive the partial-quarter management fee.

[74 words]

Editorial commentary: First, my version is easier to follow, and speaks directly to the reader. Instead of applying to a generic "client's account," the rewritten paragraph applies to "your account." Second, I cannot tell from the first version whether this adviser waives a prorated fee of less than $250, or just shifts it to the next quarter's bill. My rewrite assumes the fee is waived, but the original raises a question that it fails to answer.

Before

The total assets under management are determined when the first Portfolio Management Contract is signed. The fee schedule is 1.5% to 2% of total assets under management per year. Fees are due and payable on the first day of the month that begins a new calendar quarter. Fees are charged and drawn on the accounts on January 1st, April 1st, July 1st, and October 1st of each year. Fees are charged in quarterly increments of 25% of the total assets under management for the ending prior quarter balance.

For total assets under management in excess of $500,000, fees are discounted 25% per year. The management fee schedule is between 1.13% and 1.5% of total assets under management per year for assets under management in excess of $500,000.

[127 words]

After

The total assets under management are determined when the first Portfolio Management Contract is signed. The fee schedule generally is 1.5% to 2% of total assets under management per year, but fees are reduced to a range of 1.13% to 1.5% when assets under management exceed $500,000.

Fees are due on the first day of each calendar quarter. The amount charged to your account will be 25% of the total annual fee based on assets under management on the last day of the previous calendar quarter.

[86 words]

Editorial commentary: The original isn't just convoluted; it's filled with redundant language. Is there a difference between "the first day of the month that begins a new calendar quarter" and "the first day of each calendar quarter"? No, so why use five extra words? And once you say "the first day of each calendar quarter," do you really need to give the four specific dates? Again, I think not. Now look at the last sentence of the original first paragraph: they can't possibly intend to say that the fee is "25% of the total assets under management," but there it is. (Remember what I said about finding mistakes?) Finally, do they need to say that fees for accounts over $500,000 get a 25% discount and also do the math to arrive at the lower fee? I think one or the other is sufficient.

Next, distinguish critical information from unimportant details, and omit things that don't need to be said. One example is spelling out the four dates that start the four calendar quarters in Figure 4. Figure 5 illustrates another.

FIGURE 5. OMITTING THE OBVIOUS

The custodian will deliver a quarterly account statement directly to the client or client's independent representative showing all disbursements from the account. Clients are encouraged to review their account statements for accuracy. ~~Adviser will receive a duplicate copy of the statement that was delivered to the client.~~

Editorial commentary: If they think about it at all, clients assume you get their account statements.

Clean Up Your Language

Now you can bore down further into your content and think about some small but helpful revisions.

Use Everyday Words. One of the best compliments a client ever gave me was not intended to be a compliment. A CFO once told me that the way I explained a particular accounting concept in a 10-K was substantively correct, but that an accountant reading my explanation might not recognize it as an accounting concept at all. Great! The company's investors weren't all accountants, so why should the company's disclosure use accountants' unique vocabulary? Use common words rather than industry jargon, businesspeak, and legalese.

Explain Technical Terms. Figure 2 showed that it's helpful to isolate the explanation of a technical term. In that case, the original document talked about soft dollars, but the descriptive language was buried in a big paragraph that discussed a bunch of other things as well. Sometimes the explanation isn't there at all and you will need to add it. Sometimes the technical terms can be replaced with everyday words.

Personalize Things. Use your firm name rather than "the Adviser" or "the Firm" or "the Applicant," especially if the firm name is short. Some companies use personal pronouns ("*We* have adopted a strict code of ethics..."), but others are squeamish about that style. Whatever you decide, be consistent. Don't be "the Adviser" on page 3 and "ABC Advisers" on page 6. I definitely suggest speaking directly to the reader by replacing "client" with "you."

Figure 6 highlights all three of the foregoing points.

FIGURE 6. USING SIMPLE AND PERSONAL LANGUAGE

Before

SGM offers portfolio management services for traditional separately managed accounts by utilizing individual security investments. SGM's approach is intended to be a low risk strategy with every opportunity to provide above-average rewards over a medium to long-term period. SGM takes a value approach to investing. SGM seeks investments in securities that are trading at significant discounts to SGM's appraised value of the business that they represent. Market anomalies exist around the globe and SGM intends to fully utilize its knowledge in foreign markets. However, the bulk of invested funds will remain in U.S. dollar securities as the absolute number and widespread diversification of American markets create many special situations.

[109 words]

After

SGM offers portfolio management services in separately managed accounts. Unlike a mutual fund, where money from many investors is commingled, a separately managed account is a portfolio of individually-owned securities that can be tailored to fit your investing preferences.

We select securities that, we believe, have the potential to generate above-average rewards over a period of ___ to ___ years without appreciable risk. To make those decisions, we appraise a range of public companies and identify those that are trading at significantly less than our analysts think they are worth. This is known as value investing.

SGM evaluates companies worldwide, and will invest in foreign entities that meet our criteria. However, because of its size and scope, the U.S. market offers many good investment opportunities. Most of your assets will be invested domestically.

[133 words]

Editorial commentary: Yes, my version is longer, but I explain what separately managed accounts are, and use everyday words instead of buzzwords like "special situations." Also, the original talks generically about "the bulk of invested funds"; the rewrite talks about "your assets."

Let Verbs be Verbs. Turning perfectly good verbs into nouns (called *nominalization*) will make your sentences less interesting, and usually longer, as the two examples with boldfaced nominalizations in Figure 7 show.

FIGURE 7. AVOIDING NOMINALIZATIONS

Before

Services may include the Adviser's **collection** of financial data, **development** of income and net worth statements, estate **analysis,** estate tax **calculations,** income tax **analysis,** investment **analysis,** and **preparation** of a formal financial plan.

[33 words]

After

The Adviser may collect financial data; develop income and net worth statements; analyze your estate, estate taxes, income taxes, and investments; and prepare a formal financial plan.

[27 words]

Before

Our process begins with the **specifying** of client needs and objectives.

[11 words]

After
First we determine your needs and objectives. [7 words]

Shorten Your Sentences. When you pack too much information into a single sentence, your reader may miss a key point. Long sentences also make the reader run out of breath, at least figuratively. Read your document to find sentences that address more than one issue and consider whether they would be better as two or three sentences. See Figure 8.

FIGURE 8. BREAKING UP RUN-ON SENTENCES

Before
Although ABC is typically responsible for directing trades to brokers or dealers that it believes are capable of providing best price and execution, trades for asset-based wrap fee accounts which cover trades executed by a broker-dealer Sponsor or a broker-dealer affiliate of the Sponsor are generally executed by the Sponsor or its affiliate so that the Client is not charged commissions on the trades, as would be the case if the trades were directed to other broker-dealers for execution. [79 words, 1 sentence]
After
ABC typically directs trades to brokers or dealers we believe are capable of providing best price and execution. However, trades for asset-based wrap fee accounts, including trades executed by a broker-dealer Sponsor or a broker-dealer affiliate of the Sponsor, generally are executed so that the client is not charged a commission. If these trades were directed to other broker-dealers for execution, the client would incur a commission. [67 words, 3 sentences]
Before
SG Management offers two value investment objectives: the Value Equity Portfolio (includes both foreign and domestic equities) and the Water Sector Portfolio (Companies whose primary revenues and growth derive from some aspect of the global potable water industry: Water supply, pumps and pipes, machinery and equipment, filtration and purification, compliance and testing, utilities, metering and distribution, construction and engineering, and wastewater treatment and recycling.) [64 words, 1 sentence]

After

SG Management offers two value investment portfolios: the Value Equity Portfolio and the Water Sector Portfolio. The Value Equity Portfolio includes both foreign and domestic equities. The Water Sector Portfolio focuses on companies whose primary revenues and growth derive from some aspect of the global potable water industry, such as water supply, pumps and pipes, machinery and equipment, filtration and purification, compliance and testing, utilities, metering and distribution, construction and engineering, and wastewater treatment and recycling.

[76 words, 3 sentences]

Prefer the Active Voice. Using the active voice rather than the passive voice is helpful for two reasons. First, your sentences likely will be shorter. Second, it will be obvious who did what, or who is charged with doing something. This is particularly critical for policies and procedures: it should be clear who (which job title) is responsible for completing every required task. See Figure 9.

FIGURE 9. AVOIDING PASSIVE VOICE

Before

A review of your income and expenses will be conducted to determine your current surplus or deficit along with advice on prioritizing how any surplus should be used. *[A review "will be conducted" by whom? And where does that advice fit in?]*

After

ABC Advisers will review your income and expenses to determine your current surplus or deficit, and help you prioritize ways to use any surplus.

Before

Many prepackaged forms and financial planning software packages are used to determine the client's current financial position, as well as to define and quantify long-term goals and objectives. Once long-term financial and non-financial objectives have been defined and detailed, shorter-term, yearly, targeted objectives are derived. Assets under management are then allocated to complement the overall objectives of the client. *[Again, who is determining, defining, deriving, and allocating?]*

After

ABC Advisers will use forms and financial planning software packages to determine your current financial position and to define and quantify your long-term goals and objectives. Once we specify long-term objectives (both financial and non-financial), we will develop shorter-term, yearly, targeted objectives. After we understand your goals, we will allocate assets under management accordingly.

Attend to Grammar and Other Annoyances

I could just as easily have put this section first rather than last. I am a snob; anyone trying to sell me a high-end product or professional service better know the difference between "their" and "there." I can't be the only one who is turned off by avoidable errors. If you only have a couple of hours to spare, consider using them to proofread a stack of oft-used documents. Here are some things to look for.

Spelling. I'm sure you know you can't count on spellcheck. As far as your computer is concerned, "condensation" is as good as "compensation," and "valve" as good as "value." Read carefully. Some editors recommend reading lines from the bottom of the page to the top because, without continuity and context, you are less likely to skim words. I often read out loud, which forces me to notice every word. Try something new and see if you catch an error or two.

Tricky Words. I flagged one in an example above under "Think Visually." Nothing is ever "comprised of" anything. The word comprise means "embrace." Thus, the zoo comprises the animals. The animals constitute the zoo.[24] Your board of directors *consists of* or *is composed of* or *is made up of* or *comprises* a talented team of individuals. Another common error is "it's." Spelled that way, with an apostrophe, the word means "it is." If you want the possessive form of "it," it's "its"! An online search for "commonly misused words" yields plenty of other examples, including *affect/effect, insure/ensure, principal/principle,* and *discrete/discreet.* If wordsmithing isn't your bailiwick, find a frustrated editor. Isn't there one in every office?

Should That Apostrophe Be There? You wouldn't dream of talking about fee's or your firm's leader's, right? Apostrophes are for contractions and possessive terms—not plurals.

Don't Make Your Reader Do Mental Gymnastics. Let's start with double negatives, as in "There can be no assurance that the firm's tax positions will not be challenged by relevant tax authorities." It's better to state things positively: "It is possible the firm's tax positions will be challenged by relevant tax authorities." (Besides, "there can be no assurance that..." are lawyerly weasel words.)

Using the word "respectively" can also be a problem, as in "Net income for 2010, 2011, and 2012 was \$2.6 million, \$3.1 million, and \$1.4 million, respectively." Rather than making your reader match years to numbers, just say it this way: "Net income was \$2.6 million in 2010, \$3.1 million in 2011, and \$1.4 million in 2012."

Use Consistent Language. I mentioned already that you should ensure you are not "the Adviser" on one page, "ABC Advisers" on another, and "Applicant" on a third. Use your names and defined terms consistently.

---

24 William Strunk, Jr. and E. B. White, *The Elements of Style*, 3rd ed. (Needham Heights, MA: Allyn & Bacon, 1979), at 43.

In addition, make sure the tone of the writing in your document is consistent. Often when reading something written in a casual voice I am stopped cold by language that must have been lifted directly from a contract or other formal piece of writing. A good tip-off is the word "shall."

Figure 10 illustrates some of these points, with the dubious wording in bold.

FIGURE 10. REVISING A MIXED TONE

Before

Firm X has adopted and implemented a Code of Ethics to maintain the interest of **our clients,** in accordance with its fiduciary duties under the Investment Advisers Act of 1940. Firm X's policy allows employees to maintain personal securities accounts provided any personal investing by an employee in any accounts in which the employee has a beneficial interest, including any accounts for any immediate family or household members, is consistent with Firm X's fiduciary duty to **its clients** and consistent with regulatory requirements. *["our clients" or "its clients"? Be consistent.]*

Since Firm X is a small investment adviser, each employee of Firm X is considered an **access person** *[if you need to use the term, it should be explained]* and must identify any personal investment accounts and report all **reportable transactions** *[this too]* and investment activity on a quarterly basis to the firm's *[are they "Firm X," or "the firm"?]* Compliance Officer.

Each access person **shall not buy or sell securities** *[some mental gymnastics here]* for their personal portfolio(s) where their decision is substantially derived, in whole or in part, by reason of his or her employment unless the information is also available to the investing public on reasonable inquiry. No person of Firm X **shall prefer** his or her own interest to that of the advisory client. *[This paragraph looks like it was lifted directly from the (poorly written) code of ethics.]*

[187 words]

After

Firm X has implemented a Code of Ethics to protect the interests of our clients and to comply with our fiduciary duties under the Investment Advisers Act of 1940. The Code of Ethics allows employees to maintain personal securities accounts. However, any investing by an employee for a personal account, or for the account of an immediate family or household member, must be consistent with regulatory requirements and with Firm X's fiduciary duty to our clients. In general, Firm X employees may not prefer their own interests to the interests of our advisory clients.

A Firm X employee may not trade for a personal (or family) account if the trading decision is based on information the employee obtained by reason of his or her employment unless the information is also available to the investing public on reasonable inquiry. All employees must identify their personal investment accounts and report all transactions and investment activity on a quarterly basis to Firm X's Compliance Officer.

[162 words, explaining the key concepts without using the technical terms or the exact language from the code of ethics]

V. CONCLUSION

There are so many other things I could cover here—parallel construction, subject-verb agreement, introductory sentences—but instead I will return to my original argument. There are many reasons to adopt plain language techniques when you draft documents anew (or supervise others who are doing the drafting), and just as many reasons to devote some time to revising existing documents. Any improvement that makes it easier for your clients, your colleagues, or your regulators to understand what they are reading is worth your time. Choose a document, choose one of the problem areas I identified, and see what you can accomplish.

ABOUT THE AUTHOR

Lois Yurow formed Investor Communications Services in 1997 to help public companies use plain English principles in the disclosure documents they file with the Securities and Exchange Commission and distribute to the public. Combining her background as a corporate and securities attorney and her experience as a writer and editor, she crafts disclosure documents that investors, analysts, regulators, and even lawyers, can appreciate.

Ms. Yurow was managing editor of *Wall Street Lawyer,* a monthly newsletter focused on securities law, for seven years, and managing editor of RealCorporateLawyer.com, a website serving corporate and securities lawyers, for five. She now writes and speaks frequently about plain English, disclosure, and other securities law matters. Her articles, most of which are available on her website, www.securitieseditor.com, have appeared in *IR Update*, *The M&A Lawyer*, *Law Practice Magazine*, *Accountability Central*, *Sustainability Update*, and *New Jersey Law Journal*. *Mutual Fund Regulation and Compliance Handbook,* a book Lois coauthored and has updated annually since 2009, is published by Thomson West.

Before forming Investor Communications Services, Ms. Yurow practiced corporate and securities law, first in Chicago and then in New Jersey. She graduated from Brandeis University with a degree in economics and legal studies, and received her law degree, with high honors, from The George Washington University. She recently completed a Master's degree in Communication and Information Studies at Rutgers University.

Chapter 27

The Seven Deadly Sins: Common Ways Investment Advisers Violate their Fiduciary Duty

By David H. Lui, *Galliard Capital Management*
Jason K. Mitchell, *Summit Creek Advisors*

I. INTRODUCTION[1]

Forget the 50 ways to leave your lover and the 10 plagues of ancient Egypt. Trusting "your" gut is key for securities compliance professionals, and no matter how they are dressed up, the ways to steal money in the investment advisory arena can be boiled down to a few fairly straightforward categories. If a chief compliance officer (CCO) can learn how to look for them and understand how these simple concepts might underlie very complex financial transactions, a CCO will understand the underpinnings of compliance.

So what are the "seven deadly sins" that mar the investment advisory landscape? What are the taproots that are most often behind schemes by which a disreputable adviser can misappropriate client money? Although some are based on outright fraud, most relate to breaches of the investment adviser's standard of care: the fiduciary duty that an investment adviser owes to a client. Most often, these deadly sins reflect the existence of a profound conflict of interest between a firm and its clients.

When looking at the ways that investment advisers have used to betray a client's trust, most seasoned compliance professionals would agree that the main vehicles for misappropriation can be distilled into certain simple categories. They are:

- Excessive fees;
- Abusive principal transactions and transactions among affiliates;
- Duplicative services;
- Insider trading;

[1] Special thanks to one of the most respected practitioners of our industry, Elizabeth M. Knoblock, whose help, encouragement, and insightful comments brought this chapter from being a loose collection of random ideas to a single, integrated vision. She is a gifted and skilled editor, and has been the mentor and teacher of an entire generation of compliance professionals.

- Valuation issues;
- Misdirecting income and expenses among client accounts; and
- Fraud and Ponzi schemes.

This chapter will discuss the special characteristics that distinguish each of the seven deadly sins.

Virtually all the detail of the federal securities laws, in all of their various incarnations through the broker-dealer arena, the investment advisory space, pooled funds, private funds, and other relationships with individual clients, tend to circle back to the basic questions about the ways that a trusted adviser's oversight and relationship to its clients can be abused, and what forms that the abuse might take.[2] Although these forms of abuse can be "dressed up" in a seemingly endless number of ways, they often employ a small number of simple methodologies—because they are the easiest ways to misappropriate other people's money when a fiduciary has been entrusted with management of client assets.

Of these seven deadly sins, six represent mechanisms through which assets can be taken in ways that are ultimately unethical, but superficially done in accordance with formal legal requirements—out-and-out fraud and theft being the exception. This dynamic can be seen as "taking under color of law," because the misappropriation of the client's assets to the adviser is ultimately accomplished under a veneer of legal formality. But in each of these situations, the underlying rationale for the fee, transfer, or other transaction is flawed because it is executed in the interest of the adviser rather than the client's best interest, and thus violates the adviser's fiduciary duty.

This is fundamental to identifying compliance issues in the securities space: looking for the thoughtful exercise of the underlying standard of care, whether that standard is a fiduciary duty or otherwise, rather than the satisfaction of superficial legal formalities. Many of the most profound issues that a compliance person can identify involve the taking of client assets in a relatively open way, under color of law.

In looking at these sins, it may seem strange to say, but intent to do harm is not necessarily even required. At times, actions that give rise to the perception that they constitute a wrongful taking of client assets might not even represent an act done to willfully harm a client, but rather represent an act that, knowingly or unknowingly, breaches the duty of care owed to the client by the firm. Although this chapter discusses these sins mainly in the context of misappropriation, breaches of a firm's standard of care that may lead

---

[2] Although this chapter looks to the "fiduciary" standard of care applicable to investment advisers as the primary yardstick to use in analyzing the situations described herein, it is important to note that the duties owed by broker-dealers in each of these contexts are substantially analogous. There has been significant regulatory activity in harmonizing broker-dealers with the standard of care used by investment advisers, but the harmonization of those standards has not yet been adopted. Thus, compliance practitioners in the broker-dealer arena should be mindful that, while the lesser "suitability" standard might apply rather than the "fiduciary" standard used by advisers, the concepts described by this chapter with respect to the seven deadly sins still provide good guidance no matter which standard of care is applicable.

to a wrongful taking of client assets may also stem from an incorrect perception that the wrongful act was thought to be in the client's best interest.

The test is ultimately one of whether the act meets the applicable standard of care, not a test of intention. A well-intentioned act that does not meet the applicable standard of care is not immune from the notion that it led to a wrongful taking, even if that wrongful act was done without the intention of causing harm. Sometimes, advisers who are bending the rules too far, working too hard to "help" a client, can do the most harm.

This chapter is not designed as a treatise on the intricacies of each of these activities—that would require its own multivolume work on the law of securities. It is more of a call to action for compliance professionals on how to keep their "antenna up" for situations that contain elements of these abuses. If a CCO learns to ask themselves questions related to the seven deadly sins and look for these forms of taking under color of law, the professionals will be well on their way to developing a gut sense of knowing what "smells" wrong. Failure to see the big picture, and just focusing on the details of each applicable rule or transaction, could stunt the development of gut instincts to the point that the CCO is never able to spot potential problems. However, looking at these seven categories of concern, one would have to conclude that they are exactly the type of abuses that the Securities and Exchange Commission (SEC) is trying to govern under the various rules it has adopted.

Thus, the chapter looks at the seven deadly sins of the investment management business.

II. EXCESSIVE FEES

Charging excessive fees for investment management and other services is the first of the deadly sins. Payments of fees are the bread and butter of investment management business: when fully disclosed, reasonable, and transacted at arm's length, receipt of fees for services rendered is fully appropriate.

It is easy to see, however, that reasonable people might differ on when a fee may be considered appropriate and when it may be considered "over-reaching." If a fee is charged and paid without appropriate disclosure, the lack of disclosure and consequent impairment of the client's ability to understand and consent to the fee renders payment of the fee problematic. Moreover, even if the fee is fully disclosed, conflicts of interest in the approval process and the amount of the fee, if unreasonable for the services provided, may render the fee inappropriate. In either context, the apparently legal mechanism for charging and paying a fee that has been authorized by a client may still be viewed as a stratagem to unfairly misappropriate client assets. Even an extra one percent, paid annually over the course of years, will equal a substantial amount of the client's principal being ultimately transferred to the adviser.

Payment of excessive fees is a time-tested methodology to misappropriate client assets, as surely as if they had just been transferred from one account to another—except that this transfer is effected under the color of a seemingly valid management agreement, with an apparently valid consent by the client. So, what are the key elements involved in analyzing whether a fee is excessive?

Effective Disclosure

Advisory fees of any kind must be fully disclosed.[3] For example, mutual fund fees must be fully disclosed to fund shareholders in a prospectus or statement of additional information. Similarly, individual advisory account fee schedules must be disclosed in the adviser's Form ADV and account agreements, along with information concerning whether or not such fees may be negotiated or reduced by certain factors such as account stacking or volume discounts. Absent this disclosure, payment may be subject to reimbursement.

In addition, the description of advisory fees must be pointed and specific. Although it may be factually correct to say that a fee "may" be paid under certain circumstances, if the fee is always paid under a more narrow set of facts by a group of clients and then only paid at times by others, the disclosure may be deemed ineffective, as it could have more clearly set out the circumstances surrounding the charge—if, for example, it is mandatory for some clients and may only be charged to others.[4]

Likewise, the SEC regularly notes that "plain English disclosure" is more than merely "nice to have." It is a key element of conveying the information necessary to level the playing field and arm clients with the information necessary to come to a well-reasoned decision that the services being provided are desirable and in the client's best interest to obtain at the quoted price.[5] Without having conveyed this information effectively and fairly, there can be no real agreement, or "meeting of the minds," and payment of the fee may be merely viewed as a form of taking assets under the color of law.

Consent

Fee disclosure is essential, but it is not the only required element. There must also be an effective consent to pay the fee.

Effective consent, where two unrelated parties enter into a contract, can be reasonably straightforward to determine. When there is an arm's length negotiation between two parties, the question of effective consent focuses on the adequacy of documentation. When the two parties to the transaction are affiliates, and one party effectively controls the assets of the other, the question becomes more complex. If an adviser is both providing

---

3 *See* Form ADV, Part 2, Item 5, https://www.sec.gov/about/forms/formadv-part2.pdf

4 *In re The Robare Group, Ltd. et al.*, 1934 Act Rel. No. 72950; Advisers Act Release No. 3907 (Sept. 2, 2014), https://www.sec.gov/litigation/opinions/2016/ia-4566.pdf

5 SEC, *A Plain English Handbook: How to Create Clear SEC Disclosure Documents*, https://www.sec.gov/pdf/handbook.pdf

the service and authorizing the payment of the fee for the service on behalf of the client, the safeguards that generally exist on a negotiated fee are not necessarily present.

The mutual fund arena provides a good example of how the question of approving fees between affiliates can be effectively addressed through process. How can a mutual fund, as a large pool of money the creation of which is generally sponsored by the same investment adviser who is providing it with investment management services, effectively approve the fee that it will pay? Who is the intermediary who works on behalf of the fund's shareholders to ensure that the fee is not abusive—even if that fee is fully disclosed?

Before the Investment Company Act of 1940 (the "1940 Act") was passed, abuses related to excessive fees were commonplace. In those years, mutual funds were viewed as a dumping ground for less desirable securities, and sponsors could extract the payment of fees at will, as long as those fees were paid under the color of a validly executed contract. The mutual fund sponsor (generally an investment adviser) organized the fund and then approved the contract between the fund and itself for the payment of its investment management fee. Needless to say, there were few safeguards to prevent the adviser from charging an excessive fee. The fund had no structure guaranteeing independent governance.

The 1940 Act addressed this issue by requiring fund fees to be reasonable under Section 36(b). In 2010, the Supreme Court upheld the longstanding test for determining whether a fund advisory fee is "reasonable."[6] A fee violates 1940 Act Section 36(b) only when it is "so disproportionately large that it bears no reasonable relationship to the services rendered and could not have been the product of arm's-length bargaining."[7]

In addition, the 1940 Act requires each fund to have a board of directors,[8] a majority of whom are independent from the adviser,[9] to act as an "independent watchdog".[10] Fund boards are obligated to approve fees paid to various fund affiliates, including fund advisers, on a periodic basis.[11] Using a board approval structure helps to ensure that the interests of fund shareholders are represented even if deals are struck between two related parties—for example, the fund and its affiliated investment adviser.

Every year, mutual fund boards gather to discuss the electronic equivalent of reams of fund data, service provider presentations, and contract analyses to determine the reasonability of fees paid to affiliates. Failure to adequately consider the reasonableness

---

6 *Jones* v. *Harris Associates L.P.*, 559 U.S. 335 (March 30, 2010), upholding *Gartenberg* v. *Merrill Lynch Asset Management, Inc.*, 694 F.2d 923 (2d Cir. 1982).

7 *Gartenberg*, at 928.

8 1940 Act, §7. A mutual fund cannot transact business unless it has a board of directors and is registered with the SEC.

9 1940 Act, §10(a). At least 60 percent of board must be independent by law. By rule, 75 percent of boards of mutual funds that rely on certain exemptive rules must be independent. See *Investment Company Governance: Final Rule*, SEC Rel. No. IC-26520) (Sept. 7, 2004).

10 Mary Jo White, "The Fund Director in 2016: Keynote Address at the Mutual Fund Directors Forum 2016 Policy Conference" (Mar. 29, 2016), note 9, https://www.sec.gov/news/.../chair-white-mutual-fund-directors-forum-3-29-16.html

11 1940 Act, §15.

of fund fees can put the personal assets of the independent directors at risk if a fund shareholder successfully challenges fund fees as being unreasonable.

Outside of the mutual fund world, payment of excessive fees often takes a keen eye to spot. When there is no "independent watchdog," such as the mutual fund structure outlined above, an investment adviser's ability to charge excessive fees is primarily limited by its fiduciary duty, as discussed next.

Fiduciary Duty

The final bulwark against the adviser's ability to charge excessive fees as a mechanism to gain ownership over client assets is its status as a fiduciary of the client under the Investment Advisers Act of 1940 ("Advisers Act"). So, what does it mean to be a "fiduciary"? A fiduciary obligation is the "highest obligation known to the common law."[12] A fiduciary is obligated to place the interests of the client before its own. To put this in context, one could compare an adviser's fiduciary obligation to its clients to those of certain relationships such as:

- A parent's relationship to a minor child;
- The relationship of an adult child in caring for an aged parent;
- The relationship of a guardian to a child whose natural parents have died; and
- The relationship of a caretaker to an infirm person under the caretaker's protection.

Each of these examples underlines the gravity of what it means to be a fiduciary. Obviously, it is not a relationship to be taken lightly. But what relevance does the notion of a fiduciary obligation have to a person who is paying an adviser for investment guidance? Isn't the mere act of taking money for a management fee outside of the notion of "putting the client's interest first?"

The Supreme Court has defined an adviser's fiduciary duty in the following terms:

> The Investment Advisers Act of 1940 reflects a congressional recognition "of the delicate fiduciary nature of an investment advisory relationship," as well as a congressional intent to eliminate, or at least to expose, all conflicts of interest which might incline an investment adviser—consciously or unconsciously—to render advice which was not disinterested.[13]

It is obvious that advisory services would not be made available without some fee. Thus, it is in the client's interest to pay something. However, the amount of that fee must be reasonable. If not, it is a breach of the adviser's fiduciary duty and the adviser's contract is subject to rescission and the fee subject to reimbursement.

---

[12] Legal Information Institute, Cornell Law School, "Fiduciary Duty," https://www.law.cornell.edu/wex/fiduciary_duty

[13] *Securities and Exchange Commission v. Capital Gains Research Bureau, Inc.*, 375 U.S. 180, 191-192 (1963).

The application of concepts of fiduciary duty in the context of the paying a fee relate, more than anything else, to the impact of conflicts of interest on the payment of fair compensation. Fairness and reasonability can be measured only in relation to what others would charge for similar services. So, the question of the satisfaction of fiduciary duty in this vein involves whether the fees charged by a firm are "in the ballpark" of similar fees charged by other companies.

Closely related and also essential in evaluating the fairness of fees is the question of whether the overall profitability for the services provided are so great as to again make the fee unreasonable. Thus, a whole segment of the market may be charging fees that place it beyond the requirements of its fiduciary duty. Mutual fund directors use the notion of reasonable profit to ascertain the fairness of fees.[14] So, in assessing the reasonableness of fees, one must ask where the fees charged by the adviser fall in relation to the fees charged by others. By addressing these questions, the reviewer can get to the heart of issues regarding the reasonability of fees and the exercise of fiduciary duty in approving them.

Other benefits an adviser may receive under a contract may have bearing, too. The impact of all "fallout" benefits to affiliates—such as fees paid to affiliated custodians, recordkeepers, and others, is also a piece of the puzzle. Without appropriate safeguards as mentioned throughout this section, the relationship of trust and control that most successful advisers enjoy with respect to their clients can position them perfectly to charge fees that are well beyond the value of the services being delivered.

Like the majority of the other seven deadly sins, the veneer of legality may make an abusive transaction difficult to spot. It is exactly for this reason that excessive fees are relied upon by unscrupulous advisers to unethically transfer assets from client accounts and why compliance professionals should watch out for this.

It is impossible to catalog the huge variety of contexts where such excessive fees may exist. The compliance professional must know the market and what others are charging for similar services, as well as the cost of those services to the firm. A compliance professional should include all direct payments made to an adviser and indirect payments made through a third party within the scope of their review.

Acting as a fiduciary, appropriately disclosing and documenting fees, and obtaining effective consent are the safeguards against charging clients excessive fees. It is the role of the compliance professional to test the fees charged by the adviser to ascertain whether they comport with these standards. When these safeguards are not properly implemented, it is easy for a client to quietly fall prey to excessive fees and for no one to be the wiser. That is why the charging of excessive fees is so difficult to combat and is included here among the seven deadly sins.

---

[14] *Gartenberg.*

III. ABUSIVE PRINCIPAL TRANSACTIONS AND TRANSACTIONS AMONG AFFILIATES

Generally, when an item is bought or sold, the transaction is said to be at "arm's length." That is, a willing buyer and a willing seller each come together to make the best deal possible, each party acting in its own self-interest and not subject to pressure or duress from each other.[15] The transaction is said to be at arm's length because the parties negotiating with one another are distant enough from one another to enter into a fair transaction or otherwise walk away. The parties are not so interwoven as to make them unable to reject a deal that is unfair: if the price is too low, the seller can walk. If the goods aren't the right quality or the price is too high, the buyer can walk.

In the investment management context, things are reasonably straightforward when an adviser buys a security for a client in the open market. Transactions become more complicated if an investment adviser or broker-dealer is selling its own property, such as a security, to a client (referred to as a "principal transaction"). Likewise, similar issues come into play if one client (or affiliate) enters into a transaction with another client under the adviser's direction (known as a "transaction between affiliates" or a "cross trade").

Clearly, the ability to set the price and sell whatever one might like to someone one controls or between parties one controls is an easy way to use a superficially lawful transaction to siphon a particular client's money out of his or her account. But the guise of a lawful transaction does not outweigh the duty owed to advisory clients to put their interest before one's own, and thus be mindful of the safeguards necessary to implement such a sale. Thus, abusive principal transactions and transactions with affiliates are fertile ground for one of the seven deadly sins.

The SEC has recognized the opportunities that exist for self-enrichment through the execution of principal transactions in client accounts and has promulgated rules that attempt to address this issue in various contexts. Following is an explanation of how these principal transactions are addressed in the context of mutual funds and investment advisers.

Mutual Funds

1940 Act Rule 17a-7 demonstrates the process requirements that must be satisfied to allow this type of transaction in the mutual fund arena.[16] In order for a sale of assets between a mutual fund and an affiliate (or an affiliate of an affiliate) to occur lawfully, procedures must be adopted by the fund's board of directors by which the transaction must be implemented and the determinations leading up to the execution of the transaction recorded. Secondly, the price must be fair as determined by the most recently reported market price, or through other mechanisms for thinly traded securities. Finally,

[15] Definition, "Arm's Length Transaction," Investopedia, http://www.investopedia.com/terms/a/armslength.asp

[16] 17 CFR 270.17a-7, https://www.law.cornell.edu/cfr/text/17/270.17a-7

the transaction must be approved by the fund's board of directors to provide some oversight of the adviser's activities to ensure the fairness of the transaction.[17]

Investment Advisers

In the adviser space, Section 206(3) of the Advisers Act makes it unlawful for any investment adviser, directly or indirectly, "acting as principal for his own account, knowingly to sell any security to or purchase any security from a client, or acting as broker for a person other than such client, knowingly to effect any sale or purchase of any security for the account of such client, without disclosing to such client in writing before the completion of such transaction the capacity in which he is acting and obtaining the consent of the client to such transaction"[18] Section 206(3) thus imposes a disclosure and prior consent requirement on any adviser that acts as principal in a transaction with a client, or that acts as broker (that is, an agent) in connection with a transaction for, or on behalf of, a client.[19]

Rule 206(3)-2 governs compliance with the agency cross portion of Section 206(3).[20] The rule states:

> The investment adviser, or any other person relying on this rule, sends to each such client, at least annually, and with or as part of any written statement or summary of such account, a written disclosure statement identifying the total number of such transactions during the period since the date of the last such statement or summary, and the total amount of all commissions or other remuneration received or to be received by the investment adviser or any other person relying on this rule in connection with such transactions during such period.[21]

This is, of course, a key area of focus for the SEC, which has taken action against firms for improper principal transactions, agency cross transactions, and transactions between affiliates. One case example is *In the Matter of Parallax Investments, LLC,* where the administrative summary stated: "By failing to disclose principal transactions and obtain consent, Parallax...deprived their clients of knowing in advance that their advisers stood to benefit substantially by running the trades through an affiliated account."[22]

---

[17] *Id.*

[18] Core Compliance & Legal Services, Inc. Risk Management Update (Aug. 2015), http://www.corecls.com/wp-content/uploads/2017/03/CCLS-RMU-August-2015-Principal-Trading-and-Agency-Cross-Transactions-for-Advisory-Clients-Are-Your-Policies-and-Procedures-Compliant.pdf

[19] Risk Management Update. *See also* 15 USC Section 80b-6, https://www.law.cornell.edu/uscode/text/15/80b-6

[20] Risk Management Update. *See also* 17 CFR 275.206(3)-2, https://www.law.cornell.edu/cfr/text/17/275.206%283%29-2

[21] Interpretation of Section 206(3) of the Investment Advisers Act of 1940, Rel. No. IA-1732 (July 17, 1998), https://www.sec.gov/rules/interp/ia-1732.htm

[22] *In the Matter of Parallax Investments, LLC, John P. Bott, II, and F. Robert Falkenberg,* Securities Act Rel. No. 75625, Advisers Act Release No. 4159, Company Act Release No. 31741 & Administrative Proceeding File No. 3-15626 (August 6, 2015), https://www.sec.gov/litigation/admin/2015/34-75625.pdf

In a second case, *In the Matter of Strategic Capital Group LLC,* the SEC censured an adviser who engaged in hundreds of securities transactions with advisory clients on a principal basis through its affiliated registered broker-dealer, without providing prior written disclosure to, or obtaining consent from, the clients. The affiliate purchased fixed-income securities from other broker-dealers and then resold them at a higher price to Strategic Capital clients without Strategic Capital disclosing for more than a year that it was acting as principal through the affiliate and without obtaining required transaction-by-transaction consent.[23]

These rules and cases provide guidance on how to ensure fairness in a principal transaction or transaction between affiliates. They go to the heart of what is necessary to shield a trusted adviser from a charge of self-dealing when entering into transactions with a client as a principal. For the compliance professional, the development of the appropriate policies and procedures surrounding principal and affiliated transactions is key to identifying any misappropriation of client funds in this manner. Additionally, having a process to verify that these transactions receive the appropriate pricing (potentially through the creation of a pricing committee) and adequate documentation of approval from the affected client is important.

Without appropriate governance procedures, disclosure, consent, and adherence to the requirements underlying the adviser's fiduciary duty, the conflict of interest inherent in principal transactions and transactions with affiliates is particularly susceptible to abuse. This makes these transactions an easy route to misappropriate client funds and making abusive principal transactions or transactions between affiliates one of the seven deadly sins.

IV. INSIDER TRADING

The taproot of all insider trading is the use of material, nonpublic (i.e. "inside") information to guide investment decisions. It is prohibited under Rule 10b-5 of the Securities Exchange Act of 1934 ("Securities Act") because the advantages that a person trading on material information that has not been released to the public are overwhelming. Using such knowledge, it is almost a certainty that the transaction will be profitable to the person making it. Thus, it is included here as one of the deadly sins.

Insider trading creates an uneven playing field where investment in securities is viewed as a "rigged" game. When such trading is allowed, people ultimately lose confidence in the fairness of the securities markets as a vehicle to aid capital formation, and the ability to fund public companies through securities issuance is impaired. As a result, companies don't get the investors they need, people lose their jobs, and the economy weakens. Insider trading is a fraud against the marketplace that weakens the entire society.

---

[23] *In the Matter of Strategic Capital Group, LLC and N. Gary Price,* Advisers Act Rel. No. 3924 & Administrative Proceeding File No. 3-16138 (Sept. 18, 2014), https://www.sec.gov/litigation/admin/2014/ia-3924.pdf

On their face, actions constituting insider trading are not readily apparent. The trade is a fully paid delivery versus payment transaction that rarely stands out without the benefit of 20/20 hindsight. Only in the context of the breach of duty that exists based on the use of the inside information does the unethical nature of the transaction become clear. Thus, it can be classified as one of the deadly sins because of the superficial legality of the transaction, and the effort and difficulty required to discover and prosecute the person over the offending transaction.

To qualify as "inside information," two basic elements must exist: the information must be "nonpublic;" and it must be material.

Nonpublic Information

Information is generally considered to be "nonpublic" if there is a limited audience of individuals who are aware of the activity or it is information that, if it has been recently made available to the public, has not had time to be adequately digested by the market.

Material Information

The information is generally considered "material" not only if the information has the potential to reap a substantial profit but also if the information is important enough to guide the trader's hand. The question in this regard is whether the information is material to the decision to make the trade.

When a prospective trader possesses material, nonpublic information, that trader must either disclose the information publicly, if the trader has the authority to do so; or abstain from making the trade pending the public disclosure of the information.[24] Moreover, the Advisers Act specifically prohibits the misuse of material, nonpublic information.[25]

Although it represents an illegal activity, insider trading can be very hard to spot because it is accomplished using apparently legal mechanisms. No money is ever missing from a client that has to be "found." All trades are fully paid for and are custodied in accounts that were opened with the requisite formality and documentation. One has to search beyond the superficial legalities to find the unethical activity.

So how can insider trading be vetted? It is not just the classic case of a person being tipped by a friend, or a family member or trusted adviser who knows that a "deal" is coming and wants to build influence in the community or support loved ones. The compliance professional has to be aware of systemic ways where inside information

---

[24] *In the Matter of Cady, Roberts & Company,* File No. 8-8925, (Nov. 8, 1961), insidertrading.procon.org/sourcefiles/CadyRobertsCo.pdf

[25] Advisers Act §204A. (80b–4a): "Every investment adviser subject to Section 204 of this title shall establish, maintain, and enforce written policies and procedures reasonably designed, taking into consideration the nature of such investment adviser's business, to prevent the misuse in violation of this Act or the Securities Exchange Act of 1934, or the rules or regulations thereunder, of material, nonpublic information by such investment adviser or any person associated with such investment adviser."

can tilt the scales in his or her own shop. Some examples are frontrunning, shadowing, market timing, and underwriting and trading.

Frontrunning. "Frontrunning" is the act of making a personal trade in a security when the trader knows that a client or other person will trade in the security immediately afterward. Generally speaking, this is considered to be an example of insider trading in violation of a firm's code of ethics because the trader's personal purchase, which occurs immediately before the client, benefits from the client's purchase which, depending on the size of the client's trade, can drive up the price of the security.

The trader then quickly sells his or her position in the security after the client has driven up the price, locking in the gain. With large (especially institutional) client purchases, the gain to the trader is almost assured and the transaction represents a vehicle to obtain a profit without incurring any market risk. The information regarding the client's trade is nonpublic, therefore making this one of the most common forms of insider trading.

Shadowing. Shadowing is the practice of using nonpublic information (which may be material) to trade in securities of a client or other person after a trade in the client account has been made. Generally, the purpose of this type of trading is

- To capitalize on having what the shadowing party believes to be an "inside track" on securities which key market observers believe will appreciate; and
- To avoid the payment of a management or subadvisory fee that would otherwise be due for the advice which, presumably, the client has been made to pay for.[26]

Thus, shadowing is also an inappropriate use of nonpublic information that, if the information is material, is a form of insider trading.

Market Timing. The "market timing" scandal which erupted in the mutual fund industry in 2003 was another variety of insider trading. In market timing, traders who had information on the types of securities that a mutual fund owned benefited from that knowledge as a result of the "forward pricing" practices commonly used by mutual funds.[27]

Much of the market timing that occurred during that time focused on international securities owned by mutual funds. Events affecting international securities can often occur when their local securities market is closed. The market can be closed because

---

[26] Soreide Law Group, "UBS Financial Broker Fined and Suspended by FINRA for 'Shadowing' Trades of Third Party" regarding Michael Charles Jennings (CRD #702719, Registered Representative, Wellesley, Massachusetts), in which the broker replicated the confidential strategies and trading of these money managers in customer accounts he managed on a discretionary basis. By shadowing investment managers' trades without the third-party managers' knowledge or consent, Jennings was able to misappropriate the third-party managers' trading strategies without incurring the fees that otherwise would have been due the third-party managers if Jennings had left the accounts with the third-party managers (June 20, 2013).

[27] "Eliot Spitzer Finds His Canary," *Forbes Magazine* (Sept. 3, 2003); for Original Pleadings, *see State of New York vs. Canary Capital Partners, LLC, et al.* (Sept. 3, 2003), news.findlaw.com/hdocs/docs/nys/nyscanary90303cmp.pdf

the event occurs after normal trading hours or because the market has been closed for a natural disaster, military coup, or other event. If an event occurs after the local close of trading and is likely to change the value of the foreign security, the correct valuation will not be represented by the last traded price on the local exchange. If a U.S. mutual fund, which uses valuations based on the last traded price of that foreign security (not considering the impact of the event), strikes the net asset value of its shares at 4:00 p.m. Eastern time, the valuation assigned for those mutual fund shares will be incorrect. Market timers thus have taken advantage of their nonpublic knowledge of that incorrect pricing to lock in a profit.

One solution to this problem was the implementation of valuation (also known as pricing) committees (discussed later). They are required to be convened where information that might affect the value of underlying securities held by the mutual fund becomes available in order to put forward management's best estimate as to the real value of underlying securities.[28]

Underwriting and Trading. A final variety of insider trading that can be an issue at larger firms is traders having access to underwriting information as a result of uncontrolled access by the firm's trading department to a department that focuses on underwriting securities. The issue here is whether due diligence and other information that may flow to a firm's underwriting team might be made available to that firm's trading desk. Generally, the information collected by an underwriter regarding the business activities and the commercial and financial prospects of a prospective issuer of securities is considered to be highly confidential and can be very sensitive in nature.

The type of information used to assess an underwriting is exactly the type of confidential, nonpublic information that could be used to trade in the existing securities of that issuer. Locked doors and limited access, as well as processes that call for the professional separation of underwriters and traders characterize the processes that govern these two groups when they coexist in a single firm.

All of these types of insider trading share a common root cause, which is that even though the trade was legally executed, there was some information available, somewhere in the system, that allowed the trader to have an unfair advantage. Was the game "rigged?" To find the answer to that question in the insider trading context, the savvy compliance professional has to look behind the superficial legalities and understand how nonpublic information might be employed unfairly.

How does a CCO spot this? He or she can start by asking what were the 10 most profitable trades during the year—and ask why the firm was able to make the right call. Did any of those trades suggest access to inside information? Was there is a big merger or

---

[28] *Report of the Mutual Fund Directors Forum, Practical Guidance for Fund Directors on Valuation Oversight* (June 2012), www.mfdf.org/images/Newsroom/Valuation-web.pdf; and SEC Division of Investment Management SEC Division of Investment Management, Valuation Guidance Frequently Asked Questions (Feb. 11, 2016), https://www.sec.gov/divisions/.../valuation-guidance-frequently-asked-questions.shtml for a good general discussion of this topic.

acquisition announced after any firm or employee transactions in that security? Were there any "access persons" who traded just outside a code of ethics blackout window? Does a review of the work of the firm's valuation committee show appropriate adjustments made to the prices of securities, or are issues often missed? What was the impact on clients for any "incorrect" changes to security price valuations, and can the process used by the valuation committee be improved?

To uncover insider trading—to reach below the veneer of legality—a compliance professional has to dig deep. The question is, while the trades superficially met all legal requirements—valid account, proper documentation, clean execution—underneath, was the game rigged? Like each of the other deadly sins, the essential element that compliance professionals must focus on is how a particular situation might be used to take advantage of clients and others in order to successfully monitor for insider trading.

V. DUPLICATIVE OR UNNECESSARY SERVICES

No matter how creatively it may be accomplished, charging a second fee for a service that has already been provided and paid for, transfers client money into the hands of the "service provider" under a cloak of a legally executed agreement without the work, decision making, or thoughtfulness necessary to make the second expenditure of funds worthwhile to the client. Thus, a payment made multiple times for the same service can be viewed as a form of misappropriation, and another of the seven deadly sins.

In the broker-dealer context, duplicative or unnecessary services are most clearly illustrated by the practice of "churning." In the mutual fund context, one fund buys shares of another through a strategy of "pyramiding" fees. In the investment advisory industry, the layering of fees often occurs through the use of subadvisers and other vendors who cloak distribution expenses in the "over-servicing" of an account. Each will be discussed in turn as well as special issues related to "wrap" accounts.

Churning

In the brokerage context, "churning" is a time-honored mechanism to deliver unnecessary and expensive services to a client. Churning—which in common usage refers to the preindustrial process of plunging milk in a vat for hours on end until it turns into butter—is the practice of taking the assets in a brokerage account and buying and selling the positions held for no other reason than to generate trading commissions. By analogy, this is the process of plunging the client's assets with commissions so many times that the assets have turned to "butter" in the broker's hands.

Like a majority of the deadly sins, the practice uses a superficially legal process—the receipt of trading commissions for an individual trade made pursuant to the broker's discretion—and turns the process on its head. While these commissions may be reasonable on an individual basis, the trade is made for the benefit of the broker instead of the client. Reflecting only the limitations of the broker's greed, the broker continues to make needless trades until the fees generated by the trading commissions cause the assets of the client account to "migrate" from the account of the client to fees generated by the broker—almost as effectively (if not as quickly) as if the broker had initiated a wire transfer to the firm's own account from the client account.

What's the lesson here? It is the notion that the repetitive use of an otherwise legal process, when there is no business reason to employ it, is a red flag. Compliance professionals know all too well that red flags are only ignored at their peril.

Investment Advisory Considerations

Another example of potentially duplicative fees existing in the investment advisory arena is where subadvisers and others deliver similar services to the primary service provider. The question becomes, are those services necessary and what is the business reason for their delivery?

Where a client pays a fee for a service, such as investment management, and the services of multiple subadvisers are also used, one must question the equities of paying for another investment adviser to "assist" the first manager. Is the "subadviser" actually filling a gap in the primary investment manager's expertise, or is the primary manager, as a practical matter, being paid to refer business to the subadviser as a distributor or solicitor?

While stemming from profoundly different rationales, the two models may look very much the same to the casual observer. An adviser serving the function of a distributor really might have a gap in management experience (distributors don't need to build their management prowess), especially if a subadviser is offering service in a "boutique" advisory area. Like an investment adviser, a distributor may also have a gap in its expertise to be filled by a "sub" vendor.

So, more than anything else, this situation becomes a question of characterization and function. With many different practical and legal limitations on the amount that an adviser can spend on marketing and distribution, has the entity that structured the relationship used more advantageous "positioning" to say that an adviser-subadviser relationship exists rather than a distributor-adviser relationship? Does the relationship seem to be grounded in the reality of the functions of the entities involved? Who is getting paid for what, and has the relationship been structured in a certain way to avoid legal or other consequences?

If the purpose of the fee paid has been mischaracterized as management rather than marketing, numerous compliance issues emerge. For example, the mischaracterization causes the adviser's disclosure to be inaccurate, making the client's consent to payment invalid. In addition, in the mutual fund context, the fee, given its nature as a distribution fee, may exceed legal limits; and ultimately the entire structure may cost the client more than if it had been accurately structured. The result? An unfair taking of assets.

The question that the compliance professional must ask is what added value the client is paying for, and whether the underlying premise of the relationships and the flow of monies have been appropriately disclosed? Is the purpose of the fee truly distribution, or is it sub-advisory, sub-recordkeeping, subtransfer agency, or otherwise, and has it has been accurately described in the fund's prospectus and/or statement of additional information and in the adviser's Form ADV, client agreements, and marketing materials? Typically, to help alleviate this issue, the first adviser would either volunteer, or be called upon, to waive a certain amount of its fees.

Mutual Fund Examples

Similar to the investment advisory realm, what is the benefit of one mutual fund investing in shares of another fund, especially when both funds charge hefty fees? In 2006, the SEC addressed the ability of one mutual fund to invest in the shares of another in Rules 12d1-1, 12d1-2, and 12d1-3.[29] The rules addressed issues that arose in so-called pyramiding schemes, in which a manager would invest in a mutual fund that charged its own fee, which might in turn use other funds, each charging its own fees. The rules addressed this particular context by limiting both the amount of the investment and the fees that could be charged in this context, while recognizing the legitimate needs that could exist for a client to need assistance in selecting funds.[30]

Other services can present the same questions and be subject to the same analysis. Recordkeeping can be notorious, as responsibilities flow from a transfer agent to a platform or subtransfer agent, or to a consolidating broker. The underlying question can be who is being compensated for what, and whether that compensation is actually for the "service" that is being provided or are there hidden elements of distribution involved. In other words, is the payment being made for the actual service provided, or is the payment a "fig leaf" for having brought the money to the table?

Answering these questions can be the key to identifying not only potential insufficient disclosure of the nature of the payment but also an inappropriate payment of client funds for services that are not actually provided—or provided too many times. Either way, it is a breach of fiduciary duty under the guise of otherwise seemingly valid contract payments.

Wrap Programs

Wrap agreement issues can straddle broker-dealer and investment adviser issues. A "wrap fee" is a comprehensive charge levied by an investment manager or investment adviser to a client for providing a bundle of services such as investment advice, investment research, and brokerage services. Given that comprehensive package, one could well ask when it would be appropriate to charge an investment management fee when the client is already paying a wrap fee. The potential for the duplication of services is obvious.

---

29 SEC, *Fund of Fund Investments,* Rel. Nos. 33-8713; IC-27399; File No. S7-18-03; Final Rules for Rule Nos. 12d1-1, 12d1-2 and 12d1-3, (June 20, 2006), https://www.sec.gov/rules/final/2006/33-8713.pdf

30 *Id.*

Similarly, the question of why certain trades may be charged a commission where the client has entered into a wrap agreement is also a consistent theme of duplication of services raised in SEC actions.[31] This type of situation can also cause the opposite problem. Generally, in a wrap account, the client is paying a fee that only represents a benefit if a certain amount of trading occurs. If there is little or no trading, the fee charged is not duplicative, but absolutely unnecessary because the trading being executed in the account does not support the economic value of the fee.[32] This practice is commonly referred to as "reverse churning."[33]

In 2003, FINRA's predecessor, the NASD, reminded members that they must have "reasonable grounds for believing that a fee-based program is appropriate for a particular customer, taking into account the services provided, cost, and customer preferences."[34] The SEC has tightened scrutiny on fee-based accounts and double-charging. An example is *In the Matter of Wunderlich Securities,* in which clients contracted with a firm to pay one wrap fee for advisory, execution, clearing, and custodial services except as specifically provided in their written advisory agreements. However, the SEC found that in at least 5,764 separate transactions, the firm charged commissions on a transactional basis in addition to the wrap fees.[35]

The compliance professional's takeaway here is to keep in touch with the relationship of the economics of the fees charged and their relationship to the services provided. When a CCO views the fee structure being charged to a client, the questions to ask are, "what's that fee actually for, is it necessary, and has the client already paid for those services?"

As a corollary to this, an additional question is whether the disclosure of the purpose supporting the fee matches the economic reality of why the adviser is charging the fee. Again, the common thread to the other deadly sins is that the adviser is using an otherwise legal authority and is often supported by proper documentation and client consent in a way that represents a conflict of interest and a breach of fiduciary duty. The questions that unwrap this issue are simply stated: "Didn't the client already pay for that?" or "Why does the client really need that?" Answering these questions can prevent the adviser from committing this deadly sin.

VI. VALUATION ISSUES

The accuracy of an item's valuation is a key element to the fairness of any transaction. What is true for a used car, a painting at an antique store, or a set of china at a flea

---

31 Daniel Nathan and Lauren Navarro, "SEC Intensifies Scrutiny of Fee-Based Accounts and Reverse Churning," Morrison & Foerster Client Alert (Dec. 20, 2013), http://media.mofo.com/files/uploads/Images/131219-SEC-Intensifies-Scrutiny.pdf

32 *Id.*

33 *Id.*

34 FINRA, NASD Reminds Members that Fee-Based Compensation Programs Must be Appropriate (Nov. 2003), http://www.finra.org/sites/default/files/NoticeDocument/p003079.pdf

35 SEC, *In the Matter of Wunderlich Securities, Inc., Tracy L. Wiswall, and Gary K. Wunderlich, Jr.*, SEC Rel. No. 64558 (May 27, 2011), https://www.sec.gov/litigation/admin/2011/34-64558.pdf

market is also true for the securities market. An unfair valuation results in an unfair transaction. The sale of unfairly valued stocks and bonds will result in a transaction in which one party receives too much and the other too little. When improper valuations of client assets have the effect of shifting funds away from the hands of a client or shifting funds from one client to another, they can be an effortless way to misappropriate client assets, thus earning valuation issues a well-recognized place among the seven deadly sins.

Clearly, the use of an inaccurate price to value a security can lead to inflated asset values that can:

- Burden a client by leading to the overpayment of asset management fees based on the amount of assets under management;
- Lead to an incorrect price for a transaction between affiliated (or other) parties or clients benefiting one at the expense of another;
- Result in principal transactions using self-serving valuations that unfairly benefit the adviser; or
- Provide an improper valuation for pools of securities that derive their value from the inaccurately valued securities held as underlying assets. When an interest in the pool is sold, one party is paying too much, and the other, too little.

In each of these examples, an inaccurate valuation creates unfair transactions. A disreputable adviser could use these techniques to favor preferred clients at the expense of others.

In the securities market generally, where trading volumes of publicly traded securities are measured in millions of shares traded in rapid secession over the course of a day, there can be no better indicator of the value of the security than the amount at which the market is trading at a particular moment. Few items on earth carry the notion of near-instantaneous reporting of the liquid value of securities as the reporting standards employed by the American public securities markets.

Even given this achievement, valuation issues can pose very real challenges for a compliance professional trying to understand the underlying fairness of a transaction. When a price is inaccurate, the effect is to deliver an asset for less than it's worth—or, alternatively, for more than it's worth. The fact that the transaction may have an unfair "winner" and "loser," rather than being a "fair exchange," creates the opportunity to deliver assets unfairly under the cloak of an otherwise legal transaction.

Fair Value

Although the lion's share of transactions in U.S. securities are in publicly traded securities with great liquidity and rapidly available, publicly quoted prices, not all securities fall into this category. The American Institute of CPAs' Statement of Financial Accounting Standards (FAS) No. 157 (now ASC 820) recognizes three levels of liquidity for the employment of fair value measurement. Fair value prices may be appropriate when the most recently quoted trade price does not accurately reflect the value of the security. FAS 157 defines "fair value" as the price that would be received to sell an asset in an *orderly transaction* between market participants at the measurement date. Fair value is thus distinguished from the "last traded sale price," which may require adjustment to reflect a true indication of worth. Of note, this definition of fair value requires consideration of the price in a hypothetical transaction in an orderly market (i.e., not a forced liquidation or sold under duress).[36] This point is important, as valuation issues often arise in markets that are not "orderly" purchases and sales, and thus the question becomes how to confirm or adjust the "fire sale" prices that may emerge from such situations.

So what are the circumstances in which price adjustments are appropriate, and what is the mechanism used to effect that adjustment?

Thinly Traded Securities, Special Situations, and Frozen Markets

In certain situations, an otherwise liquid security may encounter unique issues that may call into question the validity of the last reported market price. Examples include:

- Information regarding the security or the issuer is released after the close of trading, and the last trading price of the security is no longer thought to reflect the fair value of the security;
- The markets are open, but a natural disaster, military coup, revolution, or other event affecting the security has occurred, and the markets have not had the opportunity to integrate the news into the offering price of the security; or
- The markets on which the security generally trades are closed for some length of time, and although the value of the security can be fairly thought of as having changed, the value cannot be reflected in a publicly reported trade price for the security.

Frozen markets arise from different circumstances but present similar issues. In a frozen market, the market may be open for trading, but all trading has ceased in a particular security or in the securities of a particular issuer because there is widespread uncertainty of the value of a security or class of securities as a result of issues affecting the market generally. If a sale must be made as a result of the liquidity needs of the seller, and the only purchase price is far below the owner's perception of the value of the security, it is often held out as a "fire sale" price, as it is thought not to be a reflection of the real value of the security but merely a reflection of the disintegration of the marketplace. Once these prices are reported, the question becomes whether they must be adopted by all current holders of the security as the true measure of value of the securities they hold. This situation has existed in many moments of market turmoil including the 1994 bankruptcy of Orange County, California, and the Great Recession of 2008-2009.

---

[36] Financial Accounting Standards Board (FASB), Statement of Financial Accounting Standards No. 157 (as amended) "Fair Value Measurements," www.fasb.org/pdf/aop_FAS157.pdf (now known as now known as ASC 820 in the updated FASB codification).

Generally speaking, the accounting profession does not require that these fire sale prices be immediately used as a reflection of true value. The problem is that as the market coalesces around a fire sale price for a longer and longer period of time, one might fairly ask: "Is that a fire sale price, or is that merely the new market price and the marketplace is just reflecting a 'new order?'" Fire sale prices can rule the market place for a week, or even a month—but after two months or four months, or six months, when do those fire sale prices just represent the new market value for the security? Those are difficult judgment calls in which compliance needs to ensure that all sides of the discussion are represented. These discussions can be properly addressed through the use of a valuation committee.

Valuation Committees

As the publicly available information regarding a security becomes more and more tenuous, the use of a valuation committee is a time-tested solution that creates a formalized vehicle to validate the prices being used (discussed above for market timing). A valuation committee, operating pursuant to procedures that have the requisite formality, weighs additional inputs that might have a bearing on the value of an asset to ascertain the fair value of the asset. The last traded market price, if thought not to represent the true value of the asset, can be overridden as the committee sees fit, and the records of that determination and the facts supporting it are maintained to underscore the reasonableness of the action.

The reason why a valuation committee works to make trading in these securities possible, despite the many challenges that might exist in determining a fair value, is that the committee chair has a duty to act to confirm the details of a transaction whenever he or she suspects that the last traded price does not represent the true market value of a security. But what if the valuation committee is wrong?

Although the valuation committee will almost never guess the true value of the security with complete accuracy, the members' "educated guess" will generally bring the "fair value" price of the security closer to the market, and close the perceived arbitrage opportunity existing between the last reported trade price and the actual current value. This process will serve to mitigate the risk of making a trade for the benefit of some at the expense of others, because the opportunity for arbitrage is lost.

Using an unfair valuation can be reasonably difficult to discover and can be clothed as an otherwise properly executed transaction, ultimately resulting in a mechanism that, knowingly or unknowingly, may serve to shift assets from one party to another. The formalized use of the valuation committee takes valuation issues outside the realm of being a deadly sin. The transaction is no longer a fiduciary issue because the adviser has taken all steps possible to act in the client's best interest and to give full effect to the pricing impact of information that may not have been considered at the time the last reported trade price was generated. Because the opportunity to designate "winners" and "losers" is reduced, the use of a valuation committee creates an environment in which trades can be executed on a reasonable basis in spite of market dislocations without violating the adviser's fiduciary duty.

VII. MISDIRECTING INCOME AND EXPENSES AMONG CLIENT ACCOUNTS

Most people can take it as an article of faith that each person is raised to generally pay his or her own way; and there is nothing that requires the person to share income—or expenses—with strangers. Among the strangers who happen to be clients of the same investment adviser or broker-dealer, this statement is no less true-- but may sometimes be perhaps harder to implement. This leads to another of the deadly sins: misdirecting income and expenses.

In any business, there are certain overhead expenses that may need to be allocated among clients and customers. The question of how to do this fairly is always open to some interpretation. For example, should a certain fee be charged per client or in proportion to the client's assets under management?[37]

There are often two permutations of the issues that can arise out of expense allocations:

- Are the adviser's own expenses being unfairly allocated to their clients for things which the adviser should be paying for out of its own resources; and
- Have expenses more appropriately allocable to one client been shifted to another client?

This section takes a closer look at each of these issues.

Expense Shifting from the Adviser to the Client

The SEC staff has identified expense allocations as a central issue on several occasions. In particular, the staff has stressed that fund managers must ensure that they properly allocate fees and expenses among various client accounts and related vehicles they manage. For example, in 2012, Carlo di Florio, then the director of the SEC's Office of Compliance Inspections and Examinations, stated that in "cases where two funds managed by the same investment advisor coinvest in the same investment vehicle, expenses should be allocated fairly across both funds."[38] Similarly, in 2013, Bruce Karpati, then the chief of the SEC's Asset Management Unit, noted in another speech that the temptation to misallocate fund expenses is a risk the SEC frequently cites and that the SEC sees it as a form of misappropriation.[39]

---

[37] Soft dollar credits are an interesting example of issues related to the propriety of generally sharing benefits paid for by the activities of certain clients. If the trades of one client generate research that is used by all, has the benefit of the trades been improperly shared by all when the expense has been borne by others? It is for this reason that the safe harbor of Section 28(e) of the 1934 Act was developed to give guidance about which benefits generated by one client's trading expenses can be fairly and reasonably shared with other clients. *See* Section 28(e) of the 1934 Act at https://www.law.cornell.edu/uscode/text/15/78bb

[38] Carlo V. di Florio, "Speech by SEC Staff: Address at the Private Equity International Private Fund Compliance Forum (May 2, 2012), https://www.sec.gov/news/speech/2012-spch050212cvdhtm

[39] Seward & Kissel, LLP, Memorandum: Expense Allocations—A Key Issue For Examinations of Private Equity Fund Managers (Apr. 3, 2014), www.sewkis.com/pubs/xprPubDetail.aspx?xpST=PubDetail&pub=581

Several recent SEC enforcement actions have focused on the direct misallocation of expenses between managers and their funds. In both actions, the SEC claimed that:

- The manager essentially double-charged clients by allocating certain overhead expenses to its funds that should have been paid by the manager through its own management fees; and
- The manager failed to sufficiently disclose its allocation of operational expenses to the funds.

In a 2015 SEC action, *In the Matter of Lincolnshire Management, Inc.*, the SEC charged an adviser with failing to implement or follow a clear allocation policy for fees and expenses related to two merged portfolio companies held by parallel funds. Although "[t]he two companies integrated a number of business and operational functions, including payroll and 401(k) administration, human resources, marketing, and technology," and "shared numerous annual expenses," there were times when one company (or the other) would bear the entirety of what should have been a shared cost, e.g., third-party payroll expenses, certain shared overheads, and salaries and bonuses for certain shared employees. This ad hoc, and often undocumented, allocation of expenses led to more than $2.3 million in civil fines for failures "to adopt and implement written policies and procedures reasonably designed to prevent violations of the Advisers Act arising from the integration of the two portfolio companies."[40]

In April 2015, the SEC entered into settlements with Alpha Titans, LLC, regarding insufficient disclosure of allocated expenses. The SEC alleged that the manager and its chief executive officer (CEO) used fund assets to pay the manager's operational expenses without sufficient disclosure, including:

- Employee salaries and health benefits;
- Rent, parking, and utilities;
- Computer equipment and technology services; and
- Other operational costs.

Alpha Titans and its CEO agreed to pay almost $700,000 in disgorgement, interest, and penalties under the settlement; certain executive officers consented to temporary bars from the securities industry.[41]

Shifting Expenses Between Clients

Clearly, an adviser has a great deal of discretion about how expenses are shared among clients who gain a benefit from the services they buy. For example, the fees underlying a mutual fund complex for accounting and legal services are not necessarily impacted

---

[40] SEC, *In the Matter of Lincolnshire Management, Inc.*, SEC Rel. No. IA-3927 (Sept. 22, 2014), https://www.sec.gov/news/speech/2012-spch050212cvdhtm

[41] SEC, *In re Alpha Titans, LLC et al.*, SEC Rel. No. IA-4073 (Apr. 29, 2015), http://www.sec.gov/litigation/admin/2015/34-74828.pdf

by the raw amount of assets under management, but by the complexity of the structures that house them. The number of different mutual funds in the complex rather than the assets held by each fund is often the determinant of the cost.

Alternatively, although giving effect to some economies of scale, the recordkeeping, custody, and management of a fund are often more dependent on the size of the fund. The mutual fund community offers some of the most fully developed examples of structures that are designed to control this type of activity. In that context, a mutual fund board of directors is tasked with fulfilling its role as "independent watchdog" under Section 15(c) of the 1940 Act to ascertain the reasonability of the amounts paid under the fund's management and other agreements. In pursuing these discussions regarding profitability, the fund's allocation methodologies are open to a reasonable degree of interpretation and discussion.

The same is true in other contexts when an adviser is called on to employ a reasonable methodology to allocate expenses. Most advisers will endeavor to exercise this authority with great care and discretion; others will use the opportunity to decrease the expenses of some clients for the benefit of others, giving favored clients a superior investment return. Again, the ability to designate "winners" and "losers" while charging fees that superficially meet the requirements of various contractual arrangements make this area keenly susceptible to abuses and breaches of fiduciary duty.

The compliance professional's takeaway here is to take the time for a "gut-check" about whether the expense allocation structure makes intuitive sense, and to what degree independent accounting sources are helpful in validating the allocation. This check is particularly necessary when the burden of certain expenses can easily be shifted from one client to another or from the adviser itself to the client. Disclosure is generally the best litmus test. If the firm can't say, or hasn't said, what it is doing to the client in plain English disclosure, and does not have a clear reflection of that process in the firm's procedures, then the CCO probably shouldn't permit it. In this vein, a compliance professional should:

- Compare the *disclosure* in applicable fund documentation with the expenses they actually charge to their funds and accounts to ensure that none of the investment adviser's own expenses are improperly being charged to clients;
- Review *procedures* for allocating expenses among different clients and accounts to ensure that each fund or account only bears expenses attributable to its activities and that those allocations are properly documented; and
- Consider whether the adviser is sufficiently *documenting* expense allocations, particularly with respect to expenses that may not otherwise obviously tie to particular funds or accounts (e.g., "broken deal" expenses where the accounts expected to participate were not clearly identified ahead of time).[42]

---

[42] Seward & Kissel Memorandum: Expense Allocations.

Income Allocation

Implementation of any scheme that shifts income from one client to another and doesn't represent the underlying return directly attributable to the assets owned by a particular client can also be a violation of an adviser's fiduciary duty.

If a client owns securities in a segregated account, the return on investment stemming from those assets should be allocated to that account and no other. However, a permutation of this deadly sin exists when investment opportunities are unevenly allocated among various clients. Following are examples of methods used to shift income from one client to another.

Trade Allocation. The allocation of investment opportunities is an area in which income potential can be unfairly shifted from one client to another. Where the "best" trades are allocated to certain client accounts, assets haven't actually been removed, but the greater income potential represented by the "desirable" trades will make it more likely that the performance of those accounts will exceed others. An unfair trade allocation is an income-shifting mechanism. Most advisers maintain trade allocation policies to address and document these situations.

The manner in which advisers allocate investments among clients and other managed accounts is a high-risk compliance area. Currently, the SEC is highlighting certain problematic investment allocation practices by investment advisers.[43] These practices include allocating profitable trades to proprietary or other accounts that the adviser may wish to favor (e.g., accounts with a higher fee structure) or, conversely, "dumping" unprofitable trades in less-favored accounts without proper disclosure to advisory clients. Other issues exist with respect to the advisers' failure to keep proper books and records with respect to trade orders and allocations. The SEC continues to highlight and scrutinize investment advisers' trading activities and allocation practices.

The current enforcement cases brought by the SEC serve as a reminder of certain basic rules that investment advisers should follow. The key issues for maintaining practices that are deemed fair to all a firm's clients should include:

- Avoiding "cherry-picking" or other undisclosed inequitable allocation practices;
- Determining and documenting the allocation method before executing trades or, in very limited cases, immediately thereafter but before settlement;
- Ensuring that allocation methods and practices are consistent with investor disclosures;
- Maintaining proper written records with respect to all allocations, including any post-trade modifications and cancellations; and
- Reviewing any deviations from allocation guidelines, both individually and in the aggregate, for evidence of any inappropriate favoritism.

---

[43] PriceWaterhouseCoopers, FS Regulatory Brief, SEC's Current Views Related to Trade Allocation Practices (July 2011), available at http://www.pwc.com/us/en/financial-services/regulatory-services/publications/assets/fs-reg-brief-trade-allocations.pdf

Compliance testing can be a very important forensic safeguard here. Understanding why the accounts in a manager's portfolio with the largest investment return came to be that way can lead to interesting observations on the fairness of allocation procedures in an advisory practice.[44]

Diversion of Income. Diversion of income from clients to the adviser is also a fertile source of regulatory activity. Often, these issues exist in the context of a pooled investment vehicle rather than the ownership by the client of individual securities. For example, the SEC charged Taberna Capital Management for fraudulently retaining more than $15 million in "exchange fees" that belonged to the collateralized debt obligations (CDOs) that Taberna managed.[45] According to the SEC, "Taberna secretly diverted funds owed to CDO clients, and concealed that diversion and the conflicts it created." The SEC stated that this reflected a deliberate attempt to "obscure the nature of the fees." Taberna agreed to pay disgorgement of $13 million (on top of $2 million it had already paid), prejudgment interest of $2 million, and a penalty of $6.5 million. The company also agreed not to act as an investment adviser for three years.[46]

As with the previously discussed deadly sins, many strategies to shift income and expenses can rely on a thin veneer of legality by acting in accordance with the adviser's documentation—with client consent—and still represent a breach of the adviser's fiduciary duty. A compliance professional needs to ask what makes these income structures fair? Have they been adequately disclosed to all participants? A potential shifting of the benefits of an investment or the burdens associated with maintaining an account, must be done in a way that is not only consistent with existing documentation and disclosure but also comports with the applicable standard of care. For an investment adviser it is the highest standard known to law: a fiduciary duty. Otherwise, the shifting of income and expenses can be characterized as one of the seven deadly sins.

VIII. FRAUD AND PONZI SCHEMES

Of the seven deadly sins, fraud is the outlier. Although the six other deadly sins all rely on at least superficial evidence of legality, fraud makes no such pretense. The intention of fraud is to steal, and in most cases the web of lies necessary to support it leaves little space for the initiator to find cover. With fraud, there are no judgment calls to be made on the nature of the obligation, fiduciary or otherwise, that the adviser has to the client. As soon as the scheme is revealed, there is no question as to the intent.

In this regard, fraud is qualitatively different. The other deadly sins use shades of gray to achieve their goals; the focus is on breaches of fiduciary duty. Fraud, which focuses on theft, is at the far end of the compliance professional's spectrum of "bad acts," and fortunately, is the least encountered.

---

44 *Id.*

45 *In the Matter of Taberna Capital Management, LLC, Michael Fralin and Raphael Licht, 1934* Act Rel. No. 75814, Advisers Act Release No. 4186 (Sept. 2, 2015), https://www.sec.gov/litigation/admin/2015/34-75814.pdf

46 International Comparative Legal Guides, *Allocating Fees and Expenses: The SEC is Paying Close Attention* (June 6, 2016), https://www.iclg.co.uk/practice-areas/alternative-investment-funds/alternative-investment-funds-2016/5-allocating-fees-and-expenses-the-sec-is-paying-close-attention

Figure 1. Charles Ponzi will forever be remembered to history as the man who created the "Ponzi scheme." This photo has been held out for decades as being Ponzi, sitting at his desk before his fraud was discovered. The picture has been published in the newspapers and elsewhere since the 1920s. But the discerning compliance professional might want to take a closer look: the face is Ponzi's, but does his head seem a little big for his body? His photo may have been produced by an enterprising newspaperman by placing Ponzi's head on someone else's body to create an interesting picture for print. Does the fraud continue?

Charles Ponzi

Securities fraud has existed since the first security was issued. The unregulated markets prior to the securities laws of the New Deal were rife with pump-and-dump schemes, pied-piper plans, and pyramids, more commonly referred to as the "Ponzi" scheme. Before the federal government set out to regulate the securities industry, a patchwork of state laws existed. Starting with Kansas in 1911, individual states attempted to regulate the sale of securities by initiating the first of the "blue sky" laws, whose name is supposedly derived from the attempt to prevent unscrupulous promoters from selling building lots "in the clear blue sky." However, this patchwork of state laws proved ineffectual, as hucksters proceeded to jump state lines in order to pursue their fraud in "the next town over."[47]

The granddaddy, and perhaps most famous, of all securities frauds was Charles Ponzi's pyramid operation in the 1920s. The act of taking the money of new investors to pay the return on existing accounts will forever be known to investors as a "Ponzi scheme."

---

[47] Stephen M. Bainbridge, *Mergers and Acquisitions*, 3d Edition, Foundation Press, Thomson Reuters (2012), at p.7.

Ponzi (see Figure 1) was an Italian swindler and con artist in the United States and Canada. He became known in the early 1920s as a swindler in North America when he promised clients a 50 percent profit within 45 days, or 100 percent profit within 90 days by buying discounted "postal reply coupons" in other countries and redeeming them at face value in the United States as a form of arbitrage. In reality, Ponzi was paying early investors using the investments of later investors. While this type of swindle existed before Ponzi's scheme by several years, it became so identified with him that it now bears his name. His scheme ran for over a year before it collapsed, costing his "investors" $20 million.[48]

Ponzi was unapologetic about the fraud he perpetrated. Granting one last interview to an American reporter before his death, Ponzi said, "Even if [the investors] never got anything for it, it was cheap at that price. Without malice aforethought, I had given them the best show that was ever staged in their territory since the landing of the Pilgrims! It was easily worth fifteen million bucks to watch me put the thing over."[49]

Coming of Regulation

President John F. Kennedy's father, Joseph P. Kennedy (Figure 2), made his fortune in the securities markets of the 1920s. He told his friends that he needed to make this easy money before "someone makes it illegal."[50] In mid-1929, walking downstairs from his Wall Street office, Kennedy encountered a shoe shine boy, who regaled him on how—even as a shoe shine boy—he was buying stocks on margin to get rich quick. After listening to him, Kennedy returned to his office and sold his holdings. He figured that when the shoeshine boys have tips, the market is too popular for its own good.[51]

The crash followed shortly thereafter and this quick exit from the market was the basis of the legendary Kennedy family fortune. Kennedy told a friend that "in the next generation, the people who run the government will be the biggest people in America."[52] This was the beginning of the Kennedy family's infatuation with the presidency.

Kennedy was tapped by Franklin D. Roosevelt at the start of the New Deal to be the first chairman of the new SEC. When Roosevelt was asked why he chose Kennedy, who was commonly considered one of the most prominent securities operators of the 1920s, his answer was that Kennedy's experience in the markets gave him the practical knowledge of how the regulations needed to be structured. The need wasn't theoretical—it required a practitioner: a "securities operator." In this, FDR couldn't have been

---

48 "Ponzi Payment",*TIME Magazine* (Jan. 5, 1931), as reported in Wikipedia, https://en.wikipedia.org/wiki/Charles_Ponzi#cite_note-time-2

49 New England Historical Society, "Charles Ponzi and 'The Best Show Since the Landing of the Pilgrims'" (July 24, 2014), www.newenglandhistoricalsociety.com/charles-ponzi-best-show-since-landing-pilgrims/

50 David McCullough,, "The American Experience: The Kennedys (Part 1) The Father" (1992), http://www.imdb.com/title/tt0853310/

51 John Rothschild, "When the Shoeshine Boys Talk Stocks It Was A Great Sell Signal in 1929. So What Are the Shoeshine Boys Talking About Now?" *Fortune Magazine* (Apr. 15, 1996).

52 McCullough, "The American Experience," at 15:41.

Figure 2. Joseph P. Kennedy, father of President John F. Kennedy, was the first chairman of the SEC. Kennedy, shown here in 1938, was a ferocious competitor and made a fortune in securities before the markets were regulated in the 1930s. Given his reputed use of many of the tactics to make money in stocks that later became illegal, he was thought by many to have been a paradoxical choice to be the SEC's first chair.

---

more on point. Kennedy had an intimate working knowledge of how the securities markets could be abused and ultimately, Kennedy himself became that man that Kennedy feared would come: the man who made "making easy money" in securities illegal.

Key 21st Century Fraud Cases

Not surprisingly, investment fraud cases have tended to be considered the most high profile and publicized of the deadly sins. Even Hollywood has capitalized on these types of events. For example, there's *The Smartest Guys in the Room,* the documentary that describes the case against Enron, in which Kenneth Lay (Figure 3) and Jeffrey Skilling falsified financial records to exaggerate the health of the company, resulting in investors

Figure 3. Kenneth Lay, here in his U.S. Marshall's Service mugshot in 2004. Lay was the CEO and Chairman of Enron Corporation and was a central figure in the Enron scandal. He was indicted and was found guilty of 10 counts of securities fraud and died of a heart attack three months before his sentencing. One of the best movies ever made regarding securities fraud, ***The Smartest Guys in the Room,*** is a must-see for all compliance professionals.

---

losing $74 billion dollars. There's also *The Wolf of Wall Street,* the movie that portrayed the pump-and-dump scheme executed by Jordan Belfort and Stratton Oakmont, for which Belfort was sentenced to four years in federal prison and $110 million in restitution. Finally, Bernie Madoff, has become the subject of numerous books and television series documenting his $65 billion Ponzi scheme that resulted in his 150-year prison sentence and a judgment for $170 billion in restitution.

As fraud is different from the other deadly sins, so too is the necessary compliance response. The issue in ferreting out a fraud is not—as is common to the other deadly sins—how to satisfy the requirements of the adviser's fiduciary duty. Instead, detecting fraud involves how to use the compliance professional's due diligence arsenal to surface the illegal activity.

Little need be said here regarding the processes a compliance professional needs to employ in testing for a potential fraud at his or her own firm: that's covered by the requirements of compliance control and testing applicable to each CCO under the compliance rules. The practical issues related to looking for fraud experienced by most compliance professionals relate to the tools which the compliance officer has at hand to identify a fraud at a vendor.

So what basic principles should a compliance professional use to ferret out a fraud while doing due diligence at another firm?

Custodial Statements and an Independent Accountant. An important, and relatively easy, way for a CCO to detect if a third-party service provider is misleading him or her on the management of a client's assets is to consistently reconcile the holdings and transactional information provided by the service provider and an independent custodian. When a discrepancy between the information arises, the CCO contacts the service provider to provide a reasonable explanation. If attempts to receive the explanation are either rebuffed or met with resistance, the firm should proceed with caution. If unresolved, the compliance professional should escalate the situation to management, seek guidance of outside counsel, and potentially escalate the matter to regulatory authorities.

Likewise, the unqualified report of an independent auditor who stands behind the vendor's financial statements, statements of assets, and other measures of financial health is an important safeguard as to the validity of the information being provided to the reviewer. For this report to have value, however, the auditor must have a solid reputation and be known for having expertise in this field.

Although these safeguards related to custody and accounting review may seem obvious, had these questions been drilled down on by compliance professionals and regulators doing due diligence on the prominent Wall Street firm of Bernard L. Madoff Investment Securities, Madoff's fraud would have quickly unwound. All due diligence reviews of Madoff (Figure 4) relied on his accountant's affirmation that the assets Madoff managed were safely custodied. No one effectively pressed for an independent statement from an independent custodian to say that the assets he held were as Madoff had represented. It's one thing to provide management services for billions of dollars of assets, but a due diligence reviewer must always remember to pause and ask, "where are the securities held and how can I obtain independent confirmation of that?" and then seek the independent confirmation that the assets are there. That affirmation should come *directly* from the custodian.

Likewise, compliance professionals should review trading statements. Had Madoff been actually engaged in the trading necessary to support the account activity that was communicated to clients and others, huge trading reports would have been generated to support the firm's management activities. The volume of the supposed Madoff trades alone would have rivaled the daily trading volume of some of the securities in question. However, due diligence reviewers never pulled on this thread.[53]

In Madoff, the due diligence reviewers were cowed into taking the "independent" accountant's affirmation of the integrity of the assets. But had anyone cared to look, the accountant's address led to a strip mall near White Plains, New York, where an office (which was seldom used or open for business) was essentially maintained for the purpose of issuing Madoff an opinion. A CCO should always get the goods straight from the "horse's mouth," going directly to the custodian. A compliance

---

[53] Erin Arvedlund, *Too Good to Be True: The Rise and Fall of Bernie Madoff,* New York: Penguin, (2009).

Figure 4. Bernard L. Madoff in his U.S. Department of Justice mugshot in 2009. Madoff's fraud eluded almost all observers except Harry Markopolos and Erin Arvedlund. Arvedlund was a Barron's reporter whose 2001 article entitled "Don't Ask, Don't Tell," questioned why Madoff turned away clients who asked too many questions about his investment strategies ("don't ask") and why he wouldn't let his remaining clients tell others that he was investing their assets ("don't tell"). Of course, Madoff's investment strategy turned out to be a Ponzi scheme, and having too many clients might have tipped the SEC that he needed to register as an investment adviser, and thus provoking additional examinations.

---

professional always makes sure that the reputation of the accountants involved is substantial enough to be relied upon.[54]

Client Statements. In the Madoff case, client statements were another clue of the fraud: a single dot-matrix printer was maintained on a separate floor of Madoff's elite Upper East Side Manhattan office building, away from the "public face" of the firm. That antiquated printer slowly ran day-and-night for purposes of printing falsified statements that were delivered via mail to clients. Had the proper due diligence been performed, a key question might have been why was a dot matrix printer still being used years after the entire industry had turned to lightning fast laser-printed documents? [55]

The answer was simple. No one was allowed near the printing logic of the Madoff firm's statement generation process because any securities technician reaching into the statement generation subroutines would have seen that the statements were created in a way that didn't use the current prices of securities. Instead, they pulled falsified historical prices and dummy trades. Thus, the fraud continued undetected far longer than it might have.

---

[54] *Id.*
[55] *Id.*

The lesson here is for the reviewer to trust his or her gut. If a CCO sees something that isn't right, he or she must pull on the thread.

Another example emphasizes this point. A former key SEC administrator often tells a story about the early days of his career when he accompanied a senior examiner on a field exam of an investment adviser. Watching the senior examiner stare at the walls of the adviser's office for more than 10 minutes, he finally asked, "What's so interesting?" The older man said, "The artwork's not right. If they only make as much as they've told us, how can they afford all this?" That examiner had learned to trust his gut![56]

Portfolio Performance. A classic sign of most investment fraud cases involves the promise of "guaranteed" or high levels of investment performance for the investor. With ever-changing market conditions, consistent outperformance is always a goal, but it's rarely achieved. Claims of unfailingly high performance or statements of guarantee are an immediate red flag.

In fact, one of the few people who understood that Madoff must have been running a fraudulent scheme was Harry Markopolos.[57] When he was asked by his employer to "reverse engineer" Madoff's investment return so that his own firm could copy Madoff's methods, Markopolos came to the conclusion that the Madoff investment process must be either a Ponzi scheme or based on insider trading.[58] When he reported this to the SEC, the regulators did not accept his conclusion. They unfortunately figured it out later.

To help safeguard against reporting inaccurate or fraudulent performance, it is essential to employ a reasonable process to independently verify the information provided by any third-party service provider. Transactional and position information should be provided to the firm on a consistent basis for review. This information should be reconciled with the custodial statements as mentioned above, and also used to create the firm's own performance figures for the client assets, which can them be compared to the service provider figures to verify that both records are comparable.

If variances exist, the service provider needs to be able to provide a reasonable explanation for the differences. As with custodial statement discrepancies, if there's a failure to provide an adequate response, or the CCO receives a combative response, the situation could necessitate further investigation and possible escalation to authorities. This work needn't be done by the firm's own Compliance Department, or even the firm as opposed to a third-party reviewer under the supervision of the firm, but the results of any such outside vendor monitoring should be subject to compliance testing.

---

56 John H. Walsh, "Presentation to 31st Annual National Regulatory Services Conference" (Fall 2016).

57 National Public Radio, "Madoff Whistleblower: SEC Failed to Do the Math" (Mar. 2, 2010), www.npr.org/templates/story/story.php?storyId=124208012

58 Arvedlund, *Too Good to Be True,* at 195ff.

Compliance Reports, Deficiency Letters, and Reports of Third-Party Reviewers. When performing due diligence on third-party service providers, reviewing internal compliance review documents are an important piece of the puzzle to assess the strength of an another firm's compliance program. In this context, the service provider is not always anxious to provide original copies of compliance reports issued under Rule 38a-1 of the Investment Company Act or Rule 206(4)-7 under the Advisers Act, reports of internal auditors or deficiency letters from the SEC. Although it would be ideal for the compliance professional to have a copy of the documents for review, he or she generally cannot force the provider to supply them. As a fallback, a reviewer can often request to be allowed to review them onsite if the compliance professional is conducting due diligence in the provider's offices. This is often viewed by the provider as an acceptable compromise.

If that's not possible, a second fallback is to ask for affirmations as to whether the various reports set out any material violations. Characterizations of this type—made in writing—should always be within reach of a service provider to give to a reviewer. Even better, if these characterizations are given to a reviewer by a law firm, the firm is under an ethical obligation not to mislead. A reviewer relying on a legal affirmation of this sort would have recourse to the law firm if they knowingly misrepresent the reports. In this regard, the compliance professionals must be on the lookout for subtle qualifications that may limit the value of the law firm's representations.

Policies and Procedures. Compliance policies and procedures are the backbone of a compliance program.

Although most firms will not provide the compliance reviewer with their policies and procedures manual document, they typically will allow him or her to review the documents during an onsite review of their firm. The compliance professional should take this opportunity to review policies that would be deemed important to the management of client portfolios, as well as identify any areas within the firm that appear to be missing or undercovered. In addition to the review of the documents, the compliance professional may ask the responsible members of the firm if they understand how certain processes are supposed to be executed. Having policies in place to govern actions is important, but it's even more important that they are understood and being followed by the business owners.

If the compliance professional were to determine that adequate policies and procedures were in place, he or she must next ask the provider whether an effective testing program has been implemented. Are all policies and procedures within the firm being reviewed on a consistent basis? What is the process used by compliance to review each policy? What is the escalation process for any findings that are discovered during the testing process? If an adequate response to any of these questions is not provided, it could represent another red flag in relation to a possible fraud event not being discovered internally by the service provider's compliance staff.

Tone at the Top. Conducting due diligence on a third-party service provider doesn't just involve a review of the compliance program and the policies and procedures. It should also take into consideration the "tone at the top." When meeting with department heads and corporate-level executives, the compliance professional must make a determination as to how they perceive compliance within the firm, as well as their views of the regulatory landscape. How does the CEO promote compliance within the firm? Are the executives aware of the goals and objectives of the Compliance Department? Does the CCO have a "seat at the table" when discussing business objectives of the firm? These are a few of the areas that should be explored to determine how important compliance values are held and communicated within the firm.

Another aspect to consider is the tone of the message received from each significant service provider's management. The compliance professional can discern much from observing how management speaks to (or about) its own, as well as the reviewer. Do executives give the impression that they consider compliance to be an equal, or do they give the impression that they don't value compliance input or just consider the Compliance Department a "necessary evil?" What is the tone or message they convey to the reviewer? When management tries to dismiss questions without any explanation or, worse yet, when the executives provide combative responses during the meeting, they can convey the impression of the degree to which they view compliance and adherence to rules and regulations to apply to them. This could be considered another warning signal, and in the worst-case scenario, an early indicator of investment fraud.

Intimidation. Intimidation of a compliance professional deserves a special mention here. In this regard, Madoff is a perfect example. Whenever an investigator would get too close to Madoff's "sensitivities," he would throw them off the scent by belittling them publicly, making threats to call their home office regarding their "inexperience," and using his towering prestige in the industry to convince them that the compliance professional was proceeding in the wrong direction.

The message that Madoff wanted to convey was that he could "get people fired." That was all that many investigators needed to hear to back off. "Why are you wasting our time," he would say in a booming voice, "doing this type of pro-forma, elementary background work when 20 other accountants, regulators, lawyers, and far more experienced client representatives have already been over that ground?"

Compliance work demands that each professional know the feel of an unwarranted personal attack and understand that it may be a danger sign suggesting more (and not less) review is required. When he or she is attacked for the nature of the way the compliance professional is conducting due diligence, here's a formula to follow:

- Listen very carefully to the personal criticism and separate the substance of it from any emotion that may be accompanying its delivery;
- Consider whether the substance of the criticism has any merit;
- Respond to the areas that may have merit by modifying the review approach as necessary;
- In a timely manner (and in a dispassionate tone) report to supervision the nature of the energy focused at the reviewer just for doing his or her job and any unfounded substantive criticisms; and
- Together, with the supervisor, determine how the firm should respond.

At best, the compliance professional will have your management behind him or her for what might fairly be thought of as a slight against the firm. At worst, the reviewer will have the knowledge that he or she appropriately escalated an issue to the firm's management. If the managers choose not to follow up, the reviewer probably wouldn't have been able to compel the firm being reviewed to comply with the request without the compliance professional's own management's support anyway. The next question should be internal: Is the tone at the top at his or her own firm adequate?

Continuing Review. Reviews of the policies and procedures, as well as investment activity of the third-party service provider should continue to occur on a consistent basis.

Custodial statement and performance reviews should take place periodically as a verification tool to help ensure that the firm is not being provided inaccurate data. Additionally, due diligence, both in-person and through the use of questionnaires, should continue on a periodic basis to determine whether the investment process and responsible parties have changed since previous reviews. Specifically, the in-person due diligence meetings give the compliance professional an opportunity to meet with any new staff that may be involved with the investment process and determine if the atmosphere and views of the firm on compliance and the regulatory landscape have changed in any manner.

Although the overwhelming majority of the seven deadly sins are, in essence, forms of breach of fiduciary duty done under a veneer of legality, fraud is qualitatively different. It is done without regard to the forms of superficial legal requirements and only comports with industry norms to the degree that those norms can provide more time for the fraud to continue. Lapses involving breaches of fiduciary duty can continue indefinitely. Fraud generally runs to a crescendo when a triggering event reveals the scheme.

The discovery of an out-and-out fraud is thankfully a rare occurrence for most compliance professionals. Using the weapons in their due diligence arsenal to combat this most dangerous of the seven deadly sins is the highest and most important use of your compliance skills.

IX. CONCLUSION

Most seasoned compliance professionals know that although there are an endless variety of creative schemes to misappropriate client money, many of these schemes seem to circle back to a limited array of mechanisms that have existed since the first public companies were traded. This chapter has characterized these mechanisms as the "seven deadly sins."

The community of investment advisers has always been plagued by its share of out and out thieves and sociopaths, as well as other "professionals" who have no compunction about defrauding helpless elderly and relatively unsophisticated investors. Although there will always be those who steal money through Ponzi schemes or just take the money and disappear, most of the ways of "helping yourself" to client assets involve more finesse and are done under color of law. They represent breaches of the adviser's fiduciary duty: the highest standard of care known to law.

These miscreants use superficially legal techniques pursuant to which the adviser abuses its position of trust to either sell duplicative and necessary services, enter into principal transactions with clients that don't properly consider client needs, use strategies to shift income or expenses from one client to another, or incorrectly value assets owned by the client to the client's detriment. The common thread to each of these situations is that they represent conflicts of interest pursuant to which the adviser effectively places his or her interest before the interest of the client.

While each of these deadly sins can be clothed to meet the circumstances presented by a particular situation, they all partake of the same foundational structure, regardless of how they are dressed. Most are strategies designed to move client assets from the account of the client to the account of the adviser under color of law without reference to the requirements imposed by the applicable standard of care.

In each of these sins, the adviser has allowed easy access to client funds, combined with conflicts of interest, to cloud its judgment. The schemes are often clothed in highly complicated fee structures, financial transactions, and movements of funds between affiliates. But at their root, they all enjoy certain similarities. They all seek to misappropriate client assets through breaches of the applicable standard of care. In that, they are just as bad—if only more sophisticated—than the Ponzi schemes or the "take the money and run" stories.

The compliance professional who remembers to look beneath a complex transaction, understanding why it was structured the way it was, and how to identify the impact of incorrect valuations, overcharging, duplication of services, and shifting of assets will have understood the darker side of the securities profession and confronted the real reason why compliance has become a necessary part of the financial services industry. Understanding how to address these fundamental issues of fraud and misappropriation, as well as knowing that these acts can be accomplished under color of law, can add great value to a firm's compliance regimen.

Law students are taught that the spotting of issues can be even more important than the way the lawyer suggests that they should be resolved. Understanding the seven deadly sins is the foundation of enabling compliance professionals to spot important compliance issues.

So, while one may forget the 50 ways to leave your lover or the 10 plagues of ancient Egypt, a wise compliance professional will always remember the seven deadly sins of the investment management business. Asking the right questions and trusting one's gut are the essential skills of the compliance profession. If compliance professionals apply these skills, they will have the greatest impact on the profession and give their role as compliance professionals the greatest and highest meaning possible.

ABOUT THE AUTHORS

David H. Lui was chair of the industry's trade group, the National Society of Compliance Professionals, and has been a CCO for some of America's largest investment advisers, including Charles Schwab Investment Management, Franklin Advisers (Franklin Templeton), U.S. Bancorp Asset Management, and Galliard Capital Management, a $90 billion subsidiary of Wells Fargo. Mr. Lui is currently a principal with Galliard Capital Management. Mr. Lui is a graduate of Brown University with a bachelor of arts degree with honors in History and a juris doctor degree from the University of California, Hastings College of the Law. He is admitted to practice in California and Minnesota. With John Walsh and Jason Mitchell, Mr. Lui is the co-editor of the two-volume set of *Modern Compliance.*

Jason K. Mitchell serves as the CCO for Summit Creek Advisors, LLC in Minneapolis. Mr. Mitchell entered the financial services industry in 1999, and dedicated himself to the compliance profession in 2004. Prior to joining Summit Creek Advisors, Mr. Mitchell served as a senior compliance associate for Galliard Capital Management, overseeing the investment advisory functions of the firm. He also previously served as a compliance manager at U.S. Bancorp Asset Management, where he supervised the firm's compliance training program, as well as code of ethics administration and SEC examination coordination responsibilities. He graduated with a bachelor of arts degree in Economics and Management from the University of Minnesota, Morris.

Index

D

N

O

P

Q

R

S

T

U

V

W